Windows Phone 8 Development Internals

Andrew Whitechapel
Sean McKenna

Published with the authorization of Microsoft Corporation by:
O'Reilly Media, Inc.
1005 Gravenstein Highway North
Sebastopol, California 95472

ISBN: 978-0-7356-7623-7

1 2 3 4 5 6 7 8 9 LSI 8 7 6 5 4 3

Printed and bound in the United States of America.

Microsoft Press books are available through booksellers and distributors worldwide. If you need support related to this book, email Microsoft Press Book Support at mspinput@microsoft.com. Please tell us what you think of this book at *http://www.microsoft.com/learning/booksurvey.*

Acquisitions and Development Editor: Russell Jones

Production Editor: Rachel Steely

Editorial Production: Dianne Russell, Octal Publishing, Inc.

Technical Reviewer: Peter Torr

Copyeditor: Bob Russell, Octal Publishing, Inc.

Indexer: WordCo Indexing Services, Inc.

Cover Design: Twist Creative • Seattle

Cover Composition: Karen Montgomery

Illustrator: Rebecca Demarest

We would like to dedicate this book to Narins Bergstrom and Urmila Nadkarni, with thanks for their endless patience and support.

—Andrew Whitechapel and Sean McKenna

Contents at a Glance

Contents

Foreword

Given that you've picked up this book, it's probably safe to assume you're familiar with the Windows Phone operating system. Maybe you've seen a television or magazine ad showcasing unique features such as customizable Live tiles; maybe you've watched one of the "Smoked by Windows Phone" videos online; or maybe you're even carrying a Windows Phone with you right now as your daily driver. And, with a title like *Windows Phone 8 Development Internals*, it's also pretty safe to assume you're interested in developing for Windows Phone, whether for fun, education, profit, or just because your boss asked you to.

Whatever the reason for your interest in Windows Phone development, you've selected the right book to get you started (or to help take your expertise to the next level). This book is jam-packed with expert advice, best practices, design guidelines, and clear explanations of features that will teach you not just the "how" and "what" of building great Windows Phone applications, but also the "why." And, as you'd expect from any modern development book, there's a large set of sample code that serves both to illustrate the features and concepts covered within as well as to serve as the starter code for your own applications.

Released in late 2012, Windows Phone 8 is the next evolution of the Windows Phone operating system. It offers many new end-user features such as the more customizable Start Screen, family-friendly Kids Corner, background turn-by-turn directions, deeply integrated VoIP functionality, Enterprise application support, and so much more. But today's smartphone experience is defined as much, if not more, by the rich set of applications and games that are available to download—and that's where you come in!

Windows Phone 8 is an even bigger release for developers than it is for users. Whereas Windows Phone 7 and 7.1 focused strictly on managed-code development with Microsoft Silverlight and XNA, Windows Phone 8 adds native-code development with C and C++ and facilitates the creation of high-performance games with Direct3D and XAudio2. Windows Phone 8 also shares a common kernel and many APIs with its "big brother" Windows 8 operating system, making it possible for developers to share much of their code (and their development costs) across phones, tablets, laptops, and desktops.

In addition to the incremental updates to Microsoft .NET and XAML and the large number of APIs borrowed from Windows and DirectX, Windows Phone 8 also adds APIs for more than 60 brand-new scenarios such as speech synthesis and recognition, high-performance camera access, and a world-class mapping platform. Although there's no effective way to quantify the surface area of a platform as complex as Windows Phone, it would be fair to say that this release roughly doubles the amount of functionality available to developers from the previous release—that's a lot of functionality!

There's a saying in software development that it takes 80 percent of the time to do 80 percent of the work, and another 80 percent of the time to do the last 20 percent. That's because there's so much more to building a great application than just knowing which APIs to call: your application needs to be easy to use, secure, reliable, and aesthetically pleasing. It must also perform well, protect the user's privacy, and (in many cases) generate a profit. Andrew and Sean cover all these areas and more in this book, focusing not just on a long list of APIs but rather on the entirety of the application lifecycle, from design and coding, through analysis and monetization. It's that last 20 percent that turns a good app into a great app, and this is what will set your applications apart from the others in a crowded marketplace.

Finally, I want to thank Andrew and Sean for giving me the opportunity to review this book and do my part to help developers such as yourself participate in (and hopefully profit from) the burgeoning Windows Phone application ecosystem. I'll close with the same words I used in the foreword to Andrew's previous Windows Phone development book: I also learned a lot while reviewing this book, and I know you will too.

Peter Torr
Program Manager in the
Windows Phone Application Platform team

Introduction

Smartphone technology is evolving at a rapid pace. Just two short years after the release of Windows Phone 7—which itself was a major departure from the previous version—Microsoft released Windows Phone 8. This is a huge release. Almost everything in the stack, from the hardware up to the application platform layer, has changed dramatically. The operating system moves towards convergence with the Windows 8 desktop operating system via a shared core, and the app platform includes support for native development. At the same time, the app platform maintains an extremely high degree of backward compatibility, ensuring that Windows Phone 7 apps continue to work on Windows Phone 8.

The platform has been designed from the ground up to support an all-encompassing, integrated, and delightful user experience (UX). There is considerable scope for building compelling apps on top of this platform, and Windows Phone is well-positioned as an opportunity for developers to build applications that can make a real difference in people's lives.

Windows Phone 8 Development Internals covers the breadth of application development for the Windows Phone 8 platform. You can build applications for Windows Phone 8 by using either managed code (in C# or Microsoft Visual Basic) or native code (in C++). This book covers both C# managed development and C++ native development. The primary development and design tools are Microsoft Visual Studio and Microsoft Expression Blend; this book focuses on Visual Studio.

Each chapter covers a handful of related features. For each feature, the book provides one or more sample applications and walks you through the significant code. This approach can both help you understand the techniques used and also the design and implementation choices that you must make in each case. Potential pitfalls are called out, as are scenarios in which you can typically make performance or UX improvements. An underlying theme is that apps should conform not only to the user interface design guidelines, but also to the notion of a balanced, healthy phone ecosystem.

Who should read this book

This book is intended to help existing developers understand the core concepts, the significant programmable feature areas, and the major techniques in Windows Phone development. It is specifically aimed at existing C# and C++ developers who want to get up to speed rapidly with the Windows Phone platform. Developers who have experience with other mobile platforms will find this book invaluable in learning the ins and outs of Microsoft's operating system and will find that the chapters that focus on native development will foster an easy transition. For the chapters that focus on managed development, native developers will likely need additional resources to pick up the C# and XAML languages.

Chapter 1, "Vision and architecture," covers the basic architecture of the platform, while most of the chapters delve deeply into the internal system behavior. This is the type of knowledge that helps to round out your understanding of the platform and inform your design decisions, even though, in some cases, the internal details have no immediate impact on the exposed API.

Assumptions

The book assumes that you have a reasonable level of experience with developing in C# and/or in C++. The book does not discuss basic language constructs, nor does it cover the basics of how to use Visual Studio, the project system, or the debugger, although more advanced techniques, and phone-specific features are, of course, explained in detail. Previous knowledge of XAML is useful for the managed chapters, and some exposure to COM is useful for the native chapters, but neither is essential.

Although many component-level diagrams are presented as high-level abstractions, there are also many sections that describe the behavior of the feature in question through the use of UML sequence diagrams. It helps to have an understanding of sequence diagrams, but again, that's not essential, because they are fairly self-explanatory.

Who should not read this book

This book is not intended for use by application designers—that is, if designers are defined as developers who use Expression Blend—although designers might find it useful to understand some of the issues facing developers in the Windows Phone application space. Although Windows Phone 8 does maintain support for XNA, you cannot create new XNA projects in Visual Studio 2012; therefore, this book does not cover XNA development at all.

Organization of this book

This book is divided into four parts:

- **Section I** Core Features
- **Section II** Windows Phone 7 to Windows Phone 8
- **Section III** New Windows Phone 8 Features
- **Section IV** Native Development with Windows Phone 8

As of this writing, there are still many more Windows Phone 7 phones in existence than Windows Phone 8 phones. The Windows Phone Store contains well over 140,000 apps, almost all of which target Windows Phone 7. For this reason, the first eight chapters focus on the basic infrastructure, programming model, and the core features that are common to both versions. Where there are material differences, those are called out along with references to the later chapter where the version 8 behavior is explained in detail.

Next, Section II covers both the features that are significantly different between version 7 and version 8. This section also discusses the process of porting apps from version 7 to version 8, as well as how to develop new apps that target both versions.

Section III covers the major new features in version 8 that did not exist at all in version 7. These include speech functionality, wallet, in-app purchase, and enterprise applications.

Finally, whereas the first three sections concentrate on managed development, Section IV focuses purely on native development. This section includes coverage of native-managed interoperability, convergence between Windows Phone 8 and Windows 8, threading, and integration with the Windows Phone platform via native code.

Conventions and features in this book

This book presents information by using conventions designed to make the information readable and easy to follow.

- In some cases, especially in the early chapters, application code is listed in its entirety. More often, particularly later in the book, only the significant code is listed. Wherever code has been omitted for the sake of brevity, this is called out in the listing. In all cases, you can refer to the sample code that accompanies this book for complete listings.
- In the XAML listings, attributes that are not relevant to the topic under discussion, and that have already been explained in previous sections are omitted. This omission applies, for example, to *Grid.Row*, *Grid.Column*, *Margin*, *FontSize*, and similarly trivial attributes. In this way, you can focus on the elements and attributes that do actually contribute to the feature at hand, without irrelevant distractions.
- Code identifiers (the names for classes, methods, properties, events, enum values, and so on) are all italicized in the text.
- In the few cases where two or more listings are given with the explicit aim of comparing alternative techniques (or "before" and "after" scenarios), the differences appear in bold.
- Boxed elements such as Notes, Tips, and other reader aids provide additional information or alternative methods for completing a step successfully.
- Text that you should type (apart from code blocks) appears in bold.
- A plus sign (+) between two key names means that you must press those keys at the same time. For example, "Press Alt+Tab" means that you hold down the Alt key while you press the Tab key.
- A vertical bar between two or more menu items (for example, File | Close), means that you should select the first menu or menu item, and then the next, and so on.

System requirements

You can build and run the accompanying sample code, or you can create your own solutions from scratch, following the instructions in the text. In either case, you will need the following hardware and software to create the sample applications in this book:

- **Windows 8** You cannot install the Visual Studio 2012 tools for Windows Phone development on any other version of Windows.
- **The Windows Phone SDK version 8** This is a free download that includes Visual Studio 2012 Express Edition and all other standard tools, as detailed in Chapter 1.
- Some of the server-side sample projects require Visual Studio Professional, but all the Windows Phone samples work with Visual Studio Express.
- Installing the SDK requires 4 GB of free disk space on the system drive. If you use the profiler for an extended period, you will need considerably more disk space.
- 4 GB RAM (8 GB recommended).
- The Windows Phone emulator is built on the latest version of Microsoft Hyper-V, which requires a 64-bit CPU that includes Second Level Address Translation (SLAT). If you have only a 32-bit computer (or a 64-bit computer without SLAT support), you can still install the SDK, and you can test apps as long as you have a developer-unlocked phone.
- A 2.6 GHz or faster processor (4GHz or 2.6GHz dual-core is recommended).
- Internet connection to download additional software or chapter examples and for testing web-related applications.

Depending on your Windows configuration, you might require Local Administrator rights to install or configure Visual Studio 2012 and to install or configure features such as Internet Information Services, if not already installed.

For the latest requirements, visit the Windows Phone SDK download page at:

http://dev.windowsphone.com

Code samples

All of the chapters in this book include multiple sample solutions that you can use interactively to try out new material learned in the main text. You can download all the sample projects from the following page:

http://aka.ms/WinPhone8DevInternals/files

Follow the instructions to download the WP8DevInternals.zip file.

Installing the code samples

Perform the following steps to install the code samples on your computer so that you can refer to them while learning about the techniques that they demonstrate.

1. Unzip the WP8DevInternals.zip file that you downloaded from the book's website to any suitable folder on your local hard disk. The sample code expands out to nearly 200 MB, and you will need even more space for the binaries if you choose to build any of the samples.

2. If prompted, review the displayed end-user license agreement. If you accept the terms, select the accept option and then click Next.

Note If the license agreement doesn't appear, you can access it from the same webpage from which you downloaded the WP8DevInternals.zip file.

Using the code samples

When you unzip the sample code, this creates a number of subfolders, one for each chapter. Within each chapter's subfolder there are further subfolders. In most cases, there is one subfolder per application (or per version of an application), but in some cases, multiple applications are grouped together; for example, where there is a server-side application as well as a client-side application in the solution.

All of the samples are complete, fully-functioning applications. Note, however, that in some cases, you might need to update assembly references, depending on where you install the SDK as well as where you install supplementary libraries and frameworks that don't ship with the main SDK.

For samples that demonstrate the use of some supplementary framework, you will need to download and install that framework so that you can reference its assemblies. Also note that, in some cases, this requires a user ID, such as for Facebook or Google Analytics, as described in the relevant sections. In all cases, as of this writing, you can sign up for the ID without charge.

Acknowledgments

The Windows Phone development space is truly inspiring, and the Windows Phone teams at Microsoft are chock-full of smart, helpful people. The list of folks who helped us prepare this book is very long. We'd particularly like to thank Peter Torr for doing all the heavy lifting in the technical review, and Russell Jones, our intrepid editor at O'Reilly Media.

In addition, we'd like to thank all the other people who answered our dumb questions, and corrected our various misinterpretations of the internal workings of the platform, especially Tim Kurtzman, Wei Zhang, Jason Fuller, Abolade Gbadegesin, Avi Bathula, Brian Cross, Alex McKelvey and Adam Lydick.

Errata & book support

We've made every effort to ensure the accuracy of this book and its companion content. Any errors that have been reported since this book was published are listed on our Microsoft Press site at oreilly.com:

http://aka.ms/WinPhone8DevInternals/errata

If you find an error that is not already listed, you can report it to us through the same page.

If you need additional support, email Microsoft Press Book Support at *mspinput@microsoft.com*.

Please note that product support for Microsoft software is not offered through the addresses above.

We want to hear from you

At Microsoft Press, your satisfaction is our top priority, and your feedback our most valuable asset. Please tell us what you think of this book at:

http://www.microsoft.com/learning/booksurvey

The survey is short, and we read every one of your comments and ideas. Thanks in advance for your input!

Stay in touch

Let's keep the conversation going! We're on Twitter: *http://twitter.com/MicrosoftPress*

PART I

Core Features

CHAPTER 1

Vision and architecture

This chapter covers three core topics: the principles behind the Windows Phone UI and the role that Windows Phone Store apps play in it; a primer on the architecture of the Windows Phone development platform; and an overview of what is required to build and deliver Windows Phone apps. Together, these topics form a critical foundation that will support the detailed examinations of individual platform features that follow in subsequent chapters. And, just so you don't leave this chapter without getting your hands a little bit dirty, you will walk through a simple "Hello World" project to ensure that you're all set to tackle the more involved topics ahead.

A different kind of phone

When Windows Phone 7 was released in the fall of 2010, it represented a significant departure not only from previous Microsoft mobile operating systems, but also from every other mobile operating system (OS) on the market. The user interface was clean, bold, and fluid, with a strong focus on the user's content, rather than app chrome. The Start screen (see Figure 1-1) provided a level of personalization available nowhere else. Live tiles provided key information at a glance as well as the ability to start not only apps, but specific parts of those apps, such as opening a favorite website, perhaps, or checking a friend's Facebook status. The developer platform offered unrivalled efficiency and familiar tools. It also gave app developers the ability to extend core phone experiences rather than building isolated apps.

With Windows Phone 8, Microsoft has significantly expanded the capabilities of the OS, but the fundamental philosophy remains the same. Indeed, much of the original Windows Phone philosophy is now being adopted in the core Windows OS, Microsoft Office, Microsoft Xbox, and other Microsoft products, making it all the more valuable to understand its basic tenets.

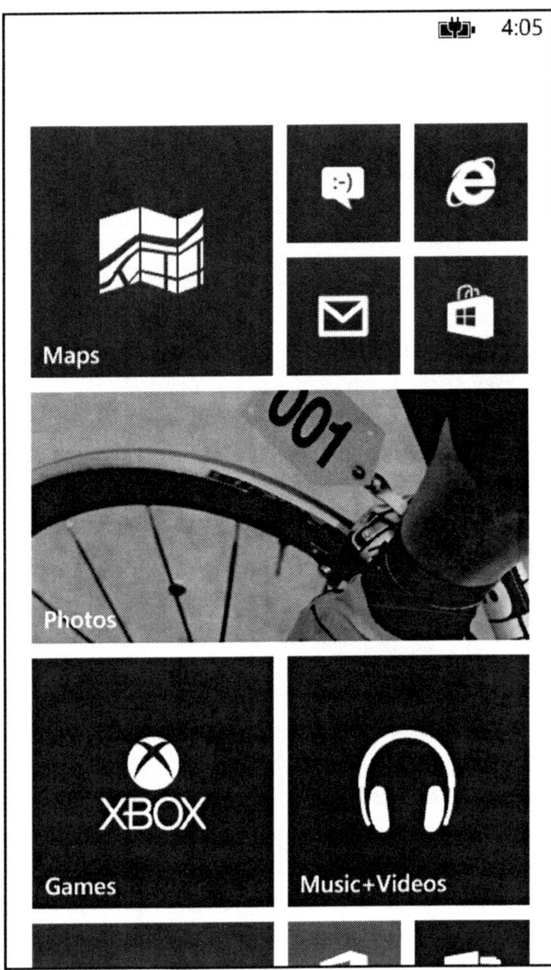

FIGURE 1-1 The distinctive Windows Phone Start screen offers unrivaled personalization.

The user interface

The distinctive Windows Phone user interface (UI) is built upon a set of core principles. Understanding these principles will help you to understand not only why the phone looks the way it does, but how you can build beautiful apps that integrate well into the overall experience. After all, in the mobile app marketplace, it is generally not the app with the most features that wins out, but the one which is the easiest and the most enjoyable to use.

For an in-depth review of these principles, watch the talk from Jeff Fong, one of the lead designers for Windows Phone on Channel9 (*http://channel9.msdn.com/blogs/jaime+rodriguez/windows-phone-design-days-metro*).

Light and simple

The phone should limit clutter and facilitate the user's ability to focus on completing primary tasks quickly. This is one of the principles that drew significant inspiration from the ubiquitous signage in major mass transit systems around the world. In the same way that a subway station uses signs that are bold and simple to comprehend in order to move hundreds of thousands of people through a confined space quickly, Windows Phone intelligently reveals the key information that the user needs among the dozens of things happening at any one time on the phone, while keeping the overall interface clean and pleasing to the eye.

Typography

One element that is common across virtually any user interface is the presence of text. Sadly, it is often presented in an uninteresting way, focusing on simply conveying information rather than making the text itself beautiful and meaningful. Windows Phone uses a distinct font, Segoe WP, for all of its UI. It also relies on font sizing as an indicator of importance. The developer platform provides built-in styles for the various flavors of the Segoe WP typeface, making it simple to incorporate into your app.

Motion

Someone who only experienced the Windows Phone UI through screenshots would be missing out on a significant part of what makes it unique: motion. Tactical use of motion—particularly when moving between pages—not only provides an interesting visual flourish at a time when the user could not otherwise be interacting with the phone, but it also is a clear connection between one experience and the next. When the user taps an email in her inbox and sees the name of the sender animate seamlessly into the next screen, it provides direct continuity between the two views such that there can be no doubt about what is happening.

Content, not chrome

If you've ever tried browsing around a new Windows Phone that has not yet been associated with a Microsoft Account, you'll find that there isn't very much to look at. Screen after screen of white text on a black background (or the reverse if the phone is set to light theme), punctuated only by the occasional endearing string—"It's lonely in here."—encouraging you to bring your phone to life. The moment when you sign in with a Microsoft Account, however, everything changes. The phone's UI recedes to the background and your content fills the device; contacts, photos, even your Xbox Live avatar all appear in seconds and help to make your phone incredibly personal.

Honesty in design

This is perhaps the most radical of the Windows Phone design principles. For years, creators of graphical user interfaces (GUIs) have sought to ease the transition of users moving critical productivity tasks from physical devices to software by incorporating a large number of *skeuomorphic* elements in their designs. Skeuomorphic elements are virtual representations of physical objects, such as a legal pad for a note-taking app or a set of stereo-like knobs for a music player. Windows Phone instead opts for a look that is "authentically digital," providing the freedom to design UI that's tailored to the medium of a touch-based smartphone, breaking from the tradition of awkwardly translating a set of physical elements into the digital realm.

The role of apps

In addition to its distinctive UI, Windows Phone takes a unique approach to the role of Windows Phone Store apps in the experience. Historically, mobile operating systems only provided simple entry points for users to start apps—Apple's iPhone is the canonical example of this, with each app able to display one and only one icon on the phone's home screen. Although this model is simple and clean, it creates a disjointed environment that obstructs how users want to interact with their content.

With Windows Phone, Microsoft made an explicit shift from the app-focused model to a content and experience-focused model, in which the user is encouraged to think primarily about what he wants to do, rather than how he wants to do it. Something as simple as making a phone call, for example, should not require remembering which cloud services your friend is a member of so that you can start the appropriate app to look up her phone number. Rather, you should simply be able to launch a unified contacts experience which aggregates information from all of your apps and services.

The content and experience-focused approach doesn't make Windows Phone Store apps less important, it just changes how they fit in the experience. Windows Phone provides an immersive "hub" experience for each of the primary content types on the phone—photos, music, people, and so on—and each of these hubs offers a rich set of extensibility points for apps to extend the built-in experience. These extensibility points offer additional ways for users to invoke your app, often with a specific task in mind for which you might be uniquely positioned to handle. Table 1-1 lists the extensibility points supported in Windows Phone 7.1 and Windows Phone 8.

Consider photos as an example. There are thousands of apps in the Windows Phone Store that can do something with photos: display them, edit them, or post them to social networks. In a purely app-focused world, the user must decide up-front which tasks he wants to perform and then remember which app would be the most appropriate for that task. In the Windows Phone model, he simply starts the Photos hub, in which he will not only see all of his photos, aggregated across numerous sources, but all of the apps that can do something with those photos. Figure 1-2 shows an example of the photos extensibility in Windows Phone, with "My Photos App" registering as a photo editor, which the user can access through the Edit entry on the app bar menu for a given photo.

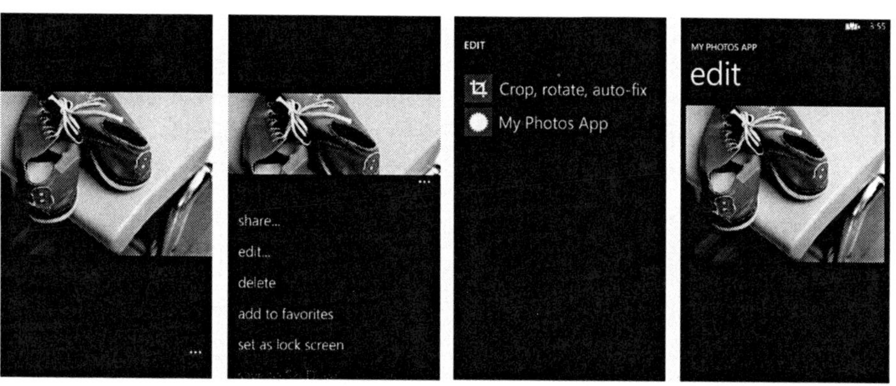

FIGURE 1-2 With Windows Phone, apps can extend built-in experiences such as the photo viewer.

TABLE 1-1 Windows Phone extensibility points

App	Extensibility point	Windows Phone 7.1	Windows Phone 8.0
Music & Videos	Now playing tile	✓	✓
Music & Videos	History list	✓	✓
Music & Videos	New List	✓	✓
Photos	Apps pivot	✓	✓
Photos	Photo viewer – share	✓	✓
Photos	Photo viewer – apps	✓	
Photos	Photo viewer – edit		✓
Search	Search quick cards	✓	✓
Wallet	Wallet items—coupons, transactions, loyalty cards		✓
Lock screen	Background photo		✓
Lock screen	Quick status		✓
Lock screen	Detailed status		✓
Speech	Voice commands		✓
People	Custom contact stores		✓
Camera	Lenses		✓
Maps	Navigation		✓

Windows phone architecture

Now that you understand the user experience (UX) philosophy that drives Windows Phone, it's time to dig a little bit deeper and review some of the core parts of the phone's architecture.

Platform stack

No chapter on architecture would be complete without the venerable block diagram, and we don't aim to disappoint. Figure 1-3 shows the basic logical components of the Windows Phone 8 platform.

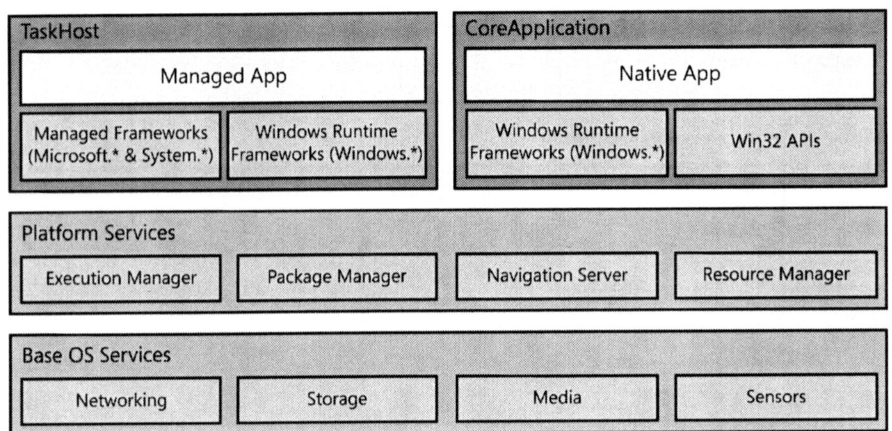

FIGURE 1-3 Windows Phone 8 layers two app models on top of a shared set of platform and OS services.

At the top of the stack sit two distinct app models. The box labeled "TaskHost" represents the XAML app model, which has been the primary model since the launch of Windows Phone 7. To its right is a box labeled "CoreApplication," a new app model for Windows Phone, which is a subset of the new Windows 8 app model. In the Windows Phone 8 release, this app model only supports pure native apps using Direct3D for UI.

Note Although Win32/COM APIs are only shown in the CoreApplication box in Figure 1-3, they are actually callable by managed apps, as well, as long as they are wrapped in a custom Windows Runtime component.

The two app models rely on a shared set of core platform services. For the most part, Store apps only ever see these services indirectly, but because they play a major role in ensuring that those apps work properly and, after all, this is an "Internals" book, we should explore them briefly.

- **Package Manager** The Package Manager is responsible for installing/uninstalling apps and maintaining all of their metadata throughout the app lifecycle. It not only keeps track of which apps are installed and licensed, it also persists information about any app tiles that the user might have pinned to the Start screen and the extensibility points for which an app might have registered so that they can be surfaced in the appropriate places in the OS.
- **Execution Manager** The Execution Manager controls all of the logic associated with an app's execution lifetime. It creates the hosting process for the app to run in and raises the events associated with app startup/shutdown/deactivation. It performs a similar task for background processes, which also includes proper scheduling of those tasks.
- **Navigation Server** The Navigation Server manages all of the movement between foreground apps on the phone. When you tap an app tile on the Start screen, you are navigating from the "Start app" to the app you chose, and the Navigation Server is responsible for relaying that intent to the Execution Manager so that the chosen app can be started. Likewise, when you press and hold the Back key and choose an app that you started previously, the Navigation Server is responsible for telling the Execution Manager which app to reactivate.
- **Resource Manager** The Resource Manager is responsible for ensuring that the phone is always quick and responsive by monitoring the use of system resources (especially CPU and memory) by all active processes and enforcing a set of constraints on them. If an app or background process exceeds its allotted resource pool, it is terminated to maintain the overall health of the phone.

All of this is built on top of a shared Windows Core, which we will describe in more detail later in this chapter.

App types

So far, we've been referring to Windows Phone apps generically, as if they were all built and run in basically the same way. In fact, Windows Phone 8 supports several different app flavors, depending on your needs. These are described in Table 1-2.

TABLE 1-2 Windows Phone 8 app types

App type	Description	Languages supported	UI framework	APIs supported
XAML	The most common app type for Windows Phone 7.x. These apps are exclusively written in XAML and managed code.	C# Visual Basic	XAML	Microsoft .NET Windows Phone API Windows Runtime API
Mixed mode	These apps follow the XAML app structure but allow for the inclusion of native code wrapped in a Windows Runtime component. This is well-suited for apps for which you want to reuse an existing native library, rather than rewriting it in managed code. It is also useful for cases in which you want to write most of the app in native code (including Direct3D graphics) but also need access to the XAML UI framework and some of the features that are only available to XAML apps such as the ability to create and manipulate Start screen tiles.	C# Visual Basic C/C++	XAML Direct3D (via DrawingSurface)	.NET Windows Phone API Windows Runtime API Win32/COM API (within Windows Runtime components)
Direct3D	Best suited for games, pure native apps using Direct3D offer the ability to extract the most out of the phone's base hardware. Also, because they are based on the Windows app model, they offer the greatest degree of code sharing between Windows and Windows Phone.	C/C++	Direct3D	Windows Runtime API Win32/COM API

What about XNA?

In Windows Phone 7.x, there were two basic app types from which to choose: Microsoft Silverlight and XNA. As described earlier, managed Silverlight applications are fully supported in Windows Phone 8, but what of XNA? In short, the XNA app model is being discontinued in Windows Phone 8. Existing Windows Phone 7.x XNA games (and new games written targeting Windows Phone 7.x), which includes a number of popular Xbox Live titles, will run on 8.0, but developers will not be able to create new XNA games or new Silverlight/XNA mixed-mode apps targeting the Windows Phone 8.0 platform. Many of the XNA assemblies, such as *Microsoft.Xna.Framework.Audio.dll*, will continue to work in Windows Phone 8.0, however. Further, Windows Phone 7.x XNA games are allowed to use some features of Windows Phone 8, such as in-app purchase, using reflection.

Background processing

When it comes to background execution on a mobile device, users often have conflicting goals. On one hand, they want their apps to continue providing value even when they're not directly interacting with them—streaming music from the web, updating their Live tile with the latest weather data, or providing turn-by-turn navigation instructions. On the other hand, they also want their phones to last at least through the end of the day without running out of battery and for the foreground app they're currently using to not be slowed down by a background process that needs to perform significant computation.

Windows Phone attempts to balance these conflicting requirements by taking a scenario-focused approach to background processing. Rather than simply allowing apps to run arbitrarily in the background to perform all of these functions, the platform provides a targeted set of multitasking features designed to meet the needs (and constraints) of specific scenarios. It is these constraints which ensure that the user's phone can actually last through the day and not slow down unexpectedly while performing a foreground task.

Background OS services

Windows Phone offers a set of background services that can perform common tasks on behalf of apps.

Background transfer service The Background Transfer Service (BTS) makes it possible for apps to perform HTTP transfers by using the same robust infrastructure that the OS uses to perform operations such as downloading music. BTS ensures that downloads are persisted across device reboots and that they do not impact the network traffic of the foreground app.

Alarms With the Alarms API, apps can create scenario-specific reminders that provide deep links back into the app's UX. For example, a recipes app might provide a mechanism for you to add an alarm that goes off when it's time to take the main course out of the oven. It might also provide a link that, when tapped, takes the user to the next step in the recipe. Not only does the Alarms API remove the need for apps to run in the background simply to keep track of time, but they can take advantage of the standard Windows Phone notification UI for free, making them look and feel like built-in experiences.

Background audio agents

Background audio playback is a classic example of scenario-based background processing. The simplest solution to permitting Windows Phone apps to play audio from the background would be to allow those apps to continue running even when the user navigates away. There are two significant drawbacks to this, however:

- Windows Phone already includes significant infrastructure and UI for playing and controlling background audio using the built-in Music & Video app. Leaving every app to build this infrastructure and UI itself involves a significant duplication of effort and a potentially confusing UX.

- A poorly written app running unconstrained in the background could significantly impact the rest of the phone

To deal with these drawbacks, Windows Phone reuses the existing audio playback infrastructure and invokes app code only to provide the bare essentials of playlist management or audio streaming. By constraining the tasks that an audio agent needs to perform, it can be placed in a minimally invasive background process to preserve both the foreground app experience and the phone's battery life.

Scheduled tasks

Scheduled tasks offer the most generic solution for background processing in Windows Phone apps, but they are still ultimately driven by scenarios. There are two types of scheduled tasks that an app can create, each of which is scheduled and run by the OS, based on certain conditions:

- **Periodic tasks** Periodic tasks run for a brief amount of time on a regular interval—the current configuration is 25 seconds approximately every 30 minutes (as long as the phone is not in Battery Saver mode). They are intended for small tasks which benefit from frequent execution. For example, a weather app might want to fetch the latest forecast from a web service and then update its app tiles.
- **Resource-intensive tasks** Resource-intensive tasks can run for a longer period, but they do not run on a predictable schedule. Because they can have a larger impact on the performance of the device, they only execute when the device is plugged in, nearly fully charged, on Wi-Fi, and not in active use. Resource-intensive agents are intended for more demanding operations such as synchronizing a database with a remote server.

Continuous background execution for location tracking

In the case of background music playback described earlier, there is very little app code that needs to execute after the initial setup is complete. The built-in audio playback infrastructure handles outputting the actual sound, and the user generally performs tasks such as play, pause, and skip track by using the built-in Universal Volume Control (UVC) rather than reopening the app itself. For the most part, all the app needs to do is provide song URLs and metadata (or streaming audio content) to the audio service.

This is not the case for location tracking and, in particular, turn-by-turn navigation apps. These apps generally need to receive and process up-to-date location information every few seconds to determine whether the user should be turning left or right. They are also likely to offer a rich UX within the app such as a map showing the full route to the destination and the time/distance to go, which will encourage the user to frequently relaunch it. As a result, the audio playback model of using a constrained background task is less suitable in this case. Instead, Windows Phone 8 introduces a concept known as Continuous Background Execution (CBE), which simply refers to the ability of the current app to continue running even if the user navigates away, albeit with a restricted API set.

Security model

Modern smartphones are by far the most personal items that people have ever owned—in the palm of your hand are the names, phone numbers, and addresses of all of your family and friends, thousands of photos, location history, email correspondence, and, increasingly, financial information stored in mobile wallet apps. Ensuring that all of this information remains safe while the phone moves between physical locations and navigates a variety of websites and apps requires a robust security model.

The Windows Phone security model is based on the notion of *security chambers*, which are isolated containers in which processes are created and executed. The chamber is the security principal to which access rights are granted in the system. The system grants those rights based on the longstanding security principle of *least privilege*, which holds that an app should not be granted the rights to do anything beyond what is strictly necessary to perform its stated functions. For example, the email app should not have the ability to arbitrarily start the camera and take a picture, because that is clearly not necessary to perform its core function.

So, how does Windows Phone ensure this principle of least privilege? Every security chamber, whether it contains code owned by Microsoft or by an external software developer, starts out with a limited set of privileges—enough to write a self-contained app such as a calculator or a simple game, but not enough to enable the full range of scenarios consumers expect from a modern smartphone. If an app wants to access resources that reside outside of its chamber, such as sending traffic over the network or reading from the user's contacts, it must be explicitly granted that access via *capabilities*. Capabilities act as a set of access control mechanisms that gate the usage of sensitive resources. The system must explicitly grant capabilities to a chamber.

Windows Phone developers encounter these capabilities directly when building their apps because accessing any privileged resource from your app requires including the appropriate capability in your app manifest. The graphical manifest editor includes a Capabilities tab that lists all of the available options, as shown in Figure 1-4.

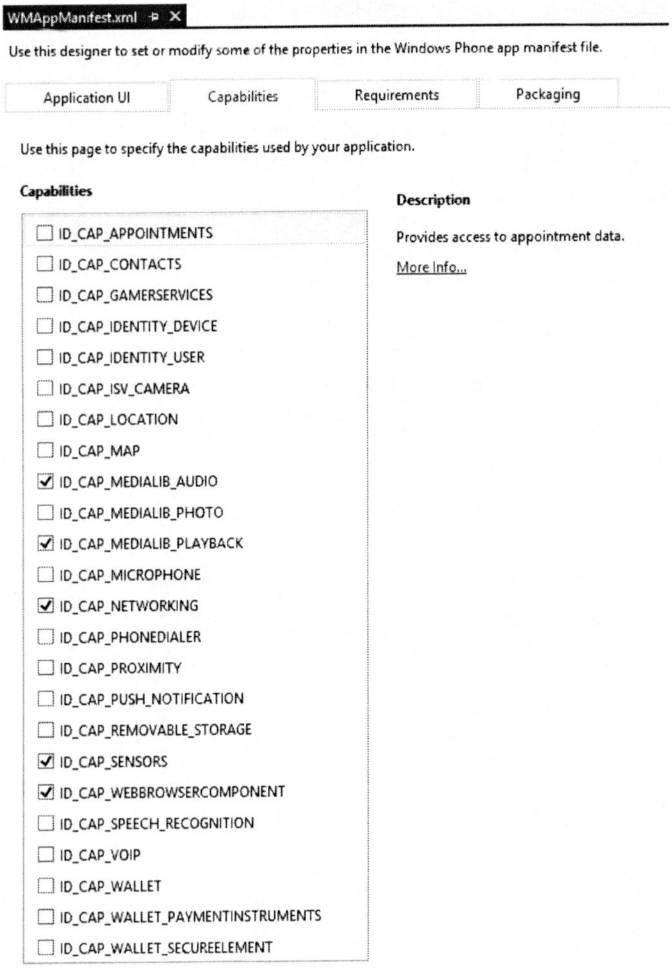

WMAppManifest.xml

Use this designer to set or modify some of the properties in the Windows Phone app manifest file.

Application UI | Capabilities | Requirements | Packaging

Use this page to specify the capabilities used by your application.

Capabilities

- [ ] ID_CAP_APPOINTMENTS
- [ ] ID_CAP_CONTACTS
- [ ] ID_CAP_GAMERSERVICES
- [ ] ID_CAP_IDENTITY_DEVICE
- [ ] ID_CAP_IDENTITY_USER
- [ ] ID_CAP_ISV_CAMERA
- [ ] ID_CAP_LOCATION
- [ ] ID_CAP_MAP
- [x] ID_CAP_MEDIALIB_AUDIO
- [ ] ID_CAP_MEDIALIB_PHOTO
- [x] ID_CAP_MEDIALIB_PLAYBACK
- [ ] ID_CAP_MICROPHONE
- [x] ID_CAP_NETWORKING
- [ ] ID_CAP_PHONEDIALER
- [ ] ID_CAP_PROXIMITY
- [ ] ID_CAP_PUSH_NOTIFICATION
- [ ] ID_CAP_REMOVABLE_STORAGE
- [x] ID_CAP_SENSORS
- [x] ID_CAP_WEBBROWSERCOMPONENT
- [ ] ID_CAP_SPEECH_RECOGNITION
- [ ] ID_CAP_VOIP
- [ ] ID_CAP_WALLET
- [ ] ID_CAP_WALLET_PAYMENTINSTRUMENTS
- [ ] ID_CAP_WALLET_SECUREELEMENT

Description

Provides access to appointment data.

More Info...

FIGURE 1-4 You select the required capabilities for a chamber in the manifest editor.

Because all of the capabilities listed in the manifest editor are available for Windows Phone Store apps to use, you might ask how the principle of least privilege is being maintained. The answer is that it is the user who decides. The capabilities listed in the manifest are translated into user-readable line items on the Windows Phone Store details page for the app when it's eventually published. The user can then decide whether he feels comfortable installing an app which requires access to a given capability—for example, the user should expect that an app that helps you find nearby coffee shops will need access to your location, but he would probably be suspicious if a calculator app made the same request. Figure 1-5 presents the user-readable capabilities for a weather app. As you can probably guess, "location services" corresponds to ID_CAP_LOCATION, and "data services" is the replacement for ID_CAP_NETWORKING.

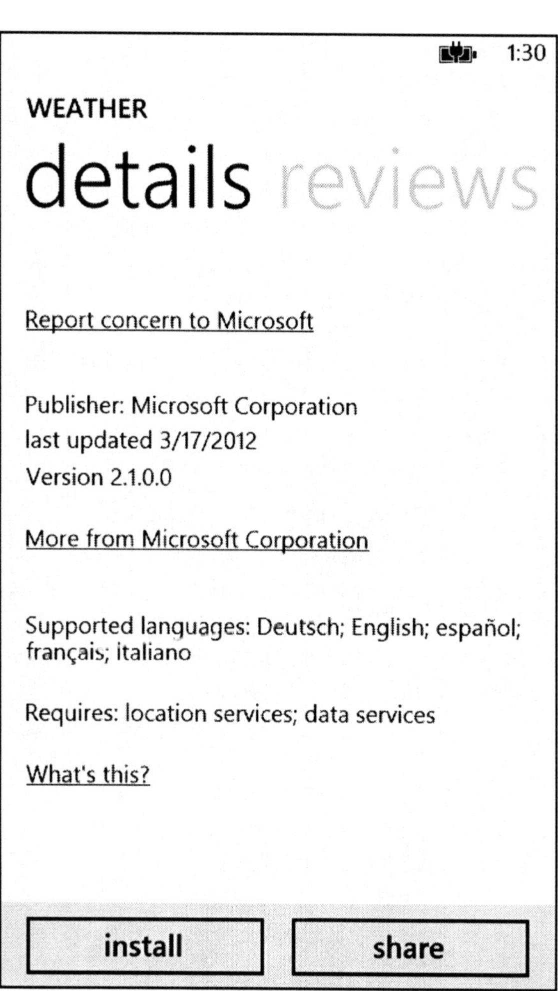

FIGURE 1-5 Security capabilities are displayed as user-readable strings in an app's details page.

Capability detection in Windows Phone 8

It's worth mentioning that Windows Phone 8 has introduced a subtle but important change in how capabilities are detected during app ingestion. In Windows Phone 7.x, the capabilities that the app developer included in the manifest that was submitted to the Store were discarded and replaced with a set determined by scanning the APIs used in the app code. In other words, if you included the ID_CAP_LOCATION capability in your manifest but never used any of the location APIs in the *System.Device.Location* namespace, that capability would be removed from the final version of your XAP package (XAP [pronounced "zap"] is the file extension for a Silverlight-based application package [.xap]) and the Store details page for your app would not list location as one of the resources it needed. Given this Store ingestion step, there was no reason for a developer to limit the capabilities that her app was requesting during development. Anything that she didn't end up using would simply be discarded as part of her submission.

With the introduction of native code support in Windows Phone 8, this approach is no longer feasible, and developers are now responsible for providing the appropriate list of capabilities in their app manifests. If an app fails to list a capability that is required for the functionality it is providing, the associated API calls will simply fail. On the other hand, if an app requests a capability that it doesn't actually need, it will be listed on its Window Phone Store details page, potentially giving the user pause about installing it.

Note For managed code apps, developers can continue to use the CapDetect tool that ships with the Windows Phone SDK to determine which capabilities they need.

Windows and Windows Phone: together at last

Even though the distinctive UX described earlier in this chapter did not change significantly between Windows Phone 7 and Windows Phone 8, there have been dramatic shifts happening below the surface. For the first time, Windows Phone is built on the same technology as its PC counterpart. In this section, we describe the two core parts of that change which impact developers: the shared Windows core, and the adoption of the Windows Runtime.

Shared core

By far the most significant architectural change in Windows Phone 8 is the adoption of a shared core with Windows, but you might be wondering what a "shared core" actually means. In fact, it contains two distinct components. At the very bottom is the Windows Core System, the most basic functions of the Windows OS, including (among other things) the NT kernel, the NT File System (NTFS), and the networking stack. This minimal core is the result of many years of architectural refinement, the goal of which was to provide a common base that could power multiple devices, including smartphones.

Above the Core System is Mobile Core, a set of Windows functionality that is not part of Core System but which is still relevant for a smartphone. This includes components such as multimedia, CoreCLR, and Trident, the rendering engine for Internet Explorer. Figure 1-6 illustrates some of the shared components on which Windows and Windows Phone rely. Note that Mobile Core is only a distinct architectural entity in Windows Phone. Windows contains the same components as Mobile Core, but they are part of a larger set of functionality. This is depicted by a dashed line around the Mobile Core components in the Windows 8 portion of the diagram.

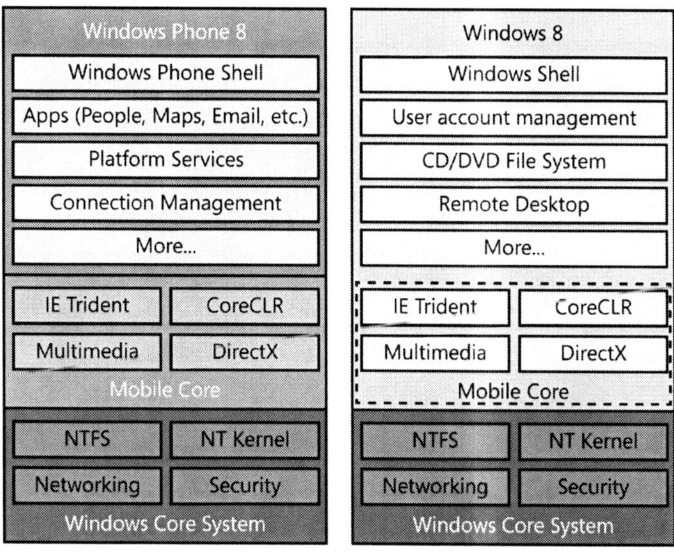

FIGURE 1-6 Windows 8 and Windows Phone 8 share a common core.

Core System and Mobile Core only represent the alignment of Windows and Windows Phone where the two operating systems are running exactly the same code. There are numerous other areas where APIs and behavior are shared, albeit with slightly different implementations to account for the different environments. For example, the location API in Windows Phone automatically incorporates crowd-sourced data about the position of cell towers and Wi-Fi access points to improve the accuracy of location readings, an optimization which is not part of the Windows 8 location framework.

Windows Runtime

For consumers, the most radical change in Windows 8 is the new UI. For developers, it is the new programming model and API set, collectively known as the Windows Runtime. Although Microsoft has delivered a variety of new developer technologies on top of Windows over the years (most notably .NET), the core Windows programming model has not changed significantly in decades. The Windows Runtime represents not just a set of new features and capabilities, but a fundamentally different way of building Windows apps and components.

The Windows Runtime platform is based on a version of the Component Object Model (COM) augmented by detailed metadata describing each component. This metadata makes it simple for Windows Runtime methods and types to be "projected" into the various programming environments built on top of it. In Windows Phone, there are two such environments: a CoreCLR-based version of .NET (C# or Visual Basic), and pure native code (C/C++). We will discuss the Windows Runtime throughout the book, covering both consumption of Windows Runtime APIs from your apps as well as creation of new Windows Runtime components.

Note Even though the core architecture of the Windows Runtime and many of the APIs are the same for Windows and Windows Phone, the two platforms offer different versions of the API framework which sits on top of it. For instance, Windows Phone does not implement the *Windows.System.RemoteDesktop* class, but does add some phone-specific namespaces such as *Windows.Phone.Networking.Voip*. The term Windows Phone Runtime is sometimes used in documentation and in Visual Studio project templates to highlight this difference. However, since the core technology is the same and the differences are obvious in context, we will use the term Windows Runtime throughout the book.

Building and delivering apps

Now that you understand the fundamentals of Windows Phone, it's time to start looking at how you can build and deliver apps that run on it.

Developer tools

Everything you need to get started building Windows Phone 8 apps is available in the Windows Phone 8 SDK, which is available as a free download from the Windows Phone Dev Center at *http://dev.windowsphone.com*. In particular, the Windows Phone 8 SDK includes the following:

- Microsoft Visual Studio 2012 Express for Windows Phone
- Microsoft Blend 2012 Express for Windows Phone
- The Windows Phone device emulator
- Project templates, reference assemblies (for managed code development), and headers/libraries (for native code development)

As with previous versions of the Windows Phone SDK, Visual Studio Express and Blend Express can be installed on top of full versions of Visual Studio and Blend, seamlessly merging all of the phone-specific tools and content directly into your existing tools. Throughout the book, we will refer to Visual Studio Express 2012 for Windows Phone as the primary development environment for Windows Phone 8, but everything we describe will work just as well with any other version of Visual Studio as soon as you have the Windows Phone 8 SDK installed.

Note Visual Studio 2012, including Visual Studio 2012 Express for Windows Phone, can only be installed on Windows 8.

Windows Phone emulator system requirements

The Windows Phone 8 SDK includes a new version of the Windows Phone emulator for testing apps directly on your desktop. The new emulator is built on the latest version of Microsoft Hyper-V, which requires a 64-bit CPU that includes Second Level Address Translation (SLAT), a memory virtualization technology included in most modern CPUs from Intel and AMD.

To check if your CPU supports SLAT, do the following:

1. Download the Coreinfo tool from *http://technet.microsoft.com/en-us/sysinternals/cc835722.*
2. Open a command prompt as an administrator. From the Start menu, type **cmd** to find the command prompt, right-click it, and then choose Run As Administrator.
3. Navigate to the location where you downloaded Coreinfo and run **CoreInfo -v**.
4. Look for a row labeled EPT (for Intel CPUs) or NP (for AMD). If you see an asterisk, as shown in Figure 1-7, you're all set. If you see a dash, your CPU does not support SLAT and will not be capable of running the new Windows Phone emulator. Note that if you have already activated Hyper-V on your computer, you will see an asterisk in the HYPERVISOR row and dashes elsewhere. In this case, you can safely ignore the dashes because your computer is already prepared to run the Windows Phone Emulator.

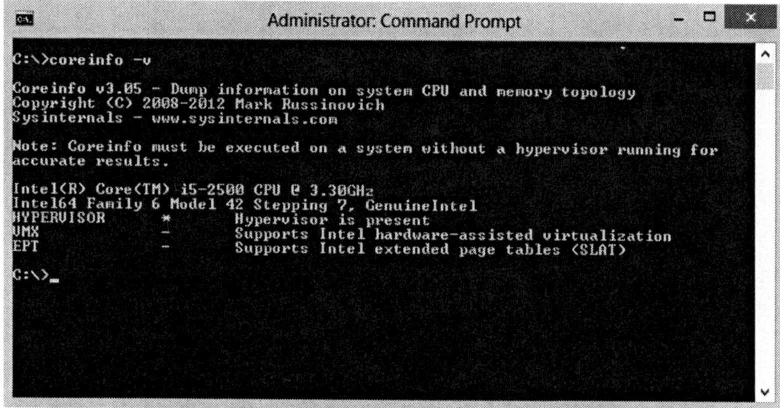

FIGURE 1-7 Use the free Coreinfo tool to determine if your computer can run the new Windows Phone emulator.

Note SLAT is required only to run the Windows Phone emulator. You can still build Windows Phone 8 apps on a non-SLAT computer; you will simply need to deploy and test them on a physical device.

Building for Windows Phone 7.x and 8.x

Because Windows Phone 8 requires new hardware, it will take some time for the installed base of Windows Phone 8 devices to surpass that of the existing Windows Phone 7.x phones. During that time, you will likely want to deliver two versions of your app, one for Windows Phone 7.x and one for Windows Phone 8.0. The Windows Phone 8 developer tools have full support for this approach.

In Visual Studio 2012 Express for Windows Phone, you can create new projects for Windows Phone 7.1 and Windows Phone 8.0, and each will be deployed to the appropriate emulator image for its target platform. You can also run your Windows Phone 7.1 apps on the Windows Phone 8 emulator to ensure that it behaves as expected—even though Windows Phone 8 is backward-compatible with Windows Phone 7.0 and 7.1 apps, it is always worth verifying that there aren't any nuances in the platform behavior for which you might want to account.

Lighting up a Windows Phone 7.1 app with new tiles

To truly take advantage of the new platform features in Windows Phone 8, you must build a version of your app which explicitly targets Windows Phone 8.0. Because there is some additional overhead to creating and managing a separate XAP for version 8.0, Windows Phone 8 allows Windows Phone 7.1 apps to create and manage the new Live tile templates available in the latest release. This approach is based on reflection and is described in detail in Chapter 13, "Porting to Windows Phone 8 and multitargeting."

App delivery

Windows Phone 7.x offered a single, broad mechanism for distributing apps: the Windows Phone Store (previously, the Windows Phone Application Marketplace). In Windows Phone 8, the Windows Phone Store will continue to be the primary source of apps for most customers. However, the distribution options have been expanded to include additional channels for distributing enterprise apps—enterprise customers will be able to deliver apps to their employees via the Internet, intranet, email, or by loading them on a microSD card and inserting the card into the phone. The options for app deployment in Windows Phone 8 are depicted in Figure 1-8.

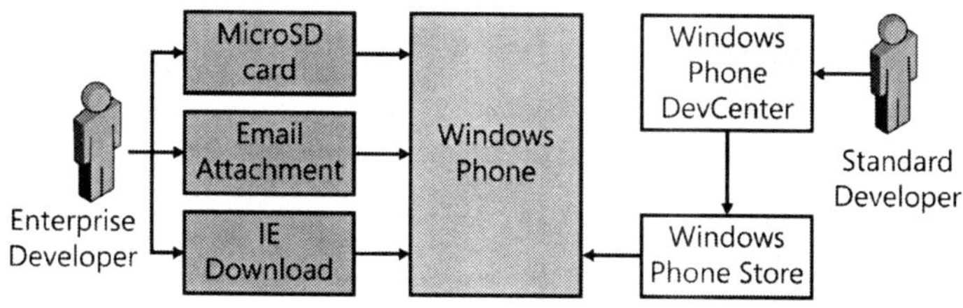

FIGURE 1-8 Windows Phone 8 adds multiple enterprise deployment options.

If you're familiar with any flavor of .NET technology, you know that building a project doesn't generally convert your code into something that's directly executable by a CPU. Rather, it is converted into Microsoft Intermediate Language (MSIL), a platform-independent instruction set, and packaged into a dynamic-link library (DLL). In the case of Windows Phone, these DLLs are then added to your app package for delivery to the phone, where it remains until the user launches the app. At that point, the just-in-time (JIT) compiler turns those DLLs into native instructions targeting the appropriate platform—ARM for physical devices and x86 for the Windows Phone emulator.

In Windows Phone 8, this process changes, such that all apps are precompiled as part of the Windows Phone Store submission process. This means that when a user downloads an app from the Windows Phone Store, the app package already contains code that is compiled for ARM. Because no "JITing" is required when the app is starting up or running, users should experience faster app load times and improved runtime performance.

Note Existing Windows Phone 7.1 apps are automatically precompiled in the Windows Phone Store. No action is required from the developers of those apps.

Getting started with "Hello World"

By now, you are well versed in the fundamentals of Windows Phone. Go ahead and file all of that knowledge away, because it's time to get into some code. Those of you who are seasoned Windows Phone developers will no doubt be tempted to skip this section, but you might want to at least ensure that your installation of the Windows Phone Developer Tools is working properly before diving into more advanced topics. In particular, you should try to launch a project in the Windows Phone emulator to ensure that Hyper-V is fully enabled and then navigate to a webpage in Internet Explorer to verify that networking is properly set up.

Creating a project

After you've installed the Windows Phone SDK from the Dev Center, begin by starting Visual Studio. The first screen you see is the Visual Studio Start Page, as demonstrated in Figure 1-9.

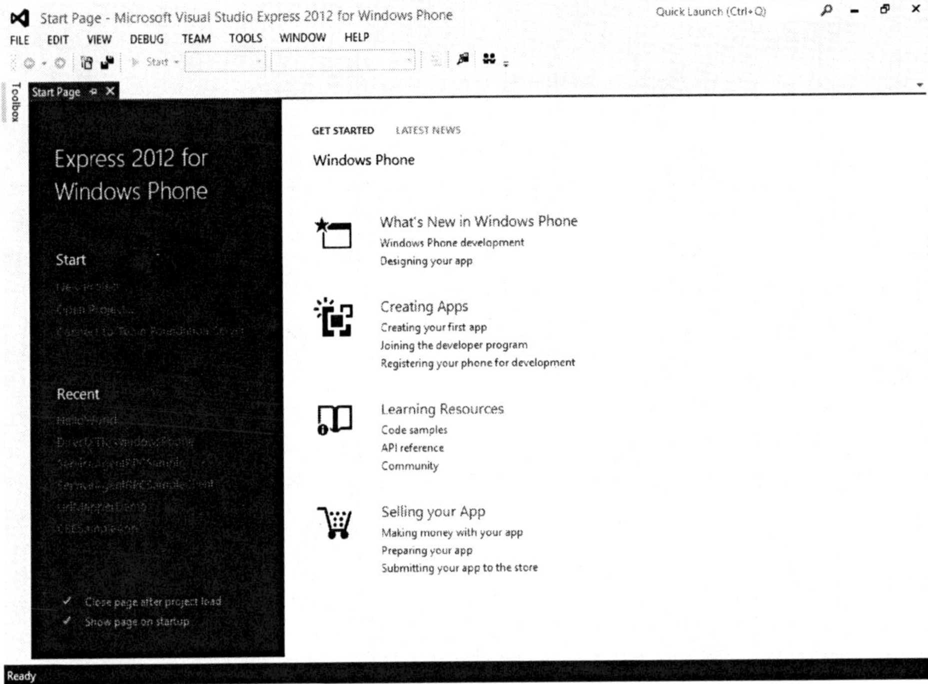

FIGURE 1-9 The first screen you see upon starting Visual Studio is the Start Page, which offers a quick way to begin a new project.

On the left side of the Start Page, in the navigation pane, click New Project. This opens the New Project dialog box in which you can choose the type of project that you want to create and the language in which you want to write it. XAML apps written in C# are the most common type on Windows Phone, so we will start there. Under Templates, click Visual C#, choose Windows Phone App, and then name it **HelloWorld**, as shown in Figure 1-10.

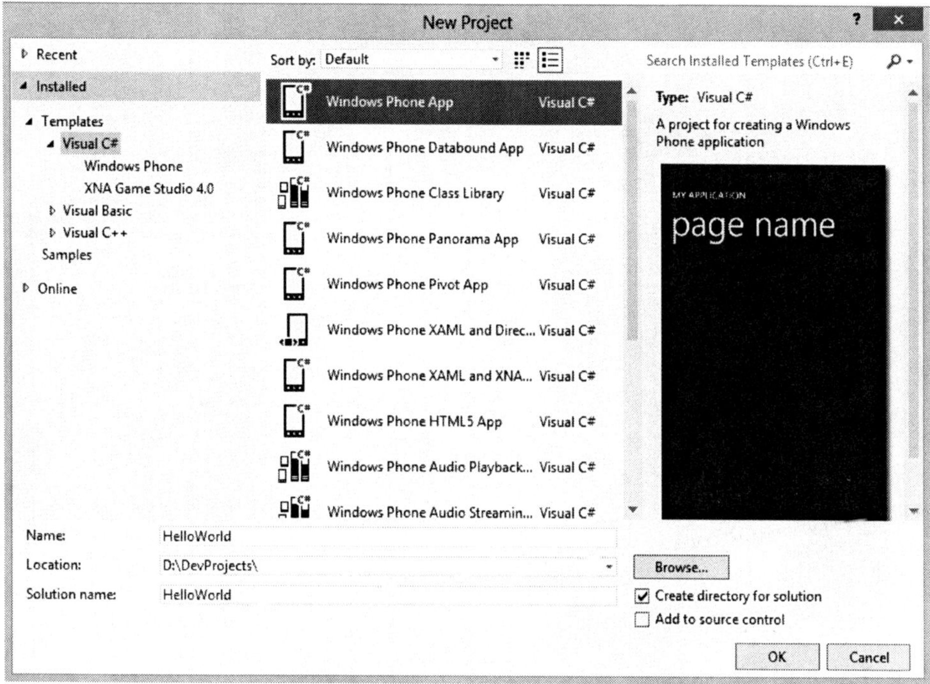

FIGURE 1-10 The New Project dialog box offers a number of templates for creating new apps, class libraries, background agents, and more. To get started, create a simple Windows Phone App in C#.

If your project was created successfully, you should be looking at a screen that resembles Figure 1-11, with *MainPage.xaml* already opened for you.

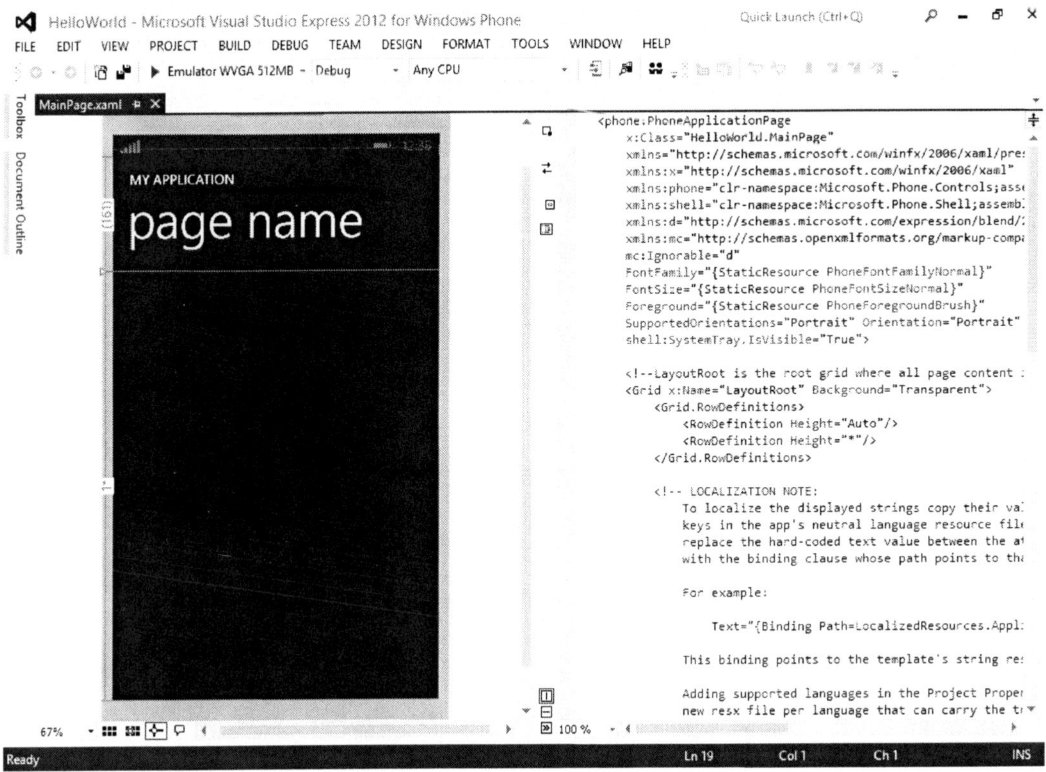

FIGURE 1-11 By default, for a Windows Phone project in C#, Visual Studio starts on *MainPage.xaml*.

Understanding the project structure

MainPage.xaml is one of a number of folders and files included in the default Windows Phone project template. Some of these have special meaning which might not be obvious at first glance, so it's worth taking a quick tour of the standard project structure while you're building your "Hello World" app. Figure 1-12 shows an expanded view of Solution Explorer for "Hello World."

> **Note** The project structure and the list of default files shown in Figure 1-12 is representative of a managed XAML app. The structure of Direct3D apps is discussed in Chapter 25, "Games and Direct3D."

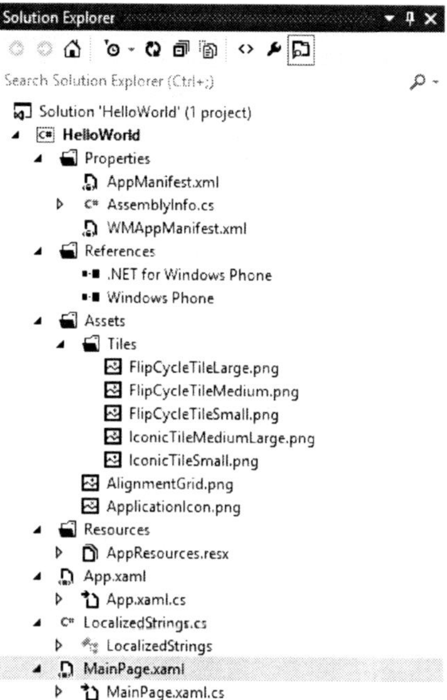

FIGURE 1-12 Windows Phone project templates include a number of special files to get you started.

The first important file is *WMAppManifest.xml*, the app manifest. The app manifest contains all of the information that the OS needs to know about the app to surface it properly on the phone. Some elements of the manifest (for example, hardware requirements) are also used during the Windows Phone Store submission process. The manifest includes (among other things) the following:

- The app name
- A reference to its app list icon and default Start tile
- Its supported resolutions (new in Windows Phone 8)
- The list of security capabilities it requires, such as location and photos, and any hardware requirements, such as NFC or a front-facing camera
- Any extensibility points for which the app is registering—for example, as an entry in the Photos share picker

In Visual Studio Express 2012 for Windows Phone, many of these manifest attributes are now configurable through a simple GUI. However, some features, such as registering for extensibility points, still require direct editing of the underlying XML file.

Tip By default, Visual Studio always displays the GUI tool when you double-click *WMAppManifest.xml*. To configure additional settings with the raw XML editor, in Solution Explorer, right-click the app manifest file. In the shortcut menu that opens, point to Open With and then click XML (Text) Editor. To return to the GUI tool, double-click the file again.

The Assets folder is provided as a location to include the core images that your app should provide. At the root of the Assets folder is a file called *ApplicationIcon.png*. This is a default icon which is shown for your app in the app list. The Tiles subfolder is prepopulated with a handful of icons for use in the FlipCycle and Iconic tile templates, which are discussed in detail in Chapter 14, "Tiles and notifications". All of these files are placeholders intended to show you which images need to be provided. You can (and should) change them to something representative of your app before submitting it to the Windows Phone Store or distributing it to others.

Together, *Resources\AppResources.resx* and *LocalizedStrings.cs* provide the initial framework for developing a fully localized app. Localization is beyond the scope of this book, but it is well documented on MSDN. See *http://msdn.microsoft.com/en-us/library/windowsphone/develop/ff637522(v=vs.105).aspx* for details on building a fully localized Windows Phone app.

App.xaml provides a convenient location to store resources that you intend to use throughout your app, such as UI styles. Its code counterpart, *App.xaml.cs*, contains critical startup code that you should generally not modify and some empty handlers for the core app lifetime events—Launching, Activated, Deactivated, and Closing. If you want to take any action when your app is opened, closed, paused, or resumed, you will need to fill these in. This is discussed in more detail in Chapter 2, "App model and navigation."

MainPage.xaml is the default starting point for your app, which we will return to momentarily to make some changes for our "Hello World" app. You can think of pages in Windows Phone as being equivalent to webpages. They contain both the definition of the UI that will be displayed to the user as well as the bridging code between that UI and the rest of the app's functionality. The role of pages in the Windows Phone navigation model is explored in depth in Chapter 2.

Tip Remember that the project templates are just a starting point for your app; you don't need to be locked in to their structure or content. For instance, if you're following a Model-View-ViewModel (MVVM) pattern, you might want to consolidate all of your views in a single subfolder. If so, don't hesitate to move *MainPage.xaml* to that folder or create a new page to act as your main page in that location. Just remember to update the Navigation Page setting in your manifest so that the system knows where to start your app.

Adding a splash screen

New Windows Phone 7.1 projects also include a file named *SplashScreenImage.jpg*, which, as the name implies, is rendered as a splash screen while the app is loading. Given the improvements in app launch time in Windows Phone 8, it is assumed that most apps will not need a splash screen, so the file has been removed from the default project template. If you believe your app could benefit from a splash screen, simply add a file named *SplashScreenImage.jpg* to the root of the project, with its Build Action set to Content.

Greeting the world from Windows Phone

Now that you understand what all the files in the default project mean, return to *MainPage.xaml*, which has been waiting patiently for you to bring it to life. By default, Visual Studio displays pages in a split view, with the Visual Studio designer on the left and the XAML markup that defines the UI on the right. You can make changes to your page by manipulating controls in the visual designer or by directly editing the XAML.

Start by using the designer to make changes to the default text that the project template has included at the top of the page. Double-click the words MY APPLICATION and change the entry to **HELLO, WORLD**. Likewise, double-click "page name" and change it to **welcome**.

Now, redirect your attention to the right side of the screen, where the XAML markup for your *MainPage* is shown. You will probably be able to spot where the changes you just made were reflected in the underlying XAML. The <StackPanel> element with the name *TitlePanel* should now look like this:

```
<StackPanel x:Name="TitlePanel" Grid.Row="0" Margin="12,17,0,28">
  <TextBlock Text="HELLO, WORLD" Style="{StaticResource PhoneTextNormalStyle}" Margin="12,0"/>
  <TextBlock Text="welcome" Margin="9,-7,0,0" Style="{StaticResource PhoneTextTitle1Style}"/>
</StackPanel>
```

Directly below the *TitlePanel*, you should find a *Grid* element called *ContentPanel*. Replace this element with the following XAML:

```
<StackPanel x:Name="ContentPanel" Grid.Row="1" Margin="12,0,12,0">
      <TextBlock
           x:Name="helloTextBlock"
           Text="Hello from Windows Phone 8!"
           Foreground="{StaticResource PhoneAccentBrush}"
           Grid.Row="0"
           HorizontalAlignment="Center"/>

     <Button
          x:Name="goodbyeButton"
          Content="Say goodbye!"
          Grid.Row="1" Click="goodbyeButton_Click"/>
</StackPanel>
```

This markup creates a simple *StackPanel* in your app, which is then filled with a *TextBlock* and a *Button*. The *TextBlock* contains the critical greeting, whereas the *Button* suggests that the meeting might not last very long. You use a *StackPanel* in this case because it is a simple and efficient way of displaying a set of visual elements in a horizontal or vertical arrangement.

As mentioned earlier, a page contains both the markup describing how the UI looks and the connective code that bridges the gap between the UI and the rest of the app's logic. In this case, the button acts as your first glimpse into that code. Double-click the *Button* in the Visual Studio designer. This opens *MainPage.xaml.cs*, which is known as a *code-behind* file because, as its name implies, it contains the code behind a given page. A code-behind file is created automatically for every page you create in a managed Windows Phone project.

You will notice that Visual Studio has not only opened the code-behind file, but it has taken the liberty of creating a click event handler (named *goodbyeButton_Click*) for the button that you added to your page. You will use this event handler to add some code that makes your app actually do something.

Note It might seem odd to be handling "click" events in an app built for an exclusively touch-based platform. The reason is that the managed UI framework for Windows Phone is primarily based on Microsoft Silverlight, which was initially built as a web browser plugin. Because a "tap" in a phone app is semantically equivalent to a click on a web page, there was no compelling reason to rename the event.

Add the following code to the click event handler:

```
helloTextBlock.Visibility = System.Windows.Visibility.Collapsed;
goodbyeButton.IsEnabled = false;
```

As you can probably discern, this code does two things: it makes your "Hello from Windows Phone 8!" text disappear, and it disables your button. To be sure, it's time to run the app.

Cross your fingers and press F5.

Within a few seconds, you should see the Windows Phone Emulator starting up. By default, Windows Phone 8 projects target the WVGA 512MB emulator, meaning a virtualized version of a Windows Phone 8 device with a WVGA (800x480) screen and 512 MB of memory. You can easily change this on a drop-down menu on the Visual Studio toolbar, as shown in Figure 1-13.

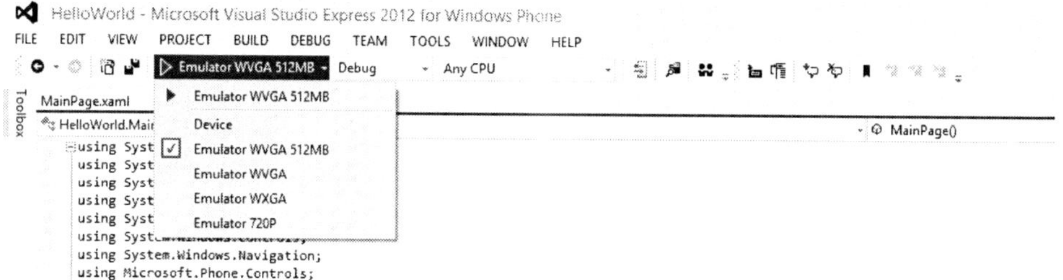

FIGURE 1-13 By default, Visual Studio deploys Windows Phone 8 projects to a WVGA 512MB emulator. You can change this target through a drop-down in the toolbar.

If all has gone according to plan, you should see your app running in the emulator, with your *MainPage* displayed and ready. Go ahead and click the Say Goodbye! button and you should see your "Hello from Windows Phone 8!" text disappear and your button become dimmed, indicating that it's been disabled.

Deploying to a Windows Phone device

The Windows Phone Emulator is sufficient for most of the app development you will do, especially while learning about the platform, as you'll be doing throughout this book. After you begin building a real app that you intend to submit to the Windows Phone Store, however, you will want to deploy it to a real device.

The first step in deploying to a device is registering as a developer in the Windows Phone Dev Center at *http://dev.windowsphone.com*. After you're registered, you can "unlock" your device for deploying apps by using the Windows Developer Registration Tool, which is included in the Windows Phone SDK. Simply connect your device to your computer via USB, run the tool, and then enter your Microsoft Account details. Within a few seconds, your device will be ready for deployment directly from Visual Studio.

The Windows Phone Toolkit

Windows Phone provides most of the core platform controls, such as *Button*, *TextBox*, *Pivot*, and *Panorama* directly in the SDK. However, some controls and UI behaviors that are commonly found in the built-in apps are not available in the SDK. For example, the SDK does not include controls that mimic the built-in time picker or context menu, which are shown in Figure 1-14.

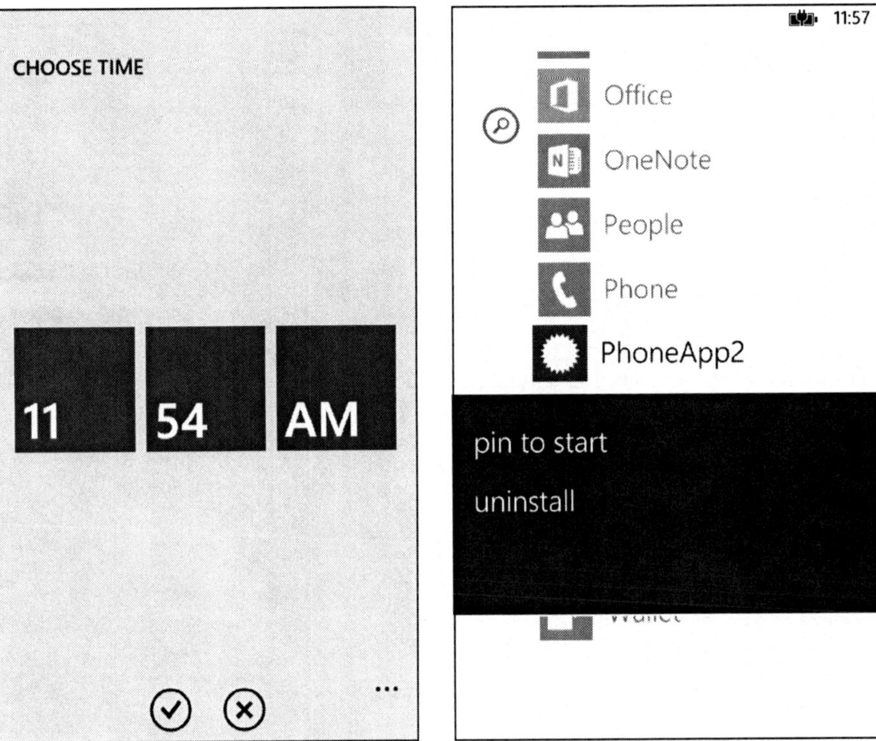

FIGURE 1-14 Many standard Windows Phone controls are not included in the SDK.

Instead, many of these controls are shipped separately from the main SDK in the Windows Phone Toolkit, which is built and maintained by the same team that creates the SDK controls. The advantage of this approach is that the toolkit can be updated more frequently than the SDK can, making it possible to fix bugs, improve performance, and add new controls on a regular basis. The toolkit is available via NuGet, a package manager included by default in Visual Studio 2012, which enables you to add libraries directly to your project. To install the Windows Phone Toolkit through NuGet, select Tools | Library Package Manager | Package Manager Console in Visual Studio. When the console has loaded, enter the following command at the prompt:

PM > **Install-Package WPToolkit**

Within a few seconds, the toolkit will be downloaded and added to your project. To begin using the toolkit controls and behaviors within your XAML, you must add a prefix for the toolkit's namespace to your page as shown:

```
<phone:PhoneApplicationPage
    x:Class="HelloWorld.MainPage"
    xmlns="http://schemas.microsoft.com/winfx/2006/xaml/presentation"
    xmlns:x="http://schemas.microsoft.com/winfx/2006/xaml"
    xmlns:phone="clr-namespace:Microsoft.Phone.Controls;assembly=Microsoft.Phone"
    xmlns:shell="clr-namespace:Microsoft.Phone.Shell;assembly=Microsoft.Phone"
    xmlns:d="http://schemas.microsoft.com/expression/blend/2008"
    xmlns:mc="http://schemas.openxmlformats.org/markup-compatibility/2006"
    xmlns:toolkit="clr-namespace:Microsoft.Phone.Controls;
                   assembly=Microsoft.Phone.Controls.Toolkit"
    mc:Ignorable="d"
    FontFamily="{StaticResource PhoneFontFamilyNormal}"
    FontSize="{StaticResource PhoneFontSizeNormal}"
    Foreground="{StaticResource PhoneForegroundBrush}"
    SupportedOrientations="Portrait" Orientation="Portrait"
    shell:SystemTray.IsVisible="True">
```

As a simple example of how the toolkit can add some visual polish to your app, we will add the tilt effect to the button in our Hello World solution. The tilt effect, found throughout the Windows Phone user experience, enables clickable controls to tilt in response to the user's touch input. To enable the tilt effect for a particular element in XAML, you simply need to set the *TiltEffect.IsTiltEffectEnabled* attached property to *true* as shown:

```
<Button
     x:Name="goodbyeButton"
     Content="Say goodbye!"
     Grid.Row="1" Click="Button_Click"
     toolkit:TiltEffect.IsTiltEnabled="True"
     />
```

Tip In most cases, you should enable the tilt effect across all clickable elements in your app. To do that, simply attach it to your app's *RootFrame* in the App.xaml.cs file:

```
TiltEffect.SetIsTiltEnabled(RootFrame, true);
```

That's it! If you've made it this far successfully, you should have everything set up correctly and you should be ready for the more detailed topics in the chapters ahead.

Summary

In this chapter, you learned about many of the principles driving the development of Windows Phone, including the distinctive UI, the architectural convergence with Windows, and the importance of developers and apps. These principles will act as the foundation as you proceed through the remainder of the book and delve into the details of specific features.

You were also introduced to the Windows Phone developer tools and SDK, so with "Hello World" in the rearview mirror, it's time to move on.

CHAPTER 2

App model and navigation

This chapter focuses on the Windows Phone app model, including lifecycle events, as well as the page-based navigation model used by the Microsoft Silverlight app framework. Users have come to expect that smartphones offer many of the same apps and overall user experience (UX) as a desktop computer. However, compared to a desktop computer, a phone has significant constraints in terms of memory, processor capacity, disk storage, screen size, input capabilities, and power.

The app platform and the underlying operating system (OS) both execute a number of services in the background, and several of these will be executing at any given period of time. Apart from services, there might also be background tasks running at the same time such as email sync or generic background agents.

Restricted processing power and system memory make it difficult for a phone to run more than one foreground app at the same time, as is common with desktop computers. By the same token, it's really not possible for the user to see multiple app windows on the phone screen at the same time because the screen real estate is so constrained. Nonetheless, the user expects to be able to run multiple apps and to switch seamlessly between them.

Windows Phone resolves these conflicting requirements by carefully managing system resources (primarily CPU and memory) so that priority is given to the app with which the user is directly interacting while simultaneously making it possible for other background tasks to continue, albeit with a smaller set of resources.

As the user navigates between pages in an app, and between apps, the app platform surfaces a number of events. The developer can use these events to make his app more robust and to integrate more closely with the system to provide a seamless UX. Be aware that the lifetime events in the native app model differ slightly (for more information on this see Chapter 23, "Native development").

The app lifecycle

One of the advantages of the Windows Phone platform is that it is extremely consistent in the way it works. All apps follow the same broad guidelines, which leads to a very predictable UX. These guidelines are as follows:

- There can be multiple apps or agents running at the same time, but only one is active in the foreground, taking over the screen.
- Only the active app (or the user) can initiate navigation from one app to another.
- There can only be one active page at a time, and the only way to activate a page is to navigate to it.
- The user can always tap the hardware Start button to switch from the current app to the Start app.
- The user can always tap the hardware Back button to return to the previous screen or dismiss temporary UI. This navigates backward—either to the previous page in the current app or to the previous app if the user is currently on the first page of an app.
- Whenever the user returns to an app after navigating forward, away from the app (including using a Launcher or Chooser), it should appear to be in the same state as when the user left it, not as a fresh instance.

Note The Continuous Background Execution (CBE) feature introduced in Windows Phone 8 adds another dimension to the app lifecycle and navigation behavior. This is discussed in more detail in Chapter 18, "Location and maps."

There are several ways by which a user can start an app, including via a toast notification, from an extensibility point, from the app list, or from a pinned tile on the Start screen. If the user navigates away from an app, and if it is not a CBE app, the app will be either deactivated or closed. Specifically, if the user navigates away by pressing the Back key, it will be closed; if he navigates away from it by any other mechanism, such as by pressing Start or launching a Chooser, it will be deactivated. The system maintains what is known as a *backstack* of recently deactivated apps as well as a minimal set of information about each app in the backstack so that it can quickly reactivate an app if called upon to do so.

Launching an app creates a new instance of the app and, by convention, always displays the same initial UX, such as a startup menu. Deactivated apps in the backstack can be reactivated by using the Back key or the Task Switcher. Reactivating apps is typically (but not always) faster than launching from scratch and preserves the app's context rather than returning to the startup page.

All Windows Phone Store apps are single-instance, so starting a fresh copy of an app always removes any previous instance from the backstack—unless you apply the resume policy (see the section "Setting a resume policy" later in this chapter). However, this is not the case with certain built-in apps, such as email, for which you can have multiple instances on the backstack.

To ensure a well-performing user interface (UI), the foreground app must be allocated the maximum amount of resources that the system can offer (after carving out a suitable reserve for the OS itself, drivers, and services). On a resource-constrained mobile device, the best way to ensure that this happens is to reclaim resources from apps that are not currently the foreground app.

Internally, an app can go through several logical states as it transitions from the foreground app to the backstack and final termination. From an app developer's perspective, there are two lifetime scenarios to be handled:

- **The Closing case** This is when an app terminates and receives the *Closing* event. This is unambiguous and simple to handle: it happens when a user presses the hardware Back button from the first page in the app, which kills the app instance and the process itself.
- **The Deactivated case** This is when an app is moved to the background and receives the *Deactivated* event. This case is a little more complicated to handle. It happens when the user leaves your app in the backstack and the system has no knowledge as to whether the user might later return to the app. The app must save sufficient transient state to recreate its current UX in case the user returns to the app instance, even if the process has been terminated in the meantime. The app must also save enough persistent state so as not to lose critical user data if the user starts a new instance of the app (for example, after it falls off the backstack). You can further divide the Deactivated case into two scenarios:
  - **Tombstoning** The app is deactivated and the process is killed, but the app instance is maintained. There's nothing actively running or even sitting in memory, but the system remembers the app's critical details and can bring it back to life if needed.
  - **Fast app resume** The app is deactivated and then immediately reactivated, without being tombstoned in between.

When you create a Windows Phone app with Microsoft Visual Studio, the templates generate code that includes stub handlers in the *App* class for the four lifecycle events: *Launching*, *Activated*, *Deactivated*, and *Closing*. To take part in navigation events, you can also optionally override the *OnNavigatedTo* and *OnNavigatedFrom* methods in your derived *Page* class or classes.

This is your opportunity to take part in your app's lifetime management and make informed decisions about when to perform certain operations. At a simple level (and for quick operations), the appropriate actions that your app should take for each lifecycle event (or virtual method override) are summarized in Table 2-1.

TABLE 2-1 Expected behavior during lifecycle events

Class	Event/override	Suitable actions
App	*Launching*	A fresh instance of the app is being started. You should not do anything here that might slow this down.
App	*Deactivated*	The app is being deactivated and the process can be killed. In sequences for which this event is raised, this is your last opportunity to save app state.
App	*Activated*	The app is activating. This is your first opportunity to reload app state.
App	*Closing*	The app is closing. In sequences for which this event is raised, this is your last opportunity to save any unsaved state and clean up. Be aware that you have limited time in which to do anything here.
Any *Page*	*OnNavigatedFrom*	The user is navigating away from this page. This is your last opportunity for this page to save transient page state.
Any *Page*	*OnNavigatedTo*	The user is navigating to this page. At this time, you can load page state.

See Table 2-2 later in this chapter for implementation details of how and where to save and load state. A naïve developer might take the *Launching/Activated/OnNavigatedTo* methods as a good time to perform initialization, and the *OnNavigatedFrom/Deactivated/Closing* events as a good time to persist state and clean up, and leave it at that. As just indicated, it is true that these trigger points are your first or last opportunity to perform such operations. However, a more sophisticated developer understands that although you can perform minimal initialization/termination functionality in these events, you should also adopt a model in which you distribute costly operations to normal running time, outside the critical lifecycle and navigation events. Again, the reason for this is the CPU/memory constraints on a mobile device.

For example, it is a Windows Phone Store certification requirement that the app must show its first screen within 5 seconds of startup, and be responsive to user input within 20 seconds. App initialization can be done in the *Launching* event handler (or even in the *App* class constructor), but you should limit this to only essential work and defer as much as possible to a later point to provide the best UX. You must also complete activation, deactivation, and navigation within 10 seconds, or you will be terminated. So, the various lifecycle events give you an opportunity to take action, but you should design your app so that whatever you do in these events, you do it quickly. The time to do lengthy operations is during normal running, not when you're handling a lifecycle event. Thus, although it might be tempting to persist all of your app state in *Deactivated*, a smart developer will persist state incrementally throughout the session, and not leave it all to the end (unless of course the state and any related computations are very small). Furthermore, your app must be robust, such that it can handle the possibility that anything you do write in your *Deactivated* handler might not complete before you're shut down, which risks leaving incomplete or even corrupt data to read when you start again.

If you need to load content, you should do this "just in time." That is to say, just before it is actually needed, and no sooner. If you need to save content, you should do this as soon as possible. This model typically means loading only enough content for the current page you are on, and saving that content when you navigate away. The data model used by an app should support this incremental load/save model, not a monolithic structure that must be serialized/deserialized in one go, because it clearly won't scale as the user adds more and more data over time.

Normal termination

When the user taps the Back button from the first page of an app, the system raises a *Closing* event on the app, and the app's hosting process is then terminated. Figure 2-1 illustrates the app lifecycle sequence, from initial launch, through loading and navigating, to the app's first (or only) page, to final termination.

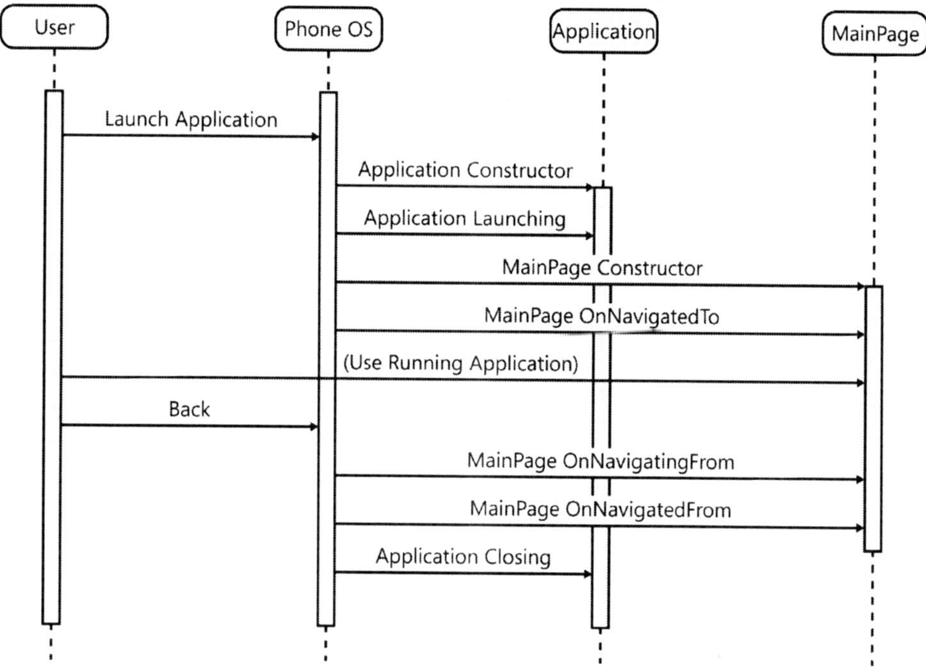

FIGURE 2-1 A diagram of the closing (normal termination) sequence.

App deactivated—fast app resume

The second lifetime scenario (see Figure 2-2) is when the user runs an app and then performs some action that navigates forward away from the app; for example, by tapping the Start button. In this sequence, the app process is not terminated; it is deactivated (and the system sends it a *Deactivated* event), and it remains in memory, taking up space. This is what makes it possible for the system to reactivate and resume the app quickly, if and when the user navigates back to it.

The deciding factor here is performance. It is not efficient for the app platform to terminate the process and bring up a new one if the old one is still viable.

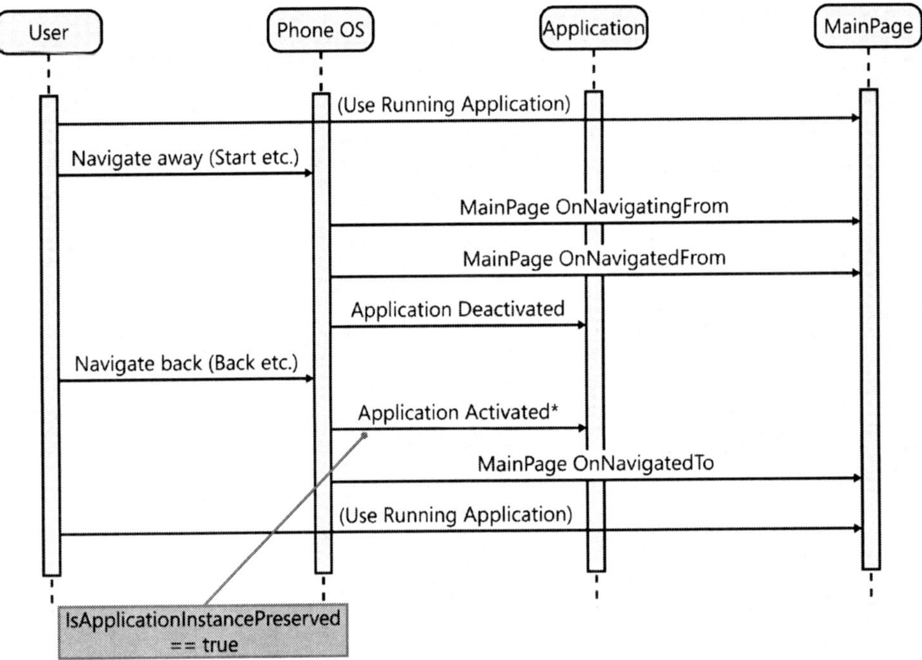

FIGURE 2-2 This diagram portrays the deactivation (fast app resume) sequence.

App deactivated—the tombstone case

The tombstone case (see Figure 2-3) is a variation on the deactivated case, in which the app's hosting process is terminated. The app instance is still valid, because the system keeps any saved state information in such a way that it can quickly reactivate the app (and send it an *Activated* event) if the user subsequently navigates back (via the Back button or the task switcher) to go back to it.

When an app is terminated in this way, all of the resources that it was consuming (CPU and memory) are taken away from it and made available to other processes. The system retains the barest minimum it needs to be able to reactivate the app at a later point, should it be called upon to do so. There will be an entry for the app in the backstack, including a note of the page within the app that the user was last viewing, the intra-app page backstack, and some limited transient state stored by the app itself (such as the state of UI controls).

If the tombstoned app is later reactivated, the lifecycle events are similar to the fast app resume case, except that the app and page constructors are called again.

Note The exact sequence of events varies according to circumstances. There are only two guarantees for a given app instance: *Launching* always happens exactly once, and *Activated* is always preceded by *Deactivated*.

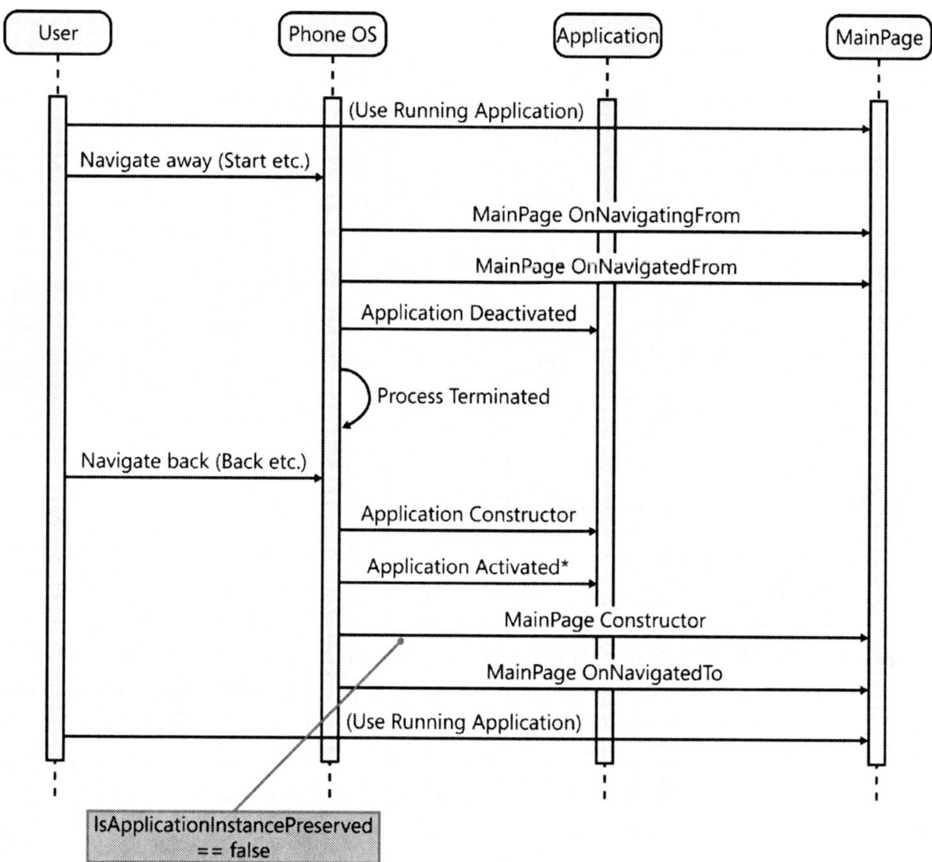

FIGURE 2-3 A typical tombstone sequence.

The sequence diagrams in Figures 2-2 and 2-3 show that there are two critical differences:

- In the fast app resume scenario, the app is maintained in memory, which means that the various app objects are not destroyed after deactivation; therefore, there is no need to run the *App*, *MainPage*, or other constructors upon subsequent activation. In the tombstone scenario, the app's memory is reclaimed by the system, so constructors must therefore be run again when the user switches back to the app.
- In the fast app resume scenario, the *IsApplicationInstancePreserved* property is *true* on *Application.Activated*, whereas in the tombstone scenario, the *IsApplicationInstancePreserved* property is *false* on *Application.Activated.*

The diagrams make the simplification that the user was on a page called *MainPage* when she navigated away from the app. In fact, the behavior holds true regardless of which page she was on. The system keeps track of the page she was on and then upon reactivation constructs the page, if necessary (that is, if the app was tombstoned), and invokes the *OnNavigatedTo* method.

The system retains only eight apps on the backstack, including the one that is currently active and including the Start screen app. As soon as the user launches the ninth app, the app at the beginning of the backstack (that is, the one that was used least recently) is discarded completely. In this situation, the discarded app would have received a *Deactivated* event when the user navigated away from it. It does not receive any further events, and there is no indication when it is discarded from the backstack. If memory pressure increases to the point at which the system needs to reclaim memory from deactivated apps, it will first start tombstoning apps from the end of the backstack (but they remain on the backstack and can be reactivated by the user).

A further consideration is resource management. Figure 2-4 shows the sequence when an app is deactivated. In this state, you don't want it consuming resources, especially hardware resources such as sensors, and most especially resources such as the camera, which can only be used by one app at a time. The standard *OnNavigatedFrom* and *Deactivated* events are your opportunity to relinquish resources. However, if you do not proactively release resources, the framework will do the job for you. It's best to keep control of this yourself so that you can track which resources you were using and reinstate them as needed, if the app is later reactivated. When an app is deactivated, its resources are detached, and threads and timers are suspended. The app enters a deactivated state in which it cannot execute code, it cannot consume runtime resources, and it cannot consume any significant battery power. The sole exception to this is memory: the deactivated app remains in memory. Note that the work of detaching resources and suspending timers and threads is done by the platform for the app as part of the app framework, but this does not surface any events to the app code itself.

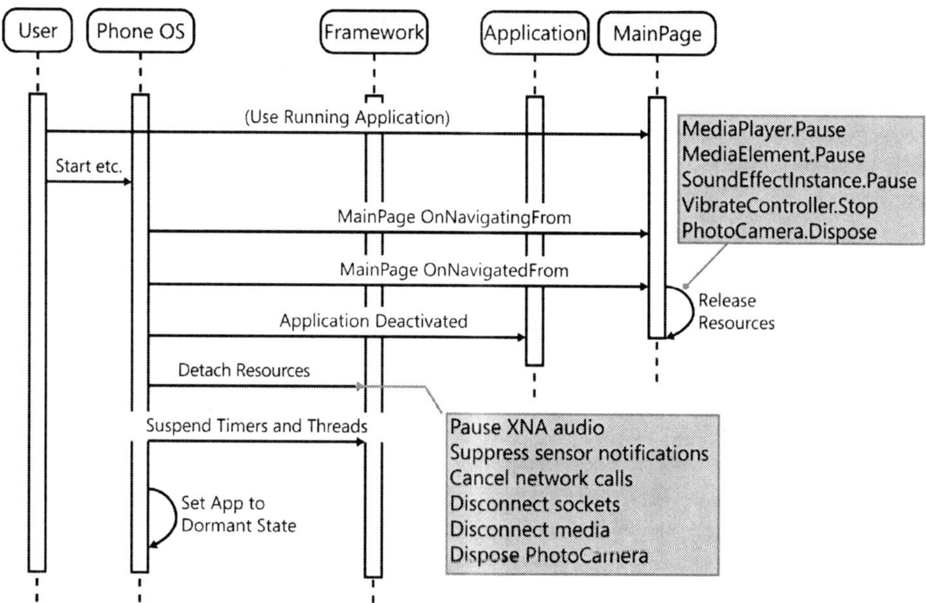

FIGURE 2-4 Bringing an app to the deactivated state.

Conversely, when an app is reactivated from the deactivated state, the framework resumes timers and threads and reattaches some (but not all) resources that it previously detached (see Figure 2-5). The developer is responsible for reconnecting/resuming media playback, HTTP requests, sockets, and the camera.

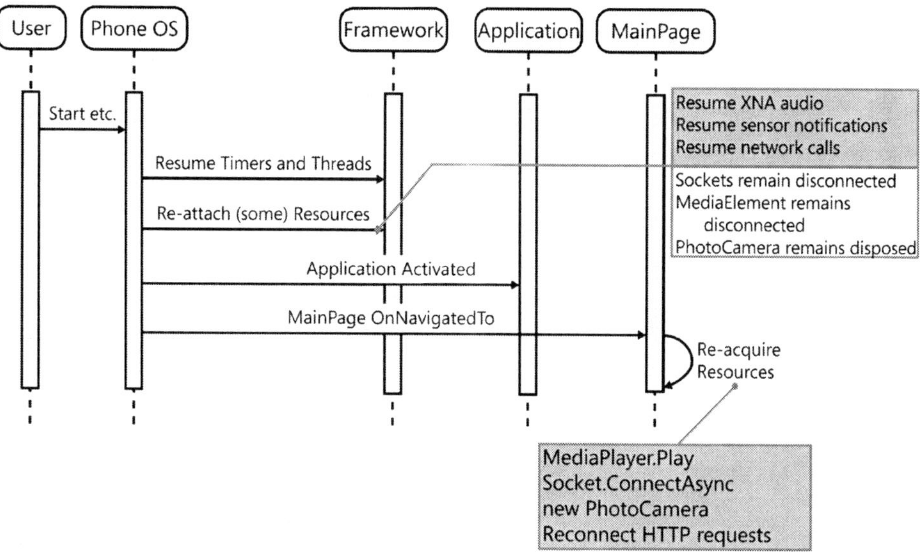

FIGURE 2-5 Resuming an app from the deactivated state.

Note There are two cases for which no lifecycle events are raised: when the app throws an exception that is not handled, and when the app calls *Application.Terminate*. If there is an *UnhandledException* handler in place—which is something the Visual Studio templates insert by default—code execution will jump there. The default handler put in place by Visual Studio merely checks to see if the app is being debugged, and if so, it invokes *Debugger.Break* to break into the debugger. If the app is not being debugged, the exception is then handled in the app platform itself, and the app is immediately terminated and removed from the backstack. *Application.Terminate* causes a rude termination—no events are sent to the app, and the process is killed instantly. This is not generally a useful mechanism for you to use.

The various sequences of lifecycle and navigation events can be challenging to keep straight in your mind. To help internalize the behavior, you can try this hands-on exercise: simply create a new app and put *Debug.WriteLine* statements into each of the interesting events or method overrides, as shown in the example that follows. You can see an example of this in the *TestLifecycle* solution in the sample code.

```
private void Application_Launching(object sender, LaunchingEventArgs e)
{
    Debug.WriteLine("Application_Launching");
}
```

The methods in the *App* class to tag like this include the *App* constructor and the handlers for the *Launching*, *Activated*, *Deactivated*, and *Closing* events. For the *MainPage* class, you can add a *Debug* statement to the constructor. You can then also override the virtual methods *OnNavigatedTo* and *OnNavigatedFrom*, as shown in the following:

```
public MainPage()
{
    Debug.WriteLine("MainPage ctor");
    InitializeComponent();
}

protected override void OnNavigatedTo(NavigationEventArgs e)
{
    Debug.WriteLine("OnNavigatedTo");
}

protected override void OnNavigatedFrom(NavigationEventArgs e)
{
    Debug.WriteLine("OnNavigatedFrom");
}
```

Build the project and then try the following operations:

1. Start the app in the debugger.
2. Tap Start in the emulator to navigate forward away from the app.
3. Tap Back to navigate back to the app.
4. Tap Back again to navigate back out of the app altogether.

This should result in the following output sequence:

```
App ctor
Application_Launching
MainPage ctor
OnNavigatedTo
OnNavigatedFrom
Application_Deactivated
Application_Activated
OnNavigatedTo
OnNavigatedFrom
Application_Closing
```

You should also then set the Tombstone Upon Deactivation While Debugging setting in your project properties (on the Debug tab) and repeat these operations. This should produce a slightly different output sequence. In particular, you will see the *App* and *MainPage* constructors invoked again.

```
App ctor
Application_Launching
MainPage ctor
OnNavigatedTo
OnNavigatedFrom
Application_Deactivated
App ctor
Application_Activated
MainPage ctor
OnNavigatedTo
OnNavigatedFrom
Application_Closing
```

Setting a resume policy

As we've already discussed, assuming your app is running on a device with sufficient memory, the system can maintain a backstack of previously running apps with sufficient context to allow the user to restart any of these apps relatively quickly. If the user taps the hardware Back button to exit from your app, your app is removed from the backstack. In this case, any attempt to start your app will cause a fresh launch. Normally, if the user starts your app explicitly, either via the main app list or via a pinned tile on the Start screen, this will also cause a fresh launch. With Windows Phone 8, you have the option to control this behavior by setting a resume policy.

Here's how this works. In your app manifest, find the entry for the *DefaultTask* and update it to include the *ActivationPolicy* attribute. Set this to *Resume*.

```
<DefaultTask  Name ="_default" NavigationPage="MainPage.xaml" ActivationPolicy="Resume"/>
```

With this change, even if there is an instance of your app in the backstack, when the user launches the app from the app list or Start screen, this forces the system to resume the previous instance. In this case, the *App* constructor is not invoked, and the *Launching* event is not raised. Instead, the first entry point into your app code will be the *Activated* event.

However, notice that the policy is applied as an attribute of the *DefaultTask*. The *DefaultTask* also specifies the *NavigationPage* attribute, and this is set to the startup page for your app. This means that even though the user might resume your app, it will start at the default startup page. In a typical multipage app, the user could have left the previous instance on any arbitrary page, but using a resume activation policy will force it to resume with the default page.

When you create an app by using Visual Studio, the starter code in the *App* class includes a handler method for the *PhoneApplicationFrame.Navigated* event. In this handler, the app checks to see if the *NavigationMode* of the navigation is *Reset*. This will be the case if the user has restarted the app when it was already in the backstack. In this case, the starter code goes on to clear the backstack.

```
private void CheckForResetNavigation(object sender, NavigationEventArgs e)
{
    if (e.NavigationMode == NavigationMode.Reset)
        RootFrame.Navigated += ClearBackStackAfterReset;
}

private void ClearBackStackAfterReset(object sender, NavigationEventArgs e)
{
    RootFrame.Navigated -= ClearBackStackAfterReset;
    if (e.NavigationMode != NavigationMode.New && e.NavigationMode
           != NavigationMode.Refresh)
        return;
    while (RootFrame.RemoveBackEntry() != null)
    {
        ; // do nothing
    }
}
```

What will happen is that the framework will re-activate the app and navigate to the page that was on the top of the backstack. It then defers to the *DefaultTask* setting and executes a second navigation to the default page. For some apps, this is actually exactly what you want; for others it isn't. Exactly what you do here depends on your business logic; for example, instead of clearing the backstack, you might want to cancel the incoming navigation and redirect to another page. Or, you might want to check whether the current state data held in the backstack is still valid, and only clear the backstack if it isn't.

You can see an example of how to work with the resume policy in the *TestResumePolicy* app in the sample code. This app has two pages. In the *App* class *InitializePhoneApplication* method (which is called from the constructor), in addition to hooking up the *Navigated* event for the root frame, this app also hooks up the *Navigating* event, and this will happen before the *Navigated* event. In this handler, in the case where the app is fast-resuming, it simply sets a flag (*isResume*) to indicate that this is a resume activation. Then, when it's invoked again, it checks to see if the navigation *Uri* indicates a navigation to the default page, and if so, it cancels the navigation.

```
private bool isResume = false;

private void RootFrame_Navigating(object sender, NavigatingCancelEventArgs e)
{
    if (e.NavigationMode == NavigationMode.Reset)
    {
        isResume = true;
    }
    else if (e.NavigationMode == NavigationMode.New && isResume)
    {
        isResume = false;
        if (e.Uri.ToString().Contains("/MainPage.xaml"))
        {
            e.Cancel = true;
            RootFrame.Navigated -= ClearBackStackAfterReset;
        }
    }
}
```

Obscured and *Unobscured*

Activation/deactivation happen when the user navigates away from the app and when the app invokes Launchers and Choosers. On the other hand, some external operations merely result in the app becoming temporarily obscured. In this scenario, there is no *NavigatedFrom* or *Deactivated* event. Instead, the system raises an *Obscured* event. A common example of such an external operation is when a notification for an incoming call or a reminder is received.

Note An incoming Short Message Service (SMS) toast does not raise the *Obscured* event.

Obscuring does not cause navigation away from the app—the app continues to run in the foreground—it's just that some higher-priority UI is obscuring the app's UI. Note that this does not cause a frozen app display; the app does actually continue running, executing whatever operations it was performing when it was interrupted.

If you want to handle the *Obscured* and *Unobscured* events, you attach event handlers to the *RootFrame* object. You should also do this in the *App* class constructor, as shown in the following example (and demonstrated in the *TestObscured* solution in the sample code):

```
public App()
{
    UnhandledException += Application_UnhandledException;
    InitializeComponent();
    InitializePhoneApplication();
    InitializeLanguage();
```

```
    RootFrame.Obscured += RootFrame_Obscured;
    RootFrame.Unobscured += RootFrame_Unobscured;
}

private void RootFrame_Obscured(object sender, ObscuredEventArgs e)
{
    Debug.WriteLine("RootFrame_Obscured");
    if (e.IsLocked)
    {
        Debug.WriteLine("IsLocked == true");
    }
}

private void RootFrame_Unobscured(object sender, System.EventArgs e)
{
    Debug.WriteLine("RootFrame_Unobscured");
}
```

The *Obscured* event does not imply that the entire app UI is obscured. In many cases, including for an incoming phone call, the UI is only partially obscured (at least until the call is accepted). Another scenario in which this event is raised occurs when the phone lock screen is engaged. An app can determine whether this is the cause of the obscuring by testing the *IsLocked* property on the *ObscuredEventArgs* object passed in as a parameter to the *Obscured* event handler, as shown in the preceding example.

Keep in mind that the app will not always receive a matching *Unobscured* event for every *Obscured* event. For example, the app does not receive matching events for the scenario in which a user navigates away from the app by pressing the Start button. It's also true in the case for which the *Obscured* event is the result of the lock screen engaging. When the user later unlocks the screen, the app is not sent an *Unobscured* event. So, if you get an *Obscured* event and then the lock screen engages, your app will be deactivated (sent the *Deactivated* event) and then later reactivated.

If you disable the lock screen, you obviously won't get any *Obscured* events for this case, because the screen will not lock. You can disable the lock screen by setting *UserIdleDetectionMode* to *Disabled*, as demonstrated in the code that follows. This statement is generated in the *App* constructor by the standard Visual Studio project templates. The Visual Studio code generation is intended only for debugging scenarios. In general, you should use this setting only after very careful consideration; it is legitimate only for an app that absolutely must continue running, even when the user is not interacting with the phone.

```
PhoneApplicationService.Current.UserIdleDetectionMode = IdleDetectionMode.Disabled;
```

The term "interacting with the phone" normally implies touching the screen, but another common use for this setting is games that are accelerometer driven as opposed to touch driven. In that case, the user is clearly interacting with the phone, even if he's not touching the screen. If you actually need to use the feature in normal situations, you should not set it globally at startup. Instead, you should turn it on only when the user is actively using the feature that requires non-locking, and then turn it off again as soon as he is done with that activity. For example, in a game, you should not disable lock while the user is on a menu screen or has already paused the game; you would turn it on only while he is actively playing the game.

A related setting is *ApplicationIdleDetectionMode*. The system's normal assumption is that if an app is running and the lock screen engages, it is reasonable to deactivate the app. By disabling *ApplicationIdleDetectionMode*, the app can continue to run under screen lock. If you do disable *ApplicationIdleDetectionMode*, the system does not deactivate idle apps. In this case, when the user eventually unlocks the screen again, the app receives the *Unobscured* event.

```
PhoneApplicationService.Current.ApplicationIdleDetectionMode = IdleDetectionMode.Disabled;
```

If you do disable *ApplicationIdleDetectionMode*, you should also do as much as possible to minimize battery consumption. Specifically, you should stop all active timers, animations, use of the accelerometer, GPS, isolated storage, and network. You would then use the *Unobscured* event to reinstate any of those things, as appropriate.

Note In Windows Phone 7.x, the technique of running under lock was used for such features as background audio and background location. Those are now first-class citizens in the platform, so they no longer require running under lock. In Windows Phone 8, therefore, there are very few valid scenarios for which you would use this technique.

The page model

Apart from Direct3D games (and legacy XNA games), Windows Phone apps employ a page-based model that offers a UX that is similar in many respects to the browser page model. The user starts the app at an initial landing page and then typically navigates through other pages in the app. Each page typically displays different data along with different visual elements. As the user navigates forward, each page is added to the in-app page backstack (also called the *journal*) so that she can always navigate backward through the stack, eventually ending up at the initial page. Although the inter-app backstack of app instances is limited to eight apps, there is no hard limit to the number of intra-app pages that can be kept in the page backstack. However, in practice it is uncommon to have more than six or so pages in the backstack; any more than that degrades the UX. Usability studies show that the optimal number is somewhere between four and ten. That doesn't mean that an app can't have dozens or even scores of pages, it just means that the navigation tree should keep each branch relatively short. You should also remember to clean up unused resources on pages in the backstack (such as images or large data context items) because they continue to consume memory and can often be recreated cheaply.

The app can support forward navigation in a wide variety of ways: through *HyperlinkButton* controls, regular *Button* controls, or indeed any other suitable trigger. An app can use the *Navigation Service* to navigate explicitly to a relative URL. Relative URLs are used for navigation to another page within the app. Absolute URLs can be used with *HyperlinkButton* controls to navigate to external web pages via the web browser (Internet Explorer). Backward navigation should typically be done via the hardware Back button on the device. If the user navigates back from the initial page, this must terminate the app, as depicted in Figure 2-6.

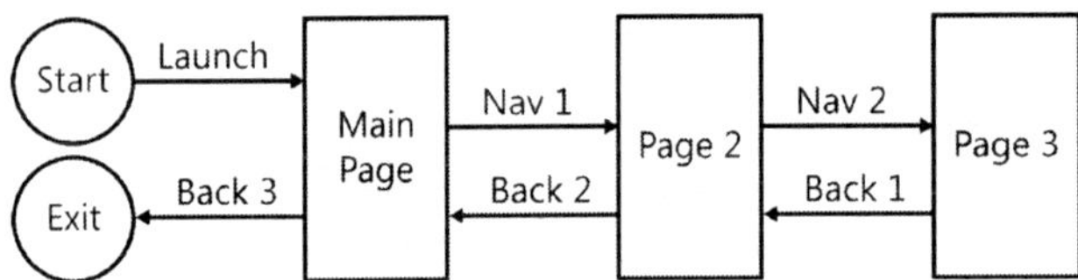

FIGURE 2-6 An overview of intra-app page navigation.

Users can also navigate forward out of an app and into another app. This can be achieved both from within the app via links with external URLs (which use the web browser) or by directly invoking Launchers and Choosers. At any time, the user can navigate away from the app by pressing the hardware Start or Search buttons on the device. Whenever the user navigates forward out of an app, that app is added to the system's app backstack. As the user navigates backward from within an app, she would move backward to that app's initial page and then back out of the app to the previous app in the backstack. Eventually, she would navigate back to the beginning of the backstack. Navigating backward from there takes her to the Start screen.

Here's a simple example. Suppose that a user starts an app. This navigates first to the default page in the app. The user then navigates to page 2 within the app. This is the second navigation. Then, the user taps the Start button. This navigates to the default page in the Start app. From there, the user starts a second app, which navigates to the default page in that second app.

Pressing the Back button from the initial page of the second app takes the user back to the Start app. Pressing Back again takes her back to page 2 in the first app. She would continue to navigate backward within the in-app page backstack until she arrives at the initial page in the first app. After that, pressing Back again takes her back to the Start app, and so on. The user's perspective of this workflow is illustrated in Figure 2-7. It's important to clarify that, internally, each app has its own internal page backstack, which is separate from the platform's app backstack.

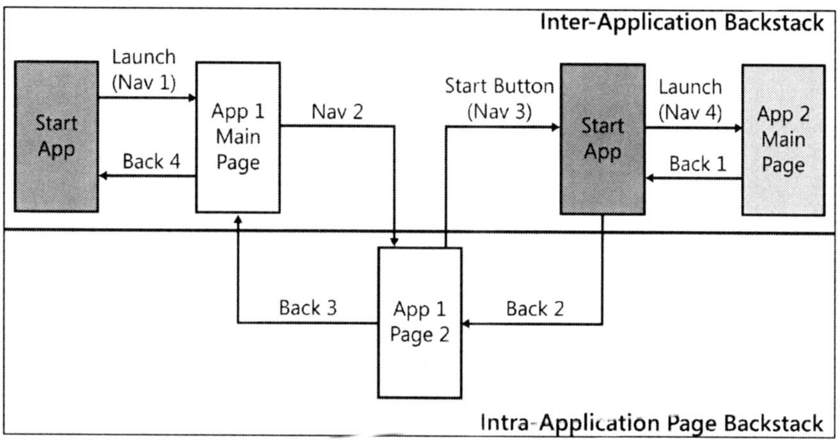

FIGURE 2-7 The inter and intra-app navigation model.

Page creation order

As part of its backstack management, the app platform keeps track of which page (in a multipage app) the user was on when he navigated away. If an app was tombstoned such that the pages need to be reconstructed if the user navigates back to the app, the order of page creation is not necessarily the same as the original order of creation. For example, if the user is on the second page when he navigates away from the app and then goes back, he will end up going back to the second page. This causes the page to be re-created. If he subsequently navigates back to the main page from there, at that point, the main page will be re-created. So, the order of page creation in the app can change according to circumstances. The main or initial page in an app is not always constructed first. In fact, if the user has navigated forward through the in-app page hierarchy and then forward to another app that uses a lot of memory (causing the original app to be tombstoned), and then navigates back to the first app, the pages will be constructed in reverse order. Figure 2-8 shows this for the tombstone behavior; Figure 2-9 illustrates it for the non-tombstone behavior. You can verify this behavior by using the *PageCreationOrder* solution in the sample code.

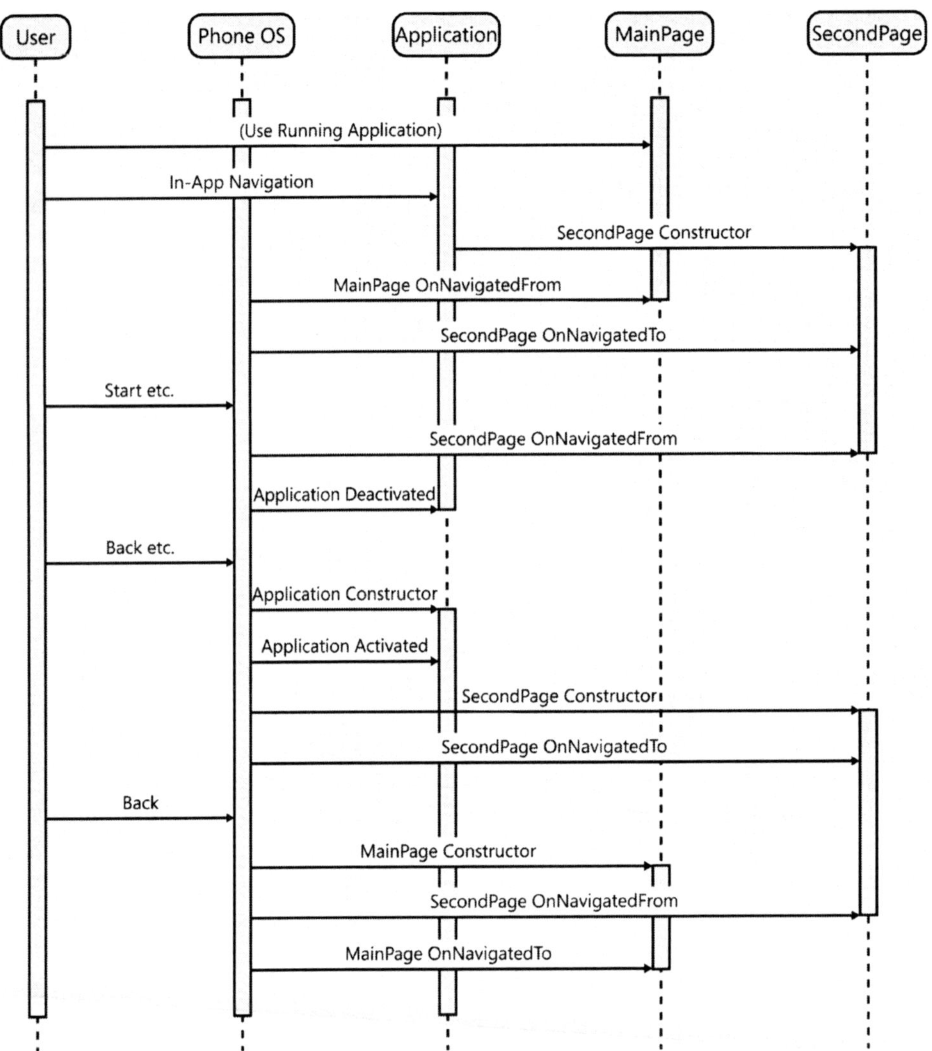

FIGURE 2-8 Unexpected page creation ordering (tombstone case). Here, *SecondPage* is constructed before *MainPage*.

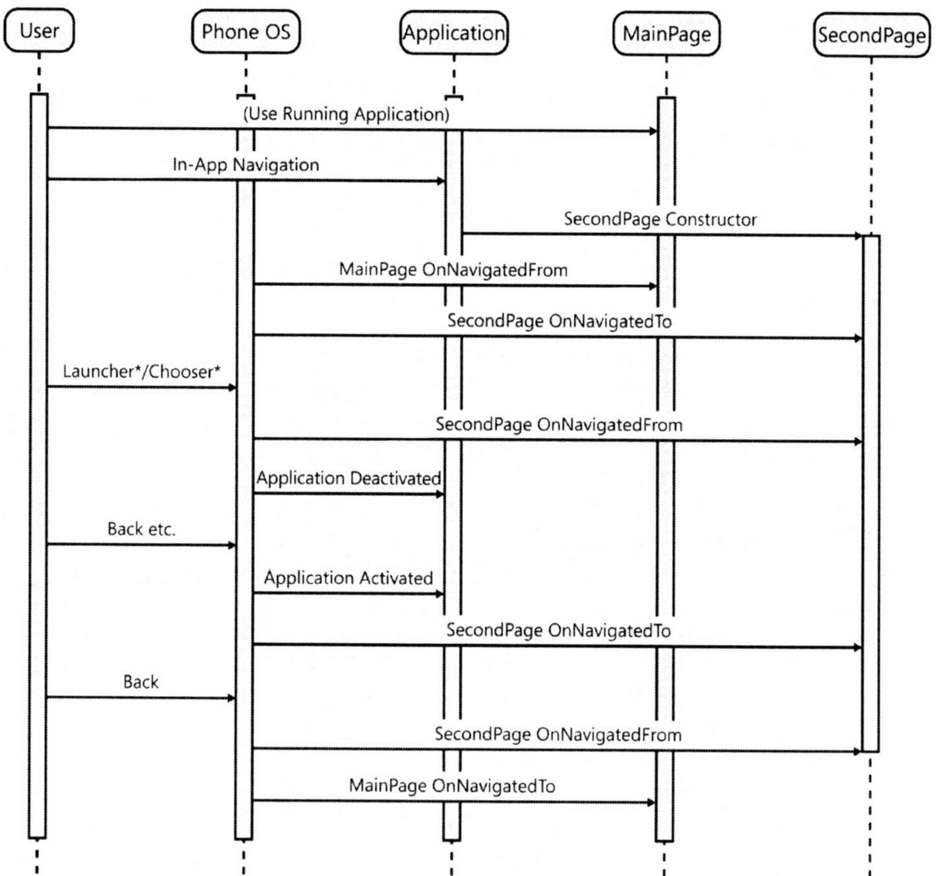

FIGURE 2-9 Page creation ordering (non-tombstone case) with no fresh page construction.

One consequence of this is that the app should not rely on a hierarchical relationship between pages in terms of object lifetime. That is, don't construct objects in Page X that are required in Page Y. Instead, all pages should be responsible for maintaining their own private state, and any state that is used across multiple pages should be held in the viewmodel (see Chapter 4, "Data binding and MVVM," for details on viewmodels). Furthermore, the viewmodel should be accessible to all pages at all times, with predictable finite lifetime characteristics, which pretty much means it should be held in the *App* class (or be declared statically and be exposed via a singleton pattern).

To ensure consistent state in the face of navigation requires that you understand the navigation sequences and that you do work to persist state where necessary.

Navigation and state

The app model presents a UX of multiple apps running concurrently, and the navigation model supports this by providing a framework for the user to navigate between pages within an app as well as between apps. At both the page level and the app level, the system raises navigation events to which you can listen to maintain your app's state. As the user navigates away from one of your pages or from your app altogether, you can persist any state you might need. Later, as the user navigates back to that page, or to your app, you can restore that state. All of this helps to support the UX of seamless switching between pages and between apps.

It is important to have a good understanding of the navigation model so that your app can integrate seamlessly with the phone ecosystem and behave in a manner that is consistent with other apps and with users' expectations. This section examines the navigation model as well as the events and methods with which you can take part in the model to provide the best possible UX.

In the contexts of app navigation (both intra-app and inter-app), app state can be divided into three categories, as summarized in Table 2-2.

TABLE 2-2 Categories of app and page state

Type of state	Description	Guidelines
Transient page state	The state specific to a page that does not need to persist between runs of the app; for example, the value of uncommitted text changes or the visual state of a page.	Store this in the *PhoneApplicationPage.State* property in the *NavigatedFrom* event, and retrieve it in the *NavigatedTo* event.
Transient application state	The state that applies across the app that does not need to persist between runs of the app; for example, cached web service data.	Store this in the *PhoneApplicationService.State* property when the app handles the *Deactivated* event, and retrieve it in the *Activated* event.
Persistent state	The state of any kind that needs to persist across runs of the app—essentially, anything that would upset the user if you didn't save it.	Store this to persistent storage incrementally during the lifetime of the app. Your last chance to do this is during the *Deactivated* and *Closing* events (the app might not return from *Deactivated*, and will not return from *Closing*), but you should not leave all persistence to these events. Also persist this during the *OnNavigatedFrom* call (for any state modified inside a page).

Navigation consists of a pair of notifications: *OnNavigatedFrom* and *OnNavigatedTo*. The former is sent to a page when it is no longer the current page; the latter is sent to a page when it becomes the current page. This is true both within an app (Page A replaces Page B) and across apps (App X replaces App Y). A page can never be navigated "from" without first being navigated "to," but the inverse is not true. A single page instance can receive an arbitrary number of to/from notifications if the user navigates into and out of the same page repeatedly.

The situation with page constructors is more complicated. This behavior can be summarized as follows:

- Navigating forward (through a hyperlink or a call to *NavigationService.Navigate*) always constructs the target page. Even if an existing instance of the page exists on the backstack, a new one will be created (this differs from desktop Microsoft Silverlight and Windows 8 XAML, in which you can configure it to reuse instances).
- Navigating backward (via the Back button or *NavigationService.GoBack*) will not construct the target page if it already exists (for instance, the process has not been tombstoned since you last visited that page). If the app has been tombstoned and the page instance does not exist, it will be constructed.

It should be clear from this that the critical times to consider state management are in the *OnNavigatedTo* and *OnNavigatedFrom* handlers, not in the page constructor. Furthermore, it is sometimes useful to handle the *Loaded* event for a page or even the *LayoutUpdated* event, but neither of these are suitable places to perform state management. Both of these are called more often than you might expect and are not intended for state management operations.

App state

The *PhoneApplicationService.State* property is an *IDictionary* object that the OS saves. All you have to do is write to the collection (or read from it) at any time during execution, or in the appropriate event handler. This dictionary is not persisted across separate instances of the app; that is, across fresh launches from the Start page, and so on. The *LifecycleState* solution in the sample code demonstrates the behavior, as illustrated in Figure 2-10.

In this app, the *App* class exposes a *MainViewModel* property. Viewmodel classes in general are discussed in detail in Chapter 4; for now, you can consider a viewmodel as a technique for encapsulating data, and a property of your *ViewModel* class is normally maintained in the *App* class. In this example, the *MainViewModel* class is trivial because it contains just one string data member and a method for initializing that data.

```
public class MainViewModel
{
    public string Timestamp { get; set; }

    public void LoadData()
    {
        Timestamp = DateTime.Now.ToLongTimeString();
    }
}
```

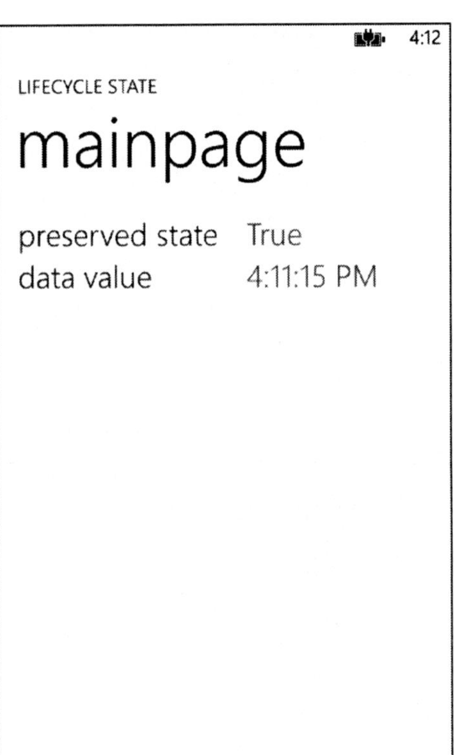

FIGURE 2-10 The *LifecycleState* solution demonstrates loading and saving app state: a fresh launch on the left, and a reactivated instance on the right.

An object of this type is exposed in the *App* class and intialized in the property *get* accessor, as shown in the example that follows. Keep in mind that this approach assumes that the *LoadData* call doesn't do a lot of work. If you do have a lot of data to load, you would want to build a separate *LoadData* method that loaded data asynchronously and incrementally.

```
private static MainViewModel viewModel;
public static MainViewModel ViewModel
{
    get
    {
        lock (typeof(App))
        {
            if (viewModel == null)
            {
                viewModel = new MainViewModel();
                viewModel.LoadData();
            }
        }
        return viewModel;
    }
}
```

The *App* class also declares a string for the name of the state data that will be persisted in the *PhoneApplicationService.State* collection, and a *bool* flag for tracking whether or not this instance of the app is a fresh instance or one that was preserved on the backstack from an earlier launch.

```
private const string appStateName = "AppViewModel";
public static bool IsAppInstancePreserved { get; set; }
```

In the *Deactivated* event handler, the app persists the *viewModel* field in the *PhoneApplication Service.State* collection. At the same time, it also writes the same value out to isolated storage by using the *IsolatedStorageSettings.ApplicationSettings* collection. The idea in the example that follows is that this data does need to be persisted across instances of the app, although this will not always be the case. In the *Closing* event handler, the app only persists to isolated storage because you can be sure at this point that the app is being terminated, so there's no point writing to *PhoneApplication Service.State*.

```
private void Application_Deactivated(object sender, DeactivatedEventArgs e)
{
    PhoneApplicationService.Current.State[appStateName] =
        viewModel;
    IsolatedStorageSettings.ApplicationSettings[appStateName] =
        viewModel.Timestamp;
    IsolatedStorageSettings.ApplicationSettings.Save();
}

private void Application_Closing(object sender, ClosingEventArgs e)
{
    IsolatedStorageSettings.ApplicationSettings[appStateName] =
        viewModel.Timestamp;
    IsolatedStorageSettings.ApplicationSettings.Save();
}
```

Conversely, in the *Activated* event handler, the app caches the value of the *IsApplicationInstance Preserved* property provided by the *ActivatedEventArgs* parameter and then tests this. If this is a preserved instance, the app then goes on to check whether the named state exists in the collection, and if so, retrieves it and overwrites the *viewModel* field, as presented here:

```
private void Application_Activated(object sender, ActivatedEventArgs e)
{
    IsAppInstancePreserved = e.IsApplicationInstancePreserved;
    if (!IsAppInstancePreserved)
    {
        if (PhoneApplicationService.Current.State.ContainsKey(appStateName))
        {
            viewModel =
                PhoneApplicationService.Current.State[appStateName]
                as MainViewModel;
        }
    }
}
```

To complete the picture, the *MainPage* class overrides the *OnNavigatedTo* virtual method to retrieve the data properties from the *App* and set them into the UI elements.

```
protected override void OnNavigatedTo(NavigationEventArgs e)
{
    stateValue.Text = App.IsAppInstancePreserved.ToString();
    dataValue.Text = App.ViewModel.Timestamp;
}
```

Page state

Just as you can use *PhoneApplicationService.State* for persisting app state, so you can also use the *PhoneApplicationPage.State* property for persisting page state. The model is identical.

You can use the phone's *NavigationService* to navigate to another page. When the user navigates back from the second page, however, the second page is destroyed. If she navigates to the second page again, it will be re-created. The main page (that is, the entry point page) is not destroyed or re-created during in-app navigation; however, it might be destroyed/recreated if the user navigates away from the app and returns back to it. The sequence of creation and navigation across two pages in an app is shown in Figure 2-11.

Now, exactly how you should save and load page state depends on what behavior you want. The normal behavior is that when the user navigates backward away from a page, that page is destroyed. So, the next time the user navigates forward to that page, it will be created from scratch. Typically, you use *PageNavigationState* if you only care about retaining state for the case when the user navigates forward, away from a page, and then back again to that page. On the other hand, you can use *PhoneApplicationService.State* if you want to preserve state that can be used by any page.

The *PageNavigationState* solution in the sample code demonstrates this behavior, as shown in Figure 2-12.

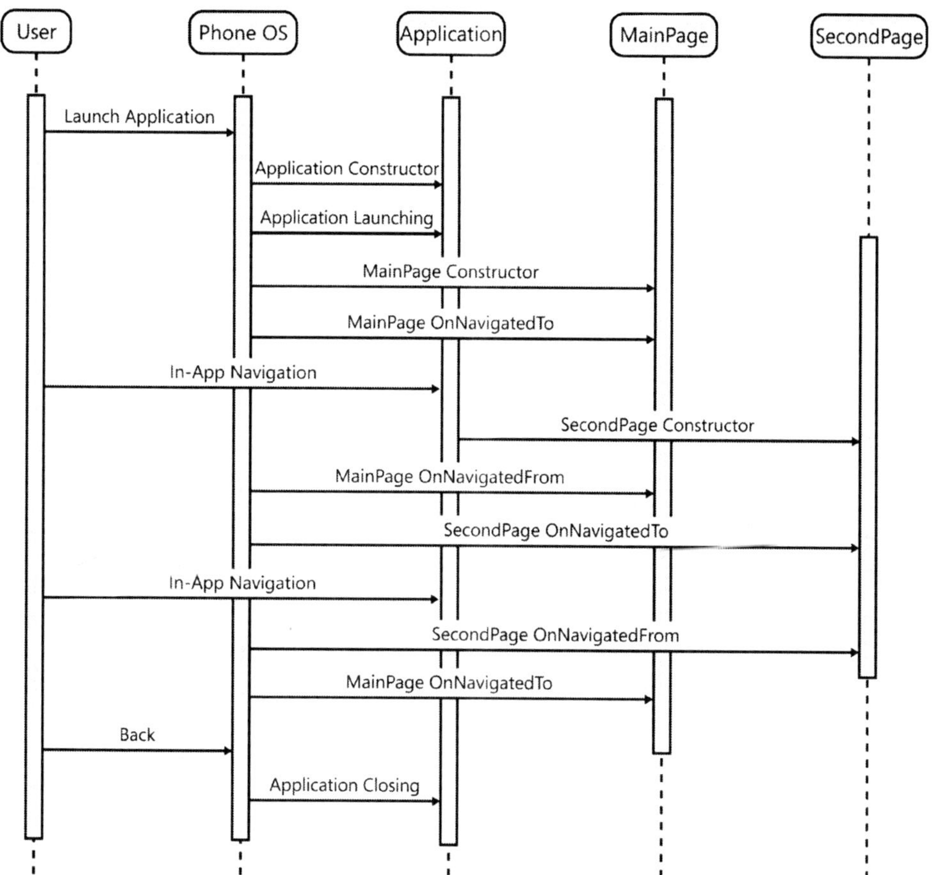

FIGURE 2-11 The sequence of page construction and navigation events.

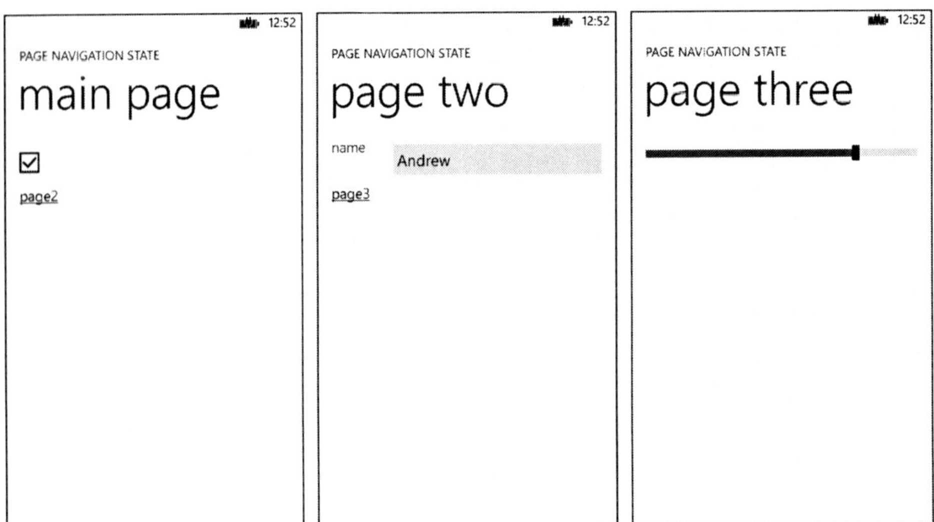

FIGURE 2-12 The *PageNavigationState* solution provides three pages. It persists state for each page in *PhoneApplicationService.State*.

The *MainPage* class declares a string field for the name of the state to be preserved in the *Phone ApplicationService.State* collection, and a *bool* flag to track whether this is a fresh instance of the page. In the *OnNavigatedFrom* override—invoked when the user navigates away from this page—the value of the UI element for this page (in this case, a *CheckBox*) is persisted in the *State* collection. Conversely, in the *OnNavigatedTo* override, the *CheckBox* state is restored from the collection if it exists. The *isNewInstance* flag is set to *true* in the page constructor, and to *false* in the *OnNavigatedTo* override. This way, state is restored if it is needed, and that code is skipped if it is not needed.

```
public partial class MainPage : PhoneApplicationPage
{
    private bool isNewInstance;
    private const string MainPageState = "CheckState";

    public MainPage()
    {
        InitializeComponent();
        isNewInstance = true;
    }

    protected override void OnNavigatedFrom(NavigationEventArgs e)
    {
        PhoneApplicationService.Current.State[MainPageState] =
            checkState.IsChecked;
    }

    protected override void OnNavigatedTo(NavigationEventArgs e)
    {
        if (isNewInstance)
        {
            if (PhoneApplicationService.Current.State.ContainsKey(MainPageState))
            {
```

```
                checkState.IsChecked = (bool)
                    PhoneApplicationService.Current.State[MainPageState];
            }
            isNewInstance = false;
        }
    }
}
```

Very similar operations are performed in each of the other pages of the app, in each case using a page-specific name for the state to be stored in the app state collection.

Note The app platform enforces limits on storing state. No single page is allowed to store more than 2 MB of data, and the app overall is not allowed to store more than 4 MB. However, these values are far larger than anything you should ever use. If you persist large amounts of state data, not only are you consuming system memory, but the time taken to serialize and deserialize large amounts of data is going to affect your app's pause/resume time. In an extreme case, the platform might identify your app as being non-responsive during a critical transition phase, at which point it will rudely terminate the app. Upon rude termination, your app might well suffer data loss or corruption. The basic guidance should be to store only simple things in the state dictionaries; you should not, for example, store the entire cache of a database.

Also, any object that you attempt to store in these dictionaries must be serializable. If the app attempts to store an object that cannot be serialized, this will throw an exception during debugging and fail silently during production runtime. Finally, note that there will be issues if you have serialized a type in an assembly that isn't loaded at startup. In this case, you need to load that assembly artificially in your *App* constructor; otherwise, you get a deserialization error. Further details on serialization/deserialization are covered in Chapter 10, "Local storage and databases."

Cancelling navigation

Navigations that are initiated by the user by interacting with your app UI can generally be cancelled, whereas navigations initiated by the user interacting with hardware buttons or initiated by the system generally cannnot be cancelled. It is common to provide navigation UI within your app, including *Hyperlink* and *Button* controls. However, there are scenarios for which, even though the user has gestured that he wants to navigate, you might want to intercept the request and prompt for confirmation. For example, if the user has edited a page or entered data, but he hasn't yet confirmed the new input or changes, you would prompt him to save first when he tries to navigate away.

One technique is to override the *OnNavigatingFrom* method. This provides a *NavigatingCancelEventArgs*, which exposes two useful properties. You can use the *Cancel* property to cancel the navigation, and the *IsCancelable* property to establish definitively whether an attempt to cancel will actually succeed. If you can't cancel the navigation, you would take other steps to handle the scenario (perhaps saving the user's input to a temporary file or other mitigating actions, depending on the context). You can see this at work in the *TestNavigating* solution in the sample code.

```
protected override void OnNavigatingFrom(NavigatingCancelEventArgs e)
{
    Debug.WriteLine("OnNavigatingFrom");

    if (e.IsCancelable)
    {
        MessageBoxResult result = MessageBox.Show(
            "Navigate away?", "Confirm", MessageBoxButton.OKCancel);
        if (result == MessageBoxResult.Cancel)
        {
            e.Cancel = true;
        }
    }
    else
    {
        Debug.WriteLine("Navigation NOT cancelable");
    }
}
```

Backstack management

The user's navigation history is maintained within an app in a history list called the backstack. The backstack is managed as a last-in, first-out (LIFO) stack. This means that as the user navigates forward through the pages of an app, each page from which she departs is added to the stack. As she navigates back, the previous page in the navigation history is popped off the stack to become the new current page. The platform includes the following API support for working with the backstack:

- The *NavigationService* class exposes a *BackStack* property, which is an *IEnumerable* collection of *JournalEntry* objects. Each page in the backstack is represented by a *JournalEntry* object. The *JournalEntry* class exposes just one significant property: the *Source* property, which is the navigation URI for that page.

- The *NavigationService* class exposes a *RemoveBackEntry* method, which is used to remove the most recent entry from the backstack. You can call this multiple times if you want to remove multiple entries.

- The *NavigationService* class exposes an *OnRemovedFromJournal* virtual method, which you can override. This is invoked when the page is removed from the backstack, either because the user is navigating backward, away from the page, or because the app is programmatically clearing the backstack. When the user navigates forward, the previous page remains in the backstack.

Here's the sequencing of the APIs, in relation to the *OnNavigatedFrom* override. When the user navigates backward, away from the page, the methods/event handlers are invoked in the following order: first, the *OnNavigatedFrom* override; next, the *JournalEntryRemoved* event handler; and then finally, the *OnRemovedFromJournal* override.

In general, your app can control forward navigation—both to new pages within the app and to external apps, Launchers, and Choosers. Conversely, backward navigation is normally left under the control of the hardware Back button.

That having been said, you can modify the user's navigation experience such that going back doesn't necessarily always take her back to the previous page. To be clear, you can still only use the *NavigationService* to navigate forward to a specific URL or back one page in the backstack. However, you can remove entries from the backstack—up to and including all entries—such that navigating back no longer necessarily takes the user back to the immediately preceding page.

Note The ability to manipulate the backstack is a powerful one that affords you a lot of flexibility, but it also gives you a way to break conformance with the Windows Phone app model. You should use this only after very careful consideration, and only if you're sure you can't avoid it.

Figure 2-13 shows the *NavigationManagement* solution in the sample code, which illustrates how you can manipulate the backstack.

FIGURE 2-13 The *NavigationManagement* sample shows how you can manipulate the backstack.

On the *MainPage* of this example, the user can choose one of two links to navigate to the public or private pages within the app. If the user chooses the public page link, the app simply navigates to that page, as normal. On the other hand, if she chooses the private page link, the app navigates to a login page. On the login page, if she taps the Cancel button, this navigates back to the *MainPage*. If, instead, she taps the Login button, this navigates forward to the first of the set of private pages. Realistically, there would be some login credential validation in there, but this example simply navigates without validation. On *PrivatePage1*, the user has a *private2* button, which navigates forward to the next private page in sequence. The idea here is that whatever page the user is on, when she presses the hardware Back button, this always skips the *LoginPage* page. The flow of navigation is presented in Figure 2-14.

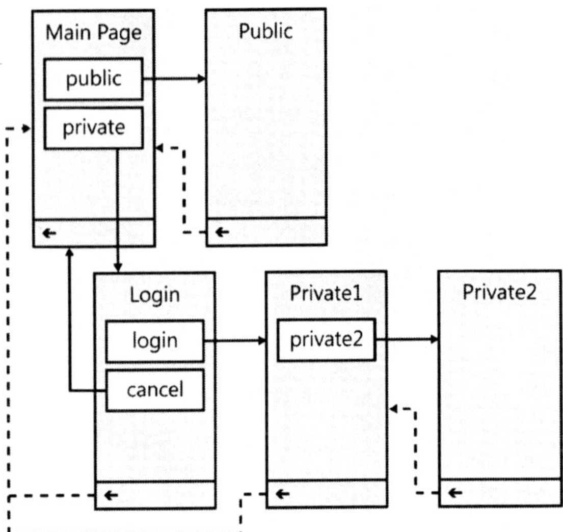

FIGURE 2-14 The navigation flow in the *NavigationManagement* sample app.

In *MainPage*, the two click handlers for the *HyperlinkButton* controls invoke the *Navigation Service.Navigate* method to navigate to explicit target pages. The Public button goes to the *PublicPage*, whereas the Private button goes to the *LoginPage*:

```
private void publicLink_Click(object sender, RoutedEventArgs e)
{
    NavigationService.Navigate(new Uri("/PublicPage.xaml", UriKind.Relative));
}

private void privateLink_Click(object sender, RoutedEventArgs e)
{
    NavigationService.Navigate(new Uri("/LoginPage.xaml", UriKind.Relative));
}
```

On the *LoginPage*, the Login button navigates to *PrivatePage1*, whereas the Cancel button invokes the *NavigationService.GoBack* method to go back one page in the backstack. The page in the back-stack immediately before the *LoginPage* is always *MainPage*:

```
private void LoginButton_Click(object sender, RoutedEventArgs e)
{
    NavigationService.Navigate(new Uri("/PrivatePage1.xaml", UriKind.Relative));
}

private void CancelButton_Click(object sender, RoutedEventArgs e)
{
    NavigationService.GoBack();
}
```

In *PrivatePage1*, the *private2* button navigates explicitly to *PrivatePage2*. Also in *PrivatePage1*, the override of *OnNavigatedTo* checks the value of the incoming *NavigationMode*. If the user navigated forward to this page, the previous page is removed from the backstack. This is done because the only way to navigate forward to this page is from the *LoginPage*, and the idea is that the user should not have to navigate back through the *LoginPage*. His perception is that the *LoginPage* is transient, and does not persist in the navigation backstack. Using this technique means that when he taps the hardware Back button, it navigates back to the page before the *LoginPage* because the *LoginPage* will no longer exist in the backstack.

Note It would be equally valid to implement the login page functionality via a true transient panel by using a *PopupControl* or a *ChildWindow* control. Such windows never persist in the backstack.

```
private void private2Link_Click(object sender, System.Windows.RoutedEventArgs e)
{
    NavigationService.Navigate(new Uri("/PrivatePage2.xaml", UriKind.Relative));
}

protected override void OnNavigatedTo(NavigationEventArgs e)
{
    if (e.NavigationMode == NavigationMode.New)
    {
        NavigationService.RemoveBackEntry();
    }
}
```

Navigation options

The Windows Phone app platform offers a number of options for navigation—both within an app and externally. In addition to the *Navigate* and *GoBack* methods on the *NavigationService* class, an app can use the *NavigateUri* property of a *HyperlinkButton* and re-route navigation by either runtime interception or static URI mapping. There are also issues to consider with regard to navigation between pages across multiple assemblies, and options for passing data between pages during navigation.

Note One question that developers often ask is, "When would you ever need to invoke the *base.OnNavigatedTo/OnNavigatedFrom*?" When you use autocomplete to create an override for these virtual methods, Visual Studio generates a call to the base class version, which seems to imply that calling the base version is useful sometimes or always. In fact, this is simply an artifact of how autocomplete works; Visual Studio will always generate a base class call. With respect to *Page.OnNavigatedTo* and *OnNavigatedFrom*, you never need to invoke the base version, because the base version is empty, so you can always safely delete these calls.

Using *NavigateUri*

The normal way to use a *HyperlinkButton* is to specify the *NavigateUri* in XAML; you do not specify a *Click* event handler. With this approach, shown in the code that follows, the link is set up declaratively, and there is no event handler in the code-behind. Note, however, that this technique only supports forward navigation; there is no way to specify the equivalent of *NavigationService.GoBack*.

```
<!--<HyperlinkButton
    x:Name="privateLink" Content="private"
    Click="privateLink_Click"
    HorizontalAlignment="Center" VerticalAlignment="Top"
    FontSize="{StaticResource PhoneFontSizeMedium}"/>-->
<HyperlinkButton
    x:Name="privateLink" Content="private"
    NavigateUri="/LoginPage.xaml"
    HorizontalAlignment="Center" VerticalAlignment="Top"
    FontSize="{StaticResource PhoneFontSizeMedium}"/>
```

Pages in separate assemblies

From an engineering perspective, it is perfectly reasonable to divide a solution into multiple assemblies—possibly with different developers working on different assemblies. This model also works with Windows Phone pages; thus, one or more pages for an app could be built in separate assemblies. This technique can also help with app startup performance because the code for the second and subsequent pages does not need to be loaded on startup, and the assembly load cost is deferred until the point when the user actually navigates to the second and subsequent pages, if ever. How does this affect navigation? Navigating back is always the same; *NavigationService.GoBack* takes no parameters. However, navigating forward requires a URI (either in the *NavigateUri* property or in the call to *Navigate*), and this URI must be able to be resolved. The simplest case is that in which the URI is relative to the app root, indicated with a leading slash. If the URI identifies a page that is in another assembly, the string format is as follows:

```
"/[assembly short name];component/[page pathname]"
```

So, for example, if you have *Page2* in a separate class library project named *PageLibrary*, to navigate to *Page2*, you would use this syntax:

```
NavigationService.Navigate(new Uri(
    "/PageLibrary;component/Page2.xaml", UriKind.Relative));
```

You can see this at work in the *NavigatingAssemblies* solution in the sample code.

Fragment and *QueryString*

To pass state values between pages on navigation, an app can use *PhoneApplicationService.State*, isolated storage, or state fields/properties on the App object. In addition, you can use *Fragment* or *QueryString*. Note that you cannot use *Fragment* to navigate within a page; you can only use it when navigating to another page. In general, *Fragment* is not particularly useful in the context of phone apps. Here is an example (the *NavigationParameters* solution in the sample code) in which the main page offers a choice between coffee and tea. The user's choice is passed down to *Page2* either via a *Fragment* or via a *QueryString*, depending on which button the user clicks. This is illustrated in Figure 2-15.

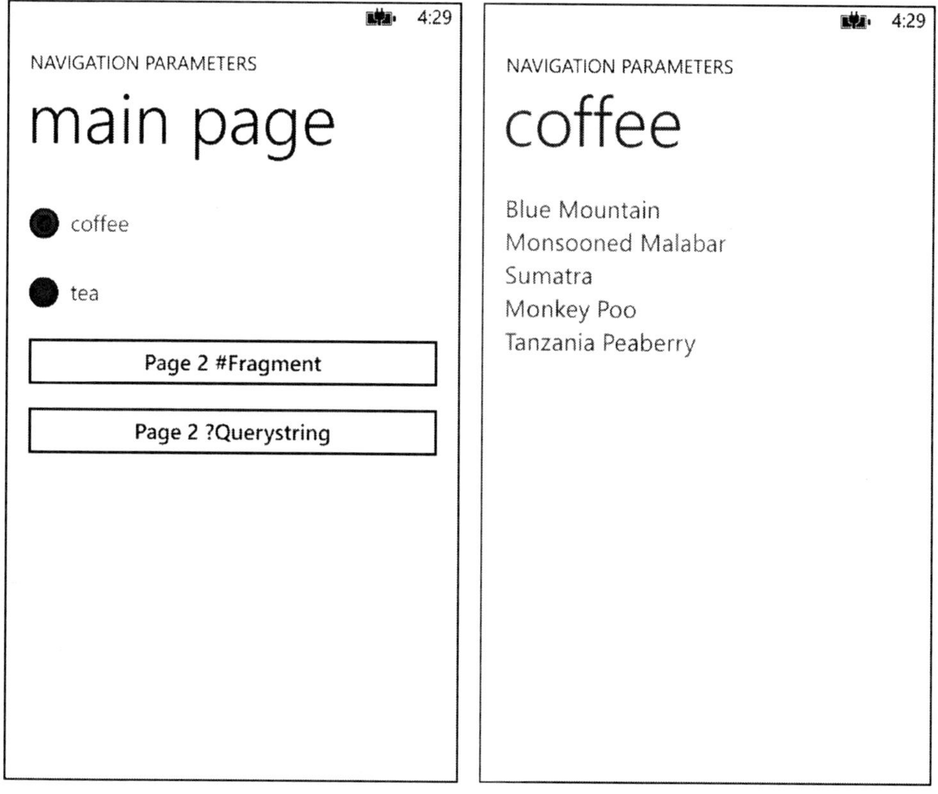

FIGURE 2-15 The *NavigationParameters* solution tests navigation by using *Fragment* and *QueryString*.

Page2 has a *ListBox* that is data-bound to one of two *ObservableCollection* objects (see Chapter 4 for details of this approach and to learn more about data binding).

```
private ObservableCollection<string> coffees =
    new ObservableCollection<string>();
private ObservableCollection<string> teas =
    new ObservableCollection<string>();

public Page2()
{
    InitializeComponent();

    coffees.Add("Blue Mountain");
    coffees.Add("Monsooned Malabar");
    coffees.Add("Sumatra");
    coffees.Add("Monkey Poo");
    coffees.Add("Tanzania Peaberry");

    teas.Add("Earl Grey");
    teas.Add("Darjeeling");
    teas.Add("Jasmine");
    teas.Add("Oolong");
    teas.Add("Chrysanthemum");
}
```

To use a *Fragment*, you simply append a "#" (hash) character to the target URI, followed by the fragment value, as demonstrated here:

```
private void buttonPage2Fragment_Click(object sender, RoutedEventArgs e)
{
    if ((bool)radioCoffee.IsChecked)
    {
        NavigationService.Navigate(new Uri(
            "/Page2.xaml#Coffee", UriKind.Relative));
    }
    else
    {
        NavigationService.Navigate(new Uri(
            "/Page2.xaml#Tea", UriKind.Relative));
    }
}
```

On the navigation destination page (*Page2* in this example), you could override *OnNavigatedTo*, but the *Fragment* is not easily accessible in that method. You could parse the string in the *Uri* property of the *NavigationEventArgs*, but that would be a fragile approach. Instead, after *OnNavigatedTo* is called, the system calls *OnFragmentNavigation*, and it is here that you can get the *Fragment*. Note that setting the *ItemsSource* property of a *ListBox* is part of the data-binding mechanism. This is explored in detail in Chapter 4. For now, you can ignore it.

```
protected override void OnFragmentNavigation(FragmentNavigationEventArgs e)
{
    switch (e.Fragment)
```

```
    {
        case "Coffee":
            SetItemsCoffee();
            break;
        case "Tea":
            SetItemsTea();
            break;
    }
}

private void SetItemsCoffee()
{
    listDrinks.ItemsSource = coffees;
    pageTitle.Text = "coffee";
    pageTitle.Foreground = listDrinks.Foreground
        = new SolidColorBrush(Colors.Brown);
}

private void SetItemsTea()
{
    listDrinks.ItemsSource = teas;
    pageTitle.Text = "tea";
    pageTitle.Foreground = listDrinks.Foreground
        = new SolidColorBrush(Colors.Green);
}
```

Conversely, you can provide a conventional query string, by appending a question mark "?" to the end of the URI, and then appending "key/value" pairs. Unlike *Fragment*, this gives you the ability to pass more than one value, in the format:

```
"/[pagename].xaml?[param1=value1]&[param2=value2]&[param3=value3]"
```

For example:

```
private void buttonPage2Querystring_Click(object sender, RoutedEventArgs e)
{
    if ((bool)radioCoffee.IsChecked)
    {
        NavigationService.Navigate(new Uri(
            "/Page2.xaml?drink=Coffee", UriKind.Relative));
    }
    else
    {
        NavigationService.Navigate(new Uri(
            "/Page2.xaml?drink=Tea", UriKind.Relative));
    }
}
```

If you use a query string, in the receiving page, this is provided as an *IDictionary* property on the *NavigationContext*, which itself is a property of the *Page* object. You can use both a query string and a fragment in the same URL, but this is not likely to be useful: it would require you to handle both, and to parse the URL in both cases to extract either one.

```
protected override void OnNavigatedTo(NavigationEventArgs e)
{
    string drinkType;
    if (NavigationContext.QueryString.TryGetValue(
        "drink", out drinkType))
    {
        switch (drinkType)
        {
            case "Coffee":
                SetItemsCoffee();
                break;
            case "Tea":
                SetItemsTea();
                break;
        }
    }
}
```

Be aware that although the *QueryString* property will not be null, it might be empty, so you should check for this before attempting to access its collection. Also, as with any *Dictionary* object, if you attempt to use an indexer that does not exist in the collection, this will throw an exception. So, rather than using the indexer, you can use the *TryGetValue* method, instead.

The *NavigationMode* and *IsNavigationInitiator* properties

Overrides of *OnNavigatedTo* and *OnNavigatedFrom* are passed a *NavigationEventArgs* object. This exposes two useful properties: *Content*, set to the instance of the destination page; and *Uri*, which will be the URI of the destination page.

Windows Phone also exposes a *NavigationMode* property on the *NavigationEventArgs* object that is passed in to the *OnNavigatedTo* and *OnNavigatedFrom* method overrides. The value of *Navigation Mode* will typically be either *New* or *Back*, which identifies the direction of navigation. The *Back* value is self-explanatory; if the value is *New*, this indicates that this is a forward navigation. The *Navigation Mode* type includes the values *Refresh* and *Reset*, which are discussed in Chapter 18. There's also a *Forward* value, but this is not used in Windows Phone. Typically, you would perform some conditional operation based on this value, such as saving or restoring state. The following code snippet merely prints a string to the debug window. The app has two pages: *MainPage* and *Page2*, and the user can navigate back and forth between them.

```
public partial class MainPage : PhoneApplicationPage
{
... irrelevant code omitted for brevity.
    protected override void OnNavigatedTo(NavigationEventArgs e)
    {
        Debug.WriteLine("MainPage.OnNavigatedTo: {0}", e.NavigationMode);
    }
```

```
    protected override void OnNavigatedFrom(NavigationEventArgs e)
    {
        Debug.WriteLine("MainPage.OnNavigatedFrom: {0}", e.NavigationMode);
    }
}

public partial class Page2 : PhoneApplicationPage
{
    protected override void OnNavigatedTo(NavigationEventArgs e)
    {
        Debug.WriteLine("Page2.OnNavigatedTo: {0}", e.NavigationMode);
    }

    protected override void OnNavigatedFrom(NavigationEventArgs e)
    {
        Debug.WriteLine("Page2.OnNavigatedFrom: {0}", e.NavigationMode);
    }
}
```

When the app starts and the *MainPage* is loaded, the following output is produced:

```
MainPage.OnNavigatedTo: New
```

As the user navigates forward from *MainPage* to *Page2*, you see the following debug output—the navigation is forward as far as both pages are concerned:

```
MainPage.OnNavigatedFrom: New
Page2.OnNavigatedTo: New
```

Then, as the user navigates back from *Page2* to *MainPage*, you would expect to see the following debug output—again, for both pages, the navigation is backward:

```
Page2.OnNavigatedFrom: Back
MainPage.OnNavigatedTo: Back
```

If the user is on *Page2* and then navigates forward out of the app by tapping the Start button, and then navigates back into the app again, you would see the following output (the *New* [forward] navigation out of the app, followed by the *Back* navigation back into the app):

```
Page2.OnNavigatedFrom: New
Page2.OnNavigatedTo: Back
```

Finally, consider another new property of both the *NavigationEventArgs* and the *NavigatingCancelEventArgs*: the *IsNavigationInitiator* property. This is a Boolean value that notifies you whether the navigation is from an external source; that is, the user navigated from outside the app into the app. This is designed so that you can avoid custom page-to-page animations in the case of an external navigation, because in that scenario, the platform will perform animation for you. In the following, you're going to modify the debug output statements to include this property value:

```
Debug.WriteLine("Page2.OnNavigatedTo: {0}, {1}", e.NavigationMode, e.IsNavigationInitiator);
```

Now, if the user starts the app (which loads *MainPage*), navigates internally to *Page2*, taps Start to navigate forward out of the app, taps the Back button to return into the app, and then finally, back from *Page2* to *MainPage*, you will see the output that follows. When the navigation is to or from an external source (including the initial launch of the app from the Start page), the value of *IsNavigation Initiator* is *False*. For internal navigation, the value is *True*.

```
MainPage.OnNavigatedTo: New, False
MainPage.OnNavigatedFrom: New, True
Page2.OnNavigatedTo: New, True
Page2.OnNavigatedFrom: New, False
Page2.OnNavigatedTo: Back, False
Page2.OnNavigatedFrom: Back, True
MainPage.OnNavigatedTo: Back, True
```

Re-routing navigation and URI mappers

It is also possible to re-route navigation from one target page to another at runtime. For example, you might build an app in which the user can navigate to an *AccountInfo* page, but if the user is not logged in (or the login has timed out), you redirect him to a *Login* page. There are two distinct ways to achieve this kind of redirection.

The first approach is navigation re-routing, as demonstrated in the *ReRouting* solution in the sample code. Suppose that you have a requirement by which most days of the week, when the user asks to navigate to *Page2*, you sent him to a default *Page2a*, but on Tuesdays, you send him instead to *Page2b*. In the *MainPage* code-behind, on the UI trigger to go to *Page2*, you navigate to *Page2*:

```
private void GotoPage2_Click(object sender, RoutedEventArgs e)
{
    NavigationService.Navigate(new Uri("/Page2.xaml", UriKind.Relative));
}
```

However, the app does not in fact contain a *Page2.xaml*. Instead, it contains a *Page2a.xaml* and a *Page2b.xaml*. In the *App* class, you hook the *Navigating* event on the *RootFrame* and perform some navigation re-routing whenever you detect that the user is attempting to go to *Page2*.

```
private void RootFrame_Navigating(object sender, NavigatingCancelEventArgs e)
{
    if (e.Uri.ToString() == "/Page2.xaml")
    {
        Uri newUri = null;
        if (DateTime.Now.DayOfWeek == DayOfWeek.Tuesday)
        {
            newUri = new Uri("/Page2a.xaml", UriKind.Relative);
        }
        else
        {
            newUri = new Uri("/Page2b.xaml", UriKind.Relative);
        }
```

```
            RootFrame.Dispatcher.BeginInvoke(() =>
                RootFrame.Navigate(newUri));
            e.Cancel = true;
        }
    }
```

Note that the handler uses *Dispatcher.BeginInvoke*. This is because the *Navigating* event is being handled during navigation, and the system does not allow overlapping navigations. Therefore, you must ensure that the second navigation is queued up. Meanwhile, you terminate the current navigation by setting *NavigatingCancelEventArgs.Cancel* to *true*.

The second technique you can use is URI Mapping (demonstrated in the *TestUriMapping* solution in the sample code). With this approach, instead of handling the *Navigating* event and manually cancelling and re-routing the navigation, you can simply provide a mapping from the original URI to a new URI. This can be either statically declared in XAML or dynamically determined in code. For example, here is a static mapping from *Page2* to *Page2b*:

```
<Application.Resources>
    <nav:UriMapper x:Name="mapper">
        <nav:UriMapping
            Uri="/Page2.xaml"
            MappedUri="/Page2b.xaml"/>
    </nav:UriMapper>
</Application.Resources>
```

This assumes that you have declared a *nav* namespace in the *App.xaml*.

```
xmlns:nav="clr-namespace:System.Windows.Navigation;assembly=Microsoft.Phone"
```

As this namespace indicates, the *UriMapper* and *UriMapping* types are declared in the *System.Windows.Navigation* namespace in the *Microsoft.Phone.dll*. Having declared the mapper and at least one mapping entry, you can use it in the app—typically after the standard initialization code.

```
RootFrame.UriMapper = (UriMapper)Resources["mapper"];
```

That would suffice for a static mapping. If you need a dynamic mapping—as you do in the following example you need to modify the *MappedUri* property before using it:

```
Uri newUri = null;
if (DateTime.Now.DayOfWeek == DayOfWeek.Tuesday)
{
    newUri = new Uri("/Page2a.xaml", UriKind.Relative);
}
else
{
    newUri = new Uri("/Page2b.xaml", UriKind.Relative);
}
UriMapper mapper = (UriMapper)Resources["mapper"];

// dynamic mapping, overwrites any MappedUri set statically in XAML.
mapper.UriMappings[0].MappedUri = newUri;
RootFrame.UriMapper = mapper;
```

Note Additional navigation techniques are discussed in Chapter 14, "Tiles and notifications," and in Chapter 22, "Enterprise apps."

Of these approaches, the *UriMapper* approach is preferred in general because it can be done mostly in XAML and doesn't rely on manipulating the navigation system. On the other hand, if you need very dynamic redirection (such as the login timeout scenario), cancelling the navigation might be better for specific/isolated cases.

File type and URI associations

Windows Phone 8 introduces the ability for apps to launch other apps via file type and URI associations, a feature that has been present in desktop Windows for many years but was not supported in Windows Phone 7. Using file type associations, you can launch the appropriate handler for a file based on its file extension and register it to be launched as the handler for types that you can support. Similarly, apps can launch and be launched for custom URI associations (also referred to as custom protocols or schemes).

Starting an app based on a file or URI

To start an app based on a file or URI, use the *Windows.System.Launcher* class, which offers *LaunchFileAsync* and *LaunchUriAsync* to handle each respective scenario. For instance, to start Microsoft Excel to view a spreadsheet stored in your app's local folder, you would get the file as a *StorageFile* and then pass it to *LaunchFileAsync*, as shown in the following:

```
StorageFile spreadsheet =
    await ApplicationData.Current.LocalFolder.GetFileAsync("spreadsheet.xlsx");

Launcher.LaunchFileAsync(spreadsheet);
```

Similarly, if you wanted to start an app to handle a URI by using the custom "contoso" URI scheme, you would pass a URI instance to *LaunchUriAsync*, as demonstrated here:

```
Launcher.LaunchUriAsync(new Uri("contoso:viewProducts?productCategoryId=12345"));
```

When the system receives these launch requests, it performs a resolution of the file type extension or the URI scheme name with the list of apps that have registered for that association. There are three possible results of that resolution:

- **No handlers installed** The user is prompted to go to the Windows Phone Store to acquire an app that handles the association.

- **Exactly one handler installed** The handler is launched immediately.
- **Two or more handlers installed** The user is shown a list of available handlers from which she can choose which one to start.

Note Windows 8 supports additional overloads of *LaunchFileAsync* and *LaunchUriAsync* that enable launching apps to customize the behavior of the *Launcher* class to do things such as falling back to a HTTP URI if no file or URI association handler is installed on the device. These overloads are not supported in Windows Phone 8.

Acting as a file type or URI handler

Registering your app as a handler for a particular file type or URI scheme makes it possible for it to be started by other Windows Phone Store apps and by many built-in experiences. For example, when you register as a file type handler, the user will be able to start your app to handle an attachment received in the email app. Similarly, when you register a custom URI scheme, the user will be able to start your app to handle a URI that he sees in the browser or in SMS.

Manifest registration

To register as the handler for a file type or URI scheme, you must first declare the file types and URI schemes that you want to support as an extension in the app manifest. For custom URI schemes, registration is straightforward. The only value that the system really needs you to define is the name of the scheme; that is, the portion that comes before the colon in the URI. In the case of *contoso:viewProducts?productCategoryId=12345*, the URI scheme name is simply "contoso". The *NavUriFragment* and *TaskID* values should always be set as shown in the following:

```
<Extensions>
  <Protocol Name="contoso" NavUriFragment="encodedLaunchUri=%s" TaskID="_default" />
</Extensions>
```

Registration of file type associations is only slightly more complex. For each file type, you have the opportunity to register a set of images to act as the icons for the file type when it is displayed in the built-in experiences. You can register three sizes of images: small, medium, and large. The use of each asset within the system as well as the recommended size for each is shown in Table 2-3. The recommended sizes are designed to appear crisp on WXGA devices, the highest resolution supported for Windows Phone 8. The system will automatically scale the images down appropriately for WVGA and 720P phones.

TABLE 2-3 Apps can specify three icon assets for display in the built-in experiences

Icon type	Usage	Recommended size
Small	Email attachments	33x33
Medium	Office Hub file listing	69x69
Large	Internet Explorer file downloads	176x176

For each file type registration, you have the opportunity to register multiple file extensions. This enables scenarios in which you have multiple file extensions mapping to a common code path and user experience in your app. The Microsoft Office apps provide a good illustration of this: although .doc and .docx are two different file extensions and file formats, the Microsoft Word app represents them as a single file type to the system. It is important that you register each file extension that you want to handle because this is the only key that the system uses to query for apps based on file types. The *ContentType* attribute is not currently used.

```
<Extensions>
     <FileTypeAssociation
          Name="MyCustomFileType"
          TaskID="_default"
          NavUriFragment="fileToken=%s">

          <Logos>
               <Logo Size="small" IsRelative="true">Assets/smallIcon.png</Logo>
               <Logo Size="medium" IsRelative="true">Assets/mediumIcon.png</Logo>
               <Logo Size="large" IsRelative="true">Assets/largeIcon.png</Logo>
          </Logos>
          <SupportedFileTypes>
               <FileType ContentType="application/contoso">.cst</FileType>
               <FileType ContentType="application/contoso">.csto</FileType>
          </SupportedFileTypes>
     </FileTypeAssociation>
</Extensions>
```

It is important to note that certain file types and URI schemes are not eligible for registration by Windows Store apps. First, any file type or URI scheme that is handled by one of the built-in experiences, such as .png or .mp3, are reserved by those apps. This restriction is designed to ensure a consistent experience for common scenarios, such as receiving a set of photos as email attachments. Second, any file type or URI scheme that is used internally by the system, such as the .xap file extension used for app packages or the "app" URI scheme used for system navigation, are also reserved. You can find a full list of reserved file types and URI schemes at *http://msdn.microsoft.com/en-us/library/windowsphone/develop/jj207065(v=vs.105).aspx.*

Handling activation

The URI-based navigation model that we looked at earlier in this chapter also applies when navigating between apps, meaning that when you get activated to handle a file type or URI association, you learn about the activation type and acquire the accompanying input parameters by parsing the navigation URI. When you are activated to handle a file type association, the navigation URI fragment will look like this:

```
/FileTypeAssociation?fileToken=[file_token]
```

The *file_token* is a GUID generated by the system to represent the file being provided to your app. We will look at how you can use it to retrieve the actual file in the next section. When you are launched to handle a URI association, the navigation URI fragment looks like this:

```
/Protocol?encodedLaunchUri=[encoded_Launch_URI]
```

The *encoded_Launch_URI* is the original URI invoked by the starting app. Because the original URI is being passed within a URI, it is URI-encoded by the system to ensure that its special characters, such as equal signs, colons, and ampersands, are not accidentally interpreted by the system as belonging to the navigation URI. Because the navigation URIs passed to the app for file type and URI associations do not include a XAML page, you must use a custom URI mapper, as shown earlier in this chapter. Note that you should URI decode the launch URI parameter before parsing it by using the *UrlDecode* method in *System.Web.HttpUtility* class.

Accessing launched files

Because all app-to-app navigation happens through URIs, it is clearly not possible to directly pass a file into an app. Consequently, file type handlers must use the file token provided as a query string parameter during file type activation to retrieve the actual file. The *SharedStorageAccessManager* class provides this functionality. The class includes two methods. The *GetSharedFileName* method synchronously returns the file name of the file being passed to the app. The synchronous nature of the API ensures that you have an opportunity to direct the user to the appropriate page of your app by using your custom *UriMapper* for cases in which you wish to provide a different experience for different file types. After you are ready to retrieve the file, you use the *CopySharedFileAsync* method to create a copy of the file in a specific folder within your app's local storage. Windows Phone does not currently support editing a file in its original location.

```
string filename = SharedStorageAccessManager.GetSharedFileName(fileToken);

StorageFolder launchedFilesFolder =
      await ApplicationData.Current.LocalFolder.GetFolderAsync("RetrievedFiles");

StorageFile sharedFile =
     SharedStorageAccessManager.CopySharedFileAsync
                                 (launchedFilesFolder,
                                  filename,
                                  NameCollisionOption.ReplaceExisting,
                                  fileToken);
```

Summary

This chapter examined the app model, and in particular, the app lifecycle and related events. The tight resource constraints inherent in all mobile devices offer challenges for app developers, particularly with regard to CPU, memory, and disk space. The Windows Phone platform presents a seamless UX with reasonably fast switching between apps to provide an experience that appears to users as if multiple apps are running at the same time. More important, the system exposes just the right number and type of events so that you can hook into the system and use the opportunities presented to make the most of the phone's limited resources. If you pay attention to these events and take the recommended actions in your event handlers, your app takes part in the overall phone ecosystem, gives users a great experience, and cooperates with the system to maintain system health.

The Windows Phone navigation model is page-based and very intuitive. Although it is possible for you to provide a navigation experience that is different from other apps on the phone, this is discouraged unless you have a very unique and compelling experience. Instead, you are strongly encouraged to take part in the standard navigation model, to respond to the standard navigation events, and to maintain navigation behavior that is consistent with users' expectations. All but the simplest apps will have some state on both a page basis and an app-wide basis that needs to be persisted across navigation. The app platform on the phone provides targeted support for persisting limited volumes of page and app state.

CHAPTER 3

UI visuals and touch

When you build an app, you have to consider the user interface (UI) both in terms of the visuals and the input mechanisms, which, in Windows Phone, means primarily touch input. The chapters in Part IV, "Native apps and games," look at the UI from the perspective of the native-code developer. In this chapter, we'll look at the UI from the managed-code perspective. The physical constraints of a smartphone screen impose some challenges for app developers. At the same time, the Windows Phone UI paradigm combined with the very nature of touch input offer considerable opportunity for building a compelling, attractive, and delightful user experience (UX) into your app. The Windows Phone platform offers a wide range of standard controls, from the humble *TextBlock* to the all-singing, all-dancing *Panorama* control. These controls have been designed to be powerful and easy to develop against, and they're all well-documented, so we will not spend too much time on these. Instead, this chapter will examine the fundamental UI infrastructure in the Windows Phone app platform, how that platform exposes significant support for mobile developers, and some of the less-understood aspects of visual and touch UI.

Phone UI elements

In the following sections, you will be introduced to the primary elements that make up the Windows Phone support for the visual UI.

Standard UI elements

The Windows Phone shell provides a couple of standard UI elements: the notification area and the app bar, both of which are optionally available for use in your apps. The standard app UI model for managed apps is to use an outermost Frame which represents the entire screen. On top of this, the app itself defines one or more Pages. Each Page typically occupies the entire Frame (allowing for the notification area and app bar). Only one Page is visible at a time.

- The notification area (or status bar) runs across the top of the screen and provides indicators for cell/wireless/bluetooth strength, data connection, roaming, battery level, and the system clock. Just to give you an idea, this is the top 32 pixels in portrait mode, or, 72 pixels in landscape mode. This is represented in code by the *SystemTray* class.

- The app bar is always displayed on the same edge as the device hardware buttons. This means that in portrait mode it's at the bottom of the screen, and in landscape mode it's on the left or right side (72 pixels in height in portrait mode, and 72 pixels wide in landscape mode). Your app can use this space to provide up to four icon buttons, plus a short menu. You can use standard icons or custom icons, but these are constrained to be white only in a 26x26-pixel area within the overall 48x48-pixel icon area. This is represented in code by the *ApplicationBar* class.
- The Frame is the top-level UI container for a Windows Phone app, represented in code by the *PhoneApplicationFrame* type. Within that, your app can have one or more *Page* elements, represented by the *PhoneApplicationPage* type, whose size varies according to how you're showing the notification area and app bar.

Windows Phone 8 supports three screen resolutions:

- WVGA = 480x800 pixels, aspect ratio 1.6 (more normally represented as 15:9). This is the only resolution supported in Windows Phone 7.
- 720p = 720x1280 pixels, aspect ratio 1.5 (or 16:9).
- WXGA = 768x1280 pixels, aspect ratio 1.6 (or 15:9).

Both WVGA and WXGA have the same aspect ratio. When you're designing your screen layouts, you should generally assume the lowest common denominator, which is WVGA. In the emulator, you'll see that WVGA and WXGA are both scaled to WVGA; that is, 480x800 pixels. In other words, you don't get a 768x1280 canvas in WXGA—you get a 480x800 canvas that is auto-scaled. The system takes care of scaling, so in general, you don't have to do anything special to target both WVGA and WXGA. There are two caveats to this:

- The images you use are scaled along with the controls. So, you have a choice of using either lower-resolution WVGA images which will be scaled up for WXGA, or higher-resolution WXGA images which will be scaled down for WVGA. If you want to do a bit more work, your other option is to use both and either dynamically select at runtime or package separate XAPs for each resolution.
- When you define your layout, you should use relative or dynamic positioning (see the section "Screen layout" later in this chapter). If you use absolute layout coordinates, although these will still be scaled, your layout will look different on devices with different aspect ratios.

The situation is slightly different with 720p because the aspect ratio is different. Therefore, although your layout is scaled, the screen is taller (in portrait mode) than WVGA/WXGA. To be clear, scaling is still uniform, there's no "stretching" involved here. The simplest approach is always to target a screen size of 480x800. That way, you can take full advantage of auto-scaling, and the only questionable side-effect is that you'll have some spare screen space at the bottom of a 720p screen.

Just to give you an indication of how much real estate is available to play with in your app, the Microsoft Visual Studio templates generate code that provides for a standard *TitlePanel* and a *ContentPanel*. You can use this as a useful reference point for the general shape of the real estate you'll have at your disposal. The *FramePageSizes* app in the sample code exercises the visibility and opacity of the *SystemTray* and *ApplicationBar*, as shown in Figure 3-1.

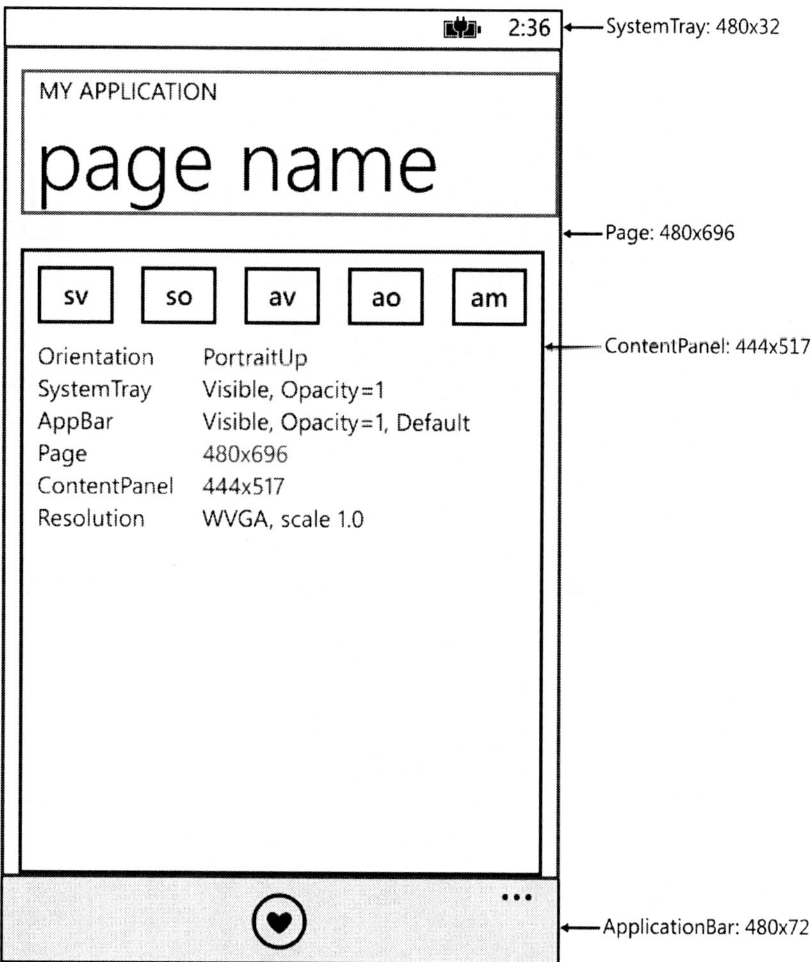

FIGURE 3-1 You should assume a page size of 480x800, which will be auto-scaled for different target screen resolutions.

Tables 3-1 and 3-2 show the width and height values (for WVGA/WXGA and 720p, respectively) for the page and the standard *ContentPanel*, given different values for *SystemTray* and *ApplicationBar* visibility, opacity, and mode.

TABLE 3-1 Page sizes for WVGA and WXGA

Orientation	*SystemTray*	*ApplicationBar*	*ApplicationBar* mode	*Page*	*ContentPanel*
Portrait	Visible and Opacity==1	Visible and Opacity==1	Default	480x696	444x517
Portrait	Hidden or Opacity <1	Visible and Opacity==1	Default	480x728	444x549
Portrait	Visible and Opacity==1	Hidden or Opacity <1	Default or Minimized	480x768	444x589
Portrait	Hidden or Opacity <1	Hidden or Opacity <1	Default	480x800	444x621
Portrait	Visible and Opacity==1	Visible and Opacity==1	Minimized	480x738	444x559
Portrait	Hidden or Opacity <1	Visible and Opacity==1	Minimized	480x770	444x591
Landscape	Visible and Opacity==1	Visible and Opacity==1	Default	656x480	620x301
Landscape	Hidden or Opacity <1	Visible and Opacity==1	Default	728x480	692x301
Landscape	Visible and Opacity==1	Hidden or Opacity <1	Default or Minimized	728x480	692x301
Landscape	Hidden or Opacity <1	Hidden or Opacity <1	Default	800x480	764x301
Landscape	Visible and Opacity==1	Visible and Opacity==1	Minimized	698x480	662x301
Landscape	Hidden or Opacity <1	Visible and Opacity==1	Minimized	770x480	734x301

TABLE 3-2 Page sizes for 720p

Orientation	*SystemTray*	*ApplicationBar*	*ApplicationBar* mode	*Page*	*ContentPanel*
Portrait	Visible and Opacity==1	Visible and Opacity==1	Default	480x749	444x570
Portrait	Hidden or Opacity <1	Visible and Opacity==1	Default	480x781	444x602
Portrait	Visible and Opacity==1	Hidden or Opacity <1	Default or Minimized	480x821	444x642
Portrait	Hidden or Opacity <1	Hidden or Opacity <1	Default	480x853	444x674
Portrait	Visible and Opacity==1	Visible and Opacity==1	Minimized	480x791	444x612
Portrait	Hidden or Opacity <1	Visible and Opacity==1	Minimized	480x823	444x644
Landscape	Visible and Opacity==1	Visible and Opacity==1	Default	709x480	673x301
Landscape	Hidden or Opacity <1	Visible and Opacity==1	Default	781x480	745x301
Landscape	Visible and Opacity==1	Hidden or Opacity <1	Default or Minimized	781x480	745x301
Landscape	Hidden or Opacity <1	Hidden or Opacity <1	Default	853x480	817x301
Landscape	Visible and Opacity==1	Visible and Opacity==1	Minimized	751x480	715x301
Landscape	Hidden or Opacity <1	Visible and Opacity==1	Minimized	781x480	745x301

If you want to determine the resolution of the screen at runtime, you can use the *ScaleFactor* property exposed from the App object, as shown in the following code snippet. Notice that the *ScaleFactor* value corresponds to the simplest representation of the scaling (for example, 150 for 1.5 scaling rather than 16:9).

```
switch (App.Current.Host.Content.ScaleFactor)
{
    case 100: resolution = "WVGA, scale 1.0"; break;
    case 150: resolution = "720p, scale 1.5"; break;
    case 160: resolution = "WXGA, scale 1.6"; break;
}
```

In Visual Studio, you can select a different emulator for each resolution (see Figure 3-2). This makes it possible for you to test that your app works correctly in all available resolutions.

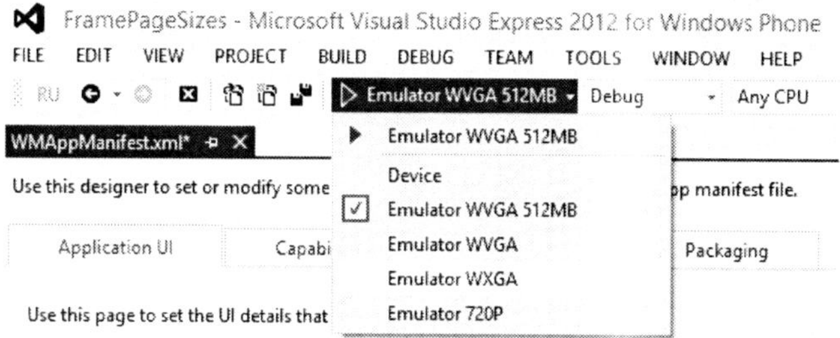

FIGURE 3-2 You should test your app on each of the emulator resolutions offered in Visual Studio.

If after testing you decide that your app doesn't work well enough in all resolutions, you can explicitly opt out of selected resolutions. To do this, you can edit your app manifest to clear the check boxes associated with the resolutions at which you don't want your app to run. This will prevent the Windows Phone Store from offering your app to a device with an excluded resolution. This will also prevent your app from installing on a development device or emulator image with an excluded resolution. This option is shown in Figure 3-3.

FIGURE 3-3 You can exclude your app from devices with selected screen resolutions.

The visual tree

The normal state of affairs is that most or all of the visual aspects of your UI are defined in XAML, with only UI logic in the code-behind. The XAML for a Windows Phone app is hierarchical in nature. At the root is a *PhoneApplicationFrame*, set as the *RootVisual* property in the *Application* base class. Each *PhoneApplicationPage* in the app becomes a child of the *RootVisual* when the user navigates to that page and the corresponding page class is instantiated. Finally, a page typically has children of its own.

At runtime, the layout engine parses the XAML and creates a set of objects to help correctly construct and maintain the UI. Some of these objects are visual, some are not—some are merely helper objects that have no visual representation. For example, a *ListBox* holds a collection of *ListBoxItems*, but the collection object itself has no visual representation. The visual hierarchy, or *tree*, is that subset of the object hierarchy that has a visual representation. You can think of it as a "parallel" tree to the XAML hierarchy. Some things don't appear in it (such as resources or *ListBox* item data), but it also contains all the expanded control templates and the like. This applies regardless of whether the object is actually visible. By default, *Grid* and *StackPanel* controls have no visual representation, but they determine the visual layout of their respective child objects, so they are part of the visual tree.

Quite often, visual objects that are not directly defined in the app's XAML are created as part of the tree. For example, a *Button* is actually made up of a number of other elements. You can see this if you examine the default template for the *Button* control. The default template is in the *System.Windows.xaml* file, which you can find in the install folder for the Windows Phone SDK, typically located at %ProgramFiles(x86)%\Microsoft SDKs\Windows Phone\v8.0\Design\System.Windows.xaml. An abstract of this template is listed in the following:

```
<ControlTemplate TargetType="ButtonBase">
    <Grid Background="Transparent">
        <Border x:Name="ButtonBackground">
            <ContentControl x:Name="ContentContainer"/>
        </Border>
    </Grid>
</ControlTemplate>
```

You can see that the *Button* is made up of a *Grid*, a *Border*, and a *ContentControl*. Now, the derivation hierarchy for the *Button* control includes the *Control* class—and the *Control* class has a *Content* field of type *object*, which means it can hold anything. In the case of the *Button* control, the default *Content* type is a *TextBlock*.

If at any time you need to gain access to any element in the tree, you can use the *VisualTreeHelper* class to walk the tree. The *VisualTreeHelper* class includes both *GetChild* and *GetParent* methods so that you can walk the tree in either order. If you want to get to an element that you have declared in XAML, you can also declare a name for it, which means you'll have a field that you can use in code. However, it should be clear from the foregoing that sometimes you have visual elements that you might want to work with but which were implicit in some composite control—and for which, therefore, you have no opportunity to define a field. If the implicitly defined element is exposed as a property of one of your code elements, there's also no problem. Sometimes, however, such a nonexplicit element is also not exposed as an accessible property of any of your explicit elements.

One scenario for which the *VisualTreeHelper* technique is useful is when you want to access elements in a dynamic visual collection, such as a *ListBox*. In this scenario, you don't necessarily have fields defined for the controls within the *ListBoxItem* template. Another scenario is when you want to carry out some common processing for multiple elements of the same type all at once, even though you might or might not have fields for each element, and the elements might be in arbitrary control hierarchies on your page.

The Windows Phone Toolkit contains a number of custom controls as well as helper utilities including extension methods for working with the visual tree. Details are available at *http://phone.codeplex.com/*. Although the controls are public, the visual tree extensions are internal to the Toolkit, so if you want to use these directly, you can download the Toolkit source code and add the relevant extension classes to your project.

Here's a simple example to illustrate this scenario. The *GlobalElementChange* solution in the sample code (see Figure 3-4), has two separate groups of controls. The *Button* at the bottom toggles the *IsReadOnly* state of all of the *TextBox* controls, in both groups.

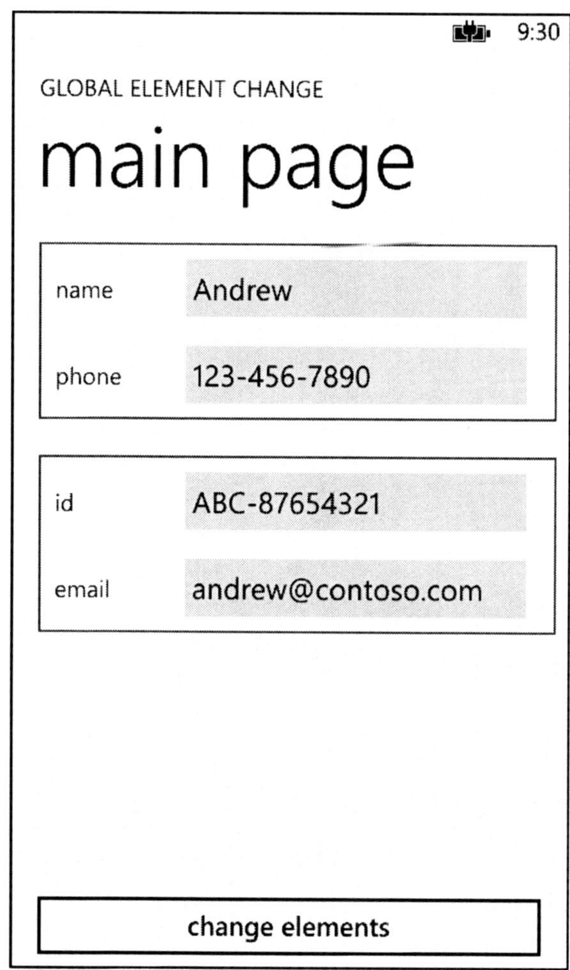

FIGURE 3-4 You can use the Windows Phone Toolkit extensions to work with the visual tree.

The *Click* handler for the *Button* invokes the *GetLogicalChildrenByType<T>* extension method. This returns an *IEnumerable<T>*, which we then enumerate and set each element's *IsReadOnly* property to *true*.

```
private void ChangeElements_Click(object sender, RoutedEventArgs e)
{
    var textBoxes = LayoutRoot.GetLogicalChildrenByType<TextBox>(false).ToList();
    foreach (TextBox t in textBoxes)
    {
        t.IsReadOnly = !t.IsReadOnly;
    }
}
```

Screen layout

The standard layout system supports three different layout models: absolute, relative, and dynamic. These are actually fairly arbitrary categorizations, but they do map to the layout characteristics of the primary control container types (the *Panel* control and its derivatives). With absolute layout, you specify absolute values for the size and position of all the visual elements. With relative layout, you specify some values for elements, relative to one another. With dynamic layout, you specify very little; instead, the system sizes and positions elements based on calculations of the elements' contents. In all cases, you can specify explicit values in the app XAML or the code-behind and/or values that are specified elsewhere in style resources. Per Windows Phone guidelines, you are encouraged to use the standard style resources for elements such as fonts, font sizes, margins, padding, and stroke thicknesses. You're also free to specify your own custom layouts by using whatever behavior you like.

The three types of layouts are represented by three container controls, all derivatives of the base *Panel* class:

- *Canvas*, for absolute layout, for which you specify absolute values for position and/or size.
- *Grid*, for dynamic layout, for which sizing depends on the relative container and item sizes.
- *StackPanel*, for relative layout, for which each item is laid out relative to the others.

It's worth mentioning that *Canvas* should generally be avoided because it makes it difficult to accommodate orientation changes and to share code with a Windows version of your app. The screenshots in Figure 3-5 show the *SimpleLayout* solution in the sample code. This app uses all three standard types of layout. Observe that the *Grid* control on the *MainPage* has its *ShowGridLines* property set to *true*, which is a useful visual aid during development.

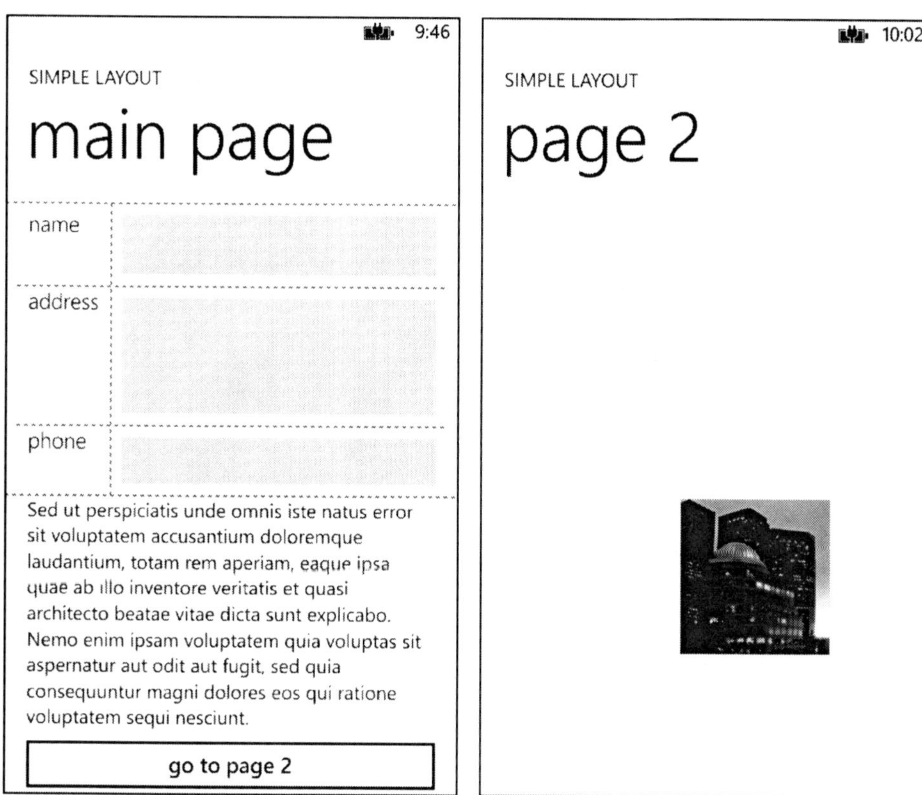

FIGURE 3-5 Use *Grid* and *StackPanel* controls (left) for controlled positioning, and *Canvas* (right) for maximum freedom.

The *MainPage* uses dynamic layout overall and is divided into three areas vertically: the top area uses relative layout, the middle area uses dynamic layout, and the bottom area again uses relative layout. *Page2* uses absolute layout. The *MainPage* XAML has an outer *Grid* (named *LayoutRoot*), within which it defines three areas: one represented by a *StackPanel*, the second by a *Grid*, and the third by another *StackPanel*.

```
<Grid x:Name="LayoutRoot" Background="Transparent" ShowGridLines="True">
    <Grid.RowDefinitions>
        <RowDefinition Height="Auto"/>
        <RowDefinition Height="300"/>
        <RowDefinition Height="*"/>
    </Grid.RowDefinitions>
```

```
    <StackPanel x:Name="TitlePanel" Grid.Row="0" Margin="12,17,0,28">
        <TextBlock
            x:Name="ApplicationTitle" Text="SIMPLE LAYOUT"
            Style="{StaticResource PhoneTextNormalStyle}"/>
        <TextBlock
            x:Name="PageTitle" Text="main page" Margin="9,-7,0,0"
            Style="{StaticResource PhoneTextTitle1Style}"/>
    </StackPanel>

    <Grid x:Name="ContentPanel" Grid.Row="1" Margin="12,0,12,0" ShowGridLines="True">
        <Grid.RowDefinitions>
            <RowDefinition Height="85"/>
            <RowDefinition Height="2*"/>
            <RowDefinition Height="*"/>
        </Grid.RowDefinitions>
        <Grid.ColumnDefinitions>
            <ColumnDefinition Width="100"/>
            <ColumnDefinition Width="*"/>
        </Grid.ColumnDefinitions>

        <TextBlock Text="name" Style="{StaticResource PhoneTextTitle3Style}" Margin="12,6,12,0"/>
        <TextBlock
            Grid.Row="1" Text="address"
            Style="{StaticResource PhoneTextTitle3Style}" Margin="12,6,12,0"/>
        <TextBlock
            Grid.Row="2" Text="phone"
            Style="{StaticResource PhoneTextTitle3Style}" Margin="12,6,12,0"/>

        <TextBox Grid.Column="1"/>
        <TextBox Grid.Row="1" Grid.Column="1"/>
        <TextBox Grid.Row="2" Grid.Column="1"/>
    </Grid>

    <StackPanel Grid.Row="2" Margin="{StaticResource PhoneHorizontalMargin}" >
        <TextBlock
            TextWrapping="Wrap" Style="{StaticResource PhoneTextNormalStyle}"
            Margin="{StaticResource PhoneHorizontalMargin}"
            Text="Sed ut perspiciatis unde omnis iste natus error sit voluptatem accusantium
doloremque laudantium, totam rem aperiam, eaque ipsa quae ab illo inventore veritatis et quasi
architecto beatae vitae dicta sunt explicabo. Nemo enim ipsam voluptatem quia voluptas sit
aspernatur aut odit aut fugit, sed quia consequuntur magni dolores eos qui ratione voluptatem
sequi nesciunt. "/>
        <Button Content="go to page 2" x:Name="Page2" Click="Page2_Click"/>
    </StackPanel>
</Grid>
```

StackPanel controls use relative layout, and the platform computes the layout for each element based on the size of the contents. The two *TextBlock* controls in the first *StackPanel* contain different text values and use different fonts and sizes. The default stacking mode in a *StackPanel* is vertical; therefore, the second *TextBlock* starts wherever the first one left off. As it happens, the second *Grid* starts wherever the first *StackPanel* (and the second *TextBlock*) left off, but for a different reason. The *StackPanel* and *Grid* are both children of an outer *Grid*, and the outer *Grid* specifies row heights. In this example, the first row height is set to *Auto*, so it takes up whatever space is needed by the child *StackPanel*. This is why the second *Grid* effectively starts where the *StackPanel* ended. Using the same mechanism, the *Button* in the second *StackPanel* is pushed down by the size of the *Text* value above it. So, the *Button* positioning is relatively arbitrary, and the result might or might not end up being aesthetically pleasing.

In contrast, grids use dynamic layout with which you have more explicit control over the sizes and positions of each child element. Consider the first *Grid*, which specifies three *RowDefinitions*, with their heights set to Auto, 300, and *, respectively.

```
<Grid.RowDefinitions>
    <RowDefinition Height="Auto"/>
    <RowDefinition Height="300"/>
    <RowDefinition Height="*"/>
</Grid.RowDefinitions>
```

- Auto specifies that the row height will be whatever it needs to be for the height of the content. In this case, the content is a *StackPanel* made up of two *TextBlock* controls, with their heights, margins, and padding determined by the style resources defined for them.
- 300 is the height in pixels of the second grid row, which is occupied by an inner *Grid*. This will be constrained to 300 pixels, regardless of the sizes of its children.
- * indicates that this row will be allocated whatever height is left after the first two rows. That is, (Page Height – (*ApplicationTitle* + *PageTitle* + *Margins*) – 300).

The inner *Grid* (named *ContentPanel*) is divided into three rows and two columns.

```
<Grid.RowDefinitions>
    <RowDefinition Height="85"/>
    <RowDefinition Height="2*"/>
    <RowDefinition Height="*"/>
</Grid.RowDefinitions>
<Grid.ColumnDefinitions>
    <ColumnDefinition Width="100"/>
    <ColumnDefinition Width="*"/>
</Grid.ColumnDefinitions>
```

Row 0 is 80 pixels in height. Rows 1 and 2 are allocated heights using a weighting of 2 and 1, respectively. This is a 2:1 ratio of the remaining space, that is, 300 – 80 = 220, giving values of 147 and 73. To target the widest range of devices of varying screen resolutions and aspect ratios, you should generally use relative or dynamic layout as much as possible and avoid specifying explicit values for absolute positioning.

Notice that it is not necessary to specify *Grid.Row* and *Grid.Column* property values when you want these to be zero; this is the default value for these properties. Indeed, setting these values explicitly causes unnecessary work and has a tiny performance impact. However, the benefits of explicit declarations and the symmetry of every item having a row and a column defined might be easier to work with from an engineering perspective. Also notice that while the *PhoneTextTitle3Style* includes settings for *Margin*, in this example we're overriding the *Margin* on some of our *TextBlock* controls because the values defined in the style are not what we want.

Finally, *Page2* has the traditional outer *Grid* and inner *StackPanel* for the *ApplicationTitle* and *PageTitle*. Beyond that, however, the remaining space is taken up by a simple *Canvas*. The *Image* control is positioned by using absolute values for the X and Y coordinates, specified as values for the *Canvas.Left* and *Canvas.Top* properties. The upper-left corner of the phone screen is X,Y coordinate 0,0. These are attached properties, which are discussed later in this chapter (as are the *Grid.Row* and *Grid.Column* properties).

```
<Canvas x:Name="ContentPanel" Grid.Row="1" Margin="12,0,12,0">
    <Image Canvas.Left="200" Canvas.Top="300">
        <Image.Source>
            <BitmapImage UriSource="Assets/SeattleEvening.jpg"/>
        </Image.Source>
    </Image>
</Canvas>
```

A *Canvas* clearly gives you absolute control over the layout of the child elements. The corollary is that you must specify layout values explicitly because nothing is done for you. If none of the standard *Panel* classes gives you the layout control you want, you can consider creating a custom panel.

Note As discussed in Chapter 11, "App publication," you should minimize the work that you do on the UI thread wherever possible to avoid impacting the UX. Windows Phone supports background image decoding, which minimizes the work done on the UI thread. To use this feature, you set the *CreateOptions* attribute on each image for which you want it to apply. You can do this in XAML, as shown in the following:

```
<Image Canvas.Left="200" Canvas.Top="300">
    <Image.Source>
        <BitmapImage UriSource="Assets/SeattleEvening.jpg"
            CreateOptions="BackgroundCreation"/>
    </Image.Source>
</Image>
```

Alternatively, you can also do this in code:

```
BitmapImage bmp = new BitmapImage();
bmp.CreateOptions = BitmapCreateOptions.BackgroundCreation;
bmp.UriSource = new Uri("Assets/SeattleEvening.jpg", UriKind.Relative);
theImage.Source = bmp;
```

Working with *UserControls* vs. custom controls

Both *UserControls* and custom controls are commonly used in phone apps, but the difference between them is a common source of confusion. Both are control types that you define, both are based on a standard type in the base class library, and you can use either or both in a Windows Phone app. So much for the commonalities; the major differences are listed in Table 3-3.

TABLE 3-3 *UserControl* vs. custom control

Feature	*UserControl*	Custom control
Derivation	You typically derive a class from *UserControl*. Visual Studio will only generate a type derived from *UserControl*, but you can derive from another type such as *ChildWindow* or *PhoneApplicationPage* (which is itself a *UserControl*) by manually editing the generated XAML and code files.	For complete freedom, you typically derive from *Control*. You can also derive from *ItemsControl* if you're building a custom control for a collection (think, *ListBox*). You can derive from *ContentControl* if your custom control will have only one piece of content (think, *Button*). You can derive from *Panel* if your control will be used as a layout container (think, *StackPanel*). A custom panel is still considered a "custom control" even though *Panel* does not derive from *Control* (it derives from *FrameworkElement*).
Tool support	Visual Studio provides a project item template for a Windows Phone *UserControl*.	Visual Studio provides a project item template for a class.
Starter code	Visual Studio generates the same code as for a desktop Silverlight *UserControl*; there's nothing phone-specific about in the starter code.	Visual Studio generates the same code as for a desktop Silverlight class; there's nothing phone-specific about in the starter code.
Designer support	You get a XAML file and a standard code-behind code file. This means that you get XAML visual designer support.	You get only a code file. There is no visual designer support. Note that you can create the template visually in Microsoft Expression Blend.
Canonical use case	Use when you want a composite control that contains other controls, which you can declare in XAML (or programmatically).	Use when you want to separate the UI of the control from its behavior via re-templating. Also used when you want completely custom behavior that might or might not include any other controls. Typically used to extend the behavior of a standard control via subclassing.

Figure 3-6 is a screenshot of the *CustomPanel* solution in the sample code, which uses a custom layout panel.

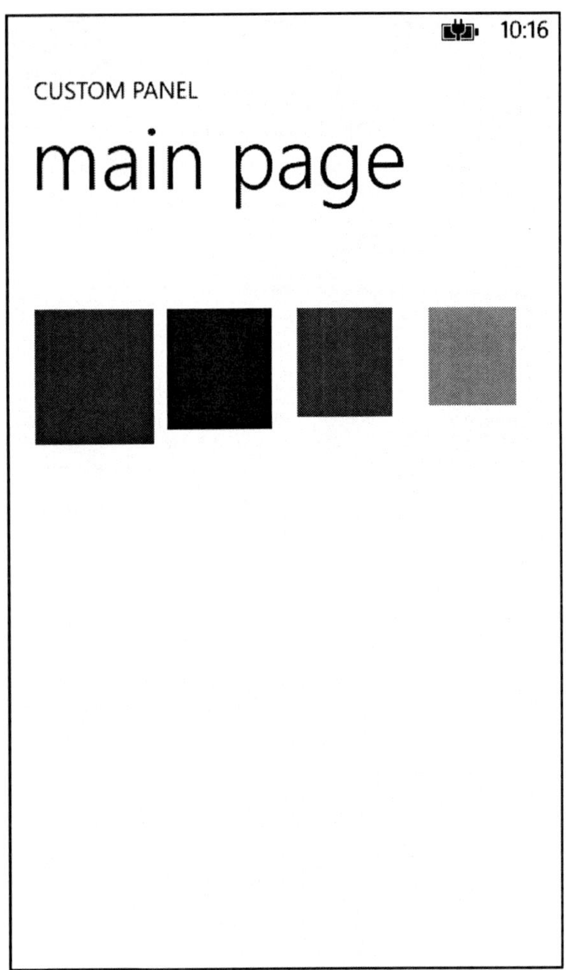

FIGURE 3-6 You can create a custom panel to achieve any kind of layout.

The behavior of this control becomes more apparent if you examine the XAML for the app in which it is being consumed.

```
<local:SizingPanel Background="Transparent" >
    <Rectangle Fill="#FFFF0097"/>
    <Rectangle Fill="#FFA200FF"/>
    <Rectangle Fill="#FF00ABA9"/>
    <Rectangle Fill="#FF8CBF26"/>
</local:SizingPanel >
```

You can see that the custom control named *SizingPanel* contains four *Rectangle* controls. None of the children defines a value for *Width* or *Height*, yet the control lays out the children by using a scaling factor so that they decrease in size from left to right. If you want this kind of full control over layout, you must override the *MeasureOverride* and *ArrangeOverride* methods. These are called in sequence. First *MeasureOverride* is called—this is your opportunity to specify the size available for each of the element's children. If a child already has a width and height defined, it is common to specify the smaller of the defined size and the available size. Of course, this is only a guideline; there's nothing to stop you from specifying any arbitrary size that you like, including a zero size. If you specify a zero size for any child, that child will not be displayed. It might even be appropriate to specify a size that is larger than the available size if the intended purpose of the control is, for example, to provide a viewport onto a larger item.

The implementation of *MeasureOverride* depends on the desired behavior of the container, but typically, it progresses by the following steps:

1. Estimate the amount of space available to each child
2. Call *Measure* on each child with the estimated size to see what their desired size will be
3. Compute any additional space needed by the container itself (for example, spacing between children) to get a final desired size

Sometimes, this is an iterative process, where the estimates improve after each layout pass (for example, in the case of a *Grid* for which the size of "*"-sized rows and columns depend on the sizes of the other rows and columns.

Finally, you must return the overall size desired for the control itself, which should be equal to or less than the available size that the system passes in to *MeasureOverride*.

After the measure pass (or passes) are complete, the system calls *ArrangeOverride*. This is your opportunity to specify the position and size of each child—by calling *Arrange* on them—and the final size of the control itself. During this call, you would typically calculate the position of the children by using their desired sizes as a factor. The desired sizes were set previously in the *MeasureOverride*. You are free to lay out your children in any way you like, including overlapping, off the screen, and not at all.

In this custom control, we define a scale factor, which is applied in the *MeasureOverride* to the size of the first child and progressively reduced for each subsequent child. In the *ArrangeOverride*, we simply lay out all the children in a single row.

```
public class SizingPanel : Panel
{
    private double childSize = 0;
    private Size desiredSize;
    private const double BaseScaleFactor = 0.9;
    private List<Size> computedSizes;
    private const double DefaultSize = 480;

    protected override Size MeasureOverride(Size availableSize)
    {
        int childCount = Children.Count;
        if (childCount == 0)
            return new Size(0, 0);
```

```
        double availableWidth = double.IsNaN(availableSize.Width) ? DefaultSize : availableSize.
Width;
        double availableHeight = double.IsNaN(availableSize.Height) ? DefaultSize :
availableSize.Height;
        computedSizes = new List<Size>();
        childSize = Math.Min(availableWidth, availableHeight) / childCount;

        double currentScaleFactor = 1.0;
        foreach (var child in Children)
        {
            currentScaleFactor *= BaseScaleFactor;
            Size size = new Size(childSize * currentScaleFactor, childSize *
currentScaleFactor);
            child.Measure(size);

            if (child.DesiredSize.Width == 0 || child.DesiredSize.Height == 0)
                computedSizes.Add(size);
            else
                computedSizes.Add(child.DesiredSize);
        }

        desiredSize = new Size(availableWidth, availableHeight);
        return desiredSize;
    }

    protected override Size ArrangeOverride(Size finalSize)
    {
        if (finalSize != desiredSize)
            MeasureOverride(finalSize);

        for (int i = 0; i < Children.Count; i++)
        {
            Rect rect = new Rect(childSize * i, 0, computedSizes[i].Width, computedSizes[i].
Height);
            Children[i].Arrange(rect);
        }

        return finalSize;
    }
}
```

Re-templating controls

An alternative to building a custom control or *UserControl* is re-templating existing controls. For example, suppose that you want to use a *Panorama* control, but you want to customize the title with a nonstandard *FontSize*, and also include your organization's logo in the title block. If you explicitly set a *FontSize* for the *Title* property (or indeed, the *Header* property of a *PanoramaItem*), this will be ignored. However, it is possible to re-template these, instead. The following code provides a custom *DataTemplate* for the panorama *Title*, using a stacked *Image* and *TextBlock*, with custom text attributes:

```
<controls:Panorama Name="MyPano" Title="My Panorama App">
    <controls:Panorama.TitleTemplate>
        <DataTemplate>
            <StackPanel Orientation="Horizontal" Margin="12,80,0,0">
                <Image
                        Source="/Assets/rocket-logo.png" Height="190" Width="190"/>
                <TextBlock
                        Text="rocket fuel"
                        FontSize="{StaticResource PhoneFontSizeHuge}"
                        VerticalAlignment="Center"/>
            </StackPanel>
        </DataTemplate>
    </controls:Panorama.TitleTemplate>
... irrelevant code omitted for brevity.
</controls:Panorama>
```

Figure 3-7 shows the result (see the *RetemplatedPanorama* solution in the sample code).

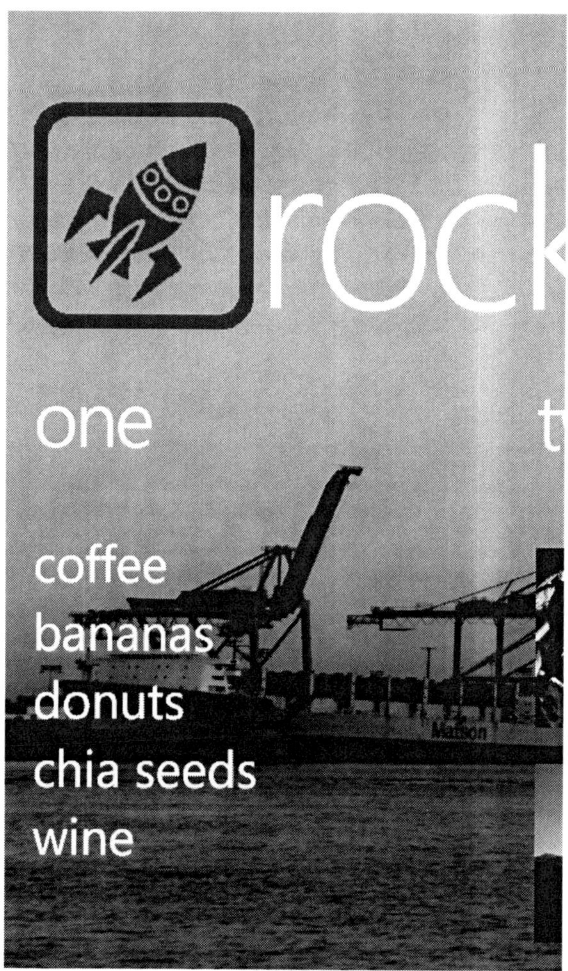

FIGURE 3-7 You can re-template any standard or custom control to customize its appearance.

Another scenario in which you typically provide a custom template is for items within list controls such as the *ListBox* and *LongListSelector* (see Chapter 4, "Data binding and MVVM," for more details on this).

Resources

In Windows Phone development, there are two different concepts of resources:

- Data resources, such as images, text files, and audio and video files
- Reusable XAML or code resources, such as styles, templates, brushes, colors, animations, and so on

In the following sections, you'll see the different ways of packaging your data resources, and your options for defining XAML resources.

Data resources

There are two ways to include data resources in a Windows Phone project: with the build action set to *Content*, or with the build action set to *Resource*. The key differences are listed in Table 3-4, using as an example an image resource named *MyImage.jpg* in the folder Assets, at the root of a project with the assembly name *MyAssembly*. Also, you can select multiple items in the Visual Studio Solution Explorer and set the value for all of them in one go. Finally, there are several other build actions available, as listed in the Visual Studio property grid, but none of the other actions are relevant for phone applications.

TABLE 3-4 Content vs. resource

Issue	Content	Resource
Location in the XAP	Loose in the XAP, in the specified folder	Embedded in the assembly itself
Source path (current assembly)	/Assets/MyImage.jpg (the leading slash is optional)	Assets/MyImage.jpg (note NO leading slash)
Source path (external assembly)	n/a	/MyAssembly;component/Assets/MyImage.jpg (note the leading slash)
Performance	Faster startup, slower to load the image	Slower startup, faster to load the image
Performance (media)	Faster startup, faster to play the media	Slower startup, slower to play the media
Assembly size	Smaller	Bigger
Loading behavior	Asynchronous	Synchronous
XAP size	(Same)	(Same)
Optimal use case	App	Library
Used for system UI (*ApplicationBar*, *SplashScreen*, LiveTile, and so on)	Required	Not supported

The following XAML shows valid syntax for loading both *Content* and *Resource* images from the current assembly and a *Resource* image from an external assembly.

```
<!-- Content resource -->
<Image Width="200" Height="150" Source="/Assets/Palms1.jpg"/>

<!-- Internal Resource resource -->
<Image Width="200" Height="150" Source="Assets/Palms2.jpg"/>

<!-- External Resource resource -->
<Image
    Width="200" Height="150" Source="/ImageLibrary;component/Assets/Coconuts.jpg"/>
```

After a resource has been read into memory, it can be cached—this is especially true of image resources. So, if you only have a few small resources, it might be worth taking the load-time performance hit incurred when you embed them as resources in the dynamic-link library (DLL). You need to balance this against the marketplace certification requirement that your app must show its first screen within 5 seconds of startup and be responsive to user interaction within 20 seconds. If you embed too many resources, you can easily exceed these startup limits. There's an additional twist in the case of media (audio and video) resources: if these are embedded in the assembly, they will nevertheless be copied out to files in isolated storage before they are played back. The underlying reason for this is because the media functionality on the phone is optimized for playback from network streaming and from disk file but not from memory. In general, therefore, you should never mark audio/video as Resource.

Note Windows Phone 7.0 devices supported image rendering of 16 bits per pixel (bpp). In Windows Phone 7.1, this was increased to 32 bpp (although the actual hardware screen might still be 16 bpp or some other value less than 32). Rendering at 16 bpp results in obvious banding in image gradients. This is significantly reduced or eliminated at 32 bpp. To select 32 bpp in a Windows Phone 7.1 app, you could add the *BitsPerPixel* attribute to the *App* element in your app manifest. In Windows Phone 8, the default is 32 bpp and the *BitsPerPixel* attribute is ignored.

XAML resources and resource dictionaries

XAML resources are a convenience designed for code reuse. For example, consider the case for which you define a *Brush* for the *Foreground* in a *TextBlock*. The simple approach is to define this *Brush* in line with the definition of the *TextBlock*. You can see this at work in the *SimpleResources* app in the sample code.

```
<TextBlock Text="Monday" FontSize="42.667" Margin="12">
    <TextBlock.Foreground>
        <LinearGradientBrush>
            <GradientStop Color="#FF339933" Offset="0"/>
            <GradientStop Color="#FFF09609" Offset="1"/>
        </LinearGradientBrush>
    </TextBlock.Foreground>
</TextBlock>
```

If, however, you find that you're using the same *Brush* for multiple *TextBlock* controls, it makes sense to define it as a shared resource. Typically, you would define this in a Resources section at the page level. When you define a resource it must have a *Key* value. It is common to use the explicit "x:" prefix, where "x" is defined in the app as the namespace for the standard XAML schema. A resource can have a *Name* instead of, or in addition to, a *Key*. If *Key* is not specified, *Name* is used as the key. When you declare a *Name* for an element in XAML, this generates a corresponding class member as well as code in the *Initialize* method to call *FindName* to match up the named element with the code variable. In the case of a resource, this won't work, because the resource isn't in the visual tree—which is why you should generally use a *Key* and not a *Name* for resources.

```
<phone:PhoneApplicationPage.Resources>
    <LinearGradientBrush x:Key="MyGradientBrush">
        <GradientStop Color="#FF339933" Offset="0"/>
        <GradientStop Color="#FFF09609" Offset="1"/>
    </LinearGradientBrush>
</phone:PhoneApplicationPage.Resources>
```

Having defined the resource, you would then consume it by using the *{StaticResource}* syntax. The following code consumes the *Brush* resource and also consumes two other resources: a *Margin* and a *FontSize*.

```
<TextBlock
    Text="Tuesday" Foreground="{StaticResource MyGradientBrush}"
    Margin="{StaticResource PhoneMargin}"
    FontSize="{StaticResource PhoneFontSizeExtraExtraLarge}"/>
```

The two standard resources used here are defined in the standard theme resources. These are loaded automatically by the system at runtime. If you want to view these same standard resources, you can find a copy of them in the install folder for the Windows Phone SDK, which is typically at %ProgramFiles(x86)\Microsoft SDKs\Windows Phone\v8.0\Design\ThemeResources.xaml.

```
<Thickness x:Key="PhoneMargin">12</Thickness>
<!--54pt-->
<System:Double x:Key="PhoneFontSizeExtraExtraLarge">72</System:Double>
```

Note that *PhoneApplicationPage.Resources* is of type *ResourceDictionary*. A *ResourceDictionary* is a *DependencyObject* that implements *IDictionary*, so it contains a regular collection of key-value pairs. The key is an arbitrary string that the app defines. The value is the resource itself. Note that there is a finite list of types that can be put into a resource dictionary. For an object to be defined in a resource dictionary, it must be shareable. This is required because when the object tree of an app is constructed at runtime, any given object cannot exist at multiple locations in the tree. So, it must exist at one location in the tree and therefore be shareable from that location to all its consumers in the tree. The following types are supported:

- Styles and templates
- Brushes and colors

- Animation types, including storyboards
- Transforms, Matrix, Matrix3D, and Point structure values
- Custom types defined in the app code and instantiated in XAML as a resource, including resource and value converters
- Strings and basic numeric values such as *double* and *int*

It's worth mentioning that any type of *UIElement* (such as a *Control*) is not supported.

Although you typically define such resources at the page level, you can in fact define resources for any *FrameworkElement*; that is, for any element in the logical tree as well as for the *Application* class. For example, we could define the resource at the level of the *StackPanel* that contains the *TextBlock*. To illustrate the point, the following definition uses different colors:

```
<StackPanel.Resources>
    <LinearGradientBrush  x:Key="MyGradientBrush">
        <GradientStop Color="#FFA200FF" Offset="0"/>
        <GradientStop Color="#FF00ABA9" Offset="1"/>
    </LinearGradientBrush>
</StackPanel.Resources>
```

Note, however, that this definition specifies the same *Key* name. If a different *Key* name is used, the consuming code could choose to use either of the two resources. If the same resource *Key* value is defined at two or more different levels in the tree, the system uses the one that is most local to the consuming element. In the current example, the visual tree is essentially *Page* → *StackPanel* → *TextBlock*. So, if the same resource is defined at both *Page* and *StackPanel* levels, the system will use the more local *StackPanel* version.

In addition to *FrameworkElements*, you can also define resources for the *Application* class. Application-level resources are available to all pages within the app. In the following example, we define a *Brush* resource with the key *"MyAppGradientBrush"*:

```
<Application.Resources>
    <LinearGradientBrush x:Key="MyAppGradientBrush">
        <GradientStop Color="#FFE671B8" Offset="0"/>
        <GradientStop Color="#FF8CBF26" Offset="1"/>
    </LinearGradientBrush>
</Application.Resources>
```

To resolve a resource reference, the runtime walks the logical tree outward in scope, from child to parent, starting with the consuming element. Thus, it will start with the object where the actual usage is applied and that object's own *Resources* property. If that resource dictionary is not null, the system searches in that dictionary for the specified resource, based on its key. If it is found, the lookup stops and the resource is applied. Keep in mind that it is not generally useful to define a resource within the object where it is consumed; the value is only accessible within that object; thus, you might as well define the values in line instead of taking the performance hit of resource resolution. If the resource is not found in the immediate object's resource dictionary, the lookup then proceeds to the next outer (parent) object in the tree and searches there. This sequence continues until the root element of the XAML is reached, exhausting the search of all possible immediate (that is, page or frame-level) resource locations. If the requested resource is not found in the page-level resources, the runtime checks the *Application* resources. If the resource is not found there, you'll get a XAML parse error.

It makes sense to define your resources at a level that provides the reuse that you want. Typically, this means at the page level if the resource is used by multiple elements on that page, or at the app level if it is used across multiple pages. In addition, you can define resources in external files and then merge those files into your app-level or page-level resource dictionaries. For example, we could add a new XML file to the project, naming it perhaps *MyResources.xaml.* The default build action for a XAML file is *Page*, which is what we need in order to have the external resources built into the assembly. In this file, we can define one or more resources in a *ResourceDictionary.* In the following example, we define a *Brush* resource with the key *"MyOtherBrush:"*

```
<ResourceDictionary
    xmlns="http://schemas.microsoft.com/winfx/2006/xaml/presentation"
    xmlns:x="http://schemas.microsoft.com/winfx/2006/xaml">
    <LinearGradientBrush x:Key="MyOtherBrush">
        <GradientStop Color="#FFFF0097" Offset="0"/>
        <GradientStop Color="#FFA05000" Offset="1"/>
    </LinearGradientBrush>
</ResourceDictionary>
```

In the app, we instruct the XAML parser to merge this resource dictionary into any of the resource dictionaries in the app—either for any *FrameworkElement* or at the *Application* level.

```
<Application.Resources>
    <ResourceDictionary>
        <LinearGradientBrush x:Key="MyAppGradientBrush">
            <GradientStop Color="#FFE671B8" Offset="0"/>
            <GradientStop Color="#FF8CBF26" Offset="1"/>
        </LinearGradientBrush>
        <ResourceDictionary.MergedDictionaries>
            <ResourceDictionary Source="MyResources.xaml" />
        </ResourceDictionary.MergedDictionaries>
    </ResourceDictionary>
</Application.Resources>
```

Then, we can consume this just like any other accessible resource in the project.

```
<TextBlock
    Text="Thursday" Foreground="{StaticResource MyOtherBrush}"
    Margin="{StaticResource PhoneMargin}"
    FontSize="{StaticResource PhoneFontSizeExtraExtraLarge}"/>
```

Be aware that using merged resource dictionaries affects both the lookup sequence and also the key uniqueness requirements. In the lookup sequence, a merged resource dictionary is checked only after checking all the resources of the local resource dictionary.

You can specify more than one *ResourceDictionary* within *MergedDictionaries*. After the lookup behavior exhausts the search in the main dictionary and reaches the merged dictionaries, each item in *MergedDictionaries* is checked, but in the inverse order that they are declared in the *MergedDictionaries* property; that is, in last-in, first-out (LIFO) order. Why is this? You might expect that a more logical sequence would be first-in, first-out (FIFO), in the order in which dictionaries are declared. The order is reversed to accommodate dynamic additions to the collection. The classic scenario for which this is employed is user preferences. These would be known only at runtime and would need to take precedence over any static resources. For this reason, you must search the user preferences first, and for that to happen, the search order must be LIFO.

Also, the key uniqueness requirement does not extend across merged dictionaries. This means that you could define the same key in multiple merged dictionaries. As always, the search for keys stops when a match is found, so any duplicate keys later in the search sequence are irrelevant.

A resource can reference another resource, but only if that other resource has already been encountered in the lookup sequence. Forward references are illegal, and you need to understand the lookup sequence in order to avoid forward references. So, any resources that will be referenced by other resources need to be defined at an earlier point in the lookup sequence—which translates to a wider scope.

Finally, you can consume resources that are defined in an external assembly. This takes the reuse aspect of resource dictionaries to its logical conclusion. Beyond defining resources in an external XML file, you can build that file (or multiple such files) into a separate library assembly. The definition of the resources doesn't change; you could build the exact same *MyResources.xaml* file into a separate assembly. The consumption of these resources does change, which means that you must use the "/<AssemblyName>;component/<path-to-resource-XAML>" syntax, as demonstrated here:

```
<Application.Resources>
    <ResourceDictionary>
        <ResourceDictionary.MergedDictionaries>
            <ResourceDictionary Source="/ResourceLibrary;component/MyLibraryResources.xaml" />
        </ResourceDictionary.MergedDictionaries>
    </ResourceDictionary>
</Application.Resources>
```

Implicit styles

The preceding example focused on the various ways to define resources. We can continue with this example and focus instead on styles. Typically, you define *Style* resources the same way you define other resources: use a unique *Key* that can later be referenced by the elements that want to consume it. The following code defines a named style that can be applied to *TextBlock* elements:

```
<Style x:Key="GradientTextStyle" TargetType="TextBlock">
    <Setter Property="FontSize" Value="{StaticResource PhoneFontSizeLarge}"/>
    <Setter Property="Margin" Value="{StaticResource PhoneHorizontalMargin}"/>
    <Setter Property="TextWrapping"  Value="Wrap"/>
    <Setter Property="Foreground">
```

```
            <Setter.Value>
                <LinearGradientBrush StartPoint="0,1" EndPoint="1,0">
                    <GradientStop Offset="0" Color="#FFD80073"/>
                    <GradientStop Offset="1" Color="#FF00ABA9"/>
                </LinearGradientBrush>
            </Setter.Value>
        </Setter>
</Style>
```

Having defined the style, you could then go ahead and apply it to any element of the specified target type by specifying the key name in the *Style* attribute for that element.

```
<TextBlock Text="Saturday" Style="{StaticResource GradientTextStyle}"/>
```

Such styles are known as *explicit* or *named* styles. Windows Phone supports these as well as implicit styles, which are defined in almost the same way as named styles; the difference is that you do not define a key value for the style. Without a key value, the style will be applied implicitly to all elements of the specified target type, without an explicit *Style* reference. Simply remove the key from the style definition, as shown here:

```
<Style TargetType="TextBlock">
... unchanged definition omitted for brevity.
</Style>
```

Then, apply the style implicitly, like so:

```
<TextBlock Text="Saturday"/>
```

At any time, for any element of the target type, you can override the implicit style if you need to. To do this, you can set the *Style* to null (using the *{x:Null}* syntax), or you can simply apply an explicit style, instead. You can also retain the implicit style, but override one or more of the style's properties.

```
<TextBlock Text="Sunday" Style="{x:Null}"/>
<TextBlock Text="Sunday" Style="{StaticResource PhoneTextLargeStyle}"/>
<TextBlock Text="Sunday" FontSize="60" />
```

Finally, you can define style hierarchies. To do this, you use the *BasedOn* attribute. Of course, this attribute requires a key name, so if you define a style hierarchy, only the last style in the tree can be implicit; all the others must have key values.

```
<Style x:Key="GradientTextStyle2" TargetType="TextBlock">
    <Setter Property="Foreground">
        <Setter.Value>
            <LinearGradientBrush StartPoint="0,1" EndPoint="1,0">
                <GradientStop Offset="0" Color="#FFD80073"/>
                <GradientStop Offset="1" Color="#FF00ABA9"/>
            </LinearGradientBrush>
        </Setter.Value>
    </Setter>
</Style>
```

```
<Style TargetType="TextBlock" BasedOn="{StaticResource GradientTextStyle2}">
    <Setter Property="FontSize" Value="{StaticResource PhoneFontSizeLarge}"/>
    <Setter Property="Margin" Value="{StaticResource PhoneHorizontalMargin}"/>
    <Setter Property="TextWrapping"  Value="Wrap"/>
</Style>
```

Dependency and attached properties

The Common Language Runtime (CLR) supports a code design by which a class can expose properties. The system adds two additional features on top of CLR properties: dependency properties and attached properties. You can use these features to make your classes interoperate more seamlessly with the XAML framework, and they're especially useful if you have highly customized UI requirements.

Dependency properties

Dependency properties are designed to augment basic CLR properties with features such as visual hierarchy, animation, and data-binding. They provide a structured way to give properties a default, inherited, or animated value, and to provide callbacks that are invoked when the value of the property changes. Almost all Windows Phone platform class properties in the XAML framework are dependency properties. If you want to create a custom control that exposes properties, and you want those properties to be settable in styles, templates, transforms, data bindings, or as targets of animation, they must be set up as dependency properties.

In the *DependencyProps* sample, we implement a custom *Button* that exposes a *Direction* dependency property. This *Direction* property is used internally to govern which one of two different images to use for the *Button* content.

Any class that implements dependency properties must derive from *DependencyObject*. The custom class derives from *Button*, which has *DependencyObject* in its hierarchy. Our class has a regular property, *Direction* (of type *Direction*, which might be a little confusing to humans, but not to the compiler), which uses the *DependencyObject.GetValue/SetValue* methods. The regular property is not backed by a private field; instead, it is backed by a Silverlight-maintained property repository. A dependency property has a public static field of type *DependencyProperty*, which has the same name as the underlying regular property but with "Property" appended to it. You set up a dependency property by registering its property name, type, the type of the enclosing class, the default value, and the callback to be invoked when the property value changes, as demonstrated in the code that follows. Note that this class is also theme-aware.

```
public enum Direction { Up, Down }
public enum Theme { Dark, Light }

public class CustomButton : Button
{
    private static Image upArrow;
    private static Image downArrow;

    public Direction Direction
    {
        get { return (Direction)GetValue(DirectionProperty); }
        set { SetValue(DirectionProperty, value); }
    }

    public static readonly DependencyProperty DirectionProperty =
        DependencyProperty.Register("Direction", typeof(Direction), typeof(CustomButton),
            new PropertyMetadata(Direction.Up, OnDirectionChanged));

    internal Theme CurrentTheme
    {
        get
        {
            Visibility v = (Visibility)Resources["PhoneDarkThemeVisibility"];
            Theme theme = (v == System.Windows.Visibility.Visible) ? Theme.Dark : Theme.Light;
            return theme;
        }
    }
}
```

In the constructor, we initialize two alternative *Image* objects that correspond to the two possible *Direction* property values (using either black or white image resources, depending on the current theme).

```
public CustomButton()
{
    BitmapImage upBitmap = null;
    BitmapImage downBitmap = null;
    if (CurrentTheme == Theme.Dark)
    {
        upBitmap = new BitmapImage(new Uri("/Assets/arrow_up_white.png", UriKind.Relative));
        downBitmap = new BitmapImage(new Uri("/Assets/arrow_down_white.png", UriKind.Relative));
    }
    else
    {
        upBitmap = new BitmapImage(new Uri("/Assets/arrow_up_black.png", UriKind.Relative));
        downBitmap = new BitmapImage(new Uri("/Assets/arrow_down_black.png", UriKind.Relative));
    }

    upArrow = new Image();
    upArrow.Source = upBitmap;
    downArrow = new Image();
    downArrow.Source = downBitmap;
    Content = upArrow;
}
```

In the *OnDirectionChanged* callback, we fetch the new *Direction* property value from the *EventArgs* provided in the call and switch the *Content* to the up or down image, accordingly.

```
static void OnDirectionChanged(DependencyObject sender, DependencyPropertyChangedEventArgs e)
{
    CustomButton button = sender as CustomButton;
    Direction d = (Direction)e.NewValue;
    if (d == Direction.Up)
        button.Content = upArrow;
    else
        button.Content = downArrow;
}
```

In the XAML, we set up a namespace for the current assembly so that we can access the types in the XAML itself.

```
<phone:PhoneApplicationPage
...
    xmlns:local="clr-namespace:TestDependencyProps"
>
```

There are various ways in which we can use our custom dependency property. One is to set up a *Style* resource, as shown here:

```
<phone:PhoneApplicationPage.Resources>
    <Style x:Key="DownButtonStyle" TargetType="local:CustomButton">
        <Setter Property="Direction" Value="Down"/>
    </Style>
</phone:PhoneApplicationPage.Resources>
```

We can also set the property directly at the point where we declare an instance of the custom button. In the following example, the first *Button* has its *Direction* property set directly, the second one falls back on the default value (*Up*), and the third one uses the custom style:

```
<StackPanel x:Name="ContentPanel" Grid.Row="1" Margin="12,0,12,0">
    <local:CustomButton Width="100" Direction="Down"/>
    <local:CustomButton Width="300"/>
    <local:CustomButton Width="150" Style="{StaticResource DownButtonStyle}"/>
</StackPanel>
```

Figure 3-8 shows the results of these three custom buttons. This is the *TestDependencyProps* solution in the sample code. This might seem like a lot of work to expose a property, but it does allow the property to be used in ways that are not possible for a standard CLR property. For example, you cannot use a standard CLR property in the *Setter* element of a *Style*. Plus, of course, you cannot use it directly in data-binding or animation.

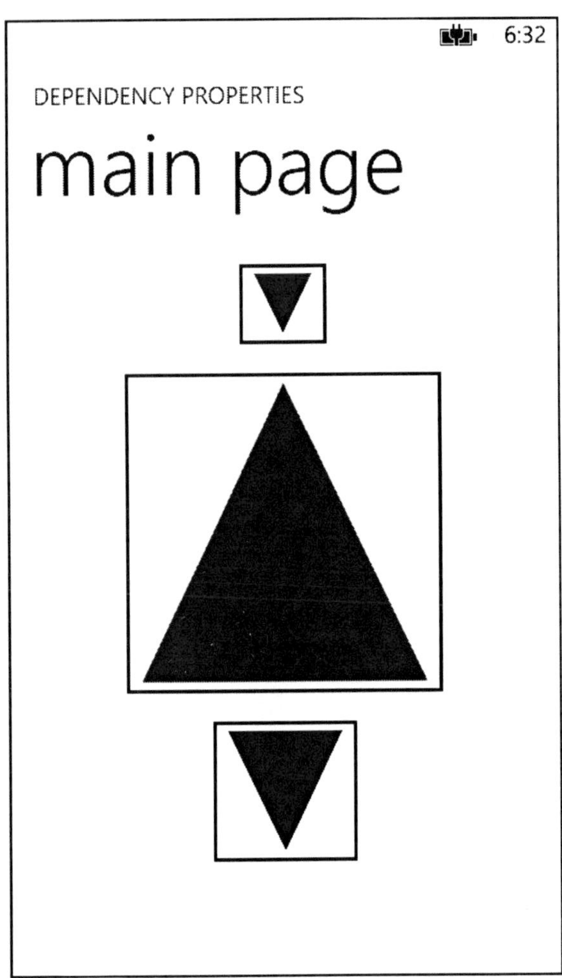

FIGURE 3-8 Dependency properties augment basic CLR properties with support for visual inheritance, animation, and data-binding.

Attached properties

Earlier in this chapter, we looked at how to create a custom *Panel* type that lays out its child controls by using a decreasing scale factor. It is often useful to be able to define the value of a parent control's property in the definition of the child. This is especially applicable to custom *Panel* types. To continue the earlier example, suppose that instead of having a fixed scaling factor, we want to allow each child to specify its own scale factor. Figure 3-9 shows the effect we're looking for (see the *CustomPanel_AttachableProperty* solution in the sample code).

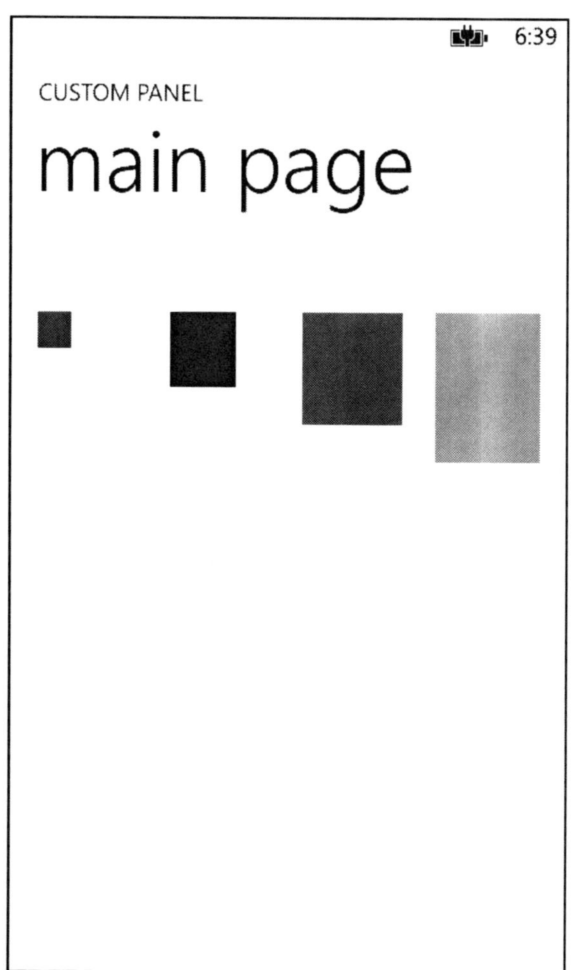

FIGURE 3-9 An application with a custom panel, using attached properties.

The listing that follows shows how we want to use the modified custom *Panel* in the app code. In this scenario, we don't want to specify a scaling factor for the control itself, because then it would apply to all children. Instead, we want to specify a different scaling factor for each child. In XAML, we can provide a value for the *ScaleFactor* for each child as though it were a property of the child itself. We're effectively attaching the *ScaleFactor* property of the parent control to the child element.

```
<Grid x:Name="ContentPanel" Grid.Row="1" Margin="12,0,12,0">
    <local:SizingPanel Background="Transparent" Width="456" Height="500">
        <Rectangle Fill="#FFFF0097" local:SizingPanel.ScaleFactor="0.25"/>
        <Rectangle Fill="#FFA200FF" local:SizingPanel.ScaleFactor="0.5"/>
        <Rectangle Fill="#FF00ABA9" local:SizingPanel.ScaleFactor="0.75"/>
        <Rectangle Fill="#FF8CBF26" local:SizingPanel.ScaleFactor="1.0"/>
    </local:SizingPanel >
</Grid>
```

To use this scale factor value in the control's layout computations, we can make a simple change to the *MeasureOverride* so that it uses the *ScaleFactor* dependency property for the child instead of the previous fixed value.

```
protected override Size MeasureOverride(Size availableSize)
{
    if (Children.Count > 0)
    {
        double childWidth = Width / Children.Count;
        double childHeight = Height / Children.Count;

        maxSize = new Size(childWidth, childHeight);
        int i = 0;
        double currentScaleFactor = 1.0;
        foreach (FrameworkElement child in Children)
        {
            child.Width = maxSize.Width;
            child.Height = maxSize.Height;

            currentScaleFactor =
                //baseScaleFactor;
                (double)child.GetValue(ScaleFactorProperty);

            child.Measure(new Size(
                childWidth * currentScaleFactor, childHeight * currentScaleFactor));
            i++;
        }
    }
    return new Size(Width, Height);
}
```

To make the property attachable in the first place, we need to enhance the custom control class with an additional public static field of type, *DependencyProperty*. For a regular dependency property, you would invoke the *Register* method to register this with the runtime. For an attachable dependency property, you instead invoke the *RegisterAttached* method. Also, instead of a regular CLR property backing this dependency property, you need to specify a pair of *GetXXX* and *SetXXX* methods.

```
public static readonly DependencyProperty ScaleFactorProperty =
    DependencyProperty.RegisterAttached(
    "ScaleFactor", typeof(double), typeof(SizingPanel), null);

public static double GetScaleFactor(DependencyObject obj)
{
    return (double)obj.GetValue(ScaleFactorProperty);
}

public static void SetScaleFactor(DependencyObject obj, double sf)
{
    obj.SetValue(ScaleFactorProperty, sf);
}
```

Passing null as the last parameter to *RegisterAttached* means that the panel will show items as zero width and height if you omit the attached property. This might be acceptable, but it is generally more useful to provide a non-zero default value, especially where the property relates to some size variable. So, a better registration would be the following:

```
public static readonly DependencyProperty ScaleFactorProperty =
    DependencyProperty.RegisterAttached(
    "ScaleFactor", typeof(double), typeof(SizingPanel), new PropertyMetadata(1.0));
```

With this updated registration, the following two lines of XAML would then be effectively identical:

```
<Rectangle Fill="#FF8CBF26" local:SizingPanel.ScaleFactor="1.0"/>
<Rectangle Fill="#FF8CBF26"/>
```

The model of attachable properties makes it possible for you to extend existing controls with custom characteristics. In the preceding example, we could use any control type (*Button*, *CheckBox*, *ListBox*, and so on) as a child within the custom *Panel* and define a value for the attached property. In fact, we could use any *DependencyObject* type. But, what is the thinking behind this slightly unusual model? We want a property of some parent control to be attached to its children and definable in the definition of the child instances. How else could this be achieved? Consider the alternatives. Inheritance wouldn't work because we'd have to define the required property in some base class so that all children would inherit it. For example, perhaps provide the property in the base *Control* class. This might serve the purpose where child controls such as *Button* and *CheckBox* would inherit it. It would not work for *Panels* or shapes such as *Rectangle* because *Panel* and *Shape* derive from *Framework Element* not *Control*. One problem is that the parent-child visual relationship has nothing to do with the parent-child inheritance relationship. For inheritance to be a suitable solution, we'd have to ensure that all properties we want to include in the model are defined on all base classes of all types that could be used as visual children. We'd end up with an inverted hierarchy in which base classes are stuffed with properties that are only used by some subset of children. Worse, the system would not be extensible.

In addition to the logical perspective, attachable properties are actually physically attached to the object for which they're defined. So, in our example, the memory for the *Rectangle* objects includes their attached properties. However, the attached properties do not form part of the object type. To illustrate this, you could declare the XAML that follows, in which the *ScaleFactor* property is attached to a *Rectangle*, but that *Rectangle* does not live in the context of a *SizingPanel*. This will compile and run quite happily, but it's possible that nothing will ever read the attached property value.

```
<Grid Grid.Row="2" Margin="12,0,12,0" Width="456" Height="200">
    <Rectangle Fill="#FFA05000" local:SizingPanel.ScaleFactor="0.25"/>
</Grid>
```

This is validation of the extensibility of the model: to attach a property, we don't have to make any changes to the target type, and nothing breaks if we attach a property, regardless of whether it is actually used.

The app bar and notification area

Windows Phone offers an app bar represented by the *ApplicationBar, ApplicationBarIconButton* and *ApplicationBarMenuItem* classes. The Application Bar—more commonly known as the app bar—is only minimally customizable: you can place up to four buttons on it (using standard or custom images). You can also have a single, flat menu. These should be short items in a short menu. There's actually no technical limit imposed on the number of items that you can have, but the menu slides up to show only five items completely. If you have more, the user would need to scroll to see the rest, and this compromises the UX.

An *ApplicationBar* property is exposed from the *PhoneApplicationPage* class, so you can define app bar items on a per-page basis. Note, however, that this is a virtualization on top of what under the hood is really a singleton object, managed by the Phone shell.

Microsoft supplies a suitable set of icons for use in the app bar. These are installed as a part of the Windows Phone Developer Tools (typically, in %ProgramFiles(x86)%\Microsoft SDKs\Windows Phone\v8.0\Icons). You can use these directly or as a base for your own images. Both light and dark-themed versions are provided. You should use the dark-themed version (white images); the platform will convert on the fly, as needed, if the user changes the theme on the device. The light-themed versions (black images) are provided not for use in the app bar, but in case you want to use them elsewhere in your app, outside of the app bar. The total image size is 48x48 pixels, and the customizable area within that is 26x26 pixels. The black versions are shown in Table 3-5.

TABLE 3-5 Standard app bar icons

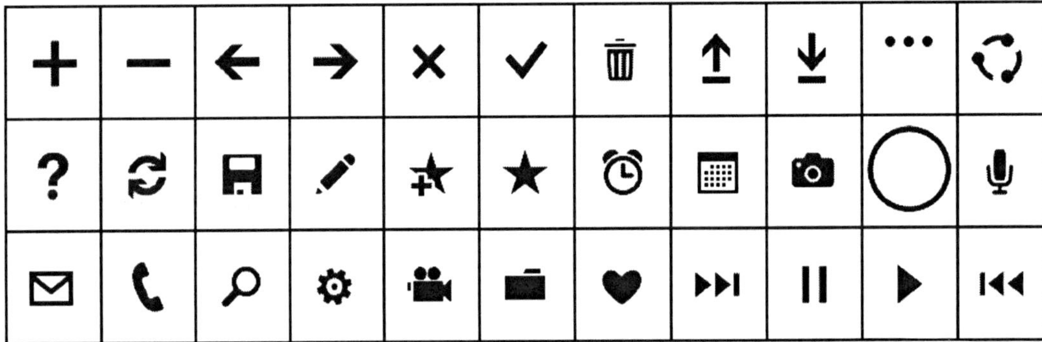

You can optionally set the opacity for the app bar. If you do so, you should limit yourself to values of 0, 0.5, and 1. If opacity <1, the app bar will overlay the UI. If opacity==1, the page size is reduced by the 72-pixel size of the app bar. If you don't provide images, the app will work just fine without explicit images (showing the default "x in a circle" image). If you attempt to provide more than four buttons, or if your buttons do not have text specified, the *ApplicationBar* will throw an exception on startup—which will typically crash your app unless you handle this exception.

The *ApplicationBar* also exposes a *Mode* property, which can be set to either *Default* or *Minimized*. The minimized mode is intended for use in scenarios for which you want to optimize your use of screen real estate, most particularly on panorama pages. If you must use an app bar on a panorama page, you should consider the minimized mode and also perhaps set *Opacity* to zero. Using this approach, the app bar ellipsis will always be visible, but the rest of the app bar only takes up space if the user taps the ellipsis to open it.

The *SystemTray* class exposes five properties: *IsVisible*, *BackgroundColor*, *ForegroundColor*, *Opacity*, and *ProgressIndicator*. Figure 3-10 shows the *AppBarSysTray* solution in the sample code, which utilizes these properties via four app bar buttons.

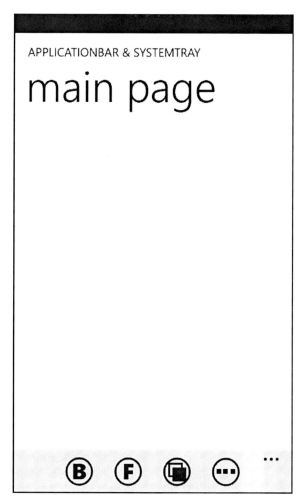

FIGURE 3-10 You can configure the *SystemTray* and *ApplicationBar* programmatically.

When you create a new app project in Visual Studio, the starter code includes a commented-out method named *BuildLocalizedApplicationBar* (invoked in the *MainPage* constructor) which illustrates how you can build an app bar in code by using localizable resource strings. For example, you might create an *ApplicationBarIconButton* with a custom image, localized text, and hook up its *Click* event to a method in your class, as shown in the following code snippet:

```
private ApplicationBarIconButton setBackColor;

private void BuildLocalizedApplicationBar()
{
    ApplicationBar = new ApplicationBar();

    setBackColor = new ApplicationBarIconButton(new Uri("/Assets/B.png", UriKind.Relative));
    setBackColor.Text = AppResources.AppBarButtonBack;
    setBackColor.Click += setBackColor_Click;
    ApplicationBar.Buttons.Add(setBackColor);

...etc
}
```

Alternatively, you can define your app bar in XAML, as shown in the snippet that follows. If you define the app bar in XAML, you can optionally declare a name for each button or menu item—in which case, of course, you don't need to declare these explicitly in your code. Also, only in code can you use localized resources for app bar items; you cannot do so in XAML.

```
<phone:PhoneApplicationPage.ApplicationBar>
    <shell:ApplicationBar IsVisible="True">
        <shell:ApplicationBarIconButton
            x:Name="setBackColor" IconUri="Assets/B.png" Text="back" Click="setBackColor_Click"/>
    </shell:ApplicationBar>
</phone:PhoneApplicationPage.ApplicationBar>
```

By default, if you try to access app bar elements by name, they will be null. When you build a C# project, the build system produces an interim C# code file for each XAML page named <*page*>.g.cs—for example, mainpage.g.cs. Note that the interim version of a page that defines app bar elements includes code in the *InitializeComponent* to retrieve XAML-declared objects into code objects, including the app bar buttons and menu items.

```
this.setBackColor = ((Microsoft.Phone.Shell.ApplicationBarIconButton)(this.
FindName("setBackColor")));
```

However, remember that the app bar is not in the app's visual tree, and you cannot retrieve app bar buttons or menu items by name (you can retrieve them only by index), so the fields will still be null after these assignments. The *FindName* method walks the visual tree to find a *UIElement* with the specified name, and, of course, it won't find any app bar elements in the tree. Keep in mind that this only applies to the app bar controls and resources; other fields will be successfully assigned in *Initialize Component*. If you need programmatic objects for the app bar buttons (for example, if you need to dynamically enable/disable them), you must fetch them from the collection by index:

```
this.setBackColor = ApplicationBar.Buttons[0] as ApplicationBarIconButton;
```

So, why is the app bar not in the app's visual tree? The answer is that under the covers, the app bar is really a part of the phone's shell. It's just that the app platform provides convenient managed classes to represent it so that you can work with it easily in your app code. It is also designed to bridge your app and the standard phone chrome in a way that appears seamless to the user. Note that the *ApplicationBar* class that you use in your code implements the *IApplicationBar* interface, which is used internally and is not intended for you to use directly.

The app bar buttons in this example perform the following operations:

- Toggle the *BackgroundColor* of the notification area between the current accent color and the default background color.
- Toggle the *ForegroundColor* of the notification area between the current accent color and the default foreground color.
- Cycle the *Opacity* between 1.0, 0.5, and 0.0.
- Attach a *ProgressIndicator* and then toggle it between determinate and indeterminate mode.

There's a slight quirk in the way the *SystemTray* color properties work. The *BackgroundColor* defaults to transparent (00000000) and the *ForegroundColor* defaults to white (FFFFFFFF), regardless of the current theme (dark or light). In other words, the exposed *BackgroundColor* and *ForegroundColor* properties of the *SystemTray* object are not used unless they are explicitly set. Also be aware that the transparent value is not the same as *Colors.Transparent* (00FFFFFF or "transparent white"). To allow for this, the sample app first determines which theme is in use and then caches suitable black or white colors for later use.

```
private Color ForegroundColor;
private Color BackgroundColor;
private Color AccentColor;
private Color HighlightColor = new Color() { A = 255, R = 106, G = 0, B = 255 };


private Color TransparentBlack = new Color() { A = 0, R = 0, G = 0, B = 0 };

public MainPage()
{
    InitializeComponent();

    Visibility v = (Visibility)Resources["PhoneDarkThemeVisibility"];
    if (v == Visibility.Visible)
    {
        BackgroundColor = TransparentBlack;
        ForegroundColor = Colors.White;
    }
    else
    {
        BackgroundColor = Colors.White;
        ForegroundColor = TransparentBlack;
    }
}
```

To toggle the notification area background and foreground colors between two colors, we have to allow for the initial default property (that is, a third color—either true black or white).

```
private void setBackColor_Click(object sender, EventArgs e)
{
    if (SystemTray.BackgroundColor == TransparentBlack ||
        SystemTray.BackgroundColor == BackgroundColor)
        SystemTray.BackgroundColor = HighlightColor;
    else
        SystemTray.BackgroundColor = BackgroundColor;
}
```

Although *Opacity* is typed as a double, as it relates to the notification area, it affects page layout more like a Boolean in the sense that you get a 32-pixel high space at the top of the page if the notification area *Opacity* is 1.0. If the notification area *Opacity* is <1.0, you don't get the 32-pixel space (and the acceptable range is 0.0 to 1.0).

```
private void setOpacity_Click(object sender, EventArgs e)
{
    if (SystemTray.Opacity == 1.0)
        SystemTray.Opacity = 0.0;
    else if (SystemTray.Opacity == 0.0)
        SystemTray.Opacity = 0.5;
    else
        SystemTray.Opacity = 1.0;
}
```

If you enable the *ProgressIndicator* on the *SystemTray* object, this occupies space right at the extreme outer edge of the notification area (at the top of the screen, when the device is in portrait orientation). An indeterminate progress bar displays a repeating pattern of dots to indicate that progress is ongoing but that the current percentage completion is undefined. On the other hand, a determinate progress bar shows a colored indicator bar within the overall control, whose length is proportional to the total length of the control and represents the percentage of progress completed thus far. You set the length of this colored indicator by setting the *Value* property. If you set *IsIndeterminate* to *true*, any *Value* property you assign will be ignored. In this example, we toggle between indeterminate and determinate mode and set the *Value* to an arbitrary number between 0.0 and 1.0.

```
private ProgressIndicator progress;

private void setProgress_Click(object sender, EventArgs e)
{
    if (progress == null)
    {
        progress = new ProgressIndicator();
        progress.IsVisible = true;
        progress.IsIndeterminate = true;
        progress.Text = "working...";
        SystemTray.ProgressIndicator = progress;
    }
```

```
        else
        {
            progress.IsIndeterminate = !progress.IsIndeterminate;
            progress.Value = 0.5;
        }
    }
```

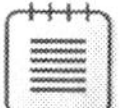

Note You can optionally set some text to display just below the progress bar. If you do, and the user then taps the notification area to display the regular system icons, your text will be hidden (regardless of the opacity setting). Also note that the progress bar in the notification area uses the current accent color; thus, if you set the notification area *BackgroundColor* to the accent color, any progress bar would be invisible.

Transient panels

In addition to using controls on a page, you can also create transient panels. These include pop-up windows, child windows, and other visual elements that are transient in nature. They can also take up the entire screen (but typically merely obscure part of it) and can all be dismissed in a consistent manner.

First, why is there no *Dialog* class in Windows Phone? When developers think of traditional dialog boxes, they are generally thinking of *modal* dialog boxes. A modal dialog is anathema in the Windows Phone world because modal means that you can't interface with whatever is underneath the modal dialog. Even if the dialog is not modal, there's a problem with real estate. The phone's small form factor simply doesn't accommodate the pattern by which an app shows the arbitrary dialog-like visuals that are so common in desktop applications.

That being said, there is one obvious modal dialog in Windows Phone: the *MessageBox*. This blocks until the user dismisses it via one of its buttons, presses the hardware Back key, or switches away from the app. Again, we see that the Back key is used in a consistent manner to back out of a situation in which the user doesn't want to be. The system *MessageBox* can be used for prompts, warnings, informational dialogs, error reports, and the like. However, you should never call it within the startup of your app or during any navigation sequences; otherwise, the system might terminate the app for being unresponsive. It supports arbitrary text and a restricted set of buttons. If the app needs something similar to a *MessageBox*, but with more scope for customizing the visual controls, there are at least four other choices:

- ***Popup*** A standard class used for hosting arbitrary content, typically composed of custom *UserControls*
- ***System.Windows.Visibility*** Any visual (including *UserControls*) that is part of the page, but with its *Visibility* toggled conditionally at runtime

- ***ChildWindow*** A standard class in the Silverlight Toolkit (note: this is not the same as the Windows Phone Toolkit) that can be used in place of *UserControl* to develop custom visuals

- ***CustomMessageBox*** An enhanced version of the standard *MessageBox* behavior, implemented as a custom control in the Windows Phone Toolkit

The *TransientPanels* solution in the sample code illustrates all four approaches. The first approach utilizes a *Popup*. This typically hosts a custom *UserControl*. So, you add a *UserControl* item to the project and define its visual elements in XAML. To make this as close to the standard *MessageBox* as possible, we simply provide a *TextBlock* and a *Button*. Obviously, if that's all you want, you would use the *MessageBox*, instead. The point of a *UserControl* is that you can put any custom visuals you want on it. However, for this illustration, we'll make it similar to the standard *MessageBox*.

```
<UserControl x:Class="TransientPanels.PopupControl"
...

    <StackPanel
        Width="480" Height="226"
        Background="{StaticResource PhoneChromeBrush}" >
        <TextBlock
            Text="hello popup" Margin="22,110,0,0"
            Style="{StaticResource PhoneTextTitle3Style}"/>
        <Button
            x:Name="PopupClose" Content="close"
            Margin="12,0,0,0" Width="150" HorizontalAlignment="Left"/>
    </StackPanel>
</UserControl>
```

To use this control, we declare a *Popup*, instantiate the control, and set it as the child of the *Popup*. We then show the *Popup* by setting *IsOpen* to *true*. The position of the *Popup* defaults to 0,0—that is, the upper-left corner of the screen.

There are two ways to close this transient visual: the obvious technique is to set *IsOpen* to *false* in the *Click* handler for the button. To make the UX consistent, we ensure that the hardware Back button also dismisses the *Popup*. To do this, we override the *OnBackKeyPress* for the page, and if the *Popup* is open, set *IsOpen* to false. It is important to be careful when handling the Back key and to ensure that the behavior is always consistent with the standard behavior. Dismissing a modal dialog is one case for which it is legitimate to handle this key. It is absolutely not appropriate to handle the Back key to prevent the user from backing out of an app.

```
private Popup p = new Popup();
private void ShowPopup_Click(object sender, RoutedEventArgs e)
{
    if (p.Child == null)
    {
        PopupControl pup = new PopupControl();
        pup.PopupClose.Click += new RoutedEventHandler(PopupClose_Click);
        p.Child = pup;
    }
    p.IsOpen = true;
}
```

```
private void PopupClose_Click(object sender, RoutedEventArgs e)
{
    if (p != null)
        p.IsOpen = false;
}

protected override void OnBackKeyPress(CancelEventArgs e)
{
    if (p != null && p.IsOpen)
    {
        p.IsOpen = false;
        e.Cancel = true;
    }
}
```

The second approach uses a transient window with its *Visibility* property toggled. Again, this could be a *UserControl* or simply some parent control (*Grid*, *Panel*, and so forth) on the page itself. In this example, we want to make it a child of the *Grid* on the *MainPage*. One of the reasons a developer might want to take this approach instead of using a *MessageBox* is that this kind of visual can easily be animated. To implement this, we need a couple of *Storyboards*: one for animating the visual as it opens, and the other for animating it as it closes. In both cases, the target property is *RotationX*, which means that the visual will be rotated on its X axis.

```
<phone:PhoneApplicationPage.Resources>
    <Storyboard x:Name="AnimatedPanelOpenStory">
        <DoubleAnimation
            Storyboard.TargetName="AnimatedPanelPlaneProjection"
            Storyboard.TargetProperty="RotationX"
            From="-80" To="0" Duration="0:0:0.4"/>
    </Storyboard>
    <Storyboard x:Name="AnimatedPanelCloseStory">
        <DoubleAnimation
            Storyboard.TargetName="AnimatedPanelPlaneProjection"
            Storyboard.TargetProperty="RotationX"
            From="0" To="-80" Duration="0:0:0.4"/>
    </Storyboard>
</phone:PhoneApplicationPage.Resources>

<Grid x:Name="LayoutRoot" Background="Transparent">
...
    <StackPanel
        x:Name="AnimatedPanel" Visibility="Collapsed"
        Width="480" Height="226" VerticalAlignment="Top"
        Background="{StaticResource PhoneChromeBrush}">
        <StackPanel.Projection>
            <PlaneProjection x:Name="AnimatedPanelPlaneProjection" />
        </StackPanel.Projection>
        <TextBlock
            Text="hello animated panel" Margin="22,110,0,0"
            Style="{StaticResource PhoneTextTitle3Style}"/>
        <Button
            x:Name="AnimatedClose" Content="close"
            Margin="12,0,0,0" Width="250"
            HorizontalAlignment="Left"/>
    </StackPanel>
</Grid>
```

The actual declaration of the *StackPanel* must be at the bottom of the XAML so that it sits above everything else in the Z-order. We need to set the *VerticalAlignment* to position the visual at the top of the page, and set the background to the same brush that the *MessageBox* uses. This is represented in user-code by the *PhoneChromeBrush* resource. Also observe that the control's *Visibility* is set to *Collapsed* initially.

To show this control, we first set its *Visibility* to *Visible*, hook up the "close" button *Click* event, and then start the "opening" animation. When the user taps the "close" button, we hook up the *Completed* event on the "closing" animation and start that animation. Only when the animation has completed do we make the control *Collapsed* again.

```
private bool isAnimatedConnected;
private bool isAnimatedOpen;
private void ShowAnimatedPanel_Click(object sender, RoutedEventArgs e)
{
    AnimatedPanel.Visibility = Visibility.Visible;
    AnimatedClose.Click += AnimatedClose_Click;
    AnimatedPanelCloseStory.Completed += AnimatedPanelCloseStory_Completed;
    AnimatedPanelOpenStory.Stop();
    AnimatedPanelOpenStory.Begin();
    isAnimatedOpen = true;
}

private void AnimatedClose_Click(object sender, RoutedEventArgs e)
{
    ClosePanel();
}

private void ClosePanel()
{
    AnimatedPanelOpenStory.Stop();
    AnimatedPanelCloseStory.Begin();
    isAnimatedOpen = false;
}

private void AnimatedPanelCloseStory_Completed(object sender, EventArgs e)
{
    AnimatedPanel.Visibility = Visibility.Collapsed;
}
```

To replicate the Back button behavior, we must ensure that the same close method is called in the override of *OnBackKeyPress*.

```
protected override void OnBackKeyPress(CancelEventArgs e)
{
...
    if (isAnimatedOpen)
    {
        ClosePanel();
        e.Cancel = true;
    }
}
```

The third approach is the *ChildWindow*. This is a class in the Silverlight Toolkit. Recall that this is not part of the Windows Phone SDK; rather, it is a separate download, which you can get at *http://silverlight.codeplex.com/releases/view/78435*. Having installed the Toolkit, we need to add a reference to the *System.Windows.Controls.dll* assembly, which will typically be in a location such as %ProgramFiles(x86)%\Microsoft SDKs\Silverlight\v4.0\Libraries\Client\System.Windows.Controls.dll.

Next, we add a namespace declaration for this in the XAML, as shown in the following:

```
xmlns:sltk="clr-namespace:System.Windows.Controls;assembly=System.Windows.Controls"
```

Then, we add another *UserControl* to the project, but this time, change the definition to *ChildWindow*. That is, we change the following (where *TestPopup* is the name of the project, and *ChildControl* is the name of the custom *UserControl*).

```
<UserControl x:Class="TransientPanels.ChildControl"
```

to this:

```
<sltk:ChildWindow x:Class="TransientPanels.ChildControl"
```

The entire XAML file is listed in the code that follows. Notice that the *Width*, *Height*, *Background*, and *Margin* of the control itself are set rather than the child *StackPanel*. The *StackPanel* offers the same *TextBlock* and *Button*, but this time, we handle the button *Click* event in the control itself rather than in the parent page.

```
<sltk:ChildWindow x:Class="TransientPanels.ChildControl"
    xmlns="http://schemas.microsoft.com/winfx/2006/xaml/presentation"
    xmlns:x="http://schemas.microsoft.com/winfx/2006/xaml"
    xmlns:d="http://schemas.microsoft.com/expression/blend/2008"
    xmlns:mc="http://schemas.openxmlformats.org/markup-compatibility/2006"
    xmlns:sltk="clr-namespace:System.Windows.Controls;assembly=System.Windows.Controls"
    mc:Ignorable="d"
    FontFamily="{StaticResource PhoneFontFamilyNormal}"
    FontSize="{StaticResource PhoneFontSizeNormal}"
    Foreground="{StaticResource PhoneForegroundBrush}"
    d:DesignHeight="480" d:DesignWidth="480"
    Width="480" Height="226"
    Background="{StaticResource PhoneChromeBrush}"
    Margin="0,-576,0,0"
>

    <StackPanel>
        <TextBlock
            Text="hello childwindow" Margin="22,80,0,0"
            Style="{StaticResource PhoneTextTitle3Style}"/>
        <Button
            x:Name="ChildClose" Content="close" Click="ChildClose_Click"
            Margin="12,0,0,0" Width="150" HorizontalAlignment="Left"/>
    </StackPanel>

</sltk:ChildWindow>
```

The code-behind also defines the inheritance to be *ChildWindow*, not *UserControl*. The only other thing we need do is to set the control's *DialogResult* to *true* when the user presses the "close" button.

```
public partial class ChildControl : ChildWindow
{
    public ChildControl()
    {
        InitializeComponent();
    }

    private void ChildClose_Click(object sender, RoutedEventArgs e)
    {
        DialogResult = true;
    }
}
```

Back in the *MainPage* code-behind, we display this control by instantiating it and calling its *Show* method. We also set a flag so that we can determine whether it is open. Thus, we need the following in the *OnBackKeyPress* override:

```
private ChildControl cc = new ChildControl();
private bool isChildOpen;
private void ShowChildWindow_Click(object sender, RoutedEventArgs e)
{
    cc.Show();
    isChildOpen = true;
}

protected override void OnBackKeyPress(CancelEventArgs e)
{
...

    if (isChildOpen)
    {
        cc.DialogResult = false;
        isChildOpen = false;
        e.Cancel = true;
    }
}
```

The fourth and final approach is to use the *CustomMessageBox* class in the Windows Phone Toolkit. This provides significant scope for customization, including any custom content that you might want. The following example incorporates a *ListPicker* control within the *CustomMessageBox*, sets other properties, and then hooks up the *Dismissing* and *Dismissed* events to inline delegates—this code should give you a good idea of the level of customization available with this control.

```
private void ShowCustomMessageBox_Click(object sender, RoutedEventArgs e)
{
    ListPicker listPicker = new ListPicker()
    {
        Header = "Snooze for:",
        ItemsSource = new string[] { "5 minutes", "15 minutes", "1 hour", "8 hours", "1 day" },
        Margin = new Thickness(12, 42, 24, 18)
    };

    CustomMessageBox messageBox = new CustomMessageBox()
    {
        Title = "Appointment Alert",
        Caption = "Something Exciting",
        Message = "main campus: " + DateTime.Now.AddDays(2),
        Content = listPicker,
        LeftButtonContent = "snooze",
        RightButtonContent = "dismiss",
        IsFullScreen = false
    };

    messageBox.Dismissing += (s1, e1) =>
    {
        if (listPicker.ListPickerMode == ListPickerMode.Expanded)
        {
            e1.Cancel = true;
        }
    };

    messageBox.Dismissed += (s2, e2) =>
    {
        switch (e2.Result)
        {
            case CustomMessageBoxResult.LeftButton:
                // Do something.
                break;
            case CustomMessageBoxResult.RightButton:
            case CustomMessageBoxResult.None:
                break;
            default:
                break;
        }
    };

    messageBox.Show();
}
```

Figure 3-11 shows two of these transient panels, the animated panel is on the left, and the *CustomMessageBox* is on the right.

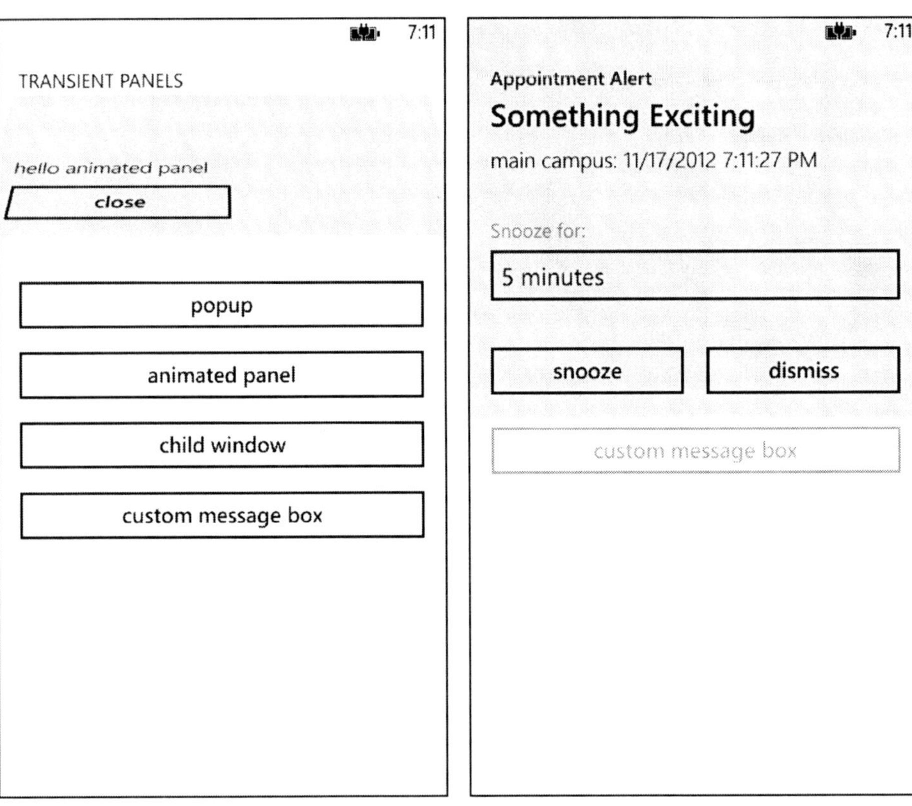

FIGURE 3-11 You can implement transient panels in four different ways.

For all types of custom transient visuals, instead of overriding *OnBackKeyPress*, an alternative approach is to define a handler for the *BackKeyPress* event on the page.

```
<phone:PhoneApplicationPage
...
    BackKeyPress="PhoneApplicationPage_BackKeyPress">
```

Adding this to the XAML in the designer will add a stub for the handler in the code-behind (if you use Tab to invoke auto-complete; otherwise, you need to right-click and select Navigate To Event Handler). This could be implemented to execute exactly the same code as the previous override of *OnBackKeyPress*. If the app were to implement both methods (which would be unnecessary), the *OnBackKeyPress* is called first followed by the event handler. Keep in mind that neither method is ever called when the user presses Back to dismiss a simple *MessageBox* or the Software Input Panel (SIP).

Although you can achieve *MessageBox*-like behavior up to a point, there are two key reasons that make *MessageBox* so different from the other approaches:

- *MessageBox* blocks the caller until the user makes a selection; all the other mechanisms are asynchronous.
- *MessageBox* offers very limited scope for customization, unlike all the other approaches.

The *MessageBox* also implements an interaction guard—that is, it dims (grays out) the rest of the app UI and suppresses touch input. You could implement this in any of the custom approaches described earlier by simply overlaying a full-screen rectangle filled with the *PhoneSemitransparentBrush*.

Routed events

UI events in Windows Phone are represented by the *RoutedEvents* class. They can be divided into events that are fully routed and events that are only partially-routed. If you take the perspective of events that are surfaced for the app code to handle, a good example of a routed event is the *MouseLeftButtonDown* event. A good example of a partially-routed event is the *Click* event on a *Button*. In fact, as you'll see shortly, the events surfaced to app code are often a façade for other events. Figure 3-12 is a screenshot of the *SimpleEvents* solution in the sample code, which responds to tap events. The page has a standard "starter" layout. That is to say, it consists of a hierarchical structure with an unnamed *PhoneApplicationPage* at the base (outermost) level of the visual tree, which contains the following:

- a *Grid* named *LayoutRoot*, which in turn contains
- a *StackPanel* named *TitlePanel* (with two *TextBlock* controls that are not interesting for this exercise)
- a *StackPanel* named *ContentPanel* (with a green background), and finally
- a *Button* named *MyButton*.

If the user taps the *Button*, this raises a non-routed *Click* event. If the user taps anywhere else, it raises a routed *MouseLeftButtonDown* event. On the emulator, of course, this will actually be a physical mouse left-button down, but on the device, it will be a tap touch event. In fact, under the hood, for both the emulator and device—and for both the button and non-button areas—the initial event raised as a result of user input is a *MouseLeftButtonDown* event. The *Button* class handles this internally and then raises the *Click* event as a result. Technically, the sequence is slightly more complicated, in that it requires a down gesture followed by an up gesture, with optional movement between, so long as the "up" is within the hit-test area. The *Click* event is not routed; rather, it is dispatched to the class where the *Button* instance is declared, and there is no automatic routing.

Contrast this with the raw *MouseLeftButtonDown* event raised when the user taps any of the other visual elements. Unlike the *Button* class, neither the *StackPanel* nor *Grid* nor *PhoneApplicationPage* have any special logic to handle this event.

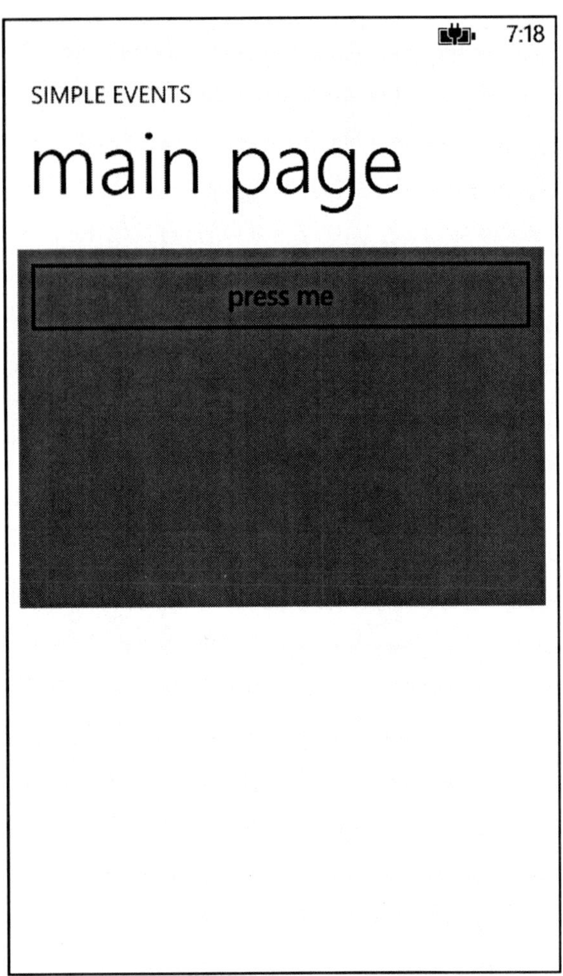

FIGURE 3-12 This simple app demonstrates event routing and the visual tree.

In the *page* class, in this example, there are event handlers at every level in the visual tree. However, if you examine the debug output from these handlers, you'll see that when the user taps the *Button*, only the *MyButton_Click* handler is invoked. Conversely, if the user taps in the *StackPanel* outside the *Button*, the event is first handled in the *ContentPanel*'s handler. After that, it is automatically routed to the next handler in the tree (the *LayoutRoot*); from there, it is routed to the outermost *Page* handler. At any time, you could stop the routing by setting the *Handled* property of the *MouseButtonEventArgs* to *True*. In contrast, the *RoutedEventArgs* that is passed in the *Click* event does not expose a *Handled* property; there is no need to because the event is not automatically onward-routed.

```
private void MyButton_Click(object sender, RoutedEventArgs e)
{
    Debug.WriteLine("{0} - {1}: MyButton_Click\n",
        sender.GetType(), e.OriginalSource.GetType());
}
```

```
private void MyButton_MouseLeftButtonDown(object sender, MouseButtonEventArgs e)
{
    Debug.WriteLine("{0} - {1}: MyButton_MouseLeftButtonDown",
        sender.GetType(), e.OriginalSource.GetType());
}

private void ContentPanel_MouseLeftButtonDown(object sender, MouseButtonEventArgs e)
{
    Debug.WriteLine("{0} - {1}: ContentPanel_MouseLeftButtonDown",
        sender.GetType(), e.OriginalSource.GetType());
}

private void LayoutRoot_MouseLeftButtonDown(object sender, MouseButtonEventArgs e)
{
    Debug.WriteLine("{0} - {1}: LayoutRoot_MouseLeftButtonDown",
        sender.GetType(), e.OriginalSource.GetType());
    //e.Handled = true;
}

private void PhoneApplicationPage_MouseLeftButtonDown(object sender, MouseButtonEventArgs e)
{
    Debug.WriteLine("{0} - {1}: PhoneApplicationPage_MouseLeftButtonDown\n",
        sender.GetType(), e.OriginalSource.GetType());
}
```

Also note that the event handler signature follows the Microsoft .NET standard. The first parameter is an object that represents the current source of the event—that is, the current source in the routing path. The second parameter is the *EventArgs* (or *EventArgs*-derived) object that carries any interesting payload. In the case of routed events, it exposes the *Handled* property. To be clear, although *MouseButtonEventArgs* derives indirectly from *RoutedEventArgs*, it is the *MouseButtonEventArgs* where the *Handled* property is defined, not in the *RoutedEventArgs* class. The only additional information that the *RoutedEventArgs* provides over and above its base *EventArgs* type is the *OriginalSource* property, which is the original source of the event.

So, if the user taps in the *ContentPanel* outside the *Button*, the *OriginalSource* is always the *ContentPanel*, and the sender will be the object where the event is being handled. Depending on where in the routing path the event has reached, this will vary.

It is also interesting to note that you have choices about how to connect event handlers. So far, this example has hooked up the *MouseLeftButtonDown* event at the level of the *ContentPanel* in XAML, as shown in the following:

```
<StackPanel Background="#FF339933"
    x:Name="ContentPanel" Grid.Row="1" Margin="12,0,12,0" Height="300"
    MouseLeftButtonDown="ContentPanel_MouseLeftButtonDown">
```

Instead, you could hook it up in code, as shown in the snippet that follows, which would achieve exactly the same behavior:

```
ContentPanel.MouseLeftButtonDown += ContentPanel_MouseLeftButtonDown;
```

However, hooking up events in code gives you one further option: you could use the explicit *AddHandler* method instead of the += approach, and if you do so, you can then pass an additional parameter, as shown here:

```
ContentPanel.AddHandler(UIElement.MouseLeftButtonDownEvent,
    new MouseButtonEventHandler(ContentPanel_MouseLeftButtonDown), true);
```

The difference this makes is in the final parameter; if this is true, the framework will invoke the handler for routed events that have already been marked as handled by another element along the event route; for example, the *MouseLeftButtonDown* event that was "handled" by the *Button* to produce the *Click* event.

It is important to note that the routing path follows the visual tree, from the most local (leaf-node) object to the outermost (root-node). As a performance optimization, therefore, it makes sense to set *Handled=true* when you're sure that you have in fact handled the event and want to prevent any unnecessary onward routing. Also, remember that some visual elements in an app are not part of the visual tree (pop-up windows, and the app bar are the common examples), so they will not be involved in event routing. Another quirk to note is that if you don't explicitly set a *Background* on a *Panel* (including *StackPanel* and *Grid*), the event is not routed to the *Panel*. It is sufficient to set the *Background* to *Transparent*—it doesn't need to be visible—but you do also need *IsHitTestVisible* set to *True* (which is the default). In this sample, the *ContentPanel* has an explicit background and receives events, but the *TitlePanel* does not.

Logical touch gestures

Windows Phone supports a range of touch gestures. Table 3-6 provides the list of logical gestures from a user's perspective.

TABLE 3-6 Logical touch gestures

Gesture	Description
Tap	A finger touches the screen and then releases with minimal movement.
DoubleTap	Two taps in quick succession.
Hold	A finger touches the screen and remains in place for some minimum period of time.
Pan/Drag	A finger touches the screen and then moves in any direction. Dragging moves some recognizably discrete content around the screen. Panning is really the same as dragging, except that the content is larger than the screen.
Flick	A finger drags across the screen and then lifts up without stopping the movement.
Pinch	Two fingers press on the screen and are then moved toward one another.
Stretch	Two fingers press on the screen and are then moved apart, relative to one another.

The Windows Phone chassis specification used by phone manufacturers dictates that all Windows Phones must support a true multitouch input system capable of sensing and reporting a minimum of 4 and a maximum of 10 distinct touch points simultaneously. The baseline for a finger touch is a circle 7 mm in diameter. There's also a recommendation that the touch screen should not support touches by objects that are not shaped like a finger (especially a palm touch), or which are greater than 30x30 mm. These measurements represent the boundary limits for any touch targets that you might include in your app.

Microsoft provides comprehensive guidelines on the use and usability of touch gestures, including the following:

- When designing your visual UI, keep in mind that touch targets (controls, shapes, and so on) should not be smaller than 9x9 mm or 34x34 pixels. You should also provide at least 2 mm or 8 pixels between touch targets. For elements that are frequent touch targets in your app, you should actually make them larger—for these, a minimum size of 72x72 pixels is recommended. Note that the default height and width for all built-in controls follows this rule and you never have to explicitly set the height or width on any of them. Controls smaller than 34 pixels are not categorically forbidden, although you might make it difficult for your app to pass certification testing. In any event, no touch target should ever be smaller than 7x7 mm or 26x26 pixels in area. With touch targets for which hitting the wrong target by mistake would have a severe negative effect, you should make them even bigger.
- It is acceptable to make the touch target larger than the touch element, but you should not exceed 40 percent larger, and it should not be smaller. If you make it larger, don't forget that the minimum 8-pixel gap should be maintained between touchable targets, not between the elements. For standard controls, the touch target size relative to the control size is set and cannot be configured; this guideline is only relevant if you're building custom controls or re-templating existing controls.

You can handle the logical user gestures at any of five levels by handling four types of events and a set of virtual methods. These are summarized in Table 3-7, presented from the lowest level to the highest. The app is responsible for determining which touch gestures the user is performing by tracking the number, timing, and permutation of events. Internally, the platform takes the raw input messages and converts them to low-level *ManipulationXXX* events. Next, these are used to synthesize higher-level events such as the *MouseXXX* events and *FrameReported* events.

TABLE 3-7 Touch events and overrides

Event type	Description
Low-level *ManipulationXXX* events, raised for each element, individually.	These are typically the first events to be raised, so handling them is the fastest approach. Most useful for composite gestures—that is, pinch and stretch, drag and flick—rather than single Tap or DoubleTap gestures. Can be scoped to individual elements or set page-wide.
OnManipulationXXX virtual methods (not events).	If you override these, they are called before the corresponding *ManipulationXXX* event handlers (if any). You would typically override these in your *Page* class, so they will be used for all such events on the page, rather than being scoped to any individual element or panel. Using these overrides is typically quicker than the event handlers: internally; if no event handler is connected in the delegate, it is null and that set of work is skipped.
Slightly higher-level mouse events such as *MouseLeftButtonDown* and *MouseLeftButtonUp* that all UIElement types support.	They are routed events, so you need to be aware of the way routing works and know when to prevent onward routing and when not to. You should only use these events if you're building a cross-platform (for example, windows and/or web, plus phone) app.
Virtual methods (not events) such as *OnMouseLeftButtonDown* and *OnMouseLeftButtonUp*.	If you override these, they are always called after the lower-level *MouseXXX* event is raised. As with the *OnManipulationXXX* overrides, you would typically override these in your *Page* class. You should only use these events if you're building a cross-platform app.
Higher-level *FrameReported* events, which are raised for touch anywhere in the frame.	This is an app-wide event that cannot be more finely scoped. It is useful for handling multiple touch points, but not useful for individual elements or individual pages.

Note The Windows Phone Toolkit for Windows Phone 7 included a *GestureService* which provided an alternative mechanism for handling touch input. This was less than perfect because it was based on the XNA *TouchPanel*, which made it less suitable for non-XNA apps. It has since been deprecated. The Windows Phone Toolkit for Windows Phone 8 does not include this feature, and you should not use this for Windows Phone 8 apps.

Manipulation events

At the lowest level exposed to applications, you can handle the *ManipulationXXX* events. You can use these events for all the Windows Phone manipulation types, both single-touch and multitouch. You would typically handle a group of *ManipulationStarted*, *ManipulationDelta*, and *Manipulation Completed* events. Consider the *ManipulationDemo* app in the sample code, illustrated in Figure 3-13.

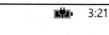

FIGURE 3-13 You can handle touch input by using the *ManipulationXXX* events.

This app presents an *Image* control positioned arbitrarily on a *Canvas*, below the usual title *TextBlock* controls. This is how the app handles touch input:

- **Single-tap** If the tap is inside the *Image*, the app increments the *Image* size by an arbitrary scaling factor. If the tap is on the page itself, outside the *Image* and the *Canvas*, the app decrements the *Image* size by the same scaling factor. In both cases, the scaling factor is applied to a scale transform applied to the *Image* control.
- **Drag** The user can drag the *Image* around the screen. The app responds to the drag gesture by updating a translate transform on the *Image* control.

- **Pinch and stretch** Using two fingers, the user can decrement the *Image* size by using a pinch gesture, and increment its size by using a stretch gesture. This is implemented in code via the same scale transform used in the single-tap gestures.
- **Flick** The user can flick the *Image*, and the app responds by starting an animation that rotates the image around both the X and Y axes.

Here's a summary of the XAML, showing the rotate animation storyboards and the how the various UI elements are laid out on the page. Notice that the storyboard target is the *PlaneProjection* property of the Image control.

```
<phone:PhoneApplicationPage.Resources>
    <Storyboard x:Name="rotateX">
        <DoubleAnimation
            Storyboard.TargetName="imagePlane" Storyboard.TargetProperty="RotationX"
            From="0" To="360" Duration="0:0:3" RepeatBehavior="Forever" />
    </Storyboard>
    <Storyboard x:Name="rotateY">
        <DoubleAnimation
            Storyboard.TargetName="imagePlane" Storyboard.TargetProperty="RotationY"
            From="0" To="360" Duration="0:0:3" RepeatBehavior="Forever" />
    </Storyboard>
</phone:PhoneApplicationPage.Resources>

<Canvas
    x:Name="MainCanvas" Background="Transparent"
    ManipulationCompleted="MainCanvas_ManipulationCompleted">
    <StackPanel x:Name="TitlePanel" Margin="12,17,0,28">
        <TextBlock
            Margin="12,17,0,28" Text="MANIPULATION DEMO" Style="{StaticResource
PhoneTextNormalStyle}"/>
        <TextBlock
            Text="main page" Margin="9,-7,0,0" Style="{StaticResource PhoneTextTitle1Style}" />
    </StackPanel>

    <Image
        Canvas.Left="24" Canvas.Top="200" Width="210" Height="175"
        HorizontalAlignment="Center" VerticalAlignment="Center"
        Name="myImage" Source="Assets/KerryPark.png"
        ManipulationDelta="myImage_ManipulationDelta"
        ManipulationCompleted="myImage_ManipulationCompleted">
        <Image.RenderTransform>
            <CompositeTransform x:Name="myCompositeTransform" />
        </Image.RenderTransform>
        <Image.Projection>
            <PlaneProjection x:Name="imagePlane"/>
        </Image.Projection>
    </Image>

</Canvas>
```

The *Image* control inside the *Canvas* is initially positioned just below the usual title block and declares handlers for the *ManipulationDelta* and *ManipulationCompleted* events. It also defines a *CompositeTransform*—this will include both a scale (size) transform and a translate (position) transform—to support the sizing and moving operations. Let's build up the required functionality in steps. First, the single-tap gestures: the *ManipulationCompleted* event handler simply increments the *ScaleX* and *ScaleY* properties of the transform by 10 percent.

```
private const double sizeIncrement = 0.1;
private void myImage_ManipulationCompleted(object sender, ManipulationCompletedEventArgs e)
{
    myCompositeTransform.ScaleX += sizeIncrement;
    myCompositeTransform.ScaleY += sizeIncrement;
    e.Handled = true;
}
```

We also override the virtual *OnManipulationCompleted* method on the page itself. The effect of this is that if the user taps the page outside the main *Canvas*, we'll decrement the *Image* scale transform by the same 10-percent value. Notice that the *ManipulationCompleted* handler sets the *Handled* property on the incoming *ManipulationCompletedEventArgs* to *true* to prevent further routing of this event. Without this, the page-level *OnManipulationCompleted* method would be called after the *Image*-level *ManipulationCompleted* event handler—in our sample, this would effectively nullify the size increment. Observe that the *OnManipulationXXX* override is always called before any *ManipulationXXX* event for the same element—in this app, we're overriding the *OnManipulationCompleted* for the page, not the *Image*. We could use the *ManipulationCompleted* event just as well as the *OnManipulationCompleted* method override; there's no difference here.

```
protected override void OnManipulationCompleted(ManipulationCompletedEventArgs e)
{
    myCompositeTransform.ScaleX -= sizeIncrement;
    myCompositeTransform.ScaleY -= sizeIncrement;
}
```

If we want to distinguish taps in the *Image* control from taps in the parent *Canvas*, we can declare a *ManipulationCompleted* event handler at the *Canvas* level, too. However, notice that for panel controls, manipulation events are only raised if the panel has an explicit *Background* value (including *Transparent*).

```
<Canvas
    x:Name="MainCanvas" Background="Transparent"
    ManipulationCompleted="MainCanvas_ManipulationCompleted">
```

If we wanted to distinguish single-tap from double-tap or hold, we would need to watch sequential *ManipulationStarted* and *ManipulationCompleted* events, and the elapsed time between them.

Note For the purposes of responding to a simple single-tap gesture, we could alternatively handle the *ManipulationStarted* event. However, in this app, we care about multiple gestures, and if we were to handle only *ManipulationStarted*, we wouldn't know if this gesture was in fact a single-tap gesture or the start of a drag or pinch/stretch operation. The only way we can determine that is if we wait for the *ManipulationCompleted* event. Nonetheless, if you only want to handle single-tap gestures, *ManipulationStarted* is perfectly valid, and if you choose this approach, you should then also call the *Complete* method on the *ManipulationCompletedEventArgs* object at the end of the handler. Calling *Complete* directs the system not to process any more events for this manipulation. If you don't care about any subsequent *ManipulationDelta* events that might arise from non–single-tap gestures, you can instruct the system that after you have the initial *ManipulationStarted* event, you don't want to be notified about anything else in this manipulation group.

Next, consider the drag operation. To implement this, we handle the *ManipulationDelta* event. When the user puts his finger on the screen, this raises a *ManipulationStarted* event. When he takes his finger off again, this raises a *ManipulationCompleted* event. In between, if the user moves his finger while still touching the screen, this raises multiple *ManipulationDelta* events. We handle these by updating the *TranslateX* and *TranslateY* properties of the transform. When this is applied to the *Image* control, it changes the horizontal and vertical position.

```
private void myImage_ManipulationDelta(object sender, ManipulationDeltaEventArgs e)
{
    myCompositeTransform.TranslateX += e.DeltaManipulation.Translation.X;
    myCompositeTransform.TranslateY += e.DeltaManipulation.Translation.Y;
}
```

The pinch and stretch gestures require the user to use two fingers. To implement this, we need to update the *ManipulationDelta* event handler, to test whether the *DeltaManipulation* includes any changes to the X or Y scale—that is, any non-zero value in the *Scale.X* or *Scale.Y* properties. If so, the user must be resizing the image. In fact, the user could be doing both dragging and pinching/stretching at the same time, so they are not treated as mutually exclusive in the code.

```
private void myImage_ManipulationDelta(object sender, ManipulationDeltaEventArgs e)
{
    if (e.DeltaManipulation.Scale.X != 0 || e.DeltaManipulation.Scale.Y != 0)
    {
        myCompositeTransform.ScaleX *= e.DeltaManipulation.Scale.X;
        myCompositeTransform.ScaleY *= e.DeltaManipulation.Scale.X;
    }
    myCompositeTransform.TranslateX += e.DeltaManipulation.Translation.X;
    myCompositeTransform.TranslateY += e.DeltaManipulation.Translation.Y;
}
```

The app only uses the X property to modify the scale factor, which ensures that we keep the aspect ratio constant. However, there's nothing in the code to prevent the user from shrinking the image beyond the point at which he could get two fingers on it to enlarge it again; nor do we prevent him from moving it off the screen such that he can't get it back; nor do we prevent him flipping the image around the X or Y axis. In a more sophisticated solution, you might also want to accelerate the drag, based on the zoom factor.

The final gesture to consider is the flick gesture. When the user flicks the *Image*, we'll start it moving by using a couple of simple animations. We'll keep the animations moving until the user taps the *Image* again to stop it. To support this feature, we first need to set up a few more class fields: a pair of doubles for the initial width and height of the *Image*, and a *bool* for whether or not the *Image* is moving.

```
private double initialWidth;
private double initialHeight;
private bool isMoving;

public MainPage()
{
    InitializeComponent();
    initialWidth = myImage.ActualWidth;
    initialHeight = myImage.ActualHeight;
}
```

When the user flicks the *Image*, this raises a *ManipulationCompleted* event, which we handle by first checking to see if the gesture was an inertial gesture. If so, the user must be flicking the *Image*. To keep things simple, we reset the transform (scale and translate). We then start the two animations. At the same time, we set the *isMoving* flag so that we can later distinguish between the user tapping the image while its stationary (in which case we increment its size) or while it is moving (in which case we stop the movement).

```
private void myImage_ManipulationCompleted(object sender, ManipulationCompletedEventArgs e)
{
    if (e.IsInertial)
    {
        myCompositeTransform.ScaleX = 1.0;
        myCompositeTransform.ScaleY = 1.0;
        myCompositeTransform.TranslateX = 0;
        myCompositeTransform.TranslateY = 0;
        rotateX.Begin();
        rotateY.Begin();
        isMoving = true;
    }
    else
    {
        if (isMoving)
        {
            rotateX.Stop();
            rotateY.Stop();
            isMoving = false;
        }
        else if (e.TotalManipulation.Scale.X == 0 && e.TotalManipulation.Scale.Y == 0
            && e.TotalManipulation.Translation.X == 0 && e.TotalManipulation.Translation.Y == 0)
```

```
        {
            myCompositeTransform.ScaleX += sizeIncrement;
            myCompositeTransform.ScaleY += sizeIncrement;
        }
    }
    e.Handled = true;
}
```

Of the different *ManipulationXXXEventArgs* types, only *ManipulationCompletedEventArgs* provides the *IsInertial* property. *IsInertial* will also be true in the context of a drag or pinch manipulation involving inertia, but we're not interested in that context in this example.

Mouse events

At a slightly higher level, simple one-finger user input can be handled by handling the *MouseXXX* events: *MouseEnter, MouseLeave, MouseLeftButtonDown, MouseLeftButtonUp,* and *MouseMove.* For each of these events, the handler is passed a *MouseEventArgs.* With a little effort, you could use the *MouseLeftButtonDown, MouseMove,* and *MouseLeftButtonUp* events to model the user performing drag or flick gestures. These events are not, however, sufficient to model the pinch/stretch multitouch gestures. Even for single-touch gestures, you'd have to handle the relevant events both within the element of interest and outside of it, as well. Plus, they have performance issues, so you should never use mouse events in your code.

This is because although the mouse down/up and enter/leave events occur in pairs, a given visual element doesn't necessarily receive paired events. For example, when the user holds the touch over the *TextBlock*, this raises a *MouseEnter* event, followed by *MouseLeftButtonDown.* If she continues to hold the touch and move her finger, this will raise *MouseMove* events—another event every time she moves more than a few pixels. If she leaves the area of the *TextBlock* (still keeping the touch on), this will raise a *MouseLeave* event but no further *MouseMove* events while they're outside of the *TextBlock.* If she moves back into the *TextBlock* area (still keeping the touch on), this will raise a *MouseEnter,* followed by further *MouseMove* events. If instead, she keeps the touch on and leaves the area but then releases the touch, there will be a *MouseLeftButtonUp* event—but just for the *ContentPanel* (or the page), not for the *TextBlock*—because this action happened outside of the *TextBlock* area.

Observe that the *Control* class (from which most visual elements derive) provides virtual methods *OnMouseEnter, OnMouseLeftButtonDown,* and so on. So, instead of declaring event handlers directly, you could instead override any of these methods. The *OnMouseXXX* methods will always be called after the corresponding event handlers. Another difference is that while all the raw *MouseXXX* events are cancelable routed events, only some of the *OnMouseXXX* overrides are cancelable events; some are passed a *MouseEventArgs* parameter, which does not expose a *Handled* property, because it is not needed. In fact, the *MouseButtonEventArgs* type that the raw event handlers receive is actually derived from *MouseEventArgs*, and the only additional feature it exposes is the *Handled* property. Also note that even though there is a raw *MouseWheel* event and an *OnMouseWheel* virtual method in the *Control* class, you will never receive this event in a Windows Phone app.

It is not normally useful to combine *ManipulationXXX* events with *MouseXXX* events. However, there's nothing to prevent you from doing this, and it is instructive to see how the various events at one level correspond to related events at another level. For example, if you were to handle both *ManipulationStarted* and *MouseLeftButtonDown* events on the same element, they will both be raised, in that order. Setting *e.Handled* and/or calling *Complete* makes no difference to this. That is, *Handled* affects the onward routing up the visual tree; it does not affect the way the system internally raises both *ManipulationXXX* and *MouseXXX* events for the same physical touch input. As far as the app is concerned, the two event schemes are independent of one another.

FrameReported events

At a very low level, you can handle the *FrameReported* event. This is not applicable to individual visual elements. Rather, it is app-wide; the name does not refer to the Phone *ApplicationFrame*; instead, it refers to a discrete "frame" of input in a sequence of events. It is therefore also not a routed event and doesn't traverse the visual tree. You handle this event anywhere in the app. You would typically put the code in one or more of your pages, because although this is app-wide, the resultant processing is very much UI-related. The *FrameReported* event is exposed from the static *Touch* class. If you want to handle this event, you must hook it up in code, not XAML, because the XAML parser doesn't support statics. The code that follows (the *FrameReportedDemo* solution in the sample code) is for an app that increments/decrements the size of a *TextBlock* and changes its foreground color, depending on which UI element is associated with the event.

In this version, we implement the *FrameReported* event handler to obtain the collection of touch points. We're actually not interested in multitouch here, so we only care about the first touch point in the collection. We can examine the *TouchDevice* property of the *TouchPoint* to determine which visual element the touch was directly over. Be aware that the *TouchDevice* does not refer to a physical device; rather, it refers to a touch gesture instance for which each gesture instance consists of a group that can include a touch-down operation, and possibly also includes one or more touch-move operations and a touch-up operation.

```
protected override void OnNavigatedTo(NavigationEventArgs e)
{
    Touch.FrameReported += Touch_FrameReported;
}

protected override void OnNavigatedFrom(NavigationEventArgs e)
{
    Touch.FrameReported -= Touch_FrameReported;
}
```

```
private void Touch_FrameReported(object sender, TouchFrameEventArgs e)
{
    TouchPointCollection tpc = e.GetTouchPoints(this);
    TouchPoint tp = tpc.FirstOrDefault<TouchPoint>();
    if (tp.TouchDevice.DirectlyOver == HelloText)
    {
        HelloText.FontSize++;
    }
    else if (tp.TouchDevice.DirectlyOver == ContentPanel)
    {
        HelloText.FontSize--;
    }
    else
    {
        if (HelloText.Foreground == orangeBrush)
        {
            HelloText.Foreground = limeBrush;
        }
        else
        {
            HelloText.Foreground = orangeBrush;
        }
    }
}
```

Because this example only cares about the first touch point in the collection, we could use *GetPrimary TouchPoint* instead of *FirstOrDefault*. However, although we don't make use of it in this app, we could examine multiple *TouchPoints* within the *TouchPointCollection* to work with multitouch operations. Also note that the *TouchPoint* exposes both a *Position* and *Size* property. The *Position* provides the X,Y coordinates of the center of the *TouchPoint*, relative to the object passed in to the *GetXXXPoint* method. This allows for changes in orientation. On Windows Phone, the *Size* will always be 1x1 pixels—both on the emulator using a mouse, and on the device, regardless of how fat your fingers are. Also note that the technique of using *DirectlyOver* works nicely with a *TextBlock* because this is a primitive type; however, it won't work with more complex templated types such as the *Button* control.

Note Many controls—such as the *Button*, *CheckBox*, *RadioButton*, and so on—handle the *MouseXXX* events internally and then surface them as *Click* events for the app to consume. This is part of the package you buy into when you use any standard control: life is made easier for you, but at the cost of flexibility. If you use a standard *Button*, you can handle the *Click* event, but you will not receive *MouseXXX* events, nor will your *OnMouseXXX* overrides be called.

Keyboard input

A hardware keyboard is an optional component in the standard Windows Phone chassis specification. On the other hand, the SIP is a part of the platform itself and, therefore, available on all Windows Phone devices. The SIP was also previously known as the On-Screen Keyboard (OSK). Just to complete the list of TLAs, the auto-correct and word suggestion features are collectively known as the Input Method Editor (IME). The SIP is popped up at appropriate times on your behalf—such as when the user taps an editable *TextBox*. When displayed, the SIP pushes your visual elements up and off the top of the screen. Exactly how much space it takes up on the screen depends on whether it is in portrait or landscape orientation, whether the word suggestions feature is engaged, the specific *InputScope* that you're using, and whether there's anything in the clipboard. In landscape orientation, the SIP occupies more space horizontally but less space vertically (because there is less vertical real estate overall in landscape). It's also important to remember that even if you detect that a hardware keyboard has been deployed (through the *DeviceStatus.KeyboardDeployedChanged* event), you can't assume that there's no SIP-related UI on screen, because for example, there might be something in the clipboard, and that requires SIP-related UI.

The Windows Phone SIP actually has a lot of very useful features, including auto-correction, word suggestion, visual and audio feedback, accent key pickers, shift and shift-lock management, compensation for finger shake, and so on. However, these are all user features rather than developer features. Relatively little functionality is exposed to developers. Partly, this is because there is very little need for developers to program the SIP directly, and partly it is to ensure a consistent UX by not enabling arbitrary programmatic manipulation.

You can configure the input scope of the SIP by setting the *InputScope* property on the element (for example, the *TextBox*) itself. There are 64 possible values for *InputScope*, but many of these are synonyms, and they map to 11 distinct modes. Why is this? There are a couple of reasons:

- To allow the developer to declare the intent of the scope. For example, the *CurrencyAmount InputScope* is synonymous with the *Number InputScope*, but the developer can specify *CurrencyAmount* to make his intentions clear.
- To allow for future tuning of the input scopes. For example, right now Bopomofo is synonymous with Default, but in some future release, there might be a distinct Bopomofo SIP.

The following app (the *SipDemo* solution in the sample code) provides a *ListBox* of the full set of input scopes and data-binds the *TextBox InputScope* to the selected item from that list. Figure 3-14 shows the *Chat* input scope on the left and the *TelephoneNumber* input scope on the right.

FIGURE 3-14 The SIP with *Chat* (left) and *TelephoneNumber* input scopes.

The *ListBox* declaration in XAML is trivial; the *TextBox* declaration includes data-binding the *Input Scope* property to the currently selected item in the *ListBox* element.

```
<StackPanel x:Name="ContentPanel">
    <ListBox x:Name="ScopeList" Height="300"/>
    <TextBox InputScope="{Binding ElementName=ScopeList, Path=SelectedItem}"/>
</StackPanel>
```

To populate the *ListBox*, we need to do a little reflection. Internally, the input scope values are declared as an *enum* named *InputScopeNameValue* in *System.Windows.dll*. We use *Type.GetFields* to get each *enum* value, and extract the *FieldInfo.Name* to populate a simple list, which is then sorted alphabetically and set as the *ItemsSource* of the *ListBox*, as demonstrated here:

```
public MainPage()
{
    InitializeComponent();
```

```
    List<string> inputScopeNames = new List<String>();
    FieldInfo[] inputScopeEnumValues = typeof(InputScopeNameValue).GetFields(
        BindingFlags.Public | BindingFlags.Static);
    foreach (FieldInfo fi in inputScopeEnumValues)
    {
        inputScopeNames.Add(fi.Name);
    }
    inputScopeNames.Sort();
    ScopeList.ItemsSource = inputScopeNames;
}
```

Keep in mind that tuning the SIP display to the keys that you want the user to use doesn't prevent her from using other keys. If she has a hardware keyboard, or if she uses the clipboard, she can ignore the *InputScope*, altogether. You can emulate a hardware keyboard on the emulator by pressing the Pause key on the computer keyboard. This toggles the keyboard to act as the hardware keyboard for the phone emulator; it remains set until you press Pause again. The emulator window must have focus before you do this—you need to click inside the emulated screen (not on the chrome) for the keystroke to work (the same applies for other special keys such as F1 for back, F2 for start, and so on). If you want to filter out unacceptable keystrokes, you can handle the *LostFocus* event to remove unwanted characters after they've been entered. For example, the following code removes anything that's not a numeric digit:

```
private void MyTextBox_LostFocus(object sender, TextChangedEventArgs e)
{`
    MyTextBox.Text = Regex.Replace(MyTextBox.Text, "[^0-9]", "");
}
```

Summary

This chapter explored the basic UI infrastructure on the phone and looked at the various options for layout, controls, resources, and coding approaches to building UIs. We examined some of the subtleties involved in using resource dictionaries, dependency properties, attachable properties and behaviors, all of which make it easier for designers and developers to work on the same project. We also looked at the developer's choices for customizing standard controls, building custom controls of various kinds, and implementing transient panels.

We looked at how you can work with the software app bar, system tray, and progress indicators, which are not conventional UI elements; they are instead part of the system chrome. Windows Phone supports a range of touch gestures, and the app platform provides a rich set of choices for interacting with touch at five different levels. Finally, we looked at the SIP and your choices for configuring this aspect of the UI.

CHAPTER 4

Data binding and MVVM

Sooner or later, your app will need to present data in the user interface (UI). Most modern programming frameworks provide mechanisms to make rendering data in the UI simple and robust. At the same time, these frameworks promote better engineering practices by cleanly separating the data from the UI, establishing standard mechanisms for connecting the data and UI in a loosely coupled manner, and ensuring that components consuming the data are conveniently notified of any changes (either initiated in the UI or from the underlying data source) so that the app can take appropriate action. The feature that carries out all this cool behavior is called *data binding*. This chapter examines the data-binding support in the platform, the rationale for its existence, the various ways that it supports both the functionality of mapping data and UI, and the engineering excellence of loose coupling between layers.

Simple data binding and *INotifyPropertyChanged*

In a Windows Phone app, you can move data between a backing data source and UI elements manually if you want. Taking this approach, you might declare a field for each UI element (by using the *x:Name=""* syntax in XAML) and get/set the displayed value of the element in code. If the data is simple, this is a reasonable approach.

However, with more complex data or where you need to perform additional processing on the data between the source and the UI, this manual back-and-forth propagation rapidly becomes a burden. It involves a lot of manual code, which inevitably increases the chance of introducing bugs. Furthermore, the data is very tightly coupled to the UI. This is a problem because as requirements or the data model change over time, this will necessitate corresponding changes to the UI. Additionally, it will entail changes to all the code that's doing the manual change propagation. Similarly, even if only the UI changes, you will still need to change the propagation code. Such tight coupling makes the entire app very fragile in the face of ongoing requirements changes.

Fortunately, the Windows Phone platform includes support for automatically initializing the UI from backing data and for automatically propagating changes, in both directions. The goals of data binding include the following:

- Enable a range of diverse data sources to be connected (web service calls, SQL queries, business objects, and so on). The underlying data sources are represented in the app code by a set of one or more data classes.

- Simplify the connection and synchronization of data so that you do not need to maintain propagation code manually.
- Maintain the separation between the UI design and the app logic (and therefore between design tools such as Microsoft Expression Blend and development tools such as Microsoft Visual Studio).

One way to think of data-binding is as a pattern with which you can declare the relationship between your app's data and the UI that displays the data *without* hard-coding the specifics of how and when the data is propagated to the UI. By doing this, you can maximize the Separation of Concerns (SoC). This is an important principle in modern app engineering, in which you maintain clear boundaries between different functional parts of your app. Specifically, this means that the UI components are solely responsible for UI, the data components handle the data source, and so on with minimal overlap between the different responsibilities. Figure 4-1 illustrates the pattern.

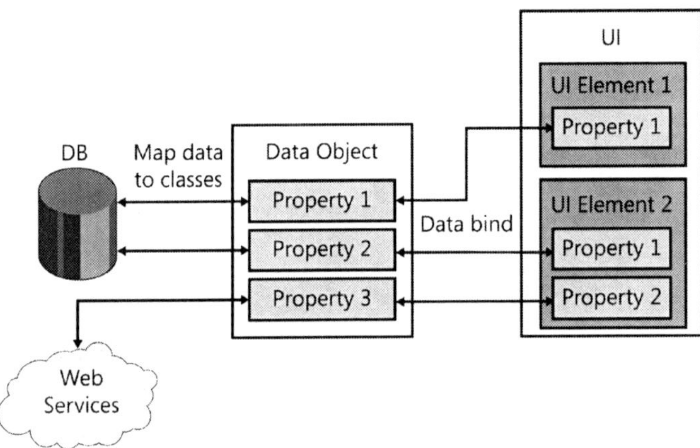

FIGURE 4-1 The data-binding pattern helps maintain the SoC.

In addition to separating concerns, the declarative relationship also takes advantage of change notifications. That is, when the value of the data changes in the underlying data source, the app does not need to take explicit action to render the change in the UI. Instead, it relies on the class that represents the data source raising a change notification event, which the app platform picks up and uses to propagate the change to the UI. The same happens in reverse; when the user changes the data interactively in the UI, that change is propagated back to the data source.

The *SimpleDataBinding* solution in the sample code (see also Figure 4-2) demonstrates the basic mechanics of data binding.

FIGURE 4-2 You can data-bind UI elements to underlying data objects.

The app provides two *TextBox* controls, each data-bound to properties of an underlying data class; in this example, it's a simple *Player* class. One *TextBox* is set to the player's *Name* property; the other is set to the *Score*. The user can edit the contents of either *TextBox*. However, when he taps the corresponding Get button, this retrieves the current value of the underlying data source. From this, it becomes clear that edits to the *Name TextBox* are propagated back to the data source, but edits to the *Score TextBox* are not. Conversely, the user can tap the Inc button, and the app will increment the *Score* value programmatically.

The UI declarations in the XAML specify the binding for each *TextBox* by using the *{Binding}* syntax. In this example, the *Score* has a *one-way binding*, which means that the data is pulled from the data class into the UI only. Any changes made to the underlying data are propagated to the UI. However, any changes made to the value in the UI are propagated back to the data source. On the other hand, the *Name TextBox* has a *two-way binding*. This means that changes are propagated in both directions. Note that *OneWay* mode is the default; thus it's unnecessary to specify it (the listing that follows only includes it to emphasize that the two *TextBox* controls have different binding modes). Also note that it would make sense in this example to set the *TextBox* control for the *Score* value to be read-only to prevent the user from editing the contents. However, it is left as read-write here to make it more obvious that, even if the user does change the *TextBox* contents, the one-way binding prevents these changes from being propagated back to the underlying data source.

Note The data-binding mechanism does not require UI elements to have defined names. Without data binding, you would need to declare element names in XAML (by using the *x:Name=""* syntax) so that the system can generate class fields for these elements. The app would then use these fields to get/set the field values. Avoiding these field declarations has the added benefit of saving a little memory and initialization time.

```
<TextBox Text="{Binding Name, Mode=TwoWay}"/>
<TextBox Text="{Binding Score, Mode=OneWay}"/>
```

To connect the data object to the UI, you instantiate the data class and assign it to the *DataContext* of the *FrameworkElement* that you want to data-bind. You can specify an individual *FrameworkElement* such as a single control or some containing parent control. At its simplest, this *FrameworkElement* might even be the main page itself, as in this example. Setting the *DataContext* at the page level is a common strategy. All child elements of the page will inherit the same *DataContext*; however, it can also be overridden at any level, if required.

Notice that the *DataContext* property is typed as object, which is why you can assign an object of a custom type such as *Player*—you can, of course, assign anything to an object. Assigning the *Player* object to the *DataContext* of the page is how the data-binding system resolves the references to *Score* and *Name* in the binding declarations of the individual elements, because these elements inherit the *DataContext* of the page. The target (UI element) of the binding can be any accessible property or element that is implemented as a *DependencyProperty* (the *DependencyProperty* mechanism is described in Chapter 3, "UI visuals and touch"). The source can be any public property of any type.

In the *Click* handler for the *getScore and getName Button* controls, the app merely displays the value of the underlying data in a message box. On the other hand, whenever the user taps the Inc button, the *Score* is incremented on the underlying data, and data-binding propagates that value to the UI on your behalf.

```
public partial class MainPage : PhoneApplicationPage
{
    private Player player;
```

```
    public MainPage()
    {
        InitializeComponent();
        player = new Player { Name = "Kim Akers", Score = 12345 };
        DataContext = player;
    }

    private void getScore_Click(object sender, RoutedEventArgs e)
    {
        MessageBox.Show(player.Score.ToString());
    }

    private void getName_Click(object sender, RoutedEventArgs e)
    {
        MessageBox.Show(player.Name);
    }

    private void incScore_Click(object sender, RoutedEventArgs e)
    {
        player.Score++;
    }
}
```

If you want the system to propagate changes in data values for you, your data class needs to implement *INotifyPropertyChanged*. This defines one member: an event of type *PropertyChanged EventHandler*. For data-binding to work, you must expose public properties (not fields) for the data values that you want to be data-bindable. You implement your property setters to raise this event, specifying by name the property that has changed. You can also factor out the invocation of the *PropertyChangedEventHandler* to a custom method, as shown in the code that follows. The more properties you have in the data class, the more useful this becomes.

```
public class Player : INotifyPropertyChanged
{
    public event PropertyChangedEventHandler PropertyChanged;

    private long score;
    public long Score
    {
        get { return score; }
        set
        {
            if (score != value)
            {
                score = value;
                NotifyPropertyChanged("Score");
            }
        }
    }

    private string name;
    public string Name
    {
        get { return name; }
        set
```

```
        {
            if (name != value)
            {
                name = value;
                NotifyPropertyChanged("Name");
            }
        }
    }

    private void NotifyPropertyChanged(string propertyName)
    {
        PropertyChangedEventHandler handler = PropertyChanged;
        if (null != handler)
        {
            handler(this, new PropertyChangedEventArgs(propertyName));
        }
    }
}
```

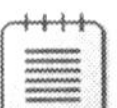

Note The custom *NotifyPropertyChanged* method doesn't raise the *PropertyChanged* event directly through the class field. Instead, it declares a local *PropertyChangedEventHandler* variable and raises the event through that local variable. This seems redundant, but this is a deliberate technique to make the code more robust in the face of multithreaded calls. Behind the scenes, the app code does not explicitly instantiate the *PropertyChanged* event; rather, this is done for you by the C# compiler. By the same token, removing event handlers is also done for you. When the last event handler is removed, the handler field becomes null, as a housekeeping strategy. Declaring a local variable doesn't protect against the field becoming null before or after you assign it; however, it does protect against it being non-null before you assign it and then null after you assign it, but before you invoke it.

The ability to specify data-binding in XAML confers significant benefits, but it is also possible to specify it in code. This might be appropriate if the binding is conditional upon some runtime behavior. For example, you could remove the *{Binding}* specifiers in your XAML and replace them with calls to *BindingOperations.SetBinding* in your code. For this to work, you must declare names for the UI elements in XAML because these are required parameters in the *SetBinding* method.

```
public MainPage()
{
    InitializeComponent();
    player = new Player { Name = "Kim Akers", Score = 12345 };
    DataContext = player;

    Binding binding = new Binding("Name");
    binding.Mode = BindingMode.TwoWay;

    // Either of these lines works.
    //BindingOperations.SetBinding(nameText, TextBox.TextProperty, binding);
    nameText.SetBinding(TextBox.TextProperty, binding);

    binding = new Binding("Score");
    binding.Mode = BindingMode.OneWay;
    //BindingOperations.SetBinding(scoreText, TextBox.TextProperty, binding);
    scoreText.SetBinding(TextBox.TextProperty, binding);
}
```

If you want to control UI formatting as part of data binding, you can use the *StringFormat* attribute in the binding definition. Figure 4-3 shows a minor enhancement of the previous app (the *SimpleData Binding_Format* solution in the sample code), in which the *Player* class exposes an additional *DateTime* property to represent the last time the player participated in the game, and two additional *String* properties (*Note* and *Motto*).

```
player = new Player
    { Name = "Kim Akers", Score = 12345, LastPlayed=DateTime.Now, Note="hello world",
Motto=null};
```

The *LastPlayed* property is displayed with custom binding formatting, as is the *Note*. In addition, the *Score* has been formatted (somewhat incongruously) with a thousands-separator and displays to two decimal places.

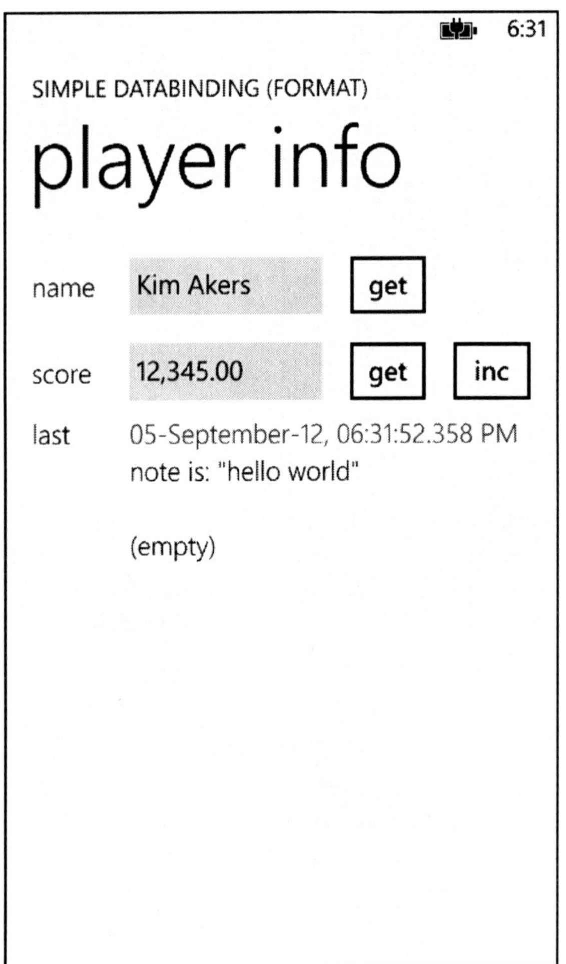

FIGURE 4-3 A demonstration of the *StringFormat* data-binding attribute.

Compare the screenshot in Figure 4-3 with the XAML in which these *StringFormat* values are declared. Observe the use of the backslash to escape the meaning of special characters in the formatting string such as the open "{" and close "}" brackets and the comma (,). Also note that you cannot use the backslash to escape double quotation marks; instead, you must use the XML *"* entity.

```
<TextBox
    Text="{Binding Score, Mode=OneWay, StringFormat=\{0:n2\}}"/>
<TextBlock
    Text="{Binding LastPlayed, StringFormat='dd-MMMM-yy, hh:mm:ss.fff tt'}"
    Foreground="{StaticResource PhoneAccentBrush}"/>

<TextBlock
    Text="{Binding Note, StringFormat='note is: &quot;\{0\}&quot;'}"/>
```

The *Motto* property makes it possible for the value to be null by using the *TargetNullValue* and/or *FallbackValue* attributes. At the bottom of the page are three more *TextBlock* controls, each bound to the same *Motto* property. In this case, the string property is set to null in code. The first variation does not specify what to do in the case of a null value, so nothing is displayed. The second specifies that the string "(empty)" should be used, via the *TargetNullValue* attribute. The third variation uses the *FallbackValue* attribute to specify that the string "unknown" should be displayed if something goes wrong with the data-binding. In the screenshot in Figure 4-3, only the second variation results in displayed text, in this instance.

```
<TextBlock Text="{Binding Motto}"/>
<TextBlock Text="{Binding Motto, TargetNullValue=(empty)}"/>
<TextBlock Text="{Binding Motto, FallbackValue=unknown}"/>
```

Data-binding collections

It is very common to have collections of items that you want to data-bind to UI lists. For example, multiple rows from a data set are commonly bound to some *ItemsControl*, such as a *ListBox*, *ListPicker*, or *LongListSelector*. To bind to a collection, at a minimum, you need to do the following:

- Maintain your individual data objects in an *IEnumerable* collection object of some type.
- Use an *ItemsControl* (or derivative) element as the display container for your list, such as the *ListBox* control.
- Set the *ItemsSource* property of the *ItemsControl* to the collection object.

Where you are displaying one or more properties of a complex data source, you should use a data template. This affords much greater control in formatting the UI. For example, to render a collection of *Player* items, you could have two columns—one for the *Name* and one for the *Score*—and you could use different fonts, colors, styles, backgrounds, and so on for each column, for each row, and so forth. Figure 4-4 presents an example (the *CollectionBinding* solution in the sample code) that demonstrates a *ListBox* bound to a collection of *Player* objects.

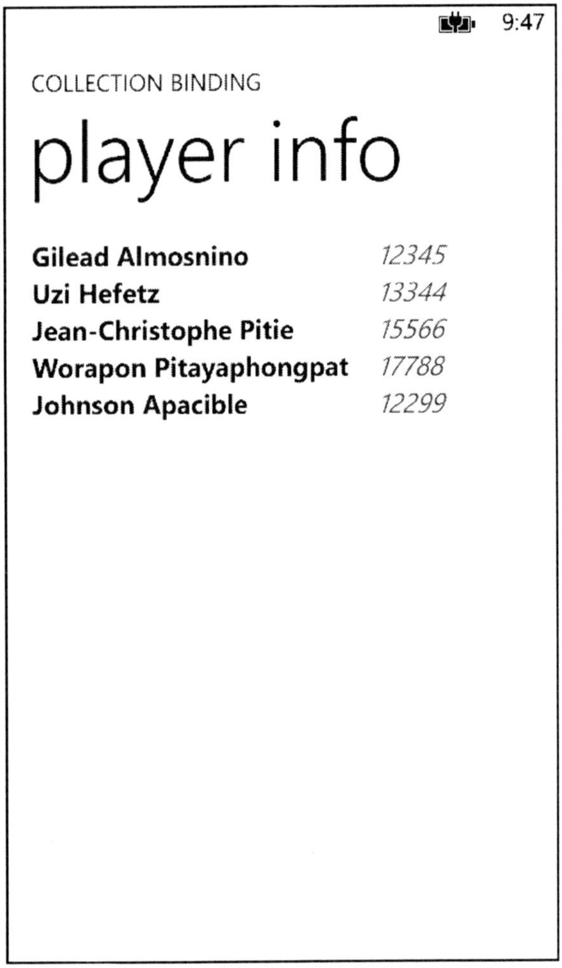

9:47

COLLECTION BINDING

player info

Gilead Almosnino 12345
Uzi Hefetz 13344
Jean-Christophe Pitie 15566
Worapon Pitayaphongpat 17788
Johnson Apacible 12299

FIGURE 4-4 Data-binding to a collection.

In this example, the data collection itself is initialized in the *MainPage* constructor. To establish the data-binding, you assign the collection to the *ItemsSource* property of an *ItemsControl* object; in this example, this is a *ListBox*.

```
private List<Player> players;

public MainPage()
{
    InitializeComponent();

    players = new List<Player>();
    players.Add(new Player { Name = "Gilead Almosnino", Score = 12345 });
    players.Add(new Player { Name = "Uzi Hefetz", Score = 13344 });
```

```
    players.Add(new Player { Name = "Jean-Christophe Pitie", Score = 15566 });
    players.Add(new Player { Name = "Worapon Pitayaphongpat", Score = 17788 });
    players.Add(new Player { Name = "Johnson Apacible", Score = 12299 });

    playerList.ItemsSource = players;
}
```

Observe that there is no need to assign the *DataContext* in this case, because you are explicitly assigning the collection data to the *ItemsSource*. You might do both because you might be data-binding one or more collections (with explicitly assigned *ItemsSource* properties) and also individual items (which would rely on the *DataContext* to resolve their bindings). It is also possible to assign a more specific *DataContext* on a per-element basis (at any level in the visual tree). However, it is more common to set the *DataContext* at a page level, allowing each element in the page to inherit this, and then simply assign individual *ItemsSource* collections, as required.

Note Data-binding large collections has a negative effect on performance because of all the housekeeping that the runtime's data-binding framework does in the background. Chapter 12, "Profiling and diagnostics," discusses mitigation strategies for this.

The data template is defined in XAML and assigned to the *ItemTemplate* property of the *ListBox*. In this example, the template is made up of a *Grid* that contains two *TextBlock* controls, each formatted slightly differently. This is easier to do in Blend than in Visual Studio, but it's still pretty simple in Visual Studio. These use a pair of *{Binding}* attributes: one for the *Name* property of the *Player* item, and one for the *Score*. Technically, these are bound to the *Name* and *Score* property of any object that exposes those properties, not specifically to the *Player* type; although, of course, this app only provides a *Player* type.

```
<ListBox x:Name="playerList" VerticalAlignment="Top" Margin="12,0,12,0" >
    <ListBox.ItemTemplate>
        <DataTemplate>
            <Grid>
                <Grid.ColumnDefinitions>
                    <ColumnDefinition Width="300"/>
                    <ColumnDefinition Width="*"/>
                </Grid.ColumnDefinitions>
                <TextBlock
                    Grid.Column="0" Text="{Binding Name}"
                    FontSize="{StaticResource PhoneFontSizeMedium}"
                    FontWeight="Bold"/>
                <TextBlock
                    Grid.Column="1" Text="{Binding Score}"
                    FontSize="{StaticResource PhoneFontSizeMedium}"
                    FontStyle="Italic"
                    Foreground="{StaticResource PhoneAccentBrush}"/>
            </Grid>
        </DataTemplate>
    </ListBox.ItemTemplate>
</ListBox>
```

Dynamic data-bound collections

With simple data binding, you want a class that implements *INotifyPropertyChanged* so that changes in value can be notified. If you're binding to a static collection, for which the number of elements in the collection doesn't change, you can use a simple collection type such as a *List<T>*. However, if you're binding to a dynamic collection, you should use a collection that implements *INotifyCollection Changed* so that additions and deletions to the collection can be notified. If you want to be notified of changes both to the collection and to the values of the properties of the items within the collection, you need something like this: *CollectionThatImplementsINotifyCollectionChanged<ItemThatImplements INotifyPropertyChanged>*.

The following example uses just such a collection. The individual items are a variation on the *Player* class that exposes *Name* and *LastPlayed* properties, and implements *INotifyPropertyChanged. Player* items are collected in a custom collection class that derives from *ObservableCollection<T>*, which itself implements *INotifyCollectionChanged.* This custom class exposes an *AddPlayer* method, which adds a new *Player* to the underlying collection using the supplied name and the current *DateTime.*

```
public class Players : ObservableCollection<Player>
{
    public void AddPlayer(string name)
    {
        Player player = new Player { Name = name, LastPlayed = DateTime.Now };
        this.Add(player);
    }
}
```

The app provides a *TextBox* in which the user can enter the name of a new player, and a "+" *Button* to add the player to the collection. Adding a player triggers the *NotifyCollectionChangedEvent* on the collection. The collection, in turn, is bound to a *ListBox*. The template for the *ListBox* specifies a *Text Block* for the *Name* and *LastPlayed* properties as well as a *Button* with which the user can update the *LastPlayed* value for the currently selected item. This triggers the *NotifyPropertyChangedEvent* on the item. The finished app (the *DynamicCollectionBinding* solution in the sample code) is shown in Figure 4-5.

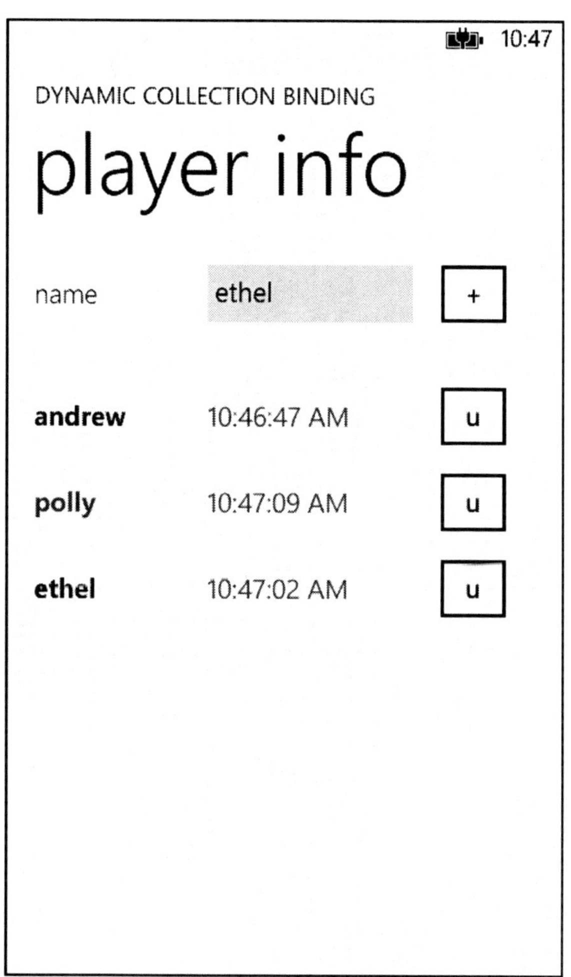

FIGURE 4-5 Data-binding works with collections that change dynamically.

The *MainPage* code-behind initializes the collection and binds it to the *ItemsSource* property of the *ListBox*. The *Click* handler for the update *Button* is interesting. This is defined inside the *Data Template*, as demonstrated in the following:

```
<ListBox
    Grid.Row="2" Grid.Column="0" Grid.ColumnSpan="3"
    x:Name="playerList" VerticalAlignment="Top" Margin="12,0,12,0">
    <ListBox.ItemTemplate>
        <DataTemplate>
            <Grid>
                <Grid.ColumnDefinitions>
```

```
                    <ColumnDefinition Width="150"/>
                    <ColumnDefinition Width="188"/>
                    <ColumnDefinition Width="80"/>
                </Grid.ColumnDefinitions>
                <TextBlock
                    Grid.Column="0" Text="{Binding Name}"
                    FontSize="{StaticResource PhoneFontSizeMedium}"
                    FontWeight="Bold" VerticalAlignment="Center"/>
                <TextBlock
                    Grid.Column="1" Text="{Binding LastPlayed, StringFormat=hh:mm:ss,
                                                   Mode=TwoWay}"
                    FontSize="{StaticResource PhoneFontSizeMedium}"
                    Foreground="{StaticResource PhoneAccentBrush}"
                    VerticalAlignment="Center"/>
                <Button
                    Grid.Column="2" x:Name="update" Content="u" Click="update_Click"/>
            </Grid>
        </DataTemplate>
    </ListBox.ItemTemplate>
</ListBox>
```

When the user taps one of the *Button* controls in the list, this does not change the selected item—the *ListBox.SelectionChanged* event is not raised. So, to obtain of the correct data object, the *Click* handler retrieves the sending *Button* object and extracts that object's *DataContext*. This will be the bound data object for the whole item; in this case, it's a *Player* object.

```
private Players players;

public MainPage()
{
    InitializeComponent();

    players = new Players();
    playerList.ItemsSource = players;
}

private void addPlayer_Click(object sender, RoutedEventArgs e)
{
    players.AddPlayer(nameText.Text);
}

private void update_Click(object sender, RoutedEventArgs e)
{
    Button button = (Button)sender;
    Player player = (Player)button.DataContext;
    player.LastPlayed = DateTime.Now;
}
```

Command binding

The *ICommand* interface gives you a way to set up your viewmodel to expose commands that can be data-bound as properties to view controls. By using this approach, you don't need to supply additional code behind your view in order for it to interoperate with your viewmodel, because the binding can be done entirely in XAML. This increases the decoupling between view and viewmodel. Consider Figure 4-6, which shows the *TestCommandBinding* solution in the sample code.

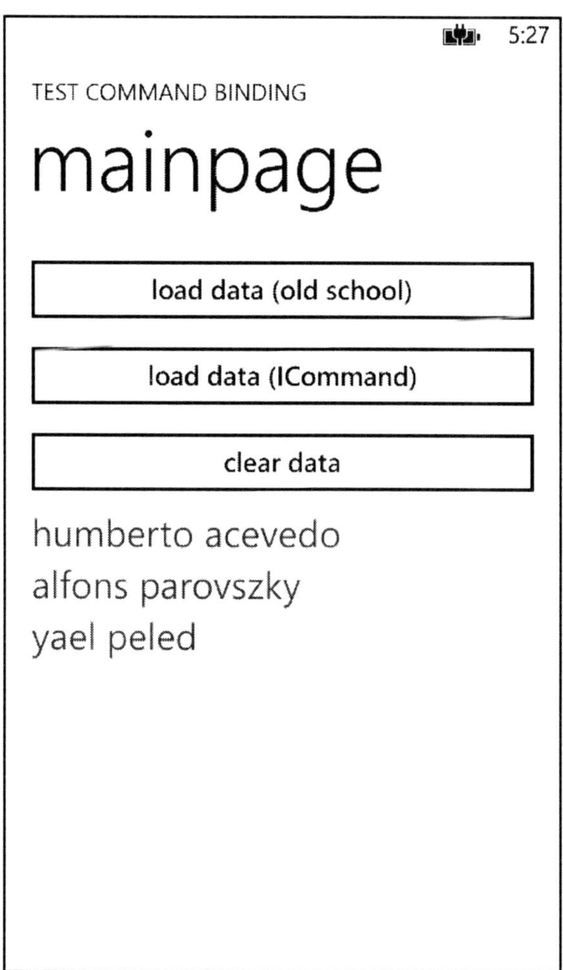

FIGURE 4-6 Data-binding and command-binding.

The app offers three buttons: one to load data into the viewmodel by using the traditional approach with a custom button *Click* handler; a second button to load data by using the *ICommand* approach; and a third button to clear the data (also using *ICommand*). Below that is a *ListBox* that is data-bound in the normal way to a collection of employee data held in the viewmodel. The application model uses a view (the page) and a viewmodel (*EmployeesViewModel*), backed by a model (*EmployeeModel*). In the traditional approach, the first button is defined with a *Click* handler, as shown in the following:

```
<Button x:Name="loadData" Content="load data (old school)" Click="loadData_Click"/>
```

This requires a corresponding handler method in the view code-behind, as demonstrated here:

```
private void loadData_Click(object sender, RoutedEventArgs e)
{
    App.ViewModel.LoadDataOldSchool();
}
```

This in turn calls into a method on the viewmodel to load the data (in this case, simulating a more realistic data source). The viewmodel is set up with an *ObservableCollection<T>*, initialized in the constructor. The traditional method to load data simply creates some dummy employees.

```
private ObservableCollection<EmployeeModel> data;
public ObservableCollection<EmployeeModel> Data
{
    get { return data; }
    private set { }
}

public EmployeesViewModel()
{
    data = new ObservableCollection<EmployeeModel>();
}

public void LoadDataOldSchool()
{
    data.Add(new EmployeeModel { Name = "humberto acevedo" });
    data.Add(new EmployeeModel { Name = "alfons parovszky" });
    data.Add(new EmployeeModel { Name = "yael peled" });
}
```

All this works just fine, but it does mean that the view has to have a method to handle the *Click* event on the button, and this in turn must invoke some functionality on the viewmodel. The alternative approach, using *ICommand*, is slightly more decoupled, which is generally a good thing for maintainability and testability. To set this up, you need a class that implements the *ICommand* interface. *ICommand* defines two methods—*Execute* and *CanExecute*—and one event—*CanExecuteChanged*. This class is a façade between the consumer (the page) and the implementation (the viewmodel).

The *Execute* delegate can be set to a method on the viewmodel that performs the desired operation when the user taps the button. The *CanExecute* delegate can be set to another method on the viewmodel that determines whether or not the button can be executed, and if not, the system disables the button automatically. The *CanExecuteChanged* event is raised when the value of the executability of the command changes.

```
public class Command : ICommand
{
    private Func<object, bool> canExecuteDelegate;
    private Action<object> executeDelegate;
    public event EventHandler CanExecuteChanged;

    public Command(Action<object> executeDelegate)
    {
        this.canExecuteDelegate = (e) => true;
        this.executeDelegate = executeDelegate;
    }

    public Command(
        Func<object, bool> canExecuteDelegate, Action<object> executeDelegate)
    {
        this.canExecuteDelegate = canExecuteDelegate;
        this.executeDelegate = executeDelegate;
    }

    public bool CanExecute(object parameter)
    {
        return canExecuteDelegate(parameter);
    }

    public void Execute(object parameter)
    {
        if (executeDelegate != null)
        {
            executeDelegate(parameter);
        }
    }
}
```

Following is a description of how you use the *Command* class in the viewmodel. First, the constructor is enhanced to initialize two *ICommand* objects: one for loading the data, and the other for clearing the data. The first initialization passes both a *CanExecute* delegate and an *Execute* delegate. If the *CanExecute* delegate returns true, the *Execute* delegate will be invoked; otherwise, it will not. The *Execute* delegate, named *LoadDataDelegate* here, simply parallels the old-school behavior of creating some dummy employees. The *CanExecute* delegate in this example always returns true; realistically, it would be doing something meaningful such as checking the availability of network connectivity so that the Execute delegate can download data from the web, and so on.

The second *ICommand* object is used to clear the collection of data. You initialize this one by using the constructor overload that takes only an *Execute* delegate. This *ICommand* object will therefore have a null *CanExecute* delegate. The *Command* class is implemented always to return true in this case.

```
public EmployeesViewModel()
{
    data = new ObservableCollection<EmployeeModel>();
    loadDataCommand = new Command(CanLoadData, LoadDataDelegate);
    clearDataCommand = new Command(ClearDataDelegate);
}

private void LoadDataDelegate(object parameter)
{
    data.Add(new EmployeeModel { Name = "humberto acevedo" });
    data.Add(new EmployeeModel { Name = "alfons parovszky" });
    data.Add(new EmployeeModel { Name = "yael peled" });
}

private ICommand loadDataCommand;
public ICommand LoadDataCommand
{
    get
    {
        return loadDataCommand;
    }
}

private bool CanLoadData(object parameter)
{
    return true;
}

private void ClearDataDelegate(object parameter)
{
    Data.Clear();
}

private ICommand clearDataCommand;
public ICommand ClearDataCommand
{
    get
    {
        return clearDataCommand;
    }
}
```

The final piece of this puzzle is to command-bind the UI. The second and third buttons are bound by using the *Command={Binding}* syntax, binding the first to the *LoadDataCommand* object in the viewmodel, and the second to the *ClearDataCommand* object, both of which are *ICommand* objects.

```
<Button x:Name="loadData" Content="load data (old school)" Click="loadData_Click"/>
<Button Content="load data (ICommand)" Command="{Binding LoadDataCommand}"/>
<Button Content="clear data" Command="{Binding ClearDataCommand}"/>
<ListBox ItemsSource="{Binding Data}" >
    <ListBox.ItemTemplate>
        <DataTemplate>
            <TextBlock
                Text="{Binding Name}"
                FontSize="{StaticResource PhoneFontSizeLarge}"
                Margin="{StaticResource PhoneHorizontalMargin}"
                Foreground="{StaticResource PhoneAccentBrush}"/>
        </DataTemplate>
    </ListBox.ItemTemplate>
</ListBox>
```

Template resources

As you can do with other things such as styles (discussed in Chapter 3), you can define a data template as a resource. This is useful if it's the kind of template that lends itself to reuse or if you're working with a team in which one developer works on the template while another developer works on the page. The mechanism is straightforward. First, you define the template just as you would normally. The only difference is that when implemented as a resource, the template must have a defined *Key*. The resource definition resides in the *Resources* section of the XAML element where you want it to be visible. This could be in the *App.xaml* if you want to use the template across multiple pages, or locally in the XAML for the page in which it will be used, either at the page level or at the level of any child element which is at or above the level where it will be used.

```
<phone:PhoneApplicationPage.Resources>
    <DataTemplate x:Key="playerTemplate">
        <Grid>
            <Grid.ColumnDefinitions>
                <ColumnDefinition Width="300"/>
                <ColumnDefinition Width="*"/>
            </Grid.ColumnDefinitions>
            <TextBlock
                Grid.Column="0" Text="{Binding Name}"
                FontSize="{StaticResource PhoneFontSizeMedium}"
                FontWeight="Bold"/>
            <TextBlock
                Grid.Column="1" Text="{Binding Score}"
                FontSize="{StaticResource PhoneFontSizeMedium}"
                FontStyle="Italic"
                Foreground="{StaticResource PhoneAccentBrush}"/>
        </Grid>
    </DataTemplate>
</phone:PhoneApplicationPage.Resources>
```

Next, in the element to which you want this template to apply, specify the template by its *Key* name. You can see this at work in the *CollectionBinding_Resource* solution in the sample code.

```
<ListBox x:Name="playerList" VerticalAlignment="Top" Margin="12,0,12,0"
            ItemTemplate="{StaticResource playerTemplate}"/>
```

Sorting and grouping bound collections

As part of data-binding a collection, you can sort or group the data by using the *CollectionViewSource* class and the *SortDescriptions* and *GroupDescriptions* collection properties. Figure 4-7 shows the *GroupBinding* solution in the sample code. When the user selects a store item from the list of stores in the first column, the view updates the second column with those products that are associated with the selected store. The key here is that this is all done via data binding—there is no *SelectionChanged* event handler in the code, for instance.

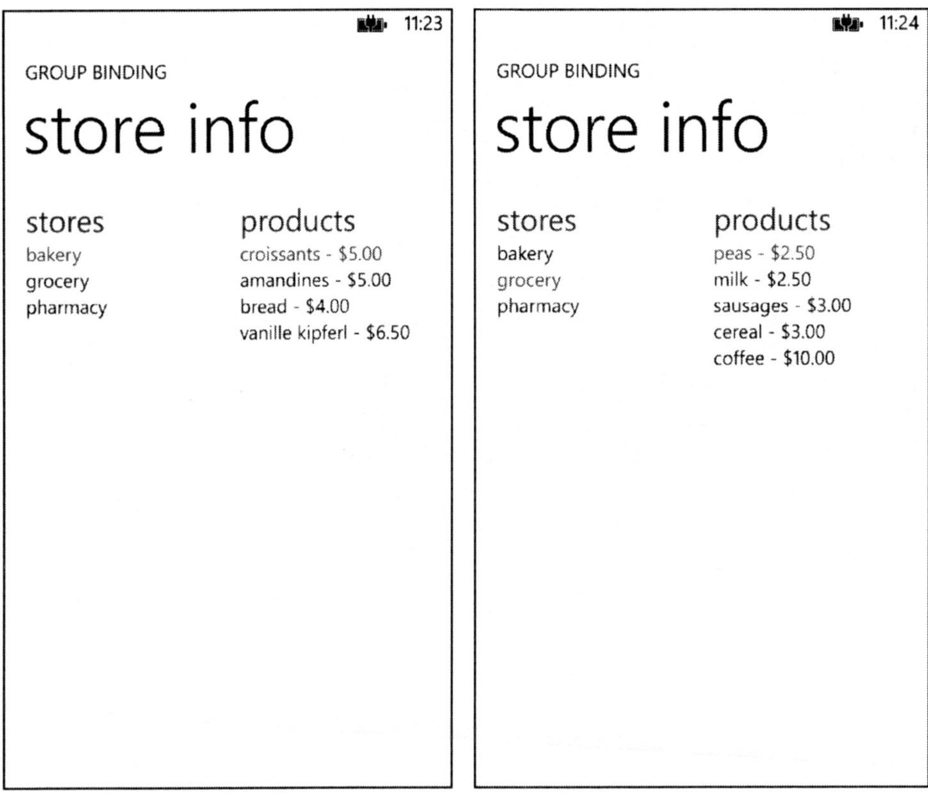

FIGURE 4-7 Data-binding with *CollectionViewSource* objects, and sorting and grouping collections.

A *Store* class represents an individual store, with a string property for the store name and a collection property for the store products. The *Product* class, in turn, consists of a string for the name and a double for the price.

```
public class Store
{
    public String Name { get; set; }
    public ObservableCollection<Product> Products { get; set; }

    public Store(String name)
```

```
    {
        Name = name;
        Products = new ObservableCollection<Product>();
    }
}

public class Product
{
    public String Name { get; set; }
    public double Price { get; set; }

    public Product(String name, double price)
    {
        Name = name;
        Price = price;
    }

    public override string ToString()
    {
        return String.Format("{0} - {1:C2}", Name, Price);
    }
}
```

The app maintains a collection of stores in an instance of the *Stores* class, where the constructor creates some demonstration data (this is an arbitrary collection of stores and products, in no particular order).

```
public class Stores : ObservableCollection<StoreModel>
{
    public Stores ()
    {
        Store grocery = new Store("grocery");
        grocery.Products.Add(new Product("peas", 2.50));
        grocery.Products.Add(new Product("sausages", 3.00));
        grocery.Products.Add(new Product("coffee", 10.00));
        grocery.Products.Add(new Product("cereal", 3.00));
        grocery.Products.Add(new Product("milk", 2.50));
        this.Add(grocery);

        Store pharmacy = new Store("pharmacy");
        pharmacy.Products.Add(new Product("toothpaste", 3.99));
        pharmacy.Products.Add(new Product("aspirin", 5.25));
        this.Add(pharmacy);

        Store bakery = new Store("bakery");
        bakery.Products.Add(new Product("croissants", 5.00));
        bakery.Products.Add(new Product("bread", 4.00));
        bakery.Products.Add(new Product("vanille kipferl", 6.50));
        bakery.Products.Add(new Product("amandines", 5.00));
        this.Add(bakery);
    }
}
```

The XAML defines two additional namespaces: one for the current assembly (where the *Stores* type is defined), and one to resolve the definition of the standard *SortDescription* type.

```
xmlns:local="clr-namespace:GroupBinding"
xmlns:scm="clr-namespace:System.ComponentModel;assembly=System.Windows"
```

The page also defines two *CollectionViewSource* objects as resources. The first is bound to the *Stores* collection; that is to say, all stores. The second *CollectionViewSource* is bound to the first *CollectionViewSource*, specifying the *Products* within that collection as the path. This effectively provides a pivot mechanism on the stores.

```
<phone:PhoneApplicationPage.Resources>
    <local:Stores x:Key="shoppingItems" />
    <CollectionViewSource x:Key="cvs1" Source="{StaticResource shoppingItems}"/>
    <CollectionViewSource x:Key="cvs2" Source="{Binding Source={StaticResource cvs1},
Path=Products}"/>
</phone:PhoneApplicationPage.Resources>
```

For the UI display itself, the XAML defines two *ListBox* controls. For the first one, its *ItemsSource* property is set to the first *CollectionViewSource*; the *TextBlock* in the item template is bound to the store *Name* property. For the second *ListBox*, its *ItemsSource* is set to the second *CollectionView Source*; the *TextBlock* in the item template is bound implicitly to the whole *Product* item. Recall that the *Product* item overrides *ToString* to render both the product name and price.

```
<ListBox ItemsSource="{Binding Source={StaticResource cvs1}}">
    <ListBox.ItemTemplate>
        <DataTemplate>
            <TextBlock Text="{Binding Name}"/>
        </DataTemplate>
    </ListBox.ItemTemplate>
</ListBox>
<ListBox ItemsSource="{Binding Source={StaticResource cvs2}}">
    <ListBox.ItemTemplate>
        <DataTemplate>
            <TextBlock Text="{Binding}"/>
        </DataTemplate>
    </ListBox.ItemTemplate>
</ListBox>
```

This results in the experience shown in the screenshots in Figure 4-7; the first column lists all stores, and the second column lists only those products for the currently selected store. There are also two further enhancements: sorting and grouping. The stores are sorted alphabetically, and the products within each store are grouped according to price. This is achieved very simply in XAML by specifying a *SortDescription* for the first *CollectionViewSource*, and a *GroupDescription* for the second.

```
<CollectionViewSource x:Key="cvs1" Source="{Binding Source={StaticResource shoppingItems}}">
    <CollectionViewSource.SortDescriptions>
        <scm:SortDescription PropertyName="Name"/>
    </CollectionViewSource.SortDescriptions>
</CollectionViewSource>
<CollectionViewSource x:Key="cvs2" Source="{Binding Source={StaticResource cvs1},
                                            Path=Products}">
    <CollectionViewSource.GroupDescriptions>
        <PropertyGroupDescription PropertyName="Price" />
    </CollectionViewSource.GroupDescriptions>
</CollectionViewSource>
```

Both *SortDescriptions* and *GroupDescriptions* are collection properties. This means that you can specify multiple sorting and grouping definitions for each *CollectionViewSource*, if required.

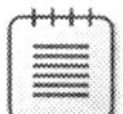

Note Another useful class for data-binding collections is the *DataServiceCollection<T>* class. This provides simplified binding for data returned by Windows Communications Foundation (WCF) Data Services. The key to this class is that it derives from *ObservableCollection<T>*, which implements *INotifyCollectionChanged* and *INotifyPropertyChanged*, allowing it to update bound data automatically. *DataServiceCollection<T>* is discussed in Chapter 8, "Web services and the cloud."

Type/value converters

In addition to formatting, grouping, and sorting, it is also possible to convert a data value from one type to another as part of the data-binding process. For example, suppose that you have a collection of *Player* objects that expose two properties, *Name* and *Score*. You want to bind the data values of these properties in the conventional way (each one to a *TextBlock.Text* element). However, you also want to format the *Score* differently depending on its data value; that is, if the value is greater than 10,000, it is rendered as *FontWeights.Black*; otherwise, it's rendered as *FontWeights.Normal*.

Figure 4-8 shows this implementation in action (the *BindingConverter* solution in the sample code).

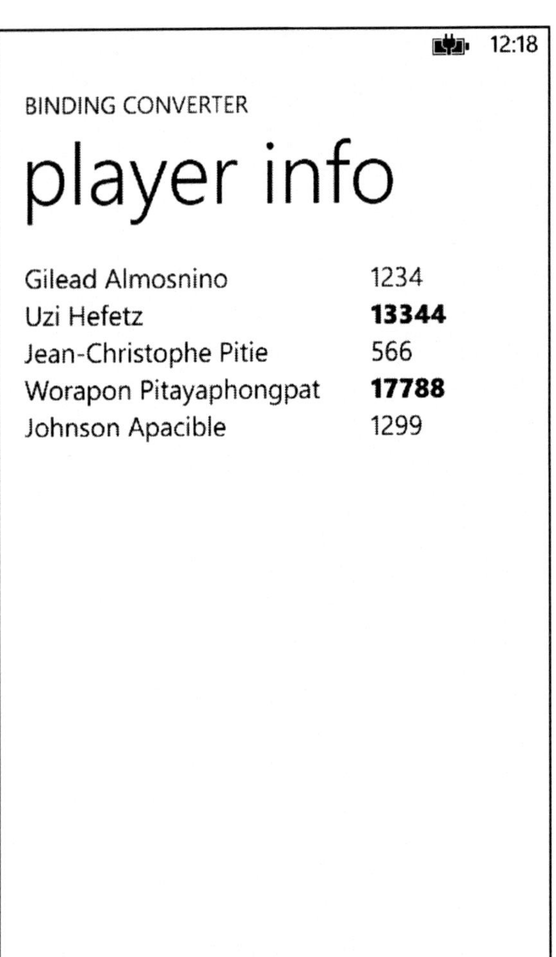

FIGURE 4-8 You can convert data values from one type to another when binding data.

The interesting code is the class that implements *IValueConverter*. This interface declares two methods: *Convert* and *ConvertBack*. If you only want one-way binding, you only need to implement the *Convert* method. For two-way binding, you would also need to implement *ConvertBack*. This example implements the *Convert* method to return a *FontWeight* whose value is computed based on the incoming value parameter. This will be used in the data-binding for the *Score* property. In this way, you convert a *Score* value into a *FontWeight* value.

```
public class ScoreLevelConverter : IValueConverter
{
    public object Convert(
        object value, Type targetType, object parameter, CultureInfo culture)
    {
        if ((long)value > 10000)
        {
            return FontWeights.Black;
        }
```

```
        else
        {
            return FontWeights.Normal;
        }
    }

    public object ConvertBack(
        object value, Type targetType, object parameter, CultureInfo culture)
    {
        throw new NotImplementedException();
    }
}
```

The converter is implemented within the app code, and you want to use it in the XAML for the same app. To make the converter accessible in the XAML, you need to declare a new XML namespace for this assembly. (In this example, this is part of the *PhoneApplicationPage* declaration, alongside all the other namespace declarations. This makes sense in this simple example, but things such as converters tend to be at the app level so that they can easily be shared across many pages.) Then, specify an *ItemsControl* (in this case, a *ListBox*) with a *ScoreLevelConverter* resource. Bind the *TextBlock.Text* to the *Player.Name* in the normal way. The interesting piece is binding the *TextBlock.FontWeight* to the *Player.Score* via the converter, as shown here:

```
<phone:PhoneApplicationPage.Resources>
    <local:ScoreLevelConverter x:Key="scoreConverter"/>
</phone:PhoneApplicationPage.Resources>
...

<ListBox x:Name="playerList" VerticalAlignment="Top" Margin="12,0,12,0" >
    <ItemsControl.ItemTemplate>
        <DataTemplate>
            <Grid>
                <TextBlock
                    Grid.Column="0" Text="{Binding Name}"
                    FontSize="{StaticResource PhoneFontSizeMedium}"/>
                <TextBlock
                    Grid.Column="1" Text="{Binding Score}"
                    FontSize="{StaticResource PhoneFontSizeMedium}"
                    FontWeight =
                        "{Binding Score, Converter={StaticResource scoreConverter}}"/>
            </Grid>
        </DataTemplate>
    </ItemsControl.ItemTemplate>
</ListBox>
```

As before, the *ListBox.ItemsSource* property is set to the collection of *Player* objects.

Element binding

In addition to binding to data from a data source, you can also bind from one element to another within the UI. Here is an example that binds the *Text* property of a *TextBlock* to the value of a *Slider*. As the user moves the *Slider*, the value is propagated to the *TextBlock*. Notice that this also uses a simple double-to-int value converter, which takes the double values of the *Slider* position and converts them to integers for display in the *TextBlock*.

```
public class DoubleToIntConverter : IValueConverter
{
    public object Convert(
        object value, Type targetType, object parameter, CultureInfo culture)
    {
        return System.Convert.ToInt32((double)value);
    }

    public object ConvertBack(
        object value, Type targetType, object parameter, CultureInfo culture)
    {
        throw new NotImplementedException();
    }
}
```

The critical syntax in the XAML is that which associates the *ElementName* property in the *TextBlock* with the name of the *Slider* element and specifies that the name of the property on the source element to which you want to bind the *Value* property (set to the *Path* property on the *TextBlock*). The result is shown in Figure 4-9 (the *ElementBinding* solution in the sample code). Also note that forward references are not supported in XAML; thus, the *ElementName* must already be defined in the tree before you reference it.

```
<phone:PhoneApplicationPage.Resources>
    <local:DoubleToIntConverter x:Key="myConverter"/>
</phone:PhoneApplicationPage.Resources>
...
<StackPanel x:Name="ContentPanel" Grid.Row="1" Margin="12,0,12,0">
    <Slider x:Name="mySlider" Maximum="100"/>
    <TextBlock
        Text="{Binding ElementName=mySlider,
        Path=Value, Converter={StaticResource myConverter}}"
        Style="{StaticResource PhoneTextTitle1Style}"
        Foreground="{StaticResource PhoneAccentBrush}"/>
</StackPanel>
```

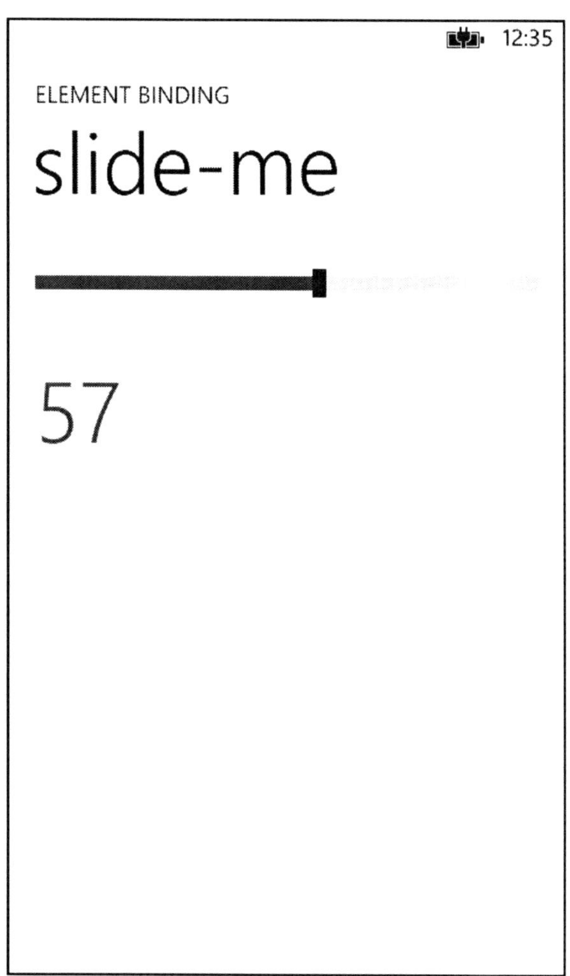

FIGURE 4-9 You can also bind data to UI elements. Here, the *Text* property of a *TextBlock* is bound to the value of a *Slider*.

Data validation

Windows Phone supports a simple level of data validation in two-way bindings. To make use of this validation, the simplest approach is to have your data class throw an exception in its property setter when it encounters invalid data (see the *BindingValidation* solution in the sample code).

```
private long score;
public long Score
{
    get { return score; }
    set
    {
        if (value >= 0)
        {
            if (score != value)
            {
                score = value;
                NotifyPropertyChanged("Score");
            }
        }
        else
        {
            throw new ArgumentOutOfRangeException();
        }
    }
}
```

In the XAML for the *MainPage*, you set the *NotifyOnValidationError* and *ValidatesOnExceptions* properties of the *Binding* for the *Score TextBox* to *true*. This directs the binding engine to raise a *BindingValidationError* event when a validation error is added to or removed from the *Validation.Errors* collection. To handle this event, you need to create an event handler either in the *TextBox* or on any of its parents in the hierarchy. It is common to handle validation errors on a per-page basis so that you can handle errors from multiple controls in a consistent manner for the entire page. Reading between the lines, it should be clear that this relies on the fact that the *BindingValidationError* is a routed event (as described in Chapter 3), which will bubble up the hierarchy from the control where the error occurs to the first parent that handles it.

In this example, however, you handle the event half-way up the hierarchy, in the parent *Grid*. The point of doing this is that you can short-circuit the routing and improve performance slightly. This is possible in this case because you know that you have no controls outside the *Grid* that have any validation that could trigger a *BindingValidationError*.

```
<Grid
    x:Name="ContentPanel"
    BindingValidationError="ContentPanel_BindingValidationError">
    <Grid.RowDefinitions>
        <RowDefinition Height="80" />
        <RowDefinition Height="80"/>
    </Grid.RowDefinitions>
    <Grid.ColumnDefinitions>
        <ColumnDefinition Width="120"/>
        <ColumnDefinition Width="*"/>
    </Grid.ColumnDefinitions>
    <TextBlock
        Grid.Row="0" Grid.Column="0" Text="name"
        Style="{StaticResource PhoneTextTitle3Style}"
        VerticalAlignment="Center"/>
```

```
    <TextBox
        Grid.Row="0" Grid.Column="1"
        Text="{Binding Name, Mode=TwoWay}"/>
    <TextBlock
        Grid.Row="1" Grid.Column="0" Text="score"
        Style="{StaticResource PhoneTextTitle3Style}"
        VerticalAlignment="Center"/>
    <TextBox
        x:Name="scoreText" Grid.Row="1" Grid.Column="1"
        Text="{Binding Mode=TwoWay, Path=Score,
        NotifyOnValidationError=True, ValidatesOnExceptions=True}"/>
</Grid>
```

The implementation of the event handler is in the *MainPage* class. If an error has been added to the collection, the *TextBox* background will display *Red*. When the error is corrected, and therefore removed from the collection, the standard background for a Phone *TextBox* is restored.

```
private void ContentPanel_BindingValidationError(
    object sender, ValidationErrorEventArgs e)
{
    Debug.WriteLine("ContentPanel_BindingValidationError");

    TextBox t = (TextBox)e.OriginalSource;
    if (e.Action == ValidationErrorEventAction.Added)
    {
        t.Background = new SolidColorBrush(Colors.Red);
    }
    else if (e.Action == ValidationErrorEventAction.Removed)
    {
        t.ClearValue(TextBox.BackgroundProperty);
    }

    e.Handled = true;
}
```

Note also the use of the *DependencyObject.ClearValue* method to reset the *Background Brush*. In this case, this is called on the *BackgroundProperty*. An alternative would be to determine manually which *Brush* you should use (as shown in the code snippet that follows)—for example, if you know you're using a standard *PhoneTextBoxBrush* resource—but that would clearly be less elegant.

```
t.Background = (Brush)Resources["PhoneTextBoxBrush"];
```

Figure 4-10 shows how the app looks in action. In this scenario, the user has typed in some invalid characters and then moved the focus to another control. This triggers the validation engine in the data-binding framework, which then invokes the error handler.

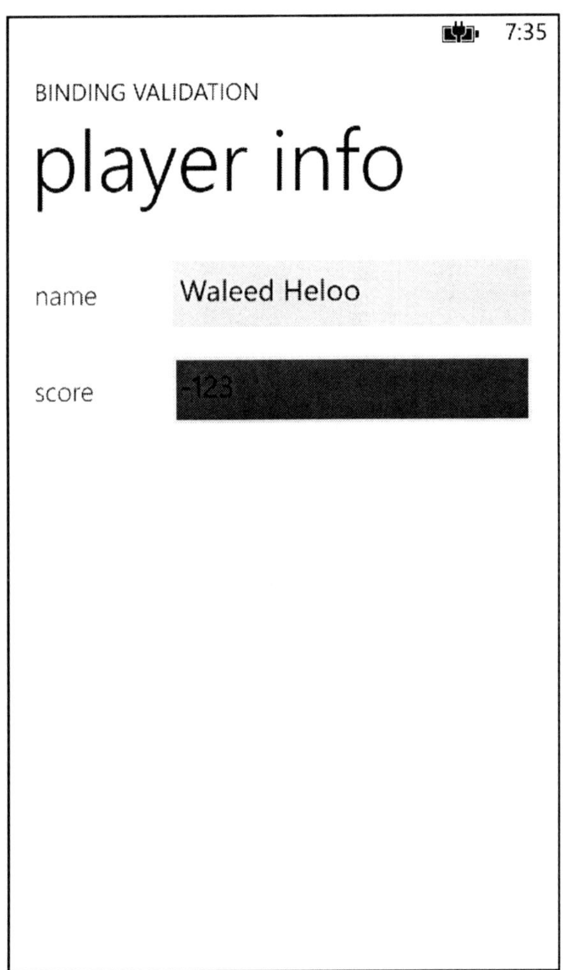

FIGURE 4-10 An invalid character triggers the validation engine in the data-binding framework.

Note that it is also not uncommon to have multiple handlers at different levels in the visual tree. For example, you might have a complex set of visual elements, perhaps several *Grid* controls each containing multiple children, for which you want to handle validation errors for each *Grid* in a different fashion. You might also want to have a catch-all handler at the page level.

```
<phone:PhoneApplicationPage
...
    BindingValidationError="PhoneApplicationPage_BindingValidationError">

        <Grid
            x:Name="ContentPanel"
            BindingValidationError="ContentPanel_BindingValidationError">
...
        </Grid>
    </Grid>
</phone:PhoneApplicationPage>
```

To ensure that the event does not continue routing up the tree, you simply need to set *Handled* to *true* in any handler for which you have in fact completely handled the event, as demonstrated in the *ContentPanel_BindingValidationError* method in the preceding example.

```
private void PhoneApplicationPage_BindingValidationError(
    object sender, ValidationErrorEventArgs e)
{
    Debug.WriteLine("PhoneApplicationPage_BindingValidationError");
}
```

Given the implementation of *ContentPanel_BindingValidationError*, the *PhoneApplicationPage_BindingValidationError* handler at the page level would never be called unless some other element outside the *Grid* also triggers a validation error.

If you want even more validation control, you can also consider using *INotifyDataErrorInfo*. You would implement this interface on your data class to signify whether there currently are any validation errors on the object. *INotifyDataErrorInfo* exposes an event that can be raised when there is a validation error. This removes the need for validation to be immediate; instead, you could perform it asynchronously (perhaps querying a web service) and then raise the event when you eventually determine the result.

By the same token, you can use this to perform validation across multiple properties for which you cannot fully determine whether an individual property is valid until you have examined other properties. This applies especially in circumstances when you need to perform not just cross-property it, but whole-entity validation. It might be that no single property is invalid but that the combination of several (or all) of the property values is invalid.

This technique is demonstrated in the *BindingValidation_Info* solution in the sample code, which is a minor variation on the *BindingValidation* sample. The new code is in the *Player* class itself. This now implements *INotifyDataErrorInfo*, which defines the *ErrorsChanged* event, the *GetErrors* method, and the *HasErrors* property. To support these, you define a *Dictionary<T>* to hold the collection of errors. When you validate one of the properties (*Score*, in this example), if there is a validation error, you add an entry to the dictionary and then raise the *ErrorsChanged* event.

```
public class Player : INotifyPropertyChanged, INotifyDataErrorInfo
{
    public event PropertyChangedEventHandler PropertyChanged;

    private long score;
    public long Score
    {
        get { return score; }
        set
        {
            if (value >= 0)
            {
                if (score != value)
                {
                    score = value;
                    NotifyPropertyChanged("Score");
                    if (errors.ContainsKey("Score"))
```

```
                {
                    errors.Remove("Score");
                }
            }
        }
        else
        {
            if (!errors.ContainsKey("Score"))
            {
                errors.Add("Score", "value cannot be negative");
            }
        }

        EventHandler<DataErrorsChangedEventArgs> handler = ErrorsChanged;
        if (handler != null)
        {
            handler(this, new DataErrorsChangedEventArgs("Score"));
        }
    }
}

}

...unchanged code omitted for brevity.

private Dictionary<String, String> errors = new Dictionary<String, String>();
public event EventHandler<DataErrorsChangedEventArgs> ErrorsChanged;

public System.Collections.IEnumerable GetErrors(string propertyName)
{
    if (String.IsNullOrEmpty(propertyName))
    {
        return errors.Values;
    }
    if (!errors.ContainsKey(propertyName))
    {
        return String.Empty;
    }
    else
    {
        return new String[] { errors[propertyName] };
    }
}

public bool HasErrors
{
    get { return errors.Count > 0; }
}

}
```

If you anticipate having to support more than one error per property, the simple *Dictionary* shown in the preceding code would not be sufficient. In that case, you'd need something like a *Dictionary<String, List<String>>*, instead.

Separating concerns

So far, the examples in this chapter have focused on data-binding by using simple objects and collections of data that are part of the *MainPage* itself. Now, it's time to pay a little more attention to engineering and to further separate the code that represents data from that which represents UI. At a minimum, the data object(s) should be abstracted from the UI code. Figure 4-11 illustrates this first level of decoupling (the *CollectionBinding_XAML* solution in the sample code).

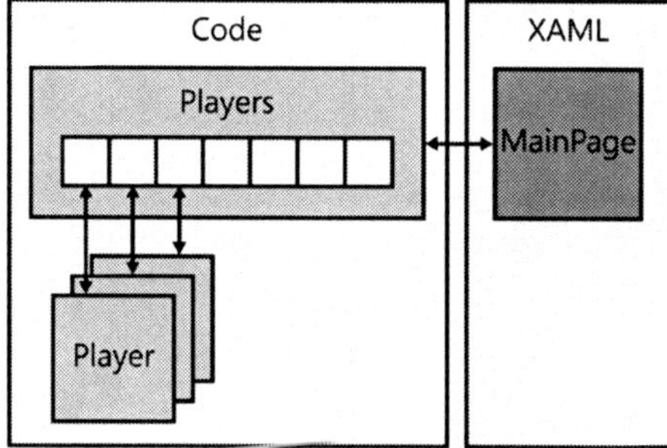

FIGURE 4-11 An example of simple SoC.

The app uses a separate *Players* collection class to represent the collection of *Player* objects. This removes the data collection from the UI class. This class exposes a collection property named *Items*. The constructor initializes its collection by calling a private *GetData* method. This is a simplified stand-in for a method that would fetch the data at runtime, perhaps from some website or from a local database.

```
public class Players
{
    public ObservableCollection<Player> Items { get; private set; }

    public Players()
    {
        Items = new ObservableCollection<Player>();
        GetData();
    }

    private void GetData()
    {
        Items.Add(new Player { Name = "Gilead Almosnino", Score = 12345 });
        Items.Add(new Player { Name = "Uzi Hefetz", Score = 13344 });
        Items.Add(new Player { Name = "Jean-Christophe Pitie", Score = 15566 });
        Items.Add(new Player { Name = "Worapon Pitayaphongpat", Score = 17788 });
        Items.Add(new Player { Name = "Johnson Apacible", Score = 12299 });
    }
}
```

The *MainPage* class initializes its *DataContext* to a new instance of the *Players* collection. This one line of code is now the only connection in the UI code to the data code, providing much cleaner separation.

```
public MainPage()
{
    InitializeComponent();
    DataContext = new Players();
}
```

One obvious advantage of SoC, even in this simple manner, is that the *ItemsSource* value can now be assigned declaratively in XAML instead of in code, as demonstrated here:

```
<ListBox ItemsSource="{Binding Items}">
```

You could take this a step further by assigning the *DataContext* in XAML, as well. To do this, you first need to add a namespace in the page's XAML for the current assembly so that you can subsequently refer to the *Players* collection class. Second, declare a keyed resource for the *Players* class. Third, set the *DataContext* to this resource in either the *ListBox* itself or in any of its parents.

```
<phone:PhoneApplicationPage
...
    xmlns:local="clr-namespace:CollectionBinding"
>
    <phone:PhoneApplicationPage.Resources>
        <local:Players x:Key="players"/>
    </phone:PhoneApplicationPage.Resources>

    <Grid
        x:Name="LayoutRoot" Background="Transparent"
        DataContext="{StaticResource players}">
    ...
        <StackPanel x:Name="ContentPanel" Grid.Row="1" Margin="12,0,12,0">
            <ListBox
                VerticalAlignment="Top" Margin="12,0,12,0"
                ItemsSource="{ Binding Items}">
                <ItemsControl.ItemTemplate>
                ...
                </ItemsControl.ItemTemplate>
            </ListBox>
        </StackPanel>
    </Grid>
</phone:PhoneApplicationPage>
```

Another benefit of SoC is that this promotes the separation of work between the design team and the development team. You can now easily set up dummy data for use by the designers. This dummy data is only used at design-time and does not form part of the final app. This gives the designers greater support in laying out the visual interface, based on realistic sample data. Here is how you do this.

First, declare the dummy data in a XAML file. In the example that follows, this is named *DesignTime Data.xaml*, but the name is arbitrary. This needs a namespace to reference the current assembly, which is where the *Players* and *Player* types are defined. In the XAML, define some *Player* items that will be in the *Items* collection in the *Players* object. The following is the entire contents of the file:

```
<local:Players
    xmlns="http://schemas.microsoft.com/winfx/2006/xaml/presentation"
    xmlns:x="http://schemas.microsoft.com/winfx/2006/xaml"
    xmlns:local="clr-namespace:CollectionBinding"
    >

    <local:Players.Items>
        <local:Player Name="Dummy Name 1" Score="22334" />
        <local:Player Name="Dummy Name 2" Score="22445" />
        <local:Player Name="Dummy Name 3" Score="22556" />
        <local:Player Name="Dummy Name 4" Score="22667" />
        <local:Player Name="Dummy Name 5" Score="22778" />
    </local:Players.Items>

</local:Players>
```

This is one of the development tasks that is much more easily done in Expression Blend than Visual Studio, and that is the primary environment in which design-time data will be used. In the Properties window for this file, set the build action to DesignData. Finally, in the *MainPage.xaml*, declare this as design-time data by using the design-time namespace *d* that has already been defined (as *http://schemas.microsoft.com/expression/blend/2008*):

```
d:DataContext="{d:DesignData DesignTimeData.xaml}"
```

You will see this data rendered in the Design view in Visual Studio (and in Expression Blend), as demonstrated in Figure 4-12. This is the *CollectionBinding_DTD* solution in the sample code. Be aware that this technique won't work if you also set the *DataContext* in XAML, because that will override the design-time setting.

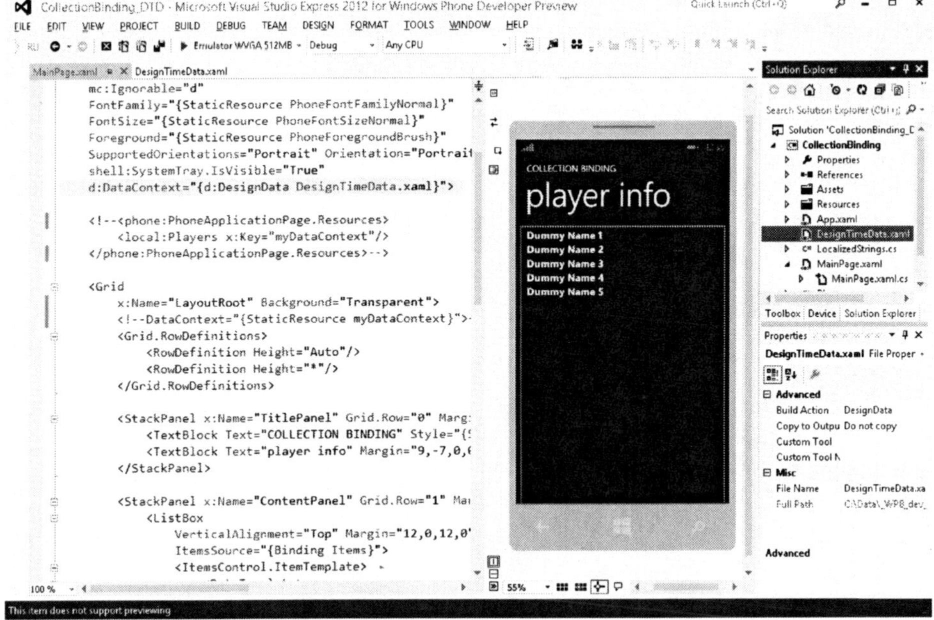

FIGURE 4-12 Viewing design-time data in Visual Studio.

The Model-View-ViewModel pattern

The Model-View-ViewModel (MVVM) pattern is extensively used in modern apps, including Windows Phone apps. This is an evolution of the Model-View Controller (MVC) pattern. One of the primary reasons to use it is to separate design from code. This supports the scenario in which app UI designers work in Expression Blend, whereas code developers work in Visual Studio—both working on the same app. It also makes testing a lot easier in that you can build automated testing independently for each logical layer (UI, Business Logic, Data Layer, and so on). The three parts of your app are decoupled, as described in the following:

- **View** This is the UI, represented by your XAML, and at a simple level by *mainpage.xaml*.
- **Model** These are the data objects, representing your connection to the underlying data source.
- **ViewModel** This part is the equivalent to the controller in MVC, which mediates between model and view. Typically, the view's *DataContext* is bound to an instance of the viewmodel. The viewmodel, in turn, typically instantiates the model (or the model graph).

Windows Phone also uses Dependency Injection (DI). With DI, when a component is dependent on another component, it doesn't hard-code this dependency; instead, it lists the services it requires. The supplier of services can be injected into the component from an external entity such as a factory or a dependency framework. In Windows Phone, DI is used to provide the glue between the view, the viewmodel, and the model so that the app does not need to hard-code the connections directly.

For example, you've seen several examples wherein you set the *DataContext* or *ItemsSource* of an element to some concrete object or collection. *DataContext* is of type *object*, and *ItemsSource* is of type *IEnumerable*. These afford extremely loose coupling—you can pretty much assign anything to a *DataContext*, and a very wide range of collection objects to an *IEnumerable*. You inject the specific concrete dependency that you want at some point, either at design-time or during unit testing with some mocked-up data, or at runtime in the final product with real data from the production source.

Figure 4-13 illustrates a high-level representation of the general case. The view, viewmodel, and model classes are all decoupled. Given the page-based UI model of Windows Phone apps, this is important to ensure that you can use the same viewmodel in multiple pages. For this reason, no view (page) is responsible for creating the viewmodel. Rather, the *App* creates the viewmodel and exposes it as a property, which is therefore accessible from any page.

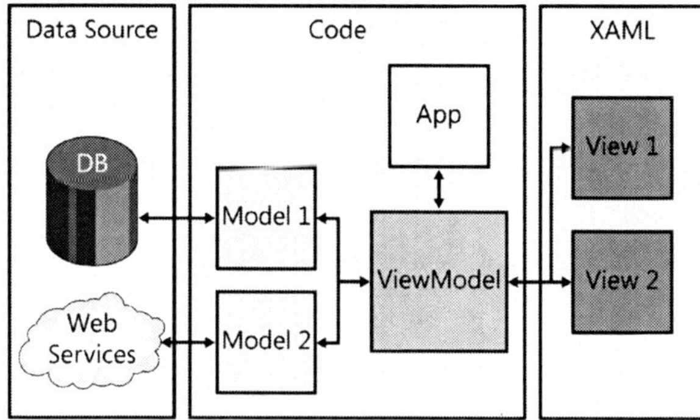

FIGURE 4-13 An overview of the MVVM layers.

The MVVM approach is encouraged in user code, and several of the Visual Studio project templates generate MVVM-based starter code.

The Visual Studio databound application project

The Databound Application template in Visual Studio generates a simple MVVM project (providing the view and viewmodel, but not the model). This is the *DataBoundApp* solution in the sample code (see Figure 4-14). Take a moment to examine the anatomy of this project type. The *MainPage* includes a *LongListSelector* whose items are made up of two *TextBlock* controls. The *DetailsPage* includes two independent *TextBlock* controls.

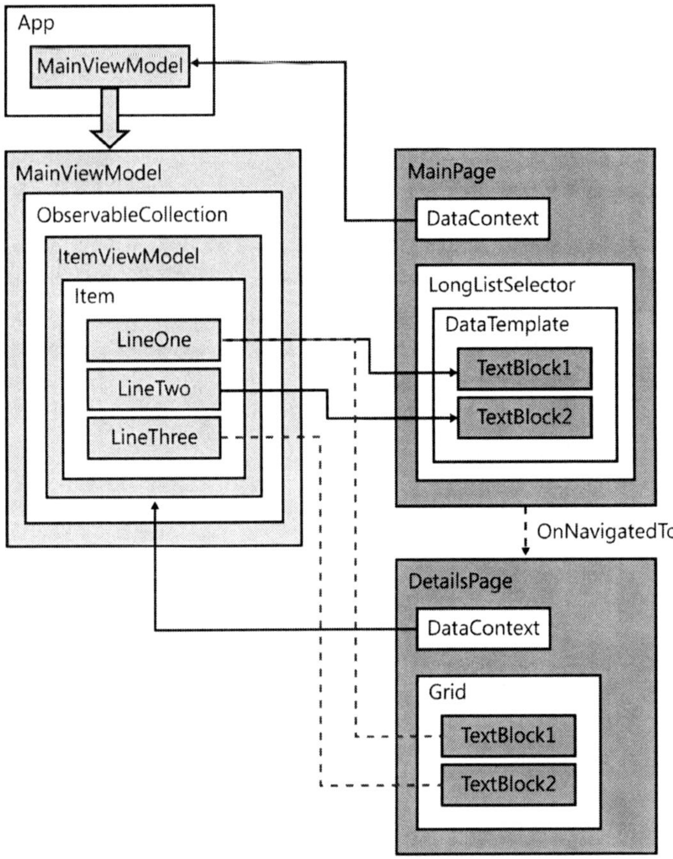

FIGURE 4-14 The Visual Studio Databound Application project template.

The *DataTemplate* for the *LongListSelector* contains two *TextBox* controls, which are bound to the *LineOne* and *LineTwo* properties in the *ItemViewModel*.

```
<phone:LongListSelector
    x:Name="MainLongListSelector"
    Margin="0,0,-12,0"
    ItemsSource="{Binding Items}"
    SelectionChanged="MainLongListSelector_SelectionChanged">
    <phone:LongListSelector.ItemTemplate>
        <DataTemplate>
            <StackPanel Margin="0,0,0,17">
                <TextBlock
                    Text="{Binding LineOne}" TextWrapping="Wrap"
                    Style="{StaticResource PhoneTextExtraLargeStyle}"/>
                <TextBlock
                    Text="{Binding LineTwo}" TextWrapping="Wrap" Margin="12,-6,12,0"
                    Style="{StaticResource PhoneTextSubtleStyle}"/>
            </StackPanel>
        </DataTemplate>
    </phone:LongListSelector.ItemTemplate>
</phone:LongListSelector>
```

The *ItemViewModel* class models the individual items of data. It also, of course, implements *INotifyPropertyChanged*. This class exposes the *LineOne* and *LineTwo* properties to which the *LongList Selector* items are bound.

```
public class ItemViewModel : INotifyPropertyChanged
{
    private string _lineOne;
    public string LineOne
    {
        get { return _lineOne; }
        set
        {
            if (value != _lineOne)
            {
                _lineOne = value;
                NotifyPropertyChanged("LineOne");
            }
        }
    }

    private string _lineTwo;
    public string LineTwo
    {
    ...
    }

    private string _lineThree;
    public string LineThree
    {
    ...
    }
...
}
```

The *MainViewModel* class contains an *ObservableCollection* of *ItemViewModel* items, and at run-time it creates an arbitrary set of items in its *LoadData* method (which you would typically replace with real data from your own model). Observe also that the *LoadData* method as supplied in the template unfortunately doesn't check to see if the data has already been loaded.

```
public class MainViewModel : INotifyPropertyChanged
{
    public ObservableCollection<ItemViewModel> Items { get; private set; }
    public MainViewModel()
    {
        this.Items = new ObservableCollection<ItemViewModel>();
    }

    public bool IsDataLoaded
    {
        get;
        private set;
    }
```

```
    public void LoadData()
    {
        this.Items.Add(new ItemViewModel() { ID = "0", LineOne = "runtime one", LineTwo =
"Maecenas praesent accumsan bibendum", LineThree = "Facilisi faucibus habitant inceptos interdum
lobortis nascetur pharetra placerat pulvinar sagittis senectus sociosqu" });
    ...//etc
        this.IsDataLoaded = true;
    }
...
}
```

The *App* class has a field that is an instance of the *MainViewModel* class. This is exposed as a property, and the property getter initializes the underlying field, if required.

```
public partial class App : Application
{
    private static MainViewModel viewModel = null;

    public static MainViewModel ViewModel
    {
        get
        {
            if (viewModel == null)
                viewModel = new MainViewModel();

            return viewModel;
        }
    }

    private void Application_Activated(object sender, ActivatedEventArgs e)
    {
        if (!App.ViewModel.IsDataLoaded)
        {
            App.ViewModel.LoadData();
        }
    }
...
}
```

At runtime, the *DataContext* of the *MainPage* is set to refer to the *MainViewModel* in the *App* class. When the page is loaded, it ensures that there is data, loading it if necessary. When the user selects an item from the *LongListSelector*, the app navigates to the *DetailsPage*, passing the selected item in the query string.

```
public partial class MainPage : PhoneApplicationPage
{
    public MainPage()
    {
        InitializeComponent();

        DataContext = App.ViewModel;
    }
```

```
    protected override void OnNavigatedTo(NavigationEventArgs e)
    {
        if (!App.ViewModel.IsDataLoaded)
        {
            App.ViewModel.LoadData();
        }
    }

    private void MainLongListSelector_SelectionChanged(
        object sender, SelectionChangedEventArgs e)
    {
        if (MainLongListSelector.SelectedItem == null)
            return;

        NavigationService.Navigate(new Uri(
            "/DetailsPage.xaml?selectedItem=" +
            (MainLongListSelector.SelectedItem as ItemViewModel).ID,
            UriKind.Relative));

        MainLongListSelector.SelectedItem = null;
    }
}
```

Down in the *DetailsPage* class, when the user navigates to the page, the code sets its *DataContext* to the item in the *MainViewModel.Items* collection that is specified in the query string.

```
protected override void OnNavigatedTo(NavigationEventArgs e)
{
    if (DataContext == null)
    {
        string selectedIndex = "";
        if (NavigationContext.QueryString.TryGetValue(
            "selectedItem", out selectedIndex))
        {
            int index = int.Parse(selectedIndex);
            DataContext = App.ViewModel.Items[index];
        }
    }
}
```

Recall that at design time, in the XAML, the page's *DataContext* is set to a design-time data file (*MainViewModelSampleData.xaml*).

```
d:DataContext="{d:DesignData SampleData/MainViewModelSampleData.xaml}"
```

Figure 4-15 shows the *MainPage* and *DetailsPage* of the standard Databound Application.

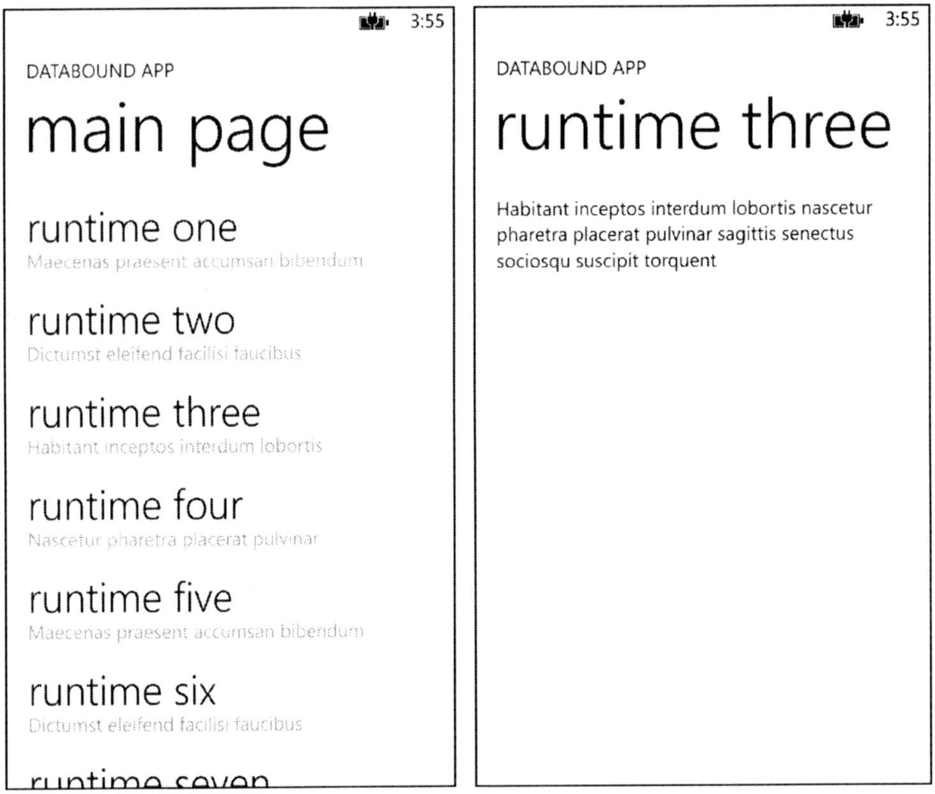

FIGURE 4-15 The Databound Application *MainPage* (on the left) and *DetailsPage* (right).

MVVM in Pivot apps

The standard Visual Studio template–generated *Pivot* and *Panorama* projects use the same MVVM approach. The *Pivot* project is especially interesting because it illustrates a useful pattern for filtering data; all pivot items are bound to the same data source, but each one has a different "column filter" applied, as represented in Figure 4-16. You can see this at work in the *PivotApp* solution in the sample code (this is an out-of-the-box Visual Studio Pivot Application project).

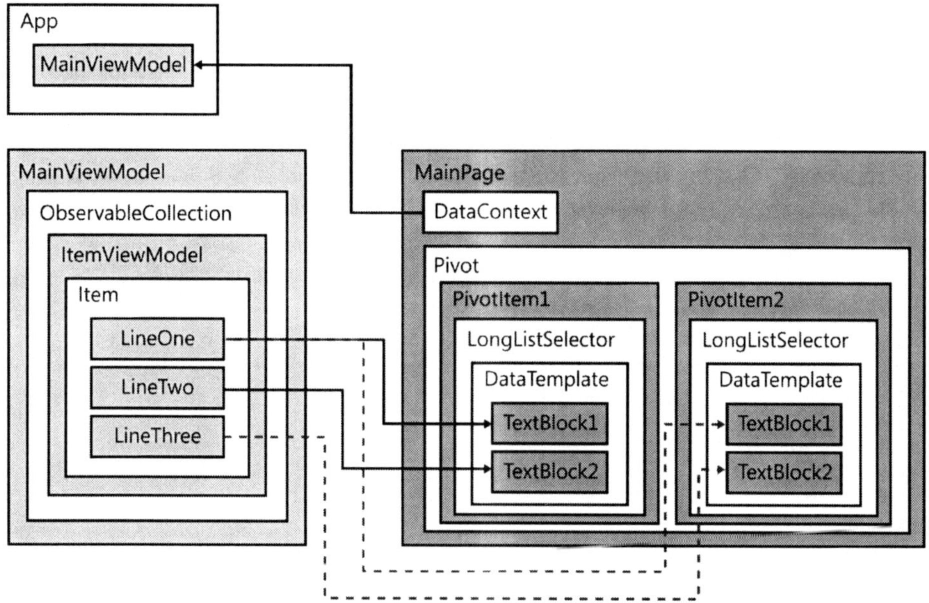

FIGURE 4-16 The Visual Studio Pivot Application.

The *column filtering* is done in the XAML. The first *PivotItem* has a *LongListSelector* whose two *TextBlock* controls are bound to *LineOne* and *LineTwo* in the viewmodel. The second *PivotItem* has a *LongListSelector* whose two *TextBlock* controls are bound to *LineOne* and *LineThree*.

```
<phone:Pivot Title="MY APPLICATION">
    <phone:PivotItem Header="first">
        <phone:LongListSelector ItemsSource="{Binding Items}">
            <phone:LongListSelector.ItemTemplate>
                <DataTemplate>
                    <StackPanel>
                        <TextBlock Text="{Binding LineOne}" />
                        <TextBlock Text="{Binding LineTwo}" />
                    </StackPanel>
                </DataTemplate>
            </phone:LongListSelector.ItemTemplate>
        </phone:LongListSelector>
    </phone:PivotItem>

    <phone:PivotItem Header="second">
        <phone:LongListSelector ItemsSource="{Binding Items}">
            <phone:LongListSelector.ItemTemplate>
                    <DataTemplate>
                        <StackPanel>
                            <TextBlock Text="{Binding LineOne}"/>
                            <TextBlock Text="{Binding LineThree}"/>
                        </StackPanel>
                    </DataTemplate>
            </phone:LongListSelector.ItemTemplate>
        </phone:LongListSelector>
    </phone:PivotItem>
</phone:Pivot>
```

Row filtering in Pivot apps

You could obviously take this further and represent the UI of each pivot item differently, according to the nature of the data that is bound to the elements in that item. You could also pivot on the data via *row filtering*. For example, suppose the *ItemViewModel* class also provided an integer *ID* property. Then, you could easily filter the *PivotItem* contents based on the value of this *ID*. Instead of simply allowing the two *LongListSelector* controls to pick up the complete data set from the viewmodel, you could explicitly set each *itemsSource* to some filtered subset of the data, as demonstrated in the *Pivot Filter* app in the sample code (see Figure 4-17). In this app, the first *PivotItem* lists only odd-numbered items; the second lists only even-numbered items.

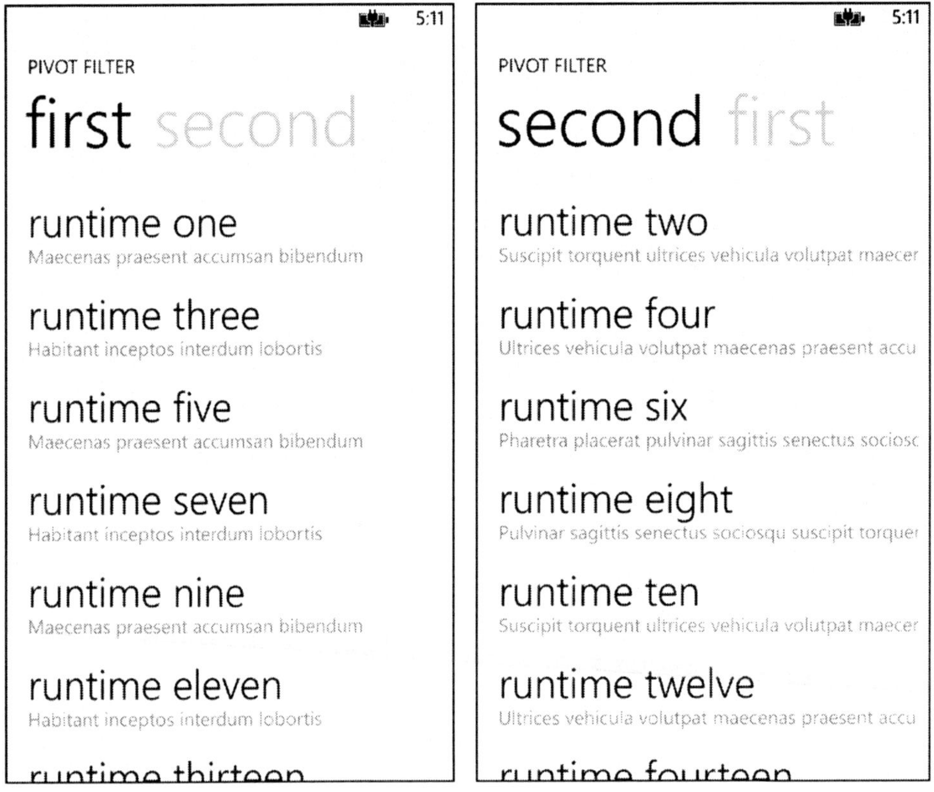

FIGURE 4-17 The row-filtered *Pivot* app.

In this app, you can use the *MainPage* class to build a collection view on top of the binding source collection that you're using in the view—that is, a layer between the view and the viewmodel. This makes it possible for you to navigate and display the collection, based on sort, filter, and grouping queries, all without the need to manipulate the underlying source collection itself.

```
private CollectionViewSource odds;
private CollectionViewSource evens;
```

```
protected override void OnNavigatedTo(NavigationEventArgs e)
{
    if (!App.ViewModel.IsDataLoaded)
    {
        App.ViewModel.LoadData();
    }

    odds = new CollectionViewSource();
    odds.Source = App.ViewModel.Items;
    odds.Filter += (s, ev) =>
    {
        ItemViewModel ivm = ev.Item as ItemViewModel;
        ev.Accepted = ivm.ID % 2 != 0;
    };

    List<object> list = new List<object>();
    foreach (var v in odds.View)
    {
        list.Add(v);
    }
    firstList.ItemsSource = list;

    evens = new CollectionViewSource();
    evens.Source = App.ViewModel.Items;
    evens.Filter += (s, ev) =>
    {
        ItemViewModel ivm = ev.Item as ItemViewModel;
        ev.Accepted = ivm.ID % 2 == 0;
    };
    list = new List<object>();
    foreach (var v in evens.View)
    {
        list.Add(v);
    }
    secondList.ItemsSource = list;
}
```

Note The mismatch between the *CollectionViewSource.View* (which is an *IEnumerable*) and the *LongListSelector.ItemsSource* (which is an *IList*) requires converting one to the other. There is no standard conversion method, so the approach taken here is to iterate the collection and construct a new *List* from the items. This would not be required if the app used a *ListBox* instead of a *LongListSelector*, because the *ListBox* implementation of *ItemsSource* is an *IEnumerable*. Of course, there are other advantages to the *LongListSelector*, which makes it the control of choice for the Visual Studio templates. The *LongListSelector* is actually an advanced *ListBox* that supports full data and UI virtualization (with the attendant performance benefits), flat lists, and grouped lists. Under the hood, the reason why the *LongListSelector* uses *IList* rather than *IEnumerable* is that to support virtualization, it needs to know how many elements there are, and there is no *Count* property on *IEnumerable*. It also needs to access the items randomly, not just in the forward-only, one-at-a-time way that enumerators do.

Improving the Visual Studio Databound Application template

If you look closely, you might notice that the Visual Studio Databound Application template is slightly suboptimal. The code to test for loaded data in the viewmodel is duplicated—it's in the *Application_Activated* handler and also in the *MainPage.OnNavigatedTo* override. Not only that, but the code is also identical, using the *App* object reference in both places, even within the *App*'s *Application_Activated* handler, where the *App* reference is clearly superfluous.

```
if (!App.ViewModel.IsDataLoaded)
{
    App.ViewModel.LoadData();
}
```

The duplication is to accommodate the fact that the entry point to the app varies, depending on circumstances. This arises from navigation and app lifecycle behavior—issues that are discussed thoroughly in Chapter 2, "App model and navigation." The lifecycle aspect that is relevant here is that the app might start on the *MainPage*, or it might start on the *DetailsPage*. In normal circumstances, the user starts the app, and the *Application_Launching* event is raised, but not the *Application_Activated* event. Shortly after that, the *MainPage.OnNavigatedTo* method is invoked. It's for this code path that you need the loading code in either the *Application_Launching* handler or the *MainPage.OnNavigatedTo* method.

The second scenario is when the user runs the app, navigates to the *DetailsPage*, and then navigates forward out of the app to another app. When he comes back to the first app, the *Application_Activated* event is raised, and the system navigates to the *DetailsPage*. The key point is that in this scenario, the *DetailsPage* is often created before the *MainPage*. This is why you need the data loading code in either the *Application_Activated* handler or in a *NavigatedTo* handler for the *DetailsPage*.

One improvement would be to remove the *MainPage.OnNavigatedTo* method (which is otherwise unused in the default code) and centralize the code to the *App* class, in the *Application_Launching* and *Application_Activated* handlers. This would at least put it all in one class, and it would afford you the ability to remove the superfluous *App* object reference. An even more elegant solution would be to remove the duplication altogether. You could achieve this by simply putting the loading code in the viewmodel property getter. This would guarantee that anytime the viewmodel is accessed, it will always have loaded data, regardless of the app's launch context and regardless of how many pages need to access the data. The slight disadvantage is the very small performance cost of doing the *IsDataLoaded* test on each access. A more significant disadvantage is that when you move to an asynchronous loading mechanism, such as from the web or from disk, this is harder to accommodate. You can see these changes in the *DataBoundApp_modified* solution in the sample code.

```
public static MainViewModel ViewModel
{
    get
    {
        if (viewModel == null)
        {
            viewModel = new MainViewModel();
        }
        // Code ported from MainPage_Loaded and Application_Activated.
```

```
        if (!viewModel.IsDataLoaded)
        {
            viewModel.LoadData();
        }
        return viewModel;
    }
}
```

Alternatively, if you decide that you always want to load the data on first initialization of the viewmodel object, you could perform both operations at the same time. Keep in mind that one reason for factoring out the viewmodel to a singleton in the *App* class is to allow access from multiple UI elements. For this reason, it is safer to protect the instantiation with a lock, as shown in the following:

```
public static MainViewModel ViewModel
{
    get
    {
        lock (typeof(App))
        {
            if (viewModel == null)
            {
                viewModel = new MainViewModel();
                viewModel.LoadData();
            }
        }
        return viewModel;
    }
}
```

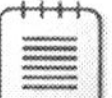

Note If your data arrives in an asynchronous manner (for example, from the web), you would probably want to raise an event when you've received new data and have the data consumers (viewmodels) subscribe to this event. You'd then have to implement a way to trigger loading, based perhaps on the first access to that event.

Although the MVVM pattern offers a number of benefits and is suitable for most apps that render data in the UI, it is not without its drawbacks. Whereas a reusable framework such as MVVM—or indeed data-binding itself—tends to make development more RAD-like in the long run, this comes at the cost of runtime complexity and performance costs. Under the hood, the Windows Phone platform is doing work to handle *NotifyPropertyChanged* and *NotifyCollectionChanged* events and then route them appropriately, including doing reflection to get the required data values (which is always a costly operation). It is also maintaining internal caches related to the data-bound objects.

You should carefully consider the size and performance costs of any technique—the threshholds at which these might become critical are generally much lower on a mobile device than in a desktop app. That said, from an engineering perspective, after you (or your organization) has gone to the effort of setting up the MVVM framework, development effort after that point for interoperating between data and UI is measurably reduced. Furthermore, the benefits increase as the complexity of the app increases.

Summary

This chapter examined the data-binding support in the Windows Phone app platform, the benefits it brings, and the various approaches you can take to customize the behavior by taking part in the data-binding pipeline. Data binding works very well in combination with the MVVM pattern. This pattern helps to ensure clean separation of concerns, such that the discrete functional parts of the app—the data, the view, and the viewmodel—can be loosely coupled, and therefore, independently engineered and independently versioned.

CHAPTER 5

Phone and media services

For app developers, a key feature of a smartphone—beyond the ability to make and receive cellular calls, of course—is the degree to which you can integrate your app with the built-in phone and media services. Windows Phone provides a set of Launchers and Choosers, which is the way that the app platform repurposes built-in apps, such as the browser, search, calendar, email, and so on. You can take advantage of these features within your own apps.

The platform also provides extensive support for media services, including audio and video playback. You can choose from several different sets of media-related application programming interfaces (APIs), depending on the specific requirements of your app. If you have a simple requirement for media playback, you can use the *MediaPlayerLauncher.* If you need more flexibility, the *MediaElement* type might suit your needs better. If you need more fine-grained control over the media file content, you can use the *MediaStreamSource* API, and so on. In this chapter, we examine the various levels of app support and your choices for integrating with—and extending—standard system features, including built-in phone apps, audio and video services, and search. This is an area where relatively little has changed between Windows Phone 7 and Windows Phone 8, so most of the programming techniques described in this chapter work on both versions of the platform.

Launchers and Choosers

Both Launchers and Choosers are API mechanisms for invoking existing apps and services on the phone. In the API, they're all called "tasks." The difference between Launchers and Choosers is that Launchers start a feature but don't return a value, whereas Choosers launch a feature and *do* return a value. Table 5-1 summarizes these tasks. The phone has a range of very useful built-in apps, exposed for programmatic integration via a very simple set of APIs.

Invoking a Launcher or Chooser causes your app (the invoking app) to be deactivated. Some Choosers run in your app session, so if you press and hold the back key, you don't see your app as a separate instance that you can activate; rather, you see the Chooser screenshot listed for your app. As you would expect, the inter-app navigation behavior is consistent with all other inter-app navigations. Users can return to the original app upon completing the task inside the Launcher/Chooser, or they can use the Back key. If the Launcher/Chooser has multiple pages, the Back key will navigate the user through the previous pages and, finally, back to the calling app. In the same manner, if the user navigates forward through multiple apps, this can result in the original calling app falling off the backstack, as normal. Also, the Chooser is auto-dismissed if the user forward navigates away from it. Table 5-1 lists the full set of available Launchers and Choosers.

TABLE 5-1 Launchers and Choosers

Type	Task	Description	New in 8
Launchers	*BingMapsDirectionsTask*	Launches the Maps app, specifying a starting and/or ending location, for which driving or walking directions are displayed (identical to the *MapsDirectionsTask*).	
	BingMapsTask	Launches the Maps app centered at the specified or current location (identical to the *MapsTask*).	
	ConnectionSettingsTask	Launches a settings dialog with which the user can change the device's connection settings.	
	EmailComposeTask	Composes a new email.	
	MapDownloaderTask	Provides a mechanism for the user to download maps for offline use.	Y
	MapUpdaterTask	Provides a mechanism for the user to update map data he has previously downloaded for offline use.	Y
	MapsDirectionsTask	Launches the Maps app, specifying a starting and/or ending location, for which driving or walking directions are displayed (identical to *BingMapsDirectionsTask*).	Y
	MapsTask	Launches the Maps app centered at the specified or current location (identical to *BingMapsTask*).	Y
	MarketplaceDetailTask	Launches the Windows Phone Store and displays the details for a specific app.	
	MarketplaceHubTask	Launches the Windows Phone Store and searches for a particular type of content.	
	MarketplaceReviewTask	Displays the Windows Phone Store review page for the current app.	
	MarketplaceSearchTask	Launches the Windows Phone Store and displays the search results from the specified search terms.	
	MediaPlayerLauncher	Launches Media Player, and plays the specified media file.	
	PhoneCallTask	Initiates a phone call to a specified number.	
	SaveAppointmentTask	Provides a mechanism for the user to save an appointment from your app.	Y
	SearchTask	Launches Microsoft Bing Search with a specified search term.	
	ShareLinkTask	Launches a dialog with which the user can share a link on the social networks of her choice. If the user does not have any social networks set up, the Launcher silently fails.	
	ShareMediaTask	Provides a mechanism for your app to share a media item with one of the media-sharing apps on the phone.	Y
	ShareStatusTask	Launches a dialog with which the user can share a status message on the social networks of her choice. If the user does not have any social networks set up, the Launcher silently fails.	
	SmsComposeTask	Composes a new text message.	
	WebBrowserTask	Launches Microsoft Internet Explorer and browses to a specific URI.	

Type	Task	Description	New in 8
Choosers	*AddWalletItemTask*	Launches the Wallet app and allows the user to add the supplied item to his wallet.	Y
	AddressChooserTask	Launches the Contacts app with which the user can find an address.	
	CameraCaptureTask	Opens the Camera app to take a photo.	
	EmailAddressChooserTask	Provides a mechanism for the user to select an email address from his Contacts List.	
	GameInviteTask	Shows the game invite screen with which the user can invite players to a multiplayer game session.	
	PhoneNumberChooserTask	Provides a mechanism for the user to select a phone number from his Contacts List.	
	PhotoChooserTask	Provides a mechanism for the user to select an image from his Picture Gallery or take a photo.	
	SaveContactTask	Launches the Contacts app with which the user can save a contact.	
	SaveEmailAddressTask	Saves an email address to an existing or new contact.	
	SavePhoneNumberTask	Saves a phone number to an existing or new contact.	
	SaveRingtoneTask	Launches the Ringtones app with which the user can save a ringtone from your app to the system ringtones list.	

Of the new tasks introduced in Windows Phone 8, maps are discussed in Chapter 18, "Location and maps," appointments are discussed in Chapter 15, "Contacts and calendar," and wallet is discussed in Chapter 20, "The Wallet." However, the general pattern for invoking Launchers and Choosers is consistent across all tasks. The *LaunchersAndChoosers* solution in the sample code demonstrates this pattern. Buttons are available to invoke a *PhoneCallTask*, *WebBrowserTask*, *SearchTask*, and *EmailAddress ChooserTask*, as shown in Figure 5-1.

In general, the app code for invoking Launchers and Choosers is very simple. The app platform provides easy-to-use wrappers for all of the app-accessible system tasks on the device. The basic steps for using a Launcher are as follows:

1. Create an instance of the type that represents the specific Launcher feature that you want to use.
2. Set properties on the object as appropriate.
3. Invoke the *Show* method.

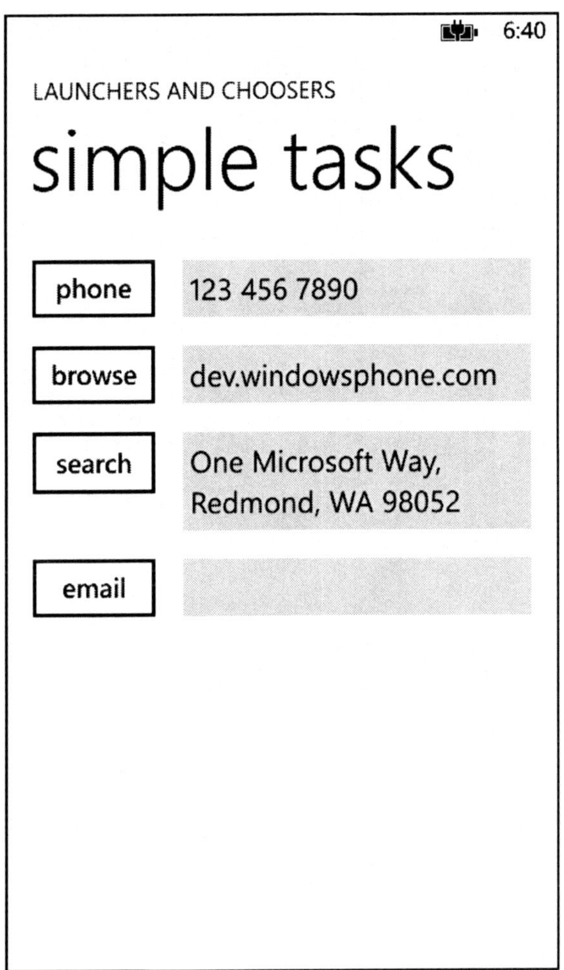

FIGURE 5-1 Many standard tasks are exposed programmatically as Launchers and Choosers.

In this example, when the user taps the Phone button, the app instantiates a *PhoneCallTask* object and calls *Show*, which prompts the user to confirm the outgoing call. This feature is protected by the *ID_CAP_PHONEDIALER* capability, so you need to update your app manifest to include this; otherwise, the attempt to invoke *PhoneCallTask.Show* will throw a security exception.

```
PhoneCallTask phone = new PhoneCallTask();
phone.PhoneNumber = phoneNumber.Text;
phone.Show();
```

The Search button invokes *SearchTask.Show*; it is equally simple to use, following the exact same pattern.

```
SearchTask search = new SearchTask();
search.SearchQuery = searchText.Text;
search.Show();
```

The first time the user selects the search feature, he gets a prompt from the system, as shown in Figure 5-2 (left). This is because the search feature can make use of the user's location, and the user must be given the option to allow access to this information. If and when the user proceeds with the search, the task displays a scrolling list that contains the Bing search results for the specified term, as illustrated in Figure 5-2 (right).

Note This happens only once on a real device, but it will happen on the emulator every time you restart it.

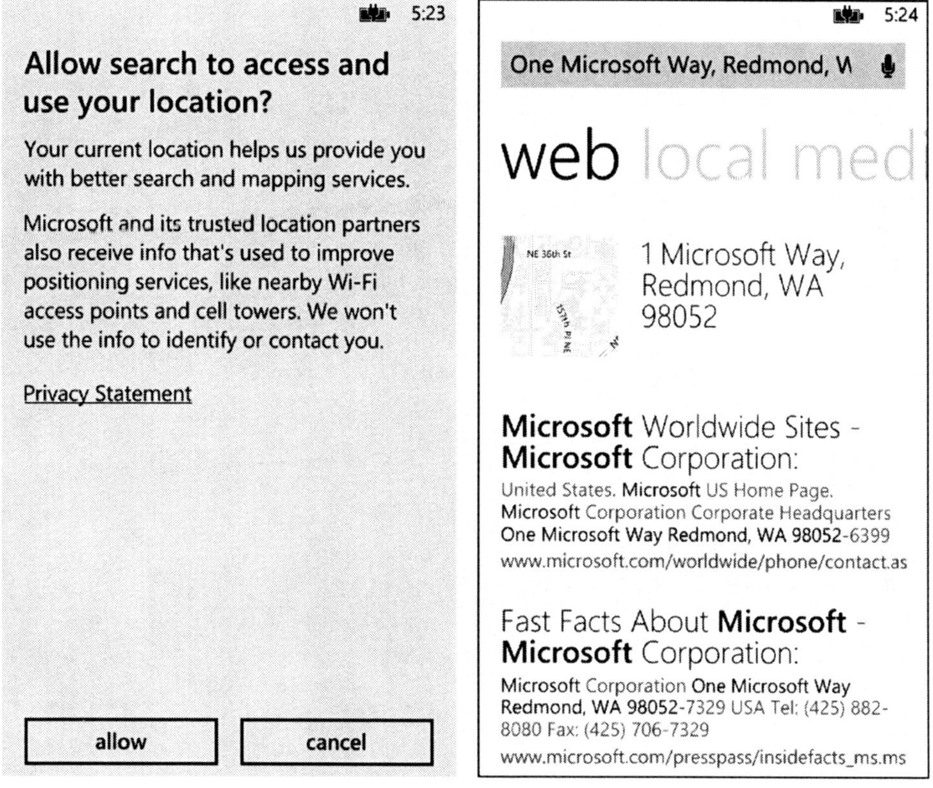

FIGURE 5-2 Invoking a search task for the first time triggers a permission request to the user.

Using the *WebBrowserTask* follows the same pattern. Windows Phone 7 developers might be accustomed to using the *URL* string property of this task, but this is now obsolete, and you should instead use the *Uri* property (of type *Uri*, and named *Uri*).

```
WebBrowserTask browser = new WebBrowserTask();
browser.Uri = new Uri("http://" +browseText.Text);
browser.Show();
```

Using the *EmailAddressChooserTask* is only marginally more involved. So far, we've shown how to use Launchers, but the *EmailAddressChooserTask* is a Chooser, which means it returns a value to the calling app. The basic steps for using a Chooser are as follows:

1. Create an instance of the type that represents the specific Chooser feature that you want to use. It is common to declare this as a field in your page class.
2. Hook up the *Completed* event on the object (or provide an inline delegate or lambda), which will be invoked when the Chooser task completes.
3. Set properties on the object as appropriate.
4. Invoke the *Show* method.
5. In your *Completed* event handler or delegate, process the return value from the Chooser.

The code snippet that follows illustrates this pattern. In this example, the email address that the user has selected from the contacts list offered by the Chooser is then pasted into the corresponding *TextBox* back in the sample app. It is important to note that you must declare the Chooser object as a class field in the page where it is used. You must also call the Chooser constructor to set up the field—and also hook up the Completed event—within the page constructor. The reason for this is to ensure that your app will be called back correctly after it has been deactivated and then reactivated for situations in which it was tombstoned and then rehydrated on return from the Chooser.

```
private EmailAddressChooserTask emailAddress = new EmailAddressChooserTask();

public MainPage()
{
    InitializeComponent();
    emailAddress.Completed += emailAddress_Completed;
}

private void emailButton_Click(object sender, RoutedEventArgs e)
{
    emailAddress.Show();
}

private void emailAddress_Completed(object sender, EmailResult e)
{
    if (e.TaskResult == TaskResult.OK)
    {
        emailText.Text = e.Email;
    }
}
```

Search extensibility

Another way that your app can communicate with standard phone services is by extending the Bing search experience with custom behavior, integrating your app seamlessly with the search results. There are two ways by which you can extend the Bing search behavior in your apps: App Connect and App Instant Answer. With both features, you can set up your app so that it shows up in the Bing search results when the user taps the hardware Search button. Table 5-2 summarizes the differences.

TABLE 5-2 Bing search extensibility

Requirement	App Connect	App Instant Answer
WMAppManifest.xml	Requires Extensions entries for each Bing category that you want to extend.	No specific changes required.
Extras.xml	Required. Specifies captions to be used in the search results apps pivot item.	Not used.
UriMapper	Recommended. Allows you to re-route to a specific page on app startup.	Not required.
Target page	You can re-route to multiple different pages, depending on the search item, if you want.	No option. Your app is launched as normal, with its default startup page.
Query string	You should parse the incoming query string for categories and item names for which you want to provide extensions.	You should parse the incoming query string for the *bing_query* value.
Search connection	Bing includes your app in the search results when the user's search matches the categories for which you registered extensions.	Bing includes your app in the search results, based on whether it thinks the query is relevant to your app.

In both cases, your app is launched with a particular query string, and you are responsible for parsing that query string to get the search context. It is then up to your app to decide what behavior to execute, based on this search context. Both approaches are discussed in more detail in the following sections.

App Connect

The App Connect approach is the more complex of the two extensibility models. You register your app in a way that gives you more fine-grained control over the criteria that Bing will use to identify it as a suitable extension. You should only register your app for the search categories—or search "extensions"—for which you believe your app has relevance.

Note It is important to choose the extensions carefully and to avoid spamming the system by registering for unrelated extensions. Apps that register excessive unrelated extensions will be removed from the Windows Phone Store.

If and when the user chooses to start your app from the search results list, your app is given a richer query string with which you can fine-tune its subsequent behavior. The overall model for App Connect is illustrated in Figure 5-3. In summary, the user initiates a Bing search and then taps one of the items in the search results. This navigates to a system-provided Quick Card, which is a pivot page that offers an "about" pivot that provides basic information, a "reviews" pivot, and an "apps" pivot. Your app can be listed in the apps pivot.

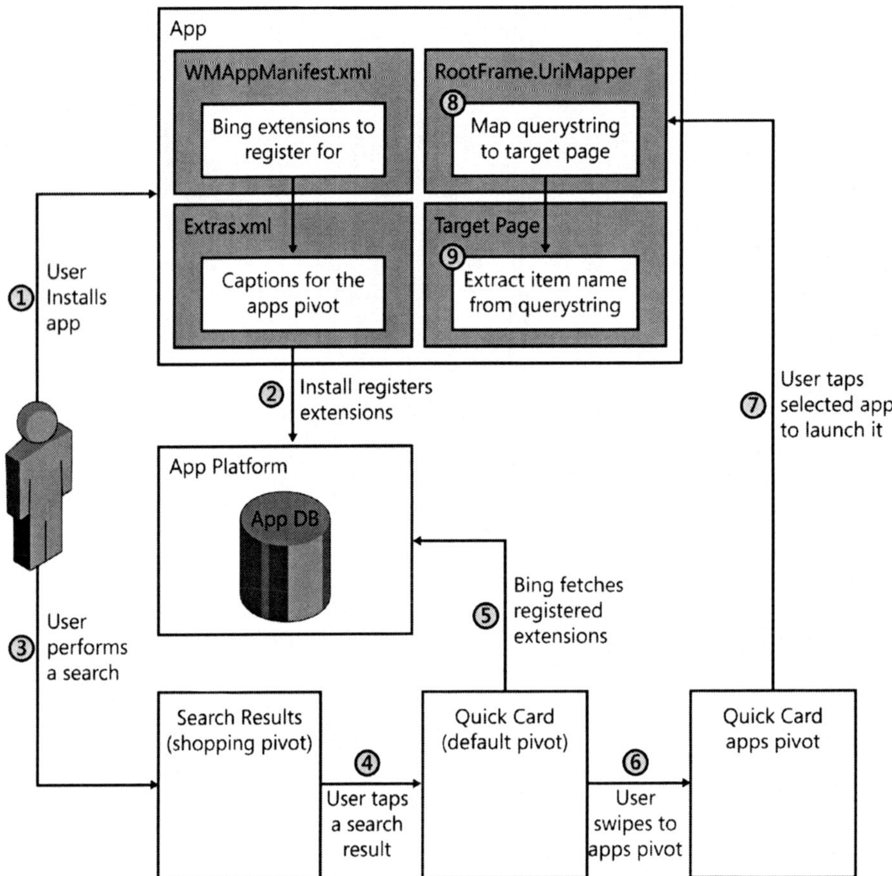

FIGURE 5-3 The App Connect extensibility model.

The following steps walk through how to create an App Connect search extension. A completed example is in the *SimplestAppConnect* solution in the sample code. Figure 5-4 (left) shows the search results page for a search on the string "coffee." Figure 5-4 (center) shows the Quick Card for one of the selected items from the search results, and Figure 5-4 (right) shows the apps pivot for that Quick Card, in which the sample app's title string and caption strings are displayed alongside the app's icon.

First, create a new Windows Phone app project. Add a second page to the project, named *MyTargetPage*. This will be the target page to which to navigate when the app is launched via App Connect. In the XAML for this page, add a simple *TextBlock*; the app will eventually set the text for this dynamically using the item information in the Bing search results.

```
<TextBlock x:Name="Target" TextWrapping="Wrap" Margin="{StaticResource PhoneHorizontalMargin}"/>
```

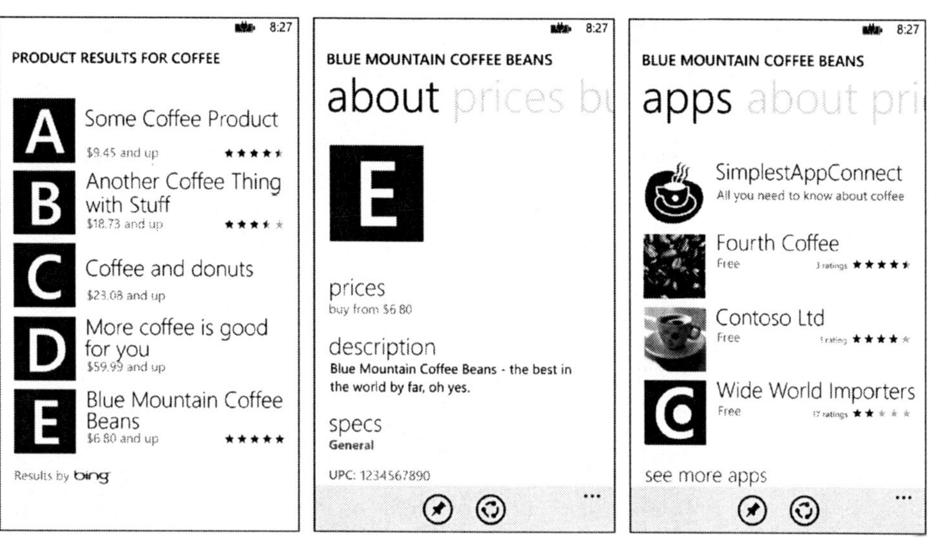

FIGURE 5-4 Search results, Quick Card, and apps list for a search on the term "coffee."

Then, add an *Extensions* section to your *WMAppManifest.xml*, within the *App* element, after the *Tokens* section. The *Extension* entry must specify one of the defined extension identifiers, as listed in the Search Registration and Launch Reference for Windows Phone, which you can find at *http://msdn.microsoft.com/en-us/library/hh202958(VS.92).aspx*. In this example, the app registers for just one extension: *Bing_Products_Gourmet_Food_and_Chocolate*. The *ConsumerID* is always the same: *{5B04B775-356B-4AA0-AAF8-6491FFEA5661}*. This specifies that the app is an extension to Bing search. The *TaskID* is always *"_default"*, and the *ExtraFile* must be a relative path to the *Extras.xml* file in your project.

```
<Extensions>
  <Extension
    ExtensionName="Bing_Products_Gourmet_Food_and_Chocolate"
    ConsumerID="{5B04B775-356B-4AA0-AAF8-6491FFEA5661}"
    TaskID="_default"
    ExtraFile="Extensions\\Extras.xml" />
</Extensions>
```

Now that you've referred to the *Extras.xml* file, you should actually create it. To do so, make a new folder in your project named *Extensions*, add a new XML file to this folder, and then name it **Extras.xml**. You should set the Build Action for this to *Content*—in Microsoft Visual Studio 2012, this will be set by default. The *Extras.xml* must be in the *Extensions* folder, but the path you specify in the *ExtraFile* attribute can omit the *Extensions* root path and just specify "Extras.xml." Either will work, so long as the file itself is in the right place. This file is where you specify the strings to be used in the Bing search results list for your app.

```xml
<?xml version="1.0" encoding="utf-8" ?>
<ExtrasInfo>
  <AppTitle>
    <default>My Search Extension</default>
  </AppTitle>
  <Consumer ConsumerID="{5B04B775-356B-4AA0-AAF8-6491FFEA5661}">
    <ExtensionInfo>
      <Extensions>
        <ExtensionName>Bing_Products_Gourmet_Food_and_Chocolate</ExtensionName>
      </Extensions>
      <CaptionString>
        <default>All you need to know about coffee</default>
      </CaptionString>
    </ExtensionInfo>
  </Consumer>
</ExtrasInfo>
```

In *Extras.xml*, you can supply an *AppTitle* with at least one string for the default language. In Windows Phone 7.1, the *AppTitle* element is used to specify the title of the app as you would like it to appear in the apps pivot page of the Quick Card; it is therefore a required field. In Windows Phone 8, however, the system uses the app title from the phone's installed Apps list, instead; so, on this platform, the *AppTitle* is not required. In the *Consumer* section, the *ConsumerID* is again the same Bing search ID. Under this, you list all the *Extensions* that you want to register for Bing search. Again, you must provide at least one default *CaptionString*. The app's icon (the 62x62-pixel image) for an extension app should not use transparency—and, as always, you should test this to ensure that it displays correctly in both light and dark themes.

The next item you need is a custom URI mapper. You need this in order to map the navigation query string that Bing search passes to your app to the correct target page within your app. For this piece, add a new class file to your project and then change the code to derive your class from *UriMapperBase*. For example, map this incoming URI

```
/SearchExtras?ProductName=coffee&Category=Bing_Products_Gourmet_Food_and_Chocolate
```

to this target page, including the original query string parameters:

```
/MyTargetPage.xaml?ProductName=coffee&Category=Bing_Products_Gourmet_Food_and_Chocolate
```

In addition to determining the correct target page, you're free to do whatever other processing you want, including modifying the parameter list according to your requirements before passing it on, if you need to. When the app has been launched via Bing search App Connect, the URI will include the *"/SearchExtras"* substring. So, if you examine the URI and find that it does not include this substring, you should immediately return because this means that the app has been launched normally, not via Bing search.

```csharp
public class MyUriMapper : UriMapperBase
{
    public override Uri MapUri(Uri uri)
    {
        String inputUri = uri.ToString();
```

```
        if (inputUri.Contains("/SearchExtras"))
        {
            if (inputUri.Contains("Bing_Products_Gourmet_Food_and_Chocolate"))
            {
                String outputUri = inputUri.Replace(
                    "/SearchExtras", "/MyTargetPage.xaml");
                return new Uri(outputUri, UriKind.Relative);
            }
        }
        return uri;
    }
}
```

A custom URI mapper must override the one and only virtual method, named *MapUri*. This takes in the search URI, as supplied by Bing. In your implementation, you typically parse the URI, and look first for the *"/SearchExtras"* substring. If this is found, you can then go on to look for the Products category. In this example, the only category of interest is "Bing_Products_Gourmet_Food_and_Chocolate." This app provides only one target page for all search requests. In a sophisticated app, you might have multiple pages; if this is the case, you would need to implement a more complex decision tree to determine which page to return from the URI mapper. You would also typically search for more than one category and one product.

To use the URI mapper in your app, you create an object of this type and then set it as the value of the *UriMapper* property in the *RootFrame*. The best place to do this is at the end of the *Initialize PhoneApplication* method in the *App* class.

```
RootFrame.UriMapper = new MyUriMapper();
```

This causes the system to load the specified target page and pass in all incoming URIs to your *UriMapper* so that they can be manipulated before navigation takes place. These incoming URIs include the query string as part of the *NavigationContext* that comes in to the page in the form of a dictionary of key-value pairs.

In the target page, you should override the *OnNavigatedTo* method so that you can examine the incoming query string. Look for an incoming *ProductName*. Having found the corresponding value for the key-value pair—in this case, "coffee"—you can then make a decision as to whether you know anything about this specific product. If so, you can then go on to do whatever domain logic you want based on this value. In this example, the app simply indicates that this is a known product by setting the *TextBlock.Text* value. The value of this string will be the full product name of the product that the user selected. Using the example in Figure 5-4, this would be "Blue Mountain Coffee Beans."

```
protected override void OnNavigatedTo(NavigationEventArgs e)
{
    String product;
    if (NavigationContext.QueryString.TryGetValue("ProductName", out product))
    {
        if (product.ToLowerInvariant().Contains("coffee"))
        {
            Target.Text = String.Format("We know about {0}.", product);
        }
```

```
        else
        {
            Target.Text = String.Format("We don't know about {0}.", product);
        }
    }
}
```

With the code complete, you can test this either in the emulator or on a physical device. Tap the Bing search button and then enter **coffee**. In the primary search results, swipe over to the *shopping* pivot item, if it's not already selected, and then scroll down to find the products list. If necessary, tap the See More Products link to get to a coffee product that contains the string "coffee." Tap any such item; this takes you to the Quick Card for that item. In the Quick Card, swipe over to the apps pivot item. Your app should be listed there. When you tap the app to launch it, the URI mapper is invoked, and the app navigates to the target page and updates the text with the Bing search information, as shown in Figure 5-5.

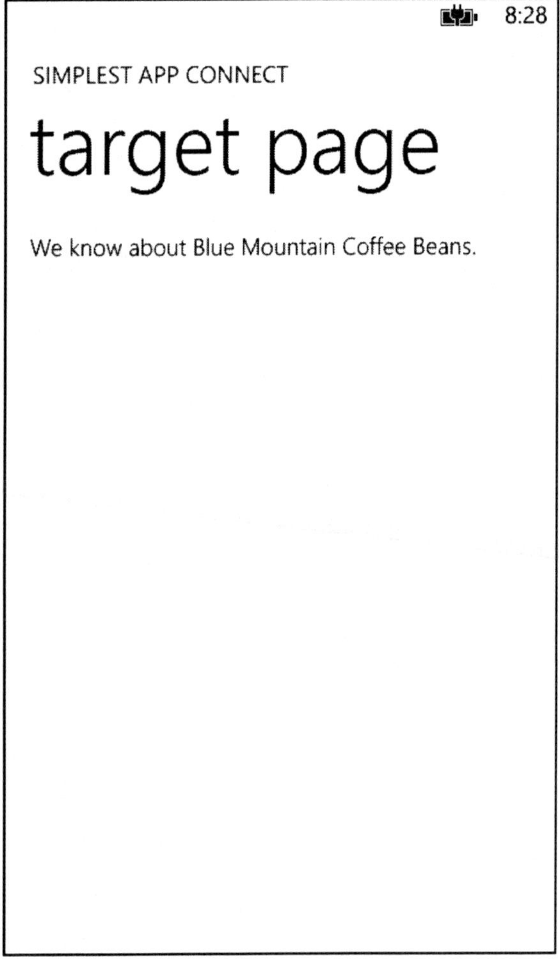

FIGURE 5-5 When the user taps your app in the apps pivot of the Quick Card, it navigates to your target page.

To test the functionality of the app in a more deterministic way, you can provide a fake launch query string in the *WMAppManifest.xml* file. For example, replace the *DefaultTask* entry with an entry that specifies a *SearchExtras* query string (without a leading slash). You can also test the negative case by providing a query string that should not result in listing your app in the search results.

Note Be aware that this technique must be used only for testing. The manifest submitted to the Store for publication must use your default page, without additional parameters.

```
<Tasks>
  <!--<DefaultTask  Name ="_default" NavigationPage="MainPage.xaml"/>-->
  <DefaultTask Name="_default" NavigationPage="SearchExtras?ProductName=coffee&amp;
      Category=Bing_Products_Gourmet_Food_and_Chocolate"/>
  <!--<DefaultTask Name="_default" NavigationPage="SearchExtras?ProductName=bananas&amp;
      Category=Bing_Products_Gourmet_Food_and_Chocolate"/>-->
</Tasks>
```

Suppose that you want to support more than one extension category and perhaps provide different caption strings for some or all of these. Or, suppose that you want to map the launch URI to one of several different target pages, according to some part of the query string. All of these behaviors are possible (see the *SimpleAppConnect* solution in the sample code). First, consider the requirement to support multiple extension categories. To do this, simply add each additional category in the Extensions section in your *WMAppManifest.xml* file. In the following listing, the app supports one of each of the three major categories, Products, Places, and Movies:

```
<Extensions>
  <Extension ExtensionName="Bing_Products_Gourmet_Food_and_Chocolate"
      ConsumerID="{5B04B775-356B-4AA0-AAF8-6491FFEA5661}" TaskID="_default"
      ExtraFile="Extensions\\Extras.xml" />
  <Extension ExtensionName="Bing_Places_Food_and_Dining"
      ConsumerID="{5B04B775-356B-4AA0-AAF8-6491FFEA5661}"
      TaskID="_default" ExtraFile="Extensions\\Extras.xml" />
  <Extension ExtensionName="Bing_Movies" ConsumerID="{5B04B775-356B-4AA0-AAF8-6491FFEA5661}"
      TaskID="_default" ExtraFile="Extensions\\Extras.xml" />
</Extensions>
```

Be aware that there's a difference between *Bing_Movies* and *Bing_Products_Movies*—the latter will include results for movies that are not found to be showing in theatres; for example, if the user is searching for movies to buy on DVD. In the *Extras.xml*, you could group multiple *ExtensionName* entries to share the same caption strings. You can also divide your supported categories into groups, each with its own caption strings.

```
<ExtensionInfo>
  <Extensions>
    <ExtensionName>Bing_Products_Gourmet_Food_and_Chocolate</ExtensionName>
    <ExtensionName>Bing_Places_Food_and_Dining</ExtensionName>
  </Extensions>
```

```
  <CaptionString>
    <default>All you need to know about coffee</default>
  </CaptionString>
</ExtensionInfo>

<ExtensionInfo>
  <Extensions>
    <ExtensionName>Bing_Movies</ExtensionName>
  </Extensions>
  <CaptionString>
    <default>Coffee in movies</default>
  </CaptionString>
</ExtensionInfo>
```

You could also enhance your URI mapper to target different pages for the different categories.

```
public override Uri MapUri(Uri uri)
{
    String inputUri = uri.ToString();
    if (inputUri.Contains("/SearchExtras"))
    {
        String targetPageName = "/MainPage.xaml";
        if (inputUri.Contains("Bing_Products"))
        {
            targetPageName = "/ProductTargetPage.xaml";
        }
        else if (inputUri.Contains("Bing_Places"))
        {
            targetPageName = "/PlaceTargetPage.xaml";
        }
        else if (inputUri.Contains("Bing_Movies"))
        {
            targetPageName = "/MovieTargetPage.xaml";
        }

        String outputUri = inputUri.Replace("/SearchExtras", targetPageName);
        return new Uri(outputUri, UriKind.Relative);
    }
    return uri;
}
```

Clearly, you could take this a step further by pivoting your decisions off any of the elements of the query string. To ensure robustness, you should also decode the incoming URI (typically, by using *HttpUtility.UrlDecode*) before processing it and then re-encode it (by using *HttpUtility.UrlEncode*) before returning from your *MapUri* method.

App Instant Answer

The second search extensibility model is simpler. It requires no special manifest entries, no *Extras.xml*, and no URI mapper. You have no choice about which page to launch based on the search results, and Bing will always launch your app using its default page. The way Bing identifies your app as being suitable for listing in the search results is internal to Bing. The overall model for App Instant Answer is summarized in Figure 5-6.

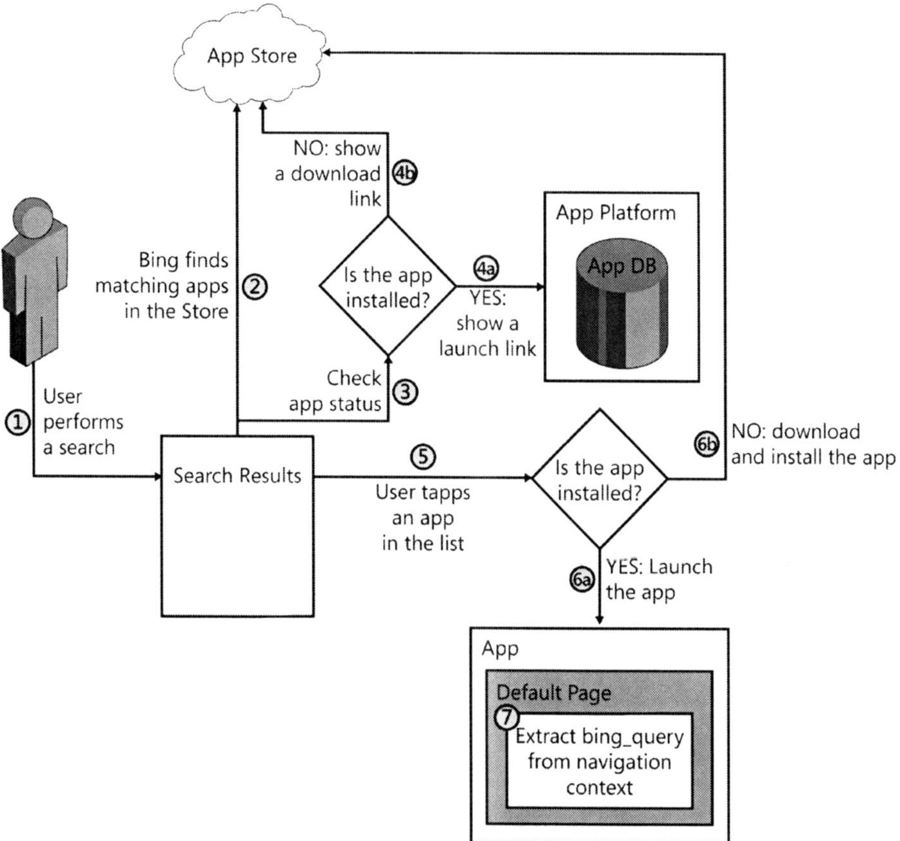

FIGURE 5-6 The App Instant Answer extensibility model.

To create an App Instant Answer app, create a Windows Phone app as normal. An example of this is in the *SimpleAppInstantAnswer* solution in the sample code. When the user performs a Bing search, it might include apps in the web pivot. For example, if the user searches for "banana," and your app name is "Banana Instant Answer," this will match, and Bing will potentially add your app to the results list. On the other hand, if your app name is "Banoffee Instant Answer," the match will fail. To set your app name, you set the *Title* attribute of the *App* element in your *WMAppManifest.xml*. Typically you set this in the project properties page in Visual Studio, although you can also edit the manifest manually, if you prefer, as follows:

```
Title="Banana Instant Answer"
```

There are two *Title* entries in the manifest: one is an attribute of the app element, the other is a subelement of the *Tokens* element. The app element's *Title* attribute is the one that you want here. Also note that even if your app name exactly matches the user's search term, there's no guarantee that your app will be listed in the search results.

If you want to allow for the possibility that you'll be included in search results for App Instant Answers, you should test for the *bing_query* parameter in the navigation query string.

```
protected override void OnNavigatedTo(NavigationEventArgs e)
{
    String query;
    if (NavigationContext.QueryString.TryGetValue("bing_query", out query))
    {
        // Do something useful with this information.
    }
}
```

As with App Connect, you can test an App Instant Answer app by providing a fake launch URI in your *WMAppManifest.xml* file. But remember, just as before, this must be removed before submitting your app to the Windows Phone Store.

```
<Tasks>
  <!--<DefaultTask  Name ="_default" NavigationPage="MainPage.xaml"/>-->
  <DefaultTask Name="_default" NavigationPage="MainPage.xaml?bing_query=Banana" />
</Tasks>
```

Finally, be aware that this is the only way that you can test your app, because even on the emulator, Bing only includes App Instant Answer apps from the published catalog in the Windows Phone Store. If it finds an app in the Windows Phone Store that is already installed on the phone, it will change the link from a Store download link to an installed app link, but it will not include an installed app unless it first finds a match for the app in the Windows Phone Store.

Audio and video APIs

Windows Phone includes a range of techniques for working with media, both audio and video, in three broad categories that are described in Table 5-3.

TABLE 5-3 Media techniques for Windows Phone

Category	Technique	Description
Media playback	*MediaPlayerLauncher*	A Launcher for playing audio or video with the built-in player experience. Primarily used for XNA videos.
	MediaElement	The primary wrapper class for audio and/or video files.
	MediaStreamSource	You can use this to work directly with the media pipeline. You use this most often to enable the *MediaElement* to use a container format not natively supported by the app platform.
	BackgroundAudioPlayer	Background audio agents use this to play music (see Chapter 9, "Background agents."
Audio input and manipulation	*SoundEffect, SoundEffectInstance, DynamicSoundEffect*	XNA classes for working with audio content.
	Microphone	The only API for the microphone on the phone is the XNA *Microphone* class.
Platform integration	*MediaHistory*	You can use this to integrate your app with the Music + Videos hub.
	MediaLibrary	XNA class that provides access to the user's songs, playlists, and pictures.

Media playback

The platform provides three main APIs for playing audio and video, each with varying levels of flexibility and control: the *MediaPlayerLauncher*, *MediaElement*, and *MediaStreamSource*. All three are described in the following sections.

The *MediaPlayerLauncher*

The *MediaPlayerLauncher*, like all Launchers and Choosers provided by the app platform, is very easy to use. It is a simple wrapper that provides access to the underlying media player app without exposing any of the complexity. To use this in your app, you follow the same pattern as for other Launchers. You can see this at work in the *TestMediaPlayer* solution in the sample code (see Figure 5-7). Observe that the media player defaults to landscape mode for videos (you can't change this).

FIGURE 5-7 You can very quickly add media player support for audio and video playback.

The following listing shows how to invoke the *MediaPlayerLauncher* with a media file that is deployed as *Content* within the app's XAP—the path will be relative to the app's install folder:

```
MediaPlayerLauncher player = new MediaPlayerLauncher();
player.Media = new Uri(@"Assets/Media/ViaductTraffic.mp4", UriKind.Relative);
player.Controls = MediaPlaybackControls.Pause | MediaPlaybackControls.Stop;
player.Location = MediaLocationType.Install;
player.Show();
```

You can assign the *Controls* property from a flags enum of possible controls. The preceding listing specifies only the *Pause* and *Stop* controls, whereas the listing that follows specifies all available controls (including *Pause, Stop, Fast Forward, Rewind*). The listing also shows how to specify a remote URL for the media file, together with the *MediaLocationType.Data.*

```
MediaPlayerLauncher player = new MediaPlayerLauncher();
player.Media = new Uri(
  @"http://media.ch9.ms/ch9/1eb0/f9621a51-7c01-4394-ae51-b581ab811eb0/DevPlatformDrillDown.wmv",
  UriKind.Absolute);
player.Controls = MediaPlaybackControls.All;
player.Location = MediaLocationType.Data;
player.Show();
```

The *MediaElement* class

The *TestMediaElement* solution in the sample code uses the *MediaElement* control. Unlike the media player, the *MediaElement* class is a *FrameworkElement* type that you can use in your app—superficially, at least—in a similar way as the *Image* type. This means that you get to choose the orientation and size of the element, apply transforms, and so on. You can set up a *MediaElement* in code or in XAML. The *MediaElement* class exposes a set of media-specific properties, including the following:

- **AutoPlay** This property defines whether to start playing the content automatically. The default is *true*, but in many cases you probably want to set it to *false* because of app lifecycle/tombstoning issues.
- **IsMuted** This defines whether sound is on (the default).
- **Volume** This property is set in the range 0 to 1, where 1 (the default) is full volume.
- **Stretch** This is the same property used by an *Image* control to govern how the content fills the control (the default is *Fill*).

The code that follows shows how to set up a *MediaElement* in XAML. This example sets up suitable properties, such as the media source file, whether the audio is muted, the audio volume, and how to render the image within the control.

```
<MediaElement
    x:Name="myVideo" Source="Assets/Media/campus_20111017.wmv" AutoPlay="False"
    IsMuted="False" Volume="0.5" Stretch="UniformToFill"/>
```

All that remains is to invoke methods such as *Play* and *Pause*; in this example, these are triggered in app bar button *Click* handlers.

```
private void appBarPlay_Click(object sender, EventArgs e)
{
    myVideo.Play();
}

private void appBarPause_Click(object sender, EventArgs e)
{
    myVideo.Pause();
}
```

This is enough to get started, but it is a little fragile: there is a very small chance in the app as it stands that the media file is not fully opened at the point when the user taps the play button, and this would raise an exception. To make the app more robust in this scenario, it would be better to have the app bar buttons initially disabled and to handle the *MediaOpened* event on the *MediaElement* object to enable them. You can set up a *MediaOpened* handler in XAML and then implement this in code to enable the app bar buttons.

```
<MediaElement
    x:Name="myVideo" Source="Assets/Media/campus_20111017.wmv" AutoPlay="False"
    IsMuted="False" Volume="0.5" Stretch="UniformToFill"
    MediaOpened="myVideo_MediaOpened" />

private void myVideo_MediaOpened(object sender, System.Windows.RoutedEventArgs e)
{
    ((ApplicationBarIconButton)ApplicationBar.Buttons[0]).IsEnabled = true;
    ((ApplicationBarIconButton)ApplicationBar.Buttons[1]).IsEnabled = true;
}
```

The *MediaStreamSource* and *ManagedMediaHelpers* classes

The *MediaPlayerLauncher* provides the simplest approach for playing media in your app. Stepping it up a notch, if you need more flexibility, the *MediaElement* class offers a good set of functionality and is suitable for most phone apps. However, if you actually need lower-level access to the media file contents, you can use the *MediaStreamSource* class. This class offers more control over the delivery of content to the media pipeline and is particularly useful if you want to use media files in a format that are not natively supported by *MediaElement*, or for scenarios that are simply not yet supported in the platform, such as RTSP:T protocol support, SHOUTcast protocol support, seamless audio looping, ID3 v1/v2 metadata support, adaptive streaming, or multi-bitrate support.

Unfortunately, the *MediaStreamSource* class is not well documented. Fortunately, Microsoft has made available a set of helper classes, which you can obtain at *https://github.com/loarabia/ManagedMediaHelpers*. These were originally designed for use in Microsoft Silverlight Desktop and Windows Phone 7 apps, but they also work in Windows Phone 8 apps. The classes are provided in source-code format and include library projects and demonstration apps for Silverlight Desktop and Windows Phone. Keep in mind that the library source code is all in the Desktop projects; the phone projects merely reference the Desktop source files. The phone demonstration app is, of course, independent.

Here's how you can use these. First, create a phone app solution, as normal. Then, add the *ManagedMediaHelpers* library projects (either take copies, so that you have all the sources available, or build the library assemblies, and then use *CopyLocal=true* to reference them in your solution). If you add the library phone projects to your solution, you then need to copy across all the source files from the Desktop projects. You need two library projects: the MediaParsers.Phone and Mp3MediaStreamSource.Phone projects. These projects provide wrapper classes for the MP3 file format. Using this approach, you must copy the four C# files from the MediaParsers.Desktop project, and the one C# file from the Mp3MediaStreamSource.SL4 project. The Mp3MediaStreamSource.Phone project has a reference to the MediaParsers.Phone project. Your app needs to have a reference to the Mp3Media StreamSource.Phone project. Figure 5-8 shows this setup, which is the *TestMediaHelpers* solution in the sample code.

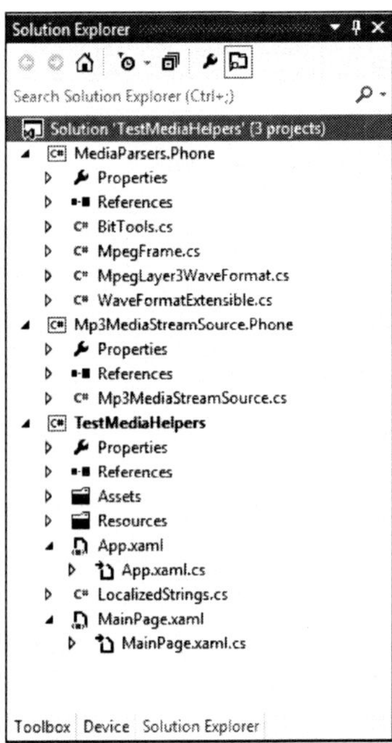

FIGURE 5-8 You can use the *ManagedMediaHelpers* for low-level control of media playback.

Having set up the projects, you can then declare an *Mp3MediaStreamSource* object. The sample app fetches a remote MP3 file by using an *HttpWebRequest*. When we get the data back, we use it to initialize the *Mp3MediaStreamSource* and set that as the source for a *MediaElement* object, which is declared in XAML.

```
private HttpWebRequest request;
private Mp3MediaStreamSource mss;
private string mediaFileLocation =
    @"http://media.ch9.ms/ch9/755d/4f893d13-fa05-4871-9123-3eadd2f0755d/
EightPlatformAnnouncements.mp3";

public MainPage()
{
    InitializeComponent();
    Get = (ApplicationBarIconButton)ApplicationBar.Buttons[0];
    Play = (ApplicationBarIconButton)ApplicationBar.Buttons[1];
    Pause = (ApplicationBarIconButton)ApplicationBar.Buttons[2];
}
```

```
private void Get_Click(object sender, EventArgs e)
{
    request = WebRequest.CreateHttp(mediaFileLocation);
    request.AllowReadStreamBuffering = true;
    request.BeginGetResponse(new AsyncCallback(RequestCallback), null);
}

private void RequestCallback(IAsyncResult asyncResult)
{
    HttpWebResponse response =
        request.EndGetResponse(asyncResult) as HttpWebResponse;
    Stream s = response.GetResponseStream();
    mss = new Mp3MediaStreamSource(s, response.ContentLength);
    Dispatcher.BeginInvoke(() =>
    {
        mp3Element.SetSource(mss);
        Play.IsEnabled = true;
        Get.IsEnabled = false;
    });
}

private void Play_Click(object sender, EventArgs e)
{
    mp3Element.Play();
    Play.IsEnabled = false;
    Pause.IsEnabled = true;
}

private void Pause_Click(object sender, EventArgs e)
{
    mp3Element.Pause();
    Pause.IsEnabled = false;
    Play.IsEnabled = true;
}
```

Observe that this code sets the *AllowReadStreamBuffering* property to *true*. If you enable buffering like this, it becomes easier to work with the stream source because all the data is downloaded first. On the other hand, you can't start processing the data until the entire file is downloaded—plus, it uses more memory. The alternative is to use the asynchronous methods and read the stream in the background. This simple example shows you how you can easily use the *MediaStreamSource* type via the *ManagedMediaHelpers*, although it doesn't really show the power of these APIs—by definition, these are advanced scenarios.

The *MediaElement* controls

When you point a *MediaElement* to a remote media source and start playing, the content is downloaded to the device, and playback starts as soon as there is enough data in the buffer to play. Download and buffering continues in the background while the previously buffered content is playing. If you're interested in the progress of these operations, you can handle the *BufferingChanged* and *DownloadChanged* events exposed by the *MediaElement* class. The standard media player app on the device, invoked via *MediaPlayerLauncher*, offers a good set of UI controls for starting, stopping, and pausing, as well as a timeline progress bar that tracks the current position in the playback, and a countdown from the total duration of the content. By contrast, the *MediaElement* class does not provide such UI controls; however, you can emulate these features by using the properties exposed from *MediaElement*, notably the *Position* and *NaturalDuration* values.

Figure 5-9 shows the *TestVideo* solution in the sample code. This uses a *MediaElement* combined with a *Slider* and *TextBlock* controls to mirror some of the UI features of the standard media player.

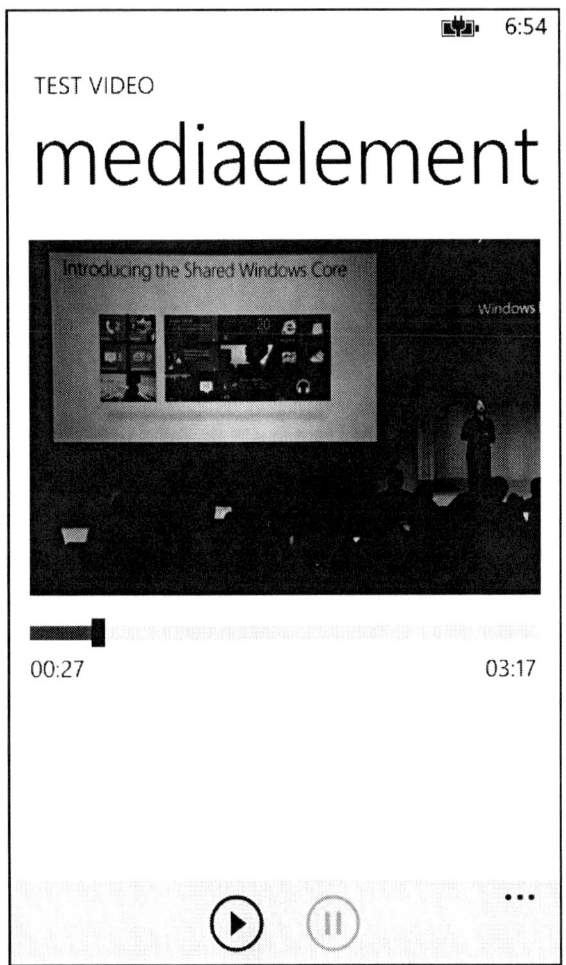

FIGURE 5-9 You can report media playback progress with custom UI.

The app XAML declares a *MediaElement*, a *Slider*, and a couple of *TextBlock* controls (to represent the playback timer count-up and count-down values).

```
<StackPanel x:Name="ContentPanel" Grid.Row="1" Margin="12,0,12,0">
    <MediaElement
        x:Name="Player" Height="297" Width="443" AutoPlay="False" Stretch="UniformToFill"
        Source="http://media.ch9.ms/ch9/b428/b746df27-e928-4306-9464-4b77c289b428/
SharedWindowsCore.wmv"/>
    <Slider
        x:Name="MediaProgress" Height="90" Margin="-5,0"
        Maximum="1" LargeChange="0.1" ValueChanged="MediaProgress_ValueChanged"/>
</StackPanel>
<TextBlock
    Grid.Row="1" x:Name="ElapsedTime" Text="00:00" IsHitTestVisible="False"
    Width="60" Height="30" Margin="19,180,0,0" HorizontalAlignment="Left" />
<TextBlock
    Grid.Row="1" x:Name="RemainingTime" Text="00:00" IsHitTestVisible="False"
    Width="60" Height="30" Margin="0,180,6,0" HorizontalAlignment="Right"/>
```

The *MediaElement* points to a video file on Channel9 (as it happens, this example is a presentation by Joe Belfiore, Microsoft vice president for Windows Phone). For the *Slider*, the important piece is to handle the *ValueChanged* event. Note that the two *TextBlock* controls are not part of the same *StackPanel*—this gives us the opportunity to specifiy *Margin* values and effectively overlay them on top of the *Slider*. Because of this, we need to be careful to make the *TextBlock* controls non–hit-testable so that they don't pick up touch gestures intended for the *Slider*.

The *Slider* performs a dual role: the first aspect is a passive role, in which we update it programmatically to synchronize it with the current playback position; the second aspect is an active role, in which the user can click or drag the *Slider* position—we respond to this in the app by setting the *MediaElement.Position* value. In the *MainPage* code-behind, we declare a *TimeSpan* field for the total duration of the video file, and a *bool* to track whether we're updating the *Slider* based on the current playback position.

```
private bool isUpdatingSliderFromMedia;
private TimeSpan totalTime;
private DispatcherTimer timer;

public MainPage()
{
    InitializeComponent();
    timer = new DispatcherTimer();
    timer.Interval = TimeSpan.FromSeconds(0.5);
    timer.Tick += new EventHandler(timer_Tick);
    timer.Start();

    appBarPlay = ApplicationBar.Buttons[0] as ApplicationBarIconButton;
    appBarPause = ApplicationBar.Buttons[1] as ApplicationBarIconButton;
}

private void Player_MediaOpened(object sender, RoutedEventArgs e)
{
    timer.Start();
}
```

Here's how to implement the first role. We implement a *DispatcherTimer* with a half-second interval, updating the *Slider* on each tick. We wait until the *MediaElement* reports that the media source is successfully opened and then start the timer. When the timer event is raised, the first thing to do is to cache the total duration of the video file—this is a one-off operation. Next, we calculate the time remaining and render this in the corresponding *TextBlock*. Assuming that the playback has actually started (even if it is now paused), we then calculate how much of the video playback is complete and use the resulting value to update the position of the *Slider*. We also need to update the current "elapsed time" value to match the playback position. Throughout this operation, we toggle the *isUpdatingSliderFromMedia* flag. This will be used in another method.

```
private void timer_Tick (object sender, EventArgs e)
{
    if (totalTime == TimeSpan.Zero)
    {
        totalTime = Player.NaturalDuration.TimeSpan;
    }

    TimeSpan remainingTime = totalTime - Player.Position;
    String remainingTimeText = String.Format("{0:00}:{1:00}",
        (remainingTime.Hours * 60) + remainingTime.Minutes, remainingTime.Seconds);
    RemainingTime.Text = remainingTimeText;

    isUpdatingSliderFromMedia = true;
    if (Player.Position.TotalSeconds > 0)
    {
        double fractionComplete = Player.Position.TotalSeconds / totalTime.TotalSeconds;
        MediaProgress.Value = fractionComplete;
        TimeSpan elapsedTime = Player.Position;
        String elapsedTimeText = String.Format("{0:00}:{1:00}",
            (elapsedTime.Hours * 60) + elapsedTime.Minutes, elapsedTime.Seconds);
        ElapsedTime.Text = elapsedTimeText;
        isUpdatingSliderFromMedia = false;
    }
}
```

In the handler for the *ValueChanged* event on the *Slider*, we check first that we're not in this handler as a result of what we did in the previous method. That is, we need to verify that we're not here because we're updating the *Slider* from the media position. The other scenario for which we'd be in this handler is if the user is clicking or dragging the *Slider* position. In this case, assuming that the media content can actually be repositioned (*CanSeek* is *true*), we reset its position based on the *Slider* position. This is the inverse of the normal behavior, for which we set the *Slider* position based on the media position.

```
private void MediaProgress_ValueChanged(
    object sender, RoutedPropertyChangedEventArgs<double> e)
{
    if (!isUpdatingSliderFromMedia && Player.CanSeek)
    {
        TimeSpan duration = Player.NaturalDuration.TimeSpan;
        int newPosition = (int)(duration.TotalSeconds * MediaProgress.Value);
        Player.Position =  TimeSpan.FromSeconds(newPosition);
    }
}
```

The app bar buttons invoke the *MediaElement Play* and *Pause* methods, each of which is very simple. In the case of *Pause*, we need to first establish that this media content can actually be paused. If you don't check *CanSeek* or *CanPause*, and just go ahead and attempt to set *Position* or call *Pause*, in neither case is an exception thrown. Rather, the method simply does nothing. So, these checks are arguably redundant, except that you should use them to avoid executing unnecessary code.

```
private void appBarPause_Click(object sender, EventArgs e)
{
    if (Player.CanPause)
    {
        Player.Pause();
    }
}
```

Audio input and manipulation

Both *MediaElement* and *MediaStreamSource* give you some ability to manipulate media during playback. For even greater flexibility, you can use the *SoundEffect* and *SoundEffectInstance* classes. You can also use the *DynamicSoundEffectInstance* class in combination with the *Microphone* to work with audio input.

The *SoundEffect* and *SoundEffectInstance* classes

As an alternative to using *MediaElement*, you can use the XNA *SoundEffect* classes, instead. One of the advantages is that you can play multiple *SoundEffects* at the same time, whereas you cannot play multiple *MediaElements* at the same time. Another advantage is that the *SoundEffect* class offers better performance than *MediaElement*. This is because the *MediaElement* carries with it a lot of UI baggage, relevant for a *Control* type. On the other hand, the *SoundEffect* class is focused purely on audio and has no UI features. The disadvantage of this is that it is an XNA type, so your app needs to pull in XNA libraries and manage the different expectations of the XNA runtime.

The *TestSoundEffect* solution in the sample code shows how to use *SoundEffect*. It also illustrates the *SoundEffectInstance* class, which offers greater flexibility than the *SoundEffect* class. A key difference is that *SoundEffect* has no *Pause* method; the playback is essentially "fire and forget." The *SoundEffectInstance* also supports looping and 3D audio effects. You can create a *SoundEffectInstance* object from a *SoundEffect*, and this does have a *Pause* method. Also, you can create multiple *Sound EffectInstance* objects from the same *SoundEffect*; they'll all share the same content, but you can control them independently.

The sample app has two sound files, built as *Content* into the XAP (but not into the DLL). In the app, we first need to declare *SoundEffect* and *SoundEffectInstance* fields. Note that this pulls in the *Microsoft.Xna.Frameworks.dll*, and in Visual Studio 2012, you don't need to add this reference manually, because it's done for you. Early in the life of the app, we load the two sound files from the install folder of the app by using *Application.GetResourceStream*. This can be slightly confusing, because we need to explicitly build the files as *Content* not *Resource*. However, *GetResourceStream* can retrieve a stream for either *Content* or *Resource*. If the sound file is a valid PCM wave file, you can use the *FromStream* method to initialize a *SoundEffect* object. For one of these *SoundEffect* objects, we create a *SoundEffectInstance*.

```
private SoundEffect sound;
private SoundEffectInstance soundInstance;

public MainPage()
{
    InitializeComponent();

    sound = LoadSound("Assets/Media/AfternoonAmbienceSimple_01.wav");
    SoundEffect tmp = LoadSound("Assets/Media/NightAmbienceSimple_02.wav");
    if (tmp != null)
    {
        soundInstance = tmp.CreateInstance();
    }
    InitializeXna();
}

private SoundEffect LoadSound(String streamPath)
{
    SoundEffect s = null;
    try
    {
        StreamResourceInfo streamInfo =
            App.GetResourceStream(new Uri(streamPath, UriKind.Relative));
        s = SoundEffect.FromStream(streamInfo.Stream);
    }
    catch (Exception ex)
    {
        Debug.WriteLine(ex.ToString());
    }
    return s;
}
```

Not only must the file be a valid WAV file, it must also be in the RIFF bitstream format, mono or stereo, 8 or 16 bit, with a sample rate between 8,000 Hz and 48,000 Hz. If the sound file was created on the phone with the same microphone device and saved as a raw audio stream (no file format headers), you could instead work with the stream directly and assume the same sample rate and *AudioChannels* values.

Also, very early in the life of the app, we must do some housekeeping to ensure that any XNA types work correctly. The basic requirement is to simulate the XNA game loop. This is the core architectural model in XNA, and most significant XNA types depend on this. XNA Framework event messages are placed in a queue that is processed by the XNA *FrameworkDispatcher*. In an XNA app, the XNA *Game* class calls the *FrameworkDispatcher.Update* method automatically whenever *Game.Update* is processed. This *FrameworkDispatcher.Update* method causes the XNA Framework to process the message queue. If you use the XNA Framework from an app that does not implement the *Game* class, you must call the *FrameworkDispatcher.Update* method yourself to process the XNA Framework message queue.

There are various ways to achieve this. The simplest approach here is to set up a *DispatcherTimer* to call *FrameworkDispatcher.Update*. The typical tick rate for processing XNA events is 33 ms. The XNA game loop updates and redraws at 30 frames per second (FPS); that is one frame every 33 ms. It's a good idea to set up timers as class fields rather than local variables. This way, you can start and stop them out of band—such as in *OnNavigatedTo* and *OnNavigatedFrom* overrides.

```
private DispatcherTimer timer;
private void InitializeXna()
{
    timer = new DispatcherTimer();
    timer.Interval = TimeSpan.FromMilliseconds(33);
    timer.Tick += delegate { try { FrameworkDispatcher.Update(); } catch { } };
    timer.Start();
}

protected override void OnNavigatedFrom(NavigationEventArgs e)
{
    timer.Stop();
}

protected override void OnNavigatedTo(NavigationEventArgs e)
{
    timer.Start();
}
```

The app provides three app bar buttons. The *Click* handler for the first one simply plays the *SoundEffect* by invoking the "fire-and-forget" *Play* method. The other two are used to *Start* (that is, *Play*) or *Pause* the *SoundEffectInstance*. If the user taps the Play button to play the *SoundEffect* and then taps the *Start* button to play the *SoundEffectInstance*, she will end up with both audio files playing at the same time.

```
private void appBarPlay_Click(object sender, EventArgs e)
{
    if (sound != null)
    {
        sound.Play();
    }
}

private void appBarStart_Click(object sender, EventArgs e)
{
    if (soundInstance != null)
    {
        soundInstance.Play();
    }
}
```

```
private void appBarPause_Click(object sender, EventArgs e)
{
    if (soundInstance != null)
    {
        soundInstance.Pause();
    }
}
```

Audio input and the microphone

The only way to work with audio input in a Windows Phone app is to use the XNA *Microphone* class. This provides access to the microphone (or microphones) available on the system. Although you can get the collection of microphones, the collection always contains exactly one microphone, so you would end up working with the default microphone, anyway. All microphones on the device conform to the same basic audio format, and return 16-bit PCM mono audio data, with a sample rate between 8,000 Hz and 48,000 Hz. The low-level audio stack uses an internal circular buffer to collect the input audio from the microphone device. You can configure the size of this buffer by setting the *Microphone.BufferDuration* property. *BufferDuration* is of type *TimeSpan*, so setting a buffer size of 300 ms will result in a buffer of 2 * 16 * 300 = 9,600 bytes. *BufferDuration* must be between 100 ms and 1000 ms, in 10-ms increments. The size of the buffer is returned by *GetSampleSizeInBytes*.

There are two different methods for retrieving audio input data:

- Handle the *BufferReady* event and process data when there is a *BufferDuration*'s-worth of data received in the buffer. This has a minimum latency of 100 ms.
- Pull the data independently of *BufferReady* events, at whatever time interval you choose, including more frequently than 100 ms.

For a game, it can often be more useful to pull the data so that you can synchronize sound and action in a flexible manner. For a non-game app it is more common to respond to *BufferReady* events. With this approach, the basic steps for working with the microphone are as follows:

1. For convenience, cache a local reference to the default microphone.
2. Specify how large a buffer you want to maintain for audio input and declare a byte array for this data.
3. Hook up the *BufferReady* event, which is raised whenever a buffer's-worth of audio data is ready.
4. In your *BufferReady* event handler, retrieve the audio input data and do something interesting with it.
5. At suitable points, start and stop the microphone to start and stop the buffering of audio input data.

You might wonder what happens if your app is using the microphone to record sound and then a phone call comes in and the user answers it. Is the phone call recorded? The answer is "No," specifically because this is a privacy issue. So, what happens is that your app keeps recording, but it records silence until the call is finished.

Figure 5-10 shows the *DecibelMeter* solution in the sample code, which illustrates simple use of the microphone. The app takes audio input data, converts it to decibels, and then displays a graphical representation of the decibel level, using both a rectangle and a text value. Note that this requires the *ID_CAP_MICROPHONE* capability in the app manifest.

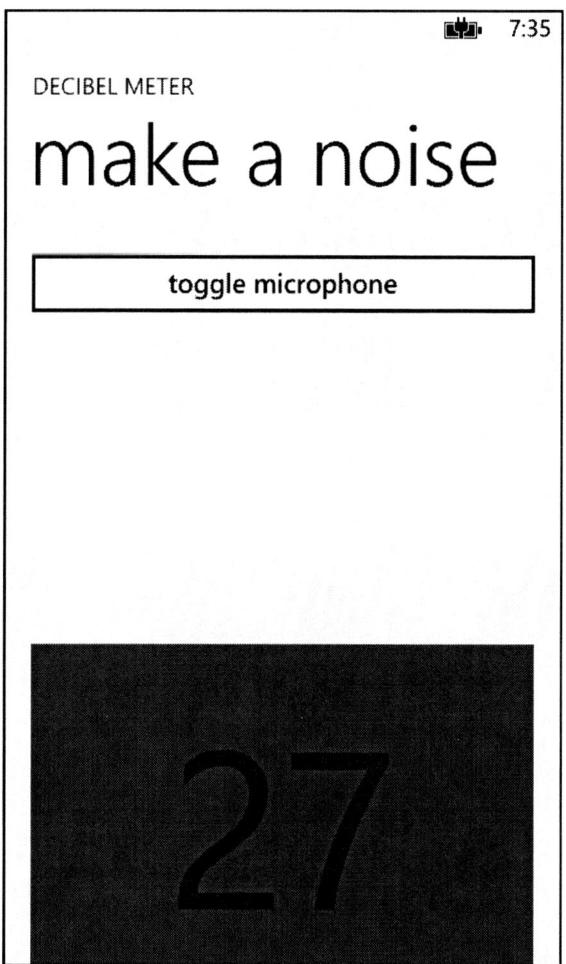

FIGURE 5-10 You can build a simple decibel meter to exercise the microphone.

The app XAML defines a *Grid* that contains a *Button* and an inner *Grid*. Inside the inner *Grid*, there's a *Rectangle* and a *TextBlock*. These are both bottom-aligned and overlapping (the control declared last is overlaid on top of the previous one).

```
<Grid x:Name="ContentPanel" Grid.Row="1" Margin="12,0,12,0">
    <Grid.RowDefinitions>
        <RowDefinition Height="Auto"/>
        <RowDefinition Height="*"/>
    </Grid.RowDefinitions>
    <Button x:Name="ToggleMicrophone" Content="toggle microphone"
            Click="ToggleMicrophone_Click"/>
    <Grid Grid.Row="1" Height="535">
        <Rectangle x:Name="LevelRect"
            Height="0" Width="432" VerticalAlignment="Bottom"
            Margin="{StaticResource PhoneHorizontalMargin}" />
        <TextBlock
            Text="0" x:Name="SoundLevel" TextAlignment="Center" Width="432"
            FontSize="{StaticResource PhoneFontSizeHuge}"
            VerticalAlignment="Bottom"/>
    </Grid>
</Grid>
```

First, we declare a byte array for the audio data and a local reference to the default microphone. We then initialize these in the *MainPage* constructor. We specify that we want to maintain a 300-ms buffer for audio input. Whenever the buffer is filled, we'll get a *BufferReady* event. We retrieve the size of the byte array required to hold the specified duration of audio for this microphone object by using *GetSampleSizeInBytes* (this is how we know what size buffer to allocate). The following code also retrieves the current accent brush and sets this as the *Brush* object with which to fill the rectangle:

```
private byte[] soundBuffer;
private Microphone mic;

public MainPage()
{
    InitializeComponent();

    Brush accent = (Brush)Resources["PhoneAccentBrush"];
    LevelRect.Fill = accent;

    mic = Microphone.Default;
    mic.BufferDuration = TimeSpan.FromMilliseconds(300);
    mic.BufferReady += Microphone_BufferReady;
    int bufferSize = mic.GetSampleSizeInBytes(mic.BufferDuration);
    soundBuffer = new byte[bufferSize];
}
```

Whenever a buffer's-worth of audio input data is received, we pull that data from the *Microphone* object and copy it into our private buffer to work on it. We process this data by determining the average sound level in decibels and rendering text and graphics to represent that level. The rectangle height and position are constrained by the height of the containing grid.

```
private void Microphone_BufferReady(object sender, EventArgs e)
{
    int soundDataSize = mic.GetData(soundBuffer);
    if (soundDataSize > 0)
```

```
    {
        SoundLevel.Dispatcher.BeginInvoke(() =>
        {
            int decibels = GetSoundLevel();
            SoundLevel.Text = decibels.ToString();
            LevelRect.Height = Math.Max(0, Math.Min(
                ContentPanel.RowDefinitions[1].ActualHeight, decibels * 10));
        });
    }
}
```

The sound pressure level ratio in decibels is given by 20*log(<actual value>/<reference value>), where the logarithm is to base 10. Realistically, the <reference value> would be determined by calibration. In this example, we use an arbitrary hard-coded calibration value (300), instead. First, we must convert the array of bytes into an array of shorts. Then, we can convert these shorts into decibels.

```
private int GetSoundLevel()
{
    short[] audioData = new short[soundBuffer.Length / 2];
    Buffer.BlockCopy(soundBuffer, 0, audioData, 0, soundBuffer.Length);
    double calibrationZero = 300;
    double waveHeight = Math.Abs(audioData.Max() - audioData.Min());
    double decibels = 20 * Math.Log10(waveHeight / calibrationZero);
    return (int)decibels;
}
```

Finally, we provide a button in the UI so that the user can toggle the microphone on or off:

```
private void ToggleMicrophone_Click(object sender, RoutedEventArgs e)
{
    if (mic.State == MicrophoneState.Started)
    {
        mic.Stop();
    }
    else
    {
        mic.Start();
    }
}
```

As before, we need to ensure that the XNA types work correctly in a Silverlight app. Previously, we took the approach of a *DispatcherTimer* to provide a tick upon which we could invoke *FrameworkDispatcher.Update* in a simple fashion. A variation on this approach is to implement *IApplicationService* and put the *DispatcherTimer* functionality in that implementation. *IApplicationService* represents an extensibility mechanism in Silverlight. The idea is that where you have a need for some global "service" that needs to work across your app, you can register it with the runtime. This interface declares two methods: *StartService* and *StopService*. The Silverlight runtime will call *StartService* during app initialization, and it will call *StopService* just before the app terminates. Effectively, we're taking the *InitializeXna* custom method from the previous example and reshaping it as an implementation of *IApplicationService*. Then, instead of invoking the method directly, we register the class and leave it to Silverlight to invoke the methods.

Following is the class implementation. As before, we simply set up a *DispatcherTimer* and invoke *FrameworkDispatcher.Update* on each tick.

```
public class XnaFrameworkDispatcherService : IApplicationService
{
    DispatcherTimer timer;

    public XnaFrameworkDispatcherService()
    {
        timer = new DispatcherTimer();
        timer.Interval = TimeSpan.FromTicks(333333);
        timer.Tick += OnTimerTick;
        FrameworkDispatcher.Update();
    }

    private void OnTimerTick(object sender, EventArgs args)
    {
        FrameworkDispatcher.Update();
    }

    void IApplicationService.StartService(AppserviceContext context)
    {
        timer.Start();
    }

    void IApplicationService.StopService()
    {
        timer.Stop();
    }
}
```

Registration is a simple matter of updating the *App.xaml* file to include the custom class in the *ApplicationLifetimeObjects* section.

```
<Application
...standard declarations omitted for brevity.
    xmlns:local="clr-namespace:DecibelMeter">

    <Application.ApplicationLifetimeObjects>

        <local:XnaFrameworkDispatcherService />

        <shell:PhoneAppservice
            Launching="Application_Launching" Closing="Application_Closing"
            Activated="Application_Activated" Deactivated="Application_Deactivated"/>
    </Application.ApplicationLifetimeObjects>
</Application>
```

Figure 5-11 shows the *SoundFx* solution in the sample code. This uses the microphone to record sound and then plays back the sound. The app uses a slider to control the sound pitch on playback. This needs the *ID_CAP_MICROPHONE* capability in the app manifest.

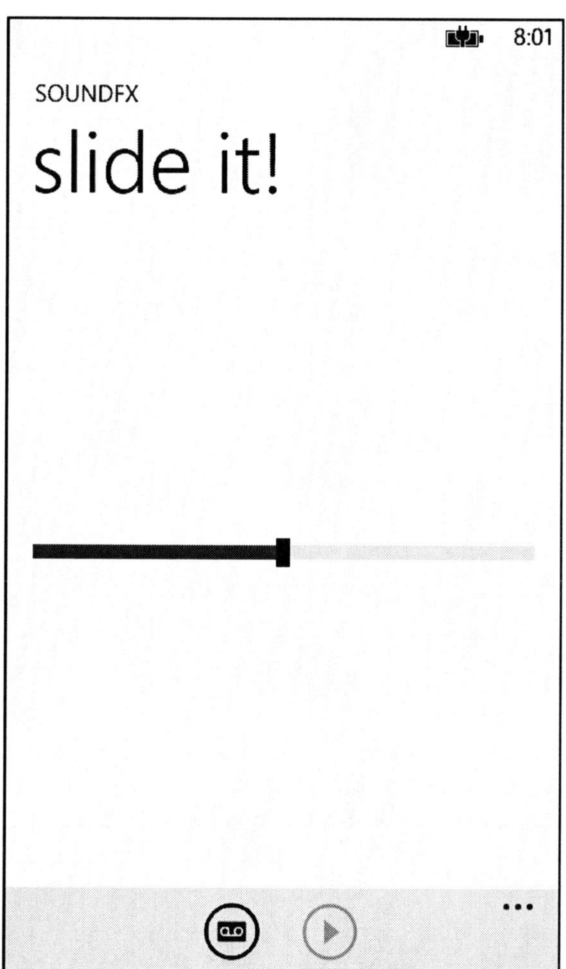

FIGURE 5-11 It's very simple to build sound recording and playback features.

In the *MainPage* constructor, we set up the XNA message queue processing, initialize the default microphone (with a 300-ms buffer), and create a private byte array for the audio data, as before. We then set the *SoundEffect.MasterVolume* to 1. This is relative to the volume on the device/emulator itself. You can set the volume in a range of 0 to 1, where 0 approximates silence, and 1 equates to the device volume. You cannot set the volume higher than the volume on the device. Each time the audio input buffer is filled, we get the data in the private byte array and then copy it to a *MemoryStream* for processing. Note that we need to protect the buffer with a *lock* object: this addresses the issue of the user pressing *Stop* while we're writing to the buffer (this would reset the buffer position to zero). The *Uri* fields and the *ButtonState* enum are used to change the images for the app bar buttons, because each one serves a dual purpose.

```
private byte[] soundBuffer;
private Microphone mic;
private MemoryStream stream;
private SoundEffectInstance sound;
private bool isRecording;
private bool isPlaying;
private DispatcherTimer timer;

private Uri recordUri = new Uri("/Assets/record.png", UriKind.Relative);
private Uri stopUri = new Uri("/Assets/stop.png", UriKind.Relative);
private Uri playUri = new Uri("/Assets/play.png", UriKind.Relative);
private enum ButtonState { Recording, ReadyToPlay, Playing };

public MainPage()
{
    InitializeComponent();

    timer = new DispatcherTimer();
    timer.Interval = TimeSpan.FromSeconds(0.33);
    timer.Tick += timer_Tick;
    timer.Start();

    mic = Microphone.Default;
    mic.BufferDuration = TimeSpan.FromMilliseconds(300);
    mic.BufferReady += Microphone_BufferReady;
    int bufferSize = mic.GetSampleSizeInBytes(mic.BufferDuration);
    soundBuffer = new byte[bufferSize];
    SoundEffect.MasterVolume = 1.0f;

    appBarRecord = ApplicationBar.Buttons[0] as ApplicationBarIconButton;
    appBarPlay = ApplicationBar.Buttons[1] as ApplicationBarIconButton;
}

private void timer_Tick(object sender, EventArgs e)
{
    FrameworkDispatcher.Update();
    if (isPlaying && sound.State != SoundState.Playing)
    {
        isPlaying = false;
        UpdateAppBarButtons(ButtonState.ReadyToPlay);
    }
}

private void Microphone_BufferReady(object sender, EventArgs e)
{
    lock (this)
    {
        mic.GetData(soundBuffer);
        stream.Write(soundBuffer, 0, soundBuffer.Length);
    }
}
```

Notice that we have to poll the *SoundEffectInstance* to see when its state changes because the class doesn't expose a suitable event for this. The user can tap the app bar buttons to start and stop the recording. We handle these by calling *Microphone.Start* and *Microphone.Stop*. When the user chooses to start a new recording, we close any existing stream and set up a fresh one and then start the microphone. Conversely, when the user asks to stop recording, we stop the microphone and reset the stream pointer to the beginning.

```
private void appBarRecord_Click(object sender, EventArgs e)
{
    if (isRecording)
        StopRecording();
    else
        StartRecording();
}

private void appBarPlay_Click(object sender, EventArgs e)
{
    if (isPlaying)
        StopPlayback();
    else
        StartPlayback();
}

private void StartRecording()
{
    if (stream != null)
        stream.Close();
    stream = new MemoryStream();
    mic.Start();
    isRecording = true;
    UpdateAppBarButtons(ButtonState.Recording);
}

private void StopRecording()
{
    mic.Stop();
    stream.Position = 0;
    isRecording = false;
    UpdateAppBarButtons(ButtonState.ReadyToPlay);
}

private void UpdateAppBarButtons(ButtonState state)
{
    switch (state)
    {
        case ButtonState.Recording:
            appBarRecord.IconUri = stopUri;
            appBarRecord.Text = "stop";
            appBarRecord.IsEnabled = true;
            appBarPlay.IsEnabled = false;
            break;
```

```
        case ButtonState.ReadyToPlay:
            appBarRecord.IconUri = recordUri;
            appBarRecord.Text = "record";
            appBarRecord.IsEnabled = true;
            appBarPlay.IconUri = playUri;
            appBarPlay.Text = "play";
            appBarPlay.IsEnabled = true;
            break;
        case ButtonState.Playing:
            appBarRecord.IconUri = recordUri;
            appBarRecord.Text = "record";
            appBarRecord.IsEnabled = false;
            appBarPlay.IconUri = stopUri;
            appBarPlay.Text = "stop";
            appBarPlay.IsEnabled = true;
            break;
    }
}
```

The only other interesting code is starting and stopping playback of the recorded sound. To start playback, we first create a new *SoundEffect* object from the buffer of microphone data. Then, we create a new *SoundEffectInstance* from the *SoundEffect* object, varying the pitch to match the slider value. We also set the Volume to 1.0 relative to the *SoundEffect.MasterVolume*; the net effect is to retain the same volume as the device itself. To stop playback, we simply call *SoundEffectInstance.Stop*, as before.

```
private void StartPlayback()
{
    SoundEffect se = new SoundEffect(stream.ToArray(), mic.SampleRate, AudioChannels.Mono);
    sound = se.CreateInstance();
    sound.Volume = 1.0f;
    sound.Pitch = (float)Frequency.Value;
    sound.Play();
    isPlaying = true;
    UpdateAppBarButtons(ButtonState.Playing);
}

private void StopPlayback()
{
    if (sound != null)
        sound.Stop();
    isPlaying = false;
    UpdateAppBarButtons(ButtonState.ReadyToPlay);
}
```

We can take this one step further by persisting the recorded sound to a file in isolated storage. You can see this at work in the *SoundFx_Persist* solution in the sample code. To persist the sound, we can add a couple of extra app bar buttons for *Save* and *Load*. To save the data, we simply write out the raw audio data by using the isolated storage APIs. This example uses a .pcm file extension because the data is in fact PCM wave data. However, this is not a WAV file in the normal sense, because it is missing the header information that describes the file format, sample rate, channels, and so on.

```
private const string soundFile = "SoundFx.pcm";

private void appBarSave_Click(object sender, EventArgs e)
{
    using (IsolatedStorageFile storage =
        IsolatedStorageFile.GetUserStoreForApplication())
    {
        using (IsolatedStorageFileStream isoStream =
            storage.OpenFile(soundFile, FileMode.Create, FileAccess.Write))
        {
            byte[] soundData = stream.ToArray();
            isoStream.Write(soundData, 0, soundData.Length);
        }
    }
}

private void appBarLoad_Click(object sender, EventArgs e)
{
    using (IsolatedStorageFile storage =
        IsolatedStorageFile.GetUserStoreForApplication())
    {
        using (IsolatedStorageFileStream isoStream =
            storage.OpenFile(soundFile, FileMode.Open, FileAccess.Read))
        {
            stream = new MemoryStream();

            isoStream.CopyTo(stream, (int)isoStream.Length);        }
    }
}
```

You've seen already that you can use the *SoundEffect* class to load a conventional WAV file (including header) from disk. There's no support in *SoundEffect*—or indeed any other Silverlight or XNA classes—for saving WAV files with header information. This is not generally a problem on Windows Phone, because if the same app is both recording the data and playing it back, it can precisely control the file contents without the need for a descriptive header. On the other hand, if you need to record audio on the phone and then transmit it externally (for example, via a web service) to a consuming user or app that is using a different device (perhaps a PC, not a phone at all), you need to save a descriptive header in the file along with the audio data.

One solution to this is the NAudio library. NAudio is an open-source Microsoft .NET audio and MIDI library that contains a wide range of useful audio-related classes intended to speed development of audio-based managed apps. NAudio is licensed under the Microsoft Public License (Ms-PL), which means that you can use it in whatever project you like, including commercial projects. It is available at *http://naudio.codeplex.com/*.

The *DynamicSoundEffectInstance* class

So far, we've used the *SoundEffect* and *SoundEffectInstance* classes to play back audio streams, either from static audio content or from dynamic microphone input. The *DynamicSoundEffectInstance* is derived from *SoundEffectInstance*. The critical difference is that it exposes a *BufferNeeded* event. This is raised when it needs more audio data to play back. You can provide the audio data from static files or from dynamic microphone input; however, the main strength of this feature is that you can manipulate or compute the audio data before you provide it. Typically, you would modify source data, or even compute the data entirely from scratch.

The *TestDynamicSounds* solution in the sample code does just that: it provides a simple sound based on a sine wave. Sound is the result of a vibrating object creating pressure oscillations—that is, variations in pressure over time—in the air. A variation over time is modeled in mathematical terms as a wave. A wave can be represented by a formula that governs how the amplitude (or height) of the signal varies over time, and the frequency of the oscillations. Given two otherwise identical waves, if one has higher amplitude it will be louder; if one has greater frequency it will have a higher pitch. A wave is continuous, but you need to end up with a buffer full of discrete items of audio data, whereby each datapoint is a value that represents a sample along the wave.

With this basic context, we can get started with dynamic sounds. First, we need to declare fields for the *DynamicSoundEffectInstance*, a sample rate set to the maximum achievable on the device (48,000), and a buffer to hold the sound data. You can get the required buffer size from the *Dynamic SoundEffectInstance* object. For the purposes of this example, set the frequency to an arbitrary value of 300.

```
private DynamicSoundEffectInstance dynamicSound;
private const int sampleRate = 48000;
private int bufferSize;
private byte[] soundBuffer;
private int totalTime = 0;
private double frequency = 300;
```

At a suitable early point—for example, in the *MainPage* constructor—you would set up your preferred method for pumping the XNA message queue. We want to initialize the *DynamicSound EffectInstance* early on, but the catch is that the constructor is too early because you won't yet have started pumping the XNA message queue. One solution is to hook up the *Loaded* event on the page and do your initialization of the XNA types there, but there is a possible race condition with that approach. The simplest approach is to just pump the XNA message queue once first, before performing initialization. Apart from the timing aspect, the key functional requirement is to hook up the *BufferNeeded* event. This will be raised every time the audio pipeline needs input data.

```
public MainPage()
{
    InitializeComponent();

    timer = new DispatcherTimer();
    timer.Interval = TimeSpan.FromMilliseconds(33);
    timer.Tick += delegate { try { FrameworkDispatcher.Update(); } catch { } };
    timer.Start();
    FrameworkDispatcher.Update();
```

```
    dynamicSound = new DynamicSoundEffectInstance(sampleRate, AudioChannels.Mono);
    dynamicSound.BufferNeeded += dynamicSound_BufferNeeded;
    dynamicSound.Play();
    bufferSize = dynamicSound.GetSampleSizeInBytes(TimeSpan.FromSeconds(1));
    soundBuffer = new byte[bufferSize];
}
```

In the handler for the *BufferNeeded* event, the task is to fill in the byte array of sound data. In this example, we fill it with a simple sine wave. The basic formula for a sine wave as a function of time is as follows:

$$y(t) = A .\sin(\omega t+\varphi)$$

Where:

- **A = amplitude** This is the peak deviation of the function from its center position (loudness).
- **ω = frequency** This is how many oscillations occur per unit of time (pitch).
- **φ = phase** This is the point in the cycle at which the oscillation begins.

In this example, for the sake of simplicity, we can default the amplitude to 1 (parity with the volume on the device), and the phase to be zero (oscillation starts at the beginning of the cycle). We loop through the whole buffer, 2 bytes (that is, 16 bits: one sample) at a time. For each sample, we compute the floating-point value of the sine wave and convert it to a short (16 bits). The double value computed from the sine wave formula is in the range –1 to 1, so we multiply by the *MaxValue* for a short in order to get a short equivalent of this.

Then, we need to store the short as 2 bytes. The low-order byte of the short is stored as an element in the sample array and then the high-order byte is stored in the next element. We fill the second byte with the low-order byte of the short by bit-shifting 8 bits to the right. Finally, we submit the newly filled buffer to the *DynamicSoundEffectInstance* so that it can play it back.

```
private void dynamicSound_BufferNeeded(object sender, EventArgs e)
{
    for (int i = 0; i < bufferSize - 1; i += 2)
    {
        double time = (double)totalTime / (double)sampleRate;
        short sample =
            (short)(Math.Sin(2 * Math.PI * frequency * time) * (double)short.MaxValue);
         soundBuffer[i] = (byte)sample;
        soundBuffer[i + 1] = (byte)(sample >> 8);
        totalTime++;
    }
    dynamicSound.SubmitBuffer(soundBuffer);
}
```

The result is a continuously oscillating tone. Figure 5-12 shows a variation on this app (*TestDynamicSounds_Controls* in the sample code), which includes an app bar button to start/stop the playback, and a *Slider* to control the frequency of the wave.

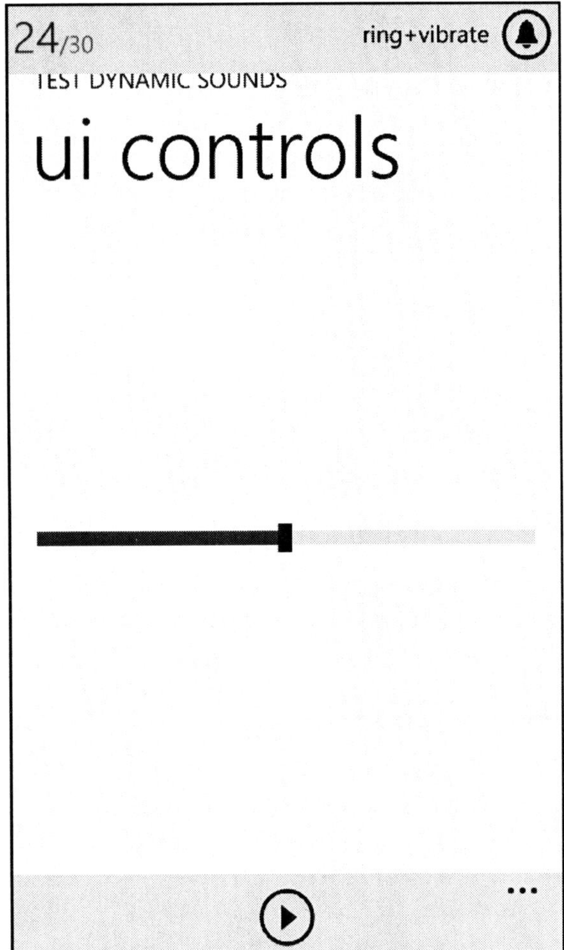

FIGURE 5-12 You can use *DynamicSoundEffectInstance* to manipulate audio data before playback.

The XAML defines a *Slider*, with its range set at 1.0 to 1000.0, and initial position set at halfway along the range, as demonstrated in the following:

```
<Slider
    Grid.Row="1" Margin="12,0,12,0"
    x:Name="Frequency" Minimum="1.0" Maximum="1000.0" Value="500.0" />
```

The implementation of the *BufferNeeded* event handler is changed slightly to use the *Slider* value instead of the fixed frequency value:

```
short sample =
    (short)(Math.Sin(2 * Math.PI * Frequency.Value * time)  * (double)short.MaxValue);
```

The only other work is to respond to button *Click* events to start and stop the playback:

```
private void appBarPlay_Click(object sender, EventArgs e)
{
    if (isPlaying)
    {
        dynamicSound.Stop();
        appBarPlay.IconUri = new Uri("/Assets/play.png", UriKind.Relative);
        appBarPlay.Text = "play";
        isPlaying = false;
    }
    else
    {
        dynamicSound.Play();
        appBarPlay.IconUri = new Uri("/Assets/stop.png", UriKind.Relative);
        appBarPlay.Text = "stop";
        isPlaying = true;
    }
}
```

When this app runs, the user can manipulate the slider to control the data that's fed into the playback buffer. Because we've tied the amplitude to the volume on the device, the user can change the volume of the playback by invoking the universal volume control (UVC), as shown in Figure 5-12. On the emulator, this is invoked by pressing F10 while audio playback is ongoing; press F10 to decrease the volume and F9 to increase it. On the device, this is invoked by the hardware volume controls.

Music and Videos Hub

The Music and Videos Hub on Windows Phone is a centralized location for accessing the phone's music and videos library. Figure 5-13 shows an app that integrates with the Music and Videos Hub to fetch a list of all songs in the library and render them in a *ListBox*. This is the *TestMediaHub* solution in the sample code. When the user selects an item from the *ListBox*, the app fetches the selected song's album art and presents buttons with which he can play/pause the selected song.

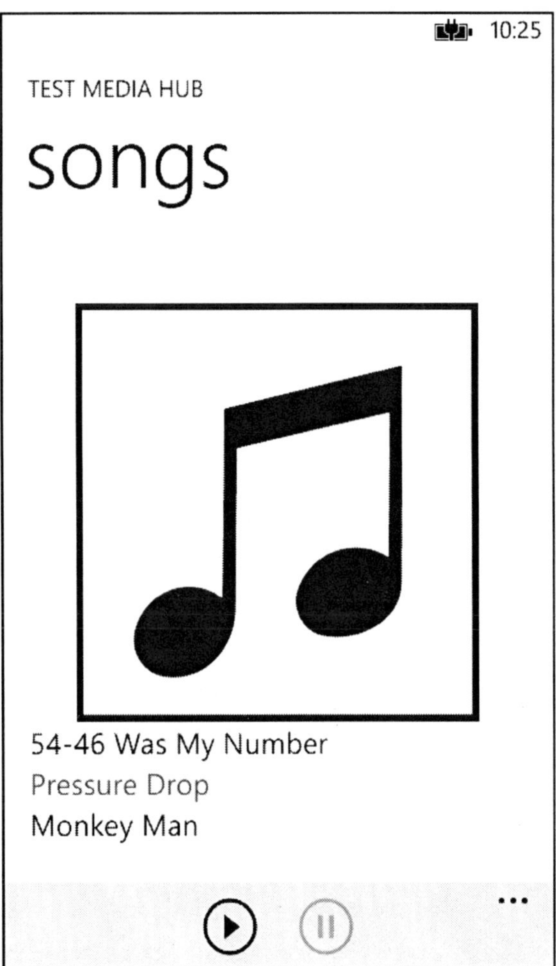

FIGURE 5-13 Your app can integrate with the Music and Videos Hub on the phone.

The *MainPage* class declares fields for the *MediaLibrary* itself and for the current *Song*. As always, you need to ensure that you pump the XNA message queue. Next, we initialize the *MediaLibrary* field and set the collection of *Songs* to be the *ItemsSource* on your *ListBox*. In the XAML, we data-bind the *Text* property on the *ListBox* items to the *Name* property on each *Song*.

```
private MediaLibrary library;
private Song currentSong;

public MainPage()
{
    InitializeComponent();
```

```
    Play = ApplicationBar.Buttons[0] as ApplicationBarIconButton;
    Pause = ApplicationBar.Buttons[1] as ApplicationBarIconButton;

    DispatcherTimer dt = new DispatcherTimer();
    dt.Interval = TimeSpan.FromMilliseconds(33);
    dt.Tick += delegate { FrameworkDispatcher.Update(); };
    dt.Start();

    library = new MediaLibrary();
    HistoryList.ItemsSource = library.Songs;
}
```

You can't effectively test this on the emulator, because it has no songs. If you test on a physical device, you would want one that has a representative number of songs. If there are very many songs on the device, initializing the list could be slow—and in this case you could restrict the test to perhaps the first album by using the following syntax:

```
HistoryList.ItemsSource = library.Albums.First().Songs;
```

The app's play and pause operations are more or less self-explanatory, invoking the *MediaPlayer Play* or *Pause* methods.

```
private void Play_Click(object sender, EventArgs e)
{
    MediaPlayer.Play(currentSong);
    Pause.IsEnabled = true;
    Play.IsEnabled = false;
}

private void Pause_Click(object sender, EventArgs e)
{
    MediaPlayer.Pause();
    Play.IsEnabled = true;
}
```

The interesting work is done in the *SelectionChanged* handler for the *ListBox*. Here, we fetch the currently selected item and fetch its album art to render in an *Image* control in the app's UI. If we can't find any corresponding album art, we use a default image built in to the app.

```
private void HistoryList_SelectionChanged(object sender, SelectionChangedEventArgs e)
{
    if (HistoryList.SelectedIndex == -1)
    {
        return;
    }

    currentSong = HistoryList.SelectedItem as Song;
    if (currentSong != null)
    {
        Play.IsEnabled = true;
```

```
            Stream albumArtStream = currentSong.Album.GetAlbumArt();
            if (albumArtStream == null)
            {
                StreamResourceInfo albumArtPlaceholder =
                    App.GetResourceStream(new Uri(
                        "Assets/AlbumArtPlaceholder.jpg", UriKind.Relative));
                albumArtStream = albumArtPlaceholder.Stream;
            }
            BitmapImage albumArtImage = new BitmapImage();
            albumArtImage.SetSource(albumArtStream);
            MediaImage.Source = albumArtImage;
        }
    }
```

The Clipboard API

Windows Phone 8 includes programmatic support for the clipboard, albeit in a constrained manner. You can set text into the system-wide clipboard, but you cannot extract text from it programmatically. This constraint is for security and privacy reasons, and it ensures that the user is always in control of where the clipboard contents might be sent. Figure 5-14 shows the *TestClipboard* application in the sample code.

This example offers a *RichTextBox* at the top with a *Button* below it, and a regular *TextBox* at the bottom. The *RichTextBox* is populated with some dummy text. The reason for this choice of controls is that you want to get your text from a control that supports selection of its contents, which the *RichTextBox* does. You also need to make an editable text control available into which the user can paste; hence, the *TextBox*. When the user taps the button, you arbitrarily select some or all of the text in the *RichTextBox* and then set this text into the clipboard by using the static *Clipboard.SetText* method.

```
private void copyText_Click(object sender, RoutedEventArgs e)
{
    textSource.SelectAll();
    Clipboard.SetText(textSource.Selection.Text);
}
```

After this, if and when the user chooses to tap the regular *TextBox*, the standard phone UI will show the Soft Input Panel (SIP) and include a paste icon, indicating that there is some text in the clipboard. If the user taps this icon, the clipboard contents are pasted into the *TextBox*. This last operation is outside your control and is handled entirely by the phone platform. Be aware that the clipboard is cleared whenever the phone lock engages.

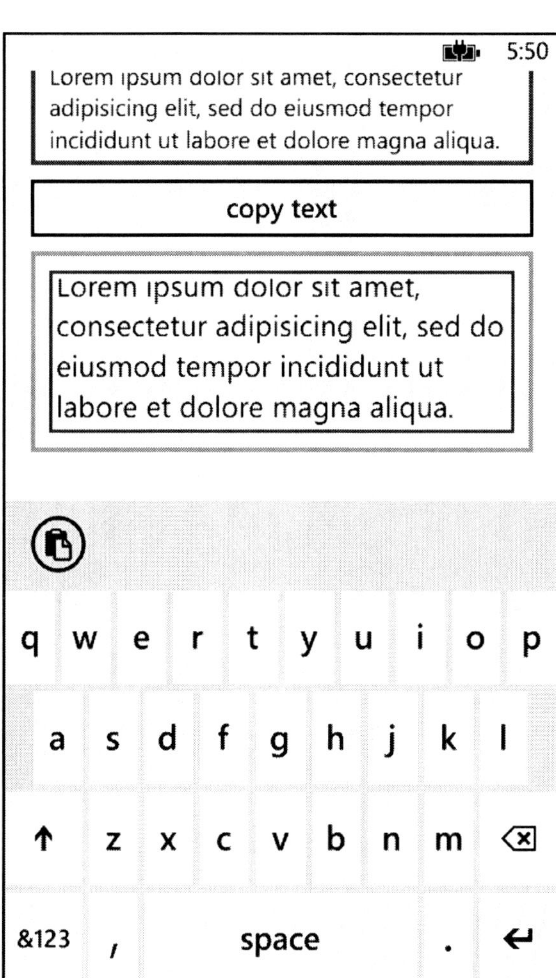

FIGURE 5-14 A simple clipboard application.

Summary

In this chapter, you examined the different levels and types of app platform support for integrating your app with standard features and services on the phone. Built-in apps such as the camera, email, browser, search, and connection to the Windows Phone Store are all exposed by a consistent set of wrapper classes that take care of the complex internal behavior and cross-app hook-ups, all while providing a developer-friendly API surface with which to work. The app platform also provides three broad categories of API support for building audio and video features into your app. There are three main classes for media playback at varying levels of flexibility. Audio input via the microphone and low-level manipulation of audio data is enabled through a second set of classes. Integration with the phone's media hub is enabled through the XNA *MediaLibrary* class. With judicious use of these APIs, you can easily build a very compelling, media-focused user experience into your app. Additional *MediaLibrary* extensibility is covered in Chapter 16, "Camera and photos."

CHAPTER 6

Sensors

In addition to the core cellular phone hardware, Windows Phone devices also support a range of additional hardware features. These features are of varying relevance to the app developer. For instance, all app developers need to be aware of and work with the constraints of the various screen resolutions. On the other hand, although the ambient light sensor is a very handy user-oriented feature, it is not programmable by app developers. The hardware features that attract the most developer focus (apart from the screen) are the camera (discussed in Chapter 16, "Camera and photos"), Near Field Communication (NFC) (Chapter 17, "Networking and proximity"), and GPS (Chapter 18, "Location and maps"). In this chapter, you'll explore the various levels of application support and your choices for using the three primary sensors: the accelerometer, the compass, and the gyroscope.

Orientation

For some apps, you design the user interface (UI) to work in portrait mode; for others, landscape is more appropriate. For some apps, you might want to support both portrait and landscape. There are no hard guidelines on which orientation(s) to support in an app, except that if your app includes keyboard input (via the Soft Input Panel [SIP] or hardware keyboard), you should allow for the user to switch to landscape. The SIP in portrait mode has very small keys and is therefore harder to use than in landscape mode. Conversely, the problem with landscape mode is that it leaves very little vertical space for your controls, which makes multiline editing especially problematic. Also, consider that the phone might have a hardware keyboard, which could be portrait or landscape, and it would clearly be quite difficult for the user to employ the landscape hardware keyboard if your application only supports portrait mode. It is also rare to support only landscape mode; the common exceptions to this are games and video-based applications.

If you want to support both portrait and landscape, you need to handle changes in device orientation. To do this, the first step is to set the *SupportedOrientations* attribute to *PortraitOrLandscape*—you'd need to do this for every page on which you want this behavior.

```
<phone:PhoneApplicationPage
...
    SupportedOrientations="PortraitOrLandscape"  Orientation="Portrait"
    >
```

If you specify *SupportedOrientations* of *Landscape* only, but at the same time set *Orientation* to *Portrait*, the *SupportedOrientations* is honored and the *Orientation* is ignored, and vice versa. Also, there are actually two landscape modes (*LandscapeLeft* and *LandscapeRight*), which function as you would expect. There is no way to force or disable either one of these. There are also two portrait modes (*PortraitUp* and *PortraitDown*), but only *PortraitUp* is used—there is no "upside-down" portrait mode. Be aware that there is no programmatic way to switch orientations. You can do this to a degree by updating your *SupportedOrientations* property in code. The device will comply with this, but you cannot force *Left* or *Right*.

If your page layout is very simple, this might be enough. More commonly, however, you'll find that you need to adjust the layout differently for the two modes. For this, you have a couple of options: either handle the *OrientationChanged* event at the page level to rearrange your controls; or use a container control that handles the change for you. Consider the *WrapOrientation* solution in the sample code, which uses a *WrapPanel* to handle orientation changes automatically.

The *WrapPanel* is one of the controls in the Windows Phone Toolkit. This is most suitable if you have a list of items that are all the same size, and you want them to rearrange themselves according to orientation changes. The screenshots in Figures 6-1 and 6-2 illustrate this. In portrait mode, the app displays two columns and three rows, whereas in landscape mode, it lays out the elements in three columns and two rows.

The app has a list of photos that are displayed in a *ListBox*, which in turn is hosted in a *WrapPanel*.

```
<ListBox
    Margin="{StaticResource PhoneHorizontalMargin}" x:Name="PhotoList">
    <ListBox.ItemsPanel>
        <ItemsPanelTemplate>
            <toolkit:WrapPanel x:Name="PhotoPanel"/>
        </ItemsPanelTemplate>
    </ListBox.ItemsPanel>
    <ListBox.ItemTemplate>
        <DataTemplate>
            <Border Width="210" Height="160" >
                <Image
                    Width="200" Height="150"
                    Source="{Binding}" CacheMode="BitmapCache"
                    Stretch="UniformToFill" HorizontalAlignment="Left" />
            </Border>
        </DataTemplate>
    </ListBox.ItemTemplate>
</ListBox>
```

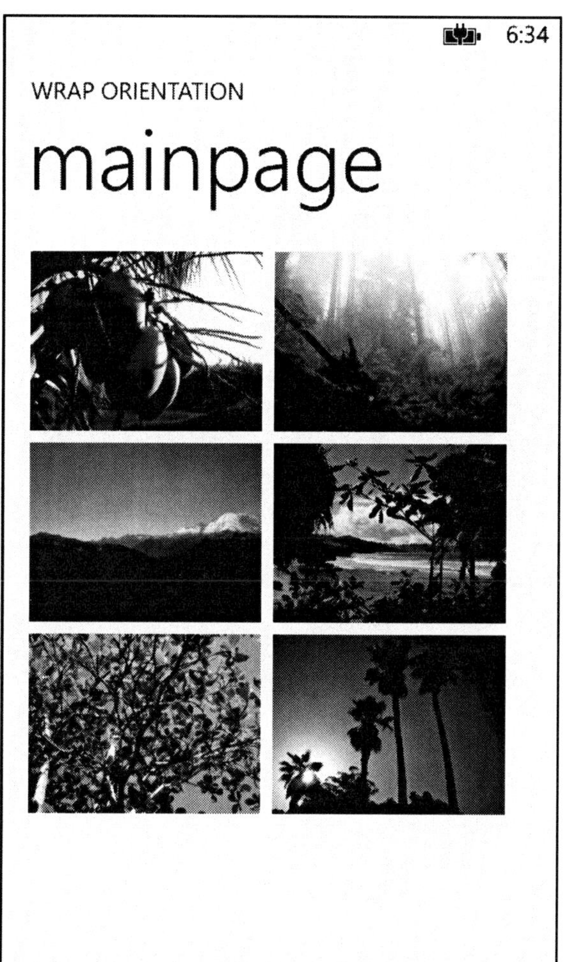

FIGURE 6-1 A *WrapPanel* in *Portrait* mode.

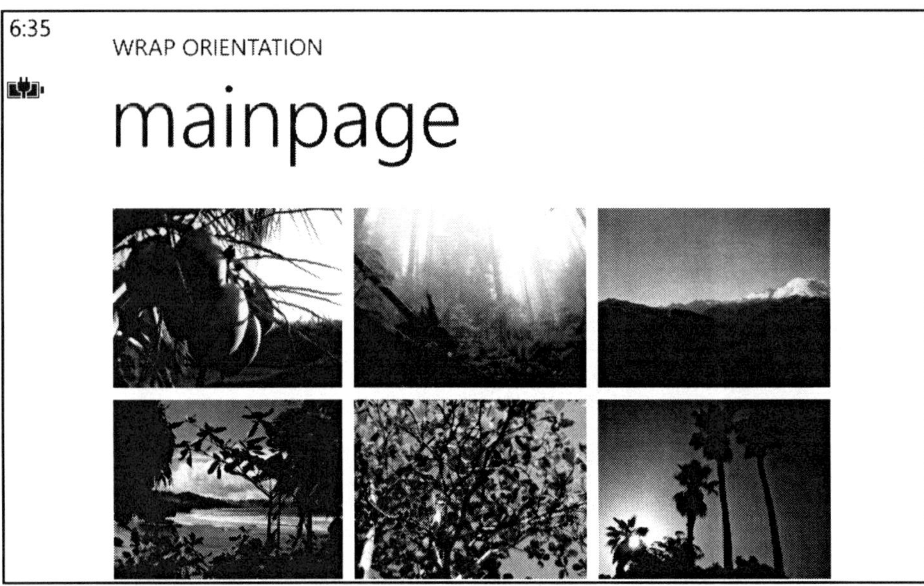

FIGURE 6-2 The same *WrapPanel* in *Landscape* mode.

There is no need to handle *OrientationChanged* events manually, because the *WrapPanel* dynamically adjusts its size according to the new *Width* and *Height* of the screen whenever the orientation changes. It also lays out its child elements within the constraints of its overall size and doesn't allow any of them to be clipped or omitted.

Phone hardware

The Windows Phone chassis specification is the set of minimum hardware standards specified by Microsoft to which all Windows Phone devices must adhere. All Windows Phone devices include a cellular radio; a true multitouch screen; vibration, accelerometer, ambient light and proximity sensors; and a GPS receiver. Table 6-1 summarizes the minimum hardware requirements. You should be aware that all devices must support the required features, and they can also support any or all of the optional features.

TABLE 6-1 Minimum hardware requirements and recommendations for Windows Phone 8

Component	Feature	Requirement	Description
Screen	Type	Required	LCD or OLED.
	Screen size	Required	One of the following: WVGA (800x400), 15:9 aspect ratio, 3.5" to 5" diagonal size 720p (1280x720), 16:9 aspect ratio, 3.5" to 7" diagonal size WXGA (1280x768), 16:9 aspect ratio, 3.5" to 7" diagonal size
	Touch support	Required	True multitouch, supporting ≥4 distinct touch points.

Component	Feature	Requirement	Description
Sensors	A-GNNS	Required	Assisted Global Navigation Satellite System receiver (helps to obtain a faster time to fix location, especially when GPS signals are weak or not available).
	Ambient light	Required	Dynamic range from 0 lux to ≥4,000 lux.
	Proximity	Required	Detects the presence of nearby objects without physical contact. This is used mainly to conserve battery power by turning off the screen when the phone senses that the user is on a call (phone is close to the ear) or that it is in a pocket/handbag.
	Vibration	Required	Motor, speaker, or haptics transducer, used to vibrate the phone as a quieter alternative to the phone's ringer.
	NFC	Optional	If implemented, peer-to-peer exchange and reader/writer mode are required; card emulation is optional.
	Accelerometer	Required	Three-axis, with hardware sampling rate up to 100 Hz.
	Magnetometer (Compass)	Optional	Three-axis, with sampling rate of 60 Hz.
	Gyroscope	Optional	Three-axis, with sampling rate from 5 Hz to ≥250 Hz. If the device has a gyroscope, it must also have a compass.

Sensor APIs

As an app developer, you must keep in mind that certain sensors are optional. You should therefore design your app to allow for the possibility that some of the sensors you expect to use might not in fact be present on a given device.

Note Some sensors, such as the magnetometer, are susceptible to environmental conditions (in particular, electromagnetic interference from nearby objects or from the phone itself), which can introduce significant errors in the reported readings. As a result, the sensors need recalibration from time to time to report meaningful values. This calibration is generally handled internally by the hardware/driver. The compass is the only sensor for which user calibration is required.

The APIs for the accelerometer, compass, and gyroscope share a high degree of consistency, and they all derive from the *SensorBase<T>* base class, where *T* is a sensor reading type. All public sensor methods are actually methods defined in *SensorBase<T>*. This is because most of the functionality required by developers is actually common to all sensors: the ability to start and stop the sensor and the *CurrentValueChanged* event, which is raised whenever the sensor data is changed. In fact, there are four derived classes: *Accelerometer, Compass, Gyroscope*, and *Motion*. The *Motion* class represents a logical compound sensor, which is discussed later in this chapter. One of the first decisions you need to make when building a sensor-based app is whether you need the fine-grained data readings provided by the lower-level sensor classes, or if the higher-level *Motion* class is sufficient for your needs. The following sections explore all four sensor classes.

The accelerometer

The accelerometer sensor detects changes in the physical acceleration of the phone and reports these as changes in X,Y,Z orientation. When it detects a change, it raises an event. You can use the accelerometer in your application to determine the phone's orientation at any point in time and therefore react to changes in orientation over time.

Be aware that the accuracy of the accelerometer at any point depends on the Earth's gravity being a constant everywhere on the planet—which it isn't—and on the user's ability to keep the phone completely steady—which is very difficult, even when it's laid flat on a table. The accelerometer assumes a baseline gravity of 9.81m/s^2, when in fact the Earth's gravity varies from 9.78 m/s^2 to 9.83 m/s^2. The effect of centrifugal force due to the Earth's rotation means that gravity increases with latitude (it's higher at the poles than at the equator). Gravity also decreases with altitude, and the density and composition of the local rocks can also affect it.

You can use the *Accelerometer* class in the *Microsoft.Devices.Sensors* namespace to start and stop the accelerometer and to respond to the events. Note that this is not the same as the *Accelerometer* class in the *Windows.Devices.Sensors* namespace. As the underlying sensor provides data readings to the application layer, these are surfaced in the form of *SensorReadingEventArgs<AccelerometerReading>* events. The *AccelerometerReading* type exposes an *Acceleration* property, which indicates the values of the force applied to the phone in the X,Y,Z planes, in the range –1.0 to +1.0, as illustrated in Figure 6-3.

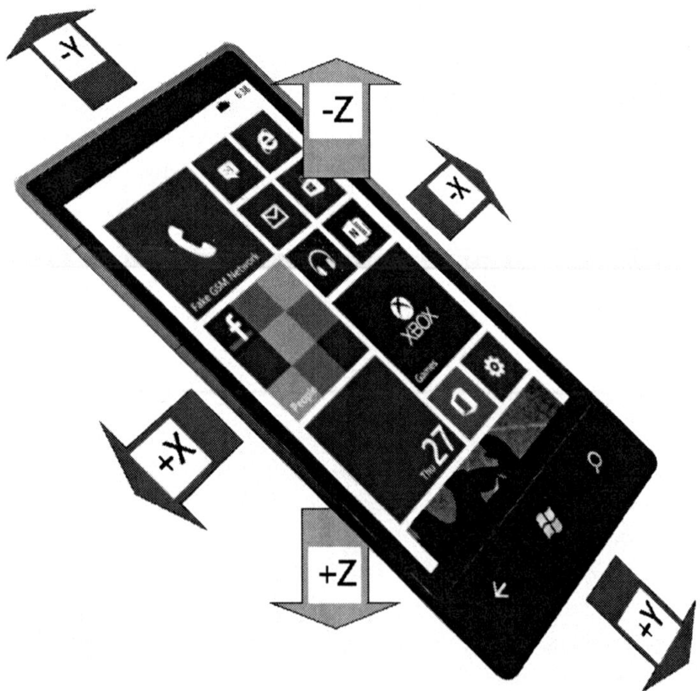

FIGURE 6-3 Accelerometer events specify the force applied in the X,Y,Z planes.

The range of values for each axis is from –1.0 to 1.0. Table 6-2 shows the X, Y, and Z minimum and maximum values for six different orientations.

TABLE 6-2 Minima and maxima for X,Y,Z planes

Orientation	X	Y	Z
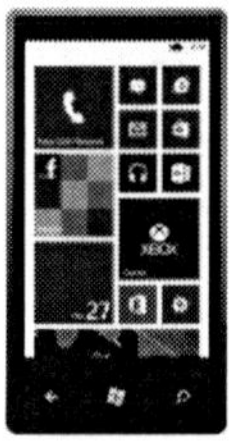	0	–1	0
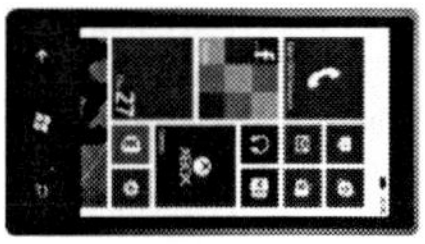	+1	0	0
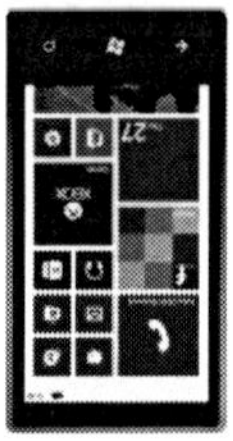	0	+1	0
	–1	0	0
Face 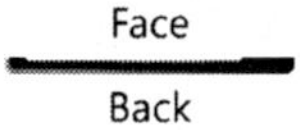 Back	0	0	–1
Back 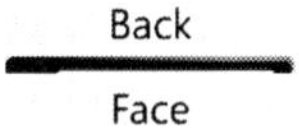 Face	0	0	+1

The *SimpleAccelerometer* solution in the sample code demonstrates the basics of programming the accelerometer. The UI offers a *TextBlock* and an app bar button. The button acts as a toggle by which the user can start or stop the accelerometer. It is important to give the user a way to control the accelerometer because running it constantly will eventually drain the battery. When the user toggles the accelerometer on, the app instantiates a new *Accelerometer* object and wires up the *CurrentValueChanged* event. When the user toggles the accelerometer off, the app unregisters the event handler, stops the accelerometer, and sets the object reference to null so that it becomes available for garbage collection.

```
private Accelerometer accelerometer;

private void appBarStopGo_Click(object sender, EventArgs e)
{
    if (accelerometer == null)
    {
        accelerometer = new Accelerometer();
        accelerometer.CurrentValueChanged += accelerometer_CurrentValueChanged;
        try
        {
            accelerometer.Start();
            appBarStopGo.Text = AppResources.AppBarStopText;
        }
        catch (AccelerometerFailedException ex)
        {
            statusText.Text = ex.ToString();
        }
    }
    else
    {
        accelerometer.CurrentValueChanged -= accelerometer_CurrentValueChanged;
        try
        {
            accelerometer.Stop();
            accelerometer = null;
            statusText.Text = "Accelerometer stopped";
            appBarStopGo.Text = AppResources.AppBarGoText;
        }
        catch (AccelerometerFailedException ex)
        {
            statusText.Text = ex.ToString();
        }
    }
}
```

When the app receives accelerometer *CurrentValueChanged* events, it extracts the X,Y,Z axis values to compose a string for the *TextBlock*. These events come in on a different thread from the UI thread, so you need to dispatch the action to the UI thread via the *Dispatcher* property on that page. You might be wondering why the *Accelerometer* uses the generic *SensorReadingEventArgs<T>* type instead of something more specific—perhaps an *AccelerometerReadingEventArgs* type. In fact, in Windows Phone 7.0, this is exactly the type that the *Accelerometer* class did use. However, this changed in Windows Phone 7.1, when all sensor classes were rationalized such that they now derive from a *SensorBase<T>* base class. For example, the *Accelerometer* class derives from *SensorBase<AccelerometerReading>*. This pattern has been brought forward to Windows Phone 8.

Another point worth mentioning here is that the *AccelerometerReading* type exposes the X,Y,Z axis values via the *Acceleration* property, which is of type *Vector3*. Sensors in Windows Phone use a 3D world coordinate system that is based on the system used in the XNA framework. *Vector3* is defined in the *Microsoft.Xna.Framework* namespace, so using this will transparently pull in the corresponding XNA assembly (in a Windows Phone 8 project—in a Windows Phone 7 project, you need to add the reference manually).

```
private void accelerometer_CurrentValueChanged(
    object sender, SensorReadingEventArgs<AccelerometerReading> e)
{
    AccelerometerReading reading = e.SensorReading;
    Vector3 acceleration = reading.Acceleration;
    Dispatcher.BeginInvoke(() =>
    {
        statusText.Text = String.Format("X={0:0.00}, Y={1:0.00}, Z={2:0.00}",
            acceleration.X, acceleration.Y, acceleration.Z);
    });
}
```

The emulator includes support for testing the accelerometer, as shown in Figure 6-4. You access this from the additional tools button on the main emulator, which brings up a window that includes an *Accelerometer* tab. To test your app's accelerometer code, drag the orange dot around the window. As you drag the dot, the X, Y, and Z coordinates are updated based on the rotation calculations, and those same values are passed into your app via the accelerometer readings.

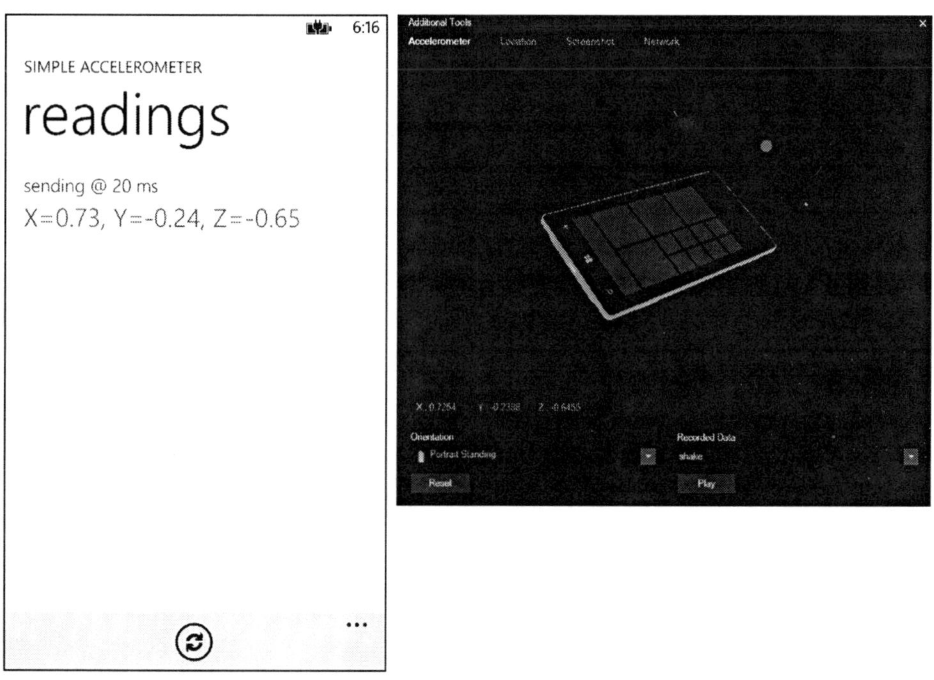

FIGURE 6-4 The accelerometer app and simulator.

The *Accelerometer* class also provides the option to specify the preferred time interval between reading updates by setting the *TimeBetweenUpdates* property. This is another property inherited from *SensorBase<T>*. In the sample solution, this additional statement continues the *CurrentValue Changed* handler.

```
Dispatcher.BeginInvoke(() =>
{
    statusText.Text = String.Format("sending @ {0} ms", accelerometer.TimeBetweenUpdates.
Milliseconds);
});
```

You should keep in mind that the specific sensor on any given device might not support the requested interval. The API layer for the sensor (that is, the *Accelerometer, Compass, Gyroscope*, and *Motion* classes) rounds the input value to the closest value that is actually permitted on the device. If you want to see the actual value used, you can examine the *TimeBetweenUpdates* property after you set it. Typical values for shipping devices as of this writing are presented in Table 6-3. In the examples in this chapter, each application is handling the incoming sensor data to display some UI. For this reason, the *TimeBetweenUpdates* property is set consistently to 33 ms, which corresponds to the optimum screen frame rate.

TABLE 6-3 *TimeBetweenUpdates* interval settings for all sensors

Sensor	*TimeBetweenUpdate* interval (minimum and multiples, thereof)
Accelerometer	20 ms
Compass	25 ms
Gyroscope	5 ms
Motion	17 ms

This illustrates the basic code requirements for working with the accelerometer, although a realistic application would do something more interesting with the X,Y,Z data.

Reactive extensions

Responding to sensor reading events is, by its very nature, reactive. That is, you write code to react to events that arrive asynchronously in your app. If you think of the wider context of mobile device software, you'll realize that almost anything non-trivial that you do involves asynchronous operations. Managing such operations manually can become complex and difficult to maintain. The Reactive Extensions for .NET (Rx), implemented in *System.Observable.dll* and *Microsoft.Phone.Reactive.dll*, is a library that you can use in your app to simplify your code.

Using Rx, you can treat sequences of events as collections rather than as independent events, which makes it possible for you to apply filter and aggregation behavior to the events. You can perform Language-Integrated Query (LINQ) operations on the sequence or compose multiple events into a higher-level virtual event. This capability is particularly useful in high-volume scenarios, such as sensor events, geo-location events, or low-level touch manipulation events. Rx ships as part of Microsoft .NET Framework 4.0 and also with the Windows Phone SDK. You can read more about it at *http://msdn.microsoft.com/en-us/data/gg577609*.

The *FilteredAccelerometer* app in the sample code is a variation on the earlier *SimpleAccelerometer* sample. This version adds a *bool* field to determine whether to apply filtering, and an additional app bar button with which the user can toggle the flag.

```
private bool isFiltered = false;

private void appBarFilterOnOff_Click(object sender, EventArgs e)
{
    isFiltered = !isFiltered;
    if (isFiltered)
    {
        appBarFilterOnOff.Text = "filter on";
    }
    else
    {
        appBarFilterOnOff.Text = "filter off";
    }
}
```

Instead of wiring up a handler for the *CurrentValueChanged* events, the app adds incoming events to an observable collection—an *IObservable<IEvent<>>*—and then subscribes to that collection. The effect of this is that your event handler is invoked when the observable collection changes. The collection changes whenever a *CurrentValueChanged* event is added to the sequence. The *Subscribe* method of the *IObservable<IEvent<>>* type returns an *IDisposable*. As a result, you can unhook the event handler and clean up when you need to by disposing of the object. To support this, you need to add a couple of *IDisposable* fields to your page class.

```
private IDisposable eventsSubscription;
private IDisposable filteredEventsSubscription;
```

The code for hooking up (and unhooking) the event handler is a little obscure.

```
accelerometer = new Accelerometer();
//accelerometer.CurrentValueChanged += accelerometer_CurrentValueChanged;
var rawEvents =
    Observable.FromEvent<SensorReadingEventArgs<AccelerometerReading>>
    (ev => accelerometer.CurrentValueChanged += ev,
        ev => accelerometer.CurrentValueChanged -= ev);
```

If you right-click *FromEvent* and go to the definition, you'll see that this makes a little more sense, with *addHandler* and *removeHandler Action<T>* parameters.

```
public static IObservable<IEvent<TEventArgs>> FromEvent<TEventArgs>(
    Action<EventHandler<TEventArgs>> addHandler,
    Action<EventHandler<TEventArgs>> removeHandler)
    where TEventArgs : EventArgs;
```

This slightly awkward-looking pattern arises because of certain constraints on events in the .NET framework that restrict the extent to which they can be used in type inference with generics. However, appearances aside, this is actually a very efficient mechanism for feeding events into the collection.

The only other change in our application is in the Start/Stop button *Click* handler. Now, when the app starts the accelerometer, it also creates an *IObservable<IEvent<>>* collection based on the *CurrentValueChanged* events. If the filter flag is off, the app simply subscribes to the full collection of events. On the other hand, if the filter flag is on, the app first samples the sequence before subscribing to it. In this example, the app samples the incoming data every second. Later, when the user asks to stop the accelerometer, the app first disposes of the subscription objects (which will unhook the events) before cleaning up the *Accelerometer* object, as done earlier.

```
private void appBarStopGo_Click(object sender, EventArgs e)
{
    if (accelerometer == null)
    {
        accelerometer = new Accelerometer();
        //accelerometer.CurrentValueChanged += accelerometer_CurrentValueChanged;
        var rawEvents =
            Observable.FromEvent<SensorReadingEventArgs<AccelerometerReading>>
            (ev => accelerometer.CurrentValueChanged += ev,
            ev => accelerometer.CurrentValueChanged -= ev);

        if (!isFiltered)
        {
            eventsSubscription = rawEvents.Subscribe(
                args => accelerometer_CurrentValueChanged(args.Sender, args.EventArgs));
        }
        else
        {
            var sampledEvents =
                rawEvents.Sample<IEvent<SensorReadingEventArgs<AccelerometerReading>>>(
                TimeSpan.FromMilliseconds(1000));
            filteredEventsSubscription = sampledEvents.Subscribe(
                args => accelerometer_CurrentValueChanged(args.Sender, args.EventArgs));
        }

        try
        {
            accelerometer.Start();
            statusText.Text = "started";
            appBarStopGo.Text = "stop";
        }
        catch (AccelerometerFailedException ex)
        {
            statusText.Text = ex.ToString();
        }
    }
    else
    {
        //accelerometer.CurrentValueChanged -= accelerometer_CurrentValueChanged;
        if (eventsSubscription != null)
        {
            eventsSubscription.Dispose();
        }
        if (filteredEventsSubscription != null)
        {
            filteredEventsSubscription.Dispose();
        }
```

```
        try
        {
            accelerometer.Stop();
            accelerometer = null;
            statusText.Text = "stopped";
            appBarStopGo.Text = "go";
        }
        catch (AccelerometerFailedException ex)
        {
            statusText.Text = ex.ToString();
        }
    }
}
```

From the user's perspective, the net result of this is that the accelerometer text value only changes every second, regardless of how fast she moves the device.

Note Developers sometimes ask what the relationship is between Rx and the task-based (*await/async*) asynchronous model in C#, because there seems—superficially at least—to be some overlap. The answer is that these are not competing technologies; rather, they are complementary. You can use task-based asynchronous operations together with Rx to orchestrate processing that is initially sourced in an event stream.

The Level Starter Kit

The Level Starter Kit for Windows Phone was first released in 2010, targeting Windows Phone 7. As of this writing, it still works just fine with Windows Phone 8 apps, although by default it uses a deprecated event. You can download this kit from *http://msdn.microsoft.com/en-us/library/windowsphone/develop/gg442298(v=vs.92).aspx*. At this time, it is not clear whether (or when) this might be updated specifically for Windows Phone 8. However, the kit is supplied in source-code format, and you can easily make minor changes to bring it up to date.

This kit provides a complete level app, which you can adapt for your own purposes. More useful, if you're not actually building a level app, you can still take advantage of the core wrapper classes: the *AccelerationHelper* and the *DeviceOrientationHelper*. The *AccelerationHelper* provides methods to calibrate the accelerometer as well as to smooth out the raw accelerometer data stream. Strictly speaking, the code does not actually calibrate the accelerometer, of course, because your application cannot write to the system's accelerometer driver. Rather, the code calibrates itself; it computes the practical values for the X and Y axes when the phone is at rest, face up on a horizontal surface. All other things being equal, this should provide X,Y values of 0,0, and the calibration allows for variations in local gravity, device shake, and so on.

Smoothing out the raw data is useful because the raw data stream comes in at 50 data points per second (50 Hz). The earlier accelerometer sample apps smoothed this out by sampling the data only every second. Sampling the data is often useful, but it is a fairly crude approach and risks losing data that might otherwise be of interest.

Exactly how you use the accelerometer depends on the specifics of the app you're building. In some cases, an *n*-second sample is exactly what you want. In other cases, you might need to see every data point in the incoming stream. Both of these are simple but inflexible. In a more sophisticated scenario, you might want to smooth the data by ignoring changes that fall below some threshold. This approach reveals a "bigger picture" trend in the data rather than focusing on the individual data points.

The *AccelerometerHelper* class includes some signal processing functionality to apply smoothing to the data stream in a number of different ways, as described here:

- **Averaging** This averages the data over time by using an arithmetic mean of the last 25 samples (the last 500 ms of data). This provides a very stable reading, but there is an obvious delay introduced by waiting for the 25 samples before computing the average. Obviously, you can adjust the number of samples, increasing the value to improve the average at the cost of increased latency, or reducing it to make the averaging less smooth but faster.
- **Low-pass filtering** This flattens the data stream to eliminate the main sensor noise. Essentially, the current value is adjusted to make it closer to the previous one.
- **Optimal filtering** This combines the low-pass filtering with a threshold-based, high-pass filter to eliminate most of the low-amplitude noise, while trending very quickly to large offsets, and with very low latency.

Here are the basic steps for reusing the *AccelerometerHelper* from the Level Starter Kit:

1. Create a Phone Application project named, for example, **TestAccelerometerHelper**.
2. Add a Class Library project to this solution. Name it **AccelerometerHelper**.
3. Add existing items to the class library: the *AccelerometerHelper.cs*, *ApplicationSettingHelper.cs*, and *Simple3DVector.cs*.
4. Build the *AccelerometerHelper* class library.
5. In the *TestAccelerometerHelper* project, add a reference to the *AccelerometerHelper* class library.
6. In the application, hook up the *ReadingChanged* event on the singleton *AccelerometerHelper* instance and then start the accelerometer by setting the *IsActive* property to *true*.

   ReadingChanged is obsolete (Windows Phone 8 apps use *CurrentValueChanged* in preference); you'll see how to change this later.
7. In your *ReadingChanged* event handler, retrieve the *AccelerometerHelperReadingEventArgs* values and then do something interesting with them.

Figure 6-5 shows the *TestAccelerometerHelper* solution in the sample code. The app fetches the X, Y, and Z values for all four of the data sets (the raw data, plus the three smoothed streams).

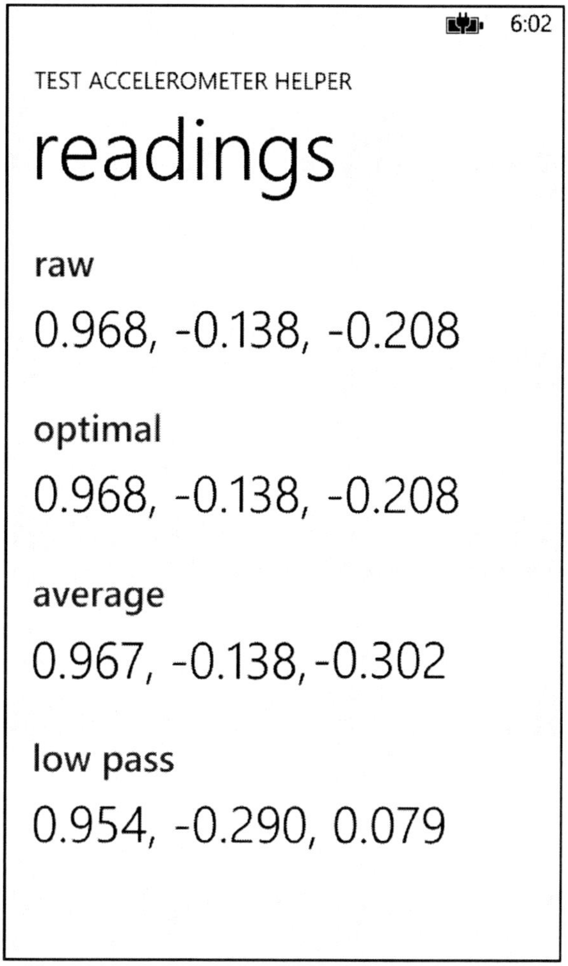

6:02

TEST ACCELEROMETER HELPER

readings

raw

0.968, -0.138, -0.208

optimal

0.968, -0.138, -0.208

average

0.967, -0.138,-0.302

low pass

0.954, -0.290, 0.079

FIGURE 6-5 You can use the *AccelerometerHelper* class to apply smoothing to the raw readings.

The XAML in this application defines a *Grid* comprising four rows of label *TextBlock* controls ("raw," "optimal," "average," and "low pass") and four rows of data *TextBlock* controls. The only custom code in the app is in the *MainPage*, which hooks up and handles the *ReadingChanged* event.

```
public MainPage()
{
    InitializeComponent();
    AccelerometerHelper.Instance.ReadingChanged += OnAccelerometerHelperReadingChanged;
    AccelerometerHelper.Instance.IsActive = true;
}

private void OnAccelerometerHelperReadingChanged(object sender,
AccelerometerHelperReadingEventArgs e)
```

```
{
    Dispatcher.BeginInvoke(() =>
    {
        raw.Text = String.Format("{0:0.000}, {1:0.000}, {2:0.000}",
            e.RawAcceleration.X, e.RawAcceleration.Y, e.RawAcceleration.Z);
        optimal.Text = String.Format("{0:0.000}, {1:0.000}, {2:0.000}",
            e.OptimallyFilteredAcceleration.X, e.OptimallyFilteredAcceleration.Y,
            e.OptimallyFilteredAcceleration.Z);
        average.Text = String.Format("{0:0.000}, {1:0.000}, {2:0.000}",
            e.AverageAcceleration.X, e.AverageAcceleration.Y, e.AverageAcceleration.Z);
        lowPass.Text = String.Format("{0:0.000}, {1:0.000}, {2:0.000}",
            e.LowPassFilteredAcceleration.X, e.LowPassFilteredAcceleration.Y,
            e.LowPassFilteredAcceleration.Z);
    });
}
```

The data sets are listed in order of latency, given the current settings for things such as the number of data points to average, and so on. The raw data stream is unprocessed, so there's effectively zero latency in rendering the data to the UI. At the other end, the processing for the low-pass data takes the longest time. Increasing the number of data points to average will generally add latency to the averaging data set. When this application runs, the raw data values stabilize rapidly, whereas the higher-latency data sets take longer to stabilize.

If you want to update the library to use *CurrentValueChanged* in place of the obsolete *Reading Changed* event, this is a simple matter; all you need do is to make a few changes to the *Accelerometer Helper* class. First, replace the *ReadingChanged*-based public event with an equivalent *CurrentValue Changed*-based event.

```
//public event EventHandler<AccelerometerHelperReadingEventArgs> ReadingChanged;
public event EventHandler<AccelerometerHelperReadingEventArgs> CurrentValueChanged;
```

Next, update the *StartAccelerometer* method to wire up the underlying *CurrentValueChanged* event instead of the old *ReadingChanged* event handler. Also do the equivalent in the *StopAccelerometer* method to unhook the *CurrentValueChanged* event.

```
private void StartAccelerometer()
{
    try
    {
        _sensor = new Accelerometer();
        if (_sensor != null)
        {
            //_sensor.ReadingChanged +=
            //  new EventHandler<AccelerometerReadingEventArgs>(sensor_ReadingChanged);
            _sensor.CurrentValueChanged += _sensor_CurrentValueChanged;

    ... unchanged code omitted for brevity.
    }
}
```

All the real work is done in the event handler. You can keep almost all the old code—just replace the definition to be your *CurrentValueChanged* event handler, dig a little deeper into the event argument to extract the X, Y, and Z values, and then invoke the exposed *CurrentValueChanged*-based event property.

```
private void _sensor_CurrentValueChanged(object sender,
                                         SensorReadingEventArgs<AccelerometerReading> e)
//private void sensor_ReadingChanged(object sender, AccelerometerReadingEventArgs e)
{
    ... unchanged code omitted for brevity.

    //Simple3DVector rawAcceleration = new Simple3DVector(e.X, e.Y, e.Z);
    Simple3DVector rawAcceleration = new Simple3DVector(
        e.SensorReading.Acceleration.X, e.SensorReading.Acceleration.Y,
            e.SensorReading.Acceleration.Z);

    ... unchanged code omitted for brevity.

    //if (ReadingChanged != null)
    if (CurrentValueChanged != null)
    {
    ... unchanged code omitted for brevity.
        //ReadingChanged(this, readingEventArgs);
        CurrentValueChanged(this, readingEventArgs);
    }
}
```

Finally, in your test app, you can wire up the new public *CurrentValueChanged* event in place of the old *ReadingChanged* event. You can see how all this comes together in the *TestAccelerometerHelper_CurrentValueChanged* solution in the sample code.

```
public MainPage()
{
    InitializeComponent();

    //AccelerometerHelper.Instance.ReadingChanged += OnAccelerometerHelperReadingChanged;
    AccelerometerHelper.Instance.CurrentValueChanged += Instance_CurrentValueChanged;
    AccelerometerHelper.Instance.IsActive = true;
}

private void Instance_CurrentValueChanged(object sender, AccelerometerHelperReadingEventArgs e)
//private void OnAccelerometerHelperReadingChanged(object sender,
AccelerometerHelperReadingEventArgs e)
{
    ... unchanged code omitted for brevity.
}
```

Figure 6-6 shows another example, this one focusing on the *DeviceOrientationHelper* class in the Level Starter Kit. This is the *TestOrientationHelper* solution in the sample code.

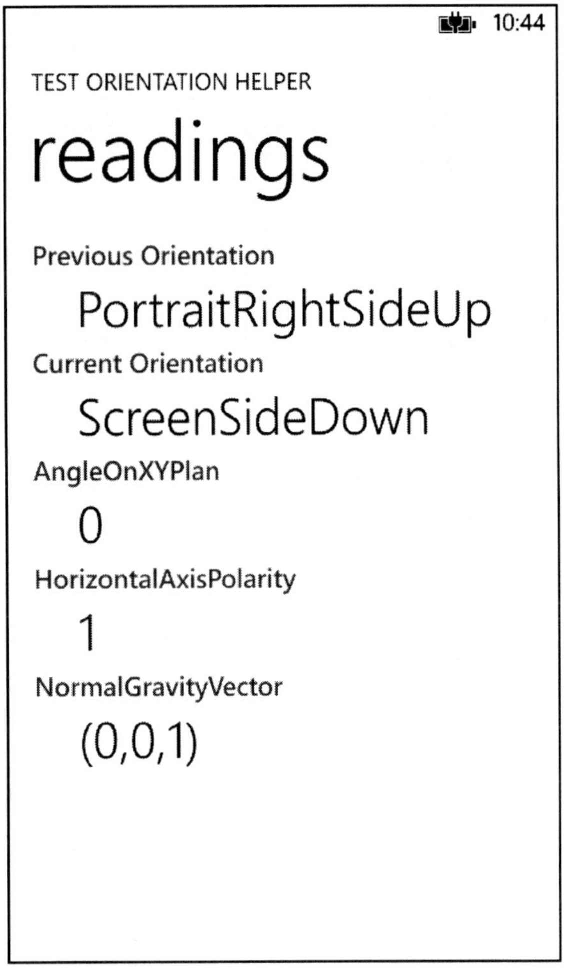

10:44

TEST ORIENTATION HELPER

readings

Previous Orientation

PortraitRightSideUp

Current Orientation

ScreenSideDown

AngleOnXYPlan

0

HorizontalAxisPolarity

1

NormalGravityVector

(0,0,1)

FIGURE 6-6 You can use the *DeviceOrientationHelper* class to smooth orientation readings.

The *DeviceOrientationHelper* uses the *AccelerometerHelper* underneath, because it also processes accelerometer reading events, taking the processed signal from the *AccelerometerHelper*.

Here are the basic steps for reusing the *DeviceOrientationHelper* from the Level Starter Kit:

1. Create a Phone Application project named, for example, **TestOrientationHelper**.
2. Add a Class Library project to this solution. Name it **OrientationHelper**.
3. Add existing items to the class library: the *AccelerometerHelper.cs*, *ApplicationSettingHelper.cs*, and *Simple3DVector.cs*, as before, plus the *DeviceOrientationInfo.cs* and *OrientationHelper.cs*.

   As before, you can either use the original *AccelerometerHelper* class or one that you have modified to use *CurrentValueChanged* instead of *ReadingChanged*.
4. Build the *OrientationHelper* class library.

5. In the *TestOrientationHelper* project, add a reference to the *OrientationHelper* class library.
6. In the application, hook up the *OrientationChanged* event on the singleton *OrientationHelper* instance.

   As before, start the accelerometer by setting the *IsActive* property on the *AccelerometerHelper* singleton instance to true.
7. In your *OrientationChanged* event handler, retrieve the *OrientationHelperReadingEventArgs* values and do something interesting with them.

If you're using an updated *CurrentValueChanged*-based *AccelerometerHelper* class, you can make corresponding changes in the *DeviceOrientationHelper* class. The first change is in the constructor, where you wire up a *CurrentChanged* event handler. The second change is to redefine the event handler to match. Everything else stays the same. Notice that this also means that the public interface for the *DeviceOrientationHelper* also stays the same.

```
private DeviceOrientationHelper()
{
... unchanged code omitted for brevity.

    //AccelerometerHelper.Instance.ReadingChanged += new
EventHandler<AccelerometerHelperReadingEventArgs>(accelerometerHelper_ReadingChanged);
    AccelerometerHelper.Instance.CurrentValueChanged += Instance_CurrentValueChanged;
}

// private void accelerometerHelper_ReadingChanged(object sender,
   AccelerometerHelperReadingEventArgs e)
private void Instance_CurrentValueChanged(object sender, AccelerometerHelperReadingEventArgs e)
{
    CheckOrientation(e.LowPassFilteredAcceleration);
}
```

The following code listing shows the simplest use of this in a client app, rendering the orientation values as strings. The client code is the same, regardless of whether you've updated the underlying *AccelerometerHelper* and *DeviceOrientationHelper* classes.

In the *OrientationChanged* event handler, the client can retrieve the current and previous orientation (an enumeration with the values: *Unknown, ScreenSideUp, ScreenSideDown, PortraitRightSideUp, LandscapeRight, LandscapeLeft, PortraitUpSideDown*), the *AngleOnXYPlan* (which will be 0° for vertical, or ±90° for horizontal), the *HorizontalAxisPolarity* (0 for vertical, or ±1 for horizontal), and the *NormalGravityVector* (X,Y,Z values).

```
public MainPage()
{
    InitializeComponent();
    AccelerometerHelper.Instance.IsActive = true;
    DeviceOrientationHelper.Instance.OrientationChanged += orientationHelper_OrientationChanged;
}
```

```
private void orientationHelper_OrientationChanged(object sender,
DeviceOrientationChangedEventArgs e)
{
    Dispatcher.BeginInvoke(() =>
    {
        previous.Text = e.PreviousOrientation.ToString();
        current.Text = e.CurrentOrientation.ToString();

        DeviceOrientationInfo doi =
            DeviceOrientationHelper.GetDeviceOrientationInfo(e.CurrentOrientation);
        angle.Text = doi.AngleOnXYPlan.ToString();
        polarity.Text = doi.HorizontalAxisPolarity.ToString();
        vector.Text = doi.NormalGravityVector.ToString();
    });
}
```

Shake

Just as low-level touch events can be modeled as more complex user-centric gestures such as pinch/stretch or flick, so too can raw accelerometer events be modeled as more complex user-centric gestures such as rotate or shake. If you analyze a shake gesture, it can be modeled as a series of accelerometer changes (typically on one axis) that oscillates between maxima in the two opposite directions of that dimension. In other words, it swings back and forth (or up and down, or left and right) with roughly the same extremes of value in both directions, and changes in the other two axes are effectively noise that should be ignored.

Microsoft provides a Shake Gesture Library, which is available at *http://aka.ms/WinPhone8DevInternals/CS*. As with the Level Starter Kit, this was originally built for Windows Phone 7, and although it has not been updated for Windows Phone 8, you can still use it successfully in Windows Phone 8 projects. You can use this to model shake gestures in your applications. This library also makes use of the *AccelerometerHelper* class available in the Level Starter Kit, primarily to smooth out the raw data stream before processing it. The core class in the Shake Gesture Library is the *ShakeGesturesHelper*, which takes the smoothed data and categorizes it into "shake" and "still" segments and then determines the signal boundaries to determine where the stream includes shake gestures.

It turns out that shake gestures are very individualized: different people shake differently, and different applications have different shake requirements. For this reason, the library includes several configuration options with which you can establish what constitutes a valid shake gesture for your application. These include settings for various thresholds, and minima/maxima for computing average.

Figure 6-7 illustrates an example application that uses the Shake Gesture Library (the *TestShakeHelper* solution in the sample code).

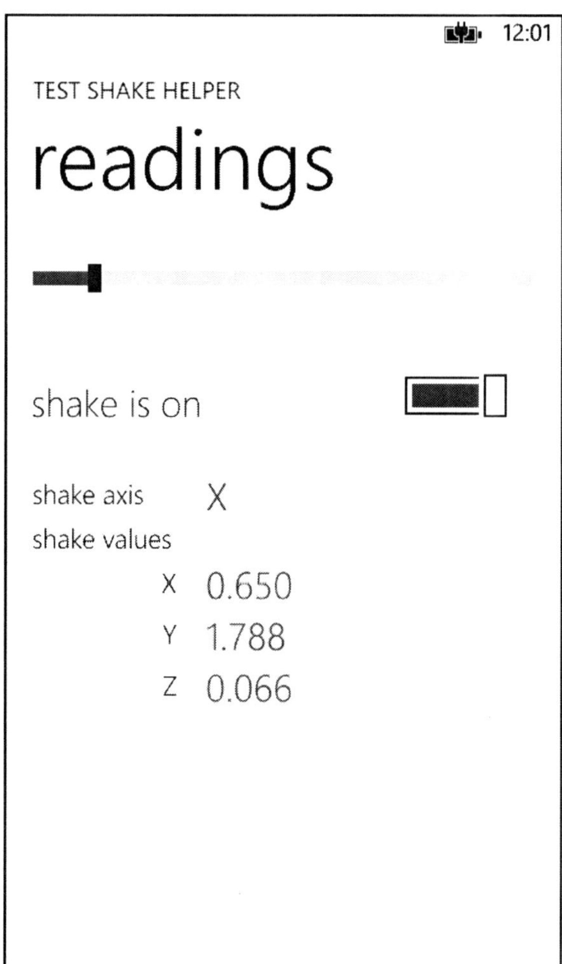

FIGURE 6-7 You can use the Shake Gesture Library to model shake gestures in your application.

Here are the basic steps for reusing the *ShakeGesturesHelper* from the Shake Gesture Library:

1. Create a Phone Application project named, for example, **TestShakeHelper**.
2. Add a Class Library project to this solution. Name it **ShakeHelper**.
3. Add existing items to the class library: the three *AccelerometerHelper* files (*Accelerometer Helper.cs*, *ApplicationSettingHelper.cs* and Simple3DVector.cs), plus the *ShakeGestureEvent Args.cs*, *ShakeGesturesHelper.cs* and *ShakeType.cs*.

   As before, you can use either the original *AccelerometerHelper* class or one that you have modified to use *CurrentValueChanged* instead of *ReadingChanged*. An additional file, *Simulation.cs*, simulates shake gestures by using a set of dummy data. If you don't want to use this, you must also comment out or remove the *Simulate* method in the *ShakeGesturesHelper* class.

4. Build the *ShakeHelper* class library.

   Note that the Shake Gesture Library is based on a slightly different version of the *Accelerometer Helper* library. If you're using your updated *CurrentValueChanged* version, you'll need to update the *ShakeGesturesHelper* class to refer to the *IsActive* property of the *Accelerometer Helper* class (instead of *Active*) and the *OptimallyFilteredAcceleration* property of the *AccelerometerHelperReadingEventArgs* (instead of *OptimalyFilteredAcceleration*).

5. In the *TestShakeHelper* project, add a reference to the *ShakeHelper* class library.

6. In the application, hook up the *OrientationChanged* event on the singleton *Orientation Helper* instance. As before, start the accelerometer by setting the *IsActive* property on the *AccelerometerHelper* singleton instance to *true*.

7. In your *OrientationChanged* event handler, retrieve the *OrientationHelperReadingEventArgs* values and do something interesting with them.

The *ShakeGestureEventArgs* that can be consumed in a client event handler only exposes one property: the *ShakeType* enum value. This is useful, but only minimally so. If you need to get more values from the underlying accelerometer readings, you can always modify the library source code for your own purposes. For example, the sample app modifies the *ShakeGestureEventArgs* to expose the underlying X, Y, Z accelerometer axis values.

```
private double _x;
public double X { get { return _x; } }
private double _y;
public double Y { get { return _y; } }
private double _z;
public double Z { get { return _z; } }

public ShakeGestureEventArgs(ShakeGestures.ShakeType shakeType, double x, double y, double z)
{
    _shakeType = shakeType;
    _x = x;
    _y = y;
    _z = z;
}
```

Then, the *ShakeGesturesHelper* class is updated to abstract the *currentVector* variable from the *OnAccelerometerHelperCurrentValue* event handler to be a class field.

```
private Simple3DVector currentVector;

//private void OnAccelerometerHelperReadingChanged(object sender,
AccelerometerHelperReadingEventArgs e)
private void OnAccelerometerHelperCurrentValueChanged(
    object sender, AccelerometerHelperReadingEventArgs e)
{
    //Simple3DVector currentVector = e.OptimallyFilteredAcceleration;
    currentVector = e.OptimallyFilteredAcceleration;

... unchanged code omitted for brevity.
}
```

This is then used in the *ProcessShakeSignal* method to construct the *ShakeGestureEventArgs* object, using the new constructor.

```
private bool ProcessShakeSignal()
{
... unchanged code omitted for brevity.
        if (localShakeGesture != null)
        {
            // localShakeGesture(this, new ShakeGestureEventArgs(shakeType.Value));
            localShakeGesture(this, new ShakeGestureEventArgs(
                shakeType.Value, currentVector.X, currentVector.Y, currentVector.Z));
        }
        return true;
    }
    return false;
}
```

The *TestShakeHelper* solution in the sample code uses a *Slider* to govern the sensitivity of the shake readings, and the *ToggleSwitch* to turn the accelerometer on and off. The *TextBlock* displays the shake axis. The app sets up the *ShakeGesturesHelper* singleton object in the *MainPage* constructor. At a minimum, you need to hook up the *ShakeGesture* event. You can optionally also set properties, and this example sets the *MinimumRequiredMovesForShake* to *4*, which means that the user will have to shake the phone four times (twice in each direction) on the same axis before the app will start processing readings.

```
public MainPage()
{
    InitializeComponent();
    ShakeGesturesHelper.Instance.ShakeGesture += ShakeHelper_ShakeGesture;
    ShakeGesturesHelper.Instance.MinimumRequiredMovesForShake = 4;
}
```

In the handler for the *ShakeGesture* event, the app extracts the *ShakeType* value and the underlying accelerometer axis values from the modified *ShakeGestureEventArgs*, to display them in the UI.

```
private void ShakeHelper_ShakeGesture(object sender, ShakeGestureEventArgs e)
{
    Dispatcher.BeginInvoke(() =>
    {
        shakeType.Text = e.ShakeType.ToString();
        xValue.Text = e.X.ToString("0.000");
        yValue.Text = e.Y.ToString("0.000");
        zValue.Text = e.Z.ToString("0.000");
    });
}
```

The app handles the *ToggleSwitch* events to toggle the *ShakeGesturesHelper* (and therefore, the underlying accelerometer) on and off. The *Slider* value is used to set the *ShakeMagnitudeWithout GravitationThreshold* property—any readings below this value are ignored for the purposes of computing the shake gesture. Higher values indicate more vigorous shaking.

```
private void ToggleSwitch_Checked(object sender, RoutedEventArgs e)
{
    ShakeGesturesHelper.Instance.Active = true;
    ShakeToggle.Content = "shake is on";
}

private void ToggleSwitch_Unchecked(object sender, RoutedEventArgs e)
{
    ShakeGesturesHelper.Instance.Active = false;
    ShakeToggle.Content = "shake is off";
}

private void SensitivitySlider_ValueChanged(
    object sender, RoutedPropertyChangedEventArgs<double> e)
{
    ShakeGesturesHelper.Instance.ShakeMagnitudeWithoutGravitationThreshold =
        SensitivitySlider.Value;
}
```

Notice that the *Slider Maximum* is set to 1.5 (in XAML). This is about the biggest threshold value that you can use realistically, and even this will generally require that the user makes shake gestures of a foot or two on each shake.

```
<Slider
    x:Name="SensitivitySlider"
    ValueChanged="SensitivitySlider_ValueChanged"
    Maximum="1.5"
    LargeChange="0.15" />
```

You can use the Accelerometer tab on the emulator to play back an arbitrary set of shake gestures, to exercise your app.

Compass

The compass feature on the phone is a magnetic sensor component that interacts with the earth's magnetic field. It can be aligned to point to magnetic north. The magnetometer device driver also incorporates the necessary code to compute the declination; that is, the variation between magnetic north and true north. The magnetic declination is different at different points on the earth and changes with time. This computation is accurate if your app has *ID_CAP_LOCATION* because it will automatically use your location to perform adjustments. If you don't have *ID_CAP_LOCATION*, it will use a cached value to perform the computation, and if there is no cached value (which should only happen if you've just cold-booted the phone), it will use zero.

The app platform encapsulates the functionality of the magnetometer sensor and exposes it through the *Compass* class via properties and methods for determining both true and magnetic north as well as the accuracy of the readings. The *Compass* class also exposes raw magnetometer readings that can be used to detect magnetic forces around the device.

Figure 6-8 shows the *SimpleCompass* solution in the sample code that uses the *Compass* class to gather magnetometer sensor readings. The app provides a button in the app bar to start/stop the compass sensor, and a simple graphical display based on the true north readings. Be aware that the emulator does not support a compass; therefore, you must test compass apps on a physical device.

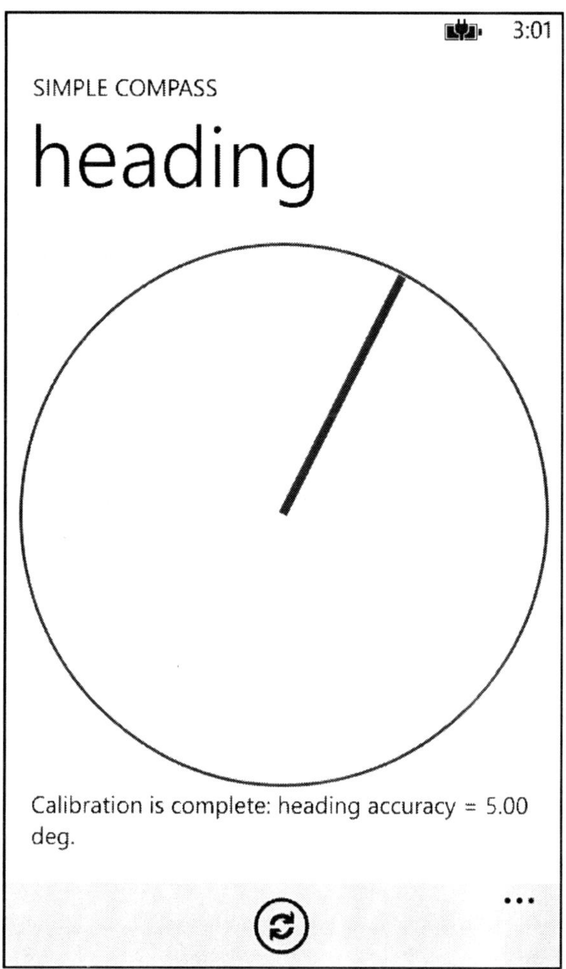

FIGURE 6-8 You can use the *Compass* class to build a compass app.

In the XAML, the app defines an inner *Grid* that contains an *Ellipse* for the compass border, and a *Line* for the compass needle. The app uses the current accent color for both the compass border and the needle. Below that is a *TextBlock* to display errors and other status messages.

```
<Grid Grid.Row="0">
    <Ellipse
        x:Name="compassBorder" Width="455" Height="455"
        StrokeThickness="3" Stroke="{StaticResource PhoneAccentBrush}"/>
```

```
    <Line
        x:Name="trueNorth" X1="228" Y1="227" X2="228" Y2="36"
        StrokeThickness="8" Stroke="{StaticResource PhoneAccentBrush}"/>
</Grid>
<TextBlock
    x:Name="status" Grid.Row="1" TextWrapping="Wrap"
    Margin="{StaticResource PhoneHorizontalMargin}" />
```

In the *MainPage* code-behind, the app declares fields for the *Compass* object and for the center point of the compass needle. Bearing in mind that the compass is an optional sensor, you should always test to see if it is actually supported on the current device before attempting to use it. In this app, the constructor performs this test and only initializes the app bar if there is a compass. Note that there is a hardware capability you can set in your app manifest if your app needs a compass to function. If you do this, your app won't even be shown to devices that don't have a compass when the user browses the Windows Phone Store.

```
private Compass compass;
private double centerX;
private double centerY;

public MainPage()
{
    InitializeComponent();

    if (!Compass.IsSupported)
    {
        status.Text = "This device does not support a compass.";
    }
    else
    {
        BuildLocalizedApplicationBar();
    }
}

private void BuildLocalizedApplicationBar()
{
    ApplicationBar = new ApplicationBar();
    appBarStopGo = new ApplicationBarIconButton(new Uri("/Assets/play.png", UriKind.Relative));
    appBarStopGo.Text = "go";
    appBarStopGo.Click += appBarStopGo_Click;
    ApplicationBar.Buttons.Add(appBarStopGo);
}protected override void OnNavigatedTo(NavigationEventArgs e)
{
    centerX = compassBorder.ActualWidth / 2.0;
    centerY = (compassBorder.ActualHeight - status.ActualHeight) / 2.0;
}
```

The page constructor is too early to calculate actual UI element sizes, so this is deferred to the *OnNavigatedTo* override. Here, the app gets the measurements needed to position the needle at the center of the grid (allowing for the status box at the bottom).

Assuming that this device does support a compass, when the user taps the app bar button, this either starts or stops the compass. There is no *IsStopped* or *IsStarted* property on the *Compass* type, but you can determine if the compass readings are ongoing by inspecting the *IsDataValid* property, which is inherited from the *SensorBase<T>* base class. In the app bar *Click* handler, if the compass is non-null and the *IsDataValid* property returns *true*, this must mean that the readings are ongoing, and, therefore, that the user must have tapped the app bar to stop the compass. In this case, the app stops acquiring sensor readings and updates the app bar accordingly.

On the other hand, if *IsDataValid* is *false*, it means that the app is not currently receiving sensor readings. This could be because the user has never started the compass in this session or because he previously started it and then stopped it. The app therefore instantiates the *Compass* object, if necessary, and specifies the required time interval between data updates. After this configuration is done, you can start the flow of compass readings.

```
private void appBarStopGo_Click(object sender, EventArgs e)
{
    if (compass != null && compass.IsDataValid)
    {
        compass.Stop();
        appBarStopGo.IconUri = new Uri("/Assets/play.png", UriKind.Relative);
        appBarStopGo.Text = "go";
    }
    else
    {
        if (compass == null)
        {
            compass = new Compass();
            compass.TimeBetweenUpdates = TimeSpan.FromMilliseconds(33);
            compass.CurrentValueChanged += compass_CurrentValueChanged;
        }

        try
        {
            compass.Start();
            appBarStopGo.IconUri = new Uri("/Assets/stop.png", UriKind.Relative);
            appBarStopGo.Text = "stop";
        }
        catch (InvalidOperationException)
        {
            status.Text = "Error starting compass.";
        }
    }
}
```

To examine the readings, the app hooks up the *CurrentValueChanged* event. In this handler, you're only interested in the *TrueHeading* (that is, the true north reading, not the magnetic north reading). You can extract this from the event arguments and convert it to radians so that you can use it to calculate the new endpoint for the needle line. These events obviously come in on a background thread, so you need to marshal the UI changes to the UI thread with a *Dispatcher*.

```
private void compass_CurrentValueChanged(
    object sender, SensorReadingEventArgs<CompassReading> e)
{
    double trueHeading = e.SensorReading.TrueHeading;
    float headingRadians = MathHelper.ToRadians((float)trueHeading);
    Dispatcher.BeginInvoke(() =>
    {
        trueNorth.X2 = centerX - centerY * Math.Sin(headingRadians);
        trueNorth.Y2 = centerY - centerY * Math.Cos(headingRadians);
    });
}
```

The preceding code is sufficient to get and render compass readings; however, there's one piece missing: calibration. After each reboot, the compass will need recalibration. Accuracy also fluctuates over time, especially if the phone is moving considerable distances (perhaps the user is flying cross-country, for example). So, if the user has not calibrated the compass recently, the readings will be inaccurate. In this case, this fact is surfaced to your code by the *Calibrate* event on the *Compass* object. So, before you can have confidence in the readings, you need to ensure that you respond to the *Calibrate* events. To do this, hook up the event when the *Compass* object itself is created.

```
if (compass == null)
{
    compass = new Compass();
    compass.TimeBetweenUpdates = TimeSpan.FromMilliseconds(33);
    compass.CurrentValueChanged += compass_CurrentValueChanged;

    // for calibration.
    compass.Calibrate += compass_Calibrate;
}
```

Also, when you get a reading, you need to cache the *HeadingAccuracy* property value, as follows:

```
private double headingAccuracy;

private void compass_CurrentValueChanged(
    object sender, SensorReadingEventArgs<CompassReading> e)
{
...unchanged code omitted for brevity.
    headingAccuracy = Math.Abs(e.SensorReading.HeadingAccuracy);
}
```

To calibrate the sensor, you need to instruct the user to rotate the phone several times over a period of a few seconds so that you can gather a range of readings for the sensor driver to compute the declination. In the *Calibrate* event handler itself, you set up a *DispatcherTimer* to update every frame. So long as the current *HeadingAccuracy* is still not within our acceptable range (≤10 degrees), you continue to update the status message to encourage the user to keep moving the phone. As you're updating the UI, you could use either a standard *Timer* and then invoke the page *Dispatcher* to marshal to the UI thread, or simply use the combined *DispatcherTimer* class, which effectively performs both aspects of the task for you.

```
private DispatcherTimer timer;

private void compass_Calibrate(object sender, CalibrationEventArgs e)
{
    Dispatcher.BeginInvoke(() =>
    {
        timer = new DispatcherTimer();
        timer.Interval = TimeSpan.FromMilliseconds(30);
        timer.Tick += timer_Tick;
        timer.Start();
    });
    compass.Calibrate -= compass_Calibrate;
}

private void timer_Tick(object sender, EventArgs e)
{
    if (headingAccuracy <= 10)
    {
        status.Text = String.Format(
            "Calibration is complete: heading accuracy = {0:00} deg.",
            headingAccuracy);
        timer.Stop();
    }
    else
    {
        status.Text = String.Format(
            "Rotate the phone to calibrate (heading accuracy is only {0:00} deg).",
            headingAccuracy);
    }
}
```

As you can see, it's very easy to use the *Compass* type to work with the compass sensor and get a flow of compass readings into your app. When building a compass-based app, you'll most likely spend far more time and effort in creating a compelling UI rather than working with the sensor itself.

Gyroscope

The gyroscope is used to determine the angular momentum of the device in each of the three primary axes. Compare this with the accelerometer, which measures acceleration in each of the three axes. So, with the accelerometer, the reading increases with the size of the rotation. With the gyroscope, on the other hand, the reading increases with the speed of the rotation. The axes are illustrated in Figure 6-9.

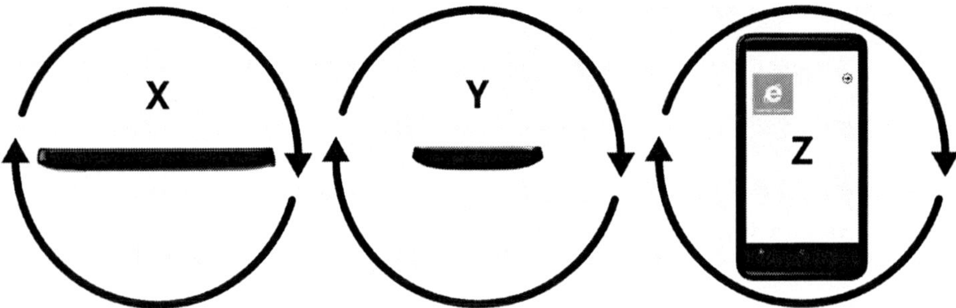

FIGURE 6-9 The gyroscope tracks rotation about the x, y, and z axes.

The sensor's reference point deliberately does not autorotate as the screen autorotates. This is to allow for apps that need to use sensors in combination with the orientation of the device as a whole in reference to the Earth, not in reference to the current viewport orientation. The rotations above are known as pitch, roll, and yaw (summarized in Table 6-4), along with their line representations in the sample application that follows.

TABLE 6-4 Descriptions of pitch, roll, and yaw

Movement	Description	Sample application line
Pitch	Rotation around the device's X axis	Red
Roll	Rotation around the device's Y axis	Green
Yaw	Rotation around the device's Z axis	Blue

A developer can use the values obtained from the gyroscope sensor to determine which way a device is facing. The rotational velocity is measured in units of radians per second. Because a gyroscope measures rotational velocity and not angle, it is susceptible to drift. Figure 6-10 shows the *SimpleGyroscope* solution in the sample code, with three colored bars, each bar representing the rotational velocity along one of the three axes. The X and Y bars are aligned with the X and Y axes on the phone; the Z bar is angled in a way that represents the 3D Z axis on a 2D surface.

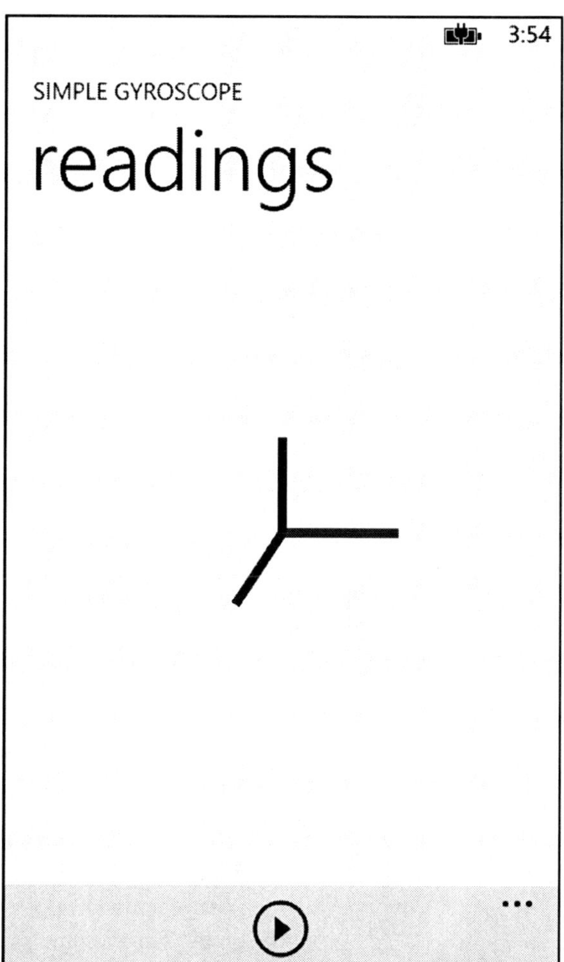

FIGURE 6-10 A gyroscope app with three axes of rotation.

As mentioned previously, all the sensor classes are based on *SensorBase<T>*, which gives them a high degree of consistency. So, the code for creating a gyroscope-based application is very similar to the code for a compass or accelerometer application—in this case, using the derived *Gyroscope* class. The sample gyroscope app sets up the XAML in a very similar way to the earlier compass app; this example has a *Grid* containing three *Lines*, and a *TextBlock* below that for status messages.

```
<Grid Height="440" Grid.Row="0">
    <Line x:Name="currentX" X1="228" Y1="240" X2="328" Y2="240" Stroke="Red"
              StrokeThickness="8"/>
    <Line x:Name="currentY" X1="228" Y1="240" X2="228" Y2="160" Stroke="Green"
              StrokeThickness="8"/>
    <Line x:Name="currentZ" X1="228" Y1="240" X2="188" Y2="300" Stroke="Blue"
              StrokeThickness="8"/>
</Grid>
<TextBlock x:Name="status" Grid.Row="1" Margin="{StaticResource PhoneHorizontalMargin}"/>
```

The *MainPage* constructor tests to verify that this device does in fact support a gyroscope sensor and then sets up the app bar accordingly. As with the compass, there's a hardware capability that you can set in your app manifest, if your app absolutely requires a gyroscope.

```
private Gyroscope gyroscope;

public MainPage()
{
    InitializeComponent();

    if (!Gyroscope.IsSupported)
    {
        status.Text = "This device does not support a gyroscope.";
    }
    else
    {
        BuildLocalizedApplicationBar();
    }
}
```

The code model in the app bar button *Click* handler is also very similar. As before, the app checks to see if the sensor is currently running and providing valid readings. If it is, it stops the sensor. If not, it instantiates the *Gyroscope* object (if necessary) and configures the time between updates. The same restrictions apply as for compass reading intervals (see Table 6-3), although the exact numbers will vary per device. As before, the critical operation is to hook up the *CurrentValueChanged* event.

```
private void appBarStopGo_Click(object sender, EventArgs e)
{
    if (gyroscope != null && gyroscope.IsDataValid)
    {
        gyroscope.Stop();
        appBarStopGo.IconUri = new Uri("/Assets/play.png", UriKind.Relative);
        appBarStopGo.Text = "go";
    }
    else
    {
        if (gyroscope == null)
        {
            gyroscope = new Gyroscope();
            gyroscope.TimeBetweenUpdates = TimeSpan.FromMilliseconds(20);
            gyroscope.CurrentValueChanged += gyroscope_CurrentValueChanged;
        }
```

```
        try
        {
            gyroscope.Start();
            appBarStopGo.IconUri = new Uri("/Assets/stop.png", UriKind.Relative);
            appBarStopGo.Text = "stop";
        }
        catch (InvalidOperationException)
        {
            status.Text = "Error starting gyroscope.";
        }
    }
}
```

In the *CurrentValueChanged* event handler, the app extracts the current rotation rate from the event arguments. This value is in radians per second, so it is a simple calculation to render a line of a suitable size for each of the axes.

```
private void gyroscope_CurrentValueChanged(
    object sender, SensorReadingEventArgs<GyroscopeReading> e)
{
    Vector3 currentRotationRate = e.SensorReading.RotationRate;
    Dispatcher.BeginInvoke(() =>
    {
        currentX.X2 = currentX.X1 + currentRotationRate.X * 50;
        currentY.Y2 = currentY.Y1 - currentRotationRate.Y * 50;
        currentZ.X2 = currentZ.X1 - currentRotationRate.Z * 50;
        currentZ.Y2 = currentZ.Y1 + currentRotationRate.Z * 50;
    });
}
```

As with the compass, the emulator does not support a gyroscope, so you can only test gyroscope applications on a physical device.

Note There's an API inconsistency between the *Compass* and *Gyroscope* classes: the *Compass* reports values in degrees, whereas the *Gyroscope* reports values in radians. This is purely for historical reasons. Most people are used to working with compasses in degrees. On the other hand, the *Gyroscope* and *Motion* types are dependent on classes in the XNA framework that internally use radians. For the same reason, the *Motion* class uses floats like the rest of the XNA framework rather than doubles as with the rest of Microsoft Silverlight.

Motion APIs

The *Accelerometer, Compass*, and *Gyroscope* APIs all expose raw sensor data for those scenarios in which the developer needs a finer level of granularity. However, the raw data can be difficult to work with, and many apps don't need the fine detail. In addition, you sometimes need to make complex geometrical calculations to convert the low-level readings into meaningful orientation information. The smoothing operations performed in the Level Starter Kit are one example of this.

Furthermore, hardware sensors are susceptible to a variety of errors, including bias (for example, as a result of temperature fluctuations), drift (loss of accuracy between calibrations), and accuracy limitations (mostly arising from the constant electromagnetic interference from outside and within the phone). Each sensor is affected by these issues to different degrees. Gyroscopes, for example, are sensitive to electromagnetic interference and are prone to drift errors because they measure angular velocity as opposed to angle. Accelerometers, on the other hand, do not suffer from drift errors, but produce poor readings while the device is in motion because the sensor is actually measuring linear acceleration along with gravitational pull.

Microsoft recognized the complexity of dealing with the low-level APIs, and introduced a logical sensor, represented by the *Motion* class. Just like the other sensor classes, this is derived from *SensorBase<T>*. This class takes advantage of multiple sensors simultaneously, which allows your app to compensate for sensor errors/noise and produce more accurate readings than can be obtained through a single sensor alone. The *Motion* class takes the raw sensor readings and surfaces a higher-level abstraction—or "fusion"—specifically the device's attitude (pitch, roll, and yaw), rotational acceleration, and linear acceleration. Augmented-reality apps benefit most from consuming this processed form of sensor data because they typically need to gather readings simultaneously across multiple sensors.

The screenshot in Figure 6-11 shows the *SimpleMotion* app in the sample code, which uses the *Motion* type to represent device rotation rate in a similar way to the earlier gyroscope example, as well as attitude (pitch, roll, and yaw).

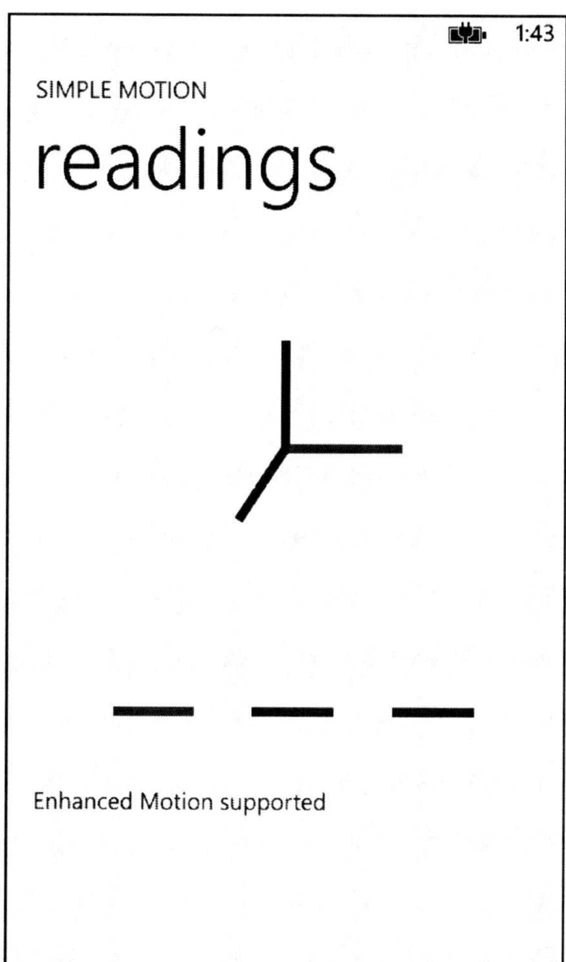

FIGURE 6-11 Using the *Motion* API.

As with the gyroscope application, the app starts off with three lines to represent the X, Y, and Z axes. Below that, there are three more lines; these represent the device's attitude (pitch, roll, and yaw, respectively). For each of the attitude lines, the app defines a *RotateTransform* so that it can rotate these lines in response to the corresponding sensor readings.

```
<Grid Height="330" Grid.Row="0">
    <Line x:Name="gyroscopeX" X1="228" Y1="170" X2="328" Y2="170" Stroke="Red"
                StrokeThickness="8"/>
    <Line x:Name="gyroscopeY" X1="228" Y1="170" X2="228" Y2="80" Stroke="Green"
                StrokeThickness="8"/>
```

```
    <Line x:Name="gyroscopeZ" X1="228" Y1="170" X2="188" Y2="230" Stroke="Blue"
                  StrokeThickness="8"/>
</Grid>

<Grid Height="120" Grid.Row="1">
    <Line x:Name="currentPitch" X1="80" Y1="60" X2="150" Y2="60" Stroke="Red"
                  StrokeThickness="8">
        <Line.RenderTransform>
            <RotateTransform CenterX="115" CenterY="60"/>
        </Line.RenderTransform>
    </Line>
    <Line x:Name="currentRoll" X1="200" Y1="60" X2="270" Y2="60" Stroke="Green"
                  StrokeThickness="8">
        <Line.RenderTransform>
            <RotateTransform CenterX="235" CenterY="60"/>
        </Line.RenderTransform>
    </Line>
    <Line x:Name="currentYaw" X1="320" Y1="60" X2="390" Y2="60" Stroke="Blue"
                  StrokeThickness="8">
        <Line.RenderTransform>
            <RotateTransform CenterX="355" CenterY="60"/>
        </Line.RenderTransform>
    </Line>
</Grid>

<TextBlock x:Name="status" Height="80" Grid.Row="2" Margin="{StaticResource
PhoneHorizontalMargin}"/>
```

The *MainPage* declares a *Motion* field and implements the constructor to test if the *Motion* API is supported on this device, configuring the app bar as in previous examples. Be aware that the *Motion* class has the following two different sensor configurations:

- *Normal Motion*, which uses the compass and the accelerometer sensor
- *Enhanced Motion*, which uses the compass, the accelerometer, and the gyroscope

These modes are configured internally and are not exposed in the API. However, if your app requires the accuracy of *Enhanced* motion, you should check to verify that the device on which the app is running supports the gyroscope sensor. Here's an additional test for this:

```
private Motion motion;

public MainPage()
{
    InitializeComponent();

    if (!Motion.IsSupported)
    {
        status.Text = "This device does not support the Motion API.";
    }
    else
    {
        if (Gyroscope.IsSupported)
```

```
        {
            status.Text = "Enhanced Motion supported";
        }
        else
        {
            status.Text = "Normal Motion supported";
        }
        BuildLocalizedApplicationBar();
    }
}
```

The app bar button *Click* handler starts or stops the *Motion* object, which under the hood will start/stop the two or three sensors that the *Motion* class is using. As you can do with all *SensorBase<T>* types, you can set the *TimeBetweenUpdates* property and hook up the *Current ValueChanged* event.

```
private void appBarStopGo_Click(object sender, EventArgs e)
{
    if (motion != null && motion.IsDataValid)
    {
        motion.Stop();
        appBarStopGo.IconUri = new Uri("/Assets/play.png", UriKind.Relative);
        appBarStopGo.Text = "go";
    }
    else
    {
        if (motion == null)
        {
            motion = new Motion();
            motion.TimeBetweenUpdates = TimeSpan.FromMilliseconds(20);
            motion.CurrentValueChanged += motion_CurrentValueChanged;
        }

        try
        {
            motion.Start();
            appBarStopGo.IconUri = new Uri("/Assets/stop.png", UriKind.Relative);
            appBarStopGo.Text = "stop";
        }
        catch (InvalidOperationException)
        {
            status.Text = "Error starting the Motion sensors.";
        }
    }
}
```

When the app receives a *CurrentValueChanged* event, it first extracts the *DeviceRotationRate* and then uses the *X, Y,* and *Z* property values to determine the endpoints of the axis rotation lines. It then extracts the *Attitude* property and sets the angle of the *RenderTransform* for each of the three attitude lines to correspond to the *Pitch, Roll,* and *Yaw* property values.

```
private void motion_CurrentValueChanged(
    object sender, SensorReadingEventArgs<MotionReading> e)
{
    Vector3 rotationRate = e.SensorReading.DeviceRotationRate;
    AttitudeReading attitude = e.SensorReading.Attitude;
    Dispatcher.BeginInvoke(() =>
    {
        gyroscopeX.X2 = gyroscopeX.X1 + rotationRate.X * 50;
        gyroscopeY.Y2 = gyroscopeY.Y1 - rotationRate.Y * 50;
        gyroscopeZ.X2 = gyroscopeZ.X1 - rotationRate.Z * 50;
        gyroscopeZ.Y2 = gyroscopeZ.Y1 + rotationRate.Z * 50;

        ((RotateTransform)currentPitch.RenderTransform).Angle =
            MathHelper.ToDegrees(attitude.Pitch);
        ((RotateTransform)currentRoll.RenderTransform).Angle =
            MathHelper.ToDegrees(attitude.Roll);
        ((RotateTransform)currentYaw.RenderTransform).Angle =
            MathHelper.ToDegrees(attitude.Yaw);
    });
}
```

The *Motion* type not only exposes gyroscopic rotation rates and device attitude, it also exposes acceleration and gravity readings. So, you could add another couple of grids comprised of three lines, with the first set to represent the accelerometer readings, and the second set to represent the gravity readings. You can see this at work in the *SimpleMotion_More* solution in the sample code.

```
<Grid x:Name="accelerometerGrid" Height="80" Grid.Row="2">
    <Line x:Name="accelerometerX" X1="225" Y1="20" X2="230" Y2="20" Stroke="Red"
                StrokeThickness="8"/>
    <Line x:Name="accelerometerY" X1="225" Y1="40" X2="230" Y2="40" Stroke="Green"
                StrokeThickness="8"/>
    <Line x:Name="accelerometerZ" X1="225" Y1="60" X2="230" Y2="60" Stroke="Blue"
                StrokeThickness="8"/>
</Grid>

<Grid Height="80" Grid.Row="3">
    <Line x:Name="gravityX" X1="225" Y1="20" X2="230" Y2="20" Stroke="Red" StrokeThickness="8"/>
    <Line x:Name="gravityY" X1="225" Y1="40" X2="230" Y2="40" Stroke="Green"
                StrokeThickness="8"/>
    <Line x:Name="gravityZ" X1="225" Y1="60" X2="230" Y2="60" Stroke="Blue"
                StrokeThickness="8"/>
</Grid>
```

You could add a center-point calculation in *OnNavigatedTo*, as in the earlier compass example. Then, in the *CurrentValueChanged* handler, you could update the UI by redrawing these two sets of lines according to the *DeviceAcceleration* and *Gravity* properties of the *SensorReading*.

```
private double centerX;

protected override void OnNavigatedTo(NavigationEventArgs e)
{
    centerX = accelerometerGrid.ActualWidth / 2.0;
}
```

```
private void motion_CurrentValueChanged(object sender, SensorReadingEventArgs<MotionReading> e)
{
    Vector3 rotationRate = e.SensorReading.DeviceRotationRate;
    AttitudeReading attitude = e.SensorReading.Attitude;
    Vector3 acceleration = e.SensorReading.DeviceAcceleration;
    Vector3 gravity = e.SensorReading.Gravity;

    Dispatcher.BeginInvoke(() =>
    {
        gyroscopeX.X2 = gyroscopeX.X1 + rotationRate.X * 20;
        gyroscopeY.Y2 = gyroscopeY.Y1 - rotationRate.Y * 20;
        gyroscopeZ.X2 = gyroscopeZ.X1 - rotationRate.Z * 20;
        gyroscopeZ.Y2 = gyroscopeZ.Y1 + rotationRate.Z * 20;

        ((RotateTransform)currentPitch.RenderTransform).Angle =
            MathHelper.ToDegrees(attitude.Pitch);
        ((RotateTransform)currentRoll.RenderTransform).Angle =
            MathHelper.ToDegrees(attitude.Roll);
        ((RotateTransform)currentYaw.RenderTransform).Angle =
            MathHelper.ToDegrees(attitude.Yaw);

        accelerometerX.X2 = centerX + acceleration.X * 200;
        accelerometerY.X2 = centerX + acceleration.Y * 200;
        accelerometerZ.X2 = centerX + acceleration.Z * 200;

        gravityX.X2 = centerX + gravity.X * 200;
        gravityY.X2 = centerX + gravity.Y * 200;
        gravityZ.X2 = centerX + gravity.Z * 200;
    });
}
```

Summary

The Windows Phone app platform provides comprehensive support for sensors, including both low-level APIs such as *Accelerometer*, *Compass*, and *Gyroscope*, and the higher-level abstraction that the *Motion* class represents. All four of the sensor classes are derived from *SensorBase<T>*; therefore, they offer a very consistent API surface. Sensor readings can be treated as just another form of user input, and you can support movement, orientation, and shake gestures in your apps to provide a richer user interface.

CHAPTER 7

Web connectivity

The Windows Phone app platform provides some basic support for connecting to the web via two core classes, *WebClient* and *HttpWebRequest*, and their supporting types. It also provides a modified version of the Microsoft Silverlight *WebBrowser* control for rendering and interacting with HTML webpages. Beyond these, there are additional SDKs available for developing with social networks such as Facebook and Twitter as well as with cloud data services such as SkyDrive. This chapter compares and contrasts the primary web connectivity mechanisms, and also explore a range of additional SDKs.

The *WebClient* and *HttpWebRequest* classes

The platform supports basic get or post web requests through two classes: *WebClient* and *HttpWebRequest*. *WebClient* is a wrapper around *HttpWebRequest*, so as you would expect, it is simpler to use but is less flexible. For a more complex request, if you need to specify headers, content type, or you need more fine-grained control over your request, *HttpWebRequest* is more useful.

Figure 7-1 shows screenshots of the *DemoWebRequests* solution in the sample code. This is a pivot app with two pivot items: the first fetches arbitrary webpages and displays their text in a *TextBlock*; the second fetches Microsoft Xbox Live avatar images and adds each image to a *ListBox*. In both cases, the user has a choice of two buttons: one uses *WebClient*, and the other uses *HttpWebRequest*.

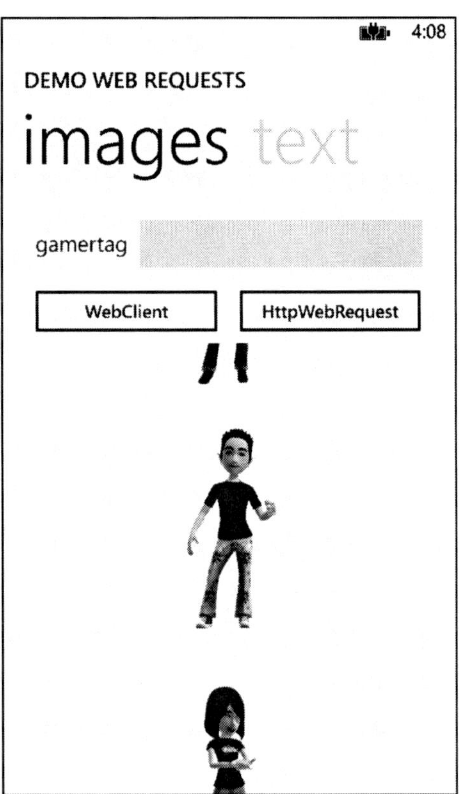

FIGURE 7-1 You can use the *WebClient* or *HttpWebRequest* classes to download or upload web data.

The *WebClient* class is part of the standard Microsoft .NET base class library (BCL), and you can use it to download or upload web content. The version that is available to you in a Windows Phone app is more constrained than the standard desktop Common Language Runtime (CLR) version, mainly because it restricts you to asynchronous calls. In general, all web calls on the phone are asynchronous. To use the *WebClient* class, you need to do the following:

- Create an instance of *WebClient*, typically as a class-level field (because the asynchronous model means that you'll most likely need to use it across more than one method).
- Wire up either the *DownloadStringCompleted* event or the *OpenReadCompleted* event (or both), implementing the event handlers to process the *Result* data returned from the service call. If you know that the target URL specifies content that can be represented as a string, you can use the handy *DownloadStringAsync* helper method. For other content, you can use *OpenReadAsync*, instead. In both cases, of course, you can use either conventional event handler methods or inline lambdas, as your coding style guidelines (or personal preferences) dictate.
- Call the *DownloadStringAsync* or *OpenReadAsync* method to start fetching data from the web.

The *WebClient* code to fetch text data is very straightforward. The app declares a *WebClient* field, and hooks up a handler for the *DownloadStringCompleted* event. Then, when the user taps the button to initiate a download, the app invokes *DownloadStringAsync*. Eventually, when the download is complete, the system invokes the *DownloadStringCompleted* event handler, which simply extracts the return value and sets it into the *TextBlock*.

```
private WebClient webClient;

public MainPage()
{
    InitializeComponent();
    webClient = new WebClient();
    webClient.DownloadStringCompleted += webClient_DownloadStringCompleted;
}

private void webGetText_Click(object sender, RoutedEventArgs e)
{
    pageText.Text = String.Empty;
    webClient.DownloadStringAsync(new Uri(urlText.Text));
}

private void webClient_DownloadStringCompleted(
    object sender, DownloadStringCompletedEventArgs e)
{
    if (e.Error == null)
        pageText.Text = e.Result;
    else
        pageText.Text = e.Error.ToString();
}
```

If you prefer to use inline lambdas, your code will be less verbose—although, of course, the results are the same.

```
public MainPage()
{
    InitializeComponent();
    webClient = new WebClient();
    webClient.DownloadStringCompleted += (sender, e) =>
    {
        if (e.Error == null)
            pageText.Text = e.Result;
        else
            pageText.Text = e.Error.ToString();
    };
}

private void webGetText_Click(object sender, RoutedEventArgs e)
{
    pageText.Text = String.Empty;
    webClient.DownloadStringAsync(new Uri(urlText.Text));
}
```

Observe that although *WebClient* operations (such as *DownloadStringAsync*) run on a background thread, the events generated (such as *DownloadStringCompleted*) are raised on the user interface (UI) thread. An advantage of this is that there's no need to dispatch any work back to the UI thread in this scenario. A disadvantage is that you're inevitably doing work on the UI thread, and you might prefer to avoid or minimize this for performance/responsiveness reasons.

The code that follows presents the *HttpWebRequest* (also part of the standard .NET BCL) equivalent. The pattern for this class is to do as follows:

- Invoke the static *Create* method to create an *HttpWebRequest* for the selected URL.
- Invoke the asynchronous *BeginGetResponse* method. When you call *BeginGetResponse*, you need to pass in the *HttpWebRequest* object (or define it as a class field) so that it is accessible in the asynchronous callback.
- When the callback is invoked, extract the *WebResponse* from the result and then fetch the embedded data stream for further processing.

Keep in mind that unlike *WebClient*, the response callbacks for *HttpWebRequest* are invoked on a background thread; hence, the use of the page's *Dispatcher* to update the UI.

```
private void httpGetText_Click(object sender, RoutedEventArgs e)
{
    pageText.Text = String.Empty;
    HttpWebRequest webRequest = (HttpWebRequest)HttpWebRequest.Create(new Uri(urlText.Text));
    webRequest.BeginGetResponse(httpGetTextCallback, webRequest);
}

private void httpGetTextCallback(IAsyncResult result)
{
    HttpWebRequest request = (HttpWebRequest)result.AsyncState;

    try
    {
        WebResponse response = request.EndGetResponse(result);
        Stream responseStream = response.GetResponseStream();
        StreamReader reader = new StreamReader(responseStream);
        Dispatcher.BeginInvoke(() => { pageText.Text = reader.ReadToEnd(); });
    }
    catch (WebException ex)
    {
        Dispatcher.BeginInvoke(() => { pageText.Text = ex.Message; });
    }
}
```

If you're using *WebClient*, and you're retrieving data that's not all strings, you can use *OpenRead Async*, instead. The second pivot item fetches user-specified avatar images from Xbox Live, adding each one to an *ObservableCollection<T>*, which is data-bound to a *ListBox* in the UI. When the user taps the *WebClient* button on this pivot item, this calls *OpenReadAsync* on the *WebClient*, using the supplied gamertag to build a URI to the corresponding Xbox Live avatar image. The *OpenReadCompleted* event handler fetches the resulting image and adds it to the collection. The magic of data-binding takes care of the rest.

```
private ObservableCollection<ImageSource> avatarImages;
public MainPage()
{
    InitializeComponent();

    avatarImages = new ObservableCollection<ImageSource>();
    avatarList.ItemsSource = avatarImages;
    webClient = new WebClient();
    webClient.OpenReadCompleted += webClient_OpenReadCompleted;
}

private void webGetImage_Click(object sender, RoutedEventArgs e)
{
    try
    {
        Uri uri = new Uri(String.Format(
            "http://avatar.xboxlive.com/avatar/{0}/avatar-body.png", gamerTagText.Text));
        webClient.OpenReadAsync(uri);
    }
    catch (Exception ex)
    {
        Debug.WriteLine(ex.ToString());
    }
}

private void webClient_OpenReadCompleted(object sender, OpenReadCompletedEventArgs e)
{
    if (!e.Cancelled && e.Error == null)
    {
        BitmapImage bmp = new BitmapImage();
        bmp.SetSource(e.Result);
        avatarImages.Add(bmp);
    }
}
```

The *HttpWebRequest* equivalent is almost identical to the code that fetches the webpage text. This highlights the more general-purpose nature of *HttpWebRequest*; that is, the app creates a new *HttpWebRequest* and invokes *BeginGetResponse*, passing in an async callback. In the callback, we can extract the data from the response stream and use it to update the UI. Observe that we can use either *BitmapImage* or *WriteableBitmap* in either the *WebClient* version or the *HttpWebRequest* version.

```
private void httpGetImage_Click(object sender, RoutedEventArgs e)
{
    try
    {

        Uri uri = new Uri(String.Format(
            "http://avatar.xboxlive.com/avatar/{0}/avatar-body.png", gamerTagText.Text));
        HttpWebRequest webRequest = (HttpWebRequest)HttpWebRequest.Create(uri);
        webRequest.BeginGetResponse(httpRequestCallback, webRequest);
    }
```

```
    catch (Exception ex)
    {
        Debug.WriteLine(ex.ToString());
    }
}

private void httpRequestCallback(IAsyncResult result)
{
    HttpWebRequest request = (HttpWebRequest)result.AsyncState;
    WebResponse response = request.EndGetResponse(result);
    Stream responseStream = response.GetResponseStream();

    Dispatcher.BeginInvoke(() =>
    {
        WriteableBitmap bmp = PictureDecoder.DecodeJpeg(responseStream, 250, 250);
        avatarImages.Add(bmp);
    });
}
```

Using the async pack

You might be wondering: if the Phone implementations of *WebClient* and *HttpWebRequest* constrain you to an asynchronous call pattern, why is it not possible to use the C# 5.0 *async* and *await* keywords. The short answer is that these classes don't expose any "awaitable" methods. The long answer is that these classes maintain a high degree of back-compatibility with Windows Phone 7.x, which is based on C# 4.0 and doesn't support the new keywords.

With that said, you can actually use this pattern by incorporating the *Microsoft.Bcl.Async* NuGet package into your project. This provides awaitable extension methods to classes such as *WebClient* and *HttpWebRequest*. To use this package, in Microsoft Visual Studio, right-click the project in Solution Explorer and then, in the shortcut menu that appears, click Manage NuGet Packages. Change the filter to Include Prerelease and then, in the Search box, type **Bcl.Async**, as shown in Figure 7-2.

Alternatively, you can open the Package Manager Console (on the Tools menu, point to Library Package Manager and then click Package Manager Console) and type the command to install the package manually:

```
install-package Microsoft.Bcl.Async
```

With this package in the project, you can streamline your code to use *async/await* and eliminate the callback method and the code to hook up the "completed" event. For example, for the *WebClient* approach to fetching text, you don't need to hook up the *DownloadStringCompleted* event. Instead of calling *DownloadStringAsync*, you can use the extension method *DownloadStringTaskAsync*. This makes it possible for you to put all your code in the same method: for setting up the web call, retrieving the result, and using the result. Another nice benefit of this is that you don't need to use a *Dispatcher*, because all your code executes on the calling (UI) thread. This is demonstrated in the *DemoWebRequests_Async* sample solution.

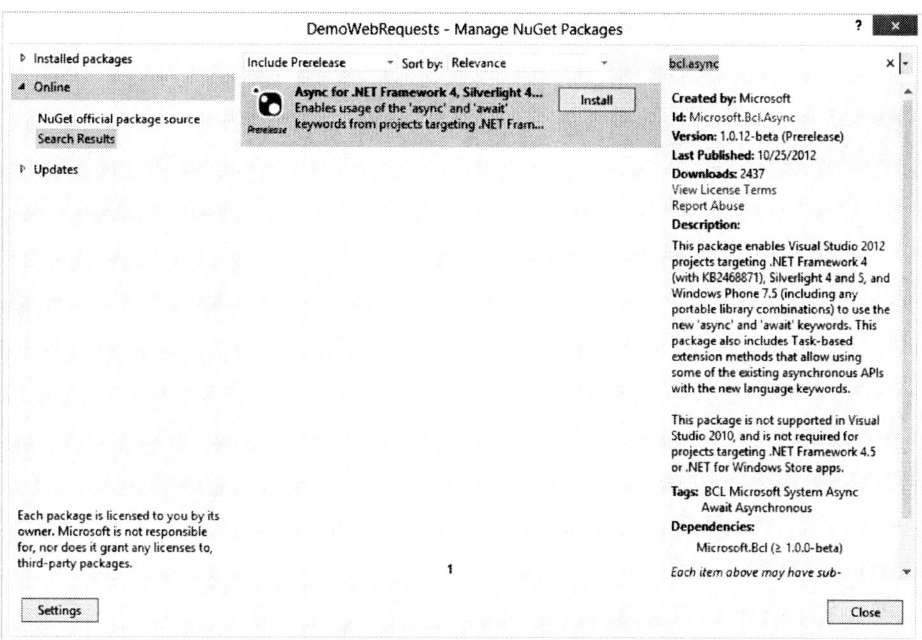

FIGURE 7-2 Install the *Microsoft.Bcl.Async* NuGet package to add async support to *WebClient* and *HttpWebRequest.*

```
private async void webGetText_Click(object sender, RoutedEventArgs e)
{
    pageText.Text = String.Empty;

    //webClient.DownloadStringAsync(new Uri(urlText.Text));
    try
    {
        string result = await new WebClient().DownloadStringTaskAsync(new Uri(urlText.Text));
        pageText.Text = result;
    }
    catch (OperationCanceledException)
    {
        pageText.Text = "(cancelled)";
    }
    catch (Exception ex)
    {
        pageText.Text = ex.Message; ;
    }
}
```

Of course, whenever you use the *await* mechanism within a method, you must mark that method as *async*. Similarly, instead of using *WebClient.OpenReadCompleted/OpenReadAsync*, you'd use *WebClient.OpenReadTaskAsync*. For *HttpWebRequest*, instead of using *BeginGetResponse* and a custom callback, you can use *GetResponseAsync*.

```
private async void httpGetText_Click(object sender, RoutedEventArgs e)
{
    pageText.Text = String.Empty;

    HttpWebRequest webRequest =
        (HttpWebRequest)HttpWebRequest.Create(new Uri(urlText.Text));
    //webRequest.BeginGetResponse(httpGetTextCallback, webRequest);

    try
    {
        WebResponse response = await webRequest.GetResponseAsync();
        Stream responseStream = response.GetResponseStream();
        StreamReader reader = new StreamReader(responseStream);
        //Dispatcher.BeginInvoke(() => { pageText.Text = reader.ReadToEnd(); });
        pageText.Text = reader.ReadToEnd();
    }
    catch (WebException ex)
    {
        //Dispatcher.BeginInvoke(() => { pageText.Text = ex.Message; });
        pageText.Text = ex.Message;
    }
}
```

Note Microsoft has provided a NuGet package for HTTP client libraries. As of this writing, this is available in prerelease format at https://nuget.org/packages/Microsoft.Net.Http. This package provides a programming interface for modern HTTP apps, and includes new classes *HttpClient* for sending requests over HTTP, and *HttpRequestMessage/HttpResponseMessage* for processing HTTP messages.

Using the Task Parallel Library

If for some reason you don't want to use the Async Pack, you have yet another alternative: you could use the Task Parallel Library (TPL), instead. For example, you can use a *TaskFactory* to invoke an *HttpWebRequest* asynchronously by using the awaitable *Task<T>* type. As with the Async Pack awaitable extensions, this allows you to collapse your code inline, avoiding the need for handling "completion" events and dispatching UI operations from another thread. You can see this at work in the *DemoWebRequests_TPL* app in the sample code.

```
private async void httpGetText_Click(object sender, RoutedEventArgs e)
{
    pageText.Text = String.Empty;
    HttpWebRequest webRequest =
        (HttpWebRequest)HttpWebRequest.Create(new Uri(urlText.Text));
    //webRequest.BeginGetResponse(httpGetTextCallback, webRequest);
```

```
        TaskFactory factory = new TaskFactory();
        Task<WebResponse> task = factory.FromAsync<WebResponse>(
            webRequest.BeginGetResponse, webRequest.EndGetResponse, null);
        try
        {
            WebResponse response = await task;
            Stream responseStream = response.GetResponseStream();
            StreamReader reader = new StreamReader(responseStream);
            pageText.Text = reader.ReadToEnd();
        }
        catch (WebException ex)
        {
            pageText.Text = ex.Message;
        }
    }
```

The *WebBrowser* control

Although Windows 8 supports HTML-based apps, Windows Phone 8 does not. However, you can create Windows Phone apps that use the embedded *WebBrowser* control, and you can even interact with JavaScript scripts on webpages. The browser in Windows Phone 8 is Internet Explorer Mobile 10, which includes support for HTML5/CSS3, Scalable Vector Graphics (SVG), ECMAScript5, IndexedDB, gesture events, and a high-performance scripting engine.

The *WebBrowser* control available for Windows Phone is based on the desktop Silverlight version. This control is not a full web browser; rather, it provides the core functionality to render HTML content, but it has no UI controls or chrome of its own. This is useful if you simply want to render local HTML (either static or dynamically generated). It is also useful if you want to navigate to remote webpages, and to provide your own custom chrome. The phone version of the *WebBrowser* control is slightly different from the desktop version in the following ways:

- It does not allow the use of ActiveX controls on webpages.
- It can invoke scripts loaded from any site. Unlike desktop Silverlight, it is not restricted to the same site as the XAP package.
- It can access isolated storage for the hosting app.
- It has the same cross-site restrictions for HTML loaded from the web, but not for HTML loaded from static or dynamic local content.
- It can be treated as a normal UI control that can have transforms and projections performed on it, and it participates in the Z-order of UI elements.

You can use the *WebBrowser* control by simply declaring it as an element in your page XAML. If you supply a *Source* URL, the browser will navigate directly to that page on load.

```
<phone:WebBrowser x:Name="browser" Source="http://dev.windowsphone.com"/>
```

Zoom (pinch and stretch) and scroll manipulations work, as do any links on the page. Embedded ActiveX controls, including Silverlight, do not work. By default, scripts do not work either, although this can be changed. The *WebBrowser* control was updated between Windows Phone 7 and Windows Phone 8, and it can now navigate directly to local HTML pages. It also exposes new *GoForward* and *GoBack* methods, which give you the basis for manipulating navigation programmatically.

Be aware that if you don't specify a name for the *WebBrowser* control in your XAML and then run the Capabilities Detection tool, this will not report any required capabilities. If you then go ahead and remove the boilerplate capabilities from your manifest, the app will fail at runtime. In fact, you need the *ID_CAP_WEBBROWSERCOMPONENT* capability for local or remote HTML content, and the *ID_CAP_NETWORKING* capability for any remote browsing.

Local webpages

The *WebBrowser* control supports HTML5, and one of the interesting new tags in HTML5 is the <video> tag. The *DemoWebBrowser* solution in the sample code includes a local HTML page. This page has a remote video link. The HTML5 <video> tag is the only standard way to embed video on webpages that is supported by multiple mobile devices and is therefore important in building cross-browser web apps. Internet Explorer 10 (and therefore the *WebBrowser* control) can play HTML5 video in H.264, which is the most commonly used video format for mobile web apps. In the example, the XAML declaration for the *WebBrowser* is simple and does not specify a *Source* URL. Instead, the work of setting up the browser is done in code by hooking up the *Loaded* event on the *WebBrowser* control. This handler fetches a local HTML page from the app install folder and then navigates the browser to that page.

```
public MainPage()
{
    InitializeComponent();
    browser.Loaded += browser_Loaded;
}

private void browser_Loaded(object sender, RoutedEventArgs e)
{
    browser.Navigate(new Uri("/VideoPage.html", UriKind.Relative));
}
```

The HTML page itself is where the video is defined. This is a simple HTML document that is added to the project, with its build action set to *Content*.

```
<!doctype html>
<html>
  <head>
    <meta name="viewport" content="width=device-width, initial-scale=1.0" />
  </head>
  <body>
    <div id="main">
      Eight Platform Announcements
      <p />
      Windows Phone 8
      <p />
```

```
        <video
        src="http://media.ch9.ms/ch9/755d/4f893d13-fa05-4871-9123-3eadd2f0755d/
EightPlatformAnnouncements.wmv"
        controls=""/>
        <p />
        Joe Belfiore, Corporate Vice President
      </div>
    </body>
</html>
```

When the app runs, it loads the HTML page, and the video element on the page provides a video button, as shown in Figure 7-3. When the user taps this button, the video element navigates to the specified video and starts playing it. Standard start/pause/forward/rewind controls are added as a semitransparent layer on top of the video.

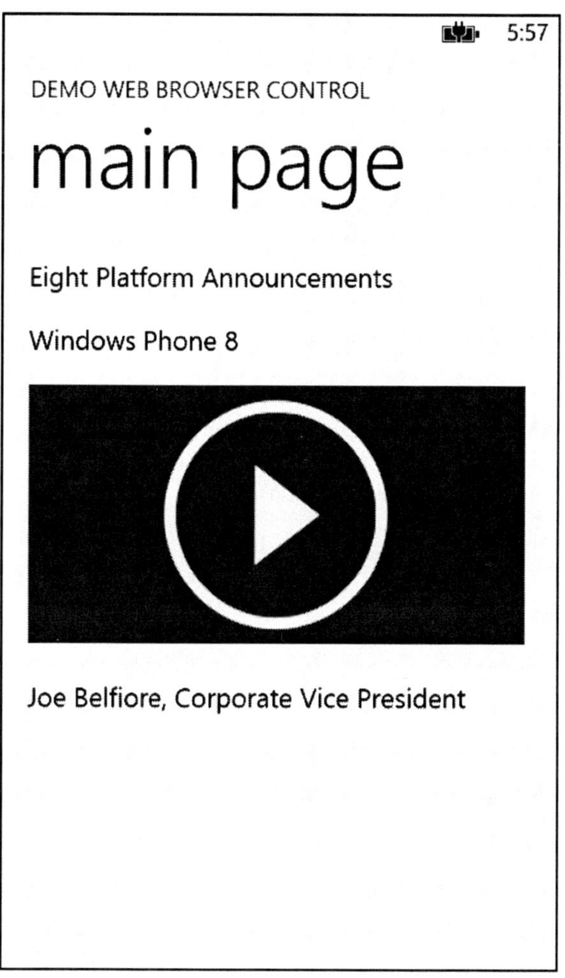

FIGURE 7-3 You can embed video links in HTML pages in your Windows Phone app.

Visual Studio includes a new Windows Phone HTML5 App project type that specifically targets Windows Phone apps where the primary content is local HTML pages. The generated code includes a CSS stylesheet, a starter HTML page, a *WebBrowser* control declaration in the *MainPage.xaml*, and two app bar buttons. These buttons are implemented to invoke the *WebBrowser* methods *GoBack*, *GoForward*, and *Navigate*. This project type is useful if your app scenario matches its intended purpose—that is, if you're making heavy use of local HTML pages. However, it's probably not generally useful to duplicate the behavior of the built-in browser on the phone. When the user wants a general-purpose browser, he'll use the general-purpose browser. Other browsing scenarios are also covered by the *WebBrowserTask*, as discussed in Chapter 5, "Phone and media services."

Integrating with JavaScript

It is possible to interoperate bi-directionally between JavaScript on an HTML page and your app code. There are three aspects to doing this:

- If you want any script on the page to run, you need to set the *WebBrowser.IsScriptEnabled* property to *true*.
- To receive data from scripts on the HTML page, you need to hook up the *WebBrowser.Script Notify* event and retrieve the data in the *NotifyEventArgs* parameter.
- To invoke script on the HTML page, you can invoke the *WebBrowser.InvokeScript* method, specifying the name of the function to invoke and passing any input data.

You can work with script on any suitable HTML page, local or remote, although you would almost certainly restrict your app to working with known pages and scripts—specifically, those that you control. For this reason, the pages are likely to be either on a server you control or local to the app. Figure 7-4 shows an app (the *DemoBrowserScript* solution in the sample code) that loads a local HTML page into a *WebBrowser* control and then interacts with the script on the page.

To make it more obvious which parts of this are in the webpage and which parts are in the client app, there is a border around the *WebBrowser* control. The HTML source for the page is listed in the code sample that follows. There are two JavaScript functions:

- **OutputFromApp** This is invoked within the app. The function takes in a text parameter and sets it into the *textFromApp* <div> on the HTML page.
- **InputToApp** This is invoked when the user taps the Send button on the HTML page. The function takes the text from the *textToApp* input textbox on the page and then sends it to anything listening to the external *Notify* event (an event that you hook up in the client phone app).

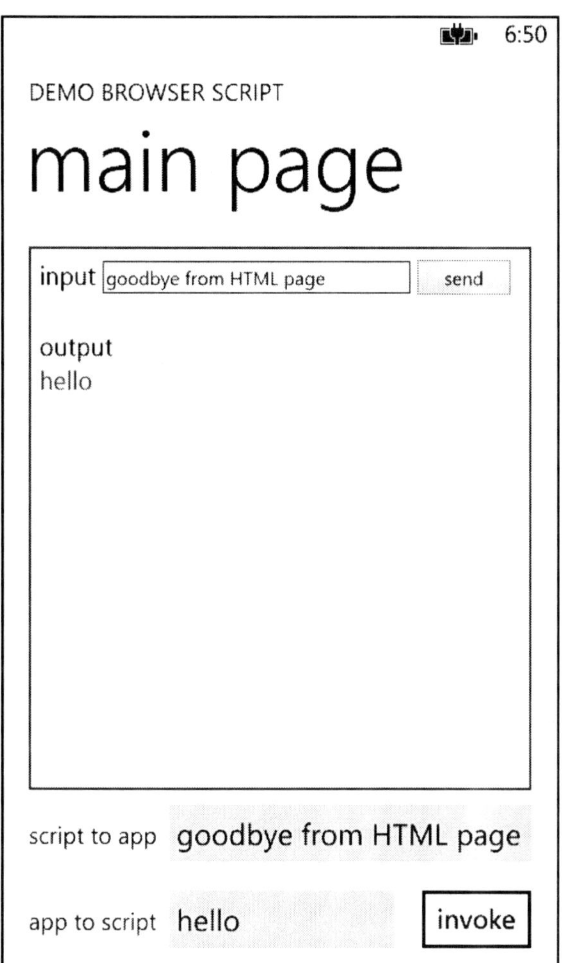

FIGURE 7-4 The *DemoWebBrowser* sample shows how you can interoperate between a phone app and | webpage script.

```
<!DOCTYPE html PUBLIC "-//W3C//DTD XHTML 1.0 Transitional//EN" "http://www.w3.org/TR/xhtml1/DTD/
xhtml1-transitional.dtd">
<html xmlns="http://www.w3.org/1999/xhtml">
  <head>
    <title>SimplePage</title>
    <meta name="mobileoptimized" content="480" />
    <script type="text/javascript">
      function OutputFromApp(text) {
      textFromApp.innerHTML = text;
      }

      function InputToApp() {
      window.external.Notify(textToApp.value);
      }
    </script>
```

```
  </head>
  <body>

    <div style="font-family: 'Segoe WP Semibold'; font-size: x-large">
      input
      <input id="textToApp" type="text"
          style="font-family: 'Segoe WP Semibold'; font-size: large; width: 292px;" />
      <input id="sendButton" type="button" value="send" onclick="InputToApp()"
          style="font-family: 'Segoe WP Semibold'; font-size: large; width: 90px;" />
      <br />
      <br />
      output
      <div id="textFromApp"
          style="font-family: 'Segoe WP Semibold'; font-size: x-large; color: #FF0000;" />
    </div>

  </body>
</html>
```

Take note of the *mobileoptimized* tag: you can use this to specify an integer value that corresponds to the intended display width of the screen. In the case of Windows Phone, this should always be 480. The browser will honor this value and force the page into a single-column layout at the specified width. Search engines also use the tag to determine whether the page is mobile-optimized.

The code for the *MainPage* first enables the *WebBrowser* control for scripting, hooks up the *ScriptNotify* event, and then navigates to the local webpage. The *ScriptNotify* event is raised when the script calls *window.external.Notify*. When the user taps Send on the webpage, the page JavaScript invokes *Notify*, which results in a callback to the *ScriptNotify* event handler. This handler fetches the incoming data from the JavaScript function and sets it into a *TextBox*. Finally, when the user taps the *Invoke* button in the client phone app, this calls *InvokeScript* on the *WebBrowser* control to invoke one of the JavaScript functions on the HTML page and pass in some data.

```
public MainPage()
{
    InitializeComponent();
}

protected override void OnNavigatedTo(NavigationEventArgs e)
{
    browser.IsScriptEnabled = true;
    browser.ScriptNotify += new EventHandler<NotifyEventArgs>(browser_ScriptNotify);
    browser.Navigate(new Uri("/SimplePage.html", UriKind.Relative));
}

private void browser_ScriptNotify(object sender, NotifyEventArgs e)
{
    scriptToApp.Text = e.Value;
}

private void InvokeScript_Click(object sender, RoutedEventArgs e)
{
    browser.InvokeScript("OutputFromApp", appToScript.Text);
}
```

Live SDK

You can use the Live SDK to connect to Windows Live, including SkyDrive. Figure 7-5 shows a very simple phone app that connects to the user's Microsoft Account and retrieves some basic profile data for the logged-on user (the *TestLive* solution in the sample code). Having fetched the data, the app displays the name in a *TextBlock* in the UI. Observe how the caption in the *SignInButton* changes dynamically from "Sign in" to "Sign out," according to the current sign-in state of the app.

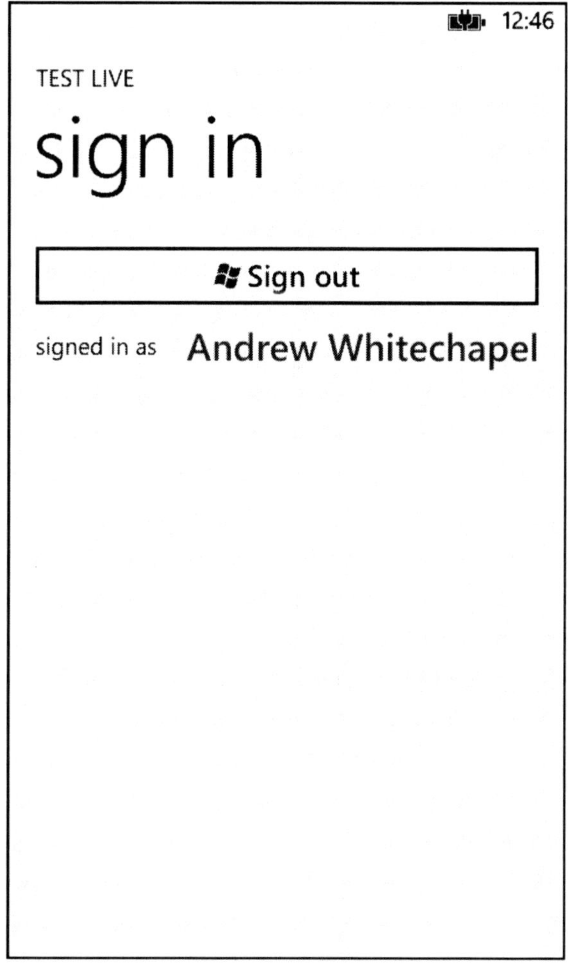

FIGURE 7-5 A phone app that connects to the user's Microsoft Account provides a sign-in/sign-out button.

Before you can successfully connect an app to a user's Microsoft Account, you must provision the app on Live itself. To do this, go to the app management site (*http://manage.dev.live.com/*) and log on with your Microsoft Account in the usual way. Then, click the Create Application link. You can give your app any arbitrary name. Live generates a Client ID and Client secret. You don't need the secret for this app, but you do need to paste the ID into your code. Be sure to select the Mobile Client App option.

To build the phone app, you need to download the Live SDK from Microsoft download. Version 5.2 is available at *http://msdn.microsoft.com/en-us/live/ff621310* (or search for Live SDK on the Microsoft Download Center). This includes a couple of critical Dynamic-Link Libraries (DLLs) that provide access to Live. Next, create a regular Windows Phone app. Add references to the *Microsoft.Live.dll* and *Microsoft.Live.Controls.dll* assemblies (these were installed with the Live SDK, typically to %ProgramFiles(x86)%\Microsoft SDKs\Live\v5.0\Windows Phone\References). You can then add a *SignInButton* control to your XAML. You can type this in manually, and you also need to add the corresponding namespace declaration. Alternatively, you can add it to the ToolBox in Visual Studio and then drag it from the there to the design surface. Using this approach, the namespace is added for you. Here's the XAML declaration for the sample app:

```
xmlns:live="clr-namespace:Microsoft.Live.Controls;assembly=Microsoft.Live.Controls"
...
<live:SignInButton
    x:Name="liveSignIn" SessionChanged="liveSignIn_SessionChanged" />
```

In the code-behind, initialize the *Scopes* and *ClientId* properties of the *SignInButton* control. *Scopes* are the permissions that your app needs when connecting to Live. These are similar in concept to the capabilities that you specify for a phone app, but they are specific to Live. When the app runs, the user is shown the list of scopes that your app is requesting so that he can make an informed decision as to whether to allow the app to connect to Live on his behalf, as shown in Figure 7-6.

The three basic scopes are *wl.signin, wl.basic*, and *wl.offline*_access. There are extended scopes for accessing birthday information, photos, emails, contacts, and so on, but those are not used in this app. Also, you need to keep in mind that if you do want to access the user's Live contacts/calendar, that information is available directly from the phone. See Chapter 15, "Contacts and calendar," for details.

```
private LiveConnectClient liveClient;

public MainPage()
{
    InitializeComponent();

    liveSignIn.Scopes = "wl.signin wl.basic wl.offline_access";
    liveSignIn.ClientId = "<< CLIENT ID >>";
}
```

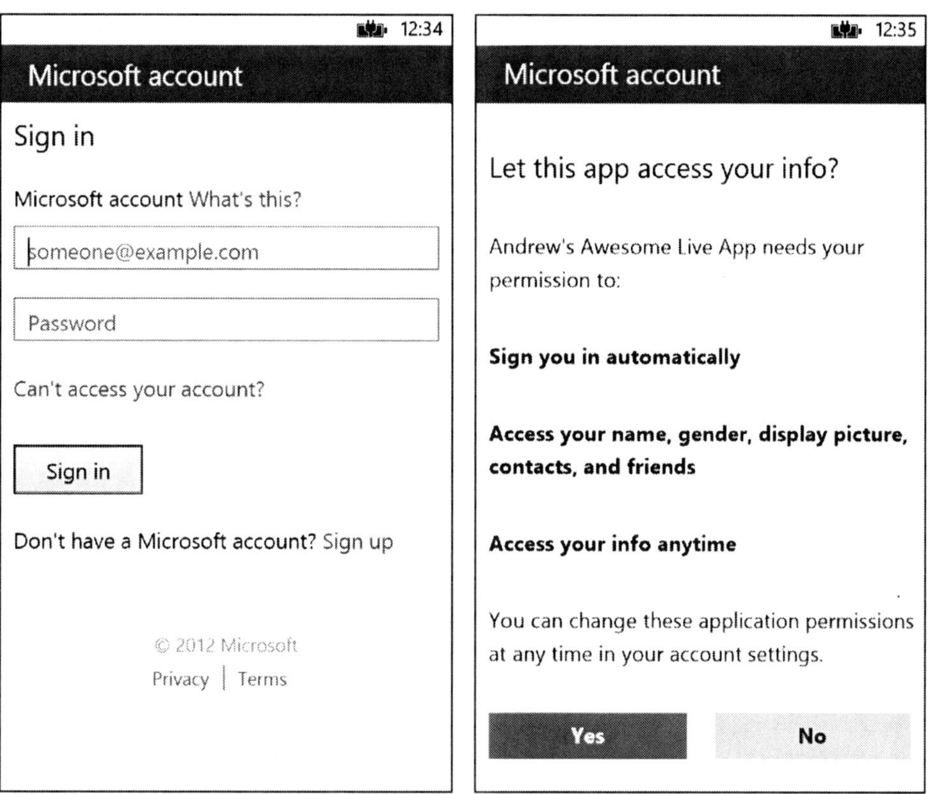

FIGURE 7-6 When you log on to Windows Live, you're presented with a scopes access prompt.

In the XAML, the *SessionChanged* event is hooked up on the *SignInButton*. The implementation for this handler constructs a *LiveConnectClient* object from the event arguments. This event handler will be invoked first when the *SiglnButton* is loaded, at which point there will be no session. After that, it will be invoked after the user has clicked the *SignInButton* to log on to Live and he has accepted the proposed scopes. At this point, the app hooks up the *GetCompleted* event and invokes the asynchronous *GetAsync* method. This calls the Windows Live REST API, with a specific entity request. In this case, the app is retrieving the user data, as specified by the "*me*" identifier.

```
private void liveSignIn_SessionChanged(
    object sender, LiveConnectSessionChangedEventArgs e)
{
    if (e.Session != null)
    {
        liveClient = new LiveConnectClient(e.Session);
        liveClient.GetCompleted += OnGetLiveData;
        liveClient.GetAsync("me", null);
    }
    else
    {
        liveClient = null;
        liveResult.Text = e.Error != null ? e.Error.ToString() : string.Empty;
    }
}
```

When the *GetAsync* call returns, the custom *OnGetLiveData* event handler is invoked. Assuming this was successful, you'll now have a set of user data that includes name, id, profile page link, birthday, employer, gender, emails, and so on. This simple app is only interested in the *name* property, which it retrieves from the result set and places into the UI of the app.

```
private void OnGetLiveData(object sender, LiveOperationCompletedEventArgs e)
{
    if (e.Error == null)
    {
        liveResult.Text = e.Error.ToString();
        return;
    }
    else
{
        object name;
        if (e.Result.TryGetValue("name", out name))
        {
            liveResult.Text = name.ToString();
        }
        else
        {
            liveResult.Text = "name not found";
        }
    }
}
```

SkyDrive

Figure 7-7 shows an enhanced version of this app (the *LivePhotos* solution in the sample code), which fetches photos from a SkyDrive album for the logged-on user. SkyDrive photos are also available through the standard photo picker feature on the phone.

The app defines a *SkyDrivePhoto* class to represent the key data that we want to fetch for each photo from SkyDrive. Note that the Live/SkyDrive REST API returns more properties (such as *Description*, *ID*, and so on), but we're only interested in the *Title* and *Url*. In a more complex app, you might want to support changes to the data by implementing *INotifyPropertyChanged*, but we don't need that feature here.

```
public class SkyDrivePhoto
{
    public string Title { get; set; }
    public string Url { get; set; }
}
```

FIGURE 7-7 You can use the Windows Live API to download photos from SkyDrive.

The XAML for the page defines a *ListBox* with an *ItemTemplate* that includes an Image for the photo itself, plus a *TextBlock* for the *Title*. These two controls are data-bound to the SkyDrive properties.

```
<StackPanel x:Name="ContentPanel" Grid.Row="1" Margin="12,0,12,0">
    <live:SignInButton
        x:Name="liveSignIn" SessionChanged="liveSignIn_SessionChanged" />
    <TextBlock x:Name="albumName" Height="80" Style="{StaticResource PhoneTextAccentStyle}"
FontSize="{StaticResource PhoneFontSizeLarge}"/>
    <ListBox
        x:Name="PhotoList" Height="460" Margin="{StaticResource PhoneHorizontalMargin}">
        <ListBox.ItemTemplate>
            <DataTemplate>
                <Grid>
                    <Grid.RowDefinitions>
                        <RowDefinition Height="180"/>
                    </Grid.RowDefinitions>
```

```
                    <Grid.ColumnDefinitions>
                        <ColumnDefinition Width="200"/>
                        <ColumnDefinition Width="*"/>
                    </Grid.ColumnDefinitions>
                    <Image
                        Grid.Row="0" Grid.Column="0" Width="200" Height="175"
                        Source="{Binding Url}" CacheMode="BitmapCache" Stretch="UniformToFill" />
                    <TextBlock
                        Grid.Row="0" Grid.Column="1" Text="{Binding Title}"
                        TextWrapping="Wrap" VerticalAlignment="Center"
                        Style="{StaticResource PhoneTextTitle3Style}" />
                </Grid>
            </DataTemplate>
        </ListBox.ItemTemplate>
    </ListBox>
</StackPanel>
```

In the page code-behind, we declare a *LiveConnectSession* field so that we can cache this between method calls. As before, we'll get the session value in the *SessionChanged* event handler. Previously, we only needed to use this in the one handler, but now we'll need it in a second handler. This is because we need to make two calls to retrieve SkyDrive data: one for the collection of albums, and a second call for the collection of photos within a given album. We also declare an *ObservableCollection* of *SkyDrivePhoto* objects. This will represent all the photos to be downloaded for the photo album that the app targets. Observe how the *Scopes* in this instance must be set to a string that includes "*wl.photos*" and "*wl.skydrive*".

```
private LiveConnectClient liveClient;
private LiveConnectSession liveSession;
private ObservableCollection<SkydrivePhoto> photos =
    new ObservableCollection<SkydrivePhoto>();
public ObservableCollection<SkydrivePhoto> Photos
{
    get { return photos; }
    private set { }
}

public MainPage()
{
    InitializeComponent();
    PhotoList.ItemsSource = Photos;
    liveSignIn.Scopes = "wl.signin wl.photos wl.skydrive";
    liveSignIn.ClientId = "<< CLIENT ID >>";
}
```

In the *SessionChanged* event handler, we hook up the *GetCompleted* event, as before, and invoke *GetAsync* to fetch the collection of albums for this user. Just for good housekeeping, when the user signs out of Live, we also clear the album and photos data from the UI.

```
private void liveSignIn_SessionChanged(
    object sender, LiveConnectSessionChangedEventArgs e)
{
    if (e.Session != null)
    {
        liveSession = e.Session;
        liveClient = new LiveConnectClient(e.Session);
        liveClient.GetCompleted += OnGetLiveData;
        liveClient.GetAsync("me/albums", null);
    }
    else
    {
        liveClient = null;
        albumName.Text = String.Empty;
        photos.Clear();
    }
}
```

The implementation of the *OnGetLiveData* callback is rather different from the previous version. Instead of retrieving a simple string value, we're now fetching a collection of albums, indicated by the *"data"* prefix in the result set. In this example, we're only interested in the first album in the collection. We extract the name so that we can display it in the UI (in place of the user name that was displayed before). We also extract the *ID* because we need to pass this to the second *GetAsync* call, appending *"/files"*, to fetch the collection of photos within this album.

```
private void OnGetLiveData(object sender, LiveOperationCompletedEventArgs e)
{
    if (e.Error != null)
        return;
    if (!e.Result.ContainsKey("data"))
            return;
    List<object> data = (List<object>)e.Result["data"];
    IDictionary<string, object> album = (IDictionary<string, object>)data[0];
    albumName.Text = (string)album["name"];
    String albumId = (string)album["id"];
    LiveConnectClient albumClient = new LiveConnectClient(liveSession);
    albumClient.GetCompleted +=
        new EventHandler<LiveOperationCompletedEventArgs>(
            albumClient_GetCompleted);
    albumClient.GetAsync(albumId + "/files", null);
}
```

Finally, in the second *GetCompleted* handler, we extract the collection of photos, again identified by the *"data"* prefix. For each photo, we extract the name and source properties. The source property is the URL of the photo on SkyDrive.

```
private void albumClient_GetCompleted(object sender, LiveOperationCompletedEventArgs e)
{
    if (e.Error == null)
    {
        List<object> data = (List<object>)e.Result["data"];
        foreach (IDictionary<string, object> item in data)
        {
            SkyDrivePhoto photo = new SkyDrivePhoto();
            photo.Title = (string)item["name"];
            photo.Url = (string)item["source"];
            photos.Add(photo);
        }
    }
}
```

Facebook

The Facebook C# SDK is available as a NuGet package, named *Facebook*. (See the instructions earlier in this chapter for the Async Pack for how to install a NuGet package.) The package supports web, desktop Silverlight, and Windows Phone apps that are designed to integrate with Facebook. Facebook uses OAuth 2.0 for authenticating your app and authorizing your app to perform operations on behalf of a valid user. To create a Phone app that integrates with Facebook, you must first provision the app on Facebook, which really just means that you create a Facebook App ID for it.

To do this, you need to go to the Facebook developer page (*http://developers.facebook.com/*), log on with a valid Facebook account, and then create an application. The tool will present you with a form with an application name as well as a captcha challenge. It will then allocate you a Facebook App ID and App Secret.

Figure 7-8 shows the *TestFacebook* solution in the sample code. The app has three pages: *MainPage*, *LoginPage*, and *DetailsPage*. *MainPage* simply shows a *Button* to navigate to the *LoginPage*. This is a separate page because it hosts a *WebBrowser* set to navigate to the Facebook login page, which takes up an entire page (Figure 7-8, left). When the user has successfully logged in, this redirects to the *DetailsPage*. The *DetailsPage* gathers some simple data from the user's profile (Figure 7-8, right).

The XAML and code for *MainPage* is trivial. In the XAML for the *LoginPage*, note that it is important to set the *WebBrowser* control's *IsScriptEnabled* property to *true*; otherwise, the connection will fail because the Facebook login mechanism includes JavaScript for redirection.

```
<phone:WebBrowser
    x:Name="browser" Margin="{StaticResource PhoneHorizontalMargin}"
    IsScriptEnabled="True" Navigated="browser_Navigated" />
```

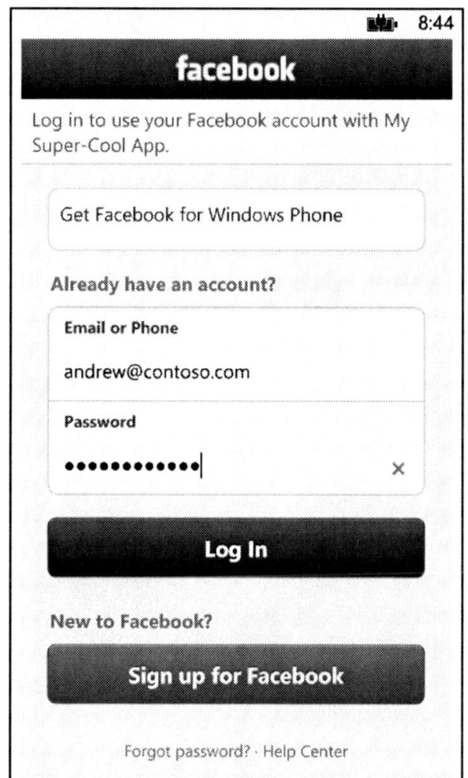

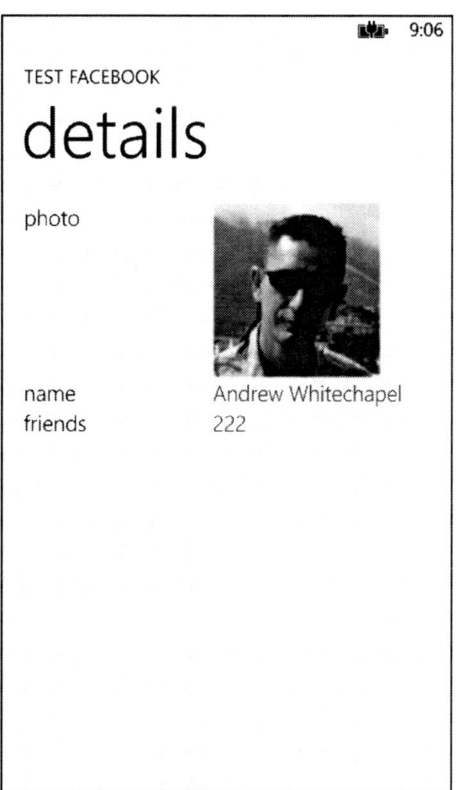

FIGURE 7-8 To connect to Facebook, your app must provide the Facebook login page. After the user logs in, your app can fetch Facebook data.

In the *LoginPage* code-behind, we declare a string for the App ID and comma-separated set of strings for the permissions that this app will request from the user when she logs in. You should request only those permissions that you actually need. The more permissions you ask for, the greater the likelihood that the user will reject the request to connect. This example requests only the ability to read basic profile data for the user and to read the user's data stream; it does not include the ability to post to the user's wall, for example.

To set up the Facebook login page, you must provide a collection of parameters that include your App ID, any extended permissions you're asking for (beyond the public profile data), the default Facebook redirect page for successful login, and, for mobile devices, the "touch" display type. Notice that the "scope" parameter is only added if you're requesting extended permissions. For more information, read the Facebook API documentation for login at *http://developers.facebook.com/docs/reference/login/*. Having built up a URL from these parameters, we can then invoke the *FacebookClient.GetLoginUrl* method. This method returns a valid URL that we can then pass on to the *WebBrowser* control for navigation.

```
private const string appId = "<< APP ID >>";
private const string extendedPermissions = "user_about_me,read_stream";
private readonly FacebookClient fbClient = new FacebookClient();

protected override void OnNavigatedTo(NavigationEventArgs e)
{
    if (e.NavigationMode == NavigationMode.New)
    {
        var parameters = new Dictionary<string, object>();
        parameters["client_id"] = appId;
        parameters["redirect_uri"] = "https://www.facebook.com/connect/login_success.html";
        parameters["response_type"] = "token";
        parameters["display"] = "touch";

        if (!string.IsNullOrEmpty(extendedPermissions))
        {
            parameters["scope"] = extendedPermissions;
        }

        Uri loginUrl = fbClient.GetLoginUrl(parameters);
        browser.Navigate(loginUrl);
    }
}
```

In this example, the URL returned by *GetLoginUrl* looks something like the following listing (with the dummy "<< APPID >>" replaced, of course), which can be useful to know in case you ever need to either compose or decompose the URL manually:

```
"https://www.facebook.com/dialog/oauth?client_id=<<APPID>>&redirect_uri=https%3A%2F%2Fwww.
facebook.com%2Fconnect%2Flogin_success.html&response_type=token&display=touch&scope=user_about_
me%2Cread_stream"
```

The app handles the *WebBrowser.Navigated* event, and after the user successfully logs in, the *FacebookOAuthResult.IsSuccess* property will be set to *true*. At this point, we can extract the *AccessToken* and use it to construct a new *FacebookClient* object. In this example, we request the user ID from the logged-in user profile data by passing "me?fields=id" to the *FacebookClient GetAsync* method.

```
private void browser_Navigated(object sender, NavigationEventArgs e)
{
    FacebookOAuthResult oauthResult;
    if (!fbClient.TryParseOAuthCallbackUrl(e.Uri, out oauthResult))
    {
        return;
    }

    if (!oauthResult.IsSuccess)
    {
        Debug.WriteLine(oauthResult.ErrorDescription);
        return;
    }

    var accessToken = oauthResult.AccessToken;
    var fb = new FacebookClient(accessToken);
```

```
    fb.GetCompleted += (o, e) =>
    {
        if (e.Error != null)
        {
            Dispatcher.BeginInvoke(() => MessageBox.Show(e.Error.Message));
            return;
        }

        var result = (IDictionary<string, object>)e.GetResultData();
        var id = (string)result["id"];
        var url = string.Format("/DetailsPage.xaml?access_token={0}&id={1}", accessToken, id);
        Dispatcher.BeginInvoke(() => NavigationService.Navigate(new Uri(url, UriKind.Relative)));
    };

    fb.GetAsync("me?fields=id");
}
```

When *GetAsync* returns, we extract the *id* value, and forward this on to the *DetailsPage*, along with the access token previously extracted. In the *DetailsPage*, we override *OnNavigatedTo* and extract the access token and user ID from the query string. We then fetch Facebook data, via three custom methods, each one using a different API. Facebook supports three different APIs:

- **REST** You can use this API to interact with Facebook via HTTP requests. Be aware, however, that Facebook is in the process of deprecating the REST API, so if you are building a new Facebook app, you are advised to use the Graph API, instead.
- **Graph** We used the Graph API to extract the user ID. Using the *GetAsync* and *PostAsync* methods, you can access all exposed Facebook data from what it calls the "social graph," for either reading or writing.
- **Facebook Query Language (FQL)** With this API, you can use a SQL-style query to access the data exposed by the Graph API. It provides for some advanced features not available in the Graph API, such as using the results of one query in another.

In the *DetailsPage*, we fetch the user's profile photo by using the HTTP URL, the user's name via the Graph API, and the count of the user's Facebook friends by using the FQL API.

```
protected override void OnNavigatedTo(System.Windows.Navigation.NavigationEventArgs e)
{
    if (e.NavigationMode == NavigationMode.New)
    {
        accessToken = NavigationContext.QueryString["access_token"];
        userId = NavigationContext.QueryString["id"];

        GetHttpData();
        GetSocialGraphData();
        GetFqlData();
    }
}
```

We could get the user's profile photo by using any of the three APIs, but in this example, we're using a simple HTTP URL, specifying the user ID and the app access token. There are several choices for the size of photo to retrieve; here, we're requesting the "large" format photo, which is 200 pixels wide and up to 600 pixels tall.

```
private void GetHttpData()
{
    string profilePictureUrl =
        string.Format("https://graph.facebook.com/{0}/picture?type={1}&access_token={2}",
        userId, "large", accessToken);
    fbPhoto.Source = new BitmapImage(new Uri(profilePictureUrl));
}
```

To get social graph data, we use the Graph API, which is the most commonly used API for Facebook. As with the user ID, you pass in the appropriate parameter to *GetAsync* and get back a collection of properties, which you can index by property name. In this example, we fetch the user name and display it in a *TextBlock* in the UI. If you're using the *FacebookClient* object in many places in your app, it might be worthwhile making it a static field in your *App* class.

```
private void GetSocialGraphData()
{
    FacebookClient fb = new FacebookClient(accessToken);

    fb.GetCompleted += (o, e) =>
    {
        if (e.Error != null)
        {
            Dispatcher.BeginInvoke(() => MessageBox.Show(e.Error.Message));
            return;
        }
        var result = (IDictionary<string, object>)e.GetResultData();
        Dispatcher.BeginInvoke(() => { fbName.Text = (string)result["name"]; });
    };

    fb.GetAsync("me");
}
```

To get a better idea of the data that's available, you can use Facebook's Graph API Explorer, with which you can select properties and execute a query to fetch data for the current logged-in user (see Figure 7-9). If you select a field that requires additional permissions, you must supply a valid access token. You can use the Get Access Token button to generate one, and this will prompt you to select the specific permissions that you want.

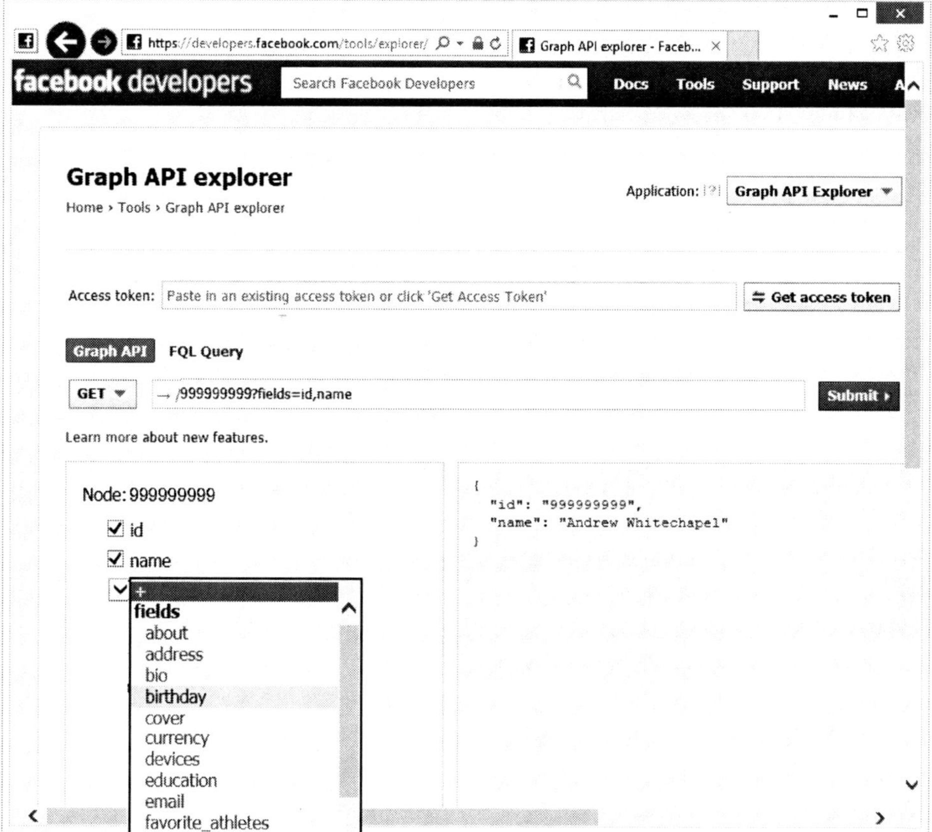

FIGURE 7-9 You can use the Facebook Graph API Explorer to investigate the data available through the Graph API.

The final custom method fetches the count of the user's Facebook friends by using the FQL API. In this example, the query selects the user IDs of all friends of the current user and then extracts the *Count* property of the collection that is returned. Unfortunately, FQL doesn't support a direct COUNT query mechanism.

```
private void GetFqlData()
{
    FacebookClient fb = new FacebookClient(accessToken);

    fb.GetCompleted += (o, e) =>
    {
        if (e.Error != null)
        {
            Dispatcher.BeginInvoke(() => MessageBox.Show(e.Error.Message));
            return;
        }
```

```
        var result = (IDictionary<string, object>)e.GetResultData();
        var data = (IList<object>)result["data"];
        var count = data.Count;
        Dispatcher.BeginInvoke(() => { fbFriends.Text = count.ToString(); });
    };

    var query = "SELECT uid FROM user WHERE uid IN (SELECT uid2 FROM friend WHERE uid1=me())";
    fb.GetAsync("fql", new { q = query });
}
```

For full details on the FQL API, go to *http://developers.facebook.com/docs/reference/fql/*.

Twitter

Twitter is another social media provider that supports programmatic interaction via a public SDK. As with Facebook, you must first provision an application on the Twitter website. Although Facebook uses OAuth 2.0 for authentication and authorization, Twitter uses the older OAuth 1.0a protocol, which is far more involved and much more difficult to get right.

If all you want to do is to read tweets, you can actually achieve this very simply and without any special security requirements. The *TwitterReader* app in the sample code prompts for a Twitter user name and then sends a *WebClient.DownloadStringAsync* call to the Twitter REST service, requesting an arbitrary number of the latest tweets from that user, as shown in Figure 7-10.

The app uses a simple *Tweet* class to represent the user's photo as well as the text and timestamp of the post.

```
public class Tweet
{
    public string TweetText { get; set; }
    public string TweetDate { get; set; }
    public string UserImage { get; set; }
}
```

FIGURE 7-10 You can read tweets very simply by using the Twitter REST APIs.

The format of the REST URL is very simple, and the data is returned in XML format, which makes it possible for the app to load it into an *XElement*.

```
private void getTweets_Click(object sender, EventArgs e)
{
    string url = string.Format(
        "https://api.twitter.com/1/statuses/user_timeline.xml?include_entities=true&include_
rts=true&screen_name={0}&count=10",
        nameText.Text);
    WebClient webClient = new WebClient();
    webClient.DownloadStringCompleted += client_DownloadStringCompleted;
    webClient.DownloadStringAsync(new Uri(url));
}
```

```
private void client_DownloadStringCompleted(object sender, DownloadStringCompletedEventArgs e)
{
    if (e.Error != null)
        return;

    XElement tweets = XElement.Parse(e.Result);
    var tweetItems = from tweet in tweets.Descendants("status") select new Tweet
    {
        UserImage = tweet.Element("user").Element("profile_image_url").Value,
        TweetText = tweet.Element("text").Value,
        TweetDate = tweet.Element("created_at").Value
    };
    tweetsList.ItemsSource = tweetItems;
}
```

If you want to do more than this—and especially if you want to access protected parts of the user's data or to post tweets on the user's behalf—you'll have to do a lot more work, most of it related to correctly constructing the OAuth security headers for the web request.

The Twitter development documentation, which you can view at *http://dev.twitter.com,* details several alternative ways to connect to the Twitter APIs, depending on the type of app and how you want to use the Twitter APIs. For mobile phones, the standard approach is to use pin-based authorization. Here's how this works—and note that this complexity is not restricted to Twitter, the same general pattern also applies for other OAuth 1.0 scenarios:

- To use most of the Twitter APIs, you must supply an Access Token.
- To acquire an Access Token, you must first get a Verifier PIN, which is the user's permission for your app to access the Twitter APIs on his behalf.
- To obtain a Verifier PIN, you must navigate the user to a Twitter login page with information in the web request that specifies your app.
- To navigate to the correct URL, you must first get a Request Token.
- To acquire a Request Token, you must supply a Consumer Key and Consumer Secret.
- To get a Consumer Key and Consumer Secret, you must create a Twitter application on the Twitter website.

Thus, the first task is to create a Twitter application on the Twitter website, as demonstrated in Figure 7-11.

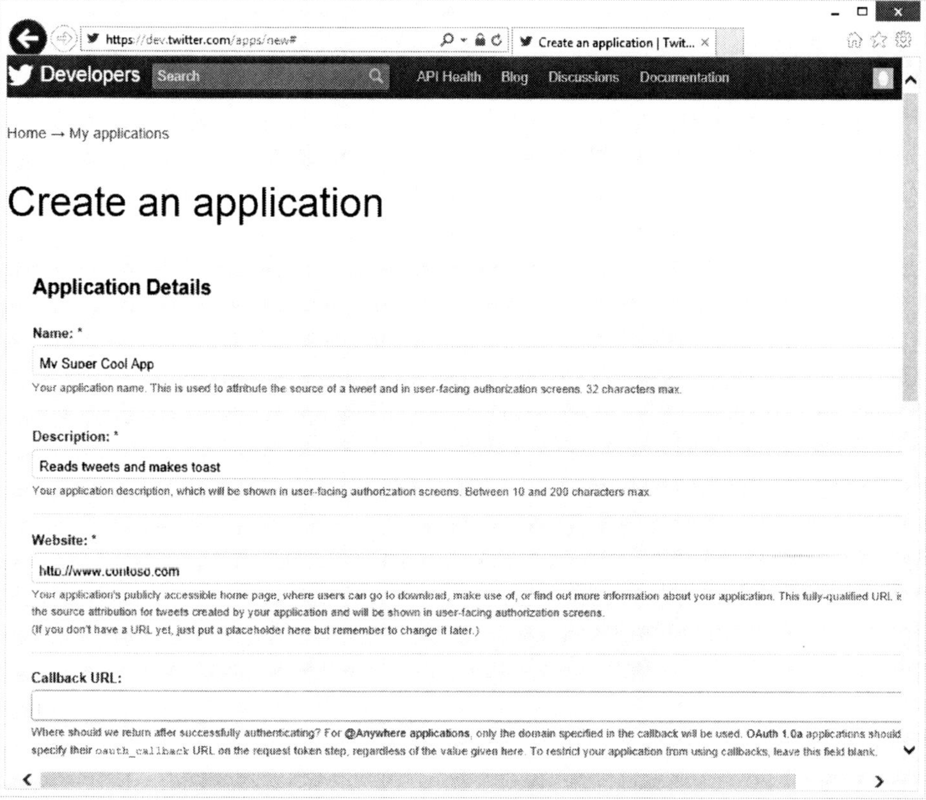

FIGURE 7-11 You must create a Twitter application on the Twitter website before you can call secured Twitter APIs.

As you fill in the details for your app, don't specify a callback URL: this is the URL to which Twitter returns after authenticating the user's login credentials. In a phone app, you typically close the browser after user login, so there's no point returning anywhere (unless you use a custom scheme). When you confirm your new application, Twitter assigns you a Consumer Key and Consumer Secret, as illustrated in Figure 7-12. These are the first two pieces of data you need to construct a secured Twitter web request.

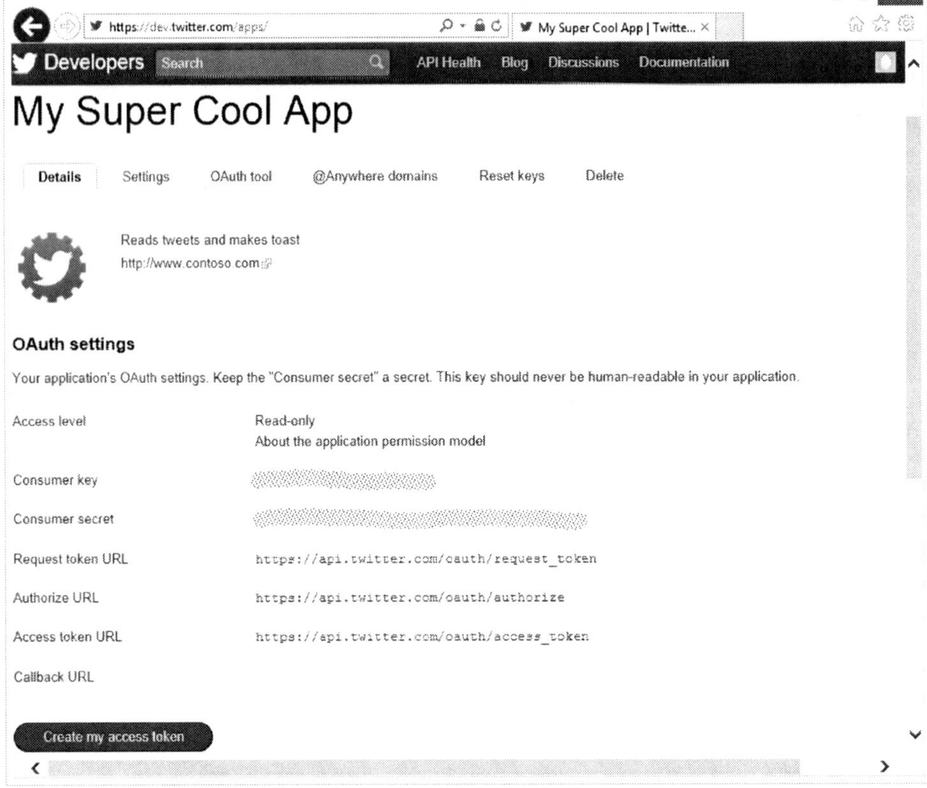

FIGURE 7-12 When you create a Twitter application, you are be given a Consumer Key and Consumer Secret.

The remaining work is done in your app code. The high-level tasks are as follows:

1. Acquire a Request Token and a Login URL.
2. Go to to the Login URL.
3. When the user logs in, from the resulting webpage, extract the Verifier PIN.
4. Get an Access Token.
5. Use the Access Token in secured API calls.

The *TwitterWriter* app in the sample code (see Figure 7-13) demonstrates all these steps. The remainder of this section describes the main points of each task; for full details, refer to the sample code.

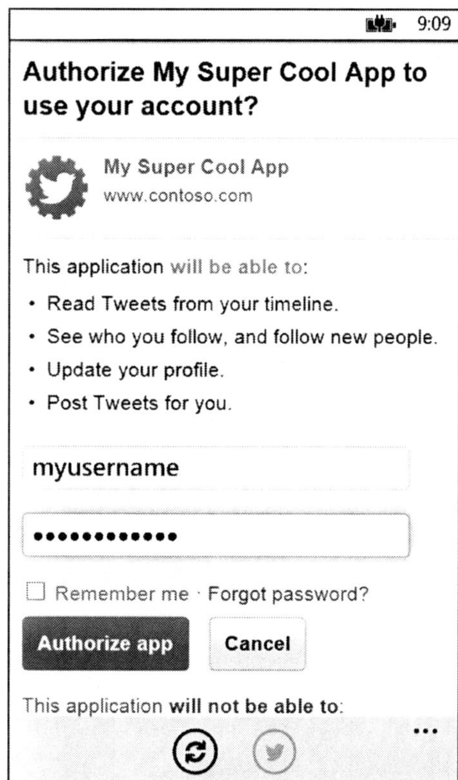

FIGURE 7-13 The *TwitterWriter* app posts tweets on behalf of the user and provides a Twitter login page so that the user can authorize the app.

The app's main page includes an app bar with four buttons. The idea is that these four buttons—plus the login page—correspond to the five high-level tasks that you must perform to successfully invoke secured Twitter APIs. Each button is enabled in turn, as the previous task succeeds. In a realistic app, you wouldn't provide such UI feedback of the underlying mechanism, but it serves here to illustrate each task more clearly.

The *Click* handlers for each button are very simple: they're focused on tracking the enabled state of the buttons and providing *MessageBox* feedback on progress. All the real work is done by a custom helper class named *TwitterHelper*. For example, the first task is to obtain a Request Token and the Login URL.

```
private TwitterHelper Twitter = new TwitterHelper();
private async void getRequest_Click(object sender, EventArgs e)
{
    bool success = await Twitter.GetRequestTokenAndLoginUrl();
    if (success)
```

```
    {
        MessageBox.Show("Got Request Token");
        login.IsEnabled = true;
        getRequest.IsEnabled = false;
    }
    else
    {
        MessageBox.Show("Cannot get Request Token");
        login.IsEnabled = false;
        getRequest.IsEnabled = true;
    }
}
```

Observe that the *TwitterHelper.GetRequestTokenAndLoginUrl* method is awaitable, and returns a simple *bool* result. An app normally doesn't do anything with the Request Token except to pass it on as part of the next stage in the request, so we really only need to know whether the call succeeded. The definition of this method executes an asynchronous *WebRequest* with a complex authorization and then extracts the token information from the response. All this is done asynchronously behind a *TaskCompletionSource* object, defined in the Task Parallel Library. The remaining tasks follow the same pattern.

For simplicity in this app, the Consumer Key and Consumer Secret are hard-coded. Bearing in mind that all apps are now encrypted in the Windows Phone Store, you might consider this sufficient security. If you want additional obscurity, you could explicitly encrypt the keys on the phone, or keep them behind a web service on a server that you control This last approach also makes it possible for you to update/revoke them as necessary.

```
private const string ConsumerKey = "<< CONSUMER_KEY >>";
private const string ConsumerSecret = "<< CONSUMER_SECRET >>";
private const string RequestUrl = "http://api.twitter.com/oauth/request_token";
public const string AuthorizeUrl = "http://api.twitter.com/oauth/authorize";
private const string AccessUrl = "http://api.twitter.com/oauth/access_token";
private const string PostUrl = "http://api.twitter.com/1/statuses/update.json";

public  Task<bool> GetRequestTokenAndLoginUrl()
{
    TaskCompletionSource<bool> source = new TaskCompletionSource<bool>();
    WebRequest request = BuildRequest(RequestUrl);
    request.BeginGetResponse(result =>
    {
        try
        {
            HttpWebRequest requestResult = result.AsyncState as HttpWebRequest;
            using (WebResponse response = requestResult.EndGetResponse(result))
            using (Stream stream = response.GetResponseStream())
            using (StreamReader reader = new StreamReader(stream))
            {
                string responseText = reader.ReadToEnd();
                ExtractTokenFromResponse(responseText);
                if (!string.IsNullOrEmpty(token))
```

```
                {
                    LoginUrl = new Uri(AuthorizeUrl + "?oauth_token=" + token);
                    source.SetResult(true);
                }
                else
                {
                    source.SetResult(true);
                }
            }
        }
        catch (Exception ex)
        {
            Debug.WriteLine(ex.ToString());
            source.SetResult(false);
        }
    }, request);
    return source.Task;
}
```

Each time you make a call to the Twitter APIs, the authorization headers must include certain specific parameters, which are listed in Table 7-1.

TABLE 7-1 Each Twitter request must include specific parameters in the headers

Parameter	Header key	Description
Consumer Key	*oauth_consumer_key*	Identifies which application is making the request.
Nonce	*oauth_nonce*	A unique token that your app must generate for each unique request. Twitter uses this value to determine whether a request has been submitted multiple times. You can use any approach which produces a relatively random string.
Signature	*oauth_signature*	Contains a value which is generated by running all of the other request parameters and two secret values through a signing algorithm. The purpose of the signature is so that Twitter can verify that the request has not been modified in transit, verify the application sending the request, and verify that the application has authorization to interact with the user's account.
Signature method	*oauth_signature_method*	This must always be HMAC-SHA1.
Timestamp	*oauth_timestamp*	Indicates when the request was created. This value should be the number of seconds since the Unix epoch (Jan 1, 1970), at the point the request is generated.
Token	*oauth_token*	Represents a user's permission to share access to their account with your app.
Version	*oauth_version*	This must always be 1.0 for any request sent to the Twitter API.

The first step within the phone app is to obtain a Request Token and an associated Request Token Secret. To do this, you need to build a request string which includes your Consumer Key and Consumer Secret, compute a hash of that string, and then build a web request that uses this hash in the headers. In the code snippet that follows, there's no particular reason for the chosen range of random numbers—the point is simply to produce a relatively random string. To generate the signature, the sample app creates an *HMACSHA1* object, sets its key to the Consumer Secret, and then uses the *HMACSHA1.ComputeHash* method to compute the hash on the request string. We then add the signature to the request parameters and set the combined request string to the request authorization header. An example OAuth header is shown here (with the Consumer Key and Signature obfuscated):

```
{oauth_consumer_key="XXXXXXXXXXXXXXXXXXXXXX",oauth_version="1.0",oauth_nonce="6444853",oauth_
timestamp="1359926196",oauth_signature_method="HMAC-SHA1",oauth_signature="XXXXXXXXXXXXXXXXXXX
XXXXXXXXXXXXXXX"}
```

```
private WebRequest BuildRequest(
    string requestUrl, IDictionary<string, string> requestParameters = null)
{
    if (requestParameters == null)
    {
        requestParameters = new Dictionary<string, string>();
    }

    if (!string.IsNullOrEmpty(token))
    {
        requestParameters["oauth_token"] = token;
    }

    if (!string.IsNullOrEmpty(verifierPin))
    {
        requestParameters["oauth_verifier"] = verifierPin;
    }

    Uri url = new Uri(requestUrl);
    string signature = BuildOAuthSignature(requestUrl, url.Query, requestParameters,
tokenSecret);
    requestParameters["oauth_signature"] = Uri.EscapeDataString(signature);
    HttpWebRequest request = WebRequest.CreateHttp(requestUrl);
    request.Method = HttpMethod;

    StringBuilder builder = new StringBuilder();
    foreach (var param in requestParameters)
    {
        if (!param.Key.StartsWith("oauth_"))
            continue;
        if (builder.Length > 0)
            builder.Append(",");
        builder.Append(param.Key + "=\"" + param.Value + "\"");
    }
    request.Headers[HttpRequestHeader.Authorization] = "OAuth " + builder;
    return request;
}

private string BuildOAuthSignature(string requestUrl, string queryString,
    IDictionary<string, string> requestParameters, string tokenSecret = null)
{
    requestParameters["oauth_consumer_key"] = ConsumerKey;
    requestParameters["oauth_version"] = "1.0";
    requestParameters["oauth_nonce"] = nonceRandom.Next(123456, 9999999).ToString();
```

```
    DateTime now = DateTime.UtcNow;
    TimeSpan timespan = now - new DateTime(1970, 1, 1, 0, 0, 0, 0);
    requestParameters["oauth_timestamp"] = Convert.ToInt64(timespan.TotalSeconds).ToString();
    requestParameters["oauth_signature_method"] = "HMAC-SHA1";

    string requestString = BuildRequestString(requestUrl, queryString, requestParameters);

    HMACSHA1 hmacsha1 = new HMACSHA1();
    string key = string.Format("{0}&{1}", Uri.EscapeDataString(ConsumerSecret),
        string.IsNullOrEmpty(tokenSecret) ? string.Empty : Uri.EscapeDataString(tokenSecret));
    hmacsha1.Key = Encoding.UTF8.GetBytes(key);

    byte[] dataBuffer = Encoding.UTF8.GetBytes(requestString);
    byte[] hashBytes = hmacsha1.ComputeHash(dataBuffer);
    return Convert.ToBase64String(hashBytes);
}
```

When building the request string, the parameters must be in alphabetical order. The simplest way to achieve this is by first passing them through a *SortedDictionary.*

```
private string BuildRequestString(
    string requestUrl, string queryString, IDictionary<string, string> requestParameters)
{
    var parameters = new SortedDictionary<string, string>();
    parameters.Add("oauth_version", requestParameters["oauth_version"]);
    parameters.Add("oauth_nonce", requestParameters["oauth_nonce"]);
    parameters.Add("oauth_timestamp", requestParameters["oauth_timestamp"]);
    parameters.Add("oauth_signature_method", requestParameters["oauth_signature_method"]);
    parameters.Add("oauth_consumer_key", requestParameters["oauth_consumer_key"]);

... etc
}
```

When you've built the authorization header, you can then execute the web request. The response from the web request will be in the form of key-value pairs. You can extract the Request Token and Request Token Secret by using the "oauth_token" and "oauth_token_secret" keys. At the same time, you can build the Login URL from the Twitter authorization URL base, concatenated with the Request Token, and show the user a *WebBrowser* control configured to navigate to that URL.

```
LoginUrl = new Uri(AuthorizeUrl + "?oauth_token=" + token);
```

This provides the user with a Twitter webpage, where he can log in with his Twitter credentials. We use the browser control in two scenarios. First, for the Twitter login page, which we show to the user so that he can provide his Twitter account credentials (see Figure 7-14). Upon successful login, Twitter then loads a response page which includes the Verifier PIN. So, the second time we use the browser control is for this Verifier PIN page, and we don't want to show this to the user, because we intend to extract the Verifier PIN programmatically.

```
private void browser_Navigated(object sender, NavigationEventArgs e)
{
    if (e.Uri.AbsoluteUri.ToLower().Replace("https://", "http://") != Twitter.AuthorizeUrl)
        browser.Visibility = Visibility.Visible;
    else
        browser.Visibility = Visibility.Collapsed;
}
```

If you'd like, you can examine the hidden HTML content during debugging by using Visual Studio's HTML visualizer, as shown in Figure 7-14.

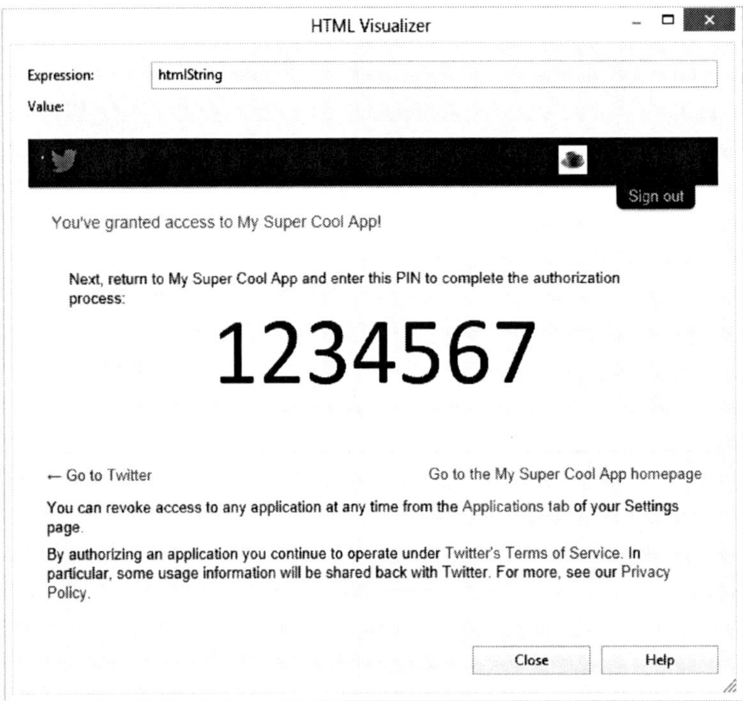

FIGURE 7-14 Upon successful login, the user is sent to a page with a Verifier PIN.

The *Navigated* event can be too early to get the HTML content, so we use the *LoadCompleted* event instead for this purpose.

```
private void browser_LoadCompleted(object sender, NavigationEventArgs e)
{
    if (e.Uri.AbsoluteUri.ToLower().Replace("https://", "http://") != Twitter.AuthorizeUrl)
        return;

    string htmlString = browser.SaveToString();
    bool success = Twitter.ExtractVerifierPin(htmlString);
```

```
    if (success)
    {
        MessageBox.Show("Login successful");
        getAccess.IsEnabled = true;
        login.IsEnabled = false;
    }
    else
    {
        MessageBox.Show("Login failed");
        getAccess.IsEnabled = false;
        login.IsEnabled = true;
    }

}
```

After you've acquired the Request Token, Request Token Secret, and Verifier PIN, you can pass these to Twitter with another web request to get an Access Token. This follows the same pattern as obtaining the Request Token: build a request string of all the required parameters, compute a hash, and set it into the authorization header. For the Access Token, you add the same parameters as for the Request Token request (Consumer Key, OAuth version, and so on). On top of that, also add the Token and Verifier PIN to the request string. This time, use both the Consumer Key and the Token Secret for the HMACSHA1 key. Compute the hash on the new request string as before, add the resulting signature to the request parameters, and then set the combined request as the request authorization header.

```
public Task<bool> GetAccessToken()
{
    TaskCompletionSource<bool> source = new TaskCompletionSource<bool>();
    WebRequest request = BuildRequest(AccessUrl);
    request.BeginGetResponse(result =>
    {
        try
        {
            HttpWebRequest requestResult = result.AsyncState as HttpWebRequest;
            using (WebResponse response = requestResult.EndGetResponse(result))
            using (Stream stream = response.GetResponseStream())
            using (StreamReader reader = new StreamReader(stream))
            {
                ResponseText = reader.ReadToEnd();
                ExtractTokenFromResponse(ResponseText);
                source.SetResult(true);
            }
        }
        catch (Exception ex)
        {
            Debug.WriteLine(ex.ToString());
            source.SetResult(false);
        }
    }, request);
    return source.Task;
}
```

Finally, with the Access Token, you can now go ahead and perform Twitter operations on behalf of the logged-in user; for example, to post a new tweet.

```
public Task<bool> PostTweet(string tweetString)
{
    TaskCompletionSource<bool> source = new TaskCompletionSource<bool>();
    var requestParameters = new Dictionary<string, string>();
    string body = "status=" + Uri.EscapeDataString(tweetString);
    requestParameters["post_body"] = body;
    WebRequest request = BuildRequest(PostUrl, requestParameters);
    request.BeginGetRequestStream(req1 =>
    {
        HttpWebRequest requestResult = req1.AsyncState as HttpWebRequest;
        using (Stream requestStream = requestResult.EndGetRequestStream(req1))
        using (StreamWriter writer = new StreamWriter(requestStream))
        {
            writer.Write(body);
        }
        requestResult.BeginGetResponse(req2 =>
        {
            try
            {
                HttpWebRequest responseResult = req2.AsyncState as HttpWebRequest;
                using (WebResponse response = requestResult.EndGetResponse(req2))
                using (Stream responseStream = response.GetResponseStream())
                using (StreamReader reader = new StreamReader(responseStream))
                {
                    ResponseText = reader.ReadToEnd();
                    source.SetResult(true);
                }
            }
            catch (Exception ex)
            {
                Debug.WriteLine(ex.ToString());
                source.SetResult(false);
            }
        }, requestResult);
    }, request);
    return source.Task;
}
```

The Data Sense feature

As part of their cellular phone service, users can sign up for different data plans. These plans range from unrestricted use through metered, or pay-as-you-go, to disabled (none). The exact status can also vary over time. For example, a user with an unrestricted data plan in the United States might travel frequently to Canada and might or might not have roaming turned on at any given time. If your app makes use of network data transfer—including web service calls, SkyDrive, Bing Maps, and any use of *WebClient* or *HttpWebRequest*—you should be prepared to deal with varying connectivity states. Further, you should be proactive about policing your app's network data usage so that you reduce or eliminate it, depending on connectivity states. Windows Phone 8 introduced the Data Sense feature with which the user can specify the limits of his data plan.

The Data Sense APIs include methods for checking connectivity status, the nature of the connection, whether the phone is currently roaming, and whether the user is approaching or has already exceeded his set data limits. If you want your app to help the user to control network usage costs, you should check these details at key intervals, such as on launch or activation, whenever the network status changes, and before any operation which you know transfers a large volume of data over the network.

> **Note** Although Data Sense is a standard feature of Windows Phone 8, its availability on any given phone or phone service plan is controlled by the mobile operator. This means that it might not be available on a given phone. If the feature is not available, the user cannot set his data limits, and in this case, the Data Sense APIs can only return "unknown" when you query the limits. You can, however, still use the APIs to ascertain the type of network connection and the roaming status. It's also not available on the emulator.

The *DemoDataSense* app in the sample code illustrates the basic techniques. The app first defines an *enum* type for the three types of network usage that we want to apply.

```
public enum NetworkUsage { Unrestricted, Reduced, Stopped }
```

In the main page, the app wires up a handler for the *NetworkStatusChanged* event. This will be raised whenever the user goes in or out of roaming mode, in and out of cellular connection or Wi-Fi connection, and so on—in fact, whenever any public property of the *NetworkInformation* type changes. In this app, the handler invokes a custom *UpdateNetworkInformation* method, which can also be called at other critical times (launch, activation, page navigation, and so on). The Internet Assigned Names Authority (IANA) defines 272 values for the network types, but only a subset of these are used in Windows Phone. The emulator uses a Software Loopback connection (24), and a device can use either Wi-Fi (71) or one of the cellular connection types such as 3GPP2 WWAN (244).

This method gets the current Internet *ConnectionProfile* and examines the connection status. If the phone is currently on a Wi-Fi connection, we don't need to apply any restrictions to network data usage. Otherwise, we should check the current *ConnectionCost*: if the phone is roaming or if the user is already over her set data limit, we should set a flag to prevent any further network data usage until the status changes again. If you use this technique in your app, you should also alert the user that this is what you're doing and provide a mechanism for the user to override this behavior if she wants to. By the same token, if the data limit has not yet been reached, but is approaching, we can proactively reduce network usage without stopping it altogether. Again, you should alert the user and provide an override mechanism. Also keep in mind that by default the phone does not provide a connection when roaming; the user must enable this feature explicitly.

```
private const uint InterfaceTypeWiFi = 71;
private NetworkUsage networkUsage = NetworkUsage.Unrestricted;

public MainPage()
{
    InitializeComponent();
    NetworkInformation.NetworkStatusChanged += NetworkInformation_NetworkStatusChanged;
    UpdateNetworkInformation();
}

private void NetworkInformation_NetworkStatusChanged(object sender)
{
    UpdateNetworkInformation();
}

private void UpdateNetworkInformation()
{
    ConnectionProfile profile = NetworkInformation.GetInternetConnectionProfile();
    if (profile.NetworkAdapter.IanaInterfaceType == (uint)InterfaceType.WiFi)
    {
        networkUsage = NetworkUsage.Unrestricted;
    }
    else
    {
        ConnectionCost cost = profile.GetConnectionCost();
        if (cost.Roaming || cost.OverDataLimit)
        {
            networkUsage = NetworkUsage.Stopped;
        }
        else if (cost.ApproachingDataLimit)
        {
            networkUsage = NetworkUsage.Reduced;
        }
    }
}
```

Be aware that some members of the *ConnectionProfile* class are used only in Windows and are not implemented in Windows Phone. These include *GetDataPlanStatus*, *GetNetworkConnectivityLevel*, and *ProfileName*.

Summary

This chapter examined the basic support that the app platform provides for connecting to the web. This included specifically the *WebClient* and *HttpWebRequest* classes as well as the *WebBrowser* control. We looked at the additional support that is available for connecting to Facebook, SkyDrive, and Twitter. Whenever your app transfers data across the Internet, you should consider ways to optimize responsiveness and performance. In addition, the Data Sense APIs give you the tools to implement your app to reduce network traffic, which is especially important when there is a cost implication to the user.

CHAPTER 8

Web services and the cloud

Many of the standard techniques for connecting to web services, including Windows Communication Foundation (WCF) data services, are directly supported on the phone. This chapter examines each of these techniques, some particular issues with testing an end-to-end web service–based mobile app, and some of the choices you have in transferring data over the network. We also look at the additional support for connecting to Microsoft Windows Azure.

Web services

Windows Phone can consume web services, including Microsoft ASP.NET and WCF. The following example uses a simple WCF service that provides a "quote of the day." The *ServiceContract* is listed in the code that follows shortly. It defines just one method, *GetQotd*, which returns an array of strings. This is the *QotdService* solution in the sample code. The service implementation contains a static two-dimensional array of strings, initialized to arbitrary quotations and their corresponding source (play, act, and scene). For each *GetQotd* call, the service returns a (pseudo-)random pair of strings from the array.

```
[ServiceContract]
public interface IQotdService
{
    [OperationContract]
    string[] GetQotd();
}

public class QotdService : IQotdService
{
    public string[] GetQotd()
    {
        Random rand = new Random();
        int i = rand.Next(Quotations.GetLength(0) - 1);
        string[] result = new string[] { Quotations[i, 0], Quotations[i, 1] };
        return result;
    }
```

```
    private static string[,] Quotations = new string[,]
    {
        {"To be, or not to be: that is the question," "Hamlet, III.i"},
        {"Neither a borrower nor a lender be; for loan oft loses both itself and friend, and
borrowing dulls the edge of husbandry," "Hamlet, I.iii"},
... etc
    };
}
```

The phone client has a single *ListBox* and an app bar button, as shown in Figure 8-1.

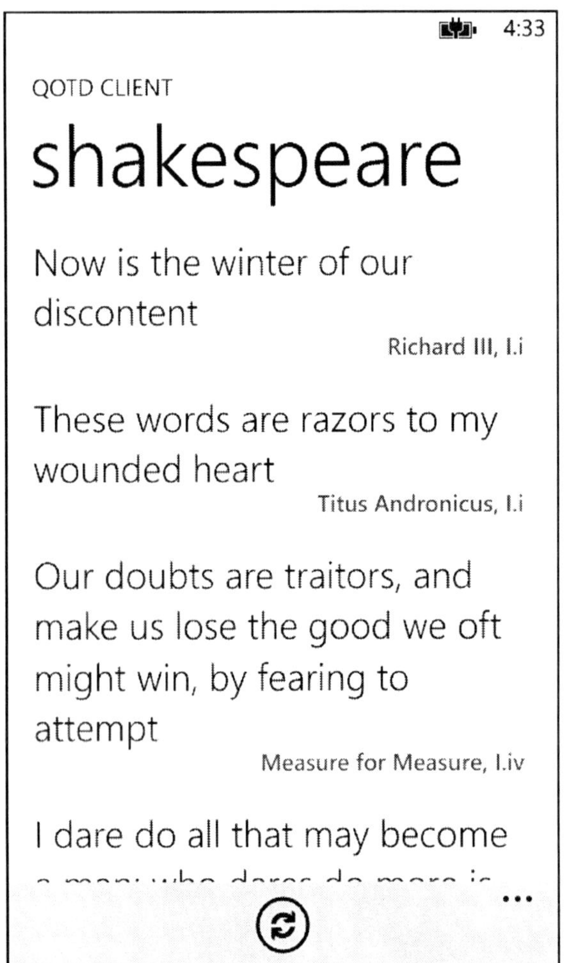

FIGURE 8-1 It's common for a phone client app to access web services.

Before we go ahead and examine the phone solution, we need to step back and consider some changes in the emulator between Windows Phone 7 and Windows Phone 8, because these changes affect the way you build both the web service and the phone client app.

Localhost and the emulator

Localhost is the standard hostname given to the address of the loopback network interface, and therefore always refers to this computer. It is useful for testing apps during development, but in production, this is always replaced with real server hostnames or IP addresses. The Windows Phone 7 emulator was based on Virtual-PC and did not have its own networking stack; it just piggy-backed off the networking stack of the host computer. One consequence of this was that "localhost" meant the same thing on both the host and the emulator, and the emulator could even access resources that were only bound to localhost on the host computer. By contrast, in Windows Phone 8, the emulator is based off Hyper-V which virtualizes the machine right down to the hardware. It is a completely separate networking entity; it has its own MAC addresses, gets its own IP addresses, and when a client app attempts to go to "localhost" on the Windows Phone 8 emulator, it reaches the emulator, not the host. Your web service, of course, is not running on the emulator, it's running on the host.

Also, by default, Microsoft Visual Studio hosts the website inside of IIS Express, which again only binds to localhost by default. Another major difficulty (or "enhanced security feature," depending on your point of view) is that if you're developing within an enterprise that uses domain security, your computer is typically part of your enterprise domain. The emulator, on the other hand, is not domain-joined. Domain network security will generally prevent a non–domain-joined device from accessing a domain computer. If you have administrator rights to your computer, you can resolve this by allowing anonymous access to your local websites. If your organization requires domain computers to use IPSec, this is a harder problem. To resolve this issue, you need to configure your computer with a boundary exception; that is, the domain administrator needs to set up your computer so that it can be reached by non-domain computers, specifically the emulator.

If you're working within a tightly-controlled enterprise environment and cannot set up your development computer appropriately, another alternative is to deploy your web services to a separate development web server, or to the cloud (or even to a separate HyperV virtual machine on the same physical machine). For details on cloud deployment, see the Windows Azure section, later in this chapter.

Finally, no matter what you do, you will not be able to use Internet Explorer on the emulator to browse to the web service URL on the local computer. The browser in Windows Phone 8 lacks the functionality that the desktop browser has when it comes to displaying the results of service requests, so even if the service is available, the browser will only ever appear to time out.

We'll go over the basic tasks for setting up a WCF web service and phone client app, including how you can actually get the solution to work in the face of the emulator's inability to connect to localhost. For comparison, here are the steps required for a Windows Phone 7 solution:

1. Run Visual Studio Professional or above, as administrator, and create a WCF service solution. By default, this will use IIS Express and localhost.
2. Build the WCF service solution and then, in Solution Explorer, select View In Browser.

   This starts the service, and opens a client browser window navigated to the service URL (on localhost).

3. In Visual Studio (Express or above, with the Windows Phone SDK, as a normal user), create a Windows Phone project.

4. Run the Visual Studio Add Service Reference tool and specify the (localhost) URL to the running web service.

   This generates the client-side proxy classes for the service contract. It also generates a *ServiceReferences.ClientConfig* file which defines the service endpoint, including a localhost-based URL.

   Use the proxy classes in your phone project to invoke the service.

For a Windows Phone 8 solution, the steps are different. Apart from running the service on a separate computer (or in the cloud), the steps vary according to whether you're running the service on IIS Express or on full IIS on your development computer. For IIS Express, the steps are as follows:

1. Run Visual Studio Professional or above, as administrator, and create a WCF service solution.

2. Build the WCF service solution. In Solution Explorer, right-click the SVC file and then, on the shortcut menu that appears, select View In Browser.

   This starts the service and opens a client browser window navigated to the service URL (on localhost).

3. Run a command window and then run the ipconfig tool to get the IP address of your development computer. If you have the emulator on this computer, make sure that you pick the physical computer's address and not just the first one in the list (which is most likely the emulator).

4. Using Notepad, open the IIS Express configuration file. This is named *applicationhost.config* and resides in the folder %USERPROFILE%\Documents\IISExpress\config\. The %USERPROFILE% environment variable expands out to your current logged-in user name on the computer.

5. Edit the *applicationhost.config* to add a new *<binding>* element for your web service, which specifies your computer's IP address. In the example that follows (for the *QotdService*), we've added the additional *<binding>* element that specifies an IP address instead of *localhost*. This example uses the string "00.000.000.00" as a placeholder for the real IP address on your computer. Be aware that there won't be an entry in the file for your service unless you've deployed it at least once. Also, the port number (8001 in this example) is more or less arbitrary (except that you cannot use port numbers below 1024 because these are reserved for system use). If you're allowing Visual Studio to generate the port number, this will vary from project to project.

```
            <site name="QotdService" id="6">
                <application path="/" applicationPool="Clr4IntegratedAppPool">
                    <virtualDirectory path="/" physicalPath="C:\Temp\Samples08\
QotdService\QotdService" />
                </application>
                <bindings>
                    <binding protocol="http" bindingInformation="*:8001:localhost" />
                    <binding protocol="http" bindingInformation="*:8001:00.000.000.00" />
                </bindings>
            </site>
```

6. If IIS Express is still running, close it. One way to do this is to find its icon in the notification area and select Exit.

7. Build the service again and browse to it to ensure that it is correctly started. The URL in the browser should include your computer's IP address instead of localhost.

8. To create (or modify) your phone project, you must run Visual Studio (Express or above, with the Windows Phone SDK) as administrator.

   Administrator permissions are required to connect to a web service at a non-localhost address.

9. Run the Visual Studio Add Service Reference tool and specify the (IP-specific) URL to the running web service, as illustrated in Figure 8-2. You can copy and paste the URL from the browser window.

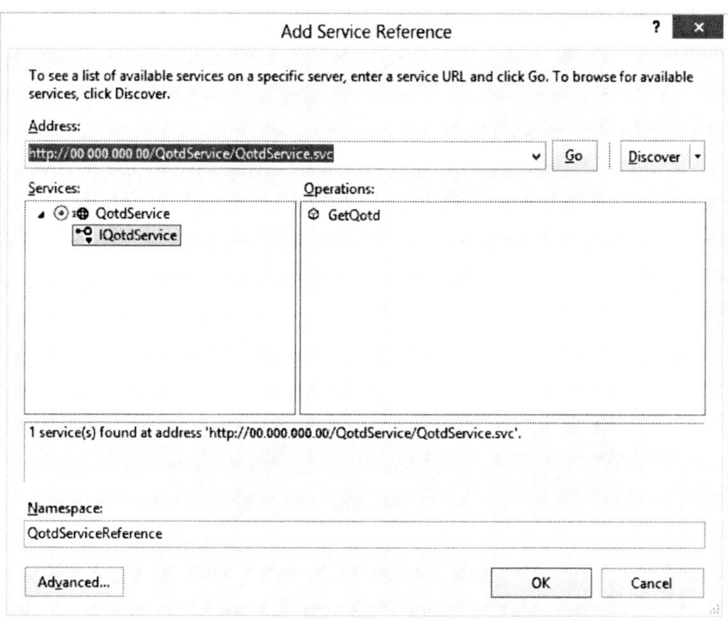

FIGURE 8-2 Use the Add Service Reference feature in Visual Studio to generate client proxy code for a web service.

10. This generates the client-side proxy classes for the service contract. It also generates a *ServiceReferences.ClientConfig* file that defines the service endpoint, including a URL that contains the specific IP address of the computer where the service is running.

11. Use the proxy classes in your phone project to invoke the service.

Note When generating client-side service proxies, you should use *System.Array* as the collection type. The default *ObservableCollection<T>* will work in most cases, but not all. To make this change, click the Advanced button and go to the Data Type settings options. You should also clear the Reuse Types In Referenced Assemblies check box so that the generated code doesn't use server-side types in the client proxies. If you have already created the reference and need to go back and change it, you can right-click it in Solution Explorer and then, on the shortcut menu that appears, click Configure Service Reference.

Note If you're having trouble connecting with the emulator, try connecting with another physical computer on your network to ensure that the service is accessible. If it can't be seen by another computer, you likely need to troubleshoot the firewall/IIS settings rather than worry about the emulator.

Alternatively, you can use full IIS. You can install this on the Add/Remove Programs page in Control Panel by selecting the option to turn Windows features on/off. If you're using full IIS on your development computer, the steps are as follows:

1. In Windows 8, WCF HTTP activation is typically enabled by default, but just to be sure, go to the Windows Start screen and type **Turn Windows features on or off** (or the first part of this phrase) to initiate a search for the Windows Features utility that is part of Control Panel. In the Windows Features dialog, navigate to .NET Framework 4.5 Advanced Services | WCF Services and then select the check box next to HTTP Activation.

2. Create a firewall exception for calls to the web service. To do this, from the Windows Start screen, type **Allow an app through Windows Firewall**. In the Allowed Apps dialog box, click Change Settings. Select the check box next to World Wide Web Services (HTTP).

3. Run a command window and then use the ipconfig tool to get the IP address of your development computer.

4. Run Visual Studio Professional or above, as administrator, and create a WCF service solution. Go to the project properties and click the Web tab. Ensure that the service is set to use the local IIS web server and clear the option to use IIS Express. Set the Project Url to specify your computer's IP address instead of localhost and then click the button to create a virtual directory for this service. If Visual Studio complains that it can't create the virtual directory, leave the Project Url as localhost but check the Override application root URL option, and specify your computer's IP address there, instead.

5. Build the WCF service solution and select View In Browser from Solution Explorer.

   This will start the service and open a client browser window navigated to the service URL (using the specified IP address in the path).

6. Run Visual Studio (Express or above, with the Windows Phone SDK), as a normal user, and create or open your Windows Phone project.

7. Run the Visual Studio Add Service Reference tool and specify the (IP-specific) URL to the running web service, as illustrated in Figure 8-9. You can copy and paste the URL from the browser window.

   This generates the client-side proxy classes for the service contract. It also generates a *ServiceReferences.ClientConfig* file which defines the service endpoint, including a URL that contains the specific IP address of the computer where the service is running.

8. Use the proxy classes in your phone project to invoke the service.

Whichever of the three approaches you've used, you should end up with a running service to which you can browse, and proxy classes in your phone client project that specify the correct running URL (localhost or IP-specific, as appropriate). The remaining steps that follow explain how to make use of these classes in your app.

Connecting to the web service

The proxy classes include a definition of the service contract *IQotdService*, a class that implements this contract *QotdServiceClient*, plus supporting classes for the service channel and event args. You have no reason to change anything in these classes, and they're normally hidden. If you want to examine them, you can click the Show All Files button in Solution Explorer and navigate to the *Reference.cs* file for the selected service reference.

```
public partial class QotdServiceClient : System.ServiceModel.ClientBase<QotdClient.
QotdServiceReference.IQotdService>, QotdClient.QotdServiceReference.IQotdService
{
...
    public event System.EventHandler<GetQotdCompletedEventArgs> GetQotdCompleted;

    private void OnGetQotdCompleted(object state)
    {
        if ((this.GetQotdCompleted != null))
        {
            InvokeAsyncCompletedEventArgs e = ((InvokeAsyncCompletedEventArgs)(state));
            this.GetQotdCompleted(this, new GetQotdCompletedEventArgs(
                e.Results, e.Error, e.Cancelled, e.UserState));
        }
    }

    public void GetQotdAsync()
    {
        this.GetQotdAsync(null);
    }
}
```

In addition to the proxy classes, you get a *ServiceReferences.ClientConfig* file, which specifies the endpoint URL, the binding type (*basicHttpBinding*), and the contract, which is based on the service interface.

```
<configuration>
    <system.serviceModel>
        <bindings>
            <basicHttpBinding>
                <binding name="BasicHttpBinding_IQotdService" maxBufferSize="2147483647"
                    maxReceivedMessageSize="2147483647">
                    <security mode="None" />
                </binding>
            </basicHttpBinding>
        </bindings>
        <client>
          <endpoint
              address="http://00.000.000.00/QotdService.svc"
              binding="basicHttpBinding"
              bindingConfiguration="BasicHttpBinding_IQotdService"
              contract="QotdServiceReference.IQotdService"
              name="BasicHttpBinding_IQotdService" />
        </client>
    </system.serviceModel>
</configuration>
```

For simplicity in this app, we data-bind the user interface (UI) to the result of the web service call. To support this model, we define a custom *Quotation* class, with properties for the *Quote* and the *Source* returned from the web service call. The *DataTemplate* for the *ListBox* declares two *TextBlock* controls, one bound to the *Quote*, the other bound to the *Source*.

```
public class Quotation
{
    public string Quote { get; set; }
    public string Source { get; set; }
}
```

We set the *ItemsSource* for the *ListBox* to an *ObservableCollection<Quotation>*. Each time the app makes a web service call, the return value is added as a new *Quotation* to this collection; data-binding takes care of the rest. To make the call, the user taps the app bar button, and the *Click* handler invokes the service method.

```
private QotdServiceClient serviceClient;
public ObservableCollection<Quotation> Quotations { get; set; }

public MainPage()
{
    InitializeComponent();
    Quotations = new ObservableCollection<Quotation>();
    qotdList.ItemsSource = Quotations;
}
```

```
private void appbarGetQotd_Click(object sender, EventArgs e)
{
    if (serviceClient == null)
    {
        serviceClient = new QotdServiceClient();
        serviceClient.GetQotdCompleted += serviceClient_GetQotdCompleted;
    }
    serviceClient.GetQotdAsync();
}
```

All phone app calls to web services are asynchronous—only asynchronous client proxies are generated, and we need to wire up the *GetQotdCompleted* event and call *GetQotdAsync*. In this example, the *GetQotdCompleted* handler constructs a new *Quotation* object for each quotation received from the web service and then adds it to the data-bound collection.

```
private void serviceClient_GetQotdCompleted(object sender, GetQotdCompletedEventArgs e)
{
    String result = String.Empty;
    if (e.Error != null)
    {
        Debug.WriteLine(e.Error.Message);
        return;
    }

    Quotations.Add(new Quotation() { Quote = e.Result[0], Source = e.Result[1] });
}
```

SOAP vs. REST

A quick Bing search will bring up any number of articles on the Simple Object Access Protocol (SOAP) versus Representational State Transfer (REST) discussion. A Windows Phone app can consume both SOAP and REST web services. So far, we've looked at consuming the more traditional SOAP web services. SOAP is commonly used for web services that expose some level of logic to the consumer and provide multiple input points that correspond to methods on an interface. This is why a strongly typed client-side proxy class is useful in SOAP clients. On the other hand, you can think of REST web services as a way of exposing data rather than logic, using a single input point, where the interface is constrained to a set of standard operations, such as GET, POST, PUT, and DELETE.

Because of the strong typing, a SOAP-based client-side proxy to a web service is easy to use; on the other hand it is also considerable work and disruption if the contract ever changes. If your server is updated to serve up additional types, the client proxy must be regenerated and the consuming code has to adapt to this. In contrast, a REST service is minimalist: this typically means a lower volume of data is transferred, but it also means that you have to do a little more work to figure out exactly what data you want to transfer. A REST service is considerably easier to update.

The *RestQotdService* and *RestQotdClient* solutions in the sample code demonstrate REST web services. The key point in the client app is that you don't use a client-side proxy to the service. REST clients can be much simpler than SOAP clients; they can use *WebClient* or *HttpWebRequest* objects to make calls to the service. The following code is from the *RestQotdClient* app. As before, the app maintains an *ObservableCollection<Quotation>* for the results of each web service call, data-bound to a *ListBox* in the UI. There is no client-side service proxy; instead, the app uses a *WebClient* and calls *OpenReadAsync*, passing the URI to the REST service. The URI specifies the *GetQotd* method. When the call returns, the results are in XML format. Other REST services are implemented to return data in JavaScript Object Notation (JSON) format (more on this in the WCF Data Services section later in the chapter). The return is handled in the *OpenReadCompleted* delegate, which extracts the two strings from the XML, creates a new *Quotation* object, and then adds it to the collection.

```
public ObservableCollection<Quotation> Quotations { get; set; }
private WebClient client;
private static string RestQotdUrl =
    "http://00.000.000.00/RestQotdService.svc/GetQotd";
private static XNamespace RestQotdNs =
    @"http://schemas.microsoft.com/2003/10/Serialization/Arrays";
private static string element = "string";

public MainPage()
{
    InitializeComponent();
    Quotations = new ObservableCollection<Quotation>();
    qotdList.ItemsSource = Quotations;

    client = new WebClient();
    client.OpenReadCompleted += (o, r) =>
    {
        if (r.Error == null)
        {
            using (StreamReader reader = new StreamReader(r.Result))
            {
                XDocument doc = XDocument.Parse(reader.ReadToEnd());
                string q = doc.Descendants(RestQotdNs + element).First().Value;
                string s = doc.Descendants(RestQotdNs + element).Last().Value;
                Quotations.Add(new Quotation() { Quote = q, Source = s });
            }
        }
    };
}

private void appbarGetQotd_Click(object sender, EventArgs e)
{
    client.OpenReadAsync(new Uri(RestQotdUrl +"?nocache=" +Guid.NewGuid()));
}
```

Notice that the call to *OpenReadAsync* specifies the web service URI, the method name, and an additional name/value parameter pair. This is set to a dummy query identifier *(nocache)* and an arbitrary GUID. The reason for this is that Windows Phone has caching behavior based on looking at the URI and seeing if it matches a previous request. So, if you invoke exactly the same URI repeatedly, the platform doesn't actually make the call; instead, it returns the cached value of the previous result. To ensure that a fresh call is always made, you can work around the caching behavior by differentiating each call. The simplest way to do this is to add a unique dummy query string to each request—hence, the fresh GUID on each call. Of course, the better solution is to have the server disable caching by setting a caching policy in the *web.config*, but this might not be under your control.

WCF data services

A data service is an HTTP-based web service that exposes server-side data by using the Open Data (OData) web protocol. WCF data services make it possible for you to publish data from a server app by using a REST-based interface in either XML or JSON format. This is particularly interesting for mobile clients, because OData formats involve significantly less overhead than traditional SOAP formats.

Figure 8-3 illustrates the high-level architecture of a generic WCF data service client/server solution. In the server app, you can define an Entity Data Model (EDM). This is a set of classes that represent some backing data, typically tables and rows in a database. Then, you would define a WCF data service to consume the EDM and expose your selected data to the web. On the client, you would typically generate a service proxy and data-bind the proxied entities to your UI.

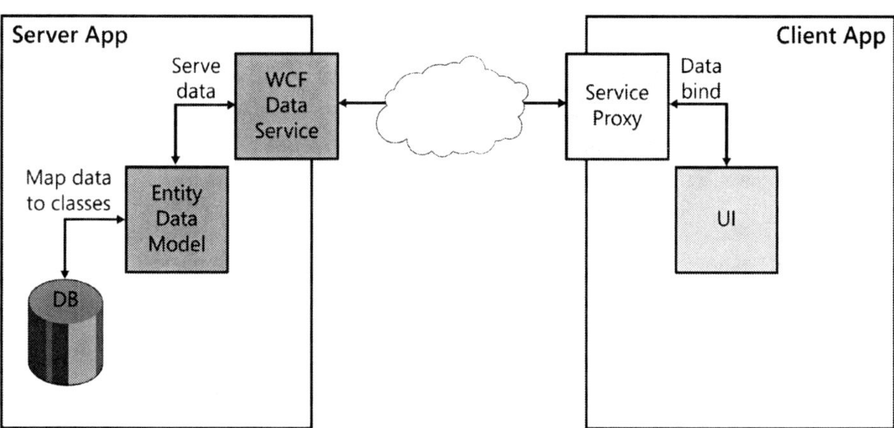

FIGURE 8-3 At a high level, there are five major components in a WCF data service client/server solution.

Here are the basic steps for building an end-to-end OData solution with a Windows Phone client:

Server

1. Create an ASP.NET app (by using either the regular ASP.NET Visual Studio project template or the empty ASP.NET template).
2. Using Visual Studio's Add Item project wizard, add an ADO.NET Entity Data Model item, mapped to the database tables/views that you want to expose.
3. Add a WCF Data Service item and then connect it to your EDM per the "TODO" comment in the generated code.

Client

1. Run the server and then generate the client-side proxy classes by running either the DataSvcUtil tool from a command window, or the Add Service Reference tool (if available) in Visual Studio.
2. In the client XAML, data-bind UI elements to the proxied data entities.
3. In the page code-behind, execute the service queries to fetch the data you need.

Creating the OData-specific server-side pieces in an end-to-end OData solution is actually very simple and involves no more work than the bare bones that we just listed. The following sections concentrate instead on the client-side pieces.

Note To build the client-side piece, you need to use the OData client tools for Windows Phone. The OData client tools for Windows Phone 7.1 were released as part of the SDK, but the version for Windows Phone 8 is a separate download, which is available at *http://msdn.microsoft.com/en-us/jj658961*.

Creating an OData client

The *NwindODataClient* solution in the sample code connects to a public OData service provided by Microsoft for testing purposes. This is backed by the familiar *Northwind* database. The first version of the client defines a *ListBox* with an *ItemTemplate* which contains *TextBlock* controls that are data-bound to the service data, as shown in Figure 8-4.

To consume this service in a Windows Phone 8 app, we have two choices: either run the DataSvcUtil command-line tool to generate the client-side proxy classes; or use the Add Service Reference option in Visual Studio.

If you want to use DataSvcUtil, be aware that there are multiple versions of the tool; the tool used for Windows Phone 7 projects (named *DataSvcUtil.exe*) is not the same as the one for Windows Phone 8 projects (named *DataSvcUtil_WindowsPhone.exe*). Here's a suitable command line for the Windows Phone 8 version, assuming that you have installed the OData client tools to the default location (typically, in %ProgramFiles(x86)%):

```
"%Program Files(x86)%\Microsoft WCF Data Services\5.0\tools\Phone\DataSvcUtil_WindowsPhone.exe"
/version:2.0 /dataservicecollection /language:CSharp /out:NorthwindEntities.cs /uri:http://
services.odata.org/Northwind/Northwind.svc/
```

FIGURE 8-4 All the hard work is in talking to the data service. After that, it's just a question of doing something useful with the data that's returned.

The */language*, */out*, and */uri* switches are self-explanatory. You need the */version* and */dataservice collection* switches to generate classes suitable for data binding.

Having executed this tool, we can then add the generated *NorthwindEntities.cs* to the phone app project. We also add a reference to the OData client library (*System.Services.Data.Client.dll* for Windows Phone 7 projects, and *System.Services.Data.Client.WP80.dll* for Windows Phone 8 projects). Then, we can consume the data service proxy in our client code.

Instead of using the command-line tool, you can also generate the proxy code by using the Add Service Reference option in Visual Studio. This approach is the same as for adding any other service reference. In this case, the generated class file and the OData client library are both added to the project automatically.

The proxies include an entities class derived from *DataServiceContext*. This loosely represents the set of tables in the database. We also get a class to represent each table or view, and this simply implements *INotifyPropertyChanged*. Then, the entities class encapsulates a property of type *DataServiceQuery<T>* for each table or view, where *T* is the table/view class type. So, in this example, there will be a *NorthwindEntities* class that exposes properties for database tables and views, such as *Customer, Employee, Order, Product*, and so on. Each of the classes that represent a table/view define a property for each column.

The following is the definition of the *ItemTemplate* and the *ListBox* in the XAML. Each *ListBox* item is made up of a two-column *Grid* with two *TextBlock* controls, one bound to the *Name*, and the other bound to the *PhoneNumber* property.

```
<ListBox x:Name="CustomerList">
    <ListBox.ItemTemplate>
        <DataTemplate>
            <Grid>
                <Grid.ColumnDefinitions>
                    <ColumnDefinition Width="310"/>
                    <ColumnDefinition Width="*"/>
                </Grid.ColumnDefinitions>
                <TextBlock
                    Grid.Column="0" Text="{Binding CompanyName}"
                    Style="{StaticResource PhoneTextAccentStyle}"
                    FontSize="{StaticResource PhoneFontSizeMedium}"/>
                <TextBlock
                    Grid.Column="1" Text="{Binding Phone}"/>
            </Grid>
        </DataTemplate>
    </ListBox.ItemTemplate>
</ListBox>
```

The code that follows is in the *MainPage* code-behind. This overrides *OnNavigatedTo* to call a custom method *RefreshData*, which sets up the query (in this example, we query for all *Customer* items) and makes an asynchronous call to execute the query. The callback retrieves the data results and dispatches them on the UI thread to the *ListBox*. This same *RefreshData* method is also invoked by the app bar button handler so that the user can trigger the refresh directly. While the web call is in progress, the app shows a progress indicator to apprise the user that something is happening.

Notice that the app defers instantiation of the entities object until the *OnNavigatedTo* override rather than as part of page construction. This is a deliberate strategy to ensure that the app is as responsive as possible on startup. Also, in a production-strength app, you would typically check to see if invoking the query is actually necessary. Specifically, you could test to see if this is a fresh start or if the app is being resurrected after tombstoning. For scenarios in which you have already done this (and persisted some or all of the data to isolated storage), you can avoid the expensive server call.

```
private NorthwindEntities entities;
private ProgressIndicator progress;

protected override void OnNavigatedTo(NavigationEventArgs e)
{
    if (entities == null)
    {
        entities = new NorthwindEntities(
        new Uri("http://services.odata.org/Northwind/Northwind.svc/"));
    }
    RefreshData();
}

private void appbarRefresh_Click(object sender, EventArgs e)
{
    RefreshData();
}

private void RefreshData()
{
    if (progress == null)
    {
        progress = new ProgressIndicator();
        progress.IsIndeterminate = true;
        progress.Text = "refreshing...";
        SystemTray.ProgressIndicator = progress;
    }
    progress.IsVisible = true;

    DataServiceQuery<Customer> query = entities.Customers;
    query.BeginExecute(query_Callback, query);
}

private void query_Callback(IAsyncResult result)
{
    DataServiceQuery<Customer> query =
        (DataServiceQuery<Customer>)result.AsyncState;
    var c = query.EndExecute(result);
    Dispatcher.BeginInvoke(() =>
    {
        CustomerList.ItemsSource = c;
        progress.IsVisible = false;
    });
}
```

Filtered queries

In the enhanced version shown in Figure 8-5 (the *NwindODataClient_Filtered* solution in the sample code), a filter capability is provided. There's an additional *ListBox* data-bound to an array of strings to represent the alphabet. The user can scroll the list to find a specific letter; the app then filters the query on the data service to return only those customers for which the *CompanyName* starts with that letter.

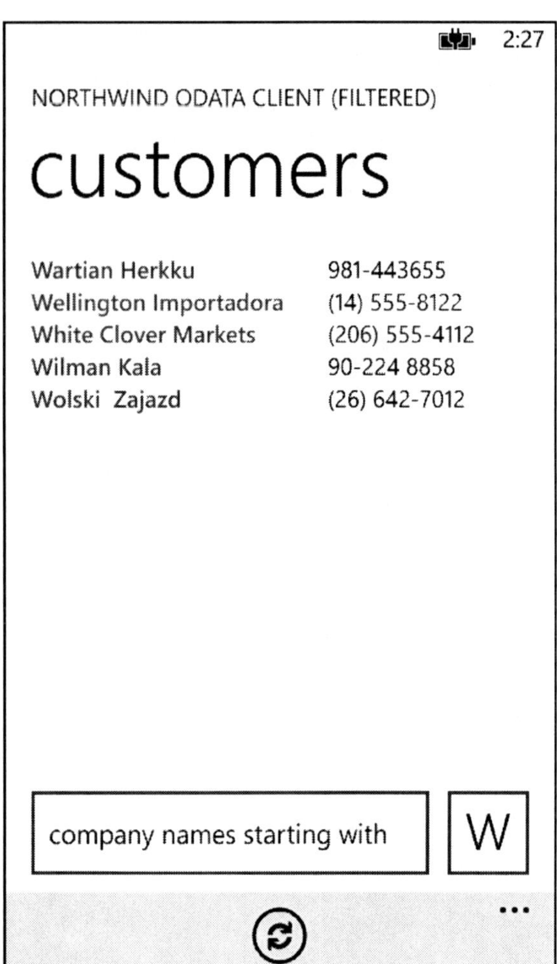

FIGURE 8-5 It is common to offer client-side filtering features for remote data services.

You can examine the sample code if you're interested in the specifics of the UI and how the filter selection works. The only interesting enhancement in the data service query is a modification to the *Refresh* method, where the filter is applied. Notice that the inner LINQ query has a *where* clause that returns an *IQueryable<T>*, which we then have to cast to the *DataServiceQuery<T>* that we need to execute against the data service.

```
DataServiceQuery<Customer> query = null;
if (filter == "*")
{
    query = entities.Customers;
}
```

```
else
{
    var innerQuery =
        from c in entities.Customers
        where c.CompanyName.StartsWith(filter)
        select c;
    query = (DataServiceQuery<Customer>)innerQuery;
}
query.BeginExecute(query_Callback, query);
```

Dynamic query results

Rather than using a *DataServiceQuery<T>* as we did previously, we could instead use a *DataService Collection<T>*. For an example of this, see the *NwindODataClient_Collection* solution in the sample code. This provides greater flexibility for composing complex queries. It also uses a more formalized *LoadAsync/LoadCompleted* model rather than the generic *IAsyncResult* callback of the *DataService Query* approach. The most significant feature, however, is that *DataServiceCollection<T>* is derived from *ObservableCollection<T>*. This means that it provides notifications when items are added to—or removed from—the collection, which makes it eminently suitable for data binding.

```
private DataServiceCollection<Customer> customers;

private void RefreshData()
{
    if (progress == null)
    {
        progress = new ProgressIndicator();
        progress.IsIndeterminate = true;
        progress.Text = "refreshing...";
        SystemTray.ProgressIndicator = progress;
    }
    progress.IsVisible = true;

    //DataServiceQuery<Customer> query = entities.Customers;
    //query.BeginExecute(query_Callback, query);

    customers = new DataServiceCollection<Customer>(entities);
    customers.LoadCompleted += query_LoadCompleted;
    var query = from c in entities.Customers select c;
    customers.LoadAsync(query);
}

//private void query_Callback(IAsyncResult result)
//{
//    DataServiceQuery<Customer> query =
//        (DataServiceQuery<Customer>)result.AsyncState;
//    var c = query.EndExecute(result);
//    Dispatcher.BeginInvoke(() =>
//    {
//        CustomerList.ItemsSource = c;
//        progress.IsVisible = false;
//    });
//}
```

```
private void query_LoadCompleted(object sender, LoadCompletedEventArgs e)
{
    if (e.Error == null)
    {
        CustomerList.ItemsSource = customers;
        progress.IsVisible = false;
    }
}
```

The *LoadCompleted* event is raised on the UI thread, so we no longer need to marshal UI operations via a *Dispatcher* object. The preceding changes to the code should produce exactly the same results as before.

Paging the data

Another optimization that is commonly used is to support paging of the data. You might have noticed with all the variants of the client app so far that we only seem to receive at most 20 records. This is not the full set of records in the *Customers* table; rather, the server has been sending the data in "pages" (or blocks of records). Typically, the server will send only one page of data. Then, it will only send subsequent pages if the client explicitly asks for more. None of our clients so far have asked for any more than the first page of records.

To support this behavior requires changes on both the server (to send the data in pages) and on the client (to handle paged data coming in). If you control the server-side piece, to implement paging on the server, you would add a call to *DataServiceConfiguration.SetEntitySetPageSize*, specifying the number of records for each page on a per-table or per-view basis, as illustrated in the following code snippet (this specifies a 20-record page size for the *Customers* table):

```
config.SetEntitySetPageSize("Customers", 20);
```

The public Northwind data service is already set up with a 20-record page size. In the client app, we need to check whenever we've received data whether there's any more available; in this case, we call *LoadNextPartialSetAsync*. For an example of this, see the *NwindODataClient_Paged* version of the client solution in the sample code. Here, the page defines an extra *TextBlock* below the title panel, and above the *ListBox*. This reports the current count of data records received, updated dynamically.

```
<TextBlock Grid.Row="1" x:Name="customerCount" Text="count = " Margin="24,0,12,12"/>
```

So far, the client has initialized the *ListBox.ItemsSource* from the set of *Customer* records returned in the *LoadCompleted* handler. Now that we know that this is not necessarily the full set of records, we need to move this initialization to the *OnNavigatedTo* override. We can also change the *Load Completed* handler to update the count of records as they come in from the service. The critical piece is to check the value of the *Continuation* property: if this is not null, it means that there is more data available, in which case, we make a call to *LoadNextPartialSetAsync*. When the server sends more data, this results in another callback to the same *LoadCompleted* event handler, so we check for more data on each call, until *Continuation* evaluates to null. At that point, we know we're done, and we can turn off the progress indicator. In this example, we're automatically calling for more data until we get all of it. Of course, in a more sophisticated app, you might defer fetching more data, perhaps placing it under user control.

```
protected override void OnNavigatedTo(NavigationEventArgs e)
{
    customers = new DataServiceCollection<Customer>(entities);
    customers.LoadCompleted += customers_LoadCompleted;
    var query = from c in entities.Customers select c;
    customers.LoadAsync(query);
    CustomerList.ItemsSource = customers;
}

private void query_LoadCompleted(object sender, LoadCompletedEventArgs e)
{
    if (e.Error != null)
        return;
    if (customers.Continuation != null)
    {
        customers.LoadNextPartialSetAsync();
        customerCount.Text =
            String.Format("count = {0}", CustomerList.Items.Count);
    }
    else
    {
        progress.IsVisible = false;
    }
}
```

By using paged data, the app is more responsive to user interaction; for example, the user can start working with the data, including scrolling through it before it has all arrived from the server.

Caching the data

Another optimization that we can use is to avoid loading the data on every navigation, as we've done so far. To achieve this, we can serialize the data in the app or page state dictionaries, if the data is very small; otherwise of course, we should use isolated storage (see Chapter 10, "Local storage and databases"). The key to this is the *Serialize* and *Deserialize* methods exposed by the *DataServiceState* class. The *NwindODataClient_Cached* variation of the sample solution illustrates this behavior, as depicted in Figure 8-6. This solution offers three app bar buttons: one to refresh the data (either from the service or from persisted cache), one to save the data to persisted state, and one to delete the saved data.

FIGURE 8-6 You can improve responsiveness if you page and cache the data from the web service.

To add this functionality to the app, we can add a *bool* field in the page class to track when data is loaded and set this to *true* in the *LoadCompleted* handler when all pages of the data have been received.

In the *OnNavigatedTo* override, if we haven't yet loaded the data, we first try to fetch it from storage, and if that fails, we go out and get it from the remote service. If we find the state we're looking for, we can deserialize the *DataServiceState* object to memory, extract the persisted entities and customer data, and then load the data into the UI. The *DataServiceState.Serialize* method takes an entities (that is, a *DataServiceContext*) object and a dictionary of all the table class object data. Observe how there are two overloads of this method, which you can use to serialize either the *DataServiceContext* object alone or the object with all its *DataServiceCollections*. If you choose the second option, you must serialize *all* the collections. In this example, there is only one: the *Customers* collection.

```
protected override void OnNavigatedTo(NavigationEventArgs e)
{
    if (isAllDataReceived)
        return;
    object tmp;
    if (State.TryGetValue("DataServiceState", out tmp))
    {
        DataServiceState state = DataServiceState.Deserialize(tmp as String);
        var stateEntities =
            (NorthwindEntities)state.Context;
        var stateCustomers =
            (DataServiceCollection<Customer>)state.RootCollections["Customers"];
        LoadDataFromPageState(stateEntities, stateCustomers);
    }
    else
    {
        LoadDataFromService();
    }
}

public void LoadDataFromPageState(
    NorthwindEntities stateEntities, DataServiceCollection<Customer> stateCustomers)
{
    loadStatus.Text = "loading from page state";
    entities = stateEntities;
    customers = stateCustomers;
}

private void LoadDataFromService()
{
    loadStatus.Text = "loading from service";

    if (entities == null)
    {
        entities = new NorthwindEntities(
            new Uri("http://services.odata.org/Northwind/Northwind.svc"));
    }

    if (progress == null)
    {
        progress = new ProgressIndicator();
        progress.IsIndeterminate = true;
        progress.Text = "refreshing...";
        SystemTray.ProgressIndicator = progress;
    }
    progress.IsVisible = true;

    customers = new DataServiceCollection<Customer>(entities);
    customers.LoadCompleted += query_LoadCompleted;
    var query = from c in entities.Customers select c;
    customers.LoadAsync(query);
    CustomerList.ItemsSource = customers;
}
```

There's an additional complication if the data is paged: it is not possible to know how many rows of data the server is going to send you at any given time. The only way to determine if all the data is received is if the *Continuation* object is null in the *LoadCompleted* handler. When the app persists the data received, it's simpler if this is only done if all the data has been received rather than trying to deal with partial data sets. For this reason, this version of the app verifies that all of the data is received before trying to persist it. If not, we should remove the corresponding state dictionary so that the app does not attempt to read in partial data at a later stage. This example performs the state persistence (and deletion) in app bar button handlers, but you could obviously do this work at other reasonable times. As always, you should avoid leaving all your state persistence work to the critical lifecycle events such as *Closing* or *Deactivated* (or even *OnNavigatedFrom*).

```
private void appbarSave_Click(object sender, EventArgs e)
{
    if (isAllDataReceived)
    {
        Dictionary<String, Object> data = new Dictionary<String, Object>();
        data.Add("Customers", customers);
        State["DataServiceState"] = DataServiceState.Serialize(entities, data);
    }
    else
    {
        State.Remove("DataServiceState");
    }
}

private void appbarClear_Click(object sender, EventArgs e)
{
    if (State.ContainsKey("DataServiceState"))
    {
        State.Remove("DataServiceState");
    }
}
```

There's one final caveat with this approach. It is entirely possible that the data set returned from the server is just too big to persist to state storage. Recall from Chapter 2, "App model and navigation," that no single page is allowed to store more than 2 MB of data, and the app overall is not allowed to store more than 4 MB. The simplest way to test this is to serialize representative (and boundary) volumes of data and then just measure the length. If the data is too big for state storage, the alternative is to use isolated storage, instead, for which there is no enforced cap. Best practices suggest that anything over a few hundred bytes is too big for state storage. This also assumes that you have already trimmed the query to return only the data in which you're interested so that you're not retrieving or storing redundant data.

JSON-formatted data

Data formatted by using JSON is significantly smaller than XML-formatted data for the same web service call. There's no proxy-generation tools support for JSON, but the code you need to write is simple enough. Instead of generating a proxy with the *DataSvcUtil* tool (or the Add Service Reference option), you need to write a class manually that corresponds to the data received. You can see this at work in the *JsonNwndClient* solution in the sample code.

Here's a class that maps to the *Customer* data. All mappable fields are set up as public properties (they need to be serializable). We only need to define the fields that we care about (in this case, *CompanyName* and *Phone*). Note that the data in a typical JSON-formatted payload is wrapped in an enclosing element named *results*, which in turn is wrapped in an outer enclosing element named *d*. The purpose of this is to mitigate a security vulnerability by preventing the data from being treated as valid script. So, our client-side class models this structure with an outermost *d* property that encapsulates an array of *Customer* results, which is the data that we ultimately care about.

```
public class ResultSet
{
    public Data d { get; set; }
}

public class Data
{
    public Customer[] results { get; set; }
}

public class Customer
{
    public String CompanyName { get; set; }
    public String Phone { get; set; }
}
```

The revised version of the *RefreshData* method now creates an *HttpWebRequest* manually. It also specifies in the HTTP Accept header that we want to receive JSON-formatted data.

```
private void RefreshData()
{
    if (progress == null)
    {
        progress = new ProgressIndicator();
        progress.IsIndeterminate = true;
        progress.Text = "refreshing...";
        SystemTray.ProgressIndicator = progress;
    }
    progress.IsVisible = true;

    HttpWebRequest request = (HttpWebRequest)HttpWebRequest.Create(
        "http://services.odata.org/Northwind/Northwind.svc/Customers?$format=json");
    request.BeginGetResponse(query_Callback, request);
}
```

The callback extracts the data stream from the response and uses the *DataContractJsonSerializer* (defined in *System.ServiceModel.Web.dll*) to deserialize it into a *ResultSet* object, from which we can access the innermost *Customer* results for data-binding to the *ListBox*.

```
private void query_Callback(IAsyncResult result)
{
    HttpWebRequest request = (HttpWebRequest)result.AsyncState;
    HttpWebResponse response = (HttpWebResponse)request.EndGetResponse(result);
    DataContractJsonSerializer deserializer =
        new DataContractJsonSerializer(typeof(ResultSet));
    Stream responseStream = response.GetResponseStream();
    ResultSet resultSet = (ResultSet)deserializer.ReadObject(responseStream);

    Dispatcher.BeginInvoke(() =>
    {
        CustomerList.ItemsSource = resultSet.d.results;
        progress.IsVisible = false;
    });
}
```

Table 8-1 provides a detailed comparison of the code in XML format and JSON format for the *Customers* data, showing just the first *Customer*.

TABLE 8-1 A comparison of XML and JSON format

XML	JSON
<?xml version="1.0" encoding="utf-8" standalone="yes"?><feed xml:base="http://services. odata.org/Northwind/Northwind.svc/" xmlns:d="http:// schemas.microsoft.com/ado/2007/08/dataservices" xmlns:m="http://schemas.microsoft.com/ado/2007/08/ dataservices/metadata" xmlns="http://www.w3.org/2005/ Atom"><title type="text">Customers</title><id>http:// services.odata.org/Northwind/Northwind.svc/Customers</ id><updated>2012-10-27T00:30:56Z</updated><link rel="self" title="Customers" href="Customers" /><entry><id>http://services.odata.org/Northwind/ Northwind.svc/Customers('ALFKI')</id><title type="text"></ title><updated>2012-10-27T00:30:56Z</updated><author><name /></author><link rel="edit" title="Customer" href="Customers('ALFKI')" /><link rel="http://schemas. microsoft.com/ado/2007/08/dataservices/related/ Orders" type="app/atom+xml;type=feed" title="Orders" href="Customers('ALFKI')/Orders" /><link rel="http:// schemas.microsoft.com/ado/2007/08/dataservices/related/ CustomerDemographics" type="app/atom+xml;type=feed" title="CustomerDemographics" href="Customers('ALFKI')/ CustomerDemographics" /><category term="NorthwindModel. Customer" scheme="http://schemas.microsoft.com/ ado/2007/08/dataservices/scheme" /><content type="app/ xml"><m:properties><d:CustomerID>ALFKI</d:CustomerID>< d:CompanyName>Alfreds Futterkiste</d:CompanyName><d:Co ntactName>Maria Anders</d:ContactName><d:ContactTitle> Sales Representative</d:ContactTitle><d:Address>Obere Str. 57</d:Address><d:City>Berlin</d:City><d:Region m:null="true"""""""" /><d:PostalCode>12209</ d:PostalCode><d:Country>Germany</d:Country><d:Phone>030- 0074321</d:Phone><d:Fax>030-0076545</d:Fax></ m:properties></content></entry></feed>	{d:{results: [{__metadata: {uri: http://services.odata.org/Northwind/ Northwind.svc/Customers('ALFKI'), type: NorthwindModel.Customer}, CustomerID: ALFKI, CompanyName: Alfreds Futterkiste, ContactName: Maria Anders, ContactTitle: Sales Representative, Address: Obere Str. 57, City: Berlin, Region: null, PostalCode: 12209, Country: Germany, Phone: 030-0074321, Fax: 030-0076545, Orders: {__deferred: {uri: http:// services.odata.org/Northwind/Northwind. svc/Customers('ALFKI')/Orders}}, CustomerDemographics: {__deferred: {uri: http://services.odata.org/Northwind/ Northwind.svc/Customers('ALFKI')/ CustomerDemographics}}}]}}

Web service security

In many cases, your app is fetching data from the Internet that is public and non-sensitive, and in this scenario you don't need to apply any special security. However, if you're transferring data that is private, sensitive, or otherwise valuable, you have a responsibility to protect the data from interception or tampering during the transfer as well as protecting any security credentials that your app uses. There are three types of web service authentication that are relevant to Windows Phone apps:

- **Basic authentication** This is a simple protocol, supported by virtually all servers. With Basic authentication, the user must supply a valid user name and password, which are returned to the server via an authentication service.
- **Forms authentication** With this approach, requests to the server from unauthenticated users are redirected to a logon page defined by the server app. The user experience is therefore very similar to using basic authentication; the difference being that this is an application-level authentication mechanism versus a protocol-level authentication mechanism. That is, the app can decide to get the credentials however it wants (for example, via a webpage with text controls, via a web service with parameters, and so on), and then the authenticated state is managed via a cookie or some other token. This is often implemented via a custom server-side logon page instead of a standard client browser dialog.
- **Windows authentication (NTLM)** This also employs user name and password credentials, but the difference is that this mechanism never passes the credentials over the wire: it uses a challenge-response mechanism, instead. For these credentials to be useful, the current user must have a valid account on the server or in the server's trusted domain. This is only really useful in intranet scenarios.

Both Basic authentication and Forms authentication have the vulnerability that, if used with an unsecured channel (such as the default HTTP), the user credentials are passed across the wire in clear text. An attacker could intercept the communication and gain access to the user credentials. Both types of authentication should only be used in production systems in combination with Secure Sockets Layer (SSL).

SSL is a standard for securing Internet connections. Its main purpose is to encrypt HTTP communications. Each session creates its own encryption key; key setup is executed via SSL certificates, also known as Transport Layer Security (TLS) certificates—typically, X.509 documents—which are used by both the client and the server. SSL provides two critical assurances: first, that the server is authentic (that you are connecting to the server to which you intended to connect), and second, that an attacker cannot intercept and read or tamper with the data being exchanged between the client and the server (so long as you don't use a null cipher for the connection). It is an effective defense against server spoofing, channel tampering, and man-in-the-middle attacks.

The server provides the SSL certificate for the session and sends the certificate to the client in the handshake phase of establishing the communication channel. The server's certificate must be valid and issued by a trusted authority. It must chain to one of the certificate authorities (CAs) in the phone's trusted authorities list.

During development, you can create a self-signed root certificate and install this on the phone. Of course, you must not use a self-signed certificate in production, but this is a common approach during development. There is no certificate management UI on the phone, but installing a certificate on the phone can be done in two ways, as described in the following:

- Send the certificate to yourself by as an attachment and then open the email and the attachment on the phone. This approach only works on the phone, not the emulator.
- Make the certificate available on a website accessible to the phone. This approach works with both the emulator and a physical phone.

In both cases, you would tap the certificate to open it. The default behavior when opening a certificate file on the phone is to install it into the trusted authorities list.

Note SSL mutual authentication (by which the client sends its certificate to the server) is not supported, because you cannot add a client certificate to the phone's trusted authorities list.

Windows Azure

Windows Azure is a cloud services platform hosted through Microsoft data centers. Customers who have active Windows Azure accounts (including free trial accounts) can build and deploy apps to the cloud. The apps are hosted in virtual machines running on geographically distributed data centers. Customer data can be hosted in SQL Azure databases and/or in Windows Azure tables and blob containers. You would then typically deploy headless components—called "worker roles"—and Internet-facing web services and web apps—called "web roles." When you build a Windows Azure app, you can build one or more web roles and/or one or more worker roles. Each web or worker role runs in a virtual machine on top of the Windows Azure operating system, which itself sits on top of Windows Internet Information Services (IIS). Figure 8-7 summarizes the high-level architecture of Windows Azure apps, as it relates to Windows Phone apps. In this diagram, the round-cornered blocks are custom-defined, whereas the rectangular blocks are part of Windows Azure. A phone client app can work with the exposed web role (either a web app and/or one or more web services), and it can optionally use the Windows Azure API on the client-side to invoke cloud app features.

Microsoft provides a web-based management portal with which you can manage your server-side app, including starting and stopping, specifying the number of instances to run, and so on. Your web role can consist of headless web services or it can include web UI. If your web role includes web UI, the user can connect to it via a browser. The Windows Azure SDK is available as a free download from *http://www.windowsazure.com/en-us/develop/downloads/* (or search for Windows Azure SDK on the Microsoft Download Center). It includes project templates for Visual Studio as well as the client-side libraries.

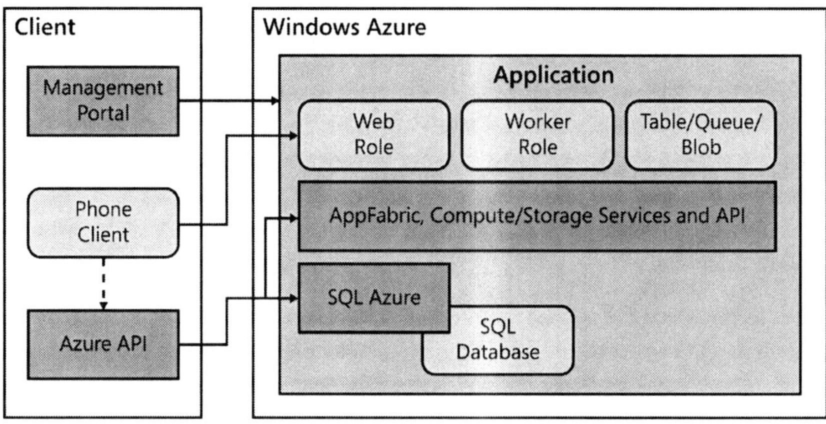

FIGURE 8-7 The Windows Azure app architecture offers a comprehensive set of cloud features.

Windows Azure web services

From the perspective of the Windows Phone app, consuming a web service exposed by Windows Azure is no different from consuming a web service exposed in any other way. Setting up the Windows Azure web service, however, does require specific steps, including an Azure account registration. For reference, you can examine the *CloudQotdService* solution in the sample code. This is a Windows Azure equivalent of the *QotdService* WCF web service sample examined earlier. If you're creating the entire client/server end-to-end solution from scratch, the main development and deployment tasks are as follows:

1. Create the service project in Visual Studio.
2. Provision the service in Windows Azure.

   To do this, you must log on to the Windows Azure management portal (*http://windows.azure.com*), create an affinity group and a storage account, and then deploy your compiled service package to the cloud.
3. Create the client.

   With the service running, create a Windows Phone app and then add a service reference to the service. Write code to exercise the service methods. All this is the same as for regular WCF web services client; you can even reuse the same *QotdClient* solution from the sample code that was used with the standard WCF *QotdService*. You just need to change the target endpoint address.

The first step is to create the web service. Having downloaded and installed the Windows Azure SDK, we can create a Windows Azure Cloud Service project, specifying .NET 4.0 Framework. We then add a WCF Service Web Role and give it a suitable name, for example *QotdServiceWebRole*.

We rename the generated *IService1.cs, Service1.svc,* and *Service1.svc.cs* files—in this example, rename them *IQotdService.cs, QotdService.svc,* and *QotdService.svc.cs*, respectively. Then, we edit the contents of each file to define our service. Most of this is the same as for regular WCF services. We can use the Refactor/Rename option in Visual Studio (right-click the name to open the shortcut menu). If we were to make the changes manually, it's easy to overlook the *Service1.svc*, because when you double-click this in Visual Studio, it takes you to the *Service1.svc.cs* file, instead. In particular, we must ensure that the *Service* attribute inside this file is set to the name of our service, for example, *QotdServiceWebRole.QotdService.*

The second step is to provision the service in Windows Azure. As of this writing, two versions of the Windows Azure management portal are available, as the new version is being rolled out. All major features are available in both versions. The only significant differences lie in the exact naming and placing of the various command links/buttons.

The first task in provisioning the service is to create a new affinity group. Affinity groups are used as a way of ensuring that all cloud-based components of a solution are deployed together (recall that cloud services can be physically executed in multiple geographical locations). Deploying all the pieces to the same location ensures high bandwidth and low latency between the app and the data on which it depends. The link to create a new affinity group is in the management portal, navigated via the Networks link, and then the Affinity Groups link. In this example, we'll set the new affinity group name to *qotd.*

The second cloud task is to create a storage account. This is a general requirement: even if you don't have explicit data to store, you need a storage account for diagnostics logs. In the management portal, we get to this option via the Data Services link and then the Storage link. On this page, we can create a new storage account—for simplicity, we'll use the same name as the affinity group (*qotd*).

The third provisioning task is to create our cloud service, as shown in Figure 8-8. In this example, the service account name is *qotdservice*, and it is set to deploy to the *qotd* affinity group.

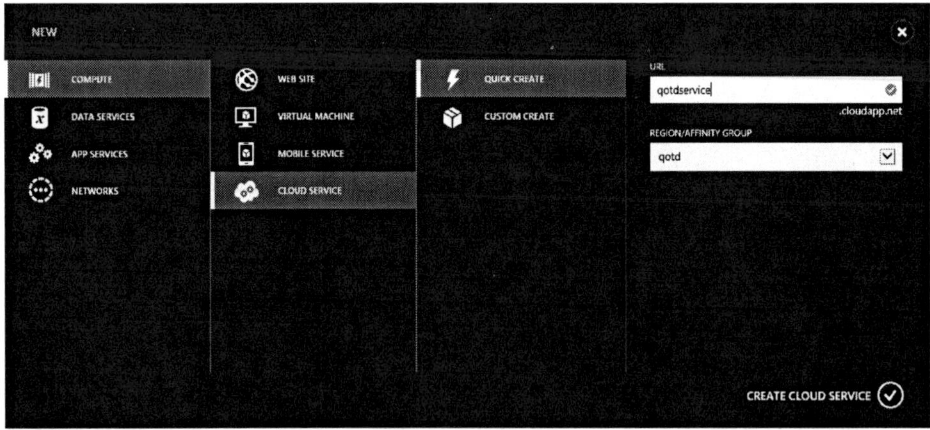

FIGURE 8-8 You can easily create a cloud service in Windows Azure to host your WCF web service.

When we confirm this dialog, the provisioning process starts—this usually takes a few minutes. As soon as provisioning is complete, we need to copy the generated access keys for use in our code. We can get these keys from the View Access Keys (or Manage Keys) button on the management portal toolbar. Alternatively, we can also get them in the Diagnostics Connection Strings section, on the Configure tab.

In Visual Studio, we need to open the *ServiceConfiguration.cscfg* file located in our service and replace the developer diagnostics connection string value with our account information. That is, replace this

```
<Setting name="Microsoft.WindowsAzure.Plugins.Diagnostics.ConnectionString"
value="UseDevelopmentStorage=true" />
```

with this (using our own account name and key, as copied to the clipboard in an earlier step):

```
<Setting name="Microsoft.WindowsAzure.Plugins.Diagnostics.ConnectionString"
value="DefaultEndpointsProtocol=https;AccountName=qotdservice;AccountKey=XXXXXXXXXXXXXXXXXXXXXX
XXXXXXXXXXXXXXXXXXXXXXXXXXXXXXXXXXXXXXXXXXXXXXXXXXXXXXXXXXXXXXXX" />
```

While we're in editing this file, it's generally a good idea to set the *count* property of the *Instances* element to *2*. The default that Visual Studio generates is *1*, but a realistic cloud service will always have at least two instances, for load-balancing and availability/robustness (of course, in a paid Azure account, there's a cost implication for each instance). It's also a good idea to increase the level of debugging support so that we get verbose error information. To do this, we add a *customErrors* element to the *web.config* inside the *system.web* element. We also set the *includeExceptionDetailInFaults* attribute of the *serviceDebug* element to *true*. If you use this technique, you must not forget to reset this to *false* before final deployment to production.

```
<system.web>
  <customErrors mode="Off"/>
</system.web>
<system.serviceModel>
  <behaviors>
    <serviceBehaviors>
      <behavior>
        <serviceDebug includeExceptionDetailInFaults="true"/>
      </behavior>
    </serviceBehaviors>
  </behaviors>
</system.serviceModel>
```

With both configuration files correctly set up, we can right-click the cloud project (not the Web Role) and then select Package to generate a deployment package for the solution. Visual Studio also offers a Publish option with which we can publish the solution directly to the cloud. However, it is generally more useful to deploy the solution in phases: build the package first, deploy it to staging, and then finally, switch it to production.

This creates the packaged solution and its configuration file. By default, these are located in the *app.publish* subfolder of the solution target folder. In this example, they are named *CloudQotdService.cspkg* and *ServiceConfiguration.Cloud.csfg*.

Back in the management portal, we can select the cloud service and then create a New Staging Deployment. A cloud service has two separate deployment slots: staging and production. With the staging deployment slot, we can test your service in the Azure environment before we deploy it to production. We specify an arbitrary name for this deployment (for example, *v1.0*) and then browse to the location for the package and configuration files.

After we've uploaded the deployment, we need to link the storage account we created with the service. To do this, we click the Link Resources link, and specify the qotd storage account. After confirming the deployment and the linked storage resources, the service is provisioned, and we can then test it by using the temporary URL provided in the service dashboard. When we have verified that the service is working correctly in the staging environment, we can promote it to final production.

To switch between staging and production, we select your service, and then on the management portal toolbar, click Swap. This brings up the Virtual IP Address (VIP) Swap dialog box. In this dialog box, we click Yes to swap the deployments between staging and production. When you deploy the app to production, Azure reconfigures its load balancers so that the app is available at its production URL—in this example, that will be *http://qotdservice.cloudapp.net/QotdService.svc*. The promotion process completes in a few seconds or minutes, and the portal reports that the deployment is running, as shown in Figure 8-9.

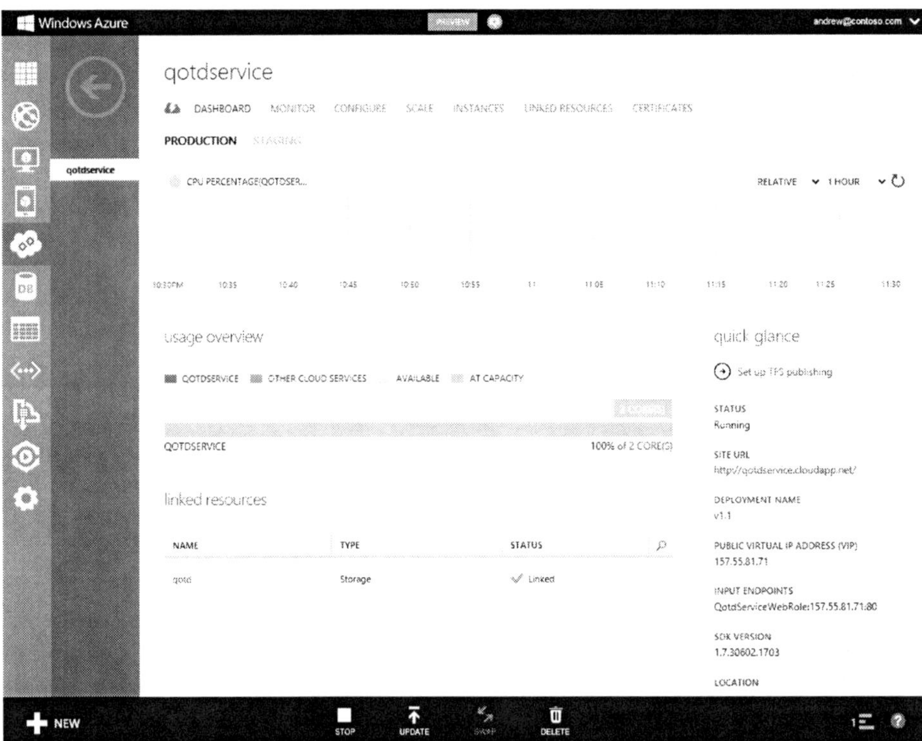

FIGURE 8-9 You can create, deploy, configure, start, and stop cloud solutions in the Windows Azure management portal.

We can then test the client phone app again. The final result on the client is exactly the same as the version illustrated back in Figure 8-4. The only difference between this version of the client and the earlier version is that we now target an Azure-hosted web service instead of a web service hosted on a non-Azure server. This difference is almost completely transparent to the client. To redirect the client to point to the Azure web service, all we need to do is to change the endpoint address in the *ServiceReferences.ClientConfig* file, as follows:

```
<endpoint
    address="http://qotdservice.cloudapp.net/QotdService.svc"
    binding="basicHttpBinding"
    bindingConfiguration="BasicHttpBinding_IQotdService"
    contract="QotdServiceReference.IQotdService"
    name="BasicHttpBinding_IQotdService" />
```

Windows Azure Mobile Services for Windows Phone

The Developer Platform Evangelism team at Microsoft publishes and maintains a set of support libraries, Visual Studio project templates, and tools to support development scenarios with Windows Azure and clients such as Windows and Windows Phone. The toolkit for Windows Phone is available for download at *http://www.windowsazure.com/en-us/develop/mobile/*. You can think of this as the Windows Phone 8 incarnation of a similar toolkit that is available for Windows Phone 7, which you can download from *http://watwp.codeplex.com/*. However, Windows Azure Mobile Services has been designed and built from the ground up with a clear mission to make the development of mobile-cloud solutions as quick and painless as possible, and in reality it bears only a passing resemblance to the earlier toolkit.

There's even a tutorial online, which takes you through the steps of creating a new Mobile Services app which will then actually run for real in Windows Azure. At the end of the tutorial, there's a button to download the solution source code for a fully-functioning client app that connects to the cloud app.

The first step for creating this end-to-end solution is to log on to the management portal and go to the Mobile Services tab. Then, click the "+" button to create a new Mobile Service. This brings up the New Mobile Service dialog box. Here, you supply a suitable name for your service, for example, **DemoMobileService**. You can use an existing SQL Azure database if you have one already set up, or you can allow Azure to create one for you. If you opt to create a new database, you'll be given the opportunity to supply a name for this and to create an administrator user name and password. You can also configure other database settings or accept the defaults.

It typically takes only a few seconds to create your Mobile Service, including the database. When this is complete, you're presented with the Quick Start page. On this page, there are links to connect this service to an existing client app or to create a new one (Windows Store or Windows Phone).

If you click the link to create a new Windows Phone app, this will create an app with which the user can add items to a "todo" list. Notice that you haven't yet configured the tables in the database. What happens is that when the user adds an item to the list, the table schema is created at that point to match the data that the client app passes to the service. This is the default behavior in the sample app, but clearly you have the option to design your own database schema or to use an existing database. Finally, you're offered a button to download the client solution code. Figure 8-10 shows the *TestMobileServices* client app that connects to the *DemoMobileService* cloud app. This allows the user to create new "todo" items and reports a list of the current items, including check boxes with which the user can mark them as complete.

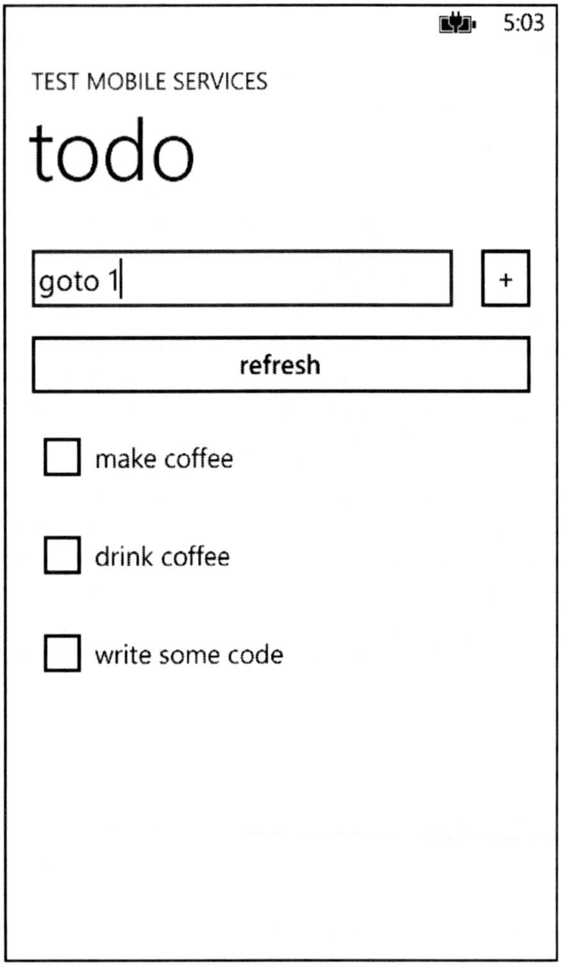

FIGURE 8-10 Connecting to a Windows Azure Mobile Services app is very similar to connecting to a regular web service.

The interesting pieces of code are as follows. First, the project has a reference to the *Microsoft.WindowsAzure.MobileServices.Managed.dll*, which contains the client-side API to Mobile Services. Second, the *App* class declares a public *MobileServiceClient* field, which establishes the connection to the cloud app. You can retrieve the identifier for your cloud app from the management portal (shown here as "XXX").

```
public static MobileServiceClient MobileService = new MobileServiceClient(
    "https://demomobileservice.azure-mobile.net/",
    "XXXXXXXXXXXXXXXXXXXXXXXXXXXXXXXX"
);
```

The app defines a custom *TodoItem* class with just two simple properties, both serializable: a *string* for the text of the item, and *bool* for the status (complete or not). There's also a third property for the *Id*; this will be supplied from the server-side and is not used on the client in this example.

```
public class TodoItem
{
    public int Id { get; set; }

    [DataMember(Name = "text")]
    public string Text { get; set; }

    [DataMember(Name = "complete")]
    public bool Complete { get; set; }
}
```

The *MainPage* declares a collection of *TodoItem* objects by using the *MobileServiceCollectionView* class, which implements *ICollectionView* (designed for data-binding to lists). When the user enters a new item in the UI and taps the *Save* button, this constructs a new *TodoItem* and calls the Mobile Services app to insert this into the database. When the operation completes and Mobile Services has assigned an ID, the item is added to the collection. The hard work of connecting to the cloud service and invoking its operations to perform the database insert is all done for you by the Mobile Services client API. As you can see from the following code, this is extremely easy to use:

```
private MobileServiceCollectionView<TodoItem> items;
private IMobileServiceTable<TodoItem> todoTable = App.MobileService.GetTable<TodoItem>();

private void save_Click(object sender, RoutedEventArgs e)
{
    TodoItem todoItem = new TodoItem { Text = TextInput.Text };
    InsertTodoItem(todoItem);
}

private async void InsertTodoItem(TodoItem todoItem)
{
    await todoTable.InsertAsync(todoItem);
    items.Add(todoItem);
}
```

When the user checks off an item to indicate that this is complete, this item is passed back to the cloud app to update the database with the new status. When the Mobile Service responds, the item is removed from the client-side collection, which subsequently updates the data-bound *ListBox* in the UI.

```
private void complete_Checked(object sender, RoutedEventArgs e)
{
    CheckBox cb = (CheckBox)sender;
    TodoItem item = cb.DataContext as TodoItem;
    item.Complete = (bool)cb.IsChecked;
    UpdateCheckedTodoItem(item);
}

private async void UpdateCheckedTodoItem(TodoItem item)
{
    await todoTable.UpdateAsync(item);
    items.Remove(item);
}
```

Finally, when the user taps the *Refresh* button, this again talks to the Mobile Services app, fetches the current list of items from the database, and then updates the collection for the UI. The query excludes items that are marked complete.

```
private void refresh_Click(object sender, RoutedEventArgs e)
{
    items = todoTable
        .Where(todoItem => todoItem.Complete == false)
        .ToCollectionView();
    ListItems.ItemsSource = items;
}
```

Although this tutorial sample is obviously very simple, you can see that it is extremely easy to get started with Mobile Services, and even in this starter example, you still have considerable flexibility for configuring both server and client parts of your solution.

Summary

This chapter examined the many different ways by which you can connect a phone app to web services, including WCF data services and Windows Azure–hosted services. You've seen that there are some challenges in setting up the emulator to test development web services, and we looked at ways to resolve these. We also compared the various options for formatting data transfers, where the aim for a mobile solution is generally to minimize volume wherever possible. Connecting mobile solutions to cloud services, and in particular Microsoft Windows Azure, is an increasingly common solution pattern, and developing such solutions is made easier with the Windows Azure Mobile Services SDK.

CHAPTER 9

Background agents

Compared to the environment in which a desktop app operates, resources on the phone (memory, CPU, screen real-estate, and power) are significantly constrained. For this reason, the user experience (UX) is optimized by giving the foreground app priority access to these resources. That said, certain other applications, notably system services such as incoming phone calls, SMS messages, or toasts, will continue to run even when an app is running in the foreground and are allowed to impinge partially on the foreground user interface (UI). Developers can also build Windows Phone Store apps where some part of the app is enabled to run in the background even while the user is interacting with another app in the foreground. This chapter examines multiple methods by which you can build background tasks, and the particular constraints and best practices you should adopt in these scenarios.

Background tasks

The platform support for background tasks is designed to enable two broad user scenarios:

- The user wants to start some app in the foreground and then switch to another app, yet have some features of the initial app continue to run in the background. An example of this is audio: you might start playing audio and then switch to email, but you want the audio to continue running in the background.
- You configure an app to perform tasks in the background independent of which app the user is using. Examples of this are alarms and reminders.

These scenarios are supported by four different types of background task, as listed here:

- **Alarms and reminders** A simple programmatic way to invoke one-off or periodic alerts that run independently of your app.
- **Background Transfer Service** A simple service for performing downloads and uploads in the background.
- **Generic Background Agents** A general-purpose mechanism for you to run code in the background when your main app is not running in the foreground.
- **Background audio** A mechanism by which your app can initiate audio playback while it is in the foreground and have the audio continue to run, even when the user navigates away from the app.

The ability of user apps to run code both in the foreground and in the background clearly runs an increased risk of contention for resources such as CPU and memory. In designing the rules governing background execution, considerable thought went into achieving the best possible overall UX. Consider this possible scenario: app A runs in the foreground while at the same time app B is running multiple resource-intensive operations in the background, to the point where the performance, responsiveness, and UX in app A is noticeably degraded. App A might be playing by the rules and using resources conservatively, whereas app B is being reckless. However, the user's perception is that app A is performing poorly, which might negatively impact the developer's ratings and thus profitability. To mitigate these issues and maintain the health of the phone as well as the overall UX, there are a number of constraints with respect to how you can set up and run background tasks. One critical constraint is that certain types of background features are actually prohibited from running while any foreground app is running. Further limitations for each class of background feature are described in the following sections.

Note Chapter 18, "Location and maps," discusses a fifth type of background task behavior, the Continuous Background Execution (CBE) app, which can run either in the foreground or in the background.

Alarms and reminders

Alarms and reminders are two forms of the same type of UX. In both cases, they trigger a notification to the user according to some schedule defined in your app. The notification is presented to the user in the form of a dialog box that appears on the screen at a specified time. The dialog box can display some text that you determine and offer buttons with which the user can dismiss the notification or postpone it until later. For reminders, if the user taps the notification, this launches your app. You can set up alarms and reminders to be either single events or recurring.

There are minor differences between alarms and reminders. For instance, with an alarm, you can specify a sound file to play when the notification is launched. On the other hand, with a reminder, you can specify a page in your app to go to when the user taps the reminder UI. One caveat is that there is a limit of 50 alarms and/or reminders at a time per app, and they are accurate only to within 60 seconds.

Alarms

There has been an alarms app built in to the phone since Windows Phone 7.0, and you can use the same underlying mechanisms in your app. From a user's perspective, custom alarms are very similar to the built-in alarms app insomuch as the alarm alert UX is the same, the options to snooze or dismiss are the same, both adhere to user settings, and so on. Here's the basic usage:

1. Create an *Alarm* object.
2. Set its properties.
3. Add it to the *ScheduledActionService*.

These steps are demonstrated in the following code snippet:

```
Alarm alarm = new Alarm("Coffee");
alarm.BeginTime = DateTime.Now.AddMinutes(30);
alarm.Content = "Time for a break.";
ScheduledActionService.Add(alarm);
```

Figure 9-1 shows the *IntervalTraining* app in the sample code: this is an interval training tool. The idea is that the user enters each interval item into a list and then starts the training session. At the start of the session, the app creates an *Alarm* for each item that starts at the end of the previous item. In this way, the user is notified when to stop the current item and start the next one. This is a very primitive demonstration; for example, it doesn't make any allowances by offsetting the other alarms if the user chooses to "snooze" an alarm. However, it serves to illustrate the core alarm mechanism.

The code is very simple. First, we declare a class to hold the session item data, including the *Alarm* for each item. Notice how in the following example each *Alarm* has a unique name:

```
public class SessionItem
{
    public int Minutes { get; set; }
    public string Name { get; set; }
}
```

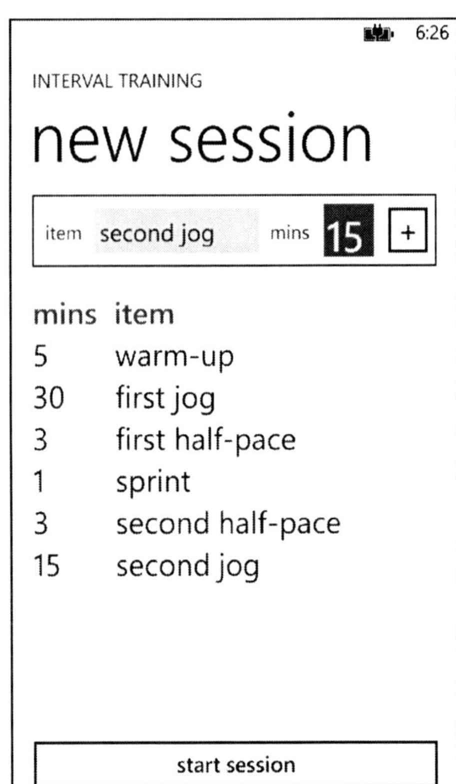

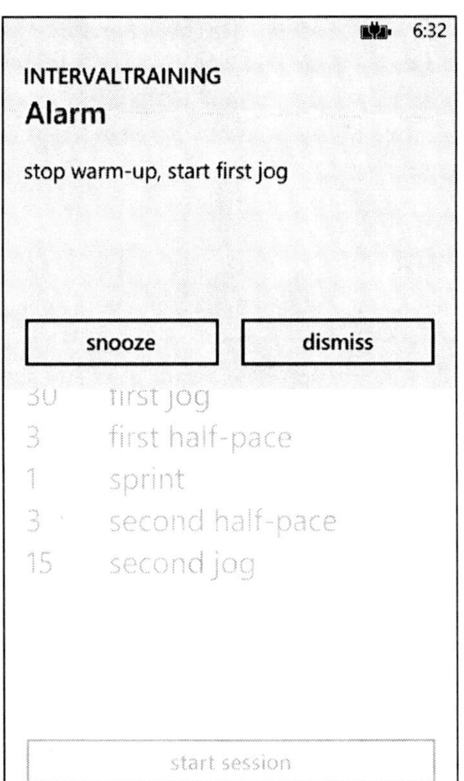

FIGURE 9-1 There are many app scenarios for which it can be useful to schedule alarms.

On the main page, we set up a collection of session items in the constructor (in this example, this is a very small amount of work, and could also be done in the *OnNavigatedTo* override) and data-bind these as the *ItemsSource* for a *ListBox*. We're also taking this opportunity to clean up any old alarms for this app that haven't already been triggered. Calling *ScheduledActionService.GetActions* retrieves the scheduled actions of the specific type for this app only; there's no danger that we'd interfere with alarms/reminders for any other app. So far, we're only considering *Alarm* and *Reminder* types, but note that *GetActions* also gets other scheduled actions for this app such as periodic or resource-intensive background tasks (discussed later in this chapter). We're using a *LoopingSelector* from the Windows Phone Toolkit for the time selection. This uses a custom *IntLoopingDataSource*. You can examine the accompanying sample code for the implementation of this, although it is not important for the current context.

```
private IntLoopingDataSource timeData = new IntLoopingDataSource();
public ObservableCollection<SessionItem> SessionItems { get; set; }
```

```
public MainPage()
{
    InitializeComponent();
    ItemMinutes.DataSource = timeData;
    SessionItems = new ObservableCollection<SessionItem>();
    SessionItemsList.ItemsSource = SessionItems;

    var oldAlarms = ScheduledActionService.GetActions<Alarm>();
    foreach (Alarm alarm in oldAlarms)
    {
        if (alarm.ExpirationTime < DateTime.Now)
        {
            ScheduledActionService.Remove(alarm.Name);
        }
    }
}
```

When the user taps the "+" button, we add a new session item to the list. Finally, when the user taps the Start Session button, we walk through the collection and schedule an *Alarm* for the end of each item. There's a conditional statement in there that affects the timing of each alarm. This is because, while testing, you can reduce the time of the alarm so that you don't have to wait so long for it to be raised. Be aware, however, that the alarm scheduling system does not work well with alarms scheduled within a very short time of one another. The finest granularity that is guaranteed is 60 seconds, and you can be pretty sure that alarms within approximately 30 seconds of one another might not be scheduled in the correct order.

```
private void AddButton_Click(object sender, RoutedEventArgs e)
{
    SessionItems.Add(new SessionItem
        { Minutes = (int)timeData.SelectedItem, Name = ItemName.Text });
    timeData.SelectedItem = 1;
    ItemName.Text = String.Empty;
}

private void StartButton_Click(object sender, RoutedEventArgs e)
{
    DateTime startTime = DateTime.Now;
    for (int i = 0; i < SessionItems.Count; i++)
    {
        SessionItem currentItem = SessionItems[i];
        Alarm alarm = new Alarm(Guid.NewGuid().ToString());
        if (i + 1 == SessionItems.Count)
        {
            alarm.Content = String.Format("stop {0}", SessionItems[i].Name);
        }
        else
        {
            alarm.Content = String.Format("stop {0}, start {1}",
                SessionItems[i].Name, SessionItems[i + 1].Name);
        }
```

```
#if DEBUG
        // For debug purposes, we'll divide the times by 10.
        startTime = startTime.AddMinutes(currentItem.Minutes / 10);
#else
        startTime = startTime.AddMinutes(currentItem.Minutes);
#endif
        alarm.BeginTime = startTime;
        try
        {
            ScheduledActionService.Add(alarm);
        }
        catch (Exception ex)
        {
            MessageBox.Show(ex.Message);
        }
    }
}
```

Reminders

Reminders are also very similar to the standard calendar reminders that are built in to the phone: they behave like standard reminders, and will stack with all the other reminders in the system from the user's calendar. They are slightly richer than alarms, with more scope for providing additional data (and UI) for the reminder. Standard calendar reminders provide for a navigation target; that is, when the user clicks a reminder, it takes her to the corresponding item in the calendar. With custom reminders, you have the same behavior: you can specify to navigate to a page in your app when the user responds to the reminder. Figure 9-2 shows an example (the *TrailReminders* app in the sample code). This represents a trail app (which in a real application would have a database of trails) and offers a reminder feature that the user can set for when she has identified a trail she's planning to hike.

To represent the trail data, the app implements a simple *Trail* class to encapsulate basic data, as shown in the following:

```
public class Trail
{
    public string Title { get; set; }
    public string Photo { get; set; }
    public string Description { get; set; }

    public Trail(string title, string photo, string description)
    {
        Title = title;
        Photo = photo;
        Description = description;
    }
}
```

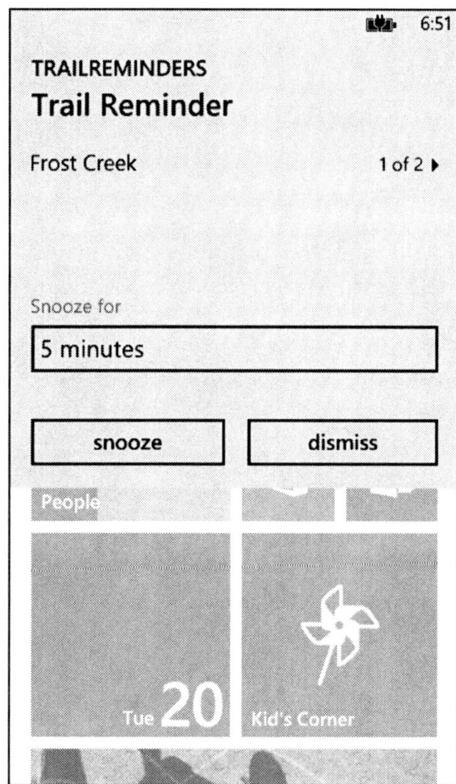

FIGURE 9-2 Using the *TrailReminders* app, the user can add a reminder for a selected trail, which later triggers a reminder alert.

The *App* class holds the data (as a simple viewmodel) with a new method, *InitializeData*, which is called at the end of the constructor. In this method, we set up a few trail data items. For debugging, we clear out any old reminders. Realistically, you might want to keep an independent list of the reminders for this app within the app itself, which you could then manage appropriately (removing expired reminders, providing a list to the user of all remaining reminders, and so on).

```
public static ObservableCollection<Trail> Trails { get; set; }

private void InitializeData()
{
    Trails = new ObservableCollection<Trail>();

    Trails.Add(new Trail("Frog Ridge", "images/FrogRidge.jpg", "This is a 16-mile roundtrip 
hike, set deep in the North Cascades forests. It boasts a wide range of wildlife, including 
black and grizzly bears, mountain lions, elk, deer and marmots - but no frogs."));
    Trails.Add(new Trail("Frost Creek", "images/FrostCreek.jpg", "Frost Creek is almost never 
free of snow and ice, as it is at 7000ft elevation in the Olympics, on the east-facing side, so 
it gets very little sun, and only for half an hour or so, once a year."));
    Trails.Add(new Trail("Blue Divide", "images/BlueDivide.jpg", "Trappers and loggers in 
the early 1800s first mapped this trail. The name comes not from the blue-tinted snow-capped 
mountains, nor from the slate-blue mists that surround them, but from the meanies that live 
here."));
```

```
#if DEBUG
    var oldReminders = ScheduledActionService.GetActions<Reminder>();
    foreach (Reminder r in oldReminders)
    {
        ScheduledActionService.Remove(r.Name);
    }
#endif
}
```

The main page offers a *ListBox* populated with trail *Titles* via data binding (through the *App.Trails* property) and implements the *SelectionChanged* handler to navigate to the corresponding individual trail page.

```
public MainPage()
{
    InitializeComponent();
    TrailList.ItemsSource = App.Trails;
}

private void TrailList_SelectionChanged(object sender, SelectionChangedEventArgs e)
{
    if (TrailList.SelectedIndex == -1)
    {
        return;
    }
    String navigationString =
        String.Format("/TrailPage.xaml?Title={0}", ((Trail)TrailList.SelectedItem).Title);
    NavigationService.Navigate(new Uri(navigationString, UriKind.Relative));
    TrailList.SelectedIndex = -1;
}
```

The interesting work is done in the *TrailPage*. In the XAML, we data-bind UI elements to the properties on the *Trail* class. To give the user an easy way to pick a date for her reminder, we use the *DatePicker* from the Windows Phone Toolkit.

```
<Grid x:Name="LayoutRoot" Background="Transparent">
...
    <StackPanel Grid.Row="0" Margin="12,17,0,28">
        <TextBlock
            Text="TRAIL REMINDERS" Style="{StaticResource PhoneTextNormalStyle}"/>
        <TextBlock
            Text="{Binding Title}" Margin="9,-7,0,0"
            Style="{StaticResource PhoneTextTitle1Style}"/>
    </StackPanel>

    <StackPanel x:Name="ContentPanel" Grid.Row="1" Margin="12,0,12,0">
        <Image Source="{Binding Photo}" Height="300" Width="410"/>
        <TextBlock
            Text="{Binding Description}" Height="210" Width="410"
            Style="{StaticResource PhoneTextNormalStyle}" TextWrapping="Wrap"/>
        <StackPanel Orientation="Horizontal">
            <toolkit:DatePicker x:Name="ReminderDate" Width="220" Margin="12,0,0,0"/>
            <Button
```

```
                x:Name="AddButton" Content="add reminder" Click="AddButton_Click"/>
        </StackPanel>
    </StackPanel>
</Grid>
```

In the code-behind, we override *OnNavigatedTo* to extract the trail *Title* from the navigation *QueryString*. We use this to find the corresponding *Trail* data from the viewmodel collection and set it as the *DataContext* for the page:

```
private string thisTitle;
private string thisPageUri;

protected override void OnNavigatedTo(NavigationEventArgs e)
{
    thisTitle = NavigationContext.QueryString["Title"];
    thisPageUri = e.Uri.ToString();


    DataContext = App.Trails.FirstOrDefault(t => t.Title == thisTitle);
}
```

Finally, we implement the Add Reminder button to create a new *Reminder* using data from the *Trail* object, and the user's selected *DateTime* from the *DatePicker*.

```
private void AddButton_Click(object sender, RoutedEventArgs e)
{
    Reminder reminder = new Reminder(Guid.NewGuid().ToString());

#if DEBUG
    reminder.BeginTime = DateTime.Now.AddSeconds(5);
#else
    reminder.BeginTime = (DateTime)ReminderDate.Value;
#endif
    reminder.Content = thisTitle;
    reminder.Title = "Trail Reminder";
    reminder.RecurrenceType = RecurrenceInterval.None;
    reminder.NavigationUri = new Uri(thisPageUri, UriKind.Relative);
    try
    {
        ScheduledActionService.Add(reminder);
    }
    catch (Exception ex)
    {
        MessageBox.Show(ex.Message);
    }
}
```

Later, when the reminder is triggered, the user can tap it to navigate directly to the corresponding trail page, regardless of which app is running at the time. There are two caveats to this: first, if the phone is locked, nothing happens; second, if the app that owns the reminder is currently the active (foreground) app, nothing happens.

From these simple examples, you can see that custom alarms and reminders are integrated with built-in alarms and calendar reminders. They even survive reboots, just like the built-in versions.

The Background Transfer Service

When deciding on a technique for network data transfer, for low-latency network requests (such as images or data in your app) you typically use *HttpWebRequest* or *WebClient*, but for larger uploads or downloads that don't have strict time requirements, you can use the Background Transfer Service (BTS). This provides benefits such as continuation/restart of transfers as necessary beyond app termination and even across reboots, built-in retries, and the ability for your app to stop and restart requests or delete them from the queue. The BTS exposes a very simple API to use: you make a *BackgroundTransferRequest*, specifying the source and destination URLs, and then add that request to the *BackgroundTransferService* queue. You can also subscribe to progress events on the operation. Then, the service takes over and executes your request asynchronously, continuing even if your app terminates or the phone reboots.

Behind the scenes, the *BackgroundTransferService* uses the same infrastructure as that used by Xbox Live, and therefore applies the same constraints. That is, file downloads are limited to 20 MB maximum for any one request over the cell network. You can download bigger files (up to a maximum of 100 MB), but the request will be queued until the phone switches from a cell network to Wi-Fi. If you know (or suspect) that the file you're downloading exceeds 100 MB, you must set the *Transfer Preferences* property of the transfer to *None*. Without this, the transfer will fail unless the phone is on a Wi-Fi connection and also is connected to an AC power source. File uploads are limited to 5 MB. In addition to the filesize limits, the system allows a maximum of two concurrent transfers across all apps on the phone, a maximum of 25 queued transfers per app, and a maximum of 500 queued transfers across all apps.

Note Chapter 7, "Web connectivity," discusses the Data Sense feature introduced in Windows Phone 8. This feature makes it possible for users to request that apps limit data transfers as they approach the limits set for their data plan. If the user turns on Data Sense and the user is either over their limit or roaming, the system will suspend background transfers.

Figure 9-3 illustrates a simple example (the *BackgroundTransferDemo* app in the sample code), in which the UI has two *Button* controls: a *ProgressBar* and a *MediaElement*. The scenario is that the user taps the Download button to initiate a background download of an arbitrary video file. While this is ongoing, we report progress in the *ProgressBar*. Then, when the download is complete, we make the Play button available so that the user can play the newly downloaded video. After initiating the download, the user is free to navigate away from the app, if he so wishes; the download will continue to run in the background.

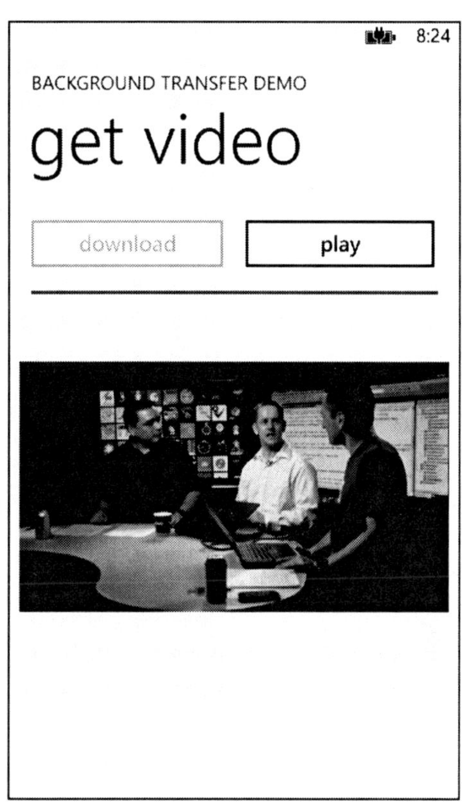

FIGURE 9-3 Starting a background transfer (on the left) and completing it (right).

In the code, we first set up some fields for the *BackgroundTransferRequest* and the target *IsolatedStorageFile*. We also initialize the storage file in the page constructor. When you download a file, it must be stored in the app's isolated storage, and it must be in the shared/transfers folder (or a subfolder thereof). You can move the file subsequently, if you need to.

```
private static readonly Uri remoteFileUri =
    new Uri(
        @"http://media.ch9.ms/ch9/4b58/de9f7501-2a51-4875-8b2f-9f4d014b4b58/
IWP22PtorrBkgrndAgnt_ch9.wmv",
        UriKind.Absolute);
private static readonly Uri localFileUri =
    new Uri("/shared/transfers/movie.wmv", UriKind.Relative);
private IsolatedStorageFile isf;
private BackgroundTransferRequest btr;

public MainPage()
{
    InitializeComponent();
    isf = IsolatedStorageFile.GetUserStoreForApplication();
}
```

When the user taps the Download button, we create a new *BackgroundTransferRequest* and hook up the progress and status events. We'll get progress events while the transfer is ongoing, and status events when the status changes (for example, from ongoing transfer to completed, or error). The app goes a bit further by disabling the download button to prevent the user from starting the transfer again while it is already in progress.

Note Additional publication requirements apply for any app that uses the BTS. The primary requirement is that such an app must not start a background transfer without the user's direct participation.

```
private void downloadButton_Click(object sender, RoutedEventArgs e)
{
    btr = new BackgroundTransferRequest(remoteFileUri, localFileUri);
    BackgroundTransferService.Add(btr);
    btr.TransferProgressChanged += btr_TransferProgressChanged;
    btr.TransferStatusChanged += btr_TransferStatusChanged;
    downloadButton.IsEnabled = false;
}
```

In the *TransferProgressChanged* event, the app takes care to update the *ProgressBar* to match its maximum value to the total file size, and its current value to the number of bytes received at that point.

```
private void btr_TransferProgressChanged(object sender, BackgroundTransferEventArgs e)
{
    Dispatcher.BeginInvoke(() =>
    {
        progressBar.Maximum = btr.TotalBytesToReceive;
        progressBar.Value = btr.BytesReceived;
    });
}
```

In the *TransferStatusChanged* event, we check to see if the new status is *Completed*; if it is, we open the downloaded file and attach it to the *MediaElement*. At the same time, we ensure that the *ProgressBar* value is set to the number of bytes received on the download. This is necessary because if the user switches away from the app and then back again, if by the time he switches back the download has completed, the app won't get any more transfer events (to indicate that we need to update the *ProgressBar*). For this example, we're going to ignore all other status events—in a more sophisticated app, you would probably handle other cases, as well.

```
private void btr_TransferStatusChanged(object sender, BackgroundTransferEventArgs e)
{
    if (btr.TransferStatus == TransferStatus.Completed)
    {
        UpdateUi();
    }
}
```

```
private void UpdateUi()
{
    Dispatcher.BeginInvoke(() =>
    {
        progressBar.Value = btr.BytesReceived;
        using (IsolatedStorageFileStream file = isf.OpenFile(
            btr.DownloadLocation.ToString(), FileMode.Open, FileAccess.Read))
        {
            mediaElement.SetSource(file);
        }
    });
}
```

When we attach the file to the *MediaElement*, this triggers the *MediaOpened* event. When this event fires, we enable the Play button. The user can then tap the Play button to start the video. Observe how the *MediaOpened* event is hooked up in the XAML.

```
private void mediaElement_MediaOpened(object sender, RoutedEventArgs e)
{
    playButton.IsEnabled = true;
}

private void playButton_Click(object sender, RoutedEventArgs e)
{
    mediaElement.Play();
}
```

Finally, we need to override *OnNavigatedTo* and check to see if we're coming back to the app with an existing transfer request. If so, this indicates that the user must have started the request and then navigated forward away from the app. In this scenario, we hook up the transfer status event handlers again, check to see if the transfer has already completed (in which case, no events will be raised), and then update the UI if it has. For fit-and-finish, we also want to set the *IsEnabled* state of the Download button according to whether there is a transfer in progress.

```
protected override void OnNavigatedTo(NavigationEventArgs e)
{
    btr = BackgroundTransferService.Requests.FirstOrDefault();
    if (btr == null)
    {
        downloadButton.IsEnabled = true;
        return;
    }

    downloadButton.IsEnabled = false;
    btr.TransferProgressChanged += btr_TransferProgressChanged;
    btr.TransferStatusChanged += btr_TransferStatusChanged;
    if (btr.TransferStatus == TransferStatus.Completed)
    {
        UpdateUi();
    }
}
```

As you can see, the BTS adds to the existing techniques for asynchronous web requests by providing for requests that can continue beyond the lifetime of the app that initiated them, and even beyond a phone reboot.

Generic Background Agents

Alarms, reminders, background transfers, and background audio are all specific types of background activity. There is also a class of background activity known as Generic Background Agents (GBAs). These are not limited to one specific set of functionality; rather, you can implement them to perform a general-purpose range of functionality per your specific domain requirements. Windows Phone supports two types of GBA:

- **Periodic** Represented by the *PeriodicTask* class, this type of agent runs for a short time on a regular recurring interval. It is only allowed a maximum of 25 seconds to run, roughly every 30 minutes (the exact timing is unpredictable because the system will attempt to align the execution of periodic agents with other system activities; the interval will be in the range of 20 to 40 minutes). There is a hard limit on the number of periodic agents that can be scheduled on the phone. This varies per device, but it can be as low as 6 and no more than 18. Also note that if the user has enabled battery-saver mode on his phone, this can effectively prevent periodic agents from running during the period when the phone enters that mode (typically at 20-percent battery power).
- **Resource-intensive** Represented by the *ResourceIntensiveTask* class, this type of agent runs for a relatively long period of time, and it is only executed when a specific set of conditions is satisfied. A *ResourceIntensiveTask* can run for a maximum of 10 minutes at a time but only when all of the following conditions are met:
    - The phone is on external power
    - The phone has network connectivity over Wi-Fi
    - Battery power is greater than 90 percent
    - The device screen is locked
    - There is no active phone call

Keep in mind that it is quite possible that these conditions will never be met on a given phone, so you must allow for the possibility that your agent never in fact has the opportunity to run. Finally, be aware that if all the above conditions are met, and a resource-intensive agent is started but then something changes such that one or more of the conditions no longer holds true, the agent will be terminated immediately. Because of these constraints, resource-intensive agents are best used for opportunistic operations that will improve the foreground app experience if they can be done in the background but which are not strictly required for the app to work properly.

Here's how the platform schedules resource-intensive tasks: the scheduler runs them in a round-robin manner for 10 minutes each until the task calls *NotifyComplete*. So, suppose that you have 25 minutes' worth of work to do. At the appropriate time, the platform starts the task, and then terminates it after 10 minutes. The platform can then run other scheduled tasks, and will eventually return to the task that was terminated. The platform then runs that task again. When another 10 minutes elapses, the task is again terminated so that the platform can run other scheduled tasks. Finally, the first task runs again, and after 5 more minutes of work, the task completes and calls *NotifyComplete*. At this point, the platform will no longer schedule this task until the original conditions are met again. For such a long-running task, it is clearly important that it is resilient to being terminated and that it performs checkpoints on the progress of work completed so that it can pick up and carry on the next time it is invoked.

Under the hood, the app platform treats both periodic and resource-intensive tasks as the same kind of background agent. The only distinction internally is that each task happens to follow a different schedule and have different resource constraints. The task type implicitly defines the schedule and resource set.

A GBA has a default expiry of 14 days, which also happens to be its maximum. That is, you cannot create a GBA with an expiration date beyond 14 days. However, you can renew the agent any time your app runs in the foreground. So, if the user keeps running your app, you can keep renewing your background agents indefinitely. Conversely, if the user doesn't run your app for a while, they're probably also not interested in the app's background agents—hence, the limited expiry. There are three exceptions to this general rule:

- If the user has pinned your app's tile to the Start screen, your GBA is automatically extended by 14 days whenever your agent updates the tile.
- If the user selects your app to display notifications on the lock screen or provide lock screen wallpaper, your GBA is automatically extended by 14 days whenever your agent updates the lock screen.
- If you implement a resource-intensive agent that uploads photos, your GBA schedule will not expire as long as the user has enabled this feature for your app on the Photos+Camera settings page.

Recall that your agent should always call *NotifyComplete* when it has completed its intended task, and in this case, the *LastExitReason* property on the task object will have the value *Completed*. If your agent is unable to complete its intended task, it should call *Abort*, and in this case, the *LastExitReason* will be *Aborted*, and the *IsScheduled* property for the associated *ScheduledTask* will be set to *false*. If your agent crashes twice in a row, the system will not reschedule it unless and until your foreground app reapplies the schedule.

There are also memory limitations: a GBA cannot take up more than 11 MB of memory on Windows Phone 8 (6 MB on Windows Phone 7). Recall that Windows Phone 8 introduced support for high-resolution screens. This presents a conundrum for GBAs: if your GBA dynamically generates images, it can exceed the memory cap if it generates high-resolution images. For this reason, you're advised to generate only WVGA-resolution images in a GBA, and allow the system to auto-scale these for higher-resolution screens. Furthermore, there are restrictions as to the types of operation your background agent can perform. These restrictions are summarized in Table 9-1.

TABLE 9-1 Permitted and prohibited operations in GBAs

Permitted operations	Prohibited operations
Create and show Tiles and Toast	Display arbitrary UI
Use location functionality	Use of the XNA libraries
Access the network	Use sensors, including microphone and camera
Read/write isolated storage	Play audio
Use sockets	Schedule alarms, reminders, or background transfers
Use most framework APIs	

Finally, the phone also includes user settings that indicate which applications have registered background agents. The user can turn off/on background agents on a per-app basis.

To make use of GBAs in your app, you produce a XAP file that contains both your main app assembly (or assemblies) and an additional assembly for your background agent. By dividing your code in this manner, the phone system services can launch your background agent in a separate process, independent of your main app. This makes it possible for your background agents to run in the background when your main app is not running. An app can have only one GBA; this can be a *PeriodicTask*, a *ResourceIntensiveTask*, or both. The two parts of your app are associated via the main app's manifest, which defines the background agent(s), including the assembly and entrypoint type for your agent.

In addition, the app and agent can optionally be connected in two other ways:

- Your agent can create a *ShellToast* object and show it. At this point, the user can click the toast, which will navigate to the page in your main app that you specified when you created it.
- Both the app and agent have access to the same app isolated storage; therefore, they can share files.

The relationships are summarized in Figure 9-4.

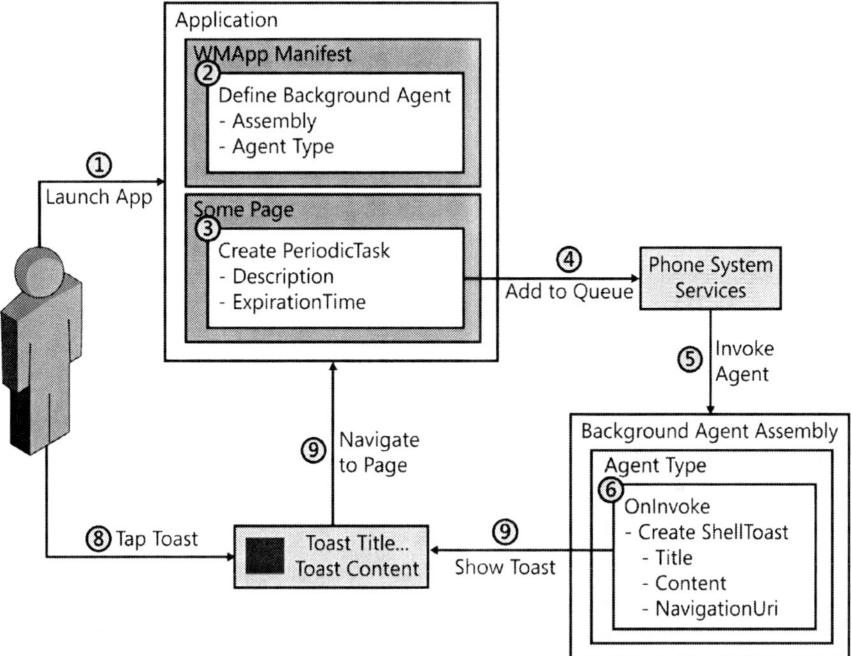

FIGURE 9-4 The relationships between background agent components.

The basic steps for setting up a GBA are as follows:

1. Create your main app project, as normal.
2. Add a Windows Phone Scheduled Task Agent project to the solution. In your main app project, add a reference to this agent project. This is merely to get the assembly into your XAP; you don't actually invoke the agent code from your app directly.
3. Update your main app manifest to include an *ExtendedTask* entry that defines your background agent.
4. In your main app, at some suitable point, call *ScheduledActionService.Add* to register your agent with the system scheduler.
5. (Optionally) invoke *ScheduledActionService.LaunchForTest* to trigger a test run of your agent sooner than it might otherwise be scheduled.
6. In your agent project, the code-gen provides a class derived from *ScheduledTaskAgent*. You must implement the *OnInvoke* override to perform whatever background operations you want. At this point, you can also test to see if this agent is a periodic agent (that is, it is of type *PeriodicTask*) or resource-intensive agent (*ResourceIntensiveTask*).
7. In your agent, ensure that you call *NotifyComplete* when done (taking care to wait for any async operations to complete).

GBA components

Microsoft Visual Studio includes project template support for adding GBAs to your app. Figure 9-5 presents a simple "geo-tracking" example (the *BackgroundAgentDemo* solution in the sample code). The main app offers Start and Stop *Button* controls to start and stop its background agent. The middle of the screen is taken up with a *ListBox* that will be populated with time-stamped location information. This data will come from the background agent. Every time it wakes up on schedule, it will find the current location and add the information to a collection, persist it to isolated storage, and then stop. Each time the user enters the main app, it will fetch the location data from isolated storage and then data-bind it to the *ListBox*.

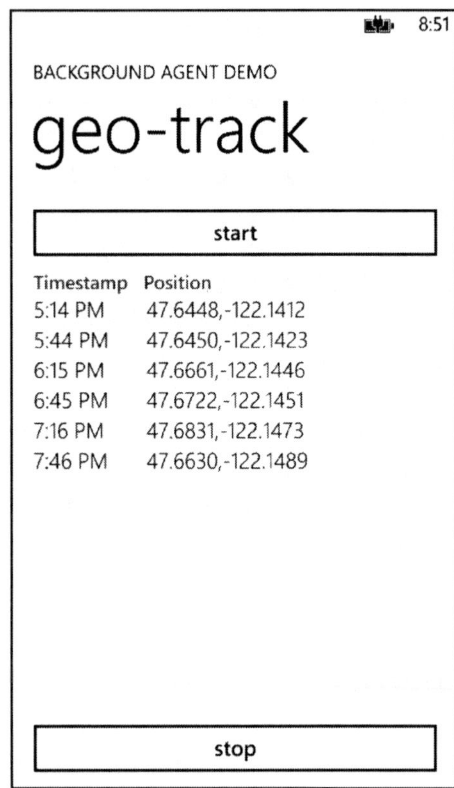

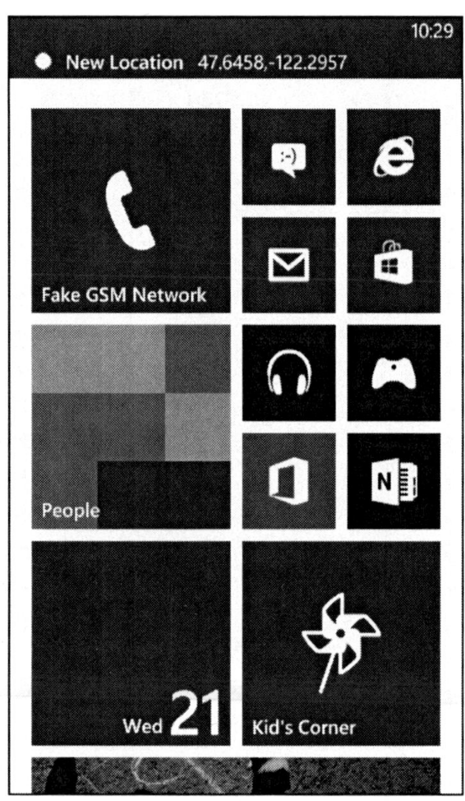

FIGURE 9-5 A foreground app (on the left) that controls a periodic background agent, and toast from the background agent (right).

To be clear, the list of locations is not updated in real time in the UI; this kind of synchronization is difficult to get right. Figure 9-5 (right) depicts the situation when the main app is not running. In this case, because there is no app in the foreground, the platform allows up to six background agents to run. In this example, the background agent pops a toast message with each new set of location data. The user can tap this, and it will launch the main app, which in turn will fetch the latest list of location data.

Note If you want the UI to be updated by the background agent in real time while the foreground app is running, you'd need to implement some kind of polling mechanism. For example, the foreground app could check every few seconds (or minutes, depending on the nature of the app) to fetch updated data from the file. Polling is always a difficult technique to get right: poll too frequently, and you're wasting time and resources (which is especially critical on a mobile device); poll too infrequently, and your UX suffers because the user is often looking at stale data.

In the example code that follows, the data is represented by a custom *PositionLite* class, which exposes *Timestamp* and *Location* properties. This class is defined in an independent class library, which is shared by both the main app and the agent. We'll be fetching the raw data by using a *GeoCoordinateWatcher*. This fetches data in the form of *GeoPosition<GeoCoordinate>* objects, which contain more information than we need. We only want to extract the specific data items that we need (latitude, longitude, and timestamp) and use them to initialize a *PositionLite* for each set. From the *PositionLite* objects, we'll be using the *Timestamp* and *Location* properties for data binding. However, we will serialize (and deserialize) only the raw *Latitude*, *Longitude*, and *Timestamp* values.

```
public class PositionLite
{
    public double Latitude { get; set; }
    public double Longitude { get; set; }

    public DateTime Timestamp { get; set; }

    [XmlIgnore]
    public String Location
    {
        get
        {
            return String.Format("{0:N4},{1:N4}", Latitude, Longitude);
        }
    }
}
```

In the *MainPage* code-behind, we initialize an *ObservableCollection* of these objects, fetching it from isolated storage in the *OnNavigatedTo* override. Of course, the first time the app is run, there will be no previous storage. At some point after that first run, the data will have been written out by the background agent.

```
public ObservableCollection<Utilities.PositionLite> Positions;
private string storageFile = "positions.xml";
```

```
protected override void OnNavigatedTo(NavigationEventArgs e)
{
    if (Positions == null)
    {
        Positions = Utilities.StorageHelper.ReadFromStorage<
            ObservableCollection<Utilities.PositionLite>>(storageFile);
    }
    if (Positions == null)
    {
        Positions = new ObservableCollection<Utilities.PositionLite>();
    }
    PositionList.ItemsSource = Positions;
}
```

This code uses a helper library, which implements a few useful utilities, including methods for reading and writing isolated storage. This same helper is used by both the main app and the background agent. The helper is genericized so that it can read and write objects of any serializable type. It is important to note that it also uses a named *Mutex* to ensure exclusive access to the file. This is required to accommodate situations in which both the foreground app and the background agent are attempting to read or write the same file at the same time.

It's worth calling out that the system doesn't do anything special with respect to GBAs when the foreground app is launched. They are not pushed to the front of the scheduling queue, nor are they stopped or paused. That is, whether or not the foreground and background code for a solution is running concurrently is effectively random.

```
public class StorageHelper
{
    private static Mutex StorageMutex = new Mutex(false, "StorageMutex");

    public static void SaveToStorage<T>(T data, string storageFile)
    {
        try
        {
            StorageMutex.WaitOne();
            using (IsolatedStorageFile isoFile =
                IsolatedStorageFile.GetUserStoreForApplication())
            {
                using (IsolatedStorageFileStream isoStream =
                    isoFile.OpenFile(storageFile, FileMode.OpenOrCreate))
                {
                    XmlSerializer xs = new XmlSerializer(typeof(T));
                    xs.Serialize(isoStream, data);
                }
            }
        }
        finally
        {
            StorageMutex.ReleaseMutex();
        }
    }
```

```
    public static T ReadFromStorage<T>(string storageFile)
    {
        T data = default(T);

        try
        {
            StorageMutex.WaitOne();
            using (IsolatedStorageFile isoFile =
                IsolatedStorageFile.GetUserStoreForApplication())
            {
                using (IsolatedStorageFileStream isoStream =
                    isoFile.OpenFile(storageFile, FileMode.OpenOrCreate))
                {
                    XmlSerializer xs = new XmlSerializer(typeof(T));
                    data = (T)xs.Deserialize(isoStream);
                }
            }
        }
        finally
        {
            StorageMutex.ReleaseMutex();
        }
        return data;
    }
}
```

The Start button creates a new *PeriodicTask* and adds it to the *ScheduledActionService*. You should use a suitable name (the name is internal to the app, so it can be anything you like), a suitable description, and (optionally) a time after which you no longer want the agent to be scheduled. It is generally considered best practice to set the *ExpirationTime* in those scenarios when you know the useful life of the agent. The description is required for periodic agents: this is the string that the user will see in the background services Settings page on the phone. The Stop button removes the task from the service.

Notice that this code is careful to put the call to the *Add* method in a *try/catch* block. This protects you in the event that the user has disabled background agents for this app—in this case, the system throws an *InvalidOperationException*. Another reason you might get an *InvalidOperationException* is if you've reached the maximum number of scheduled agents: in this case, the system prompts the user when that limit is reached, so you don't have to take any action in your code (beyond catching the exception). The only other exception you're likely to encounter is a *SchedulerServiceException*, which can be thrown if the device has just booted and the Scheduled Action Service hasn't started yet.

Also observe the call to *LaunchForTest*: this is a test-only method. The idea is that you can cause the agent to be invoked faster and/or more frequently than it would be normally, just for testing purposes. You also need to use this method during debugging, because the system does not launch periodic agents when a debugger is attached. This method must not be used in your published version, or it will fail certification. In this example, we cause the agent to be invoked for the first time only 10 seconds after we set it up.

```
private void StartButton_Click(object sender, RoutedEventArgs e)
{
    PeriodicTask task = new PeriodicTask(agentId);
    task.Description = "Collects location data at regular intervals in the background for
Windows Phone Development Internals book sample";
    task.ExpirationTime = DateTime.Now.AddDays(1);
    if (ScheduledActionService.Find(agentId) != null)
    {
        ScheduledActionService.Remove(agentId);
    }
    try
    {
        ScheduledActionService.Add(task);
#if AUTO_LAUNCH_AGENT
        ScheduledActionService.LaunchForTest(agentId, TimeSpan.FromSeconds(10));
#endif
    }
    catch (InvalidOperationException ex)
    {
        if (ex.Message.Contains("BNS Error: The action is disabled"))
        {
            MessageBox.Show(
                "The user has disabled background agents for this application.");
        }
        if (ex.Message.Contains(
            "BNS Error: The maximum number of ScheduledActions of this type have already been
added."))
        {
            Debug.WriteLine(ex.Message);
        }
    }
    catch (SchedulerServiceException ex)
    {
        Debug.WriteLine(ex.Message);
    }
}

private void StopButton_Click(object sender, RoutedEventArgs e)
{
    if (ScheduledActionService.Find(agentId) != null)
    {
        ScheduledActionService.Remove(agentId);
    }
}
```

Note The catch block for *InvalidOperationException* parses the message for a particular "magic" string. You might think that this is questionable coding—and you'd be right: it is! Unfortunately, this was an early placeholder in the implementation in the platform, which we were fully intending to clean up later in the cycle, but we simply ran out of time. The existing mechanism works, although it is not code we're particularly proud of.

The UI makes use of a custom type converter, which is used during data-binding to convert the *Timestamp* value (which is a *DateTime*) to a simple string.

That takes care of the main app; now, on to the background agent. In Visual Studio, you need to add a new project to the same solution: specifically, a Windows Phone Scheduled Task Agent project. This will generate a class library project with a starter class derived from *ScheduledTaskAgent*. The constructor for this class hooks up an *UnhandledException* handler—the same behavior that you get in the standard *App* class for a phone app. Apart from that, the class has just one other method: a skeleton override of the base class *OnInvoke* method.

In this app, we implement the *OnInvoke* to start a *GeoCoordinateWatcher* for just long enough to gather location information. The agent uses an *ObservableCollection* of *PositionLite* objects, mirroring the data model in the main app. The agent will gather the data and save it to isolated storage. Clearly, both the agent and the main app are part of a single installation and share the same isolated storage. As before, we have a debug-only call to *LaunchForTest*, which ensures that the agent is invoked again 10 seconds after the current invocation.

Notice the call to *NotifyComplete*. It is the developer's responsibility to do all work in the agent within 25 seconds and to notify the system when its work is complete. If you don't do this, the system will terminate the agent after 25 seconds, anyway. Furthermore, if the system is forced to terminate your agent very often, it might decide that your agent is badly-behaved and choose not to schedule it again. We must stop the *GeoCoordinateWatcher* as soon as we've obtained the information that we need. In this code, we can rely on the *Dispose* pattern (with a *using* statement) to take care of this for us. Be aware that when used in a background agent, the *GeoCoordinateWatcher* uses a cached location value instead of real-time data. This cache is primed just before the first agent runs. It is then updated every 10 minutes if agents are still running.

```
private ObservableCollection<PositionLite> positions;
private string storageFile = "positions.xml";

protected override void OnInvoke(ScheduledTask task)
{
    positions = StorageHelper.ReadFromStorage<
        ObservableCollection<PositionLite>>(storageFile);
    if (positions == null)
        positions = new ObservableCollection<PositionLite>();

    GetPosition();
#if DEBUG
    ScheduledActionService.LaunchForTest(task.Name, TimeSpan.FromSeconds(10));
#endif
    NotifyComplete();
}

private void GetPosition()
{
    using (GeoCoordinateWatcher watcher =
        new GeoCoordinateWatcher(GeoPositionAccuracy.High))
```

```
    {
        if (!watcher.TryStart(false, TimeSpan.FromSeconds(5)))
            return;
        if (watcher.Position == null)
            return;

        PositionLite newPosition = new PositionLite
        {
            Latitude = watcher.Position.Location.Latitude,
            Longitude = watcher.Position.Location.Longitude,
            Timestamp = watcher.Position.Timestamp.DateTime
        };
        positions.Add(newPosition);
        StorageHelper.SaveToStorage<
            ObservableCollection<PositionLite>>(positions, storageFile);
    }
}
```

The same starter code is used for either a *PeriodicTask* or a *ResourceIntensiveTask*. If you want both types of agent, you don't add multiple agent projects to your app; instead, you use the single class for both types. You can use the *ScheduledTask* parameter passed into the *OnInvoke* method and check its type to determine which type of agent is being invoked. Your code then takes the appropriate path.

If you want to notify the user when your background agent runs, and perhaps allow the user to link back easily to your main app, you can provide a toast at the end of the *OnInvoke* (or, in this example, at the end of the *GetPosition* helper method), as shown in the following snippet:

```
private void GetPosition()
{
... unchanged code omitted for brevity

        ShellToast toast = new ShellToast();
        toast.Title = "New Location";
        toast.Content = newPosition.Location;
        toast.NavigationUri = new Uri("/MainPage.xaml", UriKind.Relative);
        toast.Show();
    }
}
```

In Visual Studio 2010, with Windows Phone 7 projects, when you add the agent project to your solution, the main app manifest is automatically updated with an *ExtendedTask* element that defines the agent. Visual Studio 2012 does not perform this auto-update, so you must add the entry manually. The *ExtendedTask* element is a child of the *Tasks* element and should follow the *DefaultTask*. The key attributes are the *Source* assembly and the *Type* of the agent. Of course, if you change the name and/or namespace of your agent class or the assembly name, everything will break until you manually update this file.

```
<ExtendedTask Name="BackgroundTask">
  <BackgroundServiceAgent
     Specifier="ScheduledTaskAgent" Name="GeoAgent"
     Source="GeoAgent" Type="GeoAgent.ScheduledAgent" />
</ExtendedTask>
```

The agent assembly should be added as a reference in the main app project. This ensures that the two assemblies are packaged together in one installation XAP. It would be nice if Visual Studio were to add this reference at the point where you add the agent project to the solution, but this is not done. You should not actually use the agent assembly in your main app. If you were to do so, you would not be communicating with the agent process but with another copy of the same code in the app process.

The Visual Studio debugger provides additional support for background agents. When you debug a solution which contains a main app and a background agent, Visual Studio lets you to step seamlessly between the two projects. You can also show the Debug Location toolbar, which indicates whether you're in the main app or the background agent, as shown in Figure 9-6. In the figure, you can see that the current process is *HeadlessHost* (the hosting process for background agents), and the stack frame shows that the current method is the *GetPosition* method in the agent. Also, observe that in the Windows Phone 8 SDK, the Visual Studio debugger will stay attached, waiting for process launches until you explicitly select the Stop Debugging menu option. This is a significant improvement over the Windows Phone 7 SDK.

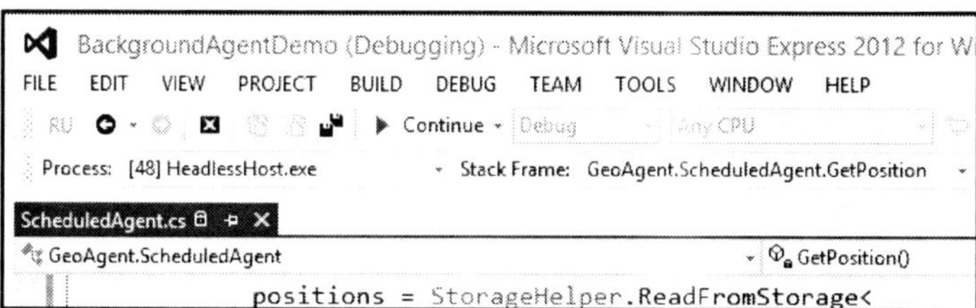

FIGURE 9-6 Visual Studio includes a Debug Location toolbar that indicates which part of your app is executing.

Updating tiles

The *SimpleWeather* app in the sample code demonstrates another common reason for deploying background agents: updating tiles. The tile features of Windows Phone are discussed in detail in Chapter 14, "Tiles and notifications." For now, all you need to know is that an app can create a tile and pin it on the Start screen. A background agent for this app can keep the tile updated periodically, as shown in Figure 9-7.

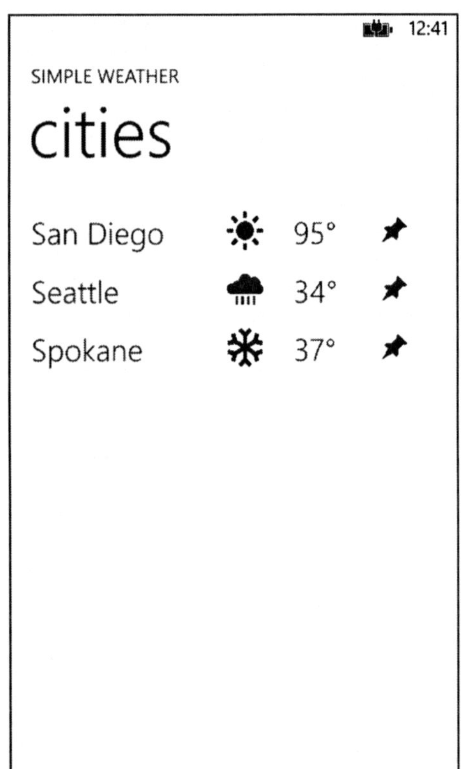

FIGURE 9-7 The user can pin a Live Tile for your app (on the left) on the Start screen, which your background agent can then update (right).

In this example, the main app offers a *ListBox* whose items include various *TextBlock*, *Image*, and *Button* controls, which in turn are data-bound to a custom *CityWeather* data type.

```
<ListBox x:Name="CityList">
    <ListBox.ItemTemplate>
        <DataTemplate>
            <Grid>
                <TextBlock Text="{Binding Name}"/>
                <Image Grid.Column="1" Source="{Binding WeatherImage}"/>
                <TextBlock Grid.Column="2" Text="{Binding Temperature, StringFormat=\{0\}°}"/>
                <Button Grid.Column="3" Click="PinUnpin_Click" BorderBrush="Transparent">
                    <Button.Background>
                        <ImageBrush ImageSource=
                        "{Binding IsPinned, Converter={StaticResource pinConverter}}"/>
                    </Button.Background>
                </Button>
            </Grid>
        </DataTemplate>
    </ListBox.ItemTemplate>
</ListBox>
```

The *Button* fills its *Background* with an *ImageBrush*, which is data-bound to the Boolean *IsPinned* property of *CityWeather*. The value of *IsPinned* is modified during rendering via a custom value converter that converts from the *bool* value to one of two image file *Uri* values.

```
public object Convert(
    object value, Type targetType, object parameter, CultureInfo culture)
{
    if ((bool)value == true)
        return new Uri("Assets/Pins/Unpin.png", UriKind.Relative);
    else
        return new Uri("Assets/Pins/Pin.png", UriKind.Relative);
}
```

The *CityWeather* data class implements *INotifyPropertyChanged* so that updates to its property values are propagated through the data-binding system. As before, we'll persist the latest data to isolated storage so that it can be shared between the foreground app and the background agent. The *Uri* class is not serializable to XML, because it doesn't have a default constructor and all its properties are read-only. To mitigate this, the *CityWeather* class provides a secondary string property which acts as a façade between the real *Uri* and the *XmlSerializer*. Alternatively, you could use the *DataContract Serializer* or *DataContractJsonSerializer*.

```
public class CityWeather : INotifyPropertyChanged
{
    private Uri weatherImage;
    [XmlIgnore]
    public Uri WeatherImage
    {
        get { return weatherImage; }
        set
        {
            if (weatherImage != value)
            {
                weatherImage = value;
                NotifyPropertyChanged("WeatherImage");
            }
        }
    }

    [XmlElement("WeatherImage")]
    public string WeatherImageAsString
    {
        get
        {
            return WeatherImage != null ? WeatherImage.OriginalString : null;
        }
        set
        {
            WeatherImage = value != null ? new Uri(value, UriKind.Relative) : null;
        }
    }
```

```
    public string Name { ...etc}
    public int Temperature { ...etc }
    public bool IsPinned { ...etc }

...irrelevant code omitted for brevity
}
```

The app reads the data from isolated storage during *OnNavigatedTo* and writes it out again in *OnNavigatedFrom*. In the interim, of course, the app would realistically be fetching updated weather data from some web service (although this sample doesn't do this). The interesting work in the main app is in the *Click* handler for the Pin/Unpin button. This first determines the *CityWeather* object that corresponds to the data item in the list for the sending *Button* object and then searches for a matching tile. Note that this demo looks for simple substrings, so, for example, if we had cities for "York" and "New York", the tile for "New York" would match both, which is an obvious limitation. If we don't find a tile, we create a new one by using the *IconicTileData* template and filling in the properties we care about from the *CityWeather* data. We then start the background agent, create the tile, and pin it on the Start screen (this will deactivate the app). The custom *StartBackgroundAgent* method creates a new *PeriodicTask* and adds it to the *ScheduledActionService*, as before. On the other hand, if the tile already exists, we must be in this *Click* handler because the user wants to unpin it, so we go ahead and delete it, at the same time, updating the *CityWeather.IsPinned* property so that the correct Pin/Unpin image can be used next time the button is rendered. This demo app includes "unpin" behavior to illustrate the use of the API; however, be aware that this is not considered good practice. You should normally leave unpinning to the user and not attempt to do so programmatically.

Note For the purposes of illustrating the technique in a simple manner, this example uses the current temperature for the *Count* property on the tile, which isn't realistic, because it doesn't allow for negative values or places with temperature extremes, especially if the temperature is measured in Fahrenheit rather than Celsius. Also, in most cases, you should use the *Count* property for a count of items rather than a value that doesn't represent a count.

```
private void PinUnpin_Click(object sender, RoutedEventArgs e)
{
    CityWeather city = (CityWeather)((Button)sender).DataContext;

    ShellTile tile = ShellTile.ActiveTiles.FirstOrDefault(
        x => x.NavigationUri.ToString().Contains(city.Name));


    if (tile != null)
    {
        tile.Delete();
        city.IsPinned = false;
        return;
    }
    IconicTileData tileData = new IconicTileData()
    {
        Title = city.Name,
```

```
        Count = city.Temperature,
        BackgroundColor = Colors.Transparent,
        IconImage = city.WeatherImage,
        SmallIconImage = city.WeatherImage,
        WideContent1 = "",
        WideContent2 = "",
        WideContent3 = ""
    };

    city.IsPinned = true;
    StartBackgroundAgent();
    ShellTile.Create(new Uri(String.Format(
        "/MainPage.xaml?city={0}", city.Name), UriKind.Relative), tileData, true);
}
```

In the agent, we deserialize the weather data from isolated storage so that we can update it. Realistically, you'd probably fetch the latest weather conditions from one of the public weather web services. In this app, we'll just simulate this by using random numbers for the temperature. Then, we write out the updated data to the shared data file, so that the main app can pick up the changes when it next runs. At the same time, we can check to see if the user has pinned any tiles for this app, and if so, update them from the latest weather conditions.

```
protected override void OnInvoke(ScheduledTask task)
{
    Cities = StorageHelper.ReadFromStorage<List<CityWeather>>(storageFile);
    if (Cities == null)
        return;

    Random rand = new Random();
    foreach (CityWeather city in Cities)
        city.Temperature = rand.Next(30, 99);

    StorageHelper.SaveToStorage<List<CityWeather>>(Cities, storageFile);

    foreach (ShellTile tile in ShellTile.ActiveTiles)
    {
        foreach (CityWeather city in Cities)
        {
            if (tile.NavigationUri.ToString().Contains(city.Name))
            {
                IconicTileData tileData =
                    new IconicTileData(){ Count = city.Temperature };
                tile.Update(tileData);
                break;
            }
        }
    }

#if DEBUG
    ScheduledActionService.LaunchForTest(task.Name, TimeSpan.FromSeconds(10));
#endif
    NotifyComplete();
}
```

The lock-screen background

One of the new features introduced in Windows Phone 8 is the ability for an app to update the lock screen. In the phone settings, the user can choose from a list of lock-screen providers—any app can register itself to be added to this list. The app requests permission from the user to become the lock-screen background provider, and if granted, this allows the app to set the background image at any time. The app can set the image either when it is running in the foreground, or, more usefully, when it has an agent running in the background. By using a background agent to set the image, the app can generate dynamic images that can be kept up-to-date. The basic steps are as follows:

1. Update the app manifest to declare the app as a lock-screen background provider. This adds the app to the list of providers in the phone settings.
2. Add code to the foreground app to request that it be the current provider. There can only be one provider at a time, and the user can change this either by responding to a request from the app or by selecting one of the registered providers in the settings list.
3. Set the background from your main app, preferably using a default image which you can be sure is always available. Also note that the user can set your app as the default lock-screen background image provider in the phone lock-screen Settings screen *before* your app has had a chance to set up the image. Therefore, you should include a default lock-screen background image at the root of your main project's XAP package, named *DefaultLockScreen.jpg*.
4. Implement a GBA to update the background periodically, typically by using a dynamically generated image.

Figure 9-8 shows the *LockScreenDemo* app in the sample code, which illustrates the general pattern. The main app offers three buttons: one to request permission to become the current lock-screen background provider; one to set the current background image; and a third to start the GBA for subsequent updates.

First, the app manifest. This app has two custom entries: an *ExtendedTask* entry to define the background agent, and an *Extension* entry to register as a lock-screen background provider. For the latter, the *ExtensionName*, *ConsumerID*, and *TaskID* values are always the same for every app, and you can't change them. The *ExtendedTask* entry is a child of the *Tasks* entry, and the *Extensions* entry must come after the *Tokens* entry.

```
<ExtendedTask Name="BackgroundTask">
  <BackgroundServiceAgent
     Specifier="ScheduledTaskAgent" Name="LockScreenAgent"
     Source="LockScreenAgent" Type="LockScreenAgent.ScheduledAgent" />
</ExtendedTask>
...
<Extensions>
  <Extension
     ExtensionName="LockScreen_Background"
     ConsumerID="{111DFF24-AA15-4A96-8006-2BFF8122084F}" TaskID="_default" />
</Extensions>
```

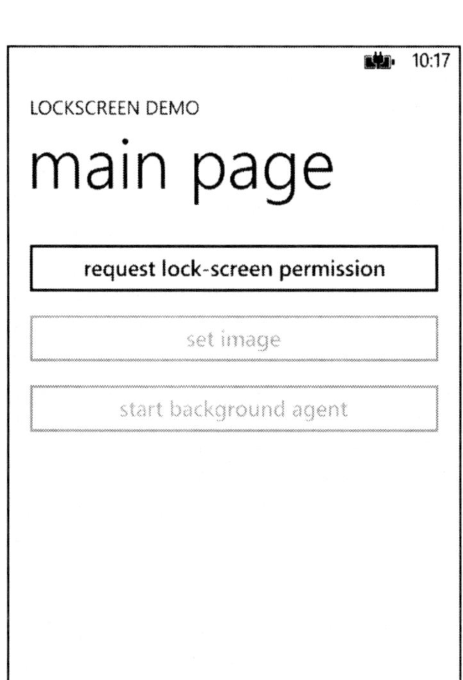

FIGURE 9-8 You can build an app to update the lock-screen background.

In the *MainPage* constructor, we check to see if we're the current lock-screen background provider, and conditionally enable the buttons based on this. If we're not the current provider, the Request button is enabled, and when the user taps this, we request permission by using *LockScreenManager.RequestAccessAsync*. This will return a *LockScreenRequestResult* of either *Granted* or *Denied*.

```
private bool isLockScreenProvider;

public MainPage()
{
    InitializeComponent();
    isLockScreenProvider = LockScreenManager.IsProvidedByCurrentApplication;
    if (isLockScreenProvider)EnableButtons();
}

private void EnableButtons()
{
    SetImage.IsEnabled = true;
    StartAgent.IsEnabled = true;
    Request.IsEnabled = false;
}
```

```
private async void Request_Click(object sender, RoutedEventArgs e)
{
    if (!isLockScreenProvider)
    {
        LockScreenRequestResult lockscreenAccess =
            await LockScreenManager.RequestAccessAsync();
        isLockScreenProvider =
            (lockscreenAccess == LockScreenRequestResult.Granted) ? true : false;
    }
    if (isLockScreenProvider)
        EnableButtons();
}
```

The simple button mechanism that this app provides for the user to set the lock-screen image is useful for demonstration purposes, but in a realistic app, you'd set this according to some other internal logic, most likely not directly related to user input. There are two alternative schemes for specifying the location of the image that you want to set:

- **ms-appdata:///local/** This points to the root of the local app data folder (in isolated storage).
- **ms-appx:///** This points to the local app install folder, to reference resources bundled in the XAP package.

This example uses the second scheme, and the image file itself is set as *Build Action = Content*, and *Do Not Copy to Output*. The file is at the root of the project rather than in the usual *Assets* folder. Having set the image, we can also get the *Uri* of the current image and report this to the debug window for information. Realistically, you might want to get the current image before you do some processing to determine what to set as the new image.

```
private void SetImage_Click(object sender, RoutedEventArgs e)
{
    if (LockScreenManager.IsProvidedByCurrentApplication)
    {
        LockScreen.SetImageUri(new Uri("ms-appx:///DefaultImage.jpg", UriKind.Absolute));
        Uri currentImage = LockScreen.GetImageUri();
        Debug.WriteLine(currentImage);
    }
}
```

The tasks of setting up the GBA project and launching it for test are the same as in the previous examples. This background agent uses some image resources and some arbitrary text to compose a fresh background image dynamically each time it runs. Having generated the image, it writes it out to a file in isolated storage. When it subsequently specifies the file path in order to set the lock-screen image, it uses the *ms-appdata:///* scheme. All the UI work is done via the current *Dispatcher* because, of course, the agent is invoked on a non-UI thread.

```
protected override void OnInvoke(ScheduledTask task)
{
    if (!LockScreenManager.IsProvidedByCurrentApplication)
        return;

    Deployment.Current.Dispatcher.BeginInvoke(() =>
    {
        Image background = new Image();
        background.Source = new BitmapImage(new Uri(
            "/Assets/LockScreen/Sunny.jpg", UriKind.Relative));
        background.Width = 480;
        background.Height = 800;

        Image icon = new Image();
        icon.Source = new BitmapImage(new Uri(
            "/Assets/LockScreen/Sunny.icon.png", UriKind.Relative));
        icon.Width = 100;
        icon.Height = 100;

        TextBlock report = new TextBlock();
        Random rand = new Random();
        int nextValue = rand.Next(75,95);
        report.Text = String.Format("{0}°{1}sunny", nextValue, Environment.NewLine);
        report.FontSize = 48;
        report.Foreground = new SolidColorBrush(Colors.White);
        report.FontFamily = new FontFamily("Segoe WP");

        string fileName = "LockBackground.jpg";
        using (IsolatedStorageFile store = IsolatedStorageFile.GetUserStoreForApplication())
        {
            using (IsolatedStorageFileStream stream = store.CreateFile(fileName))
            {
                WriteableBitmap bitmap = new WriteableBitmap(480, 800);
                bitmap.Render(background, new TranslateTransform());
                bitmap.Render(icon, new TranslateTransform() { X = 24, Y = 40 });
                bitmap.Render(report, new TranslateTransform() { X = 24, Y = 160 });
                bitmap.Invalidate();
                bitmap.SaveJpeg(stream, 480, 800, 0, 100);
            }
        }

        Uri lockImageFile = new Uri(string.Format(
            "ms-appdata:///local/{0}", fileName), UriKind.Absolute);

        LockScreen.SetImageUri(lockImageFile);

        ShellToast toast = new ShellToast();
        toast.Title = "LockScreenDemo";
        toast.Content = "(lock screen was updated)";
        toast.Show();
        NotifyComplete();
    });
}
```

At the end of the *OnInvoke*, the agent uses a toast to notify the user that it has just updated the lock-screen background. This can be a useful technique during development, although it is less useful in a production app. Also, during debugging, you can set the emulator (and the phone) to have a shorter timeout for the lock screen so that you can readily see your changes take effect. On the emulator, you can also press F12 twice to bring up the lock screen.

Lock-screen notifications

In addition to setting the lock-screen background image, you can also provide information from your app for the system to incorporate in the lock-screen status. Specifically, you can provide an icon, count, and text to be used on the lock screen in the same way that, for instance, Microsoft Outlook shows an icon and the count of new emails.

Unlike the lock-screen background, you can't make a request to show lock-screen status; instead, the user must go to the phone settings and select your app as one of the apps that can provide status. To have your app appear in the list of choices (a maximum of five can be displayed), you provide additional *Extension* entries in your app manifest. Even if the user chooses your app as one of the five to provide status, this only fetches your specified icon and count. If you want your tile text to appear on the lock screen, as well, the user must make a further selection to make your app the provider for detailed status—as with the background image, only one app at a time can provide this information.

Figure 9-9 shows an enhanced version of the *LockScreenDemo* app in the sample code. On the left in the figure is the standard phone Settings page for the lock screen. In this case, the user has chosen the *LockScreenDemo* app as one of the providers for quick status and also as the provider for detailed status. On the right is an example of the lock screen, showing the tile text below the current date, and the app icon and count below that.

The required enhancements to the solution are as follows.

First, we must update the app manifest (for the main app) to include the additional *Extension* entries for icon/count and for tile text. As you can see, the *ConsumerID* and *TaskID* are identical across all three lock-screen extensions.

```
<Extensions>
  <Extension
    ExtensionName="LockScreen_Background"
    ConsumerID="{111DFF24-AA15-4A96-8006-2BFF8122084F}" TaskID="_default" />
  <Extension
    ExtensionName="LockScreen_Notification_IconCount"
    ConsumerID="{111DFF24-AA15-4A96-8006-2BFF8122084F}" TaskID="_default" />
  <Extension
    ExtensionName="LockScreen_Notification_TextField"
    ConsumerID="{111DFF24-AA15-4A96-8006-2BFF8122084F}" TaskID="_default" />
</Extensions>
```

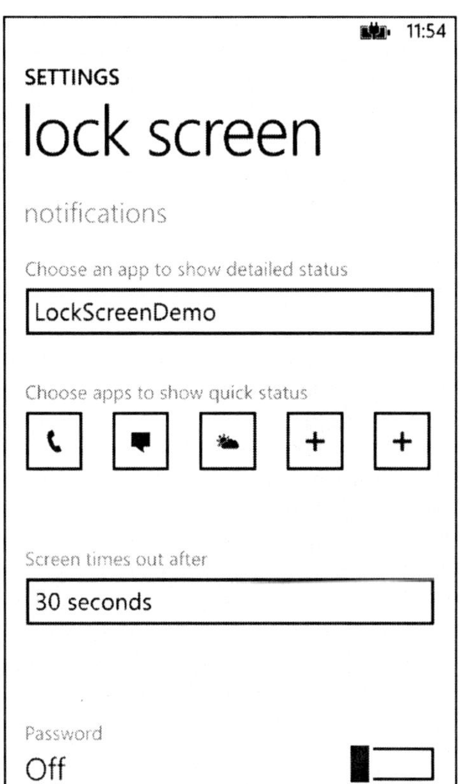

FIGURE 9-9 The user has control over which apps provide quick and detailed status on the lock screen.

Next, we must specify the icon we want to use on the lock screen. The app manifest includes a *DeviceLockImageURI* element as a child of the icon template. Although you can change the icon template by using the graphical manifest editor, you can only change the *DeviceLockImageURI* element by editing the manifest manually. The general format and attribute values for this element follow the same pattern as for the other image resources in the tile template. Keep in mind that you have an alternative option: if you're happy for this icon file to be named *LockIcon.png* and for it to be located at the root of your project, you can simply provide a blank *DeviceLocImageURI* element.

```
<PrimaryToken TokenID="LockScreenDemoToken" TaskName="_default">
  <TemplateFlip>
  ...
    <DeviceLockImageURI
        IsRelative="true" IsResource="false">Assets\LockScreen\Weather.small.png/>
  </TemplateFlip>
</PrimaryToken>
```

There are no other changes required to the main app. To implement periodic updates to the lock-screen status, we must enhance our agent's *OnInvoke* behavior. At the end of this method, we can add a call to a custom method that updates the app's primary tile. As before, this uses resources from the agent project, not from the main app. The system will pull the icon, count, and text from this tile. Using a GBA in this way makes it possible for you to generate dynamic data for the lock-screen status.

```
private void UpdateLockScreenCountAndText(int nextValue)
{
    ShellTile.ActiveTiles.First().Update(
        new FlipTileData()
        {
            Count = nextValue,
            WideBackContent = "sunny all day!",
            SmallBackgroundImage = new Uri(
                @"Assets\LockScreen\Weather.small.png", UriKind.Relative),
            BackgroundImage = new Uri(
                @"Assets\LockScreen\Weather.medium.png", UriKind.Relative),
            BackBackgroundImage = new Uri(
                @"Assets\LockScreen\Weather.medium.png", UriKind.Relative)
        });
}
```

Note In this example, only the *Count* is actually changing, and we're simply resetting all the other properties to the same values each time. In a real app, however, you could of course vary any or all of the property values.

Background audio

As with GBAs, you can set up an agent to play audio in the background. You would typically start the audio playing from your foreground app and then have the audio continue playing, even after the user navigates away from your main app (including via the Back or Start buttons). Background audio agents share some similarities with GBAs: you create a background audio agent in much the same way, and the architecture is very similar. In both cases, you build a main phone app with a UI and then add a background agent project to the solution and ensure that it is referenced in the app manifest. In the case of a GBA, you add a Windows Phone Scheduled Task Agent project, and your agent class is derived from *ScheduledTaskAgent*. In the case of a background audio agent, you add a Windows Phone Audio Playback Agent project, and your agent class is derived from *AudioPlayerAgent*.

All media on Windows Phone is actually played through the Zune media queue (ZMQ). However, your app does not interact directly with the ZMQ; instead, it uses the *BackgroundAudioPlayer* class, which acts as a kind of proxy to the ZMQ. Typically, your main app would set up and maintain the playlist of tracks (including optionally both files in isolated storage as well as files at remote URLs) and save this playlist to isolated storage. Then, you would provide suitable UI with which the user can play, pause, skip, fast-forward, rewind, and so on. You would implement the handlers for these UI elements to invoke the corresponding *Play*, *Pause*, and other related methods on the *BackgroundAudioPlayer*.

However, this does not play the audio directly; rather, the *BackgroundAudioPlayer* negotiates with your background audio agent. Your agent fetches the playlist and confirms the action to be taken. The *BackgroundAudioPlayer* works with the ZMQ to actually play the audio tracks. The *Background AudioPlayer* also feeds state change events back to both the main app (if it is running) and to the agent.

Your app does not directly launch the agent. This is done implicitly by the *BackgroundAudioPlayer* when your app makes calls to *Play*, *Pause*, and so on. The *BackgroundAudioPlayer* launches the correct agent, based on its association with your app defined in the app manifest.

If you start audio playing in your main app and the user then navigates away, the audio will continue, under the control of your agent. While your app is not in the foreground (or even if it is), the user can use the Universal Volume Control (UVC) to control both the volume and the tracks. On a physical device, the UVC is invoked when the user taps the hardware volume controls. On the emulator, you can display the UVC by pressing F10. Figure 9-10 illustrates the relationships between these components. Note that a background audio agent is capped at 20 MB of memory in Windows Phone 8 (15 MB in Windows Phone 7) and no more than 10 percent of CPU time.

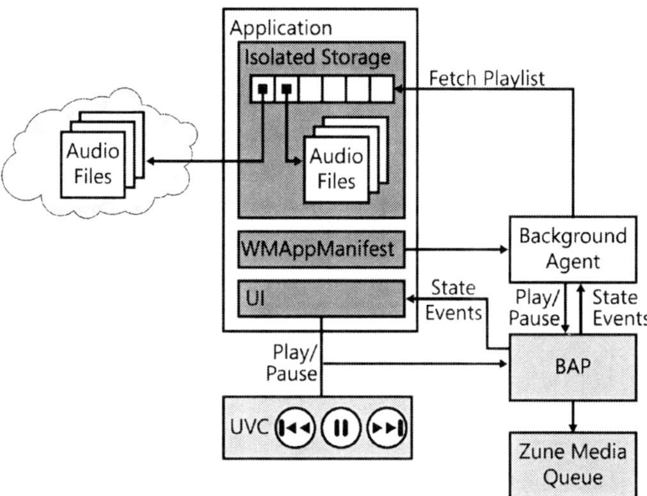

FIGURE 9-10 The relationships between background audio agent components.

The sequence of operations between these various components involves a fairly straightforward handshake. Figure 9-11 illustrates the sequence for playing tracks.

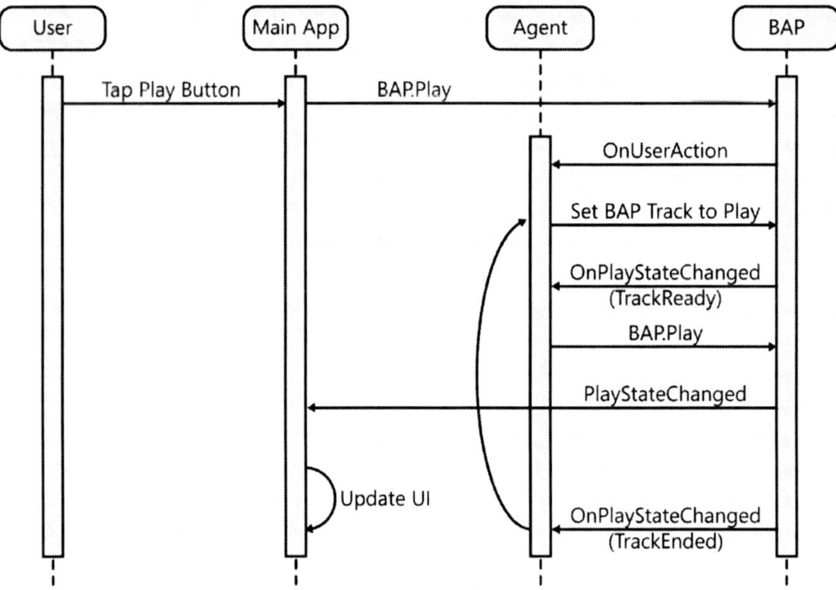

FIGURE 9-11 Playing audio tracks with the *BackgroundAudioPlayer.*

When you add an Audio Playback Agent project to your solution, the wizard-generated code in the class derived from *AudioPlayerAgent* includes almost everything you might need for playing, pausing, skipping, rewinding, and so on. The two main methods that are generated for you are the *OnUserAction* override and the *OnPlayStateChanged* override. *OnUserAction* is called as a result of user action, either from your main app, or from the UVC. You would typically implement this to invoke the *BackgroundAudioPlayer* method that corresponds to the required action. For example, if you get a *UserAction.Play,* you would typically invoke *BackgroundAudioPlayer.Play.* Alternatively, you can set the track to be played, which will cause an *OnPlayStateChanged* event to be raised. You can then handle this event by calling *BackgroundAudioPlayer.Play.*

If your main app is running, you'll also receive state change events; this is your opportunity to update your UI, typically to show the current track information. Figure 9-12 shows the pause sequence.

The pause sequence follows the same model as the play sequence: the user indicates that he wants to pause; you invoke the *BackgroundAudioPlayer.Pause*, which invokes your agent's *OnUserAction*, and so on. It is important to note that your foreground app should not directly update its UI based on user action; rather, it should wait for the associated event from the *BackgroundAudioPlayer* to ensure that everything proceeded as you planned.

Figure 9-13 shows a simple app (the *BapApp* solution in the sample code) that has an associated background audio agent. The first screenshot shows the main app running in the foreground; the second shows the UVC displayed when the user has navigated away from the app, and the background audio agent is running. The section that follows describes how to create this app.

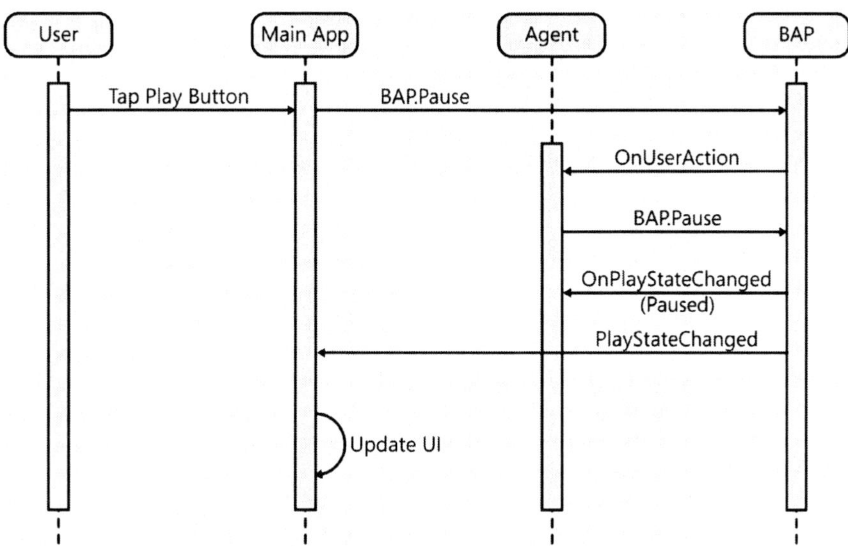

FIGURE 9-12 Pausing audio with the *BackgroundAudioPlayer*.

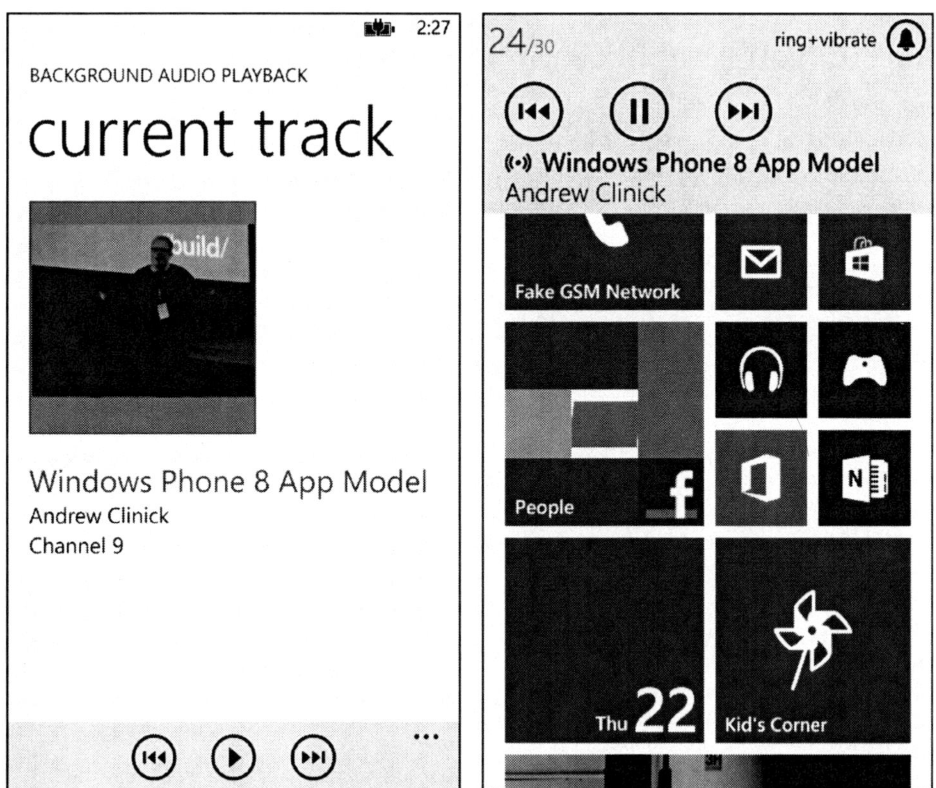

FIGURE 9-13 A foreground app (on the left) running background audio, and the background audio agent continuing to run in the background (right).

Here's a summary of the main tasks:

1. Create a regular Windows Phone app.
   a. Add one or more audio files as content files to be deployed as part of the main app XAP. Also, add code to copy these files from the app install folder to isolated storage.
   b. Add UI elements such as regular buttons or app bar buttons so that the user can play audio. In the *Click* handlers, call into the *BackgroundAudioPlayer* methods to play, pause, and so on.
   c. Respond to *BackgroundAudioPlayer* state change events and update the UI accordingly.
2. Add a Windows Phone Audio Playback Agent project.
   a. Reference this project in the main app and ensure that you define an *Extension* for the agent in the app manifest.
   b. Define a list of *AudioTrack* items as the playlist for this agent. The items in this list must be either audio files in the app's isolated storage or remote audio files specified by absolute URI, or a mixture of both. In this example, the playlist is not maintained by the main app.

Background audio application

The main app has an *Image* control for displaying the album art for the current track as well as three *TextBlock* controls for displaying the track title, artist, and album name. We also provide three app bar buttons, for skip-back, play, and skip-forward. We'll double-up the play button to also serve as the pause button.

```
<Grid x:Name="LayoutRoot" Background="Transparent">
...
    <StackPanel x:Name="ContentPanel" Grid.Row="1" Margin="12,0,12,0">
        <Border
            BorderBrush="{StaticResource PhoneAccentBrush}"
            BorderThickness="2" Height="240" Width="240">
            <Image x:Name="albumArt" />
        </Border>
        <TextBlock x:Name="track" Foreground="{StaticResource PhoneAccentBrush}"/>
        <TextBlock x:Name="artist"/>
        <TextBlock x:Name="album"/>
    </StackPanel>
</Grid>

<phone:PhoneApplicationPage.ApplicationBar>
    <shell:ApplicationBar IsVisible="True">
        <shell:ApplicationBarIconButton
            x:Name="appBarPrev" IconUri="Assets/AppBar/previous.png"
            Text="prev" Click="appBarPrev_Click"/>
```

```
        <shell:ApplicationBarIconButton
            x:Name="appBarPlay" IconUri="Assets/AppBar/play.png"
            Text="play" Click="appBarPlay_Click"/>
        <shell:ApplicationBarIconButton
            x:Name="appBarNext" IconUri="Assets/AppBar/next.png"
            Text="next" Click="appBarNext_Click"/>
    </shell:ApplicationBar>
</phone:PhoneApplicationPage.ApplicationBar>
```

For the purposes of this demonstration, we'll have just one local audio file and one remote audio file. In a more sophisticated app, you would provide a way for the user to add and remove items from the playlist via the UI, perhaps downloading files to isolated storage from the Internet. If you want to follow along and build this app from scratch, you can just copy any suitable audio file from your local computer into the project and then set its Copy To Output Directory property to Copy If Newer. This will be deployed as a loose file in the app's install folder, and we then need to copy it to the app's isolated storage. We'll do this in the *OnNavigatedTo* override in the *MainPage*, with a suitable test to ensure that we only do this once.

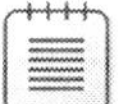

Note On a standard Windows-based computer, you can find the file *Kalimba.mp3* in the public music folder, which is typically in this path: %SystemDrive%\Users\Public\Music\Sample Music\. Alternatively, you could add any arbitrary audio file to the project and replace "Kalimba.mp3" with the correct name.

```
private bool isMediaLoaded;
protected override void OnNavigatedTo(NavigationEventArgs e)
{
    if (!isMediaLoaded)
    {
        using (IsolatedStorageFile storage =
            IsolatedStorageFile.GetUserStoreForApplication())
        {
            String fileName = "Kalimba.mp3";
            if (!storage.FileExists(fileName))
            {
                StreamResourceInfo sourceFile =
                    Application.GetResourceStream(new Uri(fileName, UriKind.Relative));
                using (IsolatedStorageFileStream targetFile = storage.CreateFile(fileName))
                {
                    byte[] bytes = new byte[sourceFile.Stream.Length];
                    sourceFile.Stream.Read(bytes, 0, bytes.Length);
                    targetFile.Write(bytes, 0, bytes.Length);
                }
            }
        }
        isMediaLoaded = true;
    }
}
```

Next, we can implement the app bar button *Click* handlers in the *MainPage* code-behind. These are trivial to implement; we just need to call into the *BackgroundAudioPlayer* methods to *Play, Pause*, and so on. Notice that the *BackgroundAudioPlayer* is a singleton object.

```
private void appBarPlay_Click(object sender, EventArgs e)
{
    if (BackgroundAudioPlayer.Instance.PlayerState == PlayState.Playing)
        BackgroundAudioPlayer.Instance.Pause();
    else
        BackgroundAudioPlayer.Instance.Play();
}

private void appBarNext_Click(object sender, EventArgs e)
{
    BackgroundAudioPlayer.Instance.SkipNext();
}

private void appBarPrev_Click(object sender, EventArgs e)
{
    BackgroundAudioPlayer.Instance.SkipPrevious();
}
```

In the *MainPage* constructor, we hook up the *PlayStateChanged* event for the *Background AudioPlayer*—we'll get these events when the state changes from *Playing* to *Paused* or *Stopped*, and so forth. This is our opportunity to update the UI; we'll toggle the icon and text for the dual-purpose play/pause button. At the same time, we'll fetch the current track information to display in our *Image* and *TextBlock* controls, which we abstract to a separate custom *UpdateTrackDisplay* method. Note that you can check either the *BackgroundAudioPlayer.Instance.PlayerState* or the *CurrentPlayState* of the incoming *PlayStateChangedEventArgs*—both produce the same results.

```
private void Bap_PlayStateChanged(object sender, EventArgs e)
{
    switch (BackgroundAudioPlayer.Instance.PlayerState)
    // switch ((e as PlayStateChangedEventArgs).CurrentPlayState)
    {
        case PlayState.Playing:
            appBarPlay.IconUri = new Uri("Assets/AppBar/pause.png", UriKind.Relative);
            appBarPlay.Text = "pause";
            break;
        case PlayState.Paused:
        case PlayState.Stopped:
            appBarPlay.IconUri = new Uri("Assets/AppBar/play.png", UriKind.Relative);
            appBarPlay.Text = "play";
            break;
    }

    UpdateTrackDisplay();
}
```

```
private void UpdateTrackDisplay()
{
    AudioTrack currentTrack = BackgroundAudioPlayer.Instance.Track;
    if (currentTrack != null)
    {
        albumArt.Source = new BitmapImage(currentTrack.AlbumArt);
        track.Text = currentTrack.Title;
        artist.Text = currentTrack.Artist;
        album.Text = currentTrack.Album;
    }
    else
    {
        albumArt.Source = null;
        track.Text = String.Empty;
        artist.Text = String.Empty;
        album.Text = String.Empty;
    }
}
```

We do need to initialize the app bar button fields. Recall from Chapter 3, "UI visuals and touch," that these need to be initialized explicitly, and this kind of one-time setup should be done in the page constructor (not in the *OnNavigatedTo* override, which is called more frequently). We should also add code to *OnNavigatedTo* to allow for the user returning back to the app after navigating away from it. In this scenario, we need to determine if background audio is still playing and then update the UI accordingly. Again, we can simply call our abstracted *UpdateTrackDisplay* method.

```
public MainPage()
{
    InitializeComponent();
    BackgroundAudioPlayer.Instance.PlayStateChanged
        += new EventHandler(Bap_PlayStateChanged);

    appBarPrev = ApplicationBar.Buttons[0] as ApplicationBarIconButton;
    appBarPlay = ApplicationBar.Buttons[1] as ApplicationBarIconButton;
    appBarNext = ApplicationBar.Buttons[2] as ApplicationBarIconButton;
}

protected override void OnNavigatedTo(NavigationEventArgs e)
{
...previously-listed code omitted for brevity.

    UpdateTrackDisplay();
}
```

Background audio agent

That's it for the main app; now, it's time for the agent. We can add an audio playback agent project to the solution and then reference this project in the main app. We also need to add the *ExtendedTask* element for this agent to the *Tasks* node in the app manifest.

```
<ExtendedTask Name="BackgroundTask">
  <BackgroundServiceAgent Specifier="AudioPlayerAgent" Name="BapAgent" Source="BapAgent"
Type="BapAgent.AudioPlayer" />
</ExtendedTask>
```

The wizard generates a great deal of placeholder code, including overrides of *OnPlayStateChanged* and *OnUserAction*. The main thing we need to do is to define the playlist. This simple example is not retrieving the playlist itself from isolated storage; instead, it hard-codes the list, which consists of just two *AudioTrack* items (one local file in isolated storage, and one remote URL). In this example, you'll notice that both the album art images are stored as part of the main app, not as part of the agent. This might seem confusing, but remember that the main app is responsible for the UI; the agent does not work directly with the UI at all. Also, it is the main project that is deployed (not the agent independently), so you need to have all your content in that project. User input is fed from either the main app or the UVC via the *BackgroundAudioPlayer* to the agent, and conversely, any UI updates are fed from the agent via the *BackgroundAudioPlayer* to the main app. Of course, in a realistic app, if you're fetching remote audio tracks, you're probably also fetching remote album art.

```
private static List<AudioTrack> playList = new List<AudioTrack>
{
    new AudioTrack(new Uri("Kalimba.mp3", UriKind.Relative),
        "Kalimba",
        "Mr. Scruff",
        "Ninja Tuna",
        new Uri("Assets/AlbumArt/NinjaTuna.jpg", UriKind.Relative)),
    new AudioTrack(new Uri(
        "http://media.ch9.ms/ch9/3430/45a1e37f-f582-4be6-8ee8-a2e6fc0b3430/2-013.mp3",
        UriKind.Absolute),
        "Windows Phone 8 App Model",
        "Andrew Clinick",
        "Channel 9",
        new Uri("Assets/AlbumArt/Clinick.png", UriKind.Relative)),
};
```

We also need to make minor changes to the *GetNextTrack* and *GetPreviousTrack* methods because the placeholder code simply returns null in each case.

```
static int currentTrack = 0;
private AudioTrack GetNextTrack()
{
    //AudioTrack track = null;
    //return track;
    if (++currentTrack >= playList.Count)
    {
        currentTrack = 0;
    }
    return playList[currentTrack];
}
```

```
private AudioTrack GetPreviousTrack()
{
    //AudioTrack track = null;
    //return track;
    if (--currentTrack < 0)
    {
        currentTrack = playList.Count - 1;
    }
    return playList[currentTrack];
}
```

Also, we need to carry out a minor modification to the *OnUserAction* method. The wizard-generated code for the *UserAction.Play* case calls the *Play* method; however, we're relying on the fact that every time the *Track* property changes, we'll get a *PlayStateChanged* event. That's where we actually invoke the *Play* method. So, we need to replace the two lines of code in this case to simply set the current track.

```
protected override void OnUserAction(
    BackgroundAudioPlayer player, AudioTrack track, UserAction action, object param)
{
    switch (action)
    {
        case UserAction.Play:
            //if (player.PlayerState != PlayState.Playing)
            //{
            //    player.Play();
            //}
            player.Track = playList[currentTrack];
            break;
        case UserAction.Stop:
            player.Stop();
            break;
        case UserAction.Pause:
            player.Pause();
            break;
        case UserAction.FastForward:
            player.FastForward();
            break;
        case UserAction.Rewind:
            player.Rewind();
            break;
        case UserAction.Seek:
            player.Position = (TimeSpan)param;
            break;
        case UserAction.SkipNext:
            player.Track = GetNextTrack();
            break;
        case UserAction.SkipPrevious:
            player.Track = GetPreviousTrack();
            break;
    }

    NotifyComplete();
}
```

Finally, we need to make one correction to the *OnPlayStateChanged* method. The wizard-generated code in the *PlayState.TrackEnded* case gets the previous track; however, the user would probably normally expect that when a track ends, the player moves on to play the *next* track, not the previous one.

```
case PlayState.TrackEnded:
    //player.Track = GetPreviousTrack();
    player.Track = GetNextTrack();
    break;
```

Note Additional publication requirements apply for any app that plays background audio. These are mostly centered around the need for your app to provide UI (typically buttons) through which the user can start, stop, and pause playback. An app must not start background audio without the user's direct participation.

Summary

The multitasking features in the platform provide a range of options for an app to divide work into multiple processes, with part of the functionality running in the background. Alarms and reminders give you a very simple mechanism for raising notifications to the user in a way that is very consistent with the built-in behavior. Thus, they are consistent across all apps. Using generic background agents, you can write code that will wake up periodically and perform an arbitrary operation, either on a schedule or opportunistically. You can use background transfers to initiate network uploads or downloads, have them continue even when the user navigates away from your app, and have them even survive phone reboots. Finally, with background audio, you can take advantage of much the same model but with audio playback in place of network transfers.

CHAPTER 10

Local storage and databases

Across the wide surface area of a modern smartphone platform, relatively few APIs are used by virtually all applications. Local storage APIs are one such set. Whether you're building a game or simple utility that only needs to keep track of user settings or a dictionary app that needs to store 100,000 words in an offline database, most developers need to understand how to persist data between invocations of their apps. This chapter reviews the ways that you can read and write settings, files, and structured data in both managed and native code.

Local storage

There are multiple options for reading and writing files in a Windows Phone 8 app, depending on whether you're writing managed or native code, whether you're bringing forward an existing Windows Phone 7 app or starting fresh, and whether you intend to target Windows 8 and Windows Phone 8 simultaneously. We will review all the options and tradeoffs in this section. It is worth noting, however, that all the file system APIs available in Windows Phone 8 operate on the same isolated data store, so you are welcome to combine their usage within your app, depending on your needs.

Isolated storage APIs

Windows Phone 7 provided only one option for reading and writing local settings and files, the *Sytem.IO.IsolatedStorage* namespace. The isolated storage APIs provide a way for apps to store simple objects and settings by using the *IsolatedStorageSettings* class. They also provide the ability to perform most standard file system operations within their chamber, such as creating and managing files and directories.

Isolated storage settings

Although virtually all apps need to persist some data between invocations, there are a number of categories of apps that only need to keep track of basic settings or simple data structures. For example, a game might only need to store a list of high scores or the most recent level that the user has completed. The *IsolatedStorage* namespace provides a class called *IsolatedStorageSettings* with which apps can store simple key/value pairs to be persisted without having to deal with files directly or worry about serializing objects. Keep in mind that even though the class includes the word "settings" in its name and is a good option for storing app settings, there is nothing stopping you from storing other types of data in it. Indeed, the *IsolatedStorageSettings* class is nothing more than a wrapper over the other *IsolatedStorage* APIs that automatically handles serialization/deserialization and the process of reading and writing the underlying file. There are certain performance and robustness concerns to keep in mind, however, and we will discuss these later in this section.

The *IsolatedStorageSettingsReaderWriter* solution in the sample code illustrates the use of the *IsolatedStorageSettings* class for storing both simple platform types such as integers and strings, and for storing custom app types such as, in this case, a *Person* class. The app contains two pivots. With one of them, the user can enter a set of basic types, with the other, the user can enter details about a person, which will be turned into an instance of the *Person* class. Each pivot contains a Read button and a Write button. When the user taps the Write button, the data currently entered is written to *IsolatedStorageSettings* and then cleared. When a user taps the Read button, the data is read from *IsolatedStorageSettings* and re-entered into the user interface (UI). Figure 10-1 shows the UI for the platform types pivot.

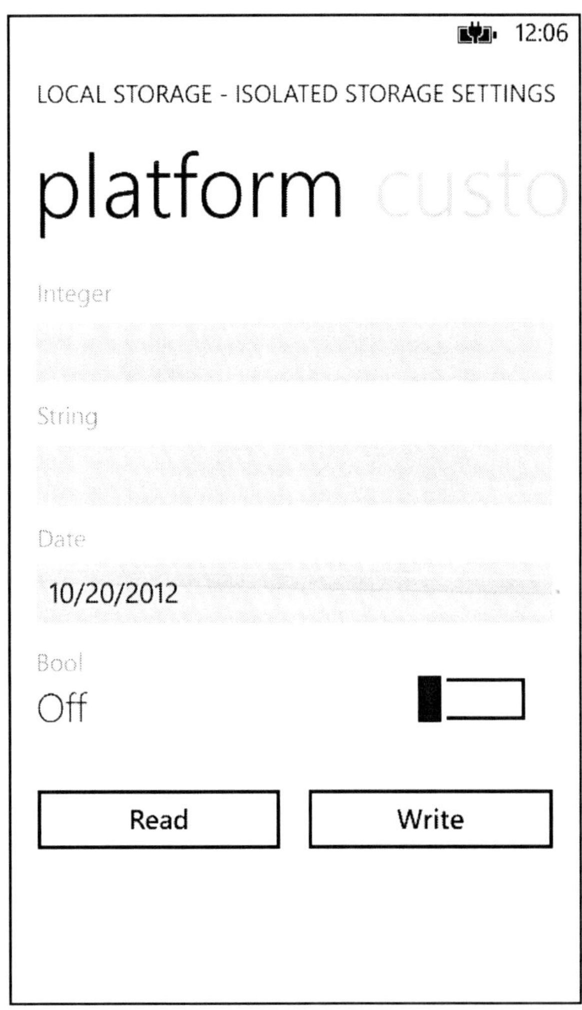

FIGURE 10-1 The *IsolatedStorageSettings* class makes it easy to persist simple key/value pairs.

The reading and writing of data for both pivots is handled in the *Click* event handlers for the respective buttons. The read and write methods for the platform pivot are shown in the following:

```
private void writePlatformTypesSettingsButton_Click(object sender, RoutedEventArgs e)
{
     System.IO.IsolatedStorage.IsolatedStorageSettings isoStoreSettings =
          System.IO.IsolatedStorage.IsolatedStorageSettings.ApplicationSettings;

     int integerValue;
     int.TryParse(integerTextBox.Text, out integerValue);

     isoStoreSettings["IntegerValue"] = integerValue;
     isoStoreSettings["StringValue"] = stringTextBox.Text;
     isoStoreSettings["DateValue"] = datePicker.Value.Value;
     isoStoreSettings["BoolValue"] = (bool)toggleSwitch.IsChecked;

     isoStoreSettings.Save();

     // code to clear out UI removed for brevity
}
private void readPlatformTypesSettingsButton_Click(object sender, RoutedEventArgs e)
{
     IsolatedStorageSettings isoStoreSettings =
          IsolatedStorageSettings.ApplicationSettings;

     int integerValue;
     string stringValue;
     DateTime dateValue;
     bool boolValue;

     if (isoStoreSettings.TryGetValue("IntegerValue", out integerValue))
          integerTextBox.Text = integerValue.ToString();

     if (isoStoreSettings.TryGetValue("StringValue", out stringValue))
          stringTextBox.Text = stringValue;

     if (isoStoreSettings.TryGetValue("DateValue", out dateValue))
          datePicker.Value = dateValue;

     if (isoStoreSettings.TryGetValue("BoolValue", out boolValue))
          toggleSwitch.IsChecked = boolValue;
}
```

Note The nature of this app is such that we should only need to call *TryGetValue* on one property to determine whether the set of properties was saved. We have used it to fetch each of the values as a reminder that it is generally preferable to code defensively.

The code for storing and retrieving a custom type such as the *Person* class is basically the same. In both cases, we take advantage of the fact that the *IsolatedStorageSettings* object is an *IDictionary* by using the *TryGetValue* method to simultaneously check for the existence of and retrieve the value in which we're interested.

```
private void writeCustomTypeSettingsButton_Click(object sender, RoutedEventArgs e)
{
    Person p = new Person();
    p.FirstName = firstNameTextBox.Text;
    p.LastName = lastNameTextBox.Text;
    p.Birthday = birthdayPicker.Value.Value;
    p.Gender = (bool)maleRadioButton.IsChecked ? Gender.Male : Gender.Female;

    IsolatedStorageSettings isoStoreSettings = IsolatedStorageSettings.ApplicationSettings;

    isoStoreSettings["Person"] = p;
    isoStoreSettings.Save();

    // code to clear out UI omitted for brevity
}

private void readSettingsPlatformTypesButton_Click(object sender, RoutedEventArgs e)
{
    Person p;

    IsolatedStorageSettings isoStoreSettings = IsolatedStorageSettings.ApplicationSettings;

    if(isoStoreSettings.TryGetValue("Person", out p))
    {
        firstNameTextBox.Text = p.FirstName;
        lastNameTextBox.Text = p.LastName;
        birthdayPicker.Value = p.Birthday.Date;
        maleRadioButton.IsChecked = p.Gender == Gender.Male;
        femaleRadioButton.IsChecked = !maleRadioButton.IsChecked;
    }
}
```

There are several important points to keep in mind when using the *IsolatedStorageSettings* class. First, because the platform is automatically serializing the key/value pairs in the *IsolatedStorageSettings* dictionary to the app's local storage, all that data must be serializable by the *DataContractSerializer*. Be aware that there are a number of common platform types, such as *ObservableCollection*, that cannot be serialized by the *DataContractSerializer*. Second, the *IsolatedStorageSettings* class serializes all the key/value pairs in its dictionary down to a single XML file, so as the dictionary grows larger, it can risk impacting the startup and shutdown performance of your app. You should limit your usage of *Isolated StorageSettings* to storing primitives and very simple types to which your app needs easy access. For larger data sets, such as the core types of your model layer, you should perform custom serialization using flat files or consider using a database. Finally, we do not recommend using *IsolatedStorage Settings* for any data that needs to be shared between a foreground app and a background agent, because it's possible for simultaneous access to result in corrupt data.

Isolated storage files

The isolated storage APIs for managing files are all contained within the *IsolatedStorageFile* class. A quick review of the surface area exposed by the *IsolatedStorageFile* class reveals that it is effectively just a thin wrapper over the underlying file system APIs—there are methods for creating, opening, moving, and deleting files and directories. The only real difference between *IsolatedStorageFile* and the Win32 APIs underneath is that *IsolatedStorageFile* is, as the name implies, designed for isolation of local storage between apps. The APIs provide no mechanism for attempting to create a file outside of the app's local storage folder. Instead, everything is relative to the root of the app's folder.

Note Although the *IsolatedStorageFile* APIs provide no direct means of reading or writing outside of the app's local folder, they are not actually responsible for enforcing isolation between apps. The security system ensures isolation between chambers regardless of which APIs an app uses to read or write data.

Even though the isolated storage file APIs support reading and writing arbitrary data, the more common usage involves serializing and deserializing part of the app's object graph so that it can survive beyond a single invocation of the app. In the *IsolatedStorageFileReaderWriter* solution, we illustrate the serialization and deserialization of a simple *Person* class. The UI for the *IsolatedStorage FileReaderWriter* is shown in Figure 10-2.

Again, the interesting code is found in the click event handlers for the two buttons.

```
private void writePersonButton_Click(object sender, RoutedEventArgs e)
{
    IsolatedStorageFile isoStore = IsolatedStorageFile.GetUserStoreForApplication();

    using(IsolatedStorageFileStream fileStream =
              isoStore.OpenFile(personFilePath, FileMode.CreateNew))
    {
        DataContractJsonSerializer dcjSerializer =
            new DataContractJsonSerializer(typeof(Person));

        Person person = new Person();

        person.FirstName = firstNameTextBox.Text;
        person.LastName = lastNameTextBox.Text;
        person.Gender = (bool)maleRadioButton.IsChecked ? Gender.Male : Gender.Female;

        dcjSerializer.WriteObject(fileStream, person);
    }

    // code to clear out the UI removed for brevity
}
```

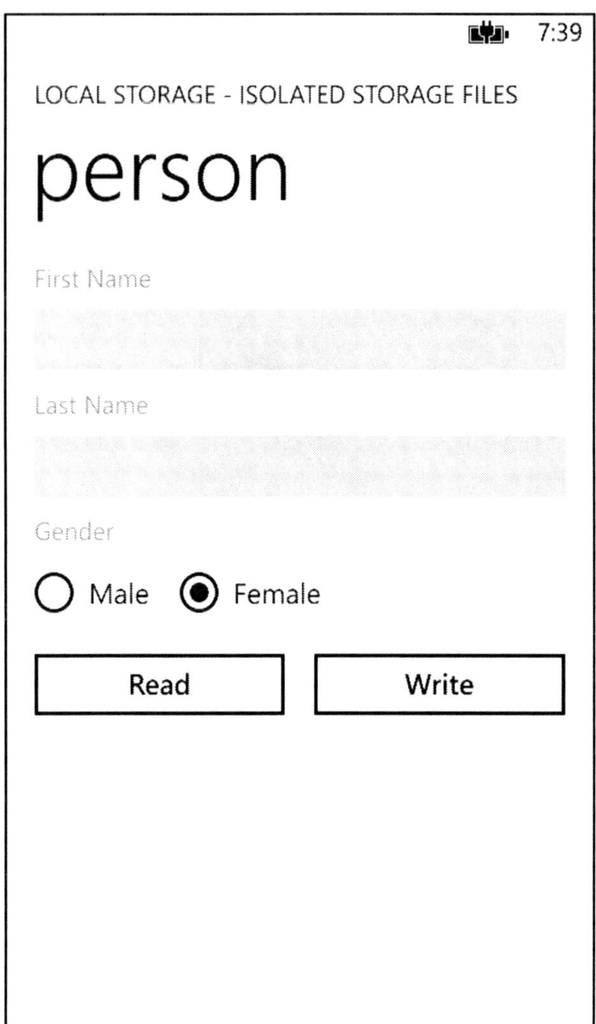

FIGURE 10-2 Storing and retrieving serialized app objects is a common usage of the file system APIs.

The app uses the *DataContractJsonSerializer* to serialize the content into a stream of JavaScript Object Notation (JSON) that can be written to a file. The platform also provides *XmlSerializer* and *DataContractSerializer*, both of which serialize objects into XML. In most cases, the XML-serialized version of an object is significantly larger than the JSON-serialized version, so if you are only looking to read and write objects in your own app code, the *DataContractJsonSerializer* offers the best performance.

Accessing your storage folder with Isolated Storage Explorer

Even though Windows Phone is built on the NT file system (NTFS), just like Windows, the phone user experience (UX) does not include any equivalent to Windows Explorer for doing general-purpose browsing of the file system's contents. As a result, there is no built-in way for an app developer to quickly inspect the contents of her local storage folder, which is often necessary to debug issues with reading and writing files. The Windows Phone SDK provides a solution to this problem in the form of the Isolated Storage Explorer (ISE).

The ISE is a command-line tool with which you can read from or write to the local storage folder of any app that has been deployed from Microsoft Visual Studio or the application deployment tool. You can find it in the Windows Phone SDK folder at *%ProgramFiles(x86)%\Microsoft SDKs\v8.0\Tools\IsolatedStorageExplorerTool*. The command-line syntax for the ISE tool is as follows:

```
ISETool <ts | rs | dir | EnumerateDevices> <xd | de | deviceindex:n> <productId>
<desktop-path>
```

The command-line arguments are described in Table 10-1.

TABLE 10-1 ISE command-line arguments

Argument	Description
ts	Takes a snapshot of the specified app's isolated-storage folder and copies it to your computer.
rs	Restores a snapshot to the app's isolated-storage folder. This option is especially useful if you need to test your app with a significant amount of user-generated data. Simply build up that data set once and then take a snapshot of it to be stored safely on your computer. When you want to test a new version of your app, restore the snapshot and begin testing immediately.
dir[:devicePath]	Lists the files and directories in the specified app's isolated storage folder. To see only the files and directories within a specific folder, provide the relative path to that folder like this: `dir:.\My Folder\Documents\.`
EnumerateDevices	Lists the available device targets, including both physical devices and emulator instances. Each device is given an index that you can use with the deviceindex parameter.
xd	Indicates that you want to perform the operation on the emulator.
de	Indicates that you want to perform the operation on an attached physical device.
deviceindex[:n]	Indicates that you want to perform the operation on the device with the index n (as returned by the EnumerateDevices option).
productId	The ProductId for the app with which you want to interact. You can find the ProductId in the app manifest.
desktop-path	Specifies the directory on your computer from which you want to read files or to which you want to write files.

For example, the command to read the full contents of the local folder for the *Isolated StorageReaderWriter* app from the emulator and write it to C:\IsolatedStorageReaderWriter is as follows:

```
Isetool.exe ts xd 56da939f-99fb-4b2b-ba84-a67769c9823d c:\IsolatedStorageReaderWriter
```

When copying from the phone onto your computer, the ISE creates a subdirectory in the one that you specify, called IsolatedStore. If you run the copy operation multiple times and the IsolatedStore folder already exists, the ISE will overwrite any files that were already there. Similarly, if you copy files from your computer to the device, all the existing files on the phone will be replaced with the contents of the directory you specify.

Note Although it is called the "Isolated Storage Explorer," the ISE tool is not specific to apps written by using the *IsolatedStorage* APIs.

Windows Runtime storage

The Windows Runtime storage APIs are contained in the *Windows.Storage* namespace, with the *IStorageFile* and *IStorageFolder* interfaces and their corresponding concrete types providing the core building blocks. In Windows Phone 8, the only portions of the *Windows.Storage* namespace that are supported are those with which developers can manage files and directories in their local storage folder and read files from their app package. Windows Phone 8 does not support the notions of roaming or temporary data that are present in Windows, nor does it provide access to user content such as photos or music as an *IStorageFolder*, as Windows does through the *KnownFolders* class.

The *WindowsRuntimeStorageReaderWriter* solution in the sample code shows usage of the Windows Runtime storage APIs for reading and writing files, including reading a file that is included in the application package. Figure 10-3 shows the UI for *WindowsRuntimeStorageReaderWriter*.

The app package includes a file named *inputfile.txt*, which contains the famous opening sentence of Charles Dickens's novel, *A Tale of Two Cities*. When the user taps the "Read File From Package" button, the app loads that file from the package, reads its contents as a string, and sets the content of the large *TextBox* on the page to that string. The code for the *Click* event handler of the *readInputFile Button* is shown here:

```
private async void readInputFileButton_Click(object sender, RoutedEventArgs e)
{
    StorageFile inputFile =
        await StorageFile.GetFileFromApplicationUriAsync(new Uri("ms-appx:///InputFile.txt"));

    using (IRandomAccessStreamWithContentType readStream = await inputFile.OpenReadAsync())
    using (StreamReader reader = new StreamReader(readStream.AsStream()))
    {
            fileContentTextBox.Text = await reader.ReadToEndAsync();
    }
}
```

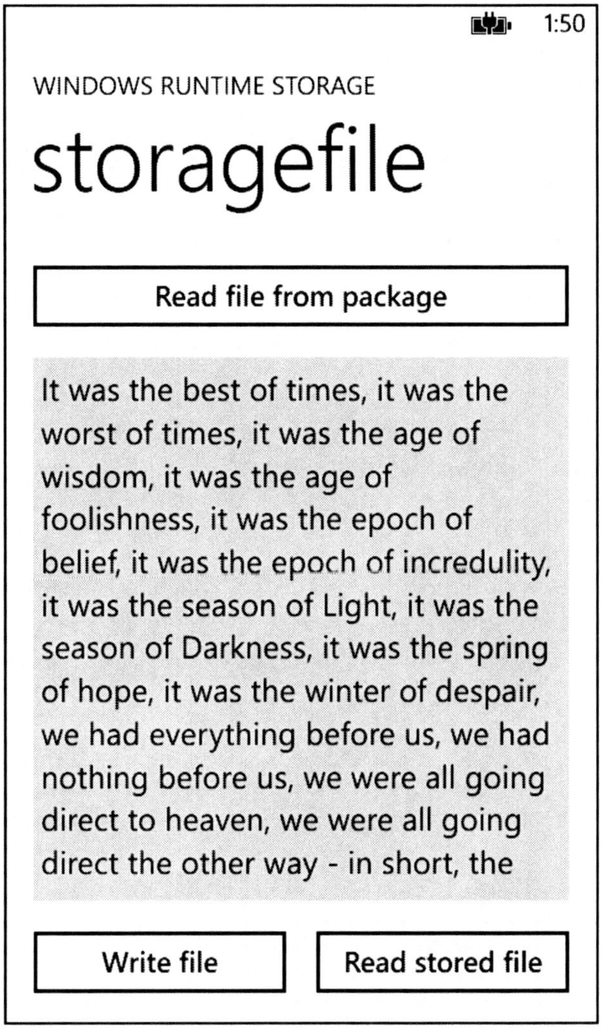

FIGURE 10-3 The *WindowsRuntimeStorageReaderWriter* solution uses the Windows Runtime storage APIs for file access.

There are two points worth noting in this code. First, like the rest of the Windows Runtime API surface, any potentially long-running operation is asynchronous, so you need to include the *await* keyword to ensure that the operation is complete before moving on to the next line of code. Second, Windows Runtime APIs support special URI schemes for addressing the app's install folder and its data folder. In this case, we use the *ms-appx* scheme (followed by three slashes) with the static *StorageFile* API *GetFileFromApplicationUriAsync* to represent the app's install folder. When the *ms-appx* scheme is encountered, the platform performs a simple substitution for the full path to the app's installation folder, which looks like this:

C:\Data\Programs\{0281B669-11F7-46D8-B373-2161FEFA0D94}\Install

As you can probably guess, the prominent GUID in the middle of the path is the *ProductId* from the app manifest. You can also interact with the app package as a *StorageFolder* via the *InstalledLocation* property. The following code is equivalent to the use of *GetFileFromApplicationUriAsync* in the previous example:

```
StorageFile inputFile = await Package.Current.InstalledLocation.GetFileAsync("InputFile.txt");
```

Note In general, when an app is installed, its install folder is marked as read-only, even to the app itself. Among other reasons, this ensures that apps cannot accidentally write content into that folder, only to have it wiped away when the app is updated. For apps in development that are deployed from Visual Studio or the app deployment tool, however, this read-only status is not conferred on the install folder. You should ensure that you never write content to the install folder during your development, because those calls will not work when the app is submitted to the Windows Phone Store.

After the text from the *inputfile.txt* has been written to the *TextBox*, the user has the opportunity to make edits to it and then save it to a new file in its local storage folder. Finally, he can then read that file back and write its content back to the *TextBox*. The *Click* event handlers for *writeFileButton* and *readStoredFileButton* are shown in the following code:

```
private async void writeFileButton_Click(object sender, RoutedEventArgs e)
{
      StorageFolder localFolder = Windows.Storage.ApplicationData.Current.LocalFolder;
      StorageFile outputFile = await localFolder.CreateFileAsync("newtale.txt",
                                    CreationCollisionOption.ReplaceExisting);

      using (Stream writeStream = await outputFile.OpenStreamForWriteAsync())
      using (StreamWriter writer = new DataWriter(writeStream))
      {
            await writer.WriteAsync(fileContentTextBox.Text);
      }

      fileContentTextBox.Text = string.Empty;
}

private async void readStoredFileButton_Click(object sender, RoutedEventArgs e)
{
     try
     {
         StorageFile storedFile = await StorageFile.GetFileFromApplicationUriAsync
              (new Uri("ms-appdata:///local/newtale.txt"));

         using (IRandomAccessStreamWithContentType
                readStream = await storedFile.OpenReadAsync())
         using (DataReader reader = new DataReader(readStream))
         {
              ulong streamSize = readStream.Size;
              UInt32 totalBytesRead = await reader.LoadAsync((UInt32)streamSize);

              fileContentTextBox.Text = reader.ReadString(totalBytesRead);
```

```
            }
        }
        catch (FileNotFoundException)
        {
            MessageBox.Show("Please write a file first.", "File not found", MessageBoxButton.OK);
        }
}
```

The two event handlers demonstrate different ways of referencing the same file within the app's local storage folder. The *writeFileButton_Click* event handler gets a reference to the *LocalFolder* property on the *ApplicationData* class, whereas the *readStoredFileButton_Click* event handler uses the *GetFileFromApplicationUriAsync* method shown previously, except in this case with the *ms-appdata* URI scheme to represent the app's storage folder rather than *ms-appx* for the install folder. Note that you must always include the "local" subdirectory with the *ms-appdata* scheme because you cannot write directly to the root data folder, and Windows Phone 8 only supports the local folder.

In the *writeFileButton_Click* event handler, we use the *CreateFileAsync* method to create a new file, specifying a member of the *CreationCollisionOption* enumeration to indicate what should happen if the file already exists. In this case, we want to replace the existing file. In the simpler overload of *CreateFileAsync*, the value defaults to *FailIfExists*, so your app receives an exception when trying to create a file with the same name as one that is already present in your storage folder.

File storage and the app lifecycle

For apps with a small amount of local data, it is generally easiest to store that data in just a few files and then perform a single set of reads when the app starts and a single set of writes when the app is closed. There are a number of potential pitfalls to watch out for with this approach, however.

First, you must always persist important data when the app is deactivated as well as when it is closed. Recall from Chapter 2, "App model and navigation," that deactivation is the last opportunity your app has to run code before being sent to the background and that it is always possible that your app's process will be terminated by the system before it is able to return to the foreground again.

Second, the operating system (OS) does not guarantee that any file write operations started during app deactivation or closing will complete before the app's process is terminated. As a result, you must ensure that any write operations done during deactivation or closing do not leave your data files in a corrupt state. If you are using the Windows Runtime storage APIs, you should use the transacted write functionality exposed by the *OpenTransactedWriteAsync* method on the *StorageFile* class to ensure that any file writes are complete before being persisted. If you are using the *IsolatedStorage* APIs (which do not supported transacted writes), consider saving your data in a new file and then replacing the existing file with it rather than immediately overwriting the existing data. This ensures that you will maintain a consistent (if somewhat stale) copy of your app state even if you are unable to complete writing out the new data before your app is terminated.

Finally, you should take particular care when using the asynchronous Windows Runtime storage APIs during deactivation and closing. The OS will terminate your app process as soon as the *Deactivated* or *Closing* event handlers have completed, with no accomodation for any outstanding asynchronous operations. Thus, you should perform any critical deactivation work synchronously. To illustrate this, consider the following implementation for the *Closing* event handler, in which the app creates the file and opens a transacted write stream asynchronously:

```
private async void Application_Closing(object sender, ClosingEventArgs e)
{
    StorageFile savedFile =
        await ApplicationData.Current.LocalFolder.CreateFileAsync
            ("savedData.dat", CreationCollisionOption.ReplaceExisting);

    using (StorageStreamTransaction saveDataStream =
        await savedFile.OpenTransactedWriteAsync())
    {
        // serialize state and write to file
    }
}
```

The *await* keyword instructs the compiler that the method will run asynchronously and that any code that follows should only be executed after it returns. In other words, it ensures that the code contained within the *using* statement should only run after *CreateFileAsync* returns. However, what the *await* keyword does not do is block the containing method from returning, because that would defeat the purpose of asynchrony. Instead, the presence of the *async* modifier allows the containing method, in this case *Application_Closing*, to return very quickly while asynchronous operations proceed in the background. As a result, the OS is able to shut down the app almost immediately, usually before any of the data persistence can complete. To avoid this, you should use a technique that is not recommended in most other circumstances: blocking until the asynchronous operation completes by treating it like a *Task* and fetching its return value using the *Result* property.

```
private async void Application_Closing(object sender, ClosingEventArgs e)
{
    Task<string> saveFileTask =
        ApplicationData.Current.LocalFolder.CreateFileAsync
            ("savedData.dat", CreationCollisionOption.ReplaceExisting).AsTask();

    StorageFile savedFile = saveFileTask.Result;

    Task<StorageStreamTransaction> saveDataStreamTask =
        savedFile.OpenTransactedWriteAsync().AsTask();

    using (StorageStreamTransaction saveDataStream =
        saveDataStreamTask.Result)
    {
        // serialize state and write to file
    }
}
```

For apps that deal with larger data sets, you should consider a more sophisticated approach. First, try to separate the data into multiple files, based on when the data is needed in the app. For example, consider creating a small file that contains the data required for the main page of the app that can be read quickly on app startup, and then larger files containing data for other pages that can be read on demand as the user progresses through the app UI. You will also need to take a different approach to writing changes to persistent storage. If you wait until your app is deactivated to write a large set of changes, there is a very good chance that the write will not complete and you will lose a significant amount of user data. In general, you should persist data when the app has completed a logical operation; for example, an RSS reader that persists a list of stories for a given feed should wait until it has completed parsing the entire feed before persisting the changes, rather than saving one story at a time. This limits the impact of file IO on app performance.

Win32 APIs

Both the isolated storage APIs and the Windows Runtime storage APIs are built on a set of core file system APIs, most of which have been part of Windows for years. In Windows Phone 8, a subset of these APIs is now also accessible by Windows Phone Store apps. The primary scenario for using the Win32 APIs rather than the Windows Runtime APIs discussed in the previous section is the case for which you have existing native libraries written for desktop Windows that you want to reuse in your Windows Phone app or game. If you are writing new native code and need to perform file operations, we recommend that you use the Windows Runtime storage APIs. Even for cases in which you intend to reuse an existing Win32 library, you might need to make some small modifications to account for modest differences between the traditional Windows APIs and their Windows 8/Windows Phone 8 equivalents. The key differences are presented in Table 10-2.

TABLE 10-2 A comparison of Windows Phone APIs and some traditional Win32 APIs

Traditional API(s)	Windows 8/Windows Phone 8 API	Key differences
CopyFile/CopyFileEx	*CopyFile2*	*CopyFile2* moves the extended properties of *CopyFile* and *CopyFileEx* into a single structure, *COPYFILE2_EXTENDED_PARAMETERS*.
CreateFile	*CreateFile2*	*CreateFile2* only allows apps to open files and directories, not physical devices, pipes, and other IO channels as with *CreateFile*. The *dwFlagsAndAttributes* parameter has been split into *dwFileAttributes*, *dwCreateFlags*, and *dwSecurityQosFlags*. As with *CopyFile2*, *CreateFile2* moves advanced properties into a unified structure, *CREATEFILE2_EXTENDED_PARAMETERS*.
GetOverlappedResult	*GetOverlappedResultEx*	*GetOverlappedResultEx* adds a timeout interval, *dwMilliseconds*, and the option to wait on an alertable thread by setting *bAlertable* to *true*.

The *Win32ReaderWriter* solution in the sample code demonstrates the use of basic Win32 file APIs. The UI (written in XAML) contains two *ListBox* controls, each of which corresponds to a subfolder of the app's local storage folder, named "folder1" and "folder2." The user can create, open, or delete files in either folder, or move them from one folder to the other, with all the file IO being done by using Win32 file APIs wrapped in a simple Windows Runtime component. The UI for *Win32Reader Writer* is shown in Figure 10-4. Observe that we use the *Ticks* property of the Microsoft .NET *DateTime* class to provide uniqueness for the file names.

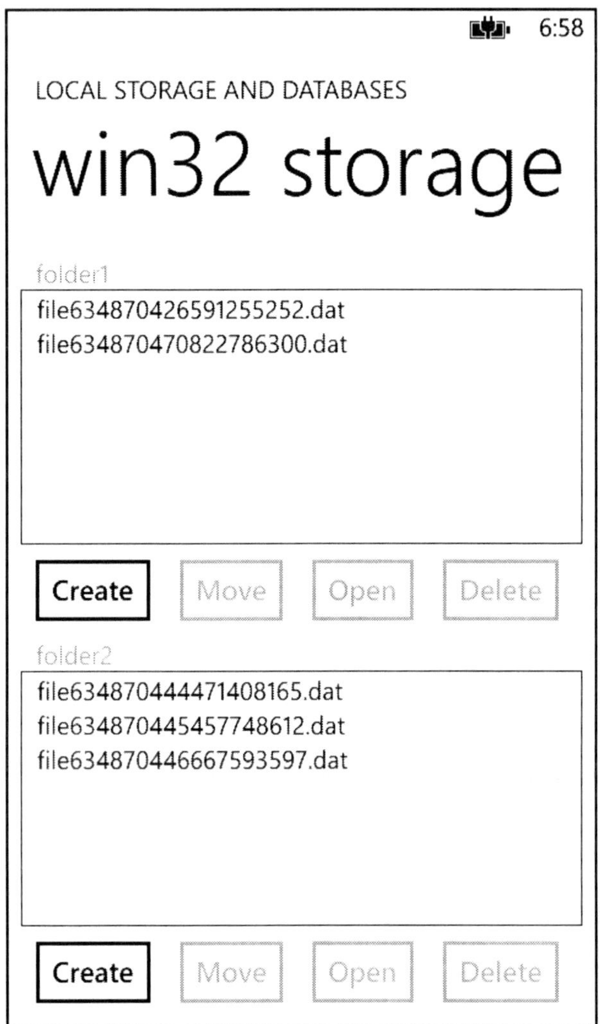

FIGURE 10-4 The *Win32ReaderWriter* solution uses a XAML UI to drive Win32 file operations.

The Windows Runtime component that wraps the Win32 APIs, named *Win32StorageWrapper*, contains four methods corresponding to the four buttons shown below the *ListBox* controls in the UI.

```
namespace Win32StorageComponent
{
    public ref class Win32StorageWrapper sealed
    {
    public:
        Win32StorageWrapper();

        void Win32CreateFile(Platform::String^ parentFolderPath, Platform::String^ filename);
        void Win32MoveFile(Platform::String^ sourceFolderPath,
                           Platform::String^ targetFolderPath,
                           Platform::String^ filename);
Platform::String^ Win32OpenFile(Platform::String^ filePath);
        void Win32DeleteFile(Platform::String^ filePath);
    };
}
```

We will review two of these APIs in detail. The *Win32CreateFile* method takes the path of the folder that will contain the newly created file and the file name. Note that the folder path is absolute, not relative, because the Win32 file APIs are not inherently aware of the app's storage location and thus cannot resolve a relative path. The API first checks whether the directory exists by querying its file attributes and creates it if necessary. It then creates a file handle by using the *CreateFile2* method described earlier. Finally, it writes a short string that includes the local system time to the newly created file.

```
void Win32StorageWrapper::Win32CreateFile(String^ parentFolderPath, String^ filename)
{
     const wstring parentFolderPathString = parentFolderPath->Data();
     const wstring filenameString = filename->Data();

     BOOL createDirectorySucceeded = CreateDirectory(parentFolderPathString.c_str(), NULL);

     if(!createDirectorySucceeded)
     {
          DWORD errorCode = GetLastError();

          if(errorCode != ERROR_ALREADY_EXISTS)
          {
               throw ref new Platform::FailureException("Failed to create directory");
          }
     }

     const wstring fullFilePathString = parentFolderPathString + L"\\" + filenameString;
     HANDLE fileResult =
          CreateFile2(fullFilePathString.c_str(), GENERIC_WRITE, 0, CREATE_NEW, NULL);

     SYSTEMTIME systemTime;
     GetLocalTime(&systemTime);

     wstringstream timeOutputStream;
     timeOutputStream << L"This test data was written at "
          << setfill(L'0') << setw(2) << systemTime.wHour << ":"
          << setfill(L'0') << setw(2) << systemTime.wMinute << endl;

     unsigned long totalBytesWritten;
```

```
    BOOL writeFileSucceeded = WriteFile(fileResult, timeOutputStream.str().c_str(),
        sizeof(timeOutputStream), &totalBytesWritten, NULL);

    if(!writeFileSucceeded)
    {
        CloseHandle(fileResult);
        throw ref new Platform::FailureException("Failed to create file");
    }

    CloseHandle(fileResult);
}
```

The string we're creating (and persisting) is of type *wstring*, which means that it is made up of wide characters rather than single-byte characters. This makes it straightforward to read the contents of the file back and return them to the app by using the Windows Runtime *String* type, which is likewise made up of wide characters. Even though we could also choose to store single-byte characters in the file and perform a conversion to wide characters at the time that we want to return the *String* type, using wide characters throughout ensures maximum flexibility for the app, should we need to support additional character sets in the future. Now that we've created a file, we can read it back by using the *Win32OpenFile* method.

```
String^ Win32StorageWrapper::Win32OpenFile(String^ filePath)
{
    const wstring filePathString = filePath->Data();

    HANDLE fileHandle = CreateFile2(filePathString.c_str(), GENERIC_READ, 0, OPEN_EXISTING,
                                    NULL);

    if(fileHandle == INVALID_HANDLE_VALUE)
    {
        throw ref new Platform::FailureException("Failed to open file");
    }

    DWORD totalBytesRead = 0;

    const int bufferSize = 100;
    wchar_t fileData[bufferSize] = {0};

    BOOL readFileSucceeded = ReadFile(fileHandle, fileData, bufferSize-1, &totalBytesRead, NULL);
    if(!readFileSucceeded)
    {
        CloseHandle(fileHandle);
        throw ref new Platform::FailureException("Failed to open file");
    }

    String^ returnString = ref new String(fileData);

    CloseHandle(fileHandle);
    return returnString;
}
```

The returned contents of the file are displayed in a *MessageBox* in the app, as shown in Figure 10-5.

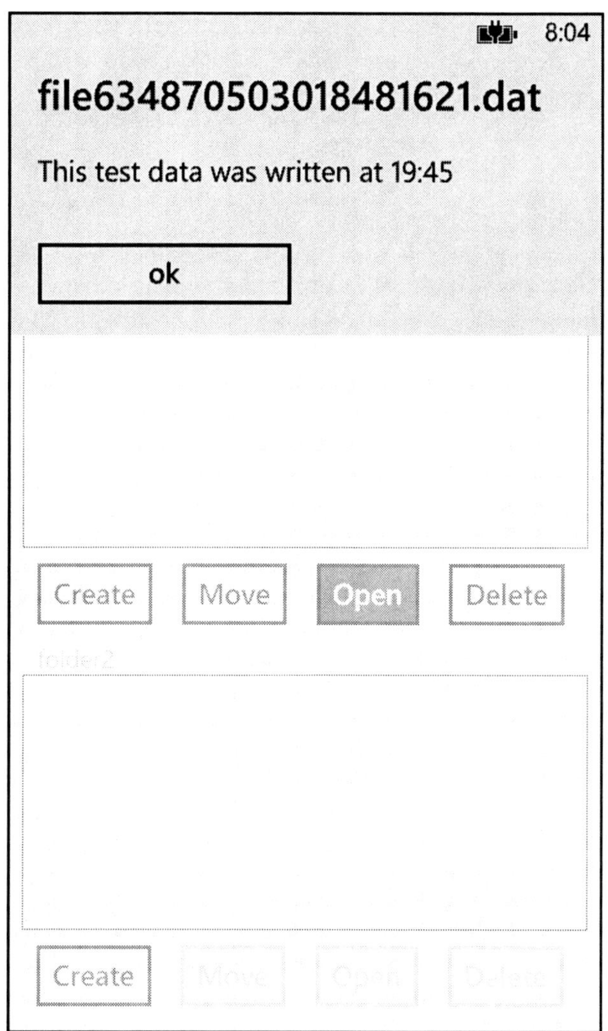

FIGURE 10-5 The contents of the file read by using the Win32 *ReadFile* API are displayed in a *MessageBox*.

LINQ-to-SQL

The Windows Phone 7.1 SDK added support for local databases in Windows Phone Store apps by using the LINQ-to-SQL API and the SQL Server Compact Edition (SQLCE) database engine. The primary advantage of a database is that it makes it possible for you to perform complex queries on potentially large data sets without requiring that you load all that data into memory.

Introduced in Microsoft .NET Framework 3.5, LINQ-to-SQL is an object-relational mapping (ORM) API based on the Language-Integrated Query (LINQ) framework. It makes it possible for apps to perform queries and create, read, update, and delete (CRUD) operations on strongly typed managed objects, just as it would on data stored in memory, while taking advantage of the underlying database engine to load only the data that's required.

Note LINQ-to-SQL is a large framework, so there is an up-front memory cost to adding a database to your app. You should consider the tradeoffs carefully and be able to clearly articulate why storing your app data in a database will yield a better app. If the amount of data in your app is small, or if you find that you're actually loading all your data into memory anyway, you might be better off simply reading and writing your data collections to files, as demonstrated earlier in this chapter.

Defining the database in code

ORM strategies fall into two categories: *data-first* and *code-first*. A data-first approach starts from a database schema and builds app classes which can represent that schema, whereas a code-first strategy uses app classes to create a database schema. LINQ-to-SQL supports both approaches, but in the desktop and server environment, it has historically been more common to use it in a data-first strategy, often because the API layer was being added on top of an existing database. In a Windows Phone app, code-first makes more sense because there is no existing database to which you must adapt. Indeed, the opposite is often the case; an app will graduate from another persistence strategy (such as serializing objects to files) and need to adapt the database to its existing object model.

The critical class involved in mapping managed classes to a database schema is *System.Data.DataContext* (not to be confused with *FrameworkElement.DataContext*, which is used in data binding). The *DataContext* acts as the bridge between the object layer and the underlying database file. Apps create a custom *DataContext* class that inherits from the base *DataContext* and that specifies the tables that they wish to create by using the generic type *Table*. The types specified in the *Table* collections are referred to as *entities*. The entity classes are decorated with attributes indicating the structure of the table, including columns, primary and foreign keys, and indexes. In addition to defining the database, the *DataContext* is used throughout the app's lifetime to query data from the database, to track changes made to that data by the app, and ultimately to submit those changes back to the database file.

Using the *LinqToSQL_BookManager* solution in the sample code, the user can create and manage a list of books in a home library. The UI of its main page is shown in Figure 10-6.

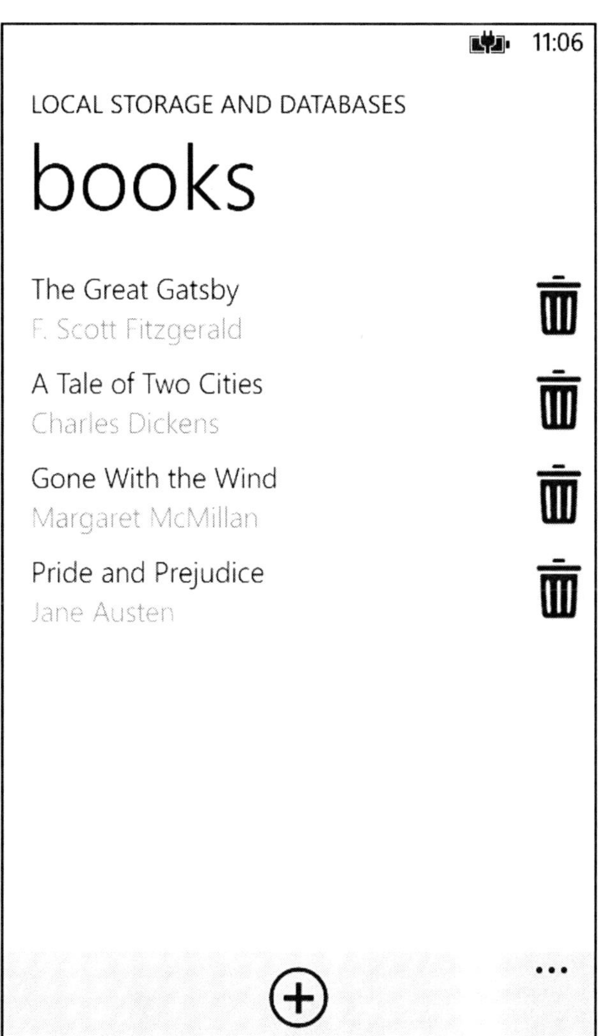

FIGURE 10-6 The *LinqToSQL_BookManager* solution maintains a single table to manage a user's library.

The *LinqToSQL_BookManager* solution defines a custom *DataContext* (named *BooksManagerData Context*) along with a single entity, *Book*. You can find the definitions of each class in the following code:

```
public class BooksManagerDataContext : DataContext
{
     public Table<Book> Books;
     public BooksManagerDataContext(string connectionString) : base(connectionString) { }
}
```

```
[Table]
public class Book : INotifyPropertyChanged, INotifyPropertyChanging
{
    [Column(DbType = "INT NOT NULL Identity", IsDbGenerated = true, IsPrimaryKey = true)]
    public int BookId { get; private set; }

    private string title;

    [Column]
    public string Title
    {
        get
        {
            return title;
        }
        set
        {
            if(title != value)
            {
                 NotifyPropertyChanging();
                 title = value;
                 NotifyPropertyChanged();
            }
        }
    }

    private string author;

    [Column]
    public string Author
    {
        get
        {
            return author;
        }
        set
        {
            if(author != value)
            {
                 NotifyPropertyChanging();
                 author = value;
                 NotifyPropertyChanged();
            }
        }
    }

    public event PropertyChangingEventHandler PropertyChanging;
    public event PropertyChangedEventHandler PropertyChanged;

    private void NotifyPropertyChanged([CallerMemberName] string propertyName = "")
    {
        var propertyChangedCopy = PropertyChanged;
        if (propertyChangedCopy != null)
        {
            propertyChangedCopy(this, new PropertyChangedEventArgs(propertyName));
        }
    }
```

```
    private void NotifyPropertyChanging([CallerMemberName] string propertyName = "")
    {
        var propertyChangingCopy = PropertyChanging;
        if (propertyChangingCopy != null)
        {
            propertyChangingCopy(this, new PropertyChangingEventArgs(propertyName));
        }
    }
}
```

The definition of the *Book* class makes it clear that LINQ-to-SQL entities are nothing more than Plain Old CLR Objects (POCOs) decorated with attributes that can be used by the framework to link them to the database. Indeed, the entities themselves play no direct role in the persistence of their data. The *Table* attribute denotes that the class maps to a database table, whereas the *Column* attributes denote the relationship to the individual database columns within that table. For basic data columns, simply including the *Column* attribute is sufficient to persist and query the data. LINQ-to-SQL automatically names the column the same as the associated property and performs the appropriate translation between .NET data types and SQLCE data types; for example, from *string* to *nvarchar*. For the *BookId* property, however, we have added a number of additional properties on the *Column*, including setting it as the table's primary key and marking it as an identity column such that the database engine will automatically generate its value for each newly inserted row.

Note You might be wondering about the *INotifyPropertyChanging* interface that parallels the well-known *INotifyPropertyChanged* interface used in data binding. The intent of the interface is to notify the LINQ-to-SQL framework when an entity is about change so that it can prepare to track those changes. For more details, see the section "Maximizing LINQ-to-SQL performance" later in this chapter.

With the schema defined, it is simple to create the database. We start by creating an instance of the *DataContext*, passing in a string indicating the name of the database. Then, we check if the database already exists and finally create it. As with any data persistence strategy, it is a good idea to decouple the data model and the app UI. If you are using the Model-View-ViewModel (MVVM) pattern as described in Chapter 4, "Data binding and MVVM," the viewmodel will provide the bridge between these two layers and is therefore a good place to manage your *DataContext*. In the *LinqToSQL_BookManager* solution, we maintain a singleton instance of the *MainViewModel* in the *App* class and perform all operations on the database through that viewmodel object. The *MainViewModel* constructor checks whether the database exists and creates it if it does not.

```
public MainViewModel()
{
     booksManagerDb =
          new BooksManagerDataContext("Data source=isostore:/books.sdf");

     if (!booksManagerDb.DatabaseExists())
     {
          booksManagerDb.CreateDatabase();
     }
}
```

Note The "isostore" scheme used in the connection string refers to the root of the app's local storage folder.

Performing queries

If you have done any development using LINQ, LINQ-to-SQL queries should look very familiar to you. The *DataContext* provides the base collections (linked to database tables) that you can query, but otherwise, the syntax is the same. For instance, the following query returns the list of book titles in ascending order:

```
var orderedBookTitles = from Book b in booksManagerDb.Books
                        orderby b.Title
                        select b.Title;
```

On the surface, this query looks just like it would if the collection of books were an in-memory collection, but, in fact, the selection and ordering defined in the statement are carried out in the database engine with a SQL select statement, as shown in the code snippet that follows. For large data sets or complex queries, this has significant memory and performance benefits.

```
SELECT Title
FROM Books
ORDER BY Title
```

For the *LinqToSQL_BookManager solution*, the query is quite basic; we simply read in all the books in the table and add them to an *ObservableCollection* called *Books* that is then bound to the UI. The query is encapsulated in a helper method, *LoadData*. As a result, we can delay loading the data until the initial UI has loaded to keep the app responsive.

```
public void LoadData()
{
     if (Books == null)
     {
          Books = new ObservableCollection<Book>(booksManagerDb.Books);
     }
}
```

Create/update/delete

As a query syntax, LINQ itself does not understand the notion of adding, updating, or removing items in a collection. LINQ-to-SQL includes support for these functions through the *DataContext*. You can think of the *DataContext* as an object cache that maintains context about the corresponding entries in the database. Thus, when you need to make changes to the database, you start by registering those changes with the *DataContext* and then you submit them to the database by using the *SubmitChanges* method.

Adding an item is simple; you only need to create a new instance of the entity and add it to the *DataContext* by using the *InsertOnSubmit* method, as demonstrated in the code that follows. Note that we also add it to the *Books ObservableCollection* maintained in the viewmodel so that the new item shows up in the UI.

```
public void AddBook(Book newBook)
{
      booksManagerDb.Books.InsertOnSubmit(newBook);

      Books.Add(newBook);
}
```

Note This approach adds the book to the UI-bound collection before it has been successfully committed to the database. If you would prefer to wait until the data has been saved to the database before adding the item in the UI, simply call *SubmitChanges* immediately after *InsertOnSubmit*.

Delete operations function in a similar way. You simply pass the entity to be deleted to the *DeleteOnSubmit* method, once again also updating the *Books* collection to ensure that the change is reflected in the UI.

```
public void DeleteBook(Book currentBook)
{
     booksManagerDb.Books.DeleteOnSubmit(currentBook);
     Books.Remove(currentBook);
}
```

Given the model for create and delete, you might expect LINQ-to-SQL to provide an *Update OnSubmit* method to round out its set of core operations, but it does not. Instead, the framework implicitly tracks changes made to entities in the *DataContext* so that those changes can ultimately be submitted back into the database.

```
public void UpdateBook(Book currentBook, string title, string author)
{
     currentBook.Title = title;
     currentBook.Author = author;
}
```

After you have added, removed, or edited entries in the *DataContext*, there is one more step required to actually persist those changes in the database: calling the *SubmitChanges* method. *SubmitChanges* consolidates all the operations performed on the *DataContext*, translates them into the appropriate SQL statements, and then executes them against the database in a single transaction, ensuring that they are atomically applied.

Tip Avoid letting the number of changes in your *DataContext* grow too large before submitting. For simple apps like the *LinqToSQL_BookManager solution*, it is feasible to call *SubmitChanges* only during *Deactivation*, but as with files, if the amount of content to write is large, the operation might not complete before the process is destroyed. The database will ensure data integrity in that case, but you will still lose potentially valuable user data.

Associations

One of the most powerful properties of a relational database is the ability to link records together through join operations. Although it is possible to perform SQL-style joins by using LINQ syntax, LINQ-to-SQL provides the ability to define associations between entities in advance so that you can use the familiar "dot" notation to navigate seamlessly between the tables, with the framework performing the join for you automatically.

We will continue with the book theme to illustrate associations. The *LinqToSQL_LendingLibrary* solution in the sample code provides management for a library. The user can add and delete borrowers, add books and loans, and mark loans as returned. The UI is focused on a main page containing pivots for each of the three entities: books, borrowers, and loans. The loans pivot is shown in Figure 10-7.

The *LinqToSQL_LendingLibrary* solution defines a *DataContext* (named *LibraryDataContext*) that includes three tables: *Books*, *Borrowers*, and *Loans*. The *Books* table contains the list of books that the library owns, whereas the *Borrowers* table contains the list of people who are able to borrow books from the library. Finally, the *Loans* table includes all loans that the library has made (both active and closed) and includes foreign keys to the other two tables. The database schema diagram is shown in Figure 10-8.

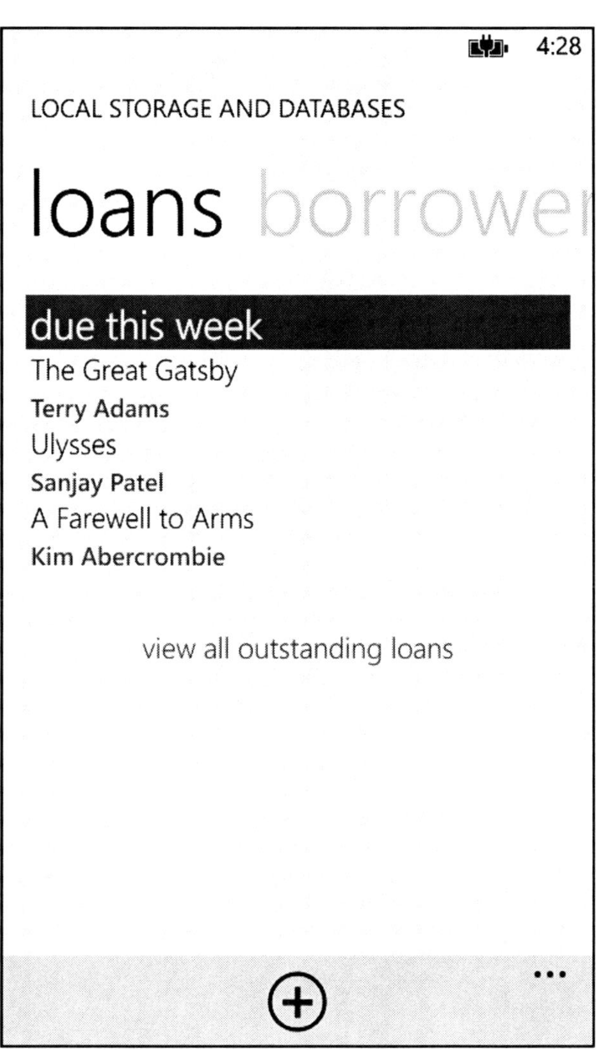

FIGURE 10-7 The lending library app uses a database to keep track of books, borrowers, and loans.

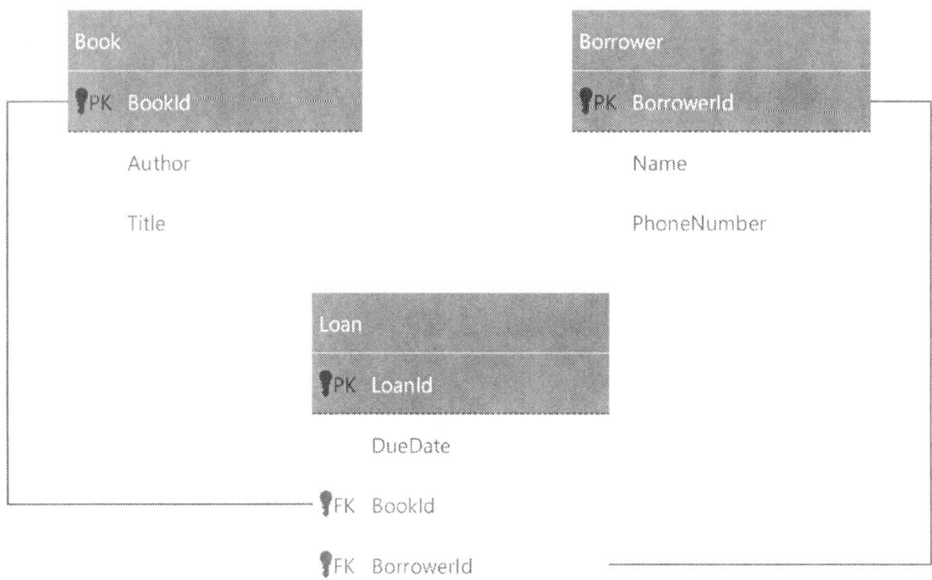

FIGURE 10-8 The *Loans* table contains foreign keys to the *Books* and *Borrowers* tables.

Like the *Book* entity in the *LinqToSQL_BookManager solution*, the *Borrower* entity includes a *Table* attribute and a set of *Column* attributes to define the core structure of the associated database table. However, it also includes an *EntitySet* collection of *Loan* entities that is decorated with an *Association* attribute.

```
[Table]
public class Borrower: INotifyPropertyChanged, INotifyPropertyChanging
{
   [Column(IsPrimaryKey = true,
           DbType = "INT NOT NULL Identity",
           IsDbGenerated = true)]
   internal int BorrowerId { get; private set; }

   private string name;

   [Column]
   public string Name
   {
       get
       {
           return name;
       }
       set
       {
           NotifyPropertyChanging();
           name = value;
           NotifyPropertyChanged();
       }
   }
```

```
    [Association(OtherKey = "BorrowerId")]
    public EntitySet<Loan> Loans
    {
        get;
        private set;
    }

    // constructor and property notification code omitted for brevity
    // ...
}
```

The *EntitySet* collection represents the "many" side of a one-to-many database relationship. In this case, every borrower is associated with a set of loans, so the *Borrower* entity includes an *EntitySet* of *Loan* entities. The *OtherKey* property instructs the framework as to which property to match in the entity on the other side of the relationship to create the association, which in this case is the *Loan* entity. The corresponding type representing the "one" side of the one-to-many relationship is *EntityRef*. Each loan has exactly one *Borrower*, so we use an *EntityRef* of type *Borrower* to represent that relationship. In this case, the *Association* attribute includes a *ThisKey* property that maps to the same field as the *OtherKey* property defined earlier. Also, observe the use of the *IsForeignKey* property. As the name suggests, this creates a foreign key constraint in the database. If you attempt to delete the *Borrower* associated with a *Loan* without first deleting the *Loan*, you will get an exception.

```
[Table]
public class Loan: INotifyPropertyChanging, INotifyPropertyChanged
{
     [Column(DbType="INT NOT NULL Identity", IsDbGenerated=true, IsPrimaryKey=true)]
     internal int LoanId { get; private set; }

     private DateTime? dueDate;
     [Column]
     public DateTime? DueDate
     {
          get
          {
               return dueDate;
          }
          set
          {
               NotifyPropertyChanging();
               dueDate = value;
               NotifyPropertyChanged();
          }
     }

     private bool isReturned = false;

     [Column]
     public bool IsReturned
     {
         get
         {
             return isReturned;
         }
```

```
            set
            {
                NotifyPropertyChanging();
                isReturned = value;
                NotifyPropertyChanged();
            }
        }

        [Column]
        private int BorrowerId;

        private EntityRef<Borrower> borrower;

        [Association(Storage = "borrower", IsForeignKey=true , ThisKey="BorrowerId")]
        public Borrower Borrower
        {
            get
            {
                return borrower.Entity;
            }
            set
            {
                borrower.Entity = value;
                BorrowerId = value.BorrowerId;
            }
        }

    // constructor and property notification code omitted for brevity
    // ...
}
```

With these associations in place, you can perform natural LINQ queries in your object layer that span the two tables. For example, the following sets the *CurrentLoans* list to the set of unreturned loans for a given *Borrower*:

```
CurrentLoans = Borrower.Loans.Where(loan => loan.IsReturned == false).ToList();
```

Of course, just because one entity has a relationship with another does not mean that you always need both sets of data at the same time. For instance, you might want to simply view and edit the properties of a *Book* without needing to see the *Loan* entities associated with it, so it would be inefficient to proactively load them whenever you loaded a *Book* entity. To accommodate this, LINQ-to-SQL follows a pattern of *deferred loading*. If you query an entity that has an association, the contents of that association will not be loaded until the app actually needs them. On the other hand, if you know in advance that you will always need the associated data, you can instruct LINQ-to-SQL to perform *eager loading* by using the *DataLoadOptions* class, like so:

```
using(LibraryDataContext library = new LibraryDataContext(LibraryDataContext.ConnectionString))
{
    DataLoadOptions dlo = new DataLoadOptions();
    dlo.LoadWith<Borrower>(borrower => borrower.Loans);
    library.LoadOptions = dlo;

    var Borrowers = library.Borrowers;
}
```

In this case, the query for all *Borrower* entities will also read in all the associated *Loan* entities, as well. It is a good idea to perform eager loading when you know that you will need the associated data because it avoids an additional roundtrip to the database.

LINQ-to-SQL: phone vs. desktop

LINQ-to-SQL is a large, powerful framework, and we cannot possibly cover it fully here. Whereas most in-depth content covering LINQ-to-SQL will reference the desktop .NET implementation, it is important to understand some of the differences in the phone implementation.

The most obvious difference is that LINQ-to-SQL on Windows Phone does not support passing explicit Transact-SQL commands directly through to the underlying database via methods such as *DataContext.ExecuteQuery*. These methods are available in desktop LINQ-to-SQL primarily as a way of accessing advanced database functionality, such as stored procedures, most of which is not supported in SQLCE. Similarly, Windows Phone does not expose any ADO.NET objects (such as *DataReader*) through the LINQ-to-SQL interface.

The other major differences you are likely to encounter are actually differences between SQLCE and its server-based counterparts. Although LINQ-to-SQL is supported with SQLCE databases on the desktop, it is more common to see LINQ-to-SQL used with full versions of SQL Server, so you should be aware of some differences between the database engines that surface through the LINQ-to-SQL framework. First, SQLCE does not support the full set of data types available in SQL Server. For instance, the SQL Server *Date* type is not supported. Second, the LINQ extension method *Take* cannot accept a computed value as a parameter. In other words, you cannot say the following:

```
var topTenPercent = (from Item item in myDb.Items
                     orderby item.Name
                     select item).Take(myDb.Items.Count() / 10);
```

Rather, you should simply compute the value that you want to pass into the *Take* method in advance, like so:

```
int takeSize = myDb.Items.Count() / 10;
var topTenPercent = (from Item item in myDb.Items
                     orderby item.Name
                     select item).Take(takeSize);
```

Handling schema changes

Over the course of an app's lifetime in the Store, it is likely that you will need to make some changes to its database schema, perhaps to add a new table or column as the result of supporting a new feature or to add an index to an existing table to improve performance. The core LINQ-to-SQL framework does not provide a way to execute these types of upgrades. The structure of the database is set when the app calls *CreateDatabase* on the *DataContext* and can no longer be changed. In a desktop LINQ-to-SQL app, you could perform the upgrade operations by passing Data Definition Language (DDL) statements through the *ExecuteQuery* API. Because this option is not available in Windows

Phone, the platform includes the *DatabaseSchemaUpdater* class as an alternative. The *DatabaseSchemaUpdater* supports adding tables, columns, indexes, and foreign keys and includes the ability to track the schema version number so that you can determine at runtime whether an upgrade is required.

Accurately emulating the app upgrade experience during development requires some care. We recommend the following approach:

1. Make a copy of the current project before starting to work on your upgrades.

   This provides a way of generating data that matches what current users of your app have.

2. Implement the changes that you want to make to the project.

3. Run the project and ensure that it works as you expect. There is no use trying to upgrade to a version of the app that doesn't work correctly yet.

4. Implement the schema upgrade functionality by using the steps listed later in this section.

5. Clean and rebuild the old version of the app that you copied to a new location in step 1. Deploy it to the emulator/device and generate data that mimics what you expect a real user would have.

6. Run the new version of the app without rebuilding.

   This deploys the app without wiping the isolated storage contents from the old version, which matches the real world update process.

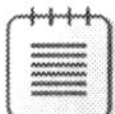

Note Depending on the complexity of your app, the process of generating a representative set of data in step 4 can take some time. In those cases, you might want to consider taking a snapshot of the database by using the ISE tool after you have built up sufficient data. This ensures that you can return to the original state quickly if you need to test the upgrade again after making further changes.

The *LinqToSQL_UpdatedBookManager* solution in the sample code takes the simple *LinqToSQL_BookManager solution* shown earlier and updates it to include the length of the book in pages, which we include in the details of the book (if available), as shown in Figure 10-9.

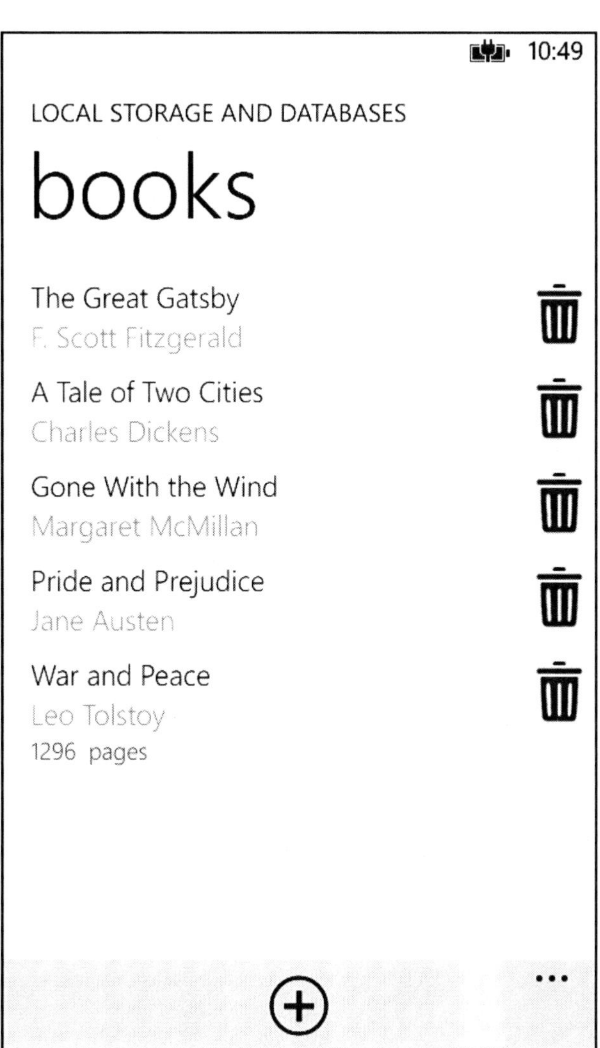

FIGURE 10-9 The updated book manager can show the number of pages in the book.

We begin by updating the *Book* entity to include a *NumberOfPages* property as a nullable *int*. When upgrading an existing table with a new column, you must use nullable types so that the database has a way of dealing with any existing records that will not have a value for that column.

```
private int? numberOfPages;

[Column(CanBeNull=true)]
public int? NumberOfPages
{
    get
    {
        return numberOfPages;
    }
    set
    {
        NotifyPropertyChanging();
        numberOfPages = value;
        NotifyPropertyChanged();
    }
}
```

If we ran the new app with an existing database file at this point, we would get an exception the first time that we tried to create a *DataContext* because the structure of the database schema would no longer match what is found in the *DataContext*. Therefore, the remaining step is to explicitly update the database schema so that it understands the new column by using the *DatabaseSchema Updater*. The *DatabaseSchemaUpdater* exposes a *DatabaseSchemaVersion* property that refers to the database schema version of the current database file. When the database is created, the value is set to 0 by default but thereafter is completely managed by the app. The platform does not enforce any constraints on how the version is incremented, as long as it is always increasing. A simple but generally effective approach is to maintain a constant value in your *DataContext* class for the version. You can compare that value to the *DatabaseSchemaVersion* to determine whether an upgrade is needed and then use one of the add methods exposed by the *DatabaseSchemaUpdater* class to complete the upgrade, as demonstrated in the following code with *AddColumn*:

```
public MainViewModel()
{
    booksManagerDb = new BooksManagerDataContext(BooksManagerDataContext.ConnectionString);

    if (!booksManagerDb.DatabaseExists())
    {
        booksManagerDb.CreateDatabase();

        DatabaseSchemaUpdater schemaUpdater = booksManagerDb.CreateDatabaseSchemaUpdater();
        schemaUpdater.DatabaseSchemaVersion = booksManagerDb.SchemaVersion;
        schemaUpdater.Execute();
    }
    else
    {
        DatabaseSchemaUpdater dbUpdater = booksManagerDb.CreateDatabaseSchemaUpdater();
        if (dbUpdater.DatabaseSchemaVersion < booksManagerDb.SchemaVersion)
        {
            dbUpdater.AddColumn<Book>("NumberOfPages");
            dbUpdater.DatabaseSchemaVersion = booksManagerDb.SchemaVersion;
            dbUpdater.Execute();
        }
    }
}
```

Observe that in addition to adding the code to upgrade the database when it's out of sync, we also added logic to update the version of a newly created database. It might seem odd to instantiate a *DatabaseSchemaUpdater* immediately after creating the database, but it's important that you match the schema version in the database file to the hardcoded version set in your *DataContext*. Otherwise, the next time the user runs the app, it will attempt to add a column that already exists, and thus will fail.

Prepopulating a reference database

Reference data refers to a set of data that is common to all users of an app. For small reference data sets, such as the list of states in the United States or a set of genres for books, it is reasonable to populate the database during the app's first run, either from a file in the app package or from the cloud. For some apps, however, reference data sets can be quite large. A dictionary app, for example, might have 100,000 words or more, each with a pronunciation, a definition, and an example sentence. In those cases, it is not feasible to load the database during the app's initialization process, because it will likely take significant time to complete, especially if the data is being loaded from the cloud. Instead, you should create the database file in advance and then include it in the app package. In this section, we will review how to create and package a prepopulated database file.

In most cases, a SQL Server Compact 3.5 database created in a desktop Windows app will work on Windows Phone. For maximum compatibility, however, we recommend creating your reference database in a phone app that is exclusively tasked with creating the database file. The *LinqToSQL_ReferenceDBCreator* solution in the sample code provides an example of this. It loads a comma-separated values (CSV) file from the United States Geological Survey containing all the earthquakes recorded around the world in the last week that registered 1.0 or higher on the Richter scale. Neither the UI nor the code is particularly interesting—the app consists of a button that triggers the parsing of the file and the creation of the database. When the app has completed parsing the file, it writes how many rows it created in the database, as shown in Figure 10-10.

After the database file is created, we can use the *IsolatedStorageExplorer* tool (described earlier) to fetch it from the app's isolated storage folder and then include it in our real app for use as reference data. The *LinqToSQL_ReferenceDBConsumer* solution shows an example of such an app, incorporating the reference database in its app package. The app simply groups the earthquakes by date and displays the total number of recorded events for each day, as shown in Figure 10-11.

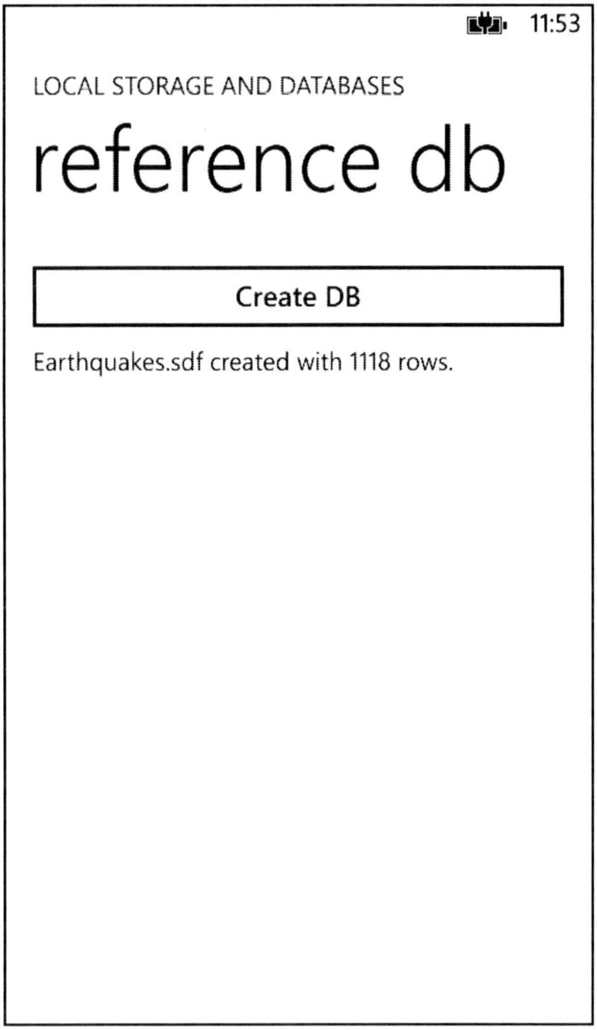

FIGURE 10-10 There's no need to spend much time building a beautiful UI for apps that create reference databases.

9:53

LOCAL STORAGE AND DATABASES

earthquakes

October 23, 2012 126
October 24, 2012 142
October 25, 2012 156
October 26, 2012 170
October 27, 2012 115
October 28, 2012 207
October 29, 2012 174
October 30, 2012 28

FIGURE 10-11 Reference databases can be referenced directly from the app package.

The code to display this data is shown in the snippet that follows. Note that we are able to reuse the same *DataContext* and entity classes from the *LinqToSQL_ReferenceDbCreator* project because they refer to the same database schema.

```
protected override void OnNavigatedTo(NavigationEventArgs e)
{
     EarthquakeDataContext earthquakeDb =
          new EarthquakeDataContext("Data Source=appdata:/Earthquakes.sdf");

     var earthquakeDates = from Earthquake eq in earthquakeDb.Earthquakes
                           group eq by eq.DateTimeRecorded.Date into Dates
                           select new EarthquakeDate { EarthquakeDateTime = Dates.Key,
                                                       EarthquakeCount = Dates.Count() };

     earthquakesLongListSelector.ItemsSource = earthquakeDates.ToList();
}
```

You can use the *appdata* scheme in the *DataContext* constructor to refer to the app package, rather than the app's local storage. Be aware that because the app package location is read-only, you can only perform queries from this location; you cannot insert, update, or delete rows. There might be cases for which you want to deliver the bulk of the reference database in the app package to avoid loading it at run time, but you might also want to make updates to it based on user actions or changes in your cloud service. In those situations, you should copy the database from the app package location into your local storage folder and then open it from there. This can be done in two lines of code by using the Windows Runtime storage APIs.

```
StorageFile sf =
      await Package.Current.InstalledLocation.GetFileAsync("Earthquakes.sdf");

await sf.CopyAsync(ApplicationData.Current.LocalFolder);
```

Note The names of the schemes used to reference well-known app directories in some of the .NET APIs for Windows Phone have some confusing overlaps with the schemes used in Windows Runtime APIs. In .NET APIs like LINQ-to-SQL, the *isostore* scheme refers to the app's local storage, whereas the *appdata* scheme refers to the app package. In the Windows Runtime, *ms-appdata* refers to local storage, whereas *ms-appx* refers to the app package.

Again, because the app package location is read-only, you can only copy the database file from the package into the app's local storage. It is not possible to move it. This means that the original copy of the database file remains in the app package, unused and taking up space, so you should avoid copying reference databases into local storage unless you actually believe you will need to update it.

Reference databases and encryption

Windows Phone makes it possible for apps to specify a password when creating the database. The password is passed as a parameter in the constructor for the *DataContext* instance used to initially generate the database file.

```
SecretDataContext sdc =
      new SecretDataContext("Data Source=isostore:/secret.sdf;Password=pw.");
```

After a database has been created with a password, all subsequent *DataContext* objects used to connect to it must provide the same password to access its data. In addition, the inclusion of a password in the connection string automatically triggers encryption of the database file using a key that is based on the password. In Windows Phone 7.1, it was possible to create a password-protected (and thus encrypted) database and include it in an app package as a reference database.

However, as part of the migration to Windows Phone 8, the Natural Language Support (NLS) version changed, requiring SQLCE to recompute database indexes to ensure proper sorting across all Windows Phone languages. Because index information is stored within the database file itself, it is not possible to perform these updates without access to the app password. As a result, reading an encrypted database directly from the app package is no longer supported. Instead, apps should copy those databases to their local storage folder, as shown earlier.

Maximizing LINQ-to-SQL performance

As an API which originated in the .NET Framework, the original execution environment for LINQ-to-SQL was fairly different from the context that it runs in on Windows Phone. For example, in desktop and server environments, it is quite common for multiple callers to be accessing the database at the same time, so it was important for LINQ-to-SQL to provide a robust solution for dealing with conflicts. At the same time, the resource constraints are not generally as tight in desktop and server environments as they are on the phone. As a result, it is common for app developers getting started with LINQ-to-SQL on the phone to see higher than expected memory usage and slower than expected query performance. Thankfully, there are numerous ways to optimize the memory usage and performance of your LINQ-to-SQL code by using a few simple techniques.

Minimizing memory usage

The key to minimizing the amount of memory used by LINQ-to-SQL in your app is to limit the number and lifetime of materialized entities as much as possible. In particular, it is important to understand how to use the *DataContext* object.

Recall that the *DataContext* is both a bridge to the database and a cache for the entities that have been queried from the database (or are about to be added to it). On the surface, the *DataContext* simply exposes a set of object collections for the entities that have been queried, but in the background it is maintaining detailed information about changes that the app has made to those entities so that those modifications can be persisted back to the database correctly when the app calls *SubmitChanges*. The *DataContext* keeps track of those changes by maintaining two copies of a given entity, the original version and the modified version. When the app calls *SubmitChanges*, the *DataContext* can simply compare the two objects and generate the appropriate SQL Update statement to persist the changes to the database. Of course, in many cases, the app will only modify a handful of the entities returned from a query, so it would be inefficient to keep two copies of every object just in case a change might be made. It would be much better to only create the copy when it is known that a change is going to be made. Providing this notification is the role of the *INotifyPropertyChanging* interface that was presented earlier. If an entity implements *INotifyPropertyChanging*, the *DataContext* will wait for the *PropertyChanging* event before starting to track changes for that entity, cutting memory consumption significantly.

In some cases, there might be no opportunity for edits at all. For instance, a weather app might read a cached forecast from a database and display it on screen. Because we haven't yet figured out how to reliably change the weather, there isn't much need to support edits in this case. In such situations, you can simply set the *ObjectTrackingEnabled* property of the *DataContext* to false and turn off all change tracking.

```
LibraryDataContext library = new LibraryDataContext(LibraryDataContext.ConnectionString);

library.ObjectTrackingEnabled = false;
var readOnlyBooks = library.Books;
```

If you do need to perform updates, you should focus on keeping your *DataContext* objects highly scoped so that any queried entities can be garbage-collected as soon as you finish making your changes. Where possible, we recommend encapsulating database updates within a *using* statement so that the *DataContext* and associated entities are always automatically disposed.

```
using(LibraryDataContext library = new LibraryDataContext(LibraryDataContext.ConnectionString))
{
    // query entities
    // perform updates
}
```

Speeding up batch updates

A common task for apps using a database is to download new data from a cloud service, parse it, and then update the local database to reflect the changes. You can improve the performance of these updates by several orders of magnitude by adding a version column to your entities, like so:

```
[Table]
class VersionedBook
{
     [Column(IsPrimaryKey = true, DbType = "INT NOT NULL Identity", IsDbGenerated = true)]
     internal int BookId { get; private set; }

     [Column(IsVersion = true)]
     private Binary Version;

     [Column]
     public string Author { get; set; }

// remainder of Book definition omitted
}
```

Because LINQ-to-SQL follows a model of optimistic concurrency, any given *DataContext* can never be sure that there have not been changes made to the database since the last query was performed. As a result, the *DataContext* needs to verify the state of its cache whenever an update is performed so that it can raise a *ChangeConflictException* to the app if something has changed. By default, the framework performs this check through brute force by comparing every property of every impacted entity. As you might imagine, this can be slow. The version column instructs the database to track a version for the database record that corresponds to the entity being updated. Because the version is incremented every time the record is modified in any way, LINQ-to-SQL can simply compare the version on the cached entity to the version in the database to determine if anything has changed, which is a much faster operation.

The *LinqToSQL_Performance* solution in the sample code includes a direct comparison of running the same update operation on an entity with the version attribute and one without it. As you can see in Figure 10-12, the difference is dramatic.

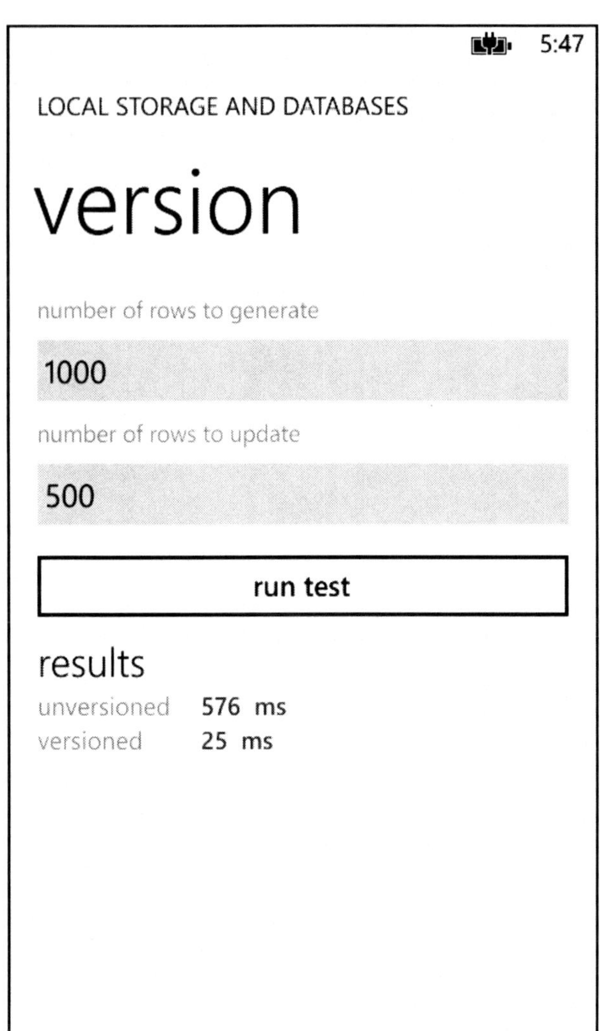

FIGURE 10-12 You can add a version column to all your entities for an easy performance gain on large updates.

SQLite

Windows Phone 8 adds support for the popular open-source database engine, SQLite. SQLite offers several key advantages over LINQ-to-SQL and SQLCE, such as the following:

- SQLite is accessible from native code.
- It is supported on most modern operating systems, allowing for code reuse across platforms.
- It provides higher performance for certain types of operations.

Acquiring SQLite for Windows Phone

Even though the SQLite component is not built in to the core platform, it can be added easily to your app package directly from Visual Studio. On the Tools menu, choose Extension And Updates to open the Extensions And Updates dialog box. Use the search box in the upper-right corner of the dialog box to search for "SQLite", as shown in Figure 10-13. Click the download button and complete the short installation process. You will be required to restart Visual Studio when the installation is complete.

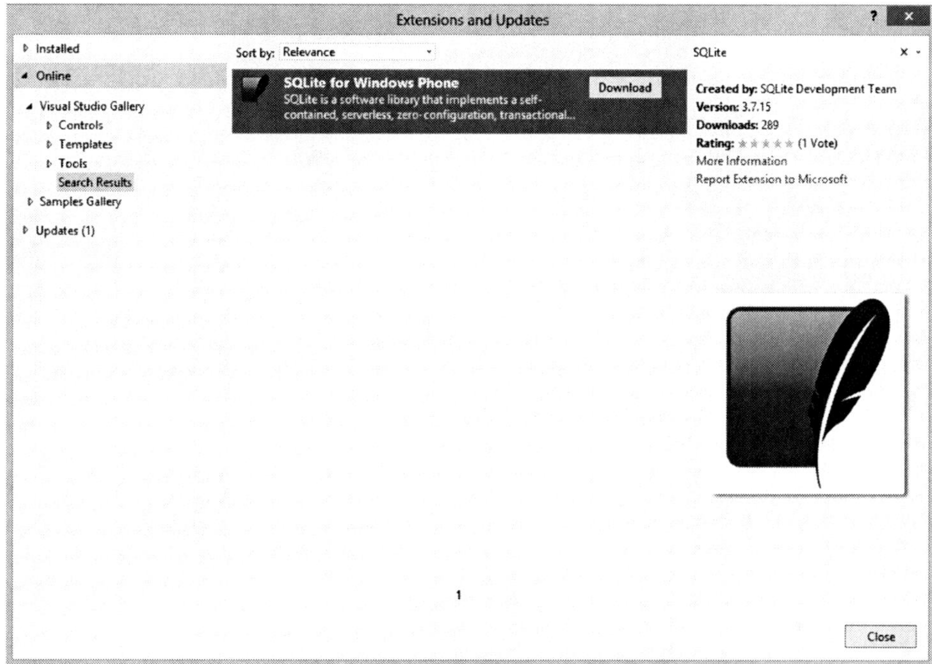

FIGURE 10-13 SQLite for Windows Phone is available as a free download through the Extensions And Updates dialog box.

The SQLite for Windows Phone package includes all the native headers and libraries required to use the SQLite database engine in a Windows Phone project.

Note As with LINQ-to-SQL, the SQLite framework is far too large to cover in any depth here. Unlike LINQ-to-SQL, however, the version of the SQLite engine available for Windows Phone does not differ in any significant ways from the latest versions available on other platforms. Thus, any documentation, code samples, or best practices that you find for SQLite should apply on Windows Phone.

Using SQLite from managed code

Because the core SQLite engine only provides native APIs, you will need to wrap database access in a C++ Windows Runtime component if you want to use it from managed code. There are several high-quality generic wrappers available on CodePlex, so you should consider using one of these unless you have a specific need to write the logic yourself. The following blog post walks through using the SQLite WinRT wrapper library: *http://blogs.windows.com/windows_phone/b/wpdev/archive/2013/05/30/sqlite-winrt-wrapper-for-windows-phone.aspx*.

Summary

The data that an app creates and manages is what makes it personal to the user. Although web services are increasingly the provider of that data, there are virtually no apps on the phone that do not need to create and manage some amount of data locally. In this chapter, you learned about the different options for storing settings, files, and structured data in Windows Phone apps, including the isolated storage APIs and the Windows Runtime storage APIs for files, and LINQ-to-SQL and SQLite for structured data.

PART II

Windows Phone 7 to Windows Phone 8

CHAPTER 11

App publication

Developing an app obviously runs through various phases, and you should be designing and adjusting your app with the final certification process in mind throughout the development cycle. This chapter walks you through the final preparation tasks before submitting your app to the Windows Phone Store, as well as the submission and certification process itself. We then look at how to submit updates, beta releases, multiversion issues and selective device targeting. Finally, we consider the feedback mechanisms available to you, especially in the form of Windows Phone Store reports and analytics.

Preparing for publication

Before submitting your app to the Windows Phone Store for certification and publication, you are strongly encouraged to prepare for publication by using the Store Test Kit. This helps to ensure that you have all the right pieces in place that are required for publication and that your app is in a fit state for certification. The Store Test Kit is available on the Project menu in Microsoft Visual Studio (see Figure 11-1). You must have your app solution open and the project (or any node under the project) selected in Solution Explorer. You must also have built a Release-build XAP before running the Store Test Kit; this mirrors the real Windows Phone Store publication process for which a Release-build XAP is required.

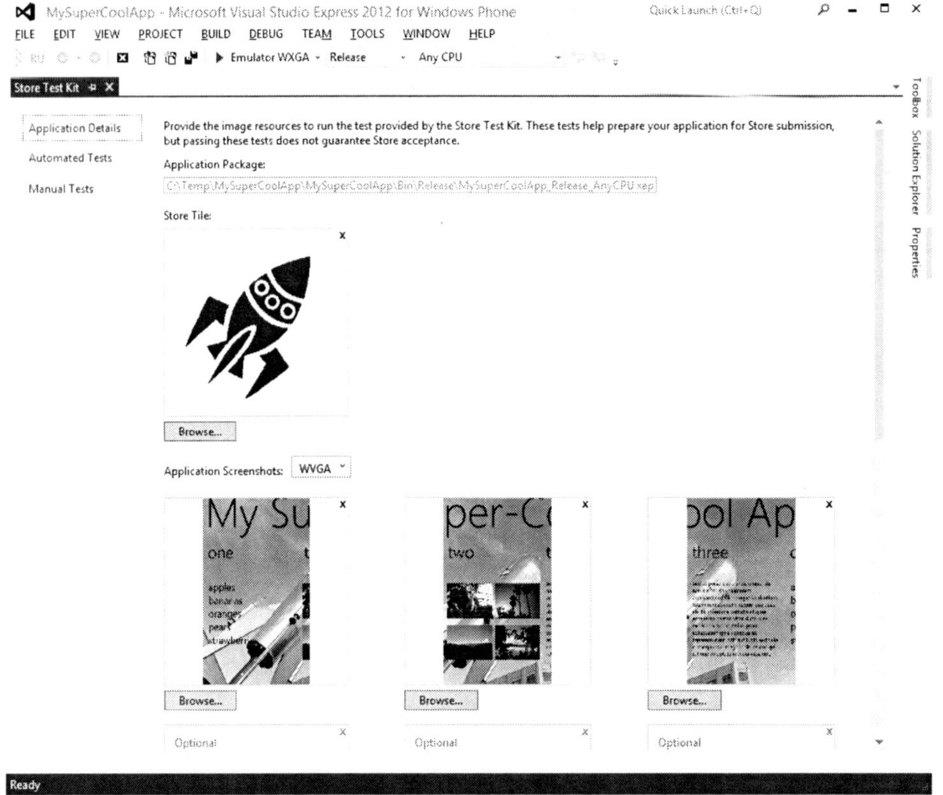

FIGURE 11-1 You are strongly encouraged to use the Store Test Kit in Visual Studio prior to publication.

The Store Test Kit uses rules and test cases that are periodically synchronized with the rules and test cases used in the full Windows Phone Store publication process. Upon startup, the Store Test Kit makes a web service call to the Windows Phone Store to check for updated rules or test cases, and if needed, it will prompt you to install the updates if it finds any. There are four parts to the Store Test Kit:

- **Application Details** This is where you provide a set of required and optional image files for the Windows Phone Store.
- **Automated Tests** These tests validate your XAP and the size and type of image files you provided.
- **Application Analysis** The Store Test Kit provides a link to run a monitoring session on your app.
- **Manual Tests** You can use this tab to track your manual testing results against a set of test cases.

On the Application Details tab, you specify the app tile and screenshot images used in the Windows Phone Store. These must all be in PNG format, without transparency, and with the sizes as noted in Table 11-1. You must supply the Windows Phone Store tile and at least one screenshot for each resolution your app supports (as defined in the app manifest). You can also supply up to seven additional (optional) screenshots.

TABLE 11-1 The Windows Store image requirements

Image	Required size in pixels
Store tile	300x300
Application screenshot WVGA	480x800
Application screenshot 720p	720x1280
Application screenshot WXGA	768x1280

When you have completed the Application Details, you can run the Automated Tests. These tests validate the static Windows Phone Store requirements; that is, they validate the size of your XAP and any additional content files, the app icon, tile images, and screenshots. Your XAP package must contain the following:

- A valid Windows Phone app manifest file, named *WMAppManifest.xml*. This must contain a *Title* attribute within the *App* element. The *Title* attribute must not be empty, and it must be the same as the title you subsequently specify during the final submission process.
- For managed apps, a valid Microsoft .NET app manifest file, named *AppManifest.xaml*, and the assembly files as specified in the *AppManifest.xaml* file.
- Support for at least one screen resolution.

The maximum size of the XAP package file is 225 MB for Windows Phone 7.1, and 1 GB for Windows Phone 8.

The Automated Tests tab also provides a button for running app analysis. Chapter 12, "Profiling and diagnostics," discusses this tool in detail, and you should use all three features of the tool (execution, memory, and monitoring) at multiple stages during development. When you reach the end of the cycle prior to publication, you should run the monitoring feature of the tool one last time. This feature examines your app as you run it and exercise its functionality. Its focus is on app performance and quality. The tests look for certain specific behaviors, including that your app starts up within the published maximum required time (5 seconds to first screen, 20 seconds to user interface (UI) responsiveness); the peak memory is within published limits (90 MB); you handle all exceptions so that they do not propagate out of your app; you do not interfere with the Back button behavior in an unexpected way; and the battery consumption of your app is within reasonable limits.

You can run these tests either on the emulator or on a connected device; however, not surprisingly, performance on the emulator is not a good representation of physical device performance, so you should ultimately run these tests on a device. In fact, you should ideally test on several different devices, if you can, because there can be variability in the user experience across different devices. You can also run the tool on either a Release or Debug build, but again, for the purposes of preparing for publication, you should run it on a Release build.

This is an opportunity to test your app thoroughly. You should exercise all code paths, navigate to all pages, and perform all operations that the user might perform. This especially includes scenarios at the edges of your app's control, such as the use of Launchers and Choosers, the behavior when there's an incoming phone call or Short Message Service (SMS), fast app switching, and tombstoning. Testing at this stage should be destructive; your aim is to try to cause failures in the app so that you can catch them before submitting to the Windows Phone Store. Each time you run the monitoring tests, a fresh set of test results is persisted to hard disk in a subfolder of your solution folder that is named with the current date/time, making it easy for you to open any of them subsequently. This is useful for historical comparisons and correlation with bug fixes. Keep in mind that when the tool parses the logs, it requires a Release build of your app for reference. If you run the monitoring tool and subsequently delete the targets, you can always rebuild your app to provide this reference when you later open the log.

The Manual Tests tab provides about 60 specific test cases, which you are asked to work through manually. Each test case has a link to the specific certification requirement on MSDN. The Store Test Kit does not monitor these tests; rather, they are for your benefit to help guide you through a comprehensive set of scenarios for which you should be testing. These tests are designed to match the tests performed during Windows Phone Store publication. Be aware that some of the tests might not apply to your app (for example, your app might not make use of game-specific or media-specific features, background audio, background transfers, and so on). For tests that don't apply, simply leave them as pending. The aim here is to ensure that you test all cases that do apply and that your app passes these tests. It is obviously in your own interests to flag tests as failed until you fix the cause of the failure. Thus, you should use the test kit here as a bug-tracking tool, as demonstrated in Figure 11-2.

Note Visual Studio Update 2 includes unit testing support for Windows Phone solutions. As of this writing, this is available in Community Technology Preview (CTP) form. Check the Microsoft downloads site for details regarding the latest release.

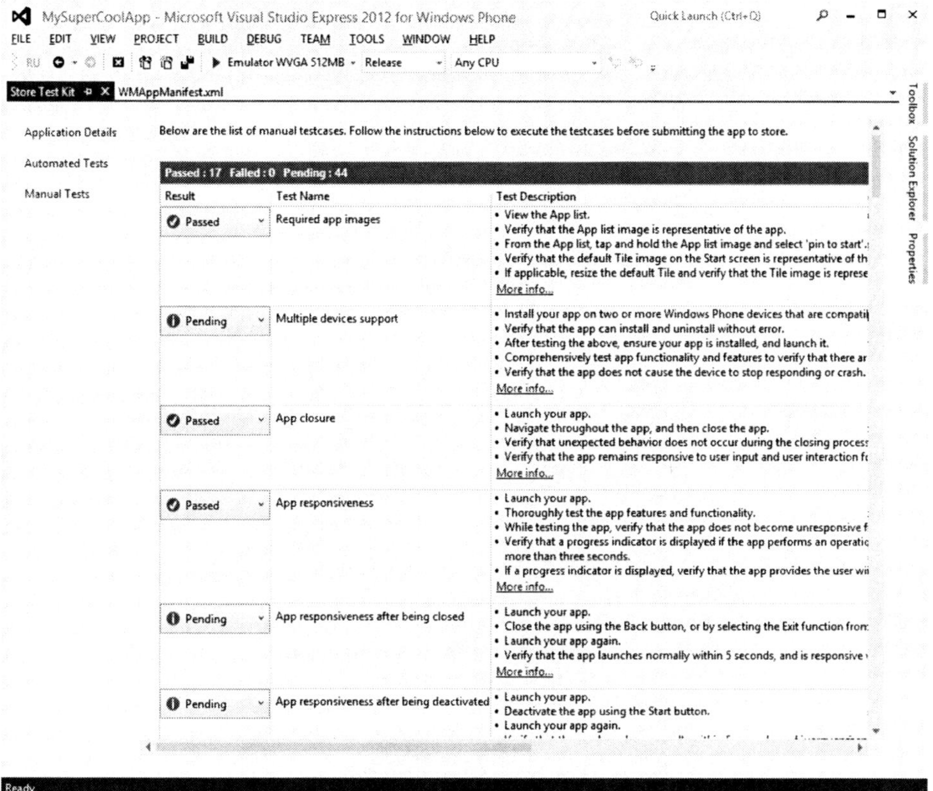

FIGURE 11-2 You can use the Manual Tests tab as a bug-tracking tool.

When you run the test kit, it creates a folder named SubmissionInfo in your project and then copies any Windows Phone Store image files you specified into this folder. It also creates two XML files: *Settings.xml* (a simple list of the image files), and *ManualTestResults.xml* (logs the results of all manual tests run for the app). After you have added an image to the list in the Application Details tab, you can't remove it via the UI, although you can replace it with another image (so long as the new image has a different name). Alternatively, you can close the Test Kit, and edit the *Settings.xml* file directly, or you can simply delete it altogether so that the Store Test Kit can recreate it from scratch the next time you run it. When you've completed all tests, you can also use the SubmissionInfo folder as your source for images when you finally submit your app to the Windows Phone Store.

The publication process

During development, you typically deploy your app to developer-unlocked phones, but normal users will install your app on retail phones. There are actually two supported ways to install an app onto a retail phone (that is, a phone that has not been developer-unlocked): via the Windows Phone Store, and via a company hub app. Company hub apps are discussed in Chapter 22, "Enterprise apps." The standard mechanism is via the Windows Phone Store. For developers, the portal to the Windows

Phone Store is called the Windows Phone Dev Center, which you can access by going to *http://dev.windowsphone.com*. When you submit your app to the Windows Phone Store, it goes through multiple stages, and you can track the progress of the submission through eight reported stages on your dashboard, as indicated in Figure 11-3. The textual and graphical data you supply as part of your submission is validated up front when you submit it. Therefore, failures at any later stage will be the result of certification failures. If the submission does fail any of these tests, you need to resubmit your XAP and start the process again.

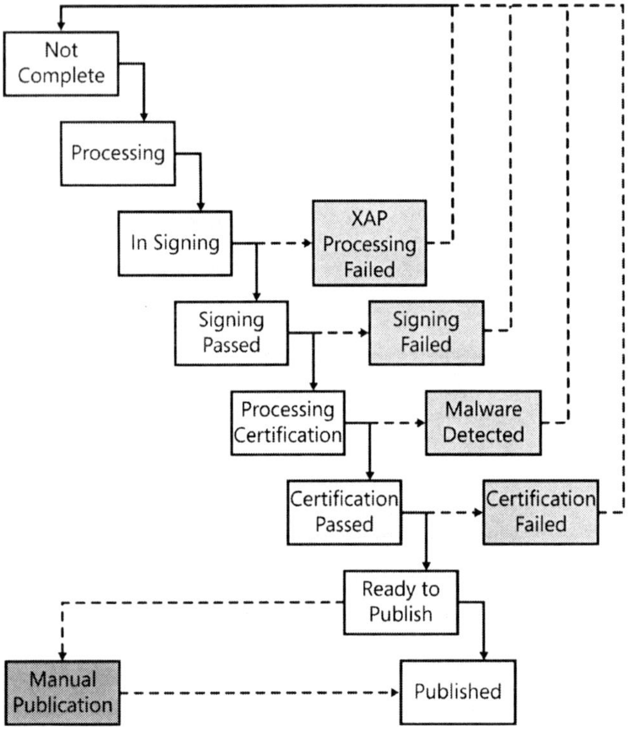

FIGURE 11-3 There are eight distinct stages in the publication process.

You can't resubmit a XAP after it has already started going through testing. If you resubmit a XAP at any other time, this will obviously restart the certification process. There are other data changes which will also trigger recertification, including anything which requires re-evaluating your data for acceptable content, including the following:

- Changes to your app category
- Changes to any game rating certificates or to target markets that have more strict content rules
- Changes to any descriptions, tiles, or screenshots

Note When your app is published, the XAP is encrypted. This applies to all apps, both 7.1 and 8.0 versions. Prior to the release of Windows Phone 8 and the new version of the Windows Phone Store, XAPs were not encrypted, so developers often mitigated the risk to their intellectual property by obfuscating their code. This is no longer necessary. Also, for managed apps, your assemblies are precompiled in the Windows Phone Store to high-quality ARM code before they are downloaded and deployed on end-user devices. This avoids the need to just-in-time (JIT) compile the assemblies at runtime, which therefore improves startup and execution speed on the device, while at the same time reducing battery consumption. This also applies to all Windows Phone Store apps, both 7.1 and 8.0 versions. Another new Windows Phone Store feature is that each app now gets a link by which users can download the XAP to their computer and then install it locally. The purpose of this is to support installing apps to removable microSD cards, which some Windows Phone devices support.

When you're ready to submit your app to the Windows Phone Store, you must log on to the Dev Center by using your Microsoft Account (formerly known as your Windows Live ID). On your dashboard, you'll find a button to submit an app. If you're continuing a previously saved submission, you can select the submission from the list on your dashboard, as shown in Figure 11-4.

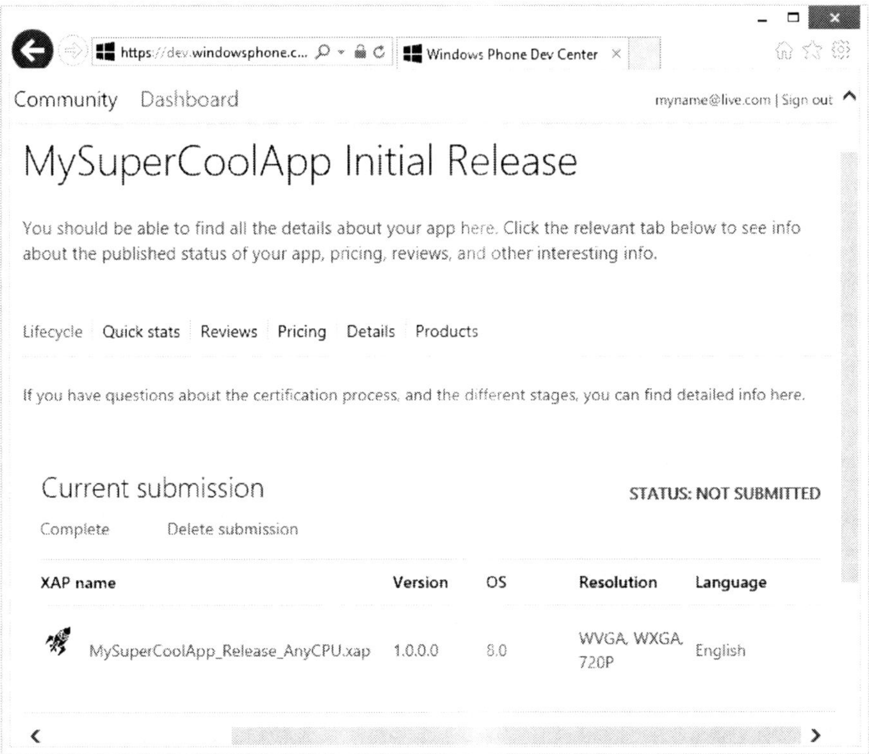

FIGURE 11-4 You can select any of your published or in-progress app submissions from your dashboard.

The submission tool is mostly intuitive. There are two forms for required information (basic app info, your XAP and the Windows Phone Store images), and three further forms for optional information (in-app advertising, market selection and custom pricing, and map services tokens).

As you fill in the forms, you can save at any point. This gives you the opportunity to pause if you need to and go back to complete the submission later. Or, you can abandon the process at any point before final submission. If you need to, you can completely delete the submission. If you want to start again from scratch and use the same app alias, you can also delete the old entry for the app alias from your Dev Center dashboard. Everything remains editable and under your control until you click the Submit button.

The first page (see Figure 11-5) asks you to provide the following information:

- **App alias** This is not the app title, and it is not a name that customers will see. Rather, it is a name that you can use to identify this specific app in the Dev Center. This is required, and it is useful if you have many apps.
- **Category and subcategory** These are the groupings under which you want your app to be listed. Click the respective list boxes to choose from the categories supplied on the Windows Phone Store at the time of submission. For some categories, such as the tools + productivity category, there are no subcategories. If your app is a game, you must specify the games category.
- **Pricing** The pricing section and primary offer currency (the default is United States dollars). You can choose $0.00 if your app is free.

Figure 11-6 depicts the bottom half of the first page, on which you specify the market distribution and publishing details. For distribution, the default is to publish to all markets except those with stricter content rules. However, if you're sure your app meets all certification requirements of all markets, you can specify distribution to all markets, instead. This relates to section 3 of the certification requirements, that covers formal certification for games as well as potentially offensive content for all apps. Your app must not contain any content that could be deemed offensive in any market you target for distribution. Content might be offensive in certain countries/regions because of local laws or cultural norms. Examples of potentially offensive content in certain countries/regions include, but are not limited to, the following:

- People in revealing clothing or sexually suggestive poses, sexual, or bathroom humor
- Religious references
- Alcohol, tobacco, weapons, and drug references
- Defamatory, libelous, slanderous, threatening or discriminatory content, or excessive profanity
- Simulated or actual gambling

- Disputed territory or region references
- Enabling access to content or services that are illegal in the country or region
- Realistic or gratuitous violence, sexual violence, glorification of crimes

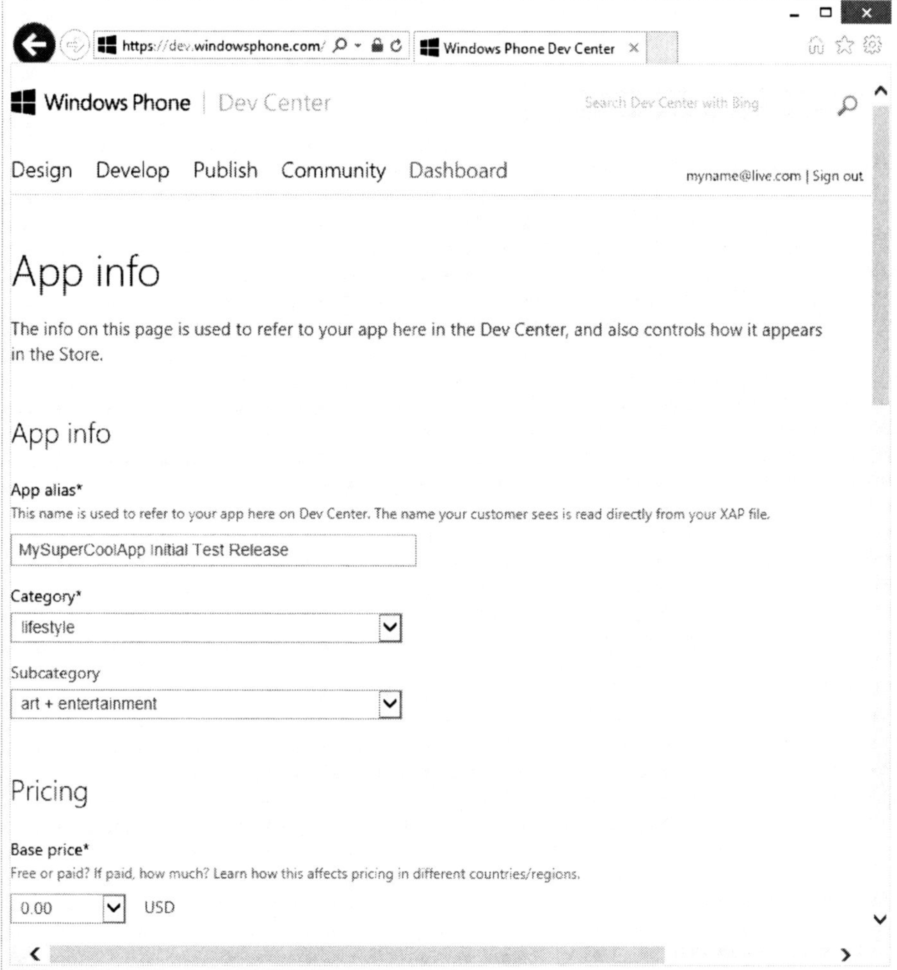

FIGURE 11-5 The first page of the submission tool, on which you enter basic app info.

Note that the default is to publish your app automatically as soon as it passes certification. If you want to control when your app becomes public, you can specify that on this page. The final option on this page is for setting up an authenticated web service for sending push notifications (this is discussed in Chapter 14, "Tiles and notifications").

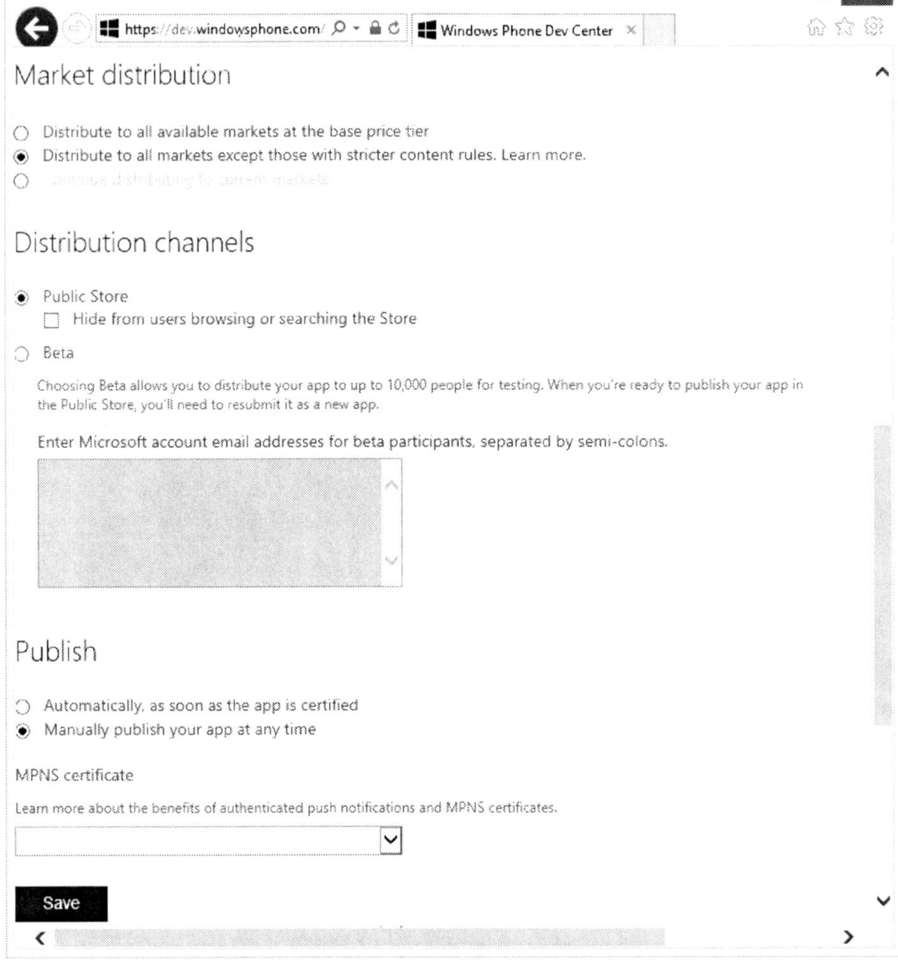

FIGURE 11-6 You also specify market distribution and publishing details on the App Info page.

On the second page, you upload your XAP and provide a Windows Phone Store description. When you upload your XAP, the Dev Center tool parses it to extract the supported operating system (OS) version, languages, resolutions, and capabilities, as illustrated in Figure 11-7. The XAP version number is an arbitrary value that you supply manually; this is not extracted from the XAP, and it need not be the same as the version in the app manifest (nor the assembly or file versions).

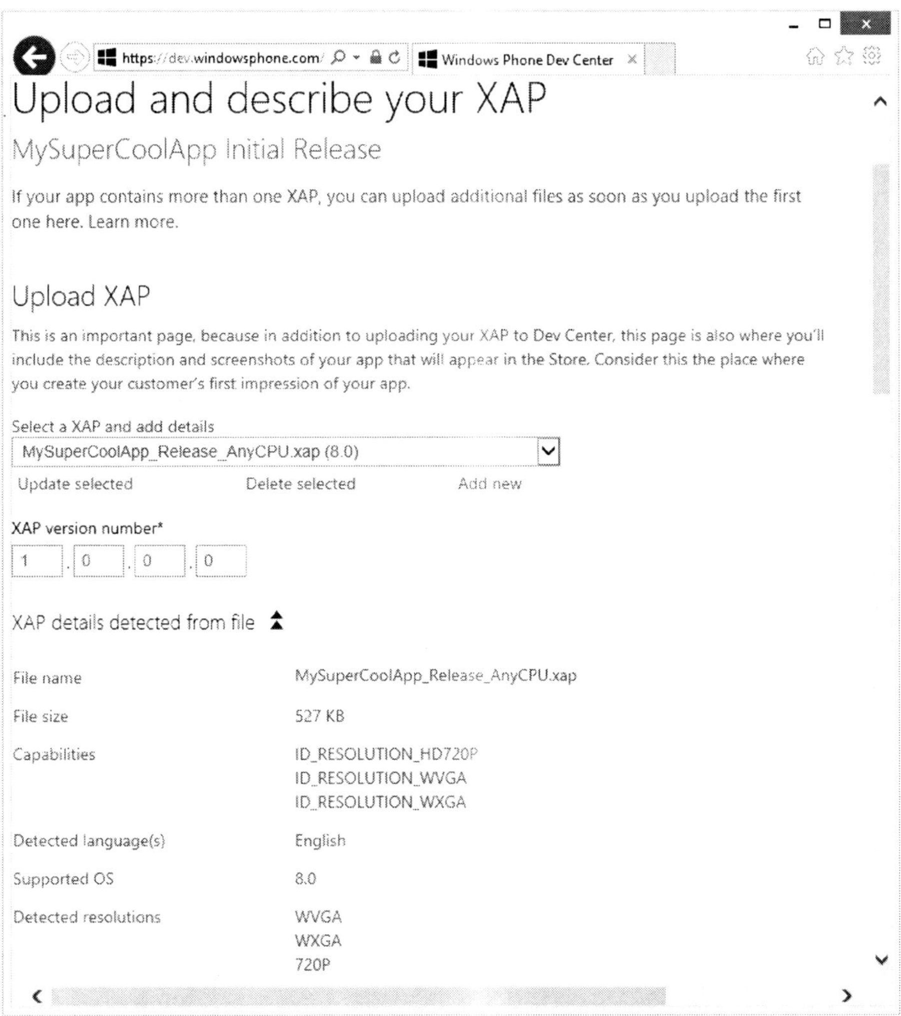

FIGURE 11-7 The Upload And Describe Your XAP page is where you upload your XAP.

A XAP can contain multiple languages. These are detected by the tool, and for each language you must then provide a description and keywords (see Figure 11-8). The description here is not the same as the description in the *WMAppManifest.xaml* (which is restricted to 255 characters). The Windows Phone Store description is limited to 2,000 characters. The keywords are arbitrary, but they should certainly reflect the topic or nature of your app. You can supply up to five, but you must supply at least one.

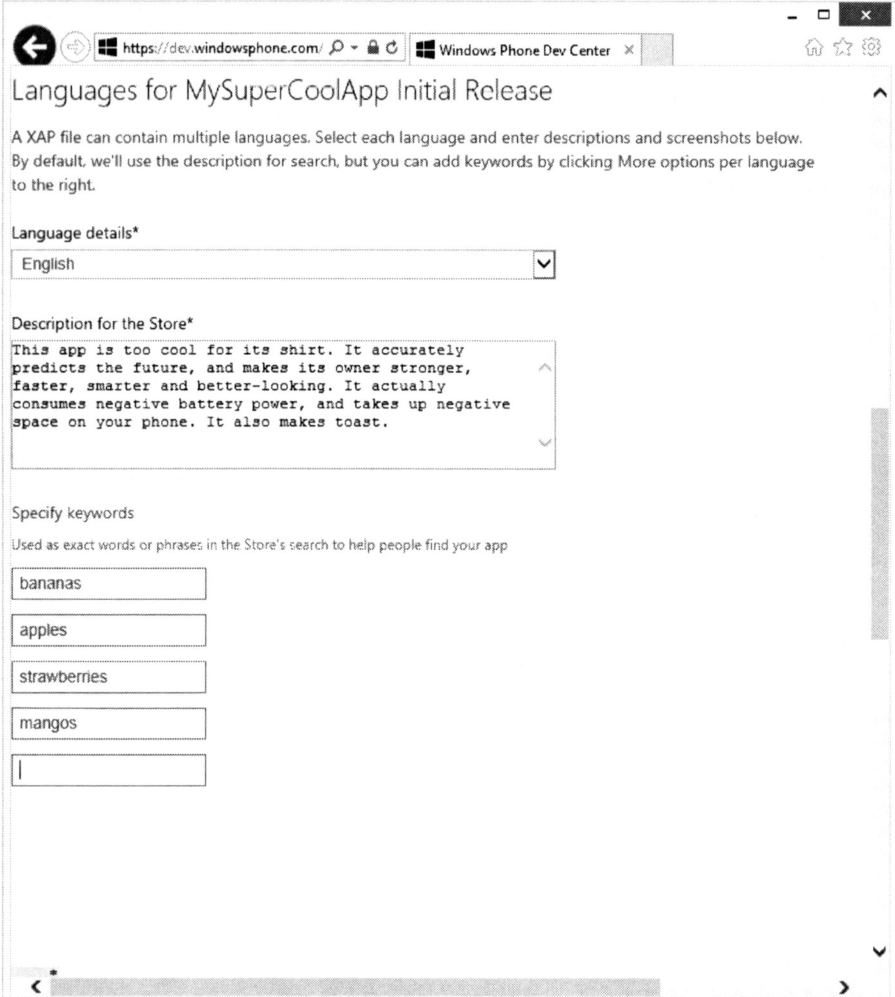

FIGURE 11-8 You must provide a description for each supported language.

Finally on this page, you upload the required artwork, which are exactly the same images you specified in the Store Test Kit: a 300x300 pixel Windows Phone Store icon and at least one screenshot for each supported resolution (these are always portrait even if your app runs only in landscape). You can also provide up to seven additional screenshots for each resolution. In addition, you can provide a 1000x800-pixel background image, which will be used if your app is designated as the feature app in the Windows Phone Store at any time. The bottom of the Upload page is depicted in Figure 11-9.

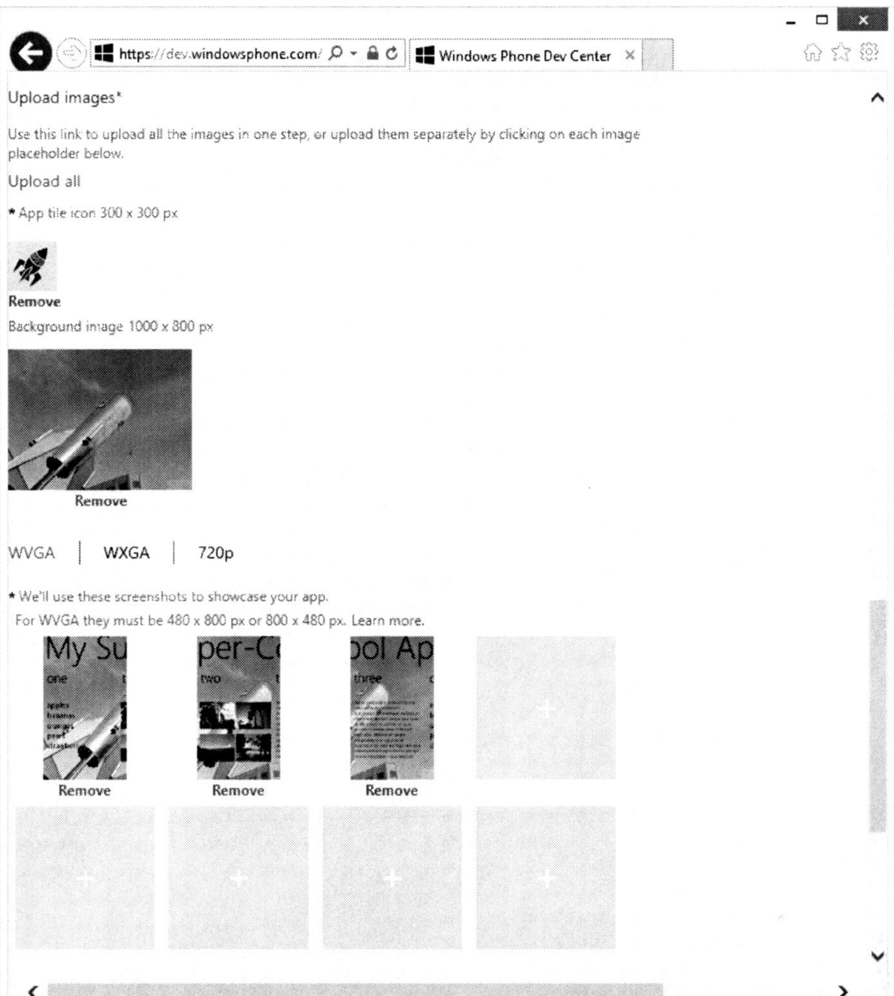

FIGURE 11-9 You upload the same images that you specified in the Store Test Kit.

Notice that the Upload page also includes two optional sections that are not immediately obvious. They're over on the right side of the page, accessed via drop-down arrows (see Figure 11-10). Select the Technical Exception check box in case your app requires an exception to the certification approval process for technical reasons. You would not normally select this option, because doing so will slow down the approval process and approval could be withheld. There are very few scenarios for which you would need to apply for a technical exception; for example, if your app interacts with third-party hardware (perhaps a media streaming device or a Bluetooth accessory).

The Certification Notes text box is where you can provide special testing instructions for the testing and certification of your application. You can use this if it is not clear from the UI. This is limited to 1,000 characters. If your app behaves in an unexpected way in any scenario, you should document it here so that the testers don't fail it simply because they don't understand how it's supposed to work. This is also the right place to provide dummy credentials if your app requires an account for any operations. The second optional section (More Options Per Language) is where you can provide legal and privacy URLs and a support email address, on a per-language basis.

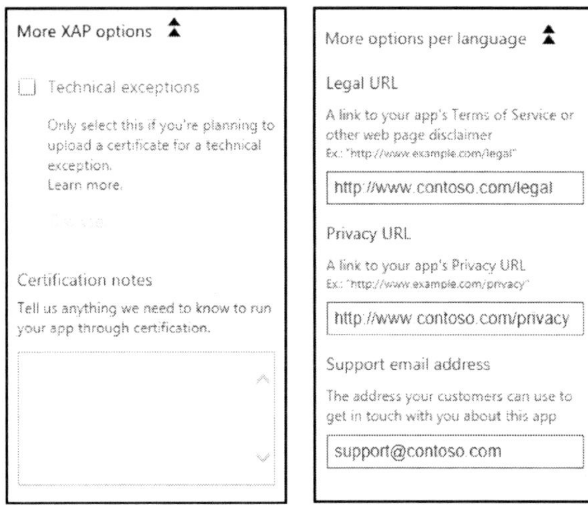

FIGURE 11-10 The Upload page includes two drop-down sections, which are optional.

When you're done filling in the submission form—assuming that you haven't missed any required field—you are returned to your dashboard, where your new app will be listed as pending certification.

When you submit your app, it goes through both static validation and automated testing, to verify that it meets all the policies and requirements. If it passes certification, it is repackaged and signed before it is made available to the Windows Phone Store. The Windows Phone Application Certification Requirements are described at *http://aka.ms/WinPhone8DevInternals/MSDN.*

You can cancel a submission before or after it has been certified, but you cannot do anything to it while it is actually going through the certification process.

Dev Center reports

The Dev Center also provides reports on your app, including the number of downloads, payment history (for non-free applications), ratings and reviews, and crash dumps (if any). To see these reports, log on to the Dev Center, go to your dashboard, and then click the Reports link. The reports page shows charts and tables of daily downloads and crash counts for all your applications, as shown in Figure 11-11. You can use the Export link, to download the report in Microsoft Excel format.

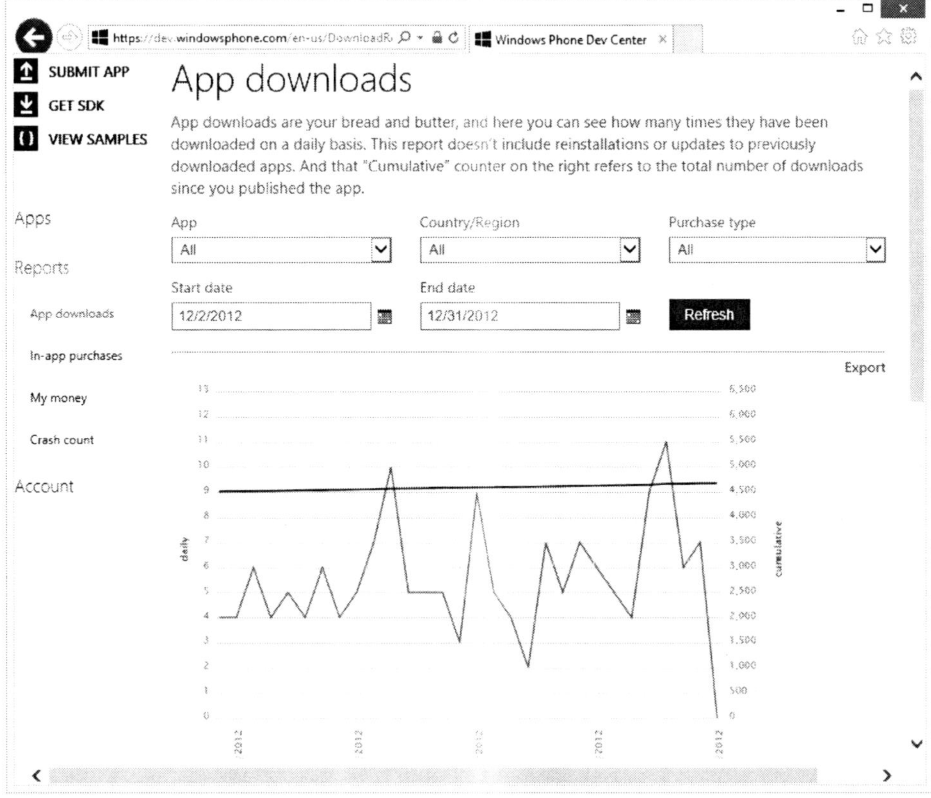

FIGURE 11-11 You can get app download reports on the Dev Center.

It is a certification requirement that your app should not allow any unhandled exceptions to propagate out of the app. However, the testing done during the ingestion process is not completely exhaustive, so it is possible to miss some code path where an exception might escape. This means that your app might pass certification even if it does throw unhandled exceptions. To assist in mitigation efforts, whenever an app crashes, a tiny crash dump is collected and sent back to Microsoft. This eventually makes its way to the Windows Phone Store servers, where a summary is produced and made available to the app publisher for retrieval. Figure 11-12 shows a crash count report in the Dev Center.

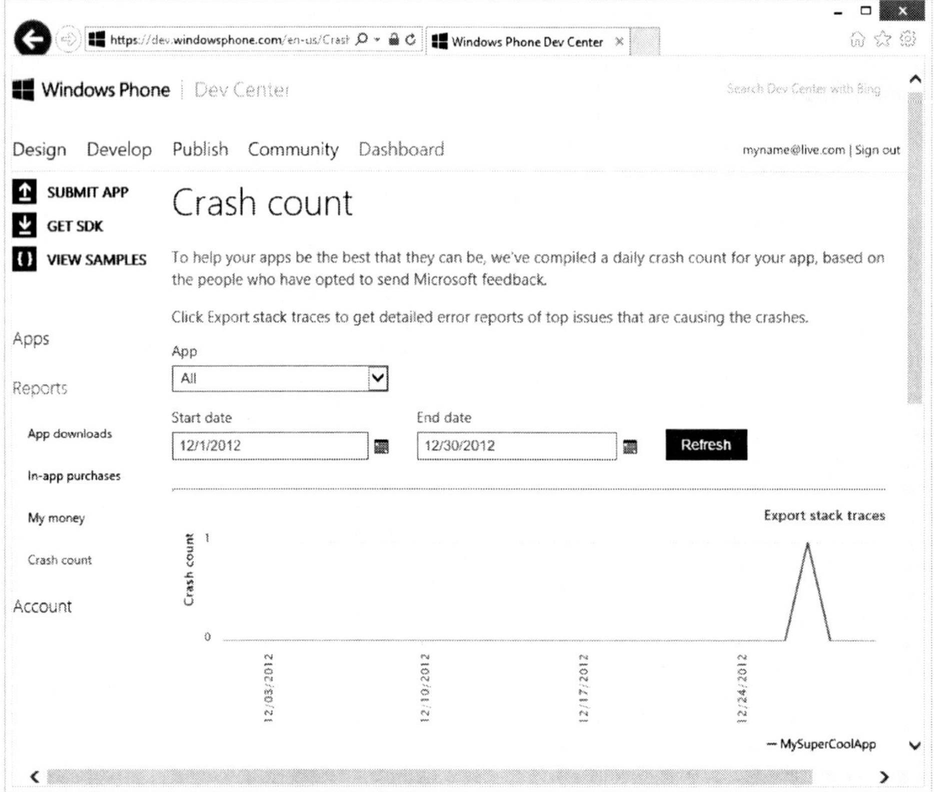

FIGURE 11-12 The Dev Center provides download and crash count reports.

You can use the Export Stack Traces link to download any crash in Excel spreadsheet format: the spreadsheets will include the stack traces for each crash. Although these don't provide very extensive information, they are still quite useful for diagnosing the cause of the crash.

Updates

You can update the Windows Phone Store catalog information for your app at any time. This includes the descriptions, artwork, keywords, pricing and regional availability, and so on. Although this goes through the same ingestion pipeline as a full submission, if you do not update the XAP, the time-consuming steps of validating and testing the XAP are skipped, so this kind of update is relatively quick. You can also upload a new version of your XAP at any time, and in all cases, you use the same submission form and upload mechanism. Just as with a full submission, you can check the progress of an update in Windows Phone Store through the portal.

When you perform an incremental build of your app in Visual Studio and run it in the emulator or on a device, the fresh XAP replaces the previous version. However, it does not replace any data stored in isolated storage. On the other hand, if you perform a clean-and-rebuild, this does wipe out isolated storage. This is because a clean-and-rebuild performs a complete uninstall/reinstall, as opposed to an update. In the Windows Phone Store, when you submit an update, this behaves the same way as an incremental build: it replaces the XAP, but does not touch isolated storage. The only way that isolated storage is automatically cleaned out is when the user uninstalls the app.

So, when you publish an update to your app, you might want to clean out isolated storage yourself upon the first run of the updated app. Alternatively, if you want to keep the old data, you might need to make allowances for any changes in data schema that you have made. For example, you might want to convert all the old data to the new format upon first run. Be aware that this only applies to data stored in isolated storage files; it does not apply to app state or page state, which are not persisted across runs of the app.

Getting updates right is not always straightforward, particularly if you accommodate users skipping an update (for example, the user goes from version 1 to version 4 without installing versions 2 or 3). To thoroughly test update permutations, one strategy is that for every released version of the app, you generate a representative snapshot of data in the app (that is, perform downloads, save data, and so on) and then use the Isolated Storage Explorer tool from the SDK to copy this data off the device and archive it with the version of your app (in a folder, or if you're using source control, put it in there). Then, whenever you update your app, you can deploy the app, update the isolated storage with the archived copy for each previous version's files, and see what happens.

The system checks for updates for installed apps periodically; thus, there little reason for the developer to perform this check independently. Nonetheless, if you do want proactively to check for updates from within your app, you have a couple of options.

The platform includes the *MarketplaceDetailTask*, *MarketplaceHubTask*, *MarketplaceReviewTask* and *MarketplaceSearchTask* classes, which all represent Launchers that access the Windows Phone Store for a set of specific operations. Each one brings up a Windows Phone Store UI page for a specific task. There is no public Windows Phone Store API with which you can fetch data programmatically, without showing UI.

With that said, it is fairly easy to construct web requests to the Windows Phone Store to fetch metadata for a given app, assuming that you know what you're looking for. That might not be as simple as it sounds, however, because some of the values in your *WMAppManifest.xml* will be modified during Windows Phone Store ingestion. This includes the *Author*, *Publisher*, *Capabilities*, and—crucially—your app's *ProductID*.

Figure 11-13 shows a simple implementation of the key techniques in this approach (the *StoreInfo* solution in the sample code). This app fetches its page in the Windows Phone Store and compares the version number there with the current version number. If the Windows Phone Store version is higher, the app then launches the *MarketplaceDetailTask* so that the user can examine the information for the update. This is a fairly crude approach which involves mining the app's HTML page for interesting data, but this page will contain most of the Windows Phone Store data for your app, so it's a good way to retrieve all this data very simplistically.

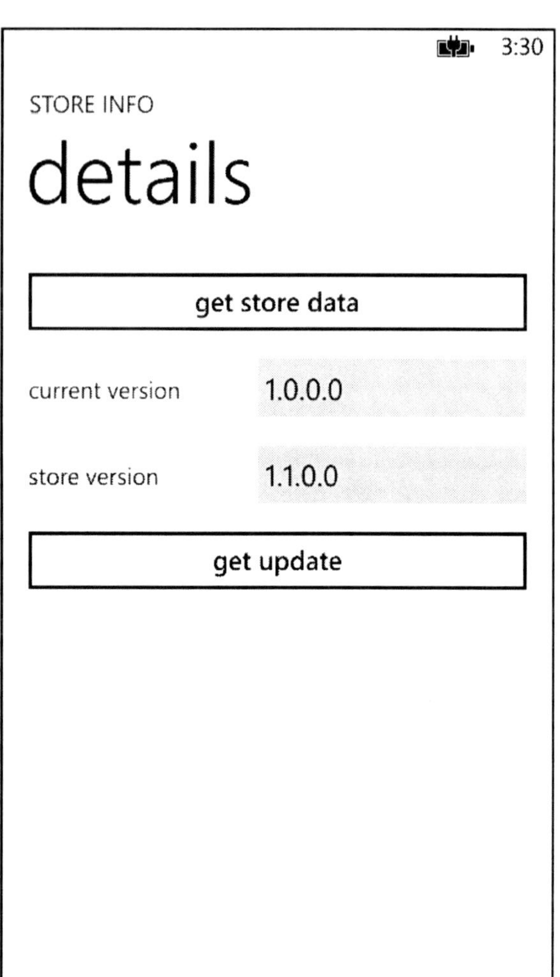

FIGURE 11-13 You can fetch information for an app from the Store with an *HttpWebRequest*.

The app constructs a simple *HttpWebRequest* for its own page in the Windows Phone Store. This is in the format "http://www.windowsphone.com/s?appid=*GUID*", where *GUID* is a placeholder for the app's *ProductId*.

```
private const string storeUrl = "http://www.windowsphone.com/s?appid=";
private const string appId = "3375b957-7d3e-4330-8bb7-3e0c28765432";

private void getData_Click(object sender, RoutedEventArgs e)
{
    HttpWebRequest webRequest =
        (HttpWebRequest)HttpWebRequest.Create(new Uri(storeUrl + appId, UriKind.Absolute));
    webRequest.BeginGetResponse(httpRequestCallback, webRequest);
}
```

This will return an HTML page for the app (assuming the *ProductId* is actually found in the Windows Phone Store). The app first gets the version of the currently-executing app. There are various ways you can achieve this, and one of the simplest is to retrieve the *AssemblyName*: of course, this assumes that your assembly version is the same as the version you specify in the app manifest. Next, the app retrieves the page HTML from the callback result and parses it for the version string.

HTML parsing is an arcane art: some developers prefer to do this via regular expressions, but this is an inherently fragile approach. Instead, there are plenty of third-party libraries to support this. An even simpler approach is to treat the HTML as a flat string, and simply scan it for the version substring. In this case, the string is in this format: "<span itemprop=\"softwareVersion\">*1.0.0.0*</span>", where *1.0.0.0* represents the version number. Keep in mind, however, that this could change, and a more sophisticated solution would be more resilient to such changes.

```
private const string versionElement = "<span itemprop=\"softwareVersion\">";
private const string spanEnd = "</span>";

private void httpRequestCallback(IAsyncResult result)
{
    AssemblyName assemblyName = new AssemblyName(Assembly.GetExecutingAssembly().FullName);
    HttpWebRequest request = (HttpWebRequest)result.AsyncState;
    using (WebResponse response = request.EndGetResponse(result))
    {
        using (StreamReader reader = new StreamReader(response.GetResponseStream()))
        {
            string htmlString = reader.ReadToEnd();
            int start = htmlString.IndexOf(versionElement) + versionElement.Length;
            int end = htmlString.IndexOf(spanEnd, start);
            if (start >= 0 && end > start)
            {
                string versionString = htmlString.Substring(start, end - start);
                Version storeVersion = null;
                Dispatcher.BeginInvoke(() =>
                {
                    if (Version.TryParse(versionString, out storeVersion))
                    {
                        current.Text = assemblyName.Version.ToString();
                        store.Text = storeVersion.ToString();
                    }
                    if (storeVersion > assemblyName.Version)
                    {
                        getUpdate.IsEnabled = true;
                    }
                });
            }
        }
    }
}
```

If the Windows Phone Store version is greater than the current version, the app enables the button to launch the *MarketplaceDetailsTask* so that the user can see the details for the update. If you don't provide the app's *ProductId* as the *ContentIdentifer* for the task, the task defaults to fetching the details page for the calling app. Obviously, for the first version of your app, in the early stages of development, your app will not be in the Windows Phone Store, so you can use an alternative *ProductId* for a published Windows Phone Store app for testing purposes in this scenario.

```
private void getUpdate_Click(object sender, RoutedEventArgs e)
{
    MarketplaceDetailTask storeTask = new MarketplaceDetailTask();
    storeTask.ContentIdentifier = appId;
    storeTask.ContentType = MarketplaceContentType.Applications;
    storeTask.Show();
}
```

Beta testing

The Windows Phone Store supports a simple beta testing mode for applications. When you first submit your app, you have the option to make it available to only a selected set of users. You choose the users by specifying their Microsoft Account email addresses in the submission form. You can enter up to 10,000 users for beta testing (a huge improvement over Windows Phone 7, for which you could only support 100 beta users). When you do this, the Dev Center sends you an email containing the download link for your app, which you can then send to your selected users. The Windows Phone Store hides the app from general availability, making it visible for download to only those users whom you selected. You need to handle test results from your beta users directly; there is no Windows Phone Store mechanism to support feedback in this scenario. There is a 90-day limit to the beta testing period, and this is enforced by installing a 90-day license for the app on the phone. After this time, your users will no longer be able to start the app. You can add more test users at any time during this period. Be aware also that there is no option to terminate your test period before the 90-day period has expired. Users who have installed the app will be able to use it up to the end of the 90-day period. However, you can delete the app from the Windows Phone Store, so that it is no longer available to any designated beta users who happen not to have installed it yet.

Submitting an app for beta distribution is free, and it does not count against your allowed number of app submissions. You cannot attach a price to a beta app. Anyone with a Windows phone (and a Microsoft Account) can be a beta tester, and he does not need to have a developer-unlocked device. The process is also fast because the app does not go through the full set of certification tests and generally becomes available to your beta testers within hours of submitting it to the program.

There is no special "beta-to-release" upgrade path, so when your beta test is complete, you need to submit a fresh, full submission to publish your app in the normal way. It might also be worth pointing out to users that any data that they create within the app during beta testing will be lost when the final app is published.

Versions

Apart from fixing bugs, improving the UI, providing fresher data, and adding features, the other main reason for updating is to take advantage of new features in the latest version of the platform and SDK. As of this writing, this means updating from version 7.1 to 8.0. However, some users will not have upgraded to version 8.0 devices. All version 7.0 and 7.1 apps will continue to work on version 8.0 devices, so if you're not adding new features, you could take the path of least resistance and simply maintain your version 7.x app.

If you are adding new features, one option is to maintain both major versions of your app in the Windows Phone Store. This means forking your source code and applying bug fixes in two places, but it does mean that users can continue to get the benefit of your updates, regardless of which platform version they use.

You can maintain multiple versions on the Windows Phone Store and submit updates to each one independently. You might want multiple XAP versions to support different target markets, or for different screen resolutions, or indeed for different device versions. Even though some of the Windows Phone Store metadata for your app is shared across both versions, most of it is independent. Specifically, the XAP itself, the catalog details (descriptions and screenshots), pricing and regional availability, the version number the published/unpublished status, and the hidden/live status are all independent per version. This means the version number of your 7.1 version doesn't need to be the same as the version number for your 8.0 version. You might submit, for example, four version updates for your 7.1 version, and only two version updates for your 8.0 version, and so on, as shown in Figure 11-14.

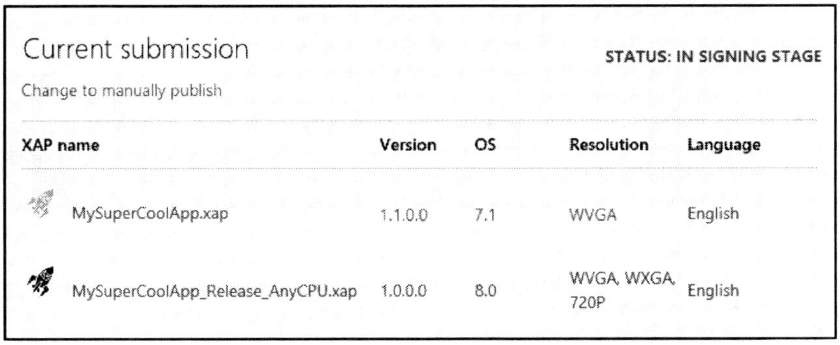

Current submission

STATUS: IN SIGNING STAGE

Change to manually publish

XAP name	Version	OS	Resolution	Language
MySuperCoolApp.xap	1.1.0.0	7.1	WVGA	English
MySuperCoolApp_Release_AnyCPU.xap	1.0.0.0	8.0	WVGA, WXGA, 720P	English

FIGURE 11-14 You can maintain multiple versions of your app in the Windows Phone Store.

One reason to publish an update for an old version 7.1 app is to enable a "light-up" scenario; that is, to take advantage of version 8.0 features if the app is running on Windows Phone 8.0. To be clear, this strategy is not the same as publishing an 8.0 version of your version 7.1 app. Rather, it means publishing a version 7.1 update to a 7.1 version app, but including version 8.0 features. For a detailed discussion of the development aspects of multitargeting, including light-up behavior, read Chapter 13, "Porting to Windows Phone 8 and multitargeting."

Selective targeting

As mentioned earlier, some markets have more strict requirements for content than others, and you have three choices for dealing with this:

- Target the lowest common denominator and tailor your content to suit all markets. This can get complicated if different markets have conflicting requirements.
- Build separate, tailored XAPs and their associated descriptions, tiles, and screenshots for each market.
- Make your app available only for a selected subset of all possible markets.

The same kinds of choices apply for different devices. That is, some devices have different capabilities than others: some support optional sensors, others have more powerful cameras or front and/or back-facing cameras. Another dimension to this is memory and processor power. Devices range from 256 MB at the low end to 2 GB (currently) at the high end, some devices have just a single-core processor, others have dual-core processors, and processor speeds vary across devices. There's also an OS dimension here in that current Windows Phone 7 devices range from 256 MB to 1 GB, whereas current Windows Phone 8 devices range from 512 MB to 2 GB.

Device capabilities

The app manifest includes a *Capabilities* section in which you must specify all the capabilities that your app requires. There are three reasons for this:

- So that the user can be informed of these capabilities by the Windows Phone Store prior to installing your app. For example, if the user sees that the app requires access to your contacts, you must specify this in the *Capabilities* section with an *ID_CAP_CONTACTS* entry.
- The security sandbox for your app is configured at runtime to include only those capabilities that the app declares it uses. So, if you don't declare a capability that you're using, the app will fail at runtime.
- For optional hardware capabilities, the Windows Phone Store will filter the app catalog to match each device. For example, if a given device does not have a compass, and your app requires one, your app will not be available to that device.

As with content and markets, you can choose to build one app for the lowest common denominator of device or multiple versions for different device configurations. Or, you can make your app available only for a selected subset of devices. You can achieve the first strategy by simply eliminating any features that do not work on all devices in the market. You can achieve the second by building and publishing multiple XAPs. You can achieve the third by declaring appropriate capabilities in your app manifest.

Another option is to adapt your code dynamically to accommodate the constraints of the device on which it's running. As discussed in Chapter 6, "Sensors," some hardware capabilities are optional, notably the gyroscope, compass, and camera (front or back-facing). You can test for the presence of each of these sensors and then take alternative code paths, depending on the results. You can use the same technique for features that the user can arbitrarily enable and disable, such as cellular data connectivity and cellular data roaming. Figure 11-15 shows the *OptionalCapabilities* app in the sample code, which makes use of these dynamic-discovery techniques. This app merely displays the test results in the UI.

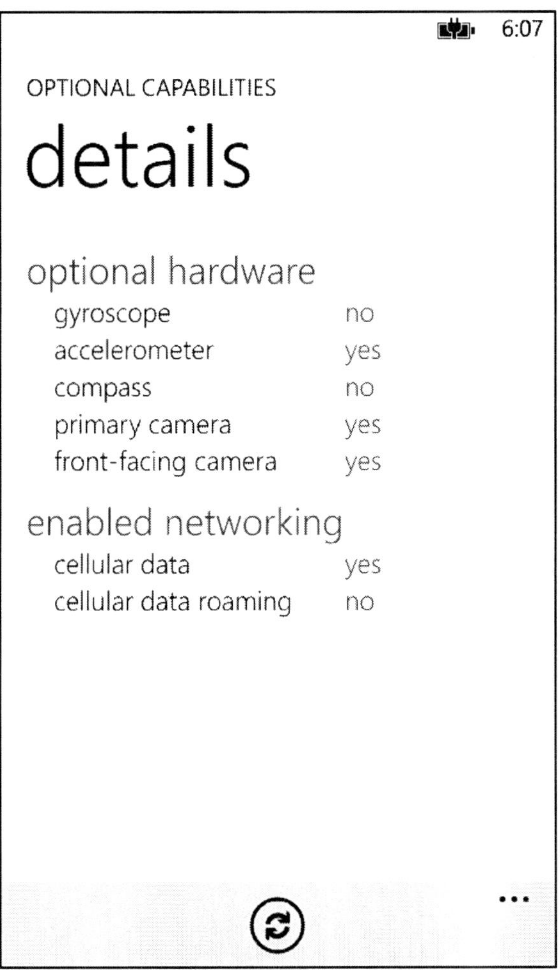

FIGURE 11-15 You can test for optional capabilities and adjust your features accordingly.

The app declares a number of data-bound *TextBlock* controls for each of the "yes/no" test results.

```
<TextBlock Text="{Binding Gyroscope, Converter={StaticResource converter}}"/>
```

Each *TextBlock* is data-bound to a property on a custom *OptionalFeatures* class, which exposes *bool* properties for whether or not the device supports a gyroscope, compass, and so on. The binding also uses a custom *BoolToStringConverter* for converting the *bool* values to "yes/no" strings.

```
public class OptionalFeatures : INotifyPropertyChanged
{
    public event PropertyChangedEventHandler PropertyChanged;
    private void NotifyPropertyChanged(string propertyName)
    {
        PropertyChangedEventHandler handler = PropertyChanged;
        if (null != handler)
            handler(this, new PropertyChangedEventArgs(propertyName));
    }

    private bool gyroscope;
    public bool Gyroscope
    {
        get { return gyroscope; }
        set
        {
            if (gyroscope != value)
            {
                gyroscope = value;
                NotifyPropertyChanged("Gyroscope");
            }
        }
    }

    ... other properties omitted for brevity.
}
```

In this app, when the user taps the app bar button, we gather all the optional capability information via tests such as *Gyroscope.IsSupported* or *DeviceNetworkInformation.IsCellularDataEnabled* and feed it into an *OptionalFeatures* object.

```
public OptionalFeatures Features { get; set; }

public MainPage()
{
    InitializeComponent();
    Features = new OptionalFeatures();
    DataContext = Features;
}

private void appbarRefresh_Click(object sender, EventArgs e)
{
    Features.Gyroscope = Gyroscope.IsSupported;
    Features.Accelerometer = Accelerometer.IsSupported;
    Features.Compass = Compass.IsSupported;
    Features.PrimaryCamera = Camera.IsCameraTypeSupported(CameraType.Primary);
    Features.FrontCamera = Camera.IsCameraTypeSupported(CameraType.FrontFacing);
    Features.CellData = DeviceNetworkInformation.IsCellularDataEnabled;
    Features.CellRoaming = DeviceNetworkInformation.IsCellularDataRoamingEnabled;
}
```

Device memory

Windows Phone 7.x apps are limited to using 90 MB of memory; that is, the app is promised that it can use up to 90 MB, and that while it might sometimes get more, there is no guarantee of this. So, 90 MB is effectively both the minimum and the maximum on which a version 7.x app can rely. In addition to that, one of the certification requirements for version 7.x apps is that they must not consume more than 90 MB. What has happened in practice is that while most apps (well over 95%) stayed well below the 90 MB cap, there were a few that did not. Even within these few, there was an extremely small number of apps that consistently exceeded the cap by a significant amount. When an app exceeds the cap, it runs the risk of running out of memory. That is, if the device is under extreme memory pressure, and the app is attempting some operation that requires the system to allocate it memory which it cannot grant, the allocation will fail. In this case, an *OutOfMemoryException* is thrown, and if the app doesn't catch this, it will crash. If you do catch an *OutOfMemoryException*, you're still faced with the dilemma of what to do with it. You must reduce your memory consumption, and you must be careful to perform this clean-up in a way that doesn't inadvertently attempt to allocate more memory; otherwise, you'll simply fail again.

The version 7.1.1 release of Windows Phone seems at first sight somewhat anomalous. Although the min/max guarantee (and Windows Phone Store certification requirement) for 7.1.1 remains at 90 MB, the OS can actually safely allocate an app up to 110 MB. The primary purpose of the 7.1.1 release was to support markets where devices with only 256 MB of total memory are common, and it's not immediately obvious why a release that targets devices with restricted memory should increase the app memory cap rather than reduce it. The reason this makes sense is that version 7.1.1 introduced paging, and could satisfy the higher cap by adding virtual memory to the physical memory allocation for an app. Paging is a technique uses by desktop and server operating systems to write out memory to a hard disk, thereby freeing up physical memory. An app can consume more memory than is physically available because the amount of memory the OS commits to the app can include space in the page file, which is therefore virtual memory. The cost of paging is slower performance, however, so it is used as a last resort. In addition, the 110 MB cap is strictly enforced on devices with only 256 MB of memory. That is, on a version 7.1.1 device with 256 MB memory, if your app attempts to allocate memory beyond 110 MB, the allocation will fail. On a version 7.1.1 device with more memory, the model is the same as for versions 7.0 and 7.1; that is, it might fail, and it might not, depending on the circumstances. The feedback from developers—strongly echoed by the Windows Phone product team—was that it would be useful to get more than 90 MB of memory. Conversely, it is not useful to provide additional memory in a nondeterministic manner. Developers seemed to prefer the 256 MB version 7.1.1 model, wherein the app is granted a deterministic 110 MB always, and no more.

Windows Phone 8 also implements paging and also makes the caps completely deterministic. There are two memory caps for all Windows Phone 8 apps: a default *MIN_CAP* and an optional *MAX_CAP*. The values of these caps vary by app type and by device configuration, as shown in Table 11-2.

TABLE 11-2 Windows Phone 8 memory cap values

Cap	Low-memory devices	High-memory devices
Default for XNA/Native aps	150 MB	150 MB
Default for non-XNA Managed apps	150 MB	300 MB
Optional higher cap for all apps	180 MB	380 MB

The labels "low memory" and "high memory" in this table need some explaining. Simplistically, "low memory" means ≥512 MB and <1 GB, whereas "high memory" means ≥1 GB. However, this is not necessarily always accurate. Internally, the computation takes into account any additional memory that is carved out for unusual hardware capabilities. For example, if a device manufacturer ships an extremely high-resolution camera and then needs to carve out a large amount of additional memory for device drivers for this camera, this will reduce the total amount of memory available to the app. If this amount falls below a certain threshold, the device will be treated as a low-memory device, even if it nominally has ≥1 GB. That being said, as of this writing, all devices with ≥1 GB memory are in fact treated as high-memory devices.

To support these caps, the Windows Phone 8 app manifest supports two new optional app manifest tags, as shown in Table 11-3.

TABLE 11-3 New Windows Phone 8 memory-related manifest entries

Manifest entry	Description	Memory cap
ID_REQ_MEMORY_300	Opts out of low-memory devices: the app will be filtered out in marketplace and will not install on a low-memory device.	The default cap (On high-memory devices, 150 MB for XNA/Native apps, and 300 MB for non-XNA Managed apps).
ID_FUNCCAP_EXTEND_MEM	Does not opt out of low-memory devices (installs on all devices) but is granted the optional higher cap instead of the default cap.	The optional higher cap (180 MB on low-memory devices; 380 MB on high-memory devices).

App memory is capped to ensure a balanced user experience, with cap values that make the following possible:

- Developers can develop for all devices, especially the high-volume, low-memory devices.
- Developers can build apps that use more memory if it is available.
- Adjusts for the fact that a non-XNA managed app's memory consumption goes up on WXGA devices due to auto-scaling of high-resolution graphics. All 720p and WXGA devices have ≥1 GB memory.

The new memory cap flags are not surfaced in the Visual Studio UI at all. You must edit the manifest manually. The order of the tags in the manifest is important, and it's different between a Windows Phone 7.1 app manifest and a Windows Phone 8.0 app manifest. For Windows Phone 7.1, the *Requirements* section should immediately follow the *Capabilities* section. The *FunctionalCapabilities* section, if present, should immediately follow the *Requirements* section. For Windows Phone 8.0, both *Requirements* and *FunctionalCapabilities* sections should be at the end, just before the closing *</App>* tag, in that order. That is, the *Requirements* section should follow the *ScreenResolutions* section.

To get the higher memory cap, add this tag inside the <App> tag:

```
<FunctionalCapabilities>
  <FunctionalCapability Name="ID_FUNCCAP_EXTEND_MEM" />
</FunctionalCapabilities>
```

To opt your app out of low-memory (512MB/768MB) devices, add this tag:

```
<Requirements>
  <Requirement Name="ID_REQ_MEMORY_300" />
</Requirements>
```

If you want both opt-out and higher-cap, your Windows Phone 8.0 manifest should look like this:

```
<App ...>
...
  <Requirements>
    <Requirement Name="ID_REQ_MEMORY_300" />
  </Requirements>
  <FunctionalCapabilities>
    <FunctionalCapability Name="ID_FUNCCAP_EXTEND_MEM" />
  </FunctionalCapabilities>
</App>
```

And, your Windows Phone 7.1 manifest would be as shown in the snippet that follows. Be aware that a Windows Phone 7.1 manifest might also include *ID_REQ_MEMORY_90* to specify behavior for 256 MB Windows Phone 7.1.1 devices.

```
<App ...>
  <Capabilities>
  ...
  </Capabilities>
  <Requirements>
    <Requirement Name="ID_REQ_MEMORY_90" />
    <Requirement Name="ID_REQ_MEMORY_300" />
  </Requirements>
  <FunctionalCapabilities>
    <FunctionalCapability Name="ID_FUNCCAP_EXTEND_MEM" />
  </FunctionalCapabilities>
  <Tasks>
  ...
  </Tasks>
  <Tokens>
  ...
  </Tokens>
</App>
```

ID_REQ_MEMORY_90 only opts the app out of 256 MB Windows Phone 7.1.1 devices, and if you additionally want to be opted out of low-memory Windows Phone 8 devices, then you must include *ID_REQ_MEMORY_300*. Keep in mind that *ID_REQ_MEMORY_300* opts the app out of both, so if you have *ID_REQ_MEMORY_300*, you don't need *ID_REQ_MEMORY_90*; if you do have both *ID_REQ_MEMORY_300* and *ID_REQ_MEMORY_90*, the *ID_REQ_MEMORY_90* is ignored.

If you opt out of low-memory devices, your app knows statically how much memory it can use, because this is dependent only on the type of app (XNA, non-XNA managed, or native) and whether or not the app manifest includes *ID_FUNCCAP_EXTEND_MEM*, both of which are known. If you don't opt out of low-memory devices, you can't completely know statically what your memory cap will be, because it also depends on what configuration of device on which the app happens to be running. In this scenario, you can determine this dynamically by using the memory-related properties on the *DeviceStatus* class. Specifically, *ApplicationMemoryUsageLimit* notifies you of the cap that this specific system is enforcing on your app, and *ApplicationCurrentMemoryUsage* informs you how much memory you're currently consuming.

```
long cap = DeviceStatus.ApplicationMemoryUsageLimit;
long current = DeviceStatus.ApplicationCurrentMemoryUsage;
```

Armed with this information, you can then make appropriate choices to conditionally enable/disable features in your app to accommodate the lower/higher memory caps. You can use the different emulator images available in Visual Studio to test your app on different device configurations. The simplest approach is to start by just running your app and check memory usage in the profiler. Then, if it needs too much and you can't reduce it, add the right flags.

Summary

The Windows Phone Store is becoming easier to use and more sophisticated at the same time, and the publication process is now very intuitive and flexible. The Dev Center portal to the Windows Phone Store is updated periodically and has added features such as private beta testing, which give you even more options for publishing your app. You should use the Store Test Kit prior to submitting your app for publication, and this will also check for updated rules. At the same time, you should also check the Windows Phone Store certification requirements because these are also kept up to date. You can maintain multiple versions of your app in the Windows Phone Store, and you have choices about where your app is available and on what devices. Finally, the Dev Center provides simple data reports on download profiles and crash statistics. This chapter examined the core publication scenarios, but you should also read Chapter 21, "Monetizing your app," for information about in-app purchases, ads, and trial-mode publication.

CHAPTER 12

Profiling and diagnostics

Modern app development platforms excel at making it very easy to build a professional-looking product quickly. Indeed, creating demo apps and prototypes has never been simpler. But, users aren't interested in buying demo apps from the Windows Phone Store. In fact, user standards for performance and reliability are higher than ever. As a result, successful app developers spend a considerable portion of their time squashing the last few bugs and eking out any performance bottlenecks that keep their apps from performing well on user devices. In this chapter, you will learn about some of the key tools and techniques for finding and fixing bugs and performance issues before you ship your app.

Debugging

Microsoft Visual Studio includes a rich set of debugging utilities, most of which are available for use in Windows Phone projects. If you press F5 or choose Start Debugging from the Debug menu, you can start the current project in a debug session and perform all of the common debugging tasks, such as setting breakpoints, stepping through code line by line, and examining the state of the app at various stages of execution, all by using the various debug windows.

Targeting different device configurations

As mentioned in the "Getting started" section in Chapter 1, "Vision and architecture," the Windows Phone SDK includes a number of different emulator images. For Windows Phone 7.1 apps, you can choose an emulator that mimics a phone with 256 MB of memory or one that emulates a device with 512 MB. For Windows Phone 8 apps, there are four choices: a 512-MB device with a WVGA (800x480) screen, a 1-GB device with a WVGA screen, a 1 GB-device with a 720P (1280x720) screen, and a 1-GB device with a WXGA (1280x768) screen. You can easily switch between the different device images by using a menu on the Visual Studio toolbar, as shown in Figure 12-1 (for a Windows Phone 8 project). For Windows Phone 8 projects, you should do the bulk of your testing on the 512-MB WVGA emulator because that provides the most constrained environment. If your app works well in that configuration, it will work well on other configurations with larger screens and more memory. Of course, if you want to specifically target the larger screen sizes with different graphical assets, you should certainly validate that your app works properly on those device images prior to submitting it to the Windows Phone Store.

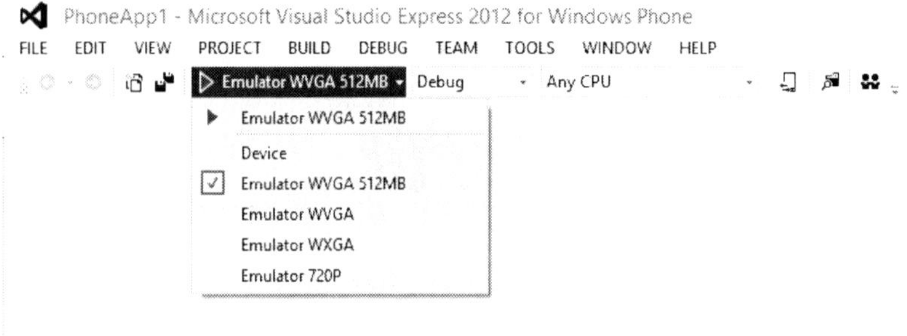

FIGURE 12-1 You can easily switch between target devices by selecting an emulator from a menu on the Visual Studio toolbar.

Troubleshooting app startup

As discussed in Chapter 1 and throughout the book, Windows Phone offers a number of extensibility points for apps. Apps can create multiple tiles on the Start screen, they can be invoked from many of the phone hubs, and they can register to handle specific URI schemes or file types, among other launch points. In most cases, these extensibility points deep-link into the app to provide a specific experience based on the context in which the user started it. In previous versions of the Windows Phone SDK, it was challenging to debug problems handling these deep links because you could only attach the debugger when the app was launched directly from Visual Studio—as soon as you navigated away from the app to start it from an extensibility point, the debugger would detach.

In the Windows Phone 8 SDK, this behavior has changed so that the debugger stays attached until you explicitly stop debugging in Visual Studio. This means that you can start the app for debugging, navigate away from it to the Start screen, a hub or any other extensibility point, and then start the app again to step through its activation code path. To end a debugging session, use the Stop Debugging button in Visual Studio or press Shift+F5 on your keyboard.

Using Fiddler with the Windows Phone emulator

Fiddler is a popular HTTP debugging tool available as a free download from *http://www.fiddler2.com/fiddler2/*. Fiddler logs all HTTP(S) traffic going in and out of your computer, making it possible to inspect and manipulate requests and responses travelling to and from the web. In most cases, the Windows Phone networking stack provides very limited error information when interacting with web services; thus, Fiddler is a useful tool that can help you to better understand what is being sent and what is being returned.

Note In Windows Phone, most HTTP failures are translated into a generic *WebException* with the message "Not found." If you see this exception in your app but are confident that the web service is available, consider using Fiddler to extract more diagnostic information about the failure.

To configure Fiddler for use from the Windows Phone emulator, perform the following steps:

1. Start Fiddler and click Tools | Fiddler Options. On the Connections tab, select the check box labeled Allow Remote Computers To Connect.
2. In the lower-left corner of the Fiddler window, click the small QuickExec window (or press Alt+Q).
3. In the QuickExec window, type the following:

   prefs set fiddler.network.proxy.registrationhostname *YourComputerNameOrIPAddress*

   Where *YourComputerNameOrIPAddress* is either the fully-qualified name of your development computer or its IPv4 address (available from ipconfig).
4. Close and restart Fiddler.
5. Start the Windows Phone emulator.
6. Open Internet Explorer in the emulator and browse to a website.

   You should see traffic being captured in the Fiddler window, as depicted in Figure 12-2. Network traffic sent to and from an app will also show up here.

Note The order in which you start Fiddler and the emulator is important. When Fiddler starts, it tweaks your computer's Internet settings to route all traffic through the Fiddler proxy. When the emulator boots, it copies the current computer settings to configure its own Internet options. If you start the emulator first, the Fiddler proxy will not be available to be copied and the emulator will send traffic through its standard path. Similarly, when you close Fiddler, it removes its proxy server, meaning that any subsequent network requests from the emulator will fail. You must restart the emulator to refresh the network settings.

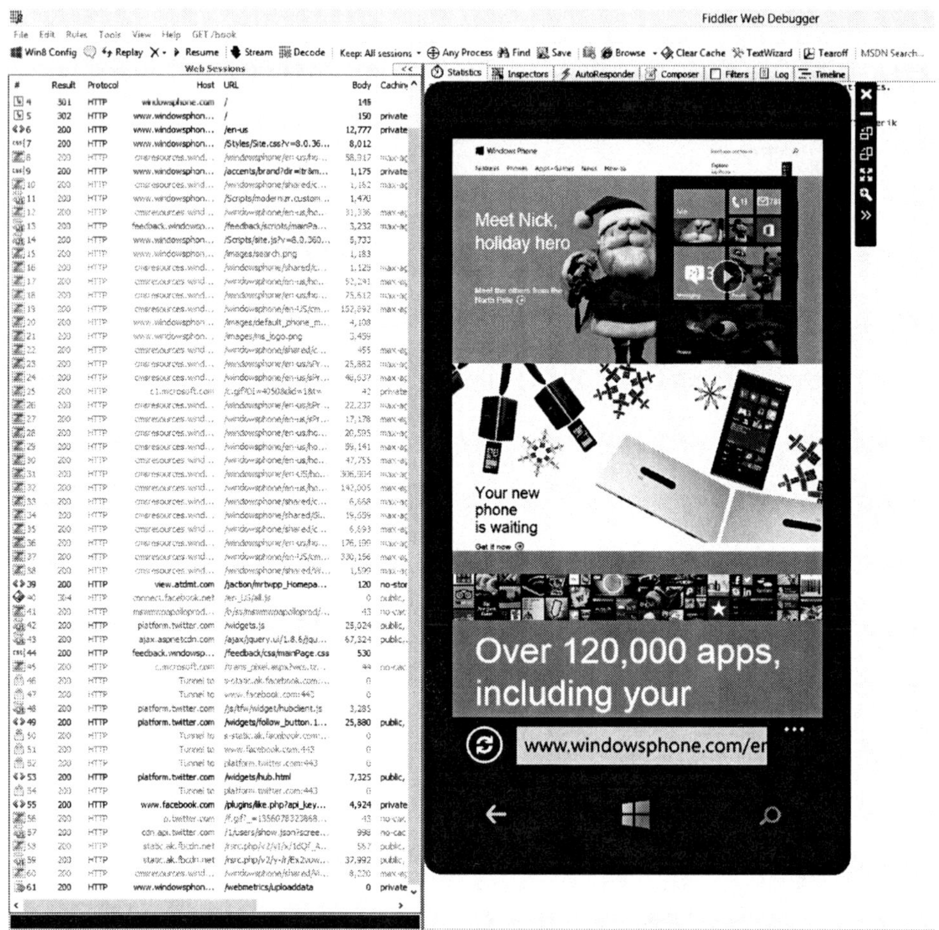

FIGURE 12-2 Fiddler provides a simple way to inspect network traffic travelling in and out of the Windows Phone emulator.

You can also use Fiddler as a proxy for network traffic originating from a real phone, as long as the computer and the phone are connected to the same Wi-Fi network. Simply configure the Wi-Fi network on the phone to point to the Fiddler proxy on your development computer, as illustrated in Figure 12-3. Just remember to turn the proxy off after you finish debugging; otherwise, you will continue to proxy all of your phone's Wi-Fi traffic through your computer, and those connections will fail if you close Fiddler.

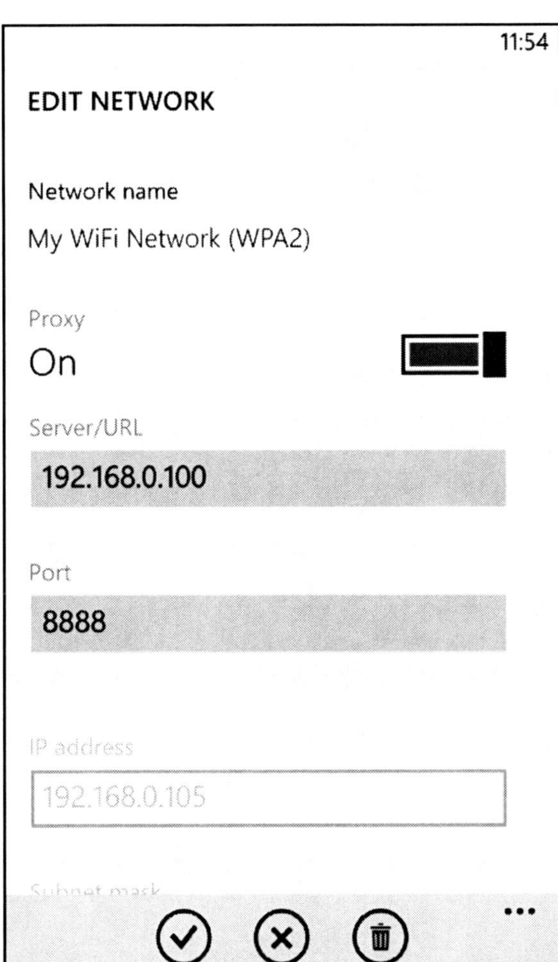

FIGURE 12-3 To debug network calls from your phone, configure your phone's Wi-Fi connection to route traffic through the Fiddler proxy on your computer.

Note If your development computer resides on a network that requires Internet Protocol security (IPsec), you will need to request a boundary exception from your IT department to route traffic from the emulator or a device through Fiddler.

Testing

It is no secret that most mobile app developers pay little attention to structured testing, seeing it as an impediment to adding new features to their apps or getting them into the Windows Phone Store. However, even a modest time investment in creating automated, repeatable tests for your app and in anticipating conditions that users might encounter in the real world can pay off significantly in the long term. Not only do well-tested apps perform better in the Windows Phone Store, the presence of a stable test foundation for your app makes it easier to refactor it and improve it quickly.

Unit testing

Unit testing is a common practice in any type of software development and is especially prominent in agile development methodologies such as extreme programming (XP) and test-driven development (TDD). It involves writing tactical test cases that exercise individual pieces of an application, such as a class or interface, or a specific method.

The Windows Phone Toolkit now includes a unit test framework for use in Windows Phone 7.1 and 8.0 apps. The *TestFrameworkApp* solution in the sample code illustrates how to use it to create simple unit tests for a Windows Phone app. The solution includes two projects: *MainApp* (the app to be tested), and *MainApp.Tests* (which contains the unit tests). The *MainApp* project provides just one simple function: it converts temperatures between the Celsius scale and the Fahrenheit scale. The user interface (UI) includes two *TextBox* controls, one for each temperature scale. When the user makes a change to one *TextBox*, the value of the other is updated with the converted value. The UI for the app is shown in Figure 12-4.

The main page of the app contains event handlers for the *KeyUp* events of the two *TextBox* controls. We use the *KeyUp* event to detect when the user has made a change to one of the temperatures and then call the *ConvertTemperatureAndUpdate* method on the *MainViewModel*, which performs the conversion and updates the data-bound property backing the opposite *TextBox*.

Note In Windows Phone 7.1, you can use the *TextInputUpdate* event to detect user-initiated changes in a *TextBox*. However, this method is not supported in Windows Phone 8.

Although this app provides very simple functionality that could easily be implemented in the code-behind of the main page, we are using a viewmodel to reiterate the importance of layering your app correctly, based on the principle of Separation of Concerns (SoC). Without a clean separation of your business logic from your UI layer, your unit test suite can end up relying on a specific UI layout, making it difficult to modify that UI layer without significantly refactoring your tests.

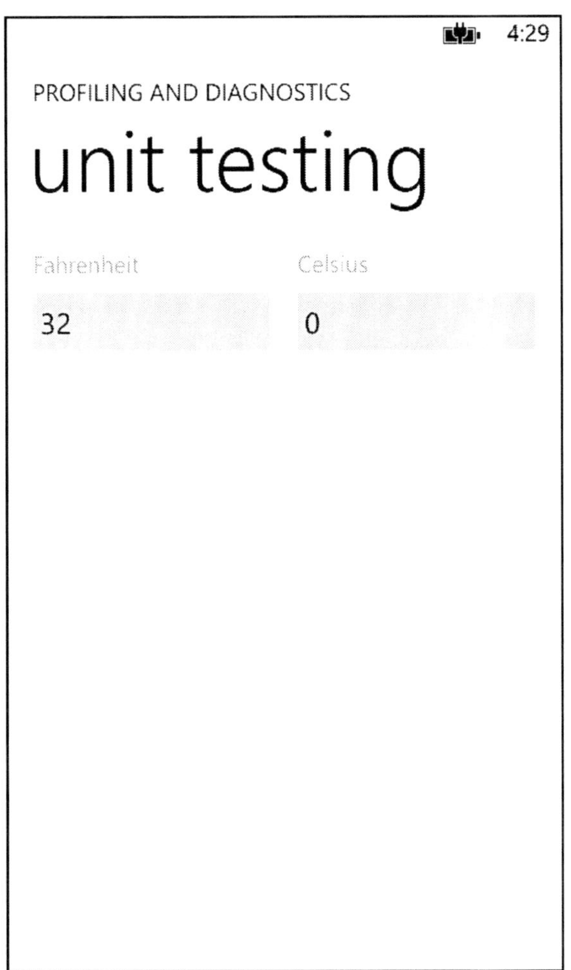

FIGURE 12-4 The *MainApp* project in the *TestFrameworkApp* solution provides simple temperature conversions.

The *MainApp.Tests* project is a standard Windows Phone app project, but its functionality is limited to defining and running the tests for *MainApp*. The test project includes three reference assemblies from the Windows Phone Toolkit: the assembly containing additional UI controls (such as *ToggleSwitch*) used throughout the book as well as two assemblies that support the unit test framework. Because the test framework assemblies should only be added to unit test projects, they are not included in the main NuGet package for the toolkit. Instead, they are included in a separate package named *WPToolkitTestFx* that you can add to a unit test project by running the following command in the Package Manager Console:

```
PM> Install-Package WPToolkitTestFx
```

Note that the default project for the NuGet Package Manager Console is the first one created in the solution. If you create the main app first, you will need to ensure that you change the default project to the unit test project before installing the test framework package by using the menu highlighted in Figure 12-5.

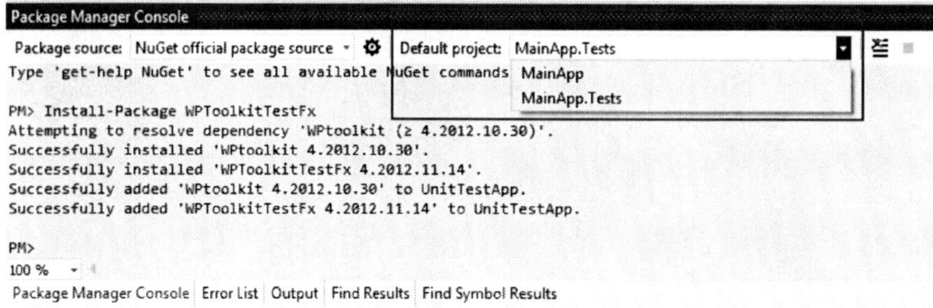

FIGURE 12-5 Remember to select your unit test project before installing the toolkit test framework.

While you're adding reference assemblies to the unit test app, be sure to add references to any assemblies in the main app that you want to test. In the case of the *TestFrameworkSolution*, the main app is contained in a single assembly, so we add a single reference to it in the *MainApp.Tests* project.

The test framework comes with a predefined UI for displaying tests and their results. You can generate this UI by calling the *CreateTestPage* method on the *UnitTestSystem* class and setting the page's *Content* property to the value returned:

```
public MainPage()
{
    this.Content = UnitTestSystem.CreateTestPage();
}
```

With everything set up, it's time to write some tests. We create two tests for the *MainApp*. One performs a Celsius to Fahrenheit conversion and the other performs the reverse calculation. Test cases within the unit test framework are contained within a test class. Test classes are decorated with the *TestClass* attribute and derive from *WorkItemTest*. The *TestClass* attribute indicates to the test framework that the class contains tests that should be executed. Within a test class, specific tests are encapsulated by methods decorated with the *TestMethod* attribute. The test method performs an operation on the code that we want to test and then uses one of the static methods on the *Assert* class to validate that the actual value meets what we expect.

```
[TestClass]
public class MainAppTests : WorkItemTest
{
    [TestMethod]
    [Tag("ConversionTests")]
    [Description("Test 1: Fahrenheit to Celsius Test")]
    public void FahrenheitToCelsiusTest()
    {
        MainViewModel viewModel = new MainViewModel();

        viewModel.ConvertTemperatureAndUpdate(70, TemperatureType.Fahrenheit);

        Assert.AreEqual(21, viewModel.CelsiusTemperature);
    }

    [TestMethod]
    [Tag("ConversionTests")]
    [Description("Test 2: Celsius to Fahrenheit Test")]
    public void CelsiusToFahrenheitTest()
    {
        MainViewModel viewModel = new MainViewModel();

        viewModel.ConvertTemperatureAndUpdate(32, TemperatureType.Celsius);

        Assert.AreEqual(89, viewModel.FahrenheitTemperature);
    }
}
```

When you start the unit test app, you are initially presented with a page labeled Test Filter (see Figure 12-6). On the Test Filter page, you can choose a subset of your suite to run, based on a specific tag. In the *MainApp.Tests* project, for instance, both tests have the tag "ConversionTests", so as the breadth of the test suite grows, we could always return to this basic test pass by using that tag.

The play button on the app bar navigates to a test results page and initiates the chosen set of unit tests. When the tests are complete, a summary of the results is shown, grouped by test class. Tapping a test class expands the list to show the tests that were run for that class, as demonstrated in Figure 12-7.

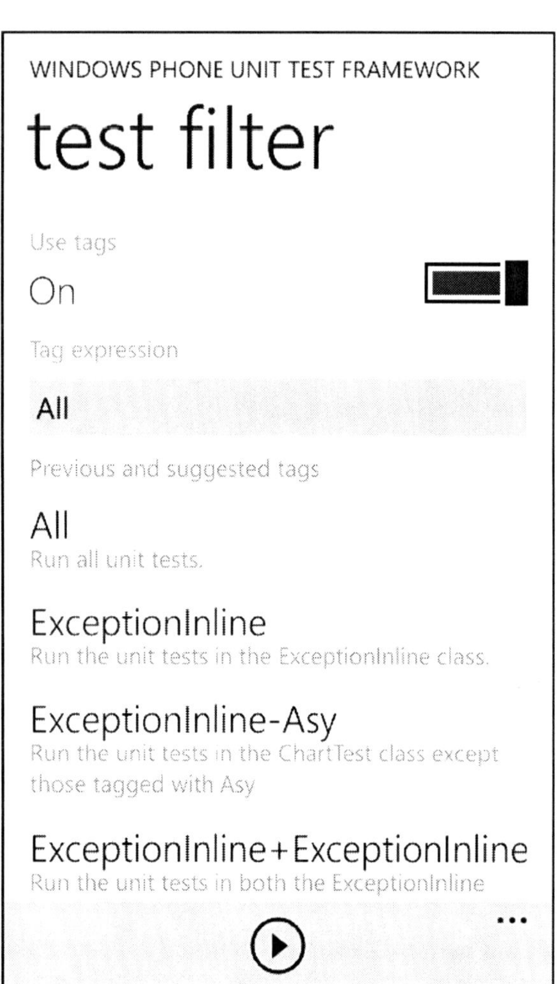

FIGURE 12-6 With this test framework, you can run only those tests that match a given tag.

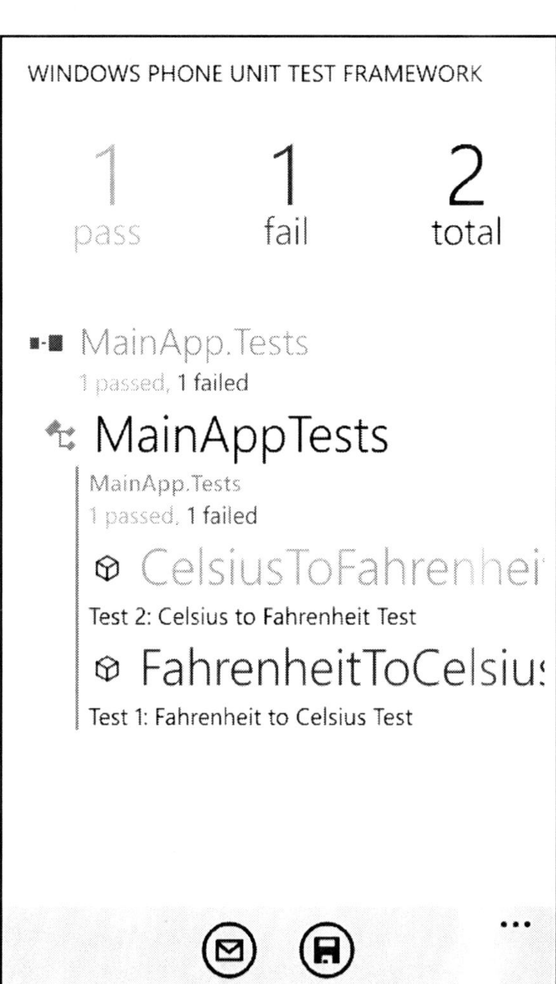

FIGURE 12-7 The test framework results page shows a summary of tests run and their pass/fail status.

Note The assert statements that perform validation in test methods throw an *AssertFailedException* when the comparison fails. If you run the unit test app under the debugger by using the default Visual Studio settings, you will see an unhandled exception message box similar to the one shown in Figure 12-8 when the exception is thrown.

FIGURE 12-8 The unhandled exception message box is expected if a test fails while running a unit test app under the debugger.

This is expected, even if the test failure might not be. If you let execution continue, the test framework will catch the exception and capture the error details to help you investigate the issue. If you want to run through a large test suite without worrying about interruptions for failed tests, you have two options: you can clear the check box at the bottom of the exception message box so that unhandled assert exceptions pass through to the framework without interruption; or you can run the unit test app without the debugger attached.

Naturally, we want to understand why one of the tests failed. By clicking it, we can view the details for the specific test including a stack trace and a comparison of the actual and expected values. The details page is shown in Figure 12-9. Notice the Email and Save buttons on the app bar, which provide ways to capture and share the diagnostics on the page for further analysis.

For such a simple method, there are very few possible explanations for the failure. The fact that the actual value returned is a non-zero number indicates that it is probably not a case of the value not being set correctly; rather, it is more likely that the calculation itself is wrong. Sure enough, when we look back at the method, there is a simple operator-precedence bug—we are performing the multiplication before the subtraction.

```
public void ConvertTemperatureAndUpdate(int newTemperature, TemperatureType tempType)
{
    if (tempType == TemperatureType.Celsius)
    {
        FahrenheitTemperature = (newTemperature * 9 / 5) + 32;
    }
```

```
        else
        {
            CelsiusTemperature = newTemperature - 32 * 5 / 9;
        }
    }
```

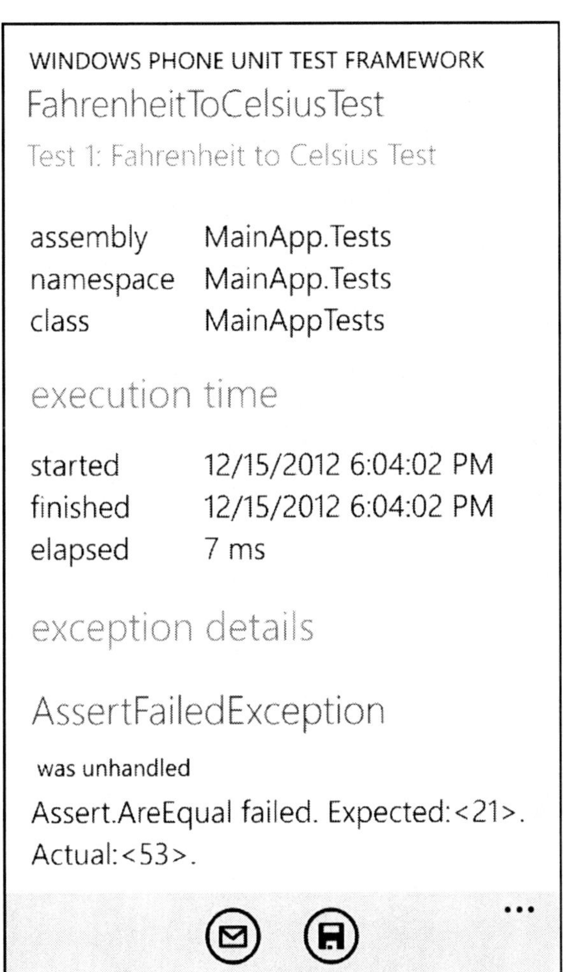

FIGURE 12-9 The test case details page provides diagnostic information to help analyze the test failure.

Unfortunately, bugs aren't always this simple to find and fix. In most cases, you will want to record the test failure in your bug tracking system and then move on to find new issues without seeing the same known failures over and over again. The unit test framework provides an option to annotate a given test with a *Bug* attribute, allowing it to "pass" with the identified issue. Returning to the unit test app, we add the *Bug* attribute to the *FahrenheitToCelsiusTest*, providing a bug number and description as well as an indication that the bug is not yet fixed.

```
[TestMethod]
[Tag("ConversionTests")]
[Description("Test 2: Celsius to Fahrenheit Test")]
[Bug("Bug 12345: Fahrenheit-Celsius conversion has incorrect operator precedence", Fixed=false)]
public void FahrenheitToCelsiusTest()
{
    MainViewModel viewModel = new MainViewModel();

    viewModel.ConvertTemperatureAndUpdate(70, TemperatureType.Fahrenheit);

    Assert.AreEqual(21, viewModel.CelsiusTemperature);
}
```

After adding this attribute, both tests pass, but now the bug is shown in the details page for the *FahrenheitToCelsiusTest*, as shown in Figure 12-10.

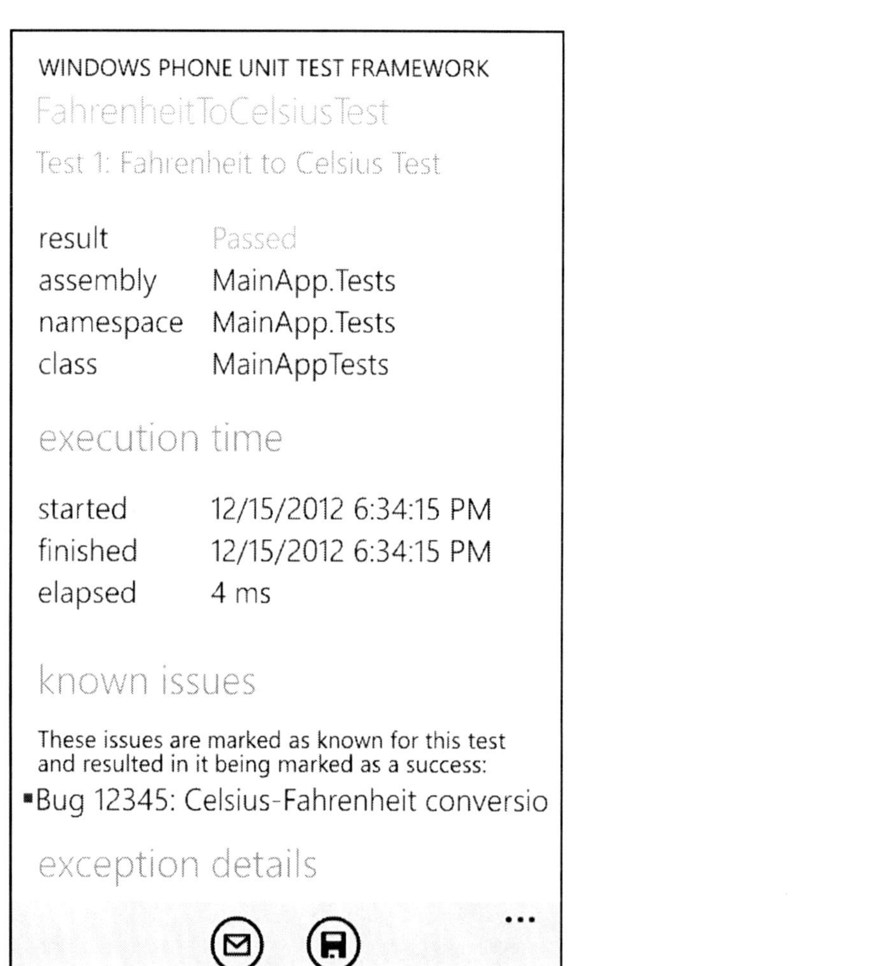

FIGURE 12-10 The *FahrenheitToCelsiusTest* details page shows known bugs that are associated with the test.

Simulating real-world conditions

There are few things in software development more frustrating than receiving persistent bug reports from customers regarding issues that you cannot reproduce yourself. In mobile app development, one of the most common causes for this problem is the difference between the environment in which the app developer tests an app and the environment in which real customers try to use it. In particular, the wide variability in the availability and performance of network connections introduces significant challenges to ensuring that your app works as expected before you submit it to the Windows Phone Store. The Windows Phone SDK now provides a tool to help deal with this challenge. The Simulation Dashboard, which is accessible on the Tools menu in Visual Studio, makes it possible for you to simulate the speed and signal strength of the different network types that your app might encounter in the real world. It is available for use in the emulator and on the phone.

Note The Simulation Dashboard also includes tools for locking and unlocking the emulator and for triggering a reminder. This is useful if your app needs to run under the lock screen and to ensure that you are properly handling the *Obscured* and *Unobscured* events that are raised for reminders and incoming phone calls. However, because a much larger proportion of apps rely on network connectivity and varying network conditions are especially difficult to re-create without the dashboard, we will focus on that feature in this section.

Figure 12-11 shows that two axes of configuration are provided: the network speed (including no connection at all) and the signal strength. The network speed setting provides the initial latency and bandwidth for the connection, with signal strength having a relative impact on those properties. Signal strength also dictates the frequency at which the connection drops packets, which ultimately has an impact on network roundtrip time for guaranteed delivery protocols such as TCP and HTTP. The system emulates the different network profiles by enabling an additional network driver that filters and manipulates packets as they move between the app and the base networking layer. In effect, the special network driver creates additional friction for packets as they move in and out of the app that is representative of the lags the app would see on the chosen network. For obvious reasons, the Simulation Dashboard is not able to simulate a network that is faster than the one to which the phone or emulator is currently connected.

Note The network emulation driver can only be activated on the emulator and on developer-unlocked phones. When you enable it on a developer-unlocked phone for the first time, Visual Studio prompts you to perform a full device reboot.

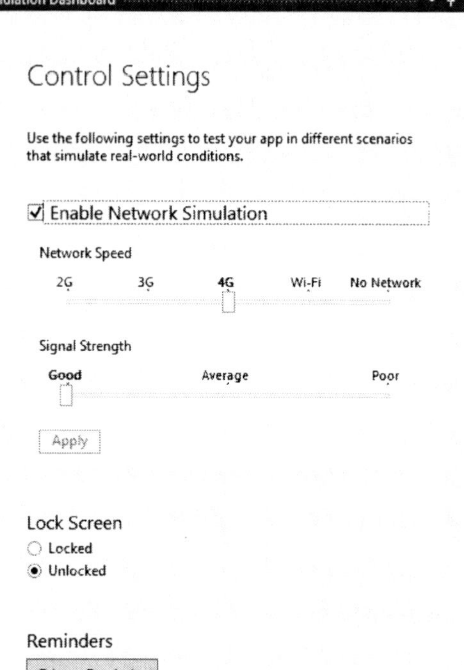

FIGURE 12-11 With the Simulation Dashboard, you can set network speed and connectivity.

The *SlowYouTube* solution in the sample code provides an example of an app that can benefit from some realistic network testing. The app contains a pivot control with four pivot items. On startup, it makes four web service requests to the public YouTube search API to retrieve metadata for videos on four topics: Windows Phone, Windows 8, Nokia Lumia, and HTC 8X. The app parses the results and creates four *ObservableCollection* objects, which are data-bound to the pivot items. Figure 12-12 shows the app UI after the search results have been filled in. Observe the bar at the bottom of the screen labeled Startup Wait. The number listed refers to the time (in milliseconds) between when the requests were sent and when all of the results were parsed and populated in the UI. We will use this box to measure the difference in app performance as we test different network conditions.

When testing an app with the Simulation Dashboard, you should always start by validating the behavior when no network is available. Failure to handle the loss of network connectivity is a very common source of app bugs and Windows Phone Store certification failures, but it is generally easily fixed. Even though cellular networks might seem ubiquitous today, users still frequently find themselves beyond network range; for example, while in a tunnel, an elevator, or at a major sporting event. Network availability also varies widely across markets, so being robust against network loss can be critical to expanding the reach of your app.

6:46
PROFILING AND DIAGNOSTICS
wp8 nokia lum

Meet Windows Phone 8
See some of the most exciting new features in Windows Phone 8, including Kid's Corner, Rooms,...

New Features in Windows Phone 8's
You may have already heard about how Microsoft made an over-the-air update available this week to...

Nokia Lumia 920 Review
Nokia Lumia 920 (AT&T) review video

Samsung ATIV S Unboxing & Hardw
It was the first Windows Phone 8 device to officially break cover, but in a strange twist of circumstance,...

Nokia Lumia 510 launched with Win
Startup wait: 3636

FIGURE 12-12 The *SlowYouTube* solution includes UI that shows how long it takes to make a set of web requests.

Running the *SlowYouTube* solution with the No Network setting enabled in the Simulation Dashboard quickly yields one bug to fix. The *UpdateVideosForUri* method in the *YouTubeViewModel* is not catching the potential *WebException* resulting from a call to the *EndGetResponse* method on *HttpWebRequest*.

```
public void UpdateVideosForUri(string searchUri, ObservableCollection<Video> videoCollection)
{
    HttpWebRequest youtubeRequest = HttpWebRequest.CreateHttp(searchUri);
    youtubeRequest.BeginGetResponse((IAsyncResult result) =>
    {
        XNamespace atom = "http://www.w3.org/2005/Atom";
        XNamespace media = "http://search.yahoo.com/mrss/";
```

```
            // WebException at this line if no network result returned
            using(XmlReader reader =
                XmlReader.Create((youtubeRequest.EndGetResponse(result)).GetResponseStream(),
                new XmlReaderSettings()))
            {
                // additional code omitted…

            }
        }
}
```

The simplest fix for this bug is to catch the *WebException* and return; although in a real app, you would want to provide the user with some notification that the network connection failed. If it makes sense for your app, implementing a local cache of network data that can be used when the network is unavailable can temporarily limit the user impact of a network failure.

Tip Network connectivity failures can occur at any time. If your app needs to connect to the network multiple times through its lifecycle, ensure that you test every potential path by using the Simulation Dashboard. For instance, if you are building an app that performs one web service request to fetch a list and then performs another to fetch the details of one particular item chosen by the user, try disabling the network between the time that you fetch the list and the time that you attempt to fetch the details. Simply update the network configuration in the Simulation Dashboard and click Apply for the updated state to take effect.

With the network-connectivity–failure bug fixed, we can move on to reviewing our app performance on networks of varying speed and quality. As shown in Figure 12-12, the *SlowYouTube* solution takes between three and four seconds to download the results of the four YouTube search queries when running on a 4G or Wi-Fi network with good signal strength. In other words, the app's startup performance is only passable on high-quality networks and we have reason for concern that the performance might become unacceptable on slower networks. When we update the network simulation settings so that the emulator behaves like an average 2G connection, the startup wait time spikes significantly; in some cases taking over 30 seconds to populate all four pivot items.

There are two common approaches to improving the startup experience for an app that must make network calls to populate its UI. One approach is to provide some form of progress UI, which can be as simple as an overlay that displays "Loading…" while the app is receiving data. Even though this obviously does not make the app start any faster, it reassures the user that *something* is happening. However, if your network testing indicates that the app is taking 10 seconds or more to become functional, a progress UI is not likely to be enough to keep the user interested. The second approach, therefore, is to seek ways to limit the amount of data that the app is downloading when it starts. Using Fiddler, we can see that just one of our YouTube search queries returns about 150 kb of data as an Atom feed. Because we are performing four queries on startup, we are requesting at least 600 kb of data in total. On a 2G network or a weak 3G signal, downloading that much data is bound to have a significant impact on app startup time. Furthermore, the vast majority of that data is ultimately discarded because we only need a few fields to populate our UI. Thus, we are not only wasting the user's time, but we are also wasting her money! Thankfully, the YouTube search API provides the ability to specify only the fields that you need in your query. If we modify our query to only ask for the video ID (used to fetch the thumbnail), its title, and description, we can reduce the size of each query by about 90 percent, making the sum of all four feeds about half the size of just one full feed. With the change, app startup time on an average 2G network drops from 20–30 seconds to about 3 seconds, equivalent to the average startup time on the fastest networks before the change.

Note The *SlowYouTube* solution in the sample code includes the original YouTube search URIs and the filtered URIs in the same project, controlled by the conditional compilation symbol *SLOW*. To see the app run in its original form, uncomment the following line from the top of the *YouTubeViewModel.cs* file:

```
// #define SLOW
```

Reading syndication feeds

The *SlowYouTube* sample uses the *SyndicationFeed* class to parse the downloaded Atom results from the YouTube service. The *SyndicationFeed* class is part of the *System.ServiceModel.Syndication* assembly that ships with the Microsoft Silverlight desktop SDK. Although it has never been included with the Windows Phone SDK, it is possible to add the Silverlight 4 version of the assembly to a Windows Phone project and use it to parse various types of syndication feeds, including RSS and Atom. The Silverlight 4 SDK libraries can be found at %programfiles(x86)%\Microsoft SDKs\Silverlight\v4.0\Libraries\Client\. Visual Studio will show a general warning about potential incompatibility between Silverlight assemblies and Windows Phone projects, but you can safely ignore it in this case.

Testing tombstoning

Chapter 2, "App model and navigation," demonstrates that an app on the backstack can be completely removed from memory if the system is running low on resources, a process known as tombstoning. When the system resumes an app from the tombstoned state, it navigates directly to the last page that the user visited without reconstructing the previous pages in the stack. If an app makes incorrect assumptions about the ordering of certain code paths, resuming from tombstoning will often cause it to crash or behave erratically. However, because many developers do most of their testing on the emulator or on a device with 1 GB of memory and rarely push the app deep enough into the backstack to force tombstoning, those bugs are often not found before the app is submitted to the Windows Phone Store. Thankfully, the Windows Phone SDK includes an option to automatically trigger tombstoning when you navigate away from the app so that you can test resuming the app from that state. To enable automatic tombstoning, open your project's Properties page, click the Debug tab, and then select the check box labeled Tombstone Upon Deactivation While Debugging, as depicted in Figure 12-13.

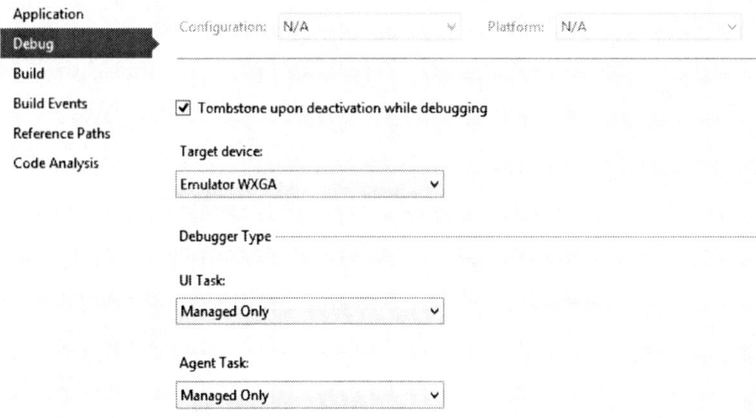

FIGURE 12-13 Be sure to test your app by using forced tombstoning; select the option on the debug properties page.

The Windows Phone emulator

The Windows Phone Emulator provides a fast, efficient way to perform most functional tests directly on your desktop.

Emulator keyboard shortcuts

The emulator supports a number of shortcuts (listed in Table 12-1) with which you can simulate hardware events that can make your testing more realistic. Be aware that the emulator must have focus in order to respond to these shortcuts.

TABLE 12-1 Windows Phone emulator keyboard shortcuts

Shortcut	Hardware equivalent
Esc/F1	Back button
F2	Start/Windows button
F3	Search/Bing button
F7	Camera button
F9	Volume up
F10	Volume down
F12	Power (press F12 twice to bring up the lock screen)
Pause/Break	Toggle between the On-Screen Keyboard and the physical keyboard

Emulator vs. device

The emulator is a great tool for performing quick iterations during app development without needing to tether a device to the computer. However, it is critical to understand the limitations of the emulator when it comes to testing your app. First, there are a number of device features that are either not available or behave differently in the emulator. These differences are captured in Table 12-2.

TABLE 12-2 Device features that are not supported or behave differently in the emulator

Feature	Emulator behavior
Camera	The emulator displays a gray rectangle that fills the screen with a small square of rotating colors moving along the edge of the viewfinder.
Near Field Communication (NFC)	The emulator behaves like a phone that does not support NFC. Calls to *ProximityDevice.GetDefault()* return null.
Gyroscope	The emulator behaves like a phone that does not include a gyroscope sensor. The *Gyroscope.IsGyroscopeSupported* method always returns false.
Compass	The emulator behaves like a phone that does not include a compass. The *Compass.IsSupported* method always returns false.
MicroSD cards	The emulator behaves like a phone that does not support microSD or does not currently have a microSD card inserted. Calls to *ExternalStorage.GetExternalStorageDevicesAsync()* will return an empty collection.
Social network integration	Facebook, Windows Live, and other social accounts linked through Windows Live (such as Twitter) cannot be set up on the emulator. If you launch a task that allows for sharing with social networks, such as *ShareLinkTask*, it will immediately return to your app.
Multitouch	Multitouch is supported if you have a touch monitor on your computer. Note, however, that some touch computers provide only two points of multitouch, whereas the emulator supports four. It is not possible to simulate touch with a mouse.
State Persistence	The emulator is refreshed to a clean state every time it is launched. Any apps that were installed, along with their associated state, is lost.

More significant than the feature differences are the differences in performance characteristics. The emulator's Hyper-V Virtual Machine does not constrain its use of your computer's hardware. Because desktop computers tend to have faster CPUs and GPUs than phones, computationally intensive tasks usually exhibit significantly better performance on the emulator than on a real phone. It is critical that you spend time testing your app thoroughly on a real device.

Profiling

By employing app profiling, a developer can capture critical metrics about how an app is performing at runtime. Profiling data is often critical to turning the general feedback of "the app is slow" into a set of actionable steps for improving app performance. Some profiling tools, such as the Windows Phone Application Analysis tool, augment the raw performance data with perceived performance bottlenecks and provide suggestions on how to fix them. In this section, we will review the key profiling tools included in the Windows Phone SDK.

Before we do that, however, it is worth recalling the famous quip from computer-science legend, Donald Knuth: "Premature optimization is the root of all evil (or at least most of it) in programming." When setting out to profile your app, you should do so with a clear set of performance goals in mind. You can then use the tools provided in the SDK to identify problems that are getting in the way of meeting those goals and fix them. If you begin profiling without clear goals, you can waste a significant amount of time and energy trying to optimize an aspect of your app that no real user will ever notice.

Frame rate counters

When running apps under the debugger, you have probably noticed a set of small white and red numbers displayed in the upper-right corner of the screen (in portrait mode) or along the top left of the screen (in landscape). These are frame rate counters that are included in the default app template and added to your app only when attached to the debugger. The frame rate counters provide valuable insight into performance problems in the UI layer, such as overly complex visual trees and expensive animations. Figure 12-14 illustrates the counters that are enabled by default, and Table 12-3 explains what each counter means.

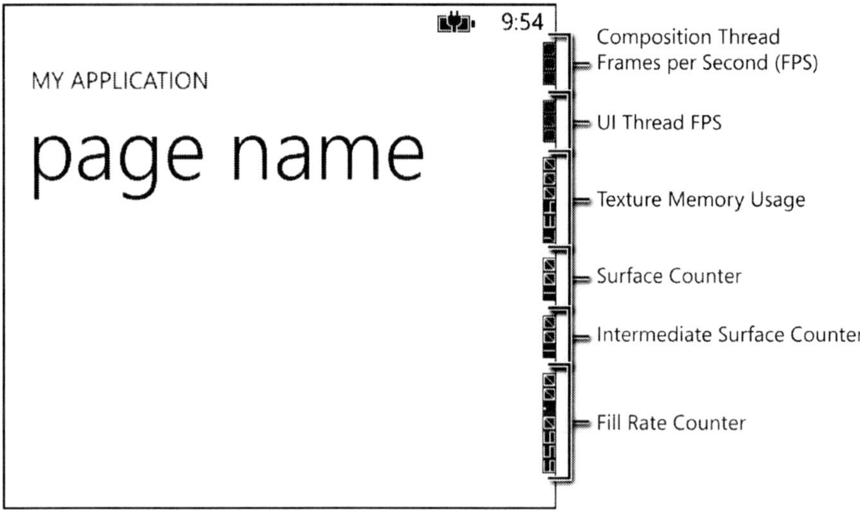

FIGURE 12-14 Frame rate counters are included by default when running under the debugger.

TABLE 12-3 The Windows Phone frame rate counters

Frame rate counter	Description
Composition thread frame rate	The frame rate (in frames per second) of the composition thread, also known as the render thread. The composition thread provides the device's graphics processor (GPU) with the types of textures and animations that it can render without support from the main processor (CPU). A value between 50 and 60 is desirable. If the number drops to 30 or lower, you will notice performance degradation in animations and the number will be rendered in red.
UI thread frame rate	The frame rate (in frames per second) of the app's UI thread. Apps have only one UI thread and it is responsible for most of their user interactivity. It is therefore important to keep this value as high as possible. As with the composition thread frame rate counter, a higher value is better and you should aim for 20 or higher. If the UI thread frame rate drops below 15, the number will be rendered in red.
Texture memory usage	The amount of video and system memory (in kilobytes) being used to store textures being created by the app. This value tends to be of little value to most apps. Note that this value only refers to memory being used to store textures, not the total memory usage for the app.
Surface counter	The total number of surfaces being provided to the GPU for processing. Most apps do not need to worry about this value.
Intermediate surface counter	The number of implicit surfaces created as a result of explicitly cached surfaces. Once again, this value is generally not actionable for most apps.
Fill rate counter	The number of logical screens being painted per frame. A value of 1 indicates that the app is painting the equivalent of just one screen of pixels. This value will rise when an app creates multiple overlapping UI elements, such as a list box on top of a panorama. You should try to keep the fill rate under 2.5. The counter will be rendered in red if it rises above 3.

The most important frame counters to watch are the composition thread frame rate, the UI thread frame rate, and the fill rate. If the composition thread frame rate drops significantly, animations will begin to appear choppy, whereas if the UI frame rate drops, the app might become less responsive to user input. The fill rate, meanwhile, provides a very clear indication when the app is trying to do too much on the screen.

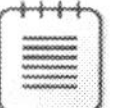

Note The frame rate counters can fall to 0 if there is nothing actively being animated on the screen. This is expected, but if you would like to display a more accurate value at all times, you can add a small repeating animation on the page. Just remember to remove it before submitting your app to the Windows Phone Store.

Redraw regions

A key part of improving UI performance is understanding what is being painted on the screen and how. Redraw regions make it possible for you to see the elements of your UI that are being drawn in software, using the CPU, rather than in hardware, using the GPU. Even though the CPU is always involved in the initial rendering of a texture, you should try to move rendering for subsequent frames to the GPU if possible. The *ExpandingEllipse* solution in the sample code illustrates the type of problem that redraw regions can help identify. The app contains two ellipses that grow and shrink by using storyboard animations. The UI for the app is shown in Figure 12-15.

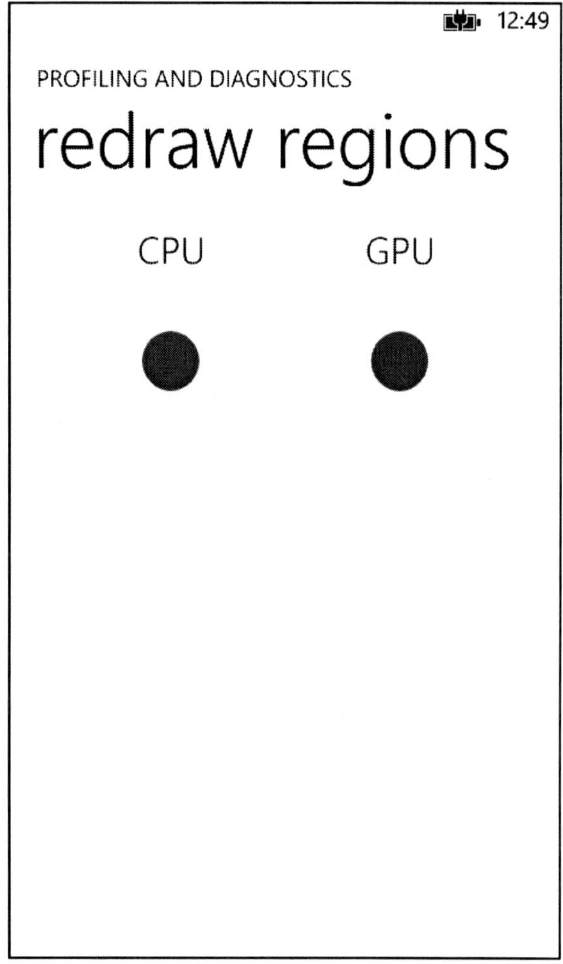

FIGURE 12-15 The *ExpandingEllipse* solution illustrates the difference between CPU and GPU rendering, which can be easily identified with the *EnableRedrawRegions* flag.

When run normally, the two animations appear to be the same; each grows and shrinks by the same amount. By enabling redraw regions, however, you can see that they are very different. To turn on redraw regions, simply set the *EnableRedrawRegions* flag to *true*, as shown in the code snippet that follows. This line of code is included in the *App.xaml.cs* file of the new project template but is initially commented out.

```
Application.Current.Host.Settings.EnableRedrawRegions = true;
```

With the flag enabled, the difference in the two animations is stark. The system draws a colored box around a texture when it is drawn in software by using the CPU, cycling through a set of colors so that each redraw is noticeable. As mentioned earlier, the CPU must be involved to render any texture for the first time, so the ellipse labeled GPU has a single box surrounding it even as it grows and shrinks. Meanwhile, the ellipse labeled CPU shows a series of overlapping boxes of different colors as it grows and shrinks, indicating that the CPU is helping to paint every single frame as it expands and contracts.

After you notice this type of pattern in your app, you can begin investigating how to fix it. In the case of the *ExpandingEllipse* sample, the ellipse labeled CPU is expanding and contracting by changing the height and width of the ellipse, which cannot be handled by the GPU, whereas the other ellipse is using a scale transform in its animation, an operation that can be handled by the GPU.

Note A scale transform can only be handed off to the GPU if the scaling factor is less than 50 percent of the original size.

DeviceStatus Memory APIs

Memory is one of the tightest constraints on a modern smartphone. As part of its overall resource management strategy, Windows Phone places a series of limits on the memory usage of apps, with different allocations for foreground apps and background tasks. Windows Phone 7.1 apps are limited to 90 MB of memory when running in the foreground and 5 MB of memory when running as a background task. In Windows Phone 8, the foreground resource allocations vary based on the amount of memory available on the device. This ranges from 150 to 180 MB for phones with less than 1 GB of memory, and up to 380 MB for higher-end devices. You should always ensure that your app can run well within the limits placed upon it by the system; apps that go beyond their memory cap are shut down immediately. The static *DeviceStatus* class in the *Microsoft.Phone.Info* namespace provides a number of simple methods with which you can query your app's memory usage. In particular, you can query the app's current memory usage by using the *ApplicationCurrentMemoryUsage* property, and its highest memory usage for the current session by using the *ApplicationPeakMemoryUsage* property. You can also query the maximum amount of memory available to the app on the current device by using the *ApplicationMemoryUsageLimit* property.

Tip The *DeviceExtendedProperties* class included in the original Windows Phone 7 platform provides many of the same values as *DeviceStatus*. However, most of the properties were deprecated in Windows Phone 7.1 in favor of *DeviceStatus*. Therefore, you should avoid using *DeviceExtendedProperties* if possible.

As with performance issues, it is important that you discover memory issues early in the development cycle. If you only discover that you are pushing the system's memory limits when your app is complete, you might find it more difficult to refactor your code to bring its memory usage down. As a result, it is useful to monitor how your app's memory usage might be changing as you develop and test it iteratively. Peter Torr's *MemoryDiagnosticsHelper* is a valuable tool for performing this type of monitoring. By adding a single source file to your project and writing one line of code, you can add a memory usage counter to the column of frame rate counters, as illustrated in Figure 12-16. You can download the tool from Peter's blog at *http://blogs.msdn.com/b/ptorr/archive/2010/10/30/that-memory-thing-i-promised-you.aspx.*

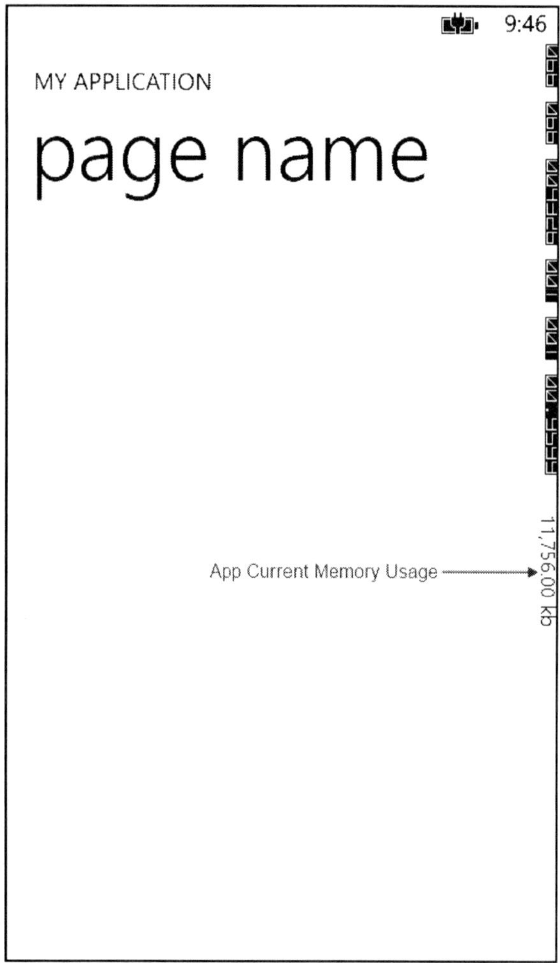

FIGURE 12-16 The *MemoryDiagnosticsHelper* puts your app's current memory usage in the list of frame rate counters.

The Windows Phone Performance Analysis Tool

The Windows Phone Performance Analysis Tool (also known as the profiler) that is built in to Visual Studio makes it possible for you to silently capture performance and app quality data while using your app and then analyze it to find areas for improvement. The tool uses a set of heuristics to detect common performance problems. It also provides raw performance data for metrics such as frame rate, CPU usage, and memory usage. The tool supports three types of profiling: app analysis, execution, and memory. The app analysis tool is the best place to start investigating performance issues in your app. It captures some of the key metrics related to startup time, responsiveness, and memory usage, and it displays a series of alerts if your app performs poorly on any of those metrics. The app analysis tool also provides information about power and data consumption, which you can use to further refine your app's resource usage. The execution and memory profiling options provide the same high-level data as the app analysis tool; however, they give you the opportunity to tweak certain settings and, in the case of the memory profiler, get more details about the specific part of your app that is causing the problem.

Tip Performance analysis is often thought of as a technique for identifying and fixing known performance issues. However, it is always a good idea to run long, thorough analysis sessions even if no problems are initially visible. This gives you an opportunity to uncover and fix hidden issues that can become more worrisome as your app grows. Memory leaks are a common example of this type of issue. App developers often don't realize how much memory their apps are using until they start receiving *OutOfMemoryException*s for exceeding their memory cap.

All performance analysis sessions are initiated in the same way. On the Debug menu, click Start Windows Phone Application Analysis. Make sure that you choose the Windows Phone–specific menu option, because there is a separate option labeled Start Performance Analysis that is not supported for phone projects. In the screen shown in Figure 12-17, you can choose from the three analysis options discussed earlier.

To begin an analysis session, at the bottom of the menu, click the Start Session link. Visual Studio then creates a special build of your project, augmented with instrumentation to capture performance data, and launches it on the current target platform (emulator or device). You then simply need to use the app as a user would, focusing on any known problem areas such as *ListBox* scrolling. When you have completed the set of steps that you want to profile in the app, click End Session to stop analyzing it.

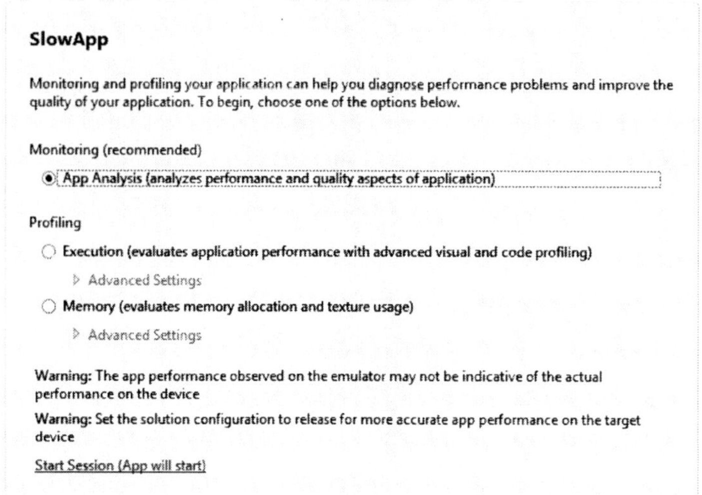
SlowApp
Monitoring and profiling your application can help you diagnose performance problems and improve the quality of your application. To begin, choose one of the options below.
Monitoring (recommended)
App Analysis (analyzes performance and quality aspects of application)
Profiling
Execution (evaluates application performance with advanced visual and code profiling)
Advanced Settings
Memory (evaluates memory allocation and texture usage)
Advanced Settings
Warning: The app performance observed on the emulator may not be indicative of the actual performance on the device
Warning: Set the solution configuration to release for more accurate app performance on the target device
Start Session (App will start)

FIGURE 12-17 With the Windows Phone Application Analysis tool, you can gather detailed profiling data for your app.

Tip As discussed earlier, you should always try to test your app in an environment that mimics as closely as possible the one that the user will experience. In particular, you should perform app analysis on a real device, using a release build with real data. For example, if your app suffers from a startup performance problem that worsens as the amount of user data it stores grows, you should ensure that you have generated a realistic amount of data before beginning an analysis session. It is also a good idea to test under different network conditions by using the network simulator tool introduced earlier in this chapter.

Each profiler session generates a new .sap file, which is automatically added to the root of your project, making it simple to reopen a profiling session at any time. Also, if you maintain multiple profiling sessions over the course of your development period, you can track performance improvements (or regressions) by using the profiler data. Be aware, however, that the SAP file is simply an XML manifest of the detailed logs that are created in the automatically generated PerfLogs folder within your project folder. These log files can grow quite large, especially for long-running profiling sessions, but because they are not actually added to your project, you don't need to worry about cleaning them up unless you are running out of storage space on your computer.

We will use the *SlowApp* solution from the sample code to walk through an app analysis report. The app includes two pages: *MainPage* and *Page2*. *MainPage*, shown in Figure 12-18, includes two buttons: one to navigate to *Page2*, and the other to invoke a slow method.

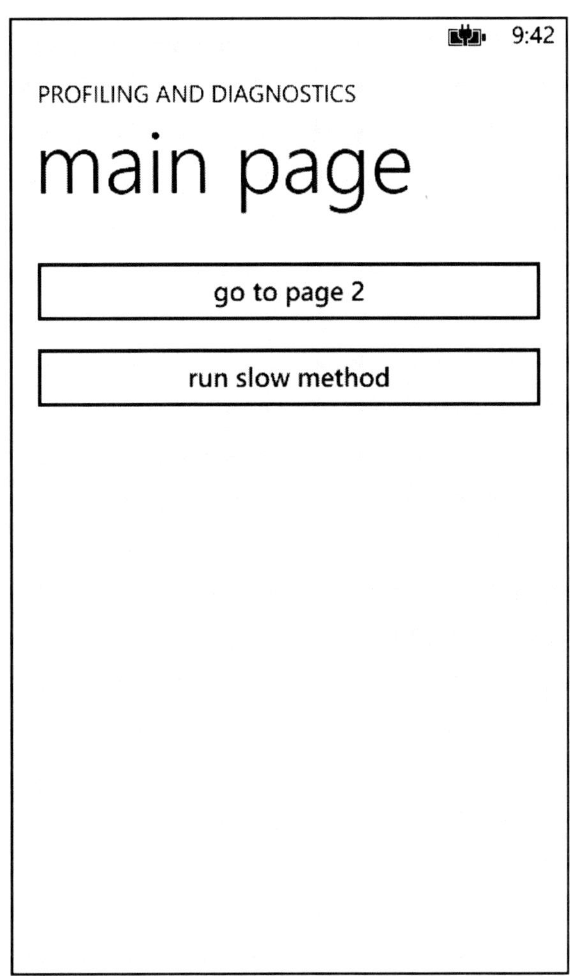

FIGURE 12-18 The *SlowApp* solution includes several problems that can be revealed by performance analysis.

Our performance analysis session involves clicking the Run Slow Method button once and navigating back and forth between *MainPage* and *Page2* four times. We will run through these steps twice, once to generate an app analysis report and again to generate a memory report. As mentioned earlier, the execution report provides the same basic data as the app analysis report, so in most cases, it is sufficient to use only the app analysis report for diagnosing issues with responsiveness and frame rate.

The app analysis report

The app analysis report includes a summary of the key quality metrics for the app, with specific areas of concern highlighted as alerts. The summary for *SlowApp* is shown in Figure 12-19.

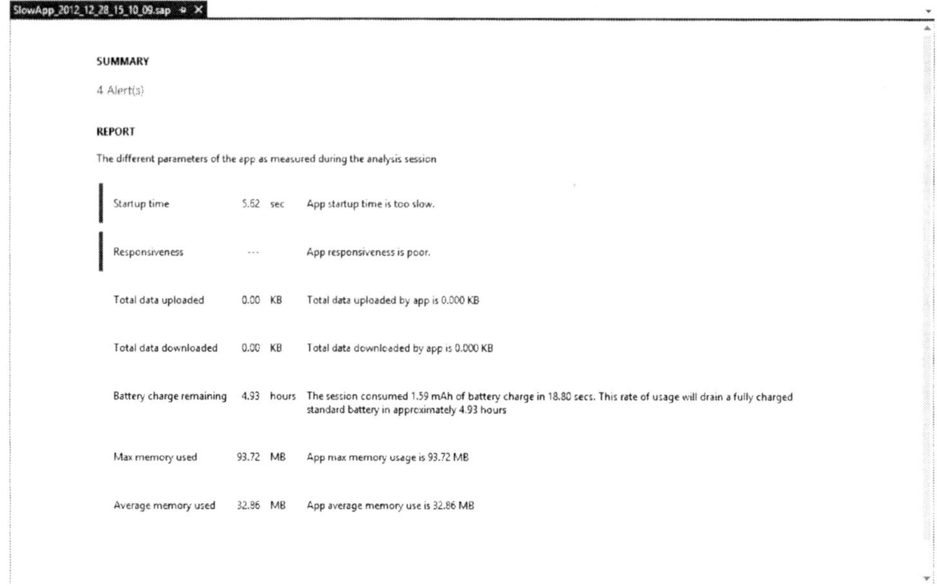

FIGURE 12-19 The app analysis summary highlights specific areas of concern for further investigation.

To open a more detailed report of app performance (see Figure 12-20), click the Alerts link in the summary report. Each of the alerts includes a start and end time, as well as a short summary of the issue and a suggestion for further investigation.

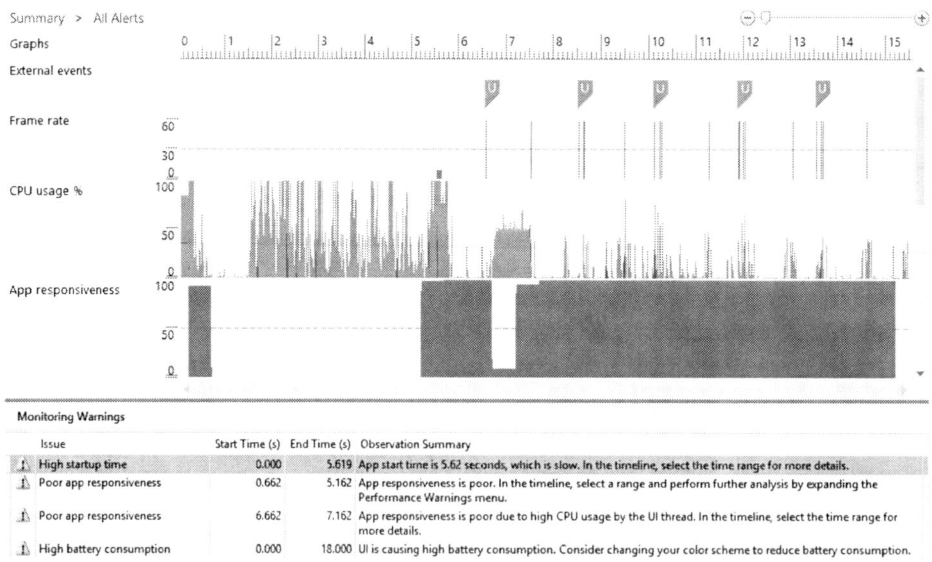

FIGURE 12-20 The detailed app analysis page provides graphical views of various quality metrics throughout the lifetime of the analysis session.

Before looking at the specific alerts in detail, it is useful to review the graphs shown in the upper half of the report. Understanding the data conveyed in these graphs will not only help you deal with the alerts raised by the profiler, but might also assist you in catching other issues that the profiler did not flag. From top to bottom, the graphs shown are as follows:

- **External Events** User-input events are marked with a "U," whereas changes in simulated network conditions are marked with an "N." In both cases, you can hover over the marker to view a ScreenTip with more detail. For example, the ScreenTip for a user-input event will show the type of gesture and its target.
- **Frame Rate** This is the rate (in frames per second) at which the compositor is redrawing the screen. As discussed earlier, if the frame rate drops below 30 Frames Per Second (FPS), you might begin to see glitches in animations. To help visualize points in the session that might be close to that point or beyond it, the graph includes a dotted line at 30 FPS. As mentioned earlier, the frame rate will usually drop to 0 if there are no active animations, so you might see large gaps between the lines.
- **CPU Usage %** This is the proportion of the phone's CPU time that is being allocated to various categories of threads, differentiated by colors.
  - Green lines represent the UI thread. As discussed earlier, significant activity on the UI thread will often lead to a drop in app responsiveness.
  - Purple lines represent all non-UI threads in your app, including the compositor threads and any background threads created by app code, directly or indirectly.
  - Gray lines are for system threads. In most cases, there isn't much your app can do to influence CPU utilization by system threads. However, it is useful to know when in the profiling session the system might have been busy doing something else, because it can help to explain app performance at that time.
  - White space indicates CPU idle time. If the CPU has nothing to do, it will be ready to immediately handle user input, thus making the app highly responsive.
- **App Responsiveness** The responsiveness of the app to user input, measured on a scale from 0 to 100, where 0 is completely unresponsive and 100 is highly responsive.
- **Network data transfer Mbps** The rate of network data transfer in megabits per second. (This graph is only shown for apps that perform network transfers.)
- **Memory usage MB** The current memory usage in megabytes.
- **Storyboards** Storyboard events are marked with an "S." CPU-bound storyboards are shown on a red marker, whereas those that can be offloaded to the GPU are shown on a purple marker. Some storyboards are embedded in the templates for platform controls and these will also be marked on the graph. For example, the default template for *Button* includes a storyboard that changes the background of the button to the device theme color when it is pressed.

- **Image loads** Image loads are marked with an "I."
- **GC events** Garbage collection events are marked with a "G." Each marker includes a ScreenTip that indicates the type of collection—ephemeral or full.

Note The last three graphs described—storyboards, image loads, and garbage collection events—are only available in the Detailed Analysis view. To access the Detailed Analysis view, simply highlight a portion of the session.

With the graphical portion of the report understood, we can return to the specific issues flagged by the profiler for the *SlowApp* solution. The first two alerts (high startup time and poor app responsiveness) are actually highlighting the same issue, namely that the app takes too long to become responsive to user input on startup. This is highlighted visually in the app responsiveness graph. The *SlowApp* solution forces this situation by putting the UI thread to sleep for five seconds in the app's *Launching* event handler. In a real app, it is more likely to be caused by performing a significant amount of file input/output, parsing complex XAML in the app's main page, or decoding a large number of images.

The report highlights another case of poor app responsiveness later in the session, suggesting high CPU usage on the UI thread. Recall that because the UI thread is responsible for handling most types of input from the user and for updating the UI, it is important to limit the amount of app code that runs on it. With the issue and its timing identified, we can begin investigating the root cause by using the timeline view.

Tip When investigating app performance issues by using the profiler, it is useful to be able to tie patterns in the timeline back to specific events in the session. The markers discussed earlier for user interactivity and storyboard events provide some guidance, but you might want to keep a more detailed record of what was happening in the app at each point, especially for profiling sessions that last 30 seconds or more. One way to do this is to open the Windows system clock from the desktop toolbar before launching the profiling session and then keeping notes about the interesting events during the session, along with the time that they occurred.

When you select a range in the timeline view, the profiler scopes the issues to those found during that period and provides additional guidance on how to proceed. In our case, we want to determine which method is running too long on the UI thread. By following the provided instructions, we eventually open the Functions table within the CPU Usage view, as illustrated in Figure 12-21.

Performance Warnings ▸ CPU Usage ▸ Functions ▸

Method Name	Inclusive Samples	Exclusive Samples	Inclusive Samples (%)	Exclusive Samples (%)
SlowApp.MainPage.runSlowMethodButton_Click(System.Object,	157	0	81.35 %	0.00 %
SlowApp.MainPage.SlowMethod()	157	3	81.35 %	1.55 %
System.Guid.ToString()	45	0	23.32 %	0.00 %
System.Guid.ToString(System.String, System.IFormatProvider)	45	0	23.32 %	0.00 %
System.String.CtorCharArrayStartLength(Char[], Int32, Int32)	28	1	14.51 %	0.52 %
System.Guid.HexsToChars(Char[], Int32, Int32, Int32, Boolean)	1	1	0.52 %	0.52 %
ManagedFunction_mdToken(100663888)	7	2	3.63 %	1.04 %
System.Collections.Generic.List`1[System.__Canon].Sort()	102	0	52.85 %	0.00 %

FIGURE 12-21 Drilling in on a specific warning in the timeline makes it possible for you to see where the app is spending its time.

The Functions table shows the list of functions called within the chosen period, whether those functions are part of the app code or part of the framework. For each function call, the profiler shows the number and proportion of inclusive and exclusive samples. Like many profiling tools, the Windows Phone profiler uses sampling to measure app performance; at regular intervals, the profiler interrupts the app's normal operation to gather session state and then combines those samples together to provide an accurate approximation of the full session. If the CPU is in the process of executing instructions for a given function when a sample is taken, the profiler increments the exclusive sample count, whereas if the CPU is in the process of executing instructions for a given function or any function called on its behalf, the profiler increments the inclusive sample count. When the profiler includes an app function in the table, it automatically creates a link to the function definition in the app code, making it easy to jump directly to the potential source of the problem. In the case of *SlowApp*, the culprit is the aptly named *SlowMethod*, which is performing a large number of string manipulations and sorting operations on a list of GUIDs. By moving this code to a background thread, we can significantly improve the app's responsiveness and thus the overall user experience (UX).

Note The last warning shown for the *SlowApp* solution concerns the impact of the app UI on battery life. Some Windows Phone devices include screens that are optimized for displaying dark content, so a brighter app UI will tend to drain the battery faster. This includes apps that allow the user theme color to act as the primary background color when the user's device is set to light theme. When faced with the tradeoff between UI consistency with the rest of the system and a slight savings in battery life, you should opt for consistency. If, on the other hand, you are creating a fully custom UI that does not incorporate the theme color and you have an opportunity to opt for a darker color scheme, you might be able to help your users squeeze a bit more life out of their batteries by dialing down the brightness.

Memory analysis report

When running an app analysis profiling session, you might see performance warnings related to memory usage, such as Excessive Allocations. However, because the additional instrumentation required to provide full details about memory allocations has an adverse impact on the profiler's ability to correctly monitor the app's execution performance, you must run a separate profiler session to fully investigate what is happening. There are several categories of problems to look out for when profiling your app's memory usage. First, you should ensure that your app is not running close to the memory limits imposed by the system, which we discussed earlier. Second, you should try to limit the number of times that the garbage collector needs to run, because it temporarily requires CPU cycles that could otherwise be allocated to your app. Finally, you should look out for any potential memory leaks. Even though the end result of a memory leak is the same as actively using too much memory, the indicators and solutions tend to be different.

The memory analysis report, shown in Figure 12-22, provides the necessary data to identify all three types of issues. Overall memory usage is tracked over the lifetime of the session so that you can see whether you are in danger of hitting the system-imposed caps. Garbage collection activity is highlighted in its own row, with a small marker shown on the timeline for each garbage collection event. Memory leaks are less obvious, but tend to be characterized by a memory usage chart that is growing gradually over time. The *SlowApp* solution, which is the basis for the memory analysis chart shown in Figure 12-20, contains a memory leak that is fairly pronounced, with a distinct increase coming at regular intervals.

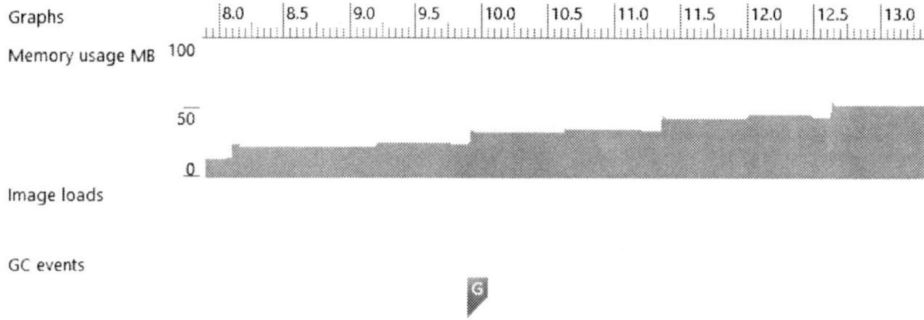

FIGURE 12-22 The memory profiler can help you identify and fix memory leaks such as this one.

If we highlight the portion of the session where the memory leak occurs, the profiler will attempt to provide more detail about what is causing it. In the case of *SlowApp*, the profiler shows a warning about excessive allocations of character arrays, suggesting that they account for 99 percent of the app's memory usage. To determine where and why those allocations are happening and, more importantly, why they are not being cleaned up by the garbage collector, we need to drill in deeper. The next level of detail, the heap summary view, shows the beginning and end state of the heap based on the part of the profiling session that was highlighted for analysis. In an app that has a memory leak, you should expect to see more new memory being allocated than is collected, and a larger amount of memory retained on the heap at the end of the session than at the start. The heap summary for the *SlowApp* solution, depicted in Figure 12-23, matches this pattern.

Performance Warnings ▸ Heap Summary ▸

Category	Instances	Total Size (KB)
Retained Allocations at Start	10221	643.742
New Allocations	3352	41117.263
Collected Allocations	5983	440.387
Retained Allocations at End	7590	41320.618
Retained Visuals at Start	31	2.035
Retained Visuals at End	55	4.270

FIGURE 12-23 The heap summary view shows an overview of heap activity during the highlighted portion of the profiling session.

For each row in the table, you can inspect the set of types that make up the values shown in the summary. For a memory leak, you should focus on retained allocations and retained visuals. For the *SlowApp* solution, it is retained allocations that is growing significantly, so we should continue the investigation there. In the Types view, a part of which is shown in Figure 12-24, you will generally see a list containing dozens of entries. Many of these are actually created by the system to perform basic platform functions and bear no relationship to app code, so you need to do a bit of searching to find the types that might actually be responsible for the problem. In the *SlowApp* solution, the offending allocations are large enough to easily stand out when the list is sorted by total size, but it is not always so obvious.

Performance Warnings ▸ Heap Summary ▸ Types ▸

Type Name	Instances	Total Size (Bytes)	Max Size (Bytes)	Avg Size (Bytes)	Total Allocated Size %	Allocating Module
System.Char[]	4	41943088	10485772	10485772	99.13 %	SlowApp.ni.DLL
System.String	865	69040	8400	79	0.16 %	mscorlib.ni.dll
System.String	794	34520	1586	43	0.08 %	N/A
System.Char[]	27	21748	4102	805	0.05 %	mscorlib.ni.dll

FIGURE 12-24 The Types view can help you to pinpoint objects that are accounting for most of your memory usage.

If you continue drilling further into the details, you can eventually analyze the object relationship for an instance of the type that is causing the problem, and specifically the relationship that the garbage collector cares about, a view labeled GC Roots. The GC Roots view (see Figure 12-25) represents the types as a tree, where the parent node cannot be cleaned up until all of its children are also ready for clean-up. We can see that the large character array is allocated in a type called *BigObject*, which in turn is held by *Page2*. The real question is why an instance of *Page2* is still around even after the user navigated away from it. Looking at the children of *Page2* provides an answer: the page is maintaining an event handler for the *Tick* event of a static *DispatcherTimer* object from *App.xaml.cs*. Because the *DispatcherTimer* object never goes out of scope and *Page2* never unhooks the event handler, the garbage collector cannot remove any instance of *Page2*, even though it is no longer accessible. This leads to a memory leak.

Performance Warnings ▸ Heap Summary ▸ Types ▸ Methods ▸ Instances ▸ GC Roots

Type Name	Instance ID	Generation	Root Kind	Create Time (s)	Allocating Module
◢ System.Char[]	10654	Gen2		8.083	SlowApp.ni.DLL
◢ SlowApp.BigObject	10653	Gen1		8.083	SlowApp.ni.DLL
◢ SlowApp.Page2	10455	Gen1		8.060	mscorlib.ni.dll
▷ System.Windows.Controls.Grid	10622	Gen1		8.079	System.Windows.ni.dll
▷ System.Collections.Generic.Dictionary`2<System.	10641	Gen1		8.082	mscorlib.ni.dll
▷ System.EventHandler	10655	Gen1		8.083	SlowApp.ni.DLL

FIGURE 12-25 The GC Roots view shows object relationships from the garbage collector's perspective.

Note The Windows Phone profiler does not support profiling background agents. To monitor memory usage in background agents, you must rely on the *DeviceStatus* APIs described earlier. Alternatively, you can create a temporary app project that includes a reference to the background agent assembly and does nothing but invoke your background agent code. Be aware, however, that the base memory usage for an app is higher than the base memory usage for an agent, so you should only use this technique to look for memory problems, not to try to optimize your agent memory usage down to a specific number.

Profiling native code

One of the significant new features in Windows Phone 8 is the ability to write apps and games as well as individual app components by using native code. Likewise, the Windows Phone profiler provides tools for developers to profile native code using the same tools and reports provided in Visual Studio for Windows 8 apps.

The first step in profiling a Direct3D game or a XAML app that uses a native component is the same as it is for a fully managed project, namely launching Start Windows Phone Application Analysis from the Debug menu in Visual Studio. For apps and games that use native code, the only profiling option is execution—app monitoring and memory profiling are not available. After you start the session, the process of running through the app is the same as it is for a managed app. You should move through all of the key paths in the app, paying special attention to any known hot spots where animations lag or responsiveness drops. When you are finished running through your tests, the profiler will display a summary report, as shown in Figure 12-26. The summary report for native profiling looks different from that shown for managed apps, although many of the concepts are the same.

The top portion of the report shows a graph of CPU usage over the course of the session. As with the managed profiler report, you can select a portion of the timeline on which to focus, either zooming in for a closer look at the CPU usage graph or actually filtering the other data to just that portion of the session. The second table in the report shows the app's hot path. The hot path is defined as the execution path that took up the greatest proportion of time during the session. The third and final table in the summary report shows the list of functions that took up the greatest proportion of time during the session. This data is based on exclusive samples, meaning that it is restricted to time spent in the function itself, not in functions that it calls.

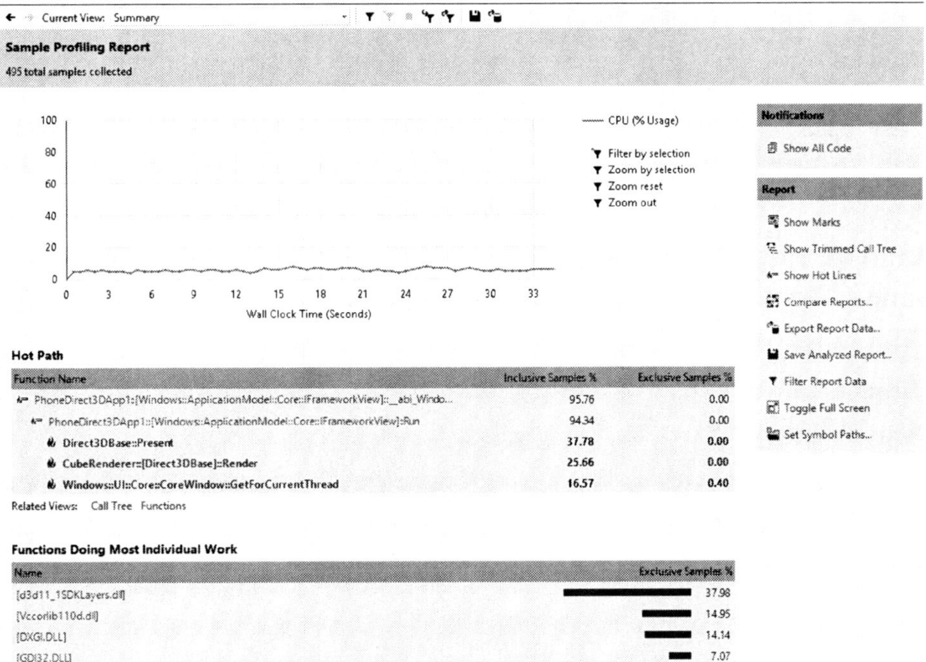

FIGURE 12-26 The native profiler report looks different from the managed version, but many concepts are the same.

The native profiler report also provides additional detail through various views, which are accessible on the menu at the top of the screen. For instance, using the Caller/Callee view, you can walk up and down the call stack, easily jumping between functions that called the current function and functions that the current function called. This makes it possible for you to more easily hone in on specific problems in your code after a general area of concern is identified.

Performance best practices

Providing general purpose performance advice can be a difficult proposition. In most cases, optimizing performance is a matter of considering tradeoffs that are unique to each app. As a result, the best way to improve performance of your app is to understand the options available so that you can decide which of them make sense to apply in a given situation. In this section, we will look at a handful of techniques that can help make your apps faster, more responsive, and less resource intensive.

More Info For a full list of performance tips, see App Performance Considerations for Windows Phone on MSDN at *http://msdn.microsoft.com/en-us/library/windowsphone/develop/ff967560(v=vs.105).aspx.*

Keep the user engaged

Recently, many major airports have sought to *increase* the distance that passengers have to walk after leaving the plane in order to retrieve their luggage. By providing something to do while luggage is delivered to baggage claim, those airports are reporting improved levels of customer satisfaction and a belief on the part of passengers that luggage is actually being delivered faster. The lesson: performance is perception. The same principle applies for apps. If users believe your app is fast, it doesn't really matter what the numbers say. One of the best ways to improve the perception of your app's performance is to ensure that the user is never left wondering what is happening or feeling that the app is stuck. Specifically, you should consider doing the following:

- Render as much of your page UI as possible immediately, with additional data filling in as it's available. Avoid blocking the page constructor or the *OnNavigatedTo* event handler waiting for data to be loaded.
- If app startup time is more than two seconds, consider adding a splash screen image. A splash screen can highlight your brand while reassuring the user that the app is loading. For apps that startup quickly, however, a splash screen image can decrease the perception of your app's performance and should generally be avoided.
- For data that does not load instantaneously, use the *ProgressIndicator* control or the *ProgressBar* control. The *ProgressIndicator* includes the familiar animating dots and a status text field and is shown in the notification area, whereas the *ProgressBar* control includes only the animation and can be placed anywhere in your UI. For Windows Phone 7.1 apps, you should use the *PerformanceProgressBar* in the Windows Phone Toolkit rather than the *ProgressBar* available in the platform. For an in-depth explanation of the performance issues in the Windows Phone 7.x ProgressBar, see Jeff Wilcox's post on the subject at *http://www.jeff.wilcox.name/2010/08/performanceprogressbar/*.

Stay off of the UI thread

As mentioned throughout the chapter, the UI thread is responsible for a large number of tasks that are out of your control, including many forms of user input and data binding. You should move any code that doesn't need to be on the UI thread to a background thread and to only return to the UI thread when you need to update the UI. The simplest way to run code in the background is to spin off a separate thread by using the *System.Threading.ThreadPool* and then use the *Dispatcher* to marshal updates back to the UI thread.

```
ThreadPool.QueueUserWorkItem((o) =>
{
    // background code

    Dispatcher.BeginInvoke(() =>
    {
        // update UI
    });

    // more background code
});
```

Windows Phone 8 apps also have the option to use the *Windows.System.Threading.ThreadPool*, which offers simple integration with the *await* keyword through the *RunAsync* method. One advantage of this approach is that if you only need to update your UI after the background operation has completed, you can do so without using the dispatcher, assuming that the call to *RunAsync* was itself made on the UI thread.

```
await Windows.System.Threading.ThreadPool.RunAsync((operation) =>
{
    // run background code

});

// update UI
```

Simplify the visual tree

The flexibility of XAML markup is incredibly powerful, but it must be used with caution. The more complex your page's XAML layout, the longer it will take it to be rendered. For example, multiple levels of nested grid controls with automatic sizing for rows and columns require the XAML layout system to do several passes over your page layout to determine the appropriate size of each element. Consider some of the following tips to speed up XAML layout:

- Use *StackPanel* rather than *Grid* for elements that can be placed in vertical or horizontal order without specific spacing requirements.
- Set exact sizes for elements that are known in advance to avoid having to calculate them at runtime.
- Avoid explicitly setting default values on XAML attributes. It is faster for the system to use the default value directly, rather than having to parse it out of XAML.
- Avoid naming XAML elements that don't need to be referenced from code. The system will create addressable objects for named XAML elements. If you never need to use those elements, you can skip that creation.
- Simplify the *DataTemplate* definition for list boxes that will have more than a handful of items and consider using a different template while the user is scrolling. List boxes in Windows Phone use UI virtualization, meaning that the system only creates the *ListBoxItem* objects for a few dozen list entries up front and then generates others on the fly as you scroll. If you have a complex *DataTemplate*, the layout system might not be able to keep up with rendering it as the user scrolls quickly through the list. One solution is to use a different, simpler *DataTemplate* definition when the item is not on the screen or while it's quickly scrolling past and only render the richer version when the user has stopped to look at it. See Peter Torr's LazyListBox sample for an idea of how to do this, which you can find at *http://blogs.msdn.com/b/ptorr/archive/2010/10/12/procrastination-ftw-lazylistbox-should-improve-your-scrolling-performance-and-responsiveness.aspx*.

Easy wins with photos

The Windows Phone platform makes it easy to load local or remote images into an app, either in XAML by using the *Image* element, or in code by using *BitmapSource* and its derivations. However, the simplicity in the programming model masks a significant amount of work happening under the surface, so certain easy performance gains might not be obvious:

- A common source of unnecessary memory usage is high-resolution images scaled down to very small UI elements on the phone. If you set the source of an *Image* element to a 2000x2000 pixel image, but set the height and width of the *Image* to 100x100, the system will first load the full size image and then scale it down, keeping far more pixels than are necessary to fill the desired space. In Windows Phone 8, you can now set properties on a *BitmapSource* that indicate the image size you need: *DecodePixelWidth* and *DecodePixelHeight*. Of course, you should be careful with this if you expect the images will have to grow larger than their original size, because they will then appear pixelated.
- The *BitmapImage* class includes a *CreateOptions* property with which you can specify how you would like the in-memory bitmap to be created from the provided source. By default, *CreateOptions* is set to *`DelayCreation*, meaning that the system will wait until the image is actually needed before initializing it, at which point it will decode it on the UI thread. In most cases, you should use *BackgroundCreation*, instead. When *BackgroundCreation* is set, the system immediately downloads and decodes the image on a background thread, ensuring that it is ready as soon as it is needed without interrupting the UI thread.

Use *LongListSelector* instead of *ListBox* for large collections

The *ListBox* control is one of the most commonly used controls on the Windows Phone platform and historically has been one of the major sources of performance issues in Windows Phone apps, especially with respect to scrolling performance. Although it has been optimized over several releases, the foundation of the *ListBox* control is still based on the original version found in desktop Silverlight, where it could assume significantly faster CPUs and GPUs. The *LongListSelector* control, by contrast, has been built from the ground up to deal with the resource constraints imposed by a mobile device. The *LongListSelector* control was previously only available in the Windows Phone toolkit, but it is now included directly in the platform. Although the *LongListSelector* includes a number of additional features beyond what is available in the basic *ListBox* control, it can (and should) also be used as a direct replacement for *ListBox* for collections that include anything more than a handful of items. To replace *ListBox* with *LongListSelector* simply change:

```
<ListBox x:Name="itemsList">
    <ListBox.ItemTemplate>
        ...
    </ListBox.ItemTemplate>
</ListBox>
```

to:

```
<phone:LongListSelector x:Name="itemsList">
    <LongListSelector.ItemTemplate>
    ...
    </LongListSelector.ItemTemplate>
</phone:LongListSelector>
```

Use panorama thoughtfully

Panorama is one of the signature controls in Windows Phone, providing the unique UX found in the built-in hubs. It is therefore no surprise that developers are eager to use panorama to power their own differentiated experiences. However, using the panorama control carries a cost. First, because one of the key elements of panorama is the subtle hint that more content is available in the next pane, the system loads and renders all panorama items up-front, adding to startup time and memory usage. Second, even though one of the ways to make panorama especially striking is to add a high-resolution background image, decoding and rendering that image can likewise add to startup time, memory usage, and fill rate. Finally, because the panorama controls tend to be used for an app's main page and offer a wide, expansive canvas for content, there is a tendency for apps to include too much information and too many features on that single page, again leading to increases in startup time, memory usage, and fill rate. Earlier in this section, we discussed how performance is often a matter of tradeoffs. Deciding how and when to use panorama is a perfect example of that. Consider some of the following tips when thinking about using a panorama:

- The standard metaphor for the panorama control is a magazine cover. The cover should be visually engaging and provide a good idea of what content will be found inside the magazine, but it should not contain much of the content itself. In the same way, a panorama should draw the user into the app and provide broad entry points into the app's functionality, but limit the amount of text and controls that are layered on top of it. In most cases, the only controls present on a panorama should be those with which the user can navigate elsewhere in the app.

- Don't force yourself to use a background image if you don't have one that significantly improves the UX. The built-in people and wallet hubs use a panorama control but do not show a background image. Not only does this improve startup time and reduce memory usage, but it ensures easy visibility of text throughout the page, something that can be challenging with an image that varies in brightness and color.

- Consider whether using the pivot control would fit your needs. If your app is focused on completing tasks rather than discovering new content serendipitously, the pivot control might be more suitable. It is also faster to load and uses less memory than panorama.

Summary

A modern mobile app cannot succeed based on features alone. The qualities that lead people to use an app frequently and tell others about it are often the least tangible. These attributes are typically referred to using expressions such as "polish" and "fit and finish." To deliver an experience that users will consider polished requires spending time testing the app, fixing bugs, and improving performance. The tools discussed in this chapter provide a solid foundation for creating a high-quality app that users will love.

CHAPTER 13

Porting to Windows Phone 8 and multitargeting

Although Windows Phone 8 represents a major step forward for the Windows Phone platform, the transition from Windows Phone 7.x is not without hurdles. Significant architectural differences between Windows CE (the basis for Windows Phone 7.x) and Windows NT (the basis for Windows Phone 8) mean that existing devices cannot be upgraded, which will keep millions of Windows Phone 7 devices in market for several years. For app developers, even though Windows Phone 8 provides backward compatibility for Windows Phone 7 apps, there are some breaking changes that must be dealt with when upgrading an app to the latest operating system (OS) version. In this chapter, we review techniques for maximizing the reach of your app across the two major OS versions and look at ways to smooth the transition of your apps to Windows Phone 8.

Lighting up a Windows Phone 7 App with Windows Phone 8 features

The fact that Windows Phone 7 devices will remain in the market for some time creates a challenge for developers seeking to maximize the reach of their apps; namely, which OS version should you target? To reach the largest possible audience, your app should target Windows Phone 7.1 because then it can run on both Windows Phone 7.1 and Windows Phone 8 devices. However, significant platform advances such as new tile functionality and in-app purchase are only available on Windows Phone 8. Ideally, you could create a Windows Phone 7.1 app that runs on both platforms, but is able to take advantage of Windows Phone 8 features when running on a Windows Phone 8 device. In fact, this is possible through a technique known as *light up*, whereby you check the OS version at runtime and dynamically invoke Windows Phone 8 APIs to take advantage of Windows Phone 8–only features. In this section, we will review how you can do this for the new tile functionality in Windows Phone 8, but it can be used for any API in the platform that does not rely on static declarations in the app manifest.

A quick introduction to reflection

Light up uses a technique called reflection with which you query type information from an assembly and invoke methods based on those types at runtime. All of the languages supported for Windows Phone development are statically typed, meaning that the compiler validates the proper usage of all types in the app during compilation. When you target a particular version of the Windows Phone OS with a managed app, the compiler checks the types that you're using against those defined in the public surface area of the platform by using metadata stored in a set of design-time assembly files, known as reference assemblies. When you deploy the app to a device or emulator running the version of the OS that you're targeting, the API surface area available at runtime matches what was available in the reference assemblies checked at runtime. However, when you run on a later version of the OS, additional types and methods might be available. Reflection makes it possible for you to dynamically create instances of those types and call their methods to perform operations that the compiler would never allow.

Creating Windows Phone 8 tiles in a Windows Phone 7 App

The Start screen and its active set of Live tiles are one of the most distinctive features of the Windows Phone user experience (UX). As is discussed in Chapter 14, "Tiles and notifications," Windows Phone 8 makes two significant changes to Live tiles:

- **Resizable tiles** All tiles are now resizable by the user and can offer different content in small, medium, and wide modes.
- **Additional tile templates** In Windows Phone 7.1, Windows Phone Store apps were only permitted to use one tile template, the equivalent of the Windows Phone 8 flip tile template. In Windows Phone 8, Windows Phone Store apps can also create iconic and cycle tiles.

Given the importance of tiles to the user experience, Windows Phone offers two ways to bridge the gap between Windows Phone 7.1 and Windows Phone 8 for users and developers. For users, the Windows Phone 7.8 release provides the new start screen functionality to a set of Windows Phone 7.x devices. For developers, the Windows Phone 8 SDK makes it possible to light up a Windows Phone 7.1 app with new tiles when running on Windows Phone 7.8 or Windows Phone 8. In this section, we will focus on the general mechanism for creating the new tile types in a Windows Phone 7.1 app. For full details on the new tile features in the Windows Phone 8 SDK, see Chapter 14.

Tip Even if you choose not to take advantage of the new tile templates in your Windows Phone 7.1 app, you should consider upgrading your existing tile image assets so that they will look sharp on all Windows Phone 8 devices, including those offering 720p and WXGA resolutions. For standard Windows Phone 7.1 tiles, you should provide an image that is 336x336 pixels because that is the size of the medium tile on a WXGA device. The system will automatically scale your images down for lower-resolution phones.

The *TileLightUp* solution in the sample code illustrates how you can enhance an app targeting the Windows Phone 7.1 SDK with the new tiles available in Windows Phone 7.8 and Windows Phone 8. The app itself is extremely simple, with the main page offering a single button to add a new secondary tile while showing the current OS version at the bottom of the page. The user interface (UI) for the main page of the app is shown in Figure 13-1.

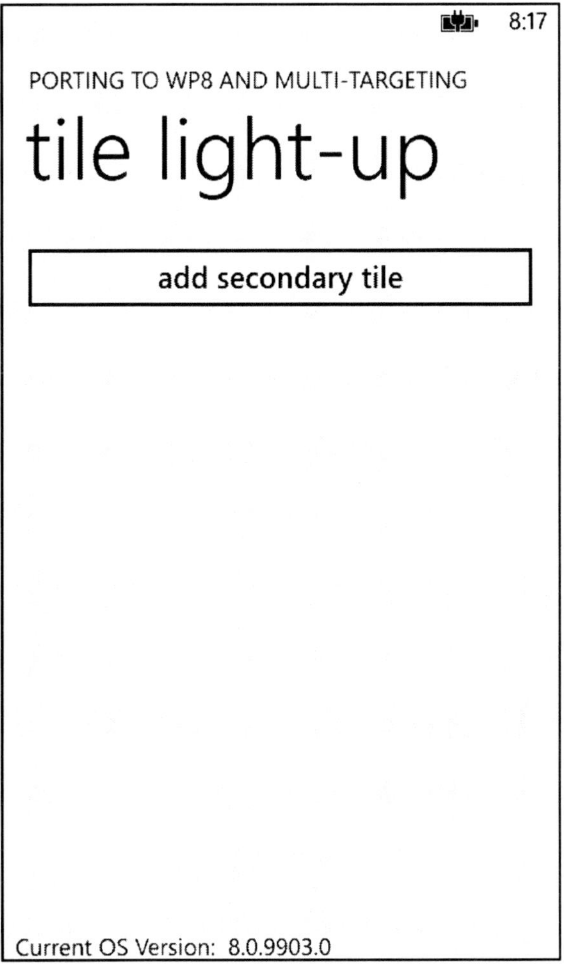

FIGURE 13-1 The main page of the *TileLightUp* solution.

Registering for the tiles *AppExtra*

To create tiles based on the new templates in a Windows Phone 7.1 app project, you must include the *AppExtra* element in the app manifest. This element is used to keep track of which apps are using the tile light-up feature in Windows Phone Store, and it should be added immediately before the existing *App* element.

```
<Deployment xmlns="http://schemas.microsoft.com/windowsphone/2012/deployment"
            AppPlatformVersion="7.1">
    <DefaultLanguage xmlns="" code="en-US"/>
    <AppExtra xmlns="" AppPlatformVersion="8.0">
        <Extra Name="Tiles"/>
    </AppExtra>
    <App xmlns=""
        ProductID="{88023d79-05d7-477f-ace5-49c89b01fbd4}"
        Title="TileLightUp"
        RuntimeType="Silverlight"
        Version="1.0.0.0"
        Genre="apps.normal"
        Author="TileLightUp author"
        Description="Sample description"
        Publisher="TileLightUp"
        PublisherID="{bb9220cd-4f83-4b7c-a66a-36188b0cfa42}">

    <!-- remainder of manifest omitted -->
    </App>
</Deployment>
```

Checking the OS version

Because the entire idea behind light-up is that your app can have different behavior on different OS versions, you need to determine the current OS version number before you can do anything else. The *TileLightUpViewModel* class includes a *CurrentOSVersion* property, which returns the current OS version from the platform's *OSVersion* class.

```
public Version CurrentOSVersion
{
    get
    {
        return Environment.OSVersion.Version;
    }
}
```

After the current OS version is known, determining which tile functionality to use in the app is just a matter of comparing the current OS version with the minimum version that supports the new tile features. As we've seen, the first release to support the enhanced tiles is Windows Phone 7.8. Technically, however, the OS version for Windows Phone 7.8 is 7.10.8858, meaning that only the build number has changed since the Windows Phone 7.1 release (7.10.8773). The reason for this discrepancy is that the platform version is only incremented when the new OS represents a distinct platform that apps can target. Apart from the tile changes, which are only accessible via reflection, Windows Phone 7.8 is exactly the same as Windows Phone 7.1 as far as apps are concerned, so the major and minor version numbers remain the same.

Note Maintaining an OS version number that is different from the brand of the consumer product is a long-standing practice in Windows. Desktop Windows has used 6 as its major version number since Windows Vista, with Windows 7 using version 6.1 and Windows 8 using version 6.2. The goal of this seemingly strange practice is avoiding unnecessary compatibility issues. Historically, many Windows apps checked the OS version number and failed to run if the version was higher than some hard-coded upper limit. Given the high degree of backward compatibility for Windows apps, these checks were usually unnecessary. By maintaining a single major OS version, these apps can continue to run on subsequent versions of Windows. Interestingly, Windows Store apps do not have the ability to query the current OS version, precisely to avoid this problem going forward.

The *TileViewModel* maintains a hard-coded instance of the *Version* class set to the OS version for Windows Phone 7.8 and a helper method to determine whether the current OS version is at least 7.8, a cue to use the enhanced tile functionality.

```
public static Version MinOSVersionForEnhancedTiles = new Version(7, 10, 8858);

public bool IsCurrentVersionEnabledForEnhancedTiles
{
    get
    {
        return CurrentOSVersion >= MinOSVersionForEnhancedTiles;
    }
}
```

Upgrading existing tiles

There are two reasons why you might want to upgrade your tiles immediately when your app is started. First, the user might have upgraded from Windows Phone 7.1 to Windows Phone 7.8 since the last time your app was started. Second, if the updated version of your app was just installed, your primary tile will be based on the properties defined in your app manifest, which are based on the version 7.1 tile definition (see Figure 13-2), which is shown in the *TileLightUp* solution in the sample code. If you want to upgrade your primary tile to take advantage of the new tile functionality, you must do so programmatically.

Note It is not necessary for your primary tile to be present on the Start screen to upgrade it. The system maintains a representation of every app's primary tile even if it has not been pinned. If you modify the properties of your primary tile before it is pinned to the Start screen, the new content will be visible immediately if the user eventually does pin it.

FIGURE 13-2 The default start tile is based on the properties defined in the app manifest.

The *TileLightUp* solution performs a check during app startup to determine whether any of the app's start tiles need to be upgraded. For tile upgrades to happen, two things must be true. First, the app must be running on a platform version that supports the enhanced tile features; that is, 7.10.8858 or later. Second, the tile upgrade must not have already taken place, as tracked by the Boolean property *AreTilesEnhanced* on the view model. The *LoadViewModel* helper simply loads and deserializes the persisted view model object and assigns it to the static member, *TileViewModel*. We do not need to worry about performing tile upgrades during app activation because both situations in which upgrades will be required—an update to the app or to the OS—will result in the app being closed.

```
private void Application_Launching(object sender, LaunchingEventArgs e)
{
    LoadViewModel();
    TryTileUpgrade();
}
```

```
private static void TryTileUpgrade()
{
    if (TileViewModel.IsCurrentVersionEnabledForEnhancedTiles &&
        !TileViewModel.AreTilesEnhanced)
    {
         TileViewModel.UpgradeTilesToFlipTemplate();
    }
}
```

The *UpgradeTilesToFlipTemplate* method on the view model iterates through all of the app's tiles on the Start screen and upgrades them to the new flip tile template. The flip tile template in Windows Phone 7.8 and Windows Phone 8 is the evolution of the only template that was available to Windows Phone Store apps in Windows Phone 7.1 and is therefore the only one that you can target when upgrading an existing tile. Because the tile type remains the same, the opportunity for upgrades is limited to the new tile sizes: small and wide.

Note Although you cannot upgrade an existing Windows Phone 7.1 tile to the iconic or cycle tile templates, it is technically possible to *remove* the existing tiles and add new ones that use the new templates. There are two significant drawbacks to this, however. First, adding a new tile always automatically navigates the user away from your app to the Start screen, making the process of replacing multiple tiles a very poor UX. Second, new tiles are always added at the bottom of the Start screen, meaning that the user must manually restore your tiles to their previous positions. In general, it is best to stick to upgrading existing tiles to the flip template and optionally expose the ability for users to create new tiles that use the other templates. The user can then make the decision regarding whether to replace the flip tiles with tiles of a different template.

In Windows Phone 8, all tiles can be resized to small, even those created by Windows Phone 7.1 apps. The system simply shrinks the medium tile and drops its title such that the only thing shown is the background image. Although this automatic resizing works for many apps, you might want to provide a different background image for the small tile; for instance, if you were using the tile to provide a rich set of live data, that content might not be legible in a small tile and might be better replaced with a simple icon. For wide tiles, the app must explicitly provide one of the types of wide content to indicate to the system that the user should be allowed to expand the tile to full size. For the flip tile template, the wide tile properties are: *WideBackgroundImage*, *WideBackBackgroundImage*, and *WideBackContent*.

As mentioned earlier, lighting up the new templates requires the use of reflection, and the *UpgradeTilesToFlipTemplate* method provides the first glimpse of it. We first acquire representations of the *FlipTileData* and *ShellTile* types from the *Microsoft.Phone* assembly. It is important to understand that these are not instances of these types, but references to the types themselves. With these references, we can access the type's constructor, properties, and members by name by using the methods of the *Type* class. For instance, we use the *GetConstructor* method to access the constructor for the *FlipTileData* class and then invoke it to instantiate an instance of that type—an operation that would have not been possible statically. The lone parameter to *GetConstructor*, an array of *Type* objects, makes it possible for you to specify the overload of the constructor that you want to use. For the default constructor, use the *EmptyTypes* array. Because all of the values on the *FlipTileData* class are exposed as properties, we create a *SetProperty* extension method to update each property's value (explained further below). Finally, we get a reference to the *Update* method on *ShellTile* and invoke it, passing the instance of the tile to update and the *FlipTileData* object containing the new data.

Note The *UpgradeTilesToFlipTemplate* method takes a simplistic approach to upgrading the app's tiles, setting each to the same content. In a real app, you would probably want to set different content on each tile. You can use the *NavigationUri* property on the *ShellTile* class to differentiate between different tiles.

```
public void UpgradeTilesToFlipTemplate()
{
    Type flipTileDataType = Type.GetType("Microsoft.Phone.Shell.FlipTileData, Microsoft.Phone");
    Type shellTileType = Type.GetType("Microsoft.Phone.Shell.ShellTile, Microsoft.Phone");

    var updatedTileData = flipTileDataType.GetConstructor(Type.EmptyTypes).Invoke(null);

    foreach (var oldTile in ShellTile.ActiveTiles)
    {
        updatedTileData.SetProperty("BackTitle", "TileLightup");
        updatedTileData.SetProperty("WideBackContent", "Wide tiles are great!");

        updatedTileData.SetProperty("BackgroundImage",
                    new Uri("/Assets/FlipBackgroundImage.png", UriKind.Relative));

        updatedTileData.SetProperty("WideBackgroundImage",
                    new Uri("/Assets/FlipWideBackgroundImage.png", UriKind.Relative));

        updatedTileData.SetProperty("SmallBackgroundImage",
                    new Uri("/Assets/SmallBackgroundImage.png", UriKind.Relative));

        shellTileType.GetMethod("Update").Invoke(oldTile, new object[] { updatedTileData });
    }

    AreTilesEnhanced = true;
}
```

Extension methods are a feature of the C# and Microsoft Visual Basic compilers with which you can create new methods callable as instance methods on types that you do not own, including framework types. This creates much cleaner code because you can use the standard "dot notation"—that is, *instance.method(parameters)* rather than having to pass the instance into the method—*method(instance, parameters)*. To create extension methods, you must define a static class containing one static method for each extension that you want. The extension method takes an instance of the type that you want to extend as its first parameter, preceded by the *this* modifier.

```
public static class LightUpExtensions
{
    private static void SetProperty(this object instance, string propertyName, object
                                    propertyValue)
    {
        instance.GetType().GetProperty(propertyName).SetValue
                                                        (propertyName, propertyValue, null);
    }
}
```

After the upgrade code has run, the app's tiles can be set to any of the three supported sizes, with each providing assets and content that are specific to the size, as shown in Figure 13-3. Observe the use of a symbolic icon for the small tile, rather than simply having the platform downsize the medium tile photo.

FIGURE 13-3 The *TileLightUpSolution* provides different content for each tile size.

Adding new tiles

You can follow a similar approach when adding new tiles from your app (check the OS version that the app is running on and provide enhanced tiles only when running on Windows Phone 7.8 or later). The difference between adding new tiles and upgrading existing tiles is that new tiles can use any of the new templates, including iconic and cycle.

The *TileLightUp* solution includes a single button to add a new secondary tile. The button's click event handler directly calls the *AddSecondaryTile* method on the view model, which in turn performs the OS version check and then either adds a standard tile (if running on Windows Phone 7.1) or uses reflection to add an iconic tile (if running on Windows Phone 7.8 or later). In the latter case, the code is nearly identical to what we showed earlier for updating existing tiles, though there are a couple of things worth pointing out about the way the tile is finally created. First, as mentioned earlier for *GetConstructor*, the *GetMethod* method on the *Type* class accepts an array of *Type* objects that make it possible for you to specify the desired overload of the method you're requesting. In this case, we want the version of the *Create* method with the following signature:

```
public static void Create(Uri navigationUri, ShellTileData initialData, bool supportsWideTile)
```

To find that specific method, we need to pass in an array containing the types for *Uri*, *ShellTileData*, and *bool*. You can reuse the existing *Type* instance for *IconicTileData* because *IconicTileData* inherits from *ShellTileData*. Next, observe that the call to *Invoke* on the returned *Create* method includes a null argument rather than an instance of the type on which you want to invoke the method. When invoking a static member of the *Type*, the instance parameter is ignored, so it is safe to set it to *null*.

```
public void AddSecondaryTile()
{
    // Make deep-links unique by using the value of DateTime.Now.Ticks
    Uri deepLinkUri = new Uri(String.Format("/SecondaryPage.xaml?deepLinkId={0}",
                                            System.DateTime.Now.Ticks), UriKind.Relative);


    if (IsCurrentVersionEnabledForEnhancedTiles)
    {
        // create iconic tile for WP7.8/WP8

        Type iconicTileType =
            Type.GetType("Microsoft.Phone.Shell.IconicTileData, Microsoft.Phone");

        Type shellTileType = Type.GetType("Microsoft.Phone.Shell.ShellTile, Microsoft.Phone");

        var newTileData = iconicTileType.GetConstructor(Type.EmptyTypes).Invoke(null);

        newTileData.SetProperty( "Count", 78);

        newTileData.SetProperty( "Title", "TileLightUp");

        newTileData.SetProperty( "WideContent1", "Wide tiles are great!");

        newTileData.SetProperty( "WideContent2", "Lots of room for content!");

        newTileData.SetProperty( "WideContent3", "Three whole lines of text!");

        newTileData.SetProperty( "SmallIconImage",
                    new Uri("/Assets/SmallBackgroundImage.png", UriKind.Relative));

        newTileData.SetProperty( "BackgroundColor", Colors.Blue);

        newTileData.SetProperty( "IconImage",
                    new Uri("/Assets/IconImage.png", UriKind.Relative));

        shellTileType.GetMethod
            ("Create", new Type[] { typeof(Uri), iconicTileType, typeof(bool) })
            .Invoke(null, new object[] { deepLinkUri, newTileData, true });
    }
    else
    {
        // create WP7.1 standard tile

        Microsoft.Phone.Shell.StandardTileData standardData = new StandardTileData();
```

```
            standardData.Count = 71;
            standardData.Title = "StandardTile";
            standardData.BackgroundImage =
                new Uri("/Assets/WP71-TileBackground.png", UriKind.Relative);

            ShellTile.Create(deepLinkUri, standardData);
        }
    }
```

Simulating OS upgrade and App update

We have now seen how you can create new secondary tiles based on the OS on which your app is running and upgrade existing tiles to use the new tile features in Windows Phone 7.8 and 8. However, the fact that your app can now add the right type of tile depending on the OS version makes it somewhat challenging to test the process of upgrading secondary tiles because you can no longer create Windows Phone 7.1–style tiles in an app running on Windows Phone 7.8 and 8. Thankfully, it is straightforward to simulate the conditions that will trigger your update logic; namely, the first run of your app following either an OS upgrade to Windows Phone 7.8 or an app update that adds the new tile functionality.

The *TileLightUp* solution includes a symbolic constant named *SIMULATE_71*, which is used to tweak the behavior of the *IsCurrentVersionEnabledForEnhancedTiles* Boolean property that indicates whether the current OS supports enhanced tile functionality. Rather than check the current OS version against the minimum version for the new tile support, the app always returns false when running with the *SIMULATE_71* directive defined.

```
#define SIMULATE_71

// ...

public bool IsCurrentVersionEnabledForEnhancedTiles
{
    get
    {
#if SIMULATE_71
        return false;
#else
        return CurrentOSVersion >= MinOSVersionForEnhancedTiles;
#endif
    }
}
```

While the directive is defined, *AddSecondaryTile* will behave like it would on Windows Phone 7.1, creating a tile by using a *StandardTileData* object. After you have created a few Windows Phone 7.1–style tiles, you can comment out the directive and return to the real version of the app, which can then perform the updates. For this technique to work, however, you need to ensure that the app is not fully uninstalled and reinstalled when you redeploy it because that will remove all of the tiles you created for testing. To do this, avoid fully rebuilding your project after commenting out the *SIMULATE_71* directive. Either build it and deploy it or start it under the debugger by pressing F5. This will mimic the process of an app update, where the app package is changed but its data (including tiles) remain on the device.

Quirks mode and breaking changes

As described in Chapter 1, "Vision and architecture," the architectural changes from Windows Phone 7.x to Windows Phone 8 are significant. The core OS was changed from Windows CE to Windows NT and the Microsoft .NET runtime was changed from the .NET Compact Framework (.NET CF) to the Core Common Language Runtime (Core CLR). In both cases, the existing component was replaced with one that shares many similarities but also contains a number of differences. Maintaining backward compatibility in light of these changes is a huge undertaking, and Windows Phone takes a very deliberate approach to how compatibility is managed.

In short, the platform aims to maintain two types of compatibility for apps. The highest priority is ensuring that unmodified Windows Phone 7.x apps behave and perform on Windows Phone 8 exactly as they did in Windows Phone 7.x. Without this assurance, it would be incumbent upon app developers to make changes to deal with compatibility breaks and ship updates for their apps prior to any of their customers starting to use a Windows Phone 8 device, which is clearly an unrealistic requirement. A secondary goal is ensuring that Windows Phone 7.x apps can be upgraded to Windows Phone 8 with few or no changes. Although it is important to limit the number of changes required to upgrade an app to Windows Phone 8, the fact that the developer has an opportunity to change her app and test it on the new platform before submitting it to the Windows Phone Store allows for a small number of breaking changes for cases in which it is impossible or undesirable to maintain the previous behavior of the platform.

Quirks mode

When a developer builds an app, she tests it thoroughly against the version of the platform that she is targeting before submitting it to the Windows Phone Store, ideally ensuring that all possible code paths are exercised and work correctly. When a new version of the platform is released, it is unrealistic to expect the developer to immediately retest her app on the new platform to ensure that it still works correctly, even though no app code changes have been made. It is the platform's responsibility to ensure that it behaves exactly as the app expects, such that the initial testing performed by the developer remains valid. Not surprisingly, keeping things exactly as they were before tends to be at odds with the goal of a new release, which is to change the platform.

To deal with these conflicting goals, platforms often have to maintain parallel code paths to serve both old and new apps. Windows Phone borrows the term *quirks mode* from web browsers, which generally use it to refer to a rendering mode that attempts to emulate the behavior of previous browser versions that supported a large amount of nonstandard HTML. When an API is "quirked," it continues to offer the previous behavior to apps targeting the previous version of the platform while providing the modified behavior for new apps. Figure 13-4 provides a simple graphical representation of how quirks mode works.

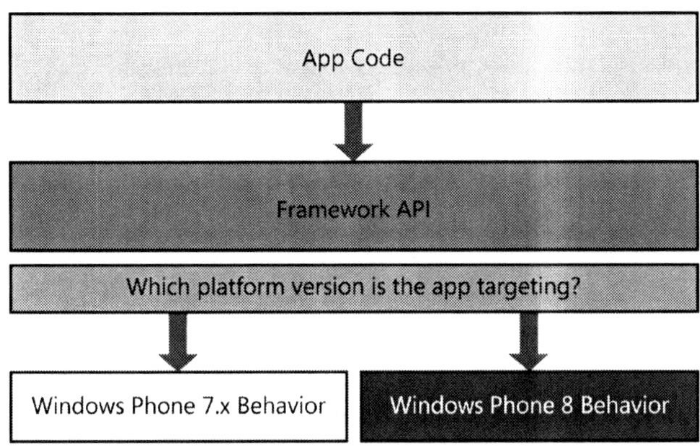

FIGURE 13-4 With quirks mode, Windows Phone can maintain previous behavior for existing apps.

Because the goal of quirks mode is to provide the app with the behavior it expects, it is entirely based on the target platform of the calling app, as specified in the app manifest, and is generally completely invisible.

Testing backward compatibility

In any large, complex platform such as Windows Phone, maintaining backward compatibility involves a significant amount of mostly manual testing by the platform vendor. Not only are there endless combinations of ways that various framework APIs can be integrated to create an app, but developers often make assumptions about behavior that is not documented or not guaranteed. Although the platform technically has no obligation to maintain compatibility for such behaviors, it is clearly not in anyone's interest for the app to behave incorrectly on the new OS version. As a result, a huge amount of time and effort is invested to make the new platform behave as closely as possible to the previous one, even if the previous behavior was arbitrary or even undesirable. Indeed, one of the biggest challenges in backward-compatibility testing is realizing that a change in behavior that resolves an app bug on the new platform is itself a compatibility break and must be "fixed" such that the app bug returns.

Breaking changes

In the previous section, we reviewed quirks mode, a means of maintaining previous behavior for existing apps when running on a new version of the platform. When you upgrade an app to explicitly target a new version of the platform, such as Windows Phone 8, quirks mode no longer applies and your app must be prepared to deal with any changes in behavior that have been introduced in the new release. In this section, we will deal with several of the key breaking changes that you should be aware of and provide suggestions on how to handle the changes.

Note A comprehensive list of breaking changes in Windows Phone 8 is available on MSDN at *http://msdn.microsoft.com/en-US/library/windowsphone/develop/jj206947%28v=vs.105%29.aspx.*

Why did some Windows Phone 7 apps temporarily disappear from the Windows Phone 8 Windows Phone Store?

When Windows Phone 8 launched, some users were surprised to see a handful of popular Windows Phone 7 apps such as Spotify and Photosynth missing from the Windows Phone Store. With more than 100,000 other apps available and running well on new Windows Phone 8 devices, it was not obvious why a handful of apps had seemingly disappeared. The reason is that these apps were built by using a set of private APIs, delivered as part of a separate package known as the Hybrid SDK and controlled by a special capability that was limited to very close partners. Partners that requested access to the hybrid SDK did so with the knowledge that it might not be supported in a future release of the platform.

The hybrid SDK satisfied two broad sets of requirements that were otherwise not available to apps delivered through the Windows Phone Store. First, it made it possible for apps to include native code in their packages. Because the Windows Runtime was not available in the Windows Phone 7.x timeframe, the mechanism for invoking native code from a managed app was COM interop, a feature of the .NET Common Language Runtime (CLR) that facilitates interaction between .NET code and interfaces exposed as Component Object Model (COM) objects. Second, in addition to enabling their own custom native code, apps could also directly call a very small set of APIs exposed by the underlying Windows CE OS to use functionality that was not available in the public API surface.

Note Although additional APIs were available through the hybrid SDK, apps that were granted access to it were still bound by the same security sandbox described in Chapter 1. For instance, they could not read or write files outside of their isolated storage container except through controlled platform APIs.

In Windows Phone 8, native code development is supported for all apps, and interaction between managed and native code is made possible by using the Windows Runtime. As a result, the hybrid SDK is not supported for Windows Phone 8 development, and partners that were using it for Windows Phone 7 apps must update their apps to account for the changes. During this brief development period, these apps were not available in the Windows Phone Store for Windows Phone 8 devices.

Use of *MessageBox* during app lifecycle events

In Windows Phone 7.x, it was possible to display a *MessageBox* in the core lifecycle event handlers, namely *Launching*, *Activated*, *Deactivated*, and *Closing*. In Windows Phone 8, this is not allowed. If you attempt to display a *MessageBox* during *Launching* or *Activated*, the system will throw an *InvalidOperationException*. If you attempt to display a *MessageBox* during *Deactivated* or *Closing*, the call will be ignored. Note that the latter change is a rare example of a change that also affects Windows Phone 7.1 apps running on Windows Phone 8—that is, it is not quirked.

A related change is that apps can no longer block the *OnBackKeyPress* event handler while waiting on user input to a *MessageBox* if the current page is the last one in the app's page stack. In Windows Phone 7.x, apps that wanted to provide the user with an opportunity to confirm exit generally did so by overriding the *OnBackKeyPress* event handler on their main page, like so:

```
protected override void OnBackKeyPress(System.ComponentModel.CancelEventArgs e)
{
     var result = MessageBox.Show
                    ("Are you sure you want to exit?", "Confirm exit",
                     MessageBoxButton.OKCancel);

     if (result == MessageBoxResult.Cancel)
     {
          e.Cancel = true;
     }
}
```

In Windows Phone 8, you must follow a different approach. First, you must cancel the Back key press to prevent it from flowing through the system's navigation service, which will close your app. You must then dispatch the call to *MessageBox.Show* so that the *OnBackKeyPress* event handler can return in time for the system to recognize that you canceled the Back key press before it navigates away from your app. If the user ultimately decides to exit by confirming in the message box, you can explicitly close your app by calling the *Terminate* method on the *Application* class. Be aware, however, that the *Terminate* method will perform a rude termination, meaning that the app will be closed immediately, without having an opportunity to run through the standard closing path, which includes the current page's *OnNavigatedFrom* event handler and the app's *Application_Closing* event handler. You should call those methods explicitly to ensure that your app is put into a consistent state before it shuts down.

```
protected override void OnBackKeyPress(System.ComponentModel.CancelEventArgs e)
{
     e.Cancel = true;

     Dispatcher.BeginInvoke(() =>
     {
          var result = MessageBox.Show
                         ("Are you sure you want to exit?", "Confirm exit",
                          MessageBoxButton.OKCancel);
```

```
            if (result == MessageBoxResult.OK)
            {
                OnNavigatedFrom(new NavigationEventArgs(null, new Uri("app://external/"),
                                                NavigationMode.Back, false));
                var app = App.Current as App;
                app.Application_Closing(PhoneApplicationService.Current, new ClosingEventArgs());
                app.Terminate();
            }
        });
}
```

Note Requiring the user to confirm that he wants to exit your app is heavily disruptive to the overall navigation experience and should only be used when leaving the app will result in a loss of critical user data.

Anonymous user ID

The Anonymous ID (ANID) available in the *UserExtendedProperties* class is a hashed version of the user's Microsoft Account ID (formerly known as Windows Live ID). In Windows Phone 7.x, the platform returned a single ANID value to all apps. In Windows Phone 8, the ANID property is replaced by ANID2, which is also based on the Microsoft Account ID, but hashed by using a key that is specific to the app publisher. This means that all apps for a given publisher will see the same identifier for the user but that value will not be common between publishers. The goal of the change was to limit the opportunity for tracking the user across a wide range of apps while still allowing apps from the same publisher to maintain a common identity for that user. The biggest impact of the change is that there is no automatic way to link the Windows Phone 7.x ANID to the Windows Phone 8 ANID2 in your app. If you were using the ANID as the sole user identity for your app and need to re-establish that relationship with the user in your Windows Phone 8 app, you will need to perform a mapping in the cloud. For a sample project that can help you to perform this conversion, go to *http://blogs.windows.com/windows_phone/b/wpdev/archive/2013/03/11/migrating-anids-to-windows-phone-8.aspx*.

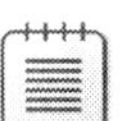

Note The *DeviceUniqueId* property has also been updated to return a publisher-specific value. However, because it does not span devices by definition, you should not need to worry about mapping it from Windows Phone 7 to Windows Phone 8.

FM radio

Unlike Windows Phone 7.x, not all Windows Phone 8 devices support FM radio hardware. As a result, you cannot use the *FMRadio* class on some Windows Phone 8 devices, either from Windows Phone 7.1 or Windows Phone 8 apps. Any attempt to interact with the *FMRadio* class will raise a *RadioDisabledException*.

Photo apps picker

In Windows Phone 7.1, apps can register for the Photo Apps Picker extension, which provides the user with the option to launch the app directly from the built-in photo viewer, as demonstrated in Figure 13-5.

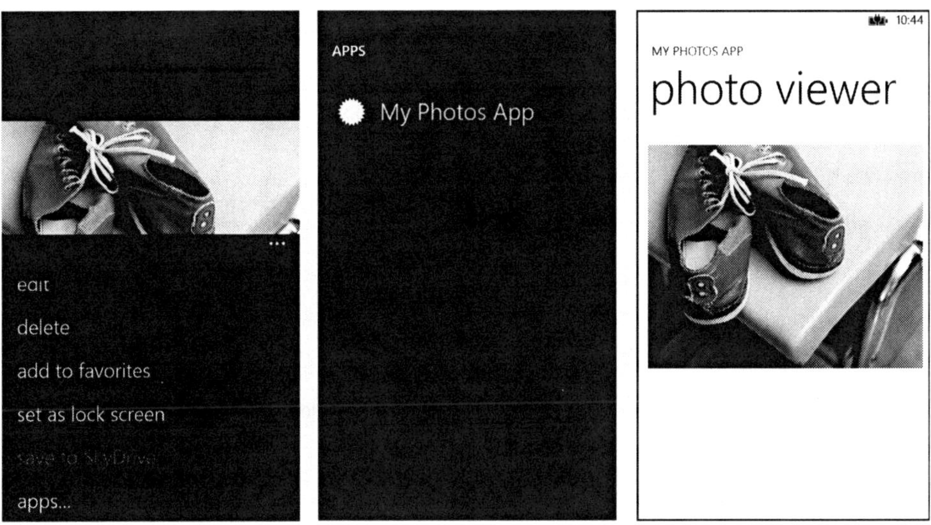

FIGURE 13-5 The Photo Apps Picker is deprecated in Windows Phone 8.

In Windows Phone 8, the Photo Apps Picker is replaced by the Photo Edit Picker, which is conceptually similar but requires a different registration in the manifest and launches the app with a navigation URI that is consistent with the other photos extensibility points, such as Lenses. The two changes are outlined in Table 13-1.

TABLE 13-1 Changes required to move from the Photos App Picker to the Photos Edit Picker

	Windows Phone 7.1	**Windows Phone 8**

Manifest registration	`<Extension`
	`ConsumerID=`
	`"{5B04B775-356B-4AA0-AAF8-6491FFEA5632}"`
	
	`ExtensionName=`
	`"Photos_Extra_Viewer"`
	`TaskID="_default" />`
		`<Extension`
		`ConsumerID=`
		`"{5B04B775-356B-4AA0-AAF8-6491FFEA5632}"`
		
		`ExtensionName=`
		`"Photos_Extra_Image_Editor"`
		`TaskID="_default" />`

Navigation URI	/MainPage.xaml? token=<PhotoFileId>	/MainPage.xaml? Action=EditPhotoContent &FileId=<PhotoFileId>

LayoutUpdated timing

The ordering of the events raised on the *PhoneApplicationPage* class differs slightly in Windows Phone 8 as compared to Windows Phone 7.1. As a result, the first time that the *LayoutUpdated* event is raised, it might not have the correct dimensions for the page. If you use *LayoutUpdated* as the cue to perform some operation that is dependent on knowing the dimensions of the screen, you should add a check to verify that the given dimensions are valid before proceeding.

```
void MainPage_LayoutUpdated(object sender, EventArgs e)
{
     if (ActualHeight == 0 || ActualWidth == 0)
          return;

     // do resolution-specific operations...
}
```

The *WebBrowser* control

The version of Microsoft Internet Explorer included with Windows Phone 7.1 was based on the Internet Explorer 9 rendering engine, whereas Windows Phone 8 is based on Internet Explorer 10. This change might result in a number of small issues if your app renders HTML content in a *WebBrowser* control, so you should test the web-based portion of your app thoroughly to ensure that it appears and behaves as you expect.

General rendering and scrolling Look for issues with text, bullet lists, and drop-down menu arrows, as well as changes in scrolling behavior within lists.

User agent string As you would expect for a new release of Windows Phone that includes an updated version of the browser, Internet Explorer's user-agent string has been updated to reflect the new version numbers. For Windows Phone 8, the user-agent string is:

```
Mozilla/5.0 (compatible; MSIE 10.0; Windows Phone OS 8.0; Trident/6.0; IEMobile/10.0; <phone
manufacturer>; <model> [;<mobile operator>])
```

Tip In many cases, what you want to know when you look at the user-agent string in your web server is the operating system and/or the browser rather than the specific version number. In those cases, you can make your logic robust against future upgrades by simply looking for "Windows Phone" or "IEMobile" in the user-agent string rather than trying to perform an exact match.

Text input events

In Windows Phone 7.1, apps can listen for the *TextInput*, *TextInputStart*, and *TextInputUpdate* events in UI elements that support text entry, such as *TextBox*. In Windows Phone 8, these events are no longer raised and apps should use the *KeyDown* event, instead.

Slider control

The behavior and XAML template of the *Slider* control have changed in Windows Phone 8, potentially causing issues for apps that created a custom control derived from the built-in version. The default Windows Phone 7.x *Slider* control, derived from the desktop Microsoft Silverlight version, allows the user to jump forward and back along the range in fixed increments by tapping on either side of the dial. Behind the scenes, the *Slider* control template enables this functionality by using two transparent *RepeatButton* controls, one on either side of the dial, and provides these controls in the template, with names like *HorizontalTrackLargeChangeDecreaseRepeatButton*, making it possible for developers to move and modify them in derived versions of *Slider*. In Windows Phone 8, tapping anywhere on the *Slider* automatically sets its value to that position immediately, eliminating the need for the *Repeat Button* controls, so they have been removed from the template.

What is more likely to cause compatibility problems, however, is the fact that the dial on the *Slider* has changed names and types. In Windows Phone 7.x, the dial is exposed as an instance of the *Thumb* primitive and named *HorizontalThumb* and *VerticalThumb* based on the two orientations supported for *Slider*. In Windows Phone 8, this is replaced with the *HorizontalCenterElement* and *VerticalCenter Element*, which are instances of the base *FrameworkElement* type. Migrating to the new template is straightforward. Simply rename the top-level XAML control that you used to re-template the *Thumb* objects to *HorizontalCenterElement* or *VerticalCenterElement* depending on the orientation. The *SliderMigration* solution in the sample code shows the same customized horizontal Slider control in both Windows Phone 7.1 and Windows Phone 8. In Windows Phone 7.1, we re-template the *Thumb*:

```
<Thumb x:Name="HorizontalThumb" Height="12" Margin="18,0" Grid.Row="1" Width="12">
    <Thumb.Template>
        <ControlTemplate>
            <Canvas Background="{StaticResource PhoneForegroundBrush}"
                    Height="12"
                    Width="12">
                <Ellipse Fill="{StaticResource PhoneForegroundBrush}"
                     Height="24"
                     Width="24"
                     IsHitTestVisible="True"
                     Canvas.Left="-18"
                     Canvas.Top="-30" />
            </Canvas>
        </ControlTemplate>
    </Thumb.Template>
</Thumb>
```

In Windows Phone 8, we simply mark the ellipse as the *HorizontalCenterElement*:

```
<Ellipse x:Name="HorizontalCenterElement"
         Fill="{StaticResource PhoneForegroundBrush}"
         HorizontalAlignment="Left"
         Height="12"
         Width="12"
         Margin="0,16,0,44">
    <Ellipse.RenderTransform>
        <TranslateTransform />
    </Ellipse.RenderTransform>
</Ellipse>
```

XML serialization

There are several changes to the rules concerning XML serialization of app types. Among them are the following:

- For a type to be serializable, it must now provide a default (for instance, *parameterless*) constructor.
- Types that contain members of type *Nullable<T>* are no longer supported.
- Attempting to deserialize an empty XML file now throws an exception.

The *LongListSelector* control

The addition of *LongListSelector* to the set of controls that ships directly in the Windows Platform will cause a compilation error for apps that were using the version that was previously available in the Windows Phone toolkit. Update your app to use the Windows Phone 8 form of the toolkit and the error will be resolved. The new version of the toolkit is available via NuGet by running the following command in the NuGet Package Manager Console:

PM > **Install-Package WPToolkit**

Read-only database connections in local storage

In Windows Phone 7.1, you could create a read-only connection to a database in local storage by using the connection string passed to the *DataContext* constructor. However, the read-only status of the database was somewhat misleading as it was limited only to that *DataContext* instance. Because there is no way to restrict write operations from other *DataContext* objects or to prevent direct write access to the underlying database file, the read-only option has been removed for databases in local storage and will throw a *NotSupportedException* in Windows Phone 8.

Managing platform-specific projects

Earlier in the chapter, we looked at how you can use light-up to take advantage new features of the Windows Phone 8 release while still targeting the Windows Phone 7.1 platform. If you want to access more functionality in the Windows Phone 8 platform, you must update your app to target the Windows Phone 8 platform explicitly.

As mentioned at the beginning of the chapter, it is expected that a large number of Windows Phone 7 devices will remain in the market for some time, so it is worthwhile thinking about how you might target both platforms simultaneously because there are several options available.

Note This section focuses on techniques for maintaining platform-specific projects during development. To see how to manage multiple app packages in the Windows Phone Dev Center, see Chapter 11, "App publication."

Create distinct apps for Windows Phone 7.1 and Windows Phone 8

The first option is to create a duplicate of your existing project and update it to target Windows Phone 8, keeping the original project untouched. Although this approach always keeps it clear which project you're working on, it does so at the cost of significant code duplication. Assuming that you want to continue to actively work on the 7.1 version of your project, any new work that you do will need to be done in two places. As a result, this approach is only recommended for cases in which you want to significantly diverge the code bases of your Windows Phone 7.1 and Windows Phone 8 projects or where you expect to make very little additional investment in your Windows Phone 7.1 app.

To duplicate an existing project as a Windows Phone 8 project within your solution, take the following steps:

1. In Windows Explorer, make a copy of the Windows Phone 7.1 project directory within your solution folder. Consider giving the new project directory a name that indicates that it contains a Windows Phone 8 project, for instance, **ParallelPlatforms.WP8**.
2. Add the project to your solution in Microsoft Visual Studio by right-clicking the solution name and then, on the shortcut menu that appears, point to Add, and then click Existing Project.
3. Upgrade the copied project to Windows Phone 8 by right-clicking the project name and then, on the shortcut menu that appears, click Upgrade To Windows Phone 8, as shown in Figure 13-6.

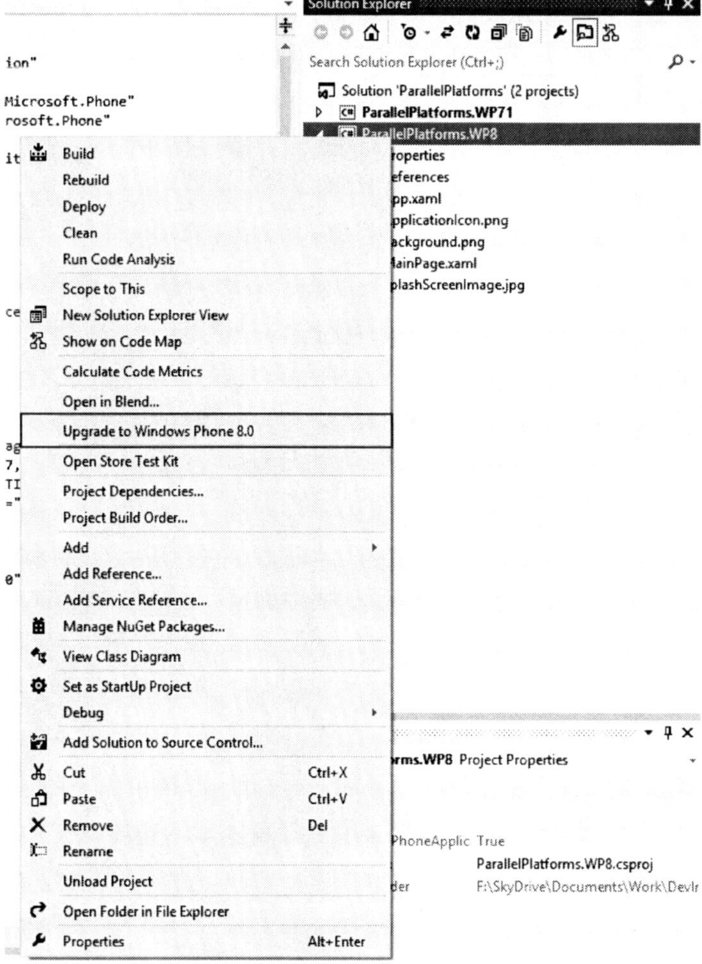

FIGURE 13-6 This shortcut menu for a Windows Phone 7.1 app provides an option to upgrade to Windows Phone 8.

Share a Windows Phone 7.1 library

If you have factored your app into distinct components based on a pattern such as Model-View-ViewModel (MVVM) as shown in Chapter 4, "Data binding and MVVM," your existing app will usually have components that you want to reuse in your Windows Phone 8 app without any platform-specific changes. For instance, if the Model layer of your app is entirely comprised of app-specific types and business logic, persistence code, and cloud interaction, there might not be any pressing need to use new Windows Phone 8–specific features in that area.

To share this type of code, simply create a new Windows Phone Class Library project in your solution and choose Windows Phone 7.1 as the target platform. Move any code that you believe to be common into the shared library project so that it will be accessible by both apps. You can then create a Windows Phone 8 app either by using the copy and upgrade technique shown earlier or by creating an entirely new Windows Phone 8 app project. To use the shared library from both apps, simply add a reference to it in both projects.

Note Although the class library itself might target Windows Phone 7.1, be aware that quirks mode behavior is applied at the app level. Thus, if a Windows Phone 7.1 class library is running in the context of a Windows Phone 8 app, the Windows Phone 8 app behavior applies. Always test shared components in the context of both apps to ensure that they work properly on both target platforms.

Link source code files

The shared library technique makes it possible for you to share exactly the same code between apps targeting Windows Phone 7.1 and Windows Phone 8. In some cases, however, you might want to share most of the code between the two platforms but have the freedom to diverge in certain places to use platform-specific functionality. By using linked source-code files, you can share a single source file across two projects, with the code in that file interpreted based on the project in which it's being viewed. This ensures that you always get the appropriate IntelliSense behavior for the current project, whether you're working on the file in a Windows Phone 7.1 project or a Windows Phone 8 project.

To use linked source files, you first need to create a Windows Phone 8 project. You can either follow the copy and upgrade technique shown earlier or you can create an entirely new project, targeting Windows Phone 8. If you choose to duplicate your existing project, you should delete any files that you want to link from the new Windows Phone 8 project. To link files, simply right-click the location in your Windows Phone 8 project folder to which you want to add the files and then, on the shortcut menu that appears, point to Add and then click Existing Item. In the Add Existing Item dialog box, choose the files that you want to add as you normally would. Rather than clicking the Add button in the dialog box, however, click the drop-down arrow next to it and select Add As Link, instead, as depicted in Figure 13-7.

Tip You can also create linked files by dragging them between projects in Solution Explorer while holding down the Alt key.

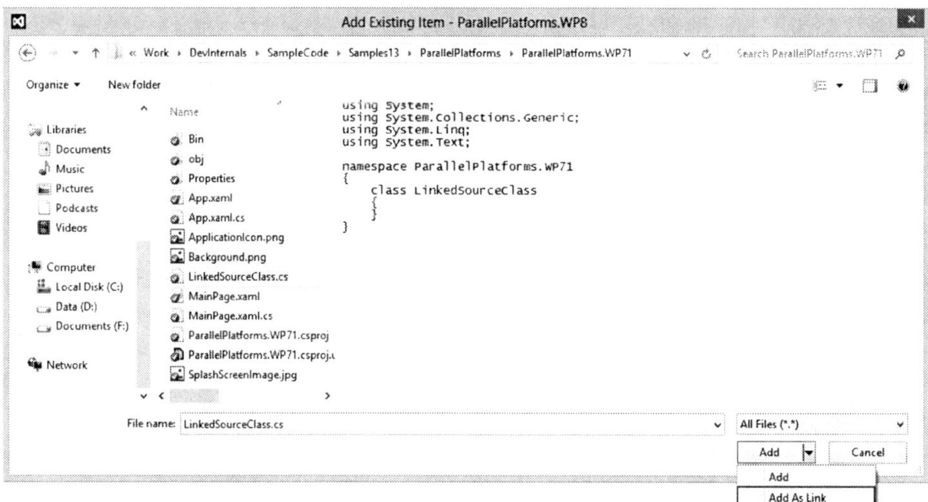

FIGURE 13-7 In the Add Existing Item dialog box, you can add a source-code file as a link.

A linked file displays a small glyph in its icon in the Solution Explorer view in Visual Studio, as shown in Figure 13-8. Otherwise, however, it functions just like a standard source file.

FIGURE 13-8 Linked files display a small glyph on their file icon in the Solution Explorer.

To isolate platform-specific functionality, you can use conditional compilation symbols that will automatically strip out any code not meant for the current target platform when the app is built. Two symbols are defined by default for Windows Phone apps—SILVERLIGHT and WINDOWS_PHONE—but because those are both defined for both Windows Phone 7.1 and Windows Phone 8 apps, you will need new symbols that can differentiate between the two platforms. You can do this on the Build tab of the project properties page as illustrated in Figure 13-9, where we have added the symbol WP8 to a Windows Phone 8 project.

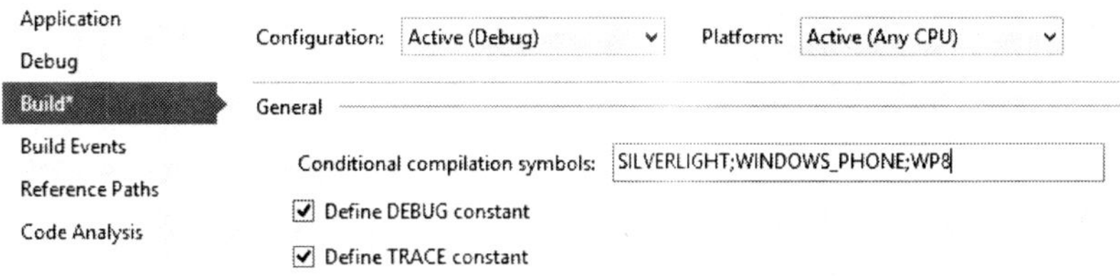

FIGURE 13-9 Create a WP8 conditional compilation symbol to differentiate between Windows Phone 7 and Windows Phone 8 code.

When code wrapped in the WP8 conditional compilation symbol is viewed in the context of a Windows Phone 8 project, it appears normal, as shown in Figure 13-10.

```
ParallelPlatforms.LinkedSourceClass                                    TestMethod()
using System;
using System.Collections.Generic;
using System.Linq;
using System.Text;

#if WP8
using Windows.Storage;
#endif

namespace ParallelPlatforms
{
    class LinkedSourceClass
    {

#if WP8
        public async void TestMethod()
        {
            StorageFile testFile =
                await StorageFile.GetFileFromApplicationUriAsync(new Uri("ms-appdata:///local/myfile.dat"));
        }
#endif
    }
}
```

FIGURE 13-10 In the context of a Windows Phone 8 app, code wrapped in the WP8 conditional compilation symbol looks normal.

However, if you look at the same code in the context of the Windows Phone 7.1 project, the code is grayed out (see Figure 13-11), indicating that it will be ignored when the project is compiled.

Conditional compilation can become unwieldy very quickly if there is a lot of platform-specific code, so you should try to maintain consistency wherever possible and isolate platform-specific functionality to helper methods that can have different implementations for Windows Phone 7.1 and Windows Phone 8.

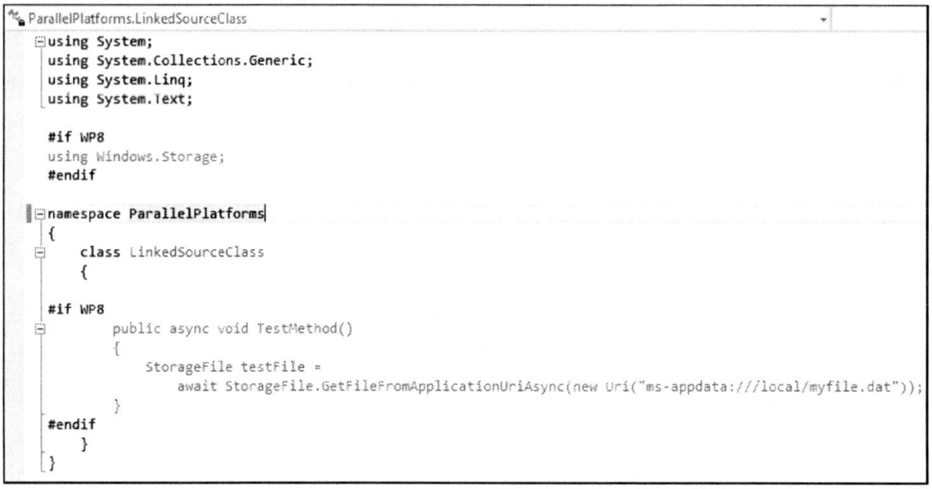

```
ParallelPlatforms.LinkedSourceClass
using System;
using System.Collections.Generic;
using System.Linq;
using System.Text;

#if WP8
using Windows.Storage;
#endif

namespace ParallelPlatforms
{
    class LinkedSourceClass
    {
#if WP8
        public async void TestMethod()
        {
            StorageFile testFile =
                await StorageFile.GetFileFromApplicationUriAsync(new Uri("ms-appdata:///local/myfile.dat"));
        }
#endif
    }
}
```

FIGURE 13-11 When the conditional compilation symbol is not defined, Visual Studio shows wrapped code in gray to indicate that it will not be compiled.

Create abstract base classes and partial classes

As mentioned in the previous section, conditional compilation can become difficult to manage if there are too many differences between your Windows Phone 7.x and Windows Phone 8 implementations. Eventually, you might want to take a more structured approach to targeting the two platforms. Abstract base classes and partial classes offer two good options. In the first approach, you create an abstract base class in a Windows Phone 7.1 shared library and provide Windows Phone 7.1–compliant implementations for code that can be common. You then create abstract definitions for methods that will be implemented in a platform-specific way, which you can implement in derived classes within the projects specifically targeting the two platforms.

```
// in WP7.1 Shared Library
public abstract class MultiTargetingClass
{
     public abstract void PlatformSpecificMethod();

     public void SharedMethod()
     {
          // shared implementation
     }
}
// In WP7.1 derived class
public class WP7ChildClass : WP71SharedLibrary.MultiTargetingClass
{
     public override void PlatformSpecificMethod()
     {
          // WP7.1 implementation of PlatformSpecificMethod
     }
}
```

```
// In WP8 derived class
public class WP8ChildClass : WP71SharedLibrary.MultiTargetingClass
{
     public override void PlatformSpecificMethod()
     {
          // WP8 implementation of PlatformSpecificMethod
     }
}
```

The abstract base class method makes sense if there is a common set of abstract functionality that you want to enable on both platforms but whose implementation varies between the two versions. For cases in which you want to enable entirely different sets of functionality between the two platforms, partial classes can offer a better solution. Using partial classes, you can split the implementation of a class between multiple source files. Combined with the linked-file approach shown earlier, partial classes provide the key benefits of conditional compilation while creating a cleaner separation of platforms-specific code.

```
// SharedCodeFile.cs in WP7.1 project - linked into WP8 project
namespace SharedCodeNamespace
{
     public partial class SharedCodeClass
     {
          public void SharedMethod()
          {
               // implementation of shared method
          }
     }
}

// WP71CodeFile.cs in WP7.1 project
namespace SharedCodeNamespace
{
     public partial class SharedCodeClass
     {
          public void WP71Method()
          {
               // implementation of WP7.1-specific method
          }
     }
}

// WP8CodeFile.cs in WP8 project
namespace SharedCodeNamespace
{
     public partial class SharedCodeClass
     {
          public void WP8Method()
          {
               // implementation of WP8-specific method
          }
     }
}
```

When the compiler builds the Windows Phone 7.1 project, it creates a version of *SharedCodeClass* that includes two methods: *SharedMethod* and *WP71Method*. Likewise, when it builds the Windows Phone 8 project, it creates a version that includes *SharedMethod* and *WP8Method*.

Note Linked source files, abstract base classes, and partial classes are also good techniques for sharing code between Windows 8 and Windows Phone 8. Read Chapter 24, "Windows 8 convergence," for additional information on these techniques, including more detailed sample code.

Windows Phone 7.8 SDK

As mentioned throughout the chapter, the Windows Phone 7.8 release brings the new Windows Phone 8 Start screen to Windows Phone 7.1 devices. With the release of the Windows Phone 7.8 update for end-user devices comes the accompanying Windows Phone 7.8 SDK, available as an optional addition to either the Windows Phone 7.1 SDK or the Windows Phone 8.0 SDK. You can download the Windows Phone 7.8 SDK at *http://www.microsoft.com/en-us/download/details.aspx?id=36474*.

As mentioned earlier, the Windows Phone 7.8 release does not change the API surface that apps can statically target, so the SDK reference assemblies have not changed. Instead, what the SDK provides is two additional emulator images on which to test your apps. One of the images emulates Windows Phone 7.8 running on a 512-MB device, whereas the other emulates the OS on a 256-MB phone. The two new OS images are available in the Target Platform list in Visual Studio for apps targeting Windows Phone 7.1, as shown in Figure 13-12 for the Windows Phone 8 SDK.

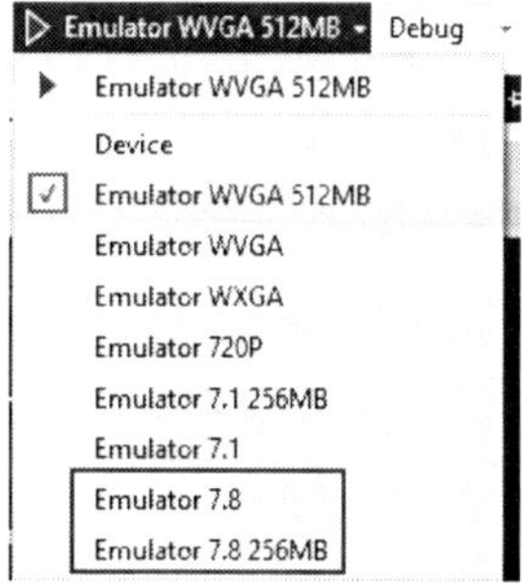

FIGURE 13-12 The Windows Phone 7.8 SDK adds two new emulator images in Visual Studio.

Test coverage for Windows Phone 7.x apps

The addition of the Windows Phone 7.8 SDK to the Windows Phone 8 SDK brings the number of emulator images available for Windows Phone 7.1 apps to Windows Phone 8. With so many emulator options to target, it is reasonable to ask whether you need to thoroughly test your Windows Phone 7.1 app on each configuration. Table 13-2 provides an outline of which images you should test on for each type of app.

TABLE 13-2 Test configurations for Windows Phone 7.x apps

App properties	Test on	Notes
■ No tile light-up ■ No background agents ■ No high-memory requirements	Emulator 7.1 256 MB Emulator WVGA 512 MB	If your app does not have background agents and is not specifying high memory requirements through the *ID_REQ_MEMORY_90* manifest entry, you can safely test only on the 7.1 256-MB emulator. Windows Phone 7.8 is exactly the same as Windows Phone 7.1 for apps not using tile light-up, so no additional testing is required. Windows Phone 8 should be nearly identical for Windows Phone 7.1 apps but should be separately tested for non-quirked breaking changes, especially in the *WebBrowser* control.
■ No tile light-up ■ Background agents ■ No high-memory requirements	Emulator 7.1 256 MB Emulator 7.1 512 MB Emulator WVGA 512 MB	Background agents are not supported on 256-MB devices, so it is worth testing that your foreground app makes no assumptions about them running on lower-memory phones.
■ No tile light-up ■ High-memory requirements	Emulator 7.1 512 MB Emulator WVGA 512 MB	If you specify *ID_REQ_MEMORY_90* in your app manifest, your app will not be available to 256-MB devices, so it is not necessary to test on that configuration.
■ Tile light-up ■ No background agents ■ No high-memory requirements	Emulator 7.1 256 MB Emulator 7.8 256 MB Emulator WVGA 512 MB	Focus your Windows Phone 7.8 testing on your tiles functionality. Also be sure to thoroughly exercise the same functionality on a Windows Phone 7.1 image to ensure that you haven't regressed the existing behavior.
■ Tile light-up ■ Background agents ■ No high-memory requirements	Emulator 7.1 256 MB Emulator 7.1 512 MB Emulator 7.8 256 MB Emulator 7.8 512 MB Emulator WVGA 512 MB	If you update your tiles from a background agent, be sure to test any light-up functionality on a Windows Phone 7.8 512-MB image.
■ Tile light-up ■ High-memory requirements	Emulator 7.1 512 MB Emulator 7.8 512 MB Emulator WVGA 512 MB	

Summary

Due to the incompatibility between Windows Phone 7 hardware and the Windows Phone 8 OS, Windows Phone 7 devices will continue to represent a significant proportion of the Windows Phone market for some time. To maximize the reach of your app, it is a good idea to target both platforms. In this chapter, you learned about several techniques for multitargeting, including simply maintaining a Windows Phone 7 app that can take advantage of new tile templates when running on Windows Phone 8. You also learned about some of the key breaking changes to be aware of when upgrading your app to Windows Phone 8 and how to deal with them. With all of these techniques in mind, you can create great apps targeting both platforms and ensure maximum coverage of the various Windows Phone devices in the market.

CHAPTER 14

Tiles and notifications

On all smartphones, apps are represented by an icon in an app list. Windows Phone 7 introduced the notion of an additional app tile that users could pin to the Start screen. This provides several benefits: it is a way for the user to customize his phone experience, prioritizing the apps that he uses most and positioning them in whatever order he chooses. Because tiles are bigger than app icons, this also introduces the opportunity for you to provide information on the tile that would not fit on an icon. Not only that, but with Windows Phone, the app can keep its tile up to date dynamically. There are multiple dimensions to this feature, including the following:

- An app can have a primary tile plus any number of secondary tiles, which can be created and updated programmatically.
- The style and size guidelines for tiles have evolved from Windows Phone 7 to Windows Phone 8, and there are now multiple tile sizes and new tile style templates available.
- Tiles can be updated either purely locally on the phone or from remote servers via the push notification system.

The push notification system can be used to update tiles. It can also be used to send toasts to the user and to send any arbitrary raw data to your app. All of this provides a highly efficient mechanism for sending up-to-date data to your app. This chapter discusses all the options that are available to you for tiles, toasts, and push notifications.

Tile sizes and templates

Windows Phone 7 supported one tile size for Windows Phone Store apps, which included front-to-back flipping. Windows Phone 8 now supports three tile sizes: small, medium, and large. It also supports three tile styles, or templates: flip, iconic, and cycle. All three tile styles are available in all three sizes. You can control the styles programmatically in your app, but only the user can set the size. The user can change the size any time he likes, and the platform does not provide any API to discover the size. For this reason, you should always be prepared to provide images and data for all tile sizes.

Flip tiles have a front and back, and the medium and large flip tiles alternate periodically between front and back. This flipping occurs every six seconds or so—the timing is slightly randomized to ensure that all the tiles on the Start screen don't all flip at the same time. Figure 14-1 presents an example of flip tiles.

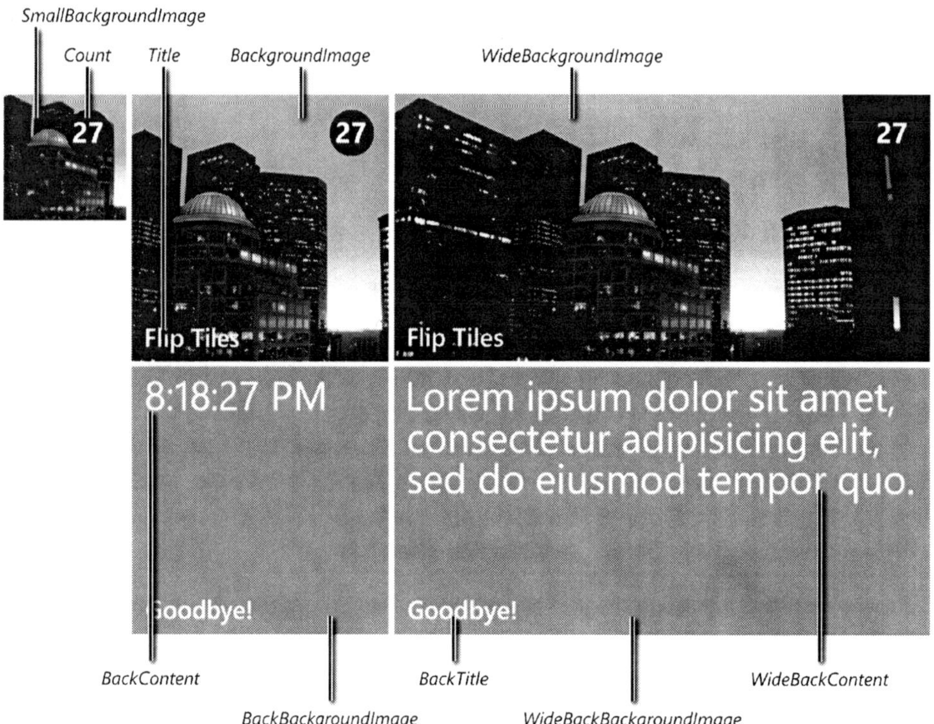

FIGURE 14-1 Flip tiles have a front (top) and back (bottom) side, and flip automatically between them.

To update a flip tile, you initialize a *FlipTileData* object and pass it to the *ShellTile.Update* method. For the primary tile, you retrieve the first tile in the *ActiveTiles* collection. You can specify values for the front and back titles, the count, three front image files, medium and large back images, and medium and large back content. For *WideBackContent*, you can specify multiple lines of text, up to about 80 characters; anything beyond that will be truncated. The number is approximate because different characters have different widths, so it depends which characters you're using. The small tile does not flip, and the count is shown only on the front.

```
ShellTile primaryTile = ShellTile.ActiveTiles.FirstOrDefault();
FlipTileData flipTileData = new FlipTileData()
{
    Title = "Flip Tiles",
    Count = now.Second,
    BackgroundImage = new Uri("/Assets/Tiles/FlipTileMedium.png", UriKind.Relative),
    SmallBackgroundImage = new Uri("/Assets/Tiles/FlipTileSmall.png", UriKind.Relative),
    WideBackgroundImage = new Uri("/Assets/Tiles/FlipTileLarge.png", UriKind.Relative),
    BackTitle = "Goodbye!",
    BackContent = now.ToLongTimeString(),
    BackBackgroundImage = new Uri("/Assets/Tiles/FlipTileMediumBack.png", UriKind.Relative),
    WideBackContent = "Lorem ipsum dolor sit amet, consectetur adipisicing elit, sed do eiusmod
tempor quo.",
    WideBackBackgroundImage = new Uri("/Assets/Tiles/FlipTileLargeBack.png", UriKind.Relative),
};
primaryTile.Update(flipTileData);
```

Cycle and iconic tiles have only a front side and don't flip. The medium and large cycle tiles sequence between multiple images every few seconds (up to nine), in a random order. When a cycle tile switches image, it does so by scrolling the new image up from the bottom, as shown in Figure 14-2, in which the top image is shown transitioning to the bottom image.

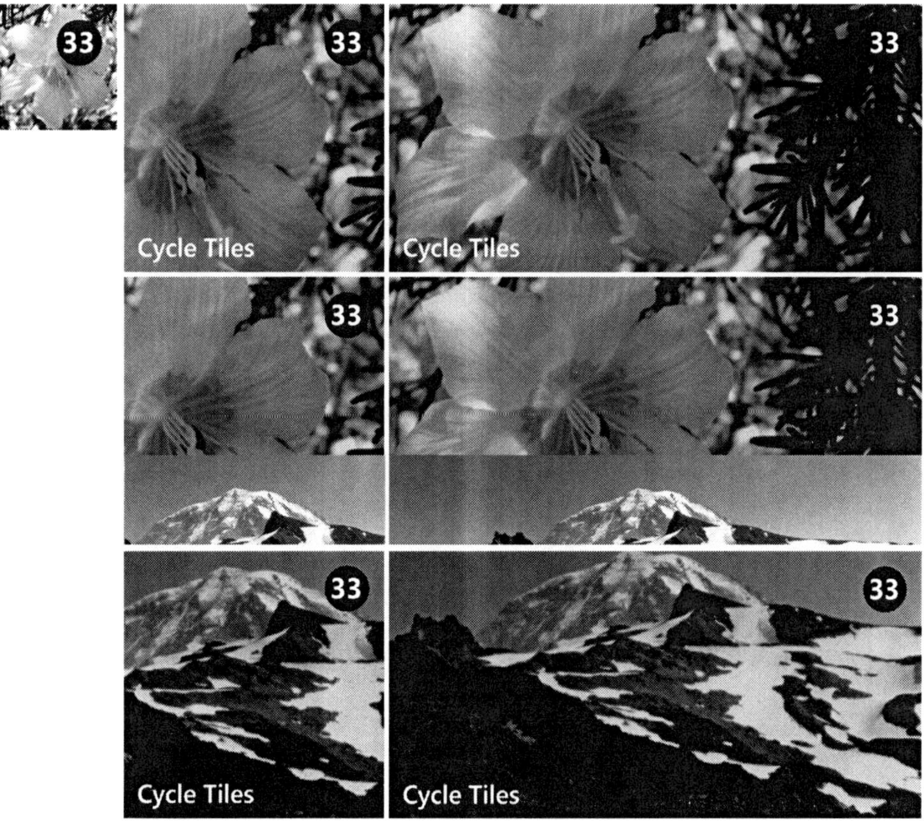

FIGURE 14-2 Cycle tiles can sequence between nine images.

To update a cycle tile, you initialize a *CycleTileData* object and pass it to *ShellTile.Update*. For cycle tiles, you specify the title, count, and the image for the small tile, plus up to nine images for the cycling medium and large tiles. The small tile does not cycle, the title is shown only on medium and large tiles, and the count is shown on all three formats.

```
ShellTile primaryTile = ShellTile.ActiveTiles.FirstOrDefault();
CycleTileData cycleTileData = new CycleTileData()
{
    Title = "Cycle Tiles",
    Count = now.Second,
    SmallBackgroundImage = new Uri("/Assets/Tiles/SprayPark3Small.png", UriKind.Relative),
    CycleImages = new List<Uri>
```

```
    {
        new Uri("/Assets/Tiles/SprayPark1.png", UriKind.Relative),
        new Uri("/Assets/Tiles/SprayPark2.png", UriKind.Relative),
        new Uri("/Assets/Tiles/SprayPark3.png", UriKind.Relative),
        new Uri("/Assets/Tiles/SprayPark4.png", UriKind.Relative),
        new Uri("/Assets/Tiles/SprayPark5.png", UriKind.Relative),
        new Uri("/Assets/Tiles/SprayPark6.png", UriKind.Relative),
        new Uri("/Assets/Tiles/SprayPark7.png", UriKind.Relative),
        new Uri("/Assets/Tiles/SprayPark8.png", UriKind.Relative),
        new Uri("/Assets/Tiles/SprayPark9.png", UriKind.Relative),
    }
};
primaryTile.Update(cycleTileData);
```

Iconic tiles use the clean, modern app style (see Figure 14-3), with a simple background color, no background images, and simple icon images that are limited to white and transparent colors. For iconic tiles, you prepare two images: small and medium. If the user selects a wide tile, the iconic style uses the small image if there is wide content; otherwise, it uses the medium image.

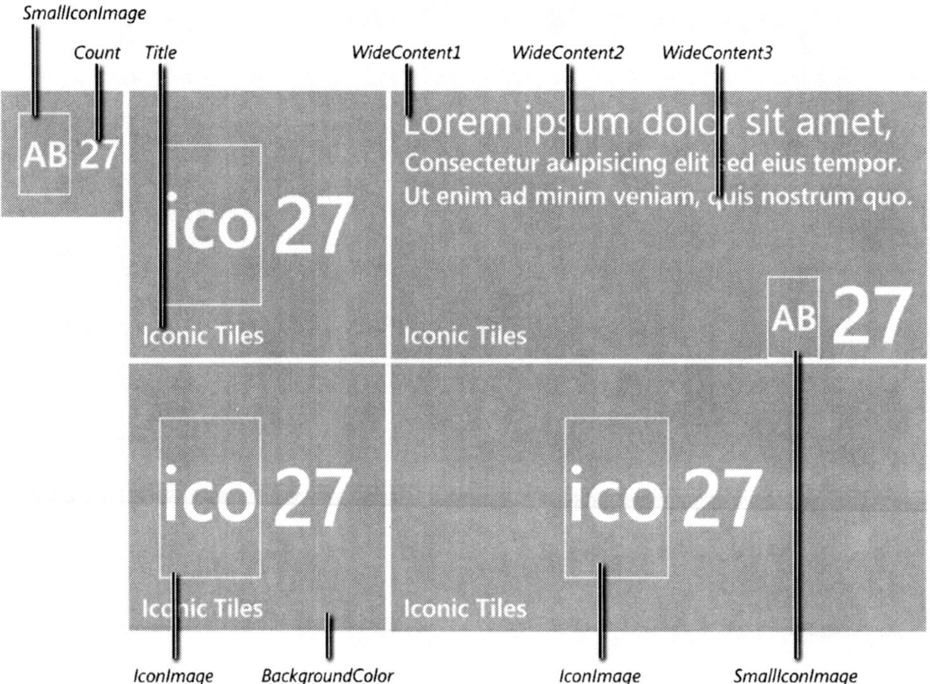

FIGURE 14-3 Iconic tiles use the clean, modern app style.

To update iconic tiles, you initialize an *IconicTileData* object and pass it to *ShellTile.Update*. If you provide *WideContent1*, you're limited to one line of about 30 characters; anything beyond that is truncated. For *WideContent2* and *WideContent3*, each is limited to one line of about 42 characters.

```
ShellTile primaryTile = ShellTile.ActiveTiles.FirstOrDefault();
IconicTileData iconicTileData = null;
if ((bool)wideContent.IsChecked)
{
    iconicTileData = new IconicTileData()
    {
        Title = "Iconic Tiles",
        Count = now.Second,
        BackgroundColor = Colors.Orange,
        IconImage = new Uri("/Assets/Tiles/IconicTileMedium.png", UriKind.Relative),
        SmallIconImage = new Uri("/Assets/Tiles/IconicTileSmall.png", UriKind.Relative),
        WideContent1 = "Lorem ipsum dolor sit amet,",
        WideContent2 = "Consectetur adipisicing elit sed eius tempor.",
        WideContent3 = "Ut enim ad minim veniam, quis nostrum quo.",
    };
}
else
{
    iconicTileData = new IconicTileData()
    {
        Title = "Iconic Tiles",
        Count = now.Second,
        BackgroundColor = Colors.Orange,
        IconImage = new Uri("/Assets/Tiles/IconicTileMedium.png", UriKind.Relative),
        SmallIconImage = new Uri("/Assets/Tiles/IconicTileSmall.png", UriKind.Relative),
        WideContent1 = "", WideContent2 = "", WideContent3 = ""
    };
}
primaryTile.Update(iconicTileData);
```

For the primary tile, the template must be specified at compile time. You do this by using the WMAppManifest graphical editor, as demonstrated in Figure 14-4. Using this, you can select each image and the title text. This is also where you specify the screen resolutions that you want to support.

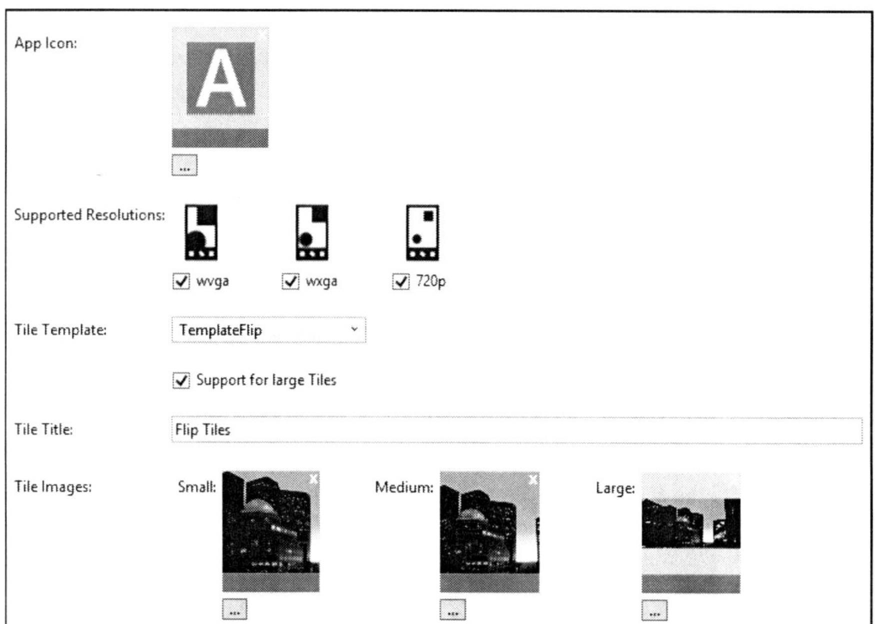

FIGURE 14-4 You can use the graphical manifest editor to set the primary tile template.

Note Windows Phone 8 supports three screen resolutions: WVGA (800x480 pixels), 720p (1280x720 pixels), and WXGA (1280x768 pixels). As you might expect, there's a performance trade-off with screen resolutions. If you want to view the highest-quality graphics at the highest resolution screen (WXGA), your images will take up more memory. You have two choices here. One option is to use high-resolution images and allow the system to scale them down when running on a device with a lower-resolution screen. The other option is to use lower-resolution images and allow the system to scale them up when running on a device with a higher-resolution screen. The automatic scaling that the platform performs produces very good results, and in most cases will be indistinguishable to the user. On the other hand, the memory cost of using high-resolution images can be significant, and you should profile your app to see if it is worthwhile, especially if you are constructing images dynamically. This becomes even more critical if you're manipulating images from a background agent, as discussed in Chapter 9, "Background agents."

When you use the manifest editor, it updates the XML for you. Alternatively, you can edit the *WMAppManifest.xml* file directly. The flip template settings from Figure 14-4 are represented in XML in the following:

```
<TemplateFlip>
  <SmallImageURI IsRelative="true" IsResource="false">Assets\Tiles\FlipTileSmall.png</
SmallImageURI>
  <Count>0</Count>
```

```
  <BackgroundImageURI IsRelative="true" IsResource="false">Assets\Tiles\FlipTileMedium.png</
BackgroundImageURI>
  <Title>Flip Tiles</Title>
  <BackContent>
  </BackContent>
  <BackBackgroundImageURI IsRelative="true" IsResource="false">
  </BackBackgroundImageURI>
  <BackTitle>
  </BackTitle>
  <LargeBackgroundImageURI IsRelative="true" IsResource="false">Assets\Tiles\FlipTileLarge.png</
LargeBackgroundImageURI>
  <LargeBackContent>
  </LargeBackContent>
  <LargeBackBackgroundImageURI IsRelative="true" IsResource="false">
  </LargeBackBackgroundImageURI>
  <HasLarge>True</HasLarge>
</TemplateFlip>
```

The *TileSizes* app in the sample code demonstrates all three template styles. The app discovers the template style in use by reading the manifest at run time and then offers user interface (UI) options to update the primary tile. The code for reading the information from the manifest is quite simple, and it relies on XML navigation using *XDocument*.

```
private TemplateType GetTemplateTypeFromManifest()
{
    TemplateType templateType = TemplateType.TemplateUnknown;
    XDocument appManifest = XDocument.Load("WMAppManifest.xml");
    if (appManifest != null)
    {
        var primaryTokenNode = appManifest.Descendants("PrimaryToken");
        if (primaryTokenNode != null)
        {
            var templateNode = primaryTokenNode.Descendants().FirstOrDefault();
            if (templateNode.Name == "TemplateFlip")
            {
                templateType = TemplateType.TemplateFlip;
            }
            else if (templateNode.Name == "TemplateIconic")
            {
                templateType = TemplateType.TemplateIconic;
            }
            else if (templateNode.Name == "TemplateCycle")
            {
                templateType = TemplateType.TemplateCycle;
            }
        }
    }
    return templateType;
}
```

When you create a new project, Microsoft Visual Studio generates six tile images, plus an image for the app icon. These are all placeholders with a default graphic, but the image files are sized appropriately, so they offer a good starting point for your own images. The usable area within the image varies according to the size of tile and the template. As a general guideline, for iconic tiles, you should configure a border of about 19 pixels all around, leaving an inner, "usable" area. This is simply a guideline to ensure that your text/data fits in with the way the system positions the icon and count data. This does not apply to cycle and flip tiles, for which you can use the entire surface of the image. Table 14-1 lists the recommended tile sizes.

TABLE 14-1 Recommended image sizes and usable areas by template and tile size

Template	Tile size	Image size	Usable area
Flip	Small	159x159	121x121
	Medium	336x336	298x298
	Large	691x336	653x298
Cycle	Small	159x159	159x159
	Medium	336x336	336x336
	Large	691x336	691x336
Iconic	Small	71x110	71x110
	Medium	134x202	134x202

You can use JPG or PNG image files. The trade-off here is that PNG supports transparency, which is especially recommended for iconic tiles. On the other hand, PNG image files are generally larger than the equivalent JPG image file for photographic content with gradients and the like. For blocks of solid color, PNG are smaller. You should try both to see what looks better and what the size trade-off is in your specific case.

Secondary tiles

In addition to the primary tile—which all apps have, even if they're not pinned to the Start screen—you can also create one or more secondary tiles. All the same properties apply to both primary and secondary tiles, but a key distinction is that when you create a secondary tile, you can choose at that point which template to apply. Another distinction is that a secondary tile can be linked to any page in your app, and this results in some interesting choices in the page navigation model. The *Secondary Tiles* app in the sample code demonstrates how to create, update, and delete secondary tiles. The app has two pages: *MainPage* and *Page2*. *MainPage* offers just a *HyperlinkButton*, set to navigate to *Page2*. *Page2* offers three buttons to create, update, and delete a secondary tile. The app uses the flip template, but the same technique can be used for cycle or iconic tiles, too. You could even create a mixture of secondary tiles that use all three of the tile templates, but this is probably not a good UI design. In general, it makes the most sense to create secondary tiles that use the same template as the app's primary tile. Again, this depends on the specifics of your app. For example, you can imagine an app such as Facebook might want an iconic tile for its primary tile, a cycle tile for any pinned albums, a flip tile for any pinned friends, and so on.

Of course, a realistic app would likely have a more sophisticated UI for triggering tile operations based on user action rather than just simple buttons. The typical scenario would be that the user opts to pin a tile to the Start screen that corresponds to some data item in your app. Then, the app would update the tile—typically without user interaction—to keep the tile fresh. Finally, deleting the tile would normally not be done in the app code; instead, it would be triggered by the user explicitly unpinning it from the Start screen.

All the interesting work is in the *Page2* button *Click* handlers. The *Click* handler for the create button initializes a *FlipTileData* object and passes it to *ShellTile.Create*. This takes two additional parameters: the navigation *Uri* for the tile, and a *bool* that indicates whether this tile supports the wide format.

```
private void createTile_Click(object sender, RoutedEventArgs e)
{
    DateTime now = DateTime.Now;
    FlipTileData tileData = new FlipTileData
    {
        Title = "Sound Sunrise",
        Count = now.Second,
        BackgroundImage = new Uri("/Assets/Tiles/sunrise_336x336.png", UriKind.Relative),
        SmallBackgroundImage = new Uri("/Assets/Tiles/sunrise_159x159.png", UriKind.Relative),
        WideBackgroundImage = new Uri("/Assets/Tiles/sunrise_691x336.png", UriKind.Relative),
        BackTitle = "Sound Sunset",
        BackContent = now.ToLongTimeString(),
        BackBackgroundImage = new Uri("/Assets/Tiles/sunset_336x336.png", UriKind.Relative),
        WideBackContent = "Lorem ipsum dolor sit amet, consectetur adipisicing elit, " +
            "sed do eiusmod tempor quo.",
        WideBackBackgroundImage = new Uri("/Assets/Tiles/sunset_691x336.png", UriKind.Relative),
    };
    ShellTile.Create(new Uri("/Page2.xaml?ID=SoundTile", UriKind.Relative), tileData, true);
    UpdateButtons();
}
```

A common pattern is to generate images dynamically according to some run-time context and then persist the images by using the *WriteableBitmap* class. The *System.Windows.Media.Imaging* namespace includes extension methods for this class to save and load JPG format images. The variation in the example that follows does just that. The custom *SaveTileImage* takes in a tile size; composes an image dynamically, with varying content according to the size of the tile; saves that image to isolated storage; and returns a corresponding *Uri*.

```
private Uri SaveTileImage(TileSize tileSize, int width, int height)
{
    string fileName = String.Format("/Shared/ShellContent/Dynamic{0}.jpg", tileSize);
    WriteableBitmap wb = new WriteableBitmap(width, height);
    TextBlock tb = new TextBlock()
    {
        Foreground = new SolidColorBrush(Colors.White),
        FontSize = (double)Resources["PhoneFontSizeExtraExtraLarge"]
    };

    switch (tileSize)
    {
        case TileSize.Small:
            tb.Text = "abc";
```

```
            break;
        case TileSize.Medium:
            tb.Text = "def ghi";
            break;
        case TileSize.Large:
            tb.Text = "jkl mno pqr stu vwx";
            break;
    }

    wb.Render(tb, new TranslateTransform() { X = 20, Y = height / 2 });
    wb.Invalidate();

    using (IsolatedStorageFile isoStore = IsolatedStorageFile.GetUserStoreForApplication())
    {
        if (isoStore.FileExists(fileName))
        {
            isoStore.DeleteFile(fileName);
        }
        using (IsolatedStorageFileStream fileStream =
            new IsolatedStorageFileStream(fileName, FileMode.Create, isoStore))
        {
            wb.SaveJpeg(fileStream, wb.PixelWidth, wb.PixelHeight, 0, 100);
        }
    }
    return new Uri("isostore:" + fileName, UriKind.Absolute);
}
```

Note If you want to generate images on the fly, and you want to include transparency, you need to save your images in PNG format. However, this is not supported in the standard library. A solution that you can consider is the *WriteableBitmapEx* third-party library, which is available on codeplex at *http://writeablebitmapex.codeplex.com/*.

In this sample app, *Page2* also has a *TextBlock* whose *Text* is set to a string that indicates whether the user navigated to this page via a pinned tile on the Start screen or via the *HyperlinkButton* on the *MainPage*. When you create a secondary tile, you can also specify the *NavigationUri* for the tile. This must include the page to which to navigate within this app, plus, optionally, a query string with whatever parameters you want. This sample app sets one *ID* parameter, which it uses subsequently to determine which tile this is. When you call the *ShellTile.Create* method, the tile is created with the specified properties and pinned to the Start screen on the phone. The Start screen is an app that is part of the system shell, so this action causes a navigation away from your app, which is therefore deactivated. The reason for this is to avoid spamming the Start screen: when you create a tile, the system makes it very obvious to the user that the tile has been created, and the user is shown where the tile is. She can then immediately interact with it, perhaps by moving it around, resizing it, or deleting it if she doesn't want it.

There are two ways to get to *Page2* in the app: through normal navigation via the hyperlink on the main page of the app, or via a pinned tile on the Start screen. So that you can determine which route was taken, you need to override the *OnNavigatedTo* method. This is where the *ID* parameter comes into play; the app can examine the query string to see which tile the user tapped to get to this page. This is also where you cache the *ShellTile* object. There's only one secondary tile in this app, so you can cache this as a *ShellTile* field in the class. If there were more tiles, it would make sense to use a collection, instead.

```
protected override void OnNavigatedTo(NavigationEventArgs e)
{
    String tmp;
    if (NavigationContext.QueryString.TryGetValue("ID", out tmp))
    {
        navigation.Text = String.Format("from Start ({0})", tmp);
    }
    else
    {
        navigation.Text = "from MainPage link";
    }

    tile = ShellTile.ActiveTiles.FirstOrDefault(
        x => x.NavigationUri.ToString().Contains("ID=" +tmp));
}
```

In this example, if the query string indicates that the user arrived at *Page2* via a pinned tile, you simply extract the parameter value and display it in a *TextBlock*. In a more sophisticated app, you would use this identifier to govern some business logic in your solution.

Updating a tile's properties and deleting a tile are both very straightforward. To update a tile, you simply find that tile and invoke the *Update* method, passing in a replacement set of data by using an object of the appropriate *ShellTileData*-derived class (*FlipTileData*, *CycleTileData*, or *IconicTileData*), as before. You don't have to provide values for all the properties, because any properties for which you don't provide values simply retain their previous values. If you want to clear a value, you can provide an empty string or a *Uri* with an empty string, depending on the item to be cleared. To delete a tile, find the tile and invoke the *Delete* method, but remember that in a real app, you should normally leave tile deletion to the user and avoid doing this programmatically. Keep in mind that neither updating nor deleting need to send the user to the Start screen, so there is no navigation away from the app in these cases.

```
private void updateTile_Click(object sender, RoutedEventArgs e)
{
    DateTime now = DateTime.Now;
    FlipTileData tileData = new FlipTileData
    {
        Count = now.Second,
        BackContent = now.ToLongTimeString(),
    };
    tile.Update(tileData);
}

private void deleteTile_Click(object sender, RoutedEventArgs e)
{
    tile.Delete();
    tile = null;
}
```

Note One technique that you should *not* adopt is to force the user to pin a secondary tile to acquire live updates as if it were the primary tile. The user will pin the primary tile if that's what he wants; secondary tiles should be for additional entry points.

Pinning tiles

The ability to pin local tiles to the Start screen becomes more interesting when the user can choose from multiple possible tiles to pin within an app. Consider a typical weather app. The user can mark individual locations as favorites and can then pin zero or more of these favorites to the Start screen. The screenshots in Figure 14-5 show the *PinTiles* solution from the sample code. This is based on the standard Visual Studio Databound Application project type.

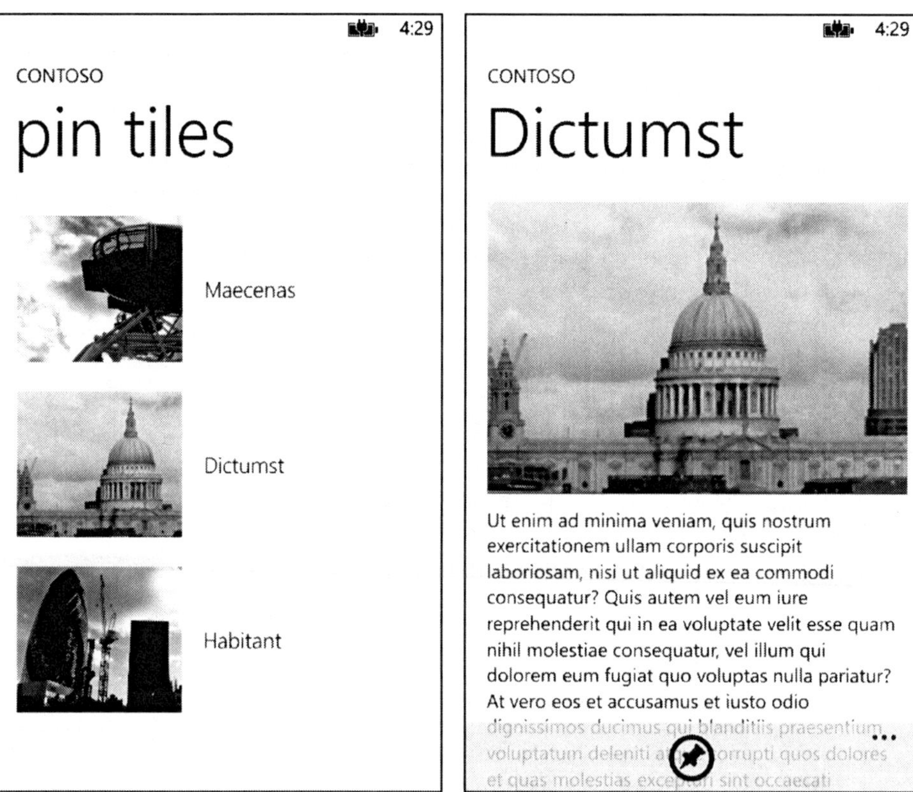

FIGURE 14-5 The *MainPage* (on the left) and *DetailsPage* (right) of the *PinTiles* sample app.

The idea here is that the app presents a list of items on the *MainPage*, and when the user taps one of these items, it navigates to the *DetailsPage*, which is data-bound to that item's viewmodel. In addition, the UI presents an app bar *Button* control that displays a "pin" image. When the user taps this control, the app creates a local tile and pins it to the Start screen. In this way, the user can tap multiple items and pin them all to the Start screen, as shown in Figure 14-6. When the user taps one of the pinned tiles, this starts the app and navigates her to that page, with the corresponding data loaded.

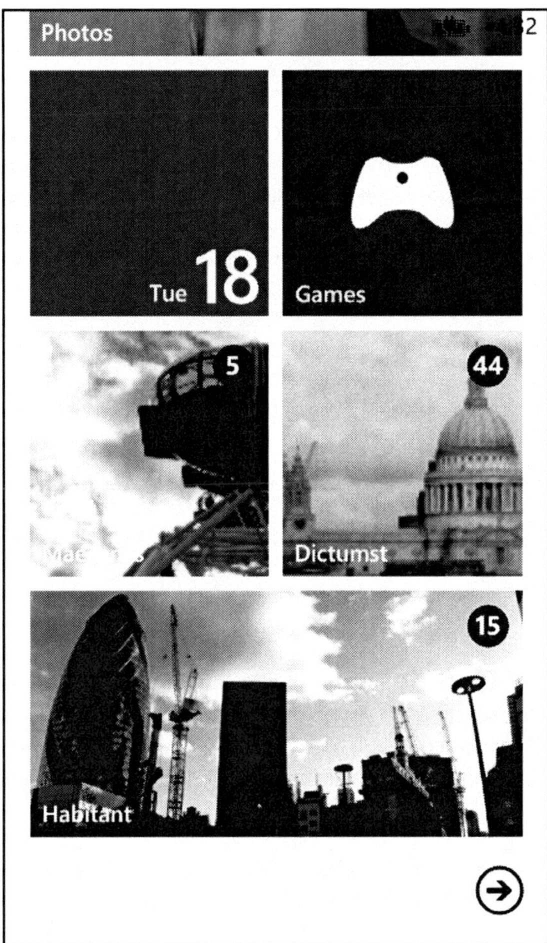

FIGURE 14-6 Pinning multiple tiles from the same app.

Some apps in the Windows Phone Store adopt the practice of providing an "unpin" feature in addition to the pin feature. As you've seen from the previous example, the platform API does expose methods for programmatically deleting (and therefore, unpinning) secondary tiles. However, this is not strictly compliant with Windows Phone app guidelines. The preferred behavior is that the user experience (UX) is always very predictable and very simple. The user knows that she can always unpin any tile that she's pinned to the Start screen; she knows that this is the standard approach for doing this. So, even though an app could provide an alternative mechanism for unpinning tiles, there's really no need. That said, one scenario for which it does make sense is when you delete tiles that the user has implicitly requested to be deleted. For example, if a weather app has a list of cities that the user is following and she's pinned some of these to the Start screen, the app should delete the corresponding tile if she removes a city from her favorites/watch list.

The viewmodel for each item is very simple: just a *Uri* for the image, and two strings.

```
public class ItemViewModel
{
    public Uri Photo { get; set; }
    public String Title { get; set; }
    public String Details { get; set; }
}
```

The *MainViewModel* is exposed as a static property of the *App* class, and some dummy data is loaded when this property is first accessed. See Chapter 4, "Data binding and MVVM," for details of this design (or examine the sample code). The *ListBox.SelectionChanged* handler in the *MainPage* navigates to the *DetailsPage* and then passes in a query string that includes an identifier for the selected item.

```
private void PhotoList_SelectionChanged(object sender, SelectionChangedEventArgs e)
{
    if (PhotoList.SelectedIndex != -1)
    {
        String targetUrl = String.Format(
            "/DetailsPage.xaml?Title={0}",
            ((ItemViewModel)PhotoList.SelectedItem).Title);
        NavigationService.Navigate(new System.Uri(targetUrl, UriKind.Relative));
        PhotoList.SelectedIndex = -1;
    }
}
```

All the interesting work is in the *DetailsPage*. The XAML defines an *Image* control for the item photo and a *TextBlock* inside a *ScrollViewer* (to accomodate large amounts of text in the item's *Details* property). The *Image* and the *TextBlock* are data-bound to the item properties. The app bar has one button that displays a "pin" image. This will be conditionally enabled depending on whether the user has already pinned this item to the Start screen.

```
<Grid x:Name="LayoutRoot" Background="Transparent" d:DataContext="{Binding Items[0]}">
...

    <ScrollViewer
        Grid.Row="1" Margin="12,0,12,0"
        VerticalScrollBarVisibility="Auto" ManipulationMode="Control">
        <StackPanel >
            <Image
                Height="300" Source="{Binding Photo}"
                Stretch="UniformToFill" Margin="12,0,0,0"/>
            <Grid Height="12"/>
            <TextBlock
                Text="{Binding Details}" TextWrapping="Wrap"
                Margin="{StaticResource PhoneHorizontalMargin}" />
        </StackPanel>
    </ScrollViewer>
</Grid>
```

```
<phone:PhoneApplicationPage.ApplicationBar>
    <shell:ApplicationBar IsVisible="True" Opacity="0.8">
        <shell:ApplicationBarIconButton
            x:Name="appBarPin" IconUri="/Images/Pin.png" Text="pin to start"
            Click="appBarPin_Click"/>
    </shell:ApplicationBar>
</phone:PhoneApplicationPage.ApplicationBar>
```

To apply this pinning behavior, you override the *OnNavigatedTo* method in the *DetailsPage*. First, you need to figure out to which item to data-bind, based on the query string parameters. In the process, you formulate a string that you can use later as the URI for this page. This is cached in a field object so that it is available across multiple methods. You also need to determine if there's an active tile for this item. If so, disable the app bar button; otherwise, you need to enable it.

```
protected override void OnNavigatedTo(NavigationEventArgs e)
{
    itemTitle = NavigationContext.QueryString["Title"];
    var pinnedItem = App.ViewModel.Items.FirstOrDefault(x => x.Title == itemTitle);
    if (pinnedItem != null)
    {
        DataContext = thisItem = pinnedItem;
    }

    thisPageUri = e.Uri.OriginalString;
    tile = ShellTile.ActiveTiles.FirstOrDefault(
        x => x.NavigationUri.ToString().Contains(thisPageUri));

    appBarPin = ApplicationBar.Buttons[0] as ApplicationBarIconButton;
    if (tile != null)
    {
        appBarPin.IsEnabled = false;
    }
    else
    {
        appBarPin.IsEnabled = true;
    }
}
```

Note To handle the scenario in which one title is a substring of another title (and thus would cause a false match), it is useful to add some kind of sentinel value to the end of the URI string, such as "&end=here" or just a relatively unique string like "|~|".

In the *Click* handler for the pin button, create the tile. In this method, you can rely on the fact that you've already performed the search for the tile in the *OnNavigatedTo* override and established that it doesn't exist (otherwise, you wouldn't be in this *Click* handler). So, go ahead and create it now by using the current item's *Photo* property and *Title* property as the *BackgroundImage* and *Title* for the tile.

```
private void appBarPin_Click(object sender, EventArgs e)
{
    DateTime now = DateTime.Now;
    FlipTileData tileData = new FlipTileData
    {
        Title = thisItem.Title,
        Count = now.Second,
        BackgroundImage = thisItem.Photo,
        SmallBackgroundImage = thisItem.Photo,
        WideBackgroundImage = thisItem.Photo,
        BackTitle = "Lorem Ipsum!",
        BackContent = now.ToLongTimeString(),
        BackBackgroundImage = new Uri("/Assets/FlipTileMediumBack.png", UriKind.Relative),
        WideBackContent = "Lorem ipsum dolor sit amet, consectetur adipisicing elit.",
        WideBackBackgroundImage = new Uri("/Assets/FlipTileLargeBack.png", UriKind.Relative),
    };
    ShellTile.Create(new Uri(thisPageUri, UriKind.Relative), tileData, true);
}
```

By doing this, the user can pin multiple tiles, with individual control over each tile and appropriate UI feedback (the pin button is conditionally enabled) so that it's clear what the pinned state of each item is. When he taps a pinned tile, the app starts and navigates to the item page specified in the tile's *NavigationUri*. This does not go through the *MainPage*; therefore, if he then taps the Back button, there are no more pages for this app in the navigation backstack, so the app terminates.

There is an alternative UX model whereby the user can always return to the main page—and therefore, to the rest of the app—regardless of whether he started the app from Start in the normal way or from a pinned tile. This model uses a "home" button, but you should use it with care because it varies from the standard, expected behavior. Normally, the user model of a Home button is not commonly employed, because it can result in a confusing navigation experience. However, the pinned tile technique gives the user two different ways to start the app. It can justify the decision, ensuring that he can always navigate from the individual item page back to the rest of the app.

Note The practice of providing a "home" feature, as demonstrated in this sample, is pushing the boundaries of Windows Phone app guidelines. A good rule of thumb is to use the built-in apps as your inspiration. For example, with the People Hub, you can pin individual people to the Start screen, but it does not provide a Home button to return you to the All People list. The same is true of "music+videos", and so on.

If you do want to implement this behavior, you can add a second app bar button to the *Details Page*, as shown in Figure 14-7. This technique is illustrated in the *PinTiles_Home* solution in the sample code.

FIGURE 14-7 You should consider carefully whether a Home button is good or bad.

You implement the *Click* handler for the Home button to navigate to the main page.

```
private void appBarHome_Click(object sender, EventArgs e)
{
    NavigationService.Navigate(new System.Uri("/MainPage.xaml", UriKind.Relative));
}
```

This ensures that the user can always consistently navigate from an item page back to the main page. However, it now introduces a different problem. Consider the following scenario. The user navigates from the Start screen, through a pinned tile to an item page, and then navigates to the main page. This means that pressing Back from the main page will go back to the item page. This is not what the user normally anticipates: her expectation is that pressing Back from the app's main page always exits the app. Fortunately, it is very easy to fix this. All you need do is to ensure that the main page is always the top of the page stack for this app by overriding the *OnNavigatedTo* in the main page to clear the in-app page navigation stack, as shown in the following:

```
protected override void OnNavigatedTo(NavigationEventArgs e)
{
    while (NavigationService.CanGoBack)
    {
        NavigationService.RemoveBackEntry();
    }
}
```

In addition to cleaning up the backstack, this app also ensures that the Home button is not available unless the user has navigated to the page via the corresponding pinned tile on the Start screen. Using normal navigation within the app, the Home button is unnecessary. But, be aware that this might not be true for all apps. You can imagine an app that includes a Home button to deal with a deep navigation stack. Enforcing this behavior helps to maintain the UX, where home navigation is a recognizable exception to the normal navigation behavior, and that it only applies in the specific scenario of a pinned tile. Although you can programmatically set the *IsEnabled* state of an *ApplicationBarIconButton*, this class does not expose a *Visibility* property, as do regular controls. Disabling the button is not really good enough; under normal navigation, you should not make this button available at all, not even in a disabled state. This means that you need to implement this additional button programmatically, not in XAML. To do this, you can update the *OnNavigatedTo* method. First, when creating the tile, enhance the page URI to include an additional parameter which indicates that the user navigated to this page from a pinned tile. Then, you can check if the current *NavigationContext* does include this parameter in the query string. If so, you can create the additional Home button and add it to the app bar.

```
private ApplicationBarIconButton appBarHome;

protected override void OnNavigatedTo(NavigationEventArgs e)
{
    itemTitle = NavigationContext.QueryString["Title"];
    var pinnedItem = App.ViewModel.Items.FirstOrDefault(x => x.Title == itemTitle);
    if (pinnedItem != null)
    {
        DataContext = thisItem = pinnedItem;
    }

    thisPageUri = String.Format("/DetailsPage.xaml?Title={0}&Nav=FromPinned", itemTitle);
    tile = ShellTile.ActiveTiles.FirstOrDefault(
        x => x.NavigationUri.ToString().Contains(thisPageUri));

    appBarPin = ApplicationBar.Buttons[0] as ApplicationBarIconButton;
    if (tile != null)
    {
        appBarPin.IsEnabled = false;
    }
    else
    {
        appBarPin.IsEnabled = true;
    }
```

```
    // Did the user get here from a pinned tile?
    if (NavigationContext.QueryString.ContainsKey("Nav"))
    {
        appBarHome = new ApplicationBarIconButton();
        appBarHome.Text = "home";
        appBarHome.IconUri = new Uri("/Assets/Home.png", UriKind.Relative);
        appBarHome.Click += appBarHome_Click;
        ApplicationBar.Buttons.Add(appBarHome);
    }
}
```

Finally, keep in mind that this is one scenario in which it can be useful during debugging to change your *WMAppManifest.xml* file to have the app launched with a specific page and query string, as opposed to the default page. This is a debugging technique, and you must remember to remove the fake navigation before submitting your app to the marketplace. Notice that special characters—such as the ampersand ("&") in the query string must be escaped as "&"—because they occur within the XML.

```
<Tasks>
  <!--<DefaultTask Name="_default" NavigationPage="MainPage.xaml" />-->
  <DefaultTask Name="_default" NavigationPage="DetailsPage.xaml?Title=Dictumst&amp;Nav=FromPinn
ed"/>
</Tasks>
```

Cross-targeting Windows Phone 7

If you need to build an app that cross-targets both Windows Phone 7 and Windows Phone 8, you must restrict your code to using the lowest common denominator. In the context of tiles, this means using the old *TemplateType5* in the manifest, and the *StandardTileData* class in code, as shown in the code example that follows. You would also use the old overload of *ShellTile.Create*, which does not take the *bool* parameter for wide-format support. There is only one tile size in Windows Phone 7, 173x173 pixels, but it is capable of flipping. The flip style in Windows Phone 8 evolved from this style.

```
<TemplateType5>
  <BackgroundImageURI IsRelative="true" IsResource="false">Background.png</BackgroundImageURI>
  <Count>0</Count>
  <Title>SecondaryTiles7</Title>
</TemplateType5>

...
private void createTile_Click(object sender, RoutedEventArgs e)
{
    StandardTileData tileData = new StandardTileData
    {
        BackgroundImage = new Uri("/Assets/sunrise_173x173.jpg", UriKind.Relative),
        Title = "Sound Sunrise",
        Count = 1,
        BackTitle = "Sound Sunset",
        BackContent = "Goodnight!",
        BackBackgroundImage = new Uri("/Assets/sunset_173x173.jpg", UriKind.Relative)
    };
    ShellTile.Create(new Uri("/Page2.xaml?ID=SoundTile", UriKind.Relative), tileData);
}
```

Another option you can consider is the "light-up" scenario, in which your Windows Phone 7 app uses reflection to discover whether it is running on Windows Phone 8 and thus has new tile styles available to it. For details of this approach, see Chapter 13, "Porting to Windows Phone 8 and multitargeting."

Push notifications

Part of the delight users derive from Windows Phone is that apps keep themselves up-to-date. Not only can an app update its tiles dynamically, but it can also get updated data on demand from remote servers. This data can be used to update tiles, show toast notifications, and for any other purpose internal to the app. For remote updates, Windows Phone uses a push notification system, so named because the remote server pushes data to the phone only when it is updated rather than waiting for the app to pull the data from the server. Push notifications were introduced in Windows Phone 7, and there has been very little change in the feature set in the transition to Windows Phone 8.

The underlying philosophy of the push system is a *shoulder tap* mechanism. That is, you use a push notification as a signal to the phone/app that there is new data available and potentially provide some information which hints at what it is. In some cases, the notification contains all the data required for the scenario. In other cases, the notification contains only a minimal amount of data, and the full data payload isn't delivered until the app pulls it, which is typically done via a web service call or a *WebClient* request. This is one reason why the size of push payloads is limited (the other reason, of course, is to minimize network data usage).

The Microsoft Push Notification Service (MPNS) handles many of the common server-side features of this model, including identifying the target devices, retry and queuing logic to allow for offline targets, and per-app registration for notifications. Your server sends new data as simple HTTP messages to the MPNS, specifying which phones should receive the messages. The MPNS then takes care of propagating the messages and pushing them to all the target devices. Each client app running on the device that wants to receive notifications talks to the MPNS to establish an identity for the device. Figure 14-8 illustrates the high-level workflow.

Note Don't be confused by the fact that the push server example happens to be a Windows Store app. Windows Store apps can use the Windows Push Notification System (WNS) for sending and receiving notifications. This borrows considerably from the MPNS that has been in use for Windows Phone for a couple of years, with a very similar model. However, the WNS and MPNS are separate systems; they cannot be cross-purposed. That is, even though you can build a Windows Store app to send either WNS or MPNS notifications (or both), Windows Phone devices can only receive MPNS notifications, and Windows Store apps can only receive WNS notifications.

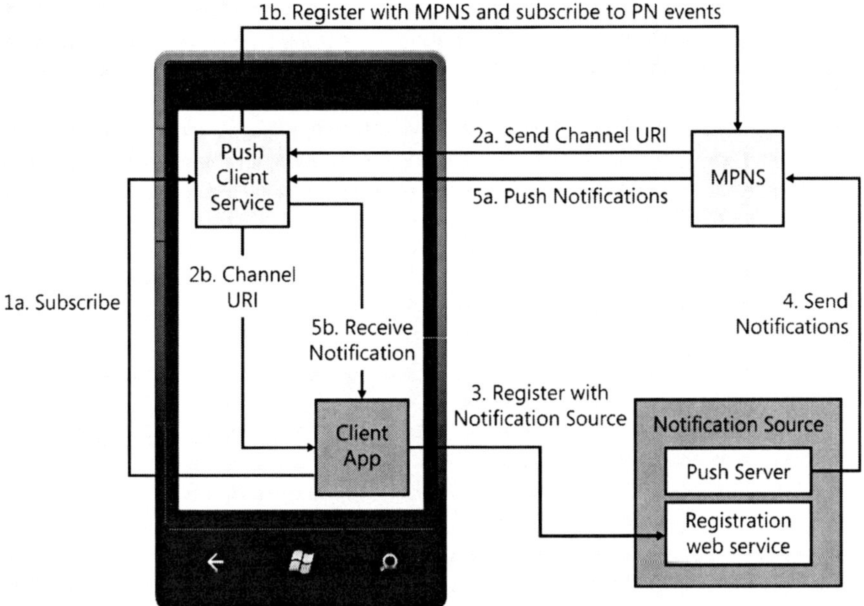

FIGURE 14-8 An overview of the Push Notification architecture.

The two darker boxes in Figure 14-8 represent pieces that you build; the two lighter boxes are supplied by Microsoft. The numbered items are described in more detail, as follows:

1. Your phone app initiates the communication by registering with the MPNS. This is a simple matter of using *HttpNotificationChannel.Open* (1a). Behind the scenes, this uses the Push Client service running on the device to communicate with the MPNS (1b).

2. The MPNS returns a channel URI back to the phone. This URI serves as a unique identifier for the phone; it will be used by the server application as the target URI for a web request. Again, the MPNS actually sends this to the Push Client service on the device (2a), which forwards it to your app (2b).

3. To register for the server's notifications, the phone must send this channel URI to the server application (the app that will send the notifications). The server application can be any kind of application that can make and receive web requests. The server application typically exposes a web service that the phone app can call to perform registration.

4. When it's ready to send a notification to a particular device, the server application makes an *HttpWebRequest* for the given channel URI (typically, it does this for multiple registered devices at the same time). This web request goes to the MPNS.

5. The MPNS pushes the corresponding notification to the specified device or devices. Again, the MPNS actually sends this to the Push Client service on the device (5a), which forwards it to your app (5b).

Whenever the server application sends a notification to the MPNS, it receives a response that provides some information about the result, including the connection status of the target device and whether the notification was actively received or suppressed.

There are three types of push notification, which are described in Table 14-2. The payload for all types of notification must be no more than 3 KB, and additional constraints apply to each type. There's a limit of one push notification channel per app, and this channel will be used for all types of notification. The MPNS has a daily limit of 500 pushes per channel—this is per app/device combination, not 500 in total. Keep in mind that this limit doesn't apply if you create an authenticated push channel, as described later in this chapter. There is no limit to the number of push notification channels per device.

TABLE 14-2 Push notification types

Type	Description	Constraints	Typical scenario
Tile	This is handled by the phone shell and rendered on the Start screen when the tile is pinned to it. The display includes multiple customizable items, all specified in the tile notification received on the phone. The images must be either local to the phone app itself or specify a reachable HTTP URL.	The title can be any length, but only the first ~15 characters of the title will be displayed. Images are scaled to the tile size chosen by the user. They can be either JPG or PNG format. The Count is capped at 99. Any remote image must be ≤150 KB and must download in ≤30 seconds.	Status updates; for example, count of unread emails for an email client, current temperature for a weather app.
Toast	Include a title, a message body and a target page URI. If your app is not running or is obscured, the phone OS will display a pop-up toast at the top of the screen for 10 seconds, including both the title and the message. The user can tap the toast to start the app. If your app is running and not obscured, there is no default display, and it's up to your app to handle the message, as appropriate.	If you supply only a title, this is capped at ~40 characters. If you supply only a body, this is capped at ~47 characters. If you supply both, the combined total is capped at ~41 characters.	Breaking news, alerts, instant messaging apps.
Raw	No default visual display. With a raw push notification, you can send any arbitrary text or binary data (up to the overall 3 KB limit) to your app on the phone.	This can only be received when the app is running.	Arbitrary data for use in your app.

To build a solution that uses push notifications, you need two main pieces: the server-side application that generates and sends the notifications, and the client-side app that runs on the phone to receive and process incoming notifications. The client-side app is an optional piece because you might send only tile notifications that do not require client-side code to process them. Both server and client pieces are explored in the following sections.

Push notification server

The *PushSimpleServer* solution in the sample code is an example of a server that sends all three types of notification, as illustrated in Figure 14-9. The server is a simple Windows Store app that offers a UI with which the user can enter suitable values for the various parts of the three notification types. The "server" in this context doesn't mean a big computer in a data center, it just means an app or service that sends push messages to the phone.

There are two broad sets of functionality that you need to expose from the server: the code that generates and sends the notifications, and the code with which client apps can register to receive notifications. Although it is possible to incorporate both features into one app, in the real world these will most likely be separate server-side components. Building and testing push-based apps can sometimes be complicated by corporate firewalls and proxies; in particular, this affects web services. For this reason, the first version of the server application does not include a registration web service. Instead, when the client first registers with the MPNS and is given a channel URI, you can copy-and-paste this from the client debug session into the running server app (into the *target device uri TextBox*). Later, you will see how to layer on a more realistic registration service. Be aware that the emulator is given a different channel URI each time you reboot it, and potentially at other times, as well.

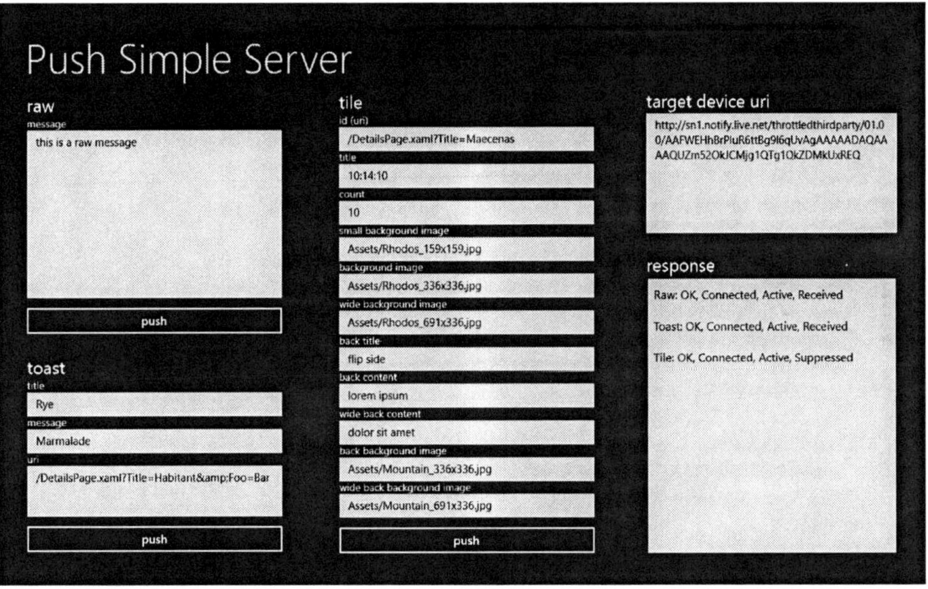

FIGURE 14-9 A simple Windows Store Push Notification server.

For some of the message elements—such as the raw message body, the tile title and count, and so on—the data is constructed entirely on the server and is independent of anything on the client. For others—such as the toast and tile target URI elements—the server data corresponds to some entity on the client. In this example, certain elements, notably the image URIs for the various tile backgrounds, the string passed from the server corresponds to resources known to exist in the client app. This will not always be the case, particularly for image paths, because the system does support remote image paths.

The app also implements a response list with which the server reports on status and responses from notifications that have been sent. The values in the response report are the response *StatusCode* and the values from the *X-DeviceConnectionStatus*, *X-SubscriptionStatus*, and *X-NotificationStatus response* headers.

In the server, the *MainPage* declares string templates for the toast and tile messages. Each type of notification is formatted as XML, with different elements and attributes for the different types of notification. This example sets up the XML payload by using simple text templates. This is useful as a learning exercise to understand the payload format and content. The templates use "{n}" placeholders for the variable data, to be completed by regular string formatting. Later on, you will see how to achieve this in a more robust manner.

```
const String toastTemplate =
    "<?xml version=\"1.0\" encoding=\"utf-8\"?>" +
    "<wp:Notification xmlns:wp=\"WPNotification\">" +
        "<wp:Toast>" +
            "<wp:Text1>{0}</wp:Text1>" +
            "<wp:Text2>{1}</wp:Text2>" +
            "<wp:Param>{2}</wp:Param>" +
            "</wp:Toast>" +
    "</wp:Notification>";

const String tileTemplate =
    "<?xml version=\"1.0\" encoding=\"utf-8\"?>" +
    "<wp:Notification xmlns:wp=\"WPNotification\" Version=\"2.0\">" +
        "<wp:Tile Id=\"{0}\" Template=\"FlipTile\">" +
            "<wp:SmallBackgroundImage>{1}</wp:SmallBackgroundImage>" +
            "<wp:WideBackgroundImage>{2}</wp:WideBackgroundImage>" +
            "<wp:WideBackBackgroundImage>{3}</wp:WideBackBackgroundImage>" +
            "<wp:WideBackContent>{4}</wp:WideBackContent>" +
            "<wp:BackgroundImage>{5}</wp:BackgroundImage>" +
            "<wp:Count>{6}</wp:Count>" +
            "<wp:Title>{7}</wp:Title>" +
            "<wp:BackBackgroundImage>{8}</wp:BackBackgroundImage>" +
            "<wp:BackTitle>{9}</wp:BackTitle>" +
            "<wp:BackContent>{10}</wp:BackContent>" +
        "</wp:Tile>" +
    "</wp:Notification>";
```

The *MainPage* constructor initializes the *TextBox* controls with some dummy data. Notice that the URI fields can include query strings, which can include name-value pairs. You can pass any name-value pairs that make sense in your client app, but the ampersand character ("&") must be escaped by using the "*&*" entity.

```
toastUri.Text = "/DetailsPage.xaml?Title=Habitant&amp;Foo=Bar";
```

The app implements suitable button *Click* handlers to trigger sending each of the three notification types. Each handler invokes a custom *SendNotification* method, which has all the common code for sending a notification of any type. The parameters that you pass to this method distinguish the different types and therefore govern how the XML payload is ultimately composed. The payload must include the notification type—this is 1 for tiles, 2 for toasts, and 3 for raw messages. It is common to define an enum for these values, but the simple numeric values are retained here to make it clear that this is what the system uses under the hood. As you can see from the following code, raw messages are simply sent directly, whereas toast and tile message data is composed by using the predefined template strings:

```
private void sendRaw_Click(object sender, RoutedEventArgs e)
{
    SendNotification(rawMessage.Text, 3);
}

private void sendToast_Click(object sender, RoutedEventArgs e)
{
    String message = String.Format(
        toastTemplate, toastTitle.Text, toastMessage.Text,
        toastUri.Text);
    SendNotification(message, 2);
}

private void sendTile_Click(object sender, RoutedEventArgs e)
{
    DateTime now = DateTime.Now;
    tileTitle.Text = now.ToString("hh:mm:ss");
    tileCount.Text = now.Second.ToString();
    String message = String.Format(
        tileTemplate, tileId.Text, tileSmallBackground.Text,
        tileWideBackground.Text, tileWideBackBackground.Text,
        tileWideBackContent.Text, tileBackground.Text,
        tileCount.Text, tileTitle.Text, tileBackBackground.Text,
        tileBackTitle.Text, tileBackContent.Text);
    SendNotification(message, 1);
}
```

The *SendNotification* method sets up an *HttpClient* for the notification and adds the required message headers. All messages must have a unique ID and must include the notification type. For toast and tile notifications, you also need to add the *X-WindowsPhone-Target* header; however, this is not used for raw notifications. The toast target specifier is "toast", whereas the tile target specifier is "token" (tiles used to be called tokens, internally). After you've composed the appropriate notification payload, you send the message to the target device via the *PostAsync* method, using the *await* keyword to wait for the return.

The return will be an *HttpResponseMessage*, in which much of the push-specific data will be in custom headers. The app extracts the notification type, status code, connection, subscription, and notification status header values so that they can be reported in the UI by adding them to the response *ListBox*.

```
private async void SendNotification(String message, short notificationClass)
{
    String responseText;
    if (message.Length > 3072)
    {
        responseText = String.Format("The message must be <= 3072 bytes: {0}", message);
    }
    else
    {
        HttpClient request = new HttpClient();

        // Add message headers.
        request.DefaultRequestHeaders.Add("X-MessageID", Guid.NewGuid().ToString());
        request.DefaultRequestHeaders.Add("X-NotificationClass", notificationClass.ToString());

        if (notificationClass == 1)
        {
            request.DefaultRequestHeaders.Add("X-WindowsPhone-Target", "token");
        }
        else if (notificationClass == 2)
        {
            request.DefaultRequestHeaders.Add("X-WindowsPhone-Target", "toast");
        }

        try
        {
            // Send the message, and wait for the response.
            HttpResponseMessage response = await request.PostAsync(
                targetDeviceUri.Text, new StringContent(message));

            IEnumerable<string> values;
            String connectionStatus = String.Empty;
            if (response.Headers.TryGetValues("X-DeviceConnectionStatus", out values))
            {
                connectionStatus = values.First();
            }
            String subscriptionStatus = String.Empty;
            if (response.Headers.TryGetValues("X-SubscriptionStatus", out values))
            {
                subscriptionStatus = values.First();
            }
            String notificationStatus = String.Empty;
            if (response.Headers.TryGetValues("X-NotificationStatus", out values))
            {
                notificationStatus = values.First();
            }

            responseText = String.Format("{0}: {1}, {2}, {3}, {4}",
                notificationClass == 1 ? "Tile" :
                notificationClass == 2 ? "Toast" : "Raw",
                response.StatusCode,
                connectionStatus, subscriptionStatus, notificationStatus);
```

```
            }
            catch (WebException ex)
            {
                responseText = ex.Message;
            }
        }
        responseList.Items.Add(responseText);
    }
```

Push notification client

In the client, raw and toast notifications are handled by the app if the app is running and not obscured. If the app is not running, toast notifications are rendered by the platform shell as pop-up windows. The shell always handles tile notifications.

Figure 14-10 (left) shows the client app running. This is the *PushSimpleClient* solution in the sample code, which is an evolution of the *PinTiles* sample discussed earlier. Here, the notification status and any incoming toast notification is reported in a *ListBox* at the bottom of the main page. Contrast this with Figure 14-10 (right), which shows the Start screen when a toast notification is received. This displays the app's icon and the incoming toast *Title* and *Message* values. When the user taps the toast, this navigates to the target URI specified in the toast notification payload. Any additional parameters in the query string are passed in to the target page in the *NavigationContext*.

When the user taps the toast, she navigates to the specified page—in this example, to the *Details Page* with the *Habitant* item loaded. The fact that there is a pinned tile for the *DetailsPage* with the *Maecenas* item is irrelevant at this point. On the client side, the *DetailsPage* code is exactly the same as in the earlier *PinTiles* sample. The existing *OnNavigatedTo* override, which was designed to meet the needs of navigation via local tiles, also meets the needs of navigation via URI-targeted toast notification, and, of course, navigation via a tile that might or might not have been updated via a push notification. The only update on the client side for this toast is to extract the additional query string values and display them in the UI, in the scenario in which the toast is received when the app is actually running.

Now, consider what happens when a tile notification is received. Figure 14-10 shows that the user has pinned a secondary tile for the *Maecenas* item. If a tile notification arrives that includes this corresponding tile ID—that is "/DetailsPage.xaml?Title=Maecenas"—the tile information will be used to update that specific tile. If the tile is not pinned, the notification is simply suppressed. If the server sends a tile notification and omits the *ID*, this will update the default (primary) tile—again, assuming that this tile is pinned to Start.

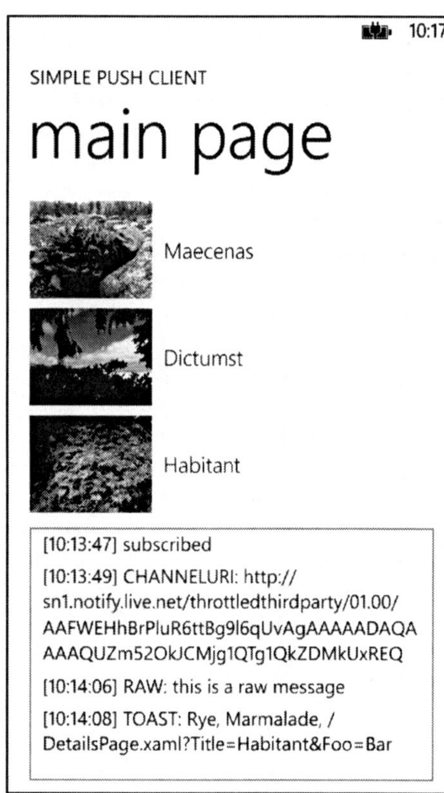

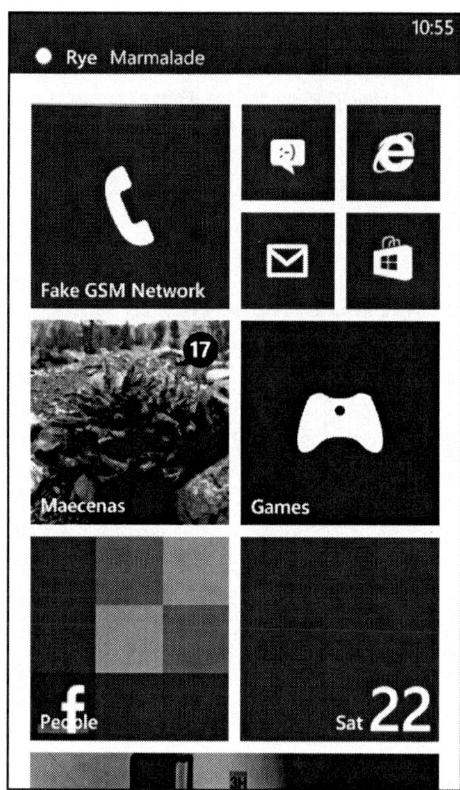

FIGURE 14-10 The client app receiving a toast notification while running (on the left), and the phone receiving a toast while the client app is not running (right).

The client app needs to perform the following tasks:

1. Subscribe to receive notifications, via the Push Client service on the phone.
2. Bind toast and tile notifications to this app so that when these are received by the shell, the shell can associate them with the app.
3. When the MPNS sends this app a unique push client ID, the app would realistically then register this with a registration web service on the server. However, this first version of the client doesn't include remote registration; instead, it relies on copy-paste during debugging.
4. Process any incoming raw and toast notifications that arrive when the app is running.

Note that an app that uses push notifications must have the *ID_CAP_PUSH_NOTIFICATION* capability declared in its app manifest. The *MainPage* declares fields for the channel name (an arbitrary string), the *HttpNotification* channel for working with the MPNS, and an *ObservableCollection<T>* to hold all the message strings and status information. This collection is data-bound to the *ListBox* in the UI. The app also declares a simple *bool* which it uses to ensure that the notification events are only hooked up to event handlers once. This is important, because the hook-up is done in the *OnNavigatedTo* override, and this method, of course, can be invoked multiple times.

```
private String channelName = "Contoso Notification Channel";
private HttpNotificationChannel channel;
private Uri channelUri;
private bool isConnected;
private ObservableCollection<String> notifications;
public ObservableCollection<String> Notifications
{
    get { return notifications; }
    private set { }
}
```

The *OnNavigatedTo* override is a reasonable place to perform initialization. The first thing to do is to try to find an existing push channel. If none is found, go ahead and create a new one now. Behind the scenes, this triggers the Push Client component on the phone to request a device identifier (channel URI) from the MPNS. When the MPNS sends the channel URI back to the device, the Push Client component raises a *ChannelUriUpdated* event. So, this is the first push event for which the client must set up a handler. Two other events the client handles are the *ShellToastNotificationReceived* (self-explanatory) and the *HttpNotificationReceived* (which is raised when a raw notification is received). If the channel hasn't already been bound to tile and toast notifications, you can bind it now by using the *BindToShellTile* and *BindToShellToast* APIs. The app reports ongoing status and other messages in the UI via an *AddNotification* method that updates the data-bound *ListBox* on the UI thread.

```
protected override void OnNavigatedTo(NavigationEventArgs e)
{
    channel = HttpNotificationChannel.Find(channelName);
    if (channel == null)
    {
        channel = new HttpNotificationChannel(channelName);
        channel.ChannelUriUpdated += channel_ChannelUriUpdated;
        channel.Open();
    }

    if (!isConnected)
    {
        channel.ShellToastNotificationReceived += channel_ShellToastNotificationReceived;
        channel.HttpNotificationReceived += channel_HttpNotificationReceived;
        isConnected = true;
    }

    if (!channel.IsShellTileBound)
    {
        channel.BindToShellTile();
    }
    if (!channel.IsShellToastBound)
    {
        channel.BindToShellToast();
    }
    AddNotification("subscribed");
}
```

```
private void AddNotification(String message)
{
    Dispatcher.BeginInvoke(() => Notifications.Add(
        String.Format("[{0:hh:mm:ss}] {1}", DateTime.Now, message)));
}
```

You should allow for the possibility of a server restart while the client has a channel open. Of course, your client app won't know when this has happened, but you can mitigate it somewhat by always registering the channel during *OnNavigatedTo*. If you were to receive a *ChannelUriUpdate* event, you would realistically call the server app's web service in order to register this client, passing it the channel URI you've been given by the MPNS. This first version of the client simply prints this out to the output window in a Visual Studio debug session. From there, you can manually copy it and paste it into the Target Device Uri *TextBox* in the server app.

```
private void channel_ChannelUriUpdated(object sender, NotificationChannelUriEventArgs e)
{
    channelUri = e.ChannelUri;
    String message = String.Format("CHANNELURI: {0}", channelUri);
    Debug.WriteLine(e.ChannelUri);
    AddNotification(message);
}
```

When the app receives a push notification (raw or toast) event, it also displays this in the UI, appropriately dispatched to the UI thread. To retrieve the data, you dig into the *Collection* property on the *NotificationEventArgs* parameter that is passed into the event handler. Notification data is sent in this collection, which is a dictionary, so the elements are key-value pairs. In this app, there will only be one pair of data, although you will allow for it being a null element (in which case, you use an empty string).

```
private void channel_HttpNotificationReceived(object sender, HttpNotificationEventArgs e)
{
    byte[] bytes;
    using (Stream stream = e.Notification.Body)
    {
        bytes = new byte[stream.Length];
        stream.Read(bytes, 0, (int)stream.Length);
    }
    String rawMessage = Encoding.UTF8.GetString(bytes, 0, bytes.Length);
    String message = String.Format("RAW: {0}", rawMessage);
    AddNotification(message);
}

private void channel_ShellToastNotificationReceived(object sender, NotificationEventArgs e)
{
    String title = e.Collection.Values.First();
    String toastMessage = e.Collection.Values.Skip(1).FirstOrDefault() ?? String.Empty;
    String toastUrl = e.Collection.Values.Skip(2).FirstOrDefault() ?? String.Empty;
    String message = String.Format("TOAST: {0}, {1}, {2}", title, toastMessage, toastUrl);
    AddNotification(message);
}
```

Registration web service

Of course, copying and pasting the client's channel URI from a debug session into the server app is only useful during development. In production, to support client registration on the server, you can expose a web service with appropriate *Register* (and *Unregister*) web methods. It is actually possible to host this web service within your push server application, but it is more likely to be hosted independently, perhaps by Internet Information Services (IIS), and potentially even on separate physical server computers. This raises the question of how to share information about registered devices between the web service and the push server. Typically this would be done via a shared database; on Windows Azure, this would be done via Azure table storage.

For test purposes, if you don't have a database server or a Windows Azure account, you can simulate a shared database by using a shared file, instead. This is the approach taken in the *Registration Service* web service in the sample code.

The web service itself is a straightforward Windows Communications Foundation (WCF) service that defines a simple *ServiceContract* named *IRegisterDeviceService* and implements it in a custom *RegisterDeviceService* class. Because the push server is a Windows Store app, it must adhere to constraints on filesystem access. The WCF service doesn't have the same restrictions, so for simplicity, the shared file is placed in the install folder for the push server—a location which is accessible to both components. Client phone apps will call *Register* to register their channel URI with this server app. The service loads the shared file (which simulates a more realistic database query), searches the list, adds the device's channel URI if not found, and then overwrites the file with the modified list, using a *DataContractJsonSerializer*. Similarly, client apps will call *Unregister* to unregister their channel URI with this server app, and in this case, the service searches the list, removes the channel URI if found, and then overwrites the file again.

```
[ServiceContract]
public interface IRegisterDeviceService
{
    [OperationContract]
    void Register(Uri deviceUri);

    [OperationContract]
    void Unregister(Uri deviceUri);
}

public class RegisterDeviceService : IRegisterDeviceService
{
    private const string DeviceListFilePath =
        @"C:\temp\Samples12\PushSimpleServer_Registration\bin\Debug\AppX\deviceList.txt";

    public void Register(Uri deviceUri)
    {
        List<Uri> devices = LoadDeviceListFromFile();
        if (devices != null & !devices.Contains(deviceUri))
```

```
        {
            devices.Add(deviceUri);
            using (FileStream writeFile = File.Create(DeviceListFilePath))
            {
                DataContractJsonSerializer serializer =
                    new DataContractJsonSerializer(typeof(List<Uri>));
                serializer.WriteObject(writeFile, devices);
            }
        }
    }

    public void Unregister(Uri deviceUri)
    {
        List<Uri> devices = LoadDeviceListFromFile();
        if (devices != null & devices.Contains(deviceUri))
        {
            devices.Remove(deviceUri);
            using (FileStream writeFile = File.Create(DeviceListFilePath))
            {
                DataContractJsonSerializer serializer =
                    new DataContractJsonSerializer(typeof(List<Uri>));
                serializer.WriteObject(writeFile, devices);
            }
        }
    }

    private List<Uri> LoadDeviceListFromFile()
    {
        if (!File.Exists(DeviceListFilePath))
        {
            using (FileStream createFile = File.Create(DeviceListFilePath)){}
            return new List<Uri>();
        }
        using (FileStream readFile = File.OpenRead(DeviceListFilePath))
        {
            DataContractJsonSerializer serializer =
                new DataContractJsonSerializer(typeof(List<Uri>));
            return (List<Uri>)serializer.ReadObject(readFile);
        }
    }
}
```

Note From Windows Vista onward, security has improved so that if you build and run a WCF service from Visual Studio, you might see this error (where "+" is a wildcard, and "8002" is the arbitrary port you specified for your service):

```
HTTP could not register URL http://+:8002/. Your process does not have access rights to
this namespace (see http://go.microsoft.com/fwlink/?LinkId=70353 for details).
```

This is because by default, every HTTP path is reserved for use by processes executed by the system administrator. If you are not running your WCF service as administrator, it will fail to start with an *AddressAccessDeniedException*. To mitigate this, you could run Visual Studio as administrator. Alternatively, you can open a command window (as administrator) and execute the *netsh* command to delegate permissions on your service's HTTP path to your regular user account (or to Everyone); for example:

```
netsh http add urlacl url=http://+:8002/RegisterDevice user=Andrew
```

The push server app can now load the device list from the shared file. You can see this at work in the *PushSimpleServer_Registration* version of the app in the sample code. The device list itself is held in a *List<Uri>* field. The known path chosen for the shared file corresponds to the *InstalledLocation* property of the current app package. During development, this will be in the bin\Debug\AppX folder of the current project. If the device list file doesn't exist, the app creates it now and returns an empty list. Otherwise, it converts the Windows Runtime input stream into a managed stream and deserializes it into the list.

```
private List<Uri> deviceList;

private async void LoadDeviceListFromFile()
{
    //C:\temp\Samples12\PushSimpleServer_Registration\bin\Debug\AppX
    StorageFolder folder = Windows.ApplicationModel.Package.Current.InstalledLocation;
    string fileName = "deviceList.txt";
    StorageFile file = await folder.GetFileAsync(fileName);

    if (file == null)
    {
        file = await folder.CreateFileAsync(fileName);
        deviceList = new List<Uri>();
    }
    else
    {
        IInputStream inputStream = await file.OpenReadAsync();
        Stream readStream = inputStream.AsStreamForRead();
        DataContractJsonSerializer serializer =
            new DataContractJsonSerializer(typeof(List<Uri>));
        deviceList = (List<Uri>)serializer.ReadObject(readStream);
    }
}
```

The app calls this custom *LoadDeviceListFromFile* method after setting up the *HttpClient* object but before invoking *PostAsync*; this is now done in a loop, within which the app iterates through all the registered devices, sending the same notification to all of them. Of course, this is also where you would perform any target client filtering, perhaps sending some notifications only to certain devices and not to others, as your domain logic dictates.

```
HttpClient request = new HttpClient();
... add message headers: unchanged code omitted for brevity.
LoadDeviceListFromFile();
foreach (Uri deviceUri in deviceList)
{
    try
    {
        HttpResponseMessage response = await request.PostAsync(
            //targetDeviceUri.Text, new StringContent(message));
            deviceUri, new StringContent(message));

... process the response: unchanged code omitted for brevity.
```

The client app can be updated to take advantage of the registration web service, as demonstrated in the *PushSimpleClient_Registration* version of the app in the sample code. First, you would add a service reference for the WCF service, in exactly the same way as for any other web service (as described in Chapter 8, "Web services and the cloud"). You can then declare an instance of the web service client proxy class as a field in the *MainPage*.

```
private RegisterDeviceServiceClient serviceClient;
```

In the *OnNavigatedTo* override, you would instantiate this service proxy and hook up a handler for the *RegisterCompleted* event that will be raised when the registration call completes. In this sample, these are implemented to report status in the UI.

```
protected override void OnNavigatedTo(NavigationEventArgs e)
{
    serviceClient = new RegisterDeviceServiceClient();
    serviceClient.RegisterCompleted += serviceClient_RegisterCompleted;
    serviceClient.UnregisterCompleted += serviceClient_UnregisterCompleted;
...unchanged code omitted for brevity.
}

private void serviceClient_RegisterCompleted(object sender, AsyncCompletedEventArgs e)
{
    if (e.Error == null)
    {
        AddNotification("registered");
    }
    else
    {
        AddNotification(e.Error.Message);
    }
}
```

```
private void serviceClient_UnregisterCompleted(object sender, AsyncCompletedEventArgs e)
{
    if (e.Error == null)
    {
        AddNotification("unregistered");
    }
    else
    {
        AddNotification(e.Error.Message);
    }
}
```

The client would typically make the registration call as soon as the channel URI is received from the MPNS, in the *ChannelUriUpdated* event handler. You could enhance this so that the app remembers its last URI (for example, by saving it in *AppSettings*), and if this differs from the latest one, send both an *UnRegister* and a fresh *Register* request.

```
private void channel_ChannelUriUpdated(object sender, NotificationChannelUriEventArgs e)
{
    channelUri = e.ChannelUri;
    String message = String.Format("CHANNELURI: {0}", channelUri);
    AddNotification(message);

    // Register the new device Uri with the server app.
    serviceClient.RegisterAsync(channelUri);
}
```

The preceding code illustrates all the core requirements for the client and server applications. However, there are a few additional features that you could incorporate to improve robustness and usability, as described in the following sections.

Additional server features

On the server side, you can use the following additional features offered by the push notification system:

- Batching intervals, with which you can group your notifications into batches
- The *XmlWriter* or *XDocument* classes, for building the notification payload instead of using string templates
- Enhanced notification response information, to implement richer message tracking and reporting

These features are described in the following subsections.

Batching intervals

The server currently uses strings 1, 2, and 3 to identify the *X-NotificationClass*, and these must be added to the request headers. However, the values 1, 2, and 3 really correspond to batching indicators, and there are nine possible values, organized into three categories, as shown in Table 14-3.

TABLE 14-3 Notification batching Intervals

Value	Notification type	Meaning
1	Tile	Send immediately
2	Toast	Send immediately
3	Raw	Send immediately
11	Tile	Batch and send within 450 seconds (7.5 minutes)
12	Toast	Batch and send within 450 seconds (7.5 minutes)
13	Raw	Batch and send within 450 seconds (7.5 minutes)
21	Tile	Batch and send within 900 seconds (15 minutes)
22	Toast	Batch and send within 900 seconds (15 minutes)
23	Raw	Batch and send within 900 seconds (15 minutes)

This makes it possible for the MPNS to batch notifications together, including from multiple apps. The primary purpose of this is to maintain an optimal balance of UX on the phone; sending notifications in batches improves battery performance because it makes maximum use of the network while it is up rather than bringing it up for every single notification. The *PushMoreServer* solution in the sample code adds a *ComboBox* to the *MainPage*, with which the user can select one of the three batching intervals. This will be applied to all notifications until it is changed.

```
<ComboBox Name="batchList" Width="350" HorizontalAlignment="Left" FontSize="16">
    <ComboBoxItem Content="immedate" Tag="0"/>
    <ComboBoxItem Content="450 sec" Tag="10"/>
    <ComboBoxItem Content="900 sec" Tag="20"/>
</ComboBox>
```

The *SendNotification* method is updated to accomodate the batching interval. Specifically, change this line

```
request.DefaultRequestHeaders.Add("X-NotificationClass", notificationClass.ToString());
```

to this:

```
int batch = Int16.Parse(((ComboBoxItem)batchList.SelectedItem).Tag.ToString()) +
notificationClass;
request.DefaultRequestHeaders.Add("X-NotificationClass", batch.ToString());
```

Be aware that the MPNS does not provide a true end-to-end confirmation that the notification was delivered. In particular, if you batch up your notifications, you will still get an immediate response notification based on the last known state of the target device and app, even though the notification might not be sent until up to 15 minutes after the fact.

XML payload

Building the XML payload from string templates is useful from a developer's perspective; it helps to make it obvious what the XML schema is and what a typical payload for each notification type looks like. However, it is a somewhat error-prone approach. For example, it is very fragile in the face of replacement values that contain reserved characters such as "<". A more robust approach is to construct the XML in code by using *XmlWriter* methods *WriteStartElement*, *WriteEndElement*, and so on. Alternatively, you can use the simpler *XDocument*.

Using *XDocument*, you can rewrite the cumbersome XML string-based code for toasts and tiles, as demonstrated in the example that follows. You can see this at work in the *PushMoreServer* solution in the sample code.

```
private static readonly XNamespace WpNs = "WPNotification";
private void sendToast_Click(object sender, RoutedEventArgs e)
{
    XDocument doc = new XDocument();
    doc.Add(
        new XElement(WpNs + "Notification",
        new XAttribute(XNamespace.Xmlns + "wp", WpNs.NamespaceName),
        new XElement(WpNs + "Toast",
            new XElement(WpNs + "Text1", toastTitle.Text),
            new XElement(WpNs + "Text2", toastMessage.Text),
            new XElement(WpNs + "Param", toastUri.Text))));
    String message = doc.ToString();
    SendNotification(message, 2);
}

private void sendTile_Click(object sender, RoutedEventArgs e)
{
    DateTime now = DateTime.Now;
    tileTitle.Text = now.ToString("hh:mm:ss");
    tileCount.Text = now.Second.ToString();
    XDocument doc = new XDocument();
    doc.Add(
        new XElement(WpNs + "Notification",
        new XAttribute(XNamespace.Xmlns + "wp", WpNs.NamespaceName),
        new XElement(WpNs + "Tile", new XAttribute(WpNs + "Id", tileId.Text),
            new XElement(WpNs + "SmallBackgroundImage", tileSmallBackground.Text),
            new XElement(WpNs + "WideBackgroundImage", tileWideBackground.Text),
            new XElement(WpNs + "WideBackBackgroundImage", tileWideBackBackground.Text),
            new XElement(WpNs + "WideBackContent", tileWideBackContent.Text),
            new XElement(WpNs + "BackgroundImage", tileBackground.Text),
            new XElement(WpNs + "Count", tileCount.Text),
            new XElement(WpNs + "Title", tileTitle.Text),
            new XElement(WpNs + "BackBackgroundImage", tileBackBackground.Text),
            new XElement(WpNs + "BackTitle", tileBackTitle.Text),
            new XElement(WpNs + "BackContent", tileBackContent.Text))));
    String message = doc.ToString();
    SendNotification(message, 1);
}
```

Response information

The server app has logic to test for connected subscribers, so for each notification sent, the results are most likely to be *status code = OK, connection status = Connected*, or *subscription status = Active*. The notification status will be either *Received* or *Suppressed*. Raw notifications are received if the app is running; otherwise, they are suppressed. Tile notifications are received if the app is pinned to the Start screen and is not running; otherwise, they are suppressed. Toast notifications are received whether the app is running or not, and the platform will show toast UI if the app is not in the foreground.

The server app reports the most useful notification response information in the UI. In a more sophisticated app, you might well want to track other information such as the message ID and time-stamp. Most of the potentially useful information is in the *Headers* property of the *HttpResponse Message* object that you get back in the server after sending a notification (as listed in the example that follows). Be aware that only the items prefixed with "X-" are specific to push notifications and that the headers include some MPNS server information that is of no practical use to the developer.

```
X-DeviceConnectionStatus - Connected
X-NotificationStatus - Received
X-SubscriptionStatus - Active
X-MessageID - cb4f3a3b-4c2c-4363-8f5f-85458d11ed56
ActivityId - c56ab764-6d73-439e-b4a1-bbc27940c5d4
X-Server - SN1MPNSM019
Cache-Control - private
Date - Tue, 25 Sep 2012 00:05:14 GMT
Server - Microsoft-IIS/7.5
X-AspNet-Version - 4.0.30319
X-Powered-By - ASP.NET
```

Additional client features

On the client side, there are several enhancements that you should consider layering on top of the basic push features, including the following:

- Handling the special *ErrorOccurred* push notification event
- Providing a mechanism for the user to opt in or out of push notifications for your app
- Implementing a custom viewmodel for push settings

The *ErrorOccurred* event

So far, the sample app has used a reasonable level of try/catch exception handling, including for standard HTTP web error codes. However, the MPNS also reports specific errors that you can consume in your app. To do this, in the *SubscribeToNotifications* method, add an event sink for the *ErrorOccurred* event, as shown in the following example (the *PushMoreClient* solution in the sample code):

```
if (channel == null)
{
    channel = new HttpNotificationChannel(channelName);
    channel.ChannelUriUpdated += channel_ChannelUriUpdated;
    channel.ErrorOccurred += channel_ErrorOccurred;
    channel.Open();
}
```

For testing purposes and for a simple implementation, the event handler could report the error—or rather, a suitably user-friendly version of the error message—to the screen. In a more sophisticated app, you would want to look at the *ErrorType* and *ErrorAdditionalData* properties and take the appropriate corrective action. For example, if you get a *ChannelOpenFailed* or *PayloadFormatError*, the channel is now useless, so you should clean it up and optionally re-create it. To support that technique, you should abstract all the notification subscription work from the *OnNavigatedTo* override out to a custom method (named *SubscribeToNofications* in the example code that follows momentarily) and then invoke this method from *OnNavigatedTo*.

On the other hand, if you get bad data from the server or too many notifications in a short span of time, there's really not much you can do on the client, beyond reporting. If you get a *PowerLevel Changed* event, this is an informative warning that the server will stop sending tile and toast notifications; if phone power drops to critical level, MPNS will stop sending even raw notifications to the device to reduce power consumption.

```
private void channel_ErrorOccurred(object sender, NotificationChannelErrorEventArgs e)
{
    String description = String.Empty;
    switch (e.ErrorType)
    {
        case ChannelErrorType.ChannelOpenFailed:
        case ChannelErrorType.PayloadFormatError:
            channel.Close();
            channel.Dispose();
            channel = null;
            SubscribeToNotifications();
            description = "Channel closed and re-initialized.";
            break;
        case ChannelErrorType.MessageBadContent:
            description = "Bad data received from server.";
            break;
        case ChannelErrorType.NotificationRateTooHigh:
            description = "Too many notifications received.";
            break;
        case ChannelErrorType.PowerLevelChanged:
            if (e.ErrorAdditionalData == (int)ChannelPowerLevel.LowPowerLevel)
            {
                description =
                    "No more toast or tile notifications will be "
                    + "received until power levels are restored.";
            }
            else if
                (e.ErrorAdditionalData ==
                (int)ChannelPowerLevel.CriticalLowPowerLevel)
```

```
            {
                description =
                    "No notifications of any kind will be received"
                    + "until power levels are restored.";
            }
            break;
        case ChannelErrorType.Unknown:
            description = "unknown";
            break;
    }
    AddNotification(String.Format("ERROR: {0} - {1}", e.Message, description));
}
```

User opt-in/out

The Windows Phone Store certification requirements include two items that are specific to push notifications. The first time your app uses the *BindToShellToast* method, you must ask the user for explicit permission to receive toast notifications. You must also provide a UI mechanism with which the user can turn off toast notifications at any time later on. The reason for this is that toast notifications use the same alert mechanism as other system notifications, such as incoming Short Message Service (SMS) messages. These alerts are executed at idle-level priority; that is, they are displayed immediately regardless of anything else the user is doing on the phone at the time, so long as the CPU is not at maximum utilization. It is beneficial for all toast notifications to use the same UI mechanism on the phone because it promotes consistency of UX. The downside is that the user might not consider your app's notifications to have the same priority as system alerts. In addition, notifications consume battery power, and even though the MPNS itself will throttle the rate at which notifications are sent, any potentially excessive use of battery power should also be under the user's control. The user must be given the choice on a per-app basis.

To accommodate this requirement, you need to prompt the user, typically with a *MessageBox*, and then persist the user's choice. You can enhance the client app with a couple of additional *bool* fields to record whether the user wants to allow toasts and whether you've already asked him once. These need to be included in the persistent app settings.

```
protected override void OnNavigatedTo(NavigationEventArgs e)
{
    bool push;
    if (IsolatedStorageSettings.ApplicationSettings.TryGetValue<bool>("IsToastOk", out push))
    {
        isToastOk = push;
    }
    bool prompted;
    if (IsolatedStorageSettings.ApplicationSettings.TryGetValue<bool>("ToastPrompted", out
        prompted))
    {
        toastPrompted = prompted;
    }
    SubscribeToNotifications();
}
```

```
protected override void OnNavigatedFrom(NavigationEventArgs e)
{
    IsolatedStorageSettings.ApplicationSettings["IsToastOk"] = isToastOk;
    IsolatedStorageSettings.ApplicationSettings["ToastPrompted"] = toastPrompted;
    IsolatedStorageSettings.ApplicationSettings.Save();
}
```

Some apps only use toast notifications. Also, some apps require both toast notifications and either raw or tile notifications. This means that the user's choice about allowing toasts might determine whether your app uses notifications at all. However, it is more common to keep the different types of notification separate. In the following example (the *PushMoreClient* app in the sample code), you go ahead with raw and tile notifications, regardless, but only use toasts if the user has explicitly agreed to them.

```
private void SubscribeToNotifications()
{
...unchanged code omitted for brevity.

    if (!channel.IsShellToastBound)
    {
        if (!isToastOk && !toastPrompted)
        {
            MessageBoxResult pushPrompt =
                MessageBox.Show(
                    "Allow toast notifications for this application?",
                    "PushMoreClient", MessageBoxButton.OKCancel);
            toastPrompted = true;
            if (pushPrompt == MessageBoxResult.OK)
            {
                isToastOk = true;
                channel.BindToShellToast();
            }
        }
    }
}
```

Note that this doesn't cover the case in which *isToastOk* is already *true*, but the channel URI has changed. In this case, you would also need to rebind.

Implementing a push viewmodel

You are only required to ask the user about toast notifications once, but you are also required to offer a mechanism by which the user can change his decision at any later stage. This pretty much mandates a settings page of some kind. As soon as you implement a settings page, the limitations of the simple client implementation you've been working with so far become more obvious, specifically because you now need to access connection information across at least two pages. The classic design solution here is to encapsulate all the connection information into a *ViewModel* class and declare a public property of that type in the *App* class, where it will be accessible to all pages in the app.

The following is an example (the *PushViewModelClient* solution in the sample code) of the *App* class declaring a static *PushViewModel* property:

```
public partial class App : Application
{
    private static MainViewModel viewModel = null;
    public static MainViewModel ViewModel
    {
        get
        {
            lock (typeof(App))
            {
                if (viewModel == null)
                {
                    viewModel = new MainViewModel();
                    viewModel.LoadData();
                }
            }
            return viewModel;
        }
    }
... irrelevant code omitted for brevity.
}
```

All of the connection-related fields and properties are moved from the *MainPage* class to the *PushViewModel* class, along with all of the server registration and notification subscription methods. Most of these methods are taken wholesale from the original implementation in *MainPage*.

```
public class PushViewModel : INotifyPropertyChanged
{
    private String channelName = "Contoso Notification Channel";
    private HttpNotificationChannel channel;
    private Uri channelUri;
    private ObservableCollection<String> notifications = new ObservableCollection<String>();
    public ObservableCollection<String> Notifications
    {
        get { return notifications; }
    }


    public void SubscribeToNotifications()
    {
    ...original code moved unchanged from MainPage class.
    }

    private void channel_ChannelUriUpdated(object sender, NotificationChannelUriEventArgs e)
    {
    ...original code moved unchanged from MainPage class.
    }

    private void channel_HttpNotificationReceived(object sender, HttpNotificationEventArgs e)
    {
    ...original code moved unchanged from MainPage class.
    }
```

```
    private void channel_ShellToastNotificationReceived(object sender, NotificationEventArgs e)
    {
    ...original code moved unchanged from MainPage class.
    }

    private void channel_ErrorOccurred(object sender, NotificationChannelErrorEventArgs e)
    {
    ...original code moved unchanged from MainPage class.
    }
}
```

This viewmodel adopts the recommended pattern where changes to the critical data are persisted at the point at which the change is made rather than waiting until some lifecycle event to load/save all the settings at once. In this particular example, the difference is negligible, but you should generally adopt this pattern by default, and it will certainly make a difference if the amount of data is large.

```
private bool isToastPrompted;
public bool IsToastPrompted
{
    get
    {
        bool prompted;
        if (IsolatedStorageSettings.ApplicationSettings.TryGetValue<bool>
            ("IsToastPrompted", out prompted))
        {
            isToastPrompted = prompted;
        }
        return isToastPrompted;
    }
    set
    {
        if (value != isToastPrompted)
        {
            isToastPrompted = value;
            PropertyChangedEventHandler handler = PropertyChanged;
            if (null != handler)
            {
                handler(this, new PropertyChangedEventArgs("IsToastPrompted"));
            }
            IsolatedStorageSettings.ApplicationSettings["IsToastPrompted"] = isToastPrompted;
            IsolatedStorageSettings.ApplicationSettings.Save();
        }
    }
}

private bool isToastOk;
public bool IsToastOk
{
    get
    {
        bool toast;
        if (IsolatedStorageSettings.ApplicationSettings.TryGetValue<bool>
            ("IsToastOk", out toast))
        {
            isToastOk = toast;
        }
```

```
            return isToastOk;
        }
        set
        {
            if (value != isToastOk)
            {
                isToastOk = value;
                PropertyChangedEventHandler handler = PropertyChanged;
                if (null != handler)
                {
                    handler(this, new PropertyChangedEventArgs("IsToastOk"));
                }

                if (isToastOk)
                {
                    if (!channel.IsShellToastBound)
                    {
                        channel.BindToShellToast();
                        AddNotification("toasts bound");
                    }
                }
                else
                {
                    if (channel.IsShellToastBound)
                    {
                        channel.UnbindToShellToast();
                        AddNotification("toasts unbound");
                    }
                }
                IsolatedStorageSettings.ApplicationSettings["IsToastOk"] = isToastOk;
                IsolatedStorageSettings.ApplicationSettings.Save();
            }
        }
    }
```

The notifications will come in on a non-UI thread, but you're data-binding the list of notifications to the UI. To avoid cross-thread exceptions, you need to marshal any updates to the notifications collection to the UI thread. The standard way to achieve this is to use the *Dispatcher* class. Every UI element—in fact, every type derived from *DependencyObject*—has a *Dispatcher* field of type *Dispatcher*. The *PushViewModel* class is not a UI element, but you can use the *Deployment.Current.Dispatcher*, which is always globally available in a phone app.

```
private void AddNotification(String message)
{
    String formattedMessage =
        String.Format("[{0:hh:mm:ss}] {1}", DateTime.Now, message);
    if (Deployment.Current.Dispatcher.CheckAccess())
    {
        Notifications.Add(formattedMessage);
    }
    else
```

```
    {
        Deployment.Current.Dispatcher.BeginInvoke(
            () => Notifications.Add(formattedMessage));
    }
}
```

Note The *CheckAccess* method on the *Dispatcher* class doesn't show up in IntelliSense or autocomplete in Visual Studio. This is because it is marked with the *[EditorBrowsable(EditorBrowsableState.Never)]* attribute. The original reason for this is because it was thought that the method would only be used in advanced scenarios. So, although it is part of the public API, it is not advertised in the tools. This is a historical hangover that is no longer really relevant. Certainly, there is no problem in your using this method.

In the *MainPage* class, the *ListBox* is data-bound to the notifications collection, as before, but in this version, the notifications collection is exposed as a property of the *PushViewModel*, which itself is a property of the *App* class. The *MainPage* class also implements an app bar button and wires its *Click* event to navigate to the new *SettingsPage*. The only work left for the *OnNavigatedTo* override to do is to invoke the *SubscribeToNotifications* method on the *PushViewModel*.

```
public MainPage()
{
    InitializeComponent();
    BuildLocalizedApplicationBar();
    PhotoList.ItemsSource = App.ViewModel.Items;
    //notifications = new ObservableCollection<String>();
    //messageList.ItemsSource = Notifications;
    messageList.ItemsSource = App.Push.Notifications;
}

private void BuildLocalizedApplicationBar()
{
    ApplicationBar = new ApplicationBar();
    ApplicationBarIconButton appBarButton = new ApplicationBarIconButton(
        new Uri("/Assets/settings.png", UriKind.Relative));
    appBarButton.Text = AppResources.AppBarButtonText;
    appBarButton.Click += appBarButton_Click;
    ApplicationBar.Buttons.Add(appBarButton);
}

private void appBarButton_Click(object sender, EventArgs e)
{
    NavigationService.Navigate(new Uri("/SettingsPage.xaml", UriKind.Relative));
}

protected override void OnNavigatedTo(NavigationEventArgs e)
{
    App.Push.SubscribeToNotifications();
}
```

The *SettingsPage* itself is trivial; it uses the *ToggleSwitch* from the Microsoft Silverlight Toolkit so that the user can turn toast notifications on or off. The *ToggleSwitch* is data-bound to the *IsToastOk* property on the *PushViewModel*.

```
<StackPanel x:Name="LayoutRoot" Background="Transparent" Margin="{StaticResource
PhoneHorizontalMargin}">
    <toolkit:ToggleSwitch
        Header="Allow toast notifications" IsChecked="{Binding IsToastOk, Mode=TwoWay}"
        FontSize="{StaticResource PhoneFontSizeLarge}"/>
    <TextBlock
        Style="{StaticResource PhoneTextTitle3Style}" TextWrapping="Wrap"
        Text="When a toast notification is received, it consumes additional battery power, and
may be distracting." />
</StackPanel>

...
public SettingsPage()
{
    InitializeComponent();
    DataContext = App.Push;
}
```

For an even richer UX, you could provide two settings: one for toggling toasts on/off, and another for toggling all notifications on/off. This won't be useful in all apps, but if your app uses toasts plus tiles and/or raw notifications, and if it can function correctly with only some or none of the notification features, a finer-grained settings option might make sense.

Push notification security

The communications between MPNS and the Push Client component on the phone are secured via Secure Sockets Layer (SSL). This is set up by Microsoft. However, there is no default security for communications between the phone and your push web service, so you'd have to implement your own. The general recommendation is the same as for any web service that can exchange sensitive data: you should protect it with SSL.

Setting up SSL authentication for your web service is no different for a push web service than for any other web service. An additional benefit of securing your service is that this eliminates the daily limit on the number of push notifications that you can send. Recall that, by default, unsecured web services are throttled at a rate of 500 notifications per app, per device, per day. To enable this feature, you must upload a TLS (SSL) certificate to the Windows Phone Store. The key-usage value of this certificate must be set to include client authentication; the Root Certificate Authority (CA) for the certificate must be one of the CAs that are trusted on the Windows Phone platform (these are listed in the documentation in the Windows Phone Store).

After you have submitted the certificate to the Windows Phone Store, you can associate any subsequently submitted apps with this certificate. This option is made available during the app submission process. There is obviously a gap between setting up your secured web service and submitting your certificate on the one hand, and having a submitted app approved and published in the Windows Phone Store on the other hand. To bridge this gap, Microsoft flags your web service as authenticated for a period of four months. This time constraint is removed when your app is successfully published to the Windows Phone Store.

To use the authenticated channel from your phone's client app, when creating the *HttpNotificationChannel*, set the service name to the Common Name in the certificate. Keep in mind that you cannot use a self-signed certificate for this purpose.

If you do authenticate your push web service in this way, you can also take advantage of a callback registration feature. Using this feature, the MPNS can call back on your registered URI when it determines that it cannot deliver a message to the device as a result of the device being in an inactive state.

It's also worth keeping in mind that the push service does not guarantee message delivery, so you should not use it in scenarios for which failure to deliver one or more messages has serious consequences.

Summary

In this chapter, you saw how you can support the user's personalization of her phone by enabling her to pin tiles to the Start screen. You can keep these fresh and relevant by using local and remote updates, and you can choose between three style templates (flip, iconic, and cycle) that each support the three tile sizes.

On top of that, you saw how the Windows Phone push notification system provides a way for you to build apps that can easily keep information on the phone up to date from remote servers. This involves a server-side application for generating notifications, a server-side web service for clients to register with, and a client-side app for receiving the incoming notifications and rendering the data appropriately on the phone. The three different notification types (raw, tile, and toast) each provide different data and behavior, appropriate for different use cases. Raw notifications are entirely under your control; tile and toast notifications integrate seamlessly with the standard phone experience.

CHAPTER 15

Contacts and calendar

In the early days of smartphones, one of the features that differentiated high-end mobile phones from their more basic counterparts was the richness of their Personal Information Management (PIM) capabilities and, in particular, their ability to provide a convenient digital replacement for physical address books and calendars. Although the emergence of mobile devices as a tool for activities like gaming, web browsing, and photography has served to pare back the supreme importance of PIM, it's nonetheless still the case that users spend a great deal of time with their phones, connecting with people and staying organized.

In this chapter, you will see how the distinctive Windows Phone contacts experience is designed and how your app can interact with it by allowing the user to create new contacts, by incorporating the user's existing contacts into your app, and by creating your own contacts store that can fit seamlessly into the People Hub. You will also learn how to integrate with the Windows Phone calendar, including finding a free time slot in the user's schedule and providing him with the ability to book a new appointment associated with your app.

Contacts

The primary marketing tagline for the Windows Phone 7.5 release was "Put people first," which is an appropriate slogan for a product that invested so heavily in its contacts experience. In Windows Phone, contacts is about so much more than an address book. With social networking integration and the ability to keep in touch with important people by pinning them to the Start screen, the contacts experience is one of the clearest examples of the ways in which Windows Phone is a "different kind of phone."

Understanding the People Hub

Contacts management has come a long way since early smartphones. Back then, users would painstakingly type in the contact information for all their family and friends, storing it either in the phone's internal storage or on a SIM card to allow for portability between phones. Over time, mobile devices added the ability to sync contacts with a computer by using software such as Microsoft Outlook or with a service such as Microsoft Exchange. Even as it became easier to get contacts on and off the phone, it remained the case that the contacts store was a single database with at most one synchronization source. With the rise of social networking and consumer smartphones, this model started to break down. For one, users wanted the list of contacts that they were already managing through social networks such as Facebook to simply be available on their phones and available for calling or text messaging. Further, the notion of a contact that existed only on the phone began to make very little sense—who might you want to call or text but not interact with in any other way? And, why should you have to go through a laborious process to move contacts to a new phone, or worse, ask all your friends to resend their contact information to you if you lose your device? Finally, it became clear that users wanted to maintain a clean separation between the lists of contacts that they managed from different facets of life—such as colleagues, friends, and family—but at the same time not have to manage multiple versions of a contact that happened to span across those categories.

The Windows Phone People Hub takes a different approach to contacts management as a means of solving some of these problems. First, there is no notion of a "phone-only contact." When you add someone new on your phone, you are prompted to add that person to one of your online address books such as Outlook.com. This ensures that your contacts are always securely stored off the device so that they can be restored easily in the event that you lose your phone or upgrade to a new phone. Second, the People Hub keeps all your address books logically separated while presenting them in a seamless integrated way. That is, if you happen to have an entry for your colleague Kim stored in both Microsoft Exchange and in Facebook, Windows Phone will display her as a single contact in the People Hub without cross-pollinating any of Kim's Facebook data into Exchange, or vice versa. This top-level view from multiple sources is referred to as an *aggregated contact*. Figure 15-1 shows an example of how the People Hub displays a contact card aggregated from multiple sources.

The contact card user interface (UI) downplays the fact that Kim's information is being derived from multiple sources because that generally has little bearing on how the user might want to interact with her. For cases in which the value of a particular field is different between the sources, as in the case of Kim's email address, the contact card shows both values and indicates the source of each, but otherwise the information is seamlessly merged in the UI. Of course, the fact that users appreciate having a single view of a contact on their phones does not mean that they want that contact's data replicated between the different sources. As a result, when the user chooses to edit a contact (by tapping the Edit button on the app bar), the People Hub displays a list of the sources for that contact and offers the user the choice as to which one to edit.

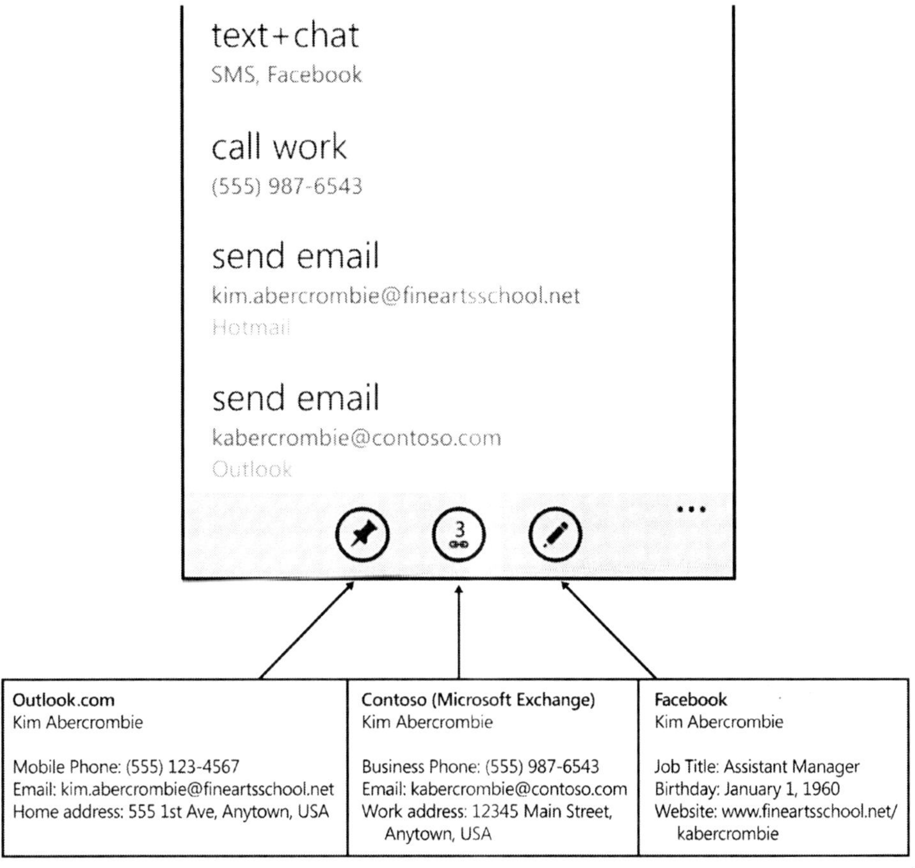

FIGURE 15-1 Aggregated contacts are presented as a single person, but their data comes from multiple sources.

Note The People Hub not only performs seamless merging of multiple sources, but of different types of sources; or, expressed broadly, address books and social networks. In the case of an address book, such as those provided by Outlook.com Contacts or Exchange, the user maintains her own version of the contact information for the people in the address book. If one of those contacts moves or gets a new phone number, it is the responsibility of the user to update the information in the address book. By contrast, in the case of social networks such as Facebook, there is one version of the contact's information, which is maintained by the contact herself. If she updates her information upon moving or getting a new phone number, everyone linked to her through the network automatically gets the new information. The result is that users can only edit address book information from the contact card, not social network information.

It is important for app developers to understand the underlying design of the People Hub because they will be exposed to many of these concepts through the contacts APIs.

Querying device contacts

Now that you understand how the contacts database in Windows Phone is structured, we can move on to writing some code. We will begin with what is likely the most common contact-related task that an app will perform, which is querying the user's existing contacts.

Single-contact choosers

A common requirement for apps is the need to ask the user to choose a single contact so that the app can do something useful with that person's phone number, physical address, or email address. Windows Phone provides built-in UI for these tasks that apps can take advantage of with just a few lines of code. The platform also provides the naturally complementary tasks for using the data that's returned—namely, making a phone call, mapping an address, or sending an email.

The *SingleContactsChoosers* solution in the sample code demonstrates the use of these three tasks, along with their natural complement. Figure 15-2 shows the UI for the main page of the app.

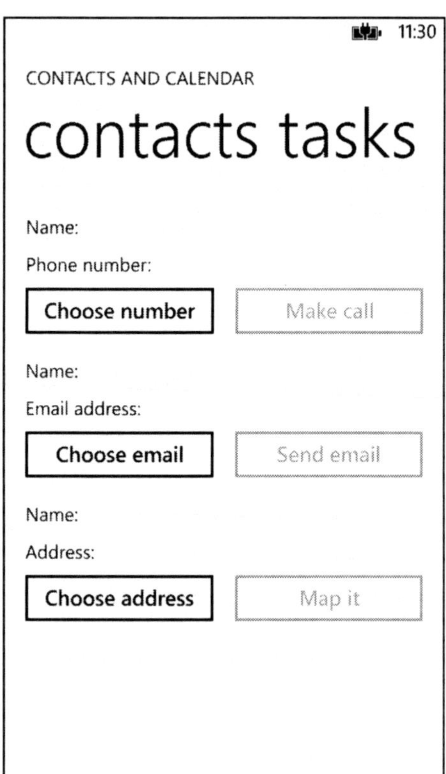

FIGURE 15-2 Each of the single-contact Chooser tasks has a natural complement with which to use the data.

All the single-contact Choosers operate in the same way. The app creates an instance of the task, registers an event handler for when it is completed, and then launches the task, based on the appropriate user action.

Tip During development, it is rare for an app to be deactivated as the result of launching a Chooser, especially on a device with 1 GB of memory. There simply isn't enough happening on the phone to cause the low-memory condition. We recommend that you always test your apps with forced tombstoning. This option is available on the Debug tab of the app properties page, as highlighted in Figure 15-3.

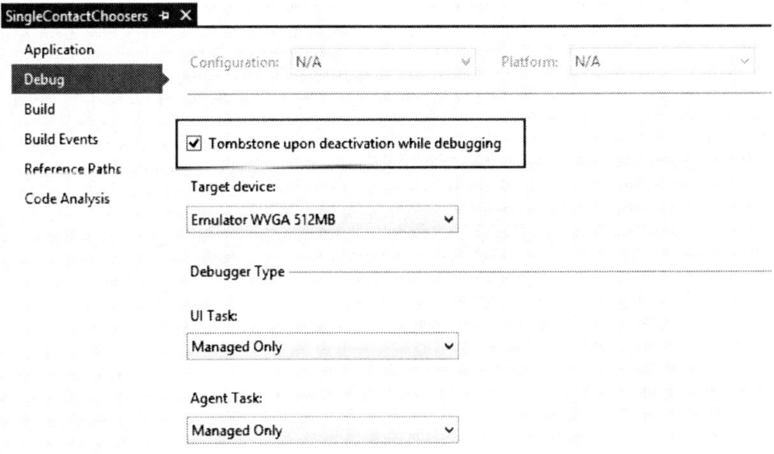

FIGURE 15-3 Always use forced tombstoning to test your app with Choosers.

The following code defines the Chooser objects, creates them in the page constructor, and then registers the event handlers:

```
private PhoneNumberChooserTask phoneNumberChooser;
private EmailAddressChooserTask emailAddressChooser;
private AddressChooserTask addressChooser;

// Constructor
public MainPage()
{
    InitializeComponent();

    phoneNumberChooser = new PhoneNumberChooserTask();
    phoneNumberChooser.Completed += phoneNumberChooser_Completed;

    emailAddressChooser = new EmailAddressChooserTask();
    emailAddressChooser.Completed += emailAddressChooser_Completed;
```

```
        addressChooser = new AddressChooserTask();
        addressChooser.Completed += addressChooser_Completed;
}
```

The Chooser is then invoked as the result of user action, in this case a *Button* click.

```
private void phoneNumberChooserButton_Click(object sender, RoutedEventArgs e)
{
    phoneNumberChooser.Show();
}
```

When the app calls the *Show* method, the system brings up the user's contacts list (see Figure 15-4). Because we are using the *PhoneNumberChooserTask*, the contact list is filtered down to only those contacts who have at least one phone number listed in their contact information.

FIGURE 15-4 The *PhoneNumberChooserTask* shows the list of contacts with at least one address.

Note By default, the emulator does not contain any contacts. You can use the *ContactsPopulator* solution included with the sample code to populate the list of sample contacts shown in Figure 15-4.

If the user chooses a contact with multiple phone numbers (for example, a home number and a mobile number), the system will ask him to choose one of them before returning the chosen number to the app. In other words, the app can assume that it will receive at most one phone number (or physical or email address) back from the task. When the Chooser returns, the platform raises the completed event, providing a *PhoneNumberResult* object which, assuming the user actually chose a contact, contains that contact's name and phone number. We can then simply update the UI with the results, as shown in the code that follows. Observe that we first check for *TaskResult.OK* because that is the indication that the user actually chose a contact and didn't simply hit the Back button to return to the app. Also note that the callback is made on the UI thread, so it is not necessary to use the dispatcher to update the UI.

```
private void phoneNumberChooser_Completed(object sender, PhoneNumberResult e)
{
    if (e.TaskResult != TaskResult.OK)
    {
        return;
    }

    phoneNumberDisplayNameTextBlock.Text = e.DisplayName;
    phoneNumberTextBlock.Text = e.PhoneNumber;
    makePhoneCallButton.IsEnabled = true;
}
```

After choosing one contact for each Chooser type, the app looks like Figure 15-5.

As mentioned earlier, each of the Chooser tasks has a complementary task in the platform which makes it easy to put together a complete scenario with relatively little code. These complementary tasks are exposed in the *SingleContactChoosers* solution through the buttons on the right side of the screen: the Make Call button launches the *PhoneCallTask*, the Send Email button launches the *EmailComposeTask*, and the Map It button launches the *MapsTask*. The code that follows shows the Send Email button's click event handler. It uses the email address to set the "To" line, the contact's name as part of the subject line, and then fills in a custom body for the message.

```
private void sendEmailButton_Click(object sender, RoutedEventArgs e)
{
    EmailComposeTask ect = new EmailComposeTask();
    ect.To = emailAddressTextBlock.Text;
    ect.Subject = "Hi " + emailAddressDisplayNameTextBlock.Text;
    ect.Body = "Hello from Windows Phone!";

    ect.Show();
}
```

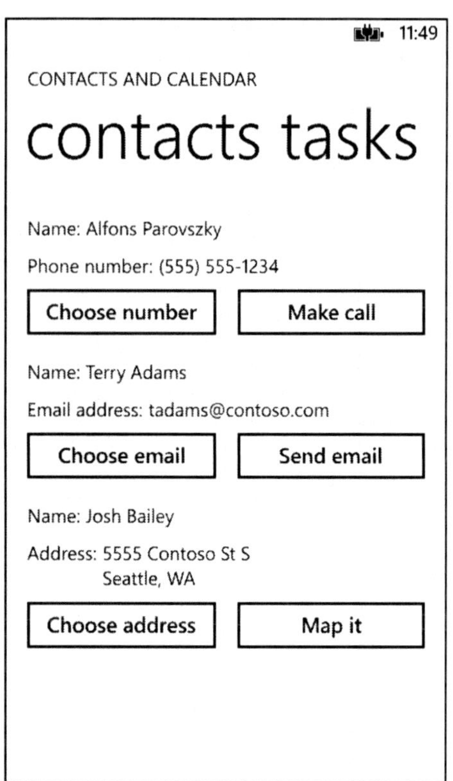

FIGURE 15-5 With all details filled in, the user is free to make a phone call, send an email, or map an address.

Note To use the *PhoneCallTask*, your app must include the *ID_CAP_PHONEDIALER* capability.

Querying contacts programmatically

The single-contact Choosers are convenient for cases in which you simply need to retrieve an address, phone number, or email address for a single contact, but in many cases, you will select multiple contacts at once or perform query operations on the contacts database. The *Microsoft.Phone.UserData* namespace provides APIs to perform such query operations on the user's existing contacts.

There are two ways of querying contacts with the *UserData* APIs. You can perform simple text-matching searches on a set of common properties for a contact, such as name or phone number, using the search capabilities built in to the address book itself. You can also perform queries on a set of contacts by using Language-Integrated Query (LINQ) syntax, which gives you the ability to use the full set of properties of the contact in your query statement. We will illustrate both of these approaches in this section.

Before you call the contacts APIs, however, you must ensure that you've given your app the *ID_CAP_CONTACTS* capability. You might wonder why this was not necessary when using the single contact choosers in the previous section. Recall from Chapter 1, "Vision and architecture," that part of the goal of capabilities is to ensure that the user is always aware of what is happening on her phone. In the case of the single-contact Choosers, the app will only receive sensitive user data if the user explicitly chooses a contact in the system-provided UI. In the case of the contacts APIs, the app is querying the data directly, so it is important that the user provide consent in advance by agreeing to the app's listed capabilities.

The *ContactsQuery* app offers the ability to search the user's contacts in three different ways: retrieving all contacts, retrieving those that match a particular name, and retrieving those which have at least one address matching a particular city. The results of those queries are displayed in a list box by using a custom *UserControl* that we will describe in more detail later in this section. The main page of the *ContactsQuery* app will look something like Figure 15-6 when a query's results have been filled in.

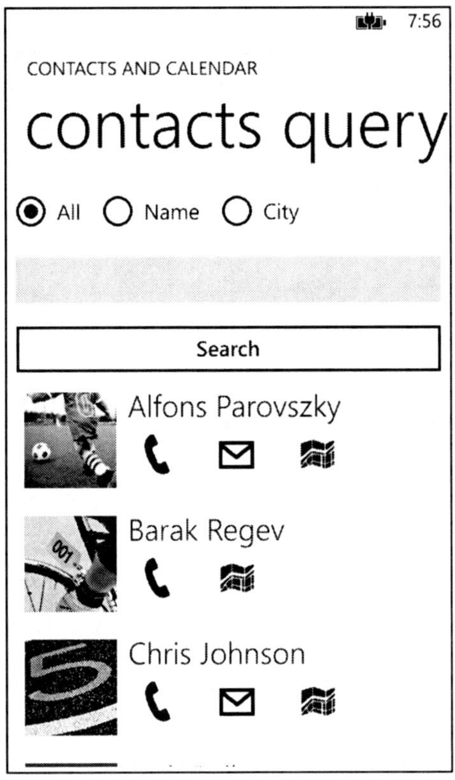

FIGURE 15-6 The *ContactsQuery* solution supports querying all contacts, querying by name, and querying by city.

All contacts queries start the same way, with a new instance of the *Contacts* object and a call to its *SearchAsync* method. The code that follows initiates a search that will retrieve all the contacts on the phone.

```
Contacts contactsDb = new Contacts();
contactsDb.SearchCompleted += contactsDb_SearchCompleted;
contactsDb.SearchAsync(string.Empty, FilterKind.None, null);
```

You can use the first two parameters of *SearchAsync* to provide filters to be performed on the search within the contacts database itself. Using the first parameter, you can specify the filtering string, whereas with the second parameter, you can choose the property of the contact on which to filter. The available filters and the type of matching performed are described in Table 15-2. You can use the third parameter to pass state to the event handler to maintain context between the invocation of the search and the asynchronous handling of the result. We will make use of this parameter later in this section.

TABLE 15-2 Built-in filters supported by *SearchAsync*

FilterKind	**Sample query**	**Matching rules**
PinnedToStart	`SearchAsync (String.Empty, FilterKind.PinnedToStart, null);`	All contacts that are pinned to Start are returned.
DisplayName	`SearchAsync ("pat", FilterKind.DisplayName, null);`	*DisplayName* matches if the search term is a prefix of either the first or last name. The following names will match "pat": Rajesh **Pat**el Pannarat **Pat**tanapitakkul **Pat**rick Sands **Pat** Coleman The following name will not: Worapon Pitayaphonogpat
EmailAddress	`SearchAsync ("tadams@contoso.com"", FilterKind.EmailAddress, null);`	*EmailAddress* matches the email address at the specified domain and any subdomains. The following email addresses match tadams@contoso.com: tadams@contoso.com tadams@exchange.contoso.com The following addresses will not match: tadams@contoso tadams@contosomail.com terry.adams@contoso.com
PhoneNumber	`SearchAsync ("555-1234", FilterKind.PhoneNumber, null)`	Last six digits must match (punctuation is ignored). The following numbers match 555-1234: (425) 555-1234 (206) 555-1234 +1 (206) 555-1234 The following numbers do not match: (425) 555-4321 (555) 123-4789

We can use the built-in *DisplayName* filter to handle the search-by-name feature in our *Contacts Query* solution. The only change we need to make from the previous code sample (for searching all contacts) is to pass in the necessary parameters to *SearchAsync*. In fact, we can build the search button's click event handler to create the *Contacts* object and set up the *SearchCompleted* event handler in the same way, regardless of what search we're doing, and then make a different call to *SearchAsync*, depending on which radio button is selected. The code for the click event handler is shown here:

```
private void searchButton_Click(object sender, RoutedEventArgs e)
{
      Contacts contactsDb = new Contacts();
      contactsDb.SearchCompleted += contactsDb_SearchCompleted;

      if (searchAllRadioButton.IsChecked == true)
      {
            contactsDb.SearchAsync(string.Empty, FilterKind.None, null);
      }
      else if (searchByNameRadioButton.IsChecked == true)
      {
            contactsDb.SearchAsync(searchTermTextBox.Text, FilterKind.DisplayName, null);
      }
}
```

Both queries ultimately raise *SearchCompleted* events, which are handled by *contactsDb_SearchCompleted*. The contacts found by the query are returned as an *IEnumerable* of *Contact* objects, which we can then easily data-bind to our *ListBox*.

```
void contactsDb_SearchCompleted(object sender, ContactsSearchEventArgs e)
{
      contactsListBox.ItemsSource = e.Results;
}
```

The *Contact* object returned is actually an aggregated contact, as described earlier; that is, it contains the consolidated view of the contact across multiple sources. The top-level list of sources is accessible through the *Accounts* property on the *Contact* class. Other *Accounts* properties exist throughout the *Contact* class in cases for which there is the possibility of the contact having multiple values for a given field from different sources. You might notice that the flexibility of the People Hub design surfaces some seeming oddities in the API; for example, the fact that a *Contact* has a collection of *Birthdays* and a collection of *SignificantOthers*. In a world of perfect data, this wouldn't be necessary, but in practice, users often have errors and inconsistencies in their various address books. Rather than forcing the user to clean up these inconsistencies for every contact, the People Hub chooses to store all values and let either the user or app decide which to choose, as needed.

A theme-aware *UserControl* for contacts

In the *ContactsQuery* solution, each of the *Contact* objects returned by the search is data-bound to a custom *UserControl* named *ContactUserControl*. This control does a couple of interesting things. First, it displays graphical buttons for calling the contact, sending him an email, or mapping his address, depending on what data is returned from the query. Second, it displays either a black or a white icon for these buttons depending on whether the phone is currently set to the dark or light theme. Figure 15-7 shows two instances of the control: one in light theme for which the contact has a phone number, email address, and physical address, and one in dark theme for which the contact has only a phone number and physical address.

FIGURE 15-7 The *ContactUserControl* shows theme-aware buttons based on the contact data.

To determine whether or not to display the buttons at all, we have used the *IValueConverter* interface, which allows an app to run custom logic to translate one data type to another during data binding. In our case, we want to translate the collection of addresses, email addresses, and phone numbers into values for the *Visibility* attributes for the three buttons. In particular, we want to make the phone call button visible if there's at least one phone number for the contact, and likewise for the email and mapping buttons. The *CollectionSizeToVisibilityConverter* class is responsible for implementing the *IValueConverter* interface in the *ContactsQuery* solution. Its implementation of the *Convert* method is shown here:

```
public object Convert
(object value, Type targetType, object parameter, System.Globalization.CultureInfo culture)
{
    IEnumerable<object> collection = (IEnumerable<object>)value;

    if (collection != null && collection.Any())
    {
        return Visibility.Visible;
    }
    else
    {
        return Visibility.Collapsed;
    }
}
```

We then need to define the *Visibility* attribute on the buttons containing the icons, using the collections from the *Contact* object as the binding property, and the *CollectionSizeTo VisibilityConverter* as the value converter, like so:

```
<Button
     Visibility="{Binding PhoneNumbers,
                  Converter={StaticResource CollectionSizeToVisibilityConverter}}">
// image definition omitted for the moment...
</Button>
```

For cases in which the button is displayed, we would like to show the appropriate image depending on the theme color so that we don't end up with white on white or black on black. This is not required for icons shown on the app bar, because the system automatically inverts the foreground color of those images depending on the device theme.

One way to present a theme-specific icon is to create dark and light theme versions of the image and then place them on top of one another by using the built-in resources *PhoneDark ThemeVisibility* and *PhoneLightThemeVisibility* to set the *Visibility* attribute of each. The XAML for this type of button is shown in the following code:

```
<Button
     Visibility="{Binding PhoneNumbers,
                  Converter={StaticResource CollectionSizeToVisibilityConverter}}">
     <Grid>
          <Image
               Source="Assets\phone.darktheme.png"
               Visibility="{StaticResource PhoneDarkThemeVisibility}" />
          <Image
               Source="Assets\phone.lighttheme.png"
               Visibility="{StaticResource PhoneLightThemeVisibility}"/>
     </Grid>
</Button>
```

Of course, there's much more to a contact than just the filters supported by *SearchAsync*. For example, you might want to query based on physical address, birthday, or employer. In those cases, you can take advantage of the fact that *SearchAsync* returns an *IEnumerable* collection to use LINQ syntax to perform the full range of possible queries on the contacts list.

You might wonder why *SearchAsync* provides filtering through its parameters at all when you can perform the same queries (and more) by using LINQ. Ultimately, it comes down to performance. The phone's contacts database has been indexed and tuned to provide high-performance queries based on the filters provided by *SearchAsync,* so you should take advantage of those optimizations whenever possible. It is also advantageous to perform as much of your query as possible in the contacts database itself, because that avoids the need to load all the contacts into your app, only to discard many of them when you actually perform your filtering. The process of marshaling all contacts into your app not only takes time, but it results in additional memory allocation. The point is not that you shouldn't use LINQ to perform richer queries on the user's contacts, but simply that you should always seek to perform initial filtering by using *SearchAsync* whenever possible.

In the case of the *ContactsQuery* solution, we want to find all the contacts matching a given city, so filtering with *SearchAsync* is not possible. Instead, we will perform a search with no filters and then perform all the filtering by using LINQ. We will add one more branches to the *if* statement in the search button's click event handler to support the search by city case.

```
private void searchButton_Click(object sender, RoutedEventArgs e)
{
    Contacts contactsDb = new Contacts();
    contactsDb.SearchCompleted += contactsDb_SearchCompleted;

    if (searchAllRadioButton.IsChecked == true)
    {
        contactsDb.SearchAsync(string.Empty, FilterKind.None, null);
    }
    else if (searchByNameRadioButton.IsChecked == true)
    {
        contactsDb.SearchAsync(searchTermTextBox.Text, FilterKind.DisplayName, null);
    }
    else if (searchByCityRadioButton.IsChecked == true)
    {
        contactsDb.SearchAsync(string.Empty, FilterKind.None, searchTermTextBox.Text);
    }
}
```

Observe that while the filters are empty, we have used the state parameter to pass in the contents of *searchTermTextBox*. This state object gives the *SearchCompleted* event handler two pieces of information: the first is that this search requires more filtering on the returned result set; and second, the actual query parameter on which the user wants to filter. By passing the value of the *TextBox* at the time that the search button was clicked to the event handler through the state object, the app ensures that it will filter the results based on the user's original request, even if the contents of the *TextBox* have changed in the interim. In this case, we are only supporting one LINQ-based query, so it is possible to assume that the presence of the state object implies that the user wants to filter by city with the value of that object. If we supported more query options, we would likely want to create a richer object to pass this context to the event handler. With the addition of the LINQ query matching the city, the event handler looks like this:

```
void contactsDb_SearchCompleted(object sender, ContactsSearchEventArgs e)
{
    if (e.State == null)
    {
        contactsListBox.ItemsSource = e.Results;
        return;
    }

    string citySearch = (string)e.State;

    var contactsInQueriedCity = from contact in e.Results
                                from address in contact.Addresses
                                where address.PhysicalAddress.City.ToUpper() ==
                                    citySearch.ToUpper()
                                select contact;

    contactsListBox.ItemsSource = contactsInQueriedCity;
}
```

The contacts APIs always return a snapshot of the data in the contacts database. After a contact object is marshaled into your app from the contacts database, it no longer contains any connection to that original contact. Changes made to the contact in the contacts database (either by the user in the People Hub or through a synchronization operation with the backing service) will not be reflected in the version of the contact that the app previously retrieved. If always having fresh data is critical to your app, it is a good idea to regularly refresh your queries.

Why don't I see all of my contact data?

If you start drilling into the results being returned by the contacts APIs, you might find that some information seems to be missing for some of your contacts. For instance, you might find that a friend's phone number from Facebook is not returned. This difference in the shape of data is the result of policy constraints set by the owners of the original data. In the case of Facebook for example, Microsoft has entered into a contractual agreement which allows the People Hub to synchronize and display Facebook data, but not to subsequently expose that full data set to other apps.

Table 15-3 describes the data returned by the contacts API for each of the account types supported by the People Hub. The *StorageKind* enumeration is found on the *Account* class, which represents one of the accounts feeding into the aggregated contact.

TABLE 15-3 The types of data available differs based on the account type

Data provider	Contact name	Contact picture	Other contact data	*StorageKind* enumeration
Windows Phone	✓	✓	✓	Phone
Windows Live Social	✓	✓	✓	WindowsLive
Windows Live Rolodex	✓	✓	✓	WindowsLive
Microsoft Exchange (local address book)	✓	✓	✓	Outlook
Mobile Operator Address Book	✓	✓	✓	Other
Facebook	✓	✓		Facebook
Windows Live Aggregated Networks (for example, Twitter, LinkedIn)				Other

Note Later in this chapter, we will look at how apps can create custom contact stores. For those stores, the creating app can choose whether other apps on the device can see only the contact's name and photo (as with Facebook) or the full contact details (as with Microsoft Exchange and Windows Live).

Adding contact information

Thus far, we've been discussing how apps can query the existing contacts on the device. In some cases, the app itself will have sufficient information about a person that it can provide the ability to create a new contact from directly within the app. In these cases, apps can use the *SaveContact Task* to prepopulate a new contact, saving the user from having to retype all the information. Note that as with the single-contact Choosers discussed earlier, the *SaveContactTask* requires that the last step in the user flow be completed in system-provided UI; that is, there is no way for an app to add a contact to one of the built-in address books without also bringing up the built-in "new contact" UI. Again, the goal is to protect the user by ensuring that malicious or poorly written apps cannot arbitrarily add contacts to the user's address book.

The *SaveContactTask* is the right solution for cases in which the app has a rich set of data about the person being added and for which the user is likely to want to add an entirely new contact. If the app only has an email address or phone number, *SaveEmailAddressTask* and *SavePhoneNumberTask* are better options. The primary advantage of these tasks is that the user can choose to either apply the new data to an existing contact or use it as the basis for creating a new contact.

The *AddContactInfo* solution in the sample code shows the use of all three of these tasks. It contains a *Pivot* control with three *PivotItems*. The first *PivotItem* contains fields for first and last name, phone number, and email address, with options to specify the types of the latter two fields. The UI for this *PivotItem* is shown in Figure 15-8.

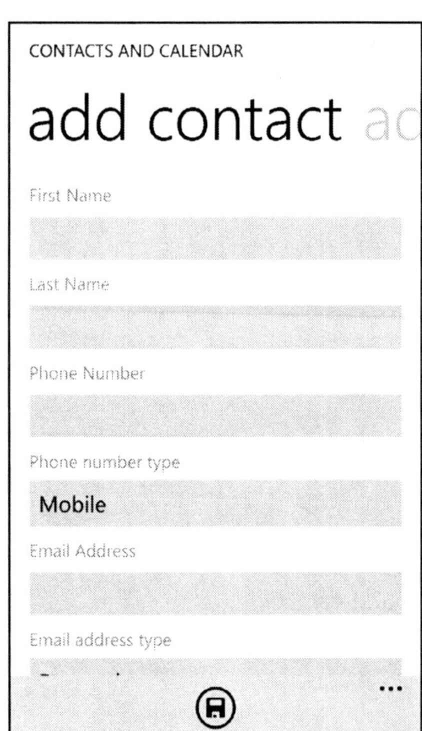

FIGURE 15-8 With the Add Contact *PivotItem*, the user can set key fields for the new contact.

The other two *PivotItems* each contain a single *TextBox* with which the user can set either a phone number or an email address, which we will provide to the *SavePhoneNumberTask* and *SaveEmailAddressTask*, respectively. After the user has entered information into the fields of one of the *PivotItems* and presses the Save button on the app bar, we check which pivot he is currently on and then prepare the appropriate task.

All three tasks follow the same basic pattern: the app creates an instance of the task, prepopulates the known contact information, and then calls the *Show* method to invoke the built-in UI, which allows the user to complete the operation. Because the *SaveContactTask* offers the most app flexibility, we will focus there. In the example that follows, the code that prepopulates the *SaveContactTask* with the user-entered fields is encapsulated in the *PrepareSaveContactTask*, which is called from the click event handler for our app bar button.

```
private void PrepareSaveContactTask()
{
    if(!String.IsNullOrWhitespace(firstNameTextBox.Text))
        saveContact.FirstName = firstNameTextBox.Text;
    if(!String.IsNullOrWhitespace(lastNameTextBox.Text))
        saveContact.LastName = lastNameTextBox.Text;

    if (!String.IsNullOrWhitespace(addContactPhoneNumberTextBox.Text))
    {
        string phoneNumberType =
            (string)((ListPickerItem)phoneNumberTypePicker.SelectedItem).Name;

        switch (phoneNumberType)
        {
             case "phoneHome":
                 saveContact.HomePhone = addContactPhoneNumberTextBox.Text;
                 break;
             case "phoneWork":
                 saveContact.WorkPhone = addContactPhoneNumberTextBox.Text;
                 break;
             case "phoneMobile":
                 saveContact.MobilePhone = addContactPhoneNumberTextBox.Text;
                 break;
             default:
                 break;
        }
    }

    if (!String.IsNullOrWhitespace(emailAddressTextBox.Text))
    {
        string emailAddressType =
            (string)((ListPickerItem)emailAddressTypePicker.SelectedItem).Name;

        switch (emailAddressType)
        {
            case "emailPersonal":
                saveContact.PersonalEmail = addContactEmailAddressTextBox.Text;
                break;
            case "emailWork":
                saveContact.WorkEmail = addContactEmailAddressTextBox.Text;
                break;
```

```
                case "emailOther":
                    saveContact.OtherEmail = addContactEmailAddressTextBox.Text;
                    break;
                default:
                    break;
            }
        }
}
```

The code is fairly self-explanatory. We check which fields the user has actually filled in and then populate an instance of *SaveContactTask* with those values. When the data has been filled in, the Save button on the app bar calls the task's *Show* method to bring up the built-in UI. With all fields populated, the built-in UI will look something like Figure 15-9. If the user has multiple accounts set up on the phone, he will get an opportunity to choose where to save this contact, just as he would if he were adding a new contact directly from the People Hub. Also note that this screen provides the ability to fill in additional details that the user might have about the contact before finally saving it to the phone.

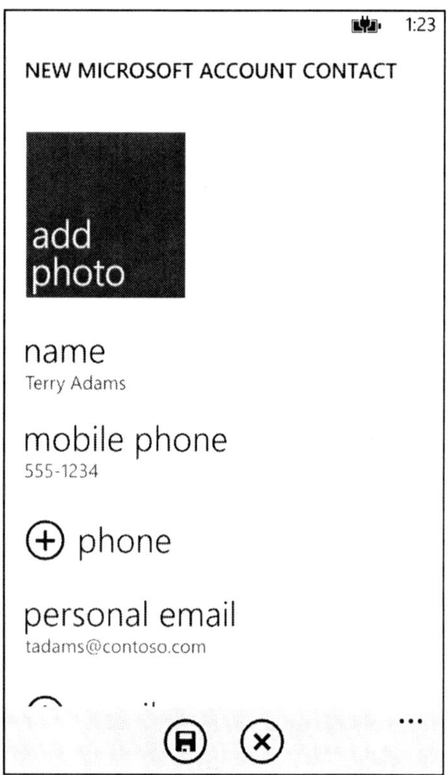

FIGURE 15-9 The user has an opportunity to fill in additional details before adding the contact.

Creating a custom contacts store

Windows Phone 8 adds the ability for apps to create custom contact stores, which are maintained within the built-in contacts infrastructure and surface naturally in the People Hub. These custom contact stores act as a natural complement to the read-only nature of the user address books; apps that maintain their own sets of rich contact information can integrate that data with the People Hub, while ensuring that the user never regrets installing an app, which is a key principle for the platform.

The *CustomContactStore* solution in the sample code creates and manages a custom contact store designed for a high school basketball coach to keep in touch with her players. This type of scenario is well-suited to a custom contact store because it makes it possible for the coach to easily get in touch with her players through the People Hub during the season, but she can just as easily remove them from her address book after the season by simply uninstalling the app. The coach can also use the built-in contacts infrastructure to store custom properties for the player, such as position and jersey number.

All the relevant classes for creating and managing a custom contact store are found in the *Windows.Phone.UserInformation* namespace. To create a custom contact store, you use a static method on the *ContactStore* class called *CreateOrOpenAsync*. As the name implies, this method will automatically create the custom store for your app if it doesn't already exist; otherwise, it will simply return a reference to the existing store.

When you create your custom store, you have the opportunity to configure how its data can be accessed by the People Hub and by other apps. By default, contacts in a custom store cannot be edited in the People Hub and have only basic information (name and photo) exposed to other apps. You can change either of these values for your store by using the overload of *CreateOrOpenAsync* that accepts two enumeration values: *ContactStoreSystemAccessMode* configures whether the user can edit the contact information through the People Hub, whereas *ContactStoreApplicationAccessMode* configures whether other apps can see limited or full details for contacts from your app. You should be thoughtful about this choice, because after the custom store is created, these values cannot be changed without deleting the store and creating it again, which requires migrating all the contact data stored within it.

Most apps that will create a custom contact store will want to populate that store by using data from their web back end. To keep things simple in our project, we will create the contacts directly in the app because the only difference is how the data is generated. The UI for the *NewContactPage* can be seen in Figure 15-10. This page is similar to what we showed earlier for the *SaveContactTask*, but with a couple of key differences. First, two properties are listed that are specific to the app, namely position and jersey number. Second, the user can choose a display picture for the contact. In the sample project, the user is able to choose a picture from the Pictures Library to set as the contact's display picture.

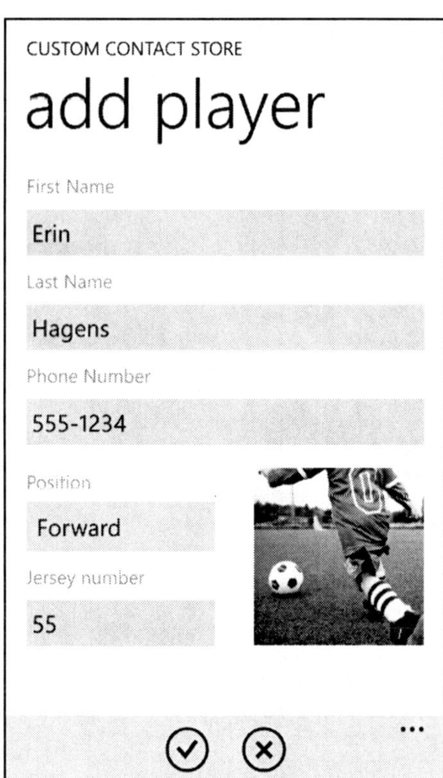

FIGURE 15-10 With a custom contact store, you can set app-specific properties and a contact photo.

All of the work to add the contact is done in the click event handler for the OK app bar button. We first need to create a new instance of the *StoredContact* class, providing a reference to the app's *ContactStore*. The *StoredContact* class contains top-level properties for the most common elements of a contact, such as given name, family name, and display picture. The majority of the properties for a contact, however, are exposed through two property bags, one for standard properties and one for app-specific extended properties. The standard properties are those that the built-in contacts database and the People Hub can natively interpret and display. It includes properties such as phone number, email address, and birthday. Extended properties are fully defined by the app by using simple name/value pairs. They are stored in the contacts database, but they are not shown in the People Hub. We will use extended properties to store the player's position and jersey number. The full code for the click event handler is shown in the following:

```
private async void okAppBarButton_Click(object sender, EventArgs e)
{
    // disable button so that the user can't hit it twice
    ApplicationBarIconButton okButton = ApplicationBar.Buttons[0] as ApplicationBarIconButton;
    okButton.IsEnabled = false;
```

```
    if (String.IsNullOrWhiteSpace(givenNameTextBox.Text) &&
        String.IsNullOrWhiteSpace(familyNameTextBox.Text))
    {
        return;
    }

    ContactStore contactsDb = await ContactStore.CreateOrOpenAsync();

    StoredContact newPlayer = new StoredContact(contactsDb);

    newPlayer.GivenName = givenNameTextBox.Text;
    newPlayer.FamilyName = familyNameTextBox.Text;

    // display name is a reference to the stream returned by the PhotoChooserTask
    if(displayPicture != null)
    {
        displayPicture.Seek(0, 0);
        await newPlayer.SetDisplayPictureAsync(displayPicture.AsInputStream());
    }

    IDictionary<string, object> knownProperties = await newPlayer.GetPropertiesAsync();
    knownProperties.Add(KnownContactProperties.MobileTelephone, phoneNumberTextBox.Text);

    IDictionary<string, object> customProperties =
        await newPlayer.GetExtendedPropertiesAsync();

    customProperties.Add("JerseyNumber", jerseyNumberTextBox.Text);
    customProperties.Add("Position", ((ListPickerItem)positionListPicker.SelectedItem).Name);

    await newPlayer.SaveAsync();

    // add a bindable contact to the PlayersList ObservableCollection to update the UI
    BindableContact bindableContact = new BindableContact();
    await bindableContact.InitializeBindableContactAsync(newPlayer);
    App.PlayersList.Add(bindableContact);

    NavigationService.GoBack();
}
```

After the app calls *SaveAsync* on the *StoredContact*, it will be persisted in the contacts database. To verify this, you can launch the People Hub and find the contact by name. For the preceding example, you should see something like Figure 15-11. Notice that the name of the app, *CustomContactStore*, displays below the contact's name.

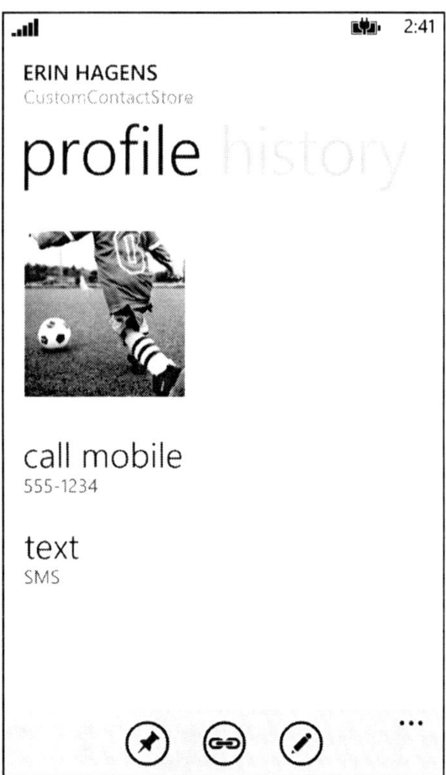

FIGURE 15-11 Contacts from custom stores are shown in the People Hub just as any other contact.

Of course, you will usually want to display the contacts in your app, as well. In the *CustomContact Store* solution, the main page includes a list of the players along with their jersey numbers, positions, and display pictures. After you've added a few contacts, the main page should look like Figure 15-12.

FIGURE 15-12 Apps can maintain both standard and custom properties in the contacts database.

The code that follows creates this UI in the *OnNavigatedTo* event handler for the main page. Note that the *PlayersList* object is simply a static *ObservableCollection* of *BindableContact* objects on the *App* object.

```
public bool isContactsStoreLoaded = false;

protected async override void OnNavigatedTo(NavigationEventArgs e)
{
    if(isContactsStoreLoaded)
        return;

    ContactStore contactsDb = await ContactStore.CreateOrOpenAsync();

    ContactQueryResult query = contactsDb.CreateContactQuery();
    IReadOnlyList<StoredContact> contacts = await query.GetContactsAsync();
```

```
    foreach (StoredContact storedContact in contacts)
    {
        BindableContact bindableContact = new BindableContact();
        await bindableContact.InitializeBindableContactAsync(storedContact);
        App.PlayersList.Add(bindableContact);
    }

    rosterListBox.ItemsSource = App.PlayersList;

    isContactsStoreLoaded = true;
}
```

We begin by getting a reference to the custom store by using *CreateOrOpenAsync*. We then create an instance of the *ContactQueryResult* class, which is what makes it possible for us to query the contacts for the store. The query API returns a list of *StoredContact* objects, the same type that we used to add a contact in the previous section. As we saw when adding a contact, relatively little information is immediately accessible on the *StoredContact* when it is first returned—mostly just the component parts of the contact's name and her local and remote IDs (which we will discuss later in this chapter). All the other properties can only be loaded by subsequent calls to *GetPropertiesAsync* and *GetExtendedPropertiesAsync*. As you can probably guess, this is a performance optimization. There is no use loading an entire copy of every contact in the custom store (of which there can be hundreds or more) if the only thing the app is going to do is display their names. It does mean, however, that if you want to data-bind the contact to your UI, you will need to load the required values into properties that can easily be found at run time. In our case, we have created a simple class called *BindableContact* that will provide the necessary details for the UI shown on the main page. The code that follows shows the *InitializeBindableContactAsync* method in *BindableContact*. Note that *DisplayName*, *JerseyNumber*, and *Position* are all string properties of *BindableContact*, whereas *DisplayPicture* is an *ImageSource* property.

```
public async void InitializeBindableContactAsync(StoredContact storedContact)
{
    if (!String.IsNullOrWhiteSpace(storedContact.DisplayName))
    {
        DisplayName = storedContact.DisplayName;
    }
    else
    {
        DisplayName =
            String.Format("{0} {1}", storedContact.GivenName, storedContact.FamilyName);
    }

    var customProps = await storedContact.GetExtendedPropertiesAsync();

    if (customProps.ContainsKey("JerseyNumber"))
    {
        JerseyNumber = (string)customProps["JerseyNumber"];
    }

    if (customProps.ContainsKey("Position"))
    {
        Position = ((string)customProps["Position"]).Substring(0, 1);
    }
```

```
        IRandomAccessStream photoStream = await storedContact.GetDisplayPictureAsync();
        if (photoStream != null)
        {
            BitmapImage bitmapImage = new BitmapImage();
            bitmapImage.SetSource((await storedContact.GetDisplayPictureAsync()).AsStream());
            DisplayPicture = bitmapImage;
        }
}
```

We've covered creating and reading contacts, so all that remains to complete the set of create, read, update, and delete (CRUD) operations is the code for updating and deleting contacts. The *CustomContactStore* solution includes an *EditContactPage*, which we launch whenever the user selects a player from the roster on the main page. On this page, she can choose to edit the position, jersey number, or phone number of the player, or delete the player altogether. The UI for the *EditContactPage* is shown in Figure 15-13.

FIGURE 15-13 With the *EditContactPage*, the user can edit or delete the contact.

The code for both the edit and delete operations is contained in their respective app bar buttons, *saveContactButton* and *deleteContactButton*. In both cases, the original contact is loaded from the custom contact store by using its local ID, which is passed from the main page to *EditContactPage* through a query string parameter. In the edit case, the app updates the information and saves it back to the store. In the delete case, the app simply calls the *DeleteContactAsync* method to remove the player altogether. The code that follows presents both click event handlers. Observe how in the delete case, we double-check that the user actually wants to delete the contact by using a *MessageBox* prior to completing the operation.

```
private async void saveContactButton_Click(object sender, EventArgs e)
{
    ContactStore contactsDb = await ContactStore.CreateOrOpenAsync();
    StoredContact player = await contactsDb.FindContactByIdAsync(localId);

    IDictionary<string, object> knownProperties = await player.GetPropertiesAsync();

    knownProperties[KnownContactProperties.MobileTelephone] = phoneNumberTextBox.Text;

    IDictionary<string, object> customProperties = await player.GetExtendedPropertiesAsync();

    customProperties["JerseyNumber"] = jerseyNumberTextBox.Text;
    customProperties["Position"] = ((ListPickerItem)positionListPicker.SelectedItem).Name;

    await player.SaveAsync();

    if(NavigationService.CanGoBack) NavigationService.GoBack();
}

private async void deleteContactButton_Click(object sender, EventArgs e)
{
    if (MessageBox.Show("Are you sure you want to delete " + CurrentPlayer.DisplayName + "?",
            "Delete contact?", MessageBoxButton.OKCancel) == MessageBoxResult.Cancel)
    {
        return;
    }

    ContactStore contactsDb = await ContactStore.CreateOrOpenAsync();
    await contactsDb.DeleteContactAsync(localId);
    if(NavigationService.CanGoBack) NavigationService.GoBack();
}
```

Staying in sync

As mentioned earlier, a common task for apps that maintain a custom contact store is to keep the contact information on the phone synchronized with their back-end service. The custom contact APIs provides some assistance in this regard. First, every *StoredContact* object has two ID properties on it: the local ID maintained by the contacts database (which we saw earlier), and the remote ID, representing the unique identifier for the contact in the app's back-end service. This makes it easy for the app to find the appropriate contact on the phone for a given ID stored in the back end by using the *FindContactByRemoteIdAsync* method on *ContactStore*.

Note Local IDs are automatically generated in the contacts database when a contact is initially added to the phone (either manually or through a sync operation). If the user moves to a new phone or performs a factory reset on his current phone and adds those contacts again, he will not have the same local IDs. As a result, you should not take any dependencies on local IDs in your cloud service.

The contacts database also keeps a record of revisions on the custom contact store, which makes it simple to determine which contacts have changed since the last time a synchronization operation occurred. As changes are made to contacts in the custom store, either from the app or from the People Hub (if enabled), the *RevisionNumber* field on the custom store is incremented. When the app begins a synchronization operation, it can iterate through the latest revisions and send the changes to its service. The following sample code shows an example of performing this type of iteration:

```
private async void SyncContacts()
{
     ContactStore contactsDb = await ContactStore.CreateOrOpenAsync();

     for (ulong i = lastRevision; i < contactsDb.RevisionNumber; i++)
     {
          var changes = await contactsDb.GetChangesAsync(i);

           foreach (ContactChangeRecord ccr in changes)
           {
                switch (ccr.ChangeType)
                {
                     case ContactChangeType.Created:
                          Service.AddNewContact
                                (await contactsDb.FindContactByIdAsync(ccr.Id));
                          break;
                     case ContactChangeType.Modified:
                          Service.EditContact
                               (await contactsDb.FindContactByIdAsync(ccr.Id));
                          break;
                     case ContactChangeType.Deleted:
                          Service.DeleteContact(ccr.RemoteId);
                          break;
                }
          }
     }

     // perform service -> client synchronization...

     lastRevision = contactsDb.RevisionNumber;
}
```

Calendar

The calendar experience in Windows Phone shares some common principles with the contacts experience discussed in the previous section. In short, the user can maintain several calendars on the device simultaneously, and these calendars are generally associated with an online service. Apps can query the contents of the user's calendar and add appointments of their own.

Querying the calendar

The *Microsoft.Phone.UserData* namespace that provides APIs for querying the user's address books also provides APIs for querying his calendar appointments. This is useful for apps that assist the user in planning events. For example, an app with which the user can reserve a table at a restaurant for dinner might want to show him a time that fits in his schedule and what appointments surround the reservation.

The *AppointmentMaker* solution in the sample code provides exactly this service. The user can choose a day and length for the appointment, and then the app finds an available time that meets those requirements. The app also shows the existing appointments before and after the suggested time so that the user has full visibility into how the new appointment will fit into his day. In the next section, we will show how to extend this app to actually add the appointment to the calendar. The main page for the *AppoinmentMaker* app is shown in Figure 15-14.

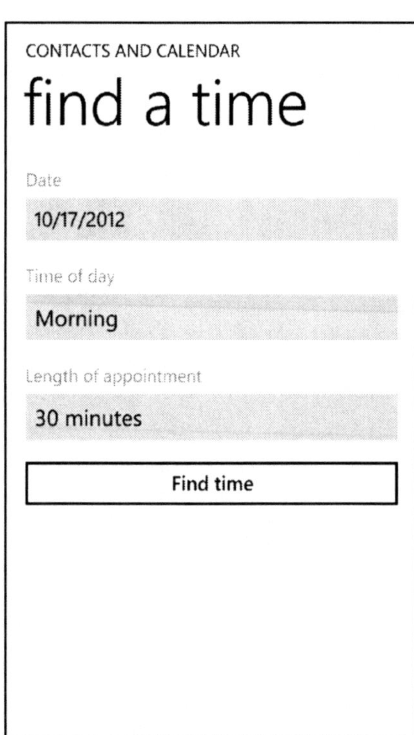

FIGURE 15-14 With the *AppointmentMaker* solution, the user can find a time for a new appointment.

After the user provides the requirements for the time slot and presses the Find Time button, the app displays a full screen *UserControl* named *AppointmentMakerControl* as a *Popup*. The *Appointment MakerControl* includes a method called *FindTimeForAppointment*, which is responsible for taking the information provided and finding a time on the calendar by using the *Appointments* class in the *UserData* namespace. The *Appointments* class is analogous to the *Contacts* class discussed in the section "Querying contacts programmatically" earlier, except that in this case, the filtering is based on a time period, with the app providing a start and end time for the search.

```
public void FindTimeForAppointment(DateTime date, string timeOfDay, int appointmentLength)
{
     DateTime startTime = date;
     DateTime endTime = date;

     lengthOfAppointmentInMinutes = appointmentLength;

     switch (timeOfDay.ToUpper())
     {
          case "MORNING":
               startTime = startTime.AddHours(7);
               endTime = endTime.AddHours(12);
               break;
         case "AFTERNOON":
               startTime = startTime.AddHours(12);
               endTime = endTime.AddHours(17);
               break;
         case "EVENING":
               startTime = startTime.AddHours(17);
               endTime = endTime.AddHours(22);
               break;
         default:
               break;
     }

     Appointments calendar = new Appointments();
     calendar.SearchCompleted += calendar_SearchCompleted;
     calendar.SearchAsync(startTime, endTime, null);
}

void calendar_SearchCompleted(object sender, AppointmentsSearchEventArgs e)
{
     List<Appointment> appointments = e.Results.ToList();

     // there are no appointments during this period
     if (appointments.Count() == 0)
     {
          AvailableTime = e.StartTimeInclusive;
          return;
     }

     Appointment firstAppointment = appointments[0];
```

```
    if ((firstAppointment.StartTime-e.StartTimeInclusive).TotalMinutes
        >=lengthOfAppointmentInMinutes)
    {
        AvailableTime = e.StartTimeInclusive;
        NextAppointment = firstAppointment;
        return;
    }

    Appointment previousAppointment = firstAppointment;

    for (int i = 1; i < appointments.Count(); i++)
    {
        Appointment nextAppointment = appointments[i];

        if ((nextAppointment.StartTime-previousAppointment.EndTime).TotalMinutes >=
            lengthOfAppointmentInMinutes)
        {
            PreviousAppointment = previousAppointment;
            NextAppointment = nextAppointment;
            AvailableTime = previousAppointment.EndTime;
            return;
        }

        previousAppointment = nextAppointment;
    }

    if ((e.EndTimeInclusive-previousAppointment.EndTime).TotalMinutes >=
        lengthOfAppointmentInMinutes)
    {
        AvailableTime = previousAppointment.EndTime;
        PreviousAppointment = previousAppointment;
        return;
    }
}
```

The method starts by determining the appropriate search range, based on the user's choice for the time of day for the meeting. Morning is between 7 A.M. and noon, afternoon between noon and 5 P.M., and evening between 5 P.M. and 10 P.M. We then set up the *SearchCompleted* event handler delegate that will handle the results of the search. Finally, we call the *SearchAsync* method to initiate the query.

Note Like contacts, accessing the user's calendar data requires the app to include a capability in its manifest. In this case, it is *ID_CAP_APPOINTMENTS*.

The logic for finding an available time is fairly simple. We start at the earliest time in the window—for example, 7 A.M. if the user selected Morning—and check if it's possible to create the appointment at that time by comparing the length of the new appointment with the amount of time available before the user's next appointment. For example, if the user requests a one hour appointment in the morning and his first appointment of the day is at 9 A.M., 7 A.M. would work. If that is not possible, we simply iterate through all the appointments returned and look for gaps between them that are large enough to fit the requested appointment. If necessary, the last check is the complement to the first one we did. That is, we check whether there is sufficient time for the appointment between the user's last appointment in the window and the end of the window. For example, if the user is busy from 7 A.M. through 11 A.M., but free after that, 11 A.M. would be sufficient for a one-hour meeting in the morning. Note that when a suitable time slot is found, we make a note of the previous and next appointments (if available) so that they can be displayed in the UI. When the available time slot is between two appointments, the UI will look something like Figure 15-15.

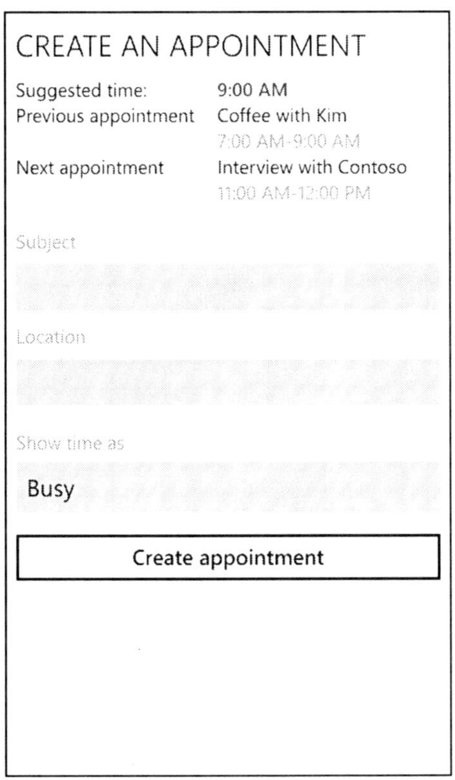

FIGURE 15-15 Using the calendar APIs, you can find available times for appointments and show what surrounds them.

As you can see, the UI includes not only the suggested time and surrounding appointments, but a few other fields to help with creating the new appointment. Completing this task is the subject of the next section.

Note In the section describing the APIs for reading the user's contacts, we mentioned that not all data available in the People Hub is returned by the APIs. The same is true for calendar data and the same rules apply. Data from calendars stored directly on the phone or synchronized with Outlook.com or Exchange is available, whereas data from Facebook and other social networks is not.

Creating a new appointment

In the previous section, we showed how to find an available time for an appointment on the user's calendar. The obvious next step after you have that data is to provide the user with the ability to create an appointment, which we can do by using the *SaveAppointmentTask*, the complement to the *SaveContactTask* that we reviewed earlier.

All the code for creating an appointment is included in the click event handler for the *createAppointmentButton*, which is shown in Figure 15-15. We set the start and end times for the appointment based on the time slot found on the calendar and then set other properties of the appointment based on the information entered by the user in the *AppointmentMakerControl*, including converting the selected status for the appointment into an element of the *AppointmentStatus* enumeration. Finally, we call the *Show* method to display the built-in UI for adding a new appointment. As with the *SaveContactTask*, the user is free to take this opportunity to fill in additional details for the appointment before saving it to her calendar. The built-in UI for adding a new appointment based on data provided by the app is shown in Figure 15-16.

FIGURE 15-16 The user has the opportunity to add final details to the appointment before adding it.

Note Unlike the *SaveContactTask*, the *SaveAppointmentTask* does not provide a result back to the app.

Summary

One of the core tenets of Windows Phone is that a smartphone should help you connect and keep in touch with the people who matter most to you. The contacts and calendar information stored on the phone are two critical components in making that possible. In this chapter, you learned about the unique design of the Windows Phone People Hub, how to query and create contacts, and how to interact with the calendar. This knowledge should help you "Put People First" in your apps.

CHAPTER 16

Camera and photos

For most people, the modern smartphone now provides a number of capabilities that were previously handled by a series of dedicated devices. The markets for Personal Digital Assistants (PDAs), MP3 players, and GPS devices are all either dead or slowly dying as consumers seek to consolidate these functions into a single product. However, none of these changes have been as dramatic as what has happened in photography. Early camera phones offered the convenience of always having a camera available to capture a moment, but with a significant quality trade-off when compared to a dedicated camera. In the past few years, however, the quality of cameras included in smartphones has risen so dramatically that it is becoming increasingly rare to see someone with a traditional point-and-shoot camera. The growth of app ecosystems has made it possible for users to combine the convenience and quality of their smartphone cameras with a wide array of photo functionality, with apps to view, edit, and share photos in rich and delightful ways. With its dedicated hardware camera button and integrated Photos Hub, Windows Phone 7 made it clear that Windows Phone devices would make photos a differentiated experience. The investment has continued in subsequent releases, with Windows Phone 8 offering an entirely new form of deep integration through "lenses."

Acquiring a single photo

Many apps need to provide the option to acquire a single photo from the user, either selected from the media library or captured by the camera. Windows Phone offers built-in tasks that make this process simple: *PhotoChooserTask* and *CameraChooserTask*.

Note Windows Phone provides a set of sample images that can be useful for testing apps that use the *PhotoChooserTask* from the emulator. However, the sample album is only initialized when you first start the Photos Hub. If you don't see the sample photos when you first invoke the *PhotoChooserTask*, simply start the Photos Hub and then restart the app.

The *SinglePhotoChooser* solution in the sample code shows a basic example of the *PhotoChooser Task*. The user taps a button to start the task and then chooses a photo from the built-in photo library user interface (UI), which is then displayed in the app's main page. The code for the *Single PhotoChooser* project is simple enough that we can include the full contents of the code-behind file for *MainPage* here:

```
public partial class MainPage : PhoneApplicationPage
{
    PhotoChooserTask photoChooser;

    public MainPage()
    {
        InitializeComponent();

        photoChooser = new PhotoChooserTask();
        photoChooser.PixelHeight = 400;
        photoChooser.PixelWidth = 400;

        photoChooser.Completed += photoChooser_Completed;
    }

    private void photoChooserButton_Click(object sender, RoutedEventArgs e)
    {
        photoChooser.Show();
    }

    private void photoChooser_Completed(object sender, PhotoResult e)
    {
        if (e.TaskResult != TaskResult.OK)
        {
            return;
        }

        BitmapImage image = new BitmapImage();
        image.SetSource(e.ChosenPhoto);

        photoChooserResultImage.Source = image;
    }
}
```

Observe that we set the *PixelHeight* and *PixelWidth* properties on the *PhotoChooserTask*. These values dictate the dimensions of the frame that the system displays in the photo chooser UI. If you have size constraints to meet, you can set these values to match those constraints and ensure that you never receive an image back that you cannot handle correctly. Finally, you should understand that the *PhotoChooserTask* returns a *Stream*, which cannot be directly displayed in the UI. Instead, you must create a new *BitmapImage*, set the source of the *BitmapImage* to the returned Stream, and then set the *Source* of the *Image UIElement* to the *BitmapImage*.

In some cases, the user might want to take a new photo rather than choosing an existing photo from the library. In those situations, there are two options. If you set the *ShowCamera* property on the *PhotoChooserTask* to *true*, the built-in photo chooser UI will show a camera icon on the app bar (see Figure 16-1), giving the user the opportunity to take a new photo rather than choosing an existing photo. In most cases, you should set this value to *true* to give the user a choice. From the app's perspective, there is no difference between a photo chosen from the user's library and a brand new photo taken with the camera.

Note In Windows Phone 8, new photos captured by using the *PhotoChooserTask* are automatically added to the user's camera roll.

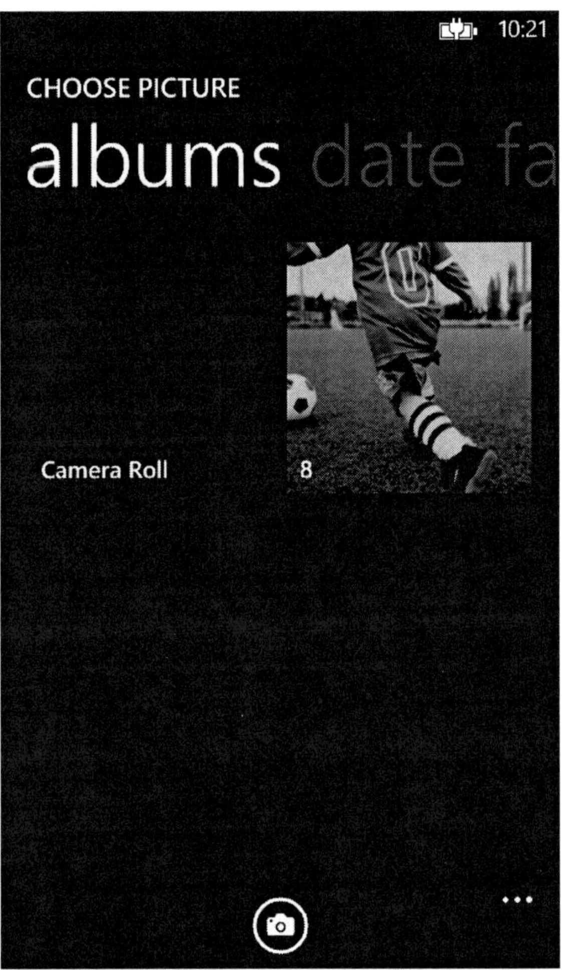

FIGURE 16-1 The *ShowCamera* property provides the flexibility to choose an existing photo or take a new one.

Some apps might want to always launch the user into the camera to take a new photo. For instance, a scavenger hunt app might require you to take a photo of each clue as you solve it. In these cases, you can use the *CameraCaptureTask* to invoke the built-in camera app directly. From the app's perspective, the *CameraCaptureTask* operates almost exactly like the *PhotoChooserTask*, apart from the inability to specify the height and width of the returned photo.

It is worth noting that the photos returned from the *PhotoChooserTask* and the *CameraCapture Task* are copies of the versions stored in the user's photo library. Any changes that you make to them are not automatically saved back to the library. Later in this chapter, we will discuss how to add a new photo to the library.

Note As is the case throughout the platform, the photo-related tasks do not require your app to declare any additional capabilities in order to use them. Because the system involves the user whenever the app requests access to a photo from the library or the camera, there is no need for the app to request an ongoing capability prior to installation.

Working with the media library

The *MediaLibrary* APIs in the XNA framework facilitate deeper integration with the user's photos collection. In particular, apps can read all of the photos directly and save new photos to the library.

Note If you are building an app that targets both Windows 8 and Windows Phone 8, you might get excited at the presence of *Windows.Storage.KnownFolders* class in Windows Phone. In Windows 8, the *KnownFolders* class provides access to a number of system storage locations, including the user's pictures library and videos library. Unfortunately, the *StorageFolder* instances exposed through *KnownFolders* are not available for Windows Phone Store apps in Windows Phone 8.

Reading photos

Although many apps only need the photo tasks described in the previous section, some can enable interesting scenarios by accessing all of the user's photos at once. The *MediaLibrary* APIs provide two ways to access the user's photos. The *Pictures* property returns all of the photos in the user's library as a single collection, whereas the *RootPictureAlbum* property returns a collection of *PictureAlbum* instances, which correspond to the individual user photo albums.

The *PhotoSlideshow* solution in the sample code provides an example of querying the list of user photo albums and then creating a simple slideshow based on a particular album of the user's choice. The main page of the app, *AlbumListPage*, simply lists the available albums (see Figure 16-2). Note that only those albums that are stored locally on the device are returned by the *MediaLibrary* APIs. Even though the Photos Hub seamlessly integrates other user photo albums, such as those from Facebook or SkyDrive, those albums are not available from the *MediaLibrary*.

MediaLibrary capabilities

Not surprisingly, access to the user's media library requires the app to declare a capability in its manifest. For Windows Phone 7.1 apps, the *ID_CAP_MEDIALIB* capability is required, whereas Windows Phone 8 apps must specify *ID_CAP_MEDIALIB_PHOTO*. Why the change? As discussed in Chapter 1, "Vision and architecture," the goal of capabilities is to provide the user with a clear idea of what data and phone services an app needs access to in order to run. As Windows Phone matured, there were simply too many disparate scenarios that required the *ID_CAP_MEDIALIB* capability, making it difficult for the user to make an informed decision about whether to grant the capability to the app. In Windows Phone 8, there are now separate capabilities for accessing the user's music, photos, and the ability to playback media content.

Note Recall that capabilities are no longer automatically added to your app manifest during the store ingestion process, so you must ensure that you manually specify the new *ID_CAP_MEDIALIB_PHOTO* capability in your app before submitting it.

This list is populated in the *OnNavigatedTo* method of the *AlbumListPage*. All of the photo albums available on the device are found under the *RootPictureAlbum* of the *MediaLibrary*.

```
protected override void OnNavigatedTo(NavigationEventArgs e)
{
    using (MediaLibrary mediaLibrary = new MediaLibrary())
    {
        albumsListBox.ItemsSource = mediaLibrary.RootPictureAlbum.Albums;
    }
}
```

Note Don't be misled by the top-level *Albums* collection in the *MediaLibrary*. This refers to albums of music. A collection of photos is actually a *PictureAlbum*.

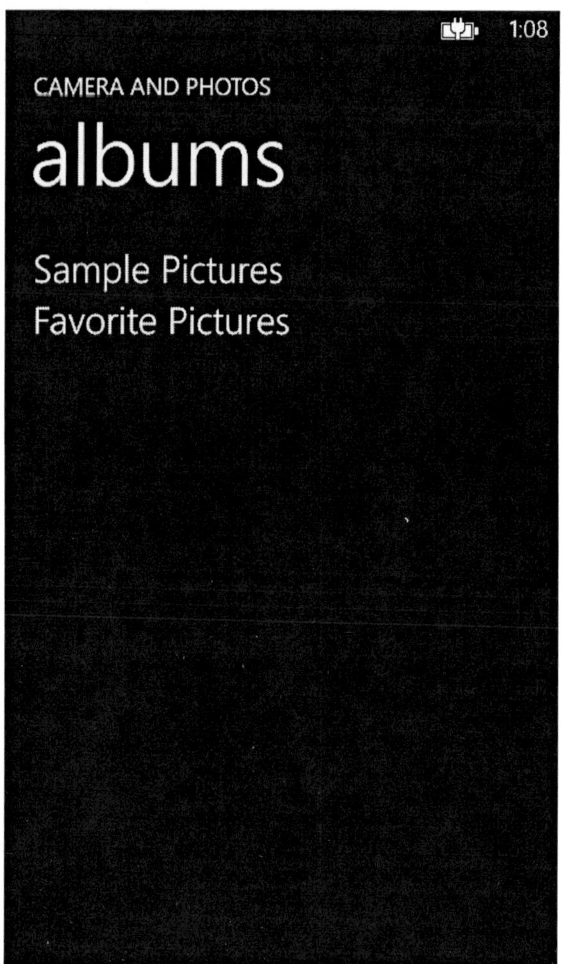

FIGURE 16-2 The *AlbumListPage* shows available albums that are stored locally on the phone.

When the user selects an album from the list, we set it as a static property of the *App* class so that it is simple to reference from the *SlideshowPage* that will actually show the slideshow.

```
private void albumsListBox_SelectionChanged(object sender, SelectionChangedEventArgs e)
{
    if (albumsListBox.SelectedItem == null)
        return;

    App.CurrentPictureAlbum = (PictureAlbum)albumsListBox.SelectedItem;
    albumsListBox.SelectedIndex = -1;
    NavigationService.Navigate(new Uri("/SlideshowPage.xaml", UriKind.Relative));
}
```

The slideshow page uses a three-item pivot control without headers to provide simple slideshow functionality, with the ability for the user to move back and forth between photos. It also includes an automatic timer to move the slideshow forward if the user would prefer to sit back and watch the photos move by on their own. The idea behind a three-item pivot control is that we can always have the next and previous photo loaded (in addition to the current photo) so that the user never sees a delay when panning back and forth at a reasonable pace. In the *InitializeSlideshow* method, we initialize the pivot control with the last photo in the album in the first position, followed by the first and second photos in the second and third positions. This is to account for the design of the pivot control, which allows the user to pan left from the first pivot item and reach the last pivot item. To actually start the user on the first photo, we set the *SelectedIndex* of the control to 1.

```
DispatcherTimer slideshowTimer;

Picture picture1;
Picture picture2;
Picture picture3;

int currentSlideIndex = 1; // track's the last index of the pivot control
int previousPhotoIndex; // the index of the previous photo in the collection
int currentPhotoIndex; // the index of the current photo in the collection
int nextPhotoIndex; // the index of the next photo in the collection
int pictureCollectionSize;

PictureCollection pictureCollection;

private bool isSlideshowInitialized = false;
private void InitializeSlideshow()
{
     pictureCollection = App.CurrentPictureAlbum.Pictures;
     pictureCollectionSize = pictureCollection.Count;

     // simplification: assume at least 3 photos
     if (pictureCollectionSize < 3)
          return;

     previousPhotoIndex = pictureCollectionSize - 1;
     currentPhotoIndex = 0;
     nextPhotoIndex = 1;

     picture1 = pictureCollection[previousPhotoIndex];
     picture2 = pictureCollection[currentPhotoIndex];
     picture3 = pictureCollection[nextPhotoIndex];

     pivotItem1Image.Source = DecodeImageInBackground(picture1);
     pivotItem2Image.Source = DecodeImageInBackground(picture2);
     pivotItem3Image.Source = DecodeImageInBackground(picture3);

     slideshowTimer = new DispatcherTimer();
     slideshowTimer.Interval = TimeSpan.FromSeconds(3);
     slideshowTimer.Tick += slideshowTimer_Tick;
     slideshowTimer.Start();
```

```
        isSlideshowInitialized = true;
    }

    void slideshowTimer_Tick(object sender, EventArgs e)
    {
        // if we're at the end of the list, wrap around; otherwise, keep moving right
        if (slideshowPivot.SelectedIndex == slideshowPivot.Items.Count - 1)
            slideshowPivot.SelectedIndex = 0;
        else
            slideshowPivot.SelectedIndex += 1;
    }
```

The *DecodeImageInBackground* helper method uses a couple of techniques to maximize the performance of the app. First, it uses the *BackgroundCreation* option for the *BitmapImage*, which ensures that the JPEG image is decoded into a bitmap on a background thread, keeping the UI responsive. Second, it sets the desired height of the decoded image by using the *DecodePixelHeight* property, based on whether the image is being shown in portrait or landscape mode. It is important that you decode images to an appropriate resolution for the device on which your app is running. If you attempt to load a large, high-resolution image into a small image control in a phone app, the system will first decode it to its full size and then scale it down, increasing image load time and bloating your app's memory usage. To maintain the correct aspect ratio, you should set either height or width but not both.

```
private BitmapImage DecodeImageInBackground(Picture pic)
{
    var bitmap = new BitmapImage();
    bitmap.CreateOptions = BitmapCreateOptions.BackgroundCreation;
    bitmap.DecodePixelHeight = Orientation == PageOrientation.Portrait ? 800 : 480;
    bitmap.DecodePixelType = DecodePixelType.Logical;
    bitmap.SetSource(pic.GetImage());

    return bitmap;
}
```

Naturally, most photo albums have more than three photos, so we need to do some work behind the scenes to make the slideshow appear to continue indefinitely, despite being just a rotation of three pivot items. We use the *slideshowPivot_SelectionChanged* event handler to fetch the next or previous photo depending on whether the user has swiped left or right. See the full sample code for *PhotoSlideshow* for the details on how this is done.

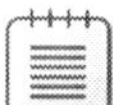

Note Because *Pivot* is an *ItemsControl*, it is technically possible to skip the explicit creation of *PivotItems* altogether and simply set its *ItemsSource* to the *PictureCollection*. However, this will result in the creation of one *PivotItem* for each photo in the collection, which will significantly increase app memory usage for a large photo collection.

Adding new images

Apps can also add new images to the user's collection through the *MediaLibrary* APIs. This is useful for cases in which your app has allowed the user to modify an existing photo, take a new photo directly in the app (described later in this chapter), or even create an entirely new, non-photographic image such as a drawing in a finger-painting app. If your new or modified image can be saved as a JPEG file, you should always offer the user the option to save it to the media library because it provides the most flexibility for sharing with other apps, devices, or cloud services. It also ensures that the file is not lost if your app is ever uninstalled.

The *GrayscalePhotoEditor* solution is a simple example of the type of app that might need to save images to the user's media library. With this app, the user can choose a photo from the photo library, convert it to a grayscale image, and then save it back. The UI for the *GrayscalePhotoEditor* (including a transformed image) is shown in Figure 16-3.

FIGURE 16-3 The *GrayscalePhotoEditor* app performs a simple conversion and saves the photo to the library.

The *choosePhotoButton* invokes the *PhotoChooserTask* described in the previous section, returning a *PhotoResult* object in its *Completed* event. The app uses the returned photo as the basis for the new grayscale image. Because converting an image to grayscale is just one of many possible transformations we could perform, we will focus on the code required to save the modified photo to the media library. If you are interested in the grayscale transformation specifically, see the sidebar at the end of this section. Otherwise, you only need to know that the *TransformToGrayscaleAsync* helper method takes a *Stream* and returns a task that asynchronously provides a *WriteableBitmap* representing the transformed image. We then set the source of the *chosenPhotoImage* image element in our UI to the transformed image and save the original file name of the chosen file to the *colorImageFilename* field to be used later in naming the new grayscale image file.

```
private async void photoChooser_Completed(object sender, PhotoResult e)
{
    if (e.TaskResult != TaskResult.OK)
        return;

    WriteableBitmap grayscaleImage = await TransformToGrayscaleAsync(e.ChosenPhoto);
    chosenPhotoImage.Source = grayscaleImage;
    colorImageFilename = e.OriginalFileName;

    savePhotoButton.IsEnabled = true;
}
```

The code required to actually save the new file to the user's library is contained in the *Click* event handler for the *savePhotoButton*. The representation of the image that we've been working with in memory is a *WriteableBitmap*, but the photo library requires that new images be saved in JPEG format, so the first thing we need to do is convert the transformed image to a JPEG. You can do this by using *SaveJpeg*, an extension method on the *WriteableBitmap* class defined in the *System.Windows.Media.Imaging.Extensions* namespace. The *SaveJpeg* method requires a *Stream* to store the resulting JPEG as well as the dimensions and desired quality of the image. Image quality is measured on a scale of 0 to 100, with 100 being the highest. The second to last parameter of *SaveJpeg*, orientation, is not currently used and should be set to zero.

After the JPEG is created, the app saves it to the media library by using the *SavePhoto* method, specifying a name for the file that simply prepends the word "gray" to the original file name for the color photo. Observe that we wrap the creation of the JPEG and the save operation into an awaitable task to keep the UI thread responsive while that code is running.

```
private async void savePhotoButton_Click(object sender, RoutedEventArgs e)
{
    if(grayscaleImage == null) return;

    savePhotoButton.IsEnabled = false;
```

```
        await Task.Run(() =>
            {
                using (var mediaLibrary = new MediaLibrary())
                using (var targetJpegStream = new MemoryStream())
                {
                    grayscaleImage.SaveJpeg(targetJpegStream, grayscaleImage.PixelWidth,
                    grayscaleImage.PixelHeight, 0, 100);

                    targetJpegStream.Seek(0, SeekOrigin.Begin);

                    string grayscaleFilename = "gray" + colorImageFilename;
                    mediaLibrary.SavePicture(grayscaleFilename, targetJpegStream);
                }
            });
}
```

Gray areas

In a color image, the color of a given pixel is made up of a mixture of several different colors. The combination of these colors at varying intensities ultimately determines the final color of the pixel. For instance, the common RGB color model involves mixing varying intensities of red, green, and blue to represent most of the color palette. In a grayscale image, there is no color, but only the varying degrees of gray between white and black. Therefore, to convert an image from color to grayscale, our goal is to determine the intensity of color in a given pixel, independent of what the actual color is; that is, a dark red should look the same when converted to grayscale as a dark blue.

A simple technique for transformation is just to average the intensities of the three core colors and then create a pixel that has that intensity for each color channel. Because each channel is equal, the color will be a shade of gray that is proportionate to the intensity. For the most accurate grayscale representation, however, you must adjust for the fact that the human eye perceives different color channels at varying intensities—in particular, we are more sensitive to green than to blue. To account for this, you simply need to create a weighted average of the three intensities rather than a simple average. For a more detailed explanation, read the Wikipedia article on grayscale at *http://en.wikipedia.org/wiki/Grayscale*.

The *TransformToGrayscale* method in the *GrayscalePhotoEditor* solution illustrates one way to translate an image from color to grayscale using this technique. The method iterates through every pixel in the original color image and determines the intensity of the color from each channel by using the bitwise AND operator ("&"). It then computes a weighted average of the intensities of each channel and sets the value of each channel in the new grayscale image to that intensity.

```
private const int ByteMask = 0xFF;
private const double RedWeight = 0.2126;
private const double GreenWeight = 0.7152;
private const double BlueWeight = 0.00722;

private Task<WriteableBitmap> TransformToGrayscaleAsync(Stream stream)
{
    BitmapImage originalBitmapImage = new BitmapImage();
    originalBitmapImage.SetSource(stream);

    colorImage = new WriteableBitmap(originalBitmapImage);
    grayscaleImage = new WriteableBitmap
                        (colorImage.PixelWidth, colorImage.PixelHeight);

    colorImage.Invalidate(); // redraw the bitmap

    return Task.Run<WriteableBitmap>(() =>
    {
        for(int imagePixel = 0; imagePixel < colorImage.Pixels.Length; imagePixel++)
        {
            int pixelColor = colorImage.Pixels[imagePixel];
            int byteMask = 0xFF;

            byte colorRed = (byte)((pixelColor >> 16) & byteMask);
            byte colorGreen = (byte)((pixelColor >> 8) & byteMask);
            byte colorBlue = (byte)(pixelColor & byteMask);

            int intensity = (byte)(colorRed * RedWeight +
                                   colorGreen * GreenWeight +
                                   colorBlue * BlueWeight);

            int opaqueAlphaChannel = 255 << 24;

            grayscaleImage.Pixels[imagePixel] =
                opaqueAlphaChannel | (intensity << 16 | intensity << 8 | intensity);
        }

        return grayscaleImage;
    });
}
```

The last line of the *for* loop, which is responsible for setting the value of the pixel in the grayscale image, deserves some explanation. Each pixel in a *WriteableBitmap* is represented as a 32-bit aRGB value. An aRGB value describes a color by using the RGB model mentioned earlier, along with an additional value for the *alpha channel*, which indicates the transparency of the pixel, with a low value indicating a highly transparent color and a high value indicating a highly opaque color. The layout of the aRGB value within each integer looks like this:

Alpha	Red	Green	Blue
8 bits	8 bits	8 bits	8 bits

Our goal is to create an image with full opacity and equal intensity in each of the RGB channels. Thus, we must use the leftward bit-shifting operator (<<) to set an alpha value of 255, and a red, green, and blue value equal to the value stored in *colorIntensity*.

Capturing photos

Earlier in this chapter, we briefly mentioned the *CameraCaptureTask* with which apps can launch the built-in camera app to acquire a photo. Windows Phone also offers the ability to build the photo preview and capture experience directly in the app, enabling camera apps that go beyond the built-in functionality. In fact, there are two primary ways to capture a photo directly in an app. The *PhotoCamera* class in the *Microsoft.Devices* namespace is supported in Windows Phone 7.1 and Windows Phone 8, but only from managed code. The Windows Runtime class *PhotoCaptureDevice*, found in the *Windows.Phone.Media.Capture* namespace, can be used from either managed or native code, but is only available in Windows Phone 8.

Note Technically, there is a third way to capture photos and videos in Windows Phone 8: the *System.Windows.Media.CaptureSource* class. However, unless you need to maintain compatibility with a desktop Silverlight project, *PhotoCamera* and *PhotoCaptureDevice* are better options for Windows Phone projects.

The *PhotoCamera* class

A common tip for composing interesting photos is to divide the image into a 3x3 grid and then line up key points of interest along its boundary lines. This guideline is commonly referred to as *the rule of thirds*. The *RuleOfThirdsCamera* solution in the sample code shows how you can build an app that helps users follow the rule of thirds by overlaying the grid on top of the viewfinder, as shown in Figure 16-4.

Note The scene you see when running a camera app on the Windows Phone emulator is a colored box that moves around the edges of the viewfinder. To build and test camera apps, you will need to use a physical device.

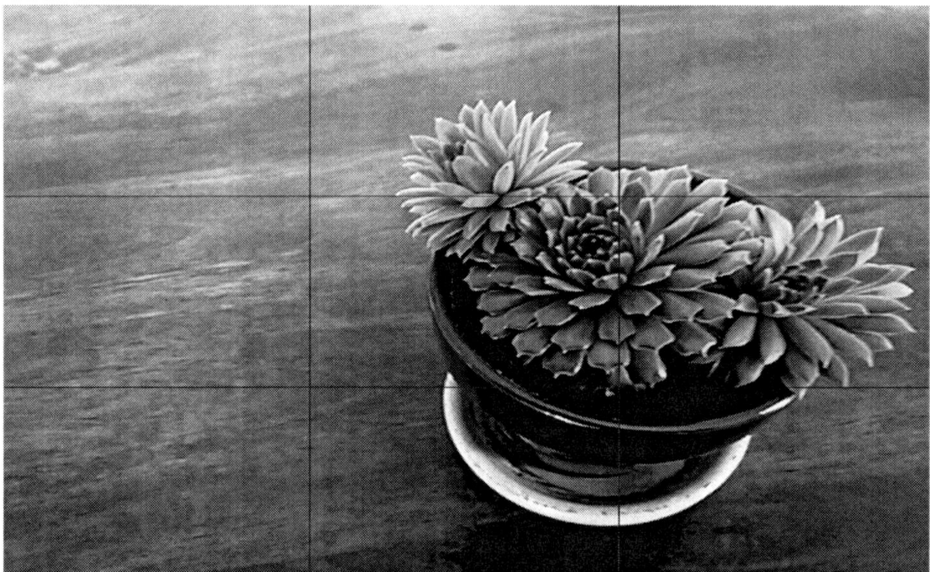

FIGURE 16-4 The *RuleOfThirds* solution demonstrates superimposing UI on the viewfinder.

The main XAML for the app is shown in the code that follows. We set the background of the grid to a *VideoBrush* element, which we will connect to the live preview from the camera in the code-behind file. The grid also includes the definition of a path that provides the 3x3 overlay. Finally, we attach an instance of the Windows Phone toolkit's *GestureListener* class to the grid. The *GestureListener* detects when the user taps and returns the location of the tap so that we can focus the camera at that point and capture a photo.

```
<Grid x:Name="capturePhotoGrid">
    <Grid.Background>
        <VideoBrush x:Name="viewFinderVideoBrush" />
    </Grid>

    <Path
        Data="M1,0 v3 m1,0 v-3 M0,1 h3 m0,1 h-3"
        Stretch="Fill"
        Stroke="{Binding GridBrush}" />

    <toolkit:GestureService.GestureListener>
        <toolkit:GestureListener x:Name="gestureListener" />
    </toolkit:GestureService.GestureListener>
</Grid>
```

In the code-behind, we declare an instance of a *PhotoCamera*, which we will use to receive the preview stream from the camera and ultimately capture the image. We also declare a *SolidColorBrush* named *GridBrush* that we will use to set the color of the gridlines—in general, it will be gray, but we will set it to the phone's accent color while the camera is focusing, which occurs either when the user presses the hardware camera button or when he taps the screen. We use the *OnNavigatedTo* method to instantiate the *PhotoCamera* class and set up two event handlers: the *Initialized* and *CaptureImage Available* events. Finally, we set the source of the *VideoBrush* defined in XAML to the *PhotoCamera* object. This is what make it possible for the app to display the preview feed directly from the camera.

```
private PhotoCamera photoCamera;
private SolidColorBrush grayBrush = new SolidColorBrush(Colors.Gray);

private SolidColorBrush gridBrush;
public SolidColorBrush GridBrush { // getter/setter omitted for brevity}

protected override void OnNavigatedTo(NavigationEventArgs e)
{
    if (!PhotoCamera.IsCameraTypeSupported(CameraType.Primary))
        return;

    photoCamera = new PhotoCamera(CameraType.Primary);
    GridBrush = grayBrush;

    photoCamera.Initialized += photoCamera_Initialized;
    photoCamera.CaptureImageAvailable += photoCamera_CaptureImageAvailable;

    viewFinderVideoBrush.SetSource(photoCamera);
}
```

Tip Always use the *IsCameraTypeSupported* method to check that the camera you want to use is supported on the device on which your app is running. If your app requires that a particular camera be present to work properly, you should declare the appropriate hardware requirements in your manifest. For Windows Phone 8 apps, use *ID_REQ_FRONTCAMERA* and *ID_REQ_REARCAMERA*. For Windows Phone 7.1 apps, use *ID_HW_FRONTCAMERA* (a rear camera is required on all Windows Phone 7.1 devices). By declaring the appropriate hardware requirements, the Windows Phone Store filters out your app when a user without appropriate hardware is browsing or searching. One caveat: because Windows Phone 7.1 apps do not have the opportunity to declare a rear-camera requirement, they will not be automatically filtered out of search results for a user with a Windows Phone 8 device that does not support a camera. Ensure that your app name and description in the Windows Phone Store make it clear if a camera is required for core functionality so that users without one can avoid it.

If you run the app with just this code in place, you will probably notice some strange behavior when you rotate the phone until the hardware buttons are facing left—an orientation known as landscape right. At some point during the rotation, the viewfinder will do a 180-degree flip and your scene will appear to be upside down. Because the viewfinder is contained within a page, it is subject to the automatic orientation changes performed by the system as the user rotates the phone. In most cases, this automatic behavior is welcome because it ensures that the app's content is always facing up regardless of which way the phone is positioned. With a viewfinder page, the main content is the world as seen through the camera's lens, which thankfully stays the right way up no matter which way the user turns his phone. Consequently, you need to counteract the automatic rotation manually. The simplest approach is to override the *OnOrientationChanged* event handler and perform a 180-degree rotation on the *VideoBrush* to offset the system's own 180-degree rotation.

```
protected override void OnOrientationChanged(OrientationChangedEventArgs e)
{
    if (Orientation == PageOrientation.LandscapeRight)
    {
        viewFinderVideoBrush.RelativeTransform
            = new CompositeTransform() { CenterX = 0.5, CenterY = 0.5, Rotation = 180 };
    }
    else
    {
        viewFinderVideoBrush.RelativeTransform
            = new CompositeTransform() { CenterX = 0.5, CenterY = 0.5, Rotation = 0 };
    }

    base.OnOrientationChanged(e);
}
```

The next step is to prepare the camera to actually take a photo. As the name suggests, the *Initialized* event is raised when the camera is ready to capture images. You should disable any mechanism by which a user can take a picture until the camera is ready; otherwise, you will get an exception.

In our app, we offer two ways of triggering image capture: the user can press the hardware camera button or tap the screen. We set up both of these in the handler for the *Initialized* event.

```
private void _photoCamera_Initialized(object sender, CameraOperationCompletedEventArgs e)
{
    CameraButtons.ShutterKeyHalfPressed += CameraButtons_ShutterKeyHalfPressed;
    CameraButtons.ShutterKeyPressed += CameraButtons_ShutterKeyPressed;
    CameraButtons.ShutterKeyReleased += CameraButtons_ShutterKeyReleased;

    gestureListener.Tap += gestureListener_Tap;
    photoCamera.AutoFocusCompleted += photoCamera_AutoFocusCompleted;
    isCameraInitialized = true;

}
```

Like the capture button on a stand-alone digital camera, the hardware camera button on Windows Phone supports two levels of pressure: a half-press, which usually instructs the camera to focus; and a full press, which usually triggers capture of the image. Each of these states has an associated event in the *CameraButtons* class, along with an event raised when the user releases the button from either the half-pressed or full-pressed state. We will use the *ShutterKeyHalfPressed* event to autofocus the camera and to set the grid lines to the phone's accent color, and the *ShutterKeyPressed* event to capture the image. The *ShutterKeyReleased* event handler will be responsible for setting the color of the grid lines back to white and cancelling the autofocus operation if it is in progress.

```
private void CameraButtons_ShutterKeyHalfPressed(object sender, EventArgs e)
{
    autoCaptureAfterFocus = false;

    if (photoCamera.IsFocusSupported)
        photoCamera.Focus();

    GridBrush = App.Current.Resources["PhoneAccentBrush"] as SolidColorBrush;
}

private void CameraButtons_ShutterKeyReleased(object sender, EventArgs e)
{
    photoCamera.CancelFocus();
    GridBrush = grayBrush;
}

private void CameraButtons_ShutterKeyPressed(object sender, EventArgs e)
{
    photoCamera.CaptureImage();
}
```

Observe that we set the Boolean value *autoCaptureAfterFocus* to *false* when the camera button is half-pressed. We use this value to differentiate the behavior between the two methods of capture; namely, pressing the hardware camera button and tapping the screen. When the user taps the screen, she is indicating exactly where she would like to focus the camera, so the standard behavior is to immediately capture the image after the focus operation completes. When she half-presses the hardware camera button, however, the user expects to be able to evaluate how well the camera has deduced the focus point before capturing the image by fully pressing the button. In the *Gesture Listener*'s *Tap* event handler, we first check whether the camera supports focusing at a specific point. If so, we get the position of the tap and call *FocusAtPoint* to focus the camera on the requested point, where the X and Y coordinates of the point are values between 0.0 and 1.0, relative to the full height and width of the screen.

```
void gestureListener_Tap(object sender, GestureEventArgs e)
{
     if (!isCameraInitialized || isCapturing)
          return;

     if (photoCamera.IsFocusAtPointSupported)
     {
          Point tapPoint = e.GetPosition(viewFinderGrid);

          double focusXPercentage = tapPoint.X / viewFinderGrid.Width;
          double focusYPercentage = tapPoint.Y / viewFinderGrid.Height;

          autoCaptureAfterFocus = true;
          photoCamera.FocusAtPoint(focusXPercentage, focusYPercentage);
     }
     else
     {
          photoCamera.Focus();
     }

     GridBrush = App.Current.Resources["PhoneAccentBrush"] as SolidColorBrush;
}
```

When the captured image is ready to be processed, the *PhotoCamera* class raises the *Capture ImageAvailable* event. We use this event to silently save the captured image to the user's camera roll and then reset the camera to capture another photo.

```
private void _photoCamera_CaptureImageAvailable(object sender, ContentReadyEventArgs e)
{
     string filename = "thirds" + DateTime.Now.Ticks.ToString() + ".jpeg";

     using (MediaLibrary mediaLibrary = new MediaLibrary())
     {
          mediaLibrary.SavePictureToCameraRoll(filename, e.ImageStream);
     }

     ResetCamera();
}

private void ResetCamera()
{
     isCapturing = false;
     photoCamera.CancelFocus();
     Deployment.Current.Dispatcher.BeginInvoke(() => GridBrush = grayBrush );
```

```
}
```

The camera draws power while active, so it is a good idea to explicitly relinquish it when it is no longer needed. In the *RuleOfThirdsCamera* solution, we perform this clean-up work in the *OnNavigatedFrom* method, but you can also handle it in the *OnRemovedFromJournal* method.

```
protected override void OnNavigatedFrom(NavigationEventArgs e)
{
    if (photoCamera != null)
    {
         photoCamera.CaptureImageAvailable -= photoCamera_CaptureImageAvailable;
         photoCamera.Initialized -= photoCamera_Initialized;
         photoCamera.Dispose();
         photoCamera = null;
    }
}
```

The *PhotoCaptureDevice* class (Windows Phone 8 only)

Windows Phone 8 includes the *PhotoCaptureDevice* class in the *Windows.Phone.Media.Capture* namespace. The primary advantages of *PhotoCaptureDevice* are that it offers advanced camera controls such as exposure compensation, which it is accessible from native code, and that it offers a set of interfaces that enable high-speed manipulation of the camera buffer in Direct3D. If you do not need any of these features in your app, you can continue to use *PhotoCamera*, which offers a simpler interface.

Note The startup performance of the *PhotoCamera* class is slower than the startup performance of *PhotoCaptureDevice* because the preview resolution for *PhotoCamera* is lower than the default resolution for *PhotoCaptureDevice* and the camera must be adjusted to account for the difference.

The *RoseColoredCamera* solution in the sample code demonstrates some of the advanced features of *PhotoCaptureDevice* as well as the ability to capture and manipulate individual frames coming from the sensor to provide a specialized viewfinder experience. The app uses an approach similar to the grayscale conversion algorithm discussed earlier to increase intensity of the red channel and present a rose-colored view of the world, which can be captured and saved to the camera roll. An example photo is shown in Figure 16-5.

FIGURE 16-5 The *RoseColoredCamera* solution previews and captures photos filtered to produce a pinkish hue.

Preparing the device and capture sequence

Taking a photo with the Windows Runtime camera APIs involves two steps: first, preparing a *PhotoCaptureDevice*, which corresponds to a specific camera on the phone (front or back) operating at a particular resolution; second, preparing a *CameraCaptureSequence*, which represents the unit of work required to capture the image from the camera. Both of the classes provide significant configurability, including whether the shutter sound plays when the user presses the camera button, to the exposure compensation on a captured frame.

We set up the *PhotoCaptureDevice* and the *CameraCaptureSequence* by using helper methods that are called from the *OnNavigatedTo* event handler on the app's main page. In *SetupCaptureDeviceAsync*, we configure the device to use the highest available capture resolution in the 16:9 aspect ratio, which refers to the ratio between the width and height of the image when the device is in landscape orientation. Windows Phone devices support capture resolutions in the 16:9 and 4:3 aspect ratios. We choose 16:9 in this example because it aligns with the standard aspect ratio of Windows Phone device screens, which are either 16:9 or 15:9.

In most cases, the camera's highest resolution will be much higher than the resolution of the phone's screen, and there is no use continually scaling down the larger image to fit the screen. Instead, when you call the *OpenAsync* method on the *PhotoCaptureDevice* class, the system automatically chooses a preview resolution that is appropriate for the size of the screen on which the app is running. You can also query the available preview resolutions by using the *GetAvailablePreviewResolutions* method and explicitly set a preview resolution by using *SetPreviewResolutionAsync* on the *PhotoCaptureDevice* instance returned by *OpenAsync*, but it must have the same aspect ratio as the capture resolution.

One of the advantages of the Windows Phone camera APIs is that they provide advanced configuration options to adjust how the camera captures an image. The *SetupCaptureDeviceAsync* method illustrates several of these. All values are configured by using the *SetProperty* method on the *PhotoCaptureDevice* class, which accepts an ID for the property and the value that you want to set for it. The list of potential IDs is available from the *KnownCameraGeneralProperties* class and the *KnownCameraPhotoProperties* class. As an example, we determine whether to play the shutter sound when the user presses the hardware camera button based on the *IsShutterSoundEnabledByUser* and *IsShutterSoundRequiredForRegion* properties. If either of these values is true, we will play the sound; otherwise, we will not. We also attempt to set two properties that directly adjust how the camera sensor captures images. First, we attempt to set the exposure compensation to 6. The integer value of the *ExposureCompensation* property represents units measured in 1/6 of an exposure value (EV), or *stop*. Thus, by setting exposure compensation to 6, we are configuring the camera to take a photo at +1EV, which causes the captured image to be brighter than normal. Next, we request to use one of the camera's built-in white balance presets to have the sensor perform the appropriate adjustments to account for a cloudy day. In a real app, you would usually provide a UI to configure these values based on the type of photo that the user wants to capture and the current lighting.

It is critical to note that the available settings vary by device. Consequently, you must always check that the value you're setting is valid for the device on which your app is running; otherwise, the system will throw an exception. We create a helper method called *TrySetValue* that first checks whether the property is supported and, if it is, sets it to the provided value. The *TrySetValue* helper includes two overloads corresponding to the range-based check performed by *GetSupportedPropertyRange* and the discrete-value check performed by *GetSupportedPropertyValues*.

```
private async Task SetupCaptureDeviceAsync()
{
    var captureResolutions =
        PhotoCaptureDevice.GetAvailableCaptureResolutions(CameraSensorLocation.Back);

    // Resolutions are ordered from highest to lowest
    var fullRes = captureResolutions.First
                   (res => Math.Round(res.Width / res.Height) == SixteenByNineAspectRatio);

    photoCaptureDevice = await PhotoCaptureDevice.OpenAsync
                         (CameraSensorLocation.Back, captureResolution);

    bool playShutterSound =
        (bool)photoCaptureDevice.
            GetProperty(KnownCameraGeneralProperties.IsShutterSoundEnabledByUser) ||
        (bool)photoCaptureDevice.
            GetProperty(KnownCameraGeneralProperties.IsShutterSoundRequiredForRegion);

    photoCaptureDevice.SetProperty(KnownCameraGeneralProperties.PlayShutterSoundOnCapture,
                                   playShutterSound);
```

```
    TrySetValue(photoCaptureDevice,
                CameraSensorLocation.Back,
                KnownCameraPhotoProperties.ExposureCompensation,
                6);
    TrySetValue(photoCaptureDevice,
                CameraSensorLocation.Back,
                KnownCameraPhotoProperties.WhiteBalancePreset,
                WhiteBalancePreset.Cloudy);

    CameraButtons.ShutterKeyPressed += CameraButtons_ShutterKeyPressed;
}

private bool TrySetValue
    (PhotoCaptureDevice device,
     CameraSensorLocation cameraLocation,
     Guid property,
     object desiredValue)
{
    var rawProperties =
        PhotoCaptureDevice.GetSupportedPropertyValues(cameraLocation, property);

    if (!rawProperties.Contains(desiredValue))
        return false;

    device.SetProperty(property, desiredValue);
    return true;
}

private bool TrySetValue
    (PhotoCaptureDevice device,
     CameraSensorLocation cameraLocation,
     Guid property,
     int value)
{
    var range =
        PhotoCaptureDevice.GetSupportedPropertyRange(cameraLocation, property);

    bool isInRange = ((int)range.Min <= value) && (value <= (int)range.Max);

    if (!isInRange)
        return false;

    device.SetProperty(property, value);
    return true;
}
```

In the *SetupCaptureSequence* helper method, we create a sequence of one frame to be captured by the camera. Note that even though the *CreateCaptureSequence* method takes a *numberOfFrames* parameter, Windows Phone 8 only supports capturing a single frame, so this value must always be set to 1. The final step in setting up the capture sequence is to give the camera a location to which to write the photo that it will eventually capture. For each *CameraCaptureFrame*, the camera supports writing to two streams: one for the full resolution image, and another for a smaller thumbnail image, which is suitable for use in your app's UI.

```
private async Task SetupCaptureSequence()
{
    roseColoredCaptureSequence = photoCaptureDevice.CreateCaptureSequence(1);

    CameraCaptureFrame captureFrame = roseColoredCaptureSequence.Frames[0];

    imageStream = new MemoryStream();
    thumbnailStream = new MemoryStream();

    captureFrame.CaptureStream = imageStream.AsOutputStream();
    captureFrame.ThumbnailStream = thumbnailStream.AsOutputStream();

    await photoCaptureDevice.PrepareCaptureSequenceAsync(roseColoredCaptureSequence);
}
```

Manipulating the preview buffer

In the *RuleOfThirdsCamera* sample presented earlier, we created a *VideoBrush* for the viewfinder and then connected the camera buffer directly to it. This creates a viewfinder that displays the world exactly as the camera sees it. But, what if you want to provide a different view of the world—in our case, a much more positive view? Both *PhotoCamera* and *PhotoCaptureDevice* offer methods to access the raw camera buffer as an array of pixels that you can manipulate before displaying them on screen, creating a viewfinder experience that can differ significantly from reality. The primary way to create this effect entirely in managed code is to create an *Image* element in your page's XAML markup and then convert the preview buffer, pixel-by-pixel, into a new *WriteableBitmap* object that can be set as the source of your page's *Image*. This approach works, but it demonstrates noticeable lag in the viewfinder compared to directly passing the camera buffer to the *VideoBrush*, as shown earlier.

Windows Phone 8 provides a solution that offers significantly better performance for manipulating the preview buffer at high speed at the cost of some additional complexity in your app. In short, there is a set of four Component Object Model (COM) interfaces that expose advanced camera functionality that is not available to managed apps consuming the Windows Runtime API projections. Of particular interest in this scenario is the *ICameraCaptureDeviceNative* interface with which apps can acquire the camera preview buffer as a Direct3D texture. The major advantage of this approach is that Direct3D textures can be manipulated at high speeds by the GPU by using a pixel shader, whereas the purely managed approach requires that the manipulation be done in the CPU, which simply cannot keep up with a requirement to display manipulated images at 30 frames per second (FPS), which is the minimum frame rate to avoid impacting the user experience (UX) in the viewfinder.

Note Several other factors contribute to the relatively poor performance of the managed solution. For one, it involves multiple copy operations to move each pixel from the preview buffer into a temporary value, and finally into the modified image. In addition, each of those copy operations requires accessing an element in an array, which in Microsoft .NET implies a range-check to ensure that the index is not outside the bounds of the array. When performed only once, the overhead of these operations is negligible, but when you need to do this tens of thousands of times to render a single frame and you are attempting to maintain a frame rate of 30 FPS, every millisecond counts.

As discussed in Chapter 1, there are two ways to incorporate Direct3D into your app. You can create a pure Direct3D app, in which case the entire UI is built by using Direct3D and all of the code is written in C++. Or, you can create a XAML app that includes a Direct3D control, such as *Drawing Surface* or *DrawingSurfaceBackgroundGrid*, and uses a Windows Runtime component to interoperate with Direct3D rendering code that can provide the input to that control. For most apps, including the *RoseColoredCamera* solution, the latter approach is preferable because you have the ability to incorporate Direct3D where you need it for performance or graphical richness while still using simpler XAML markup for other parts of your app. We review both options in more detail in Chapter 25, "Games and Direct3D."

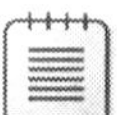

Note This section references several Direct3D concepts without explaining them in detail because they are covered more thoroughly in Chapter 25. If you are unfamiliar with Direct3D, you might want to skip this section until after you have read Chapter 25.

The *RoseColoredCamera* solution is based on the "Windows Phone XAML and Direct3D app" template in Visual Studio. This template automatically creates a XAML app that includes a *Drawing SurfaceBackgroundGrid* and a Windows Runtime component that includes the Direct3D rendering code which enables the interoperability between that rendering logic and the presentation of the result in the app. Our goal is to have the Direct3D rendering code use the *ICameraCaptureDevice Native* interface to acquire the preview buffer as a Direct3D texture, manipulate it by using a pixel shader, and then pass it back to the XAML app to be displayed in the UI. Because the camera is an exclusive resource, the app can only have one instance of it at any given time and must share that instance across the different parts of the app that need it. The *ICameraCaptureDeviceNative* interface is implemented by the COM objects behind the *PhotoCaptureDevice* class and the *AudioVideoCapture Device* class, so the instance of the *PhotoCaptureDevice* that we created in the previous section must be passed to the Windows Runtime component that will perform the Direct3D rendering. We add a new method, *SetPhotoCaptureDevice*, to the *Direct3DInterop* class created by the template to pass the *PhotoCaptureDevice* instance. We also create a method, *SetPhotoCaptureStatus*, to indicate when the managed app is using the *PhotoCaptureDevice* to actually capture a photo so that the XAML app and the Windows Runtime component do not attempt to access the camera at the same time, because that will raise an exception.

```
public ref class Direct3DInterop sealed :
    public Windows::Phone::Input::Interop::IDrawingSurfaceManipulationHandler
{
public:
    Direct3DInterop();

    Windows::Phone::Graphics::Interop::IDrawingSurfaceContentProvider^ CreateContentProvider();

    // IDrawingSurfaceManipulationHandler
    virtual void
        SetManipulationHost(Windows::Phone::Input::Interop::DrawingSurfaceManipulationHost^
                                 manipulationHost);
    void SetPhotoCaptureDevice(Windows::Phone::Media::Capture::PhotoCaptureDevice^
                                    photoCaptureDevice);

    void SetPhotoCaptureStatus(bool isCapturingPhoto);

    // unchanged code...

private:
    CameraPreview^ m_cameraPreview;
}
```

We add a single line of code to the *SetupCaptureDeviceAsync* method in the XAML app to pass the *PhotoCaptureDevice* instance to the *Direct3DInterop* class.

```
private async Task SetupCaptureDeviceAsync()
{
    // unchanged code...

    m_d3dInterop.SetPhotoCaptureDevice(photoCaptureDevice);
}
```

Ultimately, the *PhotoCaptureDevice* is passed through to the *CameraPreview* class, which uses it to acquire a pointer to the *ICameraCaptureDeviceNative* interface. As soon as we have that pointer, we set the format of the preview and then link the camera to the Direct3D device that will handle the rendering. We then create a Direct3D 2-dimensional texture and a shader resource view, which will be used to tint the preview buffer to a dark pink during the render loop. Finally, we create a new instance of the *SpriteBatch* class from the DirectXTK toolkit, which we look at in more detail in Chapter 25. The *SpriteBatch* class simplifies the process of passing a texture through a pixel shader for rendering, but it is not required for using the native camera interfaces. As soon as you have filled a 2D texture with the camera preview buffer, you can manipulate it however you choose.

```
void CameraPreview::SetPhotoCaptureDevice(PhotoCaptureDevice^ camera)
{
    ComPtr<IUnknown>(reinterpret_cast<IUnknown*>(camera)).As(&m_nativeCaptureDevice);

    m_nativeCaptureDevice->SetPreviewFormat(DXGI_FORMAT_B8G8R8A8_UNORM);
    m_nativeCaptureDevice->SetDevice(m_d3dDevice.Get(), m_d3dContext.Get());

    D3D11_TEXTURE2D_DESC desc = {};
```

```
    desc.Width = camera->PreviewResolution.Width;
    desc.Height = camera->PreviewResolution.Height;
    desc.MipLevels = 1;
    desc.ArraySize = 1;
    desc.Format = DXGI_FORMAT_B8G8R8A8_UNORM;
    desc.SampleDesc.Count = 1;
    desc.SampleDesc.Quality = 0;
    desc.Usage = D3D11_USAGE_DEFAULT;
    desc.BindFlags = D3D11_BIND_RENDER_TARGET | D3D11_BIND_SHADER_RESOURCE;
    desc.CPUAccessFlags = 0;
    desc.MiscFlags = 0;

    m_d3dDevice->CreateTexture2D(&desc, NULL, &m_previewTexture);

    D3D11_SHADER_RESOURCE_VIEW_DESC shaderResourceViewDesc;

    shaderResourceViewDesc.Format = DXGI_FORMAT_B8G8R8A8_UNORM;
    shaderResourceViewDesc.ViewDimension = D3D11_SRV_DIMENSION_TEXTURE2D;
    shaderResourceViewDesc.Texture2D.MostDetailedMip = 0;
    shaderResourceViewDesc.Texture2D.MipLevels = 1;

    auto result = m_d3dDevice->CreateShaderResourceView
                  (m_previewTexture.Get(), &shaderResourceViewDesc, &m_shaderResourceView);

    m_sprites.reset(new SpriteBatch(m_d3dContext.Get()));
    m_loadingComplete = true;
}
```

In the *Render* method of the *CameraPreview* class, we use the *GetPreviewBufferTexture* method on the *ICameraCaptureDeviceNative* interface to fill our 2D texture, *m_previewTexture*, with the camera preview buffer. We then render the preview by using the *SpriteBatch* class, which accepts the shader resource view that we created earlier along with the location of the top-left point of the image and an optional color with which to tint it. Observe that before doing anything, we acquire a named mutex to avoid potential contention for the camera sensor between managed and native code. We will acquire the same mutex later when we attempt to capture the photo in managed code. During that brief period when the camera is performing the capture, the render loop blocks and waits for the mutex to be released before proceeding.

```
void CameraPreview::Render()
{
    WaitForSingleObject(m_cameraMutexHandle, INFINITE, false);

    const float black[] = { 0.0f, 0.0f, 0.0f, 1.000f };
    m_d3dContext->ClearRenderTargetView(
        m_renderTargetView.Get(),
        black
        );
```

```
    m_d3dContext->ClearDepthStencilView(
        m_depthStencilView.Get(),
        D3D11_CLEAR_DEPTH,
        1.0f,
        0
        );

    if (!m_loadingComplete)
        return;

    m_d3dContext->OMSetRenderTargets(
        1,
        m_renderTargetView.GetAddressOf(),
        m_depthStencilView.Get()
        );

    m_nativeCaptureDevice->GetPreviewBufferTexture(m_previewTexture.Get());

    m_sprites->Begin();
    m_sprites->Draw(m_shaderResourceView.Get(), XMFLOAT2(0,0), nullptr, Colors::DeepPink);
    m_sprites->End();
}
```

Capturing a photo

When the user indicates that he would like to capture a photo by pressing the hardware camera button or tapping the screen, we call the *StartCaptureAsync* method to actually take the picture. We then kick off two asynchronous methods: one converts the full-resolution image into a JPEG that we can save to the media library and the other converts the lower-resolution thumbnail image into a bitmap that can be displayed to the user as a preview. Because we only need to loop through the pixels once each for the thumbnail and the full image to generate their rose-colored equivalents, it is reasonable to perform that translation in managed code, much like what we showed earlier for converting images to grayscale. Observe that we choose not to *await* the asynchronous method that translates the full-resolution image. Instead, we capture the task in the *imageConversionTask* member variable and proceed immediately to preparing the thumbnail image, the translation of which *is* awaited because it is required to show the preview UI. Later, when the user attempts to save the final image, we can *await* the completion of the *imageConversionTask*, though in most cases the result will already be available.

Note We are intentionally limiting the amount of functionality that is provided by the Windows Runtime component and Direct3D rendering because it adds complexity to the app and is not required unless you need to manipulate the preview buffer at high speed. In particular, we are performing the translation of the final captured image into its rose-colored equivalent in managed code by mimicking the translation performed by the pixel shader in Direct3D. In a real app, it would be cleaner and slightly faster to perform all translations (including the final ones) in Direct3D by using a common shader.

When the translated thumbnail image is ready, we bring up an app bar with Save and Cancel buttons. The code to prepare the preview UI and switch to it from the viewfinder is contained in the *CapturePhoto* method, which is invoked from either *ShutterKeyPressed* event handler or the gesture listener's *Tap* event handler.

```
private Task<MemoryStream> imageConversionTask;

private async void CapturePhoto()
{
    Mutex cameraMutex = new Mutex(false, "RoseColoredCameraMutex");
    cameraMutex.WaitOne();
    await roseColoredCaptureSequence.StartCaptureAsync();
    cameraMutex.ReleaseMutex();

    imageStream.Seek(0, SeekOrigin.Begin);
    thumbnailStream.Seek(0, SeekOrigin.Begin);

    var finalBitmapImage = new BitmapImage();
    finalBitmapImage.SetSource(imageStream);
    var finalImage = new WriteableBitmap(finalBitmapImage);

    imageConversionTask = CreateRoseJpegAsync(finalImage);

    var thumbnailBitmapImage = new BitmapImage();
    thumbnailBitmapImage.SetSource(thumbnailStream);

    var thumbnailWriteableBitmap = new WriteableBitmap(thumbnailBitmapImage);
    await TransformCapturedImageToRoseAsync(thumbnailWriteableBitmap.Pixels);
    thumbnailImage.Source = thumbnailWriteableBitmap;

    saveImageGrid.Visibility = Visibility.Visible;
    viewFinderGrid.Visibility = Visibility.Collapsed;
    ApplicationBar.IsVisible = true;
}
```

After the user has reviewed the photo and pressed the Save button on the app bar, we again use the *SavePictureToCameraRoll* method on the *MediaLibrary* class to save the photo to the camera roll. Whereas we used the thumbnail photo for the preview, we choose to save the full-resolution image to the camera roll, from which it can be shared with social networks, sent by email, or transferred to a computer.

```
private async void saveAppBarButton_Click(object sender, EventArgs e)
{
    foreach (ApplicationBarIconButton button in ApplicationBar.Buttons)
    {
        button.IsEnabled = false;
    }

    finalImageJpegStream = await imageConversionTask;
```

```
        using (MediaLibrary mediaLibrary = new MediaLibrary())
        {
            mediaLibrary.SavePictureToCameraRoll
                ("rose" + DateTime.Now.Ticks + ".jpeg", jpegMemoryStream);
        }

        FlipToViewfinder();

        foreach (ApplicationBarIconButton button in ApplicationBar.Buttons)
        {
            button.IsEnabled = true;
        }
    }
```

Capturing video

Windows Phone also provides APIs to capture MP4 video within an app. As with photos, there are two options available. Windows Phone 7.1 and 8.0 apps written in managed code can use the *CaptureSource* class in the *System.Windows.Media* namespace, which offers simple *Start* and *Stop* methods to begin and end a recording. Apps can also write the resulting video to disk by using the *FileSink* class found in the same namespace.

Windows Phone 8 introduces a new way of capturing video that works only in Windows Phone 8 apps but is accessible from native code. The *AudioVideoCapture* class is very similar to the *PhotoCaptureDevice* class described earlier—the app can set specific properties on the device (such as turning on the phone torch) and can access the raw video stream coming from the camera by using methods like *GetPreviewBufferArgb*. Like the *ICameraCaptureDeviceNative* interface described earlier for photos, the *IAudioVideoCaptureDeviceNative* enables high-performance sampling of the video preview that can be manipulated by using Direct3D. One important difference between captured videos and captured photos is that captured videos cannot be written to the user's video library.

Note Because capturing video involves capturing audio, apps must declare the *ID_CAP_MICROPHONE* capability in their manifest, in addition to the *ID_CAP_CAMERA* capability, even if they are not using the microphone APIs.

Extending the Photos Hub

As discussed in Chapter 1, the Windows Phone UI is primarily content-focused rather than app focused. The idea behind the content-centric model is that users should never have to think about which app to launch to view or manipulate a particular set of content such as photos or music. Rather, there should be a single entry point for that content, with the system and Windows Phone Store apps plugging in various actions for it. These single entry points are referred to as *hubs*, and each provides its own set of extensibility points for Windows Phone Store apps, with the Photos Hub providing the richest set of options. In this section, you will see the different ways that your app can augment the photos experience through these extensibility points.

Apps pivot

The simplest form of Photos Hub extensibility is the ability to be included in the apps pivot. The apps pivot provides a list of photo-related apps directly in the main page of the Photos Hub, as shown in Figure 16-6.

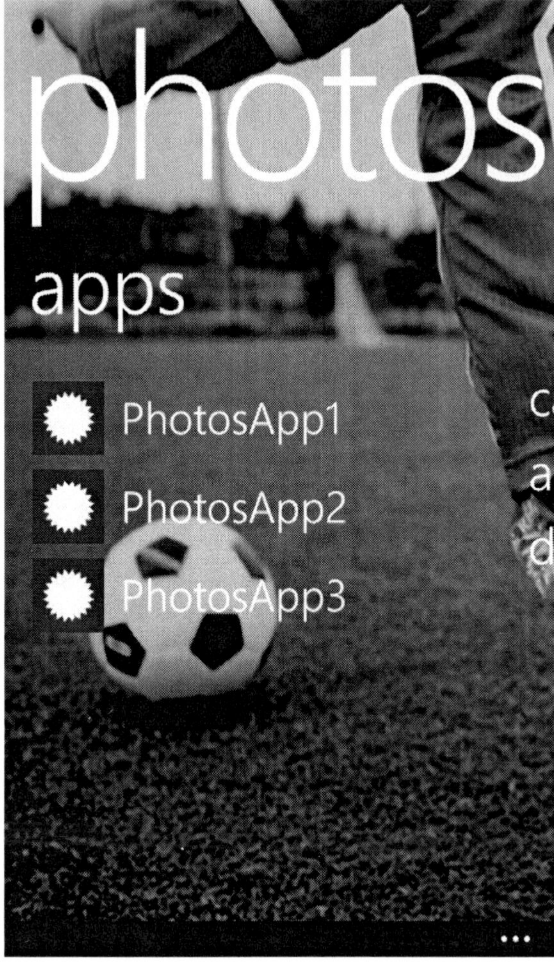

FIGURE 16-6 The apps pivot provides a launching point for photo apps.

Registration for the apps pivot is done declaratively in the app manifest. Like other extensibility points in Windows Phone 8, photos extensibility registration is not currently available in the manifest GUI tool, so you will need to edit the manifest XML directly by right-clicking the WMAppManifest.xml and then, on the shortcut menu that appears, choosing View Code. In the XML editor, you simply add the following XML after the *Tokens* element:

```
<Extensions>
    <Extension ExtensionName="Photos_Extra_Hub"
               ConsumerID="{5B04B775-356B-4AA0-AAF8-6491FFEA5632}"
               TaskID="_default" />
</Extensions>
```

The *ConsumerID* identifies the built-in app that is providing the extensibility point, in this case the Photos Hub. The *ExtensionName* refers to the specific extensibility point for which the app is registering, in this case the *Photos_Extra_Hub*, which refers to the apps pivot.

Tip Apps pivot extensibility provides another entry point in your app in a location that is specific to photos. Because no code changes are required, every camera and photos related app should register for this extensibility point.

The photo apps picker and photo edit picker

The built-in photos app provides a core set of functions for viewing and editing photos on the phone. For more advanced and creative functionality, however, users look to apps. Whether it's applying a filter to make a photo taken moments ago look old and worn or dressing up a friend's photo with a pirate hat and a huge mustache, the Windows Phone Store is full of apps that can do interesting and delightful things with a user's photo collection. Windows Phone provides a way for users to open a photo from their library in an app to view or edit it. The registration mechanism for this extensibility point has changed between Windows Phone 7.1 and Windows Phone 8, so we will describe them each in turn.

The photo apps picker (Windows Phone 7.1 only)

Windows Phone 7.1 apps can register to act as a viewer and/or editor of a photo from the user's photo library through an "apps" link on the app bar menu of the photo viewer, as shown in Figure 16-7.

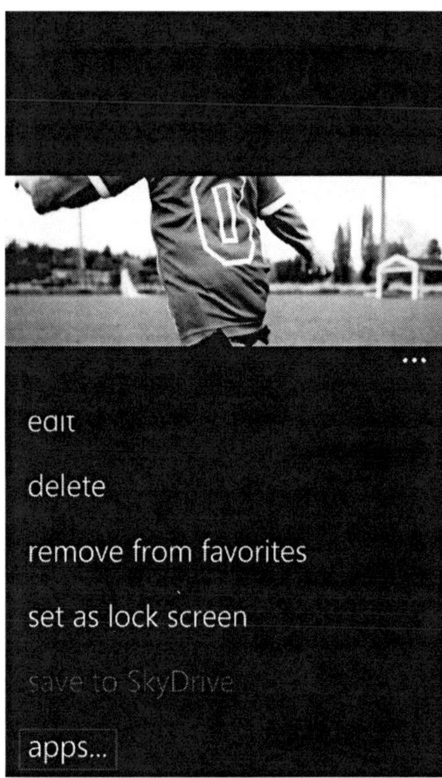

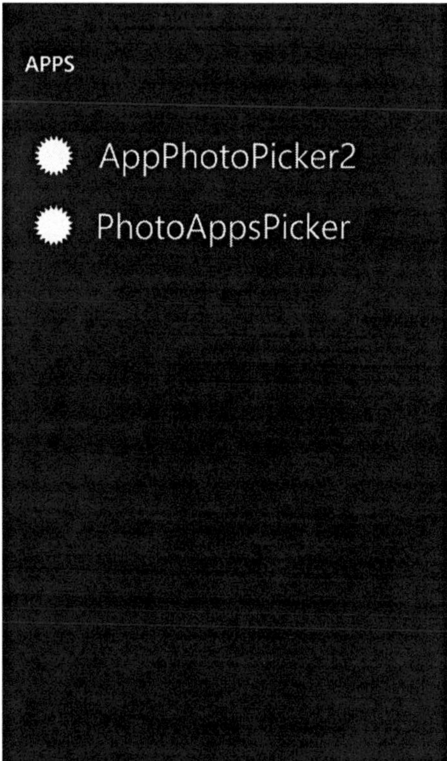

FIGURE 16-7 You can discover Windows Phone 7.1 photo apps through the apps link in the photo viewer.

As with the apps pivot extensibility discussed in the previous section, registration for the photo apps picker involves making a small change to the app manifest. Indeed, registration for the two extensibility points only differs in the name of the extension.

```
<Extensions>
    <Extension ExtensionName="Photos_Extra_Viewer"
               ConsumerID="{5B04B775-356B-4AA0-AAF8-6491FFEA5632}"
               TaskID="_default" />
</Extensions>
```

When an app is launched from the photo apps picker, the system needs to provide some reference token to the photo that it is being launched to handle. Recall from Chapter 2, "App model and navigation," that the Windows Phone navigation model is URI-based, so it is natural for this token to be included as a query string parameter in the main app navigation URI. By default, the system will launch the app to its primary navigation page (as defined in the app manifest) with the token appended, as shown here (assuming MainPage.xaml was the primary navigation page):

```
/MainPage.xaml?token={3637f67d-ad2e-491b-a60b-70c3ae0c88c9}
```

With this token in hand, the app can then retrieve the photo from the media library. The *PhotoApps Picker* solution in the sample shows an example of how to do this. To use the media library APIs, we must include a reference to the *Microsoft.Xna.Framework* assembly and specify the *ID_CAP_MEDIALIB* capability, in addition to registering the *Photos_Extra_Viewer* extension, as shown earlier. Then, we simply need to add the code to the *OnNavigatedTo* method of the *MainPage* to retrieve the photo based on the token and create a *BitmapImage* that we can use in the UI.

```
protected override void OnNavigatedTo(System.Windows.Navigation.NavigationEventArgs e)
{
    string token;

    if (NavigationContext.QueryString.TryGetValue("token", out token))
    {
        using (MediaLibrary mediaLibrary = new MediaLibrary())
        {
            Picture chosenPicture = mediaLibrary.GetPictureFromToken(token);

            BitmapImage chosenPictureBitmapImage = new BitmapImage();
            chosenPictureBitmapImage.SetSource(chosenPicture.GetImage());
            photoAppsPickerImage.Source = chosenPictureBitmapImage;
        }
    }
}
```

Of course, you're probably wondering, "What if I don't want to display the photo on my main page?" The solution, as in many of the types of Windows Phone extensibility, is to use a *UriMapper* to redirect the user to a different page of your app, based on the presence of the photo token. This technique is discussed in detail in Chapter 2 and is illustrated in the *MappedPhotoAppsPicker* solution in the sample code. The *MappedPhotoAppsPickers* solution is effectively the same app as the previous example, but in this case, we are redirecting the user to a page named *PhotoViewerPage.xaml* to see the selected photo rather than displaying it on the main page.

The photo edit picker (Windows Phone 8 only)

In Windows Phone 8, the photo apps picker has been replaced with the photo edit picker, but the process and UI has not changed significantly. Now, the user can choose an app to edit a photo by using the edit link on the app bar menu of the photo viewer, as shown in Figure 16-8.

FIGURE 16-8 With the photo edit picker, apps can extend the edit link in the photo viewer.

Registration of the extension is very similar to the photo apps picker. In the case of the photo edit picker, the app must register the following extension:

```
<Extension ExtensionName="Photos_Extra_Image_Editor"
           ConsumerID="{5B04B775-356B-4AA0-AAF8-6491FFEA5632}"
           TaskID="_default" />
```

Finally, the notion of passing in a reference to the photo in the navigation URI has not changed, though the term *token* has been replaced with *FileId*. In addition, the navigation URI now contains an *Action* parameter, describing the type of task that the app is being invoked to perform. In the case of the photo edit picker, the value of the *Action* parameter is *EditPhotoContent*. (We will look at another type of action in the next section, "Lenses").

```
/MainPage.xaml?Action=EditPhotoContent&FileId="{3637f67d-ad2e-491b-a60b-70c3ae0c88c9}"
```

The *PhotoEditPicker* solution in the sample code shows how to handle being launched from the photo edit picker. As with the photo apps picker, the app simply needs to redeem the token for a *Picture* object from the media library, as shown in the *OnNavigatedTo* method here:

```
protected override void OnNavigatedTo(NavigationEventArgs e)
{
    string fileId, action;

    if(NavigationContext.QueryString.TryGetValue("Action", out action)
        && NavigationContext.QueryString.TryGetValue("FileId", out fileId))
    {
        using (MediaLibrary mediaLibrary = new MediaLibrary())
        {
            Picture chosenPicture = mediaLibrary.GetPictureFromToken(fileId);

            BitmapImage chosenPictureBitmapImage = new BitmapImage();
            chosenPictureBitmapImage.SetSource(chosenPicture.GetImage());
            photoEditPickerImage.Source = chosenPictureBitmapImage;
        }
    }
}
```

Lenses

Earlier this chapter, you saw how you can build a camera app by using the *PhotoCamera* class. Windows Phone 8 introduces a special kind of camera app called a lens. Lenses are camera apps that can be launched directly from the built-in camera app and which naturally complement it by using the camera sensor to provide a specialized experience.

All lenses must provide a viewfinder-based experience when launched from the built-in camera app, though it is not necessary that they actually offer a capture experience—an app providing an augmented reality view of nearby coffee shops would be a perfectly valid lens, for instance. Lenses that do capture photos, however, also have the opportunity to go well beyond simply saving a JPEG file to the user's camera roll. By generating or aggregating additional content to associate with the photo, lenses can create a rich and engaging experience for the user. The system also keeps track of the app that created the photo to make it easy for the user to return to that experience from the photo viewer by using a link on the app bar menu.

The *LocationLens* solution in the sample code provides a simple example of a specialized capture and viewing experience. The solution retrieves the device's current location when a photo is taken and stores the name of the city in its local folder. If the user subsequently invokes the app to view one of the photos that it took, it can display the stored information about where the photo was taken.

Launching from the camera

As with the other extensibility points reviewed in this chapter, the way that an app declares itself as a lens is through an extension in its manifest. In the case of lenses, the extension looks like this:

```
<Extension ExtensionName="Camera_Capture_App"
           ConsumerID="{5B04B775-356B-4AA0-AAF8-6491FFEA5631}"
           TaskID="_default" />
```

The system UI for displaying lens apps is different from some of the other extensibility points discussed in the chapter; rather than displaying a list of apps, the camera app shows a list of tiles, as in Figure 16-9.

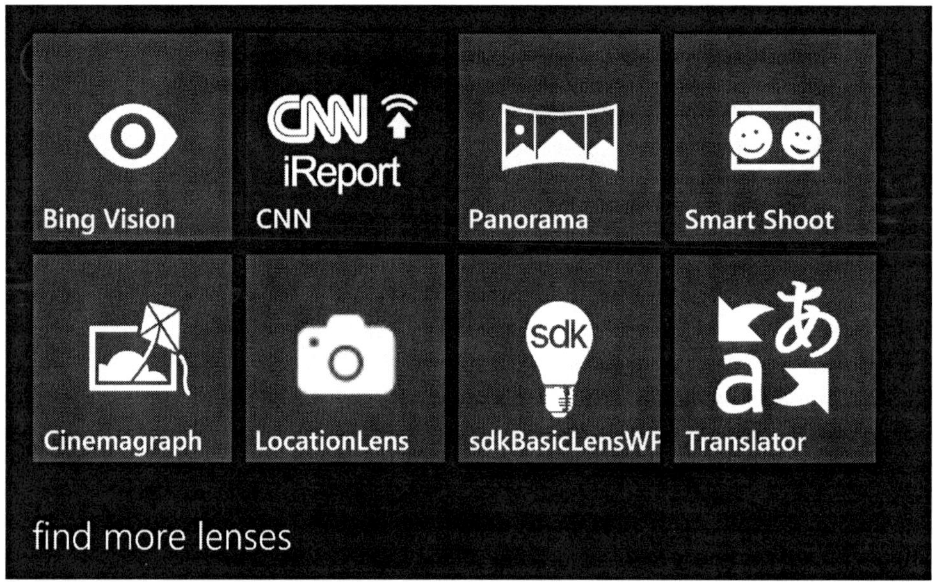

FIGURE 16-9 With the Lens Picker, the user can start a lens app directly from the camera viewfinder.

The icon for the tile must be supplied by the app in its Assets folder using a defined naming scheme depending on the target device resolution, as shown in Table 16-1.

TABLE 16-1 Naming convention and resolution for lens icons

Resolution	Icon size (in pixels)	File name
WVGA	173x173	Lens.Screen-WVGA.png
720p	259x259	Lens.Screen-720p.png
WXGA	277x277	Lens.Screen-WXGA.png

As usual, the system notifies the app that it is being launched as a lens through the navigation URI. For lenses, the URI looks like this:

```
/MainPage.xaml?Action=ViewfinderLauncher
```

One of the critical requirements for a lens is that it launch directly into the viewfinder, to provide a smooth transition from the built-in camera app. If the app's primary navigation page (in this case MainPage.xaml) provides the viewfinder UI, there is nothing further required to properly handle being launched as a lens. In most cases, however, the app will provide the viewfinder experience on a different page, in which case it will need to perform URI mapping to redirect the launch to that page, as shown earlier in the chapter. In the case of the *LocationLens* solution, we redirect the user to CameraCapturePage.xaml. In the *OnNavigatedTo* event handler, we set up a *PhotoCamera* as shown earlier and add a query to the device's location service to determine its current location and a reverse geocoding query to determine the closest city to that location.

Tip Keep in mind that lens apps are just standard Windows Phone apps that integrate with extensibility points provided in the camera and the photo viewer. If you limit yourself to frameworks that are supported in Windows Phone 7.1, such as *PhotoCamera* and *GeoCoordinateWatcher*, you can reuse virtually all of your code in an app targeting that version of the platform.

```
protected override void OnNavigatedTo(NavigationEventArgs e)
{
    SetupAppBar();
    camera = new PhotoCamera(CameraType.Primary);
    camera.Initialized += CameraInitialized;

    viewFinderVideoBrush.SetSource(camera);

    CameraButtons.ShutterKeyPressed += CameraButtons_ShutterKeyPressed;

    FindLocationAsync();
}

private void CameraInitialized(object sender, CameraOperationCompletedEventArgs e)
{
    CameraButtons.ShutterKeyPressed += ShutterKeyPressed;
    camera.CaptureImageAvailable += CaptureImageAvailable;
}

private async Task FindLocationAsync()
{
    var geoCoordinateWatcher = new GeoCoordinateWatcher(GeoPositionAccuracy.Default);
```

```
        GeoCoordinate currentLocation = await Task.Run(() =>
        {
            if (geoCoordinateWatcher.TryStart(false, TimeSpan.FromSeconds(10)))
                return geoCoordinateWatcher.Position.Location;
            else
                return null;
        });

        if(currentLocation = null)
        {
            currentLocationTextBlock.Text = "Unknown";
            locationQueryEvent.Set();
            return;
        }

        var reverseGeocodeQuery = new ReverseGeocodeQuery();
        reverseGeocodeQuery.GeoCoordinate = currentLocation;

        reverseGeocodeQuery.QueryCompleted += ReverseGeocodeQueryCompleted;
        reverseGeocodeQuery.QueryAsync();

    }

    private void ReverseGeocodeQueryCompleted(object sender,
                                              QueryCompletedEventArgs<IList<MapLocation>> e)
    {
        if (e.Result.Count() > 0)
        {
            currentAddress = e.Result[0].Information.Address;
            if(currentAddress != null)
                currentLocationTextBlock.Text = currentAddress.City;

            locationQueryEvent.Set();
        }
    }
```

Again, we give the user an opportunity to view a preview of the captured image before saving it to his camera roll. When he is ready to proceed, he can tap the Save button on the app bar to keep the photo. As in previous examples, we use this as a cue to call the *SavePictureToCameraRoll* API on the *MediaLibrary*, but in this case, we add code to also save the current city to a *Dictionary* maintained in the app class. The key in the dictionary is the full path to the photo, which can be queried by using the *GetPath* extension method, which is available in the *Microsoft.Xna.Framework.Media.PhoneExtensions* namespace. Finally, the app calls the *SaveDictionary* helper method on the *App* class, which simply serializes the current state of the dictionary and saves it to disk.

```
private void saveAppBarButton_Click(object sender, EventArgs e)
{
    imageStream.Seek(0, SeekOrigin.Begin);

    using (MediaLibrary mediaLibrary = new MediaLibrary())
    {
        Picture savedPicture = mediaLibrary.SavePictureToCameraRoll
                                ("LocationLens" + DateTime.Now.Ticks + ".jpeg",
                                imageStream);

        App.PhotoCityMapping.Add(savedPicture.GetPath(), currentAddress.City);
        App.SaveDictionary();
    }
}
```

Rich media editing

Although lens apps will generally save captured photos to the user's camera roll so that they can be viewed in the Photos Hub, the lens app itself can often provide a richer experience for interacting with the photo, using additional data and app functionality. Indeed, some lens apps can capture something significantly more immersive than a standard photo and save only an approximation of that richer artifact as a JPEG image to the user's camera roll. An example of this is the Microsoft Photosynth app. Photosynth uses a collection of captured images to create a 3D model of the scene. The user can see a simple 2D representation of the Photosynth in the Photos Hub but must start the app to interact with the full 3D panorama. With the *Photos_Rich_Media_Edit* extension, lens apps can maintain a strong affiliation with photos saved to the camera roll so that the user can quickly return to the app experience for a given photo directly from the Photos Hub, as shown in Figure 16-10. Note that the photo viewer automatically labels the photo with an attribution to the capturing app and provides a deep link to the app from the app bar menu.

The manifest declaration for the *Photos_Rich_Media_Edit* extension is shown in the code that follows. Observe that the *ConsumerID* is different from the one listed for the *Camera_Capture_App*. In that instance, we were extending the camera app, whereas the *Photos_Rich_Media_Edit* extension is associated with the Photos Hub.

```
<Extension ExtensionName="Photos_Rich_Media_Edit"
           ConsumerID="{5B04B775-356B-4AA0-AAF8-6491FFEA5632}"
           TaskID="_default" />
```

The navigation URI looks just as you would expect:

```
/MainPage.xaml?Action=RichMediaEdit&token={2fad1162-7f85-4d6c-bbd6-aee6f10e501d}
```

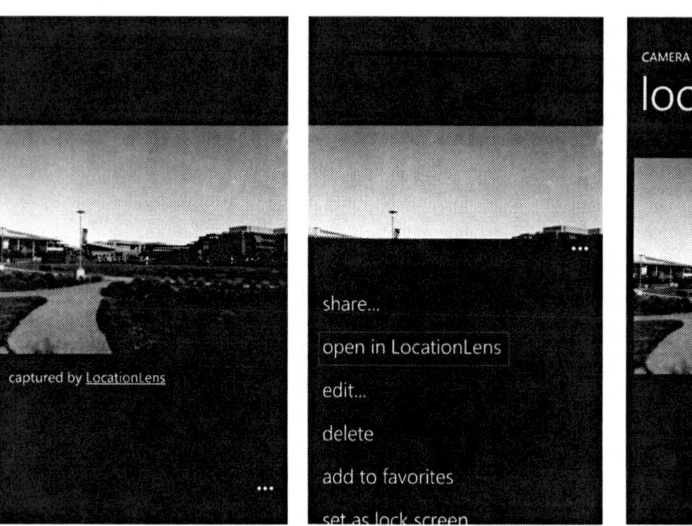

FIGURE 16-10 The *LocationLens* stores the location where a photo was taken and can display that information when launched as a Rich Media Edit app.

In the *LocationLens* solution, we retrieve the image from the media library by using the token and then look up the city where the photo was captured from the *PhotoCityMapping Dictionary* object maintained by the app.

```
protected override void OnNavigatedTo(NavigationEventArgs e)
{
    string action;
    string fileId;
    string city;

    if (NavigationContext.QueryString.TryGetValue("Action", out action)
        && action == "RichMediaEdit")
    {
        using (MediaLibrary mediaLibrary = new MediaLibrary())
        {
            fileId = (string)NavigationContext.QueryString["token"];

            Picture launchedPicture = mediaLibrary.GetPictureFromToken(fileId);

            WriteableBitmap launchedBitmap =
                new WriteableBitmap(launchedPicture.Width, launchedPicture.Height);

            launchedBitmap.SetSource(launchedPicture.GetImage());

            lensImage.Source = launchedBitmap;

            if (App.PhotoCityMapping.TryGetValue(launchedPicture.GetPath(), out city))
            {
                imageLocationTextBlock.Text = city;
            }
        }
    }
}
```

Emulating the built-in camera

A good lens app should feel like a natural extension of the built-in camera app. The requirement that lenses provide a viewfinder-based experience when launched from the camera app's viewfinder is just one part of meeting this goal. The built-in camera also makes it possible for the user to easily switch back and forth between front and back cameras (if available), to control the flash mode with a single app bar button, and to view recently captured images by swiping in from the left. The Basic Lens Sample on MSDN supports all of these behaviors and provides a great starting point for emulating the built-in camera in a new lens. The sample is available for download at *http://code.msdn.microsoft.com/wpapps/Basic-Lens-sample-359fda1b*.

Sharing photos

Users don't want to just take photos; they want to share them, too. With Windows Phone, apps can participate in this sharing flow, whether the user is explicitly sharing a photo through the *Share MediaTask* or automatically uploading them to the cloud by using auto-upload.

Share picker

The share picker makes it possible for the user to quickly share a photo from the photo viewer, using built-in apps such as email or messaging, or by using an app that has registered for the share picker extensibility point. Figure 16-11 shows the invocation point for the share picker, a link on the app bar menu of the photo viewer. The app highlighted in the share picker is the *PhotoSharePicker* solution in the sample code.

The process of registering for and being invoked by the share picker is effectively the same as it was for the photo edit picker described earlier. Again, the app must register an extension in the app manifest. In this case, the extension name is *Photos_Extra_Share*.

```
<Extension ExtensionName="Photos_Extra_Share"
           ConsumerID="{5B04B775-356B-4AA0-AAF8-6491FFEA5632}"
           TaskID="_default" />
```

As with the photo edit picker, the system informs the app that it is being launched for a specific task (in this case, sharing) through the navigation URI. In this case, the navigation URI looks something like this:

```
/MainPage.xaml?Action=ShareContent&token={3637F67D-AD2E-491B-A60B-70C3AE0C88C9}
```

The process for redirecting the invocation to a different page in the app and for retrieving the file from the *FileId* is the same as we discussed earlier for the photo edit picker.

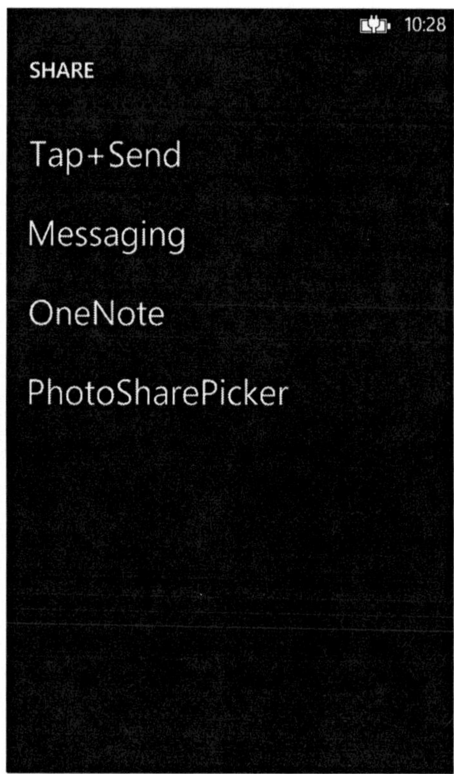

FIGURE 16-11 Apps can register to appear in the share picker for quick access from the photo viewer.

Auto-upload

In Windows Phone 8, apps that have an associated photo storage cloud service can register to automatically upload new user photos to that service in the background. In practice, building an auto-upload app involves combining two platform features already discussed: resource-intensive tasks (reviewed in Chapter 9, "Background agents"), and the media library (discussed earlier in this chapter). The app simply schedules a resource-intensive task to run based on the conditions described in Chapter 9 and then uses the media library APIs to retrieve any new photos that need to be uploaded.

So what makes auto-upload apps special? First, the resource-intensive tasks associated with auto-upload apps do not require an expiration date. As discussed in Chapter 9, the platform generally makes an assumption that if the user has not launched an app for some period (currently 14 days), she is probably not that interested in it or what it might want to do in the background. With auto-upload apps, it is reasonable to assume that the user might only care about the app for its ability to upload her photos to the cloud, so its tasks should not be subject to the same expiration period. Similar exemptions are provided for apps with tiles pinned to the Start screen and for apps that are providing lock-screen notifications. The other way in which auto-upload apps are special is that they show up in the Photos+Camera section of the Settings app, as shown in Figure 16-12.

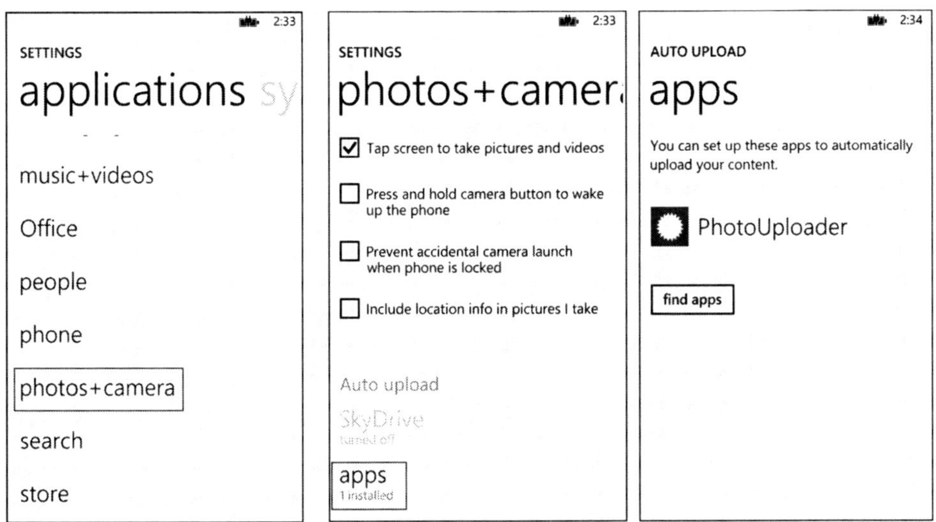

FIGURE 16-12 Apps that auto-upload photos appear in the photos+camera section of the Settings app.

It should come as no surprise by now that the way an app can appear in this list is by adding an extension to the app manifest. For auto-upload apps, the extension declaration looks like this:

```
<Extension ExtensionName="Photos_Auto_Upload"
          ConsumerID = "{5B04B775-356B-4AA0-AAF8-6491FFEA5632}"
          TaskID="_default"/>
```

When an app is started from the Settings app, it should show its own sync settings UI. At a minimum, this settings page should provide the user with the ability to disable auto-upload of photos from the app, although it could also include configuration details such as the user name and password required for the app and its background agent to reach its corresponding cloud service. The UI for the *PhotoUploader* solution available in the sample code (shown in Figure 16-13) includes a simple *ToggleSwitch* (from the Windows Phone toolkit) with which the user can turn auto-upload on and off.

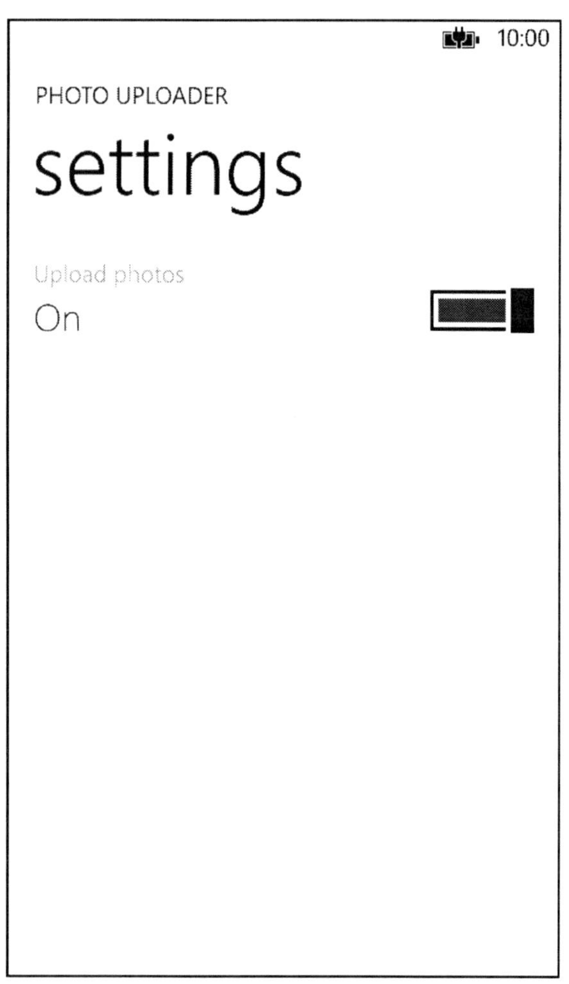

FIGURE 16-13 The Settings page for an auto-upload should include the ability to turn upload on and off.

Again, it should come as no surprise at this point that the way in which the system informs the app that it is being launched to handle a specific task is by including an *Action* query string parameter in the navigation URI. In this case, the interesting part of the navigation URI looks like this:

```
/MainPage.xaml?Action=ConfigurePhotosUploadSettings
```

Note As discussed in the Chapter 9, a *ResourceIntensiveTask* runs opportunistically based on the device's power and network state, among other factors. You should not rely on it running on a set interval.

Summary

For many people, smartphones are now the primary way by which they create, consume, and share photos. With a dedicated camera button and a vibrant Photos Hub aggregating photos from the cloud and the phone, Windows Phone has always made a great camera and photos experience a priority. The platform matches that great experience with a rich set of extensibility options for developers. In this section, you saw how you can perform simple tasks such as choosing a photo from the user's media library, all the way to creating a custom camera app.

CHAPTER 17

Networking and proximity

With the exception of games, there are few compelling mobile apps that do not rely in some way on a network connection, whether it is to retrieve data from or send it to the cloud, or to enable real-time interaction with other people and devices near and far. In Chapter 7, "Web connectivity," and Chapter 8, "Web services and the cloud," we cover the support in Windows Phone for HTTP and how you can build cloud services to support your app. In this chapter, we will round out our discussion of networking by covering the phone's support for socket communication and for connecting to nearby devices through Bluetooth and Near Field Communication (NFC), an area referred to as *proximity*.

Sockets

One of the significant gaps in the original Windows Phone platform was the lack of a socket API. Sockets support was added in Windows Phone 7.1, but it was limited to outbound connections—apps could not bind to a port and listen for incoming connections. Windows Phone 8 not only adds the ability to listen, it also supplements the Microsoft .NET socket API with the new Windows Runtime sockets API surface and the native Windows Sockets (WinSock) API. Each option has its advantages, depending on the platform you're targeting and whether you need to reuse existing networking libraries. The three options are outlined in Table 17-1.

TABLE 17-1 Socket API options for Windows Phone 8

API	Best usage
Windows Runtime sockets (*Windows.Networking.Sockets*)	■ New Windows Phone 8 apps ■ Apps using code targeting Windows 8/Windows Phone 8
.NET sockets (*System.Net.Sockets*)	■ Windows Phone 7.x apps ■ Apps using libraries with .NET socket dependencies
WinSock (*winsock2.h* and *ws2tcpip.h*)	Windows Phone 8 native apps using libraries with WinSock dependencies

All three types of API support both Transmission Control Protocol (TCP) and User Datagram Protocol (UDP) sockets. Table 17-2 provides a quick overview of the differences between TCP and UDP. In short, TCP is best suited in scenarios for which reliability and data integrity are more important than speed, whereas UDP is a better choice when you are willing to sacrifice some data loss and incorrect ordering of packets to obtain maximum performance.

TABLE 17-2 A comparison of TCP and UDP sockets

Property	TCP	UDP
Connection style	Connection-oriented. You must establish a connection with the endpoint with which you want to communicate before beginning to send data.	Connectionless. You do not need to establish a connection before sending data.
Reliability	Reliable. TCP endpoints always send ACK messages to acknowledge when messages are received, and TCP clients will attempt to resend lost packets.	Unreliable. Packets can be lost, and the protocol does not define a means for clients to learn about such losses.
Transmission type	Stream. Data is sent as an ordered stream of bytes, and the protocol guarantees that the ordering is maintained when the data is received at the endpoint.	Datagram. Data is sent as a series of individual messages, and the protocol provides no guarantees on the order in which they are delivered.
Delivery modes	Unicast. Each connection has exactly two endpoints, and only they can share data on the socket.	Unicast or Multicast. In a multicast socket, multiple endpoints can join in a multicast group and broadcast all data to all endpoints.

Tip The unreliable nature of UDP can be especially noticeable when transferring data over a cellular network because a significant proportion of transmitted packets can be dropped. If you use UDP sockets, consider testing with the Simulation Dashboard in Microsoft Visual Studio to validate how your app handles poor network conditions. For more information about the Simulation Dashboard, see Chapter 12, "Profiling and diagnostics."

The Windows Runtime sockets API

Windows Phone 8 includes the same Windows Runtime sockets API that is available in Windows 8. In addition to being available for both native and managed code, the Windows Runtime sockets API simplifies many of the common tasks involved in connecting and using sockets; it should be your default choice if you are starting a new Windows Phone 8 app.

To highlight the fact that Windows Runtime sockets are available on both Windows and Windows Phone, the *BasicSockets* app in the sample code shows a simple client/server socket scenario with a Windows 8 app acting as the server and a Windows Phone app acting as the client. The solution makes it possible for the two apps to exchange messages back and forth as you would see in an instant messaging app.

Note As mentioned earlier, Windows Phone 8 adds the ability for an app to bind to a socket and listen for incoming connections while the app is in the foreground, so the server role played by the Windows 8 app in this example could also be played by another Windows Phone app. However, if you want to create a connection between two Windows Phone devices that are in the same location—such as for a multiplayer game between two players in the same room—you should consider using proximity to establish the initial connection, as we will show later in this chapter.

Figure 17-1 shows the UI of the Windows 8 app, *SocketServer*. The left side of the screen contains configuration information for the listening socket. The IP address of the host machine is naturally fixed, but the user can specify the listening port and then click the Bind button to begin listening. On the right side of the screen are the conversation window and a *TextBox* for the user to enter new messages.

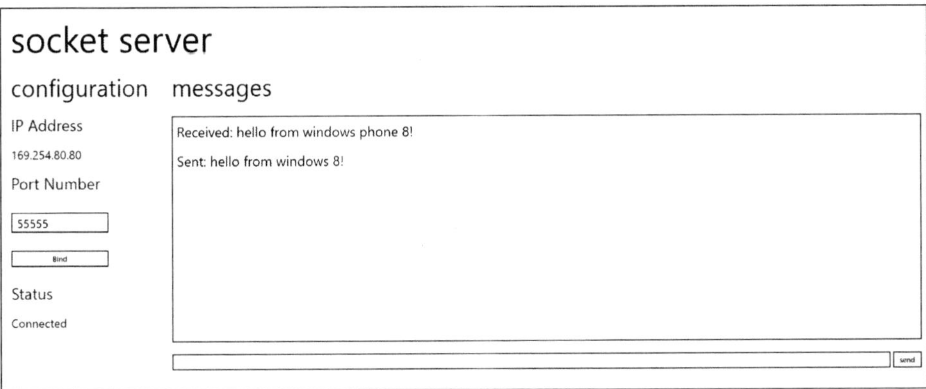

FIGURE 17-1 The Windows 8 app acts as the server for the instant messaging service.

Figure 17-2 shows the UI for the phone app, *SocketClient*. When the app starts, it shows a user control named *ConfigurationUserControl* within a pop-up message box in which the user can enter the connection details for the socket; that is, the IP address and port number shown on the left side of the screen in the *SocketServer* app. Of course, in a real app, you would not expect the user to enter this information manually. It might be hard-coded into the client, queried from a web service, or shared by proximity, as we will discuss later. After the user taps the connect button, the client app connects to the socket by using the configuration details provided, and the app is ready to start sending messages.

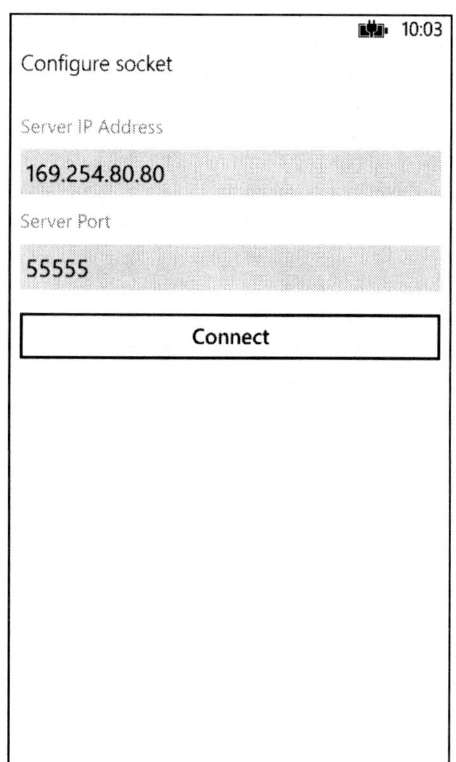

FIGURE 17-2 With the *SocketClient* app, the user can specify the connection and then start chatting.

The process of creating a socket between the client app and the server app begins when the server binds to a port and begins listening for incoming connections. Before the server app can do that, however, it needs two pieces of information: the host IP address and port. The server app queries the host IP address from the *NetworkInformation* class when the user initially navigates to the page, using the first available network adapter with a valid IP address. The port, on the other hand, is entered by the user through the UI. After the IP address is acquired and the port is entered, the user can click the Bind button to create the listener socket. The button's click event handler calls a helper method called *SetupSocketServer* to perform the binding.

Note We explicitly choose an IPv4 hostname because the *SocketServer* app needs to support both a Windows Phone 7 client and a Windows Phone 8 client. Although Windows Phone 8 supports IPv6, Windows Phone 7 does not.

```
private StreamSocketListener listener;
private StreamSocket serverSocket;
private HostName ipAddress;
private DataWriter dataWriter;
private DataReader dataReader;
private Guid internetProfileNetworkId;
```

```
protected override void OnNavigatedTo(NavigationEventArgs e)
{
     internetProfileNetworkId =
         NetworkInformation.GetInternetConnectionProfile().NetworkAdapter.NetworkItem.NetworkId;

     ipAddress = NetworkInformation.GetHostNames().FirstOrDefault
                                                  (host => IsIpv4NetworkHostName(host));

     ipAddressTextBlock.Text = ipAddress.CanonicalName;
}

private bool IsIpv4NetworkHostName(HostName host)
{
     var ip = host.IPInformation;
     if(ip == null)
         return false;

     if(ip.NetworkAdapter.NetworkItem.NetworkId != internetProfileNetworkId)
          return false;

     return host.Type == HostNameType.Ipv4;
}

private async Task SetupSocketServer()
{
     statusTextBlock.Text = "Initializing";

     listener = new StreamSocketListener();
     listener.ConnectionReceived += ConnectionReceived;

     await listener.BindEndpointAsync(ipAddress, portNumberTextBox.Text);

     statusTextBlock.Text = "Waiting for connection";
}
```

As you can see, very little code is required to set up the listener. We simply instantiate a *StreamSocketListener* object and bind it to a local endpoint by specifying the local IP address and port. After a connection is received, the system raises a *ConnectionReceived* event indicating that we are registered to handle with the *ConnectionReceived* method.

Note In a real app, you would probably want to perform some validation on your incoming connections.

The *ConnectionReceived* event arguments provide a *StreamSocket* object that acts as the Windows Runtime manifestation of the underlying TCP socket. The *StreamSocket* class includes properties for both the input and output streams of the socket. We use these streams to create a *DataReader* object and a *DataWriter* object, which will handle reading and writing bytes on the socket. These classes are part of the *Windows.Storage.Streams* namespace, and they are useful for dealing with any type of stream, not just sockets. Also notice that we are using the *CoreWindow* dispatcher to marshal updates to the UI thread—in this case, the Boolean *IsConnected* property that controls whether the Send button is enabled. This is conceptually equivalent to the *Dispatcher* in the *System.Windows.Deployment* class in Windows Phone.

```
private async void ConnectionReceived
    (StreamSocketListener sender, StreamSocketListenerConnectionReceivedEventArgs args)
{
    SendStatusUpdateToUIThread("Connected");

    serverSocket = args.Socket;

    dataReader = new DataReader(serverSocket.InputStream);
    dataWriter = new DataWriter(serverSocket.OutputStream);

    CoreApplication.MainView.CoreWindow.Dispatcher.RunAsync
        (CoreDispatcherPriority.Low, () =>
        {
            IsConnected = true;
        });

    WaitForMessage();
}
```

The *WaitForMessage* method called at the end of the *ConnectionReceived* event handler is responsible for listening for incoming messages on the input stream, reading them from the stream, and then posting them to the messages list in the UI. Because TCP itself does not dictate how data passed across the socket should be interpreted, the client and server need to agree on an application-level protocol in order to understand what each is sending to the other. For the *BasicSockets* solution, the apps send messages that begin with the length of the subsequent string in bytes, represented as an unsigned 32-bit integer, followed by the message itself. This makes the process of accepting a message straightforward: simply read the first four bytes of the stream to determine the length of the string and then use that length to determine how many additional bytes to read to acquire the full message. Note that reading from the stream is a two-step process. First, we must read a specific number of bytes into the *DataReader*. Then, we need to use one of the methods to read a particular data type, such as *ReadUInt32* or *ReadString*. Also note that calls to the *LoadAsync* method returns the number of bytes that were successfully read from the stream, so we can check whether that number matches the number we expected to receive. If not, something went wrong.

```
private async Task WaitForMessage()
{
    string receivedString = String.Empty;
    uint numBytesRead;

    try
    {
        while (true)
        {
            numBytesRead = await dataReader.LoadAsync(sizeof(uint));

            if (numBytesRead != sizeof(uint))
                return;

            // if we received a large number of bytes, it's probably a bug
```

```
                // log it and read the next message
                if (numBytesRead > 1000)
                    // log the bug
                    continue;

                uint numBytesInMessage = dataReader.ReadUInt32();

                numBytesRead = await dataReader.LoadAsync(numBytesInMessage);

                if (numBytesRead != numBytesInMessage)
                    return;

                receivedString = dataReader.ReadString(numBytesInMessage);

                await SendMessageToUIThread(receivedString);
            }
        }
        catch (Exception)
        {
            // something went wrong in the socket connection
        }
}

private async Task SendMessageToUIThread(string receivedString)
{
    CoreDispatcher dispatcher = CoreApplication.MainView.CoreWindow.Dispatcher;

    await dispatcher.RunAsync(Windows.UI.Core.CoreDispatcherPriority.Low, () =>
    {
        Messages.Add(String.Format("Received: {0}", receivedString));
    });
}
```

To send a message from the server app, the user must enter a message in the *TextBox* provided and then click the Send button. To send a message, the app must simply reverse the process shown for receiving messages, adhering to the protocol described earlier. In this case, we use the *Data Writer* to write an unsigned 32-bit integer representing the length of the message and then add the message itself. To transfer the data from the *DataWriter* buffer to the socket, we only need to call *StoreAsync*.

```
private void sendMessageButton_Click(object sender, RoutedEventArgs e)
{
    SendMessage(newMessageTextBox.Text);
    newMessageTextBox.Text = String.Empty;
}

private void SendMessage(string message)
{
    Messages.Add(String.Format("Sent: {0}", message));

    dataWriter.WriteUInt32(dataWriter.MeasureString(message));
    dataWriter.WriteString(message);

    dataWriter.StoreAsync();
}
```

Now that we've covered sending and receiving from the server app, we can briefly look at what is required from the client app. In short, because the Windows Runtime socket API surface is the same for the Windows 8 server app and the Windows Phone 8 client app, the code is mostly the same. The only significant difference between the two is the fact that the client app performs an explicit connection step rather than waiting for another app to connect. The *OnNavigatedTo* event handler for the phone app's main page instantiates the *ConfigurationUserControl* and displays it as a pop-up box. It also sets up an event handler that is raised when the user clicks the Connect button in the user control, indicating that she has provided the necessary information to connect to the server. The event handler uses the configuration information provided by the user to connect to the remote endpoint by using a *StreamSocket*, the same class used by the server app to send and receive data.

```
private StreamSocket clientSocket;
private ConfigurationUserControl configurationControl;
private Popup configurationPopup;
public ObservableCollection<string> Messages { get; private set; }

public MainPage()
{
    InitializeComponent();
    Messages = new ObservableCollection<string>();
    this.DataContext = this;
}

protected override void OnNavigatedTo(NavigationEventArgs e)
{
    configurationPopup = new Popup();
    configurationControl = new ConfigurationUserControl();
    configurationControl.SocketConfigurationComplete +=
        configurationControl_SocketConfigurationComplete;
    configurationPopup.Child = configurationControl;
    configurationPopup.IsOpen = true;
}

private async void configurationControl_SocketConfigurationComplete(object sender, EventArgs e)
{
    clientSocket = new StreamSocket();

    try
    {
        await clientSocket.ConnectAsync(new HostName
            (configurationControl.ServerIPAddress), configurationControl.ServerPort);
    }
    catch(Exception)
    {
        // connection failed - user will have to retry
        return;
    }

   configurationPopup.IsOpen = false;
   WaitForMessage();
}
```

Again, because the Windows Runtime sockets API is common between Windows and Windows Phone, the code to send and receive messages in the client is the same as we showed for the server.

Enabling Secure Sockets Layer

Windows Phone supports Secure Sockets Layer (SSL) for secure transmission of data over any network connection. To establish an SSL-protected socket, the client and server go through an elaborate handshaking procedure in which they use public key encryption to agree on a shared secret key that will be used for encrypting subsequent transmissions sent by the application layer. The Windows Runtime sockets framework hides the implementation of SSL to the app, so all that is required to encrypt a socket is to use the *ConnectAsync* overload that accepts a value from the *SocketProtectionLevel* enumeration, as shown in the following:

```
await secureSocket.ConnectAsync(hostName, hostService, SocketProtectionLevel.Ssl);
```

Keep in mind that SSL only protects data while it passes over the network. As soon as it reaches its destination, it is automatically decrypted. If you need to ensure that data is protected beyond the network, you must encrypt it separately before transmitting it.

.NET sockets

If you are building an app that targets Windows Phone 7.1, your only option for sockets support is the .NET sockets API found in the *System.Net.Sockets* namespace. The *DotNetSocketClient* project, included in the *BasicSockets* solution, is a Windows Phone 7.1 app that uses the .NET sockets API to connect to the same Windows 8 server app described in the previous section.

The app follows the same pattern as its Windows Phone 8 equivalent: a configuration screen is shown first and the app waits for the user to enter the necessary configuration details before attempting to connect. After the socket is connected, the app simultaneously waits for incoming messages and sends messages in response to user input in the provided *TextBox*. We will focus our attention on the process of connecting and receiving messages on the socket, because the code for sending messages is straightforward and not particularly different from the Windows Runtime socket APIs.

Like the Windows Runtime socket APIs, the .NET socket APIs are asynchronous, which means that you can avoid blocking the calling thread while you wait for bytes to arrive from the other party. There are two key differences of which you should be aware, however. First, the asynchronous .NET socket APIs are not implemented as "awaitable" tasks, so you cannot take advantage of the *await* keyword. Second, the .NET APIs are not *guaranteed* to operate asynchronously. For example, if you call *ReceiveAsync* to receive four bytes from a socket and those four bytes are already available, the *ReceiveAsync* call will return immediately, rather than raising an asynchronous event. As a result, you must always check the Boolean return value of the asynchronous methods to determine whether the operation completed synchronously or whether you should expect an asynchronous event to be raised. If the operation completed synchronously, you must invoke your event handler explicitly.

In the *DotNetSocketClient* project, the *ConfigurationComplete* event handler is called when the user finishes entering the details for the remote endpoint in the initial dialog. It uses the IP address and port provided to create an instance of the *SocketAsyncEventArgs* class, which represents an asynchronous socket operation and makes it possible for you to transfer state between invocation of an asynchronous method and its corresponding event handler. To initiate a socket operation, you pass the *SocketAsyncEventArgs* instance to one of the asynchronous methods such as *ConnectAsync* or *ReceiveAsync*. Rather than invoking those methods directly, however, we define the extension methods *ConnectAsyncEx* and *ReceiveAsyncEx*. As mentioned, the asynchronous .NET socket APIs have the potential to return synchronously in certain circumstances. The extension methods simply abstract that possibility away from the caller.

```
private void ConfigurationComplete(object sender, EventArgs e)
{
    var configurationControl = sender as ConfigurationUserControl;
    var ipAddress = IPAddress.Parse(configurationControl.ServerIPAddress);
    var ipEndpoint = new IPEndPoint(ipAddress, Int32.Parse(configurationControl.ServerPort));
    var clientSocketEventArgs = new SocketAsyncEventArgs();

    clientSocketEventArgs.RemoteEndPoint = ipEndpoint;
    clientSocketEventArgs.Completed += SocketEventCompleted;
    clientSocketEventArgs.UserToken = ReceivingMessageState.Uninitialized;

    clientSocket = new Socket(AddressFamily.InterNetwork, SocketType.Stream, ProtocolType.Tcp);
    clientSocket.ConnectAsyncEx(clientSocketEventArgs, SocketEventCompleted);
}

public static class SocketHelpers
{
    public static void ReceiveAsyncEx(
        this Socket socket,
        SocketAsyncEventArgs args,
        EventHandler<SocketAsyncEventArgs> handler)
    {
        var isAsync = socket.ReceiveAsync(args);
        if (!isAsync)
            Deployment.Current.Dispatcher.BeginInvoke(() => handler(socket, args));
    }

    public static void ConnectAsyncEx(
        this Socket socket,
        SocketAsyncEventArgs args,
        EventHandler<SocketAsyncEventArgs> handler)
    {
        var isAsync = socket.ConnectAsync(args);
        if (!isAsync)
            Deployment.Current.Dispatcher.BeginInvoke(() => handler(socket, args));
    }
}
```

Whether the socket operation completes synchronously or asynchronously, we always invoke the *SocketEventCompleted* event handler to handle it. Because *SocketEventCompleted* is a common event handler for a number of socket operations, it uses the *LastOperation* property on the *SocketAsync EventArgs* class to determine how to route the event. If the socket has just connected, for instance, we can close the configuration pop-up box and begin listening for incoming messages from the server by using the *HandleIncomingMessage* method.

```
private void SocketEventCompleted(object sender, SocketAsyncEventArgs e)
{
    if (e.SocketError != SocketError.Success)
    {
        Dispatcher.BeginInvoke(delegate
        {
            MessageBox.Show(e.SocketError.ToString());
            CloseSocket(e);
            return;
        });
    }

    switch (e.LastOperation)
    {
        case SocketAsyncOperation.Connect:
            Dispatcher.BeginInvoke(() => configurationPopup.IsOpen = false);
            HandleIncomingMessage(e);
            break;
        case SocketAsyncOperation.Receive:
            HandleIncomingMessage(e);
            break;
        case SocketAsyncOperation.Send:
            AddMessage(String.Format("Sent: {0}", e.UserToken.ToString()));
            break;
        default:
            break;
    }
}
```

The *HandleIncomingMessage* method implements a small state machine to manage the two-step process required to receive a message—namely, determining the size of the message and reading the message itself. State is managed by using the *UserToken* property of the *SocketAsyncEventArgs* class, which we set to a value in the custom *ReceivingMessageState* enumeration. When in the uninitialized state, we prepare to receive the size of the first message by creating a buffer that can receive an unsigned 32-bit integer and then listen on the socket for that message by using the *ReceiveAsyncEx* extension method. As soon as the message size is retrieved, we prepare the buffer to retrieve a message of that size and call *ReceiveAsyncEx* again. After the actual message is received and displayed in the UI, we reset the state and the buffer and prepare to receive another message.

```
private const uint BufferSize = 100;

private void HandleIncomingMessage(SocketAsyncEventArgs args)
{
    var state = (ReceivingMessageState)args.UserToken;

    switch (state)
    {
        case ReceivingMessageState.Uninitialized:
            args.SetBuffer(new byte[BufferSize], 0, sizeof(UInt32));
            args.UserToken = ReceivingMessageState.ExpectingSize;
            clientSocket.ReceiveAsyncEx(args, SocketEventCompleted);
```

```
                break;
            case ReceivingMessageState.ExpectingSize:
                if (args.BytesTransferred < sizeof(UInt32))
                {
                    CloseSocket(args);
                    return;
                }

                var textSize =
                    (int)IPAddress.NetworkToHostOrder(BitConverter.ToInt32(args.Buffer, 0));

                if (textSize >= BufferSize)
                {
                    CloseSocket(args);
                    return;
                }

                args.SetBuffer(0, textSize);
                args.UserToken = ReceivingMessageState.ExpectingText;
                clientSocket.ReceiveAsyncEx(args, SocketEventCompleted);

                break;
            case ReceivingMessageState.ExpectingText:
                if (args.BytesTransferred < args.Count)
                {
                    CloseSocket(args);
                    return;
                }

                string message = Encoding.UTF8.GetString(args.Buffer, 0, args.Count);
                AddMessage(String.Format("Received: {0}", message));

                args.SetBuffer(0, sizeof(UInt32));
                args.UserToken = ReceivingMessageState.ExpectingSize;
                clientSocket.ReceiveAsyncEx(args, SocketEventCompleted);

                break;
        }
    }

    public enum ReceivingMessageState
    {
        Uninitialized,
        ExpectingSize,
        ExpectingText,
        Error
    }
```

Which end(ian) is up?

A keen eye likely will have noticed this line of code in the *HandleIncomingMessage* method shown in the preceding example:

```
var textSize = (int)IPAddress.NetworkToHostOrder(BitConverter.ToInt32(args.Buffer, 0));
```

To understand the purpose of this code, we must discuss the notion of *endianness*, as it is critical to any type of network programming.

Endianness refers to the ordering of the bytes that make up a value within a stream or file. Consider the unsigned 32-bit integer that we've been using as a prefix to all messages to indicate message size. When represented in memory and in the stream passed to the socket, that value is broken down into four distinct bytes. To correctly interpret the value of that integer, it is important to know the order of those bytes. In big-endian ordering, the most significant byte—the one that contributes the largest proportion of the number's value—is stored first, at the lowest byte address. For example, the number 542 would be stored as follows (using hexadecimal notation):

00	00	02	1E
Byte 0	Byte 1	Byte 2	Byte 3

Big-endian ordering is consistent with the way that humans represent numbers in daily use. In the number 542, the most significant digit is the 5 and it is written in the left-most position. Little-endian ordering is exactly the opposite, with the most significant byte occupying the last byte address, meaning that the number 542 would be represented as follows:

1E	02	00	00
Byte 0	Byte 1	Byte 2	Byte 3

The main benefit of little-endian ordering is that you can read a number with a varying number of bits from a single memory address. For instance, suppose that you wanted to interpret 542 not as a 32-bit integer, but a 16-bit integer. In little-endian ordering, you could read the 16-bit version of 542 from the same address as the 32-bit version by simply taking fewer bits, whereas in big-endian ordering, you would need to jump ahead before starting to read. The Intel x86 architecture, which has been the primary basis for the Windows operating system for decades, uses little-endian ordering.

It should be obvious by now why the apps on either end of a socket connection must be aware of the endianness of the data that they are receiving. If you were to read the little-endian representation of 542 assuming big-endian ordering, you would get a result of 503,447,552. In common practice, network protocols transfer data by using big-endian ordering. The *DataReader* and *DataWriter* classes shown in the *SocketServer* code also use big-endian by default, though they can be configured to use little-endian through the *ByteOrder* property. On the other hand, most .NET APIs reflect the endianness of the underlying platform, which is usually little-endian. The *NetworkToHostOrder* method on the *IPAddress* class makes it possible for you to convert values from network byte order (big-endian) to the byte order that is appropriate for the platform where the app is running.

The WinSock API

The WinSock API dates back to the early 1990s and has been a core part of desktop Windows for numerous releases. Because the Windows Runtime APIs discussed earlier are available for use in native code and are generally easier to use, the WinSock API was not originally intended to be part of the supported API surface for Windows Phone 8. However, based on feedback from developers that were using a prerelease SDK to the Windows Phone 8 SDK—many of whom were looking to port existing native libraries with WinSock dependencies—it was added to the list of available Win32 APIs in the Windows Phone platform. The full list of available WinSock APIs are available at *http://msdn.microsoft.com/en-us/library/windowsphone/develop/jj662956(v=vs.105).aspx.*

Note WinSock is not available for Windows 8 store apps, so if you intend to use the same code to target both platforms, use Windows Runtime sockets.

Finding your app on nearby devices

The primary challenge in enabling peer-to-peer socket communication between apps running on different devices is discovery. The fact that an app on another device is bound to a socket and ready to accept connections is of little use if you don't know the IP address and the port on which it is listening. In the *BasicSockets* solution shown earlier, we used a rudimentary solution to this problem, whereby the server app displays its socket configuration data in the app UI, which can then be manually entered in the client app. Clearly, that is not a viable solution in a real app.

Windows Phone 8 takes advantage of two short-range wireless protocols to solve this problem when devices are nearby one another. The *PeerFinder* class in the *Windows.Networking.Proximity* namespace seamlessly combines Bluetooth and NFC to enable ad hoc discovery across devices. By default, the *PeerFinder* is configured to look for instances of the app that is calling it on nearby devices, using the app's *ProductId* as the key. However, as we will see later in the chapter, the app has the ability to expand the scope of what the system considers a peer to enable discovery of its equivalent app in Windows or to connect to other Bluetooth devices.

Note To use any of the APIs in the *Windows.Networking.Proximity* namespace, your app must declare the *ID_CAP_PROXIMITY* capability.

Although both are wireless standards designed to enable communication between nearby devices, Bluetooth and NFC have some significant differences, which are summarized in Table 17-3. The *PeerFinder* class accounts for these differences in the way that it uses each technology, as we will see later in this section.

TABLE 17-3 Summary of differences between Bluetooth and NFC

Property	Bluetooth	NFC
Range	About 10 meters for mobile phones	2–4 centimeters
Max transfer rate	2.1 Mbps	424 Kbps (actual transfer rate is 30–60 Kbps)
Max power usage	30 milliamps	15 milliamps
Max pairing time	6 seconds (not including user input)	0.1 seconds
Security	Shared key encryption using a key generated during pairing	None: extremely short range limits the practicality of man-in-the-middle attacks

Note The Windows Phone emulator does not support emulation of either a Bluetooth radio or an NFC radio. To test apps by using APIs in the *Windows.Networking.Proximity* namespace, you must use a real device.

The *SimplePeerFinder* solution in the sample code illustrates how an app can search for and connect to peers nearby with Bluetooth and NFC. The app includes one button to toggle its visibility to nearby peers and another to proactively search for peers. When peer devices are found, they are shown in a *ListBox*, in which the user can choose one and establish a socket connection. The UI for the app is shown in Figure 17-3.

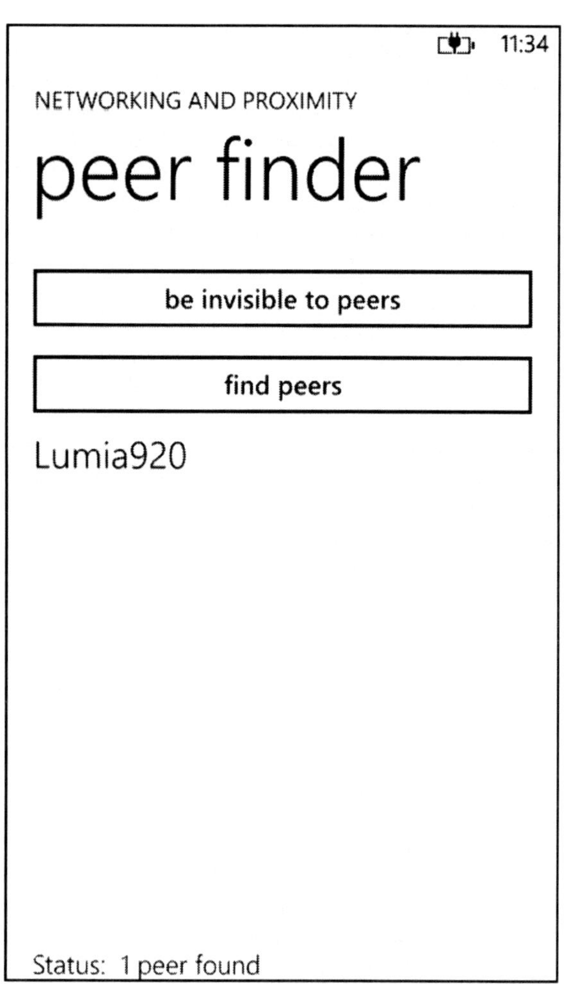

FIGURE 17-3 The *SimplePeerFinder* app can toggle visibility to other devices and search for peers.

All of the core logic and state for the app is maintained in the *PeerFinderViewModel*. To search for peers or allow peers to find the current device, the app must start the *PeerFinder* service. When the user presses the top button in the app, the main page calls *SetPeerVisibility* to toggle the *PeerFinder* service on and off as well as setting up and tearing down two event handlers: one for the *Connection Requested* event, which will be raised if the app receives an incoming Bluetooth request from a peer, and one for the *TriggeredConnectedStateChanged* event, which will be raised for each of the states associated with tap-to-connect, a feature that we will see later in this section.

```
public void SetPeerVisibility(bool visible)
{
    if (visible && !IsVisibleToPeers)
    {
        PeerFinder.ConnectionRequested += ConnectionRequested;
        PeerFinder.TriggeredConnectionStateChanged += TriggeredConnectionStateChanged;
        PeerFinder.Start();
        ConnectionStatus = "Visible to peers";
        IsVisibleToPeers = true;
    }
    else
    {
        PeerFinder.Stop();
        PeerFinder.ConnectionRequested -= ConnectionRequested;
        PeerFinder.TriggeredConnectionStateChanged -= TriggeredConnectionStateChanged;
        ConnectionStatus = "Invisible to peers";
        IsVisibleToPeers = false;
    }
}
```

After the *PeerFinder* service is started, the app can discover peers in either of two ways: browsing nearby devices by using Bluetooth or by asking the user to tap his device to another to exchange information through NFC.

Finding peers through Bluetooth

The *FindAllPeersAsync* method automatically discovers nearby devices where the app is running in the foreground and advertising its availability through the *PeerFinder* service. It returns a collection of *PeerInformation* objects that we can provide to the user from which he can choose. Note that browsing for nearby peers by using *FindAllPeersAsync* requires that Bluetooth be enabled on the calling device, so you should always wrap it in a try/catch block and provide an appropriate error message to the user.

Tip If *FindAllPeersAsync* fails because Bluetooth is disabled on the device, consider providing a button or hyperlink that takes the user directly to Bluetooth settings so that she can turn it on. You can do this by using the *Launcher* class:

```
Windows.System.Launcher.LaunchUriAsync(new Uri("ms-settings-bluetooth:"));

private const uint BluetoothDisabledHResult = "0x8007048F";

public async Task FindPeersAsync()
{
    ConnectionStatus = "Searching for peers";
    IReadOnlyList<PeerInformation> peers = null;

    try
    {
        peers = await PeerFinder.FindAllPeersAsync());
    }
    catch (Exception ex)
    {
        if ((uint)ex.HResult == BluetoothDisabledHResult)
        {
            ConnectionStatus = "Bluetooth is turned off";
            return;
        }
        else
        {
            ConnectionStatus = "Connection failed";
            return;
        }
    }

    if (peers.Count > 0)
    {
        // update peersListBox
        Peers = (List<PeerInformation>)peers;
        ConnectionStatus = peers.Count == 1 ? "1 peer found"
                                            : String.Format("{0} peers found",
                                                            peers.Count);
    }
    else
    {
        ConnectionStatus = "No peers found";
    }
}
```

Note The *PeerInformation* class includes a *DisplayName* property that can be used to represent the peer device in the app. By default, *DisplayName* is the name of the device, but you can provide a custom value by setting the *DisplayName* property on the *PeerFinder* class.

The app displays the list of returned peers and allows the user to choose a device to which he would like to connect. In the *SelectionChanged* event handler, we get the *PeerInformation* instance associated with the selected item and pass it to the *ConnectToPeerAsync* method in the view model.

```
// MainPage.xaml.cs
private async void peersListBox_SelectionChanged(object sender, SelectionChangedEventArgs e)
{
    if(peersListBox.SelectedItem == null)
        return;

    peersListBox.IsEnabled = false;

    PeerInformation peer = (PeerInformation)peersListBox.SelectedItem;
    await App.PeerFinderViewModel.ConnectToPeerAsync(peer);

    peersListBox.IsEnabled = true;
}

// PeerFinderViewModel.cs
public async Task ConnectToPeerAsync(PeerInformation peerInfo)
{
    PeerSocket = await PeerFinder.ConnectAsync(peerInfo);
    OnSocketStateChanged
        (new SocketStateChangedEventArgs { SocketState = SocketState.Connected });
}
```

The call to *ConnectAsync* causes the *ConnectionRequested* event to be raised on the peer device. The *PeerInformation* instance for the device initiating the connection is passed in the event arguments and can be used to acquire the socket by using the same *ConnectAsync* method. In the *ConnectAsync* call, the *PeerFinder* will simultaneously try to create a connection by using both Wi-Fi and Bluetooth, if both are available. If it is able to create a Wi-Fi connection within a short timeout period (currently 500 milliseconds), it will opt for that transport; otherwise, it will take the first successful connection.

```
private async void ConnectionRequested(object sender, ConnectionRequestedEventArgs args)
{
    PeerInformation peer = args.PeerInformation;
    StreamSocket peerSocket = await PeerFinder.ConnectAsync(peer);
}
```

With the socket connection established, the two apps can operate just as they would if they had created the connection by any other means. Note that you can only maintain one active connection per peer device, so a successful connection will immediately cause the device to stop broadcasting availability to that peer. If you need to create a new connection for any reason, you will need to dispose of the socket and reconnect.

Finding peers through tap-to-connect

The ability to perform peer discovery through Bluetooth is significantly easier than asking the user to enter an IP address and port number in the app, but it still has certain drawbacks. First, it requires that the app be running in the foreground on both devices, with each broadcasting its availability to potential peers. It also requires that the user choose a peer from a list of options that might not be immediately recognizable. Both of these requirements are intended to deal with the possibility that people who happen to be nearby each other with the same app installed on their devices are not necessarily interested in creating a connection between them. The extremely short range of NFC offers a convenient solution to this problem: by requiring that the two people interested in creating a peer-to-peer connection between devices bring them to within 4 cm of one another, the system can make strong assumptions about their intent.

When the *SimplePeerFinder* app is in the foreground and the *PeerFinder* service has been started, tapping the device to another device with *SimplePeerFinder* installed triggers the receiving device to display a prompt asking the user whether she would like to start the app running on the sending phone, as demonstrated in Figure 17-4. If the app is not installed on the receiving device, the prompt provides the option to go to the Windows Phone Store to get it.

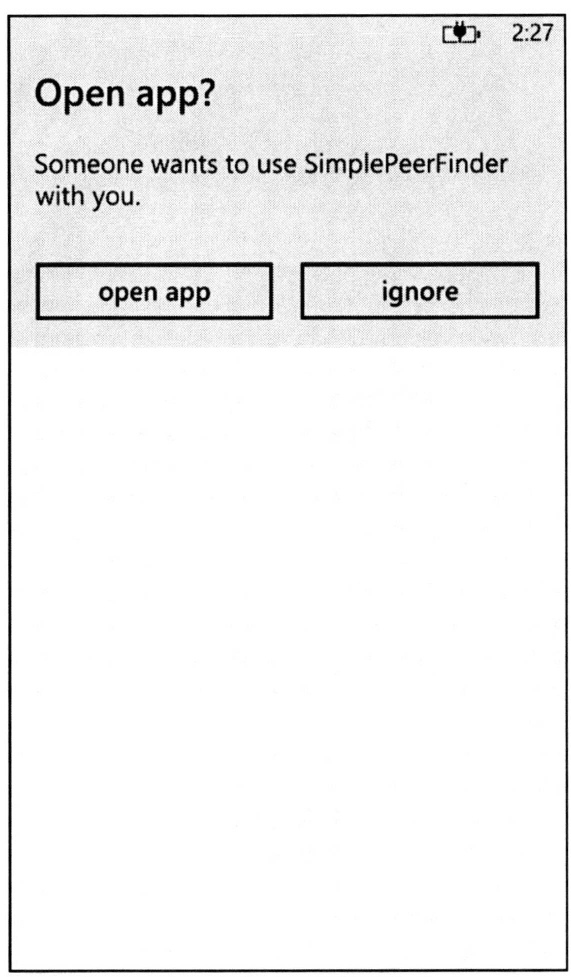

FIGURE 17-4 You can tap devices together to start an app by using NFC.

Tip If you do not see a prompt like the one shown in Figure 17-4 within one to two seconds of tapping devices, try pulling them apart and tapping again.

When the user opens the app on the target device, it is launched to its primary navigation page (as defined in the app manifest) but with an additional query string parameter indicating that it was launched by tap-to-connect and should prepare to connect. Assuming that the app's primary page is default *MainPage.xaml*, its navigation URI would look like this:

```
/MainPage.xaml?ms_nfp_launchargs=Windows.Networking.Proximity.PeerFinder:StreamSocket
```

Seeing this string in the navigation URI is a cue to the app to immediately start the *PeerFinder* service and prepare to establish a connection with the initiating device. In fact, by the time the dialog shown in Figure 17-4 appears on screen, all of the necessary information to establish a connection between the two devices has been shared, so the only thing remaining is for the app on the receiving device to accept it. In the *OnNavigatedTo* event handler, we add a check for the *ms_nfp_launchargs* query string parameter and, if it is found, call the *HandleLaunchByTap* method on the view model. Handling the tap gesture involves turning on the *PeerFinder* service and setting up a handler for the *TriggeredConnectionStateChanged* event, which is raised for the various states involved in the tap gesture.

```
// MainPage.xaml.cs

protected override void OnNavigatedTo(NavigationEventArgs e)
{
    if (NavigationContext.QueryString.ContainsKey("ms_nfp_launchargs") &&
        e.NavigationMode == NavigationMode.New)
    {
        App.PeerFinderViewModel.HandleLaunchByTap();
    }
}

public void HandleLaunchByTap()
{
    SetPeerVisibility(true);
    OnSocketStateChanged
        (new SocketStateChangedEventArgs { SocketState = SocketState.Connecting });
}

private void TriggeredConnectionStateChanged
    (object sender, TriggeredConnectionStateChangedEventArgs args)
{
    if(args.State == TriggeredConnectState.Completed)
        StreamSocket peerSocket = args.Socket;
}
```

In the *SimplePeerFinder* app, we are primarily concerned with the *Completed* state, which actually provides the *StreamSocket* instance. However, the other states can be useful for establishing the client/server relationship between the devices. They are also useful if you plan to create UI in your app that guides the user through the tap-to-connect gesture—a good idea given the novelty of NFC in mobile devices. The following states are the most important:

- **PeerFound** Raised when the tap gesture is complete. At this point, all information required to establish the connection has been transferred, so you can provide a UI cue that the users can pull their devices apart.
- **Connecting** Raised on the device that initiated the tap gesture and will act as the client.
- **Listening** Raised on the device that received the tap gesture and will act as the server.

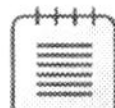

Note The determination of which device initiated the tap gesture is based on the way that the two NFC radios come into contact with one another and is effectively arbitrary as far as the user is concerned. However, because many peer-to-peer apps require that each device assume either a client role or a server role, the *Connecting* and *Listening* events are provided as a convenience for establishing this relationship.

Reconnecting without retapping

After the user has established a connection with another device by tapping, you want to avoid asking her to perform that step again if the socket happens to drop, which sometimes happens on a mobile device. In addition to the inherent network challenges introduced by mobility, the app process is always subject to termination when it goes to the background if the system needs to repurpose its resources, a process known as *tombstoning*, which we discuss in Chapter 2, "App model and navigation." Even though the system keeps a record of the app's existence in the backstack, its entire process space and any allocated memory are destroyed, meaning that any active sockets are lost.

The proximity service provides mitigation to this problem by allowing apps that temporarily lose connectivity due to network fluctuations or tombstoning to reconnect to a previous peer without having to ask the user to tap again. When two users perform the initial tap gesture, the proximity service on each device stores the configuration information for the other device in a lookup table indexed by a unique identifier for the peer device. When connectivity drops temporarily, each app can attempt to reconnect by providing the identifier and allowing the proximity service to run through the available connection options that it originally received from the peer. Because the proximity service maintains all possible connection routes, it is entirely possible that two apps connected over a Bluetooth socket could be reconnected over Wi-Fi in an instant with just one call to *ConnectAsync*.

Note Reconnection without retapping is only available in Windows Phone. It will not work in Windows 8.

The first step in re-establishing a connection is of course to determine that the connection has dropped in the first place. We define the *BeginListeningOnSocket* method to run a loop that listens for incoming messages on a background thread and call it every time the app successfully creates a socket connection to a peer.

```
private void HandleSocketStateChanged(object sender, SocketStateChangedEventArgs args)
{
    switch (args.SocketState)
    {
        case SocketState.Connected:
            UpdateConnectionStatus
                (SocketState.Connected,
                 String.Format("Connected to {0} on port {1}",
                 PeerSocket.Information.RemoteAddress.CanonicalName,
                 PeerSocket.Information.RemotePort));

            ThreadPool.QueueUserWorkItem(BeginListeningOnSocket);
            break;
        case SocketState.Connecting:
            UpdateConnectionStatus(SocketState.Connecting, "Establishing connection...");
            break;
        case SocketState.Disconnected:
            UpdateConnectionStatus(SocketState.Disconnected, "Disconnected");
            ConnectSocketAsync(remoteRawHostName, remoteService);
            break;
        case SocketState.Failed:
            UpdateConnectionStatus(SocketState.Failed, "Failed to connect");
            break;
    }
}
```

Before it begins listening for incoming data, *BeginListeningOnSocket* captures the identity of the remote host so that we can use it to re-establish a connection later. As mentioned earlier, the proximity service maintains a lookup table of connection information based on an opaque identifier created for the peer device when the initial tap takes place. That identifier is surfaced through the *RawName* property on the *RemoteHostName* class; thus, that is the critical value to persist for any attempt to reconnect.

To exercise the communication channel established between the devices, we add the ability for the app to send a test message, a 32-bit integer representation of the number zero. On the receiving side, the app anticipates these test messages by attempting to read four bytes from the socket at a time by using *ReadAsync*. If the socket disconnects, the call to *ReadAsync* will return 0 bytes, allowing the app to begin attempting to reconnect. Keep in mind that this strategy for detecting disconnects only works if the remote endpoint gracefully closes the connection. If the remote host is abruptly terminated for some reason, *ReadAsync* might never return. If detecting abrupt disconnects quickly is important, consider implementing a heartbeat function that periodically sends a short message over the socket connection to ensure that it is still alive. When the connection is deemed to have been lost, the app closes its end of the socket and raises its *OnSocketStateChanged* event, which triggers the reconnection logic. If the app successfully receives data from the socket, it acknowledges it by using the *VibrateController* to vibrate the device.

```
private async void BeginListeningOnSocket(object state)
{
    if (PeerSocket == null || PeerSocket.Information == null) return;

    remoteRawHostName = PeerSocket.Information.RemoteHostName.RawName;
    remoteService = PeerSocket.Information.RemoteServiceName;

    DataReader socketReader = new DataReader(PeerSocket.InputStream);
    IBuffer socketCheckBuffer = new Windows.Storage.Streams.Buffer(sizeof(uint32));
    while (true)
    {
        try
        {
            var messageBuffer = await PeerSocket.InputStream.ReadAsync
                                 (socketCheckBuffer,
                                  sizeof(uint32),
                                  InputStreamOptions.None);

            if (messageBuffer.Length < sizeof(uint32))
            {
                CloseSocket();
                OnSocketStateChanged
                    (new SocketStateChangedEventArgs
                        { SocketState = SocketState.Disconnected }
                    );

                return;
            }
            else
            {
                var vibrateController = Microsoft.Devices.VibrateController.Default;
                vibrateController.Start(TimeSpan.FromMilliseconds(500));
            }
        }
        catch (Exception ex)
        {
            CloseSocket();
            OnSocketStateChanged
                (new SocketStateChangedEventArgs
                    { SocketState = SocketState.Disconnected });

            return;
        }
    }
}
```

The *ConnectSocketAsync* makes 10 attempts to re-establish a connection with the peer device. This simplistic retry strategy works fine for cases in which the socket dropped because of a temporary network fluctuation, but both apps remained in the foreground on their respective devices. However, if the reason that the socket dropped was that the app was tombstoned while the user navigated away to send an SMS or check an email, it's possible that all 10 attempts will time out before the user returns and reactivates the app. In a real app, you should consider a more sophisticated retry strategy, such as spacing out retries at ever lengthening intervals. Note, however, that there is a short window (currently six minutes) for re-establishing the connection without having to tap devices again. After that window closes, the proximity service ages out the configuration information that it was maintaining for the peer.

```
public async Task ConnectSocketAsync(string hostName, string hostService)
{
    PeerSocket = new StreamSocket();

    int attempts = 0;

    while (attempts < 10)
    {
        try
        {
            OnSocketStateChanged
                (new SocketStateChangedEventArgs { SocketState = SocketState.Connecting });

            await PeerSocket.ConnectAsync(new HostName(hostName), hostService);

            OnSocketStateChanged
                (new SocketStateChangedEventArgs { SocketState = SocketState.Connected });

            return;
        }
        catch(Exception)
        {
            attempts++;
        }
    }

    OnSocketStateChanged(new SocketStateChangedEventArgs { SocketState = SocketState.Failed });
}
```

To facilitate reconnection following tombstoning, you must store the configuration information for the peer device in the app state property bag during the app's *Deactivated* event handler and then recover it during the *Activated* event handler.

```
private void Application_Deactivated(object sender, DeactivatedEventArgs e)
{
    if (PeerFinderViewModel.PeerSocket != null)
    {
        try
        {
            PhoneApplicationService.Current.State["RemoteHostName"] =
                PeerFinderViewModel.PeerSocket.Information.RemoteHostName.RawName;
            PhoneApplicationService.Current.State["RemoteService"] =
                PeerFinderViewModel.PeerSocket.Information.RemoteServiceName;
        }
        catch (Exception) { }

        PeerFinderViewModel.CloseSocket();
    }
}
private void Application_Activated(object sender, ActivatedEventArgs e)
{
    if (PeerFinderViewModel == null)
    {
        PeerFinderViewModel = new PeerFinderViewModel();

        if (PhoneApplicationService.Current.State.ContainsKey("RemoteHostName"))
        {
            PeerFinder.Start();

            string remoteHostName =
                (string)PhoneApplicationService.Current.State["RemoteHostName"];
            string remoteService =
                (string)PhoneApplicationService.Current.State["RemoteService"];

            PeerFinderViewModel.ConnectSocketAsync(remoteHostName, remoteService);
        }
    }
}
```

With the infrastructure in place to enable reconnection following a dropped socket, we can now try it out. To simulate a temporary loss of connection, we add a Disconnect Socket button to the main page (see Figure 17-5). The button's click event handler calls the *CloseSocket* method on the view model, which sets the socket to null and causes both endpoints to initiate their reconnection logic. Observe that we have also added a button to send a test message, as described earlier.

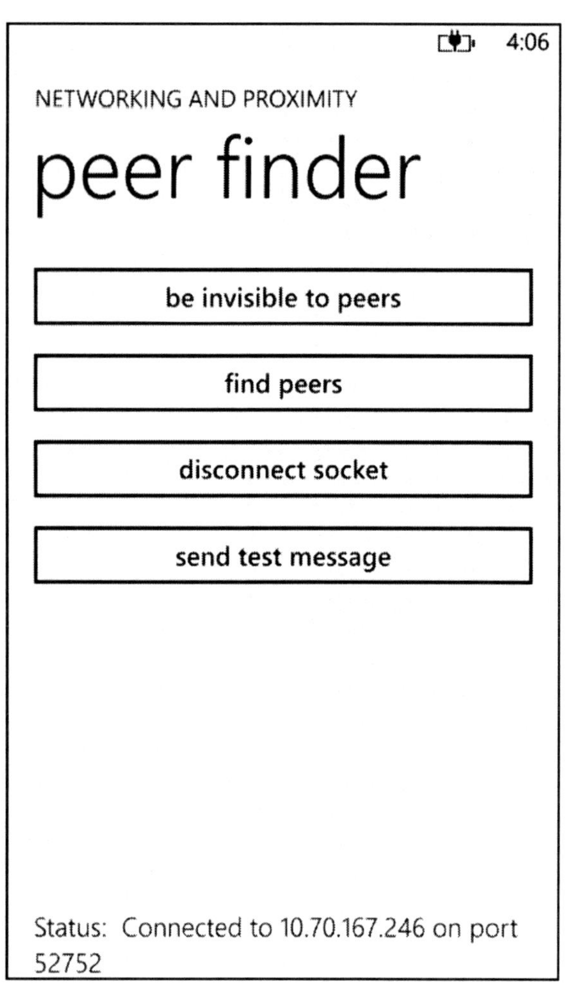

FIGURE 17-5 The Disconnect Socket button simulates a lost network connection and triggers reconnection logic.

Tap-to-connect with a Windows 8 app

As mentioned earlier, Windows Phone uses an app's *ProductId* as the key to finding other instances of the app on nearby devices. It's also possible to connect a Windows Phone 8 app to its counterpart on Windows 8; however, because the two apps do not share a common identifier, you need to give the proximity service some help.

The *PeerFinder* class includes an *AlternateIdentities* property that you can use to provide other identifiers for your app that the system should look for when browsing for peers, in addition to the built-in *ProductId*. For a Windows 8 app, the primary app identifier is known as the Package Family Name (PFN), which you can find in the app manifest. Figure 17-6 shows the PFN in the Visual Studio manifest editor.

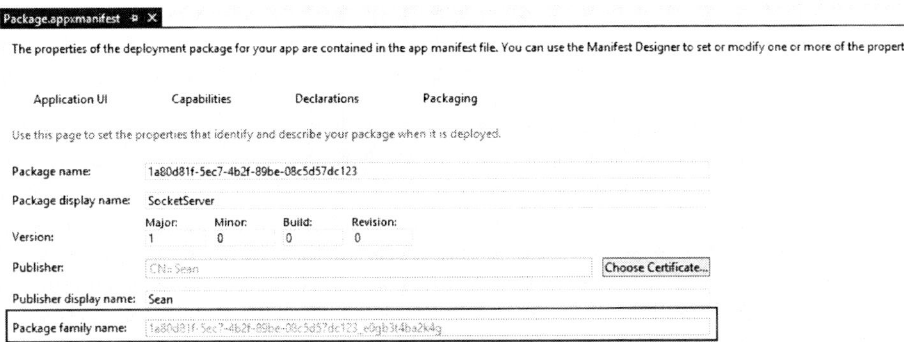

FIGURE 17-6 You can find the Package Family Name in the Windows 8 app manifest.

The *AlternateIdentities* property is a dictionary, so you must provide it with a key-value pair, matching the identity type to the identifier. For a Windows app, the identity type is simply "Windows":

```
PeerFinder.AlternateIdentities["Windows"] =
    "1a80d81f-5ec7-4b2f-89be-08c5d57dc123_e0gb3t4ba2k4g";
```

Of course, the Windows app must reciprocate the agreement by adding the *ProductId* of the Windows Phone app to its set of alternate identities.

```
PeerFinder.AlternateIdentities["WindowsPhone"] = "{64a2de20-9a89-464d-994b-8bf15585330f}";
```

Note Although both Windows and Windows Phone support browsing for nearby devices in addition to tap-to-connect, they use different mechanisms to search for and connect to peers. Windows uses Wi-Fi Direct, a short-range wireless protocol by which two Wi-Fi–enabled devices can connect with one another directly without requiring an intermediate access point. Windows Phone, as we've discussed, uses Bluetooth for this purpose; it does not support Wi-Fi Direct. Consequently, the only way to establish a connection between a Windows Phone app and a Windows app is by tap-to-connect.

Connecting to other Bluetooth devices

In the previous section, we reviewed how the proximity APIs create a degree of abstraction over the Bluetooth and NFC protocols, making it easier to find other instances of your app running on nearby devices. However, because Bluetooth is available on a wide array of devices, ranging from heart rate monitors to toy helicopters, you will occasionally need a way to connect directly over that protocol.

One of the defining characteristics of Bluetooth is that it generally requires pairing—a process of mutual authentication that creates a secure connection between the two devices. When used in the context of the proximity APIs described in the previous section, pairing is performed silently by virtue of the fact that the same app is running in the foreground and looking for peer connections on both devices. When connecting to an embedded Bluetooth device, that form of pairing is not possible. As a result, the user must go through a manual pairing process in the phone's Bluetooth settings before an app can connect to the external device. You can send the user directly to the device's Bluetooth settings and request pairing as follows:

```
Windows.System.Launcher.LauncherUriAsync(
    new Uri("ms-settings-bluetooth:pairing?AutoDismiss=true"));
```

As soon as the devices are paired, the app can use the same alternate identities mechanism described earlier for connecting to Windows 8 peers to find any nearby paired Bluetooth devices by using *FindAllPeersAsync*. There are two ways to configure *AlternateIdenties* for embedded Bluetooth devices, as described in Table 17-4.

TABLE 17-4 *AlternateIdentities* settings for embedded Bluetooth devices

Alternate identity	Results of *FindAllPeersAsync*
`PeerFinder.AlternateIdentities["Bluetooth:Paired"] = "";`	Returns all devices paired with this phone. In most cases, the *ServiceName* property of the returned *PeerInformation* instances will be empty because most embedded Bluetooth devices listen on a hardcoded port (usually port 1). You simply need to provide that hardcoded port when subsequently calling *ConnectAsync*.
`PeerFinder.AlternateIdentities["Bluetooth:SDP"] = "<service GUID>";`	Returns all devices advertising a service with the provided GUID by using the Service Discovery Protocol (SDP). In this case, returned *PeerInformation* instances will have a *ServiceName* property matching the provided service GUID.

NFC

We have already seen how you can use NFC as a fast and simple way to initiate a connection between apps running on two different devices. As with Bluetooth, though, there are a number of uses for NFC technology apart from initiating a socket connection. Indeed, NFC offers several key advantages over other short-range wireless protocols:

- NFC radios draw very little power, which means that they can remain on all the time without significantly affecting the device's battery life. This makes it possible for the user to tap her device to another NFC-enabled device without any prior setup.
- Data can be read from unpowered NFC tags, providing an inexpensive way to connect real-world objects to mobile devices. For instance, a movie poster can include an NFC tag that, when tapped, sends the user to a trailer for the film.
- Because users have to perform a deliberate tapping action to active the NFC radio, the phone's user experience can make stronger assumptions about their intent.

The *ProximityDevice* class in the *Windows.Networking.Proximity* namespace provides the entry point for interacting with the NFC radio directly. We will review two examples of NFC functionality that you might want to include in your app: reading and writing NFC tags, and sharing URIs across devices.

Note One of the nascent applications of NFC is mobile payment. See Chapter 20, "The Wallet," for a discussion of NFC mobile payment support in Windows Phone.

Reading and writing NFC tags

NFC tags are unpowered NFC chips that can be read by an NFC-enabled mobile phone or other NFC devices. Tags generally have very limited storage (usually less than 1 kilobyte), so they are best suited for storing short strings and URIs that can redirect the user to more information. They can also include the necessary details to directly start an app or redirect the user to the Windows Phone Store to acquire it if it is not already installed.

You can purchase NFC tags online fairly inexpensively—usually $1 to $2 per tag. However, you must ensure that you purchase tags that have been preformatted for the NFC Data Exchange Format (NDEF) because that is the only format supported by Windows Phone, and it is not possible to format tags from the phone.

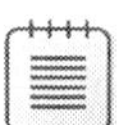

Note Windows Phone apps cannot set tags as read-only, so if you need to place the tags in a public place, you should consider purchasing an NFC accessory for your device that supports write protection.

The *NfcReaderWriter* solution in the sample code illustrates how to read and write several types of messages onto NFC tags. The app can write URIs, strings, and an app link to a tag and read back the strings. URIs and app links are automatically handled by the system and are not delivered to the app. The UI for the app is shown in Figure 17-7.

To perform any read or write operations with the NFC chip on the phone, you must first acquire a reference to it through the *GetDefault* factory method, which we do in the main page constructor.

```
ProximityDevice device;

public MainPage()
{
    InitializeComponent();
    device = ProximityDevice.GetDefault();
}
```

The *ProximityDevice* class contains a set of methods that initiate publication of a message through the NFC chip and a corresponding set of methods to stop publishing. Each publish method returns a message identifier that can be used to subsequently stop publishing the message. There are also events to indicate when the device comes within range of another NFC chip and when it leaves that range, making it easy to create UI in the app that guides the user through the tapping process.

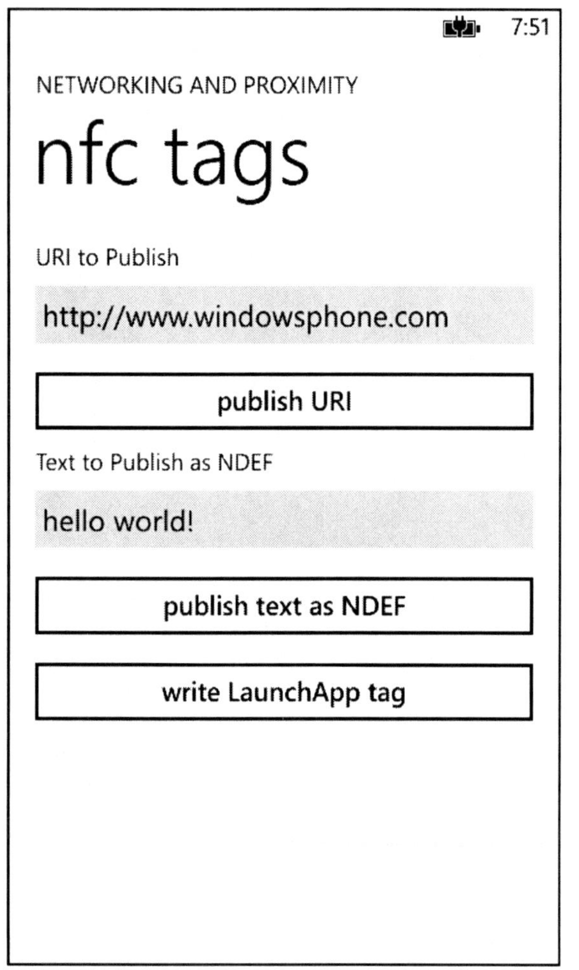

FIGURE 17-7 With the *NfcReaderWriter* solution, you can write content to unpowered NFC tags.

All messages published by NFC from Windows Phone are ultimately written in the NDEF record format, a standard for NFC data exchange. The *PublishBinaryMessage* method used to write the tags provides the flexibility to either write the NDEF record directly from the app or to use a higher level abstraction to write simple types such as strings and URIs, which can be translated to standard NDEF records by the NFC driver. The way that an app indicates which type of message it would like to publish is through its message type, which is the first parameter to the *PublishBinaryMessage* method.

Writing URIs to tags

We will first illustrate how to write a URI to the tag by using the abstraction layer. In particular, we will use the *WindowsUri* message type, which expects the content of the message to be a UTF-16LE (that is, 16-bit, Little-Endian) string containing a URI. The other high-level message types are *Windows Mime*, which expects content of the specified MIME type, such as image/jpeg, and *Windows*, which can include custom binary content. In each case, you can append "WriteTag" to the message type to indicate that you want to write the content to a static NFC tag.

```
private void publishUriToTagButton_Click(object sender, RoutedEventArgs e)
{
    if (String.IsNullOrWhiteSpace(uriToPublishTextBox.Text))
        return;

    statusTextBlock.Text = "Start tap";

    IBuffer buffer = Encoding.Unicode.GetBytes(uriToPublishTextBox.Text).AsBuffer();
    device.PublishBinaryMessage("WindowsUri:WriteTag", buffer, MessageTransmittedCallback);
}
```

When the data has been transferred, the system invokes the callback method that we specified in the original call to *PublishBinaryMessage*. This provides an opportunity to stop publishing the message and provide status to the user. Observe that the callback is done on a background thread, so any UI updates must be marshaled back to the UI thread by using the dispatcher.

```
private void MessageTransmittedCallback(ProximityDevice sender, long messageId)
{
    sender.StopPublishingMessage(messageId);

    Deployment.Current.Dispatcher.BeginInvoke(() =>
    {
        statusTextBlock.Text = "Tap completed";
    });
}
```

Note In this case, we are only stopping the publication of the message when receiving a successful callback. In a real app, you should persist the message ID returned from *PublishBinaryMessage* and stop publishing the message after a reasonable timeout period, such as 10 seconds, when it is no longer likely that the user will perform the tap.

After the tag is successfully written, tapping the device against it again will trigger a system prompt, asking the user if he would like to accept the content from the tag, as illustrated in Figure 17-8.

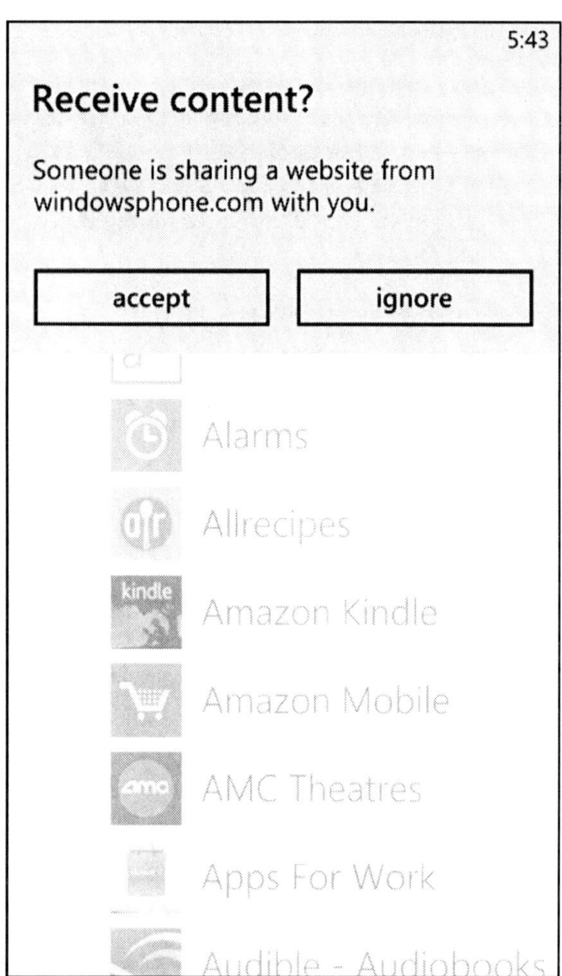

FIGURE 17-8 URI messages are intercepted by the system and result in a confirmation prompt.

Writing NDEF messages directly

Publishing an NDEF message is very similar, except that you create the NDEF records yourself. NDEF is a standard binary format defined by the NFC Forum, the primary standards body for near-field communication. An NDEF message can be made up of one or more NDEF records, each of which contains a header that includes information about the size and type of the record. The record type can be a common standard, such as a URI or a MIME type, or a custom type defined by the app. Windows Phone uses the record type to determine how to handle incoming NFC data when it is read from a tag or another device. If the content is a URI or a MIME type, the phone will display a prompt like the one shown in Figure 17-8, offering to open the appropriate app. If the type is not natively understood by the platform, it will pass it along to the foreground app if it is subscribed for messages of that type.

Because formatting binary messages can be error prone, it is preferable to use a common library whenever possible. The NDEF Library for Proximity APIs available on CodePlex (*http://ndef.codeplex.com*) is one such library for creating standard NDEF messages. The NDEF Library contains strongly typed classes for creating records based on the standard NFC record types and for custom types that are useful on the phone, such as geocoordinates and telephone numbers. In our case, we are creating a simple text-based record according to the string provided by the user, so we will create a type from the CodePlex library, *NdefTextRecord*, and add it to the message.

```
private void publishNdefMessageToTagButton_Click(object sender, RoutedEventArgs e)
{
    NdefTextRecord textNdefRecord = new NdefTextRecord();
    textNdefRecord.Text = textToPublishTextBox.Text;

    NdefMessage ndefMessage = new NdefMessage { textNdefRecord };

    ProximityDevice.GetDefault().PublishBinaryMessage
        ("NDEF:WriteTag", ndefMessage.ToByteArray().AsBuffer(), MessageTransmittedCallback);
}
```

Because the system is unable to do anything with a simple NDEF text record, it can be passed on to the app if it subscribes for it. The *NfcReaderWriter* app subscribes for NDEF messages in its *OnNavigatedTo* event handler, providing a callback to be invoked if a message is received.

```
protected override void OnNavigatedTo(NavigationEventArgs e)
{
    device.SubscribeForMessage("NDEF", NdefMessageReceived);
}
```

In the callback event, we again use the NDEF Library to parse the message read from the tag. In this case, we know that the message contains exactly one record, so we can simply operate on the first element in the array. To determine the specific type of the record, we use the *CheckSpecializedType* method on the *NdefRecord* class, which takes a Boolean parameter indicating whether to also perform the check against derived types. After we determine that the record is in fact a text-based record, we can simply create a new instance of the specific class, passing in the base record type as a parameter to the constructor. The message is then displayed in a message box in the app.

```
private void NdefMessageReceived(ProximityDevice sender, ProximityMessage message)
{
    byte[] rawMsg = message.Data.ToArray();
    NdefMessage ndefMessage = NdefMessage.FromByteArray(rawMsg);
    NdefRecord ndefRecord = ndefMessage[0];

    if (ndefRecord.CheckSpecializedType(false) != typeof(NdefTextRecord))
        return;

    NdefTextRecord ndefTextrecord = new NdefTextRecord(ndefRecord);

    Deployment.Current.Dispatcher.BeginInvoke(() =>
    {
        MessageBox.Show(String.Format("Read NDEF text record with message: {0}",
        ndefTextrecord.Text));
    });
}
```

Writing a *LaunchApp* tag

Finally, both Windows and Windows Phone support the ability to read specially formatted tags that include an app identifier and then launch that app. As with the tap-to-connect functionality shown earlier, if the user does not have the app installed, he is offered the opportunity to go to the Windows Phone Store to download it. The format of the string is shown in the code that follows. Observe that the tag format allows for the inclusion of multiple app identifiers for different platforms, so it is possible to create a single tag that refers to both your Windows app and your Windows Phone app, for example.

```
<launch arguments>[tab]<app platform 1>[tab]<app ID 1>...<app platform N><app ID N>
```

The platform identifier for Windows Phone is "WindowsPhone" and the app identifier is the *ProductId* listed in the app manifest. Launch arguments can be used to pass additional context to the app, such as the location of the tag that triggered its launch. An example string for a Windows Phone app is shown below. Note that "\t" is the escaped character for tab.

```
param1=foo\tWindowsPhone\t{9ebfb28e-0d17-4432-8fb0-f2dfbb7d4867}
```

After the required format is understood, creating the message is simple. In the code that follows, we query the *ProductId* from the *CurrentApp* singleton and then insert it into a properly formatted app tag. It is critical that you query the *ProductId* at runtime rather than hard-coding based on the value in the manifest because your app is issued a new *ProductId* when it is submitted to the Windows Phone Store, meaning that the value generated by Visual Studio will no longer be valid. Of course, that also means that you should write tags by using an instance of your app that you downloaded from the Windows Phone Store, not one that you deployed from Visual Studio.

```
private void writeLaunchAppTagButton_Click(object sender, RoutedEventArgs e)
{
    statusTextBlock.Text = "Start tap";

    string launchAppString = Windows.ApplicationModel.Store.CurrentApp.AppId.ToString();
    var fullString = String.Format("param1=foo\tWindowsPhone\t{{{0}}}", launchAppString);
    var buff = WriteStringToBuffer(fullString);
    var msgId = ProximityDevice.GetDefault().PublishBinaryMessage
                ("LaunchApp:WriteTag", buff, MessageTransmittedCallback);
}
```

Sending a URI across devices

Earlier in this chapter, we reviewed how the user can start another instance of your app on another device and set up a connection to it simply by tapping her device to it. That works well when you want to start the same app on another Windows Phone. In some cases, though, you might want to send the web-based version of the content rather than requiring the recipient to download the app, or share content with an app on a different platform such as Android. You might also want to offer a way for a tap to launch your app to a deep-link rather than having to set up a socket connection. For those scenarios, the simple URI offers the most broadly compatible solution.

In the case of content that is accessible from the web, you can share an HTTP URI, which will start the browser on the receiving device and navigate to that page. Most modern platforms, including Windows Phone, also allow apps to register a custom URI scheme that will invoke those apps, such as "fb:" for Facebook and "skype:" for Skype. The *NfcDeepLink* solution in the sample code illustrates an example of the second scenario. In the main page (see Figure 17-9), the user can enter a set of parameter values and tap Send to encode those values as a URI to be sent to another device via NFC. The URI is based on a custom scheme, *nfcdeeplink*, that the app has registered for in its manifest (described in Chapter 2).

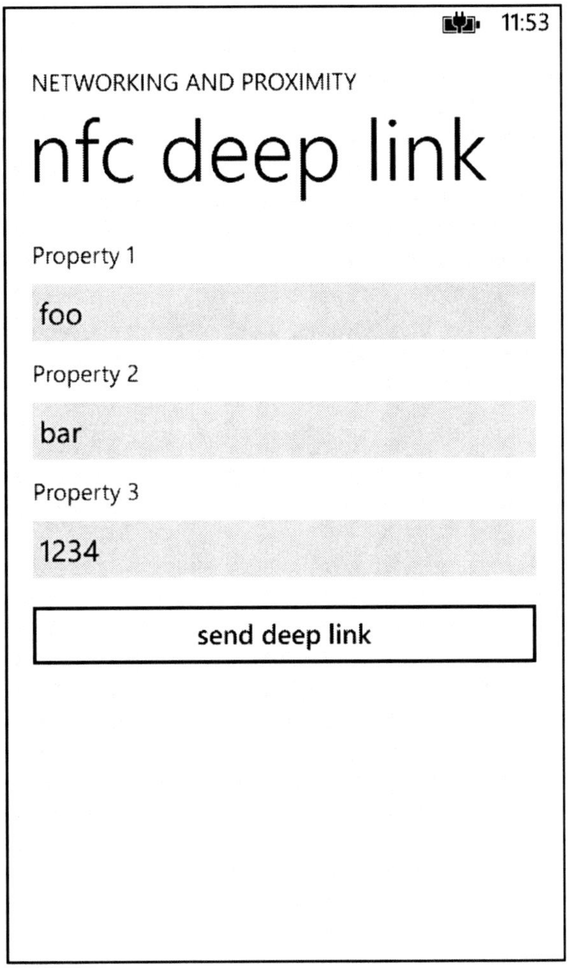

FIGURE 17-9 With the *NfcDeepLink* solution, you can send custom URIs to other devices via NFC.

The click event handler for the Send Deep Link button simply generates a URI by using the *nfcdeeplink* URI scheme and the provided values and calls *PublishUriMessage* with a callback method.

```
ProximityDevice device;

private void sendDeepLinkButton_Click(object sender, RoutedEventArgs e)
{
    string deepLinkUri = String.Format("nfcdeeplink:property1={0}&property2={1}&property3={2}",
                         property1TextBox.Text, property2TextBox.Text, property3TextBox.Text);

    device = ProximityDevice.GetDefault();
    device.PublishUriMessage(new Uri(deepLinkUri), DeepLinkTransferredHandler);
}

private void DeepLinkTransferredHandler(ProximityDevice sender, long messageId)
{
    device.StopPublishingMessage(messageId);
}
```

While the app is publishing the URI, the user can tap his device against another and transfer that URI to the receiving device. If the receiving device is a Windows Phone, it will determine the appropriate handler app for the URI based on its scheme and launch the app directly, assuming that there is only one app available to handle that scheme. From that point, the way in which the receiving app handles being launched based on the transferred URI is no different from how it would handle it if the URI were invoked from anywhere else in the system, such as an email message or the browser. Indeed, the handling app does not require the proximity capability to receive content in this way because the system is providing the intermediating control for the user to decide whether to receive it.

In the case of the *NfcDeepLink* solution, the app remaps the incoming URI to a secondary page, *DeepLinkPage.xaml* and displays the provided values there, as shown in Figure 17-10.

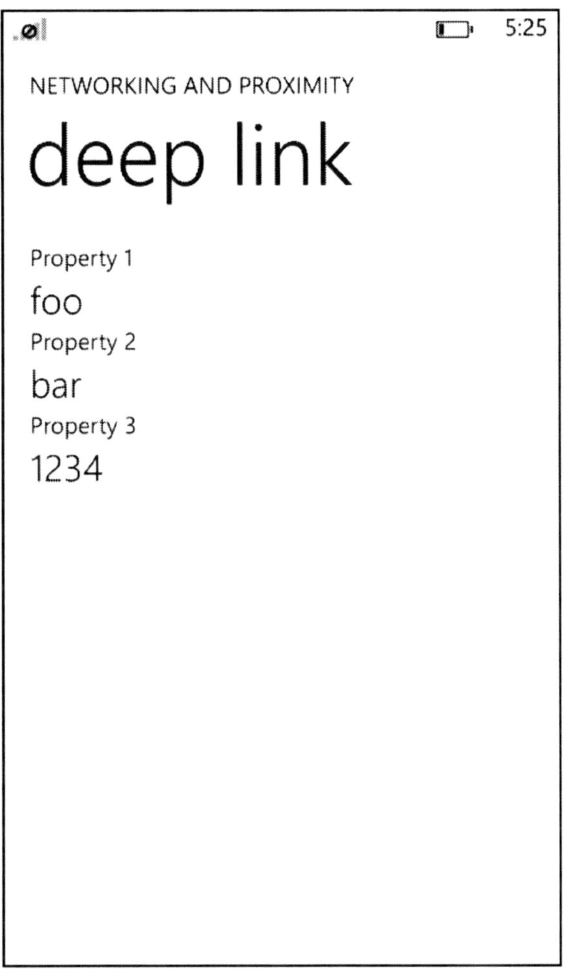

FIGURE 17-10 The *NfcDeepLink* app redirects to the *DeepLinkPage* when launched by a custom URI.

Summary

In this chapter, you learned about the various types of socket communication supported in Windows Phone as well as the tools available to easily connect to nearby devices, including devices that might also be running your app. These features provide the building blocks for creating rich and interactive experiences using the phone's networking stack, whether you are moving packets across the room or across the globe.

CHAPTER 18

Location and maps

Location and maps are supported in Windows Phone by two sets of APIs: the location APIs and the map APIs. Each of these also comes in two flavors: Windows Phone 7 and Windows Phone 8. If you want to build an app that targets both Windows Phone 7 and Windows Phone 8 (or indeed both Windows Phone and desktop Windows or web Silverlight), you should use the Windows Phone 7 APIs because those work on both versions of the platform. On the other hand, if you want to target only Windows Phone 8—taking advantage of its enhanced functionality—it is recommended that you use the Windows Phone 8 APIs. This chapter examines all approaches, starting with the Windows Phone 7 APIs to build a range of map and location-based apps, and then showing how you can build similar apps by using the Windows Phone 8 APIs. The testing and performance tips at the end of the chapter apply equally to both versions.

Architecture

Under the hood (in both versions), location information is gathered from a variety of sources, including both on-device hardware and drivers and via web service calls to cloud-based location services. A key difference in Windows Phone 8 is that both maps and location are provided by the same underlying Nokia maps platform. As well as providing a cleaner component stack that makes it a lot easier for you to work with, this also provides significantly enhanced features and improved performance. Figure 18-1 presents the architecture of the two stacks.

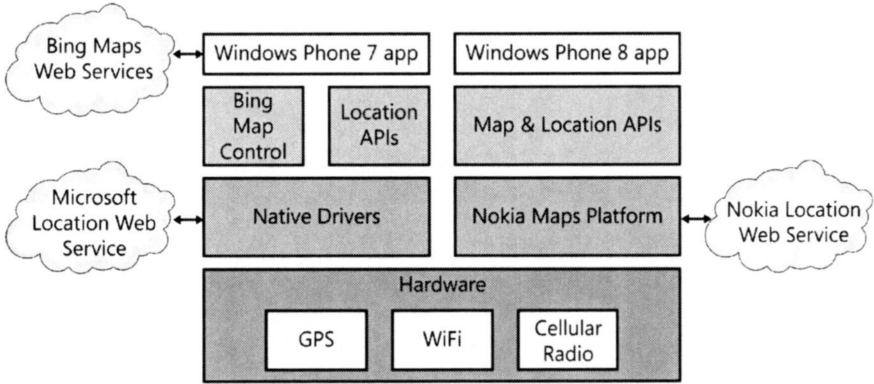

FIGURE 18-1 The support for location and maps uses two different stacks for Windows Phone 7 and 8.

The location data surfaced by the platform APIs can be sourced from any of the underlying sensors (GPS, Wi-Fi, cellular radio). With Windows Phone 7, in which data is sourced via Wi-Fi, the on-device location service also uses the Microsoft location web service to help resolve positioning. The Windows Phone 7 location APIs wrap the underlying native operating system (OS) feature that determines the best data source to feed to the API layer, depending on which source(s) is available and whether the app requires default or high accuracy. A Windows Phone 7 app might also need to set up its own client to the Bing Maps web services, for example, for geocode information. In Windows Phone 8, by contrast, the Nokia maps platform includes full geocoding, routing, and navigation capabilities, supplemented by a Nokia location web service where required. The Windows Phone 8 APIs are Windows Runtime APIs, which is where the commonality with Windows 8 comes in. A Windows Phone 8 app does not need to set up proxies to any web services, because all of this is handled at a lower level in the maps platform.

The most significant benefit of the Nokia maps platform is that it supports offline caching and preload of map data. On top of that, it also supports offline routing, which is unique among smartphones. All of this means that the phone will make far fewer calls to the server to retrieve data, and this in turn saves on network usage, which can significantly reduce the cost to users who have tariffed or pay-as-you-go data plans. The Nokia maps platform provides other benefits, too. For example, it knows about features in the landscape around the user, such as tunnels, and can predict where in the tunnel the user is, based on the speed he was going when he entered it. The Nokia maps platform also applies filtering to the raw sensor data when matching locations with maps so that it can track driving along a road and not register the location as being off the road, even when the sensors are struggling to provide accurate data.

Determining the current location (Windows Phone 7)

Windows Phone 7 exposes a *GeoCoordinateWatcher* class, which provides a simple API for determining the user's current location. Figure 18-2 illustrates an app (the *SimpleGeoWatcher* solution in the sample code) that uses location data, reporting each location event as it occurs. You can see how this could easily form the basis of a "run-tracker" or "trail-tracking" app.

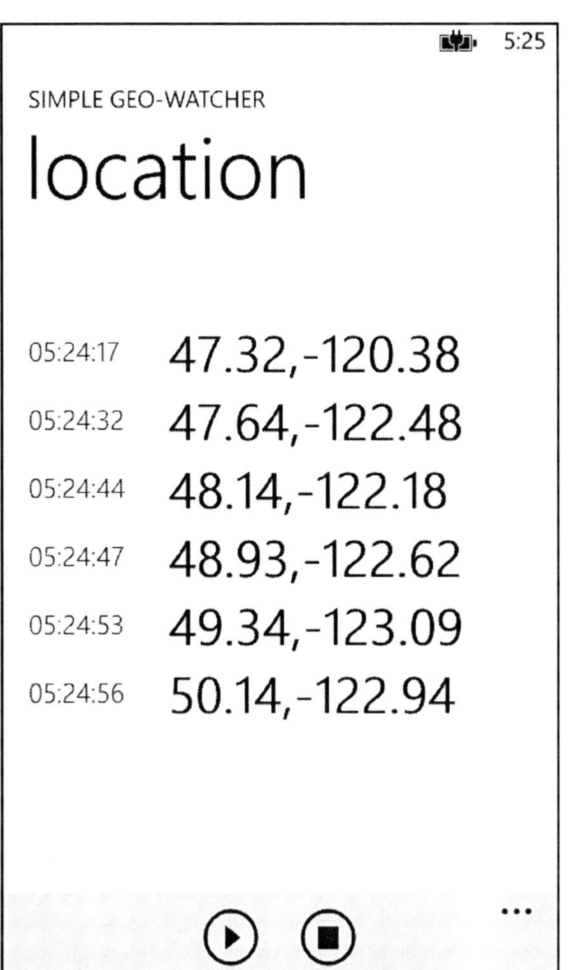

FIGURE 18-2 The *GeoCoordinateWatcher* class provides longitude and latitude readings.

In a Windows Phone 7 project, you need to add a reference to the *System.Device.dll* (this is added automatically in a Windows Phone 8 project). Then, to use location functionality, the app declares a *GeoCoordinateWatcher* object and instantiates it in the *OnNavigatedTo* override. The constructor is your only opportunity to set the required accuracy. You can subsequently retrieve this value from the *DesiredAccuracy* property, which is read-only. You also declare a collection of *GeoPosition* objects, which will be stored each time you get a location event. This is enabled by hooking up the *Position Changed* event.

```
private GeoCoordinateWatcher watcher;
public ObservableCollection<GeoPosition<GeoCoordinate>> Positions;

protected override void OnNavigatedTo(NavigationEventArgs e)
{
    InitializeCollection();
```

```
    if (watcher == null)
    {
        watcher = new GeoCoordinateWatcher(GeoPositionAccuracy.High);
        watcher.PositionChanged += watcher_PositionChanged;
    }
}
```

In the *PositionChanged* event handler, extract the *Position* value and store it in the collection. The *Position* property is of type *GeoPosition<T>*, which includes both a *DateTimeOffset* and a position of type *<T>* (in this case, a *GeoCoordinate* value). The *GeoCoordinate* type represents a geographical location with latitude and longitude coordinates. Notice that the *PositionChanged* events come in on the user interface (UI) thread, so there's no need to use *Dispatcher.BeginInvoke* when updating the UI. This is a convenience to you, but it is inconsistent with the general pattern of event handlers and has caused confusion. You should normally assume that non-UI events will arrive at the app on a non-UI thread. As you will see later in this chapter, this inconsistency was removed in the Windows Phone 8 location APIs.

Note *GeoPosition<T>* will always in fact be *GeoPosition<GeoCoordinate>*. Given that, you might be wondering why the API doesn't simply use *GeoCoordinate* directly instead of wrapping it with the seemingly redundant *GeoPosition<T>* type. The *GeoPosition* type is designed to be generic in order to support potential future expansion. However, this is actually contrary to the internal API design guidelines; this is just an anomaly in the API surface that slipped through.

```
private void watcher_PositionChanged(object sender, GeoPositionChangedEventArgs<GeoCoordinate> e)
{
    Positions.Add(e.Position);
}
```

The only other thing you need to do is to *Start* and *Stop* the *GeoCoordinateWatcher* at appropriate times. You only start it under user control, in the *Click* handler for the corresponding button. However, you stop it either when the user asks to stop or, as a good housekeeping technique, in the *OnNavigatedFrom* override. To start the watcher, you can, in theory, use either the *Start* method or the *TryStart* method. With *TryStart*, you can specify a timeout such that if the service doesn't start within that time, the method returns false. However, you should probably never use *TryStart* in this context, because this will block the UI thread, and blocking the UI thread is always considered bad practice. In fact, even the *Start* method can block the UI for up to several hundred milliseconds, but it will return relatively quickly while the service is still starting up asynchronously. You should also consider listening to the *StatusChanged* event, which among other things, can tell you when the watcher has started.

```
private void startButton_Click(object sender, EventArgs e)
{
    watcher.Start();
}


private void stopButton_Click(object sender, EventArgs e)
{
    watcher.Stop();
}

protected override void OnNavigatedFrom(NavigationEventArgs e)
{
    IsolatedStorageSettings.ApplicationSettings["Positions"] = Positions;
    watcher.Stop();
    watcher = null;
}
```

Note This example also persists the position changes in *ApplicationSettings*. This is reasonable if the number of positions is small, but it can rapidly become unreasonable as the number of positions increases. In a more realistic app, if you do want to persist location change data, you should consider doing so in isolated storage files, not in *ApplicationSettings*.

Before the location app will work, you need to ensure that your app manifest (*WMAppManifest.xml*) includes the *ID_CAP_LOCATION* in the *Capabilities* section.

```
<Capabilities>
...
  <Capability Name="ID_CAP_LOCATION" />
</Capabilities>
```

In Windows Phone 7, if you don't add this capability, when you attempt to start a *GeoCoordinate Watcher*, you'll receive a status error. In Windows Phone 8, if you don't add this capability, the app will throw an "UnauthorizedAccessException" at the point where you try to create the *GeoCoordinate Watcher*. In Microsoft Visual Studio 2012, you can edit the manifest by using the convenient graphical manifest editor, as shown in Figure 18-3.

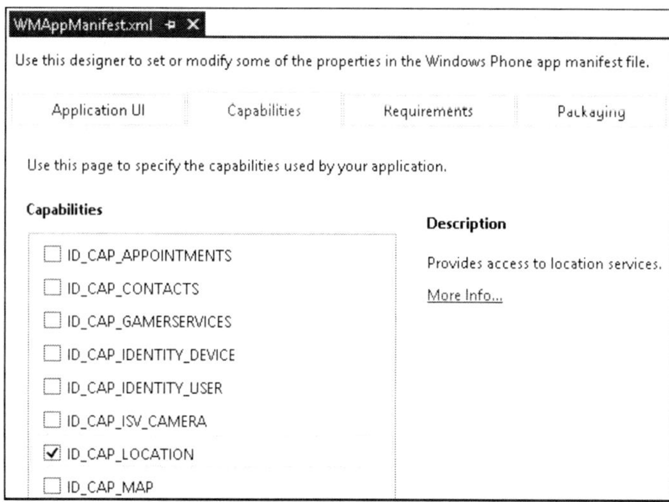

FIGURE 18-3 You can use the manifest editor in Visual Studio 2012 to configure your app's capabilities.

As well as location, the *GeoCoordinate* type provides additional values, including *Speed* and *Altitude*. Keep in mind that, in addition to the *PositionChanged* events raised on the *GeoCoordinate Watcher*, you should also handle the *StatusChanged* events. These events provide information about the location service such as whether the user has disabled location on the device, and error conditions.

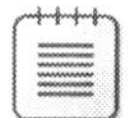

Note The location APIs also provide a *CivicAddressResolver* class. This class exposes a *Resolve* method that is intended to resolve a given *GeoCoordinate* to a civic address. However, the *Resolve* method is not implemented, so it will always return an empty address.

Bing maps (Windows Phone 7)

The Bing Maps service exposes a range of APIs for use in a wide variety of app types. These break down into three categories: the Bing *Map* control, the Bing Maps web services, and Bing-related Launchers, all of which are described in the following sections.

The Bing *Map* control

To use Bing Maps and Bing services, you need a Microsoft Account (formerly known as a Windows Live ID) and a Bing Maps developer account, both of which are free and easy to obtain. Go to *http://binged.it/eGZfqT* for terms and conditions. To get started, go to *http://www.bingmapsportal.com*, associate an account with your Microsoft Account ID, and then select the option to create keys. A Bing Maps key is required for all apps that use the Bing Maps APIs: this is a 64-character string that identifies your app, which your app passes to the Bing Maps servers with each request. You can create multiple keys, and for each one, you supply an arbitrary app name and URL (these don't have to bear any relation to your real app name/URL, but you should use names that you will recognize as being associated with the real app).

For simplicity, you can paste the key into your app code, typically as a field in the *App* class. You can see an example of this in the *SimpleBingMaps* solution in the sample code. Be aware, however, that this is not a secure approach to use for a production app. For a more secure approach, it is common to store the key on a web server, not in the app, and have the app make a web service call on startup to retrieve the key.

```
internal const string BingMapsAccountId = "<< YOUR BING KEY >>";
```

You need to incorporate this key with a *CredentialsProvider*, and for this, you need to add a reference to the Windows Phone 7 *Microsoft.Phone.Controls.Maps.dll* (*not* the *Microsoft.Phone.Maps.dll*, which is for Windows Phone 8 projects), which you will find in the installation folder for the tools. This is typically in %ProgramFiles(x86)%\Microsoft SDKs\Windows Phone\v7.1\Libraries\Silverlight\. You can then set up an *ApplicationIdCredentialsProvider* in your *MainPage* class by using this key. *ApplicationId CredentialsProvider* implements *INotifyPropertyChanged*, so you can use it for data-binding. This is useful for cases in which you want to download the key at runtime from your own web service.

```
private readonly CredentialsProvider _credentialsProvider =
    new ApplicationIdCredentialsProvider(App.BingMapsAccountId);
public CredentialsProvider CredentialsProvider
{
    get { return _credentialsProvider; }
}
```

Next, you need to put a *Map* control onto your page. In Visual Studio 2010, the Bing *Map* control is available by default in the toolbox. However, Visual Studio 2012 is geared toward the new map APIs, and for a Windows Phone 8 project, the toolbox shows the new map control, not the Bing *Map* control. If you're creating a Windows Phone 7 project in Visual Studio 2012, you won't see either the Bing *Map* control or the new *Map* control in the toolbox. Although you could add the Bing *Map* control to the toolbox, you will not be able to add the control to your page in the designer. To remedy this, you must edit your XAML manually. First, add a namespace reference for the *Microsoft.Phone.Controls.Maps.dll*, as shown here:

```
xmlns:maps="clr-namespace:Microsoft.Phone.Controls.Maps;assembly=Microsoft.Phone.Controls.Maps"
```

Next, declare an instance of the Bing *Map* control somewhere in your page, perhaps in the default *Grid* element. Data-bind the control to the *CredentialsProvider*, such as in the following:

```
<Grid x:Name="ContentPanel" Grid.Row="1" Margin="12,0,12,0">
    <maps:Map x:Name="map1" CredentialsProvider="{Binding CredentialsProvider}"/>
</Grid>
```

These few simple steps will give you map functionality in your app.

The *BingMapsLocation* solution in the sample code demonstrates how you can combine the *GeoCoordinateWatcher* with the Bing *Map* control. In the project, add a reference to the *Microsoft.Phone.Controls.Maps.dll* and set up a *CredentialsProvider*, as just described. As with the earlier location sample, if this is a Windows Phone 7 project, you must also add a reference to *System.Device.dll*. In the XAML for your main page, add a namespace reference for the *Microsoft.Phone.Controls.Maps.dll* and then declare a map object on your page, as shown earlier.

In the *MainPage* class, declare a *GeoCoordinateWatcher* field for retrieving location sensor data. In *OnNavigatedTo*, you instantiate and start the watcher and hook up a handler for the *PositionChanged* events. You stop the watcher in *OnNavigatedFrom*.

```
private GeoCoordinateWatcher watcher;

protected override void OnNavigatedTo(NavigationEventArgs e)
{
    if (watcher == null)
    {
        watcher = new GeoCoordinateWatcher(GeoPositionAccuracy.High);
        watcher.PositionChanged += watcher_PositionChanged;
    }
    watcher.Start();
}

protected override void OnNavigatedFrom(NavigationEventArgs e)
{
    if (watcher != null)
    {
        watcher.Stop();
        watcher = null;
    }
}
```

In the *PositionChanged* event handler, set the map position from the incoming *GeoCoordinate* parameter. At the same time, set the *ZoomLevel* to an arbitrary value of 16 (the valid range for the *ZoomLevel* property is 1.0 to 21.0), just to make it more obvious that the position locator is working as expected.

```
private void watcher_PositionChanged(object sender, GeoPositionChangedEventArgs<GeoCoordinate> e)
{
    map1.Center = e.Position.Location;
    map1.ZoomLevel = 16;
}
```

One area in which the Bing maps provide better programmability than the new maps API is when you want to layer arbitrary graphics and text onto the surface of the map. The simplest implementation of this in Bing maps is the pushpin feature. Figure 18-4 shows a screenshot of the *BingPushpins* solution in the sample code, in which the user has tapped the map a few times. For each tap, the app inserts a pushpin on top of the map and labels it with the selected coordinates.

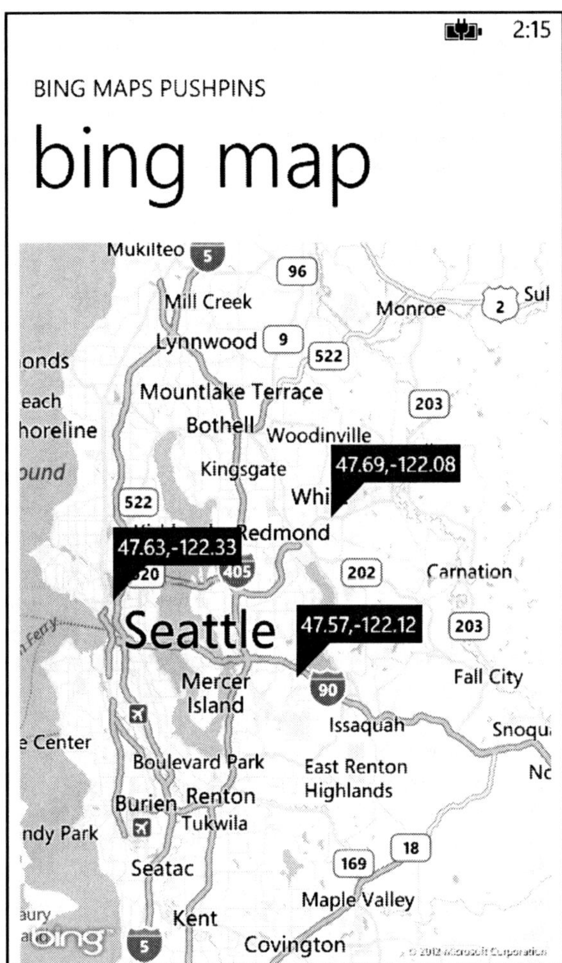

FIGURE 18-4 You can easily insert pushpins on top of the Bing *Map* control.

The code required to achieve this is very simple. The *MainPage* declares a *MapLayer* field; this layer will be used for all the pushpins. The *Tap* gesture for the *Map* control is wired up in XAML to an event handler. The handler first extracts the *Point* location of the tap gesture relative to the *Map* control and then invokes the *Map.ViewportPointToLocation* conversion method to convert this *Point* to a *Geo Coordinate*. The app uses this coordinate value for both the *Pushpin* location and its text label.

A map can have multiple layers or none at all. In this sample, even one layer is actually superfluous; you could simply add the *Pushpin* objects directly to the map, as follows:

```
private MapLayer layer;

private void map_Tap(object sender, System.Windows.Input.GestureEventArgs e)
{
    GeoCoordinate coord = map.ViewportPointToLocation(e.GetPosition(map));
    Pushpin pin = new Pushpin();
```

```
    pin.Location = coord;
    pin.Content = string.Format("{0:0.00},{1:0.00}", coord.Latitude, coord.Longitude);

    if (layer == null)
    {
        layer = new MapLayer();
        map.Children.Add(layer);
    }

    layer.Children.Add(pin);
}
```

Bing maps web services

The Bing Maps Simple Object Access Protocol (SOAP) services are listed in Table 18-1.

TABLE 18-1 Bing Maps SOAP services

Namespace	URL
GeocodeService	*http://dev.virtualearth.net/webservices/v1/geocodeservice/geocodeservice.svc?wsdl*
SearchService	*http://dev.virtualearth.net/webservices/v1/searchservice/searchservice.svc?wsdl*
ImageryService	*http://dev.virtualearth.net/webservices/v1/imageryservice/imageryservice.svc?wsdl*
RouteService	*http://dev.virtualearth.net/webservices/v1/routeservice/routeservice.svc?wsdl*

The following example (the *TestGeocodeService* solution in the sample code), which is shown in Figure 18-5, uses the *GeocodeService* to find the geocode (latitude,longitude) for a given street address.

There are, in fact, two different ways that you can use the Bing Maps web services: using the traditional SOAP approach, or using the newer REST approach. Both approaches are described here. The sample code includes two corresponding variants: *TestGeocodeService_SOAP* and *TestGeocode Service_REST*. For more information on SOAP and REST, see Chapter 8, "Web services and the cloud."

FIGURE 18-5 The *GeocodeService* is the most commonly used Bing Maps web service.

For the SOAP approach, you need to generate a client-side proxy for the web service. To do this, add a service reference to the *GeocodeService* (see Figure 18-6). In the Add Service Reference dialog box, click the Advanced button, set the Collection Type to System.Array (or IList), and then clear the Reuse Types In Referenced Assemblies check box; otherwise, the wizard generates a blank service reference. You don't want the types from the assemblies referenced by the service, because they'll be full Microsoft .NET Common Language Runtime (CLR) and not compatible with the phone. The same applies to the collection classes.

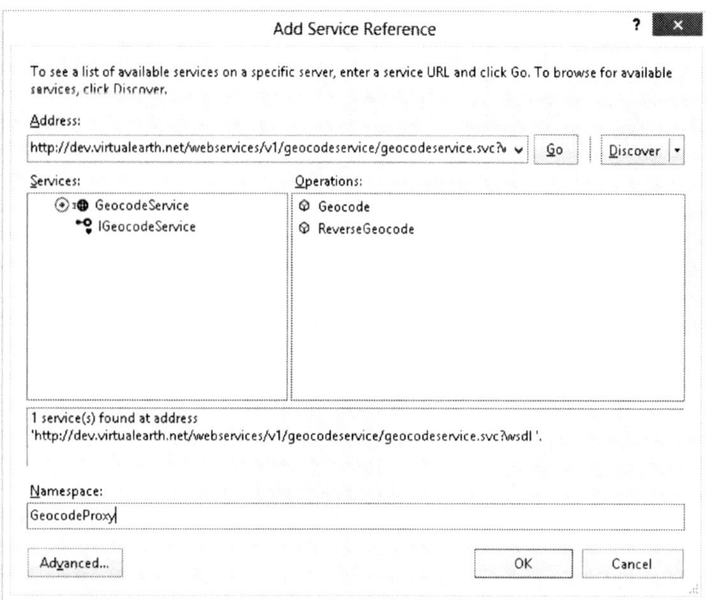

FIGURE 18-6 Use the Add Service Reference dialog box to generate proxy code for the Geocode service.

In addition to the client proxy code, this will also generate a client-side service config file, typically named *ServiceReferences.ClientConfig*. This will include declarations such as the basic HTTP binding, which you will need to reference later in your code.

```
<basicHttpBinding>
    <binding name="BasicHttpBinding_IGeocodeService" maxBufferSize="2147483647"
        maxReceivedMessageSize="2147483647">
        <security mode="None" />
    </binding>
</basicHttpBinding>
```

In the main page, you implement the button *Click* handler by creating a *GeocodeRequest*, handling its *GeocodeCompleted* event, and invoking the asynchronous web service call *GeocodeAsync*.

```
private const string BingMapsAccountId = "<< YOUR BING KEY >>";

private void getGeocode_Click(object sender, RoutedEventArgs e)
{
    if (!String.IsNullOrEmpty(streetText.Text))
    {
        GeocodeRequest request = new GeocodeRequest();
        request.Credentials = new Credentials();
        request.Credentials.ApplicationId = BingMapsAccountId;
        request.Query = streetText.Text;
        GeocodeServiceClient geocodeService =
            new GeocodeServiceClient("BasicHttpBinding_IGeocodeService");
        geocodeService.GeocodeCompleted += geocodeService_GeocodeCompleted;
        geocodeService.GeocodeAsync(request);
    }
}
```

When you receive the *GeocodeCompleted* event, extract the *Latitude* and *Longitude* values from the results and then set them into the last *TextBox*.

```
private void geocodeService_GeocodeCompleted(
    object sender, GeocodeCompletedEventArgs e)
{
    GeocodeResponse response = e.Result;
    if (response.Results.Length > 0)
    {
        geocodeText.Text = String.Format("{0:F2},{1:F2}",
            response.Results[0].Locations[0].Latitude,
            response.Results[0].Locations[0].Longitude);
    }
    else
    {
        geocodeText.Text = "not found";
    }
}
```

For the alternative REST approach, you do not need to generate a client-side web service proxy at all. Instead, you can simply use the generic *WebClient* type to invoke the REST service and then parse the resulting XML (or JSON) data. Instead of the strongly typed client-side proxy, you pass a simple query string. This version of the sample app sets up a template string with two placeholders: one for the user-supplied street address, and one for the developer Bing Maps account ID. Take note of the *o=xml* parameter in the query string. This specifies that the output (return data) should be in XML format. If you omit this parameter, the default output format is JSON. See Chapter 8 for more details on JSON.

The *Click* handler wires up the *DownloadStringCompleted* event to an inline delegate (you could alternatively use a traditional event handler method, if you prefer). This delegate parses the returned XML, extracts the *Latitude* and *Longitude* elements, and then composes these into a string to update the UI. The delegate is invoked when the call to *DownloadStringAsync* returns.

```
private const string BingMapsAccountId = "<< YOUR BING KEY >>";
private const string geoCodeTemplate =
    @"http://dev.virtualearth.net/REST/v1/Locations/{0}?o=xml&key={1}";
private static XNamespace BingRestNs =
    @"http://schemas.microsoft.com/search/local/ws/rest/v1";

private void getGeocode_Click(object sender, RoutedEventArgs e)
{
    WebClient client = new WebClient();
    client.DownloadStringCompleted += (o, r) =>
    {
        XDocument doc = XDocument.Parse(r.Result);
        double lat = double.Parse(
            (from entry in doc.Descendants(BingRestNs + "Latitude")
            select entry.Value).FirstOrDefault());
```

```
        double lon = double.Parse(
            (from entry in doc.Descendants(BingRestNs + "Longitude")
            select entry.Value).FirstOrDefault());
        Dispatcher.BeginInvoke(() => geocodeText.Text =
            String.Format("{0:0.00},{1:0.00}", lat, lon));
    };

    client.DownloadStringAsync(new Uri(String.Format(
        geoCodeTemplate, streetText.Text, BingMapsAccountId),
        UriKind.RelativeOrAbsolute));
}
```

Bing Maps Launchers

Windows Phone 7 offers two Launchers that wrap the underlying Bing maps capabilities, as described in Table 18-2. These Launchers offer a simplified programming model; however, this simplification costs the loss of some of the power of the Bing Maps API. You do not need a Bing Maps development account to use the *BingMapsTask* and *BingMapsDirectionsTask*. You therefore also do not need to set up an *ApplicationIdCredentialsProvider*.

TABLE 18-2 Bing Maps Launchers

Task	Description
BingMapsDirectionsTask	Launches the Bing Maps app, specifying a starting and/or ending location, for which driving or walking directions are displayed.
BingMapsTask	Launches the Bing Maps app centered at the specified or current location.

Figure 18-7 demonstrates the new *BingMapsDirectionsTask*. You can see this at work in the *TestBingTask* solution in the sample code. The app offers one *Button* control; the *Click* handler simply creates a *BingMapsDirectionsTask* and sets the destination location.

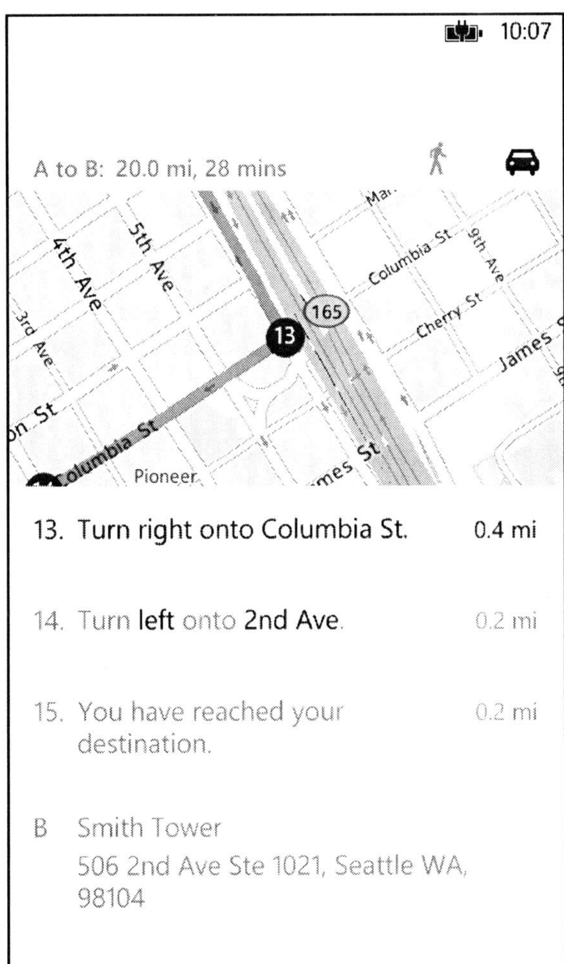

FIGURE 18-7 Using the *BingMapsDirectionsTask* Launcher.

When you instantiate the *BingMapsDirectionsTask*, you can specify a label and/or *GeoCoordinates* for the target location (the end point). If you supply a location, the label is used as a descriptive label. If you don't supply a location, the label is used as a search string. You can optionally also specify a location start point, but if you don't, the current location is used as the default starting point. Finally, invoke the *Show* method to execute the Launcher.

```
private void getDirections_Click(object sender, RoutedEventArgs e)
{
    BingMapsDirectionsTask bingTask = new BingMapsDirectionsTask();
    bingTask.End = new LabeledMapLocation("Smith Tower, Seattle", null);
    bingTask.Show();
}
```

Getting location (Windows Phone 8)

The new Windows Phone 8 maps APIs and the new location APIs form a more seamless whole. They are replacements for the old Bing Maps APIs and the old Windows Phone 7 location APIs. To use the new APIs, you do not need a Bing account and you do not use the Bing web services. The new APIs are more powerful than the old ones in some cases. They use the underlying Nokia maps platform layer, which is faster and more accurate. It is also easier to develop against the new APIs. You should use the new location APIs unless you're explicitly targeting both Windows Phone 7 and Windows Phone 8. The *Geolocator* class is the Windows Phone 8 equivalent of the *GeoCoordinateWatcher* class that was used in Windows Phone 7 projects. There are two ways by which you can use *Geolocator*:

- In "ad hoc" mode, wherein you invoke the *GetGeopositionAsync* method on demand
- In "continuous" mode, wherein you handle the *PositionChanged* events

The *SimpleGeoLocator* app in the sample code shows how to use the ad hoc approach, as shown in Figure 18-8.

All the work is done in the *Click* handler for a custom app bar button. This instantiates a *Geolocator* object and sets the *DesiredAccuracy* property. Alternatively, you could set the *Desired AccuracyInMeters* property if you want more precise control over this. Next, the app fetches the current position by using the *GetGeopositionAsync* method. As its name implies, this is an asynchronous method, so the code waits on the return from this by using the *await* keyword. Keep in mind that you can only invoke asynchronous methods in this way if the calling method itself is declared as *async*. Using the *await* keyword in this way also has the effect that the results are returned on the calling thread. In this example, this is the UI thread, so no additional thread marshaling is required here.

When the location data is retrieved, the app sets the various location properties into UI elements. Unlike the *GeoCoordinateWatcher*, the *Geolocator* always returns location data on a non-UI thread. For this reason, you must always use *Dispatcher.BeginInvoke* to marshal the UI property setters back to the UI thread.

It is also important to handle exceptions when using the *Geolocator*. In particular, you must handle the case in which the user has disabled location services on his phone; in this case, an *Unauthorized AccessException* is thrown. Finally, don't forget that the *ID_CAP_LOCATION* capability must be added to the manifest.

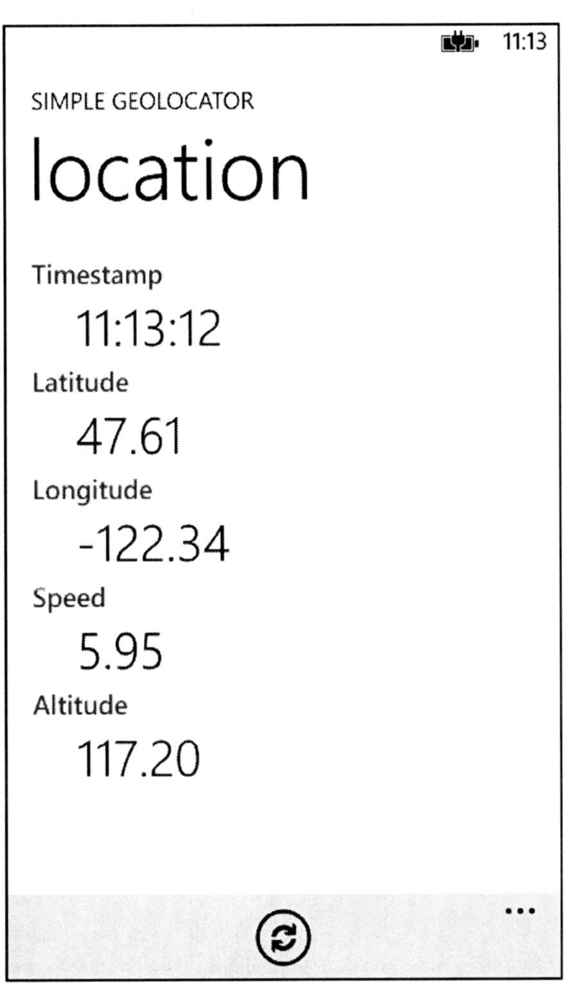

FIGURE 18-8 You can use the *Geolocator* class in ad hoc mode.

Note There is a quirk in the location simulator (which is part of the Windows Phone emulator). If you accept the default value for *DesiredAccuracy* (or if you set it to *PositionAccuracy.Default* instead of *PositionAccuracy.High*), when you test the ad hoc *Geolocator* approach, the *GetGeopositionAsync* call fetches the last location set in the simulator before you start and does not fetch any updated location. However, for real use on a real device, *PositionAccuracy.Default* is mostly what you want; it provides a good level of accuracy while still keeping battery consumption down. If you do set *PositionAccuracy.High* for the purposes of testing in the emulator, you should remember to reset it to *PositionAccuracy.Default* before shipping your app.

GetGeopositionAsync has an overload that takes two parameters: the *maximumAge* of the data to retrieve, and a *timeout* value. When you invoke this method, it gathers old data up to the point where the *maximumAge* is exceeded; thus, if you want to test rapid changes in location, you should set *maximumAge* to a low value (in seconds). This sample creates a fresh *Geolocator* each time the user taps the refresh button. You could instead set up a *Geolocator* as a class field, initialized once, and reuse it for each user request.

```
private async void refreshButton_Click(object sender, EventArgs e)
{
    try
    {
        Geolocator locator = new Geolocator();
        locator.DesiredAccuracy = PositionAccuracy.High;
        Geoposition position = await locator.GetGeopositionAsync();

        timestamp.Text = position.Coordinate.Timestamp.ToString("hh:mm:ss");
        latitude.Text = position.Coordinate.Latitude.ToString("0.00");
        longitude.Text = position.Coordinate.Longitude.ToString("0.00");
        speed.Text = String.Format("{0:0.00}", position.Coordinate.Speed);
        altitude.Text = String.Format("{0:0.00}", position.Coordinate.Altitude);
    }
    catch (UnauthorizedAccessException)
    {
        MessageBox.Show("location capability is disabled");
    }
    catch (Exception)
    {
        MessageBox.Show("unknown error");
    }
}
```

The ad hoc approach is often all you need (wherein you fetch location data only when it is actually required in the app). In other scenarios, you want the app to be fed location data continuously over a period of time. The classic example is a "run-tracker" app. In this scenario, you handle the *Position Changed* events. Unlike the *GeoCoordinateWatcher*, the *Geolocator* class does not expose *Start* and *Stop* methods; instead, the location events are raised as soon as you hook up the *PositionChanged* event handler, and stop being raised when you unhook the handler. The *ContinuousLocation* solution in the sample code demonstrates this approach, which is presented in Figure 18-9.

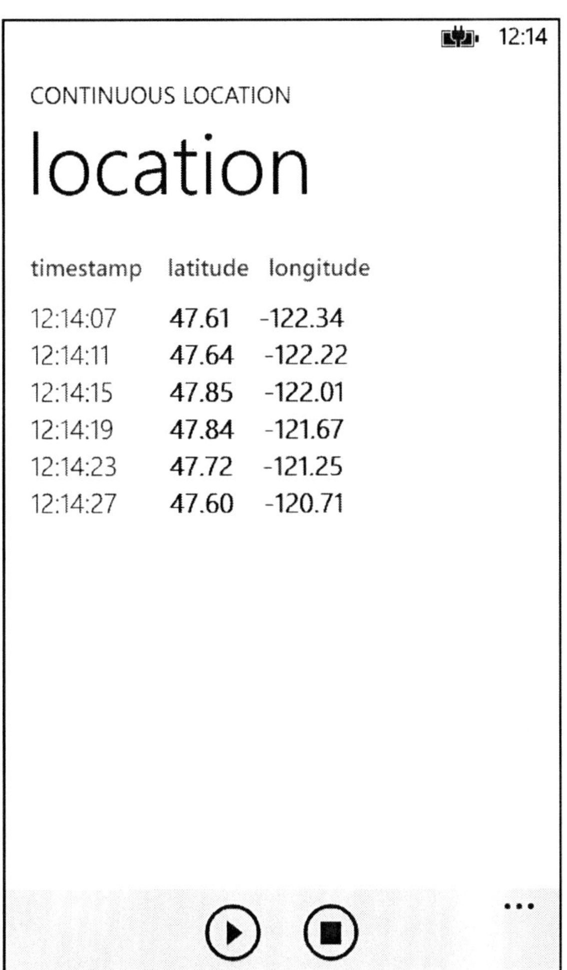

12:14
CONTINUOUS LOCATION
location
timestamp latitude longitude
12:14:07 47.61 -122.34
12:14:11 47.64 -122.22
12:14:15 47.85 -122.01
12:14:19 47.84 -121.67
12:14:23 47.72 -121.25
12:14:27 47.60 -120.71

FIGURE 18-9 You can handle *PositionChanged* events on the *Geolocator* class.

All of the interesting code is in the *MainPage* class. This sets up a *Geolocator* field and a collection of *Geocoordinate* values. The *Positions* collection is set as the *ItemsSource* for a *ListBox* in the UI. When the user navigates to the page, the app creates a *Geolocator* object and sets the *DesiredAccuracy* and *MovementThreshold* properties. Note that you must set either the *MovementThreshold* property (in meters) or the *ReportInterval* property (in seconds) before hooking up the *PositionChanged* event, or an exception will be thrown. It is also a good idea to unhook the event handler and clean up the object in the *OnNavigatedFrom* override. The *OnNavigatedTo* also enables the Start button and disables the Stop button.

```
private Geolocator locator;
public ObservableCollection<Geocoordinate> Positions;

protected override void OnNavigatedTo(NavigationEventArgs e)
{
    if (locator == null)
```

```
    {
        locator = new Geolocator();
        locator.DesiredAccuracy = PositionAccuracy.High;
        locator.MovementThreshold = 50;
        //locator.ReportInterval = 1;
    }
    stopButton.IsEnabled = false;
    startButton.IsEnabled = true;
}


protected override void OnNavigatedFrom(NavigationEventArgs e)
{
    locator.PositionChanged -= locator_PositionChanged;
    locator = null;
}
```

The user can tap the Start button to begin receiving *PositionChanged* events and then tap the Stop button to discontinue receiving them. The *Click* event handlers for these buttons also enable or disable the buttons as appropriate. This ensures that the user can't, for example, tap the Start button twice and end up with two *PositionChanged* event handlers. When the last event handler is unregistered, the events are no longer raised. When an event is received, the app extracts the *Geoposition* data and adds it to the *Positions* collection. This is a dynamic data-bound collection.

```
private void startButton_Click(object sender, EventArgs e)
{
    if (locator != null)
    {
        locator.PositionChanged += locator_PositionChanged;
        startButton.IsEnabled = false;
        stopButton.IsEnabled = true;
    }
}

private void stopButton_Click(object sender, EventArgs e)
{
    if (locator != null)
    {
        locator.PositionChanged -= locator_PositionChanged;
        stopButton.IsEnabled = false;
        startButton.IsEnabled = true;
    }
}

private void locator_PositionChanged(Geolocator sender, PositionChangedEventArgs args)
{
    Dispatcher.BeginInvoke(() => { Positions.Add(args.Position.Coordinate); });
}
```

The *MainPage* XAML declares a *ListBox* with an *ItemTemplate* set to include three *TextBlock* controls, suitably data-bound and formatted.

```
<TextBlock
    Grid.Column="0" Text="{Binding Timestamp, StringFormat='hh:mm:ss'}"
    Style="{StaticResource PhoneTextTitle3Style}"/>
<TextBlock
    Grid.Column="1" Text="{Binding Latitude, StringFormat='0.00'}"
    Style="{StaticResource PhoneTextTitle3Style}" FontWeight="Bold"/>
<TextBlock
    Grid.Column="2" Text="{Binding Longitude, StringFormat='0.00'}"
    Style="{StaticResource PhoneTextTitle3Style}" FontWeight="Bold"/>
```

Maps API (Windows Phone 8)

Windows Phone 8 introduces a new set of maps APIs that can be used in Windows Phone 8 projects in place of the old Bing Maps APIs. This includes a new *Map* control, support classes such as the *MapRoute* and *MapLayer*, and Launchers such as the *MapsTask* and *MapsDirectionsTask*. The new map system in Windows Phone 8 is faster than the old system; consumes less network bandwidth; is more accurate; has more intelligent error-correction and noise-filtering; and, in most scenarios, is also easier to develop against. However, some things are easier with the "old" Bing maps API, specifically, adding items such as pushpins to the surface of a map.

The *Map* control

In a Windows Phone 8 project, you can drag a *Map* control from the toolbox onto the XAML design surface in your app. This generates the XML namespace for the *Map* control (*Microsoft.Phone.Maps.Controls*). You must add the corresponding *ID_CAP_MAP* capability to your app manifest manually. The *MapDemo* solution in the sample code illustrates some of the features of the *Map* control by giving the user the ability to set the control properties, as shown in Figure 18-10.

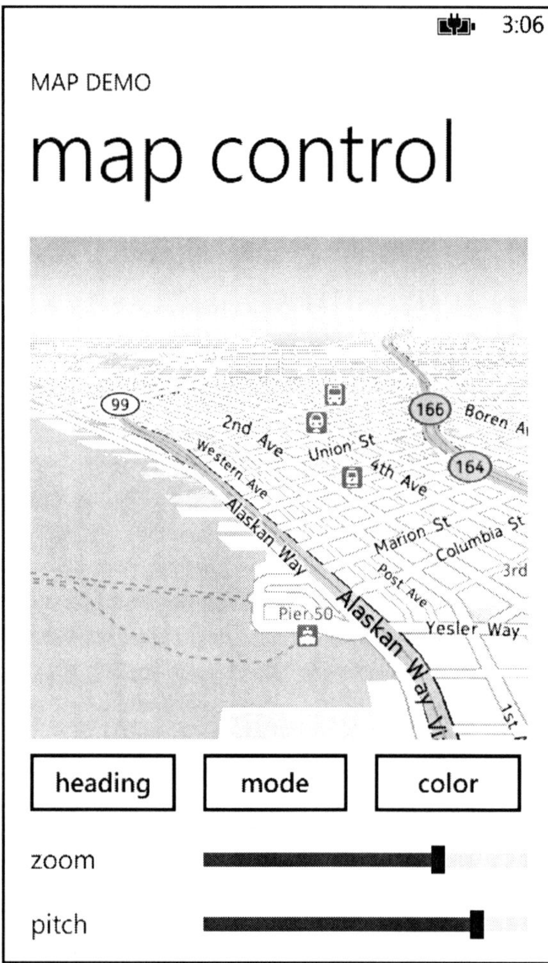

FIGURE 18-10 The new *Map* control exposes several programmable properties.

In this example, the *Map* control is initialized in the *OnNavigatedTo* override. It is also manually synchronized with the two *Slider* controls. Each public property of the *Map* control, including *Zoom Level*, and *Pitch*, is also exposed as a *DependencyProperty*, so the app could just as easily data-bind these. The user can move the *Slider* controls to adjust the *ZoomLevel* and *Pitch* properties on the map. *ZoomLevel* is self-explanatory. *Pitch* affects the user's perspective view of the map. A *Pitch* value of 0 (zero) results in a flat view (the valid range is 0 to 75). Increasing the *Pitch* has the effect of rotating the map about the X axis so that the top of the map appears further away and the bottom appears closer.

```
protected override void OnNavigatedTo(NavigationEventArgs e)
{
    map.Center = new System.Device.Location.GeoCoordinate(47.6066, -122.3386);
    map.ZoomLevel = zoomSlider.Value = 15;
    map.Pitch = pitchSlider.Value = 0;
}
private void zoomSlider_ValueChanged(object sender, RoutedPropertyChangedEventArgs<double> e)
{
    if (map != null)
    {
        map.ZoomLevel = ((Slider)sender).Value;
    }
}

private void pitchSlider_ValueChanged(object sender, RoutedPropertyChangedEventArgs<double> e)
{
    if (map != null)
    {
        map.Pitch = ((Slider)sender).Value;
    }
}
```

In a similar manner, the three *Button* controls provide the means for the user to modify the *Heading*, *MapCartographicMode*, and *ColorMode* of the map. The *Heading* property governs the orientation of the map. With a *Heading* value of 0 or 360, north is at the top of the page. As the user increments the *Heading* property, the map orientation rotates in a counter-clockwise direction about the Y axis. So, with a *Heading* value of 90, the top of the page is due east. A value of 180 would put the top of the page at due south. Due west at the top would require a value of 270. There are four discrete *MapCartographicMode* values, which are illustrated in Figure 18-11. Similarly, there are two *MapColorMode* properties.

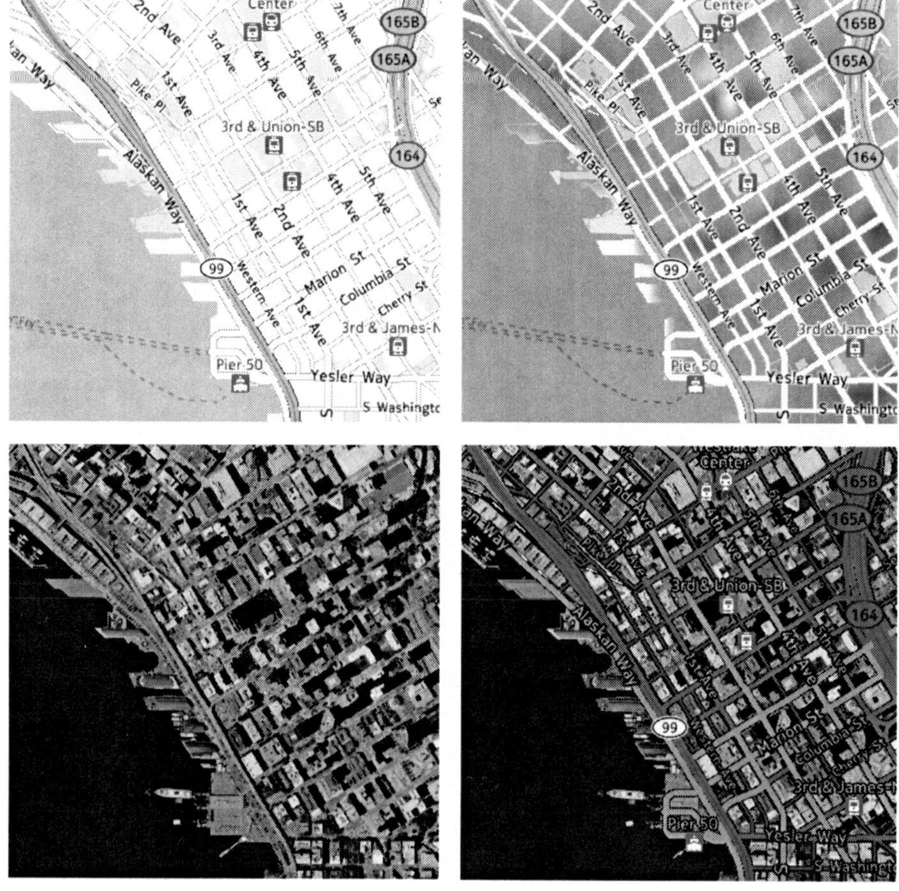

FIGURE 18-11 There are four *MapCartographicMode* values: *Road*, *Terrain*, *Aerial*, and *Hybrid*, as viewed from upper-left to lower-right.

```
private void headingButton_Click(object sender, RoutedEventArgs e)
{
    map.Heading = (map.Heading + 10) % 360;
}

private void mapModeButton_Click(object sender, RoutedEventArgs e)
{
    switch (map.CartographicMode)
    {
        case MapCartographicMode.Aerial:
            map.CartographicMode = MapCartographicMode.Hybrid; break;
        case MapCartographicMode.Hybrid:
            map.CartographicMode = MapCartographicMode.Road; break;
        case MapCartographicMode.Road:
            map.CartographicMode = MapCartographicMode.Terrain; break;
        case MapCartographicMode.Terrain:
            map.CartographicMode = MapCartographicMode.Aerial; break;
    }
}
```

```
private void colorModeButton_Click(object sender, RoutedEventArgs e)
{
    switch (map.ColorMode)
    {
        case MapColorMode.Dark:
            map.ColorMode = MapColorMode.Light; break;
        case MapColorMode.Light:
            map.ColorMode = MapColorMode.Dark; break;
    }
}
```

An alternative to setting individual properties on the *Map* control is to call the *SetView* method. This method has 10 overloads, and you can change multiple properties at once. Figure 18-12 shows the *MapDemo_SetView* solution in the sample code, which demonstrates this technique.

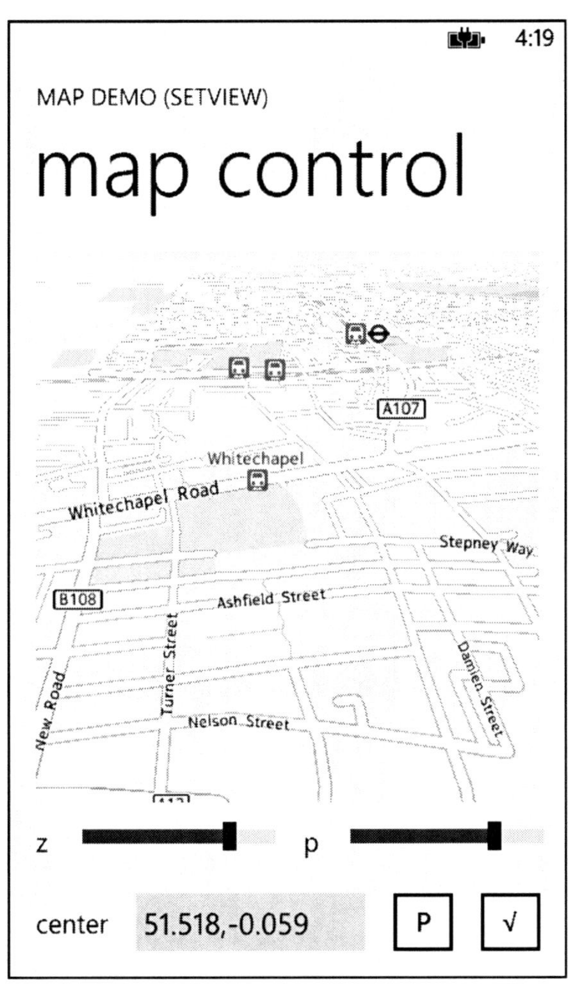

FIGURE 18-12 Using the *SetView* method, you can change multiple map properties all at once.

The two *Slider* controls govern the *ZoomLevel* and *Pitch* as before, but there are no *ValueChanged* handlers for the controls. Instead, the *Click* handler for the *updateButton* picks up the current value of each *Slider* and passes it to the *SetView* method. The *updateButton* is labelled with a tick mark (√). The *animationButton* changes its label from "P" to "L" to "N", and is backed by a *Click* handler that cycles through the three possible *MapAnimationKind* values; the *updateButton* uses the cached *animation Kind* field when it invokes *SetView*, along with a *GeoCoordinate* value for the new map *Center* value. The *MapAnimationKind* governs the visual animation that is used to transition to the new view. From the user's perspective, the effect is as follows:

- **MapAnimationKind.None** The old view snaps to the new view, with no visual animation.
- **MapAnimationKind.Linear** The user moves in a linear path from the old view to the new view, with no change in perspective.
- **MapAnimationKind.Parabolic** The user's view zooms out from the old view to a mid-point and then zooms in to the new view, describing a parabolic "flight path."

```
private MapAnimationKind animationKind = MapAnimationKind.None;

private void animationButton_Click(object sender, RoutedEventArgs e)
{
    switch (animationKind)
    {
        case MapAnimationKind.None:
            animationKind = MapAnimationKind.Linear;
            animationButton.Content = "L"; break;
        case MapAnimationKind.Linear:
            animationKind = MapAnimationKind.Parabolic;
            animationButton.Content = "P"; break;
        case MapAnimationKind.Parabolic:
            animationKind = MapAnimationKind.None;
            animationButton.Content = "N"; break;
    }
}

private void updateButton_Click(object sender, RoutedEventArgs e)
{
    string[] coordinates = centerText.Text.Split(',');
    GeoCoordinate geoCoord = new GeoCoordinate(double.Parse(coordinates[0]), double.
Parse(coordinates[1]));
    map.SetView(geoCoord, zoomSlider.Value, 0, pitchSlider.Value, animationKind);
}
```

Some of the properties of the *Map* control cannot be set in the *SetView* overloads. These include the *LandmarksEnabled* and *PedestrianFeaturesEnabled* flags. These flags govern whether recognized landmarks (such as prominent buildings and other structures) and pedestrian features (such as walk-ways, stairs, and pedestrian-only plazas) are shown on the map. A related feature is the map overlay capability, whereby you can add layers on top of the map. You can put any arbitrary UI elements in a layer and then add that layer to the collection of layers that the *Map* control maintains. You first saw this technique in the *BingPushpins* sample app. The new map APIs support the same conceptual behavior of layering text and graphics onto the map. However, the new APIs do not support *Pushpin* controls; thus, they can be slightly more cumbersome to work with in this context. The layer and overlay APIs are demonstrated in the *MapLayerDemo* app in the sample code, as shown in Figure 18-13.

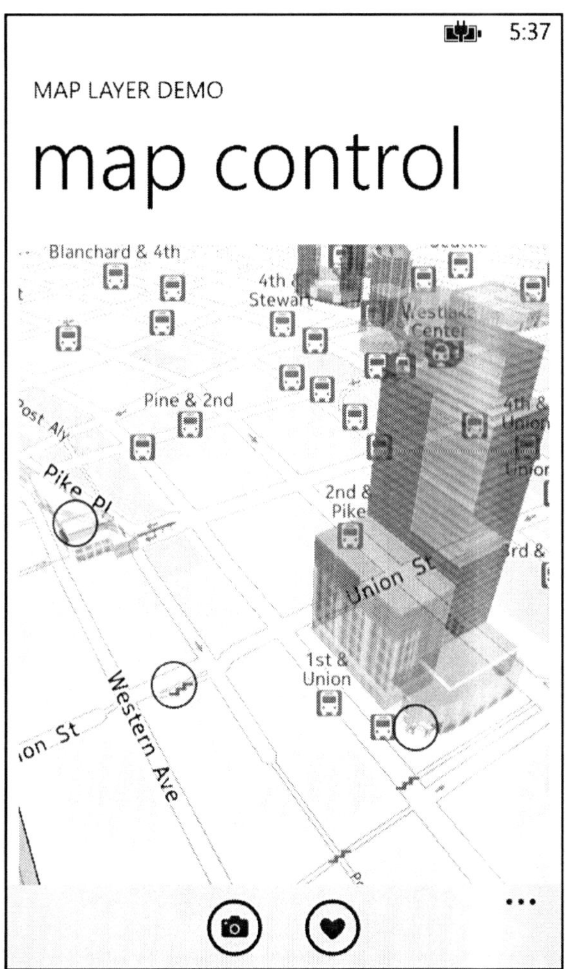

FIGURE 18-13 You can overlay multiple layers on a map.

In this app, there are two app bar buttons: one for toggling *LandmarksEnabled*, and the other for toggling *PedestrianFeaturesEnabled*. The code for the *Click* handlers is trivial.

```
private void landmarksButton_Click(object sender, EventArgs e)
{
    map.LandmarksEnabled = !map.LandmarksEnabled;
}

private void pedestrianButton_Click(object sender, EventArgs e)
{
    map.PedestrianFeaturesEnabled = !map.PedestrianFeaturesEnabled;
}
```

The overlay code is a little more complicated. The idea here is that when the user taps the map, the app will create a red circle and overlay this on the map at the point where the user tapped. A *Tap* event handler is wired up in the XAML for the map. This handler creates an *Ellipse* and adds this to a new *MapOverlay* object. To set the correct position, you first extract the position of the *Tap* event relative to the *Map* control. Next, you offset it by half the width/height of the *Ellipse* so that the point is centered around the center point of the *Ellipse* itself. Then, invoke the *ConvertViewportPointTo GeoCoordinate* method on the *Map* control and set the resulting *GeoCoordinate* into the *MapOverlay* object. Finally, add the *MapOverlay* to a *MapLayer* object and then add that object to the *Layers* collection on the *Map* control. This example only needs one *MapLayer*, so this is set up as a class field, initialized on first use. In other scenarios, you might want more than one *MapLayer*.

```
private MapLayer layer;

private void map_Tap(object sender, GestureEventArgs e)
{
    Ellipse ellipse = new Ellipse();
    ellipse.Width = 40;
    ellipse.Height = 40;
    ellipse.Stroke = new SolidColorBrush(Colors.Red);
    ellipse.StrokeThickness = 2;

    MapOverlay overlay = new MapOverlay();
    overlay.Content = ellipse;
    Point point = e.GetPosition(map);
    GeoCoordinate coordinate = map.ConvertViewportPointToGeoCoordinate(point);
    overlay.GeoCoordinate = coordinate;
    overlay.PositionOrigin = new Point(0.5, 0.5);

    if (layer == null)
    {
        layer = new MapLayer();
        map.Layers.Add(layer);
    }
    layer.Add(overlay);
}
```

Route and directions

If you want to provide route information and directions in your app, you have two choices: the *MapsDirectionsTask* is a simple, self-contained way to get directions, whereas the *GeocodeQuery*, *RouteQuery*, and *MapRoute* APIs offer more flexibility and power but at the cost of greater developer complexity. The *MapDirections* app in the sample code illustrates this more flexible approach, as depicted in Figure 18-14. Note that this app needs both *ID_CAP_MAP* and *ID_CAP_LOCATION*.

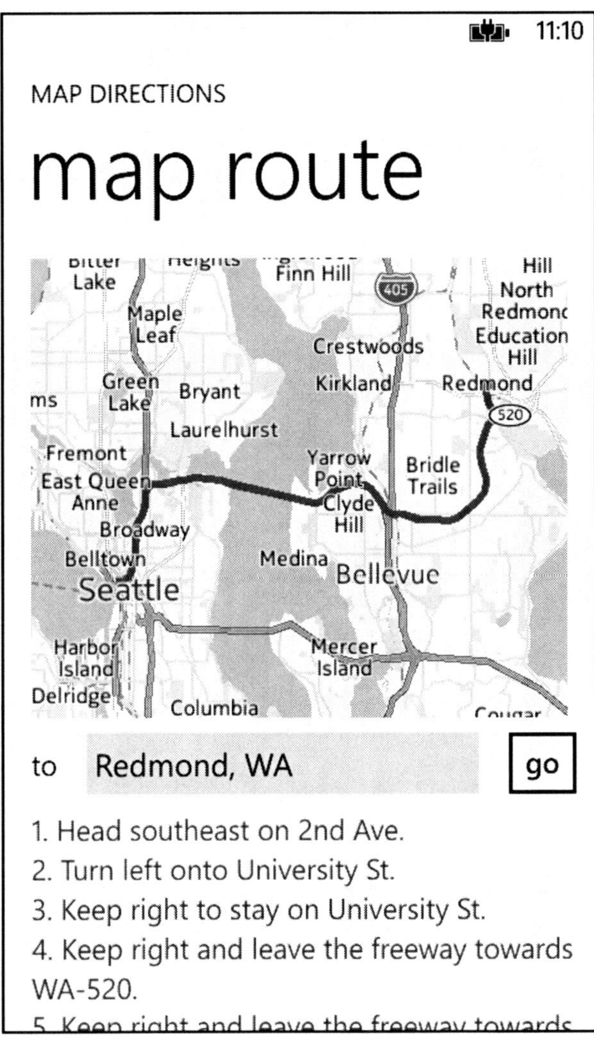

FIGURE 18-14 You can use the *RouteQuery* and *MapRoute* APIs to get route directions.

The XAML for the *MainPage* defines a *Map* control, a *TextBox* for the user to enter a destination place, and a *Button* to begin fetching the route information. Below that is a *ListBox* that will be data-bound to the route information when it is returned. The code for the page defines fields for a collection of *GeoCoordinate* values, which is used for the coordinates of the start and finish locations. The page also defines a *GeocodeQuery* for getting the coordinates for a textual finish location, and a *RouteQuery* for getting the route information. When the user taps the *getRoute* button, the *Click* handler first acquires the current location by using the *GetGeopositionAsync* method of the *Geolocator* class. Next, the user's requested finish location is fed into a *GeocodeQuery* to get the corresponding coordinates. This is done asynchronously; it raises a *QueryCompleted* event when finished.

```
private List<GeoCoordinate> coordinates = new List<GeoCoordinate>();
private GeocodeQuery codeQuery;
private RouteQuery routeQuery;

private async void getRoute_Click(object sender, RoutedEventArgs e)
{
    try
    {
        Geolocator locator = new Geolocator();
        locator.DesiredAccuracy = PositionAccuracy.High;
        Geoposition position = await locator.GetGeopositionAsync();

        GeoCoordinate coordinate = new GeoCoordinate(
            position.Coordinate.Latitude, position.Coordinate.Longitude);
        coordinates.Add(coordinate);

        codeQuery = new GeocodeQuery();
        codeQuery.SearchTerm = targetText.Text;
        codeQuery.GeoCoordinate = coordinate;
        codeQuery.QueryCompleted += codeQuery_QueryCompleted;
        codeQuery.QueryAsync();
    }
    catch (UnauthorizedAccessException)
    {
        MessageBox.Show("location is disabled");
    }
}
```

The handler for the *QueryCompleted* event for the *GeocodeQuery* adds both the start and finish coordinates to a *RouteQuery*, hooks up the *QueryCompleted* event for that query, and then invokes the query.

```
private void codeQuery_QueryCompleted(
    object sender, QueryCompletedEventArgs<IList<MapLocation>> e)
{
    if (e.Error != null)
    {
        return;
    }

    routeQuery = new RouteQuery();
    coordinates.Add(e.Result[0].GeoCoordinate);
    routeQuery.Waypoints = coordinates;
    routeQuery.QueryCompleted += routeQuery_QueryCompleted;
    routeQuery.QueryAsync();
}
```

The handler for the *QueryCompleted* event on the *RouteQuery* first extracts the *Route* object from the event arguments, converts it to a *MapRoute* object, and then adds it to the *Map* control. This results in the route being drawn on the map. Next, the handler iterates the collection of route instructions and adds each one to a list, which is then data-bound to the *ListBox* at the bottom of the page.

```
private void routeQuery_QueryCompleted(
    object sender, QueryCompletedEventArgs<Route> e)
{
    if (e.Error != null)
    {
        return;
    }

    Route route = e.Result;
    MapRoute mapRoute = new MapRoute(route);
    map.AddRoute(mapRoute);

    List<string> list = new List<string>();
    foreach (RouteLeg leg in route.Legs)
    {
        for (int i = 0; i < leg.Maneuvers.Count; i++)
        {
            RouteManeuver maneuver = leg.Maneuvers[i];
            list.Add(String.Format("{0}. {1}", i+1, maneuver.InstructionText));
        }
    }
    routeList.ItemsSource = list;
}
```

This approach is useful if you need to do further computations on the route information or if you're using it for other purposes than display. If all you want is to provide a simple set of directions, it is easier to use the *MapsDirectionsTask*. This also provides a suitable UI for you, as described in the Maps Launchers section that follows.

Note Some of the types in the new maps and location APIs are defined in the *System.Device.Location* namespace, whereas some are defined in *Windows.Devices.Geolocation*. This can be a little confusing, especially, for instance, the *GeoCoordinate* class (defined in *System.Device.Location*) and the (similar, but different) *Geocoordinate* class (defined in *Windows.Devices.Geolocation*). In Windows Phone location-based apps, it is common to use a combination of the *System.Device.Location.GeoCoordinate* class along with the *Windows.Devices.Gelocation.Geolocator* class. In practice, you're unlikely to use the *Windows.Devices.Geolocation* type, unless you're cross-targeting with Windows 8.

As an aside, if you want to streamline your code a little, you could write simple wrappers for the asynchronous *GeocodeQuery* and *RouteQuery* calls instead of setting up traditional callbacks. The following code shows how you can achieve this, via extension methods:

```
public static class GeocodeQueryExtensions
{
    public static Task<IList<MapLocation>> GeocodeAsync(this GeocodeQuery query)
    {
        TaskCompletionSource<IList<MapLocation>> source =
            new TaskCompletionSource<IList<MapLocation>>();
        query.QueryCompleted += (sender, e) =>
        {
            if (e.Error != null)
            {
                source.TrySetException(e.Error);
            }
            else
            {
                source.SetResult(e.Result);
            }
        };
        query.QueryAsync();
        return source.Task;
    }
}

public static class RouteQueryExtensions
{
    public static Task<Route> RouteAsync(this RouteQuery query)
    {
        TaskCompletionSource<Route> source =
            new TaskCompletionSource<Route>();
        query.QueryCompleted += (sender, e) =>
        {
            if (e.Error != null)
            {
                source.TrySetException(e.Error);
            }
            else
            {
                source.SetResult(e.Result);
            }
        };
        query.QueryAsync();
        return source.Task;
    }
}
```

You could then invoke these extension methods and await their return, as demonstrated in the code that follows. This eliminates the need for the *QueryCompleted* event handlers for both queries.

```
private async void getRoute_Click(object sender, RoutedEventArgs e)
{
        ... unchanged code omitted for brevity
        codeQuery = new GeocodeQuery();
```

```
        codeQuery.SearchTerm = targetText.Text;
        codeQuery.GeoCoordinate = coordinate;

        //codeQuery.QueryCompleted += codeQuery_QueryCompleted;
        //codeQuery.QueryAsync();
        IList<MapLocation> loc = await codeQuery.GeocodeAsync();
        coordinates.Add(loc[0].GeoCoordinate);
        routeQuery = new RouteQuery();
        routeQuery.Waypoints = coordinates;

        //routeQuery.QueryCompleted += routeQuery_QueryCompleted;
        //routeQuery.QueryAsync();
        Route route = await routeQuery.RouteAsync();
        MapRoute mapRoute = new MapRoute(route);
        map.AddRoute(mapRoute);

        List<string> list = new List<string>();
        foreach (RouteLeg leg in route.Legs)
        {
            for (int i = 0; i < leg.Maneuvers.Count; i++)
            {
                RouteManeuver maneuver = leg.Maneuvers[i];
                list.Add(String.Format("{0}. {1}", i + 1, maneuver.InstructionText));
            }
        }
        routeList.ItemsSource = list;
}
```

Maps Launchers

The new maps APIs in Windows Phone 8 include four Launchers, which are described in Table 18-3. The *MapsTask* and *MapsDirectionsTask* are the modern equivalent of the "old" *BingMapsTask* and *BingMapsDirectionsTask*. In fact, under the hood, these two sets of APIs are the same, they just have two different names.

TABLE 18-3 Windows Phone 8 Maps Launchers

Task	Description
MapsTask	Searches around the current or specified location for items that match the specified search text. This is a synonym for the *BingMapsTask*.
MapsDirectionsTask	Provides a map route and directions list, given the destination location (which can be in coordinate or textual form), and optionally a starting location. This is a synonym for the *BingMapsDirectionsTask*.
MapDownloaderTask	Takes the user through a series of narrowing choices to download selected maps to the phone so that later map-based apps can use these maps for faster rendering.
MapUpdaterTask	Takes the user's current set of locally downloaded maps and then fetches any updates that might be available for them.

The *TestMapsTasks* solution in the sample code illustrates the use of all four of these Launchers (invoked by four buttons), as shown in Figure 18-15.

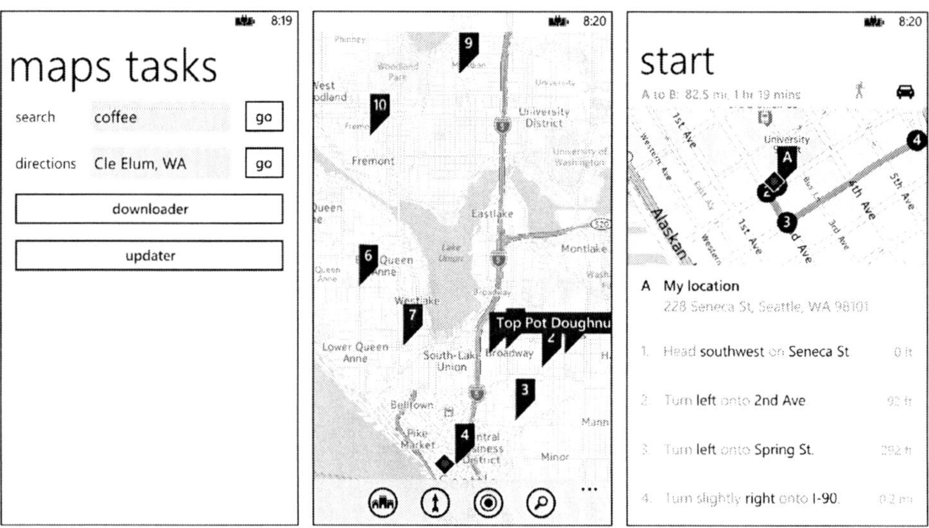

FIGURE 18-15 The *TestMapsTasks* solution (on the left), the *MapsTask* Launcher (center), and the *MapsDirectionsTask* Launcher (right).

The code is very simple; all of the interesting work is in the *Click* event handlers for the four *Button* controls. The *searchButton* invokes the *MapsTask*, the *directionsButton* invokes the *MapsDirections Task*, the *downloadButton* invokes the *MapDownloaderTask*, and the *updateButton* invokes the *MapUpdaterTask*.

```
private void searchButton_Click(object sender, RoutedEventArgs e)
{
    MapsTask mapsTask = new MapsTask();
    mapsTask.SearchTerm = searchText.Text;
    mapsTask.ZoomLevel = 15;
    mapsTask.Show();
}

private void directionsButton_Click(object sender, RoutedEventArgs e)
{
    MapsDirectionsTask directionsTask = new MapsDirectionsTask();
    directionsTask.End = new LabeledMapLocation(directionsText.Text, null);
    directionsTask.Show();
}

private void dowloadButton_Click(object sender, RoutedEventArgs e)
{
    MapDownloaderTask downloaderTask = new MapDownloaderTask();
    downloaderTask.Show();
}

private void updateButton_Click(object sender, RoutedEventArgs e)
{
    MapUpdaterTask updaterTask = new MapUpdaterTask();
    updaterTask.Show();
}
```

Continuous background execution (Windows Phone 8)

The memory and processor constraints on a mobile device mean that there is only ever one app running in the foreground with access to the full screen. As described in Chapter 2, "App model and navigation," when the user navigates away from an app, that app is suspended and might also be tombstoned. Then, there is a set of background-specific task types that are designed to run only in the background, as discussed in Chapter 9, "Background agents." Between the "fully-foreground" app and the "fully-background" agent lies the Continuous Background Execution (CBE) app, which can run either in the foreground or in the background.

The canonical use case for this app type is the "run-tracker." The idea is that the app starts in the foreground, but then when the user navigates forward away from the app, it continues to execute in the background. Of course, if the user navigates backward out of the app it is closed as normal. Taking the run-tracker case as an example, the user might start the app, and perhaps configure some settings in readiness for starting his run. Then, when he starts his run, he might navigate forward to a media-player app so that he can listen to music while he's running. Meanwhile, the run-tracker app continues to track his running progress (tracking location in real time, distance covered, average speed, altitude gain, and so on). The app might also provide intermittent feedback to the user in the form of toasts or audible prompts. If the user taps a toast, this could take him back into the app.

Although you could achieve something close to the required behavior in Windows Phone 7, this required you to handle the screen lock events; it was not very elegant, and also it didn't give you any way to continue executing if the user started another foreground app. Behind the scenes, the system imposes constraints. The reason for these constraints is that if an app is allowed to continue to run while it is not in the foreground, there is a risk that it will consume resources to an extent that might impact the foreground app and, therefore, the user's experience of the phone. The resource management model in Windows Phone 8 explicitly supports CBE apps by carefully balancing the competing requirements of the foreground app and the CBE app so that they don't conflict.

Note CBE apps are listed in the background task control panel on the phone, in the list of "apps that might run in the background." Because background execution potentially consumes more battery power, the user always has the option to block any or all of these apps from running.

If you want to build a location-tracking CBE app, there are four requirements:

- Your app manifest must specify that the app requires background execution. Without this, the app would be subject to the normal activation/deactivation model and would not be allowed to execute in the background.

- Your *App* class must handle the *RunningInBackground* event. This event is raised at the point when the user navigates forward away from your app, thereby putting your app into the background.

  Technically, you can do whatever you like in this handler (or nothing), but what you're supposed to do is to ensure that you trim your operations so that while you're running in the background, you perform only the minimal critical work that is required. At this point, of course, you can no longer access the screen, so there's no point trying to update your UI, for example.

  The Windows Phone 8 SDK documentation includes a detailed list of which APIs are permitted during background execution. It is in your own interests to minimize your background work, because behind the scenes, CBE resources are allocated opportunistically. This means that under normal circumstances, you can continue to execute in the background, so long as you don't consume resources excessively. However, for the case in which the phone is under extreme resource pressure (which is more likely on a low-memory device), priority is generally given to the foreground app (and to VoIP), whereas background tasks—including CBE—have a lower priority, and can even be starved of resources altogether. Minimizing your work in the background helps to prevent overall resource pressure.

- The app must be able to handle the restart case. The typical scenario is when your app is running in the background but surfaces toasts periodically. When the user taps a toast, this restarts your app. In the case of CBE apps, the system relaunches the app by resuming the currently running instance, complete with its internal page navigation backstack from the previous user session. In this scenario, you might want to clear the backstack to avoid confusing the user. See Chapter 2 for more details on the app lifecycle, resume model, and managing the backstack.

- Your app must be actively tracking location.

The *SimpleCbe* solution in the sample code demonstrates the behavior of a CBE app, which is demonstrated in Figure 18-16.

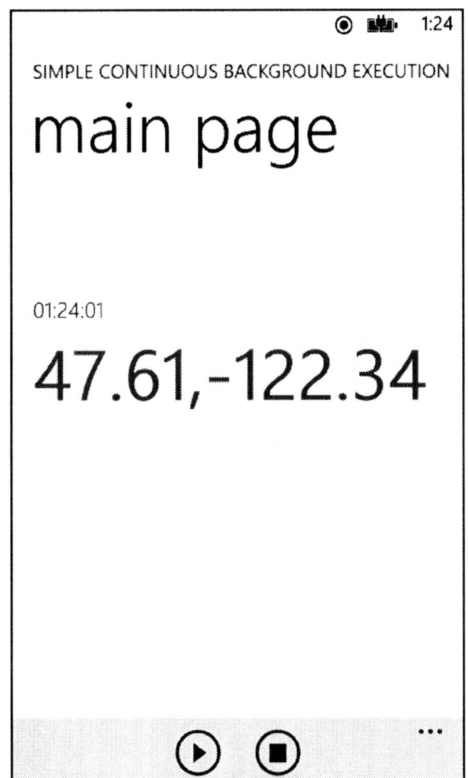

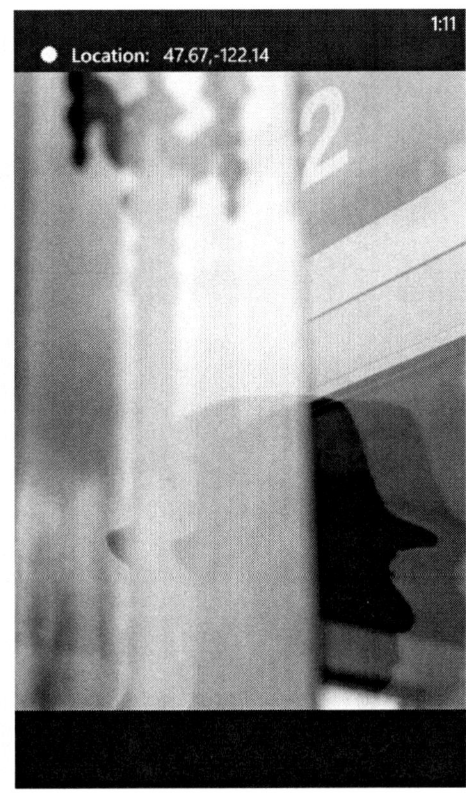

FIGURE 18-16 A CBE app has a normal UI in the foreground (on the left), and uses toasts in the background (right).

For the first requirement, the app manifest must include two items. The app requires *ID_CAP_LOCATION*, as normal, because it will be using location features. It might also require *ID_CAP_MAP* if it uses maps. In addition, it must register as a background-capable app, and this is done by adding the *BackgroundExecution* element, as shown in the code that follows. This is a child node of the *DefaultTask* element. Currently, there is only one supported *ExecutionType*, and its *Name* must be set to "LocationTracking". Keep in mind that although you can configure the *ID_CAP_LOCATION* setting by using the manifest designer, there is no designer support for the *BackgroundExecution* element, so you must edit the app manifest manually to add this.

```
<DefaultTask Name="_default" NavigationPage="MainPage.xaml">
  <BackgroundExecution>
    <ExecutionType Name="LocationTracking"/>
  </BackgroundExecution>
</DefaultTask>
```

The second requirement is that the *App* class must register to handle the *RunningInBackground* event. You do this in the *App.xaml* file, where all the other app-level event handlers are registered.

```
<shell:PhoneApplicationService
    Launching="Application_Launching" Closing="Application_Closing"
    Activated="Application_Activated" Deactivated="Application_Deactivated"
    RunningInBackground="Application_RunningInBackground"/>
```

If you use IntelliSense and the autocomplete feature in Visual Studio to register for this event, a stub method will be added to your *App.xaml.cs* file for you. In the sample app, the *App* class has just two custom data members. First, it exposes a *Geolocator* property, suitably initialized in the property getter. This will be used for getting location data. Second, it defines a *bool* property for tracking whether the app is currently running in the background. This is set to *true* in the *RunningInBackground* event handler, and to *false* in the *Activated* event handler. Because this app is registered to run in the background, when the user navigates forward away from the app, the system sends it a *RunningInBackground* event instead of the usual *Deactivated* event.

```
private static Geolocator locator;

public static Geolocator Locator
{
    get
    {
        lock (typeof(App))
        {
            if (locator == null)
            {
                locator = new Geolocator();
                locator.DesiredAccuracy = PositionAccuracy.High;
                locator.MovementThreshold = 50;
            }
        }
        return locator;
    }
}


public static bool IsRunningInBackground { get; private set; }

private void PhoneApplicationService_RunningInBackground(
    object sender, RunningInBackgroundEventArgs e)
{
    IsRunningInBackground = true;
}

private void Application_Activated(object sender, ActivatedEventArgs e)
{
    IsRunningInBackground = false;
}
```

In a CBE app, it's also a good idea to take a closer look at the *Deactivated* event. Recall that the system raises this event for the app when it is deactivating it. The *DeactivatedEventArgs* supplied with this event exposes a *Reason* property, which gives you some insight as to why the app is being terminated.

```
private void Application_Deactivated(object sender, DeactivatedEventArgs e)
{
    switch (e.Reason)
    {
        case DeactivationReason.ApplicationAction:
            Debug.WriteLine("Application_Deactivated: the app did something to cause
termination.");
            break;
        case DeactivationReason.PowerSavingModeOn:
            Debug.WriteLine("Application_Deactivated: power-saver mode is on, and the power went
below the threshold for running CBE.");
            break;
        case DeactivationReason.ResourcesUnavailable:
            Debug.WriteLine("Application_Deactivated: the phone does not have enough resources
(memory, CPU) to allow CBE to continue.");
            break;
        case DeactivationReason.UserAction:
            Debug.WriteLine("Application_Deactivated: the user did something to terminate the
app.");
            break;
    }
}
```

Note If some condition arises at run time for which you actually want to deactivate the app and not continue to run in the background, you can stop the location data events by unhooking your *PositionChanged* event handler in the *RunningInBackground* handler and then possibly hook it up again in the *Activated* event.

In the *MainPage* class, the two app bar buttons are implemented to register or unregister the event handler for the *PositionChanged* event on the *Geolocator* property in the *App* class. This handler does one of two things: if the app is running in the foreground, it extracts the latest coordinate data and sets it into the UI; if the app is not running in the foreground, it composes a toast from the coordinate data and shows that, instead.

```
private void startButton_Click(object sender, EventArgs e)
{
    App.Locator.PositionChanged += Locator_PositionChanged;
}

private void stopButton_Click(object sender, EventArgs e)
{
    App.Locator.PositionChanged -= Locator_PositionChanged;
}
```

```
private void Locator_PositionChanged(Geolocator sender, PositionChangedEventArgs args)
{
    Geocoordinate coord = args.Position.Coordinate;
    string coordText = String.Format("{0:0.00},{1:0.00}", coord.Latitude, coord.Longitude);
    if (!App.IsRunningInBackground)
    {
        Dispatcher.BeginInvoke(() =>
        {
            timeText.Text = coord.Timestamp.ToString("hh:mm:ss");
            locationText.Text = coordText;
        });
    }
    else
    {
        ShellToast toast = new ShellToast();
        toast.Content = coordText;
        toast.Title = "Location: ";
        toast.NavigationUri = new Uri("/MainPage.xaml", UriKind.Relative);
        toast.Show();
    }
}
```

The third requirement is less obvious. In the app so far, all the UI work is done in one page: the *MainPage*. However, consider the *SimpleCbe_MultiPage* solution in the sample code. This is a variation on the app in which the location UI is not done on the *MainPage* but instead on a second page named *LocationPage*. The implication of this is that when the app is running in the background and sends a toast on which the user then taps, it takes her to *LocationPage* not to *MainPage*.

When a background-enabled app is relaunched from the App List or from a toast, the system navigates to the page on the top of the stack (that is, the last page the user was on before she navigated away from the app) by using *NavigationMode.Reset*. Next, the system navigates to the page specified in the *NavigationUri* in the toast by using *NavigationMode.New*. Recall from Chapter 2 that the system maintains a stack of pages to which the user has navigated within the app. It is up to the app developer to decide whether to unload the page stack. The Visual Studio template has been updated to clear the page stack, under the assumption that this is what most people will want to do. If you don't want this behavior, you can remove or modify the code from the hidden region of *App.xaml.cs* (highlighted in bold in the example that follows), specifically, the *CheckForResetNavigation* and *Clear BackStackAfterReset* methods.

In the *Navigated* event handler, the app checks to see if the *NavigationMode* of the navigation is *Reset*. This will be the case if the user has relaunched the app when it is already running in the background. In this case, the app goes on to clear the backstack. Exactly what you do here depends on your business logic; for example, instead of clearing the backstack, you might want to cancel the incoming navigation and redirect to another page.

```
private void InitializePhoneApplication()
{
    if (phoneApplicationInitialized)
        return;
```

```
        RootFrame = new PhoneApplicationFrame();
        RootFrame.Navigated += CompleteInitializePhoneApplication;
        RootFrame.NavigationFailed += RootFrame_NavigationFailed;

        RootFrame.Navigated += CheckForResetNavigation;

        phoneApplicationInitialized = true;
    }

    private void CheckForResetNavigation(object sender, NavigationEventArgs e)
    {
        if (e.NavigationMode == NavigationMode.Reset)
            RootFrame.Navigated += ClearBackStackAfterReset;
    }

    private void ClearBackStackAfterReset(object sender, NavigationEventArgs e)
    {
        RootFrame.Navigated -= ClearBackStackAfterReset;
        if (e.NavigationMode != NavigationMode.New && e.NavigationMode != NavigationMode.Refresh)
            return;
        while (RootFrame.RemoveBackEntry() != null) { ; }
    }
```

Note You can take advantage of the CBE model in an app that doesn't track location, if you want. The reason this might be useful is if you want the "resume" behavior, where your app is relaunched with its previous backstack. In Windows Phone 7, this behavior was only available to in-box apps, but there are scenarios in which it is valid for any app. One way to achieve "resume" behavior is to mark your app *LocationTracking,* even though you don't actually track location. When an app is marked *LocationTracking* and you actively track location, the system will allow your app to run in the background and also apply the Fast App Resume (FAR) policy. If you don't actually track location or if another location-tracking app is started, the system will suspend your app as normal. The difference is that when the user taps on one of your tiles, the system resumes the app (as opposed to launching it from scratch), provided it is still in the backstack and was not tombstoned.

Testing location in the simulator

To test your location-based app, you can use the Visual Studio location sensor simulator. This is available on the Location tab in the Additional Tools window in the emulator. To use this, you start your app and start the location-tracking feature. In the simulator, toggle the Live button on. This generates location information for your current location. You can then click anywhere on the map to generate further locations. This is illustrated in Figure 18-17. You can also use the simulator to record a chain of locations, and play these back at any time. You can even save a chain of locations to a file so that it persists beyond the life of an emulator session and can be loaded in a later session.

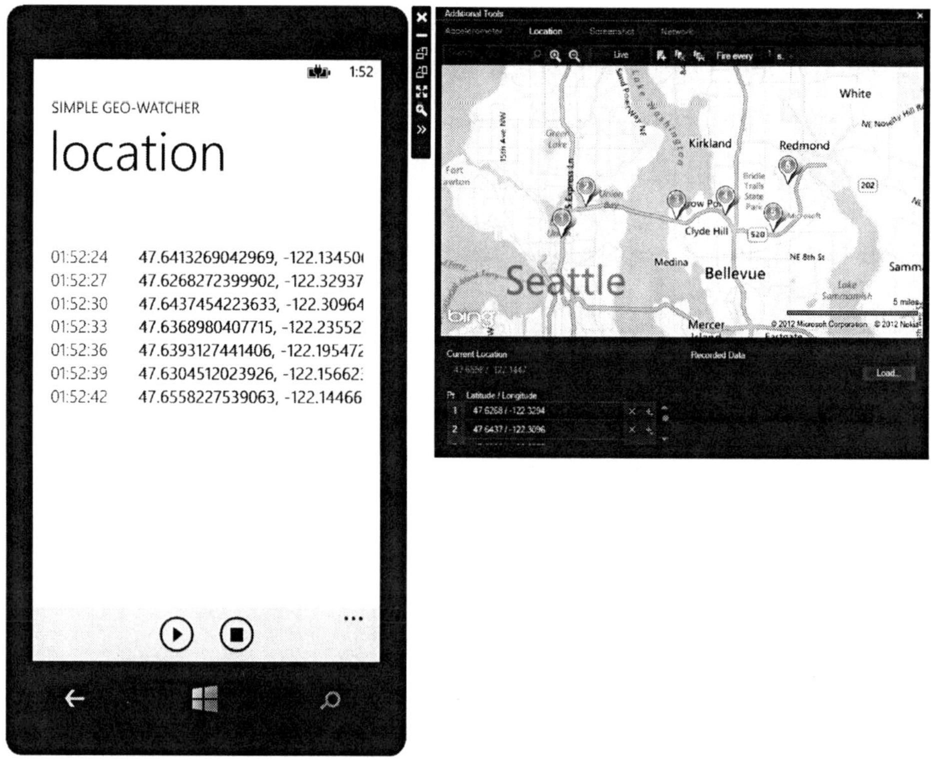

FIGURE 18-17 You can use the location sensor simulator to test your location-based app.

Location best practices

As noted in Chapter 6, "Sensors," all sensors on the phone use power, and that includes the sensors used in location services. The location sensors can consume a lot of power (reducing battery life) because of the way that they fetch and report data very frequently, and because it involves keeping the GPS radio on. You should therefore consider very carefully how you want to use classes such as the *GeoCoordinateWatcher* and the *Geolocator*. You should avoid running them without notifying the user, and you should always give the user control over starting and stopping them. When the user is running a location tracking app, the phone shell displays a corresponding "bullseye" icon in the notification area. In some apps, the use of these features is implicit and obvious from the nature of the app, but it's still a good idea to inform the user that you're doing this, and preferably to ask his permission at least once, in advance. You should also turn them off when not needed and remove all event handlers. Consider using the default accuracy setting, which is less accurate but consumes less power. For example, use the default setting if you only need a less specific location, such as the general city area for things like weather or basic personalization.

You are also encouraged to set the *MovementThreshold* property on the *GeoCoordinateWatcher* or *Geolocator* class. This is the distance in meters that the phone must move, relative to the last *PositionChanged* event, before the location provider raises another *PositionChanged* event. To optimize battery life, the recommended setting is above 20. An appropriate setting depends on the nature of your app: if you're tracking position changes for someone walking, a smaller setting might be more appropriate. On the other hand, if you're tracking movements of a car, a much higher value will probably be more useful (unless you're building a turn-by-turn feature). Setting *MovementThreshold* to a higher value will save some CPU time because the app platform does not report all values from the sensor, but it does not prevent the sensors from retrieving the data. So, although this does save on battery consumption, it doesn't save very much.

You can use the Reactive Extensions for location data in exactly the same way as for accelerometer data, discussed in Chapter 6. This way, you can sample the data stream and apply a filter of some kind. However, this also does not prevent the underlying system from sourcing the sensor data, nor does it prevent the app platform from propagating the data changed events to your app, so again, there are no battery savings with this approach.

Summary

You have an array of choices for building location-aware apps, with or without integrated maps. Your choice of the Windows Phone 7 Bing-related APIs or the new enhanced Windows Phone 8 APIs largely depends on whether you're cross-targeting Windows Phone 7 and Windows Phone 8, or cross-targeting Windows Phone 8 and Windows 8. The programming model and supported techniques are broadly similar, even though the specific classes are different. Windows Phone 8 also provides the ability to continue executing in the background. As with all sensor-based apps, you should carefully consider the battery impact of getting location data, especially if you're building a CBE app.

PART III

New Windows Phone 8 Features

CHAPTER 19

Speech

Mobile phones have always been on the cutting edge of new user interface (UI) paradigms. With limited screen real estate and the need of users to complete tasks quickly while on the run, solutions that might have worked well on a desktop computer must be rethought or thrown out entirely. Until recently, however, most of the innovation in mobile phone interaction focused on tactile input—ways for users to control the phone by using their fingers, whether via a physical keyboard, a stylus pen, or a capacitive touch screen. The advent of speech as a means of interacting with modern smartphones is exciting not just for the existing tasks it makes easier (for example, saying, "Call Terry Adams at home," to initiate a phone call) but for its potential to open up an entire new genre of apps and experiences on the phone. Of course, in some ways it's ironic that the latest craze in phones is the ability to talk into them, but as we'll show in this chapter, the possibilities of a modern speech platform are far beyond anything of which Alexander Graham Bell could have dreamt.

When it comes to speech in Windows Phone 8 apps, there are three topics of interest. First, you can register voice commands, which can then be invoked by the user from the Global Speech Experience (GSE); for example, "Movies, show what's playing now." Second, you can use APIs for Speech Recognition (SR) to accept speech input within the apps themselves, including both command-and-control and free-form dictation. Finally, you can use the phone's Text-to-Speech (TTS) framework to read out text as audio. The latter two features can also be combined to provide a responsive spoken dialog similar to what is available in the built-in Messaging app. ("Message from Kim Abercrombie." You can say, "Read it" or "Ignore.")

Voice commands

In Windows Phone 7.x, users were able to perform a number of specific tasks directly from the GSE, which is the speech dialog that is launched when the user presses and holds the hardware Start button. These tasks included making phone calls, sending text messages, and issuing Bing search queries. Users could also use the speech functionality to open Windows Phone Store apps, but nothing more. That is, you could say, "Open Weather," but not, "Open Weather and show me the forecast for Phoenix." In Windows Phone 8, developers can provide a rich set of voice commands with which users can launch Windows Phone Store apps to perform specific tasks with all of the necessary context provided by speech. This section describes how to register the actions that your app supports and how to handle being launched from speech.

The GSE

Because all of the user scenarios in this section originate from the GSE, we should start by reviewing the user experience (UX) for that component so that you understand how users will trigger your voice commands. This will help you to determine how best to expose your app to users through this UI.

As in Windows Phone 7, users can activate the GSE by pressing and holding the hardware Start button. When they do so, they see a screen that looks similar to Figure 19-1.

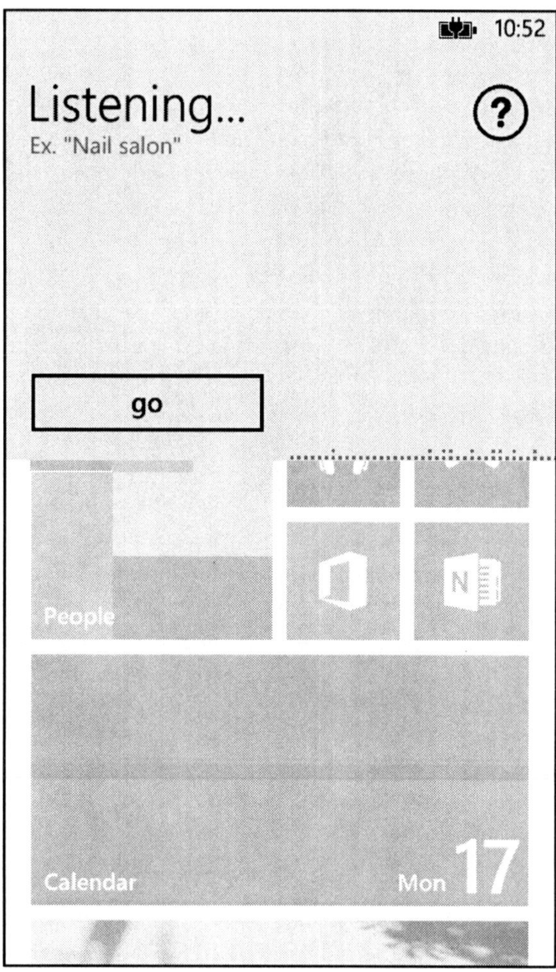

FIGURE 19-1 Users activate the GSE by pressing and holding the hardware Start button.

After the GSE displays and says that it's "Listening...," users are free to make verbal requests into the phone's microphone. The GSE is sensitive enough to know when they have completed their requests, at which point it will begin trying to match it to a valid action on the phone (or perform a Bing search).

Although most users know what they want to do when starting the GSE, a small help button is provided to show what else they can do by using speech. Tapping the Help icon in the upper right of the GSE brings up a full-screen display titled "What Can I Say?" This provides a list of valid voice commands. In Windows Phone 8, this screen includes a new pivot for Apps that lists Windows Phone Store apps that support voice commands, as shown in Figure 19-2. Tapping one of the apps provides a list of commands supported by that app.

FIGURE 19-2 The GSE's Apps pivot shows which apps support voice commands.

You will probably notice that throughout the experience, there is a considerable emphasis on providing example commands that can help users to build up a repertoire of tasks that they can complete by voice. As a developer, when you define voice commands, you also have an opportunity to provide such examples. Ensure that you take advantage of this chance to expose some of your most valuable commands.

Tip If you have a microphone set up on your computer, you can use the Windows Phone Emulator to perform all the same search commands that you can on a device. You can also use the F2 key to activate the GSE rather than pressing and holding the emulator's Start button.

Building a simple voice commands App

Now that you understand the user entry point for voice commands, it's time to build an app that can expose them. The *ToDoList* solution in the sample code demonstrates some of the capabilities of the speech API. It contains two pages, one for listing existing items and one for adding new items. Figure 19-3 shows the basic UI.

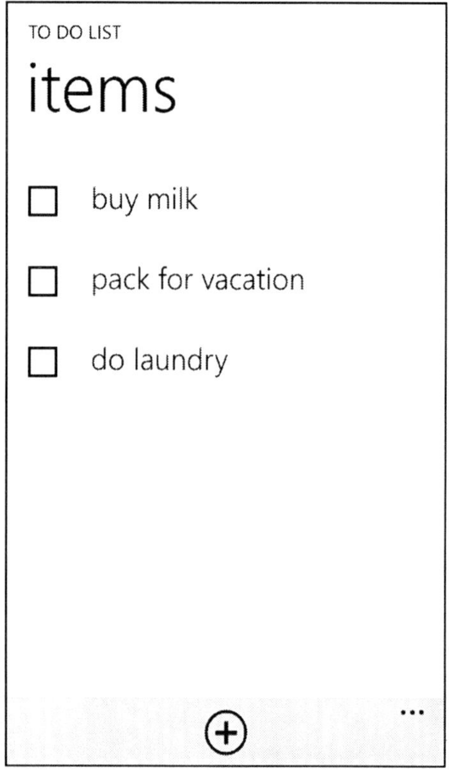

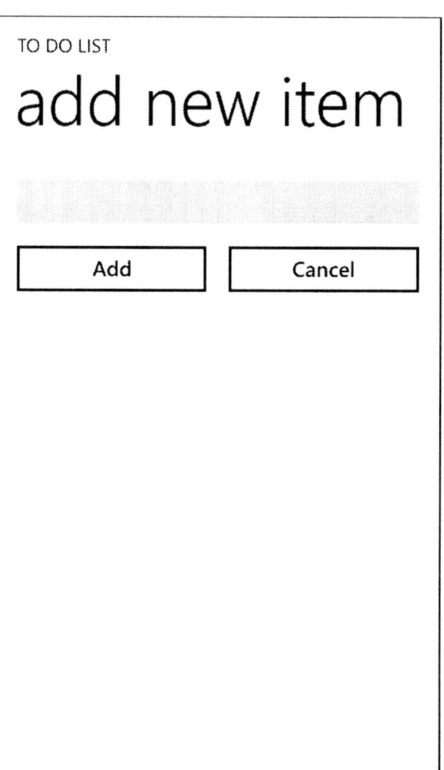

FIGURE 19-3 With the *ToDoList* solution, users can manage a simple list of to-do items.

Registering voice commands

To list the voice commands that your app supports, you first need to create a Voice Command Definition (VCD) file. The VCD file describes the format of the command that is expected, what the device should say back to you when it recognizes the command, and which page in your app should be invoked to handle it. Microsoft Visual Studio Express 2012 for Windows Phone includes a default template for VCD files, making it easy to add one to your project. Simply right-click your project, and then on the shortcut menu that appears, click Add New Item, and then click Voice Command Definition from the list of available items, as shown in Figure 19-4.

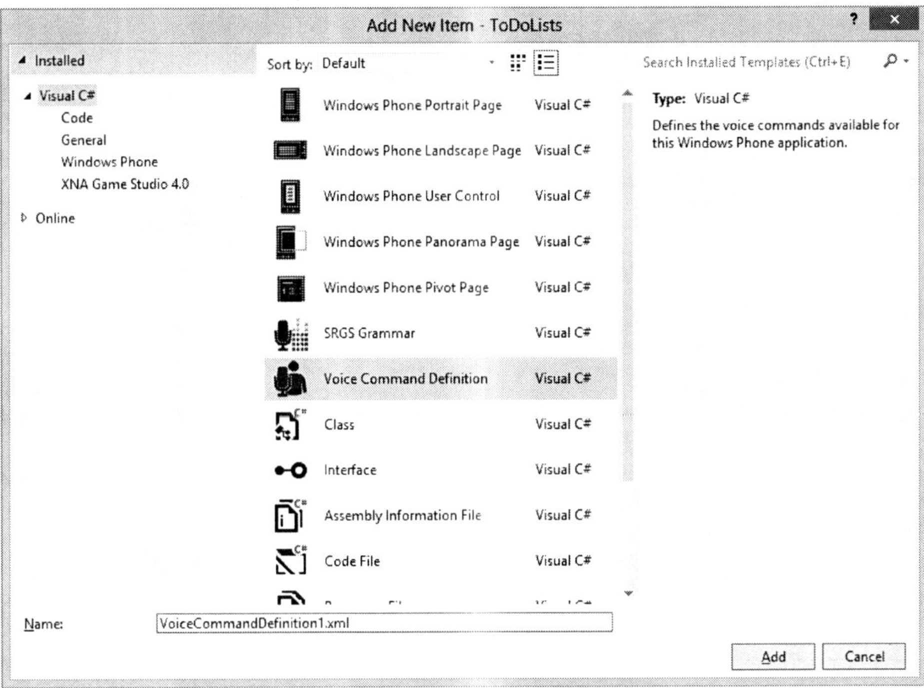

FIGURE 19-4 The Add New Item dialog box presents a default template for VCD files.

The default template includes sample commands for a game, including "play new game." For the *ToDoList* solution, we will start by defining a simple voice command which can create a new item. The full VCD file required to enable this command is shown in the following:

```
<?xml version="1.0" encoding="utf-8"?>

<VoiceCommands xmlns="http://schemas.microsoft.com/voicecommands/1.0">
  <CommandSet xml:lang="en-US">
    <CommandPrefix>To Do List</CommandPrefix>
    <Example>create new item</Example>

    <Command Name="CreateNewItem">
      <Example>create new item</Example>
      <ListenFor>create [a] new item</ListenFor>
      <ListenFor>add [an] item</ListenFor>
      <Feedback>creating a new item... </Feedback>
      <Navigate Target="/NewListItemPage.xaml" />
    </Command>
  </CommandSet>
</VoiceCommands>
```

VCD files offer a concise and powerful way to describe the voice commands that your app can support, so it is worth understanding what all of the elements mean. Table 19-1 describes the basic schema for VCD files.

TABLE 19-1 Voice commands schema

Element	Attribute	Description
VoiceCommands		Top-level element for all voice commands. This can contain many *CommandSet* children.
	Xmlns	Always *http://schemas.microsoft.com/voicecommands/1.0.*
CommandSet		Contains all voice commands for a given culture (for example, "en-us").
	xml:lang	An IETF-style culture code, such as "en-us" or "de-de." When this value matches the current culture of the phone (configurable in Settings), the speech service tries to match the given commands; otherwise, they are ignored. Keep in mind that command sets are not shared across culture codes, even when the language is the same. Thus, if you want to have the same set of voice commands supported for "en-us" and "en-gb," you need to create two copies of the *CommandSet*, one for each code.
	Name	An optional name to be used as an index into the list of installed command sets from code.
CommandPrefix		The pronunciation of app names doesn't always match up with their phonetic parts. Using this optional element, you can spell out an alternative name for your app that matches the way it sounds.
Example		A single example voice command for this *CommandSet*. This example is used in several places: ■ In the apps pivot of the GSE ■ On the "What can I say?" page for the app ■ On some error screens ■ On the "Listening..." screen—the system will cycle through examples from built-in apps and those installed from the Windows Phone Store
Command		The container for a single voice command.
	Name	This value is used to specify to your app which command it was launched to handle, so it must be unique within the *CommandSet*.
Example		An example phrase for this specific command. These example phrases will be shown in the "Did You Know?" screen for the app.

Element	Attribute	Description
ListenFor		The text for which the speech recognizer should listen when trying to match what users are saying to a specific command. You can have up to 10 *ListenFor* elements for each *Command*, which should make it possible for you to account for the different ways that a user might try to invoke the command. In the simple *ToDoList* solution that you just saw, we included two *ListenFor* elements: "create a new item" "add an item" You can denote optional words with square brackets, as we did with the indefinite articles "a" and "an" in the preceding commands. By making "a"/"an" optional, the speech recognizer will not only listen for these phrases, but also for: "create new item" "add item" By thoughtful definition of your *ListenFor* elements, you can maximize the likelihood that users will speak a command that will be correctly matched with a task that your app supports. *ListenFor* elements also support the ability to include lists of potential words within the phrase, known as *PhraseLists*, which you can even update dynamically. We'll review *PhraseLists* in detail later in the chapter.
Feedback		Where the *ListenFor* element describes what the system should listen for in what users are saying, the *Feedback* element describes what the system should say back to users when the command has been recognized. This serves to inform users whether the voice command that they uttered was correctly recognized by the system so that they can determine whether to follow through with launching the app or cancel it and try again.
Navigate		The element that defines where in your app the system should send users if this voice command is recognized.
	Target	A relative URI to the page in your app that will handle the invocation when this command is matched. You can also include custom query parameters here. Technically, this attribute is optional, because the system will launch the main page of your app if nothing is specified. This gives you the opportunity to use a custom *URIMapper* to do more granular parsing of the incoming command before determining which page will handle it.

There are actually a few more elements in the VCD schema, offering an interesting set of dynamic scenarios. You will look at those shortly.

Initializing the VCD file

Now that we've registered the voice commands that we want to support in your VCD file, there's just one more step before they will be recognized by the system through the GSE: initialization.

When the app runs for the first time, we use the *InstallCommandSetsFromFileAsync* Windows Runtime method from the *Windows.Phone.Speech.VoiceCommands.VoiceCommandService* class to pass in the VCD file for processing. For the *ToDoList* solution, we named the VCD file *ToDoListVoiceCommands.xml*, so the full command would be the following:

```
await VoiceCommandService.InstallCommandSetsFromFileAsync
    (new Uri("ms-appx:///ToDoListVoiceCommands.xml"));
```

Note the use of the "ms-appx" URI scheme prior to the file name. This scheme is shorthand for the app's install directory, which generally matches the file structure of the original project and the final XAP package. Because our VCD file resides at the root of the package, nothing else is required. If you choose to store your VCD files in a subdirectory of your project, you will need to include the entire relative path after "ms-appx:///".

After this line of code is executed, our voice commands will be registered with the speech service and ready to be recognized. To be sure, you can do the following:

1. Activate the GSE by pressing and holding the hardware Start button.
2. Tap the Help button (the question mark icon in the upper-right corner).
3. Swipe over to the Apps pivot.

You should see the app listed, along with the top-level example we provided for our *Command Set*. If you tap the app name, you will see the list of voice commands that have been registered, which so far is just one, as shown in Figure 19-5.

FIGURE 19-5 After initializing your VCD, the GSE lists your supported commands.

Handling invocation for simple voice commands

For simple voice commands, such as the "create new item" command that we just created, there's relatively little for your app to do upon invocation. Assuming that you've set the appropriate target page on the *Navigate* element in your VCD file, the system just launches your app and directs the user to the correct page.

However, although you might never notice it for simple commands, there is a significant amount of metadata about the initial voice recognition coming into your app through this invocation. This will become more interesting when you get to dynamic commands, but first, you should understand what's happening in the basic case now so that layering on the dynamic commands will be an incremental addition.

Recall from Chapter 2, "App model and navigation," that the Windows Phone navigation model is highly analogous to the web in that it is made up of a series of pages, and those pages pass data to one another through query string parameters. This is true not only between pages within an app, but also between system components and your app. In the case of the simple *ToDoList* solution and the "create new list" voice command, the part of the URI that's interesting looks like this:

```
/NewListItemPagex.xaml?
    voiceCommandName=CreateNewItem&reco=To%20Do%20List%20create%20new%20item
```

This query string has two potentially useful pieces of information:

- **voiceCommandName** This contains the name of the *Command* that was matched by the speech recognizer.
- **reco** This contains the full text of what the speech recognizer matched, including the app name.

Note that the value of *reco* includes a set of spaces that have been replaced with their percent-encoded representation of "%20". All URI values passed to your app from the system are similarly percent-encoded.

We will add more query string parameters as we delve into more advanced scenarios in the next section. For now, all you need to know is that this is how all data will be fed from the speech service into your app.

Dealing with deep links

Directly invoking app functionality via voice commands is an example of an app "deep link," whereby an app exposes a page to which the system can navigate directly rather than requiring users to start from the main page and find their way there. The most common place you will encounter deep links is in the form of secondary Start tiles, when an app creates a tile to launch directly to a specific page or piece of content, such as a particular city in a weather app.

Adding deep links to your app might require you to rethink how you move between pages. Consider the *ToDoList* solution in this example. It contains a *MainPage*, which includes a button on the app bar to add a new item. Tapping that button navigates the user forward to *NewListItemPage.xaml*. Prior to adding deep links to the app, there is exactly one way to reach *NewListItemPage*: from *MainPage*. In other words, you can safely assume that any time users find themselves on *NewListItemPage*, there must be an instance of *MainPage* right behind it on the backstack, and a simple way to leave *NewListPage* when the user is finished adding the list would be to call *NavigationService.GoBack()*. After you provide a deep link to that page from speech or elsewhere, however, that will no longer work; in fact, *NavigationService.GoBack()* will throw an exception because you cannot programmatically navigate back out of your app.

Note Although the absence of deep links in your app might guarantee that users navigated to a particular page from the main page, you cannot assume much else about the state of that main page when navigating to a secondary page. As is pointed out in Chapter 2, if the app has been resumed from a tombstoned state, the main page object will not have been instantiated yet. In general, you should not depend on a particular user flow through your app for ensuring that it is in a given state.

There are several solutions to this. Assuming that you want to keep *NewListPage* as an entirely separate page in your app (rather than, for example, making it a full-screen *Popup* over your *MainPage*), the best approach is to perform a forward navigation via *NavigationService.Navigate(Uri)* to the *MainPage*. Of course, because you probably do not want to keep that *NewListPage* instance sitting around after returning to the *MainPage*, you should use *NavigationService.RemoveBackEntry()* to clean it up. See Chapter 2 for more details on backstack management.

Adding flexibility by using labels

Now that you have a basic understanding of how to register voice commands and how those commands are received in your app, it's time to make things a little more interesting.

Those of us who are compulsive creators of to-do lists know that it isn't enough to have a list; you must have a *prioritized* list! We will create a new property on the list item to contain its priority, which will be one of three states: high, normal, or low. Users can set that priority when creating a new item. Figure 19-6 shows the new UI for the *NewListItemPage*.

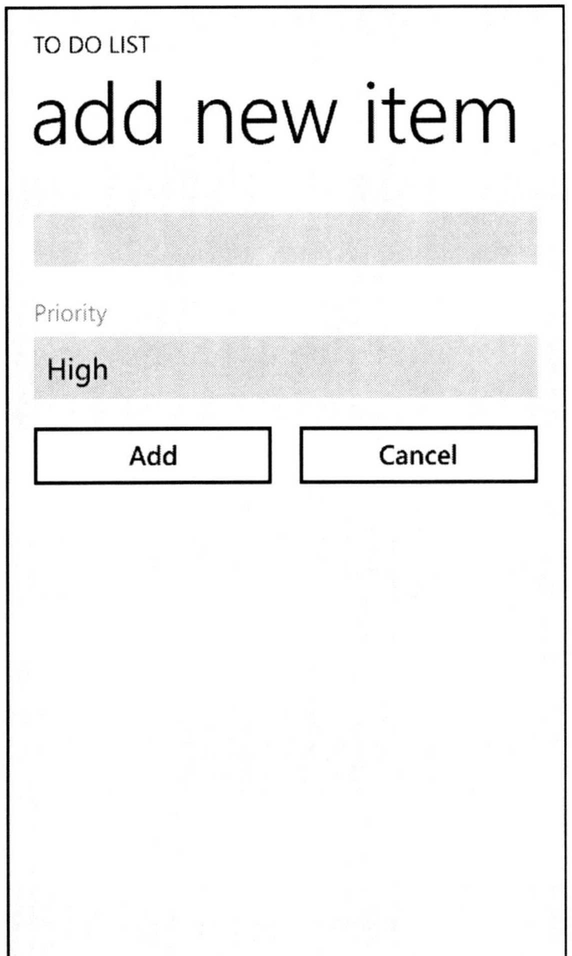

FIGURE 19-6 Lists can now be assigned a priority.

Note The Priority field here is set by using the *ListPicker* control, which is included in the Windows Phone Toolkit.

There are two ways that we can add this priority field to the VCD file. We could create new commands called *CreateNewHighPriorityItem*, *CreateNewNormalPriorityItem*, and *CreateNewLowPriority Item*, but that would culminate in a significant amount of duplication when all we really want is to add a parameter to the existing *CreateNewItem* command; enter the *PhraseList*.

With a *PhraseList*, you can specify a set of acceptable values for a given part of a command and then receive the chosen value when your app is invoked. Phrase lists are defined per *CommandSet* and then referenced within the individual commands. The following updated VCD file illustrates the addition of the priority field to the *CreateNewItem* command:

```
<?xml version="1.0" encoding="utf-8"?>

<VoiceCommands xmlns="http://schemas.microsoft.com/voicecommands/1.0">
  <CommandSet xml:lang="en-US" Name="todoVoiceCommands">
    <CommandPrefix>To Do List</CommandPrefix>
    <Example> create new high priority item </Example>

    <Command Name="CreateNewList">
      <Example> add a high priority item </Example>
      <ListenFor> create [a] new {priority} priority item</ListenFor>
      <ListenFor> add [a] {priority} priority item</ListenFor>
      <Feedback> Creating a new {priority} priority item... </Feedback>
      <Navigate Target="NewListItemPage.xaml" />
    </Command>
    <PhraseList Label="priority">
      <Item>high</Item>
      <Item>normal</Item>
      <Item>low</Item>
    </PhraseList>
  </CommandSet>
</VoiceCommands>
```

Now, the user can include any of the specified priority strings in his voice commands; for example, "create a new high-priority item." Note the addition of the priority label to the *Feedback* element. The GSE inserts the matched value for priority here when reading back to the user what it heard.

Of course, what we actually want to do is use the priority provided by the user through speech to automatically set the priority in the *ListPicker* on the *NewListItemPage*. Recall that all information coming into the app from the system is in the form of query-string parameters. As you saw earlier, the most basic commands yield query-string parameters for the name of the voice command that was matched and the full string that the speech service recognized. With phrase lists, the app receives an additional parameter for each of the phrase lists in the matched command, with the value that the speech service recognized for that phrase list. In the case of the user command "create a new low priority item," the query string looks like this:

```
/NewListItemPagex.xaml
     ?voiceCommandName=CreateNewItem
     &reco=To%20Do%20List%20create%20a%20new%20low%20priority%20item
     &priority=low%20priority
```

The app can then read that parameter in its *OnNavigatedTo* event and set the *ListPicker* appropriately, as shown in the following:

```
protected override void OnNavigatedTo(NavigationEventArgs e)
{
     string voiceCommand;
```

```
    bool launchedByVoice =
         NavigationContext.QueryString.TryGetValue
         ("voiceCommandName", out voiceCommand);

    if (launchedByVoice && voiceCommand == "CreateNewItem")
    {
          string priority;
          NavigationContext.QueryString.TryGetValue("priority", out priority);
          SetPriorityListPicker(priority);
    }
}

private void SetPriorityListPicker(string priority)
{
      /**
        * ListPicker priorities are defined in this order:
        * High: 0
        * Normal: 1
        * Low :2
        */
        switch (priority)
        {
               case "high ":
                     priorityListPicker.SelectedIndex = 0;
                     break;
               case "normal ":
                     priorityListPicker.SelectedIndex = 1;
                     break;
               case "low":
                     priorityListPicker.SelectedIndex = 2;
                     break;
               default:
                     priorityListPicker.SelectedIndex = 1;
                     break;
         }
 }
```

There is actually one small catch here. *PhraseList* tokens are not optional, nor can they contain empty values. If you include a *PhraseList* token in your *Command*, all of its values must be non-empty and the user must utter one of them in order for the *Command* to be matched. In the previous *CreateNewItem* example, this means that the addition of a priority *PhraseList* made the basic command, "create new item," no longer recognizable. Thus, if you want to have a basic version of a command as well as one that takes parameters, you need to create separate *Command* elements in your VCD file.

Note The full version of the *ToDoList* project shown in the code sample creates one voice command for non-prioritized items (*CreateNewItem*) and one for prioritized items (*CreateNewPrioritizedItem*).

Updating *PhraseLists* at run time

Adding *PhraseLists* to a VCD file is a good way to avoid creating individual *Commands* for every possible input value, but because the VCD file is a static part of the app package, it can only be updated when the user updates the app from the Windows Phone Store and cannot contain user-specific values. If you want to support voice commands based on content that the user actually created within the app, you will need to update your *PhraseLists* at run time.

Note Technically, you can also create new VCD files at run time by passing a file in your local storage to *InstallCommandSetsFromFileAsync*. However, because entirely new commands will generally require new handler code in your app, this should be rare.

For the to-do list app, the obvious candidates for dynamic commands are the to-do items themselves. This gives you the opportunity to issue a voice command to check off items as you complete them. We add a new *Command* called *MarkItemComplete*, which follows the same pattern as those shown in the previous section.

```
<Command Name="MarkItemComplete">
      <Example>mark 'buy milk' complete</Example>
      <ListenFor>mark {todoItem} complete</ListenFor>
      <ListenFor>{todoItem} is complete</ListenFor>
      <ListenFor>{todoItem} is done</ListenFor>
      <Feedback>marking "{todoItem}" complete</Feedback>
      <Navigate Target="MainPage.xaml" />
</Command>
```

Note The use of quotes around *{todoItem}* in the *Feedback* element is simply to demarcate the item itself in the feedback string shown in GSE, such that it shows something like "marking 'buy milk' complete."

The definition of the *PhraseList* we're naming *todoItem* is slightly different, however. Because we cannot know what users will add to their list at runtime, we cannot include any items in the static VCD file. Instead, it is defined as an empty set.

```
<PhraseList Label="todoItem">
</PhraseList>
```

Now, we need to add the code to update the *todoItem PhraseList* with the items the user has entered. The natural place to do this is immediately after the user has added an item to the list, so we add a small helper method called *UpdateTodoPhraseList* to the code-behind of *NewListItem Page*, which we can then call from the *addButton* click event handler.

```
private static async void UpdateTodoPhraseList()
{
      VoiceCommandSet voiceCommands =
           VoiceCommandService.InstalledCommandSets["todoVoiceCommands"];
```

```
        await voiceCommands.UpdatePhraseListAsync
            ("todoItem", App.ListItems.Select(todoItem => todoItem.ItemName));
}
```

Note You can dynamically update any *PhraseList*, even those that do contain items in the VCD file. This is useful if you have a set of default values for a phrase that you want to update from a web service or based on user input.

The first line retrieves the appropriate *CommandSet* from the speech service by using its Name attribute. The second line updates the *todoItem PhraseList* that you defined earlier in the VCD file by using an *IEnumerable* collection of strings. In our case, those strings are the item names. Notice that *UpdatePhraseListAsync* performs a complete replacement of the existing list of items in the *Phrase List*. Even if you only want to add one or two items to an existing *PhraseList*, you must remember to include the existing items in the call to *UpdatePhraseListAsync*.

Note You are limited to a maximum of 2000 items across all *PhraseLists* in a given *CommandSet*.

Speech recognition in apps

The same core technology that enables voice commands can also be used to recognize speech within apps with a great degree of flexibility in how the UX is presented and how speech is matched. There are two dimensions for which you will need to decide the level of customization that you want to provide: the speech recognition UI to show, and the grammar against which to match. We will begin by showing you an example in which the app offloads virtually all of the work to the built-in UI and speech recognizer, and then proceed to show ways that you can customize each of these. Keep in mind that the dimensions are independent; you can use the highly customized speech recognizer with the built-in UI, or vice versa.

Simple recognition with built-in UX

The easiest way to add speech recognition is to use the provided system UI and Microsoft's cloud-based speech service for converting a user's utterance to real text. This makes sense for scenarios in which you want to allow the user to enter free-form text, such as entering text into a *TextBox*. You will use this to provide a way for users to enter the name of a new to-do list item by using speech.

In Windows Phone, the standard UI cue for speech input being available in an app is a microphone icon, so we will modify the item name text box to include such an icon, as shown in Figure 19-7. To do this, we replace our standard *TextBox* control with the *PhoneTextBox* control from the Windows Phone Toolkit. The *PhoneTextBox* control enables you to specify an *ActionIcon*, which shows up at the right side of the text box, and raises the *ActionIconTapped* event when the user taps it.

Note The standard Windows Phone microphone icon is available in the set of icons installed with the Windows Phone SDK. You can find this at %PROGRAMFILES%\Microsoft SDKs\Windows Phone\v8.0\Icons\Dark\microphone.png (substitute Light for Dark to get the appropriate image for the light theme).

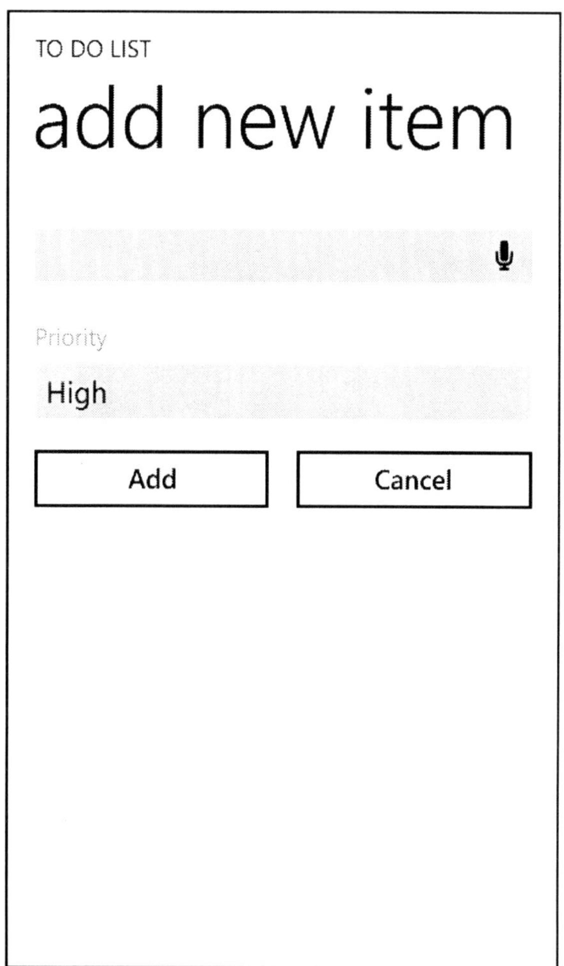

FIGURE 19-7 A microphone icon is the standard UI cue that indicates speech input is available.

Note The fact that the speech recognizer UI is now running in the context of the app is a subtle distinction from the perspective of the users (they might not even notice), but it makes a difference to the security model. Because the speech input is now being delivered directly to the app, it must include the *ID_CAP_MICROPHONE* capability, in addition to *ID_CAP_SPEECH_RECOGNITION*.

We will create a small helper method called *ReceiveItemNameBySpeech*, which we will then call from the *ActionIconTapped* event handler for the microphone button.

```
private async void ReceiveItemNameBySpeech()
{
    SpeechRecognizerUI todoItemNameRecognizer = new SpeechRecognizerUI();
    todoItemNameRecognizer.Settings.ListenText = "Add your item...";
    todoItemNameRecognizer.Settings.ExampleText = "eg. buy milk";

    SpeechRecognitionUIResult result =
        await todoItemNameRecognizer.RecognizeWithUIAsync();
    newListItemNameTextBox.Text = result.RecognitionResult.Text;
}
```

As you can see, the *SpeechRecognizerUI* class is straightforward. The *ListenText* and *ExampleText* properties set two pieces of text in the built-in speech UI control, whereas *ShowConfirmation* and *ReadoutEnabled* determine how the control behaves after the speech has been recognized, namely whether the control shows and/or reads what it recognized before passing it back to the app. The string that the speech recognizer matches is available from the *SpeechRecognitionResult* object that is returned from *RecognizeWithUIAsync*.

Customizing the recognizer UI

For most speech input scenarios, the built-in UI that is invoked by *SpeechRecognizerUI* is sufficient. Indeed, because it mimics the look-and-feel of the GSE, it can be preferable to custom UI because it is familiar and intuitive to the user. In some cases, however, it will make sense to display custom UI or no explicit listening UI at all. The *ToDoList_CustomSpeechRecognizerUI* solution shows an example of custom speech recognition UI.

Note Although it is possible to perform speech recognition without any explicit "Listening..." UI, you should always ensure that your UX makes it clear to the user when the device is listening, either through voice prompts or other UI cues.

We will repurpose the microphone icon added in the previous section to act as a subtle UI cue that speech recognition is enabled. When the user taps the microphone, it will begin rotating and continue doing so until the recognizer has stopped listening for input. To move between the two states of the UI, we create a custom version of the *PhoneTextBox* control template and add two new *VisualState* instances. The *Rotating* state contains the animation storyboard for the rotating microphone, whereas the *Stopped* state returns it to its original position. See the full sample code for the *ToDoList_CustomSpeechRecognizerUI* solution for the definition of the storyboard.

We will create a new method called *ReceiveItemNameBySpeechWithCustomUI*, which will replace *ReplaceItemNameBySpeech* from the *ToDoList* solution. The new method is shown in the code that follows. Note that the microphone button is disabled while speech is being recognized; this ensures that the user does not inadvertently stack up recognition requests. It was not necessary when using the built-in UI earlier because that UI obscures the foreground app and makes it non-interactive automatically.

Note The default template for the *PhoneTextBox* control automatically collapses its core elements when the control is disabled, causing the rotating microphone and any previously entered text to disappear. We have removed that behavior in our custom template so that the control looks the same when disabled, but does not allow for user input.

```
private async void ReceiveItemNameBySpeechWithCustomUI()
{
    newListItemNameTextBox.IsEnabled = false;

    // don't let the user tap the microphone icon again while listening
    VisualStateManager.GoToState(newListItemNameTextBox, "Rotating", true);

     using (SpeechRecognizer recognizer = new SpeechRecognizer())
     {
           SpeechRecognitionResult result = await recognizer.RecognizeAsync();

           if (result.TextConfidence != SpeechRecognitionConfidence.Rejected)
           {
                 newListItemNameTextBox.Text = result.Text;
           }
     }

     VisualStateManager.GoToState(newListItemNameTextBox, "Stopped", true);
     newListItemNameTextBox.IsEnabled = true;
}
```

Note There is a small chance that *RecognizeAsync* could throw an exception in the preceding code sample. Before the user provides speech input to the system for the first time, she must accept the speech privacy policy. Because it's unlikely that a user will use speech for the first time ever inside your app, we've chosen not to clutter the code with an additional try/catch block here. The full project that accompanies this chapter does show the handler code, however. It's also worth noting that *RecognizeAsyncWithUI* handles the acceptance of the privacy statement on the app's behalf.

Adding custom grammars

If you've tried both voice commands and simple speech recognition that you've seen in the chapter thus far, you probably noticed that the recognition accuracy is much higher for voice commands. The reason for this is simple: with voice commands, the speech recognizer has a relatively small number of possible inputs against which to match—perhaps a few hundred—and each valid command must match a specific format (an app name, followed by one of the handful of commands defined for that app). With open-ended speech, there are potentially thousands of valid matches for a given utterance and very little in guaranteed structure, making it much more difficult to match it accurately.

A good analog for this is a foreign language that you might have studied but never mastered. If you stick to checking into hotels, ordering food in restaurants, and buying postcards, your high school

French will probably be good enough for a week in Paris because each of those interactions is structured enough to limit the number of things you can expect to hear from your Parisian interlocutor. The cashier at the Louvre gift shop is much more likely to tell you how much you owe and ask whether you want a bag than to start expounding on the subtleties of Sartre, so you can hone in on those phrases and more easily decipher them.

In the case of apps, the way to provide this refinement is to provide the speech recognizer with grammars. There are two simple ways to add grammars to the speech recognizer, and one more advanced way. We will review the simpler methods first.

Adding predefined grammars

The first option is to take advantage of Microsoft's predefined grammars, of which there are two supported in Windows Phone 8: dictation and web search. The dictation grammar is the same one used by the built-in messaging app and is therefore optimized for very short messages (150 to 200 characters), which are returned as complete sentences; that is, starting with a capital letter and ending with a period. The web search grammar is also used by a built-in app (in this case, Bing) and is usually a better option for short utterances that don't map to sentences. Both of these grammars rely on cloud-based processing, so they require a network connection to work, something you should keep in mind when designing your workflow and considering error cases. You will also need to ensure that your app has the *ID_CAP_NETWORKING* capability; even though the network traffic is abstracted away by the speech framework, it is ultimately still happening on behalf of your app. The following code shows the *ReceiveItemNameBySpeech* method from the previous section updated to include loading the *WebSearch* grammar via *AddGrammarFromPredefinedType*:

```
private async Task ReceiveItemNameBySpeechWithCustomUI()
{
    newListItemNameTextBox.IsEnabled = false;
    // don't let the user tap the microphone icon again while listening
     VisualStateManager.GoToState(newListItemNameTextBox, "Rotating", true);

     using (SpeechRecognizer recognizer = new SpeechRecognizer())
     {

        recognizer.Grammars.AddGrammarFromPredefinedType
             ("websearch", SpeechPredefinedGrammar.WebSearch);
        SpeechRecognitionResult result = await recognizer.RecognizeAsync();

        if (result.TextConfidence != SpeechRecognitionConfidence.Rejected)
        {
              newListItemNameTextBox.Text = result.Text;
        }
     }

     VisualStateManager.GoToState(newListItemNameTextBox, "Stopped", true);
     newListItemNameTextBox.IsEnabled = true;
}
```

The first parameter to *AddGrammarFromPredefinedType* (and the other *AddGrammar* APIs we will discuss) is a grammar name. We can use this to reference the individual grammars that we've added to our recognizer later. You will understand the value of this after reviewing the second type of simple grammar.

Adding simple lists

Using the predefined grammars should help to improve the accuracy of recognition for free-form speech that falls into either the dictation or web search category, but most scenarios for speech in apps will be far more specialized, with commands and content that are specific to that app and the portion of its UI with which the user is currently interacting. For those cases, you can achieve significantly higher degrees of accuracy by further constraining the grammars against which the speech recognizer is matching.

In our *NewListItemPage*, the obvious candidate for a highly constrained grammar is the list of priority options. This is a simple list—just three one-word options—but it's one that is specific to this scenario within the app, so the recognizer will benefit greatly from the constraint. In this case, we will use the *AddGrammarFromList* API which allows for the creation of simple grammars from any *IEnumerable* collection of *string*. We encapsulate the recognition in a new helper method named *ListenForPriority*, which will be triggered after the user adds an item name through speech by tapping the microphone icon. We again use a subtle visual cue to indicate when the device is listening for speech input. In this case, we will show a pulsating border in the device theme color around the *ListPicker*. Once again, we move between the two states of the UI using the *VisualStateManager*—the *Pulsating* state includes a storyboard that animates the border while the speech service is listening.

```
private async Task ListenForPriority()
{
    VisualStateManager.GoToState(priorityListPicker, "Pulsating", false);

    using (SpeechRecognizer priorityRecognizer = new SpeechRecognizer())
    {
        priorityRecognizer.Grammars
            .AddGrammarFromList("priority", new string[] { "high", "normal", "low" });
        SpeechRecognitionResult result = await priorityRecognizer.RecognizeAsync();

        if (result.TextConfidence != SpeechRecognitionConfidence.Rejected)
        {
            SetPriorityListPicker(result.Text);
        }
    }

    VisualStateManager.GoToState(priorityListPicker, "Stopped", true);
}
```

Assuming that the *SpeechRecognizer* does not reject the result, we pass the result to the *Set PriorityListPicker* helper method, which was shown earlier in this chapter.

Notice again that the API for adding a new grammar (in this case, *AddGrammarFromList*) takes a name to identify it within the recognizer which, as mentioned earlier, makes it possible for you to reference the grammar later. This is important because this gives you the ability to easily enable and disable grammars as necessary on your *SpeechRecognizer* instance, which is faster and more efficient than constantly creating new *SpeechRecognizer* objects, particularly if you are using the same grammars multiple times.

Why might you want to disable a grammar? Remember that the speech recognizer is ultimately performing a probabilistic pattern matching operation when it tries to convert the user's speech input into something that the app can understand. The likelihood of it being able to correctly understand the input is inversely correlated with the number of options from which it has to choose.

To illustrate this, imagine an app for a camping store that offers speech as a way of searching for products. They might have a grammar which contains those products and includes entries for (among other things) "tent" and "boots." If the user chooses boots, the app might want to further narrow his search by asking him to provide a shoe size, in which case it will require a grammar for the valid sizes, which will naturally include the word "ten." If the app is using a common *SpeechRecognizer* instance and keeps all grammars active at the same time, that recognizer will need to discern the difference between "ten" and "tent" if the customer happens to have size-10 feet—a challenging task. However, because the app knows that the user is providing an input for shoe size, there's no need to even consider the options contained in the product grammar, and the app should disable that grammar altogether.

Note In the code samples thus far, we've elected to show a transient instance of *SpeechRecognizer* to keep things simple while you learn the basics of speech. In a real app, you would want to have a longer-lived object even in these basic scenarios because of the potential for the user to be unsatisfied with the first recognition result. Later in the chapter, we will show an example of using a long-lived *SpeechRecognizer* instance with grammars that are enabled and disabled as necessary. There is one caveat, however: a single *SpeechRecognizer* instance cannot contain a mixture of predefined grammars (that is, the Microsoft-provided dictation or web search grammars) and user grammars (either lists or the Speech Recognition Grammar Specification grammars covered in the next section).

Adding grammars by using speech recognition grammar specification

The third option for adding a grammar to the speech recognizer is through an XML file that conforms to the Speech Recognition Grammar Specification (SRGS), a W3C standard for speech recognition. Using SRGS, apps can provide much richer grammars for more complex scenarios, most of which are beyond the scope of this book. However, the *ToDoList_SRGS* solution includes a simple example of how apps can work with SRGS.

For this example, we return to the *MainPage* of the app, which shows all of our to-do items, and add a second app bar button, again taking advantage of the microphone icon to indicate speech. We add an SRGS XML file to our project through the Add Item Wizard and then replace the default template with the following XML:

```
<?xml version="1.0" encoding="utf-8" ?>
```

```
<grammar
        version="1.0" xml:lang="en-US" root="MarkTasksComplete"
        tag-format="semantics/1.0" xmlns="http://www.w3.org/2001/06/grammar"
        xmlns:sapi="http://schemas.microsoft.com/Speech/2002/06/SRGSExtensions">

  <rule id="MarkTasksComplete" scope="public">
    <one-of>
      <item>Mark</item>
      <item>Set</item>
      <item>Make</item>
    </one-of>
    <item repeat="0-1">all</item>
    <one-of>
      <item repeat="0-1"> high priority <tag>out.priority="high"</tag></item>
      <item repeat="0-1"> normal priority <tag>out.priority="normal"</tag></item>
      <item repeat="0-1"> low priority <tag>out.priority="low"</tag></item>
    </one-of>
    <one-of>
      <item>tasks</item>
      <item>items</item>
      <item>to dos</item>
    </one-of>
    complete
  </rule>
</grammar>
```

The structure and content of the file is mostly self-evident. The intent is to provide the framework of a valid utterance so that the speech recognizer can match it appropriately. By providing multiple options for a given phrase using the *one-of* element, you can make it easier for the user to succeed in speaking to the app without having to learn the exact format and wording of the accepted commands.

The portion of the XML that might not be so intuitive are the tag elements found within each item in the list of priority options. Tags allow creators of SRSG grammars to create simple key-value pairs which are set when the speech recognizer hits that portion of the grammar in a match. For the app that needs to parse the recognition result, these tags make it easier to pull out the variable portions of the utterance which might impact how the app behaves. Observe how in this example we only include tags for the priority options because that is the only part of the grammar that makes a difference in what the app will ultimately do. We've included different options for the statement's verb ("mark", "set", "make") and noun ("tasks", "items", "to-dos") to provide flexibility to the user, but it makes no difference to the behavior of the app which one of those the user chooses to say, so you don't need to create tags for them.

Note The syntax for tags is *out.key="value"*.

In this case, we do all of the work in the click event handler for the app bar button showing the microphone icon. As a means of illustrating that you can mix and match custom grammars with the built-in UI, we will once again use the *SpeechRecognizerUI* class here, rather than the *SpeechRecognizer* class that we've used for the last few examples. Note, however, that *SpeechRecognizerUI* is just a wrapper over *SpeechRecognizer,* which adds the UI-specific properties—a full-fledged *SpeechRecognizer* instance is available as a member of *SpeechRecognizerUI.* The full code for the event handler is shown in the following:

```
private async void speechAppBarButton_Click(object sender, EventArgs e)
{
    using (SpeechRecognizerUI recognizerUI = new SpeechRecognizerUI())
    {
        recognizerUI.Settings.ListenText = "Listening...";
        recognizerUI.Settings.ExampleText = "eg. Mark all high priority tasks complete";
        recognizerUI.Settings.ReadoutEnabled = false;
        recognizerUI.Settings.ShowConfirmation = false;

        recognizerUI.Recognizer.Grammars
            .AddGrammarFromUri("MarkCompleteIncomplete",
                new Uri("ms-appx:///ToDoGrammar.xml", UriKind.Absolute));

        SpeechRecognitionUIResult result = await recognizerUI.RecognizeWithUIAsync();


        if (result.RecognitionResult.TextConfidence == SpeechRecognitionConfidence.Rejected)
        {
            return;
        }

        SemanticProperty priority;

        // check if the user specified that only high, normal, or low priority
        // tasks should be marked complete
        // otherwise mark everything complete
        if (result.RecognitionResult.Semantics.TryGetValue("priority", out priority))
        {
            foreach (ToDoListItem todoItem in
                App.ListItems.Where(item => item.Priority == (string)priority.Value))
            {
                todoItem.IsCompleted = true;
            }
        }
        else
        {
            foreach (ToDoListItem todoItem in App.ListItems)
            {
                todoItem.IsCompleted = true;
            }
        }
    }
}
```

The first thing you might notice in the preceding code is that the audio readout and confirmation screen on the built-in UI are turned off. If you believe that your grammar is tightly constrained and the likelihood of misinterpretation is low, this is a good way to speed up the overall experience, especially if you are asking the user to provide multiple voice inputs.

The next thing we do is load the *ToDoGrammar.xml* file that you created earlier. Because the file resides at the top level of the app package directory, we use the *ms-appx* URI scheme to denote its path.

Preloading grammars

The *SpeechRecognizer* class includes a method called *PreloadGrammarsAsync*, with which it can parse any grammars that the app has provided prior to the first request to recognize speech. This call is optional, but because it performs an action that will need to be done regardless, it's a good idea to get it out of the way *before* the user has tapped the button to start speaking, especially for cases in which you are providing large or complex grammars that might take some time for the recognizer to ingest. By preloading those grammars, you can avoid any delays in beginning to recognize the user's speech, which will ultimately lead to higher accuracy. It is not shown in the previous code sample, because that is all running in the context of the *Button*'s click event handler.

When *RecognizeWithUIAsync* returns, you need to determine whether the user provided a priority qualifier to his request. This is where the tags that you added to the grammar file come in. Even though the recognition result contains the complete version of the string matched to the user's input, you only care about whether the user included a priority in his command and, if so, which priority it was. Recall that tags are simply a set of key-value pairs, so they naturally surface in the result as an *IReadOnlyDictionary*. You just need to check whether the priority tag is present and, if so, what its value is. Keep in mind that you can perform a simple equivalence check between the value of the tag and the *Priority* property of *ToDoListItem* because they're both defined as simple lowercase strings with possible values "high", "normal", and "low".

Text-to-Speech

So far in this chapter, we have covered topics that involve the user speaking into the phone and having that speech translated into actions or text for the app to handle. The reverse direction is also possible with Text-to-Speech (TTS), by which apps can turn text content into spoken words that can be played through the phone's audio outputs.

Simple TTS with *SpeakTextAsync*

The *ToDoList_TTS* solution shows how you can use TTS to read out the number of incomplete tasks when the app starts. The critical class in this case is *Windows.Phone.Speech.Synthesis.SpeechSynthesizer*, which offers a *SpeakTextAsync* method taking a single string. We will add a simple helper method called *ReadNumberOfIncompleteTasksAsync*, which will be invoked when the main page loads.

```
private void ReadNumberOfIncompleteTasks()
{
     SpeechSynthesizer synth = new SpeechSynthesizer();
     int numberOfIncompleteTasks = App.ListItems
                                          .Count(item => item.IsCompleted == false);
     synth.SpeakTextAsync("You have " + numberOfIncompleteTasks + " incomplete tasks.");
}
```

Taking control with speech synthesis markup language

The *SpeakTextAsync* method works well for simple strings. For more sophisticated TTS, however, you need to provide guidance to the speech synthesizer.

Crafting the speech output

Now that the user knows how many incomplete tasks she has, she will probably want to know what they are, so we will try reading those out with the *SpeechSynthesizer*, as well. We will add another button to the app bar of your *MainPage* which will provide a quick way for the user to get a read-out of her incomplete tasks. Figure 19-8 illustrates the new UI.

Note The play icon (*transfer.play.png*) is available in the Icons folder of the Windows Phone SDK.

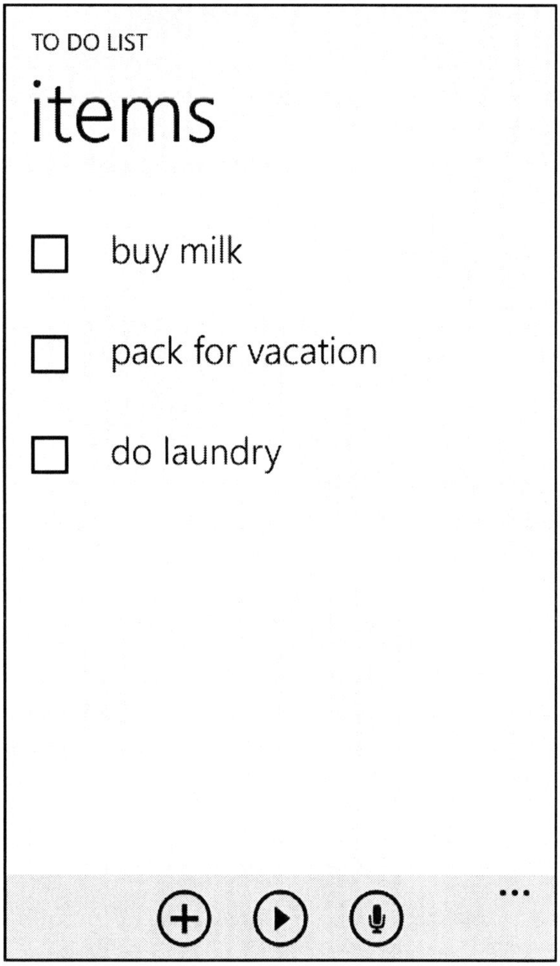

FIGURE 19-8 The app can now read out your incomplete tasks—no more excuses for putting off that laundry!

We will create a new helper method, *ReadAllIncompleteTasksAsync*, to read out the tasks, which will be invoked by the click event handler for the app bar button. Clearly, the easiest way to implement that method would be to concatenate the names of all incomplete items together into one long string and pass that to *SpeakTextAsync*. The problem is that after you translate a distinct set of to-do items into a single concatenated string, there's no notion of separation between them, and the synthesizer reads them out as if they were a single incoherent sentence.

Thankfully, there is a way to give the synthesizer some hints on how to read the text by using a W3C standard XML format known as Speech Synthesis Markup Language (SSML).

Tip You can find the W3C specification for SSML v1.0 at *http://www.w3.org/TR/speech-synthesis/*. The Windows Phone speech synthesizer supports this standard with only very minor differences.

Using SSML, apps can control the pace, pronunciation, and emphasis of spoken text. For this particular task, we use the SSML element *break* to add a one second pause between each task. The code for *ReadAllIncompleteItemsAsync* is shown in the following example:

```
private async Task ReadAllIncompleteItemsAsync()
{
      readItemsAppBarButton.IsEnabled = false;

      string incompleteItemsListWithSSML =
           "<speak version=\"1.0\" xml:lang=\"en-us\">";

      foreach (ToDoListItem item in App.ListItems.Where(item => item.IsCompleted == false))
      {
           incompleteItemsListWithSSML += item.ItemName + "<break time=\"1s\" />";
      }

      incompleteItemsListWithSSML += "</speak>";

      SpeechSynthesizer synth = new SpeechSynthesizer();
      await synth.SpeakSsmlAsync(incompleteItemsListWithSSML);

      readItemsAppBarButton.IsEnabled = true;
}
```

The SSML standard offers a high degree of customizability to TTS, most of which is beyond the scope of this book. However, Table 19-2 lists several elements worth highlighting if you are interested in adding polish to your speech output without investing significant time in creating detailed pronunciation specifications.

TABLE 19-2 SSML offers numerous ways to customize text-to-speech output

Element	Description	Example
say-as	Specifies how dates, times, numbers, and groups of characters are pronounced.	SSML input: This task is due on <say-as interpret-as="date" format="mdy">01-15-2013</say-as>. Audio output: This task is due on January fifteenth, two thousand thirteen.
emphasis	Places enhanced or reduced emphasis on a word or phrase.	This task is <emphasis level="strong">high</emphasis> priority.
voice	Sets the gender and language of the speech synthesizer voice.	<voice xml:lang="en-gb" gender="male">You have three incomplete high-priority tasks</voice> This text will be read in a male British voice (assuming that language is present on the phone).

Keeping speech and screen in sync

Apps that use speech as an alternative way to deliver content to the user will naturally run into the question of how to keep the visual output of the app synchronized with what the speech synthesizer is saying. An ebook reader app, for instance, will probably want to "turn the page" on the user's behalf as the synthesizer reads along. You can do this by using the *mark* SSML tag and the *Bookmark Reached* event on the *SpeechSynthesizer*.

We will demonstrate this in the to do list app by putting a small border around the item currently being read out in the device theme color. First, we need to make a small modification to *ReadAll IncompleteItemsAsync* to add the *mark* tags and register a handler for the *BookmarkReached* event which will be raised as the synthesizer passes over those tags. Notice how in addition to adding a tag before each item, there is one added for the end of the list; this makes it possible to clear the formatting from the final item in the list.

```
private async Task ReadAllIncompleteItemsAsync()
{
    string incompleteItemsListWithSSML = "<speak version=\"1.0\" xml:lang=\"en-us\">";
    foreach (ToDoListItem item in App.ListItems.Where(item => item.IsCompleted == false))
    {
        incompleteItemsListWithSSML += "<mark name=\"" + item.ItemName + "\" />";
        incompleteItemsListWithSSML += item.ItemName + "<break time=\"1s\" />";
    }

    incompleteItemsListWithSSML += "<mark name=\"EndOfList\" />";
    incompleteItemsListWithSSML += "</speak>";

    SpeechSynthesizer synth = new SpeechSynthesizer();
    synth.BookmarkReached += synth_BookmarkReached;
    synth.SpeakSsmlAsync(incompleteItemsListWithSSML);
}
```

The handler for *BookmarkReached* uses the name of the bookmark to find the item in the list and then uses the *ItemContainerGenerator* member of *ListBox* to find the actual *ListBoxItem* to which the *ToDoListItem* is bound, because that's the visual element you need to change.

Note A real app would do most of this visual manipulation by using data-binding and value converters. However, for the purposes of consolidating the logic in one place, we have chosen to show it in code.

```
ListBoxItem currentListBoxItem = null; // reference to the currently higlighted list box item

private void synth_BookmarkReached(SpeechSynthesizer sender, SpeechBookmarkReachedEventArgs args)
{
    Deployment.Current.Dispatcher.BeginInvoke(() =>
    {
        // reset the last item to its default state before highlighting the next one
        // this will also set the last item in the list to its default state
        // when the EndOfList bookmark is hit
        if (currentListBoxItem != null)
        {
            currentListBoxItem.BorderBrush = new SolidColorBrush(Colors.Transparent);
        }
```

```
            if (args.Bookmark == "EndOfList") return;

            ToDoListItem currentItem =
                App.ListItems.First(item => item.ItemName == args.Bookmark);

            currentListBoxItem = (ListBoxItem)toDoListItemsListBox
                                    .ItemContainerGenerator.ContainerFromItem(currentItem);

            if (currentItem != null)
            {
                currentListBoxItem.BorderBrush =
                    App.Current.Resources["PhoneAccentBrush"] as SolidColorBrush;
            }
        });
}
```

Putting it together to talk to your apps

Now that you've seen how to use SR and TTS separately, it's time to bring them together and show how to implement an experience wherein users can actually participate in an interactive dialog with apps. The *ToDoList_Dialog* solution includes the code for this section.

In the section "Voice commands" earlier in this chapter, we included a command for creating a new item in the list. We will build on that initial command to provide a completely voice-driven way of adding a new item. In particular, we will use the version of the command that did *not* accept a priority by voice command, because that will make up one part of the dialog in this example.

When the app is started, you check the incoming query string parameters to *NewListItemPage* to determine if it was launched to handle the *CreateNewItem* voice command. If so, we call a new helper method named *AddItemBySpeech*. This method implements a simple dialog, asking the user to provide the item name and priority and then confirm the addition. This method in turn relies on another helper method named *ListenForInput* to actually receive the successive commands, looping until it correctly recognizes an utterance.

```
protected async void AddItemBySpeech()
{
    this.IsEnabled = false;

    List<string> yesNoOptions = new List<string>() { "yes", "no", "cancel" };
    List<string> priorityOptions = new List<string>() { "high", "normal", "low" };

    using(SpeechSynthesizer synthesizer = new SpeechSynthesizer())
    using(SpeechRecognizer userGrammarRecognizer = new SpeechRecognizer())
    using(SpeechRecognizer dictationRecognizer = new SpeechRecognizer())
    {
        dictationRecognizer.Grammars
            .AddGrammarFromPredefinedType("dictation", SpeechPredefinedGrammar.Dictation);

        userGrammarRecognizer.Grammars.AddGrammarFromList("YesOrNo", yesNoOptions);
        userGrammarRecognizer.Grammars.AddGrammarFromList("Priorities", priorityOptions);
```

```
await userGrammarRecognizer.PreloadGrammarsAsync();

userGrammarRecognizer.Grammars["Priorities"].Enabled = false;

string newItemName =
       await ListenForInput
       ("Say the name of the item", synthesizer, dictationRecognizer);
newListItemNameTextBox.Text = newItemName;

string isItemCorrect =
       await ListenForInput
       ("Was that correct?", synthesizer, userGrammarRecognizer);

if (isItemCorrect == "no")
{
     // Start over
     AddItemBySpeech();
     this.IsEnabled = true;
     return;
}
else if(isItemCorrect == "cancel")
{
     this.IsEnabled = true;
     return;
}

userGrammarRecognizer.Grammars["Priorities"].Enabled = true;
userGrammarRecognizer.Grammars["YesOrNo"].Enabled = false;

string priority =
     await ListenForInput
     ("Set the item's priority. You can say 'high', 'normal', or 'low'",
     synthesizer, userGrammarRecognizer);

userGrammarRecognizer.Grammars["Priorities"].Enabled = false;
userGrammarRecognizer.Grammars["YesOrNo"].Enabled = true;

await synthesizer.SpeakTextAsync("Setting priority to " + priority);
SetPriorityListPicker(priority);

string isUserReady =
      await ListenForInput
      ("Are you ready to add this item?", synthesizer, userGrammarRecognizer);


if (isUserReady == "yes")
{
      await synthesizer.SpeakTextAsync
           ("Adding " + newListItemNameTextBox.Text + " to your to-do list.");
      await AddItemAndReturnToMainPage();
}
else
{
     return; // let user proceed without speech
}
```

```
        }

        this.IsEnabled = true;
}

private async Task<string> ListenForInput
      (string requestToRead, SpeechSynthesizer synthesizer, SpeechRecognizer recognizer)
{
      string input = string.Empty;
      bool inputRecognized = false;

      // keep attempting to recognize speech input until we get a match
      do
      {
            await synthesizer.SpeakTextAsync(requestToRead); // eg. "Set the item's priority"

            SpeechRecognitionResult srr = await recognizer.RecognizeAsync();
            if (srr.TextConfidence != SpeechRecognitionConfidence.Rejected)
            {
                  input = srr.Text;
                  inputRecognized = true;
            }
            else
            {
                  await synthesizer
                        .SpeakTextAsync("Sorry, didn't catch that. Please try again.");
            }
      }
      while (inputRecognized == false);

      return input;
}
```

Observe the reuse of the *userSpeechRecognizer* object for handling confirmation of the item name, the selection of priority, and the final confirmation of item addition. Recall from the speech recognition section that it is more efficient to reuse a *SpeechRecognizer* object if you intend to handle multiple inputs against the same grammar than to constantly create new instances. It is much easier for the speech service to turn grammars that have already been parsed on and off than to reparse them from scratch. On the other hand, the *SpeechRecognizer* does need to allocate memory to store the parsed grammars, so it is not advisable to maintain global static instances that contain grammars from across the app which might get used at widely varying rates. The code sample illustrates the disabling of a grammar by turning off the "Priorities" grammar after the user has chosen a priority. Also recall that user and system grammars cannot be combined in a single *SpeechRecognizer* instance; hence, the creation of a separate *dictationGrammar*.

Summary

In this chapter, you learned the three core parts of the Windows Phone speech framework:

- Voice commands
- Speech recognition
- Text-to-Speech

Some apps, such as those providing hands-free, turn-by-turn navigation, will necessarily include speech as a core part of their experience, but all developers should consider intelligently incorporating speech into their apps. In many cases, it offers a faster, more convenient, and just plain fun way to interact with smartphones that takes very little code to light up.

CHAPTER 20

The Wallet

Throughout the book, we have discussed the smartphone functionality that has replaced physical objects that people used to carry with them, such as address books, digital cameras, and maps. The next obvious candidate is the wallet, and all of the major smartphone platforms are racing to provide an experience that will encourage users to go digital. In that vein, Windows Phone 8 has introduced a new built-in app, the Wallet, along with a set of extensibility points by which apps can interact with it. In this chapter, you will learn how to create and manage payment instruments, transactions, and coupons.

Understanding the Wallet

The term "mobile wallet" can mean different things to different people, so it is worth starting the chapter by defining what it is in the context of Windows Phone.

The Wallet and Near Field Communication

In many cases, people equate the mobile wallet with the ability to make mobile payments by using Near Field Communication (NFC) technology. Although the wallet functionality in Windows Phone 8 does include the ability to make payments via NFC in some markets, it also provides the ability to manage other types of data that you might find in a physical wallet, such as membership cards and coupons. By the same token, NFC technology can be used for far more than payment, as is described in Chapter 17, "Networking and proximity." Figure 20-1 shows a Venn diagram that describes the relationship between the Wallet, NFC payment, and other NFC scenarios.

Note The diagram in Figure 20-1 is based on the one presented by Matthias Baer in his talk at the Build conference in October 2012. You can view the full talk here at *http://channel9.msdn.com/Events/Build/2012/2-020*.

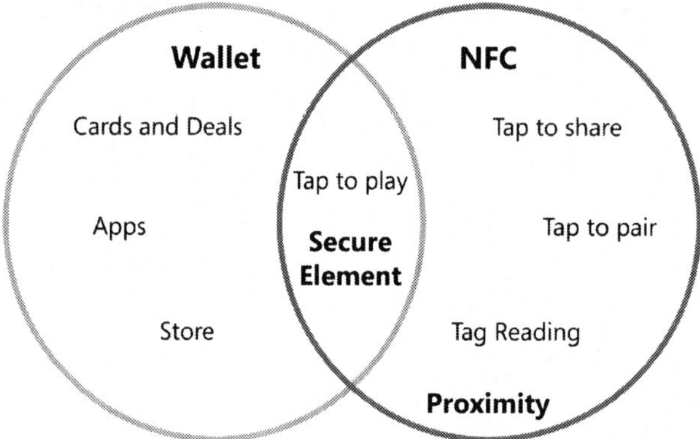

FIGURE 20-1 Even though the Wallet and NFC are linked, they each also offer distinct functionality.

In this chapter, we will focus on the features of the Wallet outside of Tap to Pay and the secure element, which is limited to highly trusted apps that have contractual arrangements with financial institutions and mobile operators. For details on NFC and proximity, see Chapter 17.

The Wallet Hub

As mentioned in Chapter 1, "Vision and architecture," and elsewhere throughout this book, Windows Phone provides a content-centric user experience (UX), with opportunities for multiple apps to contribute content to a common location where the user can easily find it. Windows Phone 7 included central hubs for photos, music, people, store, Office, and games. Windows Phone 8 introduces a new hub for Wallet content. With the Wallet Hub (see Figure 20-2), users can manage payment instruments, membership cards, and accounts, as well as coupons or deals. For membership cards and accounts, the Wallet can display account balance information and transaction history, based on data provided by associated apps. For coupons and deals, it can display information about promotions and offer ways to redeem them, such as showing a barcode.

FIGURE 20-2 Windows Phone 8 introduces a new Wallet Hub for managing wallet content.

The Wallet object model

The Wallet object model (see Figure 20-3) is rooted in the *WalletItem* class. Any object that can be stored in the user's Wallet ultimately derives from *WalletItem* and includes common properties such as *DisplayName*, *LastUpdatedTime*, and *Id*. Two classes derive from *WalletItem*: *WalletTransactionItem Base* and *Deal*. *WalletTransactionItemBase* represents any type of account associated with transactions and is further extended into a *PaymentInstrument* class and a *WalletTransactionItem* class. The *Deal* class represents a specific offer stored in the Wallet and contains properties such as *ExpirationDate* and *IsUsed* to represent its transient nature. We will review how to use each of these classes in detail later in this section.

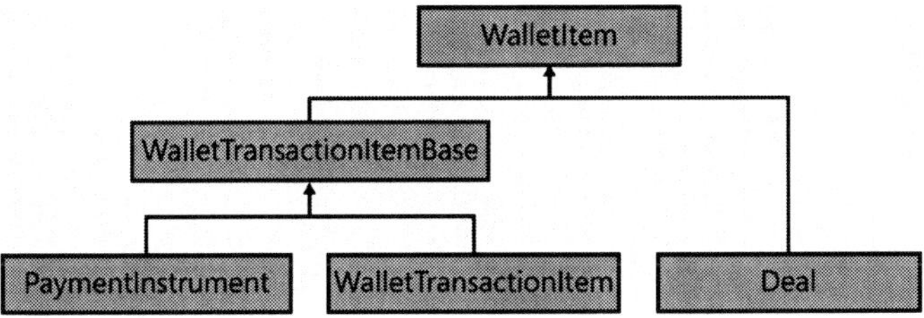

FIGURE 20-3 All items that can be added to the Wallet ultimately derive from *WalletItem*.

Note Any app that interacts with the Wallet must declare the *ID_CAP_WALLET* capability. Additional capabilities are available for apps that deal with payment instruments or that want to interact with the device's secure element (for "tap to pay") but use of these capabilities requires your developer account to be granted additional privileges by Microsoft. To request additional privileges, contact Windows Phone developer support at *http://msdn.microsoft.com/library/windowsphone/help/jj159132*.

Managing deals

For many people, the promise of an easier way to manage coupons and offers purchased from sites such as Groupon is the most exciting aspect of the mobile wallet. Many of these items end up going to waste because they're lost, forgotten, or otherwise not available when they are needed. The Wallet Hub provides a single place for the user to manage all of this content, which is collectively referred to using the term "deals." There are three ways to find deals that you can add to your Wallet. Two of those options are accessible by tapping the Add button on the app bar of the Wallet Hub. From there, you can search for local deals from providers integrated with Bing such as Yelp and Groupon. You can also enter a deal manually by typing in the necessary details, which can be useful for storing coupons from small businesses who have not yet digitized their promotions. The third option for adding deals to your Wallet is to use an app, which will be the focus of this section.

The *CouponCutter* solution in the sample code includes a set of deals that the user might be interested in adding to his Wallet, as shown in Figure 20-4. In the sample app, the coupons are hard-coded, but in a real app, they would likely be refreshed periodically from a back-end web service, based on the user's preferences and location.

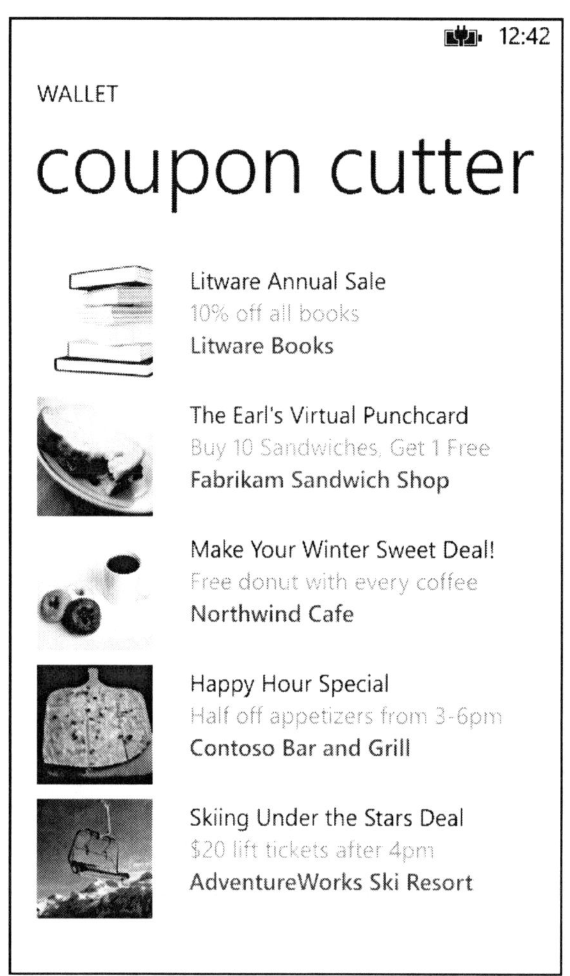

FIGURE 20-4 The *CouponCutter* solution in the sample code includes a set of coupons that the user might consider adding to his Wallet.

The main page of the app, shown in Figure 20-4, includes a *ListBox* control that is data-bound to a collection of *Coupon* objects. The *Coupon* class is defined by the app and contains most of the fields you would expect for a coupon, such as merchant name, description, and expiration date. When the user taps a coupon, the app shows the full details for the offer in the *CouponDetailsPage*, as shown in Figure 20-5.

FIGURE 20-5 The *CouponDetailsPage* provides additional details for the coupon, including a QR code.

The most obvious additional detail shown in the Details page is the Quick Response (QR) code. QR codes are a form of 2D barcode that are popular in both physical and digital coupons, primarily because they can encode more data than a traditional Universal Product Code (UPC). The QR code for the coupon is generated based on the coupon code listed below it by using ZXing.Net, a Microsoft .NET port of the popular Java barcode reader/writer API, which is available at *http://zxingnet.codeplex.com*. The ZXing.Net library provides a rich set of capabilities for both reading and writing barcodes, making it a useful tool for Wallet apps. In the *CouponCutter* app, we use the *BarcodeWriter* class to create a *BitmapSource* that can be shown directly in the app user interface (UI) and passed to the Wallet APIs. This logic is encapsulated in a helper method named *GenerateBarCodeImage*, which is called for a given coupon the first time it needs to generate the barcode.

```
public static BitmapSource GenerateBarCodeImage(string input, int height, int width)
{
    BarcodeWriter barcodeWriter = new BarcodeWriter();
    barcodeWriter.Format = BarcodeFormat.QR_CODE;
    barcodeWriter.Options = new ZXing.Common.EncodingOptions
                 { Height = height, Width = width, Margin = 0};

    WriteableBitmap barcodeWriteableBitmap = barcodeWriter.Write(input);
    return barcodeWriteableBitmap;
}
```

Of course, because this is just an app displaying some basic text and data, all of this was possible in previous versions of Windows Phone. The button at the bottom of the details page is the gateway to what is new in Windows Phone 8. When the user chooses to add the coupon to her Wallet, the *CouponCutter* app takes the critical information from the *Coupon* object and creates a *Deal* that it can add to the Wallet Hub. The *Deal* class offers a rich schema of properties to cover most of the key elements of a coupon or offer. However, the only properties that are strictly required to add a deal to the Wallet are *DisplayName* and *MerchantName*.

In addition to all of the predefined fields, apps can add their own custom fields by using the *CustomProperties* dictionary available on the *WalletItem* base class. The Wallet will not only store those custom fields in its database, it can also show the value along with an app-defined label for it. As a result, users can view app-specific information directly within the Wallet Hub.

You can find the code to convert the contents of the *Coupon* class into a *Deal* and save it to the Wallet in the *AddCouponToWalletAsync* method on the *CouponViewModel* class (shown in the code that follows). For the most part, it simply copies the values from the *Coupon* object provided as an input parameter into a new instance of *Deal*, but there are a few items worth noting.

```
public async Task AddCouponToWalletAsync(Coupon coupon)
{
    Deal deal = new Deal(coupon.Id);
    deal.MerchantName = coupon.MerchantName;
    deal.DisplayName = coupon.Name;
    deal.Description = coupon.Description;

    if (coupon.LargeLogo != null)
        deal.Logo336x336 = BitmapLogoHelper.CreateBitmapImageFromUri(coupon.LargeLogo);
    if (coupon.MediumLogo != null)
        deal.Logo159x159 = BitmapLogoHelper.CreateBitmapImageFromUri(coupon.MediumLogo);
    if (coupon.SmallLogo != null)
        deal.Logo99x99 = BitmapLogoHelper.CreateBitmapImageFromUri(coupon.SmallLogo);

    deal.IssuerWebsite = coupon.MerchantWebsite;
    deal.Message = coupon.MarketingMessage;

    deal.MessageNavigationUri =
        new Uri(String.Format("/CouponDetailsPage.xaml?CouponId={0}", coupon.Id),
            UriKind.Relative);

    deal.Notes = coupon.CustomerNotes;
    deal.StartDate = DateTime.Now;
```

```
    if(coupon.ExpirationDate != null && coupon.ExpirationDate != DateTime.MinDate)
        deal.ExpirationDate = coupon.ExpirationDate;

    if(!String.IsNullOrWhiteSpace(coupon.Token))
    {
        deal.BarcodeImage = coupon.BarcodeImage;
        deal.CustomProperties.Add("CouponCode",
                                  new CustomWalletProperty(coupon.Token, "coupon code"));
    }

    await deal.SaveAsync();

// update the app UI to reflect the coupon being added to the wallet
    coupon.IsInWallet = true;
}
```

First, the *Deal* class has both an empty constructor and one that takes a string parameter for an identifier. If you use the empty constructor, the Wallet will create an identifier for your item automatically when you save it. With the other constructor, you can handle the case in which the coupon you're creating in the Wallet is actually just a local representation of an item that is managed in your cloud service and therefore already has an identifier.

Note If you attempt to create an item by using an identifier that already exists for your app in the Wallet, you will get an exception.

Second, observe that the app can set a *MessageNavigationUri* to deep-link back into the details page for the coupon within the app directly from the Wallet. As with other Windows Phone hubs, the goal of grouping common content together in centralized hubs is not to diminish the opportunity for apps to provide a differentiated experience, but rather to provide the user with a single focal point for the type of content for which she is interacting. From those centralized points, the system provides launching points into the full richness of the app experience, including deep-links into the specific content in which the user is interested.

Note The *Deal* schema also includes an *OfferWebsite* property, which you can use to provide a URI pointing to more details about the *Deal* online

Third, notice the *CustomProperties* property with which the app can set custom fields on the item, as discussed earlier. The *CustomProperties* property is an *IDictionary* object that stores *CustomWalletProperty* objects indexed by an app-provided key. The *CustomWalletProperty* class provides two simple properties, a label and a value. The Wallet will maintain any custom values that you create for the item in its database, but for the Wallet Hub to display that value, you must set a label for it.

Finally, the *Deal* is added to the Wallet by using the *SaveAsync* method. As the name implies, the *SaveAsync* API follows the asynchronous programming model that is common through the Windows

Phone 8 API surface. Be aware, however, that unlike many of the other new Windows Phone APIs, the Wallet APIs are not based on the Windows Runtime and therefore are not accessible from native code.

Tip As you will see in Chapter 24, "Windows 8 convergence," you can get a hint about the nature of an API based on its namespace. Anything in the *System.** or *Microsoft.** namespaces is based strictly on .NET and is not available from C++. By contrast, APIs in the *Windows.** or *Windows.Phone.** namespaces are based on the Windows Runtime and are projected into C#, Microsoft Visual Basic, and C++.

After *SaveAsync* completes, the coupon is successfully added to the Wallet and we can update the UI to reflect that. In our case, this simply means flipping the Add Coupon To Wallet button to say "Remove Coupon From Wallet". Now, when the Wallet is started, the coupon that the *CouponCutter* app added is immediately visible, as shown in Figure 20-6.

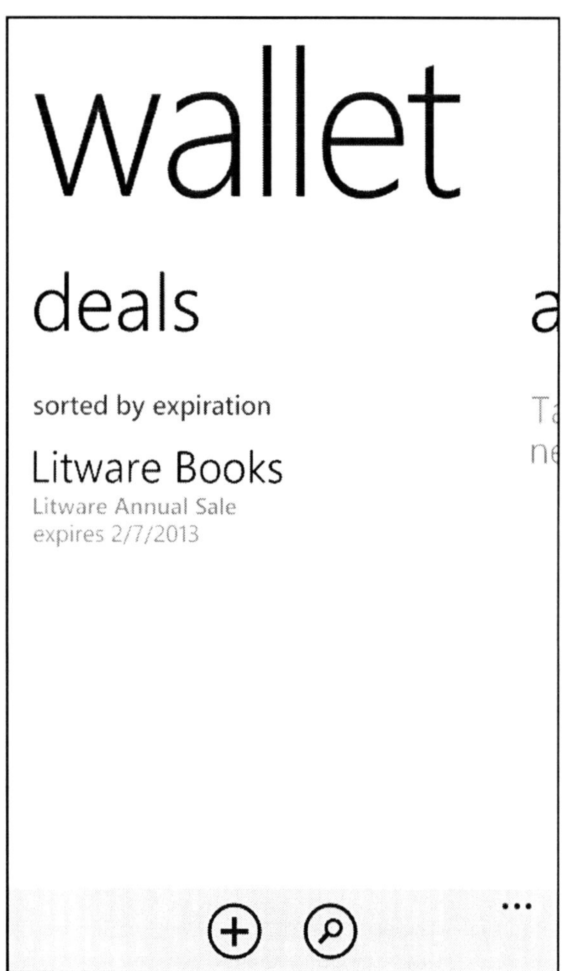

FIGURE 20-6 The Wallet Hub displays deals added by apps directly alongside deals found through the hub.

Tapping any of the saved deals in the main panorama takes the user to the Deals page, where all of the information added by the app is stored, as shown in Figure 20-7.

FIGURE 20-7 The deal Details page shows all of the information added by the app, including custom fields.

The About pivot on the Deals page provides two links back to the app that created the deal. The Open App link triggers a standard app startup, as you would see if you started the app from the Start screen or the app list. However, as mentioned earlier, the app can also provide a *Message* and associated *MessageNavigationUri*, which the Wallet shows next to the deal image. In the case of the Litware deal, the message is "All Microsoft Press books on sale!" When the user taps that message, the Wallet launches the app to the deep-link provided in the *MessageNavigationUri*.

In addition to showing the app-provided details for standard fields such as Expiration Date, the Wallet Hub also displays custom properties created by the app, as discussed earlier. In the *Coupon Cutter* solution, we created a custom field for the coupon code, which can be useful if the merchant does not have the ability to scan a QR code. That value, along with the app-provided label, is included in the Details pivot for the deal, as shown in Figure 20-8.

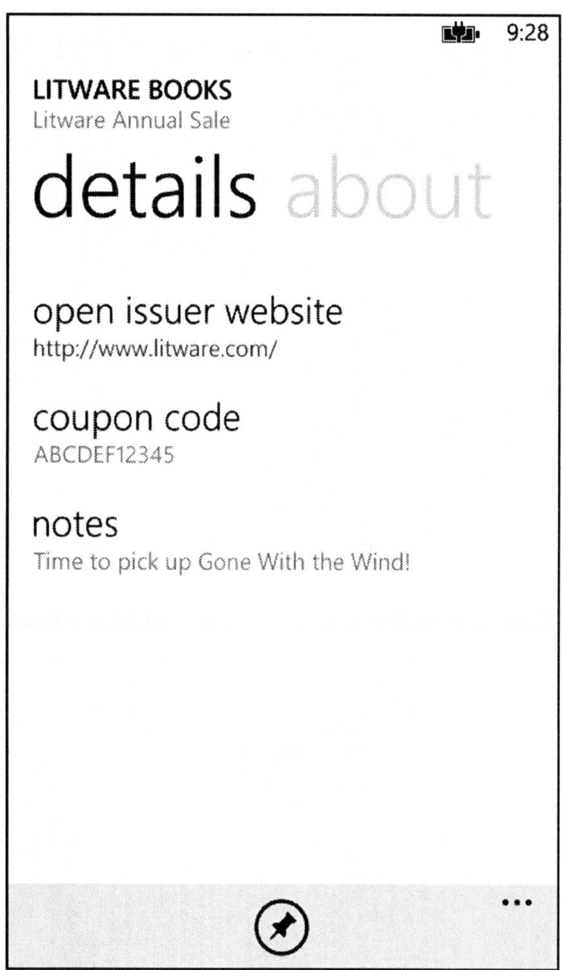

FIGURE 20-8 The Wallet Hub also displays custom properties and their labels.

Now that the deal is stored in the user's Wallet, there is the potential that some of its properties might change without the app's knowledge. Consequently, the app needs to be prepared to update its state based on any changes made in the Wallet every time it is launched. The *CouponCutter* app does this in the *UpdateCoupons* method of the *CouponViewModel* class. For each coupon in its collection, it checks if the associated deal is in the Wallet and updates the coupon accordingly. This helps to deal with two cases in particular. First, the user might delete the deal from the Wallet, in which case the app should flip the coupon's *IsInWallet* property to *false*. Second, if the user uninstalls the app and later reinstalls it, the app might lose its own state about whether the deal is stored in the Wallet. (Recall that the Wallet maintains state about the original creator of the deal even if the app is uninstalled.) By checking the state of the Wallet itself, the *CouponCutter* app can avoid showing the Add Coupon To Wallet button for an item that is already stored there. The app uses the *IsAcknowledged* property on the *Deal* as a way of keeping track of its deals as they're processed. As a result, any deals that are still marked with *IsAcknowledged* being *false* when all coupons have been processed must be deals of which the app itself is not aware. The app can then decide how it wants to handle those deals, as shown at the end of the *UpdateCoupons* method. Finally, the *UpdateCoupons* method checks whether the user has marked the deal as being used, an action that is available on the app bar menu on the Wallet Hub's Deal page. In the case of the *CouponCutter* app, both the deal and the associated coupon are deleted after the deal is used.

```
private async void UpdateCoupons()
{
    var usedCoupons = new List<Coupon>();

    foreach (Coupon coupon in AllCoupons)
    {
        Deal deal = (Deal)Wallet.FindItem(coupon.Id);

        if (deal == null)
        {
            if (coupon.IsInWallet)
            {
                coupon.IsInWallet = false;
            }

            continue;
        }
        else
        {
            deal.IsAcknowledged = true;
            coupon.IsInWallet = true;
        }


        if (deal.IsUsed)
        {
            usedCoupons.Add(coupon);
        }
    }
```

```
        foreach(Coupon usedCoupon in usedCoupons)
        {
            AllCoupons.Remove(usedCoupon);
            Wallet.Remove(usedCoupon.Id);
        }

        var unacknowledgedDeals =
            (await Wallet.GetItemsAsync()).Where(deal => deal.IsAcknowledged == false);

        foreach (Deal unknownDeal in unacknowledgedDeals)
        {
            // handle the unknown deal
            // eg. create a local coupon from it or delete it from the wallet
        }
    }
```

Transaction items

If you open your (physical) wallet and survey its contents, you will no doubt find that you manage many cards and accounts that have nothing to do with financial transactions. Membership cards, loyalty cards, and transit passes often take up more room in the wallet than credit and debit cards, and many people manage even more accounts online without physical cards. Windows Phone gives developers the tools to create digital representations of these accounts in the Wallet Hub by using the *WalletTransactionItem* class. *WalletTransactionItem* expands on the base *WalletItem* class by adding the types of properties and operations that you would associate with an account, such as balances and transaction history. Apps can populate these values so that they appear in the Wallet Hub, making it possible for the user to keep all of her accounts in a single, centralized location on the phone.

The *ContosoAirlines* solution in the sample code illustrates the type of account that you might want to have at your fingertips even if you don't carry a physical card for it in your wallet: an airline frequent-flyer program. The app includes a panorama with four items, as shown in Figure 20-9.

FIGURE 20-9 The *ContosoAirlines* app shows account deals for a frequent flier program.

When the app starts, it queries the state of the user's account from a mock web service and updates the UI with details such as the user's frequent-flier account balance, some of the recent flights that he's taken, and promotional fares for various cities. As with the *CouponCutter* app shown in the previous section, there is nothing about this app that requires new features in Windows Phone 8. By integrating with the Wallet, however, the app can provide all of this information to the user in a centralized location, alongside similar data from his other accounts.

Note Although the screenshot in Figure 20-9 uses accurate distances for the recent flights, the mock web service in the sample code has been modified to generate fake flights that are always 500 miles long, regardless of the route. Because there are always three new flights and two new redemptions returned from the service, this makes it simple to track how the app is interacting with the Wallet, especially when working with Wallet agents, which we will describe later in this chapter.

Adding and removing the account in the app

The settings panorama item includes a button labeled Add Account To Wallet, which is the app entry point for integrating the Contoso Air data with the Wallet Hub, and all of the logic is contained in that button's click event handler. Because the button flips between labeled Add Account To Wallet and Remove Account From Wallet, the click event handler's logic is split between whether it is performing an addition or a removal, with specific methods for each in the view model. Naturally, the addition step is more interesting.

```
private async void addRemoveAccountInWalletButton_Click(object sender, RoutedEventArgs e)
{
    if (App.AccountManager.IsAccountInWallet)
    {
        App.ContosoViewModel.RemoveAccountFromWallet();
    }
    else
    {
        await App.ContosoViewModel.AddAccountToWalletAsync();
    }
}

// ContosoAirlinesViewModel.cs
public async void AddAccountToWalletAsync()
{
    WalletTransactionItem walletItem = walletItem =
        new WalletTransactionItem(App.AccountManager.AccountId);
    walletItem.AccountNumber = App.AccountManager.AccountId;
    await PrepareWalletItemAsync(walletItem);

    AddWalletItemTask addWalletItemTask = new AddWalletItemTask();
    addWalletItemTask.Item = walletItem;
    addWalletItemTask.Completed += addWalletItemTask_Completed;
    addWalletItemTask.Show();
}
```

```
private async Task PrepareWalletItemAsync()
{
    walletItem.DisplayAvailableBalance = App.AccountManager.AvailableBalanceString;
    walletItem.DisplayName = "Contoso Air Frequent Traveler Program";

    walletItem.CustomProperties.Add(
        "EliteStatus",
        new CustomWalletProperty(App.AccountManager.EliteStatus, "elite status"));

    walletItem.Logo99x99 = BitmapLogoHelper.CreateBitmapImageFromUri
        (new Uri("Assets/Images/ContosoAir-Small.jpg", UriKind.Relative));
    walletItem.Logo159x159 = BitmapLogoHelper.CreateBitmapImageFromUri
        (new Uri("Assets/Images/ContosoAir-Medium.jpg", UriKind.Relative));
    walletItem.Logo336x336 = BitmapLogoHelper.CreateBitmapImageFromUri
        (new Uri("Assets/Images/ContosoAir-Large.jpg", UriKind.Relative));

    // add flights as transactions
    foreach (Flight recentFlight in App.AccountManager.RecentFlights)
    {
        WalletTransaction recentFlightTransaction =
            App.AccountManager.CreateWalletTransactionFromFlight(recentFlight);
        walletItem.TransactionHistory.Add(recentFlight.CustomerFlightReference,
                                          recentFlightTransaction);
    }

    // Add a hot fare marketing message
    HotFare currentHotFare = await contosoWebService.GetRandomHotFare();
    walletItem.Message = String.Format("{0} for ${1}",
                                       currentHotFare.DestinationName, currentHotFare.Price);

    walletItem.MessageNavigationUri = new Uri(String.Format("/HotFarePage.xaml?Id={0}",
                                              currentHotFare.Id), UriKind.Relative);

    walletItem.TransactionHistoryNavigationUri = new Uri("/TransactionHistoryPage.xaml",
                                                         UriKind.Relative);
}

public void RemoveAccountFromWallet()
{
    Wallet.Remove(App.AccountManager.AccountId);
    App.AccountManager.IsAccountInWallet = false;
}
```

The *PrepareWalletItem* helper method that creates the card is verbose but straightforward. Many of the details are pulled from the singleton *AccountManager* class stored in the *App* object, which is responsible for interacting with the mock Contoso Air web service. Again, we use the *BitmapLogo Helper* class included in the solution to convert images from the app package into *BitmapSource* objects that can be passed to the Wallet, and we take advantage of the ability to add custom properties to the Wallet item to include the user's airline status level. We also create two deep-links to the app: one for a current promotional fare, and another to the app's transactions page, which makes it possible for the user to move from the list of recent transactions in the Wallet to the full list in the app. Finally, because one of the defining features of the *WalletTransactionItem* is its ability to maintain transaction history, we use the *CreateWalletTransactionFromFlight* helper on *AccountManager* to translate the app-defined *Flight* object into a transaction that the Wallet can understand.

```
public WalletTransaction CreateWalletTransactionFromFlight(Flight flight)
{
    WalletTransaction newFlightTransaction = new WalletTransaction();
    newFlightTransaction.Description = flight.Description;
    newFlightTransaction.DisplayAmount = string.Format("{0} miles", flight.Distance);
    newFlightTransaction.TransactionDate = flight.DepartureDate;

    return newFlightTransaction;
}
```

Note It is worth pointing out how the Wallet handles key properties that you might expect to be numerical primitives, such as account balance and transaction amount. Because the Wallet itself does not need to perform any calculations on those values, and the units in which account balance and transaction amounts are maintained varies widely for membership and loyalty cards, the Wallet accepts strings for *DisplayAvailableBalance* and *DisplayAmount*. This provides maximum flexibility to the app to choose how to represent its amounts.

New items must be added through a user-mediated task, the *AddWalletItemTask*, to ensure that apps cannot arbitrarily add new items to the user's Wallet. The *AddWalletItemTask* works just like other tasks in Windows Phone. First, the app creates an instance of the task and sets key properties. It then registers an event handler for the task's *Completed* event. Finally, it calls the *Show* method to invoke it. In the case of *AddWalletItemTask*, the key property is the *WalletTransactionItem* that the app has created and wants to add to the Wallet. When the *AddWalletItemTask* is invoked, the user is presented with a pop-up message box in which he can choose whether to save the new card directly or to make some additional manual edits first, as shown in Figure 20-10.

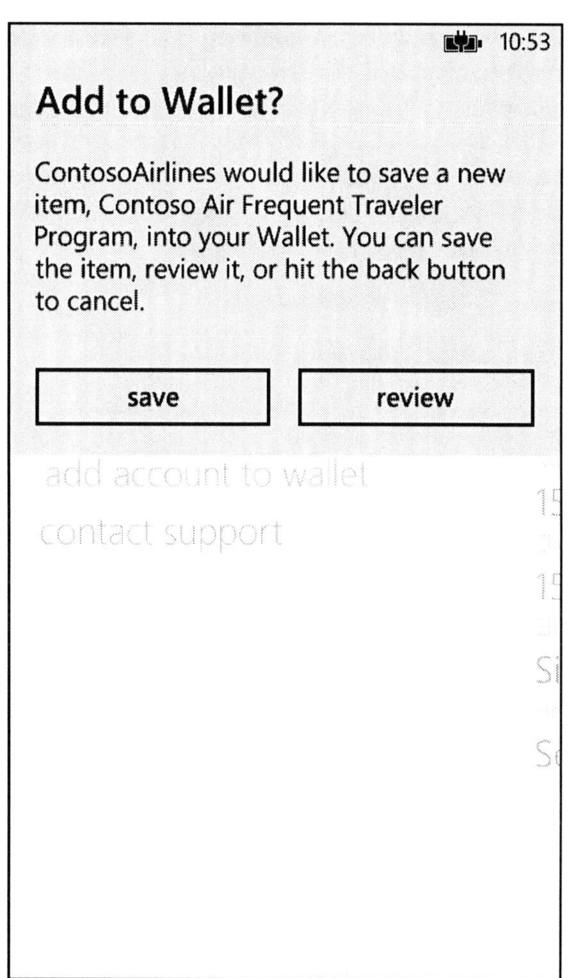

FIGURE 20-10 The *AddWalletItemTask* gives the user the chance to decide whether to add the card.

After the user completes the task, the app receives a callback to its *Completed* event handler and the card shows up prominently in the Wallet Hub, as shown in Figure 20-11.

```
private void addWalletItemTask_Completed(object sender, AddWalletItemResult e)
{
     if (e.TaskResult != TaskResult.OK)
     {
          return;
     }

     // Update the app UI to reflect the account being added to the wallet
     App.AccountManager.IsAccountInWallet = true;
     App.AccountManager.SaveAsync();
}
```

FIGURE 20-11 *WalletTransactionItem* objects can also display a photo in the Wallet Hub.

The Wallet also shows an image for *WalletTransactionItem* objects in the main panorama, using the image that the app provided in the *Logo159x159* property. All three logo sizes available on the *WalletItem* base class are required for *WalletTransactionItem* types, and their use in the Wallet Hub UI is shown in Table 20-1.

TABLE 20-1 *WalletItem* logo usage

Logo	Usage
Logo99x99	Purchase confirmation screen (payment instruments only)
Logo159x159	Small Start screen tile Wallet Hub "all" accounts list
Logo336x336	Medium Start screen tile Wallet item Details page

As with deals, when the user chooses a card, the Wallet navigates to a Details page. The card details page includes a pivot item for transactions. This is where the flights added to the *WalletTransactionItem* are shown. Both pivots are shown in Figure 20-12.

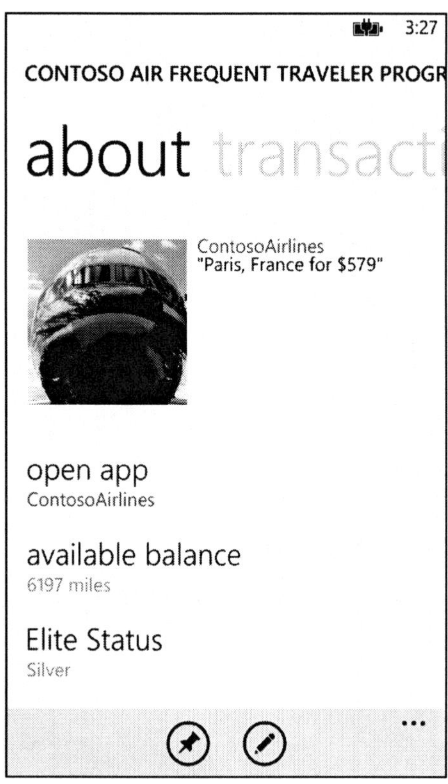

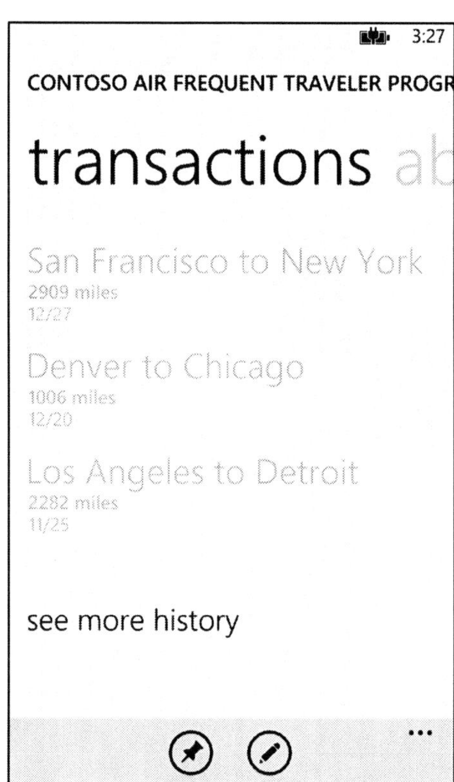

FIGURE 20-12 The card details page shows all of the details provided by the app, including detailed transactions.

Note the See More History link at the bottom of the Wallet Hub's Transactions pivot. As mentioned earlier, this is shown if the app has provided a deep-link in the *TransactionHistoryNavigationUri* property. Tapping it starts the *ContosoAirlines* app directly to its transactions page, as shown in Figure 20-13.

Handling the addition and removal of accounts in the Wallet

Thus far, we have discussed how a user can add, manage, and remove a Wallet account from within an app. However, users can also add and remove accounts from within the Wallet itself, and apps must be prepared to deal with those changes when started.

FIGURE 20-13 By specifying a transaction history deep-link, the user can get more account transactions in the app.

For the Wallet to provide an option to add an account associated with your app, you need to identify your app as a Wallet app. As with other extensibility points in Windows Phone, Wallet apps declare their intention to integrate with the Wallet Hub by adding an *Extension* element in the app manifest. Extension points cannot be added in the manifest editor, so you must add them directly in the XML, immediately after the *Tokens* element.

```
<Extensions>
     <Extension
          ExtensionName="Wallet_app_membership"
          ConsumerID="{198c3ecf-ae2a-4f0f-9288-83da0c5bf490}"
          TaskID="_default"
          />
</Extensions>
```

There are several options for the *ExtensionName* attribute, depending on whether your app supports loyalty cards, membership cards, transit cards, payment instruments, or other types of Wallet items. You can register multiple extensions if your app supports multiple types of items. By registering one or more Wallet extensions in the app manifest, your app will be indexed as a Wallet app by the Windows Phone Store when it is submitted. It will then appear in the list of available apps when the user chooses to add a card from the Wallet Hub. Figure 20-14 shows two such apps already available in the Windows Phone Store: FidMe and Ubudu.

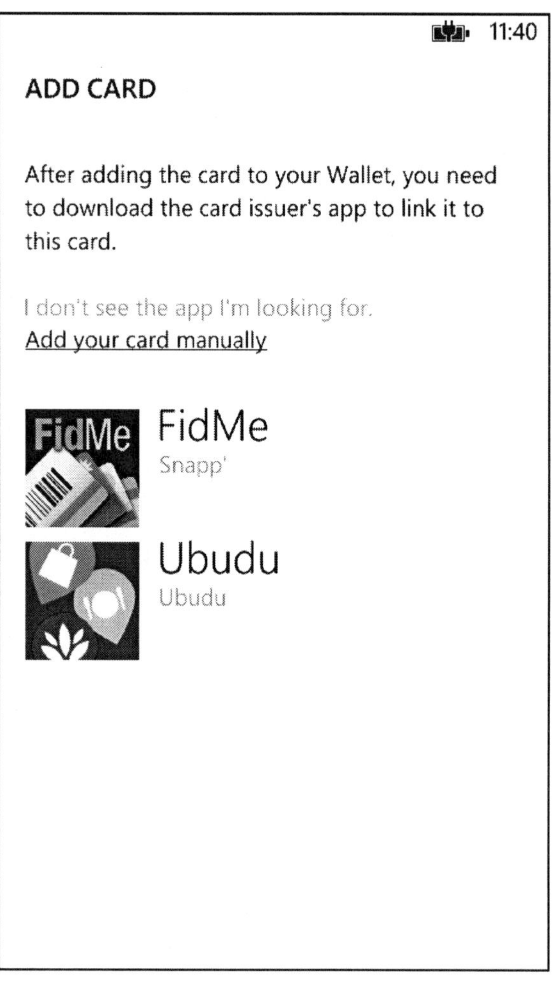

FIGURE 20-14 Apps that register for the Wallet extension are shown in the Add Card screen of the Wallet Hub.

When the user chooses one of the apps shown, the Wallet immediately adds a card for it and stamps that card with the *ProductID* of the associated app. The user can choose to go to the Windows Phone Store to download the app. When that app starts for the first time, it will find a card already in the Wallet, which it can then augment. Even after one of the apps is installed, the user can return to the Add Card UI and add another card associated with the app. In that case, rather than being given the option to go to the Windows Phone Store, the user is simply presented with the opportunity to link the app to the card. As part of linking the app to the card, the Wallet will launch the app to give it a chance to learn about its addition and supplement it with further details.

Note The *ContosoAirlines* solution does not support managing multiple frequent-flyer accounts in the Wallet. Depending on your scenario, you might want to either support multiple accounts or allow the user to change the account that the app is managing when your app is started for a second card.

Apps can also lose knowledge of user cards by being unlinked from them in the Wallet. The user can unlink cards explicitly in the Wallet Hub or implicitly by uninstalling the app. When the link between an app and a card is removed, the app no longer has access to manage the card itself, and the Wallet's query APIs will behave as if the item was removed. However, the system maintains knowledge of the creator of the card. As a result, the user can relink it later. As with creating the initial relationship between the app and the card, relinking them triggers the app to be launched, at which point the app can discover the card and update it.

Now that you understand what can happen in the Wallet without the app's knowledge, we can return to the *ContosoAirlines* app to look at how we might deal with this possibility. Recall that we maintain a Boolean value, *IsAccountInWallet*, to keep track of whether the Contoso frequent flyer account is currently stored in the Wallet. Clearly, that value is no longer sufficient given the possibility that the account's status can change outside of the app. We add a new method, *VerifyInWalletStatus*, to align the status and data for the account between the app and the Wallet. If the account exists in the Wallet but the app is not currently aware of it, we use the view model's *UpdateAcccountInWallet* method to ensure that all of the account's data is up to date. The *UpdateAccountInWallet* method calls the same *PrepareWalletItem* helper that we saw earlier to do the bulk of the work of updating the account state, but it operates on the existing *WalletTransactionItem* instance from the Wallet, rather than creating a new object. Consequently, we are able to simply call *SaveAsync* to persist the changes rather than using the *AddWalletItemTask*. On the other hand, if the user has removed the account from the Wallet or unlinked it from the app, the app update its own knowledge of the status of the account in the Wallet by using *RemoveAccountFromWallet*.

```
private void VerifyInWalletStatus()
{
    bool isAccountInWallet;

    WalletTransactionItem airlineAccountTransactionItem =
        (WalletTransactionItem)Wallet.FindItem(App.AccountManager.AccountId);

    if (airlineAccountTransactionItem == null)
        isAccountInWallet = false;
    else
        isAccountInWallet = true;
```

```
        if (isAccountInWallet != App.AccountManager.IsAccountInWallet)
        {
            if (isAccountInWallet)
                UpdateAccountInWallet();
            else
                RemoveAccountFromWallet();
        }
    }

    public async void UpdateAccountInWallet()
    {
        WalletTransactionItem walletItem =
            (WalletTransactionItem)Wallet.FindItem(App.AccountManager.AccountId);
        await PrepareWalletItemAsync(walletItem);
        await walletItem.SaveAsync();

        App.AccountManager.IsAccountInWallet = true;
        App.AccountManager.SaveAsync();
    }
```

Payment instruments

The *PaymentInstrument* and *OnlinePaymentInstrument* classes refer to accounts dealing in general purpose payments using real currency—the online version simply refers to payment instruments that were originally added through the Microsoft billing system. For the most part, payment instruments are handled like the non-payment accounts discussed in the previous section, with a few key differences:

- When the user adds a *PaymentInstrument* from an app, she can also choose to make it available for use when making purchases from the Windows Phone Store.
- When the user adds a new payment card to the Wallet, the Wallet uses the first six digits of the card number, known as the Bank Identification Number (BIN), to look up an associated app in the Windows Phone Store.

The ability to create and manage payment instruments is limited to financial institutions that have been granted permission by Microsoft.

Wallet agents

As mentioned throughout the chapter, the goal of the Wallet Hub is to provide a centralized location for all of the content associated with the user's digital deals, accounts, and payment methods, including balance and transaction information. To make the Wallet experience relevant, though, that data must be up to date, not based on the last time an app or one of its scheduled agents was able to run. To provide the freshest data possible, apps can use a new type of background agent known as a *WalletAgent*.

A *WalletAgent* operates slightly differently from the other types of agents available in Windows Phone. (To read more about agents, go to Chapter 9, "Background agents.") First, it is invoked on demand by the foreground app, namely the Wallet Hub, rather than being scheduled. Second, its resource allocation is actually carved out from the pool allotted to the foreground app rather than being provided independently, as with other agents. In Windows Phone 8, the Wallet Hub provides Wallet agents with 10 MB of memory and 5 percent CPU. This provides the Wallet Hub with the flexibility to determine how to run the agents without having to worry about impacting the rest of the system. During development, Wallet agents were often referred to internally within Microsoft as "foreground agents" because of this close relationship between the foreground app and the agent task.

Although the resource management policy and the invocation context are different for Wallet agents, their programming model is very similar to other types of agents. They are invoked through a system-defined event handler—in this case, *OnRefreshData*—and they must notify the system through the *NotifyComplete* API when they have finished their work. Unlike scheduled agents, however, the lifetime of Wallet agents is not a well-defined period. Rather, because they derive their resources from the Wallet Hub, they can continue to run so long as the Wallet Hub remains in the foreground.

We return to the *ContosoAirlines* solution in the sample code to examine how you can use Wallet agents to enhance the interaction between Wallet apps and the Wallet Hub. As with the other Windows Phone agents described in Chapter 9, Wallet agents must be hosted in a separate assembly from the primary app, so we add a new project to the solution called *ContosoAirWalletAgent*. The project contains a single class, *ContosoAirWalletAgent*, which derives from the platform base class, *WalletAgent*. For simplicity, all of the logic to perform the update to the Wallet is contained within the *OnRefreshData* event handler, which is invoked when Wallet is launched. As you might expect, the work done by the Wallet agent is very similar to the work done by the foreground app, shown earlier. The agent gets updated data from the mock web service and submits those updates to the *Account Manager*, which updates its own local cache before sending the data on to the Wallet. Observe that the *RefreshDataEventArgs* parameter provides a list of *WalletItem* objects to update. Because the app only ever adds one item to the Wallet, namely the account, it simply fetches the *WalletTransactionItem* using the first (and only) element in the collection.

```
public class ContosoAirWalletAgent : WalletAgent
{
     AccountManager accountManager;

     protected override async void OnRefreshData(RefreshDataEventArgs args)
     {
          accountManager = new AccountManager();
          await accountManager.LoadAsync();

          WalletTransactionItem walletTransactionItem = (WalletTransactionItem)args.Items[0];

          ContosoWebService contosoWebService = new ContosoWebService();

          var newFlights =
               await contosoWebService.GetFlightsForAccount(accountManager.AccountId,
                         walletTransactionItem.LastUpdated);
```

```
            foreach (Flight newFlight in newFlights)
            {
                accountManager.AddCompletedFlight(newFlight);
            }

            var newRedemptions =
                contosoWebService.GetRedemptionsForAccount(accountManager.AccountId,
                    walletTransactionItem.LastUpdated);

            foreach (Redemption newRedemption in newRedemptions)
            {
                accountManager.AddRedemption(newRedemption);
            }

            HotFare currentHotFare = await contosoWebService.GetRandomHotFare();

            walletTransactionItem.Message =
                String.Format("{0} for ${1}", currentHotFare.DestinationName,
                              currentHotFare.Price);

            walletTransactionItem.MessageNavigationUri =
                new Uri(String.Format("/HotFarePage.xaml?Id={0}", currentHotFare.Id),
                       UriKind.Relative);

            await walletTransactionItem.SaveAsync();
            await accountManager.SaveAsync();
            NotifyComplete();
        }

        // additional code omitted
    }
```

One of the key values of the Wallet Hub is the ability for the user to see all of his accounts and deals at a glance without the need to start each individual app. However, there are times when an app requires user interaction to continue providing up-to-date information, the most common example of which is incorrect or expired credentials. In those situations, apps can use the *SetUserAttentionRequiredNotification* method on the *WalletItem* base class. With this flag set, the Wallet Hub shows an Attention Required label on the item in the main panorama and then pops up a message box prompting the user to start the app if he opens the item Details page, as shown in Figure 20-15.

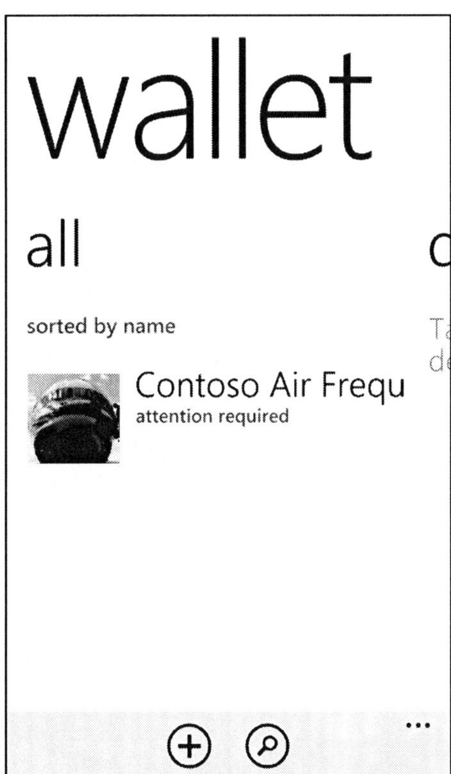

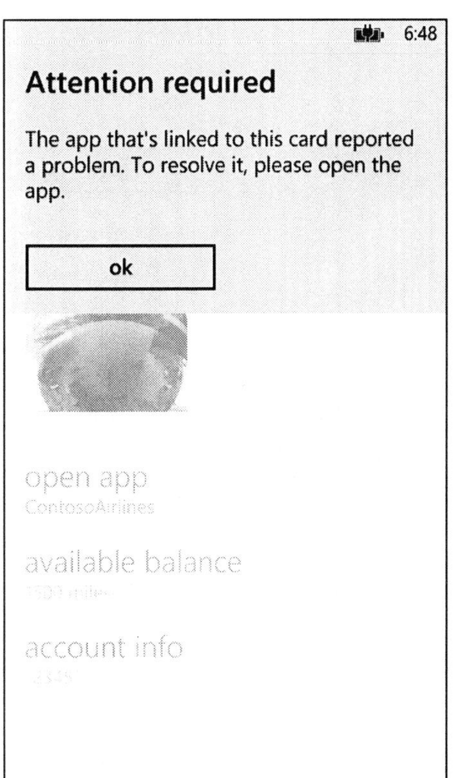

FIGURE 20-15 Use the *SetUserAttentionRequiredNotification* method to let the user know to start the app.

Summary

There is little doubt that mobile devices will eventually replace the physical wallet. It is far more convenient, scalable, and extensible to manage payment cards, transactions, and coupons in a software wallet than it is to do it in its physical counterpart. Windows Phone 8 takes a first step toward this future with the new Wallet Hub and its associated extensibility points. In this chapter, you learned how apps can take advantage of those extensibility points to create and manage Wallet items to create a rich, content-focused experience that can save users time and money.

CHAPTER 21

Monetizing your app

Even though mobile apps sell for relatively little compared to desktop software products, it can still be a challenge to convince users to part with their hard-earned money in return for your app. The explosion of mobile app development has led to a large number of high-quality free apps, making it even more difficult to persuade users to purchase your app based solely on its description, reviews, and screenshots. In this chapter, we review some of the techniques available for deriving a larger return from your app in the Windows Phone Store. Advertising and in-app purchase make it possible for you to provide the app for free but offer the opportunity to earn revenue later based on the level of user engagement; meanwhile, trial mode gives the user an opportunity to try out your app before purchasing.

Advertising

Advertising offers a great way to monetize your app while keeping the barrier to entry low for the user. Although various advertising networks provide XAML controls that you can include in your app, the Microsoft Ad Control is directly integrated with the Windows Phone SDK and has historically provided one of the highest payout rates, as measured in cost per 1,000 impressions, or CPM.

Note In this section, we will focus on integrating the Microsoft Ad Control in your Windows Phone app. However, some of the principles discussed, particularly with respect to placement of ads in your user interface (UI), also apply to other advertising controls.

The Ad Control works by retrieving text-based or graphical ads directly from the Microsoft Ad Exchange and displaying them in your app. The Microsoft Ad Exchange is a real-time auction where advertisers bid for the right to display their advertisement in your app. By always displaying the ad with the highest bid, the Ad Exchange maximizes the revenue opportunity for your app. Originally, Microsoft Advertising was only available to app developers based in the United States, but it now supports 19 different markets, with payout available in each market's local currency. Table 21-1 lists the supported markets (as of early 2013) as well as the minimum amount that you must earn before receiving a payout. The app developer receives 70 percent of the advertising revenue, minus applicable taxes.

TABLE 21-1 Supported countries for Microsoft Advertising and minimum payouts

Country/region	Currency	Minimum payout
Australia	Australian Dollar	50 AUD
Belgium	Euro	50 EUR
Canada	Canadian Dollar	50 CAD
Denmark	Danish Krone	250 DKK
Finland	Euro	50 EUR
France	Euro	50 EUR
Germany	Euro	50 EUR
Hong Kong SAR	Hong Kong Dollar	500 HKD
India	Rupee	2500 INR
Italy	Euro	50 EUR
Japan	Yen	5000 JPY
Mexico	Peso	750 MXN
Netherlands	Euro	50 EUR
Norway	Euro	50 EUR
Spain	Euro	50 EUR
Sweden	Swedish Krona	350 SEK
Switzerland	Swiss Franc	50 CHF
United Kingdom	Pound Sterling	35 GBP
United States	US Dollar	50 USD

Integrating the Ad Control

The Microsoft Advertising SDK is integrated directly with the Windows Phone SDK, so it is easy to add it to your app and see how it looks. The Ad Control offers a simulated advertising experience on the emulator and on a device so that you can try it out before going through the process of registering your app with Microsoft pubCenter, the online portal for the Microsoft Advertising network that we will discuss later in this section.

The easiest way to add the Ad Control to your app is by dragging it in from the Microsoft Visual Studio toolbox. You can find it at the bottom of the list of available controls. When you drag the Ad Control in from the toolbox, Visual Studio automatically does three things for you:

- It adds references to the two assemblies required by the *AdControl* class: *Microsoft.Advertising.Mobile.dll* and *Microsoft.Advertising.Mobile.UI.dll.*

- It adds an XML namespace prefix for the control's namespace in your page's XAML.
- It adds an instance of the *AdControl* to your page's XAML where you dropped it with default attribute values.

The only step that does not happen automatically is the provisioning of capabilities. Because the Ad Control runs in the security context of your app, you must declare the capabilities that it requires in your app manifest. The required and optional capabilities are listed in Table 21-2 along with an explanation of how they are used. Keep in mind that some of these capabilities will be displayed for your app when the user is looking at it in the Windows Phone Store, so ensure that you are comfortable requesting them before using the Ad Control.

TABLE 21-2 Capabilities used by the Ad Control

Capability	Usage
ID_CAP_PHONEDIALER	Ads can offer the ability to invoke the dialer to make a phone call when tapped. This capability is not displayed to the user in the Windows Phone Store.
ID_CAP_NETWORKING	The control needs to make network requests to the Microsoft Ad Exchange to request new ads and to record impression data.
ID_CAP_WEBBROWSERCOMPONENT	Ads are actually HTML content, so the Ad Control uses a web browser control to host them. This capability is not displayed to the user in the Windows Phone Store.
ID_CAP_IDENTITY_USER	The Microsoft Ad Exchange incorporates a small set of coarse-grained demographic properties of the user to help improve ad relevance.
ID_CAP_MEDIALIB (Windows Phone 7.x)/*ID_CAP_MEDIALIB_PHOTO* (Windows Phone 8)	If an ad shows a coupon, the user can tap it and save it to her media library for subsequent redemption.
ID_CAP_LOCATION (optional)	If the Ad Control has access to the user's location, it can provide more relevant ads and (usually) increase your CPM. Be aware that declaring the location capability in your app manifest makes you subject to additional certification requirements to protect user privacy, including adding a location consent prompt when the user runs your app for the first time.

After you have dropped the Ad Control into your app and declared the necessary capabilities, you will see a placeholder graphical ad similar to that shown in Figure 21-1. Of course, you will generally not want to display the Ad Control in the middle of your page as is shown here. We will review correct placement later in this section.

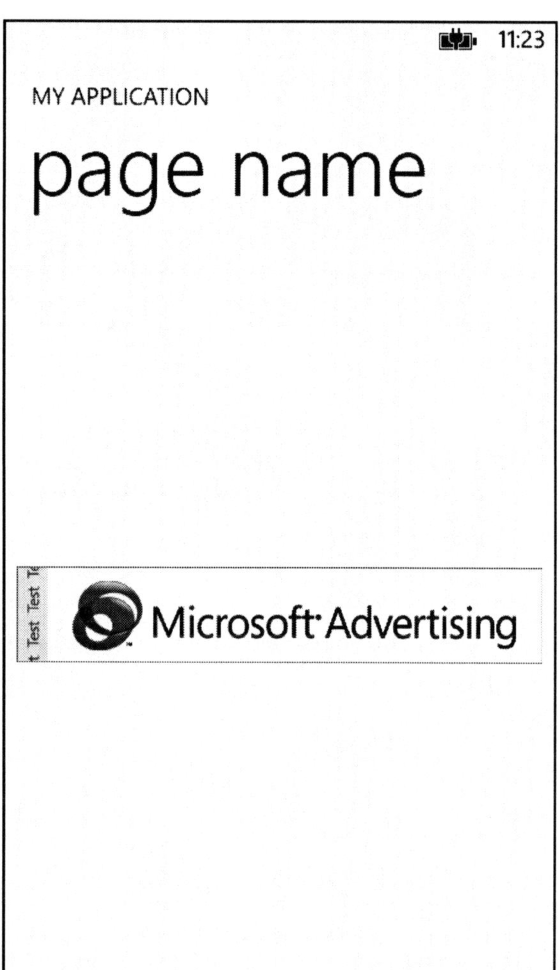

FIGURE 21-1 The Ad Control shows placeholder ads until you register with Microsoft pubCenter.

Note Even though dragging a control from the Visual Studio toolbox performs several set-up operations on your behalf, it also hard-codes a set of margins to ensure that the control appears exactly where you put it on the page. You should remove the hard-coded margins and position the control within your overall page layout based on the design guidelines found later in this chapter.

To display the placeholder ad, the control automatically sets two default attribute values: *ApplicationId* and *AdUnitId*. When you register your app in Microsoft pubCenter, you are provided with unique values for these attributes, ensuring that your app receives ads that are relevant to your content and that you receive credit for the ad impressions that your app drives. During development, however, you can use test values to get the control to display placeholder content. In all cases, the test value for *ApplicationId* is simply *test_client*, but you can modify the *AdUnitId* attribute to see different types of ad content, as shown in Table 21-3.

TABLE 21-3 Test values for the Microsoft Ad Control

Ad Type	*AdUnitId*	Size
Text ad	TextAd	480x80
Extra-large graphical	Image300_50	300x50
Extra-extra-large graphical ad	Image480_80	480x80

Although it is possible to create an extra-large (300x50) ad unit in Microsoft PubCenter, you should always explicitly set the size of your *AdControl* to the extra-extra-large size (480x80) to provide the flexibility to show both sizes of ads. The *AdControl* automatically centers smaller ads within the provided space. Ensure that you always set the size of the ad control to 480x80 explicitly: setting a smaller size or depending on automatic layout rendering will result in no ads being displayed.

Note In some cases, the Ad Control will be unable to display an ad, either because the user's device has no network connection or because he is in a location where Microsoft Advertising is not available. When that happens, the Ad Control raises the *ErrorOccurred* event with the *NoAdAvailable* error code.

In addition to the *ApplicationId* and the *AdUnitId*, there are several interesting properties on the *AdControl*.

- **IsAutoRefreshEnabled** When set to *true*, this property automatically refreshes the ad displayed in the control every 60 seconds, resulting in additional impressions. If you would prefer to refresh ad content manually, use the control's *Refresh* method.
- **IsAutoCollapseEnabled** When set to *true*, this property automatically hides the *AdControl* if there is no ad to display, either because it has not been retrieved yet or the *AdControl* failed to retrieve it.
- **CountryOrRegion and PostalCode** These properties make it possible for your app to manually set the user's general location, usually based on information that it has already collected. The Ad Control can use this information to improve ad targeting without requiring your app to declare the *ID_CAP_LOCATION* capability. For the *CountryOrRegion* property, use the two-letter code returned by *System.Globalization.RegionInfo.CurrentRegion.TwoLetterISORegionName*.
- **Latitude and Longitude** Using these properties, your app can set more specific location information for targeting. As with *CountryOrRegion* and *PostalCode*, you can use these properties to provide the Ad Control with location information that the user has provided to your app directly, perhaps by tapping a location in the map control or by viewing content that is geotagged, such as a photo or a business listing.

Ad Control design guidelines

As a business model, advertising has always struggled with the question of how to provide advertisers with sufficient exposure to warrant their spending money on ads while not distracting the consumer from the publisher's core content. In this section, we will review a set of guidelines for incorporating advertising into your app while simultaneously ensuring that users still receive a great experience that will keep them coming back.

Positioning

In most cases, the best place to position the Ad Control is at the very bottom of your page. This ensures that the ad does not interfere with the user's interaction with the core part of your UI. If your page includes an app bar, however, it is usually better to move the Ad Control to the top of the page, reducing the possibility that the user might accidentally tap the ad when he intended to use one of your app bar buttons. Figure 21-2 shows examples of pages with the Ad Control placed at the bottom and the top. This is derived from the *AdSupportedApp* solution in the sample code. The *ContentPanel* grid provided in the default page template is 456 pixels wide as a result of a 12 pixel margin on the left and right. To allow for the full width of the Ad Control, be sure to place it outside of the *ContentPanel*.

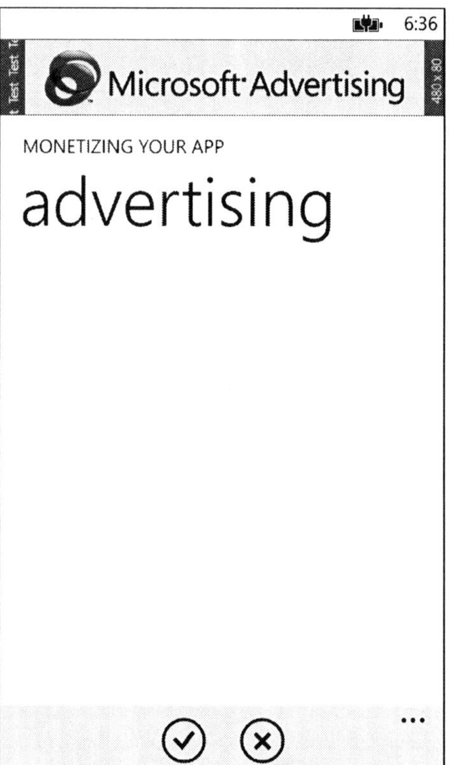

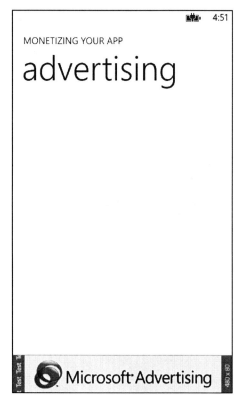

FIGURE 21-2 Place the Ad Control either at the bottom or top of your pages.

Integration with panorama and pivot controls

Special care must be taken if you want to incorporate ads into a page that includes either a panorama or pivot control. First, you should generally try to avoid using an Ad Control within a panorama control. In most cases, you should be using a panorama as a rich and engaging entry point into the rest of your app, not a place where the user spends a significant amount of time. Consequently, including an ad in your panorama has the potential to interfere with the visual effect that you're trying to achieve while not earning a significant return in terms of ad impressions. The metaphor often used for the panorama is a magazine cover—visually rich with limited text, and offering the promise of more content inside. In that respect, it is worth noting that although magazines earn a higher proportion of revenues from advertising than many other types of media, they almost never include ads on their covers.

If you do choose to include an Ad Control in a panorama or in a pivot control, the ad will no longer be visible if the user pans right or left, creating a poor user experience (UX) and limiting your ad impressions. To ensure that the ad remains visible as the user moves back and forth, always place the *AdControl* outside of the *Panorama* or *Pivot* control, as demonstrated here:

```
<Grid x:Name="LayoutRoot" Background="Transparent">
        <Grid.RowDefinitions>
            <RowDefinition Height="Auto"/>
            <RowDefinition Height="*"/>
            <RowDefinition Height="Auto"/>
        </Grid.RowDefinitions>

        <TextBlock Style="{StaticResource PhoneTextNormalStyle}"
                   Text="MONETIZING YOUR APP" Margin="24,0,0,0" />

        <phone:Pivot Grid.Row="1">
            <phone:PivotItem Header="pivot 1" />
            <phone:PivotItem Header="pivot 2" />
        </phone:Pivot>

        <UI:AdControl
             Height="80"
             Width="480"
             Grid.Row="2"
             ApplicationId="test_client"
             AdUnitId="Image480_80" />
</Grid>
```

Creating a common Ad Unit across all pages

One way to simplify the integration of advertising into your app UI is to position the Ad Control at the same place on every page. Although it is possible to enable a common placement by adding an instance of the Ad Control on each individual page, this approach results in your app loading a new ad on each page, causing the Ad Control to go blank momentarily on the new page while the new ad is fetched. It also requires that you integrate the Ad Control into each page's particular layout, as shown in the previous section for a page using the *Pivot* control.

An alternative approach is to create a custom template for *PhoneApplicationFrame*, the parent control for the entire app, which maintains a placeholder for the *AdControl* and provides the remainder of the space for the page itself. The *RootFrameAdControl* solution in the sample code shows how to implement this approach with two simple changes.

First, we define a custom template for the *PhoneApplicationFrame* in the app resources collection maintained in *App.xaml*. The template reserves 80 pixels of vertical space for a *Border* that will hold the *AdControl* at the bottom of the frame and a *ContentPresenter* that will hold the rest of the page.

```
<Application.Resources>
    <local:LocalizedStrings xmlns:local="clr-namespace:RootFrameAdControl"
                            x:Key="LocalizedStrings"/>
    <ControlTemplate TargetType="phone:PhoneApplicationFrame" x:Key="AdFrameTemplate">
        <Grid x:Name="ClientArea">
            <Grid.RowDefinitions>
                <RowDefinition Height="*"/>
                <RowDefinition Height="80"/>
            </Grid.RowDefinitions>
            <ContentPresenter Grid.Row="0"/>
            <Border x:Name="AdHolder" Grid.Row="1" />
        </Grid>
    </ControlTemplate>
</Application.Resources>
```

Then, in the *InitializePhoneApplication* method defined in *App.xaml.cs*, we apply the custom template to the app's root frame and add an instance of the *AdControl* to the *Border* that we defined in the template.

```
private Border adContainer;
private void InitializePhoneApplication()
{
    if (phoneApplicationInitialized)
        return;

    RootFrame = new PhoneApplicationFrame();

    RootFrame.Template = Resources["AdFrameTemplate"] as ControlTemplate;
    RootFrame.ApplyTemplate();

    adContainer = (Border)(VisualTreeHelper.GetChild(RootFrame, 0) as
                     FrameworkElement).FindName("AdHolder");

    adContainer.Child = new AdControl
                      {
                          AdUnitId = "Image480_80",
                          ApplicationId = "test_client",
                          Height = 80,
                          Width = 480
                      };
```

```
        RootFrame.Navigated += CompleteInitializePhoneApplication;
        RootFrame.NavigationFailed += RootFrame_NavigationFailed;
        RootFrame.Navigated += CheckForResetNavigation;
        phoneApplicationInitialized = true;
}
```

Registering with Microsoft pubCenter

After you are satisfied with how the Ad Control appears in your app, it is time to register with Microsoft pubCenter so that you can start to receive real ads prior to submitting your app to the Windows Phone Store. You can find the pubCenter portal at *http://pubcenter.microsoft.com*. After signing in by using your Microsoft Account, you are prompted to register with pubCenter by providing some basic profile information, and then you will have the opportunity to register your first app and ad unit, as shown in Figure 21-3. To register an app, you need to provide a name and a device type. The name that you provide in the Application Name text box is only used to refer to the app within the pubCenter portal, so it does not need to be the same as the name of your app in the Windows Phone Store. In the Device Type list box, you will see two options: Windows Phone 7 and Windows 8. There is only one version of the advertising control and it is built for the Windows Phone 7 platform, so choose Windows Phone 7 even if you are targeting the Windows Phone 8 SDK.

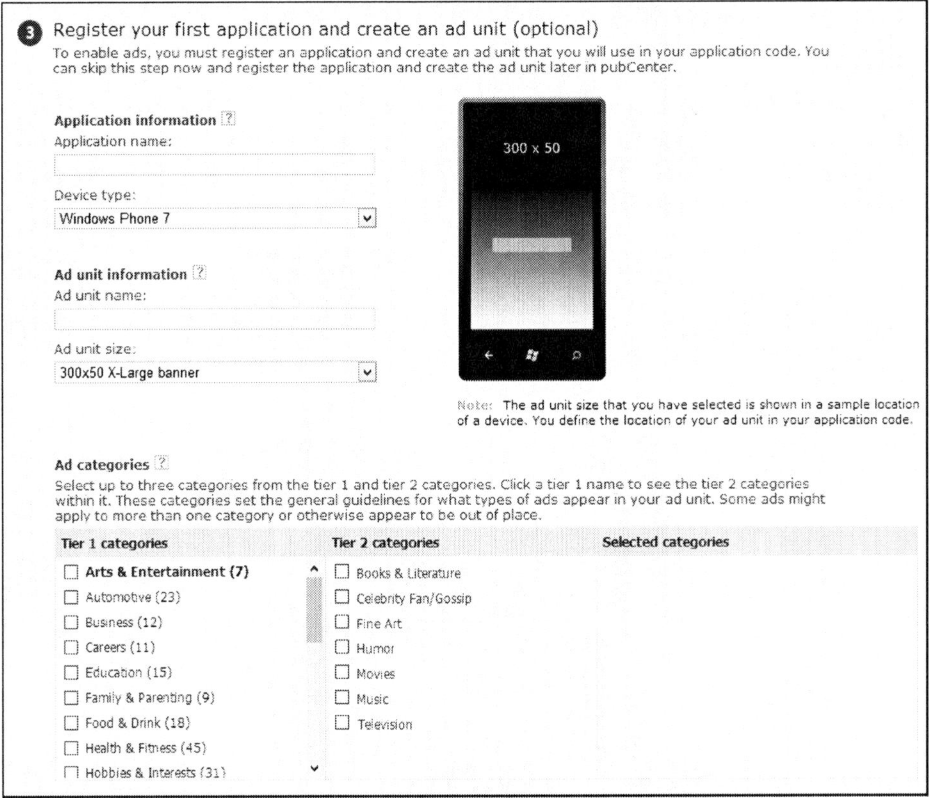

FIGURE 21-3 The pubCenter portal is where you register an app and an ad unit for use in the Ad Control.

The remainder of the registration process concerns the setup of your first ad unit. Like the app name, the Ad Unit Name is used solely for tracking your ad impressions within pubCenter, so choose something that is meaningful to you. The other aspects of ad unit configuration have a much greater impact on the types of ads that will appear in your app. First, you can choose the size of the ads that you want to display, as discussed earlier. You then have the opportunity to specify the types of ads that you want to feature in your app. In general, you should choose categories that you think will be most relevant to the users of your app. For example, if you are building a recipes app, it would make sense to choose the Food & Drink category. By displaying ads that are relevant to your users, you will make the Ad Control feel more integrated in your app and increase the likelihood that they will tap the ads, which in turn increases your click-through rate (CTR), which ultimately drives higher CPM.

The integration of the Dev Center and the pubCenter

Microsoft is in the process of integrating most of the pubCenter configuration functionality needed by phone developers directly into the Windows Phone Dev Center. In particular, developers can now create ad units directly within Dev Center by using a process that is streamlined for Windows Phone apps. Rather than choosing target categories, for instance, the Dev Center simply sends your app category to pubCenter, which automatically maps it to the appropriate ad category. To create ad units for an app within Dev Center, on the app submission page, in the Optional section, click Add In-App Advertising, as demonstrated in Figure 21-4.

There are two important tasks which still require that you visit pubCenter, however. First, to receive payment for advertising revenue earned by your app, you must provide your payment details and tax information in pubCenter, even if you have already provided them in Dev Center. Second, Dev Center does not provide any reporting for ad impressions or revenue, so to see how your ad units are doing, you still need to visit pubCenter.

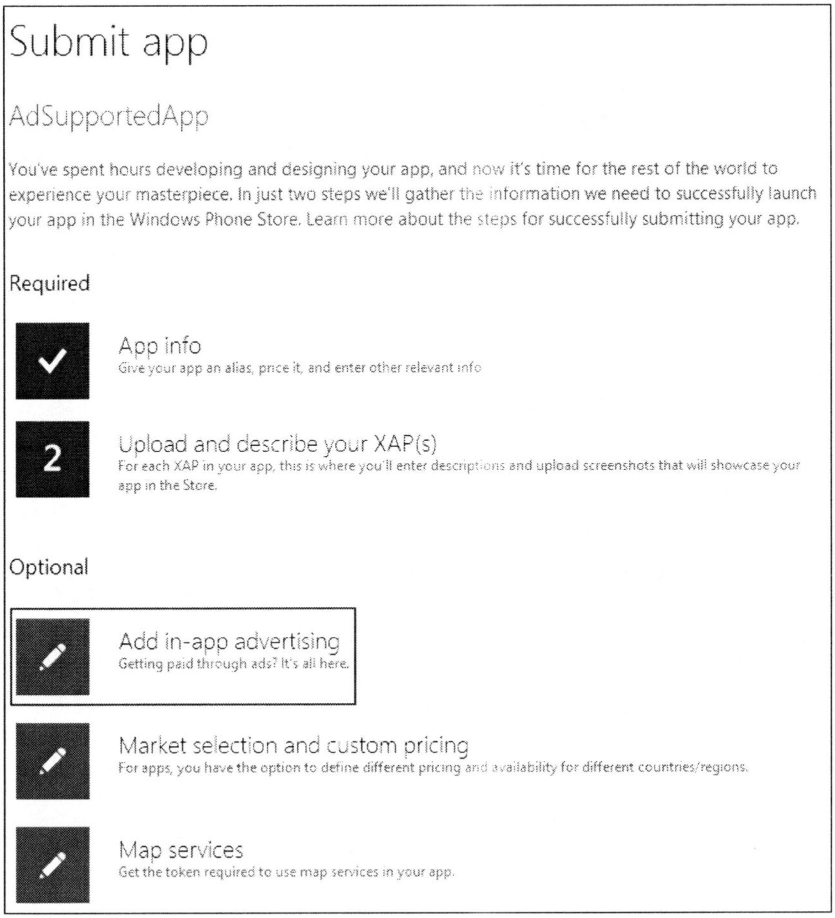

Submit app

AdSupportedApp

You've spent hours developing and designing your app, and now it's time for the rest of the world to experience your masterpiece. In just two steps we'll gather the information we need to successfully launch your app in the Windows Phone Store. Learn more about the steps for successfully submitting your app.

Required

App info
Give your app an alias, price it, and enter other relevant info

2 Upload and describe your XAP(s)
For each XAP in your app, this is where you'll enter descriptions and upload screenshots that will showcase your app in the Store.

Optional

Add in-app advertising
Getting paid through ads? It's all here.

Market selection and custom pricing
For apps, you have the option to define different pricing and availability for different countries/regions.

Map services
Get the token required to use map services in your app.

FIGURE 21-4 You can now create ad units directly in the Windows Phone Dev Center.

When you complete the registration process, you are provided with your app ID and ad unit ID, which you can then include in your app. Keep in mind that real ads are never shown in the emulator, so you might want to include a conditional compilation directive to switch back and forth between test values and real values. For instance, you could define a preprocessor directive named *SHOW_TEST_ADS* in a particular build configuration of your app and use that to control whether you use test values such as *test_client* and *Image480_80* or real values provided by pubCenter.

```
#if SHOW_TEST_ADS
     public const string pubCenterAppId = "test_client";
     public const string pubCenterAdUnitId = "Image480_80";
#else
     public const string pubCenterAppId = "myRealAppId";
     public const string pubCenterAdUnitId = "myRealAdUnitId";
#endif
```

Tip As always, it is a good idea to spend time testing your app exactly as users will see it before you publish it in the Windows Phone Store. For apps using the Ad Control, that means switching to using real ads by running your app on a real device with your actual pubCenter app ID and ad unit ID. Pay attention to whether ads are being displayed properly and consistently and whether the types of ads being shown make sense for your app. If not, you can make changes to your ad unit ID in pubCenter and generally see it take effect within about 20 minutes. Be aware that real ads displayed in your app during this test period are tracked just as they will be after you publish your app to the Windows Phone Store, so you should start to see ad impressions, estimated CPM (eCPM), and revenue being calculated in pubCenter within a few hours.

Playing by the rules

Because one of the primary factors dictating how much an app earns from advertising is the number of impressions it generates, there is a natural motivation to increase impressions in whatever way possible. The Microsoft pubCenter Publisher Agreement defines a set of rules to constrain an app's ability to artificially drive up its impression count. If you do not abide by these rules, pubCenter can stop serving your app with ads. The complete text of the Publisher Agreement can be found at *https://pubcenter.microsoft.com/CustomerManagement/Customer/TC.html.*

For Windows Phone apps, the key rules to be aware of are the following:

- You must not refresh your ad more frequently than every 30 seconds.
- You cannot display more than one Ad Control on screen at any given time.
- You cannot hide ads.

Trial mode

Although smartphone users have shown a strong willingness to pay for useful and interesting apps for their devices, it is relatively rare for them to do so without first seeing firsthand what value an app provides. A common solution for this on other platforms is to publish two versions of an app to the store—a fully-featured paid version, and a limited "lite" version that is available for free. This approach works, but has several significant downsides. For the developer, it requires managing two different app packages. For the user, it means that there is no built-in migration path from the free version to the paid version because the system treats them as two distinct apps. It also results in a significant amount of duplication in the Windows Phone Store, with two versions of the same app being available, one free and one paid.

The Windows Phone platform offers a solution to this problem: trial mode. Using trial mode, you can submit a single app package to the Windows Phone Store and have it offer that app both for trial and for purchase, as illustrated in Figure 21-5. At run time, you can differentiate the behavior of your app for trial and paid modes by calling a trusted-platform API. It is entirely up to you to determine how to restrict functionality in your app for trial mode. You might choose to disable entire features of your app or limit how deeply a user can interact with a specific feature. Alternatively, you could choose to provide full access to your app for a limited period, such as one week. Be aware, however, that there is no limitation in the Windows Phone Store or in the platform restricting how many times a user can install a trial app. If you opt for a time-limited approach, you should ensure that there is some downside to uninstalling and reinstalling the trial version of your app, such as a loss of data, to encourage users to upgrade rather than continuing to use the trial version.

The *TrialModeApp* solution in the sample code shows an example of using trial mode. The app provides simple stopwatch functionality, as depicted in Figure 21-6. When running in trial mode, the app simply limits the maximum duration of any timer to a hard-coded maximum of 10 seconds, at which point the user is prompted to consider purchasing the app.

FIGURE 21-5 The Windows Phone Store automatically provides both "try" and "buy" buttons for apps that support trial mode.

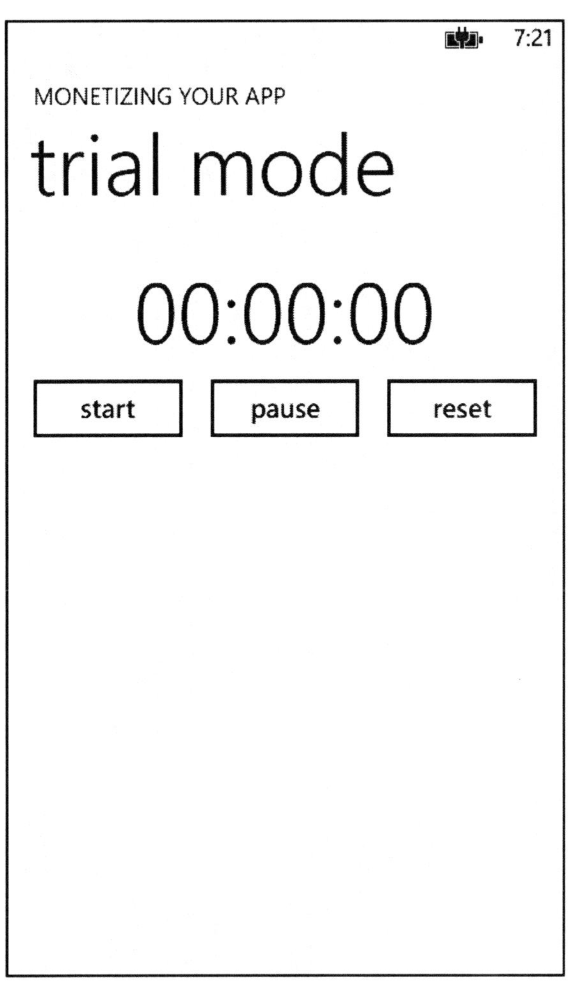

FIGURE 21-6 The *TrialModeApp* provides a stopwatch that is limited to 10-second runs when in trial mode.

When a user chooses to try an app in the Windows Phone Store, that app is installed on her phone with a trial license, so to determine whether the app is currently in trial mode at run time requires checking the *IsTrial* property on the app's *LicenseInformation* object. Querying the *IsTrial* property can take up to 60 milliseconds, which is clearly not feasible for use at high frequency within the app, such as in the *TrialModeApp* solution. Thankfully, because it is not possible for an app's license to change without the user leaving the app, we can simply check the trial mode flag during app startup and activation and then maintain a cached version of the value in the app that can be checked very quickly. The *TrialModeApp* solution does this in the *App* class by using a private helper method, *CheckTrialStatus*, and a static Boolean property, *IsTrialMode*. Because it is not possible to acquire a trial license for an app during testing, the *CheckTrialStatus* method takes advantage of a conditional compilation symbol, *TRIAL*, to emulate running in trial mode.

```
public static bool IsTrialMode
{
     get;
     private set;
}

private void CheckTrialStatus()
{
#if TRIAL
     IsTrialMode = true;
#else
     IsTrialMode = Windows.ApplicationModel.Store.CurrentApp.LicenseInformation.IsTrial;
#endif
}
```

Tip Apps targeting Windows Phone 7 can use the *IsTrial* method on the *Microsoft.Phone.Marketplace.LicenseInformation* class to provide the same information.

During the *Application_Launching* and *Application_Activated* event handlers, we call *CheckTrialStatus* to update the value of *IsTrialMode*.

```
private void Application_Launching(object sender, LaunchingEventArgs e)
{
     CheckTrialStatus();
}

private void Application_Activated(object sender, ActivatedEventArgs e)
{
     CheckTrialStatus();
}
```

Even though we could now wrap any trial-mode functionality differences in an *if*-statement that checks the value of *IsTrialMode*, it is a good practice to consolidate the management of your trial mode functionality in one location in your app. We add a new class, *EnabledFunctionality*, to serve this role in the *TrialModeApp*. It includes a single static method that checks whether the app is in trial mode and returns the appropriate maximum timer value.

```
public class EnabledFunctionality
{
    private const TimeSpan trialTimerLimit = TimeSpan.FromSeconds(10);

    public static TimeSpan GetMaxTimerTime()
    {
        if (App.IsTrialMode)
            return trialTimerLimit;
        else
            return TimeSpan.MaxValue;
    }
}
```

In the app's main page code-behind, we maintain a *DispatcherTimer* that updates a *TimeSpan* property that is data-bound to the elapsed time shown in the UI.

```
private DispatcherTimer timer;

private TimeSpan elapsedTime;
public TimeSpan ElapsedTime
{
    get { return elapsedTime; }
    set
    {
        if (elapsedTime != value)
        {
            elapsedTime = value;
            NotifyPropertyChanged();
        }
    }
}

public MainPage()
{
    InitializeComponent();
    timer = new DispatcherTimer();
    timer.Interval = TimeSpan.FromMilliseconds(10);
    timer.Tick += timer_Tick;

    ElapsedTime = new TimeSpan();

    this.DataContext = this;
}
```

Every time the *DispatcherTimer* raises a tick event, we use the *EnabledFunctionality* class to determine whether the elapsed time on the timer is greater than maximum allowance that we have set. If it exceeds the allowance, we stop the timer and display a button in the UI that prompts the user to purchase the app, as shown in Figure 21-7.

```
private void timer_Tick(object sender, EventArgs e)
{
    ElapsedTime.Add(timer.Interval);

    if (ElapsedTime >= EnabledFunctionality.GetMaxTimerTimer())
    {
        timer.Stop();
        trialUpsellStackPanel.Visibility = Visibility.Visible;
    }
}
```

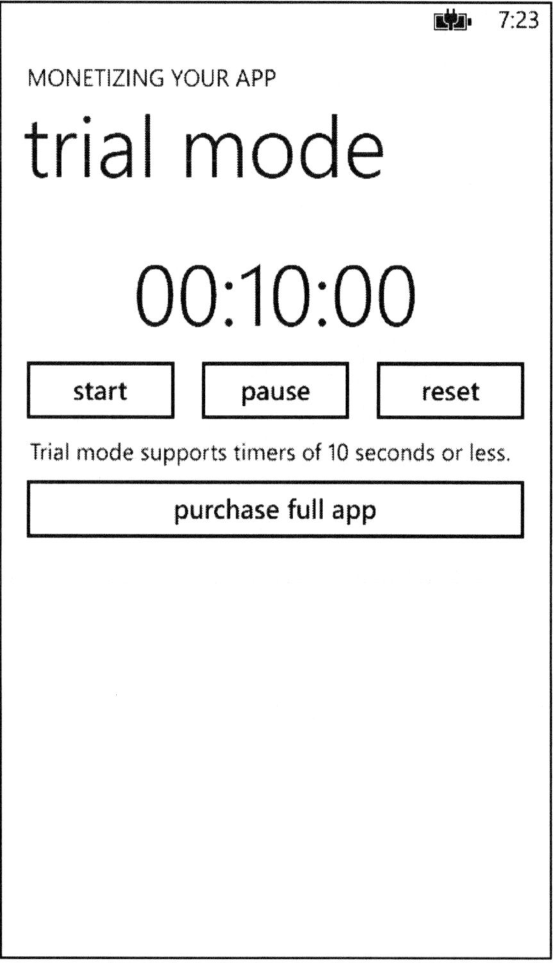

FIGURE 21-7 When the user hits the limitations of your trial mode, offer an upgrade path to the full version.

To upgrade to the full version of your app, the user must return to the app details page in the Windows Phone Store and purchase it. You can simplify that discovery by offering a direct link from your app via the *MarketplaceDetailTask*. When launched without a specific item identified, the platform automatically sends the user to the details page for your app, where she can immediately tap the Buy button. Of course, during your development phase, the Windows Phone Store will be unable to find your app and will display an error. This flow will work properly as soon as the app is published.

```
private void buyFullAppButton_Click(object sender, RoutedEventArgs e)
{
    MarketplaceDetailTask marketplaceTask = new MarketplaceDetailTask();
    marketplaceTask.Show();
}
```

Note Upgrading from the trial version of an app to the full version is very quick because the system only needs to upgrade the user's license for the app. It is not necessary to download a separate app package.

In-app purchase

Trial mode offers a good solution for apps that can segment their functionality into two states: a limited version and a full version. However, many apps have much more granular feature sets or offer content that enriches their experience, which users might be willing to pay for beyond the initial purchase price. For these scenarios, Windows Phone 8 now supports in-app purchase (IAP), also known as premium downloadable content (PDLC), providing significant additional flexibility in your monetization strategy. In fact, IAP might become the most popular business model for a large number of apps because it offers a couple of key advantages:

- You can initially distribute your app free of charge, eliminating the barrier to entry for new users and providing an opportunity to grow your base of potential paying customers. Of course, you can enable a similar model with trial mode, but users expect trials to be highly limited and temporary, whereas free apps with IAP usually offer some core functionality indefinitely with optional upgrades.

- You can benefit from ongoing revenue. In many ways, the "purchase once, use forever" model that has been the primary monetization strategy for most mobile apps to date is completely antiquated. In the past, when customers bought software on some form of physical media, they were buying exactly what came in the box—a specific version of the app with little or no guarantee of anything further to come. When the next version of the product was released, those customers could decide whether the additional value it provided was worth paying to upgrade. In the case of mobile apps, customers who pay once generally receive ongoing updates at no extra charge as developers continue to add value. If the number of customers willing to purchase the app for the first time starts to run low, the developer's revenue can begin to slow. IAP provides an opportunity to continue monetizing new features and content, fostering an ongoing revenue stream from an existing customer base.

Note IAP is only available in Windows Phone 8. However, Windows Phone 7.1 apps running on Windows Phone 8 can use IAP through a technique known as *light up*, whereby you call Windows Phone 8 methods by using reflection. See Chapter 13, "Porting to Windows Phone 8 and multitargeting," for more detail. Although the sample app in Chapter 13 uses light-up to add new start tiles, the same mechanism can be used for IAP. The only difference is that you do not need to include the *AppExtras* element in your app manifest when lighting up IAP functionality.

Division of responsibilities

Even though the term "in-app purchase" implies that the transaction happens completely within the app, it is in fact a collaborative process between the app, the Windows Phone Store (client and service), and (optionally) your app's cloud service. Figure 21-8 shows all of the steps in the process, from app submission to content fulfillment.

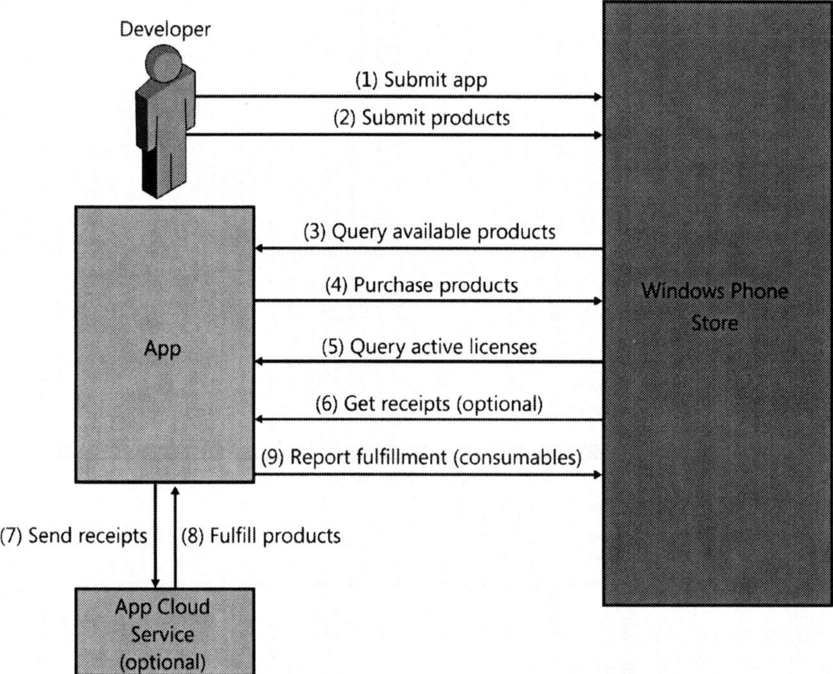

FIGURE 21-8 In-app purchase is a collaborative effort between the app, the Windows Phone operating system, and the Windows Phone Store, and (optionally) the app's cloud service.

It is important to understand the division of responsibilities between the app and the system so that you can invest your development time in the right areas. You are responsible for providing the following:

- A catalog of products that can be sold in your app
- Product details, including name, description, and icon for display in the Windows Phone Store
- An entry point in the purchase flow within the app, such as a button labeled "Buy"
- Product fulfillment, either directly within the app or from your own cloud service

In return, Windows Phone provides the following:

- Product catalog management in the Windows Phone Dev Center
- A built-in purchase experience by which the user can acquire your content with the payment instruments they have already configured
- Payment services in 190 countries/regions
- Secure purchase receipts

Note The revenue sharing arrangement for IAP content is the same as the one for app purchases—app developers receive 70 percent of the revenue.

Types of IAP content

Windows Phone enables two broad categories of IAP content, consumables and durables.

- **Consumables** As the name suggests, consumables represent content that the user can consume within the app and can replenish by making an additional purchase. For example, a role-playing game that uses virtual currency might offer the opportunity to purchase 100 gold coins as consumable content. When all 100 coins have been spent in the game, the user can choose whether to purchase more. Note that it is the app's responsibility to keep track of the state of a consumable purchase; for instance, the number of coins remaining.
- **Durables** Durable content is purchased once and lasts for the lifetime of the app. For example, an audiobook app could provide individual books as durables. When the user purchases a particular book, he can listen to it as many times as he wants without having to pay more.

IAP in Windows 8

Windows and Windows Phone use the same API for IAP, but there are several differences worth calling out:

- Windows supports the purchase of subscriptions through IAP. Windows Phone does not.
- Windows Phone supports the purchase of consumables. Windows does not.
- Windows provides the *CurrentAppSimulator* class, with which you can test your IAP code by using test items prior to submitting to the Windows Phone Store. Windows Phone does not support the *CurrentAppSimulator*, but it does provide two alternatives: the mock IAP library and beta products. We will look at each option in this section.

Configuring the mock IAP library

As with advertising, using IAP requires setup in both your client app and in a Microsoft cloud service, in this case the Windows Phone Dev Center. To provide full payment and licensing support on your behalf, the Dev Center requires that you provide an inventory of the items that you want to sell in your app prior to enabling customer purchases. As with the Ad Control, however, you will usually want to try prototyping IAP scenarios in your app prior to going through the process of configuring all of your content in Dev Center. So that you can undertake initial development and testing, Microsoft provides a mock version of the IAP library that provides an accurate simulation of the behavior of the real APIs, which you can download at *http://aka.ms/WinPhone8DevInternals/download*.

The mock IAP library download includes the library project, *MockIAPLib*, and a sample app that shows how to use it. You can either add the *MockIAPLib* project to your solution directly or build it as a Dynamic-Link Library (DLL) and then add a reference to it from your app. The library works by completely replicating the platform IAP surface area in a parallel namespace, so the first step when using it for testing is to toggle the *using* statements in any source file that needs to interact with IAP APIs with a conditional compilation symbol, such as *MOCK_IAP*.

```
#if MOCK_IAP
using MockIAPLib;
#else
using Windows.ApplicationModel.Store;
#endif
```

Tip Because you might want to run your app in both debug and release configurations against both the mock IAP library and the real service, it is a good idea to create different build configurations for each permutation. In other words, you should create a *Debug_MockIAP* configuration and a *Release_MockIAP* configuration in addition to the default *Debug* and *Release* configurations. In the *MockIAP* versions, you can define the *MOCK_IAP* conditional compilation symbol so that your code talks to the mock IAP library instead of the real service.

The only other setup required to use the mock IAP library is to create a set of products to use for testing. This is the equivalent of what you will eventually do in the Dev Center for your real catalog. There are two ways to do this. If you have a single, small catalog with which you want to test, you can add products directly in code. In *App.xaml.cs*, add a private helper method to create the products and then call that method from your *App* constructor. Naturally, you only want to run this code when testing, so ensure that you check for a symbolic constant that indicates your testing mode, such as *MOCK_IAP*, before calling the helper.

```
private void SetupMockIAP()
{
    MockIAP.Init();

    MockIAP.RunInMockMode(true);

    // Configure catalog info
    MockIAP.SetListingInformation(1, "en-us", "A description", "1", "TestApp");

    // Add some more items manually.
    ProductListing durableTestProduct = new ProductListing
    {
        Name = "My test durable",
        ImageUri = new Uri("/durableTestProductImage.jpg", UriKind.Relative),
        ProductId = "1234",
        ProductType = Windows.ApplicationModel.Store.ProductType.Durable,
        Keywords = new string[] { "books" },
        FormattedPrice = "1.99",
        Tag = "{IsOnsale : true, NumberOfPages : 500}"
    };

    MockIAP.AddProductListing(durableTestProduct.ProductId, durableTestProduct);

    ProductListing consumableTestProduct = new ProductListing
    {
        Name = "My test consumable",
        ImageUri = new Uri("/consumableTestProductImage.jpg", UriKind.Relative),
        ProductId = "5678",
        ProductType = Windows.ApplicationModel.Store.ProductType.Consumable,
        Keywords = new string[] { "music" },
        FormattedPrice = "0.99",
        Tag = "{IsOnSale : false, Genre : Folk}"
    };

    MockIAP.AddProductListing(consumableTestProduct.ProductId, consumableTestProduct);
}

public App()
{
    // standard App constructor code...

#if DEBUG
    SetupMockIAP();
#endif
}
```

Tip Product listings include a *Tag* field and a *Keywords* collection, which can be useful for determining where and how to display your products in your UI. If your app sells multiple types of content in different contexts, you can use keywords to filter the list of products that you are retrieving from the catalog. For example, if we decided to add audiobooks to the *EbookStore* solution, we might create "ebook" and "audiobook" keywords and query for those products separately depending on where the user is in the app. You can also use these techniques as a way to highlight promotions and sales within your app, as we have shown with the *IsOnSale* tag.

If you have a larger catalog or want to be able to easily switch between different catalogs for testing, you can also load your test products from an XML string that contains a collection of *ProductListing* elements, each of which contains child elements that map directly to the properties on the *ProductListing* type.

```
<?xml version="1.0"?>
<ProductListings>
    <ProductListing Key="1234" Purchased="false" Fulfilled="false">
        <Name>My test durable</Name>
        <Description>A test durable product listing</Description>
        <ProductId>1234</ProductId>
        <ProductType>Durable</ProductType>
        <FormattedPrice>$1.99</FormattedPrice>
        <ImageUri></ImageUri>
        <Keywords>books</Keywords>
        <Tag>{IsOnSale : true, NumberOfPages : 500}</Tag>
    </ProductListing>
</ProductListings>
```

After you have loaded the XML string from a file, you can pass it to the mock IAP library by using the *PopulateIAPItemsFromXml* method.

```
private void SetupMockIAP()
{
     MockIAP.Init();

     MockIAP.RunInMockMode(true);
     MockIAP.SetListingInformation(1, "en-us", "A description", "1", "TestApp");

     using(Stream xmlStream =
                App.GetResourceStream(new Uri("Assets/Products.xml", UriKind.Relative)).Stream)
     {
     using (Stream xmlStream = ... )).Stream)
     using (StreamReader fileReader = new StreamReader(xmlStream))
{
     MockIAP.PopulateIAPItemsFromXml(fileReader.ReadToEnd());
     }
}
```

Tip Microsoft also provides a mock version of the IAP service that you can host in an Internet Information Services (IIS) web server, either on your development computer or in a test environment. The mock service is available for download at *http://code.msdn.microsoft.com/wpapps/Mock-Catalog-Service-56a2b1ff.*

Although it is more complex to configure, the mock service approach facilitates testing your app by using the real IAP APIs rather than the mock library. Instead of redirecting IAP requests within the app, you configure the Windows Phone emulator to direct requests to your mock service in lieu of sending them to the real IAP service. You must be careful with this approach, however, because purchases made from the same app on a real device will incur real charges.

Purchasing durable content

As mentioned earlier, a durable IAP item is one that the user purchases once and owns for the lifetime of your app. A common example of a durable item is an ebook. This scenario is illustrated by the *EbookStore* solution in the sample code. The app's main page shows a list of books available from its cloud catalog, each of which includes a prominent Buy button next to it, as shown in Figure 21-9.

The books are contained in a *ListBox*, which is data-bound to a collection of *Ebook* instances maintained in the view model. The Ebook type contains just two properties, a *ProductListing* instance that contains all of the product information available in the catalog, and a Boolean value that acts as a cache for the indicator of whether the user has purchased the book. The list is populated in the *InitializeViewModelAsync* method, which queries and iterates the current list of available books, checking whether the user has a valid license for each one by using the *IsActive* property.

```
public async Task InitializeViewModelAsync()
{
    var listingInfo = await CurrentApp.LoadListingInformationAsync();
    LicenseInformation licenseInformation = CurrentApp.LicenseInformation;

    foreach (var product in listingInfo.ProductListings)
    {
        Ebook book = Products.FirstOrDefault
                     (prod => prod.IapProduct.ProductId == product.Value.IapProduct.ProductId)

        if (book == null)
        {
            book = new Ebook { IapProduct = listingInfo.ProductListings[product.Key] };
            Products.Add(book);
        }

        ProductLicense license = licenseInformation.ProductLicenses[product.Key];

        if(license.IsActive)
            book.IsOwned = true;
    }
}
```

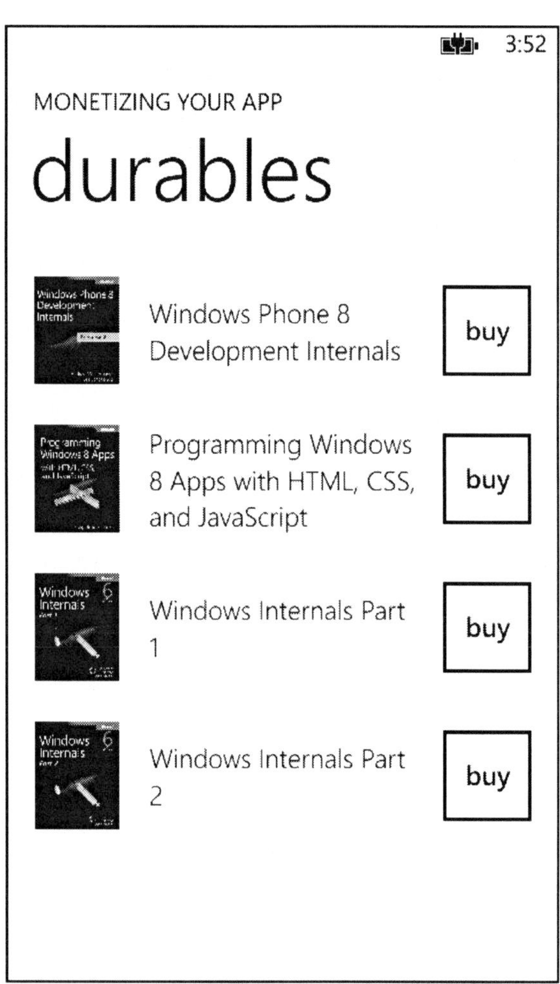

FIGURE 21-9 Ebooks are a popular type of durable content available for IAP.

You must take special care to handle license checks correctly. Validating a license by checking the *IsActive* property ensures that the user has actually purchased the content before you provide it. On the other hand, because license validation requires verification of a cryptographically strong digital signature, it is not a trivial operation and should not be called frequently within your app. Consequently, the *EbookStore* app uses the *IsOwned* Boolean to track ownership at run time. Be aware that it is possible for license state to change without your app's knowledge—for example, if the user purchases an item from another device—so it is important to check for the latest license information on every startup and activation, rather than maintaining state about what the user has purchased in the app's local storage.

As soon as all of the available products are shown in the UI, enabling purchase is straightforward. When the user taps the Buy button adjacent to a book, we acquire the associated *Ebook* by querying for the button's *DataContext*. The *Ebook* is then passed to the view model's *PurchaseProduct* method, which calls the static *RequestProductPurchaseAsync* method on the *CurrentApp* class, passing in the product identifier that was originally submitted to the catalog (or to the mock catalog if you're using the mock IAP library). The second parameter to the purchase method is a Boolean by which the app can indicate whether it wants to receive a receipt for the purchase. The receipt is an XML string containing information about the product purchased and the license acquired as a result. If set to *true*, *RequestProductPurchaseAsync* will return a string with the receipt XML.

Tip You can always request a receipt for a previous purchase by calling *GetProduct ReceiptAsync* on the *CurrentApp* class.

The final step in the purchase process involves checking the license to determine whether the user actually completed the purchase. If he did, we set the *IsOwned* property for the product to *true*.

```
public async Task PurchaseProduct(Ebook productToBuy)
{
    LicenseInformation licenseInformation = CurrentApp.LicenseInformation;

    await CurrentApp.RequestProductPurchaseAsync(productToBuy.IapProduct.ProductId, false);

    if (licenseInformation.ProductLicenses[productToBuy.IapProduct.ProductId].IsActive)
        productToBuy.IsOwned = true;
}
```

When calling the real IAP APIs and using the real IAP service, a call to *RequestProductPurchase Async* triggers the built-in purchase UI, with which the user can choose a payment instrument and complete the transaction. When you use the mock IAP library, however, the full purchase flow is replaced by a simple message box, as demonstrated in Figure 21-10.

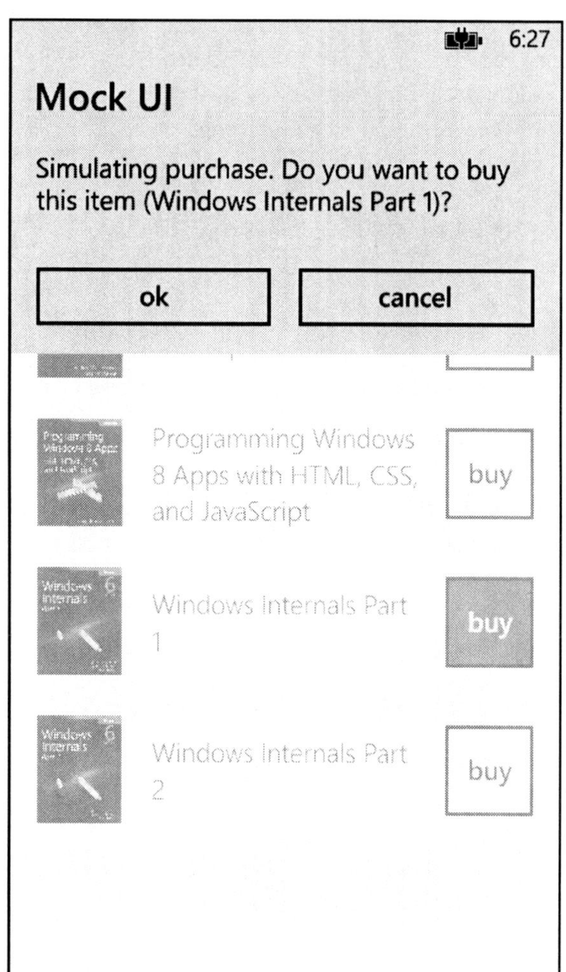

FIGURE 21-10 The mock IAP library replaces the standard purchase flow with a simple message box.

After the *IsOwned* property is set to *true* for a given book, the label for the button next to that book changes to "read" instead of "buy," indicating that it is now available for use in the app. Tapping the Read button brings the user to a page where she can begin reading the book (see Figure 21-11). When the purchase is complete, it is up to you to determine how to unlock the content. If you have a small catalog of relatively small items, you might choose to include all of those items directly in your app package so that they can be unlocked directly on the device. For larger catalogs or larger pieces of content, however, you will likely want to pull the item from your cloud service after the purchase is complete. In the *EbookStore* solution, we include the content for the test books in the app package, though a real ebooks app would naturally choose to download content on demand from the cloud.

6:47
MONETIZING YOUR APP
reader
Windows Internals Part 1
Windows
Internals
Part 1
6
In this chapter, we'll introduce the key Microsoft Windows operating system concepts and terms we'll be using throughout this book, such as the Windows API, processes, threads, virtual memory, kernel mode, and user mode, objects, handles, security, and the registry. We'll also introduce the tools that you can use to explore Windows internals, such as the kernel debugger, the Performance Monitor, and key tools from Windows Sysinternals (www.microsoft.com/technet/sysinternals). In addition, we'll explain how you can use the Windows Driver Kit (WDK) and the Windows Software Development Kit (SDK) as resources for finding further

FIGURE 21-11 After the user completes a purchase, you can unlock the content directly in the app or by downloading it from the cloud.

Validating IAP receipts

When fulfilling IAP content from your cloud service, it is a good idea to validate the digital signature associated with the purchase receipt as an additional defense against potential attacks. A sample project showing how you can verify a digital signature provided in an IAP receipt is available at *http://code.msdn.microsoft.com/wpapps/In-app-purchase-receipt-c3e0bce4*.

Purchasing consumable content

As described earlier, the primary difference between durables and consumables is that consumable content can be spent by the user and then replenished, whereas durable content lasts for the lifetime of the app. As a result, determining the set of consumable content that the user is entitled to is not as simple as enumerating the available products and checking each for an active license. Instead, your app must manage the state of the user's consumables itself and notify the IAP system when you have fulfilled a purchase by replenishing their consumable balances.

The *PaidClicks* solution in the sample code shows an example of an app that sells consumable content. The app allows users to pay for the privilege of clicking a button in a Windows Phone app, as depicted in Figure 21-12. Clicks are sold in batches of five and the app manages the click balance in its own local storage.

FIGURE 21-12 The state of consumable content, such as paid "clicks," must be managed by the app.

When the user purchases a consumable item in your app, you must do two things to complete the transaction. First, you must augment the user's balance of the item. In the case of the *PaidClicks* solution, this means adding 5 to the *AvailableClicks* property. Second, you must call the *ReportProduct Fulfillment* method, indicating that you have fulfilled the purchase. Because the IAP service plays no part in tracking the balance of the user's consumables, reporting fulfillment marks the end of the transaction from the service's perspective and enables the user to purchase the item again. If you do not report fulfillment, the IAP service will treat a subsequent attempt to purchase the product as a user retry and will authorize the transaction *without* a charge.

```
private async void buyMoreClicksButton_Click(object sender, RoutedEventArgs e)
{
    await CurrentApp.RequestProductPurchaseAsync(fiveClicksProductId, false);

    LicenseInformation licenseInfo = CurrentApp.LicenseInformation;

    if (licenseInfo.ProductLicenses[fiveClicksProductId].IsConsumable
        && licenseInfo.ProductLicenses[fiveClicksProductId].IsActive)
    {
        AvailableClicks += 5;
        CurrentApp.ReportProductFulfillment(fiveClicksProductId);
    }
}
```

Configuring IAP inventory

After you have thoroughly tested your IAP functionality by using the mock IAP library or the mock IAP service, you are ready to validate the entire process by using the real service. The first step in performing this validation is submitting your app to the Windows Phone Dev Center as a beta. For details on publishing a beta app, see Chapter 11, "App publication." As soon as the app is submitted, you can go to the Products tab on app's dashboard page to add items to its IAP catalog, as shown in Figure 21-13.

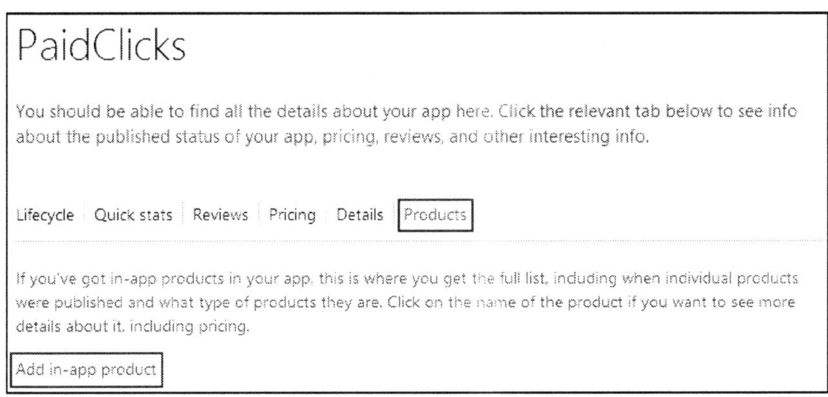

FIGURE 21-13 The Products tab on the app's dashboard is the entry point for publishing your IAP catalog.

As with app submission, the process for creating a beta IAP parallels the process for creating a real IAP, but without the ability to set prices, because all beta apps and products are free. Keep in mind that the product identifier and the product type (durable or consumable) cannot be modified after they are submitted, so ensure that you are setting the values you want to use before submitting.

When your beta app and IAP products are published in the Windows Phone Store (usually within 24 hours), you can test the complete purchase flow. Be aware, however, that Dev Center always generates a new *ProductID* for your app when it is submitted, so you must update your project to use that value to see the products that you configured in the service. You can find the new *ProductID* on the Details tab for your app in the Dev Center, as illustrated in Figure 21-14 (in the illustration, it is referred to by the synonymous term "App ID" in this context to avoid any confusion with IAP products). Simply copy this value to the *ProductID* field of the app manifest, which can be edited on the Packaging tab of the Visual Studio manifest editor.

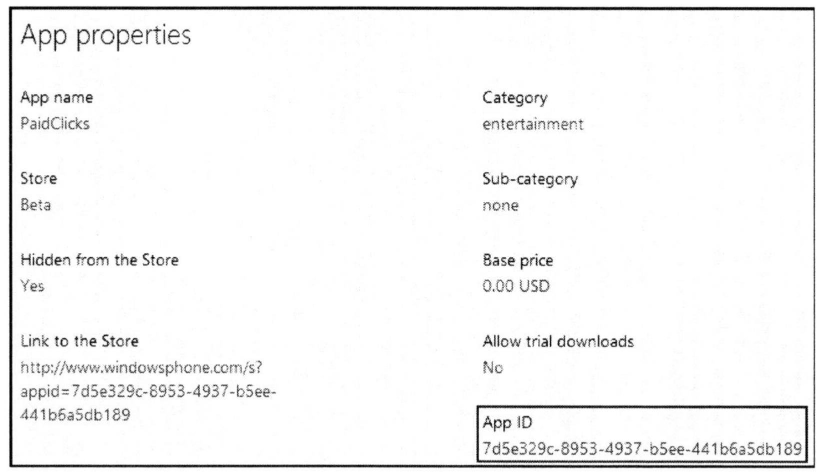

FIGURE 21-14 You must update your local XAP with the Dev Center–generated *ProductID* to test the full IAP flow.

When you have updated the *ProductID* of your app to match the beta submission, you can begin pointing directly at the real IAP service. Now, when you initiate the purchase flow, you are directed to the built-in purchase experience, as shown in Figure 21-15. Observe that for IAP products associated with beta apps, the purchase UI shows a subset of the product's metadata.

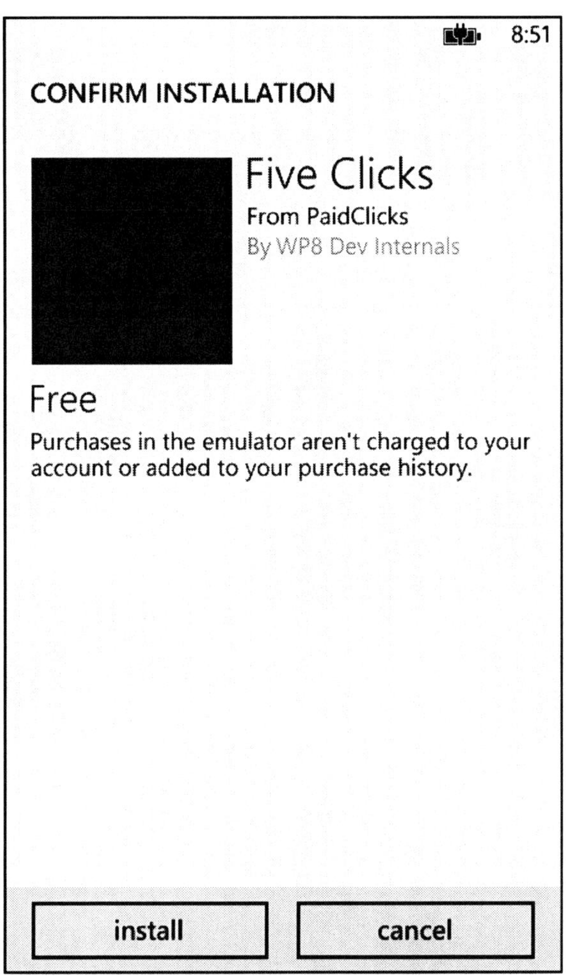

FIGURE 21-15 When testing against the real IAP service, transactions are completed in the built-in purchase UI.

Note Figure 21-15 shows that transactions in the Windows Phone emulator are always free, even if you are testing IAP of paid products of a published app. For beta apps, both the app and the associated IAP products are free in both the emulator and on real devices.

Summary

Whether you are building apps full-time or doing it as a hobby on the weekends, you are likely interested in earning some return on investment of your time and energy. Although directly selling your app in the Windows Phone Store remains the most common monetization option, it is incredibly challenging for a brand new paid app to get off the ground, so it is generally a good idea to consider alternative strategies. In this chapter, you learned how to incorporate advertising, trials, and IAP in your app, both as a means of earning additional revenue from users who would not have bought it directly, and as a way of providing a free introduction to your app that might result in conversions to paying customers.

CHAPTER 22

Enterprise apps

Windows Phone 7 was heavily focused on the consumer market. The overall user experience (UX) and target feature set were firmly targeted toward building a compelling, delightful device that users would enjoy integrating as a key part of their daily lives. With this in mind, the product focused less on the enterprise strengths of the platform. The balance shifted with Windows Phone 8, which introduced significant enterprise-focused features and capabilities such as drive encryption and XAP encryption. In this chapter, we'll look at the enterprise-focused support in the platform, the various ways that an enterprise can manage Windows Phone devices on behalf of its employees, and how you can build and deploy company hub apps and company apps.

Windows Phone for business

There are five major areas in which Windows Phone brings enterprise-focused support. Some of these features (app platform security and most of the data protection features) have been brought forward from Windows Phone 7; the rest are new in Windows Phone 8.

- **System integrity** This ensures that only validated components can execute as part of the operating system (OS) and app platform. The two key aspects of this are trusted boot and code signing. Trusted boot validates firmware images on the phone before they are allowed to load the OS. All boot components are digitally signed and cryptographically validated at boot. All code in the OS is signed by Microsoft, and this extends to drivers, services, and apps prepared by the original equipment manufacturer (OEM) or the mobile operator (MO). All apps that are added after the phone image is built (apart from side-loaded apps on a developer-unlocked phone and enterprise-signed company apps), including apps installed from the public Windows Phone Store, are also signed by Microsoft, and verified at both installation and startup. Updates to the phone OS, drivers, services (including OEM or MO software), the app platform, or any apps are only available through the Windows Phone update service.

- **App platform security** This ensures that apps are isolated from one another and cannot access one another's data. This is the same behavior as in Windows Phone 7, in which every app on the phone runs in its own isolated chamber that is defined by the capabilities that the app needs to function. These capabilities are declared in the app manifest and granted at install time; an app cannot elevate its permissions at runtime. This ensures that each app is granted only the permissions it needs and no more, thereby reducing the potential attack surface for any malicious code. Each app must disclose its required capabilities to the user on the app details page in the Windows Phone Store, which will display an explicit installation prompt for those capabilities that have requirements for explicit disclosure and specific consent collection, such as geographic location. Finally, apps are isolated from one another and cannot access memory used or data stored by other apps. Another change from Windows Phone 7 is that now even the in-box apps all run inside least-privilege chambers.

- **Browser security** This strengthens the security used by Internet Explorer and reduces the attack surface. Internet Explorer on the phone runs in an app chamber just like any other app, and is subject to the same capabilities model and lack of privilege elevation. Also, even though Internet Explorer on the phone does support JavaScript, it does not support ActiveX controls or plug-ins, further reducing the attack surface. Finally, Internet Explorer on the phone also uses the SmartScreen technology to warn users of websites that are known to be malicious.

- **Data protection** This provides mechanisms to protect the confidentiality and integrity of user data on the phone. This functions at several levels. First, the user can set a PIN or password for unlocking his phone. Next, the phone supports Exchange ActiveSync, through which an enterprise can enforce additional security policies. The phone includes a device management client component that can communicate with device management servers controlled by the enterprise, which can apply further security policies. If a user loses his phone, he can initiate a remote wipe of the device via Microsoft Outlook Web App. Enterprise IT professionals can do the same thing by using Microsoft Exchange Server. In addition, the user can locate a lost phone, map its location, make it ring, and wipe its data if necessary if he registers the phone with *windowsphone.com*. You can enable full-device encryption via device management or Exchange server policy using the same BitLocker technology as desktop Windows with strong 128-bit Advanced Encryption Standard (AES) encryption. The combination of device lock and data encryption makes it extremely difficult for any potential attacker to recover sensitive information from a device. Finally, the phone supports Information Rights Management (IRM) for email and documents. You can use this to control the type of access a user has to any given document (for example, controlling the ability to modify the document, copy/paste from the document, or forward it).

- **Secured network access** Network traffic is secured via user credentials and data encryption. Part of what makes Windows Phone so compelling is the ability to connect to email, social networks, web services, and cloud storage. Data synchronization between the phone and most cloud services or on-premises servers (including email and SkyDrive) uses a Secure Sockets Layer (SSL) connection. All network traffic for critical Windows Phone business apps, such as Exchange Server, Microsoft SharePoint, and Microsoft Office365, is encrypted by using 128-bit or 256-bit AES encryption.

Managed vs. unmanaged phones

From an enterprise-IT perspective, the first decision to consider is to what extent the enterprise wants to manage its employees' phones. If you want to maximize control and reporting capabilities, you would opt for managing the devices via a Mobile Device Management (MDM) tool such as Windows Intune or System Center Configuration Manager (SCCM). At a slightly less comprehensive level, you could manage devices via Exchange ActiveSync. At the other end of the scale, you could opt to implement only the lightest management by controlling the Line of Business (LoB) apps that can be installed on the phone.

MDM and managed phones

A Windows Phone 8 device can be configured to connect to at most one MDM server. However, it can also be connected at the same time to zero or more Exchange servers. Both MDM and Exchange servers can push security policies to the phone. In the event of potential conflict, the device management client will always select the most secure policy.

With Windows Intune, you can enroll devices into the system so that you can subsequently deploy policies to help secure corporate data, perform a hardware inventory, deploy LoB apps, and retire and wipe these devices. SCCM makes it possible for you to use the Windows Intune service over the Internet. In fact, enterprises are not restricted to these tools: Windows Phone 8 supports an MDM protocol that can be implemented by any third party. The phone includes a built-in management component that can communicate with any MDM server. This component provides two broad features:

- The enrollment client, which enrolls the device with the chosen MDM.
- The device management client, which periodically synchronizes with the MDM to check for updates and to apply the latest policies, as set by the enterprise.

For further details of Windows Intune and SCCM as well as device management in general, go to *http://aka.ms/WinPhone8DevInternals/protocol.*

Managed enrollment

The UX of device enrollment is simple and intuitive. This uses the built-in enrollment client user interface (UI), which is not extensible by third parties. To enroll, the user navigates to Settings | Company Apps. The general sequence is shown in Figure 22-1. When the user taps the Company Apps setting, this shows a simple informational page with an Add Account button. When the user taps this button, the enrollment client prompts for a corporate email address and password. The device then tries to autodiscover the MDM server and start the enrollment process. If the device cannot find the MDM server, it prompts for the user to specify the server address manually. When enrollment is complete—and in the case where the enterprise wants to deploy a company hub app—the enrollment client then prompts to install the hub app. After this is installed, it shows up on the Settings page under Company Apps.

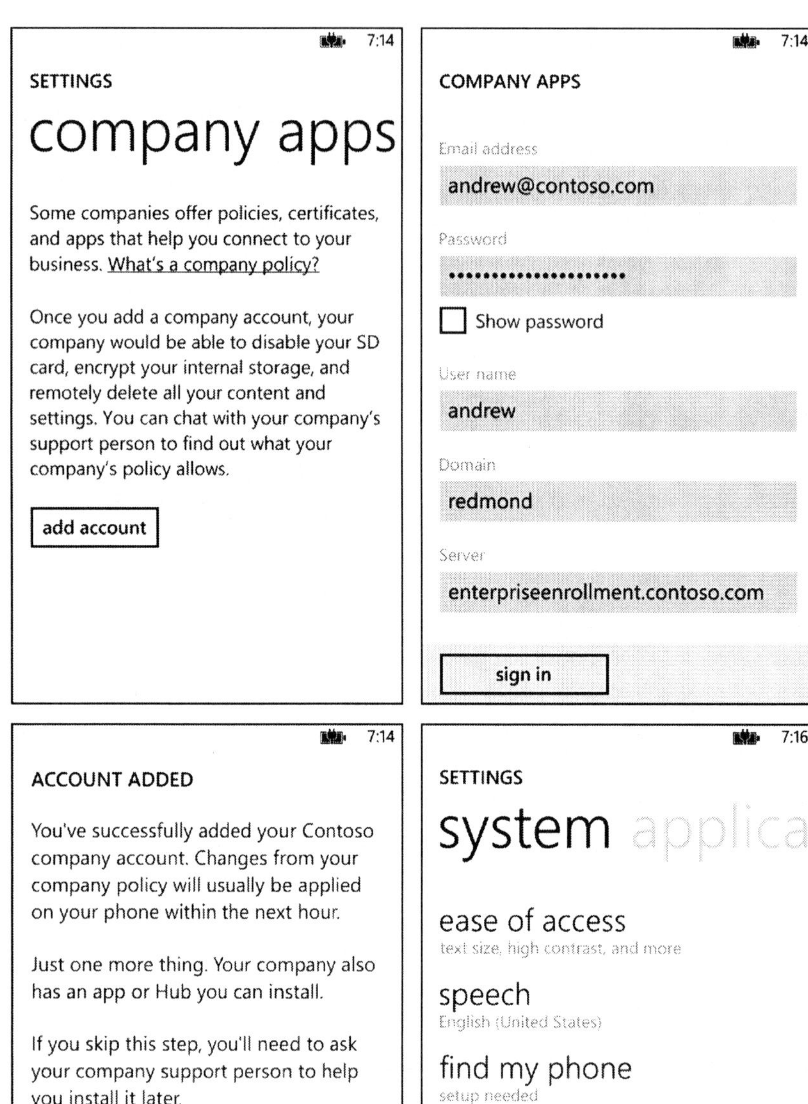

FIGURE 22-1 The built-in enrollment client takes the user through the process of enrolling the device in enterprise management.

Behind the scenes, the enrollment process performs a number of key operations, including the following:

- The MDM server generates a device certificate and deploys it to the phone.
- The enrollment client on the phone installs the certificate.
- For the case in which a hub app is deployed, the server deploys an enterprise application token to the phone, which the enrollment client installs.
- The enrollment client is configured with a scheduled maintenance task, whereby it periodically contacts the server for updates.

Unenrollment can be initiated either by the user on the device or remotely via the MDM server. For the case in which unenrollment is triggered by the MDM server, the enrollment client on the device performs the requisite clean-up operations during its next regular maintenance session. If the user initiates the unenrollment, this is done via the Settings page. During disconnection, the enrollment client performs a number of operations, as follows:

- Removes the enterprise token that allowed installing and running LoB apps
- Removes any LoB apps associated with this enterprise token
- Removes client and root certificates as configured by the MDM server
- Removes the client configuration, including the scheduled maintenance task
- In the case of server-driven unenrollment, reports successful unenrollment to the MDM server—this step is not performed if the user initiates the unenrollment locally

Unmanaged phones

You can use the Windows Phone 8 Company Apps feature regardless of whether your enterprise is managing your employees' phones via MDM. The Company Apps feature does require a lightweight enrollment process on the phone, but this is different from managed enrollment and does not involve an MDM server at all. Table 22-1 summarizes the key differences between managed and unmanaged enrollments.

TABLE 22-1 The key differences between managed and unmanaged enrollment

Feature	Managed	Unmanaged
Enrollment method	The Company Apps settings control panel item, in conjunction with an MDM server	Application Enrollment Token (AET) distributed by email or browser
Number of enrollments	One only	Unlimited
Policy management	Yes	No
App install method	MDM and/or company hub	Email, browser or company hub
App inventory	MDM	No
Silent app updates	MDM	No
Unenrollment	Remote or local	No

The managed approach clearly gives the organization a greater degree of control over the remote device and the apps and data on that device. This is suitable for larger organizations which require more comprehensive IT support. On the other hand, the unmanaged approach has a far lower IT infrastructure cost, and you can enroll the phone with multiple companies. This would be most useful, for example, for consultants or contractors who need to enroll both with their own company and with the client companies for projects on which they're engaged.

Unmanaged enrollment

Enrollment in an unmanaged environment is simpler than for managed devices, but still incorporates a high level of security. The main tasks are as follows:

1. The company registers a company account on the Windows Phone Dev Center.
2. The company acquires an enterprise certificate from Symantec and exports this as a personal information exchange (PFX) file.
3. The company uses the PFX file to create an application enrollment token (AET). Only users who have installed the company's AET can install the company's apps. Note, however, that there is no protection for the AET itself, so you can't use it for security purposes; nothing stops a rogue employee from posting the AET on the web where random people can install it.
4. The company builds one or more company apps, signs each XAP with the PFX, and deploys the signed XAPs to a suitable app repository server, or emails them to the user.
5. Optionally, the company develops a company hub app. This app typically knows how to find the company's apps from the company's app repository, install them, and start them.
6. Company users enroll for company app distribution on their phones by installing the AET.
7. Company users employ the company hub app to install the company's apps or retrieve them from email or the company's website.

When the company registers a company account on the Dev Center, this is validated by Symantec. This validation is generally very simple but can involve a phone call from Symantec to the company, and Symantec might ask for additional information at this point. For example, if you use a brand name to register, Symantec will request proof of rights in that brand name, typically via registration documents. See Figure 22-2 for an example.

FIGURE 22-2 To build and deploy company apps, you must have a company account on the Windows Phone Dev Center.

After the validation step is completed and the company account is established, the company must then acquire an enterprise mobile code signing certificate. To do this, you go to the Symantec website, *http://aka.ms/WinPhone8DevInternals/Symantec*, and provide the Symantec ID listed for your account in the Windows Phone Dev Center, as shown in Figure 22-3.

When this request is complete, Symantec delivers a certificate. You must import this intermediate certificate into the certificate store on a suitable corporate computer. Then, you must export it from the certificate store in PFX format. You must export the private key along with the certificate itself. You can perform this export via the Certificates snap-in to the Microsoft Management Console (MMC).

FIGURE 22-3 You must request an enterprise mobile code signing certificate from Symantec.

Armed with the PFX, you can now create an AET. This is done with the AETGenerator tool provided as part of the Windows Phone SDK. To run this, you must open a Microsoft Visual Studio command prompt as an administrator. Change the current directory to the folder where you've put the PFX file, and run the AETGenerator tool. For example (where *"myPFXfile.pfx"* is the name of your PFX file, and *"myPassword"* is the password for your PFX file):

```
"%ProgramFiles(x86)%\Microsoft SDKs\Windows Phone\v8.0\Tools\AETGenerator\AETGenerator.exe"
myPFXfile.pfx myPassword
```

This will generate three files, as listed in Table 22-2.

TABLE 22-2 The AETGenerator tool generates three files

File	Description
AET.xml	The raw AET in XML format.
AET.aet	A Base64-encoded version of AET.xml. This is used to configure the AET for distribution to phones through an MDM system.
AET.aetx	The AET.aet file in an XML format that can be processed on the phone through email or Internet Explorer. This is used to manually install the AET on phones for companies that are not using Windows Intune or SCCM.

The PFX is also used to sign the XAPs for any apps the company builds and wants to distribute to enrolled devices. Recall that all Windows Phone apps now go through a native-code generation process in the Windows Phone Store. Because company apps don't go through the Windows Phone Store, you must perform the equivalent native-code generation step independently, and this must be done before signing the XAP. To do this, you can either run the MDILXAPCompile tool or the *BuildMDILXap.ps1* Windows PowerShell script. Both are provided as part of the Windows Phone 8.0 SDK. The MDILXAPCompile tool involves additional manual steps (renaming the XAP to a ZIP, unzipping the ZIP, extracting the contents, and then running the tool), but it does give you finer-grained control over the output. If you use MDILXAPCompile to generate the native-code XAP, you then need to sign the XAP with the XapSignTool.

Conversely, with the *BuildMDILXap.ps1* script approach, you can both generate a native code XAP and sign it all in one go. Using this approach, you should open a Windows Powershell window and navigate to the location for the script, which is typically "%ProgramFiles(x86)%\Microsoft SDKs\Windows Phone\v8.0\Tools\MDILXAPCompile\". You would then execute a command line similar to the following (where *"myXapFile.xap"* is the path of your XAP, *"myPFXfile.pfx"* is the path of your PFX file, and *"myPassword"* is the password for your PFX file):

```
.\BuildMDILXap.ps1 -xapfilename myXapFile.xap -pfxfilename myPfxFile.pfx -password myPassword
```

Note that any spaces or special characters in either of the paths or in the password itself should be protected by surrounding the parameter in quotations. When this successfully completes, it writes out a couple of log files and a new XAP which contains native (MDIL) code and is signed. The new XAP will be named <OldXAPName>_new.xap.

After you've precompiled and signed the company XAPs, you must deploy them to some location from where they can be downloaded and installed to the target phones. Typically, you would put them on a server and then point your company hub app at that server. You would also maintain a list of current apps on the server, with details of the available apps, so that the company hub app can show this list to the user. It's up to you how much additional app metadata you want to maintain, but just as an example, you might maintain version information so that your hub app can be smart about installing updates. Or, you might maintain user role or region information so that your hub app can make decisions about which apps to offer to which users. If you have any very large apps, you might want to include this in the metadata and enhance your app download logic to check for a Wi-Fi connection before proceeding.

If you need additional behavior, you might build web services or a web app around the company app repository, but these are not required. The simplest approach is to create a virtual directory on the server by using Internet Information Services (IIS) Manager and then copy the prepared XAPs to the path that backs that virtual directory.

In an unmanaged context, the next step is to get the AETX file to your users. The simplest approach here is to send it to them via email. Alternatively, put it on your server and either send a link by email or simply tell users to navigate to the server in Internet Explorer on their phone. Either way, when the user taps the AETX file, it downloads and installs on their phone, as shown in Figure 22-4.

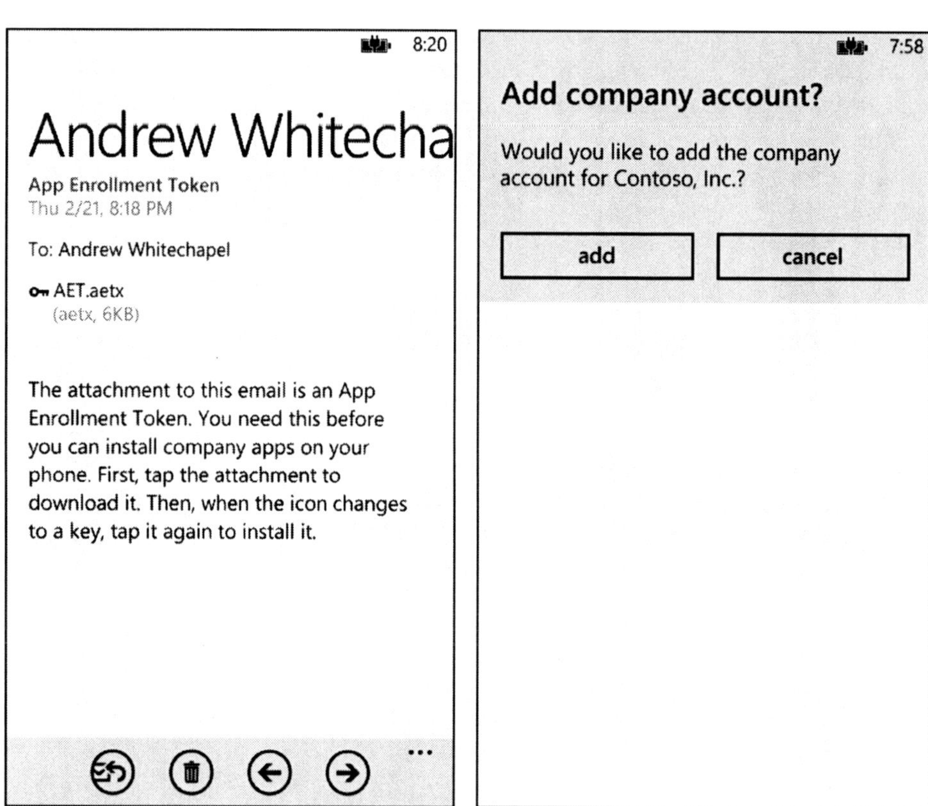

FIGURE 22-4 You can email the AET to your users so that they can add your company account.

Note If you use email to deploy your AET or company hub app to users of unmanaged phones, you should apply IRM protection to the email as an extra security measure. You should also remember that users might be accessing their email via a desktop computer, so whatever protection you apply should allow for this scenario, as well.

When the user selects Add from the message box, the installation of the AET commences. Be aware, however, that there is no further feedback in this operation, and the installed AET doesn't show up in the UI anywhere on the phone. This lack of confirmation might be a little disconcerting to some users, so you should consider this in your messaging to them.

When the user has installed the AET, you can follow this up with another email, sending your company hub app as an attachment, which she can then install. The hub app installs like a regular Windows Phone Store app and shows up in the app list as normal—it doesn't show up in the Company Apps settings list. At this point, the user is completely setup to run the hub app. The hub app can then programmatically discover, download, and install further company apps, as described in the next section.

Company Apps

Apart from Company Apps, there are only two ways to get an app onto a Windows Phone: through the Windows Phone Store, or via the SDK tools onto a developer-unlocked phone. Using the Company Apps feature, companies can deploy apps to enrolled devices without going through the Windows Phone Store and without developer-unlocked phones. This implies certain constraints:

- Company Apps can be installed and run only on phones that are enrolled with the associated company.
- The company controls the release of its apps: there's no ongoing interaction with Microsoft. The app does not go through the Windows Phone Store, does not go through the Windows Phone Store publishing and certification pipeline, and does not go through Microsoft's functional or compliance testing. The company, therefore, is responsible for the quality of its apps and the impact to the user. Even though you don't go through Windows Phone Store testing, you can of course still run your app through the Store Test Kit, as described in Chapter 11, "App publication."
- The company controls deployment and distribution. This can be achieved by setting up an app repository on a server that the company phones can access, with all the associated reliability, security, and availability considerations of a remote server. Alternatively, the company can use removable SD cards or simple email attachments as a more lightweight deployment mechanism.
- The company is responsible for securing deployment. In particular, there are no technical means to block installation of apps by unauthorized people. All they need is the AET and the XAP, both of which could be leaked (or stolen) and neither of which have any kind of authentication requirements, in and of themselves. In particular, for apps that access sensitive network data, you still need to ensure that your network end-points are well secured, require credential, and so on.
- The company controls app updates, any authorization updates, app retirement, and so on.
- App capabilities are still limited to the same set of capabilities as Windows Phone Store apps; that is, company apps do not get any additional privileges.

Another dimension to consider is that the phone is still a consumer device. It is likely that a given phone will have both company LoB apps installed as well as public Windows Phone Store apps. The user might set up email connectivity for both his corporate email account and one or more private email accounts. He can have company documents on the phone as well as private documents, photos, music, and videos. Consumer and enterprise data and apps are kept separate. That is, a company can deploy, update, and inventory its own apps, but it cannot manage Windows Phone Store apps on the device. On the other hand, if the device is enrolled in the company's MDM service, the company can wipe all data and apps on the device, both corporate and private, and reset the device to an out-of-the-box state. This does not apply to an unmanaged device, of course.

Building a company hub app

A company hub app typically serves two purposes: act as a corporate portal, providing information and links into the company's websites; and offer users a list of installable company apps. However, you might have one app for your portal, and a different app for listing available apps. As with other hub apps, it's generally appropriate to use a *Panorama*-based main page, as indicated in Figure 22-5. But, keep in mind that a company hub app is just a normal app; there's nothing special about it. The UI might be a panorama (but doesn't have to be); the app might use the deployment APIs to install apps (but it doesn't have to); and so on.

FIGURE 22-5 A company hub app can discover, download, and install other company apps.

The *ContosoHub* app in the sample code illustrates the API support for a company hub app that discovers and deploys company apps. The app is based on the standard *Panorama* app template in Visual Studio, which generates an app with a *Panorama*-based main page that is data-bound to a collection of viewmodel items. Each item, in this case, represents a company app. Here's the significant part of the item definition. The *Status* enum represents the installed status of the app, and the item constructor gives you an indication of the class properties.

```
public enum Status
{
    NotInstalled,
    Installed,
    Installing,
    InstallFailed,
    Pending,
    Cancelled
}

public class AppItem : INotifyPropertyChanged
{
    public AppItem(string title, string description, Uri imagePath, Uri xapPath, Status status,
Guid productId)
```

```
    {
        Name = title;
        Description = description;
        IconUrl = imagePath;
        XapUrl = xapPath;
        Status = status;
        ProductId = productId;
    }
... etc
}
```

The "available apps" *PanoramaItem* is data-bound to a collection of these *AppItem* objects, displaying the icon, title, and description for each app. This app metadata is retrieved from the server. The "installed apps" *PanoramaItem* is very similar, the main difference being that it is data-bound to only the installed subset of all available apps.

```
<phone:PanoramaItem  Header="available" >
    <phone:LongListSelector x:Name="AvailableItems" SelectionChanged="AvailableItems_
SelectionChanged" ItemsSource="{Binding Apps}">
        <phone:LongListSelector.ItemTemplate>
            <DataTemplate>
                <StackPanel Orientation="Horizontal">
                    <Image x:Name="ItemImage" Source="{Binding IconUrl}" />
                    <StackPanel>
                        <TextBlock Text="{Binding Name}"/>
                        <TextBlock Text="{Binding Description}" />
                        <TextBlock
                            Text="{Binding Status,
                            Converter={StaticResource InstallStateConverter}}" />
                        <ProgressBar
                            IsIndeterminate="False"
                            Visibility="{Binding Status,
                            Converter={StaticResource InstallingVisibilityConverter}}"/>
                    </StackPanel>
                </StackPanel>
            </DataTemplate>
        </phone:LongListSelector.ItemTemplate>
    </phone:LongListSelector>
</phone:PanoramaItem>
```

Notice also that each item in the displayed list also includes a *TextBlock* to indicate the current install state of the item, data-bound to the *Status* property via a custom value converter. There's also a *ProgressBar* for each item whose visibility is also data-bound to the *Status* property but using a different value converter.

```
public class InstallStateConverter : IValueConverter
{
    public object Convert(object value, Type targetType, object parameter, CultureInfo culture)
    {
        Status status;
        if (value == null)
            status = Status.NotInstalled;
        else
            status = (Status)value;
```

```
        switch (status)
        {
            case Status.Installed:
                return "Installed";
            case Status.NotInstalled:
                return "Not Installed";
            case Status.Installing:
                return "Installing...";
            case Status.InstallFailed:
                return "Installed Failed";
            case Status.Cancelled:
                return "Cancelled";
            case Status.Pending:
                return "Queued";
            default:
                break;
        }
        return value.ToString();
    }
}
public class InstallingVisibilityConverter : IValueConverter
{
    public object Convert(object value, Type targetType, object parameter, CultureInfo culture)
    {
        if (!(value is Status))
            return Visibility.Collapsed;
        Status status = (Status)value;
        return status == Status.Installing ? Visibility.Visible : Visibility.Collapsed;
    }
}
```

We maintain a list of available company apps on the server, with suitable supporting metadata.

```
<Applications>
  <App
    Name="ContosoFacilities"
    IconUrl="http://www.contoso.com/ContosoAppStore/ContosoFacilities.png"
    XapUrl="http://www.contoso.com/ContosoAppStore/ContosoFacilities_Release_AnyCPU_new.xap"
    ProductId="{8b9b06cd-509a-4c68-9b52-09c15fc6ff85}"
    Description="Office facilities requests" />
...etc
</Applications>
```

The *AppItems* viewmodel collection class fetches this app list from the server. It does this by using a simple *WebClient*. When we get the file, we load it into an *XDocument* and parse out the metadata to populate the list of available apps and the list of installed apps. It is important to note that this is just one of the user experiences you can support; there are many others.

```
private string appRepositoryUrl = "http://www.contoso.com/ContosoAppStore/applications.xml";
private WebClient webClient;
public ObservableCollection<AppItem> Apps { get; private set; }
public Dictionary<uint, Guid> PendingInstalls { get; private set; }
public ObservableCollection<AppItem> InstalledApps { get; private set; }
```

```
public void LoadData()
{
    webClient.DownloadStringCompleted += webClient_DownloadStringCompleted;
    webClient.DownloadStringAsync(new Uri(appRepositoryUrl));
}

private void webClient_DownloadStringCompleted(object sender, DownloadStringCompletedEventArgs e)
{
    if (e.Error != null)
        return;

    XDocument xdoc = XDocument.Parse(e.Result);
    var apps = from app in xdoc.Descendants("App")
               orderby app.Attribute("Name").Value
               select new AppItem(
                   app.Attribute("Name").Value,
                   app.Attribute("Description").Value,
                   new Uri(app.Attribute("IconUrl").Value),
                   new Uri(app.Attribute("XapUrl").Value),
                   Status.NotInstalled,
                   Guid.Parse(app.Attribute("ProductId").Value));
    foreach (AppItem appItem in apps)
    {
        Apps.Add(appItem);
    }

    RefreshInstallState();
}
```

The custom *RefreshInstallState* method is called in two places: from the *OnNavigatedTo* override in the main page; and from the *DownloadStringCompleted* event handler in the *AppItems* class. In this method, we use *InstallationManager.FindPackagesForCurrentPublisher* to get a list of all company apps that have already been installed. This method finds all apps that have the same *PublisherID* in the *WMAppManifest.xml*. We also call *InstallationManager.GetPendingPackageInstalls* to get the current status of all app installs. We default the status of all apps in the list to *NotInstalled*, figure out which ones have actually been installed, and then reset the status for these. In this method, we check for *AsyncStatus.Completed* and set the installed status to *Installed*, but this is more to illustrate how you can handle different *AsyncStatus* values; you could just as easily set the status in the *Completed* callback. You would probably also want to check for the status of any app when the hub app starts so that the app is in sync with the latest install status of all available apps.

```
public void RefreshInstallState()
{
    foreach (AppItem appItem in Apps)
    {
        appItem.Status = Status.NotInstalled;
    }
    var installedPackages = InstallationManager.FindPackagesForCurrentPublisher();
    foreach (Package package in installedPackages)
    {
        Guid productId = Guid.Parse(package.Id.ProductId);
        AppItem appItem = App.ViewModel.Apps.FirstOrDefault(i => i.ProductId ==productId);
        if (appItem != null)
```

```
            {
                appItem.Status = Status.Installed;
            }
        }

        var inProgressPackages = InstallationManager.GetPendingPackageInstalls();
        foreach (var item in inProgressPackages)
        {
            uint id = item.Id;
            AppItem appItem = null;
            if (PendingInstalls.ContainsKey(id))
            {
                Guid guid = PendingInstalls[id];
                appItem = App.ViewModel.Apps.FirstOrDefault(i => i.ProductId.Equals(guid));
                if (appItem != null)
                {
                    if (item.Status == AsyncStatus.Completed)
                    {
                        PackageInstallResult result = item.GetResults();
                        if (result.InstallState == PackageInstallState.Installed)
                        {
                            appItem.Status = Status.Installed;
                        }
                    }
                    else if (item.Status == AsyncStatus.Started)
                    {
                        item.Completed = InstallCompleted;
                        item.Progress = InstallProgress;
                    }
                    else
                    {
                        appItem.Status = Status.NotInstalled;
                    }
                }
            }
        }

        InstalledApps.Clear();
        foreach (AppItem appItem in Apps.Where(i => i.Status.Equals(Status.Installed)))
        {
            InstalledApps.Add(appItem);
        }
    }
```

Notice in the *RefreshInstallState* method that for each app, if the install state shows that the app is in the pending-install list and has started installing, we hook up the *Progress* and *Completed* events. In the *Progress* handler, if the install is still flagged as *Started*, we record that the app is still in the Installing status. This uses the value converter to render an appropriate string in the list. The *Progress* handler is called at four points in the install operation: when the phone displays the message box prompting the user to confirm the install; when the user accepts this prompt; when the app has been downloaded; and finally, when the app has been installed. The *progressInfo* parameter indicates which of these points is in play, and you could provide different UI feedback for each stage, if desired.

```
private void InstallProgress(IAsyncOperationWithProgress<PackageInstallResult, uint>
installResult, uint progressInfo)
{
    Guid guid = PendingInstalls[installResult.Id];
    if (installResult.Status == AsyncStatus.Started)
    {
        App.ViewModel.Apps.FirstOrDefault(i =>
            i.ProductId.Equals(guid)).Status = Status.Installing;
    }
}
```

When we get the callback informing us that an install has progressed to completion, we check whether the final result was *AsyncStatus.Completed* and set the app status accordingly. You would typically also handle the case in which the status is *AsyncStatus.Error* and take some remedial action or at least provide feedback to the user. On completion, we again update the list of installed apps via *FindPackagesForCurrentPublisher*.

```
private void InstallCompleted(
    IAsyncOperationWithProgress<PackageInstallResult, uint> installResult, AsyncStatus
asyncStatus)
{
    Guid guid = PendingInstalls[installResult.Id];
    Deployment.Current.Dispatcher.BeginInvoke(() =>
    {
        AppItem appItem = App.ViewModel.Apps.FirstOrDefault(i => i.ProductId == guid);
        if (installResult.Status == AsyncStatus.Completed)
        {
            appItem.Status = Status.Installed;
        }
        else
        {
            appItem.Status = Status.NotInstalled;
        }

        if (!InstalledApps.Contains(appItem))
        {
            InstalledApps.Add(appItem);
        }
    });
}
```

Back in the *mainpage*, when the user selects an item from the list of available apps, if the app is already installed, we start it. Otherwise, we install it. In both cases, the call goes through to the *AppItems* main viewmodel.

```
private void AvailableItems_SelectionChanged(object sender, SelectionChangedEventArgs e)
{
    if (AvailableItems.SelectedItem == null)
        return;
```

```
    AppItem appItem = (AvailableItems.SelectedItem as AppItem);
    if (appItem.Status == Status.Installed)
    {
        App.ViewModel.LaunchApp(appItem.ProductId);
    }
    else if (appItem.Status == Status.NotInstalled)
    {
        App.ViewModel.InstallApp(appItem.ProductId);
    }

    AvailableItems.SelectedItem = null;
}
```

The *LaunchApp* and *InstallApp* methods in the viewmodel also use the *InstallationManager* type, either to call *AddPackageAsync* to install the app or to call *FindPackagesForCurrentPublisher* to get the package that corresponds to the selected item and start it.

```
public void InstallApp(Guid productId)
{
    AppItem appItem = App.ViewModel.Apps.FirstOrDefault(i => i.ProductId == productId);
    if (appItem == null)
        return;
    try
    {
        appItem.Status = Status.Installing;
        var result = InstallationManager.AddPackageAsync(appItem.Name, appItem.XapUrl);
        result.Completed = InstallCompleted;
        result.Progress = InstallProgress;
        PendingInstalls.Add(result.Id, productId);
    }
    catch (Exception ex)
    {
        Debug.WriteLine(ex.ToString());
    }
}


public void LaunchApp(Guid productId)
{
    try
    {
        var packages = InstallationManager.FindPackagesForCurrentPublisher();
        Package package = packages.FirstOrDefault(p => Guid.Parse(p.Id.ProductId) == productId);
        package.Launch(string.Empty);
    }
    catch (Exception ex)
    {
        Debug.WriteLine(ex.ToString());
    }
}
```

Notice the *Package.Launch* API, used to start an app: beyond its use in company hub apps, this is available to any app that wants to start another app from the same publisher. Also, some properties of *Package* are available when discovered through the deployment APIs, but are not available when using *Package.Current* to try and get the executing app's info. All company apps show up in the regular app list when installed. This means that the user can launch a company app either from the regular app list or from the company hub app (assuming the hub app lists the installed apps). The user can also uninstall a company app via the UI just like a regular Windows Phone Store app.

Summary

In this chapter, we looked at the two main ways by which you can manage company apps for your user's phones. The managed approach is suitable for larger organizations which have a dedicated IT team and supporting server infrastructure. This uses an MDM server, and gives the company a high degree of control over remote devices and the applications and data on them. If your organization doesn't require such comprehensive management control, you can enroll your user's phones and deploy company apps in a simpler manner. In both cases, company apps can only be installed to phones that have enrolled by using appropriate credentials or tokens, and in both cases, app management covers only company apps, not Windows Phone Store apps.

PART IV

Native Development and Windows Phone 8 convergence

CHAPTER 23

Native development

The largest change in the Windows Phone 8 SDK is the addition of support for native code. The ability to include C/C++ code in a Windows Phone app makes it much simpler to port existing libraries from the desktop or other mobile platforms, and it provides the opportunity to significantly optimize performance for computationally intensive apps. In this chapter, we look at when it makes sense to include native code in your app and review the different types of native development that are available in Windows Phone 8.

Note This chapter focuses on native development in the context of a XAML app. The samples include a XAML UI layer that calls into native code through custom Windows Runtime components. The only exclusively native apps supported in Windows Phone 8 must be built by using Direct3D, which is covered in Chapter 25, "Games and Direct3D."

Native code overview

The C++ support in Windows Phone 8 is based on Microsoft Visual C++ 2012 (also known as Visual C++ 11) and is nearly identical to what is available for building Windows Store apps. The compiler, libraries, and Integrated Development Environment (IDE) are effectively the same, further reinforcing the notion that native code makes it possible for you to easily move between platforms.

For managed-code developers, the introduction of native code support to Windows Phone might inspire two concerns: first, whether the addition of C++ represents a move away from managed languages such as C# and Microsoft Visual Basic; second, whether using C++ still involves painstakingly managing memory to avoid leaks, something that they might have become accustomed to having managed by the Common Language Runtime (CLR) garbage collector. In this section, we cover each of those concerns in turn, explaining why native code support is being added and when you should use it, and providing an introduction to some of the features of modern C++ that can make you much more productive.

Note Because C is a subset of C++, we simply use the term C++ to cover both C and C++ throughout the chapter.

When to use native code

Although Windows Phone 8 introduces support for native code development, it is expected that the overwhelming majority of apps will continue to be written predominantly (if not entirely) in managed languages. There are three specific reasons why you might want to consider using native code in your application.

Portability

The days of being able to target a single platform with an app are long gone: today, most developers realize that maximizing the reach for an app requires building versions for each of the major OS vendors while also accounting for differences between mobile, tablet, and desktop platforms. Even though those platforms offer different user experiences and frameworks, there is a common foundation underlying each of them: support for C++ development. By writing most of your business logic in a C++ component, you can significantly cut down on your development cost when adding support for additional platforms, freeing up time to focus on building a great user experience (UX) that feels natural for each device.

Reusability

Related to *portability* is the notion of *reusability*—the ability to take existing native libraries, either your own or those of someone else, and drop them directly into your project with little or no change required. A common example of code reuse is a data access layer that includes the SQLite database engine. Prior to Windows Phone 8, it was not easy to incorporate such code into a Windows Phone app. You could either target one of several managed implementations of SQLite or migrate to the built-in SQL Compact Edition (SQLCE) database by using the LINQ-to-SQL API. In either case, some amount of rewriting was required to exclusively work in managed code. With the addition of native code, you can start building your app's data model from a well-understood, well-tested foundation.

Performance

Performance is often cited as one of the primary benefits of native development over managed development. In practice, however, relatively few mobile apps can derive significant performance benefits by moving from managed to native. Indeed, if you have already written your app in managed code, you are usually better off using the time that it would take to rewrite it in native to optimize the performance of the managed component by using tools such as the Windows Phone profiler, discussed in Chapter 12, "Profiling and diagnostics." However, for a set of computationally intensive tasks such as image processing, you can sometimes derive noticeable performance improvements by maintaining fine-grained control over resource management.

Note The Windows Phone SDK includes the same native profiling support that is available in desktop Windows. See Chapter 12 for more details.

An introduction to modern C++

If you started a new project on a Microsoft platform any time in the past ten years, it is very likely that you were working in some flavor of the Microsoft .NET managed-code environment. If you have not spent much time using C++ during that time, you might be worried that you will lose all of the productivity enhancements that you have come to rely on in .NET. Thankfully, C++ has not stood still and, in fact, has borrowed a number of popular features from managed environments. In this section, we review some of the most useful additions to C++ 11, the latest version of the C++ standard.

Note Visual C++ 2012 does not yet support the full set of C++ 11 features. For a list of C++ 11 features and whether they are supported in Visual Studio 2012, go to *http://blogs.msdn.com/b/vcblog/archive/2011/09/12/10209291.aspx*. More functionality will be added over time as updates to Visual Studio are released.

Smart pointers

A fundamental difference between managed and native development concerns the way that memory is allocated and reclaimed. In managed environments, the developer allocates memory for new objects but generally leaves the job of reclaiming those allocations to the runtime's garbage collector. In native environments, it is the developer's responsibility to handle cleaning up memory that is no longer used. Although the ability to directly control the resources that an app is using can provide some performance benefits if handled correctly, memory management is a very common source of bugs, especially memory leaks.

One of the biggest challenges in manual memory management is keeping track of which component is responsible for managing the lifetime of a resource. If a component assumes responsibility when it should not, it might delete a resource that another component is still using. On the other hand, if a component fails to perform a cleanup for which it is responsible, a memory leak can occur. C++ 11 includes several enhanced pointer types that can alleviate some of these challenges. This group is collectively known as *smart pointers*. Various smart pointer types were available in supplementary libraries for the previous version of the C++ standard (C++ 03), such as Boost or Technical Report 1 (TR1), but they are now included directly in the standard library.

Note C++ 03 did include one smart pointer type: *auto_ptr*. Now deprecated in favor of *unique_ptr*, the *auto_ptr* type automatically deletes the referenced object when the pointer goes out of scope. And of course, conscientious developers have been using their own custom versions of smart pointers for years.

Unique pointers

You can use unique pointers to limit ownership of a resource to a single pointer. The copy constructor and the assignment operator for *unique_ptr* are private, making it impossible to accidentally create a second pointer for the resource. The only way to explicitly change ownership of the resource is to transfer it by using the *move* function.

```
std::unique_ptr<int> uniqueIntPointer(new int(10));

// compile error - assignment operator is private
std::unique_ptr<int> uniqueIntPointerAssignment = uniqueIntPointer;

// compile error - copy constructor is private
std::unique_ptr<int> uniqueIntPointerCopy(uniqueIntPointer);

// ok - ownership explicitly transferred
std::unique_ptr<int> uniqueIntPointerMoved = std::move(uniqueIntPointer);

// does nothing - uniqueIntPointer doesn't own the resource
pUniqueIntPointer.reset();

// memory is deleted
uniqueIntPointerMoved.reset();
```

Although *move* offers the only way to explicitly transfer ownership of a unique pointer, the compiler can reassign ownership implicitly in certain cases. For example, when a function returns a *unique_ptr*, the compiler automatically moves the value created in the function to the variable specified by the caller.

Shared Pointers

In some cases, you do need to maintain multiple pointers to the same resource. In those situations, each component maintaining a pointer to the resource plays a part in managing its lifetime, and the resource should not be deleted until all of its owners are done with it. Shared pointers enable this type of relationship by maintaining a reference count to the resource. The count is incremented each time a new pointer is created, and decremented when a pointer is destroyed. Although each component can destroy its copy of the pointer normally, the resource will only be freed when the last reference is removed.

```
std::shared_ptr<int> firstSharedIntPointer(new int(10)); // refcount = 1

std::shared_ptr<int> secondSharedIntPointer(firstSharedIntPointer); // refcount = 2

firstSharedIntPointer.reset();      // refcount = 1

(*secondSharedIntPointer) += 1; // ok - resource still exists

secondSharedIntPointer.reset(); // refcount = 0 - memory freed
```

Be aware that the use of reference counting to determine when to free a resource is susceptible to problems arising from circular references. As a trivial example, if resource A has a shared pointer reference to resource B, which in turn has a shared pointer reference to resource A, neither resource can ever be destroyed. Even though it is usually not possible to detect a circular reference in advance, the C++ standard library supports the notion of a weak pointer as a way to protect against them. Use weak pointers when you want to make use of a resource for as long as it exists, but you do not want to participate in the management of its lifetime. Because weak pointers are not included in the reference count for a resource, you must temporarily convert them to shared pointers to ensure that the resource is not deleted during the period that you need access to it. You can do this either by using the shared pointer copy constructor or by calling the *lock* function on the *weak_ptr* type.

```
std::shared_ptr<int> firstSharedIntPointer(new int(10));
std::weak_ptr<int> weakSharedIntPointer(firstSharedIntPointer
if(std::shared_ptr<int> tempSharedPointer = weakSharedIntPointer.lock())
{
     // resource is temporarily protected from deletion
     (*tempSharedPointer) += 1;
}

firstSharedIntPointer.reset(); // only one shared_ptr reference remaining - resource deleted

// resource is gone - lock returns null shared_ptr
if(std::shared_ptr<int> tempSharedPointer2 = weakSharedIntPointer.lock())
{
     // this code is not executed
     (*tempSharedPointer2) += 1;
}
```

Type Inference

Type inference makes it possible for developers in strongly typed languages such as C# and C++ to avoid explicitly declaring the type of a variable, instead allowing the compiler to determine it for them. This can be useful for types that have complicated names or for types that are automatically generated by the compiler, as in lambda functions. C# developers will be familiar with type inference through the use of the *var* keyword introduced in C# 3.0. C++ 11 adds support for the same concept by repurposing the deprecated *auto* keyword. You can see the type that the compiler deduced by hovering over the variable declaration in Visual Studio, as shown in Figure 23-1.

```
void NativeClass::ShowAutoKeyword()
{
    int num1 = 10;
    double num2 = 7.5;

    auto num3 = num1 / num2;
}
            double num3
```

FIGURE 23-1 Hovering over a variable declared with the *auto* keyword displays a ScreenTip revealing the inferred type.

It is important to note that type inference is simply a syntactic convenience; the compiled version of the code will look exactly the same regardless of whether you use the *auto* keyword or you explicitly declare its type. C++ remains a strongly and statically typed language.

Foreach loops

C++ 11 adds support for ranged-based "for" loops, also known as *foreach* loops. Although C++ does not use the foreach keyword, the programming model is effectively the same.

```
int numbers[] = {0, 1, 2, 3, 4, 5};
int sum = 0;

for(int& number: numbers)
{
    sum += number;
}
```

Lambdas

Lambda functions—anonymous inline functions that have access to variables in their caller's scope—are used heavily in .NET, particularly since the introduction of Language-Integrated Query (LINQ) syntax in .NET 3.5. C++ 11 adds support for lambda functions, providing a cleaner, more powerful alternative to traditional function pointers and function objects.

In the following code, the *SumNumbers* function accepts an array of 10 integers, along with a function. The function provided is used to determine whether a given number in the array should be included in the sum. This makes it possible for the *SumNumbers* function to focus on the logic required to sum the set of numbers while supporting any number of different criteria for inclusion.

```
#include <array>
#include <functional>

int ModernCPPExamples::SumNumbers(std::array<int, 10> values, std::function<bool(int)>
candidateFunction)
{
    int sum = 0;
```

```
    for(int &i : values)
    {
        if(candidateFunction(i))
            sum += i;
    }

    return sum;
}
```

The *TestLambdas* function is then able to use the *SumNumbers* function to perform three different calculations by providing three different criteria for inclusion: even numbers, large numbers (greater than or equal to 100), and prime numbers.

```
void NativeClass::TestLambdas()
{
    std::array<int, 10> candidateValues = { 0, 2, 5, 9, 21, 29, 77, 100, 150, 200 };

    int sumOfEvenNumbers = SumNumbers(candidateValues, [](int value) -> bool
        {
            return value % 2 == 0;
        });

    int sumOfLargeNumbers = SumNumbers(candidateValues, [](int value) -> bool
        {
            return value >= 100;
        });

    int sumOfPrimeNumbers = SumNumbers(candidateValues, [](int value) -> bool
        {
            if(value == 0 || value == 1) return true;

            for(int divisor = 2; divisor < sqrt(value); divisor++)
            {
                if(value % divisor == 0) return false;
            }

            return true;
        });
}
```

The lambda syntax is defined as follows:

[optional captured variables] (optional parameters) -> return type { function body }

Of particular interest to C# developers is the captured variables block. In C#, a lambda expression automatically has access to all variables within the scope of the function that contains the lambda, and because .NET exclusively passes objects by reference, any changes made to those variables within the lambda impacts their usage elsewhere. C++ lambdas are different in two ways. First, lambdas do not have access to external variables by default; they must be added to the lambda's closure explicitly. Second, because C++ supports passing objects by reference or by value, the nature of the capture can be specified in the lambda syntax. Table 23-1 provides a summary of the different options for capturing external variables in a lambda expression.

TABLE 23-1 Summary of capture options for C++ lambdas

Capture expression	Meaning
[]	No external variables are captured.
[=]	All variables in containing scope are captured by value; in other words, they are copied.
[&]	All variables in containing scope are captured by reference, except "this," which is always captured by value.
[=, &var1]	Var1 is captured by reference. All others are captured by value.
[&, var2]	Var2 is captured by value. All others (apart from "this") are captured by reference.
[&var3, var4]	Var3 is captured by reference. Var4 is captured by value. Others are inaccessible.

Note Explicit declaration of a lambda's return type is usually optional because it can be inferred by the compiler in most cases.

Scoped, strongly typed *enums*

Prior to C++ 11, *enums* were effectively just named integer values added to the global scope of your project. Consider the following *enum* for a set of colors:

```
enum Color
{
    Blue,
    Green,
    Yellow,
    Red,
    Purple,
    Orange
};
```

An *enum* like this made it simple to create what looked like a strongly typed *Color* member on a custom type such as a *Product* and then perform checks such as this:

```
if(product.Color == Color::Blue)
{
    // do something for blue products...
}
```

On the other hand, the fact that *enum* values were just integers under the covers also made it possible to write code such as this without any complaints from the compiler.

```
int colorfulSum = Blue + Green; // what does this mean?
```

Granted, the potential impact of such errors was somewhat limited by the fact that you could not implicitly cast an integer to a variable marked as an *enum* type, but it gave developers the opportunity to be overly clever with their use of *enums*, occasionally leading to unintuitive code that was difficult to maintain. C++ 11 solves these problems by introducing *enum* classes. The only change required to the *Color enum* is the introduction of the *class* keyword, shown in bold in the following example:

```
enum class Color
{
    Blue,
    Green,
    Yellow,
    Red,
    Purple,
    Orange
};
```

This simple change helps the compiler find two problems with the ridiculous computation of *colorfulSum*. First, it is unable to resolve the terms *Blue* and *Green*, because they are no longer in global scope. This is especially helpful for large projects, in which you will often want to have multiple *enums* with the same member; for example, "Success." Second, after those values are prefixed with the class name, the compiler complains that it is unable to initialize an integer with a value of type *Color*, proving that those values are no longer just integers in disguise.

Note There are some valid uses for representing *enum* values as numbers, such as setting each value as a bitwise flag that can be XOR'd together to create a composite value, as you can do by using the *Flags* attribute on an *enum* in C#. C++ 11 gives you the opportunity to explicitly choose whether you want to have that flexibility or if you'd rather let the compiler catch unplanned uses of the *enum* values.

What about properties and events?

Two commonly used features of .NET languages not included in the previous section are properties and events. Although neither is supported in the C++ standard, both are available in the C++ Component Extensions (C++/CX) defined by Microsoft for use with the Windows Runtime. However, you should be thoughtful about how they are used because any code that depends on them will not be portable to non-Windows platforms. Also note that they can only be used within *ref* classes.

Properties offer the best aspects of fields and methods. To the caller, a property looks like a public field, with the ability to access the value directly rather than by using explicit getter and setter methods. For the implementer, however, properties continue to offer the ability to abstract away the details of how the value is retrieved or set, including providing a chance to perform custom validation of input.

C++/CX properties very closely resemble their counterparts in .NET languages. You can define automatic properties (also known as trivial properties), which depend on the compiler to provide a backing member variable and automatically implemented getter and setter methods. You can also provide a getter method, a setter method, or both. There are two small differences from .NET properties worth pointing out. First, you cannot give a getter or setter different visibility within the property. If you want to have, for example, a private setter but a public getter, you should create a separate private setter method to manipulate the backing variable. Second, the input to the setter method is not automatically provided by the compiler in the way that the *value* keyword is provided in .NET. Instead, you should define your own input variable to the setter method, as shown in the following:

```
public ref class Order sealed
{
private:
    // private backing variables

    double price;
    int quantity;

public:
    property Platform::String^ Description; // automatic/trivial property
    // read-only property

    property double Price
    {
        double get() { return price; }
    }


    // setter with custom validation logic
    property int Quantity
    {
        int get() { return quantity; }
        void set(int newQuantity)
        {
            if(newQuantity < 0)
                throw ref new Platform::InvalidArgumentException();

            quantity = newQuantity;
        }
    }
};
```

C++/CX events should also look familiar to .NET developers. The event is a property of type *delegate* and is declared by using the caret operator (^), also known as the hat operator, which we discuss in more detail later in the chapter. To listen for the event, you use the += operator, just as you would in C#.

```
namespace ModernCppExamples
{
    ref class EventRaiser;
    public delegate void MyCustomEventHandler
                        (EventRaiser^ sender, Platform::String^ eventMessage);
```

```
    public ref class EventRaiser sealed
    {
    public:
        event MyCustomEventHandler^ MyCustomEvent;
        void DoWork()
        {
            // do something

            // raise the event
            MyCustomEvent(this, L"An interesting event occurred!");
        }
    };
    public ref class EventListener sealed
    {
    public:
        void MyMethod()
        {
            auto eventRaiser = ref new EventRaiser();
            eventRaiser->MyCustomEvent += ref new
                          CppCxExamples::MyCustomEventHandler
                          (this, &EventListener::MyEventHandler);

            eventRaiser->DoWork();
        }

       void MyEventHandler(CppCxExamples::EventRaiser^ raiser,
                          Platform::String^ eventMessage)
       {
           // respond to event
       }
    };
}
```

As with properties, there are several differences worth highlighting between C# and C++/CX when it comes to events.

- Although it is possible to provide a lambda function as the delegate for an event, it is generally not recommended because of the possibility of circular references. A named function captures the "this" pointer with a weak reference, whereas a lambda function captures it with a strong reference, creating the conditions for a cycle.
- To unsubscribe from an event, you must provide a token that is returned when the event handler delegate is initially hooked up, like so:

  ```
  //subscribe
  auto token = eventRaiser->MyCustomEvent += ref new ModernCppExamples::MyCustomEventHandler
                                                  (this, &EventListener::MyEventHandler);

  //unsubscribe
  eventRaiser->MyCustomEvent -= token;
  ```

- Unlike their .NET equivalents, it is not possible to use the Windows Runtime generic base types (*TypedEventHandler* and *EventHandler*) for your own custom events. You must always declare your own delegate types, as just shown.
- In C++/CX, it is not necessary to check if an event is null before raising it, a difference that results in cleaner code.

Managed-native interop

There are two primary ways to use C++ in a Windows Phone 8 project. You can write your app entirely in C++ by using Direct3D for your UI layer or you can create a managed XAML app that wraps native code within a Windows Runtime component by using the interop capabilities of Windows Runtime to move between the managed and native layers. In this section, we focus on the Windows Runtime approach.

Note You can also create a XAML app that includes Direct3D components by using the *DrawingSurface* control. See Chapter 25 for more information.

The *FibonacciPrimes* solution in the sample code is a simple XAML app that relies on a Windows Runtime component written in C++ for its core business logic, in this case the computation of a user-defined quantity of Fibonacci prime numbers starting from a certain base, also provided by the user. The UI for the *FibonacciPrimes* solution is shown in Figure 23-2. Clearly, this functionality could be provided in managed code, likely with equivalent performance. As discussed earlier, the primary reasons why you might want to use C++ for this type of app are either that you already have the code available or that you intend to port it to another platform.

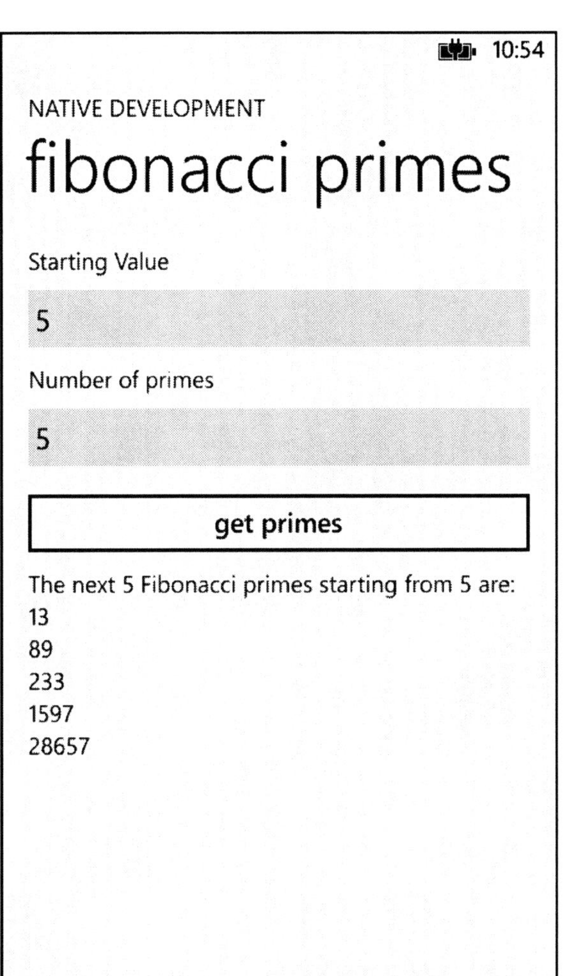

FIGURE 23-2 The *FibonacciPrimes* solution includes a XAML UI with C++ business logic.

Note This section focuses on managed-native interop in a foreground app, but you can also include native code in a background agent by using the same techniques.

Creating the Windows Runtime component

The process of adding a new Windows Runtime component to your app is effectively the same as adding a new managed library. In the Solution Explorer, right-click the name of your solution and then, on the shortcut menu that appears, point to Add and then click New Project. In the Add New Project dialog box, in the navigation pane on the left, click Visual C++ and then click Windows Phone. A list of project templates appears that includes Windows Phone Runtime Component, as illustrated in Figure 23-3.

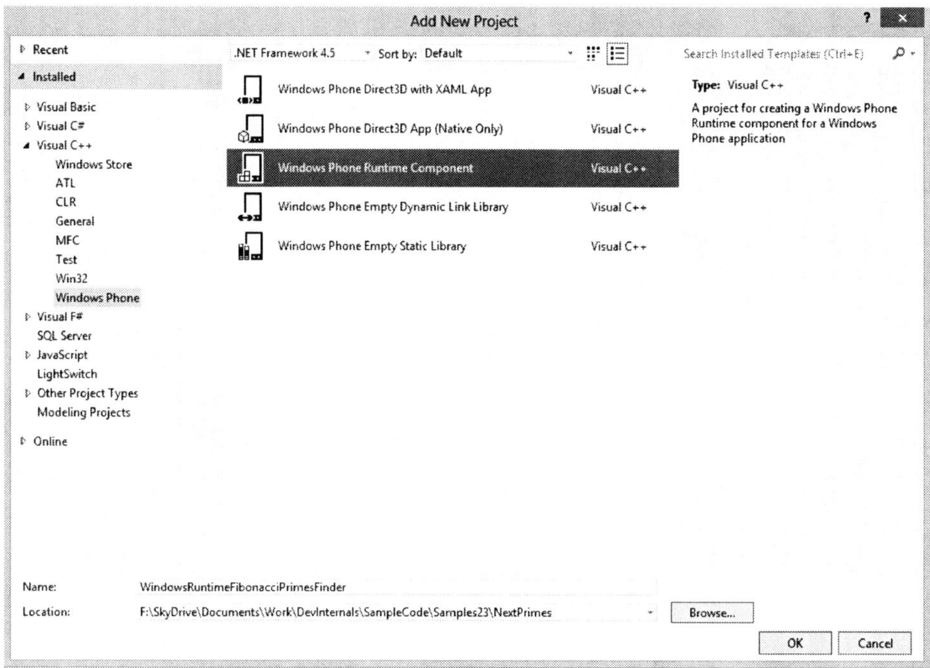

FIGURE 23-3 You can add Windows Phone Runtime components from the Visual C++ menu in the Add New Project dialog box.

The default project template for a Windows Runtime component includes four files: a header, an implementation file for your primary Windows Runtime class, and a pair of files for declaring precompiled headers.

Tip Precompiled headers can improve your build time if you have multiple source code files including a common set of headers. Rather than recompiling the common code multiple times, the compiler can simply reuse the first version of the compilation. To include a header in the set of precompiled headers, simply include it in the *pch.h* header file.

The header for a Windows Runtime header file looks mostly like a standard C++ header, but there are a few notable differences to point out. The first is that Windows Runtime types must be declared as a *public ref class* and be marked as *sealed*. Using the *ref* keyword, the platform can perform reference counting on instances of that type regardless of which language they are projecting to, enabling automatic memory management. Of course, you can still use standard C++ classes (without *ref*) within your native code, but those types will not be available in the Windows Runtime projections. The second difference is that the signatures of public Windows Runtime APIs must only use types that are either part of the core Windows Runtime type system or are custom Windows Runtime types. This allows the runtime to naturally translate those types to and from the equivalent types in the projected languages. For instance, the *GetPrimes* method returns the Windows Runtime type *IVector*, which translates to an *IList* in C#. Because private and protected members are not projected across language boundaries, the constraint does not apply to them. Finally, note that the *IVector* collection return type includes a caret (^) symbol. Combined with the *ref* keyword, the caret indicates that the type can be reference-counted for memory management.

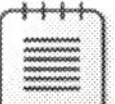

Note The *ref* keyword and the caret symbol are borrowed directly from the C++ Common Language Infrastructure (C++/CLI) specification, which is a set of C++ language extensions defined by Microsoft for use in conjunction with the Common Language Runtime (CLR). However, the Windows Runtime version of the language extensions, referred to as C++ Component Extensions (or C++/CX) generate unmanaged objects that have nothing to do with the CLR and are not garbage collected.

```
#pragma once
#include <windows.foundation.collections.h>

namespace WindowsRuntimeFibonacciPrimesFinder
{
     public ref class FibonacciPrimesFinder sealed
     {
     public:
          static Windows::Foundation::Collections::IVector<UINT64>^
                     GetPrimes(int startingValue, int numberOfPrimesToFind);
     };
}
```

Similarly, the implementation file contains mostly standard C++. The only significant difference is found in the return statement of the *GetPrimes* method. When creating an object of a reference-counted type, you must include the *ref* keyword in the instantiation.

```
#include "WindowsRuntimeFibonacciPrimesFinder.h"
#include <collection.h>
#include <vector>
#include <safeint.h>
```

```
using namespace WindowsRuntimeFibonacciPrimesFinder;

using namespace concurrency;
using namespace Windows::Foundation;
using namespace Windows::Foundation::Collections;
using namespace msl::utilities;

static bool IsPrime(const SafeInt<UINT64> candidate)
{
     if(candidate == 0 || candidate == 1) return false;

     for(UINT64 divisor = 2; divisor < sqrt(candidate); divisor++)
     {
          if(candidate % divisor == 0)
          return false;
     }

     return true;
}

IVector<UINT64>^ FibonacciPrimesFinder::GetPrimes(int startingValue, int numberOfPrimesToFind)
{
     std::vector<uint64> fibonacciPrimes;

     SafeInt<UINT64> currentFibonacciCandidate = 0;
     UINT64 lastTwoFibonacciNumbers[2];

     lastTwoFibonacciNumbers[0] = 0;
     lastTwoFibonacciNumbers[1] = 1;

     int currentFibonacciIndex = 2;
     int numberToSwitch = 0;

     while(fibonacciPrimes.size() < numberOfPrimesToFind)
     {
          // SafeInt will throw in the event of an overrun
          try
          {
               currentFibonacciCandidate = lastTwoFibonacciNumbers[0] +
                                           lastTwoFibonacciNumbers[1];
          }
          catch(SafeIntException)
          {
               break;
          }

          if((currentFibonacciCandidate > startingValue) && IsPrime(currentFibonacciCandidate))
               fibonacciPrimes.push_back(currentFibonacciCandidate);

          numberToSwitch = (currentFibonacciIndex % 2);
          lastTwoFibonacciNumbers[numberToSwitch] = currentFibonacciCandidate;

          currentFibonacciIndex++;
     }

     return ref new Platform::Collections::Vector<UINT64>(fibonacciPrimes);
}
```

Maintain portability and performance through limited use of Windows Runtime types

The fact that the public interfaces of Windows Runtime classes must be composed exclusively of Windows Runtime types might suggest that you should try to use those types throughout your native component to avoid having to convert back and forth with types from the standard library. However, although there is some overhead to this translation, it is critical to maintaining the portability of your code across platforms. In general, you should aim to move as quickly as possible into standard library types when entering a Windows Runtime API and stick to standard C++ until you need to return a value to the caller. Notice that the *GetPrimes* method maintains the in-progress set of Fibonacci primes by using the *vector* class from the C++ standard library and only creates a Windows Runtime *Vector* for the return value. Figure 23-4 provides an illustration of how you should structure your Windows Runtime APIs, with pure C++ wrapped in translation to and from Windows Runtime types.

Note There is one caveat to this general advice. For small functions that perform simple operations, portability is clearly less critical, and the benefits of translating in and out of standard types will likely be outweighed by the small impact on performance and memory usage.

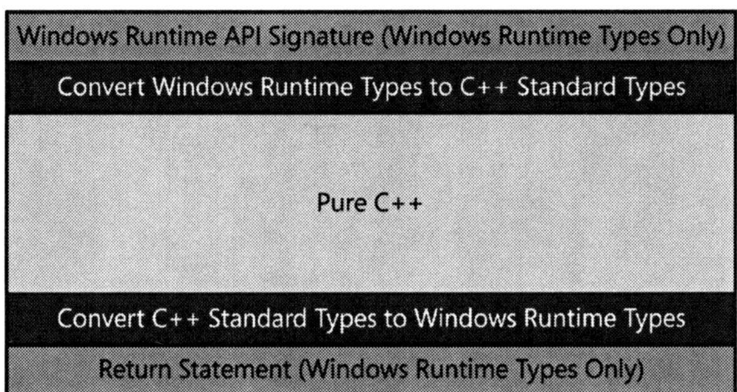

FIGURE 23-4 Aim to limit your core logic to pure C++ with translation to and from Windows Runtime types only at the boundaries of your APIs.

An important consideration when performing translation between Windows Runtime types and standard C++ types is the treatment of strings. In the Windows Runtime, all strings are UTF-16 encoded, meaning that they use two bytes per character. On the other hand, some older C++ libraries still assume that strings (or simple character arrays) are ASCII encoded, using one byte per character. Use the *MultiByteToWideChar* and *WideCharToMultiByte* functions to translate back and forth between the two encodings. The *StringConversions* solution in the sample code provides an example of this. The Windows Runtime component, *Windows RuntimeStringManipulator*, exposed a single static method, *ConvertAlternatingCharsToUpper*, which checks every second character in the string and converts it to uppercase if it is currently lowercase. To do this, it uses a static function named *ConvertAlternatingUtf8CharactersToUpper*, which only supports UTF8 strings. Think of this function as being representative of existing code that you cannot (or prefer not to) modify to support wide characters.

```
#include <functional>
#include <vector>
#include <array>
#include <windows.h>
#include <string.h>

Platform::String^ WindowsRuntimeStringManipulator::ConvertAlternatingCharsToUpper
                                                   (Platform::String^ inputString)
{
     std::string singleByteString =
          ConvertWideStringToUTF8(std::wstring(inputString->Data()));
     ConvertAlternatingUtf8CharactersToUpper(singleByteString);
     const std::wstring wideCharString = ConvertUtf8ToWideString(singleByteString);
     Platform::String^ returnString = ref new Platform::String(wideCharString.c_str());
     return returnString;
}
```

There are two ways to call the *WideCharToMultiByte* and *MultiByteToWideChar* functions. If you provide a destination character array into which they can copy, they will perform the conversion and place the result in the array. However, it is not necessarily straightforward to determine how big the destination array should be, particularly if you need to support different code pages. The safer option, then, is to call each function twice. In the first call, pass -1 instead of a character array; this will provide the required size of the destination array without performing the conversion. You can then create an appropriately sized array. Note that although *WideCharToMultiByte* and *MultiByteToWideChar* operate exclusively on character arrays, we use the safer *string* and *wstring* classes as much as possible and convert only when necessary.

```
static std::string ConvertWideStringToUTF8(const std::wstring wideString)
{
    const int sizeOfSingleByteString =
        WideCharToMultiByte(CP_UTF8, 0, wideString.c_str(), -1, 0, 0, NULL, NULL);
    std::string singleByteString(sizeOfSingleByteString, 0);
    WideCharToMultiByte(CP_UTF8, 0, wideString.c_str(), -1, &singleByteString[0],
                        sizeOfSingleByteString, NULL, NULL);
    return singleByteString;
}
```

See the sample code for listings of the *ConvertAlternatingUtf8CharactersToUpper* and *ConvertUtf8ToWideString* functions.

Consuming the Windows Runtime component from C#

One of the most powerful aspects of the Windows Runtime is that it makes it possible for you to author components in C++ and consume them in managed languages without writing any custom interop code. Indeed, from the perspective of your managed classes, Windows Runtime APIs look just like any other .NET component.

To use a custom Windows Runtime component from a managed app, you must first add a reference to it as you would with a managed Dynamic-Link Library: right-click the project name and then, on the shortcut menu, click Add Reference. After you have added the reference, you can use the component from managed code just like you would use a managed assembly. Visual Studio can even resolve references to unqualified types within the Windows Runtime component, as demonstrated in Figure 23-5. Behind the scenes, what makes this possible is the Windows metadata (winmd) file, a description of the public surface of your Windows Runtime component generated by the compiler. The winmd file format closely resembles the metadata content contained within managed .NET assemblies, making it seamless to integrate with managed code.

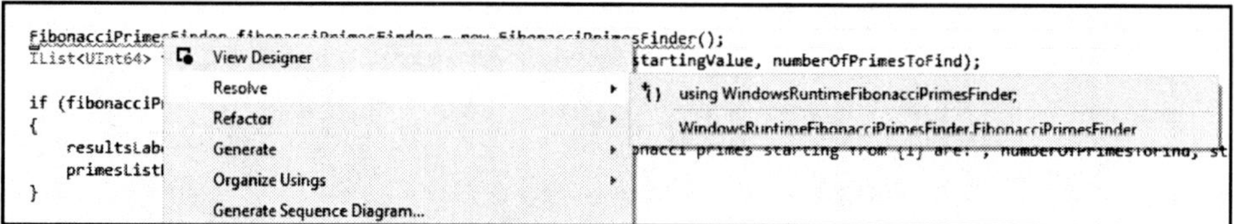

FIGURE 23-5 Visual Studio can resolve Windows Runtime types just as it does for .NET assemblies.

Simply by looking at the calling C# code, it is effectively impossible to see the difference between a Windows Runtime component and a standard .NET assembly.

```
private void getPrimesButton_Click(object sender, RoutedEventArgs e)
{
    primesListBox.ItemsSource = null; // clear previous result

    int startingValue;
    int numPrimesToFind;

    if(!int.TryParse(startingValueTextBox.Text, out startingValue) ||
       !int.TryParse(numberOfPrimesToFindTextBox.Text, out numPrimesToFind))
         return;

    if(numPrimesToFind == 0)
         return;

    FibonacciPrimesFinder fibonacciPrimesFinder = new FibonacciPrimesFinder();

    IList<UInt64> fibonacciPrimes =
         fibonacciPrimesFinder.GetPrimes(startingValue, numPrimesToFind);

    if (fibonacciPrimes.Count > 0)
    {
         resultsLabelTextBlock.Text =
              String.Format("The next {0} Fibonacci primes starting from {1} are:",
                            numPrimesToFind, startingValue);

         primesListBox.ItemsSource = fibonacciPrimes;
    }
}
```

Mapping .NET types to Windows Runtime types

As mentioned earlier, the Windows Runtime automatically maps its core type system into the languages to which it projects. Table 23-2 lists some of the key mappings between Windows Runtime types and .NET types.

TABLE 23-2 Key Windows Runtime type to .NET type mappings

Windows Runtime type (Windows.Foundation)	.NET type (System)
DateTime	*DateTimeOffset*
EventHandler<T>	*EventHandler<T>*
HResult	*Exception*
IReference<T>	*Nullable<T>*
Timespan	*Timespan*
Uri	*Uri (see note below)*
IClosable	*IDisposable*
Collections.IIterable<T>	*IEnumerable<T>*
Collections.IVectorView<T>	*Collections.Generic.IReadOnlyList<T>*
Collections.IMap<Key, Value>	*Collections.Generic.IDictionary<Key, Value>*
Collections.IMapView<Key, Value>	*Collections.Generic.IReadOnlyDictionary<Key, Value>*
Collections.IKeyValuePair<Key, Value>	*Collections.Generic.KeyValuePair<Key, Value>*

Note The Windows Runtime does not support relative URIs, only absolute URIs are allowed. For cases in which you might use a relative URI in .NET, such as identifying a resource in your app package, you must use system-provided custom schemes such as "ms-appx" and "ms-appdata," instead. For example, the relative URI path "/Assets/MyImage.jpg" in the app package should be replaced by "ms-appx:///Assets/MyImage.jpg."

Debugging mixed-mode projects

When writing a managed app that interoperates with a native component, you need the ability to debug both the managed and native portions of that app. The Windows Phone SDK provides the ability to debug either managed or native code in a given debugger session by setting an option on the Debug tab of the app properties, as depicted in Figure 23-6. Full mixed-mode debugging is not currently supported, so breakpoints in native code will not be hit when the debugger type is set to Managed Only, and vice versa.

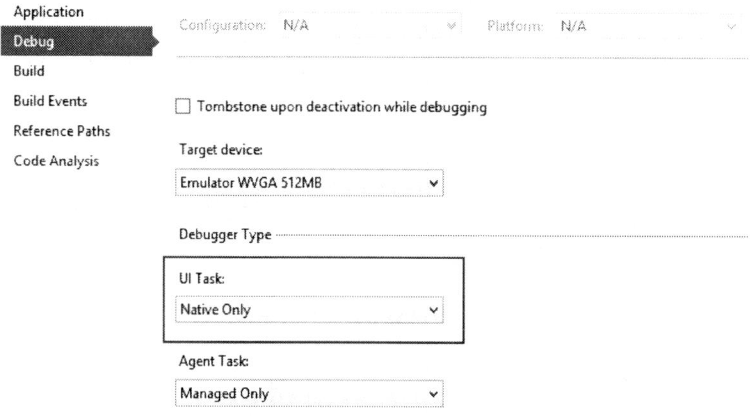

FIGURE 23-6 The debug settings menu offers an option to choose managed or native debugging.

Writing asynchronous code in C++

The Windows Runtime API makes extensive use of the asynchronous programming model to ensure that apps remain fluid and responsive even when performing long-running operations. In general, if an operation might take longer than 50 milliseconds, it should be made asynchronous. Of course, you do not always have the option or the desire to rewrite an existing native component that follows a synchronous model. Thankfully, the Windows Runtime makes it possible to wrap synchronous code such that it is callable from other components without blocking them.

Tip It is important to highlight that the guideline for making operations asynchronous is merely based on the *potential* that they might take longer than 50 milliseconds. If an operation executes quickly most of the time but might slow down in some circumstances, such as system resource pressure, it is a good idea to make it asynchronous. Even if your app only becomes unresponsive following a user action five percent of the time, that can be enough to create an impression of poor performance.

Moving synchronous code to the background

The *FibonacciPrimes* solution contains a good candidate for conversion to the asynchronous pattern. If the user enters a sufficiently high number of primes or provides a high starting value, it can take some time for the native Windows Runtime component to compute the set of numbers and return them. During that period, we do not want to block the UI from receiving additional input from the user.

The first step in creating an asynchronous version of an existing synchronous method is simply to create a copy of the original method signature, but with a couple of small changes. First, the method should return a handle to an *IAsyncOperation* of the original return type. That is, if the synchronous method returns *int*, the asynchronous version should return *IAsyncOperation<int>^*. The *IAsync Operation* interface encapsulates the asynchronous task that will potentially run in the background and eventually return a result to the calling app. It provides seamless integration with the *async/await* keywords used to simplify asynchronous programming in .NET. The second change required to the method signature is cosmetic but important: all asynchronous method names should end in *Async* as a cue that the method will execute in the background. With the changes, the declaration of the async version of *GetPrimes* looks like this:

```
IAsyncOperation<IVector<UINT64>^>^ GetPrimesAsync(int startingValue, int numberOfPrimesToFind);
```

Note You must include *windows.foundation.h* in your header file to use *IAsyncOperation*.

The key to implementing the asynchrony of the *GetPrimesAsync* method is the Parallel Patterns Library (PPL), included in the *ppltasks.h* header file. The *concurrency* namespace within the PPL provides the ability to create an asynchronous operation based on a lambda function that can satisfy the Windows Runtime *IAsyncOperation* contract. The lambda function can then simply return the result of the synchronous version of the method. By virtue of passing the lambda to *create_async*, the synchronous code will run on a background thread, allowing *GetPrimesAsync* to return immediately and not block the app UI thread.

```
IAsyncOperation<IVector<UINT64>^>^ FibonacciPrimesFinder::GetPrimesAsync
     (int startingValue, int numberOfPrimesToFind)
{
     return concurrency::create_async([=]()
     {
          return GetPrimes(startingValue, numberOfPrimesToFind);
     });
}
```

We then simply need to update our C# code to call *GetPrimesAsync* and await the result of that call by using the *await* keyword.

```
IList<UInt64> fibonacciPrimes =
     await fibonacciPrimesFinder.GetPrimesAsync(startingValue, numberOfPrimesToFind);
```

Tip After you have replaced a synchronous API with an asynchronous version, it is a good idea to make the synchronous version private so that it is only callable from its asynchronous wrapper and not from the app UI layer.

Providing progress updates

Ensuring that app UI remains responsive while long-running operations are underway is an important part of providing a great UX. In some cases, however, there isn't anything else for the user to do but wait for the results of the operation to come back before proceeding. In those situations, it is valuable to provide progress notifications in your UI so that the user knows that something is happening and so that she has a rough idea of when the operation will be complete. With the *FibonacciPrimes* solution, for instance, it might be useful to know how many primes have been calculated so far as the operation continues running.

In the previous example, we made the operation to calculate a set of Fibonacci primes asynchronous by returning an *IAsyncOperation* interface rather than directly returning the result. The Windows Runtime supports a related type, *IAsyncOperationWithProgress*, with which the caller can specify a callback function to be invoked when the asynchronous operation provides an update on its progress. In the C++ code, two changes are required. First, the lambda function passed to the *create_async* function must be declared to take a parameter of type *progress_reporter<TProgress>* that will be used to report progress back to the caller via instances of type *TProgress*. In the case of *FibonacciPrimes* solution, we simply pass back the current number of primes found as an unsigned integer.

```
IAsyncOperationWithProgress<IVector<UINT64>^, int>^ FibonacciPrimesFinder::GetPrimesAsync
     (int startingValue, int numberOfPrimesToFind)
{
     return concurrency::create_async([=](progress_reporter<int> progressReporter)
     {
          return GetPrimes(startingValue, numberOfPrimesToFind, progressReporter);
     });
}
```

In the *GetPrimes* function, we add a call to the *progress_reporter*'s *report* function, passing in the size of the list of primes each time a new one is found.

```
IVector<UINT64>^ FibonacciPrimesFinder::GetPrimes
     (int startingValue, int numberOfPrimesToFind, progress_reporter<int> progressReporter)
{
     // repeated set up code omitted...

     while(fibonacciPrimes.size() < numberOfPrimesToFind)
     {
          currentFibonacciCandidate = lastTwoFibonacciNumbers[0] + lastTwoFibonacciNumbers[1];

          if((currentFibonacciCandidate > startingValue) && IsPrime(currentFibonacciCandidate))
          {
               fibonacciPrimes.push_back(currentFibonacciCandidate);
               progressReporter.report(fibonacciPrimes.size());
          }
```

```
            numberToSwitch = (currentFibonacciIndex % 2);
            lastTwoFibonacciNumbers[numberToSwitch] = currentFibonacciCandidate;

            currentFibonacciIndex++;
        }

        return ref new Vector<UINT64>(fibonacciPrimes);
}
```

Now that *GetPrimesAsync* returns an operation that reports progress, we can provide a delegate in our C# code to relay those progress notifications to the UI. The data-bound integer property *NumPrimesFound* is used to update both a progress message and a *ProgressBar* in the UI, as shown in Figure 23-7.

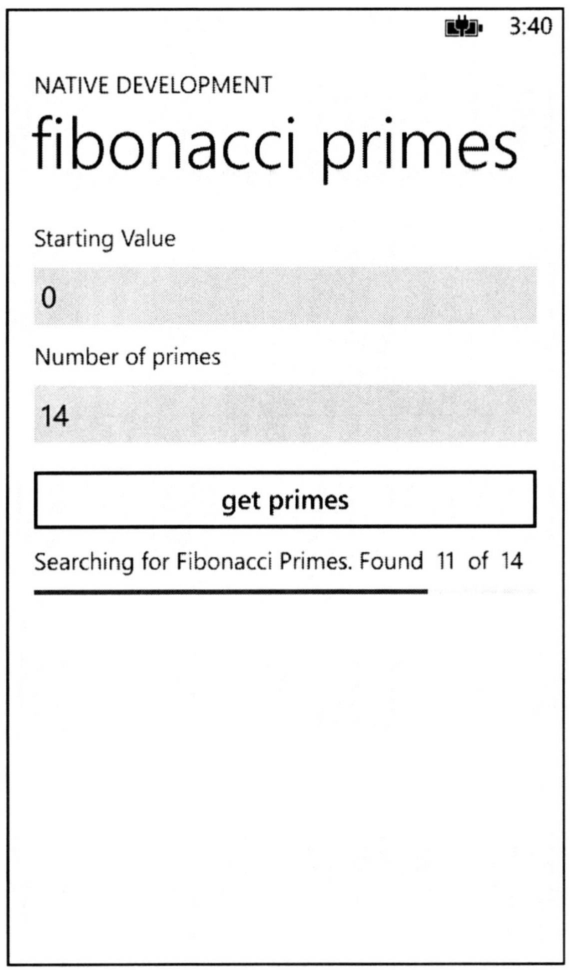

FIGURE 23-7 Returning *IAsyncOperationWithProgress* makes it possible to implement progress reporting of an asynchronous operation in the UI.

Observe that the code still begins with a call to *GetPrimesAsync*, but without the *await* keyword. This is a critical difference because it means that the return result now represents the asynchronous operation itself rather than the value returned by that operation, namely a list of Fibonacci primes. You must acquire a reference to the asynchronous operation if you want to assign a delegate for progress updates to it, as we've done. The only changes to the code support the progress UI shown in Figure 23-7. In particular, we created a simple enumeration to maintain the current state of the search operation, which can be one of *Initialized*, *Searching*, or *Completed*. The states are used to show or hide the in-progress UI and the final results UI.

```
private async void getPrimesButton_Click(object sender, RoutedEventArgs e)
{
    primesListBox.ItemsSource = null; // clear previous result

    int startingValue = 0;
    NumPrimesToFind = int.Parse(numberOfPrimesToFindTextBox.Text);

    FibonacciPrimesFinder fibonacciPrimesFinder = new FibonacciPrimesFinder();

    var fibonacciPrimesTask =
        fibonacciPrimesFinder.GetPrimesAsync(startingValue, NumPrimesToFind);

    fibonacciPrimesTask.Progress = (primes, progress) =>
    {
        Deployment.Current.Dispatcher.BeginInvoke(() =>
        {
            NumPrimesFound = progress;
        });
    };

    SearchState = PrimeSearchState.Searching;
    var fibonacciPrimes = await fibonacciPrimesTask;
    SearchState = PrimeSearchState.Complete;

    if (fibonacciPrimes.Count > 0)
    {
        resultsLabelTextBlock.Text =
            String.Format("The next {0} Fibonacci primes starting from {1} are:",
                NumPrimesToFind, startingValue);

        primesListBox.ItemsSource = fibonacciPrimes;
    }
}
```

Cancelling asynchronous operations

By adding progress notifications to asynchronous operations, you can inform the user as to how much longer a task is going to take. Often, the user might want to use that knowledge to abandon the operation entirely. To handle this, the Windows Runtime supports the notion of *cooperative cancellation* of asynchronous operations. It is cooperative because the component that initiates the cancellation does not get to control when and how it occurs. Rather, it simply informs the asynchronous operation of its desire to cancel the long-running task and then leaves it to that task to determine the best way to wrap up what it is doing. Although this can mean that the cancellation request takes some additional time to be carried out, it facilitates a graceful termination of the task, reducing the risk of corrupted state.

Again, the *FibonacciPrimes* solution offers a good example of the type of operation that the user might want to cancel. This is because the calculation of new primes slows significantly as the number of primes requested grows. In this case, we will look at the changes required in the managed code first and then see how cancellation is dealt with in the native task. We begin by adding a Cancel button to the UI that appears only while a search is in progress. When the user taps that button, we want to initiate a cancellation request on the long-running task. The *IAsyncOperation* interface includes a *Cancel* method (derived from its parent interface *IAsyncInfo*) that can be used to notify the operation that it should stop what it is doing. To access that method from the Cancel button's click event handler, we need to declare an *IAsyncOperation* instance at class-level scope and set the return value of *GetPrimesAsync* to that value.

```
private IAsyncOperationWithProgress<IList<UInt64>, int> fibonacciPrimesTask;

private async void getPrimesButton_Click(object sender, RoutedEventArgs e)
{
    primesListBox.ItemsSource = null; // clear previous result

    int startingValue = int.Parse(startingValueTextBox.Text);
    NumPrimesToFind = int.Parse(numberOfPrimesTextBox.Text);

    FibonacciPrimesFinder fibonacciPrimesFinder = new FibonacciPrimesFinder();

    fibonacciPrimesTask =
        fibonacciPrimesFinder.GetPrimesAsync(startingValue, NumPrimesToFind);

    // additional code omitted...
}

private void cancelAsyncOperationButton_Click(object sender, RoutedEventArgs e)
{
    if (fibonacciPrimesTask == null)
        return;

    if (fibonacciPrimesTask.Status == AsyncStatus.Started)
    {
        fibonacciPrimesTask.Cancel();
        SearchState = PrimeSearchState.Canceling;
    }
}
```

Observe that we have added a new value to the *PrimeSearchState* enumeration: *Canceling*. While in this state, the UI changes to show that the user's cancellation request has been received and shows an indeterminate progress bar, reflecting the fact that we do not know how long it will take to complete. The cancellation progress UI is presented in Figure 23-8.

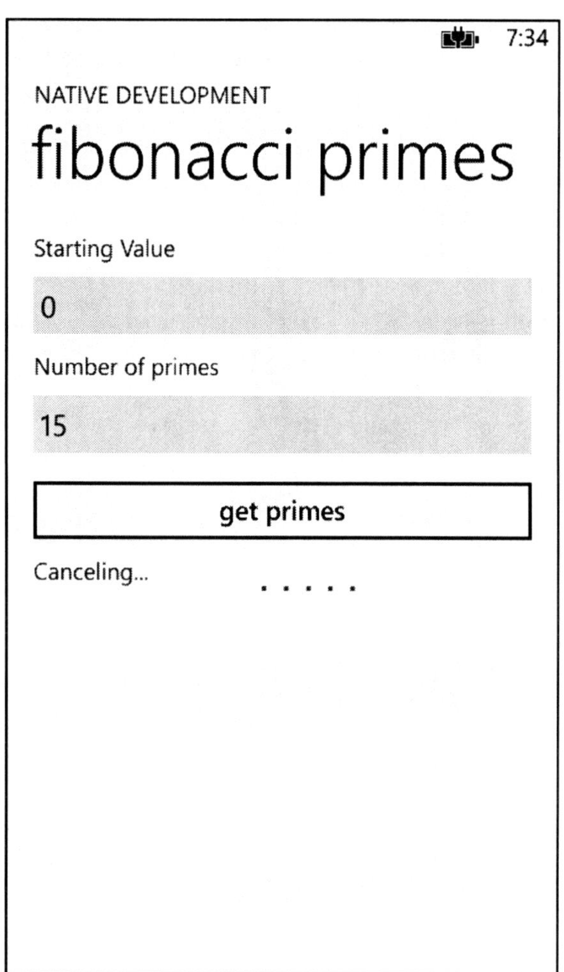

FIGURE 23-8 You should always provide some UI indication that the user's request to cancel was received.

Because cancellation is cooperative, calling the *Cancel* method by itself does not do anything to actually stop the long-running operation from continuing. The cancellation request must be acknowledged and carried out by the task itself, which it does by periodically checking the result of the *is_task_cancellation_requested* function in the *Concurrency* namespace.

```
IVector<UINT64>^ FibonacciPrimesFinder::GetPrimes(int startingValue, int numberOfPrimesToFind,
                                                  progress_reporter<int> progressReporter)
{
    // set up code omitted
    while(fibonacciPrimes.size() < numberOfPrimesToFind)
    {
        currentFibonacciCandidate = lastTwoFibonacciNumbers[0] + lastTwoFibonacciNumbers[1];
        if((currentFibonacciCandidate > startingValue) && IsPrime(currentFibonacciCandidate))
        {
            fibonacciPrimes.push_back(currentFibonacciCandidate);
            progressReporter.report(fibonacciPrimes.size());
        }
```

```
            numberToSwitch = (currentFibonacciIndex % 2);
            lastTwoFibonacciNumbers[numberToSwitch] = currentFibonacciCandidate;

            currentFibonacciIndex++;

            if(is_task_cancellation_requested())
            {
                cancel_current_task();
            }
        }

        return ref new Vector<UINT64>(fibonacciPrimes);
}
```

The call to *cancel_current_task* aborts the long-running operation and raises a *TaskCanceledException* that must be handled by the code that is awaiting its outcome.

```
private async void getPrimesButton_Click(object sender, RoutedEventArgs e)
{
    // set up code omitted
    fibonacciPrimesTask
        = fibonacciPrimesFinder.GetPrimesAsync(startingValue, NumPrimesToFind);

    fibonacciPrimesTask.Progress = (primes, progress) =>
    {
         Deployment.Current.Dispatcher.BeginInvoke(() =>
         {
              NumPrimesFound = progress;
         });
    };

    SearchState = PrimeSearchState.Searching;

    try
    {
        IList<UInt64> fibonacciPrimes = await fibonacciPrimesTask;
        SearchState = PrimeSearchState.Complete;

        if (fibonacciPrimes.Count > 0)
        {
            resultsLabelTextBlock.Text =
                String.Format("The next {0} Fibonacci primes starting from {1} are:",
                              NumPrimesToFind, startingValue);
            primesListBox.ItemsSource = fibonacciPrimes;
        }
    }
    catch (TaskCanceledException)
    {
        SearchState = PrimeSearchState.Complete;
        resultsLabelTextBlock.Text = "The operation was canceled.";
    }
}
```

Note Most of the techniques for dealing with long-running operations discussed in this section can also be applied asynchronous .NET operations built by using the *Task* class in the *System.Threading.Tasks* namespace.

Using Windows Runtime classes in C++

A key value of the ability of Windows Runtime to project into multiple languages is the ability to learn the framework in one language and then seamlessly apply that knowledge in a different environment. Throughout the book, we have shown examples of using Windows Runtime APIs from C#. In each of those cases, we could have called the same API and retrieved the same result from C++ code.

The primary difference you will find when moving from using the Windows Runtime APIs in a .NET-based language to using them in C++ is the way in which you invoke asynchronous methods. Although the heavy use of asynchrony in the Windows Runtime framework means that many developers have learned how to use the async/await pattern at the same time that they became familiar with the framework, it is important to understand that they are completely distinct. The *async/await* keywords are features of the .NET 4.5 compiler, which happen to integrate very well with the asynchronous API model promoted by the Windows Runtime framework, but they are not a part of the framework itself.

In the previous section, we reviewed how to wrap a synchronous C++ method into a lambda function that can run asynchronously. Now, we will look at how you can consume such an asynchronous method *within* C++ code. The *DistanceSpeaker* solution in the sample code uses two of the asynchronous Windows Runtime frameworks that we've looked at in the book: the geolocation APIs in *Windows.Devices.Geolocation*, and the speech synthesis APIs in *Windows.Phone.Speech.Synthesis*. The app determines the current location of the device, calculates the distance (in miles) from that point to Redmond, Washington, and then reads out the distance by using a speech synthesizer. The header file includes just one public method, along with a couple of private helper methods. Note that because the asynchronous API in this example, *CalculateDistanceAndSpeakAsync*, does not produce a result when it completes, it returns an *IAsyncAction* rather than the *IAsyncOperation* that we saw in the previous section.

Note As with *IAsyncOperation*, *IAsyncAction* has a peer interface that supports progress notifications and cancellation, *IAsyncActionWithProgress*.

```
#include <windows.foundation.h>

namespace DistanceSpeakerWindowsRuntimeComponent
{
    public ref class NativeDistanceSpeaker sealed
    {
        int GetDistanceBetweenPoints(double lat1, double lon1, double lat2, double lon2);
        double ConvertDegreesToRadians(double valueInDegrees);
    public:
        Windows::Foundation::IAsyncAction^ CalculateDistanceAndSpeakAsync();
    };
}
```

As before, the *create_async* function is used to generate and immediately return the asynchronous task to the managed caller, which can then await the completion of the lambda function. Within the lambda, we create a task that can run the call to *GetPositionAsync* asynchronously by using the *create_task* function. The *create_task* function is similar to *create_async*, except that it creates pure C++ task objects (defined in the PPL) rather than Windows Runtime interfaces such as *IAsyncOperation* and *IAsyncAction*. You should always use tasks to wrap asynchronous operations when working exclusively in C++ and only use the Windows Runtime interfaces when you need to return a reference to such an operation to the managed layer.

```
IAsyncAction^ NativeDistanceSpeaker::CalculateDistanceAndSpeakAsync()
{
    return create_async([&]()
    {
        Geolocator^ geoLocator = ref new Geolocator();
        geoLocator->DesiredAccuracy = PositionAccuracy::High;

        auto geoPositionTask = create_task(geoLocator->GetGeopositionAsync());

        geoPositionTask.then([&](Geoposition^ position)
        {
            Geocoordinate^ coordinate = position->Coordinate;
            // Redmond, WA is located at (approximately) 47.6460/-122.143
            double distance = GetDistanceBetweenPoints
                (coordinate->Latitude, coordinate->Longitude, 47.6460, -122.143);

            std::wstringstream speechStringStream;
            speechStringStream << "You are " << distance << " miles from Redmond"
                               << std::endl;
            std::wstring speechString = speechStringStream.str();

            Platform::String^ platString = ref new Platform::String(speechString.c_str());
            SpeechSynthesizer^ synthesizer = ref new SpeechSynthesizer();

            return synthesizer->SpeakTextAsync(platString);
        }).then([](task<void> distanceSpeechTask)
```

```
        {
            try
            {
                distanceSpeechTask.get();
            }
            catch(Platform::Exception^ platformException)
            {
                // handle exception
            }
        });
    });
}
```

The PPL borrows from the concept of *promises* in JavaScript to provide an easy way to both handle the results of asynchronous operations and to chain a set of operations together into something that can be read in a linear fashion, as if it were synchronous. With the *then* function on the *task* class, you can specify a lambda function, referred to as a continuation, to be called when the operation completes. If the lambda function itself returns a task, you can call *then* on that result, and so on. One advantage of chaining continuations together like this is that you can push any common error handling to the last lambda function. If an exception occurs anywhere in the chain, it is passed down to subsequent continuations that accept tasks until there is a lambda function which is prepared to handle it. Of course, all good exception handling practices should still apply: you should catch specific exceptions at their source and you should propagate outward any exceptions that would be better handled higher in the call stack.

Note The compiler performs automatic conversions between Windows Runtime interfaces representing asynchronous operations, such as *IAsyncAction* and *IAsyncOperation*, and equivalent task objects. This facilitates the creation of continuations from the return values of Windows Runtime asynchronous methods, such as *SpeakTextAsync*.

Win32 API

Prior to the Windows Runtime framework, one of the primary ways to directly interact with a Windows-based operating system was to use a set of interfaces officially called the Windows API, but colloquially referred to as *Win32*. All other platforms that support development on Windows-based devices, such as the .NET framework, ultimately sit on top of the Win32 API. Although a large proportion of Win32 API has been supplanted by the Windows Runtime framework, both Windows and Windows Phone offer a subset of the original Win32 surface area to facilitate reuse of existing Windows libraries and to bridge the gap until the Windows Runtime API set matures.

Because the primary goal of providing Win32 functionality is to enable compatibility with existing code, the API signatures and behavior are nearly identical to the versions that have been available in Windows for decades, and we will not review them in detail here. A list of the supported Win32 functionality in Windows Phone is available on MSDN at *http://msdn.microsoft.com/en-us/library/windowsphone/develop/jj662956(v=vs.105).aspx.*

Tip In general, you should only be using the Win32 API surface as a means of enabling existing native libraries. If you are writing new code, you should aim to use the equivalent Windows Runtime frameworks, instead.

Component Object Model (COM)

When the Windows Runtime was initially introduced to developers, those who had been developing for Windows for years quickly recognized that it was not an entirely new technology. The idea of a common binary interface that can be projected into multiple languages and can perform reference-counting on objects has been around for decades in the form of the Component Object Model (COM), and the Windows Runtime is indeed heavily based on COM. In fact, during early development of the Windows Runtime, it was referred to internally as Modern COM (MoCOM).

Supported platform COM libraries

Windows Phone supports a very small set of class IDs (CLSIDs) for use from C++, using either the *CoCreateInstanceFromApp* function or the *CreateFX* function. The *CoCreateInstanceFromApp* function is the modern version of the traditional *CoCreateInstanceEx* COM API for use in Windows and Windows Phone Store apps, whereas *CreateFX* is used to create objects related to the XAudio2 libraries common in native games. Table 23-3 summarizes the supported CLSIDs in Windows Phone.

TABLE 23-3 Supported activatable class IDs (CLSIDs) in Windows Phone 8

Activatable class ID (CLSID)	Activating function
CLSID_MFMediaEngineClassFactory	*CoCreateInstanceFromApp*
CLSID_FreeThreadedXMLHTTP60	*CoCreateInstanceFromApp*
AudioReverb	*CreateFX*
AudioVolumeMeter	*CreateFX*
FXEcho	*CreateFX*
FXEQ	*CreateFX*
FXMasteringLimiter	*CreateFX*
FXReverb	*CreateFX*

Note Support for the Microsoft Media Foundation APIs (*CLSID_MFMediaEngineClassFactory*) differs between Windows and Windows Phone. For more details, go to *http://msdn.microsoft.com/en-us/library/windowsphone/develop/jj681688(v=vs.105).aspx*.

Using custom COM libraries

With the Windows Runtime providing cross-language interop capabilities that were previously enabled by COM, direct support for COM is relatively limited in both Windows and Windows Phone. Although it is possible to use a COM library within a Windows Phone app, there are three key considerations to keep in mind:

- To use a COM library from managed code, it must be wrapped in a Windows Runtime component. It is not possible to directly interact with a COM interface from managed code.
- The COM library must be packaged with the app and support registration-free activation. It is not possible to invoke COM components that are registered by other apps in the system or that require registration in the registry.
- The COM library can use only Win32 APIs that are supported in the platform, as discussed in the previous section.

In practice, it is relatively rare to have a COM library that meets the latter two criteria and that would not be better rewritten as a Windows Runtime component.

Summary

The addition of native code support is the most significant change to the Windows Phone platform since the launch of Windows Phone 7. Although Windows Phone still offers predominantly a managed development environment, the ability to include pure C/C++ code in your app makes it easy to share components across multiple platforms and to reuse existing native components rather than rewriting them. For certain classes of apps, the opportunity to tightly control resource allocation can also provide appreciable performance gains. In this chapter, you learned about some of the key features of modern C++ and how you can use it in conjunction with the Windows Runtime framework to derive the greatest possible benefit from the addition of native code to your project.

CHAPTER 24

Windows 8 convergence

As mentioned in Chapter 1, "Vision and architecture," the biggest architectural change in Windows Phone 8 is the adoption of a common core platform with Windows 8. This chapter covers how to take advantage of that common core by reusing code across Windows 8 and Windows Phone 8 projects and how to deal with some of the differences that exist between the two platforms. Because development for Windows 8 would require another entire book, we will generally assume that you are familiar with the new platform for Windows Store apps and focus on sharing code between Windows Store apps and Windows Phone Store apps.

Windows 8 and Windows Phone 8 compared

When Microsoft first entered the mobile device market in the early 2000s, it aimed to provide a familiar interface for users and developers who were accustomed to using Windows on desktop computers. With the launch of Windows Phone 7, Microsoft made a dramatic shift away from alignment of its mobile operating system (OS) with its desktop OS. For users, Windows Phone 7 offered a touch-first experience that included a much greater emphasis on consumer features such as social networking and photos. For developers, the new OS offered a significant change in the platform, with a more structured and secure app model, and a common source of app distribution through the Windows Phone Store (then known as the Windows Phone Marketplace).

The launch of Windows 8 began the process of bringing Microsoft's mobile and desktop operating systems back into alignment except that this time, it was desktop Windows taking inspiration from Windows Phone. The two operating systems now share a common design philosophy centered around crisp typography, fast and fluid animation, and a focus on content over chrome. They also share a number of recognizable end-user features, most notably a vibrant Start screen that is made up of personalized *Live tiles*, as shown in Figure 24-1.

FIGURE 24-1 Windows 8 (on the left) and Windows Phone 8 (right) share a common design philosophy and many important features, such as a Start screen filled with Live tiles.

For developers, the two platforms offer a significant amount of commonality in both the app model and the frameworks, in addition to the common user experience (UX) design language. These similarities make it possible (and advantageous) to design both a Windows app and a Windows Phone 8 app at the same time so that you can deliver a consistent experience across the two platforms. Given the similarities between the core experience on Windows and Windows Phone, users will expect consistency between apps on the two platforms. There are also many opportunities for sharing code across the two platforms. We will discuss a number of techniques for code sharing in this chapter. Before doing that, however, let's review some of the key similarities and differences between the platforms.

Developer tools and supported languages

Microsoft Visual Studio is the primary development environment for both Windows and Windows Phone, and each platform's SDK includes a free Express version of the IDE. The Express editions of Visual Studio are platform-specific, so if you want to develop for both Windows and Windows Phone, you will either need to install both of the Express editions (which will work side-by-side) or install a paid version of Visual Studio (Professional or Ultimate).

Windows 8 supports three distinct app types:

- XAML apps written in C#/Visual Basic/C++
- DirectX apps written in C++
- HTML5/CSS apps written in JavaScript

Windows Phone 8 supports a subset of these. You can create XAML apps with C# or Microsoft Visual Basic and Direct3D (a subset of DirectX) apps with C++. Even though you can include C++ code in a XAML app, it must be wrapped in a Windows Runtime component and cannot interact directly with your XAML markup.

Application models

At its broadest definition, an application model encompasses everything that relates to how an operating system interacts with an application. In Chapter 2, "App model and navigation," we reviewed the portions of the app model that have the greatest impact on apps at run time, namely the run-time lifecycle events: launch, activation/deactivation, and closing. Other, less obvious portions of the app model include the way the app is packaged, how it is installed, updated, and uninstalled, as well as how its contents are described to the OS.

The Windows Phone 7.x app model inherited a number of concepts and components from Microsoft Silverlight, including the packaging format (XAP), the hosting process (TaskHost), and the page navigation model (*OnNavigatedTo*, *OnNavigatedFrom*, and so on). The Windows 8 app model contains many of the same concepts, but they are built from the ground up to support the new Windows platform and are not compatible with Windows Phone. Consequently, it is not possible for Windows and Windows Phone apps to be built and managed as a single entity. Even Windows Phone apps which share practically all of their code with their Windows counterpart, such as Direct3D games, are packaged in a .xap file and define their app metadata in a file named *WMAppManifest.xml*, whereas Windows Store apps are packaged in an .appx file and include their metadata in a file named *Package.appxmanifest*.

Direct3D games are somewhat special with respect to Windows and Windows Phone convergence because they are the only apps to use the key pieces of the new Windows app model on Windows Phone. Recall from Chapter 1 that Windows Phone 8 supports two app models in parallel: the existing Windows Phone app model (covered extensively in Chapter 2), and the new Windows app model, built around the *CoreApplication* object. The Windows app model supports apps written entirely in native code, so it was a natural fit for native games to be enabled this way on Windows Phone, too.

The surface area of the Windows app model supported on Windows Phone is significantly smaller than the version found in Windows 8. Recall from Chapter 2 that the Windows Phone app model supports only two events to indicate when an app is coming to the foreground—*Launching* when it is a brand new instance and *Activated* when it is being resumed from backstack. All other information that the system might want to provide to the app about how and why it's being invoked is delivered through its navigation URI. By contrast, the Windows app model supports a number of top-level activation types, corresponding to all of the different ways that apps can be invoked. For example, an app might be activated as a target for the Share contract or as the handler of a particular file type. In Windows Phone 8, only the basic Launch activation type is supported.

Frameworks

Three goals motivated the design of the Windows Phone 8 API surface. In order of priority, they were as follows:

1. **Compatibility with the Windows Phone 7.x API surface** It was essential to ensure that existing apps could be extended to incorporate new functionality easily rather than having to start over.
2. **Enabling native apps and games** As discussed in Chapter 23, "Native development," adding support for native code was a key goal for Windows Phone 8 and it was important to provide an intuitive set of APIs for developers who were writing native code.
3. **Windows 8 convergence** Where it did not conflict with the first two goals, the Windows Phone 8 API surface aimed to enable code sharing with apps built on Windows 8.

Windows Phone framework namespaces explained

The top-level namespace of a Windows Phone API indicates the types of components that can call it and provides a clue about its relationship with Windows. All APIs included in a namespace starting within Windows use the Windows Runtime and are available from all languages in Windows Phone: C#, Visual Basic, and C++. APIs that are in the System or Microsoft namespaces use the Common Language Runtime (CLR) of Microsoft .NET and are therefore only available from the .NET languages supported by Windows Phone: C# and Visual Basic.

APIs that are in the *Windows.Phone* or *Microsoft* namespaces are specific to Windows Phone and are not available for use in Windows. Within the *Windows* and *System* namespaces, the picture is not as clear. For the most part, the *Windows* namespace available on the desktop is a superset of what is available on the phone, whereas the *System* namespace is the opposite. Exceptions exist in each case, however, so it is safest to consult the API documentation available on MSDN to determine a framework's availability on a given platform. For classes in the *Windows* namespace, the MSDN documentation is common across Windows and Windows Phone, so there are two elements to look for to determine whether a certain method or property is supported. First, at the bottom of the page, you will find a Requirements table listing the minimum platform versions where the class is present, as shown in Figure 24-2.

Requirements	
Minimum supported client	Windows 8
Minimum supported server	Windows Server 2012
Minimum supported phone	Windows Phone 8

FIGURE 24-2 MSDN documentation shows whether a given class in the *Windows* namespace is available in Windows 8 and/or Windows Phone.

Second, you must determine whether the specific method or property that you are interested in is present. Windows Runtime APIs are made up of immutable interfaces, which means that if any member of the interface is present on the phone, all of the members of that interface must be present, even if some of them throw an exception when invoked. Furthermore, because certain interfaces have dependencies on other types, Windows Phone includes a number of types that are not implemented at all. You can determine whether a given member is available in Windows Phone by checking the Remarks section of the MSDN page for the class. The inline documentation in Visual Studio will also indicate whether a particular member is available in Windows Phone, as shown in Figure 24-3 for the *RoamingFolder* property of the *ApplicationData* class.

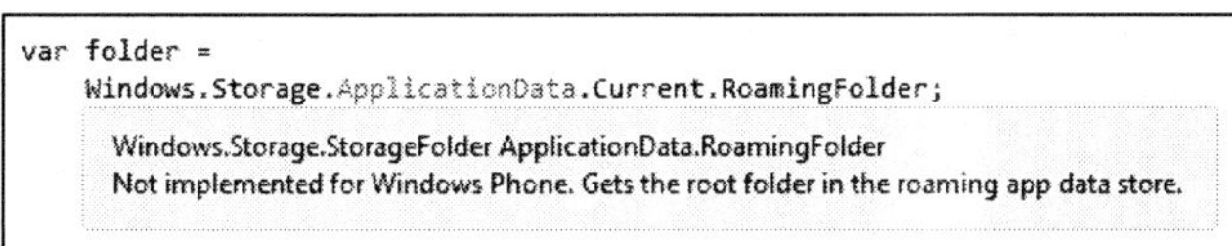

var folder =
Windows.Storage.ApplicationData.Current.RoamingFolder;
Windows.Storage.StorageFolder ApplicationData.RoamingFolder
Not implemented for Windows Phone. Gets the root folder in the roaming app data store.

FIGURE 24-3 The inline IntelliSense documentation shows whether a given class member is available in Windows Phone.

Windows Runtime API comparison

Given that you cannot immediately determine what functionality is available for a given class by glancing at it in the Object Browser or IntelliSense, it is worth quickly reviewing some of the major differences in Windows Runtime frameworks that are present on both platforms.

Note This list is not comprehensive. For a full listing of Windows Runtime APIs available in Windows Phone, go to *http://msdn.microsoft.com/en-us/library/windowsphone/develop/jj207212(v=vs.105).aspx*. For each class, use the approach described in the previous section to determine the specific functionality that is supported in Windows Phone.

- **Touch** Windows Phone supports only the raw touch events raised by the *ICoreWindow* interface for Direct3D apps, such as *PointerPressed* and *PointerRelease*. The helpers provided by Windows to recognize special types of touch input, such as gestures, are not supported on Windows Phone.

- **Contracts** Windows Phone enables simplified versions of some Windows 8 contracts as a means of allowing native apps to access existing system functionality. They do not provide the full extensibility available for store apps that is available in Windows.

  Apps can use the *Share* contract as a means of providing small amounts of text and/or a URI to the built-in sharing task, from which the user can share the content by email, Short Message Service (SMS), or via registered social networks. This is the same sharing UI available to managed apps through the *ShareLinkTask* and the *ShareStatusTask*. Store apps cannot register as sharing targets in Windows Phone 8. Also, the Share contract can only be invoked programmatically in Windows Phone; there is no global UI which is equivalent to Windows charms.

Direct3D apps can also use the *FileOpenPicker* API, which makes it possible for the user to choose a photo from his photo library and have that photo be returned to the app. As with the Share contract, the *FileOpenPicker* wraps a built-in experience, in this case the photo chooser. The API also only allows a single photo to be chosen at a time, unlike Windows, in which the user has the option to select multiple files. Finally, as with the Share contract, store apps cannot register as a target for exposing files through the picker.

Note There are two other Windows extensions which have analogs on Windows Phone: the Protocol associations and the File associations. These are not highlighted here because their associated activation types are not supported in Windows Phone 8. Only XAML apps can register to be launched for files and protocols, as shown in Chapter 2, "App Model and Navigation." The APIs used by apps which want to do the launching are aligned, however, and are discussed in the section that follows.

- **Storage** Windows 8 introduced a data model for store apps which included three system-defined categories of data: roaming, local, and temporary. The roaming and local categories include both a file system folder and a property bag for settings. Although Windows Phone 8 mimics this structure, only the local folder (not local settings) is currently supported. The basic API surface for performing file input/output (IO) operations on the local folder—that is, the *StorageFile* and *StorageFolder* classes—are supported on Windows Phone, though some advanced features, such as folder queries, are not available. Note that the root of the local folder available via the Windows Runtime *ApplicationData* class is the same as the one accessible from the *IsolatedStorage* APIs in .NET.

  The Windows 8 storage APIs also enable access to a set of file system locations outside of the app's own storage container which are not supported on Windows Phone. This includes the pictures library and removable devices, both of which are available through .NET APIs.

- **Location** The Windows Runtime location framework available on Windows Phone is nearly identical to the version on Windows, but there are two minor differences. First, Windows Phone does not support civic address resolution. That functionality is available via a much richer managed API in the *Microsoft.Phone.Maps.Services* namespace. Second, the Windows Phone version includes the source of the location information, such as GPS, Wi-Fi access point lookup, or cell-tower triangulation, as well as detailed information about the precision of the reading.

- **Bluetooth** Even though the Bluetooth API surface is identical on Windows and Windows Phone, Windows Phone supports some additional scenarios. In particular, you can communicate with various types of Bluetooth devices and you can enumerate paired Bluetooth devices by using the *FindAllPeersAsync* method on the *PeerFinder* class. Windows only supports using Bluetooth as a communication channel between peers; that is, two versions of the same app running on different Windows computers.

- **Proximity** The only difference in the proximity API is that Windows Phone does not support peer device discovery via WiFi Direct, because that standard is not currently supported on the phone. Instead, Windows Phone performs peer enumeration by using Bluetooth.
- **App launching** Windows Phone supports the same APIs for launching apps based on a file type or a custom URI scheme, namely *LaunchUriAsync* and *LaunchFileAsync*. However, Windows Phone only supports the basic versions of these APIs, not the overloads with which apps can specify options such as whether to show the Open With dialog box or where to send the user if the app is not installed.
- **CoreApplication and CoreWindow** In Windows Phone, the *CoreApplication* and *Core Window* classes are only supported in Direct3D apps, and they support a subset of the functionality in Windows. In particular, *CoreApplication* only supports the *Launch ActivationKind* and does not support requesting a deferral during the *Suspending* event. It is also not possible to create a new view in the app.
- **Sensors** The Windows Runtime classes that expose readings from the compass, gyrometer, inclinometer, and orientation sensors are identical between Windows and Windows Phone. The API surface for the accelerometer sensor is nearly identical; the only difference is that Windows Phone will not raise the *Shaken* event. Windows Phone does not support the ambient light sensor.
- **In-app purchase** Windows and Windows Phone offer the same functionality for selling durable goods, which are items that last forever such as an additional map pack for a game. Windows Phone also offers the ability to sell consumable goods, which are consumed by the user in the app, such as food or medicine in a role-playing game. Windows does not support consumables, but it does allow for the sale of subscriptions, which is not available in Windows Phone.
- **Sockets** Windows and Windows Phone have identical support for TCP and UDP sockets. Windows Phone does not support web sockets, a message-based, full-duplex communication channel that performs its initial handshake over standard HTTP/HTTPS ports (80 and 443).
- **Threading** The API surface exposed in the *Windows.System.Threading* namespace is identical on Windows and Windows Phone.
- **Data usage** In the *Windows.Networking.Connectivity* namespace, Windows Phone only supports the *ConnectionCost* class, which provides information about the type of network to which the user is currently connected and whether he is approaching or over the limit of his mobile operator's data plan. In Windows Phone, this information is derived from the built-in Data Sense app (if available).

Dealing with API overlaps

Existing Windows Phone developers will notice a number of Windows Runtime frameworks which offer similar or identical functionality to existing frameworks from Windows Phone 7.x. These new frameworks are included for access from native code and to assist developers who would like to share code between Windows and Windows Phone. As a general rule, if you are writing new code, you should opt for the Windows Runtime version over the .NET version, not only because it will help you share code now, but also because the Windows Runtime version is likely to see the bulk of the investment in future releases. Of course, if you have a significant amount of code relying on an existing framework, that will continue to be supported on Windows Phone 8.

Another consideration to keep in mind is the set of dependencies that other frameworks might have on one of the overlapping types. For example, the new Windows Phone map control described in Chapter 16, "Camera and photos," only supports the use of the *System.Device.Location.GeoCoordinate* class for adding items to the map, not the equivalent Windows Runtime type, *Windows.Devices.Geolocation.Geocoordinate*. Converting between the two types is trivial, however.

Non-converged frameworks

As mentioned earlier in this section, the highest priority in designing the Windows Phone 8 API surface was to maintain compatibility with the existing frameworks shipped in Windows Phone 7.x. Consequently, there are a number of areas for which Windows and Windows Phone offer a similar feature but expose it through an entirely different set of APIs. Table 24-1 provides a summary of the key differences between the two platforms.

TABLE 24-1 Key differences in API surface between Windows and Windows Phone

Feature	Windows	Windows Phone
Push notifications	Based on the Windows Push Notification Services (WNS) and exposed through the *Windows.Networking.PushNotifications* namespace.	Based on the Microsoft Push Notification (MPN) service and exposed through the *Microsoft.Phone.Notification* namespace.
Live tiles	Exposed through the *Windows.UI.Notifications* namespace.	Exposed through *Microsoft.Phone.Shell.ShellTile* namespace.

Feature	Windows	Windows Phone
Background transfers	The *Windows.Networking.Background Transfer* namespace offers a *BackgroundUploader* class and a *BackgroundDownloader* class. Transfers are managed by using per-app processes that run within the app's security context. Because transfers are performed within the app's security context, partially completed downloads are available to the app. This makes it possible for the app to begin reading from the file shortly after the download begins, which is useful for media download scenarios. However, if the app is terminated (not suspended), in-progress transfers are stopped.	The *BackgroundTransferService* class in the *Microsoft.Phone.BackgroundTransfer* namespace offers the ability to perform both uploads and downloads. Transfers are performed by a system-wide service running in its own security context. When downloads are completed, they are transferred to an app-specified location within the app's local data folder. Because transfers are handled centrally, they are completely independent of the app's lifetime.
Media library access	User media is exposed through the *Windows.Storage.KnownFolders* class, which includes properties for the *MusicLibrary*, *PicturesLibrary*, and *VideosLibrary*. The media content exposed through *KnownFolders* maps directly to the user libraries shown in Windows Explorer and the API surface is based on file system primitives, namely *StorageFolder* and *StorageFile*.	User media is exposed through the *MediaLibrary* class in the *Microsoft.Xna.Framework.Media* namespace. The XNA media library exposes user media content using classes that are specific to the media type; for instance, *AlbumCollection* and *PictureCollection*. Access to user videos is not available from the XNA media library.
Removable devices access	Removable storage devices are exposed through *KnownFolders.RemovableDevices*. Apps can read or write any file as long they have registered as a file type handler for that file extension and have the removable devices capability.	The only form of removable storage supported by Windows Phone is microSD. It is exposed through the *ExternalStorage* class in the *Microsoft.Phone.Storage* namespace. Windows Phone only supports read access, and like Windows, you must have registered as a file type handler for any files that you want to read.

Direct3D

The area in which Windows Phone comes closest to full alignment with Windows 8 is in Direct3D, the native framework used for high-performance graphics apps and games. See Chapter 25, "Games and Direct3D," for more details on their minor differences.

Background processing

Windows and Windows Phone adhere to very similar philosophies regarding background processing. In short, the system's highest priorities are to serve the needs of the current foreground app and to preserve battery life; background processes can take advantage of surplus resources to do their work when conditions permit. They also share a requirement that the entry point for any background processing must be contained in a separate class library from the foreground app. In Windows Phone, this library is a Dynamic-Link Library (DLL); in Windows, it is Winmd.

Generic background processing

The primary difference between the background processing models concerns how tasks are scheduled. As demonstrated in Chapter 9, "Background agents," Windows Phone supports two types of generic background tasks: periodic tasks and resource-intensive tasks. Periodic tasks run approximately every 30 minutes for 25 seconds, whereas resource-intensive tasks run only when the device is idle, connected to AC power and a Wi-Fi network, and the battery is nearly full. Windows offers developers significantly more control over the scheduling of their background tasks, including the ability to be activated by a push notification message or to only be run when certain system conditions (such as Internet connectivity) are met. The caveat is that the Windows scheduling policy is heavily weighted toward apps that the user has chosen to feature on her lock screen. These tasks can run more frequently and receive more CPU time than other background tasks.

Background audio

Recall from Chapter 9 that background audio in Windows Phone is managed by an app-owned background audio agent and played through a system service, the Zune media queue (ZMQ). In Windows, all audio is played from the main app. To make it possible for the app to continue playing audio when the user navigates away, you simply need to set the *AudioCategory* attribute on the *MediaElement* control to *BackgroundCapableMedia* and register for the system media controls, namely play, pause, stop, and the play/pause toggle.

Voice over IP

Windows and Windows Phone both provide the platform infrastructure to support Voice over IP (VoIP) apps. The following are the key differences:

- In Windows, a VoIP app can register to be awakened to handle a call based on two types of system triggers: the push notification trigger that is raised when a WNS notification is received, and the channel control trigger that is raised when traffic is detected on a socket connection. Windows Phone only supports push notifications sent through the MPN service as a means of sending a call notification.
- In Windows, the foreground app that provides all of the UI and the background task that manages the interaction with the app's cloud service run in a single process. In Windows Phone, app code runs in two processes: the foreground process that provides the app UI, and the background process that responds to incoming calls, reports call progress to the system, and sends keepalive messages to the app's cloud service.
- Windows Phone provides rich integration between VoIP apps and the built-in phone experience; this includes showing the incoming call dialog when a VoIP call is received and displaying the call progress UI at the top of the screen while there is an active call.

Note For more details on VoIP support in Windows Phone, go to *http://msdn.microsoft.com/en-US/library/windowsphone/develop/jj206983%28v=vs.105%29.aspx*.

Background location tracking

As discussed in Chapter 16, Windows Phone 8 supports a new type of background processing known as *Continuous Background Execution*, which is designed to handle background location tracking for apps providing functionality such as turn-by-turn directions. In this case, the app's ability to continue running in the background is directly tied to it continuing to listen to location events. This type of background processing is not available in Windows 8.

Authoring Windows Runtime components on Windows Phone

In addition to the differences in Windows Runtime frameworks between Windows and Windows Phone described in the previous section, there are also a handful of differences that developers who intend to write their own Windows Runtime components should understand.

The first important difference is that in Windows Phone 8, Windows Runtime components can only be written in C/C++, whereas in Windows they can be authored in C/C++, C#, and Visual Basic. For developers strictly targeting the Windows Phone platform, this is not a significant drawback, because the primary use of Windows Runtime in Windows Phone 8 is to provide a way to call native code from a managed component. If you want to reuse code from a C#-based Windows Runtime component written for a Windows Store app in Windows Phone, you can simply create a managed library project that contains the same source files but builds to a .NET assembly rather than a Windows Runtime component.

The second difference is that Windows Phone does not create JavaScript projections of Windows Runtime types, so you cannot use Windows Runtime functionality from the *WebBrowser* control.

Sharing code between Windows and Windows Phone

The introduction of the Windows Runtime to Windows Phone and the presence of a rich set of common .NET functionality offer an opportunity to share code across apps written for the two platforms. In this section, we will review strategies and techniques for maximizing code sharing while maintaining high-quality, device-specific experiences.

Deciding when and how to share code

Before considering specific techniques for sharing code between Windows and Windows Phone projects, it is worthwhile examining your goals for the two projects and determining what code sharing will help you accomplish them. Usually your goal would be to save initial development time and the cost of ongoing maintenance by being able to write code once rather than duplicating effort across two projects. Depending on the complexity of your apps and your level of familiarity with the techniques described later in this section, however, you might find that trying to maintain shared code actually leads to greater up-front and ongoing costs.

For new developers or those who have already built apps for one platform or the other, it will often be easier to simply copy code from one project to the other and then fix build or run-time issues as they arise rather than spending a significant amount of time designing (or redesigning) the app for easier code sharing. If you do choose to refactor an existing app to accommodate additional code sharing, you should work on a *copy* of the original project until you are confident that you have not regressed any existing functionality during the course of making the changes.

Tip An alternative option for safely embarking on a major refactoring effort is to use a source control system, which would make it possible for you to roll back to a previous version of your code if something goes wrong. Microsoft's primary source control product, Team Foundation Service (TFS), is now available as a cloud-based service at *http://www.tfspreview.com*.

If you believe that you will benefit from code sharing between projects, the best strategy is to build both apps at the same time, including UX and architectural design as well as development. When you add a new feature or significantly change the code for one app, you should make sure to build and test the app on the other platform to ensure that it works as you expect. By following an iterative approach across both platforms, you will reduce the likelihood of taking a dependency on a framework or design approach that is not supported in both places.

Tip Use unit tests to automate the testing of your core app logic as you iterate. In Chapter 12, "Profiling and diagnostics," we looked at one approach to creating phone unit tests by using the Windows Phone Toolkit. Unit testing support is also available for both Windows Store apps and Windows Phone Store apps in the Visual Studio 2012 Update 2, which is available at *http://www.microsoft.com/en-us/download/details.aspx?id=38188*.

Definitions of compatibility

This section covers a number of techniques for achieving compatibility between code written on Windows and code written on Windows Phone. Before we do that, however, it's worthwhile to review the different types of compatibility, because not all of the techniques shown will result in the same type of compatibility.

- **Binary compatibility** Binary compatibility refers to the ability to compile shared source code once and then run it on multiple platforms without modification.
- **Source compatibility** Source compatibility refers to the ability to share the exact same source code between two different platforms but with the requirement that it be separately compiled for each platform.

The only way to achieve binary compatibility between Windows and Windows Phone is to create a Portable Class Library (PCL) project, which we will look at later in this chapter. If you write native code or .NET code that uses Windows Runtime APIs, you can only achieve source code compatibility. A number of the Windows Runtime APIs that are supported on Windows Phone have been tweaked to work around missing Windows dependencies or to work correctly with the phone's application model, so although the caller should see the same behavior on the two platforms, the calling code is not binary-compatible with Windows.

Code sharing and Model-View-ViewModel

In Chapter 4, "Data binding and MVVM," we reviewed the Model-View-ViewModel (MVVM) pattern, a popular design pattern for building XAML apps. Recall that in MVVM, you separate your app into three distinct parts:

- **View** The app UI, made up of XAML pages and user controls and very lightweight code-behind files.
- **Model** The app data classes, which are usually responsible for interacting with a persistent data store, such as a files, databases, or the cloud.
- **ViewModel** The view model layer manages the relationship between the view and the model, making it possible for them to remain completely decoupled from one another. The view model instantiates the classes in the model layer and then translates their data into a format that can be consumed by the view, usually through data binding.

In a well-factored MVVM app, virtually all of the app logic is contained in the model and view model layers. Consequently, the code in those layers offers the best opportunity for code sharing between Windows and Windows Phone. Even though there are techniques for sharing elements of your view layer, they generally offer the lowest return on investment, given the difference in target form factors for the two platforms.

Throughout this section, we use variations of the *CityFactBook* solution in the sample code to illustrate different techniques for code sharing. The UI for the Windows and Windows Phone apps is shown in Figure 24-4.

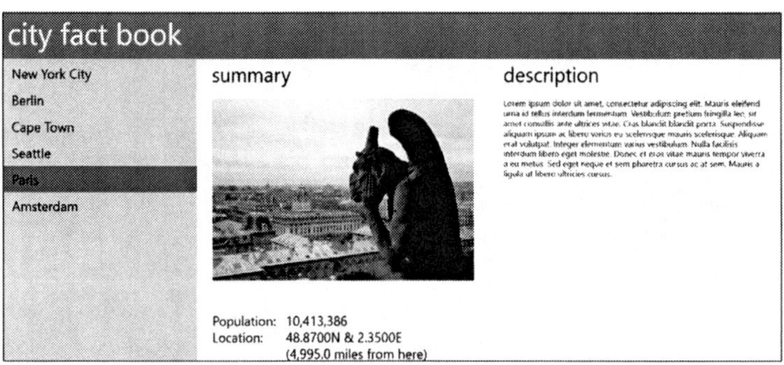

FIGURE 24-4 The *CityFactBook* solution offers good opportunities for code sharing between Windows (on the left) and Windows Phone (right).

The *CityFactBook* app adheres to the MVVM pattern with the following division of responsibilities:

- The view layer includes the definition of the UI. On Windows Phone, the view layer includes two pages: one to select the city, and one to show the information for that city. On Windows, the larger screen size makes it possible to show both the list and information about the chosen city on a single page.
- The view model layer manages the list of cities and surfaces details about each city in a format that the view can easily consume.
- The model layer maintains all of the information about the city entries, including the population, location, and description of each city.

Sharing .NET code by using the PCL

The PCL project is designed to make cross-platform development of .NET components across a number of endpoints possible, including Windows 8 and Windows Phone 8. It does this by providing a set of .NET reference assemblies which contain only the types that are supported and behave similarly on the endpoints that you're targeting. Creating a PCL assembly is recommended for code which will only ever need to be called from other managed assemblies on both platforms.

Note To create a PCL project, you need a copy of Visual Studio 2012 Professional or higher. It is not available in Visual Studio 2012 Express for Windows Phone. Alternatively, you can create a separate class library for each platform and share code between them by using linked files, a technique we will discuss later in this chapter.

Creating the project

The PCL project template is available under the Windows node for either Visual C# or Visual Basic. After you create the project, Visual Studio opens the Add Portable Class Library dialog box shown in Figure 24-5, asking you to choose which platforms you want to target.

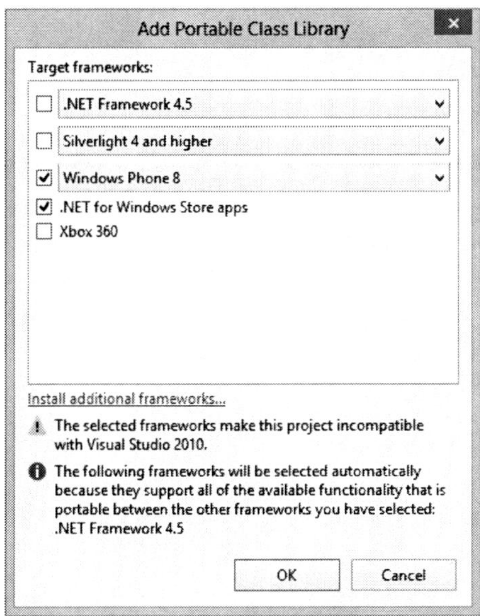

FIGURE 24-5 PCL projects provide only the assemblies supported on the chosen platforms.

The *CityFactBook_PCL* solution in the sample code illustrates how you can use PCL projects to encapsulate logic that is entirely shared between Windows and Windows Phone. We create a PCL project to encapsulate the view model and model layers of the app. The view layer—as well as any code that is specific to the target platform, including interaction with app lifecycle events—remains separate, as illustrated in Figure 24-6.

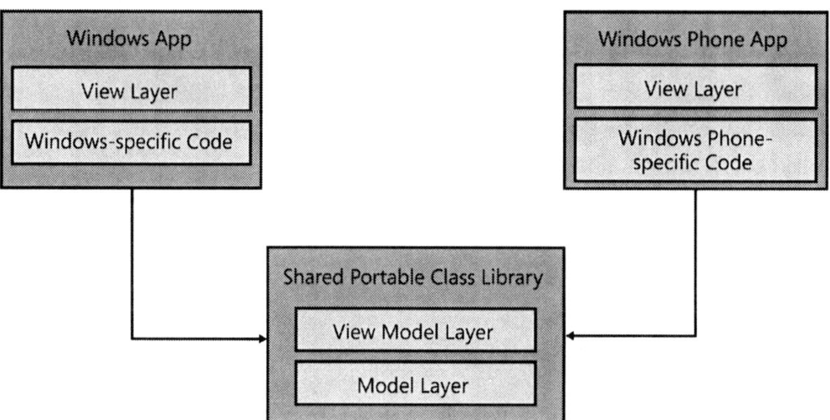

FIGURE 24-6 PCLs offer a binary-compatible way to share platform-independent .NET code.

We have not included the code for the view model or model classes here, because there isn't anything particularly interesting about them. Indeed, after the project is created, there is no real difference between building a PCL project and building any other type of .NET assembly, other than the assurance that the resulting DLL will run without modification on any of the target platforms that were selected when it was created. Likewise, you can add the PCL project to your Windows and Windows Phone apps just as you would add any other managed assembly—either by including the project directly in your Visual Studio solution and referencing the source project or by referencing the pre-built DLL.

Note As always, the full source is available in the sample projects that accompany this chapter.

Handling platform differences

Although you can encapsulate a significant amount of logic in a PCL project, you will inevitably come across a framework API that is not available because it is not common across your chosen platforms or because it is exposed through the Windows Runtime rather than as a .NET API. The location framework is one example of such a framework and one that impacts the *CityFactBook* solution because we include a feature to show the distance to the chosen city from the user's current location on each city page.

Because the PCL project cannot call non-PCL classes directly, it must do so indirectly. One approach is to create an abstract class which is then implemented in the platform-specific projects. In the *CityFactBook_PCL* solution, we define the abstract class *LocationHelper* to handle location-related functionality, some of which is handled by platform-specific subclasses. The *LocationHelper* class includes three method definitions, two of which are implemented and one of which is abstract. The concrete methods *GetDistanceBetweenPoints* and *ConvertDegreesToRadians* are both static helpers for determining the distance between two points on Earth. Because these methods are only responsible for performing basic calculations on primitive data types, their implementation can easily be shared between the Windows and Windows Phone apps. The abstract method *GetCurrentLocation Async* depends on platform-specific code to acquire the user's current location, so it must be implemented by types that live within the respective apps. Note that because there is no type representing a geocoordinate available to PCL projects, we create a simple helper type, the *Location* class, which contains *Latitude* and *Longitude* properties.

```
public abstract class LocationHelper
{
    public abstract Task<Location> GetCurrentLocationAsync();
    public static double GetDistanceBetweenPoints(Location loc1, Location loc2)
    {
        double lat1 = loc1.Latitude;
        double lat2 = loc2.Latitude;
        double lon1 = loc1.Longitude;
        double lon2 = loc2.Longitude;

        // remainder of code omitted for brevity...
    }

    private static double ConvertDegreesToRadians(double valueInDegrees)
    {
        return valueInDegrees * Math.PI / 180;
    }
}
```

We create platform-specific subclasses called *PhoneLocationHelper* and *WindowsLocationHelper* within the respective app projects. To illustrate the opportunity for using the abstract method technique for invoking platform-specific code, we use the location API in the *System.Devices.Location* namespace on Windows Phone and the version in the *Windows.Devices.Geolocation* namespace on Windows, even though Windows Phone could use exactly the same code.

```
public class PhoneLocationHelper : LocationHelper
{
    public override Task<Location> GetCurrentLocationAsync()
    {
        var taskSource = new TaskCompletionSource<Location>();
        var watcher = new GeoCoordinateWatcher(GeoPositionAccuracy.High);

        watcher.StatusChanged += (sender, args) =>
        {
            if(args.Status != GeoPositionStatus.Ready)
                return;

            var loc = watcher.Position.Location;

            taskSource.SetResult(new Location(loc.Latitude, loc.Longitude);
            watcher.Stop();
        };

        geoCoordinateWatcher.Start();
```

```
            return taskSource.Task;
        }
    }

    public class WindowsLocationHelper : LocationHelper
    {
        public async override Task<Location> GetCurrentLocationAsync()
        {
            var geolocator = new Geolocator();

            Geoposition currentLocation = await geolocator.GetGeopositionAsync();

            return new Location
                    {
                        Latitude = currentLocation.Coordinate.Latitude,
                        Longitude = currentLocation.Coordinate.Longitude
                    };
        }
    }
```

All that remains is to instantiate the subclasses of *LocationHelper* in each project and pass them into the PCL project, where they will be used to calculate the distance to the chosen city. Because the distance calculation happens in the PCL project's *CityViewModel* class, we simply pass the platform-specific implementations to its constructor.

```
// in Windows Phone app
var cityViewModel = new CityViewModel(currentCity, new PhoneLocationHelper());

// in Windows App
var cityViewModel = new CityViewModel(currentCity, new WindowsLocationHelper());

// in Shared PCL project
public CityViewModel(City selectedCity, LocationHelper locHelper)
{
    City = selectedCity;
    CalculateDistanceToCityAsync(locHelper);
}

private async Task CalculateDistanceToCityAsync(LocationHelper locHelper)
{
    double distance = LocationHelper.GetDistanceBetweenPoints
                            (City.Location,
                            await locHelper.GetCurrentLocationAsync());
    DistanceFromCurrentLocation = String.Format("({0:n1} miles from here)", distance);
}
```

PCL tradeoffs

The primary benefit of sharing code in a PCL project is that the Visual Studio editor automatically ensures that you are writing code that is portable across platforms. The technique illustrated in this section offers one way to invoke non-portable code from a PCL project when necessary, at the cost of some added complexity. If you find that you need to use this type of technique frequently in your PCL project, you should consider using shared source files (discussed in the next section), instead.

It is also worth calling out a couple of other techniques that can facilitate interaction between your portable code and platform-specific functionality. First, if the platform-specific functionality that you need to invoke from your PCL project is "fire and forget"—that is, it either does not return data or you don't need the data—consider simply creating an event in your portable code and registering for that event within your platform-specific projects. You can then include the platform-specific functionality in the app event handlers rather than defining an abstract class. Second, if you want your PCL project to perform some computation and then make a simple callback into platform-specific code, consider using a delegate type. Of course, for this technique to work, all of the inputs and outputs to the computation must be PCL-compatible types.

Linked files and conditional compilation

As we have seen, portable class libraries can only target the intersection of .NET types that are available on the platforms for which the library is created. However, because Windows Phone supports a set of the Windows Runtime frameworks available in Windows, there are cases in which you can share a significant amount of code between apps for the two platforms outside of a portable library. Visual Studio provides a useful technique to enable this type of code sharing: linked files. You can think of a linked file like a symbolic link in the file system; it makes it possible for a single physical file to logically reside in multiple projects. After a file is linked between your Windows project and your Windows Phone project, you can write code in just one place and have it automatically compiled in both projects.

To create a linked file, first create the actual file normally in one of the projects. Then, in the other project, use the standard Add Existing Item dialog and locate the file (or files) that you want to link. Rather than adding the file normally (which would create a copy), select Add As Link from the drop-down menu next to the Add button, as shown in Figure 24-7.

Tip You can also create linked files by dragging them between projects while holding down the Alt key.

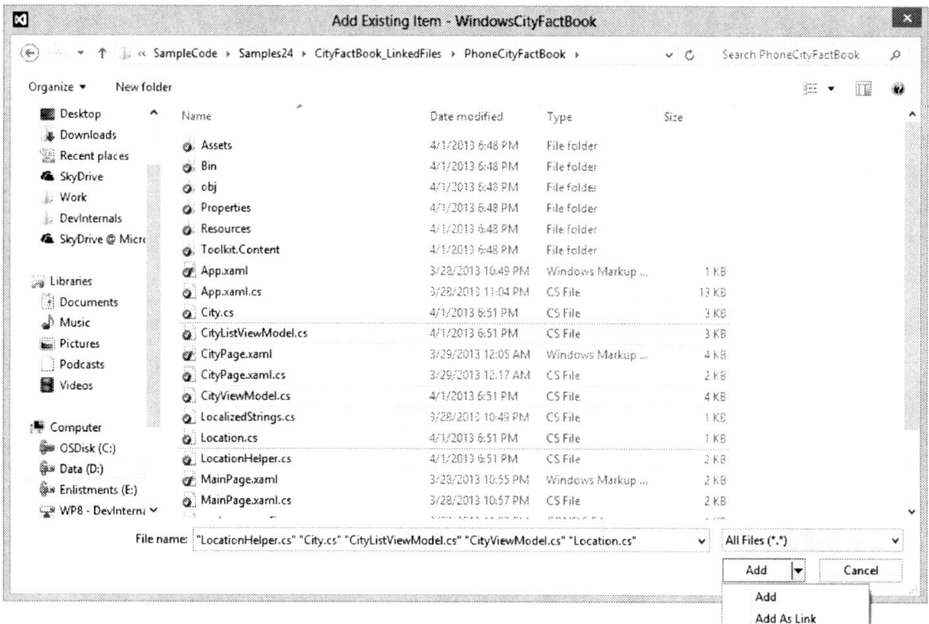

FIGURE 24-7 The Add Existing Item dialog box includes an option to add linked files to your project.

The *CityFactBook_LinkedFiles* solution in the sample code includes the same app-specific projects shown in the previous section. The only difference is that they are now sharing code via linked files rather than a portable library. Because we are no longer restricted to shared .NET types, the two apps can now share a common concrete implementation of the *LocationHelper* class that relies on the Windows Runtime Geolocation APIs, which are available on both Windows and Windows Phone.

```
public class LocationHelper
{
    public async Task<Location> GetCurrentLocationAsync()
    {
        var geolocator = new Geolocator();
        geolocator.DesiredAccuracy = PositionAccuracy.High;
        Geoposition currentLocation = await geolocator.GetGeopositionAsync();
        return new Location
                  {
                      Latitude = currentLocation.Coordinate.Latitude,
                      Longitude = currentLocation.Coordinate.Longitude
                  };
    }

    // other code unchanged...
}
```

In the case of the Windows Runtime location framework, most of the API surface is common between the two platforms, so it is possible to share simple classes like *LocationHelper* in their entirety. Sometimes, however, you will find API and behavior differences between the two platforms that require different implementations in your apps. You can add platform-specific code to linked files by using conditional compilation. Simply wrap Windows-specific code within a check for the NETFX_CORE symbol and Windows Phone–specific code within a check for the WINDOWS_PHONE symbol.

To illustrate this, we add a new feature to the app in the *CityFactBook_LinkedFiles* solution: the ability for users to add short notes for each city. In Windows, this type of small, user-specific data is a good candidate for roaming between devices because you might want to add some notes while using the app on your home computer and then view them later while using the app on your tablet. Even though Windows Phone does not support roaming data, it is still useful to add the notes feature to the Windows Phone version of the app so that users can add content for each city that is persisted across invocations of the app. Because the roaming folder and the local folder are both instances of the *StorageFolder* type, the code to read and write content to them is exactly the same; the only difference is which *StorageFolder* we acquire.

```
private async void SaveUserNotesAsync()
{
#if NETFX_CORE
    StorageFolder saveFolder = ApplicationData.Current.RoamingFolder;
#else
    StorageFolder saveFolder = ApplicationData.Current.LocalFolder;
#endif

    var filename = GetCityFilename(); // returns City[CityId]-UserNotes.dat
    var userNotesFile =
        await saveFolder.CreateFileAsync(filename, CreationCollisionOption.ReplaceExisting);

    using (var filestream = await userNotesFile.OpenStreamForWriteAsync())
    using (var writer = new StreamWriter(filestream))
    {
        await writer.WriteAsync(UserNotes);
    }
}
```

Note The conditional compilation symbols *NETFX_CORE* and *WINDOWS_PHONE* are only defined by default for managed code. In native code, you should check the value of the *WINAPI_FAMILY_APP* symbol as follows:

```
#if WINAPI_FAMILY == WINAPI_FAMILY_APP
    // Windows
#endif

#if WINAPI_FAMILY == WINAPI_FAMILY_PHONE_APP
    // Windows Phone
#endif
```

Visual Studio helps you write platform-specific code by setting up the development environment for a linked file based on the project type in which it was opened. In particular, it applies conditional compilation symbols for the current project and configures IntelliSense to use the API surface available to apps targeting that platform. Figure 24-8 illustrates this by showing the same code from the *SaveUserNotesAsync* method in the context of the Windows app and the Windows Phone app, respectively. Observe that in the Windows app, the code wrapped in the check for the *NETFX_CORE* symbol exhibits standard syntax highlighting, whereas the line of code encapsulated in the *#else* statement is dimmed (grayed out). The reverse is true in the Windows Phone app.

```
#if NETFX_CORE
            StorageFolder saveFolder = ApplicationData.Current.RoamingFolder;
#else
            StorageFolder saveFolder = ApplicationData.Current.LocalFolder;
#endif
```

```
#if NETFX_CORE
            StorageFolder loadFolder = ApplicationData.Current.RoamingFolder;
#else
            StorageFolder loadFolder = ApplicationData.Current.LocalFolder;
#endif
```

FIGURE 24-8 Visual Studio interprets linked files based on the project in which you open them.

Sharing managed code with partial classes

Despite Visual Studio's help with distinguishing the development environment for linked files based on the platform that you are targeting, when you reach a certain level of conditional compilation in your code, it is bound to become unwieldy. Partial classes offer one solution for keeping platform-specific code cleanly segmented within your projects.

Partial classes make it possible to split the definition of a class across multiple source files simply by using the *partial* keyword in each definition. For example, you can define a *Person* class across two files, *Person1.cs* and *Person2.cs*. The source file *Person1.cs* might look something like this:

```
namespace Mammals
{
    partial class Person
    {
        public void Eat()
        {
            // code...
        }

        public void Sleep()
        {
            // code...
        }
    }
}
```

The second source file, *Person2.cs*, could add further definition to the *Person* class, as follows:

```
namespace Mammals
{
    partial class Person
    {
        public void WriteCode()
        {
            // code...
        }
    }
}
```

For as long as these classes share the same namespace and visibility (public, protected, or internal), the compiler will combine them together into a single class. When combined with the technique of linking files shown earlier, partial classes offer another way to share parts of a codebase between Windows and Windows Phone while also accommodating for platform-specific differences.

The *CityFactBook_Partial* solution in the sample code illustrates the use of partial classes by adding yet another feature to the app, the ability to create secondary tiles for a given city. Even though Windows and Windows Phone share the concept and general aesthetic of Live tiles, the platform APIs to add and manage them are different. Consequently, the definition of the new *AddSecondaryTile* method in the *CityViewModel* class will also differ.

We begin by modifying the existing *CityViewModel* class to add the *partial* keyword, which makes it possible for it to be combined with platform-specific functionality in the other half of the partial class.

```
public partial class CityViewModel
{
    // other code unchanged...
}
```

In the phone project, we add a new file named *PhoneCityViewModel.cs*, which will include the definition of the phone-specific version of *AddSecondaryTile*. Keep in mind that for partial classes to be joined by the compiler, the following must be true:

- The fully qualified class name (namespace plus class name) must be the same as other partial definitions.
- The visibility of the class (public, protected, or internal) must be the same.
- The class definition must include the partial keyword.

```
namespace CityFactBook.ViewModel
{
    public partial class CityViewModel
    {
        public void AddSecondaryTile()
        {
            var tileData = new StandardTileData();
            tileData.Title = City.Name;
            tileData.BackgroundImage =
                new Uri("Assets/ApplicationIcon.png", UriKind.Relative);

            var navigationUri = String.Format("/CityPage.xaml?CityId={0}", City.CityId);
            ShellTile.Create(new Uri(navigationUri, UriKind.Relative), tileData);
        }
    }
}
```

Likewise, in the Windows project, we add a new file called *WindowsCityViewModel.cs*, which includes the Windows-specific definition of *AddSecondaryTile*.

```
namespace CityFactBook.ViewModel
{
    public partial class CityViewModel
    {
        public void AddSecondaryTile()
        {
            var secondaryTile =
                new SecondaryTile(City.CityId, // TileId
                                  City.Name, // ShortName
                                  City.Name, // LongName
                                  City.CityId, // Arguments
                                  TileOptions.ShowNameOnLogo, // TileOptions
                                  new Uri("ms-appx:///Assets/Logo.png")); // Logo

            secondaryTile.RequestCreateAsync();
        }
    }
}
```

Sharing native code

Developers who want to share native code between Windows and Windows Phone projects have several options. Even though Windows Runtime components cannot be directly shared between Windows and Windows Phone apps (see the sidebar that follows), you can create platform-specific Windows Runtime component projects and then link source files or share static libraries or DLLs as source code between them. Unlike with managed PCL projects, the Visual Studio editor will not guarantee compatibility, but if care is taken to ensure that only those frameworks which are supported on both platforms are used, Windows Runtime can offer a high degree of C/C++ code reuse. Encapsulating elements of your core app business logic in native code also makes it easier to share it with apps written for non-Windows platforms. You simply need to ensure that you do not take dependencies on specific platform features or that they are abstracted away by a well-defined platform abstraction layer (PAL).

Why can't Windows Runtime components be shared?

Even though the core technology behind the Windows Runtime is the same on Windows and Windows Phone, there are a number of differences that make it effectively impossible to directly share Windows Runtime components between the two platforms. First, Windows Runtime components are packaged and deployed differently on the phone than they are on Windows. Consequently, if you try to add a reference to a Windows Runtime project built to target Windows to a Windows Phone app, or vice versa, Visual Studio will display an error. The reason for this error is that Visual Studio is not only adding a reference to the Windows Runtime component to the app's project file, but is also adding the necessary configuration information to the app manifest such that the component can be registered properly when the app is installed. In the context of a phone app, Visual Studio only knows how to add the configuration for a phone-targeted component, and vice versa. Second, the C runtime libraries (CRT) and platform libraries are not exactly identical on the two platforms.

Instead, you should maintain separate projects for the Windows and Windows Phone versions of your component and then share all of the code between them. Even though it is possible to use a Windows Runtime project targeting either Windows or a Windows Phone as the basis for the code that will be shared, it is generally safer to start with a phone project because the phone's Windows Runtime surface area is mostly a subset of what you will find on Windows and it is obvious when you add a phone dependency, making it less likely to write code which will not be available across both platforms.

Note Visual Studio distinguishes the Windows Phone–specific type of Windows Runtime project by referring to it as a Windows Phone Runtime component.

To illustrate sharing native code in this way, the *CityFactBook_WindowsRuntime* solution in the sample code includes a Windows Runtime component that includes a native implementation of the *LocationHelper* class. As with the PCL project, there isn't much interesting code to show in the Windows Runtime component (which we've named *PhoneLocationHelper*). It contains one static public method, *GetDistanceFromCurrentLocationAsync*, which takes the latitude and longitude of the location to which we want to calculate the distance and returns that distance as a double. What's more interesting is how we can reuse this component within the Windows version of the app.

Note For more details on writing Windows Runtime components for Windows Phone, see Chapter 23.

We start by creating a Windows-targeted Windows Runtime component project, which we name *WindowsLocationHelper*. By default, the template for a Windows Runtime project will include four files: a header file, a source file like *Class1.h* and *Class1.cpp*, and the precompiled header and source files, *pch.h* and *pch.cpp*. Because we will be exclusively using files from our existing Windows Runtime project, we can safely delete all of these files. Also, because we aren't using any significant frameworks in our Windows Runtime component, we can turn off the use of precompiled headers in the Windows Runtime component's property pages, under Configuration Properties | C/C++ | Precompiled Headers. Then, we simply add the header and source files for the *LocationHelper* class from the *PhoneLocationHelper* project through the Add Existing Item dialog box or by dragging them between projects in Solution Explorer. In this case, when adding the files there is no option to add them as linked files because files in native projects are always linked. Figure 24-9 shows the final project structure.

Tip Sharing precompiled headers across multiple projects requires some additional configuration in your build process. One solution is to nominate one of the projects to be the "master project" and build the precompiled header file (pch.h) in that project. You must then add the directory containing the master project's pch.h file to the set of include directories for all other projects by opening the project properties and choosing Configuration Properties | C/C++ | General. Finally, you must set each project's precompiled header file to the master version of *pch.h* through Configuration Properties | C/C++ | Precompiled Headers.

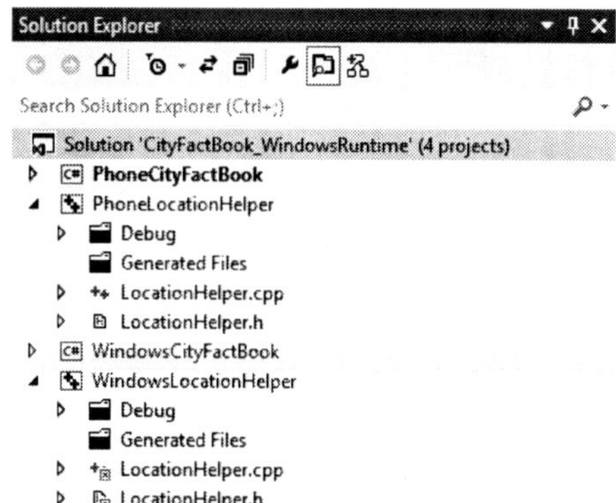

FIGURE 24-9 You can share native code across platform-specific Windows Runtime component projects.

The last step required before being able to build the Windows version of the Windows Runtime component is to align its root namespace with the one in our code. It is a requirement that Windows Runtime components expose all of their public surface area within a namespace that matches or is a subnamespace of the name of the component. By default, Visual Studio sets the root namespace to the name of the project, such as WindowsRuntimeComponent1, which will not match the namespace of the phone app. You can set the root namespace for the component in its Properties window, as shown in Figure 24-10.

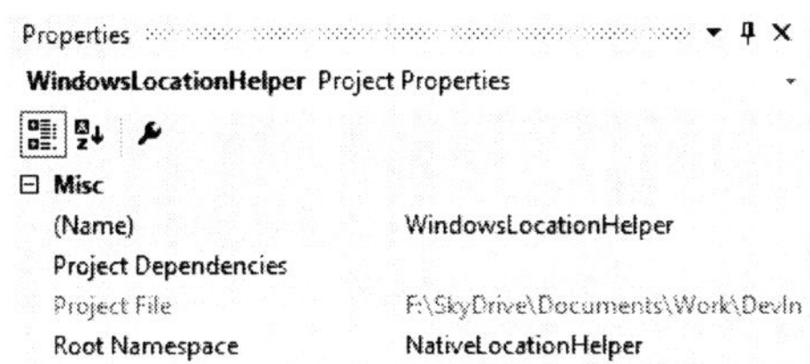

FIGURE 24-10 To share Windows Runtime component definitions, the root namespace must be the same.

Now, we can add a reference to the Windows Runtime component from our Windows app as if we had written its code from scratch.

Sharing XAML-based UI with user controls

In general, UI code is the most challenging to share between versions of an app that are targeting devices with different form factors, such as phones and computers. In most cases, you should optimize the UI for the form factor of the device that it is running so that you make the most of the screen space available. That does not mean that there aren't opportunities for code reuse, however. Although the top-level layout of a given screen will most likely be customized for the device, the individual components of the UI can often be shared.

For Windows and Windows Phone apps written primarily in XAML and C#/Visual Basic, the fundamental UI container is a page, but pages are not shareable between the two platforms because they do not share a common page class and their respective page types offer several conceptual differences. For example, the app bar on a Windows Phone page can only appear at the bottom of the screen and enforces a specific UI pattern, whereas Windows makes it possible to create an app bar at the top or bottom of the page and provides some flexibility in its UI.

One way to share UI markup and code between XAML-based apps is to create a user control. A user control encapsulates a piece of UI and its associated code-behind such that you can easily drop it into pages in both apps in ways that make sense for the form factor. For instance, you might have UI that is included on the main page in Windows but which is placed in a separate page or pop-up window on the phone due to its limited screen size.

Note You can also share UI by using custom controls. Whereas user controls facilitate wrapping a set of platform controls in a single unit, custom controls make it possible for you to extend an existing platform control with new functionality and styling.

The *CityFactBook_UserControls* solution in the sample code illustrates how you can take advantage of user controls to reuse small pieces of your UI between Windows and Windows Phone. We begin by creating four controls in the phone app project: *SectionHeaderControl*, *CitySummaryControl*, *City DescriptionControl*, and *CityNotesControl*. Then, we move the XAML defining the UI of *CityPage.xaml* from the page into the individual controls. Figure 24-11 shows how the controls are laid out on the page after the refactoring.

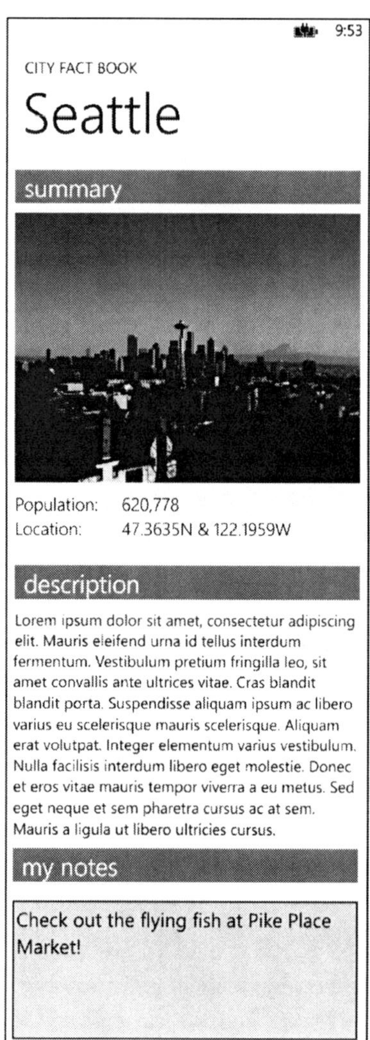

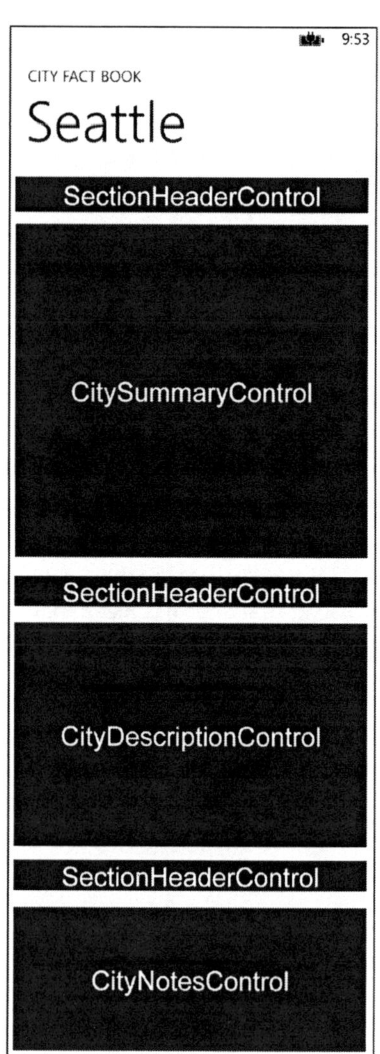

FIGURE 24-11 *UserControls* are a good way of creating small pieces of UI that are reusable across Windows and Windows Phone apps.

Dealing with built-in styles

Even though *UserControls* have fewer dependencies on the underlying platform than *Pages*, you will still see some platform-specific elements in the templates used to generate those controls in Visual Studio. For instance, if you create a phone control, you will see a number of phone-specific styles set as defaults, as highlighted in the following:

```
<UserControl x:Class="CityFactBook.Controls"
    xmlns="http://schemas.microsoft.com/winfx/2006/xaml/presentation"
    xmlns:x="http://schemas.microsoft.com/winfx/2006/xaml"
    xmlns:d="http://schemas.microsoft.com/expression/blend/2008"
    xmlns:mc="http://schemas.openxmlformats.org/markup-compatibility/2006"
    mc:Ignorable="d"
    FontFamily="{StaticResource PhoneFontFamilyNormal}"
    FontSize="{StaticResource PhoneFontSizeNormal}"
    Foreground="{StaticResource PhoneForegroundBrush}"
    d:DesignHeight="300" d:DesignWidth="480">
```

Because these styles are not defined in Windows, the control falls back to the default values for that platform, which might not be what you want. There are a few ways to handle this. If you are defining your own distinct look and feel, you can either explicitly set these values—perhaps setting the foreground color to blue—or you can create your own custom styles and reference them in your XAML. However, even apps that define most of their own look and feel will occasionally want to use some built-in styles. For instance, the text styles in Windows Phone offer a quick way to load the appropriate typeface and font size, even if you want to choose a different color. In this case, a small amount of indirection is required to set up the control for cross-platform use. Rather than using the built-in styles in the control directly, we will replace them with custom styles which we will then define in a platform-specific portion of the app and point to a built-in style.

As an example, we set the style of the *TextBlock* that shows the population and location of the city to the built-in style *PhoneTextTitle3Style*, a medium-sized, light version of the Segoe font. Rather than setting it directly, though, we will set the *TextBlock* to a style called *Text3Style*, as shown in the following.

```
<TextBlock Text="Population: " Style="{StaticResource Text3Style}" />
```

We then define *Text3Style* as a resource either on the page or at the top level of the app. Because we might want to reuse this basic style in other shared controls, we will put it in *App.xaml*, as demonstrated here:

```
<Application.Resources>
     <local:LocalizedStrings
          xmlns:local="clr-namespace:PhoneCityFactBook" x:Key="LocalizedStrings"/>
     <Style
          x:Key="Text3Style"
          TargetType="TextBlock"
          BasedOn="{StaticResource PhoneTextTitle3Style}"
          />
</Application.Resources>
```

By marking this custom style as being based on *PhoneTextTitle3Style*, it will automatically pick up all of the attributes of that style as if you had applied the built-in style directly. When we move this control to our Windows app, we define *Text3Style* there, as well.

Taking the *UserControl* cross-platform

Now that we've removed any platform-specific dependencies from our XAML markup, we can try moving our user controls to our Windows project. Again, we use the linked files to share the XAML and code-behind files for the controls defined in the phone project with the Windows project. Because we removed the phone-specific styles from the controls, their XAML definitions can now move across seamlessly. If we try to build at this point, however, we will hit a compile error because the *UserControl* base class is in a different namespace in Windows and Windows Phone. To maintain a single file across the two projects, we need to use conditional compilation for the *using* statements in the custom control's code-behind file, as shown in the following:

```
#if WINDOWS_PHONE
using System.Windows.Controls;
#elif NETFX_CORE
using Windows.UI.Xaml.Controls;
#endif
```

Note Because conditional compilation is not available in XAML, and Windows and Windows Phone use a different syntax for mapping code namespaces to XAML namespace prefixes, it is not possible to include a shared component within another shared component.

Because we have a lot more horizontal space available when targeting the full screen in Windows, we can arrange the controls differently in the Windows app than we did in the Windows Phone app. Figure 24-12 shows how the same set of controls is arranged in the Windows app. Note that the three instances of the *SectionHeaderControl* appear differently in the Windows app than they do in the Windows Phone app—the definition of the control includes dependency properties which dictate the background color and text style for the header and provide flexibility in determining how the control should appear in different circumstances.

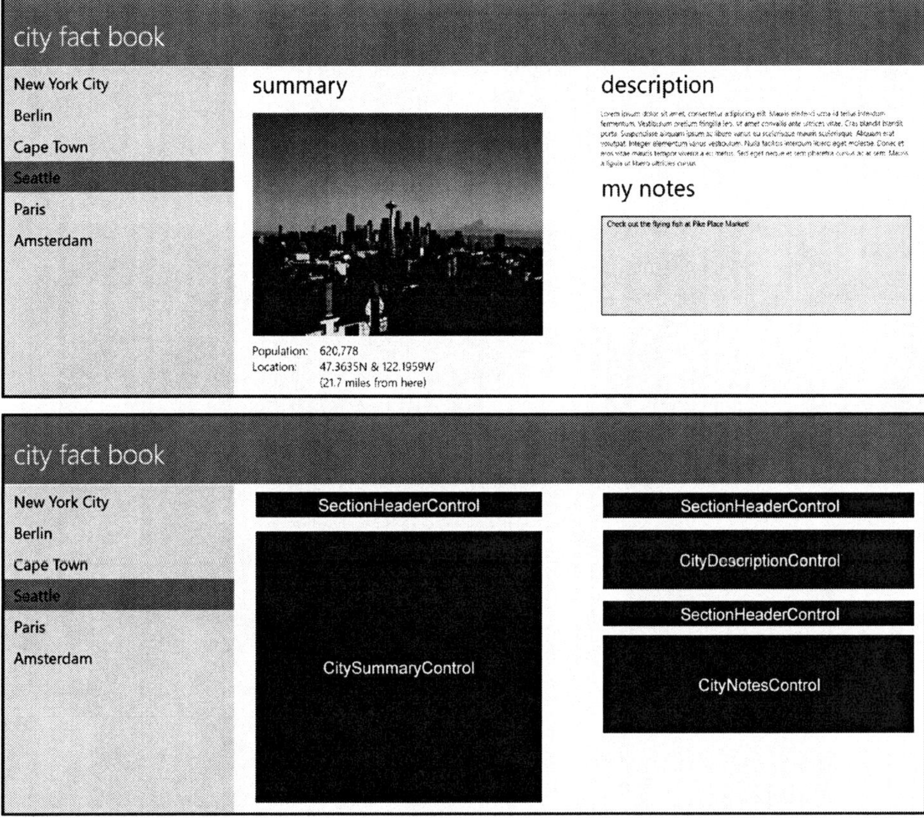

FIGURE 24-12 In Windows, you can the set of user controls to fit the full width of the screen.

Reusing phone UI in Windows snapped view

In general, you should design the user interfaces for your Windows app and your Windows Phone app without concern for how much of that UI definition you will be able to share. The two form factors are different and you will usually end up with a subpar experience on both if you attempt to design a single UI that just scales up and down, based on the screen size. However, there is one case in which you can design a very similar experience between Windows and Windows Phone: the Windows snapped view.

Windows supports showing two Windows Store apps side by side on the screen with one app receiving approximately one quarter of the horizontal screen space (320 logical pixels) and the other app receiving the rest. Because the snapped window is taller than it is wide and has a similar width to a Windows Phone portrait page, it offers a good opportunity for sharing custom user controls even if it does not make sense for your full screen view. Figure 24-13 shows the Windows version of the *CityFactBook* app in snapped view alongside the Bing Weather app.

FIGURE 24-13 Windows Store apps in snapped view can look very similar to Windows Phone apps.

Tip The Grid and Split app templates for Windows Store apps in Visual Studio illustrate how to implement snapped view by using the *VisualStateManager*. You can also find a full sample at *http://code.msdn.microsoft.com/windowsapps/Snap-Sample-2dc21ee3*.

Summary

With Windows Phone 8 and Windows 8, developers have an opportunity to target both of Microsoft's primary platforms while sharing a significant amount of code between their apps. In this chapter, you learned some of the key areas in which the platforms are alike and different, and a number of techniques for achieving maximum efficiency when targeting both platforms, including Portable Class Libraries, shared Windows Runtime components, and common user controls.

CHAPTER 25

Games and Direct3D

In this chapter, we look at the support in Microsoft Visual Studio for building games by using Direct3D. This is not a games or Direct3D tutorial; rather, it is an exploration of the different Direct3D-enabled project types that you can use and a close examination of the starter code generated for Direct3D projects. The intent is two-fold: to cover the specifics of Direct3D in the context of Windows Phone for existing game developers new to Windows Phone; and to provide a very simple overview of Direct3D development for existing Windows Phone developers. We'll look at the key classes and the component architecture as well as places where you would typically replace or enhance the starter code, and the areas where Direct3D apps for Windows Phone are different from Direct3D apps for Windows on the desktop.

Direct3D primer

The terms Direct3D and DirectX are often used interchangeably. DirectX is a collection of application programming interfaces (APIs) geared toward multimedia, especially game programming and video. Direct3D is strictly the 3D graphics API within DirectX. It is widely used in game development, especially for Windows and Xbox, and also for non-game graphics applications such as CAD/CAM engineering.

Here's a very brief introduction to the key terms and concepts in Direct3D that you'll come across in even the simplest Windows Phone Direct3D app:

- **Vertices** A vertex is another name for the corner of a geometric shape. 3D graphics are made up of many triangles (arranged in a mesh), each of which is described by three vertices (corners). Each vertex is a point in 3D space defined by using X, Y, and Z coordinates. So, the set of vertex data for an object defines its shape, size and location in space.
- **Textures** A texture is a matrix of data elements. Typically, this is used for image data, where each element in the texture stores the color of a pixel and is used to "paint" graphics on top of the simple 3D model, but a texture can also be used for storing 3D vectors instead of colors. There is a finite list of data types that can be stored in a texture, specified in the *DXGI_FORMAT* enumeration.

- **The swap chain** To provide glitch-free playback, Direct3D-based apps keep at least two screens of data (known as *frames*) at any one time. One frame represents the currently displayed screen, and the other represents a working surface where the next screen is drawn. The collection of buffers used for storing this frame data is known as a swap chain. Each time the app computes and presents a new frame for display, the first buffer in the swap chain takes the place of the displayed buffer. This buffering ensures that the app is always ready to present a new frame to the display, and that only complete frames are displayed so that the user does not see any partial frame rendering. In most cases, you only need two buffers, termed the *front buffer* (currently being displayed on the screen) and the *back buffer* (the next buffer ready to be drawn). When the image in the front buffer has been completely rendered on screen, the buffers are swapped (or rather, a pointer to the buffers is swapped) in preparation for displaying the next frame.
- **Depth buffering** A depth buffer is a texture that contains depth information about a pixel, rather than color information. The possible depth values range from 0.0 to 1.0, where 0.0 indicates the closest an object can be to the viewer, and 1.0 indicates the farthest away. There is a 1:1 mapping between the pixels in the back buffer and the depth information in the depth buffer. In the starter code, you'll see comments about a *depth stencil* buffer. Stenciling is an advanced technique that is not always used. A stencil buffer works like a stencil, making it possible for the app to block rendering of specific pixels to the back buffer. If a stencil buffer is used, it is always attached to the depth buffer.
- **Shaders** A shader is a piece of code that is used to transform an image resource, either by applying light and shade or by applying any other transformative effect. There are two primary types of shader: vertex and pixel. A *vertex shader* transforms each vertex's 3D position in virtual space to the 2D coordinate at which it appears on the screen. A *pixel shader* transforms a texture's color to apply a lighting value or special effects such as blur, sepia-tone, edge-enhancement, and so on. A shader transforms one element at a time, and there are typically a very large number of elements. Shader code is executed on the GPU which can process operations in parallel to a far greater extent than the CPU. So, using shaders for image processing provides significant throughput performance gains.
- **HLSL** Shaders are typically written in the High-Level Shader Language (HLSL). HLSL is a C-like programming language that is optimized for writing shader code. When you create a simple Direct3D native app, you'll notice that the starter project includes two HLSL files: one for a vertex shader, and the other for a pixel shader. These are compiled as part of building the project into separate compiled shader object (CSO) files, using the effect compiler (FxC.exe) tool. The app code then loads these CSO files explicitly during its initialization phase. Direct3D for the phone does not support runtime compilation of shader code.
- **Rendering pipeline** Direct3D is designed for 3D graphics, but of course the image that the user ultimately sees on the screen is a 2D image. The rendering pipeline is made up of multiple stages, each stage transforms the image data in a particular way, and the final output renders 3D geometry into a 2D image. Figure 25-1 presents a high-level view of the rendering pipeline. The input-assembler stage supplies vertex data to the pipeline. The vertex-shader stage

processes vertices, typically performing operations such as transformations, skinning, and lighting. The rasterizer prepares primitives for the pixel shader and determines how to invoke pixel shaders. The pixel-shader stage receives interpolated data for a primitive and generates per-pixel data such as color. The output-merger stage combines pixel-shader values with the contents of the render target and depth/stencil buffers to generate the final pipeline result.

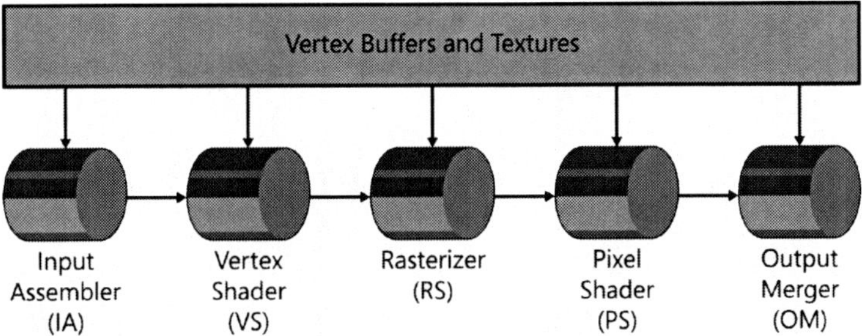

FIGURE 25-1 Each stage in the rendering pipeline transforms the image.

- **Texture resource views** A texture can be bound to different stages in the rendering pipeline. For example, the same texture can be used both as a render target (where the app writes to the texture) and as a shader resource (where the app samples the texture in a shader operation). You don't directly bind a resource to a pipeline stage. What you actually do is to create a resource view and bind that, instead.

- **Viewport** Typically, the viewport maps to the entire back buffer. That is, you usually want to draw to the entire screen. It is possible, however, to set a viewport that is either larger or smaller than the target screen. For example, you might want to set up two viewports that each take up half the screen so that you can provide two different views into your game. Or, you might set a viewport that is larger than the screen, giving the user the option to zoom in and out.

Direct3D differences on Windows Phone

In Chapter 24, "Windows 8 convergence," we discuss how Windows on the desktop and Windows Phone are converging and now share a common kernel. The area where Windows Phone comes closest to full alignment with Windows 8 is in Direct3D, but there are still a few areas of significant divergence that are worth mentioning:

- **Direct2D** Direct2D is a library built on top of Direct3D and intended for performing immediate rendering of two-dimensional shapes, images, and text. It is not supported on Windows Phone. You can use the DirectX Toolkit for 2D drawing (see the section "Direct2D and DirectXTK" later in this chapter).

- **Windows Imaging Component** Windows 8 provides the Windows Imaging Component (WIC) to assist developers in loading textures from standard formats such as PNG, BMP, and JPEG into their apps or games. WIC is not supported on Windows Phone, so developers will need to load DirectDraw Surface (DDS) files, instead. You can use the DirectXTex texture processing library for reading and writing DDS files and performing various processing operations on texture content. This is a shared-source library, available on CodePlex.
- **DirectWrite** DirectWrite helps developers with text rendering and layout, including the ability to easily adjust its typeface, size, weight, and justification. It is not supported in Windows Phone 8.
- **Input** Windows Phone doesn't support a gamepad or hardware keyboard input for games. You handle the *PointerPressed*, *PointerMoved* and *PointerReleased* events for touch on the phone. You can create a custom text box control that will cause the On-Screen Keyboard to appear, either by using the *KeyboardInputBuffer* class (which provides a buffer that contains the current text) or by using key events (where you must manage your own text buffer).

These gaps are addressed in two ways. First, via the aforementioned open-source DirectXTK and DirectXTex libraries for building pure-native Direct3D apps. Second, via the hybrid XAML-plus-DirectX model, wherein text and text input, for example, are covered by the XAML side of the hybrid.

Visual Studio project types

In Windows Phone 7, if you want to build a game, you typically choose to build it with XNA. In Windows Phone 8, even though XNA is still supported, it is no longer the recommended strategic approach to building games, and you cannot create a new Windows Phone 8 XNA project in Visual Studio 2012. Instead, Windows Phone 8 introduces extensive support for Direct3D. There are three app solution types for building Direct3D games (plus a number of other project types for building shared libraries, resources and the like), as described in Table 25-1.

TABLE 25-1 The three project types for building Direct3D games on Windows Phone

Visual Studio project node	Project type	Description
C# or Visual Basic	Windows Phone XAML and Direct3D	The solution includes a managed app and a native C++ Windows Runtime component. The *MainPage* XAML declares a *DrawingSurface* element within a *Grid*.
C++	Windows Phone Direct3D with XAML	The solution includes a managed app and a native C++ Windows Runtime component. The *MainPage* XAML declares a *DrawingSurfaceBackgroundGrid* as its root element.
C++	Windows Phone Direct3D App (Native Only)	A pure-native C++ Windows Runtime solution.

The first two solutions listed in Table 25-1 are essentially the same. In both cases, there are two projects: a managed app project, and a Windows Runtime native component project. At a high level, one significant difference is whether or not the Direct3D element is a child of some other XAML element (*DrawingSurface*) or the root XAML element itself (*DrawingSurfaceBackgroundGrid*). As it happens, Visual Studio offers these project types from different language nodes. You can get a *DrawingSurface*-based app if you choose either C# or Microsoft Visual Basic, and in both cases the Windows Runtime component will be defined in C++. However, if you want a *DrawingSurfaceBackgroundGrid*-based app, you must choose C++, and the XAML app will be C# (no Visual Basic option). There's nothing to stop you from creating a Visual Basic XAML app that uses *DrawingSurfaceBackgroundGrid*, but you'll have to do a little work to replicate what the Visual Studio template does for the equivalent C# project.

The third solution in the list is a pure-native C++ solution, containing just the one project. In all three cases, the Direct3D component renders a spinning cube, and the C++ code for this is identical across the three solution types. This is an important point because it means that the exact same native Direct3D code can be used in three different app hosting contexts. You would choose the XAML-based solution types if you want the ease of development for standardized user interface (UI) components such as *TextBox, Button, LongListSelector*, and the like, or for platform features such as Live tiles and the use of Launchers and Choosers. For example, perhaps your app presents a menu page (XAML), from which the user can navigate to a game page (XAML with Direct3D), and then to a leaderboard page (XAML again). On the other hand, you would choose a pure-native solution if you have less need of standardized UI elements, if you're focused on maximizing performance or you want to maximize code sharing with desktop Windows. It's worth emphasizing at this point that a pure-native approach is very much a bare-bones approach by which you are expected to provide the vast majority of the functionality in your own code. A pure-native solution doesn't take the size/performance hit of loading the Common Language Runtime (CLR). In either approach, of course, your Direct3D component can make use of any native libraries you might already have (so long as they only call supported APIs). This is especially useful if you're porting a native game from another platform, or if you're using native middleware libraries.

Direct3D and XAML projects

We'll look at the Direct3D specifics of all three solution types in the following sections. First though, a brief note on how you could use the two "hybrid" solution types. The advantage of using the *DrawingSurface* element is that it can slot in to your XAML as a child of any other element. This is useful if you want a Direct3D-rendered element within a "normal" XAML page, as illustrated in Figure 25-2 (left). The XAML for this is shown in the code example that follows, in which the *DrawingSurface* is a child of the usual *Grid* that you get in a standard Windows Phone app project. The full page XAML is shown here to emphasize how the *DrawingSurface* element simply lives in the tree like any other XAML element. This means that you can also perform standard operations on it, such as transforms, visibility and opacity, and so on.

```
<Grid x:Name="LayoutRoot" Background="Transparent">
    <Grid.RowDefinitions>
        <RowDefinition Height="Auto"/>
        <RowDefinition Height="*"/>
    </Grid.RowDefinitions>

    <StackPanel x:Name="TitlePanel" Grid.Row="0" Margin="12,17,0,28">
        <TextBlock Text="XAML + DRAWINGSURFACE" Style="{StaticResource PhoneTextNormalStyle}"
Margin="12,0"/>
        <TextBlock Text="main page" Margin="9,-7,0,0" Style="{StaticResource
PhoneTextTitle1Style}"/>
    </StackPanel>

    <Grid x:Name="ContentPanel" Grid.Row="1" Margin="12,0,12,0">
        <Grid.RowDefinitions>
            <RowDefinition Height="Auto"/>
            <RowDefinition Height="*"/>
            <RowDefinition Height="Auto"/>
        </Grid.RowDefinitions>
        <Grid.ColumnDefinitions>
            <ColumnDefinition Width="160"/>
            <ColumnDefinition Width="290"/>
        </Grid.ColumnDefinitions>
        <TextBlock
            Grid.Row="0" Grid.ColumnSpan="2" Margin="{StaticResource PhoneHorizontalMargin}"
            TextWrapping="Wrap" FontSize="{StaticResource PhoneFontSizeMedium}"
            Text="Lorem ipsum dolor sit amet, consectetur adipisicing elit, sed do eiusmod
                  tempor incididunt ut labore et dolore magna aliqua. Quis nostrud exercitation
                  ullamco laboris nisi ut aliquip ex ea commodo consequat."/>
        <TextBlock
            Grid.Row="1" Grid.Column="0" FontSize="{StaticResource PhoneFontSizeLarge}"
            Margin="{StaticResource PhoneHorizontalMargin}"
            VerticalAlignment="Center" TextWrapping="Wrap" Text="Ut enim ad minim veniam"/>
        <DrawingSurface Grid.Row="1" Grid.Column="1" x:Name="DrawingSurface"
            Loaded="DrawingSurface_Loaded" />
        <TextBlock
            Grid.Row="2" Grid.ColumnSpan="2" Margin="{StaticResource PhoneHorizontalMargin}"
            TextWrapping="Wrap" FontSize="{StaticResource PhoneFontSizeMedium}"
            Text="Duis aute irure dolor in reprehenderit in voluptate velit esse cillum dolore eu
                  fugiat nulla pariatur. Excepteur sint occaecat cupidatat non proident, sunt in
culpa
                  qui officia deserunt mollit anim id est laborum."/>
    </Grid>
</Grid>
```

Conversely, the *DrawingSurfaceBackgroundGrid* must be the root element of your XAML page. This is useful for the case in which you want to use other XAML elements layered on top of your background, as illustrated in Figure 25-2 (right). This example shows a grid of *TextBox* controls for reporting game attributes such as score, fuel, speed, and so on. The XAML for this is presented here:

```
<phone:PhoneApplicationPage
...>
    <DrawingSurfaceBackgroundGrid x:Name="DrawingSurfaceBackground"
       Loaded="DrawingSurfaceBackground_Loaded">
        <Grid Margin="0,650,0,0">
            <Grid.RowDefinitions>
                <RowDefinition Height="Auto"/>
                <RowDefinition Height="Auto"/>
            </Grid.RowDefinitions>
            <Grid.ColumnDefinitions>
                <ColumnDefinition Width="*"/>
                <ColumnDefinition Width="*"/>
                <ColumnDefinition Width="*"/>
            </Grid.ColumnDefinitions>
            <TextBlock Grid.Row="0" Grid.Column="0" Text="score"/>
            <TextBlock Grid.Row="0" Grid.Column="1" Text="fuel"/>
            <TextBlock Grid.Row="0" Grid.Column="2" Text="speed"/>
            <TextBlock Grid.Row="1" Grid.Column="0" Text="22,345"/>
            <TextBlock Grid.Row="1" Grid.Column="1" Text="0.4%"/>
            <TextBlock Grid.Row="1" Grid.Column="2" Text="68 mph"/>
        </Grid>
    </DrawingSurfaceBackgroundGrid>
</phone:PhoneApplicationPage>
```

FIGURE 25-2 A *DrawingSurface* element can be a child of any page element, whereas a *DrawingSurfaceBackgroundGrid* must be the root element.

Structure of the basic Direct3D app

Direct3D apps on Windows Phone use the Windows Runtime, just as Windows Phone Store apps use the Windows Runtime. Before we examine the detailed starter code for a native Direct3D app, we should step back a bit and look at the general architecture involved as well as some of the key classes. At a high level, there are two main phases in a game app:

- **Initialization** In this phase, you set up run-time and library components that your game uses, load game-specific resources such as shaders and audio files, and initialize the various buffers required for the rendering pipeline. As always, your app must render its first screen within 5 seconds of startup and be responsive to user input within 20 seconds. So, you must be careful to load only essential resources on startup, load resources asynchronously (especially if they're large), and defer loading of non-essential resources until they're actually required.
- **The game loop** After initialization, the rest of your app runs within a loop. In this loop, you update the position and appearance of any game artifacts (objects in the scene, and the scene itself), render the scene and present it to the display. It is useful to separate the game logic (update) from the display rendering code. At the same time, you respond to events, especially user input events.

The *CoreApplication* and *CoreWindow* classes

The two most important classes in the Windows Runtime are *CoreApplication* and *CoreWindow*. You don't directly instantiate either of these; instead, the runtime provides an instance of both classes for you. The app starts with the standard C/C++ *main* entry point:

```
[Platform::MTAThread]
int main(Platform::Array<Platform::String^>^)
{
    auto direct3DApplicationSource = ref new Direct3DApplicationSource();
    CoreApplication::Run(direct3DApplicationSource);
    return 0;
}
```

In *main*, the app invokes *CoreApplication::Run*, which internally creates the *CoreApplication* singleton object. This object represents the app to the Windows Runtime, for process lifetime management and window views and events. Shortly after this, the runtime calls *IFrameworkView::SetWindow*, which is your app's first opportunity to work with the *CoreWindow* object that the runtime has created. In the starter code, the class that implements *SetWindow* obtains this *CoreWindow* object via *CoreWindow::GetForCurrentThread* and hands it off to another class, which caches it as a class member variable, inside its *Initialize* method.

```
void PhoneDirect3DApp1::SetWindow(CoreWindow^ window)
{
...
    m_renderer->Initialize(CoreWindow::GetForCurrentThread());
}
```

After creating the *CoreApplication* and *CoreWindow* objects, the runtime calls into your app's implementation of *IFrameworkView::Run*. This method implements your main game loop in which you update and render your scene and process incoming Windows events. The method calls *CoreDispatcher::ProcessEvents* to check the message queue for events and dispatch them to the event handlers defined in the app. Your *CoreWindow* object includes a *Dispatcher* member of type *CoreDispatcher*. Each time you call *ProcessEvents*, this invokes the callbacks for the specific event message types in the queue.

```
void PhoneDirect3DApp1::Run()
{
    BasicTimer^ timer = ref new BasicTimer();
    while (!m_windowClosed)
    {
        if (m_windowVisible)
        {
            timer->Update();
            CoreWindow::GetForCurrentThread()->Dispatcher->ProcessEvents(
                CoreProcessEventsOption::ProcessAllIfPresent);
            m_renderer->Update(timer->Total, timer->Delta);
            m_renderer->Render();
            m_renderer->Present();
        }
        else
        {
            CoreWindow::GetForCurrentThread()->Dispatcher->ProcessEvents(
                CoreProcessEventsOption::ProcessOneAndAllPending);
        }
    }
}
```

Notice that the loop does nothing if the window is not visible. The *m_windowVisible* member variable is set in the *PhoneDirect3DApp1::OnVisibilityChanged* event handler. There's obviously no point doing any work to update and render your scene if the user can't see it.

Starter code classes

When you create a Windows Phone Direct3D App (Native Only) project, you get a set of header files, C++ class implementation files, and HLSL files, as described in Table 25-2.

TABLE 25-2 The files generated for a Windows Phone Direct3D native C++ app

File	Classes/interfaces	Description
BasicTimer.h	*BasicTimer* class	A simple helper class for tracking elapsed time in the game. After each update, it computes the total time in seconds from the start of the game, and the elapsed time in seconds since the last frame.
CubeRender.h/.cpp	*CubeRenderer* class	A class derived from *Direct3DBase*. The *CubeRenderer* class is for illustration purposes: it renders a simple spinning cube. You should replace this class with your own app-specific rendering class.
Direct3DBase.h/.cpp	*Direct3DBase* class	A helper class that initializes DirectX APIs for 3D rendering. You would typically derive a class from *Direct3DBase* with your custom rendering behavior.
DirectXHelper.h	Global methods *ThrowIfFailed* and *ReadDataAsync*	*ThrowIfFailed* converts failed *HRESULTs* into *Exception* objects. *ReadDataAsync* reads binary data from a file asynchronously. In the starter code, this is used to read the compiled shaders.
pch.h/.cpp	n/a	The standard C++ precompiled header files, used to support incremental building, where any standard (and therefore, unchanging) headers you include are only compiled the first time you build.
<ProjectName>.h/.cpp	*<ProjectName>* class; for example, *PhoneDirect3DApp1* and *Direct3DApplicationSource*	These contain your app's primary application functionality, including the main entrypoint and the required implementations of *IFrameworkView* and *IFrameworkViewSource* that are required for an app that uses the Windows Runtime.
SimplePixelShader.hlsl and *SimpleVertexShader.hlsl*	Shaders	These are extremely simple shaders, and you would typically replace them with more complex behavior. The vertex shader simply multiplies the vertices by the Model, View, and Projection matrices and then hands off the new position and color to the pixel shader. The pixel shader simply outputs the supplied colors. HLSL source files are compiled into CSO files, which the app then loads explicitly at runtime.

Here's how the starter code classes fit together. The *Direct3DApplicationSource* class implements the standard *IFrameworkViewSource* interface. When it starts, the app first instantiates a *Direct3DApplicationSource* object and hands this off to the static *CoreApplication::Run* method in the Windows Runtime. This creates a new thread for the app's main view and then invokes *IFrameworkViewSource::CreateView* on that new thread. The implementation of this method in the starter code instantiates and returns a *PhoneDirect3DApp1* object (where *PhoneDirect3DApp1* is the name you chose for your project). If you examine the code, you'll see that *Direct3DApplicationSource* is a tiny class whose only purpose is to instantiate a *PhoneDirect3DApp1*. The *PhoneDirect3DApp1* class implements *IFrameworkView*. Shortly thereafter, the runtime invokes two important callback methods: *IFrameworkView::Initialize* and *IFrameworkView::SetWindow*.

In its implementation of *Initialize*, the *PhoneDirect3DApp1* object subscribes to the three standard lifetime events for a Windows Runtime app: *Activated, Suspended*, and *Resuming*. As you might guess, you get an *Activated* event when the app is started afresh; *Suspended* when the app is moving to the background, and *Resuming* when the app is coming back from the suspended state to the foreground. The object also creates a *CubeRenderer* instance and caches a reference to this as a member variable (*m_renderer*). The runtime calls *SetWindow* when it has created a window (including a standard Windows message pump) for the app. In its implementation of *SetWindow*, the *PhoneDirect3DApp1* object subscribes to interesting window events including *VisibilityChanged* and *Closed*. This is also where you subscribe to input events such as *PointerPressed*, *PointerMoved*, and *PointerReleased*. Finally, *SetWindow* invokes the *CubeRenderer::Initialize* method. Figure 25-3 shows the key classes.

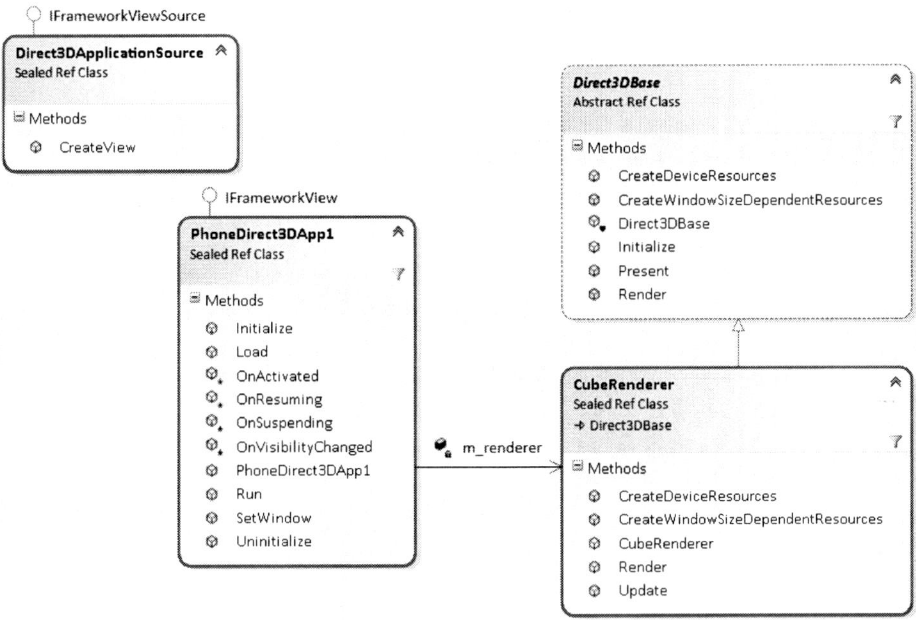

FIGURE 25-3 The key classes in a native Direct3D app.

The sequence diagram in Figure 25-4 provides more detail on the call sequence for activating a native Direct3D app and rendering the scene. This diagram somewhat simplifies the internal behavior of the Windows Runtime and uses the *CoreApplication* object to represent the runtime generally. You can think of this as two main logical phases: setup and run. All the work to connect *CoreApplication*, *CoreWindow*, and an *IFrameworkView* implementation is required for basic setup. As part of setup, you have the opportunity during the *IFrameworkView::Initialize* call to load your Direct3D resources. In the starter project, this is divided into *CreateDeviceResources* for the resources that depend on the device (such as the supported DirectX hardware feature level), and *CreateWindowSizeDependent Resources* for the resources that depend on the window size. These two methods first perform the required initialization of Direct3D and then carry out further setup for the app-specific display behavior (the spinning cube, in this case).

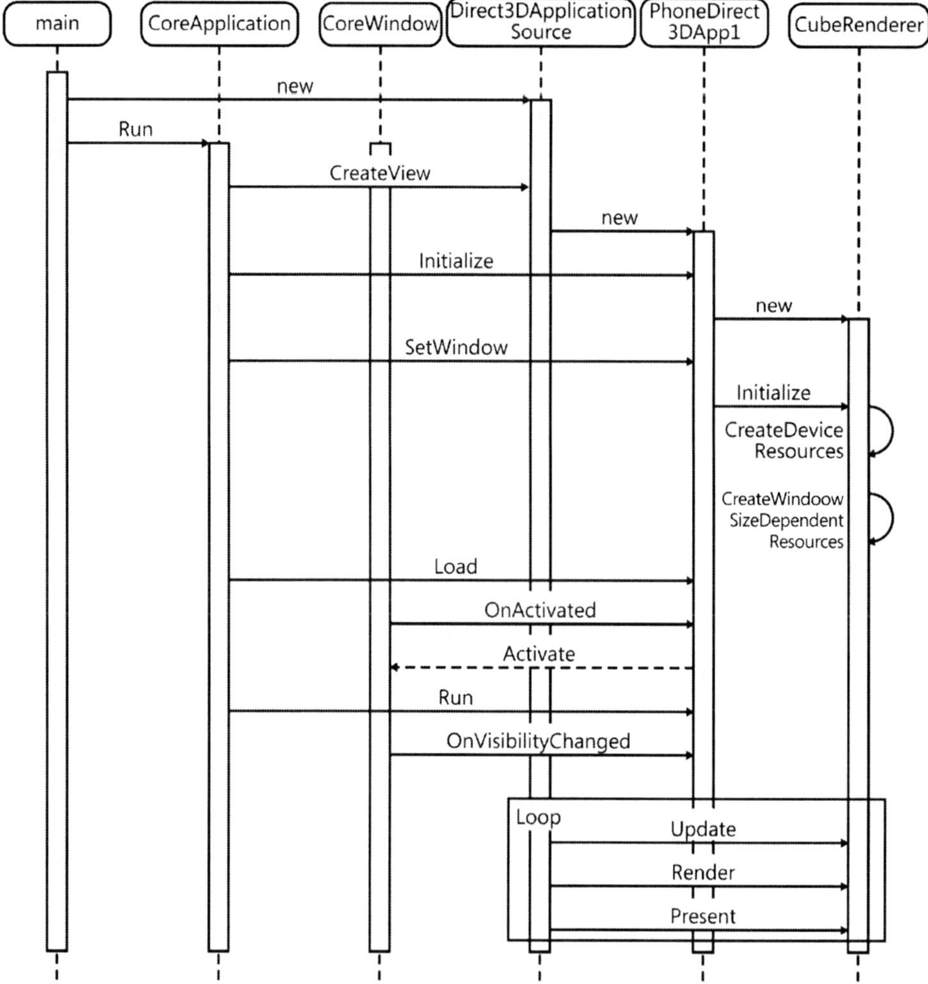

FIGURE 25-4 The call sequence for activating and rendering a native Direct3D app.

After this setup is done, the runtime calls *IFrameworkView::Run*; this is where there's a thread context switch and your app-specific work executes. At this point, your app cycles between the *Update*, *Render*, and *Present* methods to display on the screen. The *Update* method creates the model and view matrices; the *Render* method applies the shaders and renders the scene (the spinning cube, in this case); and the *Present* method delivers the final image to the display. You would also typically add code to the *OnPointerPressed, OnPointerMoved*, and *OnPointerReleased* event handlers so that you can process user input.

Initializing Direct3D

The critical work in initializing Direct3D is done in the custom *CreateDeviceResources* and *Create WindowSizeDependentResources* methods in the *Direct3DBase* class. These are the key steps:

1. Create the objects that implement *ID3D11Device* and *ID3D11DeviceContext* by using *D3D11CreateDevice*—these are the primary objects for interacting with the screen.
2. Configure and create the swap chain by using *IDXGIFactory2::CreateSwapChainForCoreWindow*. Create a render target view to the swap chain's back buffer by using *ID3D11Device::Create RenderTargetView*.
3. Create the depth buffer and configure its associated depth view to bind to the output-merger stage of the rendering pipeline by creating a *CD3D11_TEXTURE2D_DESC* object and specifying *D3D11_BIND_DEPTH_STENCIL* in the binding flags. Create the depth view by using *ID3D1 1Device::CreateDepthStencilView*.
4. Create a viewport (a *CD3D11_VIEWPORT* object) for the entire screen and bind this viewport to the rasterizer stage of the pipeline by using *ID3D11DeviceContext::RSSetViewports*.

The preceding steps are required for almost all Direct3D apps, and this is why Visual Studio generates this functionality in the *Direct3DBase* class. In most cases, you don't need to touch this code. The *CubeRenderer* class derives from *Direct3DBase* and performs additional initialization. Although the *CubeRenderer* in the *Direct3D* native project is the same as the *CubeRenderer* in the two XAML-based Direct3D apps, the *Direct3DBase* class is different. The key difference is that the low-level behavior for manipulating the device and creating the swap chain is done as part of the XAML framework. The implementation is specific to the spinning cube, but the general pattern is common to other scenarios. So, even though you'll likely replace the *CubeRenderer* class, you might well use many of the techniques:

1. Load the compiled shaders (in this case, a vertex shader and a pixel shader). Create in-memory objects for the vertex and pixel shaders by using *ID3D11Device::CreateVertexShader* and *ID3D 11Device::CreatePixelShader*.
2. Define vertex and index buffers for the various stages in the rendering pipeline—including the vertices for the cube—by using *ID3D11Device::CreateBuffer*. Each buffer stores the data plus a description of how the data should be used via a *CD3D11_BUFFER_DESC* object.
3. Create an input-layout object to describe the input buffer data for the input-assembler stage of the rendering pipeline by using *ID3D11Device::CreateInputLayout*. This tells the pipeline how to interpret the vertex data.

A brief word about the Component Object Model

DirectX is based on the Component Object Model (COM), which is a model for component reuse. A detailed discussion is beyond the scope of this book, but it is useful to have a basic understanding of a few key elements, as follows:

- **Interfaces** COM specifies that COM object writers publish and document an interface: a description of a set of functions, their parameter types, and return type. No internal implementation details of the functions are published. Therefore, clients rely only on the interface; they do not rely on any implementation details. All COM interfaces, and all classes that implement COM interfaces and are directly createable, have an associated Globally Unique Identifier (GUID). An object can implement multiple interfaces, and there are various coding techniques for switching from one interface to another on the same object.

- **Reference Counting** An object that implements a COM interface is reference-counted; that is, it keeps a count of the number of consumers that have a pointer to the object. The object stays in memory so long as the reference count is non-zero. The .NET notion of reference types—which are not available for garbage collection until there are no remaining consumers holding a reference to the object—is clearly an evolution of this concept. To ensure that an object is correctly reference-counted, you don't use *new* to instantiate a COM object; instead, you create a COM object by calling some well-known global method or a method on another COM interface.

- **HRESULTs** COM interface methods typically return *HRESULT* values; any other results from the method are returned in *out* parameters. An *HRESULT* is an integer, where a zero or positive value indicates success, and any negative value is failure.

- **Apartments** The *[Platform::MTAThread]* attribute on *main* deserves a little explanation. In COM, the threading architecture divides objects contained in a process into logical groups called apartments. An apartment is a logical boundary that contains COM object instances and one or more threads. Only those threads can have direct access to the objects in the apartment. Threads in different apartments must access the objects through marshaling.

  A single-threaded apartment (STA) has only one thread that creates and calls objects. Because there is only one thread that can access those objects in the apartment, the objects are effectively synchronized. A multithreaded apartment (MTA) makes it possible for multiple threads to reside in one apartment. MTAs provide the highest performance. In the MTA model, any thread can call an object concurrently—and the corollary, of course, is that objects written for an MTA must be thread-safe. In fact, this is how non-UI objects in .NET and plain old C++ behave: they are designed to be called on any thread at any time, and the object itself must implement a synchronization mechanism (or explicitly forbid cross-thread access).

The app's *CoreApplication* object uses a new threading model called Application Single-Threaded Apartment (ASTA) to host your app's UI views. This ASTA is like a traditional STA with a couple of differences. First, you cannot create an ASTA directly; the *CoreApplication* object creates it for you, specifically to host UI views and the UI thread. Second, the ASTA is non–re-entrant, so arbitrary calls must be dispatched by using *CoreDispatcher::ProcessEvents*. To be able to dispatch MTA thread events in this way, you must set the *[Platform::MTAThread]* attribute on *main*.

Consider the code in *Direct3DBase::CreateWindowSizeDependentResources* to create a swap chain (see the snippet that follows). The first thing to notice is the *ComPtr<T>* declaration. This creates a smart pointer type that represents the interface specified by the template parameter (in this example, *IDXGIFactory2*). The *ComPtr<T>* automatically maintains a reference count for the underlying interface pointer and releases the interface when the reference count goes to zero. We eventually want to call *IDXGIFactory2::CreateSwapChainForCoreWindow*, so we need to get an object that implements the COM interface *IDXGIFactory2*. Instead of using *new*, we get this object by calling *IDXGIAdapter::GetParent*. Notice that we wrap this call in the *ThrowIfFailed* method, which examines the *HRESULT* return, and if this is a failure, it converts it into an *Exception* and throws it. Also, the *GetParent* method is defined to take a GUID parameter, and the *__uuidof* keyword takes a COM interface and returns its corresponding GUID.

```
ComPtr<IDXGIDevice1> dxgiDevice;
DX::ThrowIfFailed(
    m_d3dDevice.As(&dxgiDevice)
    );

ComPtr<IDXGIAdapter> dxgiAdapter;
DX::ThrowIfFailed(
    dxgiDevice->GetAdapter(&dxgiAdapter)
    );

ComPtr<IDXGIFactory2> dxgiFactory;
DX::ThrowIfFailed(
    dxgiAdapter->GetParent(
        __uuidof(IDXGIFactory2),
        &dxgiFactory
        )
    );

Windows::UI::Core::CoreWindow^ window = m_window.Get();
DX::ThrowIfFailed(
    dxgiFactory->CreateSwapChainForCoreWindow(
        m_d3dDevice.Get(),
        reinterpret_cast<IUnknown*>(window),
        &swapChainDesc,
        nullptr,
        &m_swapChain
        )
    );
```

Having created the object that implements *IDXGIFactory2*, we can go ahead and call *CreateSwapChainForCoreWindow*. The definition of this method is shown in the snippet that follows. You can see that four of the five parameters are COM interfaces. The first parameter is a pointer to the Direct3D device for the swap chain. The second is a pointer to the *CoreWindow* object that is associated with the swap chain. In the preceding snippet, you can see that we get the *CoreWindow* as a strongly typed object. Windows Runtime reference types are instantiated only via reference-counted pointers, specified by using the caret (^) character (also called the hat symbol). The compiler interprets this to instruct the Windows Runtime to modify the reference count of an object when it is instantiated, copied, set to null, or goes out of scope. When the reference count becomes zero, the object's destructor is invoked. Again, you can see that this notion is an evolution of COM reference counting. For more details on the new syntax, and on modern C++, see Chapter 23, "Native development."

Having declared the *CoreWindow* object as strongly typed, we must then cast it to an *IUnknown** when passing it to *CreateSwapChainForCoreWindow*—this is the most basic of all COM interfaces. All COM interfaces derive from *IUnknown*, which means that all COM objects implement *IUnknown*, so any COM object can be cast to *IUnknown**. Finally, because COM interface methods return an *HRESULT*, the swap chain we're creating is returned in an *IDXGISwapChain* out* parameter.

```
HRESULT CreateSwapChainForCoreWindow(
  [in]    IUnknown *pDevice,
  [in]    IUnknown *pWindow,
  [in]    const DXGI_SWAP_CHAIN_DESC1 *pDesc,
  [in]    IDXGIOutput *pRestrictToOutput,
  [out]   IDXGISwapChain1 **ppSwapChain
);
```

Also notice how we create and cache the device object and how we can later use it for different purposes. Consider the *Direct3DBase::CreateDeviceResources* method, in which we call *D3D11CreateDevice* to create the primary device object. The device parameter is typed as an *ID3D11Device**, and we cache the returned pointer in the *m_d3dDevice* class variable, which is typed as *ID3D11Device1* (or, strictly, as a *ComPtr<ID3D11Device1>*. This works because *ID3D11Device1* derives from *ID3D11Device*, and the device object therefore implements both interfaces. We use *ComPtr<T>::As* to treat the object as an *ID3D11Device1* pointer.

```
ComPtr<ID3D11Device> device;
ComPtr<ID3D11DeviceContext> context;
DX::ThrowIfFailed(
    D3D11CreateDevice(
        nullptr, // Specify nullptr to use the default adapter.
        D3D_DRIVER_TYPE_HARDWARE,
        nullptr,
        creationFlags, // Set set debug and Direct2D compatibility flags.
        featureLevels, // List of feature levels this app can support.
        ARRAYSIZE(featureLevels),
        D3D11_SDK_VERSION, // Always set this to D3D11_SDK_VERSION.
        &device, // Returns the Direct3D device created.
        &m_featureLevel, // Returns feature level of device created.
        &context // Returns the device immediate context.
        )
    );
```

```
DX::ThrowIfFailed(
    device.As(&m_d3dDevice)
    );
```

Later on, however, in *Direct3DBase::CreateWindowSizeDependentResources*, as you've already seen, we use *ComPtr<T>::As* again, this time to treat the cached *ID3D11Device1* pointer as an *IDXGIDevice1* pointer. Now, there is no relationship between *ID3D11Device1* and *IDXGIDevice1*, but remember that our cached *ID3D11Device1* pointer actually refers to a device object, and this device object does in fact implement both interfaces. The *As* method is effectively doing a COM *QueryInterface* call behind the scenes to use one interface implemented by the object to obtain another interface implemented by the same object.

```
ComPtr<IDXGIDevice1> dxgiDevice;
DX::ThrowIfFailed(
    m_d3dDevice.As(&dxgiDevice)
    );
```

Note The D3D11 prefixes in the APIs indicate Direct3D level 11. The DXGI prefix indicates the DirectX Graphics Infrastructure (DXGI) API set. This is a separate set of APIs from Direct3D that provides support for swap chains, enumerating graphics hardware, enumerating display modes (for desktop Windows), and so on. The DXGI APIs are used in both Direct3D and Direct2D scenarios.

DirectX hardware feature levels

On desktop computers, there is a wide variety of supported video cards and multiple, different GPUs. Different computers can support different sets of Direct3D functionality. Direct3D version 11 introduced the concept of *feature levels*. A feature level is a well-defined set of GPU functionality. On the desktop platform, you can develop an app for Direct3D 9, Direct3D 10, or Direct3D 11 and then run it on 9, 10, or 11 hardware; your app can dynamically detect the supported feature level and tailor its functionality accordingly. On Windows Phone 8, all devices have GPUs that support feature level 9.3. Because there's no variability, there's no need to dynamically detect the level support, but you still need to set the target level in your code.

Note that the emulator uses a software rasterizer for DirectX. The Windows Advanced Rasterization Platform (WARP) is capable of Direct3D levels up to 11. One of the strengths of the Windows Phone 8 platform is that there is significant convergence with the Windows (desktop computer) Runtime. This means that you can share code across both platforms, including, obviously, the code generated by Visual Studio for a native Direct3D app. Although this is all generally a good thing, there's a slight catch in the case of Direct3D feature levels. The code in *Direct3DBase::CreateDeviceResources* sets up an array of feature levels and dynamically discovers the supported level on the current device (by walking down through the array until it finds the first level supported on the device). This is just what you want for a Windows app, but not quite what you want for a Windows

Phone app. This is because the app will use level 11 on the emulator, which will be a problem if you inadvertently introduce level 11 features in your app—these will work on the emulator but not on a real phone device. To eliminate this risk, simply reduce the array to the one supported level. That is, change this

```
D3D_FEATURE_LEVEL featureLevels[] =
{
    D3D_FEATURE_LEVEL_11_1,
    D3D_FEATURE_LEVEL_11_0,
    D3D_FEATURE_LEVEL_10_1,
    D3D_FEATURE_LEVEL_10_0,
    D3D_FEATURE_LEVEL_9_3
};
```

to this:

```
D3D_FEATURE_LEVEL featureLevels[] =
{
    D3D_FEATURE_LEVEL_9_3
};
```

Update and render

The *Update* method is where your game logic happens: this is where you update the visual objects, their shape, size, and positions, as well as the overall game scene for each frame you're going to render. In the starter app, the *CubeRenderer::Update* method simply recaculates the cube vertices and uses *XMMatrixRotationY* to rotate the cube about its Y axis. In a more sophisticated game, this is where you'd also handle things like collisions, explosions, and so on.

To update these objects, the app updates the *m_constantBufferData* member. This is a custom *ModelViewProjectionConstantBuffer* type defined in *CubeRenderer.h*. The model, view, and projection are three separate matrices. The model maps from an object's local coordinate space (essentially, the object's own geometry) into world space (how the object relates to the scene); the view maps from world space to camera space (to provide the user's view on the scene); and the projection maps from camera to screen (converting from a 3D view to a 2D view that can be rendered on the display). The *eye, at*, and *up* variables deserve a little comment: imagine that you are telling someone how to position a video camera to record a movie scene. You need to tell him where to put the camera in the room (*eye*), the direction in which to point it (*at*), and the angle at which to rotate it relative to the ground (*up*).

```
void CubeRenderer::Update(float timeTotal, float timeDelta)
{
    XMVECTOR eye = XMVectorSet(0.0f, 0.7f, 1.5f, 0.0f);
    XMVECTOR at = XMVectorSet(0.0f, -0.1f, 0.0f, 0.0f);
    XMVECTOR up = XMVectorSet(0.0f, 1.0f, 0.0f, 0.0f);
    XMStoreFloat4x4(&m_constantBufferData.view, XMMatrixTranspose(XMMatrixLookAtRH(eye, at,
up)));
    XMStoreFloat4x4(&m_constantBufferData.model, XMMatrixTranspose(XMMatrixRotationY(timeTotal *
XM_PIDIV4)));
}
```

The *Render* method binds the render target and depth stencil views, clears those views, and draws the scene. First, it defines a color (midnight blue). It then sets all the elements in the render target to this value by using *ID3D11DeviceContext:ClearRenderTargetView*. The four elements of the color array correspond to red, green, blue, alpha (RGBA) values, where each is a floating-point value from 0.0 to 1.0, computed as (RGBA element / 255). Next, it clears the depth stencil buffer—this is important to ensure that there are no visible artifacts left over from the previous frame. The only time you wouldn't do this is if you were sure that you were going to update every pixel on the screen in this frame. Having cleared the screen, we check to see if the cube data has been loaded, including the vertex and pixel shader resources (because this happens asynchronously), and if not, we just return at this point.

```
const float midnightBlue[] = { 0.098f, 0.098f, 0.439f, 1.000f };
m_d3dContext->ClearRenderTargetView(
    m_renderTargetView.Get(),
    midnightBlue
    );

m_d3dContext->ClearDepthStencilView(
    m_depthStencilView.Get(),
    D3D11_CLEAR_DEPTH,
    1.0f,
    0
    );

if (!m_loadingComplete)
{
    return;
}
```

If the cube data has been loaded, we then go ahead and set the render target and the depth stencil buffer as the current ones by using *ID3D11DeviceContext::OMSetRenderTargets*. This binds the render target and the depth stencil buffer to the output-merger stage of the rendering pipeline.

```
m_d3dContext->OMSetRenderTargets(
    1,
    m_renderTargetView.GetAddressOf(),
    m_depthStencilView.Get()
    );
```

The next step is to update the constant buffer with the model, view, and projection matrices for the scene. The *ID3D11DeviceContext::UpdateSubresource* method copies the matrix data from CPU memory to GPU memory.

```
m_d3dContext->UpdateSubresource(
    m_constantBuffer.Get(),
    0,
    NULL,
    &m_constantBufferData,
    0,
    0
    );
```

After this, we bind the vertex and index buffers to the input-assembler stage by using *ID3D11DeviceContext::IASetVertexBuffers* and *ID3D11DeviceContext::IASetIndexBuffer*.

```
UINT stride = sizeof(VertexPositionColor);
UINT offset = 0;
m_d3dContext->IASetVertexBuffers(
    0,
    1,
    m_vertexBuffer.GetAddressOf(),
    &stride,
    &offset
    );

m_d3dContext->IASetIndexBuffer(
    m_indexBuffer.Get(),
    DXGI_FORMAT_R16_UINT,
    0
    );
```

Finally, we set the vertex and pixel shaders as the current shaders for the device and set their input layout. We created the input layout in the *CreateDeviceResources* method as part of initialization. The input layout describes how the vertex data is streamed into the input-assembler stage, and we call *IASetPrimitiveTopology* to direct this stage to interpret the vertex data as a list of triangles. A 3D object is represented by a collection of triangles; any 3D surface can be approximated by using a mesh of triangles. The vertex data for our cube is stored in a vertex buffer, and the primitive topology we specify here dictates how the vertices should be assembled together to form the triangle mesh. *TRIANGLELIST* is the most appropriate format for our 3D cube from the *D3D11_PRIMITIVE_TOPOLOGY* enum.

```
m_d3dContext->IASetPrimitiveTopology(D3D11_PRIMITIVE_TOPOLOGY_TRIANGLELIST);
m_d3dContext->IASetInputLayout(m_inputLayout.Get());

m_d3dContext->VSSetShader(
    m_vertexShader.Get(),
    nullptr,
    0
    );

m_d3dContext->PSSetShader(
    m_pixelShader.Get(),
    nullptr,
    0
    );
```

The *Present* method displays the rendered image to the screen. Because this functionality is very generic, it is in the *Direct3DBase* class, where you'll likely leave it unchanged. First, this calls *IDXGISwapChain1::Present* to present the current frame to the screen. The first argument specifies the number of vertical blanks to wait before presenting the frame. This is typically set to 1, which makes the app sleep until the next vertical blank. A *vertical blank* is the time between when one frame finishes drawing to the screen and the next frame begins. This ensures that the app doesn't waste any cycles rendering frames that will never be displayed to the screen.

Next, we call *ID3D11DeviceContext1::DiscardView*, which informs the GPU that the existing content in the render target is no longer needed. In the same way, we discard the contents of the depth stencil buffer. Finally, the app tests to see if the video card has been physically removed from the system or the driver has been updated. Neither of these will happen while the app is running on a phone, so this code is redundant.

```
void Direct3DBase::Present()
{
    HRESULT hr = m_swapChain->Present(1, 0);
    m_d3dContext->DiscardView(m_renderTargetView.Get());
    m_d3dContext->DiscardView(m_depthStencilView.Get());

    if (hr == DXGI_ERROR_DEVICE_REMOVED)
    {
        HandleDeviceLost();
    }
    else
    {
        DX::ThrowIfFailed(hr);
    }
}
```

The shaders used in this app are very simple. The vertex shader executes first. If you examine the code in *SimpleVertexShader.hlsl*, you'll see that the HLSL declaration for *VertexShaderInput*, which is the input for the vertex shader, exactly matches the C++ declaration in *CubeRenderer.h* for *VertexPositionColor*, as shown in Table 25-3.

TABLE 25-3 Comparing HLSL and C++ declarations of the same type

HLSL	C++

`struct VertexShaderInput`
`{`
`    float3 pos : POSITION;`
`    float3 color : COLOR0;`
`};`
	`struct VertexPositionColor`
	`{`
	`    DirectX::XMFLOAT3 pos;`
	`    DirectX::XMFLOAT3 color;`
	`};`

Also note that the *VertexShaderOutput* is the same as the *PixelShaderInput* defined in *SimplePixelShader.hlsl*, as shown in Table 25-4.

TABLE 25-4 Output from the vertex shader must exactly match the input to the pixel shader

VertexShaderOutput	*PixelShaderInput*

`struct VertexShaderOutput`
`{`
`    float4 pos : SV_POSITION;`
`    float3 color : COLOR0;`
`};`
	`struct PixelShaderInput`
	`{`
	`    float4 pos : SV_POSITION;`
	`    float3 color : COLOR0;`
	`};`

The vertex shader operates on one element at a time and transforms the vertex position into projected space by using the model, view, projection data. In this example, it passes the color straight through without modification.

```
VertexShaderOutput main(VertexShaderInput input)
{
    VertexShaderOutput output;
    float4 pos = float4(input.pos, 1.0f);
    pos = mul(pos, model);
    pos = mul(pos, view);
    pos = mul(pos, projection);
    output.pos = pos;
    output.color = input.color;
    return output;
}
```

The pixel shader also passes the color straight through unmodified.

```
float4 main(PixelShaderInput input) : SV_TARGET
{
    return float4(input.color,1.0f);
}
```

If you want to experiment with the pixel shader, you could start by setting a grayscale effect, such as the following:

```
float4 main(PixelShaderInput input) : SV_TARGET
{
    //return float4(input.color,1.0f);
    return dot(float3(0.2 0.6, 0.1), input.color);
}
```

Minimal Direct3D app

To show how you can use the starter code for your own apps, we'll start at the bottom with the simplest possible app; this way, it will be clear where the starter code is common to all Direct3D apps, and where it is specific to the spinning cube. You can see an example of this in the *SimplestD3DApp* solution in the sample code. Recall that you're likely to use much of the starter code as is, especially in the *Direct3DBase* class. However, even in that class there's some redundant code. First, you can safely remove the code for handling window size changes because this will never happen on the phone. In the *Direct3DBase.h*, comment out or remove the declaration of the *UpdateForWindowSizeChange* method. Do the same for the definition in *Direct3DBase.cpp* and also for the one explicit invocation in *Direct3DBase::HandleDeviceLost*. You can actually go ahead and remove the *HandleDeviceLost* method altogether and clean up the *Present* method to remove the code that handles the case when the video card is removed or upgraded.

```
void Direct3DBase::Present()
{
    HRESULT hr = m_swapChain->Present(1, 0);
    m_d3dContext->DiscardView(m_renderTargetView.Get());
    m_d3dContext->DiscardView(m_depthStencilView.Get());
    DX::ThrowIfFailed(hr);
}
```

Next, strip down the *CubeRenderer* class to its bare minimum. In the header file, you can comment out or remove the *ModelViewProjectionConstantBuffer* and *VertexPositionColor* structs. These are used for computing the shape and colors for the 3D cube—you might want something similar for any 3D multicolored shape, but they're not needed for the bare minimum app. Also reduce the *Cube Renderer* class to remove the various buffer and index count variables.

```
ref class CubeRenderer sealed : public Direct3DBase
{
public:
    CubeRenderer();
    virtual void CreateDeviceResources() override;
    virtual void CreateWindowSizeDependentResources() override;
    virtual void Render() override;
    void Update(float timeTotal, float timeDelta);
};
```

In the *CubeRenderer.cpp* file, you can similarly reduce the implementation to the minimum. Having removed the buffer variables, there's nothing in the constructor to initialize; the *CreateDevice Resources*, *CreateWindowSizeDependentResources*, and *Update* methods can all be reduced to bare shells (retaining only the calls to the *Direct3DBase* parent class), and the *Render* method simply renders a midnight-blue scene.

```
CubeRenderer::CubeRenderer()
{
}

void CubeRenderer::CreateDeviceResources()
{
    Direct3DBase::CreateDeviceResources();
}

void CubeRenderer::CreateWindowSizeDependentResources()
{
    Direct3DBase::CreateWindowSizeDependentResources();
}

void CubeRenderer::Update(float timeTotal, float timeDelta)
{
}
```

```
void CubeRenderer::Render()
{
    const float midnightBlue[] = { 0.098f, 0.098f, 0.439f, 1.000f };
    m_d3dContext->ClearRenderTargetView(
        m_renderTargetView.Get(),
        midnightBlue
        );

    m_d3dContext->ClearDepthStencilView(
        m_depthStencilView.Get(),
        D3D11_CLEAR_DEPTH,
        1.0f,
        0
        );

    m_d3dContext->OMSetRenderTargets(
        1,
        m_renderTargetView.GetAddressOf(),
        m_depthStencilView.Get()
        );
}
```

You can also remove both the vertex and pixel shader HLSL files altogether. At this point, build and run the solution. This will produce an app that shows a blank midnight-blue screen. You could then use this minimal app as the basis of your own functionality.

This is all very well if all you want is a blank screen, but we'll now look at the minimum requirements if you actually want to render something on that blank screen. We'll start with the standard starter code, and modify it to draw a single-colored 2D stationary triangle on the screen in place of the multicolored 3D spinning cube. You can see this at work in the *SimpleTriangle* solution in the sample code, as shown in Figure 25-5.

As before, remove the *UpdateForWindowSizeChange* and *HandleDeviceLost* methods, and clean up the *Present* method—these are never required. Also remove the *ModelViewProjectionConstantBuffer* and *VertexPositionColor* structs—these are commonly required where your app has objects that need specifying in terms both of vertex and color, but in this example, we only care about vertex. In the *CubeRenderer* class, we need the members for vertex and pixel shaders and buffers—the only declarations we can remove are the *m_constantBuffer* and *m_constantBufferData* variables.

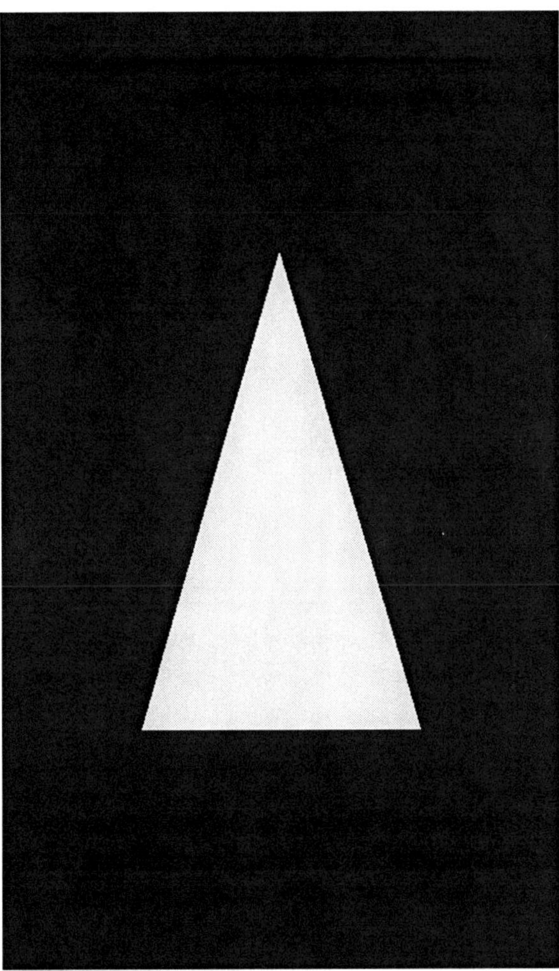

FIGURE 25-5 Most of the starter code is useful in even the simplest Direct3D app.

In the *CubeRenderer::CreateDeviceResources*, replace the input element description: because we'll have a single-color triangle, we don't need to describe a set of color data. Also, we'll draw a 2D triangle, so the position vertex data is simpler because we'll use *XMFLOAT2* instead of *XMFLOAT3*, so the vertex description uses the 2-vertex *DXGI_FORMAT_R32G32_FLOAT* format.

```
//const D3D11_INPUT_ELEMENT_DESC vertexDesc[] =
//{
//    { "POSITION", 0, DXGI_FORMAT_R32G32B32_FLOAT, 0, 0,  D3D11_INPUT_PER_VERTEX_DATA, 0 },
//    { "COLOR",    0, DXGI_FORMAT_R32G32B32_FLOAT, 0, 12, D3D11_INPUT_PER_VERTEX_DATA, 0 },
//};
const D3D11_INPUT_ELEMENT_DESC vertexDesc[] =
{
    { "POSITION", 0, DXGI_FORMAT_R32G32_FLOAT, 0, 0, D3D11_INPUT_PER_VERTEX_DATA, 0 },
};
```

Remove the code to create the constant buffer and replace the declaration of the cube vertices with a simpler declaration for our triangle vertices. To keep things simple, you can keep the *cubeVertices* variable name, even though it is no longer an accurate description.

```
//VertexPositionColor cubeVertices[] =
//{
//    {XMFLOAT3(-0.5f, -0.5f, -0.5f), XMFLOAT3(0.0f, 0.0f, 0.0f)},
      ...etc
//};
XMFLOAT2 cubeVertices[] =
{
    XMFLOAT2(-0.5f, -0.5f),
    XMFLOAT2( 0.0f,  0.5f),
    XMFLOAT2( 0.5f, -0.5f),
};
```

In the same way, replace the declaration of the *cubeIndices*.

```
//unsigned short cubeIndices[] =
//{
//    0,2,1, // -x
//    1,2,3,
..etc
//};
unsigned short cubeIndices[] =
{
    0, 1, 2,
};
```

Reduce the *CubeRenderer::CreateWindowSizeDependentResources* to the bare minimum by simply invoking the base class method. Reduce the *Update* method to do nothing. In the *Render* method, remove the code to call *UpdateSubresource* and *VSSetConstantBuffers* because we no longer have a constant buffer.

Both shaders need updating, as well. This is because the original versions worked on data for our 3D multicolored cube, and now we only have a 2D single-color triangle. First, the vertex shader. Simply remove the code that relates to the color data and the 3D model/view/projection information.

```
struct VertexShaderInput
{
    float3 pos : POSITION;
    //float3 color : COLOR0;
};

struct VertexShaderOutput
{
    float4 pos : SV_POSITION;
    //float3 color : COLOR0;
};
```

```
VertexShaderOutput main(VertexShaderInput input)
{
    VertexShaderOutput output;
    //float4 pos = float4(input.pos, 1.0f);
    //pos = mul(pos, model);
    //pos = mul(pos, view);
    //pos = mul(pos, projection);
    //output.pos = pos;
    //output.color = input.color;
    //output.pos = float4(input.pos, 0.5f, 1.0f);
    output.pos = float4(input.pos, 1.0f);
    return output;
}
```

Finally, do the same work in the pixel shader to remove the color-related code and to draw the entire triangle pink.

```
struct PixelShaderInput
{
    float4 pos : SV_POSITION;
    //float3 color : COLOR0;
};

float4 main(PixelShaderInput input) : SV_TARGET
{
    //return float4(input.color,1.0f);
    return float4(1.0f, 0.827f, 0.875f, 1.0f);
}
```

Touch input

Now, we'll see how to handle user input. You can see an example of this in the *D3DInputApp* solution in the sample code. Create another starter project, but this time, leave all the spinning cube behavior as is. We'll modify this, first to handle simple touch input, and then to handle sensor input from the user moving the device in space. First, when the user taps the screen, we'll toggle the cube between spinning and stationary. Enhance the *CubeRenderer* class with a new method to toggle the spin state, and a *bool* variable to track the state.

```
ref class CubeRenderer sealed : public Direct3DBase
{
public:
... previously-listed code unchanged

    void ToggleSpin();
private:
    bool m_isStopped;
};
```

Initialize the state variable in the constructor and implement the *ToggleSpin* method to flip the value of this variable.

```
CubeRenderer::CubeRenderer() :
    m_loadingComplete(false),
    m_indexCount(0),
    m_isStopped(false)
{
}

void CubeRenderer::ToggleSpin()
{
    m_isStopped = !m_isStopped;
}
```

Then, change the *Update* method to toggle between spinning and static, depending on the current state of the variable. You can implement this behavior very simply by making the vector matrix update code conditionally, based upon a simple test.

```
void CubeRenderer::Update(float timeTotal, float timeDelta)
{
    if (!m_isStopped)
    {
       XMVECTOR eye = XMVectorSet(0.0f, 0.7f, 1.5f, 0.0f);
       XMVECTOR at = XMVectorSet(0.0f, -0.1f, 0.0f, 0.0f);
       XMVECTOR up = XMVectorSet(0.0f, 1.0f, 0.0f, 0.0f);

        XMStoreFloat4x4(&m_constantBufferData.view,
           XMMatrixTranspose(XMMatrixLookAtRH(eye, at, up)));
        XMStoreFloat4x4(&m_constantBufferData.model,
           XMMatrixTranspose(XMMatrixRotationY(timeTotal * XM_PIDIV4)));
    }
}
```

Finally, implement the *PointerReleased* handler in the app class to invoke the *ToggleSpin* method. Now, when the app runs, the user can tap the screen to toggle the cube between spinning and stationary.

```
void D3DInputApp::OnPointerReleased(CoreWindow^ sender, PointerEventArgs^ args)
{
    m_renderer->ToggleSpin();
}
```

Another form of user input is when the user moves the phone, triggering accelerometer events. To use the accelerometer in your app, you must first update the manifest to include the *ID_CAP_SENSORS* capability. Then, add two new member variables to your *CubeRender* class: one for the *Accelerometer*, and one for the latest *AccelerometerReading* value.

```
Windows::Devices::Sensors::Accelerometer^ m_accelerometer;
Windows::Devices::Sensors::AccelerometerReading^ m_reading;
```

Initialize the *Accelerometer* in the *CubeRenderer* constructor.

```
m_accelerometer = Windows::Devices::Sensors::Accelerometer::GetDefault();
```

Finally, in the *Update* method, use the *AccelerometerReading* values to update the orientation of the camera.

```
void CubeRenderer::Update(float timeTotal, float timeDelta)
{
     if (m_isStopped)
        return;

    float x = 0.0f;
    float y = 1.0f;
    float z = 0.0f;

    if (m_accelerometer != nullptr)
    {
    m_reading = m_accelerometer->GetCurrentReading();
    x = (float)m_reading->AccelerationX;
    y = (float)m_reading->AccelerationY;
    z = (float)m_reading->AccelerationZ;
    }

    XMVECTOR eye = XMVectorSet(0.0f, 0.7f, 1.5f, 0.0f);
    XMVECTOR at = XMVectorSet(0.0f, -0.1f, 0.0f, 0.0f);
    //XMVECTOR up = XMVectorSet(0.0f, 1.0f, 0.0f, 0.0f);
    XMVECTOR up = XMVectorSet(x, -y, z, 0.0f);

    XMStoreFloat4x4(&m_constantBufferData.view,
        XMMatrixTranspose(XMMatrixLookAtRH(eye, at, up)));
    XMStoreFloat4x4(&m_constantBufferData.model,
        XMMatrixTranspose(XMMatrixRotationY(timeTotal * XM_PIDIV4)));

}
```

You can test this in the emulator by using the *Accelerometer* tab, or you can test on a real device by simply moving the phone around in space. As the user moves the phone, this adjusts the orientation of the cube.

Direct2D and DirectXTK

DirectX on Windows Phone does not include Direct2D. This means that if you want to draw 2D shapes and text, you either have to do a lot of work yourself or use the DirectX Toolkit (DirectXTK). The *HelloWorld* solution in the sample code uses this approach to render the 2D text "Hello World" on the screen, as demonstrated in Figure 25-6.

FIGURE 25-6 You can use DirectXTK for 2D rendering.

To produce this app, you first create a standard Direct3D app, and then strip it down to the bare minimum as described in earlier sections. Next, download the DirectXTK from *http://directxtk.codeplex.com/*. This comes in a source-code format, so you just need to unzip the download file to a suitable location. Then, add the *DirectXTK_WindowsPhone8* project to your *HelloWorld* solution so that you can build it. You also need to add a reference to the output from this project to your HelloWorld project. To do this, right-click your project and then, on the shortcut menu that appears, point to References, click Add New Reference in the submenu, expand the Solution node, and then select the *DirectXTK_WindowsPhone8* project. This should also automatically set up the project dependencies so that your project depends on the toolkit project in the build order.

In addition to referencing the toolkit library in your project, you also need to use some of the types defined in the toolkit. That means adding *#include* statements for the appropriate header files. For convenience, you can update your project to add the toolkit location to the search path for include folders. To do this, right-click your project and then, on the shortcut menu that appears, click Properties. In the Properties dialog box, expand the C/C++ node and select the General subnode. In the main window, click the Additional Include folders and select Edit. Click the New Folder button and navigate to the Inc folder in the DirectXTK download.

To draw text with Direct2D, you use the *SpriteFont::DrawString* method. This takes a *SpriteBatch* as its first argument as well as a string, X/Y coordinates for the string, and a color. In the *CubeRenderer.h*, add *#include* statements for the *SpriteBatch* and *SpriteFont* headers. Then, update the *CubeRenderer* class to declare *SpriteBatch* and *SpriteFont* member variables.

```
#include "SpriteBatch.h"
#include "SpriteFont.h"

ref class CubeRenderer sealed : public Direct3DBase
{
public:
    CubeRenderer();
    virtual void CreateDeviceResources() override;
    virtual void CreateWindowSizeDependentResources() override;
    virtual void Render() override;
    void Update(float timeTotal, float timeDelta);
private:
    std::unique_ptr<DirectX::SpriteBatch> m_sprites;
    std::unique_ptr<DirectX::SpriteFont> m_font;
};
```

Now, to initialize a *SpriteFont* object, you need to load suitable font data. The DirectXTK also supports this via a MakeSpriteFont tool. Because the entire toolkit is provided in source format, you have to build this tool, as well. You'll find it in the *DirectXTK_Desktop_2012* solution, so you need to load this solution independently and build it. After it is built, you can run the MakeSpriteFont tool from a command window. The command line that follows creates a suitable spritefont file from the system Consolas font, specifying a font size of 54. This will output the specified file to either the fully-qualified path or by default to the same location as the MakeSpriteFont tool. When you execute this command line, you should see output similar to the following:

```
MakeSpriteFont.exe "Consolas" consolas.spritefont /FontSize:54

Importing Consolas
Cropping glyph borders
Packing glyphs into sprite sheet
Premultiplying alpha
Writing consolas.spritefont (CompressedMono format)
```

If you didn't specify an explicit path for the output file, copy the file into the *Assets* folder of the *HelloWorld* project. Then, in Visual Studio, add the existing file to the project and set its *Content* property to *True*. Armed with suitable font data, you can now update the *CreateDeviceResources* method to initialize the *SpriteBatch* and *SpriteFont* objects.

```
void CubeRenderer::CreateDeviceResources()
{
     Direct3DBase::CreateDeviceResources();

    auto context = m_d3dContext.Get();
    m_sprites.reset(new SpriteBatch(context));
     auto device = m_d3dDevice.Get();
    m_font.reset(new SpriteFont(device, L"assets\\consolas.spritefont"));
}
```

The only remaining work is to update the *Render* method to draw the text. Do this at the end of the method, after clearing the render target view and binding the render target and the depth-stencil buffer to the output-merger stage.

```
void CubeRenderer::Render()
{
    const float backgroundColor[] = { 224.0f/255.0f, 1.0f, 102.0f/255.0f };
    m_d3dContext->ClearRenderTargetView(
        m_renderTargetView.Get(),
        backgroundColor
        );

    m_d3dContext->OMSetRenderTargets(
        1,
        m_renderTargetView.GetAddressOf(),
        m_depthStencilView.Get()
        );

    m_sprites->Begin();
    m_font->DrawString( m_sprites.get(), L"Hello World", XMFLOAT2( 10, 10 ), Colors::Violet );
    m_sprites->End();
}
```

That's about as simple as it gets. For a more realistic app, you'd obviously want to draw other shapes, load textures, and update objects in the *Update* method to simulate movement, just as you do with 3D objects.

Summary

In this chapter, we looked at the support in Visual Studio for building games with Direct3D, including the different Direct3D-enabled project types that you can use, and the starter code generated for Direct3D projects. We examined the key classes and the component architecture as well as places where you would typically replace or enhance the starter code, the areas where Direct3D apps for Windows Phone are different from Direct3D apps for Windows on the desktop, and how you can use Direct2D techniques by using the DirectXTK.

Index

Symbols

A

B

C

D

E

F

G

H

I

J

K

L

M

N

O

P

S

T

U

V

W

X

Y

Z

About the Authors

ANDREW WHITECHAPEL is a senior program manager for the Windows Phone Developer Platform team, responsible for internal components within the platform. He is the author of several books, including *Windows Phone 7 Development Internals* (Microsoft Press, 2012).

SEAN MCKENNA is a senior program manager on the Windows Phone Developer Platform team. He has been responsible for several key features, including local database support and app-to-app communication.

CPSIA information can be obtained at www.ICGtesting.com
Printed in the USA
BVOW051457170613

323264BV00007BC/7/P